W9-BVM-464

America's
TEST KITCHEN

ALSO BY THE EDITORS AT AMERICA'S TEST KITCHEN

The Cook's Illustrated Meat Book

The Complete Cooking for Two Cookbook

The America's Test Kitchen Cooking School Cookbook

The Cook's Illustrated Baking Book

The Cook's Illustrated Cookbook

The Science of Good Cooking

The America's Test Kitchen Menu Cookbook

The America's Test Kitchen Quick Family Cookbook

The America's Test Kitchen Healthy Family Cookbook

The America's Test Kitchen Family Baking Book

THE AMERICA'S TEST KITCHEN LIBRARY SERIES:

The Make-Ahead Cook

The How Can It Be Gluten-Free Cookbook

Slow Cooker Revolution Volume 2: The Easy-Prep Edition

Slow Cooker Revolution

The 6-Ingredient Solution

Pressure Cooker Perfection

Comfort Food Makeovers

The America's Test Kitchen D.I.Y. Cookbook

Pasta Revolution

Simple Weeknight Favorites

The Best Simple Recipes

THE COOK'S COUNTRY SERIES:

From Our Grandmothers' Kitchens

Cook's Country Blue Ribbon Desserts

Cook's Country Best Potluck Recipes

Cook's Country Best Lost Suppers

Cook's Country Best Grilling Recipes

The Cook's Country Cookbook

America's Best Lost Recipes

THE TV COMPANION SERIES:

The Complete Cook's Country TV Show Cookbook

The Complete America's Test Kitchen TV Show Cookbook 2001–2015

America's Test Kitchen: The TV Companion Cookbook (2002–2009 and 2011–2015 Editions)

AMERICA'S TEST KITCHEN ANNUALS:

The Best of America's Test Kitchen (2007–2015 Editions)

Cooking for Two (2010–2013 Editions)

Light & Healthy (2010–2012 Editions)

THE BEST RECIPE SERIES:

The New Best Recipe

More Best Recipes

The Best One-Dish Suppers

Soups, Stews & Chilis

The Best Skillet Recipes

The Best Slow & Easy Recipes

The Best Chicken Recipes

The Best International Recipe

The Best Make-Ahead Recipe

The Best 30-Minute Recipe

The Best Light Recipe

The Cook's Illustrated Guide to Grilling and Barbecue

Best American Side Dishes

Cover & Bake

Steaks, Chops, Roasts & Ribs

Italian Classics

American Classics

FOR A FULL LISTING OF ALL OUR BOOKS
OR TO ORDER TITLES:

CooksIllustrated.com

AmericasTestKitchen.com

or call 800-611-0759

THE NEW *Family Cookbook*

THE NEW Family Cookbook

ALL-NEW EDITION OF THE BEST-SELLING CLASSIC
WITH 1,100 NEW RECIPES

THE EDITORS AT AMERICA'S TEST KITCHEN

BROOKLINE, MASSACHUSETTS

Copyright © 2014 by the Editors at America's Test Kitchen

All rights reserved. No part of this book may be reproduced or transmitted in any manner whatsoever without written permission from the publisher, except in the case of brief quotations embodied in critical articles or reviews.

AMERICA'S TEST KITCHEN
17 Station Street, Brookline, MA 02445

Library of Congress Cataloging-in-Publication Data

The America's Test Kitchen new family cookbook : all-new edition of the best-selling classic with 1,100 new recipes / the editors at America's Test Kitchen.
    pages cm
Includes index.
ISBN 978-1-936493-85-2
1. Cooking, American. I. America's Test Kitchen (Firm)
TX715.A5496 2014
641.5973--dc23

                    2014009517

Hardcover: $40.00 US

Manufactured in the United States of America
10 9 8 7 6 5 4 3 2

DISTRIBUTED BY
America's Test Kitchen
17 Station Street, Brookline, MA 02445

America's
TEST KITCHEN

RECIPES THAT WORK®

EDITORIAL DIRECTOR: Jack Bishop
EDITORIAL DIRECTOR, BOOKS: Elizabeth Carduff
EXECUTIVE FOOD EDITOR: Julia Collin Davison
SENIOR EDITOR: Debra Hudak
EDITORIAL ASSISTANT: Rachel Greenhaus
DESIGN DIRECTOR: Amy Klee
ART DIRECTOR: Greg Galvan
ASSOCIATE ART DIRECTOR: Taylor Argenzio
DESIGNER: Jen Kanavos Hoffman
DIRECTOR OF PHOTOGRAPHY: Julie Cote
PHOTOGRAPHY: Carl Tremblay, Keller + Keller, and Anthony Tieuli
STAFF PHOTOGRAPHER: Daniel J. van Ackere
ADDITIONAL PHOTOGRAPHY: Steve Klise
ASSOCIATE ART DIRECTOR, PHOTOGRAPHY: Steve Klise
CAST PHOTOGRAPH: Christopher Churchill
FOOD STYLING: Daniel Cellucci, Catrine Kelty, Marie Piraino, and Mary Jane Sawyer
PHOTOSHOOT KITCHEN TEAM:
  ASSOCIATE EDITOR: Chris O'Connor
  TEST COOK: Daniel Cellucci
  ASSISTANT TEST COOK: Cecelia Jenkins
PRODUCTION DIRECTOR: Guy Rochford
SENIOR PRODUCTION MANAGER: Jessica Quirk
PROJECT MANAGEMENT DIRECTOR: Alice Carpenter
PROJECT MANAGER: Britt Dresser
WORKFLOW AND DIGITAL ASSET MANAGER: Andrew Mannone
SENIOR COLOR AND IMAGING SPECIALIST: Lauren Pettapiece
PRODUCTION AND IMAGING SPECIALISTS: Heather Dube and Lauren Robbins
COPYEDITOR: Jeff Schier
PROOFREADERS: Pat Jalbert-Levine and Elizabeth Wray Emery
INDEXER: Elizabeth Parson

PICTURED OPPOSITE TITLE PAGE: Cream Cheese Brownies (page 637)

Contents

Welcome to America's Test Kitchen

This book has been tested, written, and edited by the folks at America's Test Kitchen, a very real 2,500-square-foot kitchen located just outside of Boston. It is the home of *Cook's Illustrated* magazine and *Cook's Country* magazine and is the Monday-through-Friday destination for more than four dozen test cooks, editors, food scientists, tasters, and cookware specialists. Our mission is to test recipes over and over again until we understand how and why they work and until we arrive at the "best" version.

We start the process of testing a recipe with a complete lack of conviction, which means that we accept no claim, no theory, no technique, and no recipe at face value. We simply assemble as many variations as possible, test a half-dozen of the most promising, and taste the results blind. We then construct our own hybrid recipe and continue to test it, varying ingredients, techniques, and cooking times until we reach a consensus. The result, we hope, is the best version of a particular recipe, but we realize that only you can be the final judge of our success (or failure). As we like to say in the test kitchen, "We make the mistakes, so you don't have to."

All of this would not be possible without a belief that good cooking, much like good music, is indeed based on a foundation of objective technique. Some people like spicy foods and others don't, but there is a right way to sauté, there is a best way to cook a pot roast, and there are measurable scientific principles involved in producing perfectly beaten, stable egg whites. This is our ultimate goal: to investigate the fundamental principles of cooking so that you become a better cook. It is as simple as that.

If you're curious to see what goes on behind the scenes at America's Test Kitchen, check out our daily blog, The Feed, at AmericasTestKitchenFeed.com, which features kitchen snapshots, exclusive recipes, video tips, and much more. You can watch us work (in our actual test kitchen) by tuning in to America's Test Kitchen (AmericasTestKitchen.com) or Cook's Country from America's Test Kitchen (CooksCountryTV.com) on public television. Tune in to America's Test Kitchen Radio (ATKRadio.com) on public radio to listen to insights, tips, and techniques that illuminate the truth about real home cooking. Want to hone your cooking skills or finally learn how to bake—from an America's Test Kitchen test cook? Enroll in a cooking class at our online cooking school at OnlineCookingSchool.com. And find information about subscribing to Cook's Illustrated magazine at CooksIllustrated.com or Cook's Country magazine at CooksCountry.com. Both magazines are published every other month. However you choose to visit us, we welcome you into our kitchen, where you can stand by our side as we test our way to the best recipes in America.

FACEBOOK.COM/AMERICASTESTKITCHEN

TWITTER.COM/TESTKITCHEN

YOUTUBE.COM/AMERICASTESTKITCHEN

INSTAGRAM.COM/TESTKITCHEN

PINTEREST.COM/TESTKITCHEN

AMERICASTESTKITCHEN.TUMBLR.COM

GOOGLE.COM/+AMERICASTESTKITCHEN

Preface

I made my first recipe at age 8—it was an old-fashioned chocolate cake with seven-minute frosting. That recipe appeared in an old edition of the *Joy of Cooking,* the go-to cookbook for my parents' generation. Irma Rombauer, the author, was a gracious host from the very first omelet to Cock-a-Leekie Soup; she invited you into her kitchen and gave you the confidence to become a good cook.

When we published the first edition of *The America's Test Kitchen Family Cookbook* in 2005, our objective was the same as Irma's: to invite people into our test kitchen to make them comfortable with the culinary arts. But as we have learned more about teaching the culinary arts, about how to write and present recipes, and how to make anyone and everyone successful in the kitchen, we thought that it was time for a major revision. *The America's Test Kitchen New Family Cookbook* runs almost 900 pages, contains 302 finished recipe photographs, over 1,100 step-by-step photos, and 1,356 recipes, including 1,139 new recipes for this revised edition.

One thing we have learned is that teaching cooking is something quite different than just presenting recipes. Our 60 Learn How tutorials clearly set out the basics from pan sauces, pot roasts, and buttermilk biscuits to pizza, quiche, cobbler, and even stir-fried tofu. We also visually present over a dozen All About sidebars on brining, setting up the grill, Asian ingredients, cheeses, and grains.

And let's not forget the recipes. After 20 years of test kitchen work, we have developed unusual, sometimes remarkable, and always foolproof ways of making classic recipes. Our Weeknight Roast Chicken turns the oven *off* halfway through cooking. We use vodka in our Foolproof Pie Dough to make tender pie crust that is also easy to roll out. Easier French Fries start in *room-temperature,* not hot, oil and they are *less greasy* than regular fries. We reinvented Poached Salmon by using only a small amount of liquid and lemon slices to keep the fish above the water. A grated apple makes our Ultimate Blueberry Pie a winner since apples are full of pectin that gives the final pie the perfect soft but firm texture. Plus our risotto recipe is almost hands-free.

Our shopping guide has also been completely updated with the latest equipment testings and food tastings from charcoal grills and garlic presses to baking powder, chicken broth, and quick-cooking oats. No other cookbook on the market today gives you both recipes and entirely unbiased test results for 300 different products.

Even with this wealth of information, home cooks do experience failure. That brings us to the essence of this volume. Our recipes are tested dozens of times in our test kitchen just outside of Boston. When we are finished, we send our recipes to our viewers and readers to get feedback. Once approved, we then make our recipes using electric stovetops, the worst cookware, and incorrect ingredients to find out what can go wrong in your home kitchen. So when you cook from an America's Test Kitchen recipe, we let you know what you can and cannot do, which items you can substitute (and which you can't), and exactly which steps in a recipe are most important.

In other words, this cookbook will make you a good cook, and maybe a great cook. The recipes work and you will find success. Nobody has to extol the virtues of being a good cook; it guarantees a lifetime of personal rewards and happiness and you will gain in self-confidence.

That reminds me of the story about the minister and the Vermont farmer. The farmer had bought an old, run-down farm and had worked very hard to get it back into shape. The local minister stopped by one day for a call. He congratulated the farmer on the results, remarking that it was wonderful what God and man could accomplish when they worked together. "Ayuh," replied the farmer, "pr'haps it is. But you should have seen this place when God was running it alone!"

Well, there's self-confidence for you!

CHRISTOPHER KIMBALL
Founder and Editor,
Cook's Illustrated and *Cook's Country*
Host, *America's Test Kitchen* and
Cook's Country from America's Test Kitchen

Getting Started

Test Kitchen Tips That Will Make You a Better Cook

Even the best of cooks can produce disappointing results. However, there are some basic rules you can follow that will help you use recipes—successfully—in your kitchen.

READ THE RECIPE CAREFULLY: Almost everyone has embarked upon preparing a recipe only to realize midway through that the dish needed hours of chilling before it could even be served. By reading the recipe completely through before you start to cook, you will avoid any surprises along the way, including not having that special, essential ingredient.

FOLLOW DIRECTIONS, AT LEAST THE FIRST TIME: Cooking is a science, but it is also an art. Our advice is simple: Make the recipe as directed the first time. Once you understand the recipe, you can improvise the next time.

BE PREPARED: Set out and organize all of the equipment you will need for a recipe, and prep all of the ingredients for it before you start to cook. A recipe is a lot simpler to make when all the components and tools for it are at your fingertips.

START WITH GOOD INGREDIENTS: Don't expect to turn old eggs into a nicely risen soufflé. Freshness matters. When it comes to pantry items, follow our recommendations (pages 802–822) whenever possible.

PREPARE INGREDIENTS AS DIRECTED: Be sure to prepare food as instructed in the ingredient list. Food that is uniformly and properly cut will not only cook at the same rate but also be more visually appealing.

KEEP SUBSTITUTIONS TO A MINIMUM: There are certain substitutions that we have found acceptable in a pinch. But in general it is best if you use the ingredients called for in the recipe; this is especially true in baking, where even the slightest change can spell disaster. See the inside front cover of the book for the test kitchen's list of emergency substitutions.

USE THE RIGHT-SIZE EQUIPMENT: Make sure to use the cookware and bakeware specified in the recipe. If you try to cook four chicken cutlets in a 10-inch skillet, rather than in the 12-inch skillet called for in the recipe, the chicken will steam instead of brown because the pan is too crowded.

PREHEAT YOUR OVEN: Most ovens need at least 15 minutes to preheat fully. Plan accordingly. If you don't preheat your oven fully, then your food will spend more time in the oven and, as a result, will likely be dry and overcooked. Also, position the racks in the oven as directed.

MONITOR THE DISH AS IT COOKS: The cooking times in our recipes are meant as guidelines only. Because ingredients and equipment inevitably vary, it is important to follow the visual cues provided in the recipe. And don't wait until the prescribed time has elapsed to check the doneness of a particular recipe: Unless the recipe specifies otherwise, it is good practice to start checking 5 to 10 minutes before the designated time.

TASTE THE DISH BEFORE SERVING: Most recipes end by instructing the cook to adjust the seasonings. You must taste the food in order to adjust the seasonings successfully. We generally season food lightly throughout the cooking process and then add more salt as needed. Foods that will be served chilled, such as gazpacho, should be tasted again before serving because the cold mutes the effect of the seasoning.

LEARN FROM YOUR MISTAKES: Even the experienced cooks in our test kitchen often turn out less-than-perfect food. A good cook is able to analyze failure, pinpoint the cause, and then avoid that pitfall the next time. Repetition is key to any learning process, and cooking is no different. Make a dish at least once or twice a month until you master it.

ENJOY YOURSELF: The successful cook is someone who enjoys cooking. Take pride in accomplishments. If you enjoy cooking, you will get in the kitchen more often—and practice really does make perfect.

INGREDIENT ASSUMPTIONS IN OUR RECIPES

Unless a recipe in this book states otherwise, you should assume the following ingredients rules are being observed.

Flour	Unbleached, all-purpose
Sugar	Granulated
Salt	Table
Pepper	Freshly ground black
Spices	Ground
Herbs	Fresh
Broths	Low-sodium
Butter	Unsalted
Eggs	Large
Dairy	Whole milk, or full-fat (although low-fat will generally work; skim won't)

Test Kitchen Tips to Make Food Taste Better

Sometimes it's the small touches that make the biggest difference. Here are some simple tips for prepping, cooking, and seasoning designed to boost flavor in everyday cooking.

DON'T PREPARE GARLIC AND ONIONS IN ADVANCE: Chopping garlic and onions releases sharp odors and strong flavors that become overpowering with time, so it's best to cut them at the last minute. Soaking sliced or chopped onions in a solution of baking soda and water (1 tablespoon per cup of water) tames their pungency for raw applications; just be sure to rinse them thoroughly before using.

DON'T SEED TOMATOES: The seeds and surrounding "jelly" contain most of the flavor, so don't seed tomatoes unless called for in a recipe where excess moisture will ruin a dish.

KEEP FATS TASTING FRESH: The fats in butter, oils, and nuts can go rancid and impart off-flavors to your cooking. Minimize their exposure to oxygen and light to slow down this process. Store butter and nuts in the freezer, keep nut oils in the fridge, and store vegetable oils in a dark pantry.

STRIKE ONLY WHEN THE PAN IS HOT: The temperature of the cooking surface will drop the minute food is added, so don't rush the preheating step at the start of most sautés. Wait for the oil to shimmer when cooking vegetables. When cooking proteins, wait until you see the first wisps of smoke rise from the oil.

NEVER DISCARD THE FOND: Those caramelized browned bits that stick to the bottom of the pan after cooking are packed with savory flavor. Deglaze the hot pan with liquid (wine, broth, or juice) and scrape the bits free with a wooden spoon to incorporate the fond into sauces, soups, or stews.

SEASON WITH SUGAR, TOO: Browned food tastes better, and the best way to accelerate this process is with a pinch of sugar sprinkled on lean proteins (chicken and seafood) or vegetables.

BLOOM SPICES AND DRIED HERBS IN FAT: To intensify the flavor of ground spices and dried herbs, cook them for a minute or two in a little butter or oil before adding liquid to the pan. If the recipe calls for sautéing aromatics (like onions), add the spices to the fat in the pan when the vegetables are nearly cooked.

BROWN BREADS, PIES, AND PASTRIES: Browning equals flavor, so don't take breads, pies, or even cakes out of the oven until the exterior is deep golden brown. We bake all pies in a glass plate so we can track color development. When working with puff pastry or other flaky dough on a baking sheet, we lift up the bottom of individual pieces and look for even browning.

ADD A LITTLE UMAMI OR SAVORINESS: Soy sauce and anchovies contain high levels of glutamates, which give dishes a savory, meaty boost. Add a teaspoon or two of soy sauce to chili, or cook a few minced anchovies along with the vegetables in a soup or stew.

INCORPORATE FRESH HERBS AT THE RIGHT TIME: Add hardy herbs like thyme, rosemary, oregano, sage, and marjoram to dishes early in the cooking process; this way, they release maximum flavor while ensuring that their texture will be less intrusive. Save delicate herbs like parsley, cilantro, tarragon, chives, and basil for the last minute, or they will lose their fresh flavor and bright color.

WHEN SEASONINGS GO AWRY

If you've added too much salt, sugar, or spice to a dish, the damage is usually done. In mild cases, it can sometimes be masked by the addition of another seasoning from the opposite end of the flavor spectrum. Remember to account for the reduction of liquids when seasoning a dish—a perfectly seasoned stew will likely taste too salty after several hours of simmering. Your best bet: Season with a light hand during the cooking process, then adjust the seasoning just before serving.

IF YOUR FOOD IS	ADD	SUCH AS
Too Salty	an acid or sweetener	vinegar, lemon or lime juice, or canned, unsalted tomatoes; sugar, honey, or maple syrup
Too Sweet	an acid or seasonings	vinegar or citrus juice; chopped fresh herbs, dash of cayenne, or, for sweet dishes, a bit of liqueur or espresso powder
Too Spicy or Acidic	a fat or sweetener	butter, cream, sour cream, cheese, or olive oil; sugar, honey, or maple syrup

Know Your Measuring Tools

Measuring matters. In fact, accurate measuring is often the difference between success and failure in the kitchen. Using the wrong amount of any ingredient can make or break a recipe. Use our techniques to help you measure accurately and achieve consistently good results whenever you cook or bake. Here are the essential tools we use to measure when cooking. You'll need a set each of dry measuring cups, liquid measuring cups, and measuring spoons to measure wet and dry ingredients accurately. We also highly recommend a digital scale and a kitchen ruler. See Shopping for Equipment on pages 794–795 for more information and the test kitchen's buying recommendations.

DRY MEASURING CUPS

These straight-sided cups typically have flat tops that make leveling dry ingredients easy. Dry ingredients like flour and sugar should always be measured in a dry measuring cup; in a wet measuring cup, it is impossible to level the surface of the contents to obtain an exact measurement.

- Buy sturdy cups. Look for either heavy, well-constructed stainless steel models or solid and comfortable plastic cups.
- Get a complete set. Buy a set of measuring cups that also includes in-between sizes, like ¾ cup and ⅔ cup.
- Look for a long, solid handle.

LIQUID MEASURING CUPS

These cups are designed to make pouring easy and measuring liquids accurate and mess-free.

- Look for easy-to-read markings. They should be clear and easily readable (even when the cup is full), and should cover a range of gradations.
- Shop for sturdy cups. Clear cups are our preference; they make it simple to gauge how much is in the cup because the meniscus line—the bottom of the curve of the liquid's surface—is easily discernible.
- Keep your kitchen supplied with a variety of sizes. The most useful are 2- and 4-cup measures, but a 1-cup measure is worth having on hand, too.

MEASURING SPOONS

Simply eyeballing an amount won't cut it—especially when you're baking. These spoons are vital for measuring everything from granular ingredients like salt, pepper, and spices to small amounts of liquids like lemon juice and water.

- Look for a flat top. As with dry measuring cups, measuring spoons should have a handle that is flush with the rim of the bowl so that dry ingredients can be easily leveled.
- Oval-shaped spoons and deep bowls make scooping easy. The oval shape can reach into tall, narrow jars exceptionally well, while deep (not shallow) bowls keep the ingredient in the spoon, not spilling out onto the counter.

ADJUSTABLE MEASURING CUP

Sticky ingredients like peanut butter and honey can be difficult to measure and scrape out of liquid measuring cups, so we use an adjustable measuring cup.

- Look for a tight seal. The plungerlike bottom should have a tight seal and be easy (but not too easy) to push to extract ingredients.
- Get one that's dishwasher-safe since this tool can be very difficult to clean.

WHEN TO MEASURE

It addition to how you measure, it matters when you measure an ingredient. For instance, "1 cup walnuts, chopped" is not the same thing as "1 cup chopped walnuts." In the first example, "1 cup walnuts, chopped," the cook should measure, then chop the walnuts. In the second example, "1 cup chopped walnuts," the cook should chop, then measure.

Because the volume of ingredients is different when chopped, this really matters. One cup of unchopped walnuts weighs 4 ounces, while 1 cup of chopped walnuts weighs 4.8 ounces—that's 20 percent more nuts.

Apply this principle to other ingredients (such as "sifted flour" versus "flour, sifted") and you can see how this makes a significant difference in the final outcome of a recipe.

KITCHEN RULER

One often-overlooked but useful tool is the kitchen ruler. We think it is indispensable and reach for it constantly, whether we are cutting up beef for a stew, prepping vegetables, or making pastry.

- Buy stainless steel, not wood. Stainless steel is easy to clean and is dishwasher-safe.
- A size of 18 inches is best. An 18-inch ruler will handle all kitchen tasks and will fit in a kitchen drawer.

DIGITAL SCALE

When you're baking, weighing your ingredients is the most accurate method of measurement. Once you buy a scale, however, you'll find it useful in many other applications, from portioning out specific amounts of ground meat to figuring out how many apples or potatoes you'll need from the big bag you've bought. We prefer electronic kitchen scales over mechanical ones for their easy readability and incredible precision.

- Readability is key. Look for an easy-to-read display that isn't obscured when a big bowl (or anything else) is placed on the weighing platform.
- Choose by weight range. The larger the weight range (we like scales that measure from ¼ ounce up to 10 pounds at least), the more versatile your scale is and the more you'll turn to it in the kitchen.
- Make sure you can "zero" in. If your scale can be zeroed, you can automatically subtract the weight of the weighing vessel (and anything already in it) to measure only the ingredients being added—helpful when you need to make incremental additions to your mixing bowl.

How To Measure

Even though weight is a more accurate way to measure than volume, we know that most cooks will rely on measuring cups and spoons, not scales. That's fine, but there are ways to increase your accuracy when using volume measures. One note about liquid and dry measuring cups: Do not use them interchangeably—if you do, your ingredient amounts may be significantly off. Also see Conversions and Equivalencies on page 823.

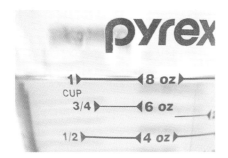

GET EYE LEVEL FOR LIQUIDS: For an accurate reading in a liquid measuring cup, set the cup on a level surface and bend down to read the bottom of the concave arc at the liquid's surface, known as the meniscus line, at eye level.

DIP AND SWEEP DRY INGREDIENTS: For accuracy, nothing beats weighing dry ingredients, but the dip-and-sweep method is also reliable. Dip the measuring cup into the ingredient, like flour or sugar, and sweep away the excess with a straight-edged object, like the back of a knife.

PACK BROWN SUGAR: Brown sugar is so moist and clumpy that it must be packed into a measuring cup to get an accurate reading. To do this, use your fingers or the bottom of a smaller cup to tap and press the sugar into the measuring cup.

Know Your Knives

Knives are the most important tools in your kitchen, and using them properly is essential. If you use the right techniques, you will encounter less risk and produce faster and better results. It is crucial to keep knives sharp so that they cut through food easier and with less slippage. It is also important to know how to grip a knife and how to position your noncutting hand. With proper cutting, your food will be evenly cut and will therefore cook at an even rate. Although there are hundreds of gadgets that claim they can help you prep ingredients more quickly, we've found that you need to invest only in three good knives: a chef's knife, a paring knife, and a serrated knife (or bread knife). If you cook a lot of roasts, we suggest buying a slicing knife as well. See Shopping for Equipment on page 788 for more information and the test kitchen's buying recommendations.

8-INCH CHEF'S KNIFE

We use a chef's knife for everything from chopping onions to mincing herbs to butchering a chicken. This one knife, with its pointed tip and slightly curved blade, will handle 90 percent of your kitchen cutting work.

- The knife should be substantial but lightweight.
- The blade should be made of high-carbon stainless steel.
- Look for a comfortable grip and a nonslip handle.

3- TO 3½-INCH PARING KNIFE

The small blade of a paring knife allows you more dexterity and precision than a chef's knife can provide. We reach for a paring knife for jobs that require a bit more accuracy and exactitude, such as coring apples, deveining shrimp, cutting citrus segments, and peeling garlic. Its small, pointed tip is also great for testing the tenderness of meat or vegetables.

- Choose a blade with agility.
- Look for a comfortable grip.

Is Your Knife Sharp?

Put your knife to the paper test. Hold a folded sheet of newspaper. Lay the blade against the top edge at an angle and slice outward. If the knife fails to slice cleanly, try steeling it (see page 7). If it still fails, it needs sharpening.

10- TO 12-INCH SERRATED KNIFE (BREAD KNIFE)

This knife features pointed serrations that allow it to glide through crusty breads and bagels, as well as through tomato skins and other foods to produce neat slices.

- A 10- to 12-inch blade is ideal. Knives shorter than 10 inches tend to catch their tips on larger loaves of bread.
- A somewhat flexible, slightly curved blade makes cutting easier.
- Go for pointed serrations that are uniformly spaced and moderately sized.

12-INCH SLICING KNIFE (CARVING KNIFE)

A slicing knife is specially designed to cut neatly through meat's muscle fibers and connective tissues. No other knife can cut through meat with such precision in a single stroke. Our holiday birds and roasts would be torn to shambles—hardly presentable—without this knife.

- A 12-inch blade about 1½ inches wide allows for a single stroke to cut through even large cuts of meat. The blade should be fairly rigid and have a rounded tip.
- Get a Granton-edged knife. These knives have oval scallops carved into both sides of the blade, creating a thinner edge on the blade.
- Tapering is important. The thickness of the blade should taper significantly from the handle to the tip.
- Look for a comfortable grip.

Holding a Knife

Much like gripping a baseball bat, how you hold a knife makes a difference in terms of control and force. And don't forget about the other hand—the one that holds the food securely in place while you cut. How you hold the food steady makes a big difference in terms of fingertip safety.

CONTROL GRIP: For more control, choke up on the handle and actually grip the blade of the knife between your thumb and forefinger.

FORCE GRIP: Holding the knife entirely by the handle allows you to use more force and is helpful when cutting through hard foods or bone.

PROTECT YOUR FINGERTIPS: Use the "bear claw" grip to hold food in place and minimize danger. Tuck your fingertips in, away from the knife, and rest your knuckles against the blade. During the upward motion of slicing, reposition your guiding hand for the next cut.

Caring for Your Knives

A sharp knife is a fast knife, and a dull knife is an accident waiting to happen. Dull knives are dangerous because a dull blade requires more force to do the job and so has a higher chance of slipping and missing the mark. Even the best knives will dull over time with regular use.

WHEN TO USE A KNIFE SHARPENER

If your knife is quite dull, you'll need to reshape its edge in order to make it sharp again. This requires removing a fair amount of metal—more than you could ever remove with a steel. To restore a very dull knife, you have three choices: You can send it out; you can use a whetstone (tricky for anyone but a professional); or—the most convenient option—you can use an electric or manual sharpener. An electric knife sharpener makes quick work of very dull knives and is easy to use. See our Equipment Guide on page 789 for further information and the test kitchen's recommendations.

WHEN TO USE A SHARPENING STEEL

A sharpening steel doesn't really sharpen a knife, but rather it hones the edge of a slightly dulled blade. Sweeping the blade along the steel realigns the edge. To safely use a steel, hold it with the tip firmly planted on the counter. Place the heel of the blade against the tip of the steel and point the knife tip slightly upward. Hold the blade at a 20-degree angle away from the steel; make sure to maintain this angle. Slide the blade down the steel, pulling the knife toward your body so that the middle of the blade is in contact with the middle of the steel. Finish the motion by passing the tip of the blade over the bottom of the steel. Four or five strokes on each side of the blade should realign the edge.

Know Your Cutting Boards

Any well-stocked kitchen needs several good cutting boards; they are hard-working and -wearing pieces of equipment. Having a solid base upon which to cut makes food preparation easier and prevents kitchen mishaps. See Shopping for Equipment on pages 788–789 for more information and the test kitchen's buying recommendations.

WOODEN AND PLASTIC CUTTING BOARDS

- The board should be sturdy but not too hard. The ideal surface should be soft enough to keep your knife in good shape but sturdy enough to absorb significant abuse. Durability is crucial.
- Look for a board with plenty of room. A cutting board should offer at least 20 by 15 inches of space. Any smaller, and you'll end up feeling cramped when breaking down a chicken or chopping vegetables.
- Look for a mid-weight (5 pounds or less) board. A cutting board shouldn't be so heavy that you hesitate to pull it out; on the flip side, a lightweight cutting board could be too flimsy to withstand much cutting.

- The weight of a cutting board contributes to its stability on the countertop. Many plastic boards, including our favorite one, have rubber strips on both sides that keep its lightweight frame anchored to the counter.

- Wooden and plastic boards must be cleaned differently. Keep in mind that wooden and bamboo boards require hand-washing and need to be oiled regularly, while a plastic board is virtually carefree and can be cleaned in the dishwasher.

Cleaning and Caring for Your Cutting Boards

Depending on the type of board, you will need to clean and care for it differently. Here are some basic tips.

SCRUB YOUR BOARD: Routine cleaning is essential; scrub your board thoroughly in hot, soapy water (or put it through the dishwasher if it's dishwasher-safe) to kill harmful bacteria, then rinse it well and dry it completely. For stubborn odors, scrub the cutting board with a paste of 1 tablespoon of baking soda and 1 teaspoon of water, then wash with hot, soapy water.

SOAK IT IN BLEACH AND WATER: To remove stubborn stains from plastic boards, mix a solution of 1 tablespoon of bleach per quart of water in the sink and immerse the board, dirty side up. When the board rises to the surface, drape a dish towel or two over its surface and sprinkle the towel with about ¼ cup bleach solution. Let it sit overnight, then wash it with hot, soapy water.

APPLY OIL: If using a wood or bamboo board, maintain it by applying a food-grade mineral oil every few weeks when the board is new, and a few times a year thereafter. The oil soaks into the fibers, creating a barrier to excess moisture. (Don't use olive or vegetable oil, which can become rancid.) Avoid leaving wood or bamboo boards in water, or they will eventually split.

Setting Up Your Cutting Station

In our test kitchen, "setting up your board" means setting up your cooking station before you begin to prep and cook. Setting up your board at home is just as important, so that you're organized and efficient.

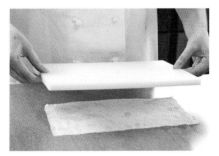  

ANCHOR YOUR BOARD: A cutting board that slides all over the counter not only is annoying, it is unsafe. If your cutting board doesn't have nonslip grips on the bottom, place either a square of wet paper towel or a small piece of shelf liner between the counter and the cutting board to hold it in place.

ORGANIZE YOUR PREP: Organizing your prepped ingredients into little bowls isn't just for TV chefs—it's a great idea for home cooks too. This setup makes it easy to grab an ingredient and add it to a hot pan at just the right moment.

KEEP IT TIDY: Don't push vegetable trimmings to one side of the cutting board. This reduces the usable work area on your board, and those trimmings always have a way of getting back under your knife. Designate a small bowl or a plastic grocery bag for trimmings.

Cutting Motions

Depending on the food being prepared, you will use different parts of the knife blade and different cutting motions. Here are four basic motions used.

SMALL ITEMS: KEEP TIP DOWN: To cut small items, such as celery, push the blade forward and down, using the blade's curve to guide the middle of the knife through smooth strokes. The tip of the blade should touch the board at all times when cutting small food.

LARGE ITEMS: LIFT BLADE UP: To cut large items, such as eggplant, lift the entire blade off the board to help make smooth strokes.

MINCING: USE BOTH HANDS: To mince herbs and garlic, grip the handle with one hand and rest the fingers of the other hand lightly toward the knife tip. This grip facilitates the up-and-down rocking motion needed for mincing. To make sure the food is evenly minced, pivot the knife as you work through the pile of food.

TOUGH ITEMS: USE THE HEEL: To cut tough foods like winter squash and bone-in chicken parts, use the heel of the knife. Use one hand to grip the handle, and place the flat palm of your other hand on top of the blade. Cut straight down into the item, pushing the blade gently. Be careful and make sure your hand and the knife are dry to prevent slippage.

Prepping Ingredients

No matter what you're cooking, you will end up prepping the same handful of ingredients again and again, so it pays to master the best and fastest techniques for chopping onions, mincing garlic and herbs, cutting up carrots, and more.

CHOPPING AN ONION

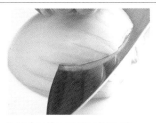  

1. Halve the onion through the root end, then peel the onion and trim the top. Make several horizontal cuts from one end of the onion to the other, but don't cut all the way through the root end.

2. Make several vertical cuts. Again, be sure to cut up to but not through the root end.

3. Rotate the onion so that the root end is in back, behind your hand, and slice the onion thinly across the previous cuts. As you slice, the onion will fall apart into chopped pieces.

PREPPING GARLIC

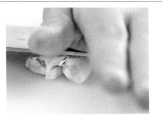  

1. Trim off the root end of the garlic clove, then crush the clove gently between the side of a chef's knife and the cutting board to loosen the papery skin. The paper skin will fall away from the garlic.

2. Using a two-handed chopping motion, run the knife over the garlic repeatedly to mince it.

3. Mincing garlic to a paste tempers its hot, raw flavor. Sprinkle minced garlic with a pinch of salt, then scrape the blade of the knife back and forth over the garlic until it forms a sticky paste.

PREPPING GINGER

1. To quickly peel a knob of ginger, hold it firmly against a cutting board and use the edge of a dinner spoon to scrape away the thin brown skin.

2. To grate ginger, peel just a small section of a large piece of ginger, then grate the peeled portion using a rasp-style grater, letting the unpeeled ginger serve as a handle to keep your fingers safely away from the grater.

3. For smashed coins of ginger, slice a peeled knob of ginger crosswise into coins, then use the corner of a heavy pan (or a mallet) to gently smash the ginger and release its flavor.

CHOPPING A TOMATO

1. Remove the tomato core using a paring knife.

2. Slice the tomato crosswise.

3. Stack several slices of tomato, then slice both crosswise and widthwise into pieces as desired.

CUTTING A CARROT

1. Using a chef's knife, cut a peeled carrot in half width-wise, separating the thick root end from the thin, tapered end.

2. Halve the carrot pieces lengthwise and, if neces-sary, halve the thicker pieces yet again until they are all roughly the same thickness.

3. Continue to cut the carrots crosswise into similar-size pieces as desired.

CUTTING BROCCOLI

1. Place the head of broccoli upside down on a cutting board and cut off the florets.

2. Slice the larger florets into bite-size pieces by slicing them through the stem.

3. Cut away the tough outer peel and square off the stalks using a chef's knife, then slice the stalks into pieces.

CUTTING A BELL PEPPER

1. Slice off the top and bottom of the pepper and remove the seeds and stem.

2. Slice down through the side of the pepper.

3. Lay the pepper flat, trim away any remaining ribs and seeds, then cut it into pieces or strips as desired.

PREPPING LEEKS

1. Trim and discard the root and dark green leaves.

2. Cut the trimmed leek in half lengthwise, then slice it crosswise.

3. Submerge cut leeks in a bowl of water and rinse thoroughly to remove dirt and sand. Drain the washed leeks.

PREPPING MUSHROOMS

1. We think that mushrooms should be rinsed under cold water just before being cooked; if this is done too far in advance, the exterior of the mushrooms will turn dark and slimy. If you are going to eat your mushrooms raw, however, don't wash them but brush the dirt away with a soft pastry brush or cloth.

2. For mushrooms with tender stems, such as white button mushrooms and cremini, the stems can be trimmed, then prepped and cooked alongside the caps. For mushrooms with tough, woody stems, such as shiitakes and portobellos, the stem should be removed and discarded.

3. When cooking portobello mushrooms in soups or stews, you may want to remove the gills on the underside of the cap or else your dish will look and taste muddy. Use a soup-spoon to scrape the gills off the underside of the mushroom cap.

PREPPING FRESH HERBS

1. To mince fresh herbs, place one hand on the handle of a chef's knife and rest the fingers of your other hand lightly on top of the knife blade. Use an up-and-down rocking motion to evenly mince the herbs, pivoting the knife as you chop.

2. For thin-stemmed thyme or rosemary sprigs, chop the stems along with the leaves, discarding the tough bottoms. If the stems are thicker, hold the sprig upright by the top and run your thumb and forefinger along the stem to release the leaves. The tender tips can be chopped along with the leaves once the woodier stems have been sheared clean and discarded.

3. To shred (or chiffonade) basil, stack several clean leaves on top of one another. Roll them up, then slice the roll crosswise into shreds.

Know Your Thermometers and Timers

Thermometers take the guesswork out of knowing when foods are done and are vital for ensuring success in the kitchen. A well-stocked kitchen will contain the three types of thermometers listed here; in addition to these three, a refrigerator/freezer thermometer is also a good idea. A kitchen timer is one of those things that most home cooks don't much think about, but precise timing is key to many aspects of successful cooking, especially baking, so a good kitchen timer is an essential piece of equipment. See Shopping for Equipment on pages 795–796 for more information and the test kitchen's buying recommendations.

INSTANT-READ THERMOMETERS

An instant-read thermometer, coupled with knowledge of how temperatures relate to doneness, will ensure success in the kitchen. And an instant-read thermometer is vital when cooking steaks or beef roasts to a specific doneness (rare, medium-rare, etc.), and for ensuring perfectly cooked chicken or pork.

- Buy a digital model. These models (as opposed to dial-face models) are easier to use because you can take a quick look and immediately know the temperature of your food.
- Look for a long stem.
- A quick response is vital.
- Water-resistant is good.

CANDY/DEEP FRY THERMOMETERS

Candy/deep fry thermometers are designed for stovetop recipes that require close monitoring of temperature. Unless you have a high-end instant-read thermometer with a range that reaches up to 400 degrees, you won't be able to monitor the temperature of very hot oil or other liquids, such as caramel sauce, without a candy/deep-fry thermometer.

- Readability is key.
- Get one that attaches to the pan.

OVEN THERMOMETERS

Since it is fairly common for ovens to run either hot or cold, the most reliable way to know the exact temperature of your oven is to use an oven thermometer. Oven thermometers are cheap and easy to use, so there is no reason to avoid relying on one to keep tabs on your oven and adjust the temperature if necessary.

- Look for a clear display with large numbers.
- It should attach securely.

KITCHEN TIMERS

While all timers are basically the same, these are the features we deem particularly important.

- It should have a lengthy time range, from 1 second to at least 10 hours.
- It should be able to count up after the alarm goes off.
- It should be easy to use and read.

CALIBRATING AN INSTANT-READ THERMOMETER

You should check your instant-read thermometer's accuracy when you first buy it and then again periodically. To do this, put a mixture of ice and cold tap water in a glass or bowl; allow this mixture to sit for several minutes to let the temperature stabilize. Put the probe in the slush, being careful not to touch the sides or bottom of the glass or bowl. On a digital thermometer, press the "calibrate" button to 32 degrees; on a dial-face thermometer, turn the dial to 32 degrees (the method differs from model to model; you may need pliers to turn a small knob on the back).

Taking the Temperature of Food

Whether cooking a burger or roasting a beef tenderloin, you should always take the temperature of the area of the meat that will be the last to finish cooking, which is the thickest part or, in some cases, the center. Bones conduct heat, so if the meat you are cooking contains bone, make sure that the thermometer is not touching it. For especially large roasts, take more than one reading to confirm you're at the right point of doneness. Also see Doneness Temperatures for Meat, Poultry, and Fish on page 15.

STEAKS, CHOPS, AND SMALL ROASTS

When taking the temperature of thin steaks or pork chops, it's easy to insert the thermometer too far or not far enough. To avoid this mistake, use tongs to hold the meat, then insert the thermometer sideways into the center, taking care not to hit any bones. You can also use this technique for pork tenderloin or rack of lamb; just lift the meat with a pair of tongs and insert the thermometer into the end, parallel to the meat.

BURGERS

Leave the burger in the pan (or on the grill), slide the tip of the thermometer into the burger at the top edge, and push it toward the center, making sure to avoid hitting the pan (or grill) with the probe. This technique keeps the burger in the pan (rather than requiring you to pick it up with tongs) and prevents it from falling apart.

POULTRY

Because breast meat cooks faster than thigh meat, you should take the temperature of both when cooking poultry. When doing so, try to avoid hitting bones, cavities, or the surface of the pan, as this will result in an inaccurate reading. When temping a whole chicken, use the following methods:

A. FOR THIGH MEAT: Insert the thermometer at an angle into the area between the drumstick and the breast, taking care not to hit the bone. It should register 175 degrees.
B. FOR BREAST MEAT: Insert the thermometer from the neck end, holding the thermometer parallel to the bird. It should register 160 degrees.
If cooking chicken or turkey pieces, use the same technique described above, while lifting the piece with tongs and inserting the thermometer sideways into the thickest part of the meat, taking care to avoid bones.

BREAD

A thermometer is useful when baking bread. First, you can use it to check the temperature of the liquid, which is crucial in many recipes. And you can use it to be sure your bread is done. Rustic breads are generally done at 200 to 210 degrees, while rich, buttery yeast breads are done when they reach 190 to 200 degrees.

A. FOR FREE-FORM LOAVES: Insert the probe through the side or bottom of the loaf, making sure the probe reaches the center.
B. FOR LOAVES BAKED IN A PAN: To avoid a hole in the top crust, insert the thermometer from the side, just above the edge of the pan, directing it downward toward the center of the loaf.

Doneness Temperatures for Meat, Poultry, and Fish

Since the temperature of beef and pork will continue to rise as they rest—an effect called carryover cooking—they should be removed from the oven, grill, or pan when they are 5 to 10 degrees below the desired serving temperature. Carryover cooking doesn't apply to poultry and fish (they lack the dense muscle structure of beef and pork and don't retain heat as well), so they should be cooked to the desired serving temperatures. The following temperatures should be used to determine when to stop the cooking process.

FOR THIS INGREDIENT...	COOK TO THIS TEMPERATURE
BEEF/LAMB	
Rare	115 to 120 degrees (120 to 125 degrees after resting)
Medium-Rare	120 to 125 degrees (125 to 130 degrees after resting)
Medium	130 to 135 degrees (135 to 140 degrees after resting)
Medium-Well	140 to 145 degrees (145 to 150 degrees after resting)
Well-Done	150 to 155 degrees (155 to 160 degrees after resting)
PORK	
Chops and Tenderloin	145 degrees (150 degrees after resting)
Loin Roasts	140 degrees (145 degrees after resting)
CHICKEN	
White Meat	160 degrees
Dark Meat	175 degrees
FISH	
Rare	110 degrees (for tuna only)
Medium-Rare	125 degrees (for tuna or salmon)
Medium	140 degrees (for white-fleshed fish)

Doneness Temperatures for Various Other Foods

We rely on temperature to gauge when many other foods are done cooking, not just meat, poultry, and seafood. Here's a partial list, including temperatures for frying oil and for water for bread baking.

FOOD	DONENESS TEMPERATURE
Oil, for frying	325 to 375 degrees
Sugar, for caramel	350 degrees
Yeast bread, rustic and lean	195 to 210 degrees
Yeast bread, sweet and rich	190 to 200 degrees
Custard, for ice cream	180 degrees
Custard, for crème anglaise or lemon curd	170 to 180 degrees
Custard, baked (such as crème brûlée or crème caramel)	170 to 175 degrees
Water, for bread baking	105 to 115 degrees (sometimes)

COOKING MEAT THOROUGHLY

The doneness temperatures in the charts represent the test kitchen's best assessment of palatability weighed against safety. In most cases, those concerns align. Rare chicken isn't very tasty, or very safe. There are a few notable exceptions, especially in regards to ground meat. If safety is your primary concern, you don't want to eat rare burgers. The U.S. Department of Agriculture has issued a complex set of rules regarding the cooking of meat and poultry. Here are the basics.

WHOLE CUTS: Cook whole cuts of meat, including pork, to an internal temperature of at least 145 degrees and let rest at least three minutes.

GROUND MEAT: Cook to an internal temperature of at least 160 degrees.

POULTRY: Cook all poultry, including ground poultry, to an internal temperature of at least 165 degrees.

Basic Food Safety

Basic sanitation practices can dramatically reduce the risk of food-borne illness. Here are the test kitchen's best practices for how to handle, defrost, cook, cool, store, and reheat food, as well as important tips for keeping your refrigerator cool and your kitchen clean.

Handling Foods Carefully

Raw meat, poultry, and eggs may carry harmful bacteria like salmonella, listeria, or E. coli. Cooking kills off these bacteria—ensuring the food is perfectly safe to eat—but it's critical to be careful about how you handle raw foods in the kitchen in order to avoid cross-contamination.

SEPARATE RAW AND COOKED FOODS: Keep raw and cooked foods separate to prevent the spread of bacteria. Never place cooked food on a plate or cutting board that has come into contact with raw food (meat or not), and wash any utensil (including a thermometer) that comes in contact with raw food before reusing it.

PUT UP BARRIERS: Items that come in contact with both raw and cooked food, like scales and platters, should be covered with aluminum foil or plastic wrap to create a protective barrier. Once the item has been used, the protective layer should be discarded—taking any bacteria with it. Similarly, wrapping your cutting board with plastic wrap before pounding meat and poultry on it will limit the spread of bacteria.

DO NOT RINSE RAW BEEF, PORK, OR POULTRY: Avoid rinsing raw beef, pork, or poultry, as doing so is likely to spread contaminants around your sink (and perhaps onto nearby foods sitting on the counter). Cooking food to a safe internal temperature will kill surface bacteria more effectively than rinsing. And our kitchen tests failed to demonstrate any flavor benefit to rinsing meat or poultry before cooking.

SEASON SAFELY: Though most bacteria can't live for more than a few minutes in direct contact with salt, they can live on the edges of a box or shaker. To avoid contamination, we grind pepper into a clean, small bowl and then mix it with salt (using a ratio of 1 part pepper to 4 parts kosher salt or 2 parts table salt). We reach into the bowl for seasoning without having to wash our hands every time. Then the bowl goes in the dishwasher.

DO NOT RECYCLE USED MARINADES: It may seem economical to reuse marinades, but used marinade is contaminated with raw meat juice and is therefore unsafe to consume. If you want a sauce to serve with cooked meat, make a little extra marinade and set it aside before adding the rest to the raw meat.

Storing Foods Safely

Within the "danger zone" of 40 to 140 degrees, bacteria double about every 20 minutes. As a general rule, food shouldn't stay in this zone for more than 2 hours (1 hour if the room temperature is over 90 degrees).

DEFROST IN THE FRIDGE: Defrosting should always be done in the refrigerator, not on the counter, where the temperature is higher and bacteria can multiply rapidly. Always place food on a plate or in a bowl while defrosting to prevent any liquid it releases from coming in contact with other foods. Most food will take 24 hours to thaw fully. (Larger items, like whole turkeys, can take far longer; count on about 4 hours per pound.)

COOL ON THE COUNTER: Do not put hot foods in the fridge right after cooking. This will cause the temperature in the refrigerator to rise, making it potentially hospitable to the spread of bacteria. The U.S. Food and Drug Administration recommends cooling foods to 70 degrees within the first 2 hours after cooking, and to 40 degrees within another 4 hours. We cool food on the counter for about an hour, until it reaches 80 to 90 degrees, then put it in the fridge.

REHEAT RAPIDLY: When food is reheated, it should be brought through the danger zone as rapidly as possible—don't let it come slowly to a simmer. Bring leftover sauces, soups, and gravies to a boil, and make sure casseroles reach at least 165 degrees, using an instant-read thermometer to determine when they're at the proper temperature.

ADDITIONAL SAFETY TIPS

Keeping Your Fridge Cool

A refrigerator thermometer will tell you if your fridge and freezer are working properly. Check the temperature of both regularly to ensure that the refrigerator is between 35 and 40 degrees and that the freezer is below zero degrees.

At right are the recommended storage temperatures for specific foods. Keep in mind that the back of a refrigerator is the coldest part, while the door is the least cold. Make sure that raw meat is stored well wrapped and never on shelves that are above other food.

Fish and Shellfish	30° to 43°
Meat and Poultry	32° to 36°
Dairy Products	36° to 40°
Eggs	38° to 40°
Produce	40° to 45°

Keeping Your Kitchen Clean

Depending on factors such as moisture, temperature, and surface porosity, microbes can live as long as 60 hours. But you don't need anything special to clean a kitchen—for the most part, we rely on old-fashioned soap and hot water or a bleach solution.

Since a wet sponge is an ideal host for bacteria, whenever possible use a paper towel or dish towel instead. If you do use a sponge, disinfect it. We tested myriad methods for disinfecting sponges, and lab results showed that microwaving and boiling were the most effective. Since sponges have been known to catch fire in high-powered microwaves, we prefer to boil them for 5 minutes.

- **Wash Your Hands**
- **Sanitize Your Sink**
- **Clean Your Sponges**
- **Clean Your Cutting Boards**
  (see page 8)

Appetizers

■ SIGNIFIES A **FAST** RECIPE (45 MINUTES OR LESS)

Herbed Spinach Dip

SERVES 4 TO 6   **TOTAL TIME** 1 HOUR 15 MINUTES

✔ **WHY THIS RECIPE WORKS:** All too often, spinach dip is the one appetizer left almost untouched when the party is over. For a spinach dip to really taste good, we found that both the ingredients and the method were key. We enriched our dip with equal amounts of mayonnaise and sour cream, while the addition of herbs and other aromatics ensured that it had bright flavor (and texture). For the mixing method, we used the food processor to help distribute the thawed spinach perfectly throughout the dip. The garlic must be minced or pressed before going into the food processor or else the dip will contain large chunks of garlic. Serve with crudités.

1 (10-ounce) package frozen chopped spinach, thawed and squeezed dry
½ red bell pepper, stemmed, seeded, and chopped fine
½ cup sour cream
½ cup mayonnaise
½ cup packed fresh parsley leaves
1 tablespoon fresh dill or 1 teaspoon dried
3 scallions, sliced thin
1 garlic clove, minced
¼ teaspoon hot sauce
   Salt and pepper

Process all ingredients with ½ teaspoon salt and ¼ teaspoon pepper in food processor until well combined, about 1 minute. Transfer to serving bowl, cover, and refrigerate until flavors have blended, at least 1 hour or up to 1 day. Season with salt and pepper to taste before serving.

VARIATIONS

Spinach Dip with Blue Cheese and Bacon

Omit red bell pepper, dill, salt, and hot sauce. Add ⅓ cup crumbled blue cheese to food processor with spinach. Sprinkle with 2 slices cooked, crumbled bacon before serving.

Spinach Dip with Feta, Lemon, and Oregano

Omit red bell pepper, dill, and salt. Add 2 tablespoons fresh oregano, ½ cup crumbled feta cheese, 1 teaspoon grated lemon zest, and 1 tablespoon lemon juice to food processor with spinach. Season with salt to taste before serving.

Cilantro-Lime Spinach Dip

This dip is good served with tortilla chips.

Omit red bell pepper, dill, and hot sauce. Add ¼ cup fresh cilantro leaves, 1 tablespoon chopped canned chipotle chile in adobo sauce, ½ teaspoon grated lime zest, 1 tablespoon lime juice, ½ teaspoon light brown sugar, and ⅛ teaspoon cumin to food processor with spinach.

French Onion Dip

SERVES 4 TO 6   **TOTAL TIME** 1 HOUR 15 MINUTES

✔ **WHY THIS RECIPE WORKS:** Stirring a packet of onion soup mix into sour cream has long been the go-to method for this popular party dip; we were determined to do better. By chopping onions instead of slicing them (for more surface area), and then starting them over medium heat, we created deep color and caramelized flavor in only 30 minutes. A base of sour cream and mayonnaise provided balanced flavor and creaminess, and a pinch of cayenne added heat, while balsamic vinegar lent sweetness and mellow tang. Serve with potato chips.

3 tablespoons unsalted butter
2 pounds onions, chopped fine
   Salt and pepper
⅛ teaspoon cayenne pepper
¼ cup water
2½ teaspoons balsamic vinegar
1 cup sour cream
½ cup mayonnaise

1. Melt butter in 12-inch skillet over medium heat. Add onions, ½ teaspoon salt, ½ teaspoon pepper, and cayenne and cook, stirring occasionally, until onions are translucent, about 10 minutes. Reduce heat to medium-low and cook until onions are golden, about 10 minutes.

2. Add 2 tablespoons water to skillet, scraping up any browned bits, and cook until water has evaporated, about 5 minutes. Add remaining 2 tablespoons water and cook until onions are caramelized and water has evaporated, about 5 minutes. Remove from heat and stir in vinegar.

3. Transfer onions to medium serving bowl and let cool for 10 minutes. Stir in sour cream and mayonnaise and season with salt and pepper to taste. Cover and refrigerate until flavors have blended, at least 30 minutes or up to 1 day. Season with salt and pepper to taste before serving.

The cool heat of wasabi paste and savory soy sauce add big flavor to this unusual dip.

Wasabi Dip

SERVES 8 TO 10   **TOTAL TIME** 1 HOUR 10 MINUTES

✔ **WHY THIS RECIPE WORKS:** For this dip, we punched up a base of tangy cream cheese with savory soy sauce and the cool heat of wasabi paste. This dip is slightly spicy; add more or less wasabi paste to make it more or less spicy. To soften cream cheese quickly, microwave it for 20 to 30 seconds. We like the clean flavor of crisp rice crackers with this dip, or serve it with crudités, potato chips, or Pita Chips (page 24).

  1 **pound cream cheese, softened**
 ¼ **cup milk**
  2 **tablespoons soy sauce**
  2 **tablespoons lemon juice**
  5 **teaspoons wasabi paste**
  4 **scallions, minced**
     Salt and pepper
  2 **tablespoons minced fresh cilantro**

Whisk cream cheese, milk, soy sauce, lemon juice, wasabi paste, and scallions together in serving bowl until well combined. Cover and refrigerate until flavors have blended, at least 1 hour or up to 1 day. Season with salt and pepper to taste and sprinkle with cilantro before serving.

Creamy Blue Cheese Dip

SERVES 8 TO 10   **TOTAL TIME** 40 MINUTES **FAST**

✔ **WHY THIS RECIPE WORKS:** The key to full-flavored blue cheese dip is to use a combination of dairy ingredients—namely, sour cream and mayonnaise. Whenever we tried to eliminate either one of these for the sake of convenience, tasters complained of seriously compromised flavor. Serve with crudités, potato chips, or Oven-Baked Buffalo Wings (page 49).

  6 **ounces blue cheese, crumbled (1½ cups)**
 ½ **cup buttermilk, plus extra as needed**
  1 **garlic clove, minced**
 ⅓ **cup sour cream**
  6 **tablespoons mayonnaise**
  2 **tablespoons white wine vinegar**
 ½ **teaspoon sugar**
     Salt and pepper

Using fork, mash blue cheese, buttermilk, and garlic together in serving bowl until mixture resembles cottage cheese. Stir in sour cream, mayonnaise, vinegar, sugar, ½ teaspoon salt, and ½ teaspoon pepper. Add extra buttermilk as needed to adjust dip consistency. Cover and refrigerate until flavors have blended, at least 30 minutes or up to 1 day. Season with salt and pepper to taste before serving.

Artichoke Dip

SERVES 6 TO 8   **TOTAL TIME** 40 MINUTES **FAST**

✔ **WHY THIS RECIPE WORKS:** Most artichoke dips are made with jarred artichokes packed in marinade. We found that these artichokes barely tasted of artichokes and could have off-flavors from the marinade. Dips made with canned artichokes were not much better. For the freshest-tasting dip, we turned to thawed frozen artichokes. And for the base a simple mixture of cream cheese and freshly grated Parmesan did the trick. To soften cream cheese quickly, microwave it for 20 to 30 seconds. Serve with crackers or Crostini (page 30).

9   ounces frozen artichokes, thawed and patted dry
8   ounces cream cheese, softened
1   ounce Parmesan cheese, grated (½ cup)
2   garlic cloves, minced
    Salt and pepper
1   tablespoon minced fresh parsley

Process artichokes, cream cheese, Parmesan, garlic, ¼ teaspoon salt, and ⅛ teaspoon pepper in food processor until mostly smooth, about 1 minute. Transfer to serving bowl, cover, and refrigerate until flavors have blended, at least 30 minutes or up to 1 day. Season with salt and pepper to taste and sprinkle with parsley before serving.

Roasted Eggplant Dip

SERVES 6 TO 8   **TOTAL TIME** 2 HOURS

☑ **WHY THIS RECIPE WORKS:** Roasting eggplant develops deep flavor and turns its texture silky-smooth; the oven makes roasting it easy. It's necessary to drain the excess liquid from the roasted eggplant to avoid a watery dip. We seasoned the dip with traditional Middle Eastern flavors of lemon, garlic, and tahini. Tahini is a sesame paste that is now widely available; be sure to stir it before measuring it. Select eggplants with shiny, taut, unbruised skin and an even shape (so they will cook evenly). Serve with fresh pita wedges or cucumber slices.

2   pounds eggplant, halved lengthwise
¼   cup extra-virgin olive oil
    Salt and pepper
2   tablespoons tahini
1   tablespoon lemon juice
1   garlic clove, minced
1   tablespoon minced fresh parsley

1. Adjust oven rack to middle position and heat oven to 400 degrees. Line rimmed baking sheet with aluminum foil. Using tip of chef's knife, score 1-inch diamond pattern into each eggplant half, making cuts about 1 inch deep. Brush with 2 tablespoons oil and season with salt and pepper.

2. Lay eggplants, cut side down, on prepared baking sheet and roast until very soft and skin is shriveled and shrunken, 45 to 60 minutes. Let eggplants cool slightly, about 5 minutes.

3. When cool enough to handle, scoop eggplant pulp, including any pulp that has stuck to foil, into mesh strainer set over bowl and let drain for 3 minutes.

4. Pulse drained eggplant pulp, remaining 2 tablespoons oil, tahini, lemon juice, garlic, ½ teaspoon salt, and ¼ teaspoon

pepper in food processor until coarsely pureed. Transfer to serving bowl, cover, and refrigerate until chilled, at least 30 minutes or up to 1 day. Season with salt and pepper to taste and sprinkle with parsley before serving.

Scoring an Eggplant

Using tip of chef's knife (or paring knife), score 1-inch diamond pattern into each eggplant half, making cuts about 1 inch deep.

Middle Eastern Roasted Red Pepper Dip

SERVES 8 TO 10   **TOTAL TIME** 40 MINUTES   **FAST**

☑ **WHY THIS RECIPE WORKS:** Our quick version of this very traditional Middle Eastern dip is simple to make and bursting with authentic flavors. Once again the food processor shines and transforms this unique collection of ingredients into a powerhouse dip. While roasted red peppers are the star, contrasting ingredients such as walnuts, molasses, and wheat crackers add complexity, revealing sweet, smoky, and savory flavors that are truly unique to this dip. Serve with Pita Chips (page 24), fresh pita wedges, or Crostini (page 30).

1½ cups jarred roasted red peppers, rinsed and
    patted dry
1   cup walnuts, toasted
¼   cup plain wheat crackers, crumbled
3   tablespoons lemon juice
2   tablespoons extra-virgin olive oil
1   tablespoon molasses
1   teaspoon honey
½   teaspoon ground cumin
⅛   teaspoon cayenne pepper
    Salt and pepper
1   tablespoon minced fresh parsley

Pulse all ingredients, except parsley, with ¾ teaspoon salt in food processor until smooth, about 10 pulses. Transfer to serving bowl, cover, and refrigerate until flavors have blended, at least 30 minutes or up to 1 day. Season with salt and pepper to taste and sprinkle with parsley before serving.

When done right, a platter of crudités gives you a fresh and healthy appetizer offering that puts those prepackaged vegetable "rings" at the supermarket to shame. Prepping the vegetables is half the battle but it's easy to prep them properly and arrange them so that the platter looks attractive. Serve vegetables on their own or with one of our dips.

TO BLANCH: In order to make appealing (and edible) crudités, some vegetables must first be blanched, then shocked in ice water. Bring 6 quarts water and 2 tablespoons salt to a boil in a large pot over high heat. Cook the vegetables, one variety at a time, until slightly softened but still crunchy at the core, following the times below. Transfer the blanched vegetables immediately to a bowl of ice water until completely cool, then drain and pat dry.

ASPARAGUS: Remove one stalk of asparagus from the bunch and bend it at the thicker end until it snaps. With the broken asparagus as a guide, trim the tough ends from the remaining asparagus bunch using a chef's knife. Blanch the asparagus for 30 to 60 seconds.

BROCCOLI AND CAULIFLOWER: Place head of broccoli or cauliflower upside down on a cutting board and use a chef's knife to trim off florets close to heads. Cut larger florets into bite-size pieces by slicing down through the stem. Blanch the broccoli and cauliflower (separately) for 1 to 1½ minutes.

GREEN BEANS: Line the beans up in a row on a cutting board and trim off the inedible stem ends with one slice. Blanch the beans for 1 minute.

SNOW AND SNAP PEAS: Use a paring knife to snip off the tip of the pod and pull along the flat side to remove the tough, fibrous string that runs along the straight side of snow and snap peas. Blanch the snow and snap peas separately for 15 seconds.

CARROTS AND CELERY: Slice both celery and peeled carrots lengthwise into long, elegant lengths rather than short, stumpy pieces.

BELL PEPPERS: Slice off the top and bottom of the pepper and remove the seeds and stem. Slice down through the side of the pepper, unroll it so that it lies flat, then slice into ½-inch-wide strips.

RADISHES: Choose radishes with their green tops still attached so that each half has a leafy handle for grasping and dipping. Trim each radish and slice in half through the stem.

TO KEEP CRUDITÉS CRISP: To prepare crudités ahead, use ice cubes to help keep cut-up vegetables bright and fresh until serving time.

Canned cannellini beans make an easy dip that's boldly flavored with olive oil, garlic, fresh rosemary, and lemon.

Rosemary and Garlic White Bean Dip

SERVES 8 TO 10   **TOTAL TIME** 40 MINUTES   **FAST**

✔ **WHY THIS RECIPE WORKS:** For a white bean dip to be really terrific, it needs to have both a little texture and a lot of flavor. We reserved a handful of beans and pulsed them in at the end for an appealingly chunky texture. To give the bland beans some flavor, we used a heavy hand with raw garlic, rosemary, and lemon juice. Serve with crackers, Pita Chips, or Crostini (page 30).

   2 **(15-ounce) cans cannellini beans, rinsed**
  ½ **cup extra-virgin olive oil**
  ¼ **cup water**
  2 **tablespoons lemon juice**
  2 **garlic cloves, minced**
  ½ **teaspoon chopped fresh rosemary**
     Salt and pepper

EASY HOMEMADE PITA CHIPS

An oil mister works best here but you can also use olive oil spray. These chips work well with any type of dip.

  4 **(8-inch) white or whole-wheat pita breads**
     Olive oil spray
  1 **teaspoon salt**

1. Adjust oven racks to upper-middle and lower-middle positions and heat oven to 350 degrees. Using kitchen shears, cut around perimeter of each pita bread to yield 2 thin rounds. Stack pita rounds and, using a chef's knife, cut them into 6 wedges each. Spread pita wedges, smooth side down, over 2 rimmed baking sheets. Spray top of each chip with oil and then sprinkle with salt.

2. Bake chips until they begin to crisp and brown lightly, 8 to 10 minutes. Flip chips over so their smooth side is facing up and continue to bake until chips are fully toasted, 8 to 10 minutes longer. Remove baking sheets from oven and let cool before serving. (Chips can be stored at room temperature for up to 3 days.)
(Makes 48 chips)

1. Process two-thirds of beans, 6 tablespoons oil, water, lemon juice, garlic, and rosemary in food processor until smooth, about 10 seconds; scrape down bowl. Add remaining beans and pulse to incorporate (do not puree smooth), about 5 pulses. Season with salt and pepper to taste.

2. Transfer to serving bowl, cover, and let sit at room temperature until flavors have blended, at least 30 minutes. (Dip can be refrigerated for up to 2 days.) Before serving, season with salt and pepper to taste, make small well in center of dip, and pour remaining 2 tablespoons oil into well.

Baked Maryland Crab Dip

SERVES 6 TO 8   **TOTAL TIME** 45 MINUTES   **FAST**

✔ **WHY THIS RECIPE WORKS:** Unlike other crab dips, ours keeps the ratio of crab to cheese high and limits the amount of mayonnaise, allowing the sweet crab flavor to come through. We softened the onions in the microwave, then gently combined them with the crabmeat and cheese. Just a bit of Old Bay seasoning, coriander, and parsley rounded out our dip, accenting the crab and allowing it to shine. Do not substitute imitation crabmeat here. To soften cream cheese quickly, microwave it for 20 to 30 seconds. Serve with crackers or Melba toast.

1 **small onion, chopped fine**
2 **tablespoons unsalted butter**
4 **ounces cream cheese, cut into 1-inch chunks and softened**
2 **ounces Monterey Jack cheese, shredded (½ cup)**
¼ **cup mayonnaise**
½ **teaspoon Old Bay seasoning**
½ **teaspoon ground coriander**
¼ **teaspoon salt**
⅛ **teaspoon pepper**
8 **ounces fresh or pasteurized crabmeat, squeezed dry and picked over for shells**
2 **tablespoons minced fresh parsley**

1. Adjust oven rack to middle position and heat oven to 425 degrees. Microwave onion and butter in bowl, stirring occasionally, until softened, about 5 minutes. Stir in cream cheese, ¼ cup Monterey Jack, mayonnaise, Old Bay, coriander, salt, and pepper until combined. Gently fold in crabmeat and parsley.

2. Transfer to greased 2-cup baking dish. Sprinkle with remaining ¼ cup Monterey Jack. (Dip can be held at room temperature for up to 2 hours before baking.) Bake until browned and bubbling, 15 to 20 minutes. Let cool for 5 minutes before serving.

VARIATION
Spicy Cajun-Style Baked Crab Dip
Microwave ¼ cup minced green bell pepper and ¼ cup minced celery with onion and butter. Substitute ¾ teaspoon Cajun seasoning and ⅛ teaspoon cayenne for Old Bay and coriander.

Fresh Tomato Salsa
SERVES 8 TO 10   **TOTAL TIME** 40 MINUTES   **FAST**

✔ **WHY THIS RECIPE WORKS:** We wanted a fresh, chunky *salsa cruda* that emphasized the tomatoes. To solve the problem of watery salsa, we drained diced tomatoes in a colander. This put all tomatoes, regardless of ripeness or juiciness, on a level—and dry—playing field. Red onions were preferred for their color and flavor and jalapeño chiles because of their slight vegetal flavor and moderate heat. Lime juice tasted more authentic (and better) than red wine vinegar or lemon juice. We found the best, and simplest, way to combine the ingredients was to layer each ingredient (chopped) on top of the tomatoes while they drained. Once the tomatoes were ready, all that was needed was just a few stirs before finishing the salsa with the lime juice, salt, and sugar. For more

This fresh chunky Mexican-style salsa can be made with any tomatoes, even ordinary supermarket ones.

heat, include the jalapeño seeds and ribs when mincing. The amount of sugar and lime juice to use depends on the ripeness of the tomatoes. This salsa is perfect for tortilla chips, but it's also nice with grilled steaks, chicken, and fish.

1½ **pounds tomatoes, cored and cut into ½-inch dice**
1 **large jalapeño chile, stemmed, seeds reserved, and minced**
½ **cup finely chopped red onion**
1 **small garlic clove, minced**
¼ **cup minced fresh cilantro**
2 **teaspoons lime juice, plus extra as needed**
  Salt and pepper
  Sugar

Let tomatoes drain in colander for 30 minutes. As tomatoes drain, layer jalapeño, onion, garlic, and cilantro on top. Shake colander to drain off and discard excess tomato juice, then transfer vegetable mixture to serving bowl and stir in lime juice. (Salsa can be refrigerated for up to 3 hours.) Season with salt, pepper, sugar, and extra lime juice to taste before serving. Add reserved jalapeño seeds to increase heat as desired.

Toasted Corn and Black Bean Salsa

SERVES 8 TO 10   **TOTAL TIME** 25 MINUTES   **FAST**

✔ WHY THIS RECIPE WORKS: Although you have to get out your skillet to make this salsa, it's a great alternative to traditional salsa and is simple to make. Toasting the corn is the key to the intense flavor of our corn and black bean salsa. Compared to boiled corn, toasted corn has a deeper, more concentrated flavor and crunchier texture. The high sugar content of the corn makes toasting incredibly easy and fast in a nonstick skillet. Do not substitute frozen corn for the fresh corn here; toasting corn works best with fresh, raw corn—frozen or cooked corn doesn't brown nearly as well, nor does it have that crisp texture. Be sure to use a nonstick skillet when toasting the corn. To make this salsa spicier, add the chile seeds. Serve with tortilla chips.

- 2 tablespoons extra-virgin olive oil
- 2 ears corn, kernels cut from cobs
- 1 (15-ounce) can black beans, rinsed
- 1 red bell pepper, stemmed, seeded, and chopped fine
- 1 tomato, cored and chopped
- ½ jalapeño chile, stemmed, seeded, and minced
- 1 scallion, sliced thin
- 2 garlic cloves, minced
- 2 tablespoons lime juice
- 2 tablespoons minced fresh cilantro
- ½ teaspoon ground cumin
  Salt and pepper

Heat 1 tablespoon oil in 12-inch nonstick skillet over medium-high heat until shimmering. Add corn and cook until golden brown, 6 to 8 minutes. Transfer corn to serving bowl and stir in remaining 1 tablespoon oil and remaining ingredients except salt and pepper. (Salsa can be refrigerated for up to 1 day.) Season with salt and pepper to taste before serving.

Cutting Corn from the Cob

Stand corn upright inside large bowl and carefully cut kernels from cob using paring knife.

VARIATION
Spicy Toasted Corn and Black Bean Salsa
Add minced seeds from jalapeño and 4 teaspoons minced canned chipotle chile in adobo sauce.

Tomatillo Salsa

SERVES 6 TO 8   **TOTAL TIME** 30 MINUTES   **FAST**

✔ WHY THIS RECIPE WORKS: For a tangy, well-balanced tomatillo salsa recipe that highlighted the green, citrusy notes of the fruit and paired nicely with a variety of Mexican dishes, we briefly boiled whole husked tomatillos to soften their firm texture and tame their acidity. A few quick pulses in a food processor, along with onion, garlic, jalapeño chile, cilantro, and lime juice, and the salsa was ready to serve. We also liked the salsa recipe made with tomatillos that were broiled—their charred skins lent the salsa subtle smoky nuances. The outer husk of a fresh tomatillo should be dry, and the tomatillo itself should be bright green, with a fresh, fruity smell. While fresh tomatillos are preferred for this recipe, canned ones will work as well; substitute two 13-ounce cans tomatillos, drained, and skip step 1. Serve as a dip with tortilla chips or with grilled meats or fish, tamales, or fajitas.

- Salt
- 1 pound tomatillos, husks and stems removed, rinsed well and dried
- ½ small onion, chopped coarse
- 1 jalapeño chile, stemmed, seeds reserved, and minced
- 1 garlic clove, minced
- ½ cup fresh cilantro leaves
- 1 tablespoon lime juice
  Sugar

1. Bring 2 quarts water to boil in large saucepan. Meanwhile, fill medium bowl with ice water. Stir 2 teaspoons salt and tomatillos into boiling water. Cook tomatillos until tender, but not mushy, and color dulls slightly, 8 to 10 minutes. Drain tomatillos and plunge immediately into ice water to stop cooking; let sit until cool, about 5 minutes.

2. Drain tomatillos (no need to pat dry) and transfer to food processor. Add remaining ingredients and ½ teaspoon salt and pulse until roughly chopped, about 7 pulses, adding sugar to taste. Add reserved jalapeño seeds and sugar to taste. (Salsa can be refrigerated for up to 5 days.) Season with salt to taste before serving.

Roasted Tomatillo Salsa

Canned tomatillos cannot be substituted for fresh tomatillos in this version.

Do not mince garlic; just peel. Do not mince jalapeño; halve lengthwise, stem, and reserve seeds. Toss jalapeño, tomatillos, onion, and garlic with 1 teaspoon vegetable oil and spread out over foil-lined baking sheet. Broil 6 inches from broiler element until vegetables are well charred, 10 to 12 minutes; let cool slightly. Transfer vegetables to food processor, add remaining ingredients, and process as directed in step 2.

Guacamole

SERVES 6 TO 8   **TOTAL TIME** 15 MINUTES   FAST

✔ **WHY THIS RECIPE WORKS:** As party dips go, it's hard to beat good guacamole, but many versions are as smooth and bland as baby food. We flavor our guacamole with red onion, cilantro, cumin, and a few other add-ins to keep it interesting. We mash two avocados into a smooth puree and then gently fold in a third diced avocado and seasonings for guacamole with just the right chunky texture. Very ripe avocados are key to this recipe. Serve with tortilla chips.

  3   **avocados, halved, pitted, and cut into ½-inch cubes**
  ½   **small red onion, chopped fine**
  ¼   **cup minced fresh cilantro**
  1   **small jalapeño chile, stemmed, seeded, and minced**
  2   **tablespoons lime juice**
  1   **garlic clove, minced**
  ½   **teaspoon cumin**
      Salt

Using fork, mash 2 avocados to smooth puree in medium bowl. Fold in remaining cubed avocado, remaining ingredients, and ¼ teaspoon salt. (Guacamole can be refrigerated for up to 1 day by pressing plastic wrap directly against its surface.) Season with salt to taste before serving.

Chile con Queso

SERVES 8 TO 10   **TOTAL TIME** 30 MINUTES   FAST

✔ **WHY THIS RECIPE WORKS:** The Tex-Mex version of chile con queso is an irresistibly creamy dip for chips. The most widespread method is to add Ro-tel diced tomatoes and chiles to Velveeta, microwave, and stir. For a dip that was similarly smooth and simple to make without the plasticky flavor and waxy texture, we nixed roux-based sauces in favor of evaporated milk, which has stabilizers built in. Colby and Monterey Jack cheeses gave us a smooth-melting base. Adding a little vegetable oil kept it dippable even after cooling down, and fortifying the canned tomatoes with onion, garlic, and chipotles in adobo added complexity and heat. You can substitute ¾ cup canned diced tomatoes (drained) and 1 tablespoon chopped canned green chiles for the Ro-tel tomatoes. Serve with tortilla chips.

Preparing Avocados

  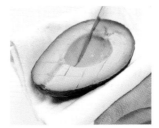 

1. After slicing avocado in half around pit, lodge edge of knife blade into pit and twist to remove.

2. Don't pull pit off with your hands. Instead, use large wooden spoon to pry pit safely off knife.

3. Use dish towel to hold avocado steady. Make ½-inch crosshatch incisions in flesh of each avocado half with knife, cutting down to but not through skin.

4. Separate diced flesh from skin with soupspoon inserted between skin and flesh, gently scooping out avocado cubes.

8 ounces Monterey Jack cheese, shredded (2 cups), room temperature
4 ounces Colby cheese, shredded (1 cup), room temperature
2 tablespoons vegetable oil
1 onion, chopped fine
1 tablespoon minced canned chipotle chile in adobo sauce
2 garlic cloves, minced
1 (10-ounce) can Ro-tel Diced Tomatoes & Green Chilies, drained
1 (12-ounce) can evaporated milk
2 tablespoons water
Salt and pepper

1. Place Monterey Jack, Colby, and 1 tablespoon oil in blender; set aside. Heat remaining 1 tablespoon oil in medium saucepan over medium-high heat until shimmering. Add onion and cook until golden brown, about 5 minutes. Stir in chipotle and garlic and cook until fragrant, about 30 seconds. Stir in tomatoes and cook until hot, about 2 minutes. Transfer to serving bowl.

2. Add evaporated milk and water to now-empty saucepan and bring to boil. Pour hot milk mixture over cheese in blender, cover, and process until smooth, about 30 seconds. Pour cheese into serving bowl with tomato mixture and stir to combine. Season with salt and pepper to taste. Let sit for 10 minutes to thicken slightly. Serve. (Dip can be refrigerated for up to 1 day. To rewarm cooled dip, microwave in 20-second bursts, stirring at each interval, until melted.)

Ultimate Seven-Layer Dip

SERVES 8 TO 10   **TOTAL TIME** 1 HOUR

✔ **WHY THIS RECIPE WORKS:** With bold Southwestern flavors and an appealing ingredient list, seven-layer dip recipes sound like a hit, but most versions of this party classic assume that guests won't notice the messy layers and tired flavors. In our version, canned black beans stood in for refried beans, while garlic, chili powder, and lime juice added flavor. We found that sour cream on its own quickly watered down our dip, but combining it with cheese gave this layer more structure. This recipe is usually served in a clear dish so you can see the layers. For a crowd, double the recipe and serve in a 13 by 9-inch glass baking dish. If you don't have time to make fresh guacamole as called for, simply mash three avocados with 3 tablespoons lime juice and ½ teaspoon salt. Serve with tortilla chips.

Fresh ingredients and bold Tex-Mex flavors form the contrasting textures and layers of this classic party dip.

4 large tomatoes, cored, seeded, and chopped fine
2 jalapeño chiles, stemmed, seeded, and minced
3 tablespoons minced fresh cilantro
6 scallions, 2 minced and 4 with green parts only, sliced thin
2 tablespoons plus 2 teaspoons lime juice (2 limes)
Salt
1 (15-ounce) can black beans, drained but not rinsed
2 garlic cloves, minced
¾ teaspoon chili powder
1½ cups sour cream
1 pound pepper Jack cheese, shredded (4 cups)
1 recipe (3 cups) Guacamole (page 27)

1. Toss tomatoes, jalapeños, cilantro, minced scallions, 2 tablespoons lime juice, and ⅛ teaspoon salt in bowl. Let stand until tomatoes begin to soften, about 30 minutes. Strain through fine-mesh strainer, discard liquid, and return to bowl.

2. Meanwhile, pulse black beans, garlic, remaining 2 teaspoons lime juice, chili powder, and ⅛ teaspoon salt in food processor until mixture resembles chunky paste, about 15 pulses. Spread bean mixture evenly over bottom of 8-inch square baking dish or 1-quart glass bowl.

3. Wipe out food processor, add sour cream and 2½ cups pepper Jack, and pulse until smooth, about 15 pulses. Spread sour cream mixture evenly over bean layer. Top evenly with remaining 1½ cups pepper Jack, followed by guacamole and, finally, drained tomato mixture. (Dip can be refrigerated for up to 1 day; bring to room temperature before serving.) Sprinkle with sliced scallion greens before serving.

VARIATION
Ultimate Smoky Seven-Layer Dip
Add 1 to 3 teaspoons minced canned chipotle chile in adobo sauce to food processor with black beans. Sprinkle with 4 slices cooked, crumbled bacon before serving.

Goat Cheese with Pink Peppercorns and Herbs
SERVES 6 TO 8   **TOTAL TIME** 15 MINUTES   FAST

✓**WHY THIS RECIPE WORKS:** Goat cheese is often sold rolled in herbs or ash, which always seems more appealing than the naked log. But why not make your own rub? We started with a base of bright, eye-catching cracked pink peppercorns. Despite being unrelated to the black peppercorn, pink peppercorn has some of the familiar pungency of its namesake, but with a much more delicate, fruity, almost floral flavor. An equal amount of minced fresh thyme and a teaspoon of toasted fennel seeds round out the flavor and texture of the rub. Serve with crackers or thinly sliced baguette.

- 1 **teaspoon fennel seeds**
- 4 **teaspoons whole pink peppercorns**
- 4 **teaspoons minced fresh thyme**
- 1 **(10-ounce) log goat cheese, well chilled**
- ¼ **cup extra-virgin olive oil**

1. Toast fennel seeds in small skillet over medium heat, shaking pan, until first wisps of smoke appear, about 2 minutes. Let cool, then place in zipper-lock bag and crush coarsely with meat pounder. Place peppercorns in zipper-lock bag with fennel seeds and crush coarsely with meat pounder.

2. Combine crushed fennel and peppercorns with thyme in shallow dish. Roll goat cheese log in mixture to coat thoroughly, pressing gently to adhere. Transfer cheese to serving plate and sprinkle with any remaining herb mixture. (Cheese can be refrigerated for up to 8 hours.) Drizzle with oil before serving.

Crushed pink peppercorns and fennel seeds transform a log of goat cheese into an impressive appetizer.

Preparing a Goat Cheese Log

1. Place toasted fennel seeds in zipper-lock bag and crush coarsely with meat pounder. Then add peppercorns to bag and crush again.

2. After combining fennel seeds, peppercorns, and minced thyme in shallow dish, roll goat cheese in mixture, pressing gently so it will adhere.

CROSTINI

Crostini make for quick and easy hors d'oeuvres. Arrange these little toasts next to a cheese platter or dip, or serve them with one of our toppings. We like to use baguettes for crostini because their narrow shape makes toasts that are the perfect size.

1 (12-Inch) baguette, sliced ½ inch thick on bias
1 garlic clove, peeled and sliced in half
2 tablespoons extra-virgin olive oil
 Salt and pepper

Adjust oven rack to middle position and heat oven to 400 degrees. Arrange bread in single layer on large baking sheet. Bake until dry and crisp, about 10 minutes, flipping slices over halfway through baking. Rub garlic clove over one side of toasted slices and brush with olive oil. Sprinkle with salt and pepper to taste. (Crostini can be stored at room temperature for several hours.) (Makes 25 to 30 toasts)

FRESH MOZZARELLA AND PESTO `FAST`
Top crostini with diced fresh mozzarella tossed with basil pesto, salt, and pepper.

GOAT CHEESE AND TOMATOES `FAST`
Spread crostini with thin layer of soft goat cheese and top with seeded, diced tomatoes seasoned with salt, pepper, and minced fresh herbs.

HUMMUS WITH ROASTED RED PEPPERS AND LEMON `FAST`
Spread crostini with hummus, top with coarsely chopped roasted red peppers, minced fresh parsley, and squeeze of fresh lemon juice.

CANNELLINI BEANS WITH LEMON AND GARLIC `FAST`
Top crostini with well-rinsed cannellini beans slightly mashed and mixed with fresh lemon juice, minced garlic, minced shallot, chopped fresh parsley, salt, and red pepper flakes.

ARTICHOKES, PARMESAN, AND BALSAMIC VINEGAR `FAST`
Top crostini with coarsely chopped canned artichoke hearts tossed with olive oil, balsamic vinegar, and chopped fresh basil. Then top with shaved Parmesan.

Baked Brie en Croûte

SERVES 6 TO 8   **TOTAL TIME** 1 HOUR 15 MINUTES

✔ **WHY THIS RECIPE WORKS:** Freezing the Brie for 20 minutes is a trick we discovered to keep the cheese from melting too much during baking. Also, while this recipe calls for apricot preserves or hot pepper jelly, other fruit preserves or chutney can be used. Use a firm, fairly unripe Brie for this recipe. It is best to thaw the puff pastry dough in the refrigerator overnight, but you can also thaw it on the counter; this can take between 30 and 60 minutes, depending upon the temperature of your kitchen. Serve with crackers or bread.

1 (9½ by 9-inch) sheet frozen puff pastry, thawed
1 large egg, lightly beaten
1 (8-ounce) wheel firm Brie cheese
¼ cup apricot preserves or hot pepper jelly

1. Line rimmed baking sheet with parchment paper. Roll puff pastry into 12-inch square on lightly floured counter. Using pie plate or other round guide, trim pastry to 9-inch circle with paring knife. Brush edges lightly with beaten egg. Place Brie in center of pastry and wrap pastry around cheese, leaving small circle of Brie exposed on top. Brush pastry with egg and transfer to prepared baking sheet. (Brie can be refrigerated for up to 1 day before freezing.)

2. Freeze Brie for 20 minutes. Adjust oven rack to middle position and heat oven to 425 degrees. Bake wrapped cheese until pastry is deep golden brown, 20 to 25 minutes.

3. Transfer to wire rack. Spoon preserves into exposed center of Brie and let cool for about 30 minutes. Serve.

Wrapping Brie in Puff Pastry

1. Lift pastry up over cheese, pleating it at even intervals and leaving opening in center where Brie is exposed.

2. Press pleated edge of pastry up into rim, which will later be filled with preserves or jelly.

Baked Goat Cheese with Olive Oil and Herbs

SERVES 6 TO 8   **TOTAL TIME** 25 MINUTES   `FAST`

✓ **WHY THIS RECIPE WORKS:** The beauty of this recipe is that it transforms a simple log of goat cheese into an impressive appetizer but requires only ingredients most people already have in the pantry. Drizzled with fragrant olive oil enhanced with honey, herbs, and lemon zest, the cheese is then baked and served warm. Serve with crackers or Crostini.

- 1 (12-ounce) log goat cheese, chilled
- ⅓ cup extra-virgin olive oil
- 2 teaspoons honey
- ½ teaspoon grated lemon or orange zest
- ½ teaspoon herbes de Provence
- ¼ teaspoon salt
- ⅛ teaspoon pepper
- ⅛ teaspoon red pepper flakes

Adjust oven rack to middle position and heat oven to 400 degrees. Using dental floss, slice goat cheese into ⅓-inch-thick rounds. Shingle cheese into small casserole dish. Whisk olive oil, honey, lemon zest, herbes de Provence, salt, pepper, and pepper flakes together in bowl, then pour over cheese. Bake until oil is bubbling and cheese begins to brown around edges, 10 to 15 minutes. Serve warm.

Caprese Skewers

SERVES 8 TO 10   **TOTAL TIME** 20 MINUTES   `FAST`

✓ **WHY THIS RECIPE WORKS:** To translate Caprese salad into a festive appetizer, we used toothpicks to stand bite-size portions upright on a halved grape tomato pedestal. We found that a quickly prepared garlic-infused oil, which we made by mincing garlic into a paste and stirring it into fruity extra-virgin olive oil, boosted the flavor of our baby mozzarella balls and tomatoes, as did a bit of salt and pepper. Basil leaves, skewered onto our toothpicks whole, completed the Caprese flavor profile and added a fresh touch. You will need about 30 sturdy wooden toothpicks for this recipe; avoid using very thin, flimsy toothpicks here. Placing a halved grape tomato, with its flat side facing down, on the bottom of the toothpick makes it easy to stand the skewers upright on a serving platter. You can use larger fresh mozzarella balls here, but they should be cut into ¾- to 1-inch pieces before marinating.

This fresh, easy appetizer requires just five simple ingredients.

- ¼ cup extra-virgin olive oil
- 1 garlic clove, minced into paste
- 10 ounces grape tomatoes, halved
- 8 ounces fresh baby mozzarella cheese balls
  Salt and pepper
- 1 cup fresh basil leaves

1. Whisk oil and garlic together in small bowl. In separate bowl, toss tomatoes and mozzarella with 2 tablespoons garlic oil and season with salt and pepper.

2. Skewer tomatoes, mozzarella, and basil leaves in following order from top to bottom: tomato half, basil leaf (folded if large), mozzarella ball, and tomato half with flat side facing down. Stand skewers upright on serving platter, drizzle with remaining garlic oil, and season with salt and pepper. Serve.

ALL ABOUT **CHEESES**

There is a vast variety of American and European cheeses, both in high-end cheese shops and at the supermarket. The selection listed here includes some of the more popular and widely available cheeses, with descriptions of their flavor and texture to help you put together a balanced cheese platter. Always consider pairing different flavors (strong to mild), textures (soft, semisoft, semifirm, and hard), and types of cheeses (such as goat's milk and cow's milk) to make the platter interesting. For accompaniments, choose mild-flavored bread and crackers that don't overshadow the cheese. Fresh and dried fruit, chutneys and jams, and olives are all good additions. As for portion size, figure on two to three ounces of cheese per person.

Cheese is best served at room temperature, as the flavors and aromas are muted by the cold. Remove cheeses from the refrigerator one to two hours before serving and keep them wrapped until serving time to prevent them from drying out. For long-term storage in the refrigerator, we find that cheeses are best wrapped in parchment paper and then in aluminum foil. The paper allows the cheese to breathe, while the foil keeps out off-flavors from the refrigerator and prevents the cheese from drying out.

Asiago
This cow's-milk cheese is sold at various ages. Fresh Asiago is firm like cheddar or Havarti, and the flavor is fairly mild. Aged Asiago is drier, almost like Parmesan, and has a much sharper, saltier flavor.

Brie
A popular soft cow's-milk cheese from France, Brie is creamy with a slight mushroom flavor, subtle nuttiness, and an edible rind. It is a classic choice for a cheese tray. With the rind removed, it's a good melting cheese.

Camembert
Camembert is a soft cow's-milk cheese from France with an edible rind. Similar to Brie in texture, Camembert is more pungent, with a stronger flavor.

Cheddar
This cow's-milk cheese is made predominantly in Great Britain and the United States. The American versions are usually softer in texture, with a tangy sharpness, whereas British cheddars are drier—even crumbly—with a nutty sharpness. Older farmhouse cheddar is best eaten by itself. Young cheddar is the quintessential melting cheese. Cheddar can also be found smoked. It is made in both white and orange forms.

Colby
Colby is a semisoft cow's-milk cheese from the United States that is very mild in flavor. One of only a few cheeses that have true American roots, Colby is a wonderful melting cheese.

Emmentaler
This semifirm cow's-milk cheese from Switzerland and France is a classic Swiss-style cheese. It has a fruity flavor with a sweet, buttery nuttiness.

Feta
A fresh cheese made from cow's, goat's, or sheep's milk (or a combination thereof), feta is a staple in many Mediterranean countries. It can be made in a variety of styles, from dry and crumbly to soft and creamy; flavors range from mild to tangy and salty. It is often eaten with fresh vegetables or crumbled over salads.

Fontina
Known more formally as Fontina Val d'Aosta, true fontina is a semisoft cow's-milk cheese from Italy with an earthy and delicately herbaceous flavor. The domestic variety (with its bright red coating) is buttery and melts well but lacks the complex flavor of the Italian original.

Goat Cheese
Produced in many countries in numerous forms, goat cheeses range from creamy fresh cheeses with a mild tanginess to aged cheeses that are firm, dry, and pungent. French goat cheeses (called chèvres) are typically more complex in flavor than most of their American counterparts.

Gorgonzola

Gorgonzola can be aged and quite crumbly or fairly young and creamy. Aged Gorgonzola has a much more potent blue cheese flavor, similar to Roquefort. In general, we like young Gorgonzola; its flavor is less overwhelming. Look for Gorgonzola dolce (sweet Gorgonzola).

Gouda

Gouda is a semifirm to firm cow's-milk cheese from Denmark. Semisoft gouda is mild and slightly sweet, whereas aged gouda is dry and crumbly, with deep caramel flavors and a sharp zing.

Gruyère

Gruyère is a semifirm cow's-milk cheese from France and Switzerland that is strong, fruity, and earthy in flavor, with a hint of honey-flavored sweetness.

Havarti

This semisoft cow's-milk cheese from Denmark is often flavored with herbs or caraway seeds due to its mild flavor.

Jarlsberg

Jarlsberg is a Swiss-style cow's-milk cheese from Norway that has a waxy texture and a straightforward Swiss cheese flavor, with a hint of fruitiness.

Manchego

Manchego is a semifirm to firm sheep's-milk cheese from Spain that is nutty, salty, and acidic. Serve it with crackers and fresh fruit.

Mozzarella

This popular cow's- or water buffalo's–milk cheese from Italy is available fresh or semisoft (the semisoft is also available smoked). The semisoft version, sold in blocks, is mild in flavor and usually shredded on top of pizza or melted. Fresh mozzarella is sold in oval-shaped balls of various sizes and is usually served on its own. Fresh mozzarella has a rich milk flavor and a good balance of brininess and sweetness.

Pecorino Romano

Pecorino Romano is a bone-white cheese with an intense peppery flavor and a strong sheepy quality. Like Parmesan, Pecorino Romano is designed for grating, but it has a much saltier and more pungent flavor. It is traditionally made entirely from sheep's milk.

Parmesan

Parmesan is a hard, grainy cheese made from cow's milk. We recommend authentic Italian Parmigiano-Reggiano, which has an unmistakable sweet, fruity, and nutty flavor. Commonly used for grating over pasta, Parmesan is excellent served on its own with fresh fruit.

Provolone

Provolone, a cow's-milk cheese from Italy, is made in two styles. The semifirm mild version is widely available and is usually sold sliced. There is also a firm, aged style that is salty, nutty, and spicy, with a light caramel sweetness. The latter makes a nice addition to any cheese platter.

Ricotta Salata

Fresh ricotta cheese is salted and pressed to make this firm but crumbly cheese with a texture that is similar to feta but with a flavor that is milder and far less salty. Ricotta salata is pleasingly piquant.

Roquefort

Roquefort is a blue-veined sheep's-milk cheese from France. Aged in specially designated caves, it's probably the oldest cheese known. Roquefort's flavor is bold but not overpowering, salty with a slight mineral tinge.

Prosciutto-Wrapped Figs with Gorgonzola

SERVES 8 TO 10   **TOTAL TIME** 20 MINUTES `FAST`

WHY THIS RECIPE WORKS: For this bite-size appetizer, we paired fresh, ripe figs with savory, salty prosciutto and bold, pungent blue cheese. We started by halving the figs so they'd be easy to eat, then we wrapped them in thin slices of the ham. For more flavor and to play off the savory notes of the prosciutto, we added a bit of honey. Briefly microwaving the honey ensured it was easy to drizzle. For the cheese, tasters preferred creamy, assertive Gorgonzola. Small mounds of the cheese, placed in the center of each fig before adding the honey, offered a rich, bold counterpoint to the fig's tender flesh and sweet flavor. To guarantee the prosciutto stayed put, we stuck a toothpick through the center of each fig. Be sure to choose ripe figs for this recipe. They will not only taste best, but also yield easily when mounding the blue cheese gently into the centers.

 2 ounces Gorgonzola cheese
16 fresh figs, stemmed and halved lengthwise
 1 tablespoon honey
 8 thin slices prosciutto (3 ounces), halved lengthwise

Mound 1 teaspoon Gorgonzola into center of each fig half. Microwave honey in bowl to loosen, about 10 seconds, then drizzle over cheese. Wrap prosciutto securely around figs, leaving fig ends uncovered. Secure prosciutto with toothpick and serve. (Figs can be refrigerated for up to 8 hours; bring to room temperature before serving.)

Assembling Prosciutto-Wrapped Figs

Mound 1 teaspoon of Gorgonzola in the center of each fig half, then drizzle honey over cheese. Wrap prosciutto around fig and secure with toothpick.

Pimento Cheese Spread

SERVES 10 TO 12   **TOTAL TIME** 25 MINUTES `FAST`

WHY THIS RECIPE WORKS: This deconstructed cheese ball is a popular Southern spread that can be slathered on anything from crackers and sandwiches to crudités. Drained jarred pimentos give the cheesy spread its name and trademark color, but we found that adding garlic, Worcestershire sauce, and hot sauce to the base gave the mixture a pleasant kick and complexity. We added just enough mayonnaise to bind everything together. Don't substitute store-bought preshredded cheese; it doesn't blend well and will make the spread dry and crumbly. If you can't find jarred pimentos, substitute jarred roasted red peppers.

 1 (4-ounce) jar pimentos, drained and
    patted dry (½ cup)
 6 tablespoons mayonnaise
 2 garlic cloves, minced
1½ teaspoons Worcestershire sauce
 1 teaspoon hot sauce, plus extra to taste
 1 pound extra-sharp cheddar cheese, shredded (4 cups)
    Salt and pepper

Process pimentos, mayonnaise, garlic, Worcestershire, and hot sauce together in food processor until smooth, about 20 seconds. Add cheddar and pulse until uniformly blended, with fine bits of cheese throughout, 20 to 25 pulses. Season with salt, pepper, and extra hot sauce to taste. Serve. (Cheese spread can be refrigerated for up to 2 weeks; bring to room temperature before serving.)

Classic Holiday Cheddar Cheese Ball

SERVES 15 TO 20   **TOTAL TIME** 30 MINUTES
(PLUS 3 HOURS CHILLING TIME)

WHY THIS RECIPE WORKS: The flavor and color of supermarket cheese balls make us wonder whether they contain any real cheese at all. We wanted a simple homemade recipe for cheese balls we'd be happy to serve as a holiday hors d'oeuvre. To achieve this, we used equal parts semisoft cheese and cream cheese for a firm yet spreadable consistency, and added a bit of mayonnaise for a silky texture. We also used small amounts of assertive ingredients like Worcestershire sauce, garlic, and cayenne to enhance our cheddar cheese ball's flavor without compromising the texture. To quickly soften cream cheese, microwave it for 20 to 30 seconds. Serve with crackers.

8 ounces extra-sharp cheddar cheese, shredded (2 cups)
8 ounces cream cheese, softened
2 tablespoons mayonnaise
1 tablespoon Worcestershire sauce
1 garlic clove, minced
¼ teaspoon cayenne pepper
½ cup sliced almonds, toasted

1. Process cheddar, cream cheese, mayonnaise, Worcestershire, garlic, and cayenne in food processor until smooth, about 1 minute, scraping down bowl as needed. Transfer mixture to center of large sheet of plastic wrap and twist plastic to shape cheese into rough ball; mixture will be somewhat loose. Refrigerate until firm, about 3 hours. (Cheese ball can be refrigerated for up to 2 days.)

2. Once cheese ball is firm, reshape as necessary until round and smooth. Unwrap, roll it in almonds, and let sit at room temperature for 15 minutes before serving.

VARIATIONS

Zesty Smoked Salmon Cheese Ball

SERVES 15 TO 20   TOTAL TIME 30 MINUTES
(PLUS 3 HOURS CHILLING TIME)

8 ounces dill Havarti cheese, shredded (2 cups)
8 ounces cream cheese, softened
2 tablespoons mayonnaise
4 ounces smoked salmon, chopped
1 shallot, minced
1 teaspoon grated lemon zest plus 1 tablespoon juice
½ cup minced fresh chives

1. Process all ingredients, except chives, in food processor until smooth, about 1 minute, scraping down bowl as needed. Transfer mixture to center of large sheet of plastic wrap and twist plastic to shape cheese into rough ball; mixture will be somewhat loose. Refrigerate until firm, about 3 hours. (Cheese ball can be refrigerated for up to 2 days.)

2. Once cheese ball is firm, reshape as necessary until round and smooth. Unwrap, roll it in chives, and let sit at room temperature for 15 minutes before serving.

Port Wine–Blue Cheese Ball

SERVES 15 TO 20   TOTAL TIME 30 MINUTES
(PLUS 3 HOURS CHILLING TIME)

4 ounces blue cheese, crumbled (1 cup)
4 ounces mozzarella cheese, shredded (1 cup)

8 ounces cream cheese, softened
2 tablespoons mayonnaise
1 tablespoon port wine
1 garlic clove, minced
½ cup pecans, toasted and chopped fine

1. Process all ingredients, except pecans, in food processor until smooth, about 1 minute, scraping down bowl as needed. Transfer mixture to center of large sheet of plastic wrap and twist plastic to shape cheese into rough ball; mixture will be somewhat loose. Refrigerate until firm, about 3 hours. (Cheese ball can be refrigerated for up to 2 days.)

2. Once cheese ball is firm, reshape as necessary until round and smooth. Unwrap, roll it in pecans, and let sit at room temperature for 15 minutes before serving.

Mexicali Cheese Ball

SERVES 15 TO 20   TOTAL TIME 30 MINUTES
(PLUS 3 HOURS CHILLING TIME)

8 ounces pepper Jack cheese, shredded (4 cups)
8 ounces cream cheese, softened
3 tablespoons salsa
2 tablespoons minced fresh cilantro
1 garlic clove, minced
½ cup blue corn tortilla chips, finely crushed

1. Process all ingredients, except tortilla chips, in food processor until smooth, about 1 minute, scraping down bowl as needed. Transfer mixture to center of large sheet of plastic wrap and twist plastic to shape cheese into rough ball; mixture will be somewhat loose. Refrigerate until firm, about 3 hours. (Cheese ball can be refrigerated for up to 2 days.)

2. Once cheese ball is firm, reshape as necessary until round and smooth. Unwrap, roll it in tortilla chips, and let sit at room temperature for 15 minutes before serving.

Tricolored Goat Cheese Terrine

SERVES 10 TO 12   TOTAL TIME 25 MINUTES   FAST

✓ **WHY THIS RECIPE WORKS:** For an impressive but easy cheese terrine, we alternated layers of a creamy goat cheese–cream cheese mixture with brightly flavored pesto, walnuts, and chopped sun-dried tomatoes. Spinach enhanced the bright color of the basil layer, while strong, tangy Pecorino Romano cheese intensified its punch. Using a plastic wrap–lined kitchen bowl for a mold made the terrine a snap to unmold as well as compose. Parmesan can be substituted for the Pecorino Romano. To quickly soften cream cheese, microwave it for 20 to 30 seconds. Serve with thinly sliced baguette or crackers.

1 pound cream cheese, softened
8 ounces goat cheese, softened
1 cup fresh basil leaves plus 1 tablespoon shredded
1 ounce (1 cup) baby spinach
1 ounce Pecorino Romano cheese, grated (½ cup)
2 garlic cloves, minced
2 tablespoons extra-virgin olive oil
½ cup walnuts, toasted and chopped
½ cup oil-packed sun-dried tomatoes, rinsed, patted dry, and chopped fine

1. Line 1-quart bowl with plastic wrap, leaving 4-inch over-hang. In separate bowl, combine cream cheese and goat cheese. Process 1 cup basil, spinach, Pecorino, garlic, and oil in food processor until smooth, about 1 minute.

2. Spread one-third of cream cheese mixture into bottom of prepared bowl. Spread half of basil mixture evenly over top. Sprinkle with half of walnuts and half of tomatoes. Repeat with half of remaining cream cheese mixture, followed by remaining basil mixture, remaining walnuts, and remaining tomatoes. Top with remaining cheese mixture. (Terrine can be refrigerated for up to 2 days.)

3. Flip terrine out of bowl onto platter and remove plastic. Sprinkle with shredded basil and serve.

Making Tricolored Goat Cheese Terrine

1. Spread plastic wrap–lined bowl with layers of cream cheese mixture, basil mixture, walnuts, and tomatoes.

2. To unmold, place platter on top of bowl, flip out terrine, and remove plastic wrap.

Easy Mushroom Pâté

SERVES 6 TO 8   **TOTAL TIME** 30 MINUTES
(PLUS 2 HOURS CHILLING TIME)

☑ **WHY THIS RECIPE WORKS:** To achieve a spread full of heady, earthy mushroom flavor without foraging the forests for wild specimens, we supplemented everyday white button mushrooms with dried porcini, which are intensely flavored but widely available year-round. Rather than aiming for a smooth texture, we found it best to pulse the mushrooms in the food processor until slightly chunky. Cream cheese and a couple of tablespoons of heavy cream provided a rich, creamy base. Sautéed shallots, thyme, and garlic contributed deep flavor, while lemon juice and parsley offset the earthy flavors with some brightness. Serve with Crostini (page 30), toast points, or crackers.

1 ounce dried porcini mushrooms, rinsed
1 pound white mushrooms, trimmed and halved
3 tablespoons unsalted butter
2 large shallots, minced
  Salt and pepper
3 garlic cloves, minced
1½ teaspoons minced fresh thyme
2 ounces cream cheese
2 tablespoons heavy cream
1 tablespoon minced fresh parsley
1½ teaspoons lemon juice

1. Microwave 1 cup water and porcini in covered bowl until steaming, about 1 minute. Let sit until softened, about 5 minutes. Drain porcini through fine-mesh strainer lined with coffee filter set over bowl. Reserve ⅓ cup liquid.

2. Pulse porcini and white mushrooms in food processor until finely chopped and all pieces are pea-size or smaller, about 10 pulses, scraping down bowl as needed.

3. Melt butter in 12-inch skillet over medium heat. Add shallots and ¾ teaspoon salt and cook until softened, 3 to 5 minutes. Add garlic and thyme and cook until fragrant, about 30 seconds. Add processed mushrooms and cook, stirring occasionally, until liquid released from mushrooms evaporates and they begin to brown, 10 to 12 minutes.

4. Add reserved porcini liquid and cook until liquid has nearly evaporated, about 1 minute. Off heat, stir in cream cheese, cream, parsley, and lemon juice and season with salt and pepper to taste. Transfer to serving bowl and smooth top. Press plastic wrap flush to surface of pâté and refrigerate until firm, at least 2 hours or up to 3 days. Before serving, bring pâté to room temperature to soften.

Chicken Liver Pâté

SERVES 6 TO 8   **TOTAL TIME** 45 MINUTES
(PLUS 6 HOURS CHILLING TIME)

⚓ **WHY THIS RECIPE WORKS:** This smooth, buttery pâté is irresistibly rich and very easy to make. Sweet shallots sautéed in butter with fresh thyme and vermouth provided an aromatic base. Searing the livers was important for developing flavor, but gently poaching them was the key to avoiding dry pâté. A bit of brandy unified the pâté's flavors. Pressing plastic wrap against the surface of the pâté helped minimize discoloration due to oxidation. Serve with Crostini (page 30), toast points, or crackers.

- 8 **tablespoons unsalted butter**
- 3 **large shallots, sliced thin**
- 1 **tablespoon minced fresh thyme**
  Salt and pepper
- 1 **pound chicken livers, rinsed, patted dry, and trimmed of fat and connective tissue**
- ¾ **cup dry vermouth**
- 2 **teaspoons brandy**

1. Melt butter in 12-inch skillet over medium-high heat. Add shallots, thyme, and ¼ teaspoon salt and cook until shallots are lightly browned, 3 to 5 minutes. Add chicken livers and cook, stirring constantly, about 1 minute. Add vermouth and simmer until livers have rosy interior, 4 to 6 minutes.

2. Using slotted spoon, transfer livers to food processor. Continue to simmer vermouth until slightly syrupy, 2 minutes.

3. Add vermouth mixture and brandy to processor. Process mixture until very smooth, about 2 minutes, scraping down bowl as needed. Season with salt and pepper to taste. Transfer to small serving bowl, smooth top, press plastic wrap flush to surface of pâté, and refrigerate until firm, at least 6 hours or up to 3 days.

4. Before serving, bring to room temperature to soften, and scrape off any discolored pâté on top.

Smoked Salmon Mousse

SERVES 4 TO 6   **TOTAL TIME** 10 MINUTES   **FAST**

⚓ **WHY THIS RECIPE WORKS:** This creamy, beautiful mousse allows the flavor of the salmon to shine because it uses just a little cream cheese and sour cream. A minced shallot added more flavor, and lemon juice added brightness. To soften cream cheese quickly, microwave it for 20 to 30 seconds. Serve with Crostini (page 30), toast points, or crackers, or, if you have more time, pipe it onto endive leaves.

- 4 **ounces smoked salmon, chopped**
- 1 **shallot, minced**
- 2 **ounces cream cheese, softened**
- 2 **teaspoons lemon juice**
- ¼ **cup sour cream**
  Salt and pepper

Process salmon and shallot in food processor until mixture is finely chopped, about 10 seconds, scraping down bowl as needed. Add cream cheese and lemon juice and process until mixture forms ball, scraping down bowl as needed. Add sour cream and pulse to incorporate, about 5 pulses. Transfer mousse to serving bowl and season with salt and pepper to taste. Serve. (Mousse can be refrigerated for up to 2 days.)

Marinated Baby Mozzarella and Olives

SERVES 8 TO 10   **TOTAL TIME** 15 MINUTES
(PLUS 4 HOURS CHILLING TIME)

⚓ **WHY THIS RECIPE WORKS:** Aromatic herbs and bright citrus notes enliven the flavor of fresh mozzarella, while briny, pungent olives offset its mildness. We liked a mix of green and black olives, which we rinsed to remove excess salt and patted dry so the olive oil and herb marinade would not be diluted. Make sure to bring the mixture to room temperature before serving, or the oil will look cloudy and congealed. Serve with toothpicks and thinly sliced baguette or crackers.

- ¾ **cup pitted green olives, halved**
- ¾ **cup pitted black olives, halved**
- 12 **ounces fresh baby mozzarella cheese balls**
- 1 **cup extra-virgin olive oil**
- 3 **shallots, sliced thin**
- 1 **garlic clove, minced**
- 1 **teaspoon grated lemon zest**
- 1 **teaspoon minced fresh thyme**
- 1 **teaspoon minced fresh oregano**
- ¾ **teaspoon salt**
- ¼ **teaspoon red pepper flakes**

Gently rinse olives and mozzarella in colander under cold running water. Drain well and gently pat dry with paper towels. Whisk oil, shallots, garlic, lemon zest, thyme, oregano, salt, and pepper flakes together in medium bowl. Add olives and cheese and toss gently to coat. Cover and refrigerate until flavors have melded, at least 4 hours or up to 2 days. Bring to room temperature before serving.

PARTY ALMONDS

Instead of just opening a can of nuts at your next party, try this quick recipe for homemade flavored almonds.

- **1 tablespoon olive oil or unsalted butter**
- **2 cups skin-on raw almonds**
- **1 teaspoon salt**
- **¼ teaspoon pepper**

Heat oil in 12-inch nonstick skillet. Add almonds, salt, and pepper, and, if desired, one of the flavor combinations below. Toast almonds over medium-low heat, stirring often, until fragrant and color deepens slightly, about 8 minutes. Transfer to paper towel–lined plate and allow to cool before serving. (Almonds can be stored at room temperature, wrapped tightly in plastic wrap, for up to 1 week.) (Makes 2 cups)

ROSEMARY ALMONDS `FAST`

Add ½ teaspoon dried rosemary to skillet with almonds.

LEMON-GARLIC ALMONDS `FAST`

Add ½ teaspoon grated lemon zest and 1 minced garlic clove to skillet with almonds. Just before serving, toss with another ½ teaspoon grated lemon zest.

BARBECUED ALMONDS `FAST`

Add ½ teaspoon cumin, ⅛ teaspoon chili powder, ⅛ teaspoon cayenne pepper, and pinch of cloves to skillet with almonds.

SPICED ALMONDS `FAST`

Use butter rather than olive oil and add 2 tablespoons sugar, ½ teaspoon cinnamon, ⅛ teaspoon cloves, and ⅛ teaspoon allspice to skillet with almonds. Serve warm.

CHINESE FIVE-SPICE ALMONDS `FAST`

Add 1 teaspoon Chinese five-spice powder to skillet with almonds.

ORANGE-FENNEL ALMONDS `FAST`

Add ½ teaspoon grated orange zest and ½ teaspoon fennel seeds to skillet with almonds. Just before serving, toss with another ½ teaspoon grated orange zest.

These spiced nuts have a delicious, cohesive shell because we coat them with an egg white before adding the spice mixture.

Spiced Nuts

SERVES 8 TO 10   **TOTAL TIME** 1 HOUR 30 MINUTES

☑ **WHY THIS RECIPE WORKS:** Most spiced nuts are made with a heavily sugared syrup that causes the nuts to clump awkwardly and leaves your hands in a sticky mess. We wanted to develop a recipe that was both tasty and neat. Tossing the nuts in a mixture of egg white, water, and salt both gave them a nice crunch when baked and helped the spices adhere. If you can't find superfine sugar, process granulated sugar in a food processor for 1 minute.

- **1 large egg white**
- **1 tablespoon water**
- **1 teaspoon salt**
- **1 pound pecans, cashews, walnuts, or whole unblanched almonds**
- **⅔ cup superfine sugar**
- **2 teaspoons cumin**
- **1 teaspoon cayenne pepper**
- **1 teaspoon paprika**

1. Adjust oven racks to upper-middle and lower-middle positions and heat oven to 275 degrees. Line 2 rimmed baking sheets with parchment paper. Whisk egg white, water, and salt together in medium bowl. Add nuts and toss to coat. Let nuts drain in colander for 5 minutes.

2. Mix sugar, cumin, cayenne, and paprika together in clean medium bowl. Add drained nuts and toss to coat. Spread nuts evenly over prepared baking sheets. Bake until nuts are dry and crisp, about 50 minutes, stirring occasionally.

3. Let nuts cool completely on baking sheet, about 30 minutes. Break nuts apart and serve. (Nuts can be stored at room temperature for up to 1 week.)

VARIATIONS

Curry-Spiced Nuts

Reduce cumin to 1 teaspoon and substitute 1 teaspoon curry powder for cayenne.

Cinnamon-Spiced Nuts

Substitute 2 teaspoons ground cinnamon, 1 teaspoon ground ginger, and 1 teaspoon ground coriander for cumin, cayenne, and paprika.

BROWN BAG MICROWAVE POPCORN

When you want a no-fuss popcorn snack, our easy microwave method fits the bill—even kids will want to try this out themselves for an afternoon snack.

Combine 1 tablespoon vegetable oil and ¼ cup popcorn kernels in clean brown paper lunch bag. Fold over top of bag several times to seal (do not tape or staple). Microwave until popping has mostly stopped, 2 to 6 minutes. Carefully open bag, watch for steam, and transfer popped corn to large bowl. Toss with 1 tablespoon melted butter and season with salt to taste. (Makes 2 quarts)

Combine paprika, sugar, salt, and pepper in large bowl; set aside. Heat oil in large Dutch oven over high heat until just smoking. Add chickpeas and cook, stirring occasionally, until deep golden brown and crisp, 12 to 15 minutes. Using slotted spoon, transfer chickpeas to paper towel–lined baking sheet to drain briefly, then add to bowl with spices and toss. Serve. (Chickpeas can be stored at room temperature for up to 1 day.)

Roasted Spiced Chickpeas

SERVES 6   TOTAL TIME 30 MINUTES   FAST

WHY THIS RECIPE WORKS: Tossed in oil and roasted, chickpeas become ultracrisp and deeply nutty in flavor, making them the perfect cocktail snack. Roasting chickpeas in the oven didn't make them crisp enough. Switching to the stovetop and frying the chickpeas in olive oil gave them a big crunch factor. A quick toss in a sweet and savory mixture of sugar and smoked paprika made our fried legumes incredibly addictive. Make sure to dry the chickpeas thoroughly with paper towels before placing them in the oil. In order to get crisp chickpeas, it is important to keep the heat high enough to ensure the oil is simmering the entire time. After about 12 minutes, test for doneness by removing a few chickpeas and placing them on a paper towel to cool slightly before tasting. If they are not quite crisp yet, continue to cook 2 to 3 minutes longer, checking occasionally for doneness.

    1   teaspoon smoked paprika
    1   teaspoon sugar
    ½   teaspoon salt
    ¼   teaspoon pepper
    1   cup olive oil
    2   (14-ounce) cans chickpeas, rinsed and patted dry

BBQ Party Mix

SERVES 10 TO 12   TOTAL TIME 1 HOUR

WHY THIS RECIPE WORKS: Crunchy, salty, and addictive, homemade party snack mix is guaranteed to disappear quickly at any gathering. But after making a back-of-the-box party mix recipe, we felt there was room for improvement. For our BBQ Party Mix recipe upgrade, tasters preferred the nutty sweetness of melted butter to margarine and olive oil, both of which left a greasy finish. Worcestershire sauce was too domineering in our recipe; barbecue sauce was more successful. Bold seasonings such as chili powder, cayenne, and dried oregano held their flavor through baking (unlike subtler spices like paprika and onion powder, whose flavor faded).

    5   cups Corn Chex cereal
    2   cups corn chips
    1   cup Melba toast rounds, lightly crushed
    1   cup pretzel sticks
    1   cup smoked almonds
    6   tablespoons unsalted butter, melted
    ¼   cup barbecue sauce
    1   teaspoon chili powder
    ½   teaspoon dried oregano
    ¼   teaspoon cayenne pepper

1. Adjust oven rack to middle position and heat oven to 250 degrees. Combine cereal, corn chips, Melba toast, pretzels, and almonds in large bowl. Whisk melted butter and barbecue sauce together in separate bowl, then drizzle over cereal mixture. Sprinkle with chili powder, oregano, and cayenne and toss until well combined.

2. Spread mixture over rimmed baking sheet and bake, stirring every 15 minutes, until golden and crisp, about 45 minutes. Let cool to room temperature. Serve. (Mix can be stored at room temperature for up to 1 week.)

VARIATIONS
Asian Firecracker Party Mix
SERVES 10 TO 12   **TOTAL TIME** 1 HOUR

- 5 **cups Rice Chex cereal**
- 2 **cups sesame sticks**
- 1 **cup wasabi peas**
- 1 **cup chow mein noodles**
- 1 **cup honey-roasted peanuts**
- 6 **tablespoons unsalted butter, melted**
- 2 **tablespoons soy sauce**
- 1 **teaspoon ground ginger**
- ¾ **teaspoon garlic powder**
- ¼ **teaspoon cayenne pepper**

1. Adjust oven rack to middle position and heat oven to 250 degrees. Combine cereal, sesame sticks, wasabi peas, chow mein noodles, and peanuts in large bowl. Whisk melted butter and soy sauce together in separate bowl, then drizzle over cereal mixture. Sprinkle with ginger, garlic powder, and cayenne and toss until well combined.

2. Spread mixture over rimmed baking sheet and bake, stirring every 15 minutes, until golden and crisp, about 45 minutes. Let cool to room temperature. Serve. (Mix can be stored at room temperature for up to 1 week.)

Fisherman's Friend Party Mix
SERVES 10 TO 12   **TOTAL TIME** 1 HOUR

- 5 **cups Corn Chex or Rice Chex cereal**
- 2 **cups oyster crackers**
- 1 **cup Pepperidge Farm Cheddar Goldfish**
- 1 **cup Pepperidge Farm Pretzel Goldfish**
- 1 **cup Melba toast rounds, lightly crushed**
- 6 **tablespoons unsalted butter, melted**
- 2 **tablespoons hot sauce**
- 1 **tablespoon lemon juice**
- 1 **tablespoon Old Bay seasoning**

This Asian-inspired party mix delivers great flavor and big crunch without seasoned salt or margarine.

1. Adjust oven rack to middle position and heat oven to 250 degrees. Combine cereal, oyster crackers, Goldfish, and Melba toast in large bowl. Whisk melted butter, hot sauce, and lemon juice together in separate bowl, then drizzle over cereal mixture. Sprinkle with Old Bay and toss until well combined.

2. Spread mixture over rimmed baking sheet and bake, stirring every 15 minutes, until golden and crisp, about 45 minutes. Let cool to room temperature. Serve. (Mix can be stored at room temperature for up to 1 week.)

Tomato and Mozzarella Tart
SERVES 4 TO 6   **TOTAL TIME** 1 HOUR

✓ **WHY THIS RECIPE WORKS:** Falling somewhere between pizza and quiche, a tomato and mozzarella tart shares the flavors of both but with a few unique problems. For starters, some sort of pastry crust is required, but the moisture in the tomatoes can make it soggy. Second, tomato tarts are often short on flavor. We set out to make a tart that would have a solid bottom crust and great vine-ripened flavor. The best results came from a two-step baking method—we parbaked the unfilled crust until golden, then baked it again once the topping had been added, which gave us a flaky yet rigid crust. Waterproofing the crust with egg wash and using two kinds of cheese in layers prevented sogginess. We also salted the sliced tomatoes for 30 minutes, then gently pressed them with paper towels to remove excess juice. For the best flavor, use authentic Parmesan cheese and very ripe, flavorful tomatoes.

- 1 **(9½ by 9-inch) sheet frozen puff pastry, thawed**
- 1 **large egg, lightly beaten**
- 1 **ounce Parmesan cheese, grated (½ cup)**
- 2 **plum tomatoes, cored and sliced ¼ inch thick**
- ½ **teaspoon salt**
- 4 **ounces mozzarella cheese, shredded (1 cup)**
- 2 **tablespoons extra-virgin olive oil**
- 1 **garlic clove, minced**
- 2 **tablespoons chopped fresh basil**

1. Adjust oven rack to lowest position and heat oven to 425 degrees. Line rimmed baking sheet with parchment paper. Lay puff pastry in center of parchment and fold over edges of pastry to form ½-inch-wide crust. Using paring knife, cut through folded edge and corners. Brush edges with egg. Sprinkle Parmesan evenly over crust bottom, then poke uniformly with fork. Bake until crust is golden brown and crisp, 15 to 20 minutes. Let cool on wire rack. (Tart shell can be stored at room temperature for up to 1 day.)

2. Meanwhile, spread tomatoes over several layers of paper towels. Sprinkle with salt and let drain for 30 minutes.

3. Sprinkle mozzarella evenly over cooled crust bottom. Press excess moisture from tomatoes using additional paper

If you are making this tart for a party, you can easily prepare the pastry shell ahead of time.

towels. Shingle tomatoes evenly over mozzarella. Whisk olive oil and garlic together, then drizzle over tomatoes. Bake until cheese has melted and shell is deep golden, 10 to 15 minutes.

4. Let cool on wire rack for 5 minutes. Gently slide tart onto cutting board, sprinkle with basil, and slice into pieces. Serve.

Preparing Tomato and Mozzarella Tart

1. FOLD PASTRY: Fold short edges of pastry over by ½ inch. Repeat with long edges.

2. CUT EDGES: Using paring knife, cut through folded edges and corners of tart shell. Brush edges with beaten egg.

3. POKE DOUGH WITH FORK: Sprinkle bottom of tart with Parmesan, then poke dough repeatedly with fork and parbake.

4. TOP WITH TOMATOES: Sprinkle mozzarella evenly over cooled crust, then shingle salted and drained tomatoes attractively over top.

These easy tarts can be made in just half an hour using prebaked naan breads and savory toppings.

Naan Tarts with Fig Jam, Blue Cheese, and Prosciutto

SERVES 6   TOTAL TIME 30 MINUTES   **FAST**

✔ **WHY THIS RECIPE WORKS:** We used baked naan (Indian flatbread) as a prebaked crust on which we could build a savory appetizer pizza. We skipped standard pizza sauce and mozzarella and instead combined the concentrated flavors of salty prosciutto and bold blue cheese against a backdrop of sweet fig jam. The toppings needed only a brief stint in the oven to warm through, so we brushed the baking sheet with olive oil and baked the tart on the lowest rack to help the naan crisp up during the short baking time. If fig jam is not available, you can substitute caramelized onion or apricot jam. Also, 1 tablespoon minced fresh parsley can be substituted for the scallions.

1 tablespoon olive oil
2 (8-inch) naan breads
¼ cup fig jam
1 teaspoon water
⅛ teaspoon pepper
2 ounces blue cheese, crumbled (½ cup)
2 ounces thinly sliced prosciutto, cut into 1-inch strips
¼ teaspoon fresh thyme leaves
2 scallions, sliced thin

1. Adjust oven rack to lowest position and heat oven to 500 degrees. Brush baking sheet with oil and lay naan on sheet. Whisk fig jam with water in bowl to loosen, then spread evenly over each naan, leaving ½-inch border around edge. Sprinkle pepper, blue cheese, prosciutto, and thyme evenly over top.

2. Bake until naan are golden brown around edges, 8 to 10 minutes, rotating sheet halfway through baking. Sprinkle with scallions, cut each tart into 6 wedges, and serve.

VARIATIONS

Naan Tarts with Ricotta and Sun-Dried Tomato, and Olive Tapenade

SERVES 6   TOTAL TIME 30 MINUTES   **FAST**

Use either whole-milk or part-skim ricotta here; do not use fat-free ricotta, which has a very dry texture and bland flavor.

¼ cup olive oil
2 (8-inch) naan breads
4 ounces (½ cup) whole-milk ricotta cheese
¼ cup Parmesan cheese, grated
1½ teaspoons lemon juice
1 garlic clove, minced
¼ teaspoon salt
⅛ teaspoon pepper
3 tablespoons sun-dried tomatoes, rinsed, patted dry, and chopped fine
3 tablespoons pitted kalamata olives, chopped fine
1½ tablespoons pine nuts
1 scallion, sliced thin

1. Adjust oven rack to lowest position and heat oven to 500 degrees. Brush baking sheet with 1 tablespoon oil and lay naan on sheet. Combine ricotta, Parmesan, 1 tablespoon oil, lemon juice, garlic, salt, and pepper in bowl. In separate bowl, combine tomatoes, olives, pine nuts, and remaining 2 tablespoons oil.

2. Spread ricotta mixture evenly over each naan, leaving ½-inch border around edge. Scatter tomato-olive mixture evenly over top. Bake until naan are golden brown around edges, 8 to 10 minutes, rotating sheet halfway through baking. Sprinkle with scallion, cut each tart into 6 wedges, and serve.

Naan Tarts with Artichokes, Pesto, and Goat Cheese

SERVES 6   TOTAL TIME 30 MINUTES   **FAST**

We prefer to use jarred marinated artichokes here rather than artichokes canned in water because they have more flavor. Either store-bought or homemade pesto will work fine here; see page 410 for our pesto recipe.

 1 **tablespoon olive oil**
 2 **(8-inch) naan breads**
 3 **ounces goat cheese, crumbled (¾ cup)**
 ½ **cup basil pesto**
 1 **tablespoon water**
 ½ **cup marinated artichokes, drained and patted dry**
 1 **tablespoon fresh parsley leaves**

1. Adjust oven rack to lowest position and heat oven to 500 degrees. Brush baking sheet with oil and lay naan on sheet. Combine goat cheese, pesto, and water in bowl.

2. Spread goat cheese mixture evenly over each naan, leaving ½-inch border around edge. Scatter artichokes evenly over top. Bake until naan are golden brown around edges, 8 to 10 minutes, rotating sheet halfway through baking. Sprinkle with parsley, cut each tart into 6 wedges, and serve.

Naan Tarts with Roasted Red Peppers, Feta, and Olives

SERVES 6   TOTAL TIME 30 MINUTES   **FAST**

Be sure to rinse and dry the roasted red peppers, as the brine can impart a sour or acidic aftertaste.

 3 **tablespoons olive oil**
 2 **(8-inch) naan breads**
 ½ **cup jarred roasted red peppers, rinsed and patted dry**
    Salt and pepper
 2 **ounces feta cheese, crumbled (½ cup)**
 3 **tablespoons pitted kalamata olives, chopped fine**
 2 **tablespoons fresh parsley leaves**

1. Adjust oven rack to lowest position and heat oven to 500 degrees. Brush baking sheet with 1 tablespoon oil and lay naan on sheet. Process red peppers and remaining 2 tablespoons oil in food processor until smooth, about 30 seconds, scraping down bowl as needed. Season with salt and pepper to taste.

2. Spread red pepper puree evenly over each naan, leaving ½-inch border around edge. Scatter feta and olives evenly over top. Bake until naan are golden brown around edges, 8 to 10 minutes, rotating sheet halfway through baking. Sprinkle with parsley, cut each tart into 6 wedges, and serve.

Filling deviled eggs close to serving time gives them a fresh, bright flavor.

Classic Deviled Eggs

SERVES 4 TO 6   TOTAL TIME 1 HOUR

✔ **WHY THIS RECIPE WORKS:** Deviled eggs often fall to the extremes, with fillings that are either pasty and monotonous or reminiscent of chunky egg salad. We wanted the deviled eggs of our childhood: perfectly cooked egg whites cradling a creamy filling made with simple ingredients and quickly whipped together. It was key to start with perfectly hard-cooked eggs. We combined the yolks with mayonnaise, mustard, cider vinegar, and Worcestershire, which gave us a full-flavored, but balanced, filling. During testing, a couple of the cooked egg whites typically ripped, which worked out well because it meant the remaining whites were very well stuffed. If all of your egg white halves are in perfect shape, discard two. For filling the eggs, a spoon works fine, but for eggs that look their Sunday best, use a pastry bag fitted with a fluted (star) tip, or make your own pastry bag by pressing the filling into the corner of a zipper-lock bag and snipping off the corner with scissors. Dust the filled eggs with paprika for a traditional look. We like the flavor of cider vinegar here, but any type will work.

Deviled eggs can easily end up with greenish yolks and bland fillings. We learned the green color appears because of prolonged heating. To make our hard-cooked eggs foolproof we start the eggs in cold water, bring the water to a boil, then turn off the heat and put the lid on the pan. The residual heat cooks the eggs in exactly 10 minutes. Plunging the eggs into ice water stops the cooking process and prevents the green ring from forming. We mash the yolks very smooth and then punch up the usual filling ingredients with cider vinegar, whole-grain mustard, and Worcestershire.

1. PUT THE EGGS IN A COLD POT: Place the eggs in a medium saucepan in a single layer and cover them with 1 inch of tap water.

WHY? With each egg resting on the bottom of the pan, they will cook evenly. If you're cooking more than seven eggs, you might want to switch to a Dutch oven. The timing will be the same as long as the eggs are kept in a single layer.

2. BRING THE WATER TO BOIL AND TAKE THE POT OFF THE HEAT: Once the water is boiling, remove the pot from the heat, cover with the pot lid, and set the timer for 10 minutes.

WHY? Since this recipe relies on residual heat to cook the eggs, the water must come to a boil. Once it's boiling, turn off the heat and use a tight-fitting lid so the water won't cool off quickly.

3. CHILL THE EGGS IMMEDIATELY AFTER COOKING: While the eggs cook, fill a medium bowl with ice water. As soon as the eggs are done, transfer them to the ice water to stop the cooking.

WHY? The ice bath stops the eggs from cooking further. If you skip this step, residual heat that's trapped inside the egg will turn a perfectly cooked egg into an overcooked egg.

4. CAREFULLY PEEL THE EGGS AND SEPARATE THE WHITES AND YOLKS: Peel the eggs and carefully slice each egg in half lengthwise. Transfer the yolks to a small bowl. Arrange the egg whites on a platter, discarding the two worst-looking halves.

WHY? For easier peeling, start at the air pocket end. No matter how careful you are, a few of the peeled cooked whites may tear. Don't worry, you can pack the remaining whites with extra filling.

5. MAKE A SMOOTH FILLING USING THE YOLKS: Mash the yolks with a fork until no large lumps remain. Add the other filling ingredients and season with salt and pepper. Mix with a rubber spatula, mashing the mixture against the side of the bowl until smooth.

WHY? Mashing the yolks smooth will take longer than you think, but having a smooth filling is important, or you'll end up with pockets of hard, powdery yolk.

6. PIPE THE FILLING ATTRACTIVELY INTO THE EGG WHITES: Fit a pastry bag with an open-star tip, then fill with the yolk mixture. Twist the top of the bag to help push the yolk mixture toward the tip, then gently pipe the mixture into the egg whites.

WHY? Using a pastry bag (or zipper-lock bag) makes filling the egg whites easy, and ensures that the filling gets evenly distributed and looks attractive

7 large eggs (cold)
3 tablespoons mayonnaise
1½ teaspoons cider vinegar
¾ teaspoon whole-grain mustard
¼ teaspoon Worcestershire sauce
Salt and pepper

1. Place eggs in medium saucepan, cover with 1 inch of water, and bring to boil over high heat. Remove pan from heat, cover, and let stand 10 minutes. Meanwhile, fill medium bowl with ice water. Transfer eggs to ice water with slotted spoon to stop cooking; let sit until chilled, about 5 minutes.

2. Peel eggs and slice each in half lengthwise with paring knife. Transfer yolks to small bowl. Arrange whites on serving platter, discarding 2 worst-looking halves. Mash yolks with fork until no large lumps remain. Add mayonnaise, vinegar, mustard, and Worcestershire and season with salt and pepper to taste. Mix with rubber spatula, mashing mixture against side of bowl until smooth. (Egg whites and yolk filling can be refrigerated, separately, for up to 2 days.)

3. Fit pastry bag with large open-star tip. Fill bag with yolk mixture, twisting top of pastry bag to help push mixture toward tip of bag. Pipe yolk mixture into egg white halves, mounding filling about ½ inch above flat surface of whites. Serve at room temperature.

VARIATIONS

Deviled Eggs with Anchovy and Basil

Add 8 anchovy fillets, rinsed, patted dry, and finely chopped, and 2 teaspoons chopped fresh basil to filling. Sprinkle eggs with 4 teaspoons shredded basil before serving.

Deviled Eggs with Tuna, Capers, and Chives

Omit Worcestershire. Add ½ cup drained and finely chopped canned tuna, 1 tablespoon rinsed and chopped capers, and 1 tablespoon minced fresh chives to filling. Sprinkle eggs with 1 teaspoon minced fresh chives before serving.

Stuffed Mushrooms with Boursin and Prosciutto

SERVES 6 TO 8   TOTAL TIME 40 MINUTES   **FAST**

✓ **WHY THIS RECIPE WORKS:** Looking for a way to make great-tasting stuffed mushrooms that were less labor-intensive, we focused on the filling, swapping in flavorful Boursin cheese for a bread-based stuffing that required lots of chopping and getting out a skillet. And for mushrooms that were properly cooked through, we microwaved them first to soften them. Once filled, these mushrooms needed only 10 minutes to bake in the oven. Be sure to buy mushrooms with caps that measure between 1½ and 2 inches in diameter.

24 (1½ to 2-inch-wide) white mushroom caps, stemmed
2 tablespoons olive oil
Salt and pepper
1 (5.2-ounce) package Boursin Garlic and Fine Herbs cheese, softened
1 ounce thinly sliced prosciutto, cut into ¼-inch strips
2 tablespoons minced fresh parsley or chives

Making Stuffed Mushrooms

1. USE LARGE MUSHROOMS: Mushrooms shrink dramatically during cooking, so look for those that measure between 1½ and 2 inches in diameter.

2. MICROWAVE MUSHROOMS: Arrange mushrooms gill side down on plate lined with 2 layers of coffee filters and microwave 10 minutes.

3. STUFF WITH CHEESE: Spoon Boursin into mushroom caps and top with thinly sliced prosciutto.

4. BAKE MUSHROOMS: Bake stuffed mushrooms in 450-degree oven until cheese is hot and prosciutto begins to crisp, about 10 minutes.

1. Adjust oven rack to lower-middle position and heat oven to 450 degrees. Toss mushroom caps with oil in bowl and season with salt and pepper. Lay mushrooms gill side down on plate lined with 2 layers of coffee filters. Microwave mushrooms until they release their moisture and shrink in size, about 10 minutes.

2. Line rimmed baking sheet with aluminum foil. Flip caps gill side up and transfer to prepared sheet. Spoon Boursin into mushroom caps and top with prosciutto. (Stuffed mushrooms can be held at room temperature for up to 2 hours.)

3. Bake mushrooms until cheese is hot and prosciutto begins to crisp, 10 to 12 minutes. Transfer to serving platter, sprinkle with parsley, and serve.

Classic Shrimp Cocktail with Horseradish Cocktail Sauce

SERVES 6   **TOTAL TIME** 35 MINUTES
(PLUS 1 HOUR CHILLING TIME)

✔ **WHY THIS RECIPE WORKS:** Shrimp cocktail should boast tender, sweet shrimp and a lively, well-seasoned cocktail sauce. To infuse the shrimp with as much flavor as possible, we cooked them in a simple mixture of water and seasonings. Old Bay seasoning delivered a perceptible depth of flavor to the shrimp. Shrimp cook very quickly. We brought the water and aromatics to a boil, took the pot off the heat, and added the shrimp, leaving them to poach for 7 minutes—a method that delivers perfectly tender, not rubbery, shrimp every time. Buy refrigerated prepared horseradish, not the shelf-stable kind, which contains preservatives and additives.

SHRIMP
- 2 **teaspoons lemon juice**
- 2 **bay leaves**
- 1 **teaspoon salt**
- 1 **teaspoon black peppercorns**
- 1 **teaspoon Old Bay seasoning**
- 1 **pound extra-large shrimp (21 to 25 per pound), peeled and deveined**

COCKTAIL SAUCE
- 1 **cup ketchup**
- 2 **tablespoons lemon juice**
- 2 **tablespoons prepared horseradish, plus extra for seasoning**

For perfectly tender and deeply flavored shrimp, we poach them off the heat.

- 2 **teaspoons hot sauce, plus extra for seasoning**
- ⅛ **teaspoon salt**
- ⅛ **teaspoon pepper**

1. FOR THE SHRIMP: Bring lemon juice, bay leaves, salt, peppercorns, Old Bay, and 4 cups water to boil in medium saucepan for 2 minutes. Remove pan from heat and add shrimp. Cover and steep off heat until shrimp are firm and pink, about 7 minutes. Meanwhile, fill large bowl with ice water. Drain shrimp and plunge immediately into ice water to stop cooking; let sit until cool, about 2 minutes. Drain shrimp and transfer to bowl. Cover and refrigerate until thoroughly chilled, at least 1 hour or up to 1 day.

2. FOR THE COCKTAIL SAUCE: Stir all ingredients together in small bowl and season with additional horseradish and hot sauce as desired. (Sauce can be refrigerated for up to 1 day.) Arrange shrimp and sauce on serving platter and serve.

Broiled Shrimp Cocktail with Creamy Tarragon Sauce

SERVES 12   **TOTAL TIME** 30 MINUTES **FAST**

✓ **WHY THIS RECIPE WORKS:** For the easiest-ever version of shrimp cocktail, we bypassed the traditional method of poaching the shrimp in a court bouillon and instead put the high heat of the broiler to work. A simple rub of salt, pepper, coriander, and cayenne infused the shrimp with flavor, while a little sugar helped caramelize the shrimp quickly under the broiler. Instead of a traditional cocktail sauce, we paired the shrimp with a mayonnaise-based creamy sauce, brightened with lemon juice and fresh tarragon. Other fresh herbs, such as dill, basil, cilantro, or mint, can be substituted for the tarragon.

SAUCE

- ¾ **cup mayonnaise**
- 2 **tablespoons lemon juice**
- 2 **scallions, minced**
- 3 **tablespoons minced fresh tarragon**
- ½ **teaspoon salt**
- ¼ **teaspoon pepper**

SHRIMP

- ¾ **teaspoon ground coriander**
- ¾ **teaspoon salt**
- ¼ **teaspoon pepper**
- ½ **teaspoon sugar**
- ⅛ **teaspoon cayenne pepper**
- 2 **pounds extra-large shrimp (21 to 25 per pound), peeled and deveined**
- 2 **tablespoons olive oil**

1. FOR THE SAUCE: Stir all ingredients together in serving bowl, cover, and refrigerate until needed. (Sauce can be refrigerated for up to 1 day.)

2. FOR THE SHRIMP: Adjust oven rack 3 inches from broiler element and heat broiler. (If necessary, set upside-down rimmed baking sheet on oven rack to get closer to broiler element.) Combine coriander, salt, pepper, sugar, and cayenne in bowl. Pat shrimp dry with paper towels, then toss with oil and spice mixture in large bowl.

3. Spread shrimp in single layer on rimmed baking sheet. Broil shrimp until opaque and edges begin to brown, about 4 minutes. Transfer shrimp to serving platter and serve with sauce.

Our fresher, easier take on crab rangoon relies on store-bought wonton wrappers and a mini muffin tin.

Easy Crab Rangoon

SERVES 4 TO 6   **TOTAL TIME** 30 MINUTES **FAST**

✓ **WHY THIS RECIPE WORKS:** Now a staple in Chinese restaurants, crab rangoon was first made famous at the Polynesian-style restaurant Trader Vic's in San Francisco. But no matter its ethnicity, the crispy fried wonton pouches, stuffed with a filling of cream cheese and crabmeat, have become a takeout favorite. Most restaurants go heavy on the cream cheese and minimize the crab, but we switched the proportions and packed our version with sweet, delicate crabmeat and a lesser amount of cream cheese. For a crispy shell, we turned to the oven instead of deep frying. Our unconventional twist was to make wonton "cups" that we baked in a mini muffin tin before filling them with our cream cheese and crab mixture. Sprinkled with sliced scallion greens, our open-faced crab rangoon were a fresher take on a typically heavy takeout dish. To soften cream cheese quickly, microwave it for 20 to 30 seconds.

Vegetable oil spray

16 wonton wrappers

4 ounces lump crabmeat, picked over for shells

3 ounces cream cheese, softened

1 scallion, white part sliced thin, green part sliced thin on bias

1 teaspoon grated fresh ginger

¾ teaspoon soy sauce

1. Adjust oven rack to middle position and heat oven to 350 degrees. Spray mini muffin tin with oil spray. Gently press wonton wrappers into tin cups, making sure bottoms and sides are flush with tin; let edges of wrappers extend out of cups. Lightly spray wrappers with oil spray and bake until lightly browned, 6 to 9 minutes; let cool slightly.

2. Combine crabmeat, cream cheese, scallion whites, ginger, and soy sauce in bowl. Using small spoon, fill each wonton cup with 2 teaspoons filling. Bake until filling is heated through, 6 to 8 minutes. Sprinkle with scallion greens. Serve warm.

Making Wonton Cups

Gently press each wonton wrapper into greased mini muffin tin cup; press out any air bubbles and folds. Lightly spray wonton cups with vegetable oil spray and bake until lightly browned.

Jalapeño Poppers

SERVES 6 TO 8   **TOTAL TIME** 30 MINUTES   **FAST**

✔ **WHY THIS RECIPE WORKS:** For a streamlined yet still flavorful version of this party favorite, we turned to cream cheese as the base for our filling. A hefty dose of shredded cheddar gave it substance and flavor, while minced deli ham gave it meaty depth. Instead of breading and frying these stuffed chiles, we found that just 20 minutes in the oven softened them and ensured the filling was hot throughout. To soften cream cheese quickly, microwave it for 20 to 30 seconds.

8 ounces cream cheese, softened

2 ounces cheddar cheese, shredded (½ cup)

2 ounces deli ham, minced

1 tablespoon lime juice

The sweet smoky flavor of ham accents the richness of the cheeses in these stuffed jalapeño chiles.

1 teaspoon chili powder

2 scallions, minced

½ teaspoon salt

12 jalapeño chiles, halved and seeded

Adjust oven rack to middle position and heat oven to 350 degrees. Line rimmed baking sheet with parchment paper. Combine cream cheese, cheddar, ham, lime juice, chili powder, scallions, and salt in bowl. Spoon cream cheese mixture into jalapeño halves and arrange on prepared baking sheet. Bake until cheese is hot, about 20 minutes. Serve warm.

Seeding Jalapeños

Most of a chile pepper's heat is in the ribs and seeds. To remove both easily, cut pepper in half lengthwise, then use a melon baller to scoop down inside of each half. (Sharp edge of melon baller can also cut off stem.)

Oven-Baked Buffalo Wings

SERVES 4 TO 6   **TOTAL TIME** 1 HOUR

✔ **WHY THIS RECIPE WORKS:** For this barroom classic, we set out to ditch the deep fryer but still turn out wings that wouldn't disappoint. Baking powder helped to dry out the skin so it became crisp when roasted in a superhot oven; baking the wings on a wire rack let the rendered fat drip away. A quick stint under the broiler crisped the skin even further and ensured a flavorful char. A spoonful of molasses added depth and richness to these oven-baked yet still finger-licking-good Buffalo wings. The mild flavor of Frank's RedHot Original Cayenne Pepper Sauce is crucial to the flavor of this dish; we don't suggest substituting another hot sauce here. Serve with Creamy Blue Cheese Dip (page 21).

3   pounds chicken wings, halved at joint and wingtips removed, trimmed
1   tablespoon baking powder
½   teaspoon salt
⅔   cup Frank's RedHot Original Cayenne Pepper Sauce
1   tablespoon unsalted butter, melted
1   tablespoon molasses

1. Adjust oven rack to middle position and heat oven to 475 degrees. Line rimmed baking sheet with aluminum foil and top with wire rack. Pat wings dry with paper towels, then toss with baking powder and salt in bowl. Arrange wings in single layer on wire rack. Roast wings until golden on both sides, about 40 minutes, flipping wings over and rotating sheet halfway through roasting.

2. Meanwhile, whisk hot sauce, butter, and molasses together in large bowl.

Baking powder and a super-hot oven help to crisp the skin on our oven-baked Buffalo wings.

3. Remove wings from oven. Adjust oven rack 6 inches from broiler element and heat broiler. Broil wings until golden brown on both sides, 6 to 8 minutes, flipping wings over halfway through broiling. Add wings to sauce and toss to coat. Serve.

Making Oven-Baked Buffalo Wings

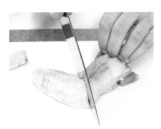

1. PREP WINGS: Using kitchen shears or sharp chef's knife, cut through wing at two joints and discard wingtip.

2. SEASON CHICKEN: Toss wings with baking powder and salt before cooking.

3. ROAST WINGS: Place wings on wire rack set inside rimmed baking sheet and roast in 475-degree oven.

4. BROIL AND ADD SAUCE: Broil wings until golden brown on both sides, flipping halfway through broiling. Toss with sauce and serve.

Dressings

Green Salads

Croutons

Main-Course and Deli Salads

■ SIGNIFIES A **FAST** RECIPE (45 MINUTES OR LESS)

Mayonnaise keeps our vinaigrettes thoroughly emulsified, so salads taste well-balanced in every bite.

Foolproof Vinaigrette

MAKES ABOUT ¼ CUP   **TOTAL TIME** 10 MINUTES   **FAST**

✔ **WHY THIS RECIPE WORKS:** Vinaigrettes often seem a little slipshod—harsh and bristling in one bite, dull and oily in the next—plus they tend to separate soon after being prepared. We found that top-notch ingredients are crucial for the best, balanced flavor. Fruity extra-virgin olive oil is preferred as an all-purpose option, while walnut oil is best for nuttier vinaigrettes. Wine vinegar (red or white) is a better match for mild greens, while balsamic vinegar is pungent enough to stand up to assertive greens. For a well-balanced vinaigrette that wouldn't separate, we whisked the vinegar together with a little mayonnaise, which acts as an emulsifier. This vinaigrette works with nearly any type of greens. For a hint of garlic flavor, rub the inside of the salad bowl with a peeled clove of garlic before adding the greens. You can use red wine, white wine, or champagne vinegar here; however, it is important to use high-quality ingredients.

1   tablespoon wine vinegar
1½   teaspoons minced shallot
½   teaspoon regular or light mayonnaise
½   teaspoon Dijon mustard
⅛   teaspoon salt
     Pepper
3   tablespoons extra-virgin olive oil

1. Combine vinegar, shallot, mayonnaise, mustard, salt, and pepper to taste in small bowl. Whisk until mixture is milky in appearance and no lumps of mayonnaise remain.

2. Place oil in small measuring cup so that it is easy to pour. Whisking constantly, slowly drizzle oil into vinegar mixture. If pools of oil gather on surface as you whisk, stop addition of oil and whisk mixture well to combine, then resume whisking in oil in slow stream. Vinaigrette should be glossy and lightly thickened, with no pools of oil on its surface. (Vinaigrette can be refrigerated for up to 2 weeks.)

Mincing a Shallot

1. Make several closely spaced parallel cuts through peeled shallot, leaving root end intact.

2. Next, make several cuts lengthwise through shallot.

3. Finally, thinly slice shallot crosswise to create mince.

Lemon Vinaigrette

This is best for dressing mild greens.

Substitute lemon juice for vinegar and omit shallot. Add ¼ teaspoon finely grated lemon zest and pinch sugar with salt and pepper.

Balsamic-Mustard Vinaigrette

This is best for dressing assertive greens.

Substitute balsamic vinegar for wine vinegar and increase mustard to 2 teaspoons. Add ½ teaspoon minced fresh thyme with salt and pepper.

Walnut Vinaigrette

Substitute 1½ tablespoons roasted walnut oil and 1½ table-spoons regular olive oil for extra-virgin olive oil.

Herb Vinaigrette

Add 1 tablespoon minced fresh parsley or chives and ½ tea-spoon minced fresh thyme, tarragon, marjoram, or oregano to vinaigrette just before use.

Thousand Island Dressing

MAKES ABOUT 1½ CUPS   TOTAL TIME 10 MINUTES   FAST

✓ WHY THIS RECIPE WORKS: For a balanced Thousand Island dressing, one that is neither too sweet nor too thick, we found the key was to include chili sauce, which helped with the texture and the flavor. Do not be tempted to use sweet relish in place of the minced sweet pickles—the resulting flavor will be muddy and overpowering. This dressing goes especially well with mild-tasting greens such as romaine and iceberg.

1 cup mayonnaise
½ cup minced sweet pickles
¼ cup chili sauce
4 green olives with pimentos, minced
2 tablespoons minced fresh parsley
1 tablespoon water
2 teaspoons lemon juice
1 garlic clove, minced
½ teaspoon salt
¼ teaspoon pepper

Whisk all ingredients together in bowl until smooth. (Dressing can be refrigerated for up to 1 week.)

All-American French Dressing

MAKES 1 CUP   TOTAL TIME 5 MINUTES   FAST

✓ WHY THIS RECIPE WORKS: The base of this easy-to-make dressing is simply equal parts ketchup and vegetable oil, spiked with white wine vinegar. We added grated onion to the vinaigrette for a sharp bite without the crunchy bits of onion that would mar its otherwise smooth texture. Some hot sauce balanced the sweetness with a little heat. Use the large holes of a box grater to grate the onion, and remember that a little bit of grated onion goes a long way. This dressing is traditionally served with iceberg or other mild lettuces such as green leaf, red leaf, romaine, Boston, and Bibb.

½ cup ketchup
½ cup vegetable oil
¼ cup white wine vinegar or distilled white vinegar
2 tablespoons sugar
1 teaspoon grated onion
¼ teaspoon hot sauce, plus extra to taste

Whisk all ingredients together in bowl until smooth. Season with extra hot sauce to taste. (Dressing can be refrigerated for up to 1 week.)

NOTES FROM THE TEST KITCHEN

Oil and Vinegar

A good extra-virgin olive oil is a must when making vinaigrettes or other dressings. But you will also need a pure olive oil and/or canola oil for recipes that call for a lot of oil, like Classic Caesar Salad (page 61), where the flavor of extra-virgin olive oil alone is too pungent and overpowering. That said, for vinaigrettes we almost always call for extra-virgin olive oil because it tastes good with all greens and vinegars; it pays to reach for a high-quality extra-virgin olive oil when making vinaigrettes. Our winning brand of extra-virgin olive oil is Columela, for its buttery flavor and peppery finish.

You will want to stock several vinegars, including red wine, white wine, balsamic, and rice vinegar. Sherry vinegar is also very nice to have on hand because it adds strong flavor to vinaigrettes. Note that vinegars can vary in acidity, which in effect measures intensity. For example, rice vinegars have a 4 percent acidity level and require less oil to make a smooth-tasting dressing; red wine vinegars can have an acidity level as high as 7 percent and so require much more oil to make a smooth dressing.

Green Goddess Dressing

MAKES 1¼ CUPS   **TOTAL TIME** 20 MINUTES (PLUS 1 HOUR CHILLING TIME)

✔ **WHY THIS RECIPE WORKS:** Our Green Goddess Dressing recipe uses a blend of mayonnaise and sour cream for its base and gets an essential flavor boost from anchovies. For the creamiest texture, we prepared the dressing in a blender. Surprisingly, we preferred the flavor of dried tarragon over fresh, because its milder flavor mingled better with the dressing's other ingredients; we just had to be sure to hydrate it in lemon juice and water first. Although a blender yields a brighter, slightly more flavorful dressing, a food processor will work, too. To appreciate the full flavor of this rich dressing, drizzle it over wedges of mild iceberg lettuce or leaves of romaine lettuce.

- 2 **teaspoons dried tarragon**
- 1 **tablespoon lemon juice**
- 1 **tablespoon water**
- ¾ **cup mayonnaise**
- ¼ **cup sour cream**
- ¼ **cup minced fresh parsley**
- 1 **garlic clove, minced**
- 1 **anchovy fillet, rinsed**
- ¼ **cup minced fresh chives**
  Salt and pepper

Combine tarragon, lemon juice, and water in bowl and let sit for 15 minutes. Process tarragon mixture, mayonnaise, sour cream, parsley, garlic, and anchovy in blender until smooth, scraping down sides of blender jar as necessary. Transfer to clean bowl, stir in chives, and season with salt and pepper to taste. Refrigerate until flavors meld, about 1 hour. (Dressing can be refrigerated for up to 1 day.)

Blue Cheese Dressing

MAKES ABOUT ¾ CUP   **TOTAL TIME** 10 MINUTES **FAST**

✔ **WHY THIS RECIPE WORKS:** We found that the secret to good blue cheese dressing lay in the creamy components, which we narrowed down to three: mayonnaise, to give the dressing body; sour cream, to supply tang; and buttermilk, both to thin out the dressing and to support the sour cream. As for the main ingredient—the cheese—we ruled out really pungent blue cheeses as too overpowering; a mild blue cheese worked best. For the right chunky consistency, we mixed the crumbled blue cheese with the buttermilk before adding any other ingredients. We dressed a variety of different salad greens and found that delicate ones, such as mesclun and butterhead lettuce, became soggy under the weight of the dressing. Sturdy romaine and curly-leaf lettuce were our two favorites. If you don't have buttermilk, substitute 3 tablespoons milk and increase the vinegar to 2½ teaspoons.

- 2½ **ounces blue cheese, crumbled (⅔ cup)**
- 3 **tablespoons buttermilk**
- 3 **tablespoons sour cream**
- 2 **tablespoons mayonnaise**
- 2 **teaspoons white wine vinegar**
- ¼ **teaspoon sugar**
- ⅛ **teaspoon garlic powder**
  Salt and pepper

Mash blue cheese and buttermilk together in bowl with fork until mixture resembles cottage cheese with small curds. Stir in sour cream, mayonnaise, vinegar, sugar, and garlic powder. Season with salt and pepper to taste. (Dressing can be refrigerated for up to 1 week.)

Creamy Peppercorn Dressing

MAKES 1 CUP   **TOTAL TIME** 30 MINUTES **FAST**

✔ **WHY THIS RECIPE WORKS:** To make a creamy peppercorn dressing that actually tastes like pepper—but without the burn—we started with a blend of mayonnaise and sour cream, thinning this creamy base with buttermilk to give it the right consistency and tang. Red wine vinegar, garlic, and Dijon mustard rounded out the flavors. To tame the fiery intensity of the pepper while still ensuring that each spoonful of the dressing had a deep peppery taste, we used the technique of blooming to temper its heat by slowly simmering the pepper in olive oil. As a bonus, the oil (with its peppery flavor) could simply be incorporated into the dressing. If you don't have buttermilk, substitute 2 tablespoons milk and increase the vinegar to 2½ teaspoons. Hardy, crisp iceberg and romaine work well with this creamy dressing.

- 1 **tablespoon coarsely ground black pepper**
- ¼ **cup extra-virgin olive oil**
- ¼ **cup sour cream**
- ¼ **cup mayonnaise**
- 2 **tablespoons buttermilk**
- 2 **teaspoons Dijon mustard**
- 2 **teaspoons red wine vinegar**
- 1 **garlic clove, minced**
  Salt

To tame the fiery heat of the peppercorns in our peppercorn dressing, we simmer them gently in olive oil.

Cook pepper and oil together in small saucepan over low heat until faint bubbles appear. Gently simmer, swirling pan occasionally, until pepper is fragrant, about 8 minutes. Remove from heat and cool to room temperature. Whisk sour cream, mayonnaise, buttermilk, mustard, vinegar, and garlic together in bowl. Gradually whisk in cooled pepper mixture until incorporated. Season with salt to taste. (Dressing can be refrigerated for up to 4 days.)

Creamy Italian Dressing

MAKES 1½ CUPS   **TOTAL TIME** 20 MINUTES   **FAST**

✔ **WHY THIS RECIPE WORKS:** For our Creamy Italian Dressing we liked mayonnaise for body and sour cream for tang, lightness, and silkiness. When it came to the herbs and aromatics, oregano and red pepper flakes made the cut, as did minced shallots (since onions tasted harsh), fresh garlic, and fresh basil. To prevent the dried oregano from tasting stale, we turned to a technique we often use in the test kitchen: "blooming" herbs and spices in warm liquid to draw out their

NOTES FROM THE TEST KITCHEN

Pairing Leafy Greens with Vinaigrette

Vinaigrettes are always the best choice for dressing leafy greens; heavier, creamier dressings should be reserved for use on sturdy lettuce such as romaine or iceberg. Most salad greens fall into one of two categories: mellow or assertive. When you're making a green salad, it's important to choose your vinaigrette recipe carefully to complement the greens you are using.

MELLOW-FLAVORED: Boston, Bibb, mâche, mesclun, red and green leaf, red oak, and flat-leaf spinach. Their mild flavors are easily overpowered and are best complemented by a simple dressing such as a classic red wine vinaigrette.

ASSERTIVE OR SPICY GREENS: arugula, escarole, chicory, Belgian endive, radicchio, frisée, and watercress. These greens can easily stand up to strong flavors like mustard, shallots, and balsamic vinegar and can also be paired with a slightly sweet or creamy vinaigrette.

flavors. We combined the dried oregano, pepper flakes, and vinegar and warmed the mixture in the microwave to get the rounder, fuller flavors we wanted. Melting the Parmesan in the microwave with the vinegar and herbs kept the dressing from being gritty. We also tossed in the minced shallot and garlic to mellow them. This creamy vinaigrette pairs best with a crisp lettuce such as iceberg or romaine.

    3   **tablespoons red wine vinegar**
    3   **tablespoons grated Parmesan cheese**
    1   **shallot, minced**
    1   **garlic clove, minced**
    2   **teaspoons dried oregano**
    ¼   **teaspoon red pepper flakes**
    ½   **cup mayonnaise**
    ¼   **cup sour cream**
    1   **tablespoon chopped fresh basil**
    ½   **cup olive oil**
        Salt and pepper

1. Whisk vinegar, Parmesan, shallot, garlic, oregano, and pepper flakes in bowl. Microwave until cheese is melted (vinegar will look cloudy) and mixture is fragrant, about 30 seconds. Let cool.

2. Process mayonnaise, sour cream, basil, and vinegar mixture in food processor until smooth. With motor running, slowly add oil until incorporated, about 1 minute. Season with salt and pepper to taste. (Dressing can be refrigerated for up to 4 days.)

Ranch Dressing

MAKES ABOUT 1½ CUPS   **TOTAL TIME** 15 MINUTES   **FAST**

✅ **WHY THIS RECIPE WORKS:** After many trials we discovered that the key to a well-rounded creamy ranch dressing—one that didn't taste dull, fatty, or overly tangy—is to use a trio of dairy ingredients: buttermilk, sour cream, and mayonnaise. When we tried to eliminate any one of them for the sake of convenience, tasters complained of seriously compromised flavor. Fresh herbs are essential for the flavor of this dressing.

½ cup buttermilk
½ cup mayonnaise
6 tablespoons sour cream
1 tablespoon minced shallot or red onion
1 tablespoon minced fresh parsley
1 tablespoon minced fresh cilantro or dill
1 garlic clove, minced
1 teaspoon lemon juice
  Pinch sugar
½ teaspoon salt
¼ teaspoon pepper

Whisk all ingredients together in bowl until smooth. (Dressing can be refrigerated for up to 1 week.)

Creamy Garlic Dressing

MAKES ABOUT 1½ CUPS   **TOTAL TIME** 10 MINUTES   **FAST**

✅ **WHY THIS RECIPE WORKS:** A combination of extra-virgin olive oil and sour cream form the creamy base for this simple dressing, while Dijon mustard and minced garlic give it an appealing bite that shines through. Do not substitute low-fat or nonfat sour cream or mayonnaise here—the dressing will become harsh. This creamy, assertive dressing pairs well with bitter greens like escarole or chicory.

¾ cup extra-virgin olive oil
6 tablespoons sour cream or mayonnaise
3 tablespoons lemon juice
4 teaspoons Dijon mustard
1 tablespoon white wine vinegar
3 garlic cloves, minced
½ teaspoon salt
½ teaspoon pepper

Whisk all ingredients together in bowl until smooth. (Dressing can be refrigerated for up to 1 week.)

Nonfat Roasted Garlic Dressing

MAKES ABOUT 1½ CUPS   **TOTAL TIME** 2 HOURS

✅ **WHY THIS RECIPE WORKS:** Roasting garlic is one way to pack a dressing, sauce, dip, or most any dish with flavor without adding any fat. The spicy sharpness of the garlic becomes mellow and subtly sweet when roasted. Once roasted, the lightly caramelized soft garlic cloves can be squeezed out of their skins and processed with a handful of other ingredients to make a rich-tasting and low-fat creamy dressing. To keep this recipe nonfat, we altered our usual technique for roasting garlic, replacing the oil we typically use with water.

2 large garlic heads
2 tablespoons water
  Salt and pepper
½ cup chicken broth
6 tablespoons cider vinegar
2 tablespoons Dijon mustard
2 tablespoons honey
2 teaspoons minced fresh thyme or ½ teaspoon dried

Roasting Garlic

1. Cut ½ inch off tip of each garlic head so that tops of cloves are exposed.

2. Place garlic heads, cut side up, in center of 10-inch square of aluminum foil. Sprinkle garlic with water and salt and seal foil tightly around garlic.

3. After garlic has roasted, let cool. With your hand or flat edge of chef's knife, squeeze garlic cloves from skins, starting from root end and working up.

1. Adjust oven rack to upper-middle position and heat oven to 400 degrees. Cut ½ inch off top of garlic heads to expose cloves. Set garlic heads, cut side up, on small sheet of aluminum foil and sprinkle with water and pinch salt. Gather up foil around garlic tightly to form packet. Place packet directly on oven rack and roast for 45 minutes.

2. Carefully open top of foil packet to expose garlic. Continue to roast until garlic is soft and golden brown, about 20 minutes. Let roasted garlic cool for 20 minutes, reserving any juices in foil packet.

3. Squeeze roasted garlic from skins. Process garlic, reserved garlic juices, broth, vinegar, mustard, honey, thyme, ¾ teaspoon salt, and ½ teaspoon pepper together in blender until thick and smooth, about 1 minute. (Dressing can be refrigerated for up to 4 days.)

Miso-Sesame Dressing

MAKES ABOUT 1 CUP   **TOTAL TIME** 15 MINUTES   **FAST**

✔ **WHY THIS RECIPE WORKS:** Miso's earthy, salty flavor as well as its viscosity enabled us to replace some of the oil in the dressing with water. We added a touch of honey to balance this assertive dressing. Several types of fresh miso—fermented soybean paste—can be found in Asian markets and in the refrigerator section of some well-stocked supermarkets. We prefer the flavor of red miso paste in this dressing. Do not use powdered miso or the dressing will be overly salty and have a watery texture. This vinaigrette also tastes great on cooked green beans.

      6 tablespoons water
      ¼ cup rice vinegar
      7 teaspoons red miso paste
      1 tablespoon soy sauce
    1½ teaspoons honey
      1 (2-inch) piece fresh ginger, peeled and
         chopped coarse
      1 small garlic clove, peeled
      ¼ cup canola oil
      1 tablespoon toasted sesame oil

Process water, vinegar, miso, soy sauce, honey, ginger, and garlic together in blender until ginger and garlic are finely chopped, about 15 seconds. With blender running, add oils in steady stream until incorporated, then continue to process until smooth, about 15 seconds. (Dressing can be refrigerated for up to 1 week.)

Orange-Lime Dressing

MAKES ABOUT 1 CUP   **TOTAL TIME** 1 HOUR

✔ **WHY THIS RECIPE WORKS:** This spa-like dressing, which uses a minimum of oil and instead relies on simmering orange juice until its flavor is concentrated and the juice is slightly thickened, tastes fresh and light. Although fresh-squeezed orange juice will taste best, any store-bought orange juice will work here. To avoid off-flavors, make sure to reduce the orange juice in a nonreactive stainless steel pan.

      2 cups orange juice
      3 tablespoons lime juice
      2 tablespoons extra-virgin olive oil
      1 tablespoon honey
      1 tablespoon minced shallot
      ½ teaspoon salt
      ½ teaspoon pepper

Simmer orange juice in small saucepan over medium heat until slightly thickened and reduced to ⅔ cup, about 30 minutes. Transfer to medium bowl and refrigerate until cool, about 15 minutes. Whisk in remaining ingredients until smooth. (Dressing can be refrigerated for up to 4 days.)

VARIATION

Cranberry-Balsamic Dressing

Omit honey. Substitute cranberry juice for orange juice and 3 tablespoons balsamic vinegar for lime juice. Whisk 1 teaspoon minced fresh thyme and ½ garlic clove, minced, into reduced and cooled juice with other ingredients.

The Simplest Green Salad

SERVES 4   **TOTAL TIME** 10 MINUTES   **FAST**

✔ **WHY THIS RECIPE WORKS:** This quick and easy way to make a simple salad requires no measuring, no whisking, and (virtually) no thought. And you need only three ingredients: greens, extra-virgin olive oil, and vinegar. It is important to use high-quality ingredients as there are no bells or whistles to camouflage old lettuce, flavorless oil, or harsh vinegar. Be sure to use interesting leafy greens, such as mesclun, arugula, or Bibb lettuce, rather than those with a more neutral flavor, such as iceberg lettuce.

½ garlic clove, peeled
8 ounces (8 cups) lettuce, torn into bite-size
   pieces if necessary
   Extra-virgin olive oil
   Vinegar
   Salt and pepper

Rub inside of salad bowl with garlic. Add lettuce. Holding your thumb over mouth of olive oil bottle to control flow, slowly drizzle lettuce with small amount of oil. Toss greens very gently. Continue to drizzle with oil and toss gently until greens are lightly coated and just glistening. Sprinkle with small amounts of vinegar, salt, and pepper to taste while tossing. Serve.

Making the Simplest Green Salad

1. RUB BOWL WITH GARLIC: For just a hint of garlic flavor, rub inside of salad bowl with half clove of peeled garlic before adding lettuce.

2. ADD WASHED GREENS: Add washed and dried salad greens to bowl. We suggest 2 lightly packed cups per person for a side salad.

3. DRIZZLE WITH OIL: Slowly drizzle greens with extra-virgin olive oil. Toss greens gently and repeat drizzling and tossing as needed until greens are lightly coated.

4. SEASON WITH VINEGAR, SALT, AND PEPPER: Finally, sprinkle greens with small amounts of vinegar, salt, and pepper to taste while tossing gently until salad tastes just right.

Arugula Salad with Figs, Prosciutto, Walnuts, and Parmesan

SERVES 6   **TOTAL TIME** 25 MINUTES **FAST**

✓ **WHY THIS RECIPE WORKS:** Arugula has a lively, peppery bite, so it's important to choose salad accompaniments that can stand up to its assertive character. We found that the sweet and salty notes of fruits and cheeses worked well as supporting players to arugula, and crunchy elements like nuts also provided a nice counterpoint. As for the dressing, a vinaigrette made with mustard turned out to be too spicy, but a surprise solution—a spoonful of jam—added fruity sweetness, pulling the flavors of the salad right in line. Although frying the prosciutto adds crisp texture to the salad, if you prefer you can cut it into ribbons and simply use it as a garnish. Honey can be substituted for the raspberry jam.

¼ cup extra-virgin olive oil
2 ounces thinly sliced prosciutto, cut into
   ¼-inch-wide ribbons
3 tablespoons balsamic vinegar
1 tablespoon raspberry jam
½ cup dried figs, stemmed and chopped into
   ¼-inch pieces
1 small shallot, minced
   Salt and pepper
8 ounces (8 cups) arugula
½ cup walnuts, toasted and chopped
2 ounces Parmesan cheese, shaved

1. Heat 1 tablespoon oil in 10-inch nonstick skillet over medium heat. Add prosciutto and cook, stirring often, until crisp, about 7 minutes. Using slotted spoon, transfer to paper towel–lined plate; let cool.

2. Meanwhile, whisk vinegar and jam together in medium bowl. Stir in figs, cover, and microwave until figs are plump, 30 to 60 seconds. Whisk in remaining 3 tablespoons oil, shallot, ¼ teaspoon salt, and ⅛ teaspoon pepper; let cool.

3. Toss arugula with cooled vinaigrette in large bowl and season with salt and pepper to taste. Divide salad among individual plates and top with prosciutto, walnuts, and Parmesan. Serve.

A surprising sweet ingredient guarantees arugula salads that are lively but not harsh.

Toasting Nuts and Seeds

Toasting nuts and seeds maximizes their flavor, so whether you are adding them to a salad or tossing them into a pasta dish or baked good it pays to spend a few minutes toasting them.

To toast a small amount (less than 1 cup) of nuts or seeds, put them in a dry skillet over medium heat. Shake the skillet occasionally to prevent scorching and toast until they are lightly browned and fragrant, 3 to 8 minutes. Watch the nuts closely because they can go from golden to burnt very quickly. To toast a large quantity of nuts, spread the nuts in a single layer on a rimmed baking sheet and toast in a 350-degree oven. To promote even toasting, shake the baking sheet every few minutes, and toast until the nuts are lightly browned and fragrant, 5 to 10 minutes.

VARIATIONS

Arugula Salad with Grapes, Fennel, Gorgonzola, and Pecans

SERVES 6   **TOTAL TIME** 25 MINUTES   **FAST**

Honey can be substituted for the apricot jam.

- 3 tablespoons white wine vinegar
- 3 tablespoons extra-virgin olive oil
- 1 small shallot, minced
- 4 teaspoons apricot jam
  Salt and pepper
- ½ small fennel bulb, fronds minced, stalks discarded, bulb halved, cored, and sliced thin
- 8 ounces (8 cups) arugula
- 6 ounces red seedless grapes, halved lengthwise (1 cup)
- 3 ounces Gorgonzola cheese, crumbled (¾ cup)
- ½ cup pecans, toasted and chopped

Whisk vinegar, oil, shallot, jam, ¼ teaspoon salt, and ¼ teaspoon pepper together in large bowl. Add fennel, toss to coat, and let sit for 15 minutes. Add arugula, fennel fronds, and grapes and toss to coat. Season with salt and pepper to taste. Divide salad among individual plates and top with Gorgonzola and pecans. Serve.

Arugula Salad with Pear, Almonds, Goat Cheese, and Apricots

SERVES 6   **TOTAL TIME** 25 MINUTES   **FAST**

Honey can be substituted for the apricot jam.

- 3 tablespoons white wine vinegar
- 1 tablespoon apricot jam
- ½ cup dried apricots, chopped into ¼-inch pieces
- 3 tablespoons extra-virgin olive oil
- 1 small shallot, minced
- ¼ small red onion, sliced very thin
  Salt and pepper
- 8 ounces (8 cups) arugula
- 1 pear, halved, cored, and sliced ¼ inch thick
- ⅓ cup sliced almonds, toasted
- 3 ounces goat cheese, crumbled (¾ cup)

1. Whisk vinegar and jam together in medium bowl. Stir in apricots, cover, and microwave until apricots are plump, 30 to 60 seconds. Whisk in oil, shallot, onion, ¼ teaspoon salt, and ⅛ teaspoon pepper; let cool.

2. Toss arugula and pear with cooled vinaigrette in large bowl and season with salt and pepper to taste. Divide salad among individual plates and top with almonds and goat cheese. Serve.

Wedge Salad

SERVES 6   **TOTAL TIME** 30 MINUTES **FAST**

✓ **WHY THIS RECIPE WORKS:** We use a quality blue cheese—English Stilton—to make the rich dressing the star of this salad. Mayo and sour cream add tang and creaminess, red wine vinegar brightens it up, and a splash of milk smooths it out to the perfect consistency—all the better to coat a crunchy wedge of iceberg. Raw onion overpowered even our robust dressing, but shallots soaked in vinegar (which we then used in the dressing) provided a mellower onion flavor. This salad is best when the iceberg wedges are cold.

4	slices bacon
1	large shallot, sliced into ⅛-inch-thick rings
¼	cup red wine vinegar
4	ounces Stilton blue cheese, crumbled (1 cup)
⅓	cup mayonnaise
¼	cup sour cream
3	tablespoons milk
1	garlic clove, minced
¼	teaspoon salt
¼	teaspoon pepper
1	head iceberg lettuce (9 ounces), cored and cut into 6 wedges
12	ounces cherry tomatoes, halved

1. Cook bacon in 10-inch skillet over medium heat until crisp, 5 to 7 minutes. Transfer to paper towel–lined plate. Combine shallot and vinegar in bowl and let sit for 20 minutes.

2. Using fork, remove shallot from vinegar; set aside. Transfer 2 tablespoons vinegar to small bowl; discard remaining vinegar. Whisk ¾ cup blue cheese, mayonnaise, sour cream, milk, garlic, salt, and pepper into vinegar until combined.

3. Arrange lettuce wedges on individual plates and top with dressing, reserved shallot, and tomatoes. Crumble bacon over top and sprinkle with remaining ¼ cup blue cheese. Serve.

NOTES FROM THE TEST KITCHEN

How to Measure Salad Greens

For a side salad we usually call for 2 cups lightly packed greens per person. To lightly pack greens, simply drop them by the handful into a measuring cup, then gently pat down, using your fingertips rather than the palm of your hand. We like to measure greens for a salad using a very large glass measuring cup.

The perfectly wilted spinach in our salads still has some bite to it.

Wilted Spinach Salad with Bacon and Red Onion

SERVES 4 TO 6   **TOTAL TIME** 30 MINUTES **FAST**

✓ **WHY THIS RECIPE WORKS:** The perfect wilted spinach salad requires a careful hand with the dressing so that the tender spinach leaves are gently wilted by the warm dressing. If you use too much dressing, the spinach will overwilt and appear lifeless. If you don't use enough dressing or, worse, if you allow the dressing to cool, the spinach will remain chewy and barely wilted. An easy trick for ensuring a properly wilted salad is to have everything at the ready before you begin— tongs and all—in close proximity to the stovetop. This way, as soon as the dressing is ready, you can pour it over the salad, toss, and serve without wasting a moment. See page 70 for our Foolproof Hard-Cooked Eggs.

10	ounces (10 cups) baby spinach
10	ounces bacon (10 slices), chopped fine
2	tablespoons extra-virgin olive oil
1	red onion, chopped fine

2 garlic cloves, minced
1 teaspoon sugar
½ teaspoon salt
½ teaspoon pepper
6 tablespoons cider vinegar
3 large hard-cooked eggs, peeled and quartered

Place spinach in large bowl. Cook bacon in 12-inch skillet over medium heat until crisp, about 5 minutes. Transfer bacon to paper towel–lined plate and pour off all but 4 tablespoons bacon fat. Add oil to fat left in skillet and return to medium heat until shimmering. Add onion, garlic, sugar, salt, and pepper and cook until onion is soft, about 3 minutes. Off heat, stir in vinegar, then pour immediately over spinach and toss to wilt. Divide salad among individual plates and top with bacon and eggs. Serve.

HOMEMADE CROUTONS FOR SALADS

Homemade croutons are easy to make and taste far better than those you can buy. You can make good croutons using nearly any type of bread, from stale pieces of baguette to the end slices of a sandwich loaf.

3 tablespoons olive oil
2 garlic cloves, minced
¼ teaspoon salt
4 cups (½-inch) bread cubes

Adjust oven rack to middle position and heat oven to 350 degrees. Whisk oil, garlic, and salt together in large bowl, add bread, and toss to coat. Spread bread onto rimmed baking sheet and bake until golden, 20 to 25 minutes. Let croutons cool before serving. (Store at room temperature in airtight container for up to 1 week.)

PARMESAN CROUTONS FAST
Increase oil to 6 tablespoons and stir 1 cup grated Parmesan cheese into oil with garlic and salt.

SPICED CROUTONS FAST
Omit garlic. Whisk ½ teaspoon cumin, ½ teaspoon coriander, ¼ teaspoon paprika, and ⅛ teaspoon cayenne pepper into oil with salt.

HERBED CROUTONS FAST
Whisk 2 teaspoons minced fresh rosemary (or ½ teaspoon dried), 2 teaspoons minced fresh thyme, sage, or dill (or ½ teaspoon dried), and ¼ teaspoon pepper into oil with garlic and salt.

VARIATION
Wilted Spinach Salad with Feta and Olives
SERVES 4 TO 6   TOTAL TIME 30 MINUTES FAST

10 ounces (10 cups) baby spinach
6 tablespoons extra-virgin olive oil
1 red onion, chopped fine
2 garlic cloves, minced
2 teaspoons minced fresh oregano or ½ teaspoon dried
½ teaspoon salt
½ teaspoon pepper
¼ teaspoon sugar
2 tablespoons lemon juice
4 ounces feta cheese, crumbled (1 cup)
½ cup kalamata olives, pitted and sliced thin

Place spinach in large bowl. Heat oil in 8-inch skillet over medium heat until shimmering. Add onion, garlic, oregano, salt, pepper, and sugar and cook until onion is soft, about 3 minutes. Off heat, stir in lemon juice, then pour immediately over spinach and toss to wilt. Divide salad among individual plates and top with feta and olives. Serve.

Classic Caesar Salad
SERVES 4 TO 6   TOTAL TIME 45 MINUTES FAST

WHY THIS RECIPE WORKS: For our Caesar salad, we wanted crisp-tender romaine lettuce napped in a creamy, garlicky dressing boasting a pleasing salty undertone, with crunchy, savory croutons strewn throughout. To start, we cut the extra-virgin olive oil in the dressing with canola oil, which made for a less harsh flavor, and we used egg yolks instead of a whole egg to add richness. For a robust, though not aggressive, garlic flavor we grated the garlic into a pulp and then steeped it in lemon juice. Incorporating a portion of the Parmesan into the dressing while saving some to serve over the salad provided a double layer of cheese flavor. We preferred chewy, crisp ciabatta bread for our croutons and tossed them with a little water before frying them in a skillet until crisp. The water ensured the interiors stayed moist and chewy while the exterior crisped. For a flavor boost, we tossed the croutons with a mixture of garlic, olive oil, and Parmesan. Tossed with pieces of crisp romaine, our Caesar is better than ever. If you can't find ciabatta, a similar crusty, rustic loaf of bread can be substituted. The eggs in this recipe are not cooked. If you prefer, ¼ cup Egg Beaters may be substituted for the egg yolks. The deep flavor of good-quality, oil-packed anchovy fillets is a must in this recipe. The fishier, flatter taste of commercial

A marriage of crisp romaine hearts, homemade croutons, and clingy, garlicky dressing, this salad, when made well, is an exercise in coaxing the most from each ingredient. Homemade croutons are a must for this recipe, and we toast them in a skillet for the best results. Mashed garlic infuses both the croutons and the dressing with flavor. Two egg yolks provide the requisite richness, and along with a mix of canola and extra-virgin olive oil, form the base for our dressing.

1. GRATE THE GARLIC: Grate 2 garlic cloves into a paste using a rasp-style grater. Measure out ½ teaspoon of the garlic for the croutons, and ¾ teaspoon of the garlic for the dressing.
WHY? Grating the garlic, rather than just mincing it, helps to bring out its flavor.

2. CUT THE BREAD INTO CROUTONS: Cut half to three-quarters of a ciabatta loaf into ¾-inch cubes to yield 5 cups.
WHY? Ciabatta bread is the best choice for the croutons, and cutting it into uniform pieces allows for even toasting.

3. SPRINKLE THE CROUTONS WITH WATER: Sprinkle the croutons with water and salt. Toss the cubes, squeezing gently so the bread absorbs water.
WHY? Tossing the croutons with a little water before toasting ensures their interiors will stay soft and tender while the exteriors turn crisp.

4. TOAST THE CROUTONS: Cook the croutons with ¼ cup olive oil in a nonstick skillet over medium-high heat until browned and crisp, 7 to 10 minutes.
WHY? The skillet toasts the croutons without drying out the interior. After toasting, we flavor the croutons with garlic and Parmesan while they are still hot.

5. MARINATE THE GARLIC IN LEMON JUICE FOR THE DRESSING: Whisk 2 tablespoons of the lemon juice and reserved ¾ teaspoon garlic paste together in a salad bowl. Let stand 10 minutes.
WHY? Marinating the minced garlic paste in lemon juice helps to temper the hot, spicy flavor of the garlic in the dressing.

6. WHISK IN THE EGGS AND FLAVORINGS: Whisk in 2 large egg yolks, 6 rinsed and dried anchovy fillets, minced and then mashed into a paste with a fork, and ½ teaspoon Worcestershire sauce.
WHY? These classic ingredients are what give Caesar salad its trademark flavor; mashing the anchovy fillets helps infuse the dressing with flavor.

7. SLOWLY WHISK IN THE OILS TO EMULSIFY: Whisking constantly, drizzle 5 tablespoons canola oil and 5 teaspoons extra-virgin olive oil into the bowl in a slow, steady stream until emulsified.
WHY? A mix of oils balances the dressing. You need only a small amount of extra-virgin olive oil; if you use more, its fruity and bitter flavors will be at odds with the other assertive ingredients.

8. ADD THE CHEESE, LETTUCE, AND CROUTONS: Whisk the cheese into the dressing until evenly incorporated, then add the lettuce and gently toss to coat. Finally, add croutons and gently toss until evenly dispersed.
WHY? Every component must be carefully handled; for an evenly dressed salad we toss the lettuce first, until completely coated, and then add the croutons.

anchovy paste won't do. Since anchovy fillets vary in size, more than 6 fillets may be necessary to yield 1 tablespoon of minced anchovies. A rasp-style grater makes quick work of turning the garlic into a paste.

CROUTONS

2	garlic cloves, grated to a paste
5	tablespoons extra-virgin olive oil
½–¾	loaf ciabatta, cut into ¾-inch cubes (5 cups)
¼	cup water
¼	teaspoon salt
2	tablespoons finely grated Parmesan cheese

SALAD

3	tablespoons lemon juice
6	anchovy fillets, rinsed and patted dry
2	large egg yolks
½	teaspoon Worcestershire sauce
5	tablespoons canola oil
5	teaspoons extra-virgin olive oil
1½	ounces Parmesan cheese, grated fine (¾ cup)
	Pepper
2	romaine lettuce hearts (12 ounces), torn into ¾-inch pieces

1. FOR THE CROUTONS: Transfer ½ teaspoon garlic paste to small bowl and combine with 1 tablespoon oil; reserve for croutons. Transfer ¾ teaspoon garlic paste to separate bowl; reserve for dressing. Discard any remaining garlic.

2. Place bread in large bowl, sprinkle with water and salt, and squeeze bread gently to absorb water. Cook bread with remaining ¼ cup oil in 12-inch nonstick skillet over medium-high heat, stirring often, until browned and crisp, 7 to 10 minutes.

3. Off heat, clear center of skillet, add reserved garlic mixture, and cook using residual heat of pan for 10 seconds. Sprinkle with Parmesan and toss to combine; transfer croutons to bowl.

4. FOR THE SALAD: Whisk reserved ¾ teaspoon garlic paste and 2 tablespoons lemon juice together in salad bowl and let stand 10 minutes. Mince anchovies, then mash into paste with fork; you should have 1 tablespoon.

5. Whisk anchovy paste, egg yolks, and Worcestershire into garlic mixture. Whisking constantly, slowly drizzle canola oil and olive oil into bowl until fully emulsified. Whisk in ½ cup Parmesan and season with pepper to taste. Add lettuce and toss gently, then add croutons and toss gently. Season with remaining 1 tablespoon lemon juice as desired. Serve with remaining ¼ cup Parmesan.

EASY SALAD COMBINATIONS

When you want to break out of the lettuce-tomato-cucumber salad doldrums, try one of these easy and interesting combinations. When making these salads, prepare all the ingredients, then toss the main ingredients and lettuces with the dressing. Add the croutons and cheese last. All of these salads serve 4 to 6.

BIBB LETTUCE, GREEN APPLES, AND CHEDDAR `FAST`

1	head Bibb lettuce
2	Granny Smith apples, peeled, cored, and cut into ½-inch pieces
½	cup Foolproof Vinaigrette (page 52)
4	ounces sharp cheddar cheese, cut into ½-inch pieces (1 cup)
½	cup dried cranberries

SPINACH, WHITE BEANS, AND RED PEPPER `FAST`

2	(5-ounce) bags baby spinach
1	(15-ounce) can white beans, rinsed
1	red bell pepper, stemmed, seeded, and chopped
½	cup Lemon Vinaigrette (page 53)
2	cups Parmesan Croutons (page 61)

ROMAINE LETTUCE, CHICKPEAS, AND FETA `FAST`

2	romaine lettuce hearts
1	head radicchio, quartered, cored, and sliced thin
1	(15-ounce) can chickpeas, rinsed
½	cup Balsamic-Mustard Vinaigrette (page 53)
3	ounces feta cheese, crumbled (¾ cup)

VARIATION

Classic Caesar Salad with Chicken

This main course salad serves 4.

Pat dry 1½ pounds boneless, skinless chicken breasts, trimmed, with paper towels and season with salt and pepper. Heat 1 tablespoon vegetable oil in 12-inch nonstick skillet over medium-high heat until just smoking. Cook chicken on first side until browned, about 3 minutes. Flip chicken, carefully add ⅔ cup water, and cover. Reduce heat to medium and cook until chicken registers 160 degrees, 6 to 8 minutes. Transfer chicken to cutting board, let cool, then cut crosswise into ½-inch thick slices. Reduce romaine to 8 ounces (1½ hearts) and add chicken to salad with croutons.

Our Greek salad dressing uses lemon juice and wine vinegar for balanced flavor, along with fresh oregano and garlic.

6 tablespoons olive oil
3 tablespoons red wine vinegar
2 teaspoons minced fresh oregano
1½ teaspoons lemon juice
1 garlic clove, minced
½ teaspoon salt
⅛ teaspoon pepper
½ red onion, sliced thin
1 cucumber, peeled, halved lengthwise, seeded, and sliced ⅛ inch thick
2 romaine lettuce hearts (12 ounces), torn into 1½-inch pieces
2 large tomatoes, each cored, seeded, and cut into 12 wedges
¼ cup minced fresh parsley
¼ cup torn fresh mint
1 cup jarred roasted red peppers, rinsed, patted dry, and cut into 2 by ½-inch strips
½ cup large pitted kalamata olives, quartered lengthwise
5 ounces feta cheese, crumbled (1¼ cups)

Whisk oil, vinegar, oregano, lemon juice, garlic, salt, and pepper together in large bowl. Add onion and cucumber and let stand for 20 minutes. Add lettuce, tomatoes, parsley, mint, and peppers and toss gently to coat. Transfer salad to serving bowl and sprinkle with olives and feta. Serve.

VARIATION
Country-Style Greek Salad
This salad made without lettuce is known as "country" or "peasant" salad and is served throughout Greece. It's excellent with garden-ripe summer tomatoes.

Omit lettuce. Reduce red wine vinegar to 1½ tablespoons and lemon juice to 1 teaspoon. Increase number of cucumbers to 2 and number of tomatoes to 6.

Greek Salad

SERVES 6 TO 8   TOTAL TIME 30 MINUTES   **FAST**

✓ **WHY THIS RECIPE WORKS:** Most versions of Greek salad consist of iceberg lettuce, chunks of green pepper, and a few pale wedges of tomato sparsely dotted with cubes of feta and garnished with one forlorn olive of questionable heritage. For our Greek salad, we aimed a little higher: We wanted a salad with crisp ingredients and bold flavors, highlighted by briny olives and tangy feta, all blended together with a bright-tasting dressing infused with fresh herbs. For a dressing with balanced flavor, we used a combination of lemon juice and red wine vinegar and added fresh oregano, olive oil, and a small amount of garlic. For our salad ingredients we chose fresh vegetables, including romaine lettuce, tomatoes, red onion, and cucumbers, as well as other ingredients, including fresh mint and parsley, roasted peppers, and a generous sprinkling of feta cheese and olives. Marinating the onion and cucumber in the vinaigrette toned down the onion's harshness and flavored the cucumber. For the sake of efficiency, prepare the other salad ingredients while the onion and cucumber marinate.

Chopped Salad with Apples, Bacon, and Smoked Turkey

SERVES 4   TOTAL TIME 20 MINUTES   **FAST**

✓ **WHY THIS RECIPE WORKS:** Chopped salads often are a hodgepodge of leftovers or pantry ingredients, aimlessly tossed together and dressed with whatever dressing is lying around. We wanted a chopped salad that made sense. We paired crispy bacon with sweet apples, rich cheddar cheese, and smoked turkey breast, a collection of ingredients that works well together and is simple to assemble. To finish this light and refreshing salad we tossed these ingredients with romaine lettuce and a simple cider vinegar and Dijon mustard vinaigrette that complemented the other ingredients but did not compete. When buying the turkey for this salad, ask the deli to slice it into a ½-inch-thick slab so that you can easily cut it into ½-inch pieces.

- 8 slices bacon, chopped
- ¼ cup extra-virgin olive oil
- 2 tablespoons cider vinegar
- 1 shallot, minced
- 1 tablespoon Dijon mustard
  Salt and pepper
- 2 romaine lettuce hearts (12 ounces), torn into bite-size pieces
- 2 apples, cored, halved, and sliced thin
- 8 ounces deli smoked turkey breast, cut into ½-inch chunks
- 4 ounces cheddar cheese, cut into ½-inch chunks

Cook bacon in 12-inch nonstick skillet over medium-high heat until crisp, 5 to 7 minutes; transfer to paper towel–lined plate. Whisk oil, vinegar, shallot, mustard, ½ teaspoon salt, and ½ teaspoon pepper together in large bowl. Add bacon, lettuce, apples, turkey, and cheese and toss to combine. Season with salt and pepper to taste. Divide among individual plates and serve.

Chicken BLT Salad

SERVES 4   TOTAL TIME 35 MINUTES   FAST

 WHY THIS RECIPE WORKS: We love the idea of enjoying a favorite sandwich in salad form. All of the expected ingredients are here—bacon, lettuce, and tomato—along with the addition of chunks of chicken. We cooked the chicken chunks right in the rendered bacon fat, giving the salad even more big bacon flavor. Instead of relying on stale-tasting store-bought croutons, we made our own in minutes using thick slices of fresh Italian bread, which we spread with mayonnaise before toasting to give them just the right hint of BLT sandwich flavor. You can substitute grape tomatoes for the cherry tomatoes here.

- ¾ cup mayonnaise
- 4 (1-inch-thick) slices Italian bread
- 1 pound bacon, chopped
- 2 (6-ounce) boneless, skinless chicken breasts, trimmed and cut into 1-inch pieces
  Salt and pepper

NOTES FROM THE TEST KITCHEN

Buying Salad Greens

Not only is there a dizzying array of greens available at the supermarket now, but in a good market you can buy the same greens more than one way: full heads, prewashed in a bag, in a clamshell, and loose in bulk bins. Which is the right choice for you? A sturdy lettuce like romaine can be washed and stored for up to a week (see page 69), making it a good option for many nights' worth of salads. Prewashed bags of baby spinach, arugula, and mesclun mix offer great convenience, but be sure to turn over the bags and inspect the greens as closely as you can; the sell-by date alone doesn't ensure quality, so if you see moisture in the bag or hints of blackened leaf edges, move on.

Don't buy bags of already cut lettuce that you can otherwise buy as whole heads, like romaine or Bibb or red leaf. Precut lettuce will be inferior in quality because the leaves begin to spoil once they are cut (bagged hearts of romaine are fine but stay away from bags of cut romaine). Endive and radicchio are always sold in heads, and because they are sturdy and will last a while, they are nice to have on hand to complement other greens and just to add more interest to a salad. And when a special salad is planned for company, for the best results you should buy the greens either the day of the party or the day before.

- 3 tablespoons red wine vinegar
- 1½ pounds cherry tomatoes, halved
- 2 romaine lettuce hearts (12 ounces), torn into bite-size pieces

1. Adjust oven rack to middle position and heat oven to 475 degrees. Spread ¼ cup mayonnaise over both sides of bread, lay on baking sheet, and bake until golden brown, 8 to 10 minutes, flipping bread halfway through cooking. Let cool 5 minutes, then cut into 1-inch croutons.

2. Meanwhile, cook bacon in 12-inch nonstick skillet over medium-high heat until crisp, 5 to 7 minutes. Transfer bacon to paper towel–lined plate and pour off all but 1 tablespoon fat left in skillet.

3. Pat chicken dry with paper towels and season with salt and pepper. Heat fat left in skillet over medium-high heat until just smoking. Cook chicken, stirring often, until golden and cooked through, 2 to 4 minutes; transfer to plate.

4. Whisk remaining ½ cup mayonnaise and vinegar together in serving bowl. Add bacon, chicken, tomatoes, lettuce, and croutons and toss to combine. Season with salt and pepper to taste and serve.

ALL ABOUT **SALAD GREENS**

Here are some of the most common salad greens you'll find at the market. With such a wide array of greens to choose from, it's good to know how to mix and match them to build interesting salads. Many are great on their own, but others are generally best used to add texture or color to other salads. No matter what type of greens you buy, make sure to select the freshest ones possible and avoid any that are wilted, bruised, or discolored.

	TYPE/DESCRIPTION	YIELD	SERVING SUGGESTIONS
	Arugula (also called Rocket or Roquette) Delicate dark green leaves with a peppery bite; sold in bunches, usually with roots attached, or prewashed in cellophane bags; arugula bruises easily and can be very sandy, so wash thoroughly in several changes of water before using.	5-ounce bag (5 cups) 6-ounce bunch (3 cups)	Serve alone for a full-flavored salad, or add to romaine, Bibb, or Boston lettuce to give a spicy punch; for a classic salad, combine with Belgian endive and radicchio.
	Belgian Endive Small, compact head of firm white or pale yellow leaves; should be completely smooth and blemish-free; slightly bitter flavor and crisp texture; one of the few salad greens we routinely cut rather than tear; remove whole leaves from the head and slice crosswise into bite-size pieces.	4-ounce head (1 cup sliced)	Add to watercress or to Bibb, Boston, or loose-leaf lettuce; combine with diced apples, blue cheese, and walnuts; use whole leaves in place of crackers with dips and flavorful soft cheeses.
	Bibb Lettuce Small, compact heads; pale to medium green leaves; soft, buttery outer leaves; inner leaves have surprising crunch and a sweet, mild flavor.	8-ounce head (8 cups)	Combine with watercress or endive, or with Boston, loose-leaf, or romaine lettuce; great tossed with fresh herbs (whole parsley leaves, chives, or dill).
	Boston Lettuce Loose, fluffy head, ranging in color from pale green to red-tipped; similar in texture and flavor to Bibb lettuce, but with softer leaves.	8-ounce head (8 cups)	Combine with baby spinach, watercress, or endive, or with Bibb or romaine lettuce; terrific as a bed for seafood salad, chicken salad, or tuna salad.
	Chicory (also called Curly Endive) Loose, feathery head of bright green, bitter leaves; texture is somewhat chewy.	10-ounce head (10 cups)	Add to bitter green salads or use sparingly to add punch to mild mixed greens; toss with warm bacon dressing; great when served with whole cloves of roasted garlic, crisp bacon, and a garlicky dressing.
	Escarole A kind of chicory with tough, dark green leaves and a mildly bitter flavor; inner leaves are slightly milder.	15-ounce head (15 cups)	Use as an accent to romaine; serve on its own with Balsamic-Mustard Vinaigrette (page 53).
	Frisée A kind of chicory; milder in flavor than other chicories, but with similar feathery leaves; pale green to white in color.	10-ounce head (4 cups)	Combine with arugula or watercress, or with Boston or Bibb lettuce; serve on its own with warm bacon dressing or warm balsamic vinaigrette; great when paired with toasted walnuts and herbed goat cheese.

TYPE/DESCRIPTION	YIELD	SERVING SUGGESTIONS
Iceberg A large, round, tightly packed head of pale green leaves; very crisp and crunchy, with minimal flavor.	1-pound head (12 cups)	Cut into wedges and top with Blue Cheese (page 54) or Thousand Island Dressing (page 53); tear into chunks and toss with Bibb, Boston, or loose-leaf lettuce.
Loose-Leaf Lettuces (specifically Red Leaf and Green Leaf) Ruffled dark red or green leaves that grow in big, loose heads; versatile with a soft yet crunchy texture; green leaf is crisp and mild; red leaf is earthier.	12-ounce head (12 cups)	Pair red leaf with romaine lettuce or watercress; pair green leaf with arugula, radicchio, or watercress; great on sandwiches and hamburgers, or as a bed for prepared salads.
Mâche (also called Lamb's Tongue or Lamb's Lettuce) Small heads of 3 or 4 stems of small, sweet, deep green leaves; very delicate; usually sold prewashed in bags; if buying heads, wash thoroughly, can be sandy.	4-ounce bag (4 cups)	Combine with arugula or watercress; perfect on its own with crumbled goat cheese and Foolproof Vinaigrette (page 52).
Mesclun (also called Mesclune, Spring Mix, Field Greens) A mix of up to 14 different baby greens, including spinach, red leaf, oak leaf, frisée, radicchio, green leaf; delicate leaves; flavors range from mild to slightly bitter depending on the blend.	4 ounces bagged or loose (4 cups)	Great as a delicate salad; terrific paired with goat cheese and Lemon Vinaigrette (page 53).
Radicchio Tight heads of red or deep purple leaves streaked with white ribs; bitter flavor.	10-ounce head (3 cups)	Cut into ribbons and mix with arugula, endive, or watercress, or with red and green leaf, Boston, or Bibb lettuce; adds color to any salad.
Romaine Long, full heads, with stiff and deep green leaves; crisp, crunchy leaves with a mild earthy flavor; also sold in bags of three romaine hearts; tough outer leaves should be discarded from full heads.	6-ounce heart (4 cups) 14-ounce head (9 cups)	A great all-purpose lettuce; mix with spinach, watercress, arugula, endive, or radicchio, or with Boston, Bibb, or red leaf lettuce; *the* lettuce for Caesar salad; good on sandwiches and hamburgers.
Spinach (Flat-Leaf and Baby) All varieties are vibrant green with an earthy flavor; choose tender flat-leaf or baby spinach for salads; tough curly-leaf spinach is better steamed and sautéed; rinse loose spinach well to remove dirt; varieties available prewashed in bags.	5-ounce bag (5 cups) 11-ounce bunch (5 cups)	Delicious mixed with arugula, watercress, or napa cabbage, or with romaine, Bibb, Boston, or loose-leaf lettuce; classic as a wilted salad with warm bacon dressing or warm lemon vinaigrette.
Watercress Delicate dark green leaves with tough bitter stems; refreshing mustardlike flavor similar to arugula; usually sold in bunches, sometimes available prewashed in bags; if buying watercress in bunches, take care to wash thoroughly.	2-ounce bunch (2 cups)	Adds flavorful punch and texture to mildly flavored or tender greens such as Bibb or Boston lettuce; delicious on its own with tart green apples, blue cheese, and a mustard-based dressing.

Our taco salad is topped with flavorful ground turkey, tomatoes, avocado, and cheese and tortilla chips for crunch.

Washing and Drying Salad Greens

To make a great salad, the only thing that is more critical than using crisp, fresh greens is using clean, dry greens. Trying to dress a salad while the greens are still wet is a losing battle—the dressing slides off, and the water from the greens will dilute the dressing. We believe that the only foolproof method for drying them is to use a salad spinner.

TO WASH GREENS: Fill a salad spinner bowl with cool water, add cut greens, and gently swish them around. Do not run water directly over the greens, as the force can bruise them. Using your hands, gently move the greens to loosen grit, which will fall to the bottom of the bowl. Use the sink if you need to clean large amounts of greens.

TO DRY GREENS: Dry greens in a salad spinner, stopping several times to dump out excess moisture. Keep spinning greens until no more moisture accumulates. After spinning them, we like to blot greens dry with paper towels; even the best salad spinners don't dry greens completely.

Turkey Taco Salad

SERVES 4   TOTAL TIME 40 MINUTES   FAST

WHY THIS RECIPE WORKS: Taco salads are a great way to enjoy the flavors of a taco with no assembly required. We make a quick, well-seasoned ground turkey mixture in a skillet—no seasoning packet required. While the turkey mixture cooks and cools, you can make the dressing; the trio of lime juice, cilantro, and jalapeño give this dressing (and salad) tons of zip. Romaine lettuce, chopped tomato, cubed avocado, and shredded cheese round out the salad, and crumbled tortilla chips provide a pleasant crunch. Be sure to use ground turkey, not ground turkey breast (labeled 99 percent fat-free) in this recipe. Salsa, sour cream, and minced cilantro also taste great on this salad.

¾ cup plus 1 tablespoon extra-virgin olive oil
1 onion, chopped fine
2 tablespoons chili powder
5 garlic cloves, minced
1 pound 93 percent lean ground turkey
1 (8-ounce) can tomato sauce
  Salt and pepper
3 tablespoons lime juice (2 limes)
1 jalapeño chile, stemmed, seeded, and chopped
½ cup fresh cilantro leaves
1 large head romaine lettuce (14 ounces), torn into bite-size pieces
2 tomatoes, cored and chopped
1 avocado, halved, pitted, and cut into ½-inch pieces
4 ounces shredded cheddar cheese or Mexican cheese blend (1 cup)
1 cup crumbled tortilla chips (2 ounces)

1. Heat 1 tablespoon oil in 12-inch nonstick skillet over medium heat until shimmering. Add onion and chili powder and cook until onion is softened, 3 to 5 minutes. Stir in 4 teaspoons garlic and cook until fragrant, about 30 seconds.

2. Stir in turkey and cook, breaking up meat with wooden spoon, until lightly browned, 6 to 8 minutes. Stir in tomato sauce and simmer until slightly thickened, about 2 minutes. Season with salt and pepper to taste.

3. Meanwhile, process lime juice, jalapeño, remaining garlic, and ½ teaspoon salt in blender until finely chopped, about 15 seconds. With blender running, add cilantro and then remaining ¾ cup oil, and continue to process until smooth and emulsified, about 15 seconds.

4. Toss lettuce with ½ cup dressing in bowl. Divide salad among individual plates, top with turkey mixture, and sprinkle with tomatoes, avocado, cheese, and tortilla chips. Drizzle with remaining dressing and serve.

Steak and Blue Cheese Salad

SERVES 4   **TOTAL TIME** 40 MINUTES   **FAST**

✓ **WHY THIS RECIPE WORKS:** Steak and sautéed mushrooms are a classic combination, and so are steak and blue cheese, so it makes perfect sense to bring all three together for a flavorful dinner salad. Cooking the mushrooms in the same skillet we used for cooking the steak allowed them to pick up the flavorful fond left behind from the meat, and adding a few tablespoons of vinaigrette, rather than the usual plain oil, while they browned gave them a tangy flavor.

> 2   (8- to 10-ounce) boneless strip steaks, 1 inch thick, trimmed
>   Salt and pepper
> ½   cup extra-virgin olive oil
> ¼   cup red wine vinegar
> 1   shallot, minced
> 1   tablespoon Dijon mustard
> 1   pound white mushrooms, trimmed and quartered
> 10 ounces (10 cups) baby spinach
> 2   tablespoons capers, rinsed and minced
> 2   ounces blue cheese, crumbled (½ cup)

1. Pat steaks dry with paper towels and season with salt and pepper. Heat 1 tablespoon oil in 12-inch skillet over medium-high heat until just smoking. Brown steaks on first side, about 5 minutes. Flip steaks over and continue to cook until meat registers 120 to 125 degrees (for medium-rare), 3 to 6 minutes. Transfer steaks to plate and tent with aluminum foil. Pour off fat but do not wipe out pan.

2. Meanwhile, whisk vinegar, shallot, mustard, and remaining 7 tablespoons oil together in large bowl and season with salt and pepper to taste.

3. Add mushrooms and 2 tablespoons vinaigrette to now-empty skillet and cook over medium-high heat, scraping up any browned bits, until mushrooms are golden, 6 to 8 minutes. Transfer mushrooms to clean bowl and let cool slightly.

4. Toss spinach and capers with remaining vinaigrette in large bowl and season with salt and pepper to taste. Divide spinach among individual plates and top with mushrooms. Slice steak thinly against grain and arrange over salad. Sprinkle with blue cheese and serve.

NOTES FROM THE TEST KITCHEN

Storing Salad Greens

Here's the best way to store the most common types of lettuce when you get home from the supermarket.

LETTUCE TYPE	HOW TO STORE
Crisp heads, such as iceberg and romaine	Core lettuce, wrap in moist paper towels, and refrigerate in plastic produce bag or zipper-lock bag left slightly open.
Leafy greens, such as arugula, baby spinach, and mesclun	If prewashed, store in original plastic container or bag. If not prewashed, wash and dry thoroughly in salad spinner and store directly in spinner between layers of paper towels, or lightly roll in paper towels and store in zipper-lock bag left slightly open.
Tender heads, such as Boston and Bibb lettuce	If lettuce comes with root attached, leave lettuce portion attached to root and store in original plastic container, plastic produce bag, or zipper-lock bag left slightly open. If lettuce is without root, wrap in moist paper towels and refrigerate in plastic produce bag or zipper-lock bag left slightly open.

24-Hour Picnic Salad

SERVES 12   **TOTAL TIME** 30 MINUTES
(PLUS 8 HOURS CHILLING TIME)

✓ **WHY THIS RECIPE WORKS:** We liked the idea of a salad recipe that could be assembled in advance, put in the fridge for a night, and simply tossed and served the next day. Salting the layers of iceberg lettuce pulled moisture out; we then used the water to thin our dressing to the perfect consistency. Crunchy vegetables like celery, bell peppers, and cucumbers stayed crisp in the salad overnight, but soft ingredients like mushrooms and spinach wilted into mush. Frank's RedHot Original Hot Sauce is our favorite brand of hot sauce. If using a hotter brand, such as Tabasco Sauce, reduce the amount to 1 tablespoon. See page 70 for our Foolproof Hard-Cooked Eggs.

SALAD

- 1 head iceberg lettuce (9 ounces), cored and coarsely chopped
- Salt
- ½ red onion, sliced thin, rinsed under cold water, and patted dry
- 6 large hard-cooked eggs, peeled and chopped
- 1½ cups frozen peas
- 4 celery ribs, sliced thin
- 1 red bell pepper, stemmed, seeded, and chopped
- 1 cucumber, halved lengthwise, seeded, and sliced thin
- 1 pound bacon, cooked and crumbled
- 6 ounces blue cheese, crumbled (1½ cups)

DRESSING

- 1½ cups mayonnaise
- 3 tablespoons cider vinegar
- 2 tablespoons hot sauce
- 2 teaspoons sugar
- 1½ teaspoons pepper

1. FOR THE SALAD: Layer ingredients into large serving bowl as follows: half of lettuce sprinkled with ½ teaspoon salt, onion, eggs, peas, celery, bell pepper, cucumber, remaining lettuce sprinkled with ½ teaspoon salt, bacon, and cheese.

2. FOR THE DRESSING: Whisk all ingredients together in bowl and spread evenly over top of salad. Refrigerate for at least 8 hours or up to 1 day. Toss until salad is evenly coated with dressing and serve.

FOOLPROOF HARD-COOKED EGGS

This simple bring-it-to-a-boil method consistently turns out perfect hard-cooked eggs with moist and creamy yolks, firm yet tender whites, and no trace of a green ring. Make as few or as many eggs as you need.

Use a pot large enough to hold eggs in a single layer, cover with 1 inch water, and bring to boil over high heat. Remove pan from heat, cover, and let sit 10 minutes. Meanwhile, fill medium bowl with 4 cups water and 1 tray ice cubes. Transfer eggs to ice water bath with slotted spoon; let sit for 5 minutes. Peel eggs.

Tender beets, halved and braised in a small amount of water for streamlined cooking, make a flavorful salad.

Beets with Lemon and Almonds

SERVES 4 TO 6   **TOTAL TIME** 1 HOUR 15 MINUTES

✔ WHY THIS RECIPE WORKS: For a streamlined recipe for beets that maximized their sweet, earthy flavor, we braised halved beets in minimal water, then reduced their cooking liquid and added brown sugar and vinegar for a flavorful thick glaze. For flavor and contrast, we added toasted nuts (or pepitas), fresh herbs, and citrus zest just before serving. To ensure even cooking, we recommend using beets of similar size— roughly 2 to 3 inches in diameter. The beets can be served warm or at room temperature. If serving at room temperature, sprinkle with almonds and herbs right before serving.

- 1½ pounds beets, trimmed and halved horizontally
- 1¼ cups water
- Salt and pepper
- 3 tablespoons distilled white vinegar
- 1 tablespoon packed light brown sugar
- 1 shallot, sliced thin

1 teaspoon grated lemon zest
½ cup whole almonds, toasted and chopped
2 tablespoons minced fresh mint
1 teaspoon minced fresh thyme

1. Place beets, cut side down, in 11-inch straight-sided sauté pan or Dutch oven. Add water and ¼ teaspoon salt and bring to simmer over high heat. Reduce heat to low, cover, and simmer until beets are tender and tip of paring knife inserted into beets meets no resistance, 45 to 50 minutes.

2. Transfer beets to cutting board and let cool. Increase heat to medium-high and reduce cooking liquid, stirring occasionally, until pan is almost dry, 5 to 6 minutes. Add vinegar and sugar, return to boil, and cook, stirring constantly with heat-resistant spatula, until spatula leaves wide trail when dragged through glaze, 1 to 2 minutes. Remove pan from heat.

3. When beets are cool, rub off skins with paper towel and cut into ½-inch wedges. Add beets, shallot, lemon zest, ½ teaspoon salt, and ¼ teaspoon pepper to glaze and toss to coat. Transfer beets to serving dish and sprinkle with almonds, mint, and thyme. Serve.

VARIATIONS

Beets with Lime and Pepitas

Omit thyme. Substitute lime zest for lemon zest, toasted pepitas for almonds, and cilantro for mint.

Beets with Orange and Walnuts

Substitute orange zest for lemon zest, toasted and chopped walnuts for almonds, and parsley for mint.

Making Beet Salad

Creamy Dill Cucumber Salad

SERVES 4   **TOTAL TIME** 1 HOUR 30 MINUTES

✔ **WHY THIS RECIPE WORKS:** Cucumbers can make a cool, crisp salad, but often they turn soggy from their own moisture. For a cucumber salad with good crunch, we found that weighting salted cucumbers forced more water from them than salting alone. After many tests, we determined that 1 to 3 hours worked best: Even at 12 hours, the cucumbers gave up no more water than they had after 3 hours. For a bit of zip, we paired cucumbers with onion—and found that salting and draining the onion along with the cucumbers removed its sharp sting. Whether we dressed them with a lively vinaigrette or a rich, creamy dressing, our cucumbers retained maximum crunch. Fresh dill is essential to the flavor of this salad; do not substitute dried.

3 cucumbers (2 pounds), peeled, halved lengthwise, seeded, and sliced ¼ inch thick on bias
1 small red onion, sliced very thin
1 tablespoon salt
1 cup sour cream
3 tablespoons cider vinegar
1 teaspoon sugar
¼ cup minced fresh dill

1. Toss cucumbers and onion with salt in colander set over large bowl. Weight cucumber mixture with gallon-size zipper-lock bag filled with water and let drain for 1 to 3 hours. Rinse cucumber mixture and pat dry.

1. BRAISE HALVED BEETS: Place halved beets, cut side down, in sauté pan or Dutch oven with 1¼ cups water and braise gently until beets are tender.

2. COOL, SKIN, AND CUT BEETS: Remove beets from pot, let cool, then rub off skins. Cut into ½-inch wedges.

3. REDUCE COOKING LIQUID AND MAKE GLAZE: Reduce braising liquid to thick, flavorful syrup. Add vinegar and sugar.

4. TOSS BEETS IN GLAZE: Return beets to pot with shallot, lemon zest, salt, and pepper and toss gently to coat.

2. Whisk sour cream, vinegar, sugar, and dill together in serving bowl. Stir in cucumbers and onion. Serve chilled. (Salad can be refrigerated for up to 1 day.)

VARIATIONS

Yogurt-Mint Cucumber Salad

Substitute following mixture for sour cream mixture in step 2: Whisk 1 cup plain yogurt, 2 tablespoons extra-virgin olive oil, ¼ cup minced fresh mint, 1 minced garlic clove, and ½ teaspoon ground cumin together in serving bowl.

Sesame-Lemon Cucumber Salad

Omit red onion and substitute following mixture for sour cream mixture in step 2: Whisk ¼ cup rice vinegar, 1 tablespoon lemon juice, 2 tablespoons toasted sesame oil, 2 teaspoons sugar, 1 tablespoon toasted sesame seeds, and ⅛ teaspoon red pepper flakes together in serving bowl.

Preparing Cucumbers for Salad

1. Peel cucumbers, halve lengthwise, and scrape out watery seeds using spoon.

2. Using chef's knife, slice cucumber into ¼-inch-thick slices on bias.

3. Toss sliced cucumbers with 1 tablespoon salt in colander, and top with gallon-size zipper-lock bag filled with water to help press out liquid. Let drain for 1 to 3 hours.

Southwestern Black Bean Salad

SERVES 6 TO 8   **TOTAL TIME** 25 MINUTES   **FAST**

✓ **WHY THIS RECIPE WORKS:** We quickly edited out the dull bell pepper and harsh onion found in traditional recipes for Southwestern black bean salad. Instead, we used scallions, which were mellow and light. Creamy avocados gave the salad richness, tomatoes lent juicy freshness, and corn added welcome sweetness. Sautéing the corn (both fresh and frozen worked well) until it was toasty and just starting to brown added a pleasant nuttiness to the kernels. To give our salad the wake-up call it needed, we turned the typical dressing ratio of 1 part acid to 3 parts oil nearly upside down, using more lime juice than olive oil. Honey balanced the citrus kick, and throwing the scallions into the dressing mellowed them even more. You will need three to four ears to yield 2 cups of fresh kernels. If using frozen corn, be sure to thaw and drain it.

⅓ cup lime juice (3 limes)
¼ cup olive oil
1 tablespoon minced canned chipotle chile in adobo sauce
1 teaspoon honey
4 scallions, sliced thin
   Salt and pepper
2 cups fresh or frozen corn
2 (15-ounce) cans black beans, rinsed
2 avocados, pitted and cut into ½-inch pieces
2 tomatoes, cored and chopped
¼ cup minced fresh cilantro

Whisk lime juice, 2 tablespoons oil, chipotle, honey, scallions, ½ teaspoon salt, and ½ teaspoon pepper together in serving bowl. Heat remaining 2 tablespoons oil in 12-inch nonstick skillet over medium-high heat until shimmering. Add corn and cook until spotty brown, about 5 minutes. Add corn to bowl with dressing. Add beans, avocados, tomatoes, and cilantro and toss to combine. Season with salt and pepper to taste and serve. (Salad can be refrigerated for up to 2 days.)

Toasting Corn

To bring out corn's flavor, toast it with oil in 12-inch nonstick skillet over medium-high heat until spotty brown, about 5 minutes.

Fresh green and yellow beans brighten a classic three-bean salad and heating the dressing intensifies its flavor.

Classic Three-Bean Salad

SERVES 8 TO 10   **TOTAL TIME** 1 HOUR 15 MINUTES (PLUS 8 HOURS CHILLING TIME)

✔ **WHY THIS RECIPE WORKS:** Recipes for that familiar picnic standby, canned green, yellow, and kidney beans tossed in a sweet, vinegary dressing, have changed little since the salad's heyday in the 1950s. We wanted an updated, fresher-tasting three-bean salad so we used a combination of canned kidney beans and fresh yellow and green beans. For the dressing, we relied on canola oil for mildness and red wine vinegar for tang. Heating the oil and vinegar with sugar, garlic, salt, and pepper intensified the vinaigrette flavor and sweetness. Refrigerating the salad overnight allows the flavors to meld so plan ahead.

1 cup red wine vinegar
¾ cup sugar
½ cup canola oil
2 garlic cloves, minced
   Salt and pepper
8 ounces green beans, trimmed and cut into 1-inch lengths
8 ounces yellow wax beans, trimmed and cut into 1-inch lengths
1 (15-ounce) can red kidney beans, rinsed
½ red onion, sliced thin
¼ cup minced fresh parsley

1. Heat vinegar, sugar, oil, garlic, 1 teaspoon salt, and pinch pepper in small saucepan over medium heat until sugar dissolves, about 5 minutes. Transfer to serving bowl and let cool to room temperature.

2. Meanwhile, bring 3 quarts water to boil in large saucepan over high heat, and fill medium bowl with ice water. Add 1 tablespoon salt, green beans, and yellow beans to boiling water and cook until beans are crisp-tender, about 5 minutes. Drain beans and plunge immediately into ice water to stop cooking; let sit until chilled, about 2 minutes. Drain well.

3. Toss green and yellow beans, kidney beans, onion, and parsley with cooled vinegar mixture. Refrigerate overnight to let flavors meld. Let stand at room temperature 30 minutes before serving. (Salad can be refrigerated for up to 4 days.)

Classic Egg Salad

SERVES 4 TO 6   **TOTAL TIME** 40 MINUTES **FAST**

✔ **WHY THIS RECIPE WORKS:** For creamy, flavorful egg salad with perfectly cooked eggs and just the right amount of crunch, we followed a few simple steps. First, we relied on our Foolproof Hard-Cooked Eggs (page 70), which yielded eggs with creamy yolks, tender whites, and no green ring. We diced the eggs then we combined them with mayonnaise (our tasters dismissed cottage cheese, sour cream, and cream cheese), lemon juice, Dijon mustard, red onion, celery, and parsley. Be sure to use red onion; yellow onion is too harsh.

6 large eggs
¼ cup mayonnaise
2 tablespoons minced red onion
1 tablespoon minced fresh parsley
½ celery rib, minced
2 teaspoons Dijon mustard
2 teaspoons lemon juice
   Salt and pepper

1. Place eggs in medium saucepan, cover with 1 inch water, and bring to boil over high heat. Remove pan from heat, cover, and let sit 10 minutes. Meanwhile, fill medium bowl with 4 cups water and 1 tray ice cubes. Transfer eggs to ice water bath with slotted spoon; let sit 5 minutes. Peel and dice eggs.

2. Mix eggs with remaining ingredients in bowl and season with salt and pepper to taste. Serve. (Salad can be refrigerated for up to 1 day.)

VARIATIONS

Egg Salad with Radish, Scallions, and Dill

Substitute minced fresh dill for parsley and 1 thinly sliced scallion for red onion. Add 3 minced radishes.

Curried Egg Salad

Substitute minced fresh cilantro for parsley and add 1½ teaspoons curry powder.

Creamy Egg Salad with Capers and Anchovies

Add 1 minced small garlic clove, 2 tablespoons rinsed and minced capers, and 1 rinsed and minced anchovy fillet.

Classic Chicken Salad

SERVES 4 TO 6   TOTAL TIME 1 HOUR

✔ **WHY THIS RECIPE WORKS:** Recipes for chicken salad are only as good as the chicken. If the chicken is dry or flavorless, no amount of dressing or add-ins will camouflage it. To ensure silky, juicy, and flavorful chicken, we used a method based on *sous vide* cooking (submerging vacuum-sealed foods in a temperature-controlled water bath). Our ideal formula was four chicken breasts and 6 cups of cold water heated to 170 degrees and then removed from the heat, covered, and left to stand for about 15 minutes. Incomparably moist, this chicken was perfect for our salad. To ensure that the chicken cooks through, don't use breasts that weigh more than 8 ounces or are thicker than 1 inch. Make sure to start with cold water in step 1. This salad can be served in a sandwich or spooned over leafy greens.

    Salt and pepper
4   (6- to 8-ounce) boneless, skinless chicken breasts,
    trimmed and pounded to 1-inch thickness
½   cup mayonnaise
2   tablespoons lemon juice

Our special poaching method ensures incredibly moist chicken for chicken salad.

1   teaspoon Dijon mustard
2   celery ribs, minced
1   shallot, minced
1   tablespoon minced fresh parsley
1   tablespoon minced fresh tarragon

1. Dissolve 2 tablespoons salt in 6 cups cold water in Dutch oven. Submerge chicken in water. Heat pot over medium heat until water registers 170 degrees. Turn off heat, cover pot, and let stand until chicken registers 165 degrees, 15 to 17 minutes. Transfer chicken to paper towel–lined rimmed baking sheet and refrigerate until cool, about 30 minutes.

2. Whisk mayonnaise, lemon juice, mustard, and ¼ teaspoon pepper together in large bowl. Pat chicken dry with paper towels and cut into ½-inch pieces. Add chicken, celery, shallot, parsley, and tarragon to mayonnaise mixture and toss to combine. Season with salt and pepper to taste. Serve. (Salad can be refrigerated for up to 2 days.)

Curried Chicken Salad with Cashews

SERVES 4 TO 6 **TOTAL TIME** 1 HOUR

    Salt and pepper
  4 (6- to 8-ounce) boneless, skinless chicken breasts,
     trimmed and pounded to 1-inch thickness
  1 teaspoon vegetable oil
  1 teaspoon curry powder
 ⅛ teaspoon cayenne pepper
 ½ cup mayonnalse
  2 tablespoons lime juice
  1 teaspoon grated fresh ginger
  2 celery ribs, minced
  1 shallot, minced
 ½ cup raw cashews, toasted and chopped coarse
 ⅓ cup golden raisins
  2 tablespoons minced fresh cilantro

1. Dissolve 2 tablespoons salt in 6 cups cold water in Dutch oven. Submerge chicken in water. Heat pot over medium heat until water registers 170 degrees. Turn off heat, cover pot, and let stand until chicken registers 165 degrees, 15 to 17 minutes. Transfer chicken to paper towel–lined rimmed baking sheet and refrigerate until cool, about 30 minutes.

2. Microwave vegetable oil, curry powder, and cayenne in bowl until oil is hot, about 30 seconds. Whisk mayonnaise, lime juice, ginger, and curry mixture together in large bowl.

3. Pat chicken dry with paper towels and cut into ½-inch pieces. Add chicken, celery, shallot, cashews, raisins, and cilantro to mayonnaise mixture and toss to combine. Season with salt and pepper to taste. Serve. (Salad can be refrigerated for up to 2 days.)

Chicken Salad with Red Grapes and Smoked Almonds

SERVES 4 TO 6 **TOTAL TIME** 1 HOUR

    Salt and pepper
  4 (6- to 8-ounce) boneless, skinless chicken breasts,
     trimmed and pounded to 1-inch thickness
 ½ cup mayonnaise
 ¼ teaspoon grated lemon zest plus 2 tablespoons juice
  1 teaspoon Dijon mustard
  2 celery ribs, minced
  1 shallot, minced
  6 ounces seedless red grapes, quartered (1 cup)

 ½ cup smoked almonds, chopped coarse
  1 tablespoon minced fresh parsley
  1 teaspoon minced fresh rosemary

1. Dissolve 2 tablespoons salt in 6 cups cold water in Dutch oven. Submerge chicken in water. Heat pot over medium heat until water registers 170 degrees. Turn off heat, cover pot, and let stand until chicken registers 165 degrees, 15 to 17 minutes. Transfer chicken to paper towel–lined rimmed baking sheet and refrigerate until cool, about 30 minutes.

2. Whisk mayonnaise, lemon zest and juice, mustard, and ¼ teaspoon pepper together in large bowl. Pat chicken dry with paper towels and cut into ½-inch pieces. Add chicken, celery, shallot, grapes, almonds, parsley, and rosemary to mayonnaise mixture and toss to combine. Season with salt and pepper to taste. Serve. (Salad can be refrigerated for up to 2 days.)

Making Chicken Salad

1. POACH CHICKEN: Heat chicken in salted water until water registers 170 degrees. Let stand until chicken registers 165 degrees.

2. REFRIGERATE CHICKEN: Transfer chicken to paper towel–lined rimmed baking sheet and refrigerate until cool, about 30 minutes.

3. CUT CHICKEN INTO PIECES: Pat chicken dry with paper towels and cut into ½-inch pieces.

4. COMBINE CHICKEN AND DRESSING: Whisk dressing, then fold in chicken along with herbs, vegetables, and any other add-ins.

Tuna Salad

SERVES 4 TO 6 **TOTAL TIME** 20 MINUTES **FAST**

✔ **WHY THIS RECIPE WORKS:** Even a simple tuna salad has its problems. It can be simultaneously watery, flavorless, drowning in mayonnaise, or overpowered by raw onion. There are nearly as many tuna choices at the supermarket as there are fish in the sea. Canned solid white tuna can be somewhat chalky and dry, so we pressed the tuna dry, then marinated it in oil for 10 minutes. Adding the oil and seasonings to the tuna before stirring in the mayo really infused the tuna with flavor. To soften the onion's harsh flavor, the easiest solution was microwaving it in the oil for a couple of minutes before adding it to the tuna. To finish, all our tuna salad needed was some celery for crunch. Do not use chunk light tuna in this recipe. Our favorite brand of canned tuna is Wild Planet Wild Albacore Tuna. If you can't find it, use canned solid white albacore tuna packed in water.

- ¼ cup finely chopped onion
- 2 tablespoons olive oil
- 3 (5-ounce) cans solid white albacore tuna
- 2 teaspoons lemon juice
- Salt and pepper
- ½ teaspoon sugar
- ½ cup plus 2 tablespoons mayonnaise
- 1 celery rib, chopped fine

1. Microwave onion and oil in bowl until onion begins to soften, about 2 minutes. Cool slightly, about 5 minutes.

2. Meanwhile, place tuna in fine-mesh strainer and press dry with paper towels. Transfer tuna to medium bowl and mash with fork until finely flaked. Stir in onion mixture, lemon juice, ½ teaspoon salt, ½ teaspoon pepper, and sugar, and let sit for 10 minutes.

3. Stir in mayonnaise and celery and season with salt and pepper to taste. Serve. (Salad can be refrigerated for up to 1 day.)

Draining Tuna

Place tuna in fine-mesh strainer and press dry with paper towels to remove excess moisture and prevent watery tuna salad. Once drained, transfer to medium bowl and mash with fork until finely flaked.

VARIATIONS

Tuna Salad with Sweet Pickle and Egg

See page 70 for our Foolproof Hard-Cooked Eggs.

Add ¼ cup sweet pickle relish to tuna with onion mixture. Stir 2 hard-cooked eggs, peeled and chopped, into salad with mayonnaise.

Tuna Salad with Roasted Red Peppers and Capers

Add ¼ cup jarred roasted red peppers, patted dry and chopped, and 2 tablespoons rinsed and minced capers to tuna with onion mixture.

Tuna Salad with Lemon and Dill

Increase lemon juice to 1 tablespoon. Add ½ teaspoon grated lemon zest and 1 tablespoon minced fresh dill to tuna with onion mixture.

Shrimp Salad

SERVES 4 **TOTAL TIME** 30 MINUTES **FAST**

✔ **WHY THIS RECIPE WORKS:** Great shrimp salad should possess firm and tender shrimp and a perfect deli-style dressing that doesn't mask the flavor of the shrimp or drown out the other ingredients. We started by adding the raw shrimp to cold court bouillon, then heating everything to a near simmer to cook the shrimp gently. We kept the traditional mayonnaise in our shrimp salad recipe, but limited the amount to ¼ cup per pound of shrimp. We preferred milder minced shallot over onion, and minced celery for its subtle flavor and crunch. This recipe can also be prepared with large shrimp (26 to 30 per pound); the cooking time will be 1 to 2 minutes less. The recipe can be easily doubled; cook the shrimp in a 7-quart Dutch oven and increase the cooking time to 12 to 14 minutes. Serve the salad over greens or on toasted, buttered buns.

- 1 pound extra-large shrimp (21 to 25 per pound), peeled, deveined, and tails removed
- 5 tablespoons lemon juice (2 lemons), spent halves reserved
- 5 sprigs fresh parsley plus 1 teaspoon minced
- 3 sprigs fresh tarragon plus 1 teaspoon minced
- 1 teaspoon whole black peppercorns
- 1 tablespoon sugar
- Salt and pepper
- ¼ cup mayonnaise
- 1 small shallot, minced
- 1 small celery rib, minced

1. Combine shrimp, ¼ cup lemon juice, reserved lemon halves, parsley sprigs, tarragon sprigs, peppercorns, sugar, and 1 teaspoon salt with 2 cups cold water in medium saucepan. Cook over medium heat, stirring often, until shrimp are pink and firm to touch, and centers are no longer translucent, 8 to 10 minutes (water should be just bubbling around edge of pan and should register 165 degrees).

2. Remove pan from heat, cover, and let shrimp sit in broth for 2 minutes. Meanwhile, fill medium bowl with ice water. Drain shrimp, discarding lemon halves, herbs, and peppercorns, and plunge immediately into ice water to stop cooking. Let sit until chilled, about 3 minutes. Remove shrimp from ice water and pat dry with paper towels. (Cooked and chilled shrimp can be refrigerated for up to 1 day before making salad.)

3. Whisk mayonnaise, shallot, celery, remaining 1 tablespoon lemon juice, minced parsley, and minced tarragon together in medium bowl. Cut shrimp in half lengthwise and then cut each half into thirds. Add shrimp to mayonnaise mixture and toss to combine. Season with salt and pepper to taste. Serve. (Salad can be refrigerated for up to 12 hours.)

VARIATIONS

Shrimp Salad with Avocado and Orange

Omit minced parsley, tarragon sprigs, minced tarragon, and celery. Add 4 halved and thinly sliced radishes; 1 large orange, peeled and cut into ½-inch pieces; ½ avocado, cut into ½-inch pieces; and 2 teaspoons minced fresh mint to mayonnaise mixture with shallot and lemon juice in step 3.

Shrimp Salad with Wasabi and Pickled Ginger

Omit minced parsley, tarragon sprigs, minced tarragon, and shallot. Add 2 thinly sliced scallions, 2 tablespoons chopped pickled ginger, 1 tablespoon toasted sesame seeds, and 2 teaspoons wasabi powder to mayonnaise mixture with celery and lemon juice in step 3.

Cutting Shrimp for Salad

1. Using sharp knife, cut shrimp in half lengthwise along back.

2. Cut each shrimp half crosswise into three pieces.

A garlicky mustard vinaigrette, poured over the potatoes while warm, gives this French-style potato salad great flavor.

French Potato Salad with Dijon Mustard and Fines Herbes

SERVES 6   **TOTAL TIME** 45 MINUTES `FAST`

✓ **WHY THIS RECIPE WORKS:** French potato salad should be pleasing not only to the eye but also to the palate. The potatoes (small red potatoes are traditional) should be tender but not mushy, and the flavor of the vinaigrette should penetrate the relatively bland potatoes. To eliminate torn skins and broken slices, a common pitfall in boiling skin-on red potatoes, we sliced the potatoes before boiling them. Then, to evenly infuse the potatoes with the garlicky mustard vinaigrette, we spread the warm potatoes out on a baking sheet and poured the vinaigrette over them. Gently folding in fresh herbs just before serving helped keep the potatoes intact. If fresh chervil isn't available, substitute an additional ½ tablespoon of minced parsley and an additional ½ teaspoon of tarragon. For best flavor, serve the salad warm.

2 pounds small red potatoes, unpeeled and
  sliced ¼ inch thick
2 tablespoons salt
1 garlic clove, peeled and threaded on skewer
1½ tablespoons champagne vinegar or
  white wine vinegar
2 teaspoons Dijon mustard
¼ cup olive oil
½ teaspoon pepper
1 small shallot, minced
1 tablespoon minced fresh chervil
1 tablespoon minced fresh parsley
1 tablespoon minced fresh chives
1 teaspoon minced fresh tarragon

1. Place potatoes and salt in large saucepan and add water to cover by 1 inch. Bring to boil over high heat, then reduce heat to medium. Lower skewered garlic into simmering water and cook for 45 seconds. Immediately run garlic under cold running water to stop cooking; set aside to cool. Continue to simmer potatoes, uncovered, until tender but still firm (thin-bladed paring knife can be slipped into and out of center of potato slice with no resistance), about 5 minutes. Reserve ¼ cup cooking water, then drain potatoes. Arrange hot potatoes close together in single layer on rimmed baking sheet.

2. Remove garlic from skewer and mince. Whisk garlic, reserved cooking water, vinegar, mustard, oil, and pepper together in bowl, then drizzle evenly over warm potatoes. Let potatoes stand for 10 minutes, then transfer to large serving bowl. (Salad can be covered with plastic wrap and refrigerated for up to 1 day. Return salad to room temperature before continuing.)

3. Combine shallot, chervil, parsley, chives, and tarragon in bowl, then mix gently into potatoes with rubber spatula. Serve.

VARIATION

French Potato Salad with Radishes, Cornichons, and Capers
Omit chervil, parsley, chives, and tarragon and substitute 2 tablespoons minced red onion for shallot. Toss dressed potatoes with 2 thinly sliced radishes, ¼ cup rinsed and minced capers, and ¼ cup thinly sliced cornichons with red onion before serving.

All-American Potato Salad
SERVES 4 TO 6   **TOTAL TIME** 1 HOUR
(PLUS 1 HOUR CHILLING TIME)

✔ **WHY THIS RECIPE WORKS:** We were looking for flavorful, tender potatoes punctuated by crunchy bits of onion and celery. We found that seasoning the potatoes while they're hot maximizes flavor, so we tossed hot russet potatoes with white vinegar. In the crunch department, celery is a must, and one rib fit the bill. Among scallions, shallots, and onions, red onion was the winner for its bright color and taste. For a pickled flavor, we decided on pickle relish, which required no preparation and gave the potato salad a subtle sweetness. Note that this recipe calls for celery seeds (which add complexity of flavor), not celery salt; if only celery salt is available, use the same amount but omit the salt in the dressing. When testing the potatoes for doneness, simply taste a piece; do not overcook the potatoes or they will become mealy and will break apart. The potatoes must be just warm, or even fully cooled, when you add the dressing. If the potato salad seems a little dry, add up to 2 tablespoons more mayonnaise. See page 70 for our Foolproof Hard-Cooked Eggs.

2 pounds russet potatoes, peeled and cut into
  ¾-inch cubes
  Salt
2 tablespoons distilled white vinegar
½ cup mayonnaise
3 tablespoons sweet pickle relish
1 celery rib, chopped fine
2 tablespoons finely chopped red onion
2 tablespoons minced fresh parsley
¾ teaspoon dry mustard
¾ teaspoon celery seeds
¼ teaspoon pepper
2 large hard-cooked eggs, peeled and cut into
  ¼-inch cubes (optional)

1. Place potatoes in large saucepan and add water to cover by 1 inch. Bring to boil over medium-high heat. Add 1 tablespoon salt, reduce heat to medium, and simmer, stirring occasionally, until potatoes are tender, about 8 minutes.

2. Drain potatoes and transfer to large bowl. Add vinegar and toss gently to combine using rubber spatula. Let stand until potatoes are just warm, about 20 minutes.

3. Meanwhile, combine mayonnaise, relish, celery, onion, parsley, mustard, celery seeds, pepper, and ½ teaspoon salt in small bowl. Using rubber spatula, gently fold mayonnaise mixture and eggs, if using, into potatoes. Refrigerate until chilled, about 1 hour. Serve. (Salad can be refrigerated for up to 1 day.)

Classic potato salad is all too often blanketed in a mayonnaise-rich dressing that results in bland flavor. We discovered a few tricks for a great-tasting potato salad with just the right texture, creaminess, and bite. Starting cubes of russet potatoes in cold water was the key to potatoes that held their shape, while tossing them with vinegar while still hot ensured depth of flavor. We kept the mayonnaise in check, too, while adding additional ingredients for flavor and crunch.

1. USE RUSSET POTATOES: Peel 2 pounds of russet potatoes.
WHY? Russets have a strong, earthy flavor that is able to shine through the mayonnaise dressing. Their starchy texture does make for a slightly crumbly salad when mixed, but tasters found this quality charming, not alarming.

2. CUT THE POTATOES INTO UNIFORM PIECES: Once the potatoes are peeled, cut them into ¾-inch cubes.
WHY? The potato cubes cook through evenly and at the same rate. Otherwise, smaller pieces of potato will overcook and begin to disintegrate before the larger cubes have time to cook through.

3. START THE POTATOES IN COLD WATER: Add cut potatoes to a large saucepan and add cold water to cover by 1 inch. Bring to a boil, reduce heat, and simmer until tender.
WHY? Bringing the water and potatoes to a boil together, then reducing the heat immediately to a simmer, ensures that the potatoes will hold their shape better.

4. TEST DONENESS BY TASTING: To test the potatoes for doneness, simply remove a piece from the pot, let it cool slightly, and taste it.
WHY? If you try to stab them with a knife or fork, the pieces of potato will simply break apart.

5. TOSS THE WARM POTATOES WITH VINEGAR: After draining the cooked potatoes, toss them gently with the vinegar and let them stand about 20 minutes.
WHY? Seasoning the potatoes while they're hot maximizes their flavor.

6. GENTLY FOLD THE POTATOES INTO THE DRESSING: Once the potatoes have cooled, gently fold in the mayonnaise dressing to coat.
WHY? It is important to handle the potatoes gently at this point, as their texture will be quite delicate.

There are a couple of things about coleslaw with buttermilk dressing that can be bothersome: the pool of watery dressing that appears in the bottom of the bowl after a few hours and the harsh flavor of buttermilk. Not only did we figure out how to keep the cabbage from watering down the dressing, but we also figured out how to make the salad piquant without tasting too sharp and one-dimensional.

1. CORE AND SHRED THE CABBAGE:
Separate the cored cabbage quarters into stacks of leaves then cut each stack into long thin pieces (you can also use the slicing disk of a food processor to do this).
WHY? Cabbage is unwieldy to cut. To easily create uniform shreds for coleslaw, press each stack of leaves flat and cut the cabbage using a chef's knife.

2. SALT THE CABBAGE: Toss the shredded cabbage with salt in a colander set over a large bowl. Let stand until the cabbage wilts, at least 1 hour or up to 4 hours.
WHY? The salt draws the moisture out of the cabbage and eliminates the problem of watery dressing. In addition, cabbage with less water in it soaks up more of the dressing's flavors.

3. RINSE THE SALTED CABBAGE WELL:
Rinse the cabbage thoroughly under cold running water.
WHY? The salting process leaves the cabbage too salty, so it needs to be thoroughly rinsed before proceeding. If you plan to eat the coleslaw immediately, rinse the cabbage in a bowl of ice water instead of under the tap.

4. DRAIN AND DRY THE WILTED CABBAGE: Press, but don't squeeze, the cabbage in the colander to drain it then blot it dry with paper towels.
WHY? The cabbage must be dry, or else the dressing will not cling to it. Also, excess moisture will dilute the dressing.

5. DRESS AND SEASON THE COLESLAW:
Transfer the cabbage and carrot to a large bowl. Whisk together the buttermilk, mayo, sour cream, and other dressing ingredients.
WHY? Once the cabbage is patted dry, combine the vegetables with the dressing and toss well to combine.

6. CHILL THE COLESLAW: Cover the coleslaw and refrigerate until chilled, about 30 minutes, before serving.
WHY? Chilling makes the coleslaw very crisp and allows the flavors to develop even more. Coleslaw is a good salad to make ahead as it keeps so well.

Buttermilk Coleslaw

SERVES 4   **TOTAL TIME** 1 HOUR 45 MINUTES

✔ **WHY THIS RECIPE WORKS:** We wanted our coleslaw recipe to produce crisp, evenly cut pieces of cabbage lightly coated with a flavorful buttermilk dressing that would cling to the cabbage instead of collecting in the bottom of the bowl. We found that salting and draining the cabbage removed excess water and wilted it to a pickle-crisp texture. For a dressing that was both hefty and tangy, we combined buttermilk, mayonnaise, and sour cream. If you are planning to serve the coleslaw immediately, rinse the salted cabbage in a large bowl of ice water, drain it in a colander, pick out any ice cubes, then pat the cabbage dry before dressing.

- ½ **medium head red or green cabbage, cored, quartered, and shredded (6 cups)**
  Salt and pepper
- 1 **carrot, peeled and shredded**
- ½ **cup buttermilk**
- 2 **tablespoons mayonnaise**
- 2 **tablespoons sour cream**
- 1 **small shallot, minced**
- 2 **tablespoons minced fresh parsley**
- ½ **teaspoon cider vinegar**
- ½ **teaspoon sugar**
- ¼ **teaspoon Dijon mustard**

1. Toss shredded cabbage and 1 teaspoon salt in colander set over large bowl and let sit until wilted, at least 1 hour or up to 4 hours. Rinse cabbage under cold running water. Press, but do not squeeze, to drain, and blot dry with paper towels.

2. Combine wilted cabbage and carrot in large bowl. In separate bowl, whisk buttermilk, mayonnaise, sour cream, shallot, parsley, vinegar, sugar, mustard, ¼ teaspoon salt, and ⅛ teaspoon pepper together. Pour dressing over cabbage and toss to combine. Refrigerate until chilled, about 30 minutes. Serve. (Coleslaw can be refrigerated for up to 3 days.)

VARIATIONS

Buttermilk Coleslaw with Green Onions and Cilantro

Omit mustard. Substitute 1 tablespoon minced fresh cilantro for parsley and 1 teaspoon lime juice for cider vinegar. Add 2 thinly sliced scallions to dressing.

Lemony Buttermilk Coleslaw

Substitute 1 teaspoon lemon juice for vinegar. Add 1 teaspoon minced fresh thyme and 1 tablespoon minced fresh chives to dressing.

Salting and draining the cabbage for this apple-cabbage salad makes it ready to absorb the flavors of the hot dressing.

Tangy Apple-Cabbage Slaw

SERVES 10   **TOTAL TIME** 30 MINUTES
(PLUS 2 HOURS SALTING AND CHILLING TIME)

✔ **WHY THIS RECIPE WORKS:** We wanted to discover the secrets to tender cabbage, crunchy apples, and the sweet and spicy dressing that brings them together in this Southern barbecue side dish. Because cabbage is relatively watery, we salted the cut cabbage to draw out excess moisture before dressing it, which prevented moisture from diluting the dressing later and leaving us with a watery slaw. Granny Smith apples worked best in this recipe—tasters loved their sturdy crunch and tart bite. We cut the apples into matchsticks so they could be easily mixed with the cabbage while retaining their crispness. Cider vinegar gave the dressing a fruity flavor, while red pepper flakes, scallions, and mustard added some punch. To help the dressing cling, we heated it—cabbage slaw absorbs a hot dressing especially well. Look for yellowish or light green Granny Smith apples—they are riper (and better-tasting) than dark green Grannies. Don't skip the step of salting the cabbage, or your coleslaw will be watery.

1 head green cabbage (2 pounds), cored and chopped fine
Salt and pepper
2 Granny Smith apples, cored and sliced into thin matchsticks
2 scallions, sliced thin
½ cup cider vinegar
½ cup sugar
6 tablespoons vegetable oil
1 tablespoon Dijon mustard
¼ teaspoon red pepper flakes

1. Toss cabbage with 1½ teaspoons salt in colander set over large bowl and let sit until wilted, at least 1 hour or up to 4 hours. Rinse cabbage under cold running water. Press, but do not squeeze, to drain, and pat dry with paper towels. Combine wilted cabbage, apples, and scallions in large bowl.

2. Bring vinegar, sugar, oil, mustard, and pepper flakes to boil in medium saucepan, then pour over cabbage mixture and toss to coat. Refrigerate until chilled, about 1 hour. Season with salt and pepper to taste. Serve. (Slaw can be refrigerated for up to 1 day.)

Cutting Apples into Matchsticks

1. To quickly remove core from apple, cut each side of apple squarely away from core.

2. Then, cut each piece of apple into ¼-inch-thick slices.

3. Finally, cut slices into thin matchsticks.

Creamy Macaroni Salad

SERVES 8 TO 10   **TOTAL TIME** 45 MINUTES **FAST**

✔ **WHY THIS RECIPE WORKS:** Our Creamy Macaroni Salad wraps pasta elbows and chopped celery and onion in a creamy dressing. We cooked the pasta until just tender—not all the way—and left a little moisture on it. The pasta absorbed the water rather than our creamy dressing (which could have left our salad dry and bland). We added a fair amount of lemon juice to the salad to balance the richness of the mayonnaise. This was one of the rare occasions in which we preferred garlic powder to fresh garlic because the flavor wasn't as sharp and the powder dissolved into the smooth dressing. Don't drain the macaroni too well before adding the other ingredients—a little extra moisture will keep the salad from drying out. The salad can become dry as it sits; just before serving, stir in a few tablespoons of warm water to bring back its creamy texture.

1 pound elbow macaroni
Salt and pepper
½ cup finely chopped red onion
1 celery rib, minced
¼ cup minced fresh parsley
2 tablespoons lemon juice
1 tablespoon Dijon mustard
⅛ teaspoon garlic powder
Pinch cayenne pepper
1½ cups mayonnaise

1. Bring 4 quarts water to boil in large pot. Add pasta and 1 tablespoon salt and cook, stirring often, until al dente. Drain in colander and rinse with cold water until cool, then drain briefly so that macaroni remains moist. Transfer to large bowl.

2. Stir in onion, celery, parsley, lemon juice, mustard, garlic powder, and cayenne, and let sit until flavors are absorbed, about 2 minutes. Add mayonnaise and let sit until salad texture is no longer watery, 5 to 10 minutes. Season with salt and pepper to taste. Serve. (Salad can be refrigerated for up to 2 days.)

VARIATION
Macaroni Salad with Sharp Cheddar and Chipotle
Stir 1½ cups shredded extra-sharp cheddar cheese and 2 tablespoons minced canned chipotle chile in adobo sauce into pasta in step 2 with vegetables and other flavorings.

BBQ Macaroni Salad

SERVES 8 TO 10   **TOTAL TIME** 45 MINUTES   **FAST**

✔ **WHY THIS RECIPE WORKS:** Most recipes for barbecue macaroni salad are much too sweet and sticky. We found that a combination of mayonnaise and barbecue sauce made the best dressing in our BBQ Macaroni Salad recipe, as the tang of the sweet, smoky-flavored barbecue sauce is balanced by the neutral creaminess of the mayonnaise. We like the sweet, smoky flavor of Texas Best or Bull's-Eye barbecue sauce here, but feel free to substitute your favorite. Don't drain the macaroni too well before adding the other ingredients—a little extra moisture will keep the salad from drying out. The salad can become dry as it sits; just before serving, stir in a few tablespoons of warm water to bring back its creamy texture.

1   pound elbow macaroni
     Salt and pepper
1   red bell pepper, stemmed, seeded, and chopped fine
1   celery rib, minced
4   scallions, sliced thin
2   tablespoons cider vinegar
1   teaspoon hot sauce
1   teaspoon chili powder
⅛   teaspoon garlic powder
     Pinch cayenne pepper
1   cup mayonnaise
½   cup barbecue sauce

1. Bring 4 quarts water to boil in large pot. Add pasta and 1 tablespoon salt and cook, stirring often, until al dente. Drain in colander and rinse with cold water until cool, then drain briefly so that macaroni remains moist. Transfer to large bowl.

2. Stir in bell pepper, celery, scallions, vinegar, hot sauce, chili powder, garlic powder, and cayenne and let sit until flavors are absorbed, about 2 minutes. Stir in mayonnaise and barbecue sauce and let sit until salad texture is no longer watery, 5 to 10 minutes. Season with salt and pepper to taste. Serve. (Salad can be refrigerated for up to 2 days.)

Rinsing Macaroni

After draining cooked macaroni, rinse under cold water for 1 minute to stop cooking and rinse away excess starch, which helps prevent sticking. Let pasta drain just briefly. It should be slightly moist when you dress it.

Mayonnaise and fresh baby spinach keep our pesto pasta salad creamy and bright green.

Pasta Salad with Pesto

SERVES 8 TO 10   **TOTAL TIME** 1 HOUR

✔ **WHY THIS RECIPE WORKS:** At its best, pesto is fresh, green, and full of herbal flavor, but it can turn dull and muddy when it's incorporated into an American-style pasta salad. We found that adding another green element—fresh baby spinach—provided the pesto with long-lasting color without interfering with the basil flavor. Adding mayonnaise to the pesto created the perfect binder, keeping the salad creamy and luscious and preventing it from clumping up and drying out. This salad is best served the day it is made; if it's been refrigerated, bring it to room temperature before serving. Garnish with additional shaved or grated Parmesan.

2   garlic cloves, peeled and threaded on skewer
1   pound farfalle
     Salt and pepper
5   tablespoons extra-virgin olive oil
3   cups fresh basil leaves
1   ounce (1 cup) baby spinach

¾ cup pine nuts, toasted

2 tablespoons lemon juice

1½ ounces Parmesan cheese, grated (¾ cup), plus extra for serving

6 tablespoons mayonnaise

12 ounces cherry tomatoes, quartered (optional)

1. Bring 4 quarts water to boil in large pot. Lower skewered garlic into simmering water and cook for 45 seconds. Immediately run garlic under cold running water to stop cooking; set aside to cool.

2. Add pasta and 1 tablespoon salt to boiling water and cook, stirring often, until al dente. Reserve ¼ cup cooking water, then drain pasta. Toss pasta with 1 tablespoon oil, spread out over rimmed baking sheet, and let cool to room temperature, about 30 minutes.

3. Meanwhile, remove garlic from skewer and mince. Process garlic, basil, spinach, ¼ cup pine nuts, lemon juice, 1 teaspoon salt, ½ teaspoon pepper, and remaining ¼ cup oil in food processor until smooth, stopping to scrape down sides of bowl as needed. Add Parmesan and mayonnaise and continue to process until thoroughly combined. Transfer mixture to large serving bowl; cover and refrigerate until ready to assemble salad.

4. Add cooled pasta to pesto and toss to combine, adding reserved cooking water as needed until pesto evenly coats pasta. Fold in remaining ½ cup pine nuts and tomatoes, if using. Serve with extra Parmesan.

Blanching Garlic

Thread peeled garlic clove(s) on skewer. Lower skewer into simmering water and cook for 45 seconds. Immediately run garlic under cold running water to stop cooking; let cool slightly, then prep as directed.

Deli meat and cheese turn pasta salad into a main course.

Fusilli Salad with Salami and Sun-Dried Tomato Vinaigrette

SERVES 8 TO 10   TOTAL TIME 1 HOUR 30 MINUTES

✓ **WHY THIS RECIPE WORKS:** This assertive pasta salad pairs deli salami and provolone with olives and capers, and coats everything in a zesty dressing. Finely minced sun-dried tomatoes added great color and flavor to the dressing. We like using fusilli for this pasta salad because its shape traps the flavorful ingredients.

1 pound fusilli
  Salt and pepper

6 tablespoons extra-virgin olive oil

8 ounces oil-packed sun-dried tomatoes, drained, patted dry, and minced

2 tablespoons red wine vinegar

1 tablespoon lemon juice

1 garlic clove, minced

8 ounces salami or pepperoni, cut into ¼-inch-thick matchsticks

8 ounces provolone, cut into ¼-inch-thick matchsticks

½ cup pitted kalamata olives, sliced

2 tablespoons capers, rinsed and minced

2 tablespoons minced fresh parsley

1. Bring 4 quarts water to boil in large pot. Add pasta and 1 tablespoon salt and cook, stirring often, until al dente.

2. Meanwhile, whisk oil, sun-dried tomatoes, vinegar, lemon juice, garlic, ½ teaspoon salt, and ½ teaspoon pepper together in large bowl.

3. Drain pasta, then toss while hot in bowl with dressing. Refrigerate until chilled, about 30 minutes. Stir in salami, provolone, olives, capers, and parsley. Season with salt and pepper to taste. Serve. (Salad can be refrigerated for up to 1 day.)

Tortellini Salad with Asparagus and Basil Vinaigrette

SERVES 8 TO 10   TOTAL TIME 45 MINUTES   **FAST**

✔ **WHY THIS RECIPE WORKS:** For this pasta salad, we pair fresh cheese tortellini with asparagus and a dressing inspired by the flavors of pesto. To keep things easy and efficient, we simply blanched the pieces of asparagus in the same water we later used to cook the tortellini. Once cooked, the cheese tortellini and some grape tomatoes were allowed to marinate in a bold dressing made of olive oil, basil, lemon juice, shallot, and garlic. To finish the salad and complete our deconstructed pesto, we added Parmesan and toasted pine nuts just before serving. Fresh tortellini is available in the refrigerated section of most supermarkets. Cooking the pasta until it is completely tender and leaving it slightly wet after rinsing are important for the texture of the finished salad.

Salt and pepper

1 pound asparagus, trimmed and cut into 1-inch pieces

2 (9-ounce) packages fresh cheese tortellini

6 tablespoons extra-virgin olive oil

½ cup chopped fresh basil

3 tablespoons lemon juice

1 shallot, minced

1 garlic clove, minced

12 ounces grape or cherry tomatoes, halved

1 ounce Parmesan cheese, grated (½ cup)

¼ cup pine nuts, toasted

A bold basil vinaigrette unites the flavors of this summery tortellini salad.

1. Bring 4 quarts water to boil in large pot. Add 1 tablespoon salt and asparagus and cook until asparagus is crisp-tender, about 2 minutes. Using slotted spoon or spider, transfer asparagus to bowl of ice water and let cool, about 2 minutes; drain and pat dry.

2. Return pot of water to boil. Add tortellini and cook, stirring often, until tender. Drain tortellini, rinse with cold water, and drain again, leaving tortellini slightly wet.

3. Meanwhile, whisk oil, basil, lemon juice, shallot, garlic, ½ teaspoon salt, and ½ teaspoon pepper together in large bowl.

4. Add tortellini and tomatoes to vinaigrette and toss to combine. Cover and let sit for 10 minutes. (Salad and asparagus can be refrigerated separately for up to 1 day; before continuing, add warm water and additional oil as needed to refresh.)

5. Before serving, stir in asparagus, Parmesan, and pine nuts and season with salt and pepper to taste.

Soups, Stews, and Chilis

■ SIGNIFIES A **FAST** RECIPE (45 MINUTES OR LESS)

Successful Soup Making

Making a great pot of soup, stew, or chili requires attention to detail, the right ingredients, well-made equipment, and a good recipe. Whether you're making a homey chicken noodle soup or an elegant pureed vegetable soup, you'll likely build a flavor base the same way, and will need a good broth, herbs and spices, and a solid, sturdy pot that can take the heat (and, in some cases, go from the stovetop to the oven).

SAUTÉ AROMATICS: The first step in making many soups is sautéing aromatic vegetables such as onion and garlic. Sautéing not only softens their texture so that there is no unwelcome crunch in the soup, it also tames any harsh flavors and develops more complex flavors in the process.

START WITH GOOD BROTH: If you're not inclined to pack your freezer with homemade stock, store-bought broth is a convenient option for soup making. Differences among packaged broths are quite significant—some are flavorful, while others taste like salty dishwater. Shop carefully. See Buying Broth on page 94 for further information.

CUT VEGETABLES TO THE RIGHT SIZE: Most soups call for chunks of vegetables. Haphazardly cut vegetables will cook unevenly—larger pieces will be underdone and crunchy, while smaller ones will be soft and mushy. Cutting vegetables to the size specified ensures that they will be perfectly cooked.

STAGGER THE ADDITION OF VEGETABLES: When a soup contains a variety of vegetables, they often must be added in stages to account for their varied cooking times. Hardy vegetables like potatoes and winter squash can withstand much more cooking than delicate asparagus or spinach.

SIMMER, DON'T BOIL: The fine line between simmering and boiling can make a big difference in your soups. A simmer is a restrained version of a boil; fewer bubbles break the surface. Simmering heats food through more gently and more evenly; boiling can cause vegetables such as potatoes to break apart, and it can toughen meat, too.

SEASON JUST BEFORE SERVING: In general, we add salt, pepper, and other seasonings—such as delicate herbs and lemon juice—after cooking, just before serving. The saltiness of the stock and of other ingredients, such as canned tomatoes and beans, can vary greatly, so it's always best to taste and adjust the seasonings once the soup is complete.

Chicken Stock

MAKES 8 CUPS   **TOTAL TIME** 1 HOUR 30 MINUTES

✔ **WHY THIS RECIPE WORKS:** Many recipes for homemade chicken stock simmer a whole chicken in water; we found that cutting the chicken parts into small pieces released the chicken flavor in a shorter amount of time since more surface area of the meat was exposed. This technique also exposed more bone marrow, which is key for both flavor and a thicker consistency. After testing a variety of vegetables, we found only onion was crucial. Sweating the chicken pieces for 20 minutes before adding the water further sped along the release of flavor, keeping our cooking time short. Use a meat cleaver or the heel of a chef's knife to cut the chicken into smaller pieces. Any chicken meat left over after straining the stock will be very dry and flavorless; it should not be eaten. Chicken thighs can be substituted for the legs, backs, and wings in a pinch. Make sure to use a 7-quart or larger Dutch oven for this recipe.

    1 tablespoon vegetable oil
    3 pounds whole chicken legs, backs, and/or wings,
       hacked into 2-inch pieces
    1 onion, chopped
    8 cups water
    2 teaspoons salt
    2 bay leaves

1. Heat oil in Dutch oven or stockpot over medium-high heat until just smoking. Brown half of chicken lightly on all sides, about 5 minutes; transfer to large bowl. Repeat with remaining chicken using fat left in pot, and transfer to bowl.

2. Add onion to fat left in pot and cook until softened, about 3 minutes. Return browned chicken and any accumulated juices to pot, cover, and reduce heat to low. Cook, stirring occasionally, until chicken has released its juices, about 20 minutes.

3. Add water, salt, and bay leaves and bring to boil. Cover, reduce heat to gentle simmer, and cook, skimming as needed, until stock tastes rich and flavorful, about 20 minutes longer.

4. Remove large bones from pot, then strain stock through fine-mesh strainer. Let stock settle for 5 to 10 minutes, then defat using wide, shallow spoon or fat separator. (Stock can be refrigerated for up to 4 days or frozen for up to 1 month.)

Nothing compares to the flavor of homemade chicken stock. Our recipe is basic, very versatile, and relatively easy to make, using just six ingredients. Stock is an important component in a wide variety of soups and stews, as well as in rice dishes. Most recipes for traditional stock require hours of cooking time to extract flavor from the chicken. We engineered an untraditional stock-making method from chicken parts that delivers maximum flavor in a minimal amount of time.

1. CUT UP THE CHICKEN: Use a meat cleaver or the heel of a chef's knife to hack the chicken legs, backs, and/or wings into 2-inch pieces.
WHY? Cutting the chicken into small pieces exposes more surface area and helps the chicken release its flavorful juices quickly. Also, the cut bones expose more bone marrow, key for both rich flavor and full body.

2. SAUTÉ THE CHICKEN TO BUILD FLAVOR: Heat the oil in a Dutch oven until it's just smoking. Lightly brown the chicken on all sides in two batches.
WHY? Browning the chicken helps fond to form on the bottom of the pot and builds flavor. Cooking the chicken in two batches is essential for it to brown properly; if the pan is crowded, the chicken will steam and no fond will form.

3. USE A MINIMUM OF FLAVOR ENHANCERS: Add chopped onion to the fat left in the pot and cook until it is softened.
WHY? With our chicken flavor strong, very little else is needed to enhance the stock. After testing a variety of vegetables, we found that only onion was crucial. It added dimension and complexity, but celery and carrot didn't add anything, so we left them out.

4. SWEAT THE CHICKEN TO EXTRACT ITS JUICES: Return the sautéed chicken and any accumulated juices to the pot, cover, and reduce the heat to low. Cook, stirring occasionally, until the chicken has released its juices.
WHY? Cooking the chicken pieces and onion over low heat helps to release the chicken's rich, flavorful juices. This takes only 20 minutes, keeping the cooking time short.

5. SIMMER GENTLY, COVERED: Add water, salt, and bay leaves and bring to a boil. Cover, reduce to a gentle simmer, and cook, skimming as needed, until the stock tastes rich and flavorful.
WHY? Covering the pot prevents evaporation, a departure from traditional recipes that say to simmer uncovered. The stock needs only 20 minutes of simmering instead of 2 hours. Boiling can result in a murky, greasy-tasting stock.

6. STRAIN THE STOCK AND REMOVE THE FAT: Remove the large bones, then pour the stock through a fine-mesh strainer into a large liquid measuring cup. Let the stock settle for 5 to 10 minutes. Use a wide, shallow spoon to remove the fat that rises to the surface.
WHY? The solids need to be separated from the liquid. For efficiency, use a large fine-mesh strainer. Since the chicken releases its fat into the stock, it must be removed.

Beef Stock

MAKES 8 CUPS   **TOTAL TIME** 2 HOURS 30 MINUTES

✔ **WHY THIS RECIPE WORKS:** We wanted a flavorful, full-bodied beef stock without the hassle of having to buy and roast pounds of big, heavy, and expensive beef bones. We found that just a pound of ground beef, a few vegetables, water, and wine—plus a few other enhancements—produced a rich, velvety stock in just 1½ hours of simmering. Most recipes sauté onions in the pot before adding the meat. We also added mushrooms with the onions to create an even more flavorful fond, resulting in stock with a deep, meaty, roasted flavor. Tomato paste and soy sauce enhanced the meaty flavor even more. We prefer 85 percent lean ground beef for this recipe; 93 percent lean ground beef will work, but the stock will be less flavorful. The fond is important for the flavor and color of the stock, so be sure to let it form on the bottom of the pot in step 1. Make sure to use a 7-quart or larger Dutch oven for this recipe.

- 1 teaspoon vegetable oil
- 1 pound white mushrooms, trimmed and quartered
- 1 large onion, chopped
- 1 pound 85 percent lean ground beef
- 2 tablespoons tomato paste
- ½ cup dry red wine
- 8 cups water
- 1 large carrot, peeled and chopped
- 1 large celery rib, chopped
- 2 tablespoons soy sauce
- 2 teaspoons salt
- 2 bay leaves

1. Heat oil in Dutch oven or stockpot over medium-high heat until just smoking. Add mushrooms and onion and cook, stirring often, until onion is browned and golden brown fond has formed on bottom of pot, 8 to 12 minutes.

2. Stir in ground beef and cook, breaking up meat with wooden spoon, until no longer pink, about 3 minutes. Stir in tomato paste and cook until fragrant, about 30 seconds. Stir in wine, scraping up any browned bits, and cook until nearly evaporated, 1 to 2 minutes.

3. Stir in water, carrot, celery, soy sauce, salt, and bay leaves and bring to boil. Cover, reduce heat to gentle simmer, and cook, skimming as needed, until stock tastes rich and flavorful, about 1½ hours.

4. Strain stock through fine-mesh strainer. Let stock settle for 5 to 10 minutes, then defat using wide, shallow spoon or fat separator. (Stock can be refrigerated for up to 4 days or frozen for up to 1 month.)

Vegetable Stock

MAKES 8 CUPS   **TOTAL TIME** 2 HOURS 30 MINUTES

✔ **WHY THIS RECIPE WORKS:** We wanted a nicely balanced, robust stock that vegetarians and nonvegetarians alike would consider making. Caramelizing plenty of onions, scallions, and garlic, plus carrots and celery in modest amounts, was a great start to ensuring depth and a sweetness that wasn't one-dimensional. We learned that our nontraditional ingredient—cauliflower—added a nutty complexity that was essential, while a single plum tomato provided the acidity and brightness that balanced the sweetness of our stock. Bay leaves and some thyme contributed the right herbal notes. The fond is important for the flavor and color of the stock, so be sure to let it form on the bottom of the pot in step 1. To prevent the stock from looking cloudy, be sure to simmer it gently (don't boil), and don't press on the solids when straining. Make sure to use a 7-quart or larger Dutch oven for this recipe.

- 3 onions, chopped
- 2 celery ribs, chopped
- 2 carrots, peeled and chopped
- 8 scallions, chopped
- 15 garlic cloves, peeled and smashed
- 1 teaspoon olive oil
- 1 teaspoon salt
- 12 cups water
- 1 head cauliflower (2½ pounds), cored and cut into 1-inch florets
- 1 plum tomato, cored and chopped
- 8 sprigs fresh thyme
- 3 bay leaves
- 1 teaspoon black peppercorns

1. Combine onions, celery, carrots, scallions, garlic, oil, and salt in Dutch oven or stockpot. Cover and cook over medium-low heat, stirring often, until golden brown fond has formed on bottom of pot, 20 to 30 minutes.

2. Stir in water, cauliflower, tomato, thyme, bay leaves, and peppercorns and bring to simmer. Partially cover pot, reduce heat to gentle simmer, and cook until stock tastes rich and flavorful, about 1½ hours.

3. Strain stock gently through fine-mesh strainer (do not press on solids). (Stock can be refrigerated for up to 4 days or frozen for up to 1 month.)

Classic Chicken Noodle Soup

SERVES 6 TO 8   **TOTAL TIME** 2 HOURS

✓ **WHY THIS RECIPE WORKS:** For a full-flavored chicken soup recipe that we could make without taking all day, we began by browning a cut-up chicken to set the foundation for a flavorful base. Sweating the browned pieces (we reserved the breast meat for shredding into the soup) with an onion allowed the meat to release its flavorful juices quickly. Then we added water and split breasts and simmered just 20 minutes longer. We cooked the breast meat in the broth to infuse both with flavor and to keep the meat moist. Egg noodles (also cooked right in the broth), celery, carrot, onion, thyme, and parsley rounded out our classic recipe. Make sure to reserve the chicken breast pieces until step 3; they should not be browned. A cleaver will enable you to cut up the chicken parts quickly, but a chef's knife or kitchen shears will also work. Be sure to reserve 2 tablespoons of chicken fat for sautéing the aromatics in step 5; however, vegetable oil can be substituted if you prefer. Make sure to use a 7-quart or larger Dutch oven for this recipe.

STOCK

- 1 tablespoon vegetable oil
- 1 (4-pound) whole chicken, breast removed, split, and reserved; remaining chicken hacked into 2-inch pieces
- 1 onion, chopped
- 8 cups water
- 2 teaspoons salt
- 2 bay leaves

SOUP

- 2 tablespoons chicken fat or vegetable oil
- 1 onion, chopped
- 1 large carrot, peeled and sliced ¼ inch thick
- 1 celery rib, sliced ¼ inch thick
- ½ teaspoon dried thyme
- 3 ounces (2 cups) egg noodles
- ¼ cup minced fresh parsley
  Salt and pepper

1. FOR THE STOCK: Heat oil in Dutch oven or stockpot over medium-high heat until just smoking. Brown half of hacked chicken lightly on all sides, about 5 minutes; transfer to large bowl. Repeat with remaining hacked chicken using fat left in pot, and transfer to bowl.

2. Add onion to fat left in pot and cook until softened, about 3 minutes. Return browned chicken and any accumulated

Browning a cut-up chicken helps create the flavorful base for a classic chicken noodle soup.

juices to pot, cover, and reduce heat to low. Cook, stirring occasionally, until chicken has released its juices, about 20 minutes.

3. Add reserved split chicken breasts, water, salt, and bay leaves and bring to boil. Cover, reduce heat to gentle simmer, and cook, skimming as needed, until stock tastes rich and flavorful, about 20 minutes longer.

4. Transfer chicken breasts to cutting board, let cool slightly, and shred into bite-size pieces, discarding skin and bones. Remove large bones from pot, then strain stock through fine-mesh strainer. Let stock settle for 5 to 10 minutes, then defat using wide, shallow spoon or fat separator, reserving 2 tablespoons fat. (Shredded chicken, strained stock, and reserved fat can be refrigerated in separate containers for up to 2 days; return broth to simmer before proceeding.)

5. FOR THE SOUP: Heat reserved fat in Dutch oven over medium-high heat. Add onion, carrot, and celery and cook until softened, about 5 minutes. Stir in thyme and strained broth and simmer until vegetables are tender, 10 to 15 minutes. Stir in noodles and shredded chicken and cook until noodles are just tender, 5 to 8 minutes. Stir in parsley and season with salt and pepper to taste. Serve.

Weeknight Chicken Noodle Soup

SERVES 6   **TOTAL TIME** 35 MINUTES   **FAST**

✔ **WHY THIS RECIPE WORKS:** Most recipes for fast home-made chicken soups are the same: Chunks of chicken and vegetables are dumped into store-bought chicken broth and hastily boiled. This cooking method yields not only a weak-flavored broth but also dry, flavorless chicken. Our goal was twofold—to build a flavorful broth and to produce chicken soup with tender, flavorful chicken. Since we were relying on packaged broth, we had to find a way to augment its mild flavor. Heating the broth with bay leaves and thyme enlivened it and lent it a homemade flavor. We also simmered the doctored broth, so that it could spend the maximum amount of time becoming infused with flavor. Next, we focused on the chicken. Boneless, skinless breasts were the obvious choice because of their short cooking time, but simply simmering cubes of meat in broth often leads to tough nuggets of chicken. We avoided this problem by browning whole breasts in the pot and poaching them whole in the broth, then shredding them once cooked. This way, the chicken remained moist and tender. Browning the chicken left behind flavorful browned bits, called fond, which helped build a complex and rich broth.

- **6 cups chicken broth**
- **1 teaspoon minced fresh thyme, or ¼ teaspoon dried**
- **2 bay leaves**
- **1 pound boneless, skinless chicken breasts, trimmed**
  Salt and pepper
- **1 tablespoon vegetable oil**
- **1 onion, minced**
- **2 carrots, peeled and sliced ¼ inch thick**
- **1 celery rib, sliced ¼ inch thick**
- **3 ounces (2 cups) egg noodles**
- **2 tablespoons minced fresh parsley**

1. Microwave broth, thyme, and bay leaves in large liquid measuring cup until just boiling, 2 to 4 minutes. Meanwhile, pat chicken dry with paper towels and season with salt and pepper. Heat oil in Dutch oven over medium-high heat until just smoking. Brown chicken lightly on both sides, about 5 minutes; transfer to plate.

2. Add onion and ½ teaspoon salt to fat left in pot and cook over medium heat until lightly browned, about 5 minutes. Reduce heat to low and stir in hot broth mixture, scraping up any browned bits. Add carrots, celery, and browned chicken and any accumulated juices. Cover and simmer gently until chicken registers 160 degrees, about 10 minutes.

3. Transfer chicken to cutting board, let cool slightly, and shred into bite-size pieces. Stir noodles into soup, increase heat to medium-high, and simmer until just tender, 5 to 8 minutes. Off heat, discard bay leaves and stir in shredded chicken and parsley. Season with salt and pepper to taste and serve.

VARIATION

Weeknight Chicken and Rice Soup

Omit egg noodles. Add 1½ cups long-grain rice to pot with vegetables and browned chicken in step 2. After removing chicken in step 3, increase heat to medium-high and cook until rice is tender, about 5 minutes.

Shredding Chicken

To shred chicken into bite-size pieces, hold a fork in each hand with tines facing down. Insert tines into cooked meat and gently pull forks away from each other, breaking meat apart and into thin, bite-size strands.

Tortilla Soup

SERVES 8   **TOTAL TIME** 1 HOUR 30 MINUTES

✔ **WHY THIS RECIPE WORKS:** We wanted a tortilla soup with authentic flavor and easy-to-find ingredients. The classic recipe has three main components—the flavor base, the chicken stock, and the garnishes; we came up with substitute ingredients and a manageable approach to each. Typically, the vegetables are charred on a *comal* (griddle), then pureed and fried. To simplify, we made a puree from smoky chipotles plus tomatoes, onion, garlic, and jalapeño, then fried the puree in oil over high heat. We poached chicken in store-bought broth infused with onion, garlic, cilantro, and oregano, which gave our base plenty of flavor without a from-scratch stock. We oven-toasted tortilla strips instead of frying them. Despite its somewhat lengthy ingredient list, this soup is very easy to prepare. For mild spiciness, trim the ribs and seeds from the jalapeño (or omit it altogether) and use 1 teaspoon chipotle chile pureed with the tomatoes in step 3. For a spicier soup, add up to 1 tablespoon adobo sauce in step 5 before you add the chicken. Although the chicken and broth can be prepared ahead of time, the tortilla strips and garnishes are best prepared the day of serving.

Packed with layers of flavorful ingredients, tortilla soup is a classic Mexican meal in a bowl.

2. Meanwhile, bring chicken, broth, 2 onion quarters, 2 garlic cloves, cilantro, oregano, and ½ teaspoon salt to boil over medium-high heat in Dutch oven. Reduce heat to low, cover, and simmer gently until chicken registers 160 degrees, about 20 minutes. Transfer chicken to cutting board, let cool slightly, and shred into bite-size pieces, discarding skin and bones. Strain broth through fine-mesh strainer.

3. Puree tomatoes, jalapeño, chipotle, remaining 2 onion quarters, and remaining 2 garlic cloves in food processor until smooth. Heat remaining 1 tablespoon oil in now-empty Dutch oven over high heat until shimmering. Add tomato-onion puree and ⅛ teaspoon salt and cook, stirring frequently, until mixture has darkened in color, about 10 minutes.

4. Stir in strained broth and bring to boil, then reduce heat to low and simmer gently until flavors have blended, 15 to 20 minutes. (Shredded chicken and broth can be refrigerated in separate containers for up to 2 days; return broth to simmer before proceeding.)

5. Stir in shredded chicken and let heat through, about 2 minutes. Place portions of tortilla strips in bowls, ladle soup over top, and serve with avocado, Cotija, cilantro leaves, and lime wedges.

Thai-Style Chicken Soup

SERVES 6   **TOTAL TIME** 1 HOUR

✔ **WHY THIS RECIPE WORKS:** For an authentic-tasting Thai chicken soup without all the exotic ingredients, we began by making a rich base with chicken broth and coconut milk. Thai curry paste from the supermarket was an easy substitution for the assortment of obscure ingredients like kaffir lime leaves, galangal, and bird's eye chiles used in from-scratch recipes. Pungent fish sauce and tart lime juice contributed the salty and sour flavors. Although we prefer the deeper, richer flavor of regular coconut milk, light coconut milk can be substituted for one or both cans. The fresh lemon grass can be omitted, but the soup will lack some complexity; don't be tempted to use jarred or dried lemon grass, as both have characterless flavor. If you want a spicier soup, add more red curry paste to taste. To make the chicken easier to slice, freeze it for 15 minutes. For more information on slicing chicken, see page 138.

8	(6-inch) corn tortillas, cut into ½-inch-wide strips
2	tablespoons vegetable oil
	Salt
2	(12-ounce) bone-in split chicken breasts, trimmed
8	cups chicken broth
1	large white onion, quartered
4	garlic cloves, peeled
8–10	sprigs fresh cilantro, plus leaves for serving
1	sprig fresh oregano
2	tomatoes, cored and quartered
½	jalapeño chile
1	tablespoon minced canned chipotle chile in adobo sauce
1	avocado, halved, pitted, and diced
8	ounces Cotija cheese, crumbled (2 cups)
	Lime wedges

1. Adjust oven rack to middle position and heat oven to 425 degrees. Toss tortilla strips with 1 tablespoon oil and bake on rimmed baking sheet until crisp and deep golden, about 14 minutes, stirring occasionally. Season lightly with salt and let cool on paper towel–lined plate.

1	teaspoon vegetable oil
3	stalks lemon grass, bottom 5 inches only, minced
3	large shallots, chopped coarse
8	sprigs fresh cilantro, chopped, plus whole leaves for serving

3 tablespoons fish sauce

4 cups chicken broth

2 (13.5-ounce) cans coconut milk

1 tablespoon sugar

8 ounces white mushrooms, trimmed and sliced thin

1 pound boneless, skinless chicken breasts, trimmed, halved lengthwise, and sliced ¼ inch thick

3 tablespoons lime juice (2 limes), plus wedges for serving

2 teaspoons Thai red curry paste

2 fresh Thai, serrano, or jalapeño chiles, stemmed, seeded, and sliced thin

2 scallions, sliced thin on bias

1. Heat oil in large saucepan over medium heat until shimmering. Add lemon grass, shallots, chopped cilantro sprigs, and 1 tablespoon fish sauce and cook, stirring often, until just softened but not browned, 2 to 5 minutes.

2. Stir in broth and 1 can coconut milk and bring to simmer. Cover, reduce heat to gentle simmer, and cook until flavors have blended, about 10 minutes. Strain broth through fine-mesh strainer. (Broth can be refrigerated for up to 1 day.)

3. Return strained broth to clean saucepan, stir in remaining can coconut milk and sugar, and bring to simmer. Stir in mushrooms and cook until just tender, 2 to 3 minutes. Stir in chicken and cook until no longer pink, 1 to 3 minutes.

4. Remove soup from heat. Whisk lime juice, curry paste, and remaining 2 tablespoons fish sauce together in bowl to dissolve curry, then stir mixture into soup. Ladle into bowls and sprinkle with cilantro leaves, chiles, and scallions. Serve with lime wedges.

Turkey Carcass Soup

SERVES 8 TO 10   **TOTAL TIME** 4 TO 5 HOURS

✔ **WHY THIS RECIPE WORKS:** Good turkey soup is one of the great things about Thanksgiving—you can still savor the holiday bird as it simmers away with herbs and vegetables. But sometimes turkey soup boasts none of the meaty, roasted flavor of the bird. We wanted to revitalize this soup—while keeping it streamlined. A great stock was key so we chose to make it from the turkey carcass. The bones provide body and gelatin when simmered, but the flavor is really dependent on having some meat and skin in the pot, too. The stock also uses the classic trio of onion, carrot, and celery for vegetal flavor, garlic for an aromatic baseline, and some white wine for brightness. For the meat, we turned to cooked turkey meat reserved from our bird. Two cups of meat proved ample for 12 cups of stock.

NOTES FROM THE TEST KITCHEN

Buying Broth

Homemade stocks taste better than packaged broth, adding unequaled depth and full-bodied flavor to soups and stews; this is why we include recipes for them (pages 88–90). But they're not always essential, and the reality is that most home cooks rely on supermarket broth for most recipes. When selecting store-bought broth, it's important to choose wisely since what you use can have a big impact on your final recipe. We prefer chicken broth to beef broth and vegetable broth for its stronger, cleaner flavor, though all have their place in our recipes. See the Ingredient Guide on page 804 for further information and buying recommendations.

CHICKEN BROTH: We like chicken broths with short ingredient lists that include a relatively high percentage of meat-based protein and flavor-boosting vegetables like carrots, celery, and onions.

BEEF BROTH: We've found the best beef broths have concentrated beef stock and flavor-enhancing ingredients such as tomato paste and yeast extract.

VEGETABLE BROTH: We've found that the top brands of vegetable broth have a hefty amount of salt and enough vegetable content to be listed on the ingredient list.

CLAM JUICE: Bottled clam juice conveniently brings a bright flavor to seafood dishes.

STOCK

1 carcass from (12- to 14-pound) roasted turkey, with a good amount of meat and skin clinging to it

18 cups water

2 cups dry white wine

1 large onion, halved

1 large carrot, peeled and chopped coarse

1 large celery rib, chopped coarse

3 garlic cloves, smashed and peeled

2 bay leaves

SOUP

1 tablespoon vegetable oil

2 carrots, peeled and sliced ¼ inch thick

1 onion, chopped fine

1 celery rib, sliced ¼ inch thick

2 teaspoons minced fresh thyme or ¾ teaspoon dried

8 ounces (3 cups) medium pasta shells

2 cups cooked, shredded turkey meat

3 tablespoons minced fresh parsley

Salt and pepper

1. FOR THE STOCK: Cut carcass into 4 or 5 pieces as needed to fit into large stockpot. Add remaining ingredients and bring to boil. Reduce heat to low, partially cover, and simmer gently until stock is rich and flavorful, 3 to 4 hours, skimming as needed. Remove large bones from pot and strain stock through fine-mesh strainer, discarding solids. (Stock can be refrigerated for up to 4 days or frozen for up to 1 month.)

2. FOR THE SOUP: Heat oil in Dutch oven over medium-high heat until shimmering. Add carrots, onion, and celery and cook until softened, 5 to 7 minutes. Stir in thyme and cook until fragrant, about 30 seconds. Stir in stock and simmer until vegetables are nearly tender, 10 to 15 minutes.

3. Stir in pasta and simmer until just tender, 10 to 15 minutes. Stir in shredded turkey and let heat through, about 2 minutes. Stir in parsley, and season with salt and pepper to taste. Serve.

Quick Beef and Barley Soup

SERVES 4 TO 6   **TOTAL TIME** 45 MINUTES   **FAST**

✔ **WHY THIS RECIPE WORKS:** Usually beef soup is made with cheap (often fatty) cuts of meat that have to be simmered for hours before they become tender and flavorful. To speed things up in our recipe, we used sirloin steak tips, a cut that is already tender and full of flavor. By cutting the meat into ½-inch pieces, we were able to brown it in a skillet while the soup base simmered, then stir it in at the end to cook through quickly. Beef broth has a tendency to add a tinny flavor to stew, so we used a mix of beef and chicken broths, which created the perfect foundation for our soup. Enhancing the broths with sautéed aromatics, porcini, and soy sauce took our soup to the next level. Look for whole steak tips (sometimes labeled flap meat) rather than those that have been cut into small pieces for stir-fries. Be careful not to overcook the beef in step 3 or it will taste dry.

3 carrots, peeled and cut into ¼-inch pieces

1 onion, chopped fine

¼ cup olive oil

1 tablespoon minced fresh thyme or 1 teaspoon dried

¼ ounce dried porcini mushrooms, rinsed and minced

2 garlic cloves, minced

2 teaspoons tomato paste

3 cups beef broth

Sirloin steak tips are tender and full of flavor and also make beef and barley soup quicker to prepare.

3 cups chicken broth

⅔ cup quick-cooking barley

2 teaspoons soy sauce

1½ pounds sirloin steak tips, trimmed and cut into ½-inch pieces

Salt and pepper

1. Combine carrots, onion, and 2 tablespoons oil in Dutch oven and cook over medium-high heat until vegetables are softened and lightly browned, about 8 minutes. Stir in thyme, porcini, garlic, and tomato paste and cook until fragrant, about 30 seconds. Stir in beef broth, chicken broth, barley, and soy sauce, scraping up any browned bits. Simmer until barley is tender, about 15 minutes.

2. Meanwhile, heat 1 tablespoon oil in 12-inch skillet over medium-high heat until just smoking. Pat beef dry with paper towels and season with salt and pepper. Brown half of beef on all sides, about 8 minutes; transfer to bowl. Repeat with remaining 1 tablespoon oil and remaining beef; transfer to bowl.

3. Add browned beef and any accumulated juices to soup and let heat through, about 1 minute. Season with salt and pepper to taste. Serve.

Asian Beef and Noodle Soup

SERVES 4 TO 6   **TOTAL TIME** 40 MINUTES   **FAST**

✔ **WHY THIS RECIPE WORKS:** Most recipes for quick Asian noodle soups yield weak-flavored broth and mushy noodles. We wanted to create a flavorful yet simple base for a quick Asian-style soup. To craft our own recipe, we kept the noodles from store-bought ramen soup, discarding the seasoning packet, which tasters found too salty. With the help of ginger, soy sauce, and sesame oil, we added significant flavor to an otherwise simple soup. For the beef, tasters preferred flavorful flank steak to other cuts of meat. You can find shredded coleslaw mix in the packaged salad aisle at the grocery store. To make the beef easier to slice, freeze it for 15 minutes. Be careful not to overcook the beef in step 2 or it will taste tough and dry.

- 1 tablespoon vegetable oil
- 5 scallions, white and green parts separated and sliced thin
- 2 tablespoons grated fresh ginger
- 2 garlic cloves, minced
- 3 cups beef broth
- 3 cups chicken broth
- 2 tablespoons dry sherry
- 2 tablespoons soy sauce, plus extra as needed
- 1 pound flank steak, sliced ¼ inch thick against grain and cut crosswise into bite-size pieces
- 2 (3-ounce) packages ramen noodles, flavoring packets discarded
- 3 cups shredded coleslaw mix
- 3 ounces (3 cups) baby spinach
- 1 tablespoon toasted sesame oil, plus extra as needed
  Salt and pepper

1. Heat vegetable oil, scallion whites, ginger, and garlic in Dutch oven over medium heat until fragrant, about 1 minute. Stir in beef broth, chicken broth, sherry, and soy sauce. Cover and simmer gently until flavors meld, about 10 minutes.

2. Stir in beef, noodles, and coleslaw mix and cook until beef is no longer pink and noodles are tender, about 4 minutes. Stir in spinach and cook until wilted, about 1 minute. Stir in scallion greens and sesame oil. Season with salt, pepper, soy sauce, and sesame oil to taste. Serve.

Steaming open the clams and using their steaming liquid for the broth gives our clam chowder maximum clam flavor.

New England Clam Chowder

SERVES 6   **TOTAL TIME** 1 HOUR 45 MINUTES

✔ **WHY THIS RECIPE WORKS:** We love homemade clam chowder about as much as we love good chicken soup, but most recipes are too time-consuming and difficult to make. For our chowder recipe, we settled on medium-size littlenecks or cherrystone clams—which offered good value and taste—that we steamed open instead of shucking. We also found that a ratio of 2 cups of homemade clam broth to 3 cups of bottled clam juice gave enough clam taste without being too salty. We chose Yukon Gold potatoes, as their moderate levels of starch and moisture blended seamlessly with this creamy chowder. We discovered that thickening the chowder with flour helped to stabilize it, as it can otherwise easily separate and curdle. Cream turned out to be essential, but our clam chowder recipe needed only a minimal amount, which provided richness without overpowering the flavor of the clams. Finally, we chose bacon rather than salt pork, a traditional component of chowder, to enrich the flavor with a subtle smokiness. Serve with oyster crackers.

3 cups water
6 pounds medium hard-shell clams, such as cherrystones, scrubbed
2 slices bacon, chopped fine
2 onions, chopped fine
2 celery ribs, chopped fine
1 teaspoon minced fresh thyme or ¼ teaspoon dried
⅓ cup all-purpose flour
3 (8-ounce) bottles clam juice
1½ pounds Yukon Gold potatoes, peeled and cut into ½-inch pieces
1 bay leaf
1 cup heavy cream
2 tablespoons minced fresh parsley
Salt and pepper

1. Bring water to boil in Dutch oven over medium-high heat. Add clams, cover, and cook for 5 minutes. Stir clams thoroughly and continue to cook, covered, until they begin to open, 2 to 7 minutes. Transfer clams to large bowl as they open; let cool slightly. Discard any clams that refuse to open.

2. Measure out and reserve 2 cups of clam steaming liquid, avoiding any gritty sediment that has settled on bottom of pot. Remove clam meat from shells and chop coarse.

3. Clean now-empty Dutch oven, add bacon, and cook over medium heat until crisp, 5 to 7 minutes. Stir in onions and celery and cook until vegetables are softened, 5 to 7 minutes. Stir in thyme and cook until fragrant, about 30 seconds. Stir in flour and cook for 1 minute.

4. Gradually whisk in bottled clam juice and reserved clam steaming liquid, scraping up any browned bits and smoothing out any lumps. Stir in potatoes and bay leaf and bring to boil. Reduce heat to gentle simmer and cook until potatoes are tender, 20 to 25 minutes. (Chopped clams and soup can be refrigerated in separate containers for up to 1 day; return broth to simmer before proceeding.)

5. Stir in cream and return to brief simmer. Off heat, discard bay leaf, stir in parsley, and season with salt and pepper to taste. Stir in chopped clams, cover, and let warm through, about 1 minute. Serve.

Quicker Clam Chowder

SERVES 6   TOTAL TIME 1 HOUR

✔ WHY THIS RECIPE WORKS: Although we love clam chowder made with fresh clams, we wanted a quick clam chowder recipe in our arsenal, one that featured a rich smokiness, so we cooked the ingredients in rendered bacon fat. We opted for using all cream for the dairy component of our chowder, but found that it could be replaced or cut with whole milk for a lighter—but still tasty—version. Flour was key to achieving the right consistency, and it also ensured that the soup didn't curdle or separate. We prefer the creamy texture of Yukon Gold potatoes in this chowder; however, red potatoes will also work. Be careful not to overcook the clams in step 3 or they will taste rubbery.

Preparing Clams for Chowder

1. SCRUB CLAMS: Before cooking clams, use soft brush to scrub away any bits of sand trapped in shell.

2. STEAM CLAMS: Cook clams in boiling water, covered, for 5 minutes. Stir and continue to cook until clams begin to open.

3. REMOVE CLAM MEAT: Carefully open clams. Remove clam meat from bottom shells and chop coarse.

4. STIR IN CLAMS: Return cooked, chopped clams to soup just before serving to warm them through.

4 slices bacon, chopped fine

1 onion, chopped fine

2 garlic cloves, minced

⅓ cup all-purpose flour

4 (6.5-ounce) cans minced clams, drained and juice reserved

3 (8-ounce) bottles clam juice

1½ pounds Yukon Gold potatoes, peeled and cut into ½-inch pieces

1 teaspoon minced fresh thyme or ¼ teaspoon dried

2 bay leaves

1 cup heavy cream

2 tablespoons minced fresh parsley

Salt and pepper

1. Cook bacon in Dutch oven over medium heat until crisp, 5 to 7 minutes. Stir in onion and cook until softened, 5 to 7 minutes. Stir in garlic and cook until fragrant, about 30 seconds. Stir in flour and cook for 1 minute.

2. Gradually whisk in reserved clam juice and bottled clam juice, scraping up any browned bits and smoothing out any lumps. Stir in potatoes, thyme, and bay leaves and bring to boil. Reduce heat to simmer and cook until potatoes are tender, 20 to 25 minutes.

3. Stir in drained clams and cream and continue to simmer gently until clams are heated through, about 2 minutes. Discard bay leaves and stir in parsley. Season with salt and pepper to taste. Serve.

Classic Corn Chowder

SERVES 6   **TOTAL TIME** 1 HOUR

✔ **WHY THIS RECIPE WORKS:** To create a classic corn chowder, we started by browning bacon in our Dutch oven, and we used the rendered fat to sauté onions and create a richly flavored base. Fresh corn makes the best chowder—frozen kernels need not apply. To pump up the fresh corn flavor, we first added grated corn and corn milk, which comes from scraping the cobs with the back of a knife, then we stirred in more whole kernels toward the end. With whole milk as our primary dairy component (tasters rejected all heavy cream as too rich), we added a few tablespoons of flour, which not only thickened our soup nicely but also helped stabilize the dairy and kept it from curdling.

10 ears fresh corn, husks and silk removed

4 slices bacon, chopped fine

1 onion, chopped fine

2 garlic cloves, minced

3 tablespoons all-purpose flour

3 cups chicken broth

2 cups whole milk

12 ounces red potatoes, unpeeled and cut into ¼-inch cubes

2 bay leaves

1 teaspoon minced fresh thyme or ¼ teaspoon dried

1 cup heavy cream

2 tablespoons minced fresh parsley

Salt and pepper

1. Working with 1 ear of corn at a time, stand 4 ears on end inside large bowl and cut kernels from cob using paring knife. Grate remaining 6 ears over large holes of box grater into separate bowl. Using back of butter knife, scrape remaining pulp from all cobs into bowl with grated corn.

2. Cook bacon in Dutch oven over medium heat until crisp, 5 to 7 minutes. Stir in onion and cook until softened, about 5 minutes. Stir in garlic and cook until fragrant, about 30 seconds. Stir in flour and cook for 1 minute. Slowly stir in broth and milk, scraping up any browned bits. Stir in potatoes, bay leaves, thyme, and grated corn and pulp mixture. Bring

Preparing Corn for Chowder

1. Stand corn upright inside large bowl and carefully cut kernels from cobs using paring knife.

2. Grate ears of corn over large holes of box grater to release both starch and more intense corn flavor.

3. Before discarding cobs, scrape remaining pulp from each using back of butter knife.

to simmer and cook until potatoes are almost tender, about 15 minutes.

3. Stir in remaining corn kernels and cream. Continue to simmer until corn kernels are tender yet still slightly crunchy, about 5 minutes. Discard bay leaves. Stir in parsley and season with salt and pepper to taste. Serve.

VARIATION

New Orleans–Style Corn Chowder

Substitute 8 ounces andouille sausage, cut into ¼-inch pieces, for bacon; reduce browning time to 3 minutes, then remove from pot. Add 1 finely chopped celery rib and 1 finely chopped green bell pepper to pot with onion. Return browned sausage to pot with cream in step 3.

Creamless Creamy Tomato Soup

SERVES 6 TO 8   **TOTAL TIME** 45 MINUTES   **FAST**

✔ **WHY THIS RECIPE WORKS:** We wanted a creamy tomato soup recipe that would have velvety smoothness and a bright tomato taste—without added cream. We started with canned tomatoes for their convenience, year-round availability, and consistent quality. When sautéing onion and garlic, we found that butter muted the tomato flavor, so we opted for olive oil. A little brown sugar toned down acidity, and a surprise ingredient—slices of white bread torn into pieces—helped give our tomato soup body without adding cream. Make sure to purchase canned whole tomatoes in juice, not in puree. If half of the soup fills your blender by more than two-thirds, process the soup in three batches. You can also use an immersion blender to process the soup directly in the pot. For an even smoother soup, pass the pureed mixture through a fine-mesh strainer after blending it. Serve with Homemade Croutons.

¼ cup extra-virgin olive oil, plus extra for serving
1 onion, chopped fine
3 garlic cloves, minced
1 bay leaf
   Pinch red pepper flakes (optional)
2 (28-ounce) cans whole peeled tomatoes
3 slices hearty white sandwich bread, crusts removed, torn into 1-inch pieces
1 tablespoon packed brown sugar
2 cups chicken broth
2 tablespoons brandy (optional)
   Salt and pepper
¼ cup minced fresh chives

HOMEMADE CROUTONS FOR SOUP

Either fresh or stale bread can be used in this recipe, although stale bread is easier to cut and crisps more quickly in the oven.

3 cups (½-inch) bread cubes from 6 slices hearty white sandwich bread, crusts removed
3 tablespoons unsalted butter, melted
   Salt and pepper

Adjust oven rack to middle position and heat oven to 350 degrees. Toss bread with melted butter, season with salt and pepper, and spread onto rimmed baking sheet. Bake until golden brown and crisp, 20 to 25 minutes, stirring halfway through baking. Let cool and serve. (Croutons can be stored at room temperature for up to 3 days.)

GARLIC CROUTONS **FAST**
Whisk 1 minced garlic clove into melted butter before tossing with bread cubes.

CINNAMON-SUGAR CROUTONS **FAST**
Toss buttered bread cubes with 6 teaspoons sugar and 1½ teaspoons ground cinnamon before baking.

---

1. Heat 2 tablespoons oil in Dutch oven over medium-high heat until shimmering. Add onion, garlic, bay leaf, and pepper flakes, if using, and cook, stirring often, until onion is translucent, 3 to 5 minutes. Stir in tomatoes and their juice. Using potato masher, mash until no pieces bigger than 2 inches remain. Stir in bread and sugar, and bring soup to boil. Reduce heat to medium and cook, stirring occasionally, until bread is completely saturated and starts to break down, about 5 minutes. Discard bay leaf.

2. Transfer half of soup to blender. Add 1 tablespoon oil and puree until soup is smooth and creamy, 2 to 3 minutes. Transfer to large bowl and repeat with remaining soup and remaining 1 tablespoon oil. Rinse out now-empty Dutch oven and return soup to pot. Stir in broth and brandy, if using. Return soup to boil and season with salt and pepper to taste. Ladle soup into bowls, sprinkle with chives, and drizzle with oil. Serve. (Soup can be refrigerated for up to 3 days; add water as needed when reheating to adjust consistency.)

Both the mini meatballs and the pasta cook right in the tomato sauce of this easy, kid-friendly pasta dish.

1	onion, chopped fine
1	carrot, peeled and chopped fine
1	tablespoon olive oil
3	garlic cloves, minced
3½	cups chicken broth
1	(28-ounce) can diced tomatoes
8	ounces meatloaf mix
¼	cup prepared basil pesto
¼	cup panko bread crumbs
	Salt and pepper
4	ounces (1 cup) ditalini

1. Cook onion, carrot, and oil in Dutch oven over medium heat until vegetables are softened, about 5 minutes. Stir in garlic and cook until fragrant, about 30 seconds. Stir in broth and tomatoes and their juice. Simmer until vegetables are tender, about 10 minutes.

2. Meanwhile, using hands, mix meatloaf mix, pesto, panko, ⅛ teaspoon salt, and ⅛ teaspoon pepper together in bowl until uniform. Pinch off heaping teaspoons of meat mixture and roll into ¾-inch meatballs (about 32 meatballs).

3. Working in batches, puree soup in blender until smooth and return to clean pot. Return to simmer, then stir in pasta and gently add meatballs. Continue to simmer, uncovered, until pasta is tender and meatballs are cooked through, 10 to 12 minutes. Off heat, season with salt and pepper to taste. Serve. (Soup can be refrigerated for up to 3 days; add water as needed when reheating to adjust consistency.)

Pasta Os with Mini Meatballs

SERVES 4   TOTAL TIME 1 HOUR

✓ **WHY THIS RECIPE WORKS:** We developed an easy, tastier homemade version of the longtime kid-favorite canned SpaghettiOs. Replicating the thick consistency of the sauce base was easy—we simmered and pureed a combination of canned tomatoes and chicken broth that we flavored with some basic sautéed aromatics. To boost the protein (and fun factor), we created some quick and easy mini meatballs by seasoning meatloaf mix with prepared basil pesto and binding the mixture with panko bread crumbs. We poached the meatballs directly in the sauce at the same time that we added the pasta, so this dish can be ready to serve hungry kids quickly. Meatloaf mix is a combination of equal parts ground beef, pork, and veal and is available at most grocery stores. If you cannot find meatloaf mix, substitute equal parts 90 percent lean ground beef and ground pork. You can also use an immersion blender to process the soup directly in the pot. You can substitute 1 cup small pasta shells or elbow macaroni for the ditalini if necessary. Serve with grated Parmesan cheese and crusty bread.

Cream of Broccoli Soup

SERVES 4 TO 6   TOTAL TIME 55 MINUTES

✓ **WHY THIS RECIPE WORKS:** Comforting creamy vegetable soups should be rich, silky-tasting, and, when done well, bursting with vegetable flavor. Add a few croutons or a dollop of something creamy, and you have a soul-satisfying meal in a bowl. Too often, however, these soups are overly rich from a heavy hand with cream and/or butter, and too much of either dilutes the vegetable's flavor and dulls its color. Our challenge, therefore, was to develop a cream of broccoli soup in which the richness of the cream wouldn't overtake the flavor of the vegetables. Because broccoli has two parts—the hardy stems and the delicate florets—it clearly requires two different approaches. We sautéed the stems with the aromatics, then simmered the florets toward the end of cooking, giving the soup deep and well-rounded flavor. We used equal parts vegetable and chicken broths, but you could certainly use all vegetable broth for a vegetarian soup. We found that ½ cup of half-and-half provided the right amount of dairy flavor and richness without eclipsing the vegetable flavor. And, as a final touch, we cut the creaminess with a little acidity in the form of white wine, which brought out the brightness of the vegetables and added a bit of depth to the soup. Be sure to use fresh broccoli in this soup; do not substitute frozen broccoli. You can use an immersion blender to process the soup directly in the pot, instead of using a blender.

1 tablespoon vegetable oil
1 onion, chopped
1½ pounds broccoli, florets cut into 1-inch pieces, stems trimmed and sliced thin
3 garlic cloves, minced
1 tablespoon all-purpose flour
¼ cup dry white wine
2 cups chicken broth, plus extra as needed
2 cups vegetable broth
1 bay leaf
½ cup half-and-half
Salt and pepper

Preparing Broccoli

1. Place broccoli head upside down on cutting board and, with large knife, trim off florets very close to their heads. Cut florets into 1-inch pieces.

2. Trim four sides of stalk, removing tough outer layer.

3. Continue to cut squared stalk into pieces as directed.

1. Heat oil in Dutch oven over medium heat until shimmering. Add onion and broccoli stems and cook until vegetables are softened, 5 to 7 minutes. Stir in garlic and cook until fragrant, about 30 seconds. Stir in flour and cook for 1 minute. Stir in wine, scraping up any browned bits, and cook until almost completely evaporated, about 1 minute.

2. Gradually whisk in chicken broth and vegetable broth, smoothing out any lumps, and bring to simmer. Stir in broccoli florets and bay leaf, reduce heat to simmer, and cook until florets are tender, 7 to 10 minutes.

3. Discard bay leaf. Working in batches, puree soup in blender until smooth and return to clean pot. Stir in half-and-half and extra chicken broth as needed to adjust consistency. Heat soup gently over low heat until hot (do not boil). Season with salt and pepper to taste and serve.

Butternut Squash Soup

SERVES 4 TO 6   **TOTAL TIME** 1 HOUR 30 MINUTES

WHY THIS RECIPE WORKS: Butternut squash soup is essentially a simple soup. Little more than squash, cooking liquid, and a few aromatic ingredients, this soup comes together fairly easily yet is creamy and deeply flavorful. But many squash soups fail to live up to their potential, often too sweet and with a porridgelike texture. We got the most flavor out of our squash by sautéing shallots and butter with the reserved squash seeds and fibers, simmering the mixture in water, and then using the liquid to steam the unpeeled squash (thereby avoiding the difficult task of peeling raw squash). To complete our butternut squash soup recipe, we scraped the squash from the skin when cooled, then pureed it with the reserved steaming liquid for a perfectly smooth texture. You can use an immersion blender to process the soup directly in the pot, instead of using a blender. Serve with Cinnamon-Sugar Croutons (page 99).

4 tablespoons unsalted butter, cut into ½-inch pieces
1 large shallot, chopped
3 pounds butternut squash, quartered and seeded, with fibers and seeds reserved
6 cups water
Salt and pepper
½ cup heavy cream
1 teaspoon packed dark brown sugar
Pinch ground nutmeg

1. Melt 2 tablespoons butter in Dutch oven over medium heat. Add shallot and cook until softened, 2 to 3 minutes. Add squash seeds and fibers and cook, stirring often, until butter turns orange, about 4 minutes.

2. Stir in water and 1 teaspoon salt and bring to boil. Reduce heat to simmer, place squash cut side down in steamer basket, and lower basket into pot. Cover and steam squash until completely tender, 30 to 40 minutes.

3. Using tongs, transfer cooked squash to rimmed baking sheet. Let squash cool slightly and scrape cooked squash from skin using soup spoon; discard skin.

4. Strain cooking liquid through fine-mesh strainer into large liquid measuring cup. Working in batches, puree cooked squash with 3 cups strained cooking liquid in blender until smooth, 1 to 2 minutes, and return to clean pot.

5. Stir in cream, sugar, nutmeg, and remaining 2 tablespoons butter. Return to brief simmer, adding additional strained cooking liquid as needed to adjust consistency. Season with salt and pepper to taste and serve.

VARIATION

Curried Butternut Squash and Apple Soup

A tart apple, such as a Granny Smith, adds a nice contrast to the sweet squash, but any type of apple may be used.

Reduce amount of squash to 2½ pounds. Add 1 large apple, peeled, cored, and quartered, to pot with squash. Substitute 2 teaspoons curry powder for nutmeg.

One of the secrets to great carrot soup is to use more carrots and sauté them first to extract maximum flavor.

Carrot-Ginger Soup

SERVES 4 TO 6   TOTAL TIME 1 HOUR 10 MINUTES

✔ **WHY THIS RECIPE WORKS:** Sweet carrots soften and mellow once cooked, making them perfect for a creamy soup. But often carrot soups range from lean, brothy concoctions marred by tiny bits of unpureed carrot to creamy ultrarich versions that taste more of butter and cream. Ginger is often added to provide depth, but too often it is out of balance. We wanted carrot soup with a bright flavor and rich, creamy body, with just the right amount of ginger. We determined that a whopping 1½ pounds of carrots to 4 cups of broth made the right ratio. Our tasters preferred chicken broth, but vegetable broth can be used instead. Whole milk provided the right amount of dairy, giving the soup a smooth texture without overwhelming the carrot. Four teaspoons of grated fresh ginger gave the soup the spicy punch we wanted. Do not substitute ground ginger for the fresh ginger. You can use an immersion blender to process the soup directly in the pot, instead of using a blender. Serve with Homemade Croutons (page 99).

2	tablespoons vegetable oil
1½	pounds carrots, peeled and chopped
1	onion, chopped
4	teaspoons grated fresh ginger
4	cups chicken broth, plus extra as needed
¾	cup whole milk
¼	cup orange juice
	Salt and pepper
1	tablespoon minced fresh chives

1. Heat oil in Dutch oven over medium heat until shimmering. Add carrots and onion and cook until vegetables are softened, 7 to 10 minutes. Stir in ginger and cook until fragrant, about 30 seconds.

2. Stir in broth and bring to boil. Reduce heat to simmer and cook until carrots are tender, 20 to 30 minutes.

3. Working in batches, puree soup in blender until smooth and return to clean pot. Stir in milk, orange juice, and additional broth as needed to adjust consistency. Heat soup gently over low heat until hot (do not boil). Season with salt and pepper to taste. Sprinkle portions with chives before serving.

Creamy Mushroom Soup

SERVES 6 TO 8   **TOTAL TIME** 1 HOUR 15 MINUTES

♥ **WHY THIS RECIPE WORKS:** Mushrooms, one of the meatiest vegetables, can make a delicious creamy soup. But often mushroom soups are too creamy and rich, and short on mushroom flavor, or they have enough flavor but rely on expensive wild mushrooms. We wanted a recipe for cream of mushroom soup that had it all: a creamy, rich base with savory mushroom flavor, achieved by using just the humble white mushroom. Sweating the mushrooms with leeks, garlic, and thyme resulted in a good earthy flavor, but we discovered we could go one step further. Cooking the mushrooms covered for 5 minutes, then uncovering and cooking them until they softened and browned, allowed the deep, rich flavor to shine. A bit of cream, some Madeira, and a touch of lemon juice rounded out the flavors. Now we had a rich, rustic mushroom soup made with simple supermarket ingredients. Brandy or dry sherry can be substituted for the Madeira here. You can use an immersion blender to process the soup directly in the pot, instead of using a blender. Serve with Garlic Croutons (page 99).

- **4** tablespoons unsalted butter
- **3** pounds white mushrooms, trimmed and sliced thin
- **2** leeks, white and light green parts only, halved lengthwise, sliced ¼ inch thick, and washed thoroughly
- **4** garlic cloves, minced
- **2** teaspoons minced fresh thyme or ½ teaspoon dried
      Salt and pepper
- **5** cups beef broth, plus extra as needed
- **½** cup Madeira, plus extra for serving
- **1** cup heavy cream
- **2** tablespoons lemon juice

1. Melt butter in Dutch oven over medium-high heat and cook, stirring constantly, until butter is dark golden brown and has a nutty aroma, 1 to 3 minutes. Stir in mushrooms,

Pureeing Soups Safely

To prevent getting sprayed or burned when pureeing hot soup, work in small batches and fill blender only two-thirds full. Hold lid in place with dish towel and pulse several times before blending continuously.

NOTES FROM THE TEST KITCHEN

Storing and Reheating Soup

Soups, stews, and chilis make a generous number of servings, and it's easy enough to stock your freezer with last night's leftovers so you can reheat them whenever you like. First you'll need to cool the soup. As tempting as it might seem, avoid transferring hot soup straight to the refrigerator; you may speed up the cooling process, but you'll also increase the fridge's internal temperature to unsafe levels, which is dangerous for all the other food stored in the fridge. We find that letting the soup cool on the countertop for an hour helps the temperature drop to about 85 degrees, at which point the soup can be transferred safely to the fridge. If you don't have an hour to cool your soup or stew at room temperature, you can divide it into a number of storage containers to allow the heat to dissipate more quickly, or you can cool the soup rapidly by using a frozen bottle of water to stir the contents of the pot.

To reheat soups and stews, we prefer to simmer them gently on the stovetop in a sturdy, heavy-bottomed pot, but a spin in the microwave works too. Just be sure to cover the dish to prevent a mess (we don't recommend using plastic wrap). And note that while most soups freeze just fine, those that contain dairy or pasta do not. In soups that contain dairy or pasta, the dairy curdles as it freezes and the pasta turns bloated and mushy. Instead, make and freeze the soup without including the dairy or pasta component. After you have thawed the soup and it has been heated through, you can stir in the uncooked pasta and simmer until just tender, or stir in the dairy and continue to heat gently until hot (do not boil).

leeks, garlic, thyme, ½ teaspoon salt, and ¼ teaspoon pepper. Cover and cook until mushrooms release their liquid, about 5 minutes.

2. Uncover and cook, stirring often, until liquid has evaporated and mushrooms begin to brown, about 15 minutes. Remove ⅔ cup mushroom mixture from pot, let cool slightly, then chop fine; reserve.

3. Stir in broth and Madeira, scraping up any browned bits, and bring to boil. Reduce heat to simmer and cook until mushrooms and leeks are tender, about 20 minutes.

4. Working in batches, puree soup in blender until smooth and return to clean pot. Stir in cream, lemon juice, reserved chopped mushrooms, and additional broth as needed to adjust consistency. Heat soup gently over low heat until hot (do not boil). Season with salt and pepper to taste. Drizzle portions with Madeira before serving.

Hearty Vegetable Soup

SERVES 6 TO 8   **TOTAL TIME** 1 HOUR 10 MINUTES

✓ **WHY THIS RECIPE WORKS:** Great vegetable soup should be hearty and satisfying, packed with fresh, tender vegetables and a modest amount of herbs. But which vegetables provided the best flavor in terms of number and cooking times? We chose russet potatoes, which broke down and added body, and canned tomatoes so we could make this soup at any time of the year. Lima beans were substantial enough for our hearty soup, though they can be omitted if desired. Escarole added visual and textural contrast. We cut the vegetables to the same size to ensure they cooked at the same rate, and we mashed some of the potatoes to thicken our soup. Now we had a hearty soup with great body, complex flavor, and tender vegetables. The flavor of this soup tastes substantially better when made with our Vegetable Stock (page 90). Serve with crusty bread.

 1 tablespoon extra-virgin olive oil
 2 leeks, white and light green parts only, halved lengthwise, sliced ¼ inch thick, and washed thoroughly
   Salt and pepper
 3 garlic cloves, minced
 6 cups vegetable broth
 1 (14.5-ounce) can diced tomatoes, drained and chopped coarse
 12 ounces russet potatoes (2 small), peeled and cut into ½-inch pieces
 ½ celery root (12 ounces), peeled and cut into ½-inch pieces
 2 carrots, peeled and cut into ½-inch pieces
 1 small head escarole (12 ounces), trimmed and cut into 1-inch pieces
 1 cup frozen baby lima beans, thawed (optional)
 2 tablespoons minced fresh parsley

1. Heat oil in Dutch oven over medium-low heat until shimmering. Stir in leeks and ½ teaspoon salt. Cover and cook, stirring occasionally, until leeks are softened, 8 to 10 minutes.

2. Stir in garlic and cook until fragrant, about 30 seconds. Stir in broth, tomatoes, potatoes, celery root, and carrots and bring to boil. Cover, reduce heat to gentle simmer, and cook until vegetables are tender, about 25 minutes.

3. Using back of wooden spoon, mash some of potatoes against side of pot to thicken soup. Stir in escarole and lima beans, if using, and cook until escarole is wilted and beans are heated through, about 5 minutes. Off heat, stir in parsley and season with salt and pepper to taste. Serve.

Low-starch red potatoes hold their shape and leave this rustic soup full of potato chunks along with plenty of leeks.

Country-Style Potato-Leek Soup

SERVES 6 TO 8   **TOTAL TIME** 1 HOUR

✓ **WHY THIS RECIPE WORKS:** We prefer a hearty, thick version of potato-leek soup, but all too often the soup ends up with potatoes that are falling apart. We found that low-starch red potatoes were the best option for a flavorful country-style potato-leek soup because they held their shape and didn't become waterlogged during cooking. In addition, we removed the pot from the heat toward the end to allow the potatoes to finish cooking in the hot broth without becoming overcooked or mushy. Sautéing plenty of leeks in butter helped pump up the flavor, and leaving our soup full of chunks of potato and pieces of leek kept up the rustic theme. Leeks can vary in size. If yours have large white and light green sections, use fewer leeks.

 6 tablespoons unsalted butter
 4-5 pounds leeks, white and light green parts only, halved lengthwise, sliced 1 inch thick, and washed thoroughly (11 cups)

1 tablespoon all-purpose flour
5¼ cups chicken broth
1 bay leaf
1¾ pounds red potatoes, peeled and cut
into ¾-inch chunks
Salt and pepper

1. Melt butter in Dutch oven over medium heat. Stir in leeks, cover, and cook, stirring occasionally, until leeks are tender but not mushy, 15 to 20 minutes (do not brown). Stir in flour and cook for 2 minutes.

2. Increase heat to high and gradually stir in broth. Stir in bay leaf and potatoes, cover, and bring to boil. Reduce heat to medium-low and simmer, covered, until potatoes are almost tender, 5 to 7 minutes.

3. Remove from heat and let stand until potatoes are tender and flavors meld, 10 to 15 minutes. Discard bay leaf and season with salt and pepper to taste. Serve. (Soup can be refrigerated for up to 2 days; add water as needed when reheating to adjust consistency.)

Preparing Leeks

1. Trim and discard root and dark green leaves.

2. Cut trimmed leek in half lengthwise, then slice into pieces sized according to recipe.

3. Rinse cut leeks thoroughly using salad spinner or bowl of water to remove dirt and sand.

Ultimate French Onion Soup

SERVES 6   **TOTAL TIME** 4 TO 5 HOURS

✔ **WHY THIS RECIPE WORKS:** Most versions of this age-old recipe hide a mediocre broth under a crust of bread and a blanket of Gruyère. What is the secret to coaxing impressive flavor out of humble onions? We found that the way to make a rich onion soup was to caramelize the onions a full 2½ hours in the oven and then deglaze the pot several times with a combination of water, chicken broth, and beef broth. For the classic crouton topping, we warded off sogginess by toasting the bread before floating it in the soup, and we sprinkled the toasts with just a modest amount of nutty Gruyère so that its flavor wouldn't overwhelm the soup. Use a Dutch oven with at least a 7-quart capacity for this recipe. Sweet onions, such as Vidalia or Walla Walla, will make this recipe overly sweet. Use broiler-safe crocks and keep the rim of the bowls 4 to 5 inches from the broiler element to obtain a proper gratinée of melted, bubbly cheese. If using ordinary soup bowls, sprinkle the toasted bread slices with Gruyère and return them to the broiler on the baking sheet until the cheese melts, then float them on top of the soup.

SOUP
4 pounds onions, halved and sliced through root end into ¼-inch-thick pieces
3 tablespoons unsalted butter, cut into 3 pieces
Salt and pepper
2 cups water, plus extra for deglazing as needed
½ cup dry sherry
4 cups chicken broth
2 cups beef broth
6 sprigs fresh thyme, tied with kitchen twine
1 bay leaf

CHEESE CROUTONS
1 small baguette, cut into ½-inch slices
8 ounces Gruyère cheese, shredded (2 cups)

1. FOR THE SOUP: Adjust oven rack to lower-middle position and heat oven to 400 degrees. Generously spray inside of Dutch oven with vegetable oil spray. Add onions, butter, and 1 teaspoon salt. Cover and bake until onions wilt slightly and look moist, about 1 hour.

2. Stir onions thoroughly, scraping bottom and sides of pot. Partially cover pot and continue to cook in oven until onions are very soft and golden brown, 1½ to 1¾ hours longer, stirring onions thoroughly after 1 hour. (Pot of onions can be cooled, covered, and refrigerated for up to 3 days before continuing with step 3.)

Our French onion soup gets its rich flavor from caramelized onions and two kinds of broth.

3. Carefully remove pot from oven and place over medium-high heat. Using oven mitts to handle pot, continue to cook onions, stirring and scraping pot often, until liquid evaporates, onions brown, and bottom of pot is coated with dark crust, 20 to 25 minutes. (If onions begin to brown too quickly, reduce heat to medium. Also, be sure to scrape any browned bits that collect on spoon back into onions.)

4. Stir in ¼ cup water, thoroughly scraping up browned crust. Continue to cook until water evaporates and pot bottom has formed another dark crust, 6 to 8 minutes. Repeat deglazing 2 or 3 more times, until onions are very dark brown.

5. Stir in sherry and cook until evaporated, about 5 minutes. Stir in chicken broth, beef broth, 2 cups more water, thyme bundle, bay leaf, and ½ teaspoon salt, scraping up any remaining browned bits. Bring to simmer, cover, and cook for 30 minutes. Discard thyme bundle and bay leaf and season with salt and pepper to taste. (Soup can be refrigerated for up to 3 days; return to simmer before proceeding.)

6. FOR THE CROUTONS: Adjust oven rack to middle position and heat oven to 400 degrees. Lay baguette slices on rimmed baking sheet and bake until dry, crisp, and lightly golden, about 10 minutes, flipping slices over halfway through baking.

7. Position oven rack 6 inches from broiler element and heat broiler. Set individual broiler-safe crocks on baking sheet and fill each with about 1½ cups soup. Top each bowl with 1 or 2 baguette slices (do not overlap slices) and sprinkle evenly with cheese. Broil until cheese is melted and bubbly around edges, 3 to 5 minutes. Let cool for 5 minutes before serving.

Classic Gazpacho

SERVES 8 TO 10   **TOTAL TIME** 15 MINUTES
(PLUS 4 HOURS CHILLING TIME)

🗸 **WHY THIS RECIPE WORKS:** A good gazpacho should showcase the brightness of fresh vegetables, yet many recipes turn out bland, thin soups. We wanted to develop a foolproof recipe for gazpacho with clearly flavored, distinct vegetables in a bright tomato broth. We started by chopping the vegetables by hand, which ensured they retained their color and firm texture. Letting them sit briefly in a sherry vinegar marinade guaranteed well-seasoned vegetables, while a combination of tomato juice and ice cubes (which helped chill the soup) provided the right amount of liquid. Chilling our soup for a minimum of 4 hours proved critical to allowing the flavors to develop and meld. Use a Vidalia, Maui, or Walla Walla onion here. This recipe makes a large quantity because the leftovers are so good, but it can be halved if you prefer. Traditionally, diners garnish their gazpacho with more of the same diced vegetables that are in the soup, so cut some extra vegetables when you prepare those called for in the recipe. Serve with Garlic Croutons (page 99), chopped pitted black olives, chopped hard-cooked eggs, and finely diced avocados. For a finishing touch, serve in chilled bowls.

1½ pounds tomatoes, cored and cut into ¼-inch cubes
2 red bell peppers, stemmed, seeded, and cut into ¼-inch dice
2 small cucumbers, 1 cucumber peeled, both sliced lengthwise, seeded, and cut into ¼-inch dice
½ small sweet onion or 2 large shallots, minced
⅓ cup sherry vinegar
2 garlic cloves, minced
   Salt and pepper
5 cups tomato juice
8 ice cubes
1 teaspoon hot sauce (optional)
   Extra-virgin olive oil

1. Combine tomatoes, bell peppers, cucumbers, onion, vinegar, garlic, and 2 teaspoons salt in large (at least 4-quart) bowl and season with pepper to taste. Let stand until vegetables just begin to release their juices, about 5 minutes. Stir in tomato juice, ice cubes, and hot sauce, if using. Cover and refrigerate to blend flavors, at least 4 hours or up to 2 days.

2. Discard any unmelted ice cubes and season with salt and pepper to taste. Serve cold, drizzling portions with olive oil.

VARIATION
Spicy Gazpacho with Chipotle Chiles and Lime
We recommend garnishing bowls of this spicy soup with finely diced avocado. If desired, reduce the amount of chipotles to make the soup less spicy.

Omit hot sauce. Add 2 tablespoons minced fresh cilantro, 1 tablespoon minced canned chipotle chile in adobo sauce, and 2 teaspoons grated lime zest plus 6 tablespoons juice (about 3 limes) with tomato juice and ice cubes.

Black Bean Soup
SERVES 6   **TOTAL TIME** 2½ TO 3 HOURS

✔ **WHY THIS RECIPE WORKS:** A great black bean soup has carefully balanced sweet, spicy, and smoky flavors. But too often we end up with watery, thin, and bland or overspiced and bitter soups instead. We wanted to create a foolproof black bean soup with beans that were tender, and we wanted it to be dark and thick. We went with dried beans, which released flavor into the broth as they cooked, unlike canned beans. Furthermore, they proved to be a timesaver: We discovered that it was unnecessary to soak them overnight or to use the "quick-soak method" to make them tender. We also found that we didn't need from-scratch stock; we maximized flavor by using a mixture of water and store-bought chicken broth enhanced with ham and seasonings. Dried beans tend to cook unevenly, so be sure to taste several beans to determine their doneness in step 1. For efficiency, you can prepare the soup ingredients while the beans simmer, and the garnishes while the soup simmers. Garnishes are essential for this soup, as they add not only flavor but texture and color as well. Serve with lime wedges, minced fresh cilantro, finely diced red onion, diced avocado, and sour cream.

BEANS
- 1 **pound (2½ cups) dried black beans, picked over and rinsed**
- 5 **cups water, plus extra as needed**
- 4 **ounces ham steak, trimmed**
- 2 **bay leaves**
- 1 **teaspoon salt**
- ⅛ **teaspoon baking soda**

SOUP
- 3 **tablespoons olive oil**
- 2 **large onions, chopped fine**
- 3 **celery ribs, chopped fine**
- 1 **large carrot, peeled and chopped fine**
- ½ **teaspoon salt**
- 5–6 **garlic cloves, minced**
- 1½ **tablespoons ground cumin**
- ½ **teaspoon red pepper flakes**
- 6 **cups chicken broth**
- 2 **tablespoons cornstarch**
- 2 **tablespoons water**
- 2 **tablespoons lime juice**
  Salt and pepper

1. FOR THE BEANS: Combine beans, water, ham, bay leaves, salt, and baking soda in large saucepan. Bring to boil, skimming any impurities that rise to surface. Cover, reduce heat to low, and simmer gently until beans are tender, 1¼ to 1½ hours. (If after 1½ hours beans are not tender, add 1 cup more water and continue to simmer until beans are tender.) Discard bay leaves. Transfer ham steak to carving board and cut into ¼-inch pieces; set aside. (Do not drain beans.)

2. FOR THE SOUP: Heat oil in Dutch oven over medium heat until shimmering. Add onions, celery, and carrot and cook until vegetables are softened and lightly browned, 12 to 15 minutes.

3. Stir in garlic, cumin, and pepper flakes and cook until fragrant, about 1 minute. Stir in broth and cooked beans with their cooking liquid, and bring to boil. Reduce heat to medium-low and cook, uncovered and stirring occasionally, until flavors have blended, about 30 minutes.

4. Puree 1½ cups of beans and 2 cups of liquid in blender until smooth, then return to pot. Whisk cornstarch and water together in small bowl, then gradually stir half of cornstarch mixture into simmering soup. Continue to simmer soup, stirring occasionally, until slightly thickened, 3 to 5 minutes. (If at this point soup is thinner than desired, repeat with remaining cornstarch mixture.) Off heat, stir in lime juice and reserved ham, season with salt and pepper to taste, and serve. (Soup can be refrigerated for up to 3 days; add water as needed when reheating to adjust consistency.)

VARIATION
Black Bean Soup with Chipotle Chiles
Chipotle chiles are spicy; for a spicier soup, use the greater amount of chipotles given.

Omit red pepper flakes. Add 1 to 2 tablespoons minced canned chipotle chile in adobo sauce to soup with chicken broth.

11TH-HOUR SOUPS

When time is tight, you can still make a quick pot of great-tasting soup. These superfast recipes put good store-bought broth, frozen vegetables, and canned beans to work for last-minute soups that can be made in 25 minutes or less. To thaw frozen vegetables quickly, heat them in a covered bowl in the microwave for a few minutes. All of these soups serve 4 to 6.

CURRIED CAULIFLOWER SOUP FAST

Cook 1 minced onion and 2 tablespoons unsalted butter in Dutch oven over medium-high heat until softened, about 5 minutes. Add 3 minced garlic cloves and 2 teaspoons curry powder and cook for 30 seconds. Add 4 cups chicken broth and 1½ pounds thawed frozen cauliflower florets, cover, and simmer until cauliflower is tender, about 10 minutes. Puree soup, return to pot, and whisk in ½ cup half-and-half. Reheat gently and season with salt and pepper to taste. Serve with chopped fresh cilantro.

GREEN PEA SOUP WITH MINT FAST

Cook 1 minced onion and 2 tablespoons vegetable oil in Dutch oven over medium-high heat until softened, about 5 minutes. Add 3 minced garlic cloves and 2 tablespoons all-purpose flour and cook for 30 seconds. Whisk in 2 cups chicken broth and 2 cups vegetable broth and bring to simmer. Add 1½ pounds thawed frozen peas and 2 tablespoons chopped fresh mint and cook until peas are tender, 2 to 5 minutes. Puree soup, return to pot, and whisk in ½ cup half-and-half. Reheat gently and season with salt and pepper to taste. Serve with extra minced fresh mint.

RED BEAN AND RICE SOUP FAST

Cook 12 ounces coarsely chopped andouille sausage, 1 minced onion, 1 minced celery rib, 1 minced green bell pepper, and 2 tablespoons vegetable oil in Dutch oven over medium-high heat until sausage is lightly browned, 5 to 7 minutes. Add 3 minced garlic cloves and 1 tablespoon Cajun seasoning and cook for 30 seconds. Add 6 cups chicken broth, 2 (14.5-ounce) cans rinsed red kidney beans, and 2 cups cooked rice and simmer for 5 minutes. Season with salt and pepper to taste and serve.

A ham steak and thick-cut bacon give this split pea soup depth and lots of meaty flavor—without a leftover ham bone.

Split Pea and Ham Soup

SERVES 6 TO 8   **TOTAL TIME** 1 HOUR 45 MINUTES

WHY THIS RECIPE WORKS: Simmering a leftover ham shank used to be a frugal way to stretch a meal. But what if you don't have a leftover ham bone? We set out to create a richly flavorful broth with tender shreds of meat, all without the old-fashioned ham bone. As it turns out, ham steak was plenty meaty and provided the soup with a fuller pork flavor without making the soup too greasy. A few strips of raw bacon added the richness and smokiness that the bone used to provide. Four ounces of regular sliced bacon can be used, but the thinner slices are harder to remove from the soup. Unsoaked peas broke down just as well as soaked and were better at absorbing the flavor of the soup. Depending on the age and brand of split peas, the consistency of the soup may vary slightly. If the soup is too thin at the end of step 2, increase the heat and simmer, uncovered, until the desired consistency is reached. If it is too thick, thin it with a little water. We like to garnish the soup with fresh peas, chopped mint, and a drizzle of aged balsamic vinegar. Serve with Homemade Croutons (page 99).

2 tablespoons unsalted butter

1 large onion, chopped fine

  Salt and pepper

2 garlic cloves, minced

7 cups water

1 pound ham steak, skin removed, cut into quarters

3 slices thick-cut bacon

1 pound (2½ cups) split peas, picked over and rinsed

2 sprigs fresh thyme

2 bay leaves

2 carrots, peeled and cut into ½-inch pieces

1 celery rib, cut into ½-inch pieces

1. Melt butter in Dutch oven over medium-high heat. Add onion and ½ teaspoon salt and cook, stirring often, until onion is softened, 3 to 4 minutes. Stir in garlic and cook until fragrant, about 30 seconds. Stir in water, ham steak, bacon, peas, thyme, and bay leaves. Increase heat to high and bring to simmer, stirring frequently to keep peas from sticking to bottom. Reduce heat to low, cover, and simmer until peas are tender but not falling apart, about 45 minutes.

2. Remove ham steak and cover with plastic wrap to prevent it from drying out; set aside. Stir in carrots and celery and simmer, covered, until vegetables are tender and peas have almost completely broken down, about 30 minutes.

3. Shred ham into small bite-size pieces. Discard thyme, bay leaves, and bacon slices. Return ham to soup and season with salt and pepper to taste. Serve. (Soup can be refrigerated for up to 3 days. Add water as needed when reheating to adjust consistency.)

Pasta e Fagioli

SERVES 8 TO 10   **TOTAL TIME** 1 HOUR 15 MINUTES

WHY THIS RECIPE WORKS: Most versions of pasta e fagioli are bland and mushy, and take hours to prepare. We wanted to get it all—great flavor and proper texture without taking all afternoon. We started by cooking some pancetta (bacon worked well, too) in a Dutch oven, then cooked our vegetables in the rendered fat. Adding the tomatoes and beans together allowed them to absorb flavor from each other, and a 3:2 ratio of chicken broth to water added richness without turning our pasta and bean soup into chicken soup. We knew that adding a Parmesan rind to the pot would give our soup depth and a slight cheese flavor throughout (the rind can be replaced with a 2-inch chunk of cheese). Finally, parsley lent the necessary bright note to our soup. You can substitute another small pasta for the orzo, such as ditalini or tubettini.

Cooking the cannellini beans with pancetta, vegetables, tomatoes, and a Parmesan cheese rind boosts their flavor.

1 tablespoon extra-virgin olive oil, plus extra for serving

3 ounces pancetta or 3 slices bacon, chopped fine

1 onion, chopped fine

1 celery rib, chopped fine

4 garlic cloves, minced

1 teaspoon dried oregano

¼ teaspoon red pepper flakes

3 anchovy fillets, rinsed and minced

1 (28-ounce) can diced tomatoes

1 Parmesan cheese rind

2 (15-ounce) cans cannellini beans, rinsed

3½ cups chicken broth

2½ cups water

  Salt and pepper

1 cup orzo

¼ cup minced fresh parsley

2 ounces Parmesan cheese, grated (1 cup)

1. Heat oil in Dutch oven over medium-high heat until shimmering. Add pancetta and cook, stirring often, until beginning to brown, 3 to 5 minutes. Stir in onion and celery and cook until vegetables are softened, 5 to 7 minutes. Stir in garlic, oregano, pepper flakes, and anchovies and cook until fragrant, about 1 minute.

2. Stir in tomatoes, scraping up any browned bits. Add Parmesan rind and beans. Bring to boil, then reduce heat to low and simmer to blend flavors, about 10 minutes.

3. Stir in broth, water, and 1 teaspoon salt. Increase heat to high and bring to boil. Add pasta and cook until al dente, about 10 minutes.

4. Discard Parmesan rind. Off heat, stir in parsley and season with salt and pepper to taste. Serve with extra olive oil and Parmesan.

VARIATION

Pasta e Fagioli with Orange and Fennel

Ditalini and orzo are especially good pasta shapes for this variation.

Add 1 finely chopped fennel bulb to pot with onion and celery. Add 2 teaspoons grated orange zest and ½ teaspoon fennel seeds to pot with garlic.

Hearty Lentil Soup

SERVES 4 TO 6   **TOTAL TIME** 1 HOUR 30 MINUTES

✔ **WHY THIS RECIPE WORKS:** Lentil soup is cheap to make, comes together quickly, and, when made well, tastes great. Could we develop a recipe that would be worthy of a second bowl instead of the tasteless variety full of overcooked lentils that we so often encounter? The soup should be brightly colored and flavored, and hearty but not too thick, with a subtle, smoky depth from meat. We sweated the lentils in a covered pan with aromatics and bacon before adding the liquid, which helped them hold their shape and boosted their flavor. Pureeing only some of the soup ensured the final result had appealing texture that was not overly smooth. Finishing with a splash of balsamic vinegar brightened the dish. *Lentilles du Puy*, also called French green lentils, are our first choice for this recipe, but brown, black, or regular green lentils are fine, too (note that cooking times will vary depending on the type used). Lentils lose flavor with age, and because most packaged lentils do not have expiration dates, try to buy them from a store that specializes in natural foods and grains. Be sure to sort through the lentils carefully to remove small stones and pebbles and then rinse them before cooking.

3 **slices bacon, cut into ¼-inch pieces**
1 **large onion, chopped fine**
2 **carrots, peeled and chopped**
3 **garlic cloves, minced**
1 **(14.5-ounce) can diced tomatoes, drained**
1 **bay leaf**
1 **teaspoon minced fresh thyme**
1 **cup lentils, picked over and rinsed**
   Salt and pepper
½ **cup dry white wine**
4½ **cups chicken broth**
1½ **cups water**
1½ **teaspoons balsamic vinegar**
3 **tablespoons minced fresh parsley**

1. Cook bacon in Dutch oven over medium-high heat, stirring often, until crisp, about 5 minutes. Stir in onion and carrots and cook until vegetables begin to soften, about 2 minutes. Stir in garlic and cook until fragrant, about 30 seconds. Stir in tomatoes, bay leaf, and thyme and cook until fragrant, about 30 seconds. Stir in lentils and ¼ teaspoon salt. Cover, reduce heat to medium-low, and cook until vegetables are softened and lentils have darkened, 8 to 10 minutes.

2. Uncover, increase heat to high, add wine, and bring to simmer. Stir in broth and water and bring to boil. Partially cover pot, reduce heat to low, and simmer until lentils are tender but still hold their shape, 30 to 35 minutes.

3. Discard bay leaf. Puree 3 cups soup in blender until smooth, then return to pot. Stir in vinegar and warm soup over medium-low heat until hot, about 5 minutes. Stir in parsley and serve. (Soup can be refrigerated for up to 3 days; add water as needed when reheating to adjust consistency.)

VARIATIONS

Hearty Lentil Soup with Spinach

Substitute 5 cups baby spinach for parsley; cook spinach in soup, stirring often, until wilted, about 3 minutes.

Hearty Lentil Soup with Fragrant Spices

Add 1 teaspoon ground cumin, 1 teaspoon ground coriander, 1 teaspoon ground cinnamon, and ¼ teaspoon cayenne to pot with garlic. Substitute lemon juice for balsamic vinegar and minced fresh cilantro for parsley.

Hearty Curried Vegetarian Lentil Soup

In this soup, we prefer the pure flavor of homemade Vegetable Stock (page 90) to store-bought vegetable broth.

Omit bacon and balsamic vinegar, and substitute vegetable broth for chicken broth. Add 2 tablespoons extra-virgin olive oil to pot and heat over medium-high heat until shimmering before adding onion and carrots. Add 1 teaspoon curry powder to pot with garlic.

Classic Beef Stew

SERVES 6 TO 8   **TOTAL TIME** 3 HOURS

✔ **WHY THIS RECIPE WORKS:** Beef stew should be rich and satisfying, with fall-apart meat and tender vegetables draped in a rich brown gravy. Sadly, many recipes result in dry, tough meat and a watery, bland sauce. We wanted to create a fool-proof recipe that would always turn out tender meat, a rich, flavorful sauce, and perfectly cooked vegetables. To begin, we chose chuck-eye roast for its great flavor and cut it into pieces. We bypassed the step of searing the meat by cooking the stew uncovered in the oven. This not only helped brown the exposed meat but also let some of the sauce evaporate, concentrating its flavor. Along with traditional stew components like onions, garlic, red wine, and chicken broth, we also added tomato paste, which is rich in glutamates—compounds that give meat its savory taste and contribute considerable flavor. Potatoes, carrots, and peas rounded out our rich-tasting yet updated take on beef stew. Use a good-quality, medium-bodied wine, such as a Côtes du Rhône or Pinot Noir, for this stew. Try to find beef that is well marbled with white veins of fat. Meat that is too lean will come out slightly dry.

Cutting Stew Meat

1. Pull apart roast at its major seams (delineated by lines of fat and silverskin). Use knife as necessary.

2. With knife, trim off excess fat and silverskin.

3. Cut meat into 1½-inch chunks.

1   (3½- to 4-pound) boneless beef chuck-eye roast, pulled apart at seams, trimmed, and cut into 1½-inch pieces
    Salt and pepper
2   tablespoons vegetable oil
2   onions, chopped fine
1   tablespoon tomato paste
2   garlic cloves, minced
¼   cup all-purpose flour
3   cups chicken broth
¾   cup dry red wine
1   teaspoon minced fresh thyme
2   bay leaves
1½ pounds Yukon Gold potatoes, unpeeled, cut into 1-inch pieces
1   pound carrots, peeled and cut into 1-inch pieces
2   tablespoons minced fresh parsley
1   cup frozen peas, thawed

1. Adjust oven rack to lower-middle position and heat oven to 325 degrees. Pat meat dry with paper towels and season with salt and pepper. Heat oil in Dutch oven over medium-high heat until shimmering. Add onions and cook, stirring often, until well browned, 8 to 10 minutes.

2. Stir in tomato paste and garlic and cook until fragrant, about 2 minutes. Stir in flour and cook for 1 minute. Whisk in broth, wine, thyme, and bay leaves, scraping up any browned bits and smoothing out any lumps. Stir in beef and bring to simmer. Transfer pot to oven and cook, uncovered, for 1½ hours, stirring halfway through cooking.

3. Stir in potatoes and carrots and continue to cook in oven, uncovered, until beef and vegetables are tender, about 1 hour, stirring halfway through cooking.

4. Remove pot from oven. Discard bay leaves. Using large spoon, skim excess fat from surface of stew. Stir in parsley and peas and let peas warm through, about 2 minutes. Season with salt and pepper to taste and serve. (Stew can be refrigerated for up to 3 days; add water as needed when reheating to adjust consistency.)

VARIATION

Guinness Beef Stew

Omit peas. Substitute 1¼ cups Guinness Draught beer for red wine; add ¾ cup beer to pot with broth, and add remaining ½ cup beer to pot with parsley. Add 1½ tablespoons packed dark brown sugar to pot with broth.

Roasted red peppers, tomato paste, and vinegar tame the large amount of paprika in this goulash.

Hungarian Goulash

SERVES 6   **TOTAL TIME** 3 TO 3½ HOURS

✓ **WHY THIS RECIPE WORKS:** Traditional Hungarian goulash is the simplest of stews, calling for little more than beef that is melded together with long-cooked onions and infused with the flavor of paprika—no sour cream, green peppers, or mushrooms allowed. We set out to recover this recipe from the overly busy American versions and restore its simplicity. Tasters overwhelmingly preferred traditional sweet paprika, but when we reached 3 tablespoons, the spice contributed a gritty, dusty texture. Consulting a few Hungarian restaurants, we discovered they used paprika cream, so we created our own by pureeing a drained jar of roasted red peppers, adding a little tomato paste, vinegar, and the paprika. We also found that searing the meat competed with the paprika's flavor, so we simply softened the onions first, then stirred in the paprika cream mixture and the meat and left everything to cook. Paprika is vital to this recipe, so it's best to use a fresh container; do not substitute hot or smoked paprika for the sweet paprika. A Dutch oven with a tight-fitting lid is crucial to the success of this dish, since there is not much braising liquid; if necessary, place a sheet of aluminum foil over the pot before covering with the lid to ensure a tight seal. Serve with sour cream and buttered egg noodles.

- 1 (3½- to 4-pound) boneless beef chuck-eye roast, pulled apart at seams, trimmed, and cut into 1½-inch pieces
  Salt and pepper
- 1½ cups jarred roasted red peppers, rinsed
- ⅓ cup sweet paprika
- 2 tablespoons tomato paste
- 3 teaspoons white vinegar
- 3 pounds onions, chopped fine
- 2 tablespoons vegetable oil
- 4 carrots, peeled and sliced 1 inch thick
- 1 bay leaf
- 1 cup beef broth, warmed

1. Adjust oven rack to lower-middle position and heat oven to 325 degrees. Pat beef dry with paper towels and season with salt and pepper. Process roasted red peppers, paprika, tomato paste, and 2 teaspoons vinegar in food processor until smooth, 1 to 2 minutes, scraping down bowl as needed.

2. Combine onions, oil, and 1 teaspoon salt in Dutch oven, cover, and cook over medium heat, stirring occasionally, until onions soften but have not yet begun to brown, 8 to 10 minutes. (If onions begin to brown, reduce heat to medium-low and stir in 1 tablespoon water.)

3. Stir in processed roasted pepper mixture and cook, uncovered, until onions begin to stick to bottom of pan, about 2 minutes. Stir in beef, carrots, and bay leaf until well coated. Using rubber spatula, carefully scrape down sides of pot. Cover, transfer to oven, and cook until meat is mostly tender and surface of liquid is ½ inch below top of meat, 2 to 2½ hours, stirring every 30 minutes.

4. Stir in warmed broth until surface of liquid measures ¼ inch from top of meat (beef should not be fully submerged). Continue to cook in oven, covered, until meat is tender, about 30 minutes longer.

5. Remove pot from oven. Discard bay leaf. Using large spoon, skim excess fat from surface of stew. Stir in remaining 1 teaspoon vinegar and season with salt and pepper to taste. Serve. (Stew can be refrigerated for up to 3 days; add water as needed when reheating to adjust consistency.)

For easier gumbo, we make a dark brown roux that starts on the stovetop and finishes in the oven.

3/4 cup plus 1 tablespoon all-purpose flour
1/2 cup vegetable oil
1 onion, chopped fine
1 green bell pepper, stemmed, seeded, and chopped
1 celery rib, chopped fine
5 garlic cloves, minced
1 teaspoon minced fresh thyme
1/4 teaspoon cayenne pepper
1 (14.5-ounce) can diced tomatoes, drained
3 3/4 cups chicken broth, room temperature
1/4 cup fish sauce
2 pounds chicken thighs, skin removed, trimmed
Salt and pepper
8 ounces andouille sausage, halved lengthwise and sliced thin
2 cups frozen okra, thawed (optional)
2 pounds extra-large (21 to 25 per pound) shrimp, peeled and deveined

Creole-Style Gumbo

SERVES 6 TO 8   **TOTAL TIME** 2 HOURS 10 MINUTES

✓ **WHY THIS RECIPE WORKS:** With chicken, sausage, shrimp, and vegetables in a rich brown sauce with a touch of heat, gumbo is a unique stew. The basis of gumbo is the roux, which is flour cooked in fat; we use the oven to make it easier. This recipe is engineered for efficiency: Get the roux in the oven and then prep the remaining ingredients. A heavy, cast-iron Dutch oven yields the fastest oven roux. If a lightweight pot is all you've got, increase the oven time by 10 minutes. The chicken broth must be at room temperature to prevent lumps from forming. Fish sauce lends an essential savory quality to the stew; don't omit it. Since the salt content of fish sauce varies among brands, taste the finished gumbo before seasoning with salt. Gumbo is traditionally served over white rice.

1. Adjust oven rack to lowest position and heat oven to 350 degrees. Toast 3/4 cup flour in Dutch oven over medium heat, stirring constantly, until just beginning to brown, about 5 minutes.

2. Off heat, whisk in oil until smooth. Cover pot, transfer to oven, and cook until mixture is deep brown and fragrant, about 45 minutes. Remove pot from oven and whisk roux to combine. (Roux can be cooled and refrigerated for up to 1 week; reheat over medium-high heat, whisking constantly until just smoking, before continuing.)

3. Stir onion, bell pepper, and celery into hot roux and cook over medium heat, stirring often, until vegetables are softened, about 10 minutes. Stir in remaining 1 tablespoon flour, garlic, thyme, and cayenne and cook until fragrant, about 1 minute. Stir in tomatoes and cook until they look dry, about 1 minute. Gradually stir in broth and fish sauce, scraping up any browned bits and smoothing out any lumps.

4. Season chicken with pepper, add it to pot, and bring to boil. Cover, reduce heat to gentle simmer, and cook until chicken registers 175 degrees, about 40 minutes.

5. Using large spoon, skim excess fat from surface of gumbo. Transfer chicken to plate, let cool slightly, then shred into bite-size pieces, discarding bones. Stir shredded chicken, sausage, and okra, if using, into stew, return to simmer, and allow to heat through, about 5 minutes.

6. Stir in shrimp and continue to simmer until cooked through, about 5 minutes. Season gumbo with salt and pepper to taste and serve. (Gumbo can be refrigerated for up to 3 days; reheat over medium-low heat, stirring often.)

This simple, hearty bean stew hails from Tuscany and showcases one of the region's favorite ingredients: cannellini beans. Since beans are the star ingredient, we started with dried beans—not canned—and looked for a cooking method that would ensure they cooked up plump, whole, creamy, and tender-skinned. Soaking the beans in salt water overnight and then cooking them in the oven did the trick. We fortify the stew with pancetta and other traditional Tuscan flavors, including kale, lots of garlic, and rosemary.

1. BRINE THE BEANS:
Dissolve 3 tablespoons salt in cold water in a large container. Add the beans and soak at room temperature for at least 8 hours.
WHY? Soaking the beans shortens their cooking time and results in creamier beans. Brining the beans fully hydrates and softens them, making them less prone to bursting during cooking.

2. PREP THE KALE: Trim the stems from 1 pound kale and chop the leaves into 1-inch pieces.
WHY? It is necessary to trim the stems from the kale, as only the leaves are used in the stew. Cut away the leafy green portion from either side of the stalk and then chop the leaves into even-size pieces.

3. BROWN THE PANCETTA AND AROMATICS: Heat the oil and pancetta and cook until the pancetta fat has rendered. Add the onion, carrots, and celery and cook until they are softened and lightly browned.
WHY? Browning the pancetta allows it to render its fat. That fat mixes with the oil and creates a flavorful base in which to cook the aromatics.

4. ADD THE BROTH AND BEANS: Stir in the garlic, then the chicken broth, water, bay leaves, and soaked beans and bring to a simmer.
WHY? The broth and water provide the liquid for the stew. They and the beans heat through before being cooked gently in a low oven.

5. TRANSFER TO THE OVEN:
Cover the pot, transfer it to the oven, and cook until the beans are almost tender, 45 minutes to 1 hour.
WHY? Gently cooking the beans in the oven is the key to perfectly cooked beans that stay intact. The even heat of the oven is more consistent and gentler than bubbling on the stovetop, which can cause the beans to blow out.

6. ADD THE GREENS AND TOMATOES: Stir in the chopped kale and drained tomatoes and return the pot to the oven. Cook until the beans and greens are fully tender.
WHY? The kale will be perfectly cooked if added partway through. The tomatoes are also added toward the end to prevent their acid from toughening the beans.

7. ADD THE FRESH ROSEMARY: Remove the pot from the oven and submerge a sprig of fresh rosemary in the stew. Cover and let stand 15 minutes.
WHY? Rosemary can be overwhelming if simmered too long, so we steep the stew with a sprig off the heat just until the broth is infused with a delicate herbal aroma.

8. MASH SOME BEANS TO THICKEN: If desired, use the back of a spoon to press some of the beans against the side of the pot.
WHY? Mashing some of the beans right in the soup pot is an easy way to give the stew body and help to thicken it.

Hearty Tuscan Bean Stew

SERVES 8　　**TOTAL TIME** 2 HOURS 15 MINUTES

✓ **WHY THIS RECIPE WORKS:** One of our favorite bean soups is Tuscan white bean soup, which boasts creamy, tender beans in a light, velvety broth. But we wanted to convert the more rustic soup version into a hearty stew. Determined to avoid tough, exploded beans in our stew, we soaked the beans overnight in salted water, which softened the skins. Then we experimented with cooking times and temperatures, discovering that gently cooking the beans in a 250-degree oven produced perfectly cooked beans that stayed intact. We added tomatoes toward the end of cooking, since their acid kept the beans from becoming too soft. To complete our stew, we chose other traditional Tuscan flavors, including pancetta, kale, lots of garlic, and a sprig of rosemary. If pancetta is unavailable, substitute 4 slices of bacon. Serve with Crostini (page 30).

- 1　pound (2½ cups) dried cannellini beans, picked over and salt-soaked
- 1　tablespoon extra-virgin olive oil, plus extra for serving
- 6　ounces pancetta, cut into ¼-inch pieces
- 1　large onion, chopped
- 2　carrots, peeled and cut into ½-inch pieces
- 2　celery ribs, cut into ½-inch pieces
- 8　garlic cloves, peeled and crushed
- 4　cups chicken broth
- 3　cups water
- 2　bay leaves
- 1　pound kale or collard greens, stemmed and leaves chopped into 1-inch pieces
- 1　(14.5-ounce) can diced tomatoes, drained
- 1　sprig fresh rosemary
  　Salt and pepper

1. Adjust oven rack to lower-middle position and heat oven to 250 degrees. Drain beans and rinse well.

2. Cook oil and pancetta in Dutch oven over medium heat, stirring often, until lightly browned and fat has rendered, 6 to 10 minutes. Stir in onion, carrots, and celery and cook until softened and lightly browned, 10 to 16 minutes.

3. Stir in garlic and cook until fragrant, about 1 minute. Stir in broth, water, bay leaves, and rinsed beans. Increase heat to high and bring to simmer. Cover, transfer to oven, and cook until beans are almost tender (very center of beans will still be firm), 45 minutes to 1 hour.

4. Stir in kale and tomatoes and continue to cook in oven, covered, until beans and greens are fully tender, 30 to 40 minutes.

5. Remove pot from oven and submerge rosemary in stew. Cover and let stand 15 minutes. Discard bay leaves and rosemary and season stew with salt and pepper to taste. If desired, use back of spoon to press some beans against side of pot to thicken stew. Drizzle portions with olive oil before serving. (Stew can be refrigerated for up to 3 days; add water as needed when reheating to adjust consistency.)

VARIATIONS

Hearty Tuscan Bean Stew with Sausage and Cabbage

This variation has much more meat and is made with crinkly savoy cabbage.

Substitute 1½ pounds sweet Italian sausage, casings removed, for pancetta, ½ head savoy cabbage, cut into 1-inch pieces, for kale, and 1 sprig fresh oregano for rosemary. In step 2, brown sausage in oil until no longer pink, breaking meat into small pieces with wooden spoon; transfer sausage to paper towel–lined plate and refrigerate. Stir browned sausage and cabbage into stew with tomatoes in step 4.

Vegetarian Hearty Tuscan Bean Stew

Omit pancetta. Substitute 3 cups vegetable broth for chicken broth, and increase amount of water to 5 cups. Add ½ ounce dried porcini mushrooms, rinsed and minced, to pot with garlic.

Italian Vegetable Stew

SERVES 6 TO 8　　**TOTAL TIME** 1 HOUR 45 MINUTES

✓ **WHY THIS RECIPE WORKS:** Italy's *ciambotta* is a ratatouille-like stew chock-full of veggies that makes for a hearty one-bowl meal with nary a trace of meat. We wanted to avoid the sorry fate of most recipes, which end in mushy vegetables drowning in a weak broth. In order to optimize the texture of the zucchini and peppers, we employed a skillet to cook off their excess water. To address the broth, we embraced eggplant's natural tendency to fall apart and cooked it until it completely assimilated into a thickened tomato-enriched sauce. Finally, we found that a potent version of pesto, a puree of olive oil, garlic, herbs, and red pepper flakes, provided the biggest flavor punch when added near the end of cooking. Serve with crusty bread.

We found a way to coax big flavor out of watery vegetables—eggplant, zucchini, peppers, and onions—for a hearty stew.

PESTO

- ⅓ cup chopped fresh basil
- ⅓ cup fresh oregano leaves
- 6 garlic cloves, minced
- 2 tablespoons extra-virgin olive oil
- ¼ teaspoon red pepper flakes

STEW

- 12 ounces eggplant, peeled and cut into ½-inch pieces
  Salt
- ¼ cup extra-virgin olive oil
- 1 large onion, chopped
- 1 pound russet potatoes, peeled and cut into ½-inch pieces
- 2 tablespoons tomato paste
- 2¼ cups water
- 1 (28-ounce) can whole peeled tomatoes, drained with juice reserved and chopped coarse
- 2 zucchini, halved lengthwise, seeded, and cut into ½-inch pieces
- 2 red or yellow bell peppers, stemmed, seeded, and cut into ½-inch pieces
- 1 cup shredded fresh basil

1. FOR THE PESTO: Process all ingredients in food processor until finely ground, about 1 minute, scraping down sides of bowl as necessary.

2. FOR THE STEW: Toss eggplant with 1½ teaspoons salt in bowl. Line surface of large plate with double layer of coffee filters and lightly spray with vegetable oil spray. Spread eggplant evenly over coffee filters and microwave until dry to touch and slightly shriveled, 8 to 12 minutes, tossing halfway through cooking.

3. Heat 2 tablespoons oil in Dutch oven over high heat until shimmering. Add eggplant, onion, and potatoes, and cook, stirring frequently, until eggplant browns, about 2 minutes.

4. Push vegetables to sides of pot. Add 1 tablespoon oil and tomato paste to clearing and cook, stirring often, until brown fond develops on bottom of pot, about 2 minutes. Stir in 2 cups water and tomatoes and their juice, scraping up any browned bits. Bring to boil. Reduce heat to medium, cover, and gently simmer until eggplant is completely broken down and potatoes are tender, 20 to 25 minutes.

5. Meanwhile, heat remaining 1 tablespoon oil in 12-inch skillet over high heat until just smoking. Add zucchini, bell peppers, and ½ teaspoon salt and cook, stirring occasionally, until vegetables are browned and tender, 10 to 12 minutes. Push vegetables to sides of skillet. Add pesto to clearing and cook until fragrant, about 1 minute. Stir pesto into vegetables and transfer to bowl. Off heat, add remaining ¼ cup water to skillet and scrape up browned bits.

6. Remove Dutch oven from heat and stir in vegetable mixture and water from skillet. Cover and let stew stand for 20 minutes to let flavors blend. Stir in basil, season with salt to taste, and serve.

Quinoa and Vegetable Stew

SERVES 6 TO 8 **TOTAL TIME** 50 MINUTES

WHY THIS RECIPE WORKS: In countries along the Andean highlands, quinoa plays a starring role in many dishes. Unfortunately, many authentic recipes call for obscure ingredients, such as annatto powder or Peruvian varieties of potatoes and corn. We set out to re-create a quinoa dish with vegetables, including potatoes and corn, aiming to keep our ingredient list easy to navigate. After realizing that paprika has

The quinoa is added after the potatoes have softened so it doesn't overcook and will still thicken the stew.

2 tablespoons vegetable oil
1 onion, chopped
1 red bell pepper, stemmed, seeded, and cut into ½-inch pieces
5 garlic cloves, minced
1 tablespoon paprika
2 teaspoons ground coriander
1½ teaspoons ground cumin
6 cups vegetable broth
1 pound red potatoes, unpeeled, cut into ½-inch pieces
1 cup prewashed quinoa
1 cup fresh or frozen corn
2 tomatoes, cored and chopped coarse
1 cup frozen peas
Salt and pepper
8 ounces queso fresco or feta cheese, crumbled (2 cups)
1 avocado, halved, pitted, and diced
½ cup minced fresh cilantro

a similar color and flavor profile to annatto powder and is a spice we already have on hand, we added cumin and coriander until the flavor was balanced and rich, blooming the mixture in the pan after sautéing the aromatics. We settled on red bell pepper, tomatoes, red potatoes, sweet corn, and frozen peas as our vegetable mix. Wary of overcooking the quinoa, we added it after the potatoes had softened. We cooked the quinoa as far as we could, until it had some chew and released starch to help give body to the stew. All that was needed now was a flurry of garnishes. We liked the traditional combination of salty queso fresco (feta cheese makes a good substitute), creamy avocado, and citrusy cilantro. Our quinoa stew was the best of both worlds: a humble ode to its authentic roots and a streamlined yet flavorful offering for modern-day tastes. If you buy unwashed quinoa, rinse the grains in a fine-mesh strainer, drain them, and then spread them on a rimmed baking sheet lined with a dish towel and let them dry for 15 minutes before proceeding with the recipe. This stew tends to thicken as it sits; add additional warm vegetable broth as needed before serving to loosen. Do not omit the queso fresco (or feta), avocado, and cilantro; these garnishes are important to the flavor of the stew.

1. Heat oil in Dutch oven over medium heat until shimmering. Add onion and bell pepper and cook until softened, 5 to 7 minutes. Stir in garlic, paprika, coriander, and cumin and cook until fragrant, about 30 seconds. Stir in broth and potatoes, and bring to boil over high heat. Reduce heat to medium-low and simmer gently for 10 minutes.

2. Stir in quinoa and simmer for 8 minutes. Stir in corn and simmer until potatoes and quinoa are just tender, 5 to 7 minutes. Stir in tomatoes and peas and let heat through, about 2 minutes.

3. Off heat, season with salt and pepper to taste. Sprinkle portions with queso fresco, avocado, and cilantro before serving. (Stew can be refrigerated for up to 2 days; add broth as needed when reheating to adjust consistency.)

VARIATION

Quinoa and Vegetable Stew with Eggs, Avocado, and Cilantro

Serving this stew with a cooked egg on top is a common practice in Peru.

Crack 6 large eggs evenly over top of stew after removing from heat and seasoning with salt and pepper in step 3; cover and let eggs poach off heat until whites have set but yolks are still soft, about 4 minutes. To serve, carefully scoop cooked egg and stew from pot with large spoon.

Classic ground beef chili, the mainstay of family dinners, potlucks, and Super Bowl parties, can be easily made with everyday supermarket ingredients and just a few tricks. For a version that is rich and balanced, we learned that the right tomato products and the simmering method make all the difference.

1. SAUTÉ THE AROMATICS: Heat the oil and cook the onions and red bell pepper until softened, then stir in the garlic. **WHY?** In addition to traditional onions and garlic, red bell pepper adds a mellow sweetness. The vegetables are sautéed together to allow the onions and bell pepper to soften and to enable their flavors to combine. The garlic needs only 30 seconds to become fragrant.

2. BLOOM THE SPICES: Stir the spice mixture, including ¼ cup of chili powder, into the aromatics and cook until fragrant, being careful not to let them burn. **WHY?** Commercial chili powder provides plenty of spice notes and heat; upping the amount boosts the flavor. Adding the spices to the aromatics helps bloom and deepen their flavor.

3. COOK THE GROUND BEEF: Add the ground beef in two batches, breaking it up as it begins to brown, until it is no longer pink. **WHY?** We found that 85 percent lean ground beef makes for a full-flavored chili. Using all beef gives the chili hearty flavor and the best texture.

4. ADD THE BEANS: Stir in the canned dark red kidney beans. **WHY?** Canned beans are quick and convenient to use. Firm, full-flavored kidney beans, a classic component of chili, hold their shape and so can spend longer in the pot. When added with the tomatoes and their juice, they have time to absorb a lot of flavor.

5. ADD 2 KINDS OF TOMATOES: Stir in the diced tomatoes with their juice and the tomato puree. **WHY?** Diced tomatoes add fresh flavor and hold up well when simmered. They add a chunky texture, which makes for a rich sauce. Tomato puree added body and the canned flavor wasn't noticeable after simmering. There is no need to add water unless the chili sticks to the bottom of the pot or gets too thick.

6. SIMMER THE CHILI GENTLY: Cover the pot, reduce to a gentle simmer, and cook for 1 hour. Uncover and continue to simmer gently, until the beef is tender and the sauce is dark and thickened. **WHY?** Cooking the chili with the lid on led to a soupy chili, while leaving it off made the chili too dense. Keeping the lid on for half the time and off for the other half helped give the chili a perfect rich and thick consistency.

Classic Beef Chili

SERVES 6 TO 8   **TOTAL TIME** 2 HOURS 20 MINUTES

✔ WHY THIS RECIPE WORKS: With the goal of developing a no-fuss chili that would taste far better than the sum of its parts, we knew that adding the spices with the aromatics would boost their potency. Commercial chili powder, backed by cumin, coriander, cayenne, oregano, and red pepper flakes, provided plenty of spice notes and heat. For the meat, 85 percent lean ground beef gave us full, deep flavor. Using both diced tomatoes and tomato puree provided chunks of tomato and a rich, thick sauce. Adding the beans with the tomatoes ensured that they cooked enough to absorb flavor but not so much that they fell apart. Finally, cooking the chili with the lid on for half the simmering time resulted in a rich, thick consistency. Serve with lime wedges, fresh cilantro, sliced scallions, minced onion, diced avocado, shredded cheddar or Monterey Jack cheese, and/or sour cream.

- ¼ cup chili powder
- 1 tablespoon ground cumin
- 2 teaspoons ground coriander
- 1 teaspoon red pepper flakes
- 1 teaspoon dried oregano
- ½ teaspoon cayenne pepper
- Salt and pepper
- 2 tablespoons vegetable oil
- 2 onions, chopped fine
- 1 red bell pepper, stemmed, seeded, and cut into ½-inch pieces
- 6 garlic cloves, minced
- 2 pounds 85 percent lean ground beef
- 2 (15-ounce) cans dark red kidney beans, rinsed
- 1 (28-ounce) can diced tomatoes
- 1 (28-ounce) can tomato puree
- Water, as needed

1. Combine chili powder, cumin, coriander, pepper flakes, oregano, cayenne, and 1 teaspoon salt in bowl.

2. Heat oil in Dutch oven over medium heat until shimmering. Add onions and bell pepper and cook until softened, 8 to 10 minutes. Stir in garlic and cook until fragrant, about 30 seconds. Stir in spice mixture and cook, stirring constantly, until fragrant, about 1 minute.

3. Stir in half of beef. Increase heat to medium-high and cook, breaking up meat with spoon, until no longer pink, 3 to 5 minutes. Add remaining beef and cook until no longer pink. Stir in beans, diced tomatoes with their juice, and tomato puree and bring to simmer. Cover, reduce heat to gentle simmer, and cook, stirring occasionally, for 1 hour.

4. Uncover and continue to simmer gently until beef is tender and sauce is dark, rich, and slightly thickened, about 45 minutes longer. (If chili begins to stick to bottom of pot or looks too thick, stir in water as needed.) Season with salt and pepper to taste. Serve. (Chili can be refrigerated for up to 3 days; add water as needed when reheating to adjust consistency.)

VARIATION
Beef Chili with Bacon and Pinto Beans
Reduce amount of salt to ½ teaspoon in step 1. Substitute 8 ounces chopped bacon for vegetable oil; cook bacon over medium heat until crisp and fat has rendered, 5 to 7 minutes. Pour off all but 2 tablespoons bacon fat (leaving bacon in pot), then add onions and bell pepper and cook as directed in step 2. Substitute 2 (15-ounce) cans rinsed pinto beans for kidney beans.

Five-Alarm Chili

SERVES 8 TO 10   **TOTAL TIME** 2 HOURS

✔ WHY THIS RECIPE WORKS: As the name implies, five-alarm chili should be spicy enough to make you break a sweat—but it has to have rich, complex chile flavor as well. We used a combination of dried anchos, smoky chipotle chiles in adobo sauce, fresh jalapeños, and chili powder to create layers of spicy flavor. Ground beef added meaty bulk, and pureeing the chiles along with canned tomatoes and corn chips added extra body and another layer of flavor. Mellowed with a bit of sugar and enriched with creamy pinto beans, our chili was well balanced and spicy without being harsh. Look for ancho chiles in the international aisle at the supermarket. Light-bodied American lagers, such as Budweiser, work best here. Serve with lime wedges, sour cream, scallions, and cornbread.

- 2 ounces (4 to 6) dried ancho chiles, stemmed, seeded, and cut into 1-inch pieces
- 3½ cups water
- 1 (28-ounce) can whole peeled tomatoes
- ¾ cup crushed corn tortilla chips
- ¼ cup canned chipotle chile in adobo sauce plus 2 teaspoons adobo sauce
- 2 tablespoons vegetable oil
- 2 pounds 85 percent lean ground beef
- Salt and pepper
- 2 pounds onions, chopped fine
- 2 jalapeño chiles, stemmed, seeds reserved, and minced
- 6 garlic cloves, minced
- 2 tablespoons ground cumin

2 tablespoons chili powder
1 tablespoon dried oregano
2 teaspoons ground coriander
2 teaspoons sugar
1 teaspoon cayenne pepper
1½ cups beer
3 (15-ounce) cans pinto beans, rinsed

1. Combine anchos and 1½ cups water in bowl and microwave until softened, about 3 minutes. Drain and discard liquid. Process anchos, tomatoes and their juice, remaining 2 cups water, tortilla chips, chipotle, and adobo sauce in blender until smooth, about 1 minute.

2. Heat 2 teaspoons oil in Dutch oven over medium-high heat until just smoking. Add beef, 1 teaspoon salt, and ½ teaspoon pepper and cook, breaking up meat with wooden spoon, until all liquid has evaporated and meat begins to sizzle, 10 to 15 minutes. Drain in colander and set aside.

3. Heat remaining 4 teaspoons oil in now-empty Dutch oven over medium-high heat until shimmering. Add onions and jalapeños with their seeds and cook until onions are lightly browned, about 5 minutes. Stir in garlic, cumin, chili powder, oregano, coriander, sugar, and cayenne and cook until fragrant, about 30 seconds. Pour in beer and bring to simmer.

4. Stir in beans, reserved chile-tomato mixture, and reserved cooked beef and return to simmer. Cover, reduce heat to low, and cook, stirring occasionally, until thickened, 50 to 60 minutes. Season with salt to taste and serve. (Chili can be refrigerated for up to 3 days; add water as needed when reheating to adjust consistency.)

Classic Turkey Chili

SERVES 6 TO 8   **TOTAL TIME** 2 HOURS 30 MINUTES

✔ **WHY THIS RECIPE WORKS:** Making good turkey chili is not as easy as replacing ground beef with ground turkey. A simple swap will leave you with measly bits of overcooked meat floating in the chili. And the texture of ground poultry can be soft and unappetizing. We discovered a few solutions. First, we sautéed just half of the ground poultry, breaking it up into little pieces, to really distribute the flavor while it simmered. For improved texture and moister meat, we pinched the remaining ground poultry into small pieces and stirred them into the chili toward the end of the simmering time. This approach enabled some of the meat to dissolve into the sauce, giving it a meaty flavor, while the rest retained its texture. Serve with diced tomato, diced avocado, sliced scallions, shredded cheddar, sour cream, lime wedges, and minced fresh cilantro.

1 tablespoon canola oil
2 onions, chopped fine
1 red bell pepper, stemmed, seeded, and cut into ½-inch pieces
6 garlic cloves, minced
¼ cup chili powder
1 tablespoon ground cumin
2 teaspoons ground coriander
1 teaspoon red pepper flakes
1 teaspoon dried oregano
½ teaspoon cayenne pepper
2 pounds 93 percent lean ground turkey
2 (15-ounce) cans kidney beans, rinsed
1 (28-ounce) can diced tomatoes
1 (28-ounce) can crushed tomatoes
2 cups chicken broth
Water, as needed
Salt and pepper

1. Heat oil in Dutch oven over medium heat until shimmering. Add onions, bell pepper, garlic, chili powder, cumin, coriander, pepper flakes, oregano, and cayenne and cook, stirring often, until vegetables are softened, about 10 minutes.

2. Add 1 pound turkey, increase heat to medium-high, and cook, breaking up meat with wooden spoon, until no longer pink, about 4 minutes. Stir in beans, diced tomatoes and their juice, crushed tomatoes, and broth and bring to simmer. Reduce heat to medium-low and simmer until chili has begun to thicken, about 1 hour.

3. Pat remaining 1 pound turkey together into ball, then pinch off teaspoon-size pieces of meat and stir into chili. Continue to simmer, stirring occasionally, until turkey is tender and chili is slightly thickened, about 40 minutes. (If chili begins to stick to bottom of pot or looks too thick, stir in water as needed.) Season with salt and pepper to taste and serve. (Chili can be refrigerated for up to 3 days; add water as needed when reheating to adjust consistency.)

Making Turkey Chili

To keep ground turkey appealingly chunky, it is important to reserve half of it and add it to the chili later. We packed the meat into a big ball, then pinched off bits and stirred them into the simmering chili

Smoky-Spicy Turkey Chili

Chipotle chiles give this chili a smoky flavor, and habaneros lend a spicy kick. To make the chili even spicier, include the habanero seeds and ribs when mincing; to make it milder, use less habanero.

Omit pepper flakes and cayenne. Add 2 habanero chiles, seeded and minced, and 2 tablespoons minced canned chipotle chile in adobo sauce to pot with vegetables in step 1. Add 1 tablespoon packed light brown sugar to pot with beans in step 2. Serve with finely chopped pickled banana peppers.

Tequila-Lime Turkey Chili

The tequila adds a noticeable zing to this chili.

Substitute 2 (15-ounce) cans rinsed pinto beans for kidney beans. Add ¼ cup tequila and 1 tablespoon honey to chili with remaining turkey in step 3.

Easy Chili con Carne

SERVES 6 TO 8   **TOTAL TIME** 2 TO 3 HOURS

WHY THIS RECIPE WORKS: Many chili con carne recipes call for toasting and grinding whole chiles. We wanted to create a simpler but nevertheless still authentic-tasting version. For the meat, we settled on beef chuck, our favorite cut for stews because its substantial marbling provides rich flavor and tender texture after prolonged cooking. To add a smoky meatiness to our chili, we browned the beef in bacon fat instead of oil. We added a jalapeño for brightness and heat and minced chipotle for smoky, spicy depth. A few tablespoons of corn muffin mix, in place of masa harina (corn flour), helped thicken our chili and give it a silky texture. If the bacon does not render a full 3 tablespoons of fat in step 1, supplement it with vegetable oil.

- 1 (14.5-ounce) can diced tomatoes
- 2 teaspoons minced canned chipotle chile in adobo
- 4 slices bacon, chopped fine
- 1 (3½- to 4-pound) boneless beef chuck-eye roast, pulled apart at seams, trimmed, and cut into 1-inch pieces
  Salt and pepper
- 1 onion, chopped fine
- 1 jalapeño chile, stemmed, seeded, and chopped fine
- 3 tablespoons chili powder
- 4 garlic cloves, minced
- 1½ teaspoons ground cumin
- ½ teaspoon dried oregano
- 4 cups water
- 1 tablespoon packed brown sugar
- 2 tablespoons yellow corn muffin mix

1. Process tomatoes and chipotle in food processor until smooth. Cook bacon in Dutch oven over medium heat until crisp, about 8 minutes; transfer to paper towel–lined plate. Pour off and reserve 3 tablespoons bacon fat.

2. Pat beef dry with paper towels and season with salt and pepper. Heat 1 tablespoon reserved bacon fat in now-empty pot over medium-high heat until just smoking. Brown half of beef well on all sides, about 8 minutes; transfer to bowl. Repeat with 1 tablespoon bacon fat and remaining beef.

3. Add remaining 1 tablespoon bacon fat, onion, and jalapeño to fat left in pot and cook over medium heat until softened, about 5 minutes. Stir in chili powder, garlic, cumin, and oregano and cook until fragrant, about 30 seconds. Stir in water, pureed tomato mixture, bacon, sugar, and browned beef and any accumulated juice. Bring to boil, then reduce heat to low and simmer, covered, for 1 hour.

4. Uncover and skim excess fat from surface of stew using large spoon. Continue to simmer, uncovered, until meat is tender, 30 to 45 minutes.

5. Ladle 1 cup chili liquid into medium bowl and stir in muffin mix; cover and microwave until mixture is thickened, about 1 minute. Slowly whisk mixture into chili and simmer until chili is slightly thickened, 5 to 10 minutes. Season with salt and pepper to taste and serve. (Chili can be refrigerated for up to 3 days; add water as needed when reheating to adjust consistency.)

Ultimate Beef Chili

SERVES 6 TO 8   **TOTAL TIME** 4½ TO 5 HOURS

WHY THIS RECIPE WORKS: Our goal in creating an "ultimate" beef chili was to determine which of the "secret ingredients" recommended by chili experts around the world were spot-on—and which were expendable. We started with the beef—most recipes call for ground beef, but we preferred meaty blade steak, which didn't require much trimming and stayed in big chunks in our finished chili. For complex chile flavor, we traded in the commercial chili powder in favor of ground dried ancho and arbol chiles; for a grassy heat, we added fresh jalapeños. Dried beans, quick-brined before cooking, stayed creamy for the duration of cooking. Beer and chicken broth outperformed red wine, coffee, and beef broth as the liquid components. To balance the sweetness of our pot of chili, light molasses beat out other offbeat ingredients (including prunes and Coca-Cola). For the right level of thickness, a small amount of ordinary cornmeal sealed the deal, providing just the right consistency in our ultimate beef chili. A 4-pound chuck-eye roast, well trimmed of fat, can be substituted for the steak. Because much of the chili flavor is held in the fat of this dish, refrain from skimming fat from the surface. Dried New Mexican or guajillo chiles make a good substitute for the anchos; each dried arbol may be replaced with ⅛ teaspoon cayenne. If you prefer not to work with any whole dried chiles, the anchos and arbols can be replaced with ½ cup commercial chili powder and ¼ to ½ teaspoon cayenne pepper, though the texture of the chili will be slightly compromised. Good choices for condiments include diced avocado, finely chopped red onion, minced fresh cilantro, lime wedges, sour cream, and shredded Monterey Jack or cheddar cheese.

    8   ounces (1¼ cups) dried pinto beans,
        picked over and rinsed
        Salt
    6   dried ancho chiles, stemmed, seeded, and torn
        into 1-inch pieces
  2–4   dried arbol chiles, stemmed, seeded, and
        split in 2 pieces
    3   tablespoons cornmeal
    2   teaspoons dried oregano
    2   teaspoons ground cumin
    2   teaspoons unsweetened cocoa powder
  2½   cups chicken broth
    2   onions, cut into ¾-inch pieces
    3   small jalapeño chiles, stemmed, seeded,
        and cut into ½-inch pieces
    3   tablespoons vegetable oil
    4   garlic cloves, minced
    1   (14.5-ounce) can diced tomatoes
    2   teaspoons molasses
  3½   pounds blade steak, ¾ inch thick, trimmed and
        cut into ¾-inch pieces
    1   (12-ounce) bottle mild lager, such as Budweiser

1. Bring 4 quarts water, beans, and 3 tablespoons salt to boil in Dutch oven over high heat. Remove pot from heat, cover, and let stand 1 hour. Drain beans and rinse well.

2. Toast ancho chiles in 12-inch skillet over medium-high heat, stirring often, until fragrant, 4 to 6 minutes; reduce heat if smoking. Transfer chiles to food processor and let cool. Add arbol chiles, cornmeal, oregano, cumin, cocoa, and ½ teaspoon salt to food processor and process until finely ground, about 2 minutes. With processor running, slowly add ½ cup

broth until smooth paste forms, about 45 seconds, scraping down bowl as needed. Transfer paste to bowl.

3. Place onions in now-empty processor and pulse until roughly chopped, about 4 pulses. Add jalapeños and pulse until consistency of chunky salsa, about 4 pulses.

4. Heat 1 tablespoon oil in Dutch oven over medium-high heat. Add onion mixture and cook until moisture has evaporated and vegetables are softened, 7 to 9 minutes. Add garlic and cook until fragrant, about 1 minute. Stir in chile paste, tomatoes, and molasses until thoroughly combined. Stir in remaining 2 cups broth and drained beans. Bring to boil, then reduce heat to simmer.

5. Meanwhile, adjust oven rack to lower-middle position and heat oven to 300 degrees. Pat beef dry with paper towels and season with salt. Heat 1 tablespoon oil in 12-inch skillet over medium-high heat until shimmering. Brown half of beef well on all sides, about 10 minutes; transfer to Dutch oven. Add half of beer to skillet and bring to simmer, scraping up any browned bits; transfer to Dutch oven. Repeat with remaining 1 tablespoon oil, remaining beef, and remaining beer.

6. Bring to simmer, cover, and transfer to oven. Cook until meat and beans are fully tender, 1½ to 2 hours. Let chili stand, uncovered, for 10 minutes. Season with salt to taste and serve. (Chili can be refrigerated for up to 3 days; add water as needed when reheating to adjust consistency.)

Colorado Green Chili

SERVES 6   **TOTAL TIME** 2 HOURS 30 MINUTES

✓ **WHY THIS RECIPE WORKS:** Unlike Texas chili, this Colorado dish is based on pork and lots of green Hatch chiles. Since you have to mail-order real Hatch chiles, we approximate the flavor with Anaheims and jalapeños. We halved the Anaheims before roasting, which means no tedious flipping, and pureed half of the chiles (along with a can of diced tomatoes) while chopping the other half by hand to create texture. Pork butt is rich and meaty, and starting it in a covered pan with water until the fat renders lets us brown it all in one batch. Using the oven to cook the chili provides gentle heat—and hands-off cooking—and we finished the stew with the chopped roasted jalapeños to add a fresh hit of heat. Serve with sour cream and minced fresh cilantro.

    1   (3-pound) boneless pork butt roast, pulled apart at
        seams, trimmed, and cut into 1-inch pieces
        Salt

More than two pounds of chiles go into this mildly spicy stew, making it as much about the green chile peppers as the pork.

2 pounds (10 to 12) Anaheim chiles, stemmed, halved lengthwise, and seeded

3 jalapeño chiles

1 (14.5-ounce) can diced tomatoes

1 tablespoon vegetable oil

2 onions, chopped fine

8 garlic cloves, minced

1 tablespoon ground cumin

¼ cup all-purpose flour

4 cups chicken broth

Cayenne pepper

Lime wedges

1. Combine pork, ½ cup water, and ½ teaspoon salt in Dutch oven. Cover and cook over medium heat, stirring occasionally, for 20 minutes. Uncover and increase heat to medium-high. Cook, stirring often, until liquid evaporates and pork browns in its own fat, 15 to 20 minutes; transfer to bowl.

2. Meanwhile, adjust 1 oven rack to lowest position and second rack 6 inches from broiler element. Heat broiler. Line rimmed baking sheet with aluminum foil and spray with vegetable oil spray. Arrange Anaheims, skin side up, and jalapeños in single layer on prepared sheet. Broil chiles on upper rack until mostly blackened and soft, 15 to 20 minutes, flipping jalapeños halfway through broiling. Place Anaheims in large bowl, cover with plastic wrap, and let skins steam loose for 5 minutes. Set aside jalapeños. Heat oven to 325 degrees. (Chiles can be refrigerated for up to 1 day.)

3. Remove skins from Anaheims. Chop half of Anaheims into ½-inch pieces; transfer to bowl. Process remaining Anaheims in food processor until smooth, about 10 seconds; transfer to bowl with chopped Anaheims. Pulse tomatoes and their juice in now-empty food processor until coarsely ground, about 4 pulses.

4. Heat oil in now-empty Dutch oven over medium heat until shimmering. Add onions and cook until lightly browned, 5 to 7 minutes. Stir in garlic and cumin and cook until fragrant, about 30 seconds. Stir in flour and cook for 1 minute. Stir in broth, Anaheims, tomatoes, and pork and any accumulated juices. Bring to simmer, scraping up any browned bits. Cover, transfer to lower oven rack, and cook until pork is tender, 1 to 1¼ hours.

5. Stem, seed, and finely chop jalapeños (do not peel), reserving seeds, and stir into chili. Season chili with salt, cayenne, and reserved jalapeño seeds to taste. Serve with lime wedges. (Chili can be refrigerated for up to 3 days; add water as needed when reheating to adjust consistency.)

White Chicken Chili

SERVES 6 TO 8   **TOTAL TIME** 1 HOUR 50 MINUTES

✓ **WHY THIS RECIPE WORKS:** Chili made with chicken promises a lighter, fresher alternative to the red kind, but most of the time the resulting chili is bland and watery and the chicken is dry and flavorless. We found not one but three solutions to boring chicken chili. To solve the problem of insufficient chile flavor, we used a trio of fresh chiles: jalapeño, poblano, and New Mexican. To fix the watery sauce, we pureed some of our sautéed aromatics (a mix of chiles, garlic, and onions) and broth with beans to thicken the base. And finally, to avoid floating bits of rubbery chicken, we browned, poached, and shredded bone-in, skin-on chicken breasts, which gave our chicken pieces a tender texture and full flavor. Adjust the heat in this dish by adding the seeds from the jalapeños as directed in step 6. If New Mexican chiles cannot be found, add an additional poblano and jalapeño to the chili. Serve with sour cream, tortilla chips, and lime wedges.

3 pounds bone-in split chicken breasts, trimmed
   Salt and pepper
1 tablespoon vegetable oil
3 poblano chiles, stemmed, seeded, and cut into large pieces
3 New Mexican chile peppers, stemmed, seeded, and cut into large pieces
2 onions, cut into large pieces
3 jalapeño chiles, stemmed, seeds reserved, and minced
6 garlic cloves, minced
1 tablespoon ground cumin
1½ teaspoons ground coriander
2 (15-ounce) cans cannellini beans, rinsed
3 cups chicken broth
3 tablespoons lime juice (2 limes)
¼ cup minced fresh cilantro
4 scallions, sliced thin

1. Pat chicken dry with paper towels and season with salt and pepper. Heat oil in Dutch oven over medium-high heat until just smoking. Brown chicken well on both sides, about 6 minutes. Transfer chicken to plate, then remove and discard skin.

2. Pulse half each of poblanos, New Mexican chiles, and onions in food processor until consistency of chunky salsa, 10 to 12 pulses, scraping down bowl as needed. Transfer mixture to medium bowl. Repeat with remaining poblanos, New Mexican chiles, and onions; combine with first batch (do not wash food processor).

3. Pour off all but 1 tablespoon fat left in Dutch oven. Add two-thirds of jalapeños, chile mixture, garlic, cumin, coriander, and ¼ teaspoon salt. Cover and cook over medium heat, stirring occasionally, until vegetables have softened, about 10 minutes. Remove pot from heat.

4. Process 1 cup beans, 1 cup broth, and 1 cup cooked vegetable mixture in now-empty food processor until smooth, about 20 seconds. Stir pureed mixture into Dutch oven. Stir in remaining 2 cups broth and browned chicken and any accumulated juices, and bring to boil. Reduce heat to medium-low, cover, and simmer gently until chicken registers 160 degrees, 15 to 20 minutes.

5. Transfer chicken to cutting board, let cool slightly, then shred into bite-size pieces, discarding bones. Stir remaining beans into pot and continue to simmer until beans are heated through and chili has thickened slightly, about 10 minutes.

6. Stir in shredded chicken, lime juice, cilantro, scallions, and remaining minced jalapeño, and let simmer gently until heated through, about 2 minutes. Season with salt, pepper, and jalapeño seeds to taste. Serve. (Chili can be refrigerated for up to 3 days; add water as needed when reheating to adjust consistency.)

A trio of fresh chiles makes this Southwestern-style chicken chili a light, bright alternative to the classic beef chili.

VARIATION
White Turkey Chili
Substitute 1 bone-in split turkey breast (2½ pounds) for chicken, browning turkey and removing skin as directed. In step 4, add turkey breast, bone side down, to pot after stirring in remaining broth and any accumulated juices, and cook until turkey registers 160 degrees, 30 to 35 minutes.

Black Bean Chili
SERVES 6 TO 8   TOTAL TIME 3 HOURS

✔ **WHY THIS RECIPE WORKS:** Black bean chili is the vegetarian's answer to hearty, satisfying chili, but so often it turns out dull and unremarkable, tasting like either warmed black beans straight from the can or a hodgepodge of vegetables. We wanted a chili that was primarily about the beans—which should be creamy, tender, and well seasoned—and that had enough complexity and depth to hold your interest for a whole bowl. With these goals in mind, we headed into the test kitchen. After discovering that dried beans supplied superior

Chopped mushrooms and two chopped bell peppers provide a hearty texture to our black bean chili.

texture, we looked for ways to boost the meaty flavor of the chili. White mushrooms, sautéed with some onions, gave a meaty texture and flavor, and plenty of body. Whole cumin seeds and minced chipotle chile added depth and smokiness, and, surprisingly, toasted mustard seeds added pungency and an additional level of complexity. Served with a spritz of lime and a sprinkle of minced cilantro, this rich, hearty chili was so satisfying that no one missed the meat. We strongly prefer the texture and flavor of mustard seeds and cumin seeds in this chili; however, ground cumin and dry mustard can be substituted—add ½ teaspoon ground cumin and/or ½ teaspoon dry mustard to the pot with the chili powder in step 3. Serve with sour cream, shredded cheddar or Monterey Jack cheese, chopped tomatoes, and/or minced onion.

1 **pound white mushrooms, trimmed and broken into rough pieces**
1 **tablespoon mustard seeds**
2 **teaspoons cumin seeds**
3 **tablespoons vegetable oil**
1 **onion, chopped fine**
9 **garlic cloves, minced**
1 **tablespoon minced canned chipotle chile in adobo sauce**
3 **tablespoons chili powder**
2½ **cups vegetable broth**
2½ **cups water, plus extra as needed**
1 **pound (2½ cups) dried black beans, picked over and rinsed**
1 **tablespoon packed light brown sugar**
⅛ **teaspoon baking soda**
2 **bay leaves**
1 **(28-ounce) can crushed tomatoes**
2 **red bell peppers, stemmed, seeded, and cut into ½-inch pieces**
½ **cup minced fresh cilantro**
  Salt and pepper
  Lime wedges

1. Adjust oven rack to lower-middle position and heat oven to 325 degrees. Pulse mushrooms in food processor until uniformly coarsely chopped, about 10 pulses.

2. Toast mustard seeds and cumin seeds in Dutch oven over medium heat, stirring constantly, until fragrant, about 1 minute. Stir in oil, onion, and processed mushrooms, cover, and cook until vegetables have released their liquid, about 5 minutes. Uncover and continue to cook until vegetables are browned, 5 to 10 minutes.

3. Stir in garlic and chipotles and cook until fragrant, about 30 seconds. Stir in chili powder and cook, stirring constantly, until fragrant, about 1 minute. Stir in broth, water, beans, sugar, baking soda, and bay leaves and bring to simmer, skimming as needed. Cover, transfer to oven, and cook for 1 hour.

4. Stir in crushed tomatoes and bell peppers and continue to cook in oven, covered, until beans are fully tender, about 1 hour longer. (If chili begins to stick to bottom of pot or is too thick, add water as needed.)

5. Remove pot from oven and discard bay leaves. Stir in cilantro, season with salt and pepper to taste, and serve with lime wedges. (Chili can be refrigerated for up to 3 days; add water as needed when reheating to adjust consistency.)

Picking Over and Rinsing Dried Beans

Dried beans often contain little pebbles, so it's necessary to pick over them carefully to find and remove all foreign matter. Rinsing the beans washes away any traces of soil.

Poultry

■ SIGNIFIES A **FAST** RECIPE (45 MINUTES OR LESS)

PAN SAUCES FOR CHICKEN

A flavorful pan sauce is a quick and easy way to dress up plain chicken breasts. Here are some of our favorite pan sauces. They can be served with our Sautéed Chicken Breasts (page 129) or Pan-Roasted Chicken Breasts (page 152). Do not wash out the pan after browning the chicken: Those browned bits remaining on the bottom of the skillet, called fond, are the key to a successful sauce; they add important flavor. See page 184 to learn how to make a pan sauce. Each of these recipes yields enough sauce for up to four boneless or bone-in chicken breasts.

Cream Sauce with Mushrooms
TOTAL TIME 30 MINUTES `FAST`

- 1 tablespoon vegetable oil
- 2 shallots, minced
  Salt and pepper
- 8 ounces white mushrooms, trimmed and sliced thin
- ⅓ cup dry sherry or white wine
- 1 cup heavy cream
- ½ cup chicken broth
- 2 tablespoons minced fresh parsley
  Pinch nutmeg or mace

Add oil to skillet and heat over medium-high heat until shimmering. Add shallots and ¼ teaspoon salt and cook until softened, about 2 minutes. Add mushrooms and cook until browned, about 8 minutes. Stir in sherry, scraping up any browned bits, and cook until liquid evaporates, about 1 minute. Stir in cream and broth and simmer until thickened, about 8 minutes. Stir in any accumulated chicken juices. Off heat, stir in parsley and nutmeg. Season with salt and pepper to taste.

Mustard and Cider Sauce
TOTAL TIME 20 MINUTES `FAST`

- 1 tablespoon vegetable oil
- 1 shallot, minced
  Salt and pepper
- 1¼ cups apple cider
- 2 tablespoons cider vinegar
- 3 tablespoons unsalted butter, cut into 3 pieces and chilled
- 2 tablespoons minced fresh parsley
- 2 teaspoons whole-grain mustard

Add oil to skillet and heat over medium-high heat until shimmering. Add shallot and ¼ teaspoon salt and cook until softened, about 2 minutes. Stir in cider and vinegar, scraping up any browned bits, and simmer until reduced and slightly syrupy, about 8 minutes. Stir in any accumulated chicken juices. Turn heat to low and whisk in butter, 1 piece at a time. Off heat, stir in parsley and mustard. Season with salt and pepper to taste.

Apricot-Orange Sauce
TOTAL TIME 15 MINUTES `FAST`

- 1 tablespoon unsalted butter
- 1 shallot, minced
- 2 garlic cloves, minced
- 1 cup orange juice
- 1 orange, peeled and chopped coarse
- 1 cup dried apricots, chopped
- 2 tablespoons minced fresh parsley
  Salt and pepper

Add butter to skillet and melt over medium-high heat. Add shallot and cook until softened, about 2 minutes. Stir in garlic and cook until fragrant, about 15 seconds. Stir in juice, chopped orange, and apricots and simmer until thickened, about 4 minutes. Stir in any accumulated chicken juices. Off heat, stir in parsley and season with salt and pepper to taste.

Sherry-Rosemary Sauce
TOTAL TIME 20 MINUTES `FAST`

- 1 tablespoon vegetable oil
- 1 shallot, minced
  Salt and pepper
- ¾ cup chicken broth
- ½ cup dry sherry
- 2 sprigs fresh rosemary
- 3 tablespoons unsalted butter, cut into 3 pieces and chilled

Add oil to skillet and heat over medium-high heat until shimmering. Add shallot and ¼ teaspoon salt and cook until softened, about 2 minutes. Stir in broth, sherry, and rosemary sprigs, scraping up any browned bits. Bring to simmer and cook until thickened and measures ⅔ cup, about 6 minutes. Stir in any accumulated chicken juices. Turn heat to low and whisk in butter, 1 piece at a time. Off heat, discard rosemary sprigs. Season with salt and pepper to taste.

Tomato, Basil, and Caper Sauce
TOTAL TIME 20 MINUTES `FAST`

- 1 tablespoon vegetable oil
- 1 shallot, minced
  Salt and pepper
- 12 ounces tomatoes, cored, seeded, and chopped (2 cups)
- 4 garlic cloves, minced
- ¼ cup dry white wine
- 2 tablespoons capers, rinsed
- 2 tablespoons chopped fresh basil

Add oil to skillet and heat over medium-high heat until shimmering. Add shallot and ¼ teaspoon salt and cook until softened, about 2 minutes. Stir in tomatoes and garlic. Cook until tomatoes have broken down, about 2 minutes. Stir in wine and capers, scraping up any browned bits, and simmer until thickened, about 2 minutes. Stir in any accumulated chicken juices. Off heat, stir in basil and season with salt and pepper to taste.

Sautéed Chicken Breasts with Vermouth and Tarragon Sauce

SERVES 4   **TOTAL TIME** 45 MINUTES   **FAST**

✔ WHY THIS RECIPE WORKS: The key to cooking a chicken breast with flavorful, moist, and tender meat is the amount of heat. Cooking over low or even moderate heat pushes the meat's moisture to the surface, and once the juices hit the exterior of the meat, it will not brown at all. The key to making a flavorful sauce is to avoid using a nonstick skillet; if you do, there won't be any tasty browned bits to flavor the sauce. Using a 12-inch skillet is crucial here so that the chicken has enough room to brown. For a cream sauce, simply replace the butter with 4 tablespoons of heavy cream and simmer it until thickened. Parsley, basil, thyme, or dill can be substituted for the tarragon. You can also pick one of the pan sauces on page 128 to accompany the chicken.

CHICKEN

- ½ cup all-purpose flour
- 4 (6- to 8-ounce) boneless, skinless chicken breasts, trimmed
- Salt and pepper
- 2 tablespoons vegetable oil

VERMOUTH AND TARRAGON SAUCE

- 1 tablespoon vegetable oil
- 1 shallot, minced
- Salt and pepper
- ¾ cup chicken broth
- ½ cup dry vermouth or white wine
- 3 tablespoons unsalted butter, cut into 3 pieces and chilled
- 2 teaspoons minced fresh tarragon

1. FOR THE CHICKEN: Adjust oven rack to lower-middle position and heat oven to 200 degrees. Spread flour into shallow dish. Pound thicker ends of breasts as needed, then pat dry with paper towels and season with salt and pepper. Dredge in flour to coat, shaking off any excess.

2. Heat oil in 12-inch skillet over medium-high heat until just smoking. Add chicken and cook, turning as needed, until chicken is golden brown on both sides and registers 160 degrees, about 10 minutes. Transfer chicken to plate and keep warm in oven.

3. FOR THE SAUCE: Add oil to now-empty skillet and heat over medium-high heat until shimmering. Add shallot and ¼ teaspoon salt and cook until softened, about 2 minutes. Stir in broth and vermouth, scraping up any browned bits, and simmer until reduced and slightly syrupy, about 8 minutes.

4. Stir in any accumulated chicken juices. Turn heat to low and whisk in butter, one piece at a time. Off heat, stir in tarragon and season with salt and pepper to taste. Spoon sauce over chicken and serve.

Spa Chicken with Carrot-Ginger Sauce

SERVES 4   **TOTAL TIME** 1 HOUR 20 MINUTES

✔ WHY THIS RECIPE WORKS: To find the best way to cook boneless, skinless chicken breasts without using oil, we tested myriad methods before finding the optimal one. Broiling left the chicken with a tough, leathery exterior. Microwaving was too unreliable, often cooking chicken unevenly. Steaming, which consistently delivered tender, moist chicken, had the disadvantages of requiring a steamer basket and imparting no additional flavor to the chicken. In the end, poaching became a favorite method. The gentle, even heat yielded tender, moist chicken every time, and the poaching liquid was easily fortified with smashed garlic cloves, thyme sprigs, and soy sauce, which infused the chicken with meaty, complex flavor. Do not let the poaching liquid boil or the chicken will be tough.

CHICKEN

- 4 (6- to 8-ounce) boneless, skinless chicken breasts, trimmed
- Salt and pepper
- 1½ cups water
- 4 garlic cloves, peeled and smashed
- 4 thyme sprigs
- 2 teaspoons soy sauce

CARROT-GINGER SAUCE

- 1 teaspoon vegetable oil
- 2 shallots, minced
- ¼ teaspoon ground coriander
- ¼ teaspoon ground turmeric
- 2 carrots, peeled, halved, and sliced thin
- 1 cup chicken broth
- ¾ cup hot water
- 1 teaspoon grated fresh ginger
- Salt and pepper

1. FOR THE CHICKEN: Pound thicker ends of breasts as needed, then pat dry with paper towels and season with salt and pepper. Combine water, garlic, thyme sprigs, and soy sauce in 12-inch skillet. Add chicken and bring to gentle simmer over medium-low heat, 10 to 15 minutes.

2. When water is simmering, flip chicken over, cover, and continue to simmer gently until chicken registers 160 degrees, 10 to 15 minutes longer.

3. Transfer chicken to carving board, tent with aluminum foil, and let rest while assembling sauce.

4. FOR THE SAUCE: Heat oil in medium saucepan over medium heat until shimmering. Add shallots and cook until softened, about 2 minutes. Stir in coriander and turmeric and cook until fragrant, about 30 seconds. Stir in carrots and cook until softened, 6 to 8 minutes.

5. Add broth, cover, and cook until carrots mash easily, 25 to 30 minutes. Uncover and continue to cook until any remaining liquid has evaporated. Transfer to blender, add water and ginger, and puree until completely smooth, about 30 seconds. Season with salt and pepper to taste.

6. Slice chicken on bias into ½-inch-thick slices. Spoon sauce over chicken. Serve.

VARIATION

Spa Chicken with Green Pea and Garlic Sauce

Omit the Carrot-Ginger Sauce and substitute following instructions for steps 4 and 5: Heat 2 teaspoons extra-virgin olive oil in small saucepan over medium heat until shimmering. Add 1 minced shallot and cook until softened, about 2 minutes. Stir in 2 minced garlic cloves and cook until fragrant, about 30 seconds. Whisk in ½ cup chicken broth and ¼ cup dry white wine and bring to boil. Stir in 1 cup frozen peas and cook until tender, about 2 minutes. Transfer to blender and puree until completely smooth, about 30 seconds. Season with salt and pepper to taste.

Pounding Chicken Breasts

To create chicken breasts of even thickness, simply pound the thicker ends of the breasts until they are all of uniform thickness. Though some breasts will still be larger in size, at least they will cook at the same rate.

Easy Orange Glazed Chicken

SERVES 4   **TOTAL TIME** 25 MINUTES **FAST**

☑ **WHY THIS RECIPE WORKS:** For a superfast but flavorful glazed chicken, we turned to orange juice and apricot preserves for flavor and body. After browning the chicken just briefly, we simply added a mixture of orange juice, the preserves, and Dijon mustard to the pan and let the chicken finish cooking through. To thicken our sauce, we whisked in cornstarch mixed with a little more orange juice for perfectly glazed chicken. Either freshly squeezed or store-bought orange juice can be used here.

> 1 **cup plus 1 tablespoon orange juice (2 oranges)**
> 2 **tablespoons apricot preserves**
> 2 **tablespoons Dijon mustard**
> 4 **(6- to 8-ounce) boneless, skinless chicken breasts, trimmed**
>   **Salt and pepper**
> 1 **tablespoon vegetable oil**
> 2 **teaspoons cornstarch**
> 1 **tablespoon minced fresh parsley**

1. Whisk 1 cup orange juice, preserves, and mustard together in bowl. Pound thicker ends of breasts as needed, then pat dry with paper towels and season with salt and pepper. Heat oil in 12-inch skillet over medium-high heat until shimmering. Brown chicken lightly on first side, about 3 minutes.

2. Flip chicken over, add orange juice mixture, and simmer gently for 8 minutes.

3. Whisk cornstarch into remaining 1 tablespoon orange juice in bowl, then stir into skillet. Continue to simmer gently until chicken registers 160 degrees and sauce thickens slightly, about 1 minute. Off heat, stir in parsley and season with salt and pepper to taste. Serve.

VARIATIONS

Easy Orange–Red Pepper Glazed Chicken

Substitute 2 tablespoons Asian chili-garlic sauce for Dijon mustard.

Easy Orange-Bourbon Glazed Chicken

Omit Dijon mustard. Substitute 3 tablespoons bourbon for 1 tablespoon orange juice in step 3; combine with cornstarch and cook as directed.

Chicken Marsala

SERVES 4   **TOTAL TIME** 50 MINUTES

✔ **WHY THIS RECIPE WORKS:** Chicken Marsala is an Italian restaurant favorite, but most home-cooked renditions come with a watery, flavorless sauce. We learned the trick to seriously flavored sauce was to eliminate any broth and use straight sweet Marsala wine, not dry. Pancetta is Italian bacon that has been cured but not smoked. If you can't find pancetta, substitute three slices bacon, chopped fine.

- ½ cup all-purpose flour
- 4 (6- to 8-ounce) boneless, skinless chicken breasts, trimmed
  Salt and pepper
- 3 tablespoons vegetable oil
- 3 ounces pancetta, chopped fine
- 8 ounces white mushrooms, trimmed and sliced thin
- 1 garlic clove, minced
- 1 teaspoon tomato paste
- 1½ cups sweet Marsala
- 1½ tablespoons lemon juice
- 3 tablespoons unsalted butter, cut into 3 pieces and chilled
- 2 tablespoons minced fresh parsley

1. Adjust oven rack to lower-middle position and heat oven to 200 degrees. Spread flour into shallow dish. Pound thicker ends of breasts as needed, then pat dry with paper towels and season with salt and pepper. Dredge in flour to coat, shaking off any excess.

2. Heat 2 tablespoons oil in 12-inch skillet over medium-high heat until just smoking. Add chicken and cook, turning as needed, until chicken is golden brown on both sides and registers 160 degrees, about 10 minutes. Transfer chicken to plate and keep warm in oven.

3. Add remaining 1 tablespoon oil, pancetta, and mushrooms to now-empty skillet and cook over medium-high heat until pancetta is crisp and mushrooms are browned, about 10 minutes.

4. Stir in garlic and tomato paste and cook until tomato paste begins to brown, about 1 minute. Stir in Marsala, scraping up any browned bits, and simmer until reduced and slightly syrupy, about 8 minutes.

5. Stir in lemon juice and any accumulated chicken juices. Turn heat to low and whisk in butter, 1 piece at a time. Off heat, stir in parsley and season with salt and pepper to taste. Spoon sauce over chicken and serve.

NOTES FROM THE TEST KITCHEN

Buying Chicken

Here's what you need to know when buying chicken.

DECIPHERING LABELS: A lot of labeling doesn't (necessarily) mean much. Companies can exploit loopholes to qualify for "Natural/All-Natural," "Hormone-Free," and "Vegetarian Diet/Fed" labeling. "USDA Organic," however, isn't all hype: The chickens must eat all organic feed without animal by-products, be raised without antibiotics, and have access to the outdoors.

PAY ATTENTION TO PROCESSING: Our research showed that processing is the major player in chicken's texture and flavor. We found brands labeled "water-chilled" (soaked in a water bath in which they absorb up to 14 percent of their weight in water, which you pay for since chicken is sold by the pound) or "enhanced" (injected with broth and flavoring) are unnaturally spongy and are best avoided. Labeling law says water gain must be shown on the product label, so these should be easily identifiable. When buying whole chickens or chicken parts, look for those that are labeled "air-chilled." Without the excess water weight, these brands are less spongy in texture (but still plenty juicy) and have more chicken flavor.

BONELESS, SKINLESS BREASTS AND CUTLETS: Try to pick a package with breasts of similar size, and pound them to an even thickness so they will cook at the same rate. You can buy cutlets ready to go at the grocery store, but we don't recommend it. These cutlets are usually ragged and of various sizes; it's better to cut your own cutlets from breasts (see page 134).

BONE-IN PARTS: You can buy a whole chicken or chicken parts at the supermarket, but sometimes it's hard to tell by looking at the package if it's been properly butchered. If you have a few minutes of extra time, consider buying a whole chicken and butchering it yourself.

WHOLE CHICKENS: Whole chickens come in various sizes. Broilers and fryers are younger chickens that weigh 2½ to 4½ pounds. A roaster (or "oven-stuffer roaster") is an older chicken and usually clocks in between 5 and 7 pounds. Stewing chickens, which are older laying hens, are best used for stews since the meat is tougher and more stringy. A 3½- to 4-pound bird will feed 3 to 4 people.

Lemon juice, lemon slices, and capers give this dish its traditional tangy flavor.

Chicken Piccata

SERVES 4   **TOTAL TIME** 45 MINUTES   **FAST**

✓ **WHY THIS RECIPE WORKS:** Chicken piccata is a simple Italian dish that highlights the incredibly tender texture of chicken cutlets (as opposed to whole chicken breast) as well as the fresh, clean flavor of lemon. The problem with most recipes, however, is that the chicken turns out rubbery and the sauce is bland, with little lemon flavor. To build the sauce, we used a whopping ¼ cup fresh lemon juice and let thin slices of lemon simmer in it to really drive home that lemon flavor. We also used plenty of capers—2 tablespoons—adding them when the sauce was nearly done so they retained their flavor and structural integrity. To make slicing the chicken easier, freeze it for 15 minutes. Make sure that the cutlets do not overcook—they take only about 4 minutes to cook through completely.

2   lemons
½   cup all-purpose flour
4   (6- to 8-ounce) boneless, skinless chicken breasts, trimmed
     Salt and pepper
¼   cup vegetable oil
1   shallot, minced
1   garlic clove, minced
1   cup chicken broth
2   tablespoons capers, rinsed
3   tablespoons unsalted butter, cut into 3 pieces and chilled
2   tablespoons minced fresh parsley

1. Adjust oven rack to middle position and heat oven to 200 degrees. Halve 1 lemon, trim ends, and slice into ¼-inch-thick half-moons. Squeeze remaining lemon for ¼ cup juice. Spread flour in shallow dish.

2. Cut chicken horizontally into 2 thin cutlets, then cover with plastic wrap and pound to even ½-inch thickness. Pat cutlets dry with paper towels and season with salt and pepper. Dredge in flour to coat, shaking off any excess.

3. Heat 2 tablespoons oil in 12-inch skillet over medium-high heat until just smoking. Brown half of cutlets until lightly golden on both sides, about 4 minutes; transfer to plate and keep warm in oven. Repeat with remaining 2 tablespoons oil and cutlets.

4. Add shallot and garlic to fat left in skillet and cook over medium heat until shallot is softened, about 2 minutes. Stir in broth and lemon slices, scraping up any browned bits, and simmer until reduced and slightly syrupy, about 8 minutes.

5. Stir in lemon juice, capers, and any accumulated chicken juices. Turn heat to low and whisk in butter, 1 piece at a time. Off heat, stir in parsley and season with salt and pepper to taste. Spoon sauce over chicken and serve.

VARIATIONS

Chicken Piccata with Prosciutto
Add 2 ounces thinly sliced prosciutto, cut into ¼-inch strips, to skillet with shallot in step 4.

Chicken Piccata with Black Olives
Stir ¼ cup chopped black olives into sauce with lemon juice in step 5.

Our easy take on chicken saltimbocca wraps prosciutto around chicken breasts and browns them to keep the ham put.

Prosciutto-Wrapped Chicken with Sage

SERVES 4   **TOTAL TIME** 40 MINUTES   **FAST**

✓ **WHY THIS RECIPE WORKS:** For a streamlined take on classic chicken saltimbocca, the Italian dish that marries tender chicken with rich prosciutto and woodsy sage, we ditched the annoying toothpicks typically required to hold the ham in place and simply wrapped it around the chicken breasts. Browning the breasts before transferring them to the oven worked to crisp the prosciutto and helped fuse it to the chicken. Finishing the chicken in the oven allowed it to cook through gently and ensured that the prosciutto didn't burn or become leathery in the meantime. To up the elegance quotient of our easy dinner, we created an effortless browned butter sauce and amped up its flavor with minced sage and a splash of lemon juice. Though sage comes in dried forms, we prefer fresh in recipes where sage's flavor is at the forefront. Make sure to buy prosciutto that is thinly sliced, not shaved.

4   (6- to 8-ounce) boneless, skinless chicken breasts, trimmed
    Salt and pepper
8   thin slices prosciutto (3 ounces)
1   tablespoon vegetable oil
4   tablespoons unsalted butter
2   teaspoons minced fresh sage
1   teaspoon lemon juice

1. Adjust oven rack to upper-middle position and heat oven to 400 degrees. Pound thicker ends of breasts as needed, then pat dry with paper towels and season with salt and pepper. Slightly overlap 2 slices of prosciutto on cutting board, lay 1 chicken breast in center, and fold prosciutto over chicken. Repeat with remaining prosciutto and chicken.

2. Heat oil in 12-inch nonstick skillet over medium-high heat until just smoking. Brown chicken lightly on both sides, 6 to 8 minutes. Transfer chicken to rimmed baking sheet and roast until chicken registers 160 degrees, 10 to 12 minutes. Transfer chicken to platter and cover to keep warm.

3. Melt butter in now-empty skillet over medium-high heat, swirling occasionally, until butter is browned and has nutty aroma, about 1½ minutes. Stir in sage and cook until fragrant, about 1 minute. Stir in lemon juice and season with salt and pepper to taste. Drizzle sauce over chicken and serve.

Chicken Parmesan

SERVES 4   **TOTAL TIME** 40 MINUTES   **FAST**

✓ **WHY THIS RECIPE WORKS:** Traditional chicken Parmesan is a minefield of potential problems: dry meat, soggy crust, and a chewy blanket of mozzarella. To keep the exterior crunchy, we replaced more than half the starchy bread crumbs with grated Parmesan. To keep the cheese topping tender, we mixed the usual shredded mozzarella with creamy fontina, and placed the mixture directly on the cutlet, forming a waterproof layer between the crust and the sauce. You can use your favorite jarred tomato sauce here, or our Small-Batch Chunky Tomato Sauce (which yields 4 cups) (page 360).

2   (6- to 8-ounce) boneless, skinless chicken breasts, trimmed
    Salt and pepper
1   large egg
1   tablespoon all-purpose flour
1½ ounces Parmesan cheese, grated (¾ cup)

½ cup panko bread crumbs
½ teaspoon garlic powder
¼ teaspoon dried oregano
⅓ cup vegetable oil
2 ounces whole-milk mozzarella cheese, shredded (½ cup)
2 ounces fontina cheese, shredded (½ cup)
1 cup tomato sauce, warmed
¼ cup shredded fresh basil

1. Cut chicken horizontally into 2 thin cutlets, then cover with plastic wrap and pound to even ½-inch thickness. Pat chicken dry with paper towels and season with salt and pepper.

Making Chicken Parmesan

1. SLICE AND POUND: Cut chicken horizontally into 2 thin cutlets, then cover with plastic wrap and pound to even ½-inch thickness.

2. DIP AND COAT: Working with 1 cutlet at a time, dip in egg mixture, then coat with Parmesan mixture, pressing gently to adhere; transfer to large plate.

3. FRY, THEN BROIL: Working in batches, fry breaded cutlets until crisp and golden brown. Transfer to baking sheet, cover cutlets with cheese, and broil until cheese is melted and browned.

4. FINISH WITH SAUCE: Before serving, top cutlets with sauce and basil.

2. Whisk egg and flour together in shallow dish until smooth. Combine Parmesan, bread crumbs, garlic powder, oregano, and ¼ teaspoon pepper in second shallow dish. Working with 1 cutlet at a time, dip in egg mixture, then coat with Parmesan mixture, pressing gently to adhere; transfer to large plate.

3. Adjust oven rack 4 inches from broiler element and heat broiler. Heat oil in 10-inch nonstick skillet over medium-high heat until shimmering. Brown 2 cutlets until very crisp and deep golden brown on both sides, 3 to 4 minutes. Transfer to paper towel–lined plate; repeat with remaining cutlets.

4. Place cutlets on rimmed baking sheet. Combine mozzarella and fontina in bowl and sprinkle evenly over cutlets, covering as much surface area as possible. Broil until cheese is melted and beginning to brown, 2 to 4 minutes. Transfer chicken to serving platter, top each cutlet with 2 tablespoons sauce, and sprinkle with basil. Serve, passing remaining sauce separately.

Crispy Chicken Breasts

SERVES 4   TOTAL TIME 35 MINUTES   **FAST**

✔ **WHY THIS RECIPE WORKS:** The secret to breaded chicken that is crisp and golden without being dull or greasy is twofold. First, make sure that the oil is hot before placing the chicken in the pan; the bread crumbs will absorb the oil if it is not hot enough. Second, don't crowd the pan. Putting more than two pieces of chicken in the pan will only result in a soggy coating; the chicken will steam instead of brown. We found that pounding the chicken ensured it would cook evenly.

1 cup all-purpose flour
2 large eggs
3 cups panko bread crumbs
4 (6- to 8-ounce) boneless, skinless chicken breasts, trimmed
  Salt and pepper
¾ cup vegetable oil
  Lemon wedges

1. Adjust oven rack to middle position and heat oven to 200 degrees. Spread flour in shallow dish. Beat eggs in second shallow dish. Spread bread crumbs in third shallow dish.

2. Cover chicken with plastic wrap and pound to even ½-inch thickness. Pat chicken dry with paper towels and season with salt and pepper. Working with 1 breast at a time, dredge in flour, dip in egg, then coat with bread crumbs, pressing gently to adhere; transfer to large plate.

3. Heat oil in 12-inch nonstick skillet over medium-high heat until just smoking. Brown half of chicken lightly on both sides, 4 to 6 minutes.

4. Drain chicken briefly on paper towels, then transfer to paper towel–lined plate and keep warm in oven. Repeat with remaining breaded chicken. Serve with lemon wedges.

VARIATIONS

Crispy Chicken Milanese

Stir ¼ cup finely grated Parmesan cheese into bread crumbs.

Crispy Chicken with Garlic and Oregano

Whisk 3 tablespoons minced fresh oregano and 8 minced garlic cloves into eggs.

Crispy Deviled Chicken

Season each chicken breast with generous pinch cayenne pepper in addition to salt and pepper. Whisk 3 tablespoons Dijon mustard, 1 tablespoon Worcestershire sauce, and 2 teaspoons minced fresh thyme into eggs.

Breading Chicken

1. Lay chicken between 2 sheets of plastic and pound with meat pounder or rolling pin until roughly ½ inch thick.

2. Coat chicken evenly with flour, then shake to remove any excess.

3. Coat floured chicken thoroughly with egg, then let excess drip back into dish. Use tongs to keep your hands clean.

4. Coat chicken thoroughly with bread crumbs, pressing gently on bread crumbs to make sure they adhere to chicken.

BETTER-THAN-STORE-BOUGHT CHICKEN FINGERS

Homemade chicken fingers are much tastier (and cheaper) than what you can buy in the supermarket. Follow the recipe for Crispy Chicken Breasts, using trimmed chicken breasts that have been sliced on the diagonal into long, finger-size pieces. For convenience, try making a big batch all at once, then freeze them in single-serving zipper-lock bags, where they will keep for up to a month. Simply reheat them either in a microwave or a 425-degree oven until hot and crisp. Serve with any of the dipping sauces on page 144.

Nut-Crusted Chicken Breasts with Lemon and Thyme

SERVES 4   **TOTAL TIME** 1 HOUR

✓ **WHY THIS RECIPE WORKS:** Adding chopped nuts to a coating is a great way to add robust flavor to otherwise lean and mild boneless, skinless chicken breasts. But nut coatings are often dense and leaden, and the rich flavor of the nuts rarely comes through. Using a combination of chopped almonds and panko bread crumbs—rather than using nuts only—kept the coating light and crunchy, and the bread crumbs helped the coating adhere. Instead of frying the breaded cutlets, we found that baking them in the oven was not only easier, but also helped the meat stay juicy and ensured an even golden crust. But it wasn't until we cooked the coating in browned butter prior to breading the chicken that we finally achieved the deep nutty flavor we sought. This recipe is best with almonds, but works well with any type of nut.

> 4   **(6- to 8-ounce) boneless, skinless chicken breasts, trimmed**
>   **Salt and pepper**
> 1   **cup almonds, chopped coarse**
> 4   **tablespoons unsalted butter**
> 1   **shallot, minced**
> 1   **cup panko bread crumbs**
> 2   **teaspoons finely grated lemon zest, zested lemon cut into wedges**
> 1   **teaspoon minced fresh thyme**
> ⅛   **teaspoon cayenne pepper**
> 1   **cup all-purpose flour**
> 3   **large eggs**
> 2   **teaspoons Dijon mustard**

Poultry Safety and Handling

It's important to follow some basic safety procedures when storing, handling, and cooking chicken, turkey, and other poultry.

REFRIGERATING: Keep poultry refrigerated until just before cooking. Bacteria thrive at temperatures between 40 and 140 degrees. This means leftovers should also be promptly refrigerated.

FREEZING AND THAWING: Poultry can be frozen in its original packaging or after repackaging. If you are freezing it for longer than two months, rewrap (or wrap over packaging) with foil or plastic wrap, or place inside a zipper-lock bag. You can keep poultry frozen for several months, but after two months the texture and flavor will suffer. Don't thaw frozen poultry on the counter; this puts it at risk of growing bacteria. Thaw it in its packaging in the refrigerator (in a container to catch its juices), or in the sink under cold running water. Count on one day of defrosting in the refrigerator for every 4 pounds of bird.

HANDLING RAW POULTRY: When handling raw poultry, make sure to wash hands, knives, cutting boards, and counters (and anything else that has come into contact with the raw bird, its juices, or your hands) with hot, soapy water. Be careful not to let the poultry, its juices, or your unwashed hands touch foods that will be eaten raw. When seasoning raw poultry, touching the saltshaker or pepper mill can lead to cross-contamination. To avoid this, set aside the necessary salt and pepper before handling the poultry.

RINSING: The U.S. Department of Agriculture advises against washing poultry. Rinsing poultry will not remove or kill much bacteria, and the splashing of water around the sink can spread the bacteria found in raw poultry.

COOKING AND LEFTOVERS: Poultry should be cooked to an internal temperature of 160 degrees to ensure any bacteria have been killed (however, we prefer the flavor and texture of thigh meat cooked to 175 degrees). Leftover cooked poultry should be refrigerated and consumed within three days.

The secret to light, crunchy breaded chicken breasts is coating them with browned panko crumbs and nuts and baking them.

1. Adjust oven rack to lower-middle position and heat oven to 350 degrees. Set wire rack in rimmed baking sheet. Pound thicker ends of breasts as needed, then pat dry with paper towels and season with salt and pepper.

2. Pulse almonds in food processor to coarse meal, about 20 pulses. Melt butter in 12-inch skillet over medium heat, swirling occasionally, until butter is browned and releases nutty aroma, 4 to 5 minutes. Add shallot and ½ teaspoon salt and cook, stirring constantly, until just beginning to brown, about 3 minutes. Reduce heat to medium-low and add bread crumbs and ground almonds. Cook, stirring often, until golden brown, 10 to 12 minutes.

3. Transfer panko mixture to shallow dish and stir in lemon zest, thyme, and cayenne. Spread flour in second shallow dish. Lightly beat eggs, mustard, and ¼ teaspoon pepper together in third shallow dish. Working with 1 breast at a time, dredge in flour, dip in egg, then coat with bread crumbs, pressing gently to adhere; place on wire rack.

4. Bake until chicken registers 160 degrees, 20 to 25 minutes. Let chicken rest for 5 minutes. Serve with lemon wedges.

VARIATIONS

Nut-Crusted Chicken Breasts with Orange and Oregano

This version works particularly well with pistachios or hazelnuts.

Substitute 1 teaspoon grated orange zest for lemon zest (cutting zested orange into wedges) and 1 teaspoon minced fresh oregano for thyme.

Nut-Crusted Chicken Breasts with Lime and Chipotle

This version works particularly well with peanuts.

Substitute 1 teaspoon grated lime zest for lemon zest (cutting zested lime into wedges). Omit thyme and add 1 teaspoon chipotle chile powder, ½ teaspoon ground cumin, and ½ teaspoon ground coriander to toasted bread crumbs with lime zest.

Indoor BBQ Chicken

SERVES 4   **TOTAL TIME** 30 MINUTES   FAST

✔ **WHY THIS RECIPE WORKS:** Barbecued chicken is an outdoor family favorite that is often disappointing when cooked indoors in the oven. After testing lots of oven-baked barbecued chicken with flabby skin and greasy sauce, we decided to lose the skin, lose the bones, and lose the oven. Using boneless, skinless chicken breasts eliminated lots of problems and made for a very easy recipe. And by cooking the entire dish in a nonstick skillet on the stovetop, we were able to build a flavorful barbecue sauce using the pan drippings after browning the chicken. Finally, simmering the chicken in the sauce gave it serious BBQ flavor. Although we far prefer the flavor of our own sauce, you can substitute 2 cups of your favorite bottled barbecue sauce for the ketchup and flavorings in step 2. Be sure to use a nonstick skillet to prevent the sweet sauce from sticking to the pan.

Our easy barbecued chicken is cooked entirely on the stovetop and includes a homemade sauce made from the pan drippings.

4   (6- to 8-ounce) boneless, skinless chicken breasts, trimmed
     Salt and pepper
1   tablespoon vegetable oil
1   onion, minced
1   cup ketchup
3   tablespoons molasses
3   tablespoons cider vinegar
2   tablespoons Worcestershire sauce
2   tablespoons Dijon mustard
2   tablespoons maple syrup
1   teaspoon chili powder
¼   teaspoon cayenne pepper

1. Pound thicker ends of breasts as needed, then pat dry with paper towels and season with salt and pepper. Heat oil in 12-inch nonstick skillet over medium heat until shimmering. Brown chicken lightly on both sides, about 4 minutes; transfer to plate.

2. Add onion and ¼ teaspoon salt to now-empty skillet and cook over medium heat until softened, about 5 minutes. Stir in ketchup, molasses, vinegar, Worcestershire, mustard, maple syrup, chili powder, and cayenne, scraping up any browned bits.

3. Reduce heat to low. Return chicken, with any accumulated juices, to skillet and coat with sauce. Cover and simmer until chicken is fully cooked and registers 160 degrees, about 10 minutes. Serve.

Gingery Stir-Fried Chicken with Broccoli and Water Chestnuts

SERVES 4   TOTAL TIME 45 MINUTES   **FAST**

✔ **WHY THIS RECIPE WORKS:** Stir-frying is a great way to put a flavorful meal on the table quickly. However, you often end up with an underwhelming dish, with poor browning and muddy flavors. Could we come up with a better recipe that would make you put down the takeout menu? We skipped the wok in favor of a large nonstick skillet, whose wide, broad cooking surface promotes good browning, which also equals more flavor. We found that using high heat cooked everything quickly, and the pan recovered heat fast enough after adding ingredients. We sautéed the chicken first, removed it, then cooked the broccoli. The aromatics needed only 30 seconds toward the end. An easy-to-make sauce with just the right amount of cornstarch brought all of the gingery and garlic flavors together, enhancing the silky chicken, tender broccoli, and crunchy water chestnuts. To make the chicken easier to slice, freeze it for 15 minutes. Be sure to rinse the water chestnuts to remove any salty or "tinny" flavors. Serve with Sticky Rice (page 142).

SAUCE

- ¾ cup chicken broth
- 2 tablespoons Chinese rice wine or dry sherry
- 4 teaspoons soy sauce
- 1 tablespoon oyster sauce
- 1 tablespoon grated fresh ginger
- 2 teaspoons cornstarch
- 1 teaspoon sugar
- ½ teaspoon toasted sesame oil
- ¼ teaspoon red pepper flakes

STIR-FRY

- 2 tablespoons toasted sesame oil
- 1 tablespoon cornstarch
- 1 tablespoon all-purpose flour
- 2 teaspoons soy sauce
- 1 pound boneless, skinless chicken breasts, trimmed, halved lengthwise, and sliced ¼ inch thick
- 1 tablespoon grated fresh ginger
- 1 garlic clove, minced
- 8 teaspoons vegetable oil
- 1 pound broccoli florets, cut into 1-inch pieces
- ⅓ cup water
- 1 (8-ounce) can water chestnuts, rinsed

1. FOR THE SAUCE: Whisk all ingredients together in bowl.

2. FOR THE STIR-FRY: Whisk sesame oil, cornstarch, flour, and soy sauce together in medium bowl until smooth, then stir in chicken. In separate bowl, combine ginger, garlic, and 1 teaspoon vegetable oil.

3. Heat 2 teaspoons vegetable oil in 12-inch nonstick skillet over high heat until just smoking. Add half of chicken mixture, breaking up any clumps, and cook, without stirring, for 1 minute. Stir chicken and continue to cook until lightly browned, about 30 seconds; transfer to clean bowl. Repeat with 2 teaspoons vegetable oil and remaining chicken mixture; transfer to bowl.

4. Add remaining 1 tablespoon vegetable oil to now-empty skillet and return to high heat until just smoking. Add broccoli and cook for 30 seconds. Add ⅓ cup water, cover, and reduce heat to medium. Steam broccoli until slightly tender, about 2 minutes. Remove lid and continue to cook until broccoli is tender and most of liquid has evaporated, about 2 minutes.

5. Clear center of skillet, add ginger-garlic mixture, and cook, mashing mixture into skillet, until fragrant, about 30 seconds. Stir ginger-garlic mixture into broccoli.

6. Return cooked chicken, with any accumulated juices, to skillet and toss to combine. Stir in water chestnuts. Whisk sauce to recombine, then add to skillet. Cook, stirring constantly, until sauce is thickened, about 30 seconds. Transfer to platter and serve.

Slicing Chicken Thinly

1. Slice breasts across grain into ¼-inch-wide strips, about 1½ to 2 inches long. Center pieces need to be cut in half so they are same length as end pieces.

2. Cut tenderloins, if necessary, on diagonal to produce pieces of meat similar in size to strips of breast meat.

Tired of underwhelming home-cooked stir-fries, with stringy chicken, muddy flavors, and a gloppy sauce, we came up with a solution. We coated the chicken in sesame oil, cornstarch, flour, and soy sauce, utilizing a classic Chinese technique called velveting. We prefer to skip the wok and instead stir-fry in a large nonstick skillet, which heats better on the flat burner of a home stove and also requires less oil for cooking.

1. PREP EVERYTHING BEFORE COOKING:
Make the sauce and prep and organize all the other ingredients and have them handy before you start cooking.
WHY? A stir-fry cooks within a matter of minutes, so it is imperative to have everything fully prepped (including the sauce) before you begin.

2. COAT THE CHICKEN: Toss the sliced chicken with toasted sesame oil, cornstarch, flour, and soy sauce.
WHY? The technique of velveting keeps the chicken from overcooking and turning out chewy and dry. The cornstarch and oil mixture forms a barrier around the meat and keeps moisture inside, making the chicken seem more tender.

3. GET THE SKILLET HOT AND COOK THE CHICKEN IN BATCHES: Heat the oil in a 12-inch skillet until just smoking. Add half of the chicken and cook, without stirring. Stir the chicken and cook until lightly browned. Transfer to a plate and repeat with the remaining chicken.
WHY? Cooking in batches ensures the pieces have room to brown well. The chicken finishes cooking in the sauce.

4. COOK THE BROCCOLI: Add 1 tablespoon oil to the now-empty pan and add the broccoli. Cook for 30 seconds, add ⅓ cup water, and cover, reducing the heat. Cook for 2 minutes, then remove the lid and continue to cook until tender.
WHY? Tougher vegetables like broccoli should always be added to the skillet first; broccoli won't become tender fast enough by stir-frying alone, so we steam it with a bit of water until tender.

5. CLEAR THE CENTER OF THE PAN AND ADD THE AROMATICS: Push the broccoli to the edges of the skillet, add the ginger-garlic mixture, and cook, mashing the mixture into the skillet, until fragrant. Stir the mixture into the broccoli.
WHY? The aromatics are added toward the end so they don't burn and their flavors won't get lost. Mashing the aromatics into the pan before mixing them into the broccoli ensures they cook through and won't taste raw and harsh.

6. FINISH WITH THE SAUCE: Return the cooked chicken along with any juices to the pan. Add the water chestnuts. Whisk the sauce, then add it to the pan. Cook, stirring constantly, until the sauce thickens.
WHY? The sauce is added last to the pan and everything is combined. The sauce is rewhisked because the cornstarch settles out. Once simmering, the sauce starts to thicken just enough to coat the chicken and vegetables.

ALL ABOUT **ASIAN INGREDIENTS**

Asian ingredients were once considered unusual, and they were not always easy to find. Now most supermarkets have an Asian foods section, and the shelves are full of options. The following list includes common Asian ingredients that you'll find in many of our recipes. See the America's Test Kitchen Shopping Guide (page 802) for buying recommendations.

Asian Chile Sauces
Used both in cooking and as a condiment, these sauces come in a variety of styles. Sriracha contains garlic and is made from chiles ground into a smooth paste. Asian chili-garlic sauce is similar to Sriracha, but the chiles are coarsely ground. Sambal oelek is made purely from ground chiles without the addition of garlic or other spices, thus adding heat but not additional flavor. Once opened, these sauces will keep for several months in the refrigerator.

Chinese Rice Wine
This rich-flavored liquid made from fermented glutinous rice or millet is used for both drinking and cooking. It ranges in color from clear to amber and tastes slightly sweet and aromatic. Chinese rice wine is also called yellow wine, Shao Hsing, or Shaoxing. If you can't find Chinese rice wine, dry sherry is a decent substitute.

Coconut Milk
Widely available in cans, coconut milk adds rich flavor and body to soups, curries, and stir-fries. Coconut milk comes in both regular and light versions. Regular coconut milk is creamier than the light, but it also contains more fat. Do not confuse coconut milk with cream of coconut, which contains added sugar and is thus much sweeter.

Fish Sauce
Fish sauce is a salty, amber-colored liquid made from fermented fish. It is used as both an ingredient and a condiment in certain Asian cuisines, most commonly in Southeast Asia. In very small amounts, it adds a well-rounded, salty flavor to sauces, soups, and marinades. The lighter the color of the fish sauce, the lighter its flavor.

Five-Spice Powder
Often called Chinese five-spice powder, this aromatic blend of spices most often contains cinnamon, cloves, fennel seed, star anise, and Sichuan peppercorns (white pepper or ginger are common substitutes). Available in the spice aisle of the supermarket, five-spice powder is great in sauces and in spice rubs for grilled foods.

Hoisin Sauce
Hoisin sauce is a thick, reddish brown mixture of soybeans, sugar, vinegar, garlic, chiles, and spices, the most predominant of which is five-spice powder. It is used in many classic Chinese dishes, including barbecued pork, Peking duck, and kung pao shrimp, and as a table condiment, much like ketchup. The ideal hoisin sauce balances sweet, salty, pungent, and spicy elements so that no one flavor dominates.

Mirin
This Japanese rice wine has a subtle salty-sweet flavor prized in Asian marinades and glazes. The most traditional method for creating mirin uses glutinous rice, malted rice, and distilled alcohol. Many supermarket brands in this country, however, combine sake or another type of alcohol with salt, corn syrup, other sweeteners, and sometimes caramel coloring and flavoring. We use mirin to brighten the flavor of stir-fries, teriyaki, and other Asian dishes. If you cannot find mirin, substitute 1 tablespoon dry white wine and ½ teaspoon sugar for every 1 tablespoon of mirin.

Miso
Made from a fermented mixture of soybeans and rice, barley, or rye, miso is incredibly versatile, suitable for use in soups, braises, dressings, and sauces as well as for topping grilled foods. This salty, deep-flavored paste ranges in strength and color from a mild, pale yellow (referred to as white) to a stronger-flavored red or brownish black, depending on the fermentation method and ingredients.

Oyster Sauce
This thick, salty brown sauce is a rich, concentrated mixture of oysters, soy sauce, brine, and seasonings. Very salty and fishy-tasting, oyster sauce is too strong to be used as a condiment. Rather, it is used to enhance the flavor of many dishes and stir-fries and is the base for many Asian dipping sauces. This sauce will keep indefinitely when refrigerated.

Rice Vinegar
Rice vinegar is made from glutinous rice that is broken down into sugars, blended with yeast to ferment into alcohol, and aerated to form vinegar. Because of its sweet-tart flavor, rice vinegar is used to accentuate many Asian dishes. It comes in an unseasoned version and a seasoned version with added sake, sugar, and salt.

Sesame Oil
Raw sesame oil, which is very mild and light in color, is used mostly for cooking, while toasted sesame oil, which has a deep amber color, is primarily used for seasoning because of its intense, nutty flavor. For the biggest hit of sesame flavor, we prefer to use toasted sesame oil. Just a few drops will give stir-fries, noodle dishes, or salad dressings a deep, rich flavor. Purchase sesame oil in tinted glass and refrigerate it to extend its shelf life.

Soy Sauce
Soy sauce is a dark, salty fermented liquid made from soybeans and roasted grain. It is used throughout Asia to enhance flavor and contribute complexity to food. Soy sauce is rich in the amino acid glutamate, which contributes potent savory, meaty flavor to dishes. Pasteurized soy sauce can be stored at room temperature, but unpasteurized soy sauce should be refrigerated.

Thai Green Curry Paste
Store-bought green curry paste is made from fresh green Thai chiles, lemon grass, galangal (Thai ginger), garlic, and other spices. It quickly adds rich herbal flavor, complexity, and a bit of heat and is most often used in poultry, seafood, and vegetable curries. It is usually sold in small jars with the other Thai ingredients at the supermarket.

Thai Red Curry Paste
Store-bought Thai red curry paste combines a number of hard-to-find, authentic Thai aromatics—including galangal (Thai ginger), bird's eye chiles, lemon grass, and kaffir lime leaves—in one, easy-to-find ingredient. It is usually sold in small jars with the other Thai ingredients at the supermarket.

Wasabi
Hot and pungent, wasabi is commonly used as a condiment for sushi and sashimi but is also useful as an ingredient in other Japanese dishes. Fresh wasabi root (also known as Japanese horseradish) is hard to find and expensive (about $8 per ounce). More widely available is wasabi that is sold in paste or powder form (the powder is mixed with water to form a paste). Because fresh wasabi root is so expensive, most pastes and all powders contain no wasabi at all, but instead comprise a mixture of garden-variety horseradish and mustard, along with cornstarch and food coloring. We advise seeking out wasabi paste made from real wasabi root for its complex flavor.

Spicy Stir-Fried Sesame Chicken with Green Beans and Shiitakes

SERVES 4   **TOTAL TIME** 45 MINUTES   **FAST**

✓ **WHY THIS RECIPE WORKS:** Stir-fried sesame chicken should feature moist, tender, perfectly cooked pieces of flavorful chicken coated with a sweet-spicy sauce. More often than not, the chicken is dry and tasteless and serves just as a vehicle for the sauce. Tired of dry, stringy meat in our chicken stir-fries, we came up with a solution: We coated the chicken in a sesame oil-cornstarch-soy mixture. The cornstarch coating, a modified version of the Chinese technique called velveting, helped the chicken stay moist even with a high-heat cooking method. We cooked the chicken in batches over high heat, then the vegetables, and finished with the aromatics and sauce. The result was a stir-fry with plump, tasty slices of chicken and tender-crisp vegetables in a spicy sauce that strikes a perfect savory-sweet balance. To make the chicken easier to slice, freeze it for 15 minutes. For a less spicy stir-fry, reduce the amount of Sriracha to 2 teaspoons. Serve with Sticky Rice.

SAUCE

- ½ cup plus 2 tablespoons chicken broth
- 2 tablespoons Chinese rice wine or dry sherry
- 5 teaspoons sugar
- 4 teaspoons Sriracha sauce
- 1 tablespoon soy sauce
- 2 teaspoons sesame seeds, toasted
- 2 teaspoons toasted sesame oil
- 1 teaspoon cornstarch
- 1 garlic clove, minced

STIR-FRY

- 2 tablespoons plus 1 teaspoon toasted sesame oil
- 1 tablespoon cornstarch
- 1 tablespoon all-purpose flour
- 4 teaspoons sesame seeds, toasted
- 2 teaspoons soy sauce
- 1 pound boneless, skinless chicken breasts, trimmed, halved lengthwise, and sliced ¼ inch thick
- 2 garlic cloves, minced
- 1 teaspoon grated fresh ginger
- 8 teaspoons vegetable oil
- 1 pound green beans, trimmed and cut on bias into 1-inch pieces
- 8 ounces shiitake mushrooms, stemmed and sliced ⅛ inch thick

1. FOR THE SAUCE: Whisk all ingredients together in bowl.

2. FOR THE STIR-FRY: Whisk 2 tablespoons sesame oil, cornstarch, flour, 1 tablespoon sesame seeds, and soy sauce together in medium bowl until smooth, then stir in chicken. In separate bowl, combine garlic, ginger, and 1 teaspoon vegetable oil.

3. Heat 2 teaspoons vegetable oil in 12-inch nonstick skillet over high heat until just smoking. Add half of chicken mixture, breaking up any clumps, and cook, without stirring, for 1 minute. Stir chicken and continue to cook until lightly browned, about 30 seconds; transfer to clean bowl. Repeat with 2 teaspoons vegetable oil and remaining chicken mixture; transfer to bowl.

4. Add remaining 1 tablespoon vegetable oil to now-empty skillet and return to high heat until just smoking. Add green beans and cook for 1 minute. Stir in mushrooms and cook until mushrooms are lightly browned and beans are crisp-tender, 3 to 4 minutes.

5. Clear center of skillet, add garlic mixture, and cook, mashing mixture into skillet, until fragrant, about 30 seconds. Stir garlic mixture into vegetables.

6. Return cooked chicken, with any accumulated juices, to skillet and toss to combine. Whisk sauce to recombine, then add to skillet. Cook, stirring constantly, until sauce is thickened, about 30 seconds. Transfer to platter, sprinkle with remaining 1 teaspoon sesame oil and remaining 1 teaspoon sesame seeds. Serve.

STICKY RICE

This Chinese-style sticky rice is just soft enough to soak up the sauce in a stir-fry and just sticky enough to be easily eaten with chopsticks.

Bring 3 cups water, 2 cups long-grain white rice, and ½ teaspoon salt to boil in large saucepan. Cook over medium-high heat until water level drops below surface of rice and small holes form in rice, about 10 minutes. Reduce heat to low, cover, and continue to cook until rice is tender, about 15 minutes. (Serves 4 to 6)

Boldly flavored ground chicken, sweet bell pepper, and water chestnuts make an easy filling for lettuce leaves.

Asian Chicken Lettuce Wraps

SERVES 4 **TOTAL TIME** 30 MINUTES **FAST**

✔ **WHY THIS RECIPE WORKS:** These easy-to-make lettuce wraps are filled with sautéed ground chicken, bell pepper, and water chestnuts seasoned with a hefty dose of fresh garlic and ginger and finished with an aromatic Asian sauce. The bold flavors and simple ingredient list of this recipe make it a great dish for an easy dinner. We sautéed the chicken first, along with a bell pepper for sweetness and water chestnuts for contrasting texture. Adding the garlic and ginger after cooking the chicken and vegetables ensured that their bright flavors didn't get muted or turn bitter. A simple sauce, added at the end, coated all the ingredients and added another layer of flavor. Buy ground chicken, not ground chicken breast (also labeled 99 percent fat-free) for this recipe. Be sure to rinse the water chestnuts to remove any salty or "tinny" flavors.

3 tablespoons hoisin sauce
2 tablespoons soy sauce
2 tablespoons water

½ teaspoon cornstarch
5 garlic cloves, minced
2 teaspoons grated fresh ginger
4 teaspoons vegetable oil
⅛ teaspoon red pepper flakes
1 pound ground chicken
1 red bell pepper, stemmed, seeded, and cut into ¼-inch pieces
1 (8-ounce) can water chestnuts, rinsed and chopped fine
3 scallions, sliced thin
Salt and pepper
1 head Bibb lettuce (8 ounces), leaves separated

1. Whisk hoisin sauce, soy sauce, water, and cornstarch together in bowl. In separate bowl, combine garlic, ginger, 1 teaspoon oil, and pepper flakes.

2. Heat remaining 1 tablespoon oil in 12-inch nonstick skillet over medium-high heat until shimmering. Add chicken, bell pepper, and water chestnuts and cook, breaking up any large pieces of chicken with wooden spoon, until no longer pink, about 5 minutes.

3. Clear center of skillet, add garlic mixture, and cook, mashing mixture into skillet, until fragrant, about 30 seconds. Stir garlic mixture into chicken mixture.

4. Whisk sauce mixture to recombine, then add to skillet. Cook, stirring constantly, until sauce is thickened, about 30 seconds. Stir in scallions and season with salt and pepper to taste. Spoon chicken mixture into lettuce leaves and serve.

Chicken Nuggets

SERVES 4 TO 6 **TOTAL TIME** 1 HOUR 15 MINUTES

✔ **WHY THIS RECIPE WORKS:** Some chicken nugget recipes take the least desirable parts of the chicken and grind them up. We opted for boneless, skinless chicken breasts so we would know exactly which parts we were eating. Brining the chicken prevented it from drying out and provided a much-needed flavor boost to the bland breast meat. Crushed panko (Japanese-style bread crumbs), combined with flour and a little baking soda, provided a crispy brown exterior. Using whole eggs to adhere the coating made the nuggets too eggy, but egg whites alone didn't have as much binding power. We resolved this dilemma by resting the nuggets briefly before frying. Don't brine the chicken longer than 30 minutes or it will be too salty. To crush the panko, place it inside a zipper-lock bag and lightly beat it with a rolling pin. This recipe can easily be doubled. Serve the nuggets with any of the dipping sauces on page 144.

4 (6- to 8-ounce) boneless, skinless chicken breasts, trimmed

2 cups water

2 tablespoons Worcestershire sauce

Salt and pepper

3 large egg whites

1 cup panko bread crumbs, crushed

1 cup all-purpose flour

2 teaspoons onion powder

½ teaspoon garlic powder

½ teaspoon baking soda

4 cups peanut or vegetable oil

1. Cut each chicken breast diagonally into thirds, then cut each third diagonally into ½-inch-thick pieces. Whisk water, Worcestershire, and 1 tablespoon salt together in large bowl to dissolve salt. Add chicken, cover, and refrigerate for 30 minutes.

DIPPING SAUCES

These easy homemade sauces beat anything out of a bottle and are the perfect dips for our chicken nuggets and chicken fingers. Whisk all the ingredients together in a bowl, season with salt and pepper to taste, and serve. (Each sauce makes ¾ cup)

BBQ DIPPING SAUCE `FAST`

¾ cup ketchup

3 tablespoons molasses

1 tablespoon cider vinegar

1 teaspoon hot sauce

⅛ teaspoon liquid smoke (optional)

Salt and pepper

HONEY-MUSTARD DIPPING SAUCE `FAST`

½ cup yellow mustard

⅓ cup honey

Salt and pepper

SWEET AND SOUR DIPPING SAUCE `FAST`

¾ cup apple jelly, apricot jelly, or hot pepper jelly

1 tablespoon distilled white vinegar

½ teaspoon soy sauce

⅛ teaspoon garlic powder

Pinch ground ginger

Pinch cayenne pepper

Salt and pepper

---

2. Remove chicken from brine and pat dry with paper towels. Whisk egg whites together in large bowl. Combine panko, flour, onion powder, garlic powder, baking soda, 1 teaspoon salt, and ¾ teaspoon pepper in shallow dish. Working with half of chicken at a time, dip in egg whites, then coat with panko mixture, pressing gently to adhere. Transfer to plate and let sit 10 minutes. (Don't discard panko mixture.)

3. Adjust oven rack to middle position and heat oven to 200 degrees. Heat oil in large Dutch oven over medium-high heat to 350 degrees. Coat chicken with panko mixture again, pressing gently to adhere. Fry half of chicken, turning as needed, until deep golden brown, about 3 minutes. Transfer chicken to wire rack set inside rimmed baking sheet and keep warm in oven.

4. Return oil to 350 degrees and repeat with remaining chicken. Serve. (Fried nuggets can be frozen in zipper-lock bag for up to 1 month; reheat on wire rack in 350-degree oven for 15 minutes.)

Cutting Chicken into Nuggets

1. Using chef's knife, cut each chicken breast on bias into thirds.

2. Working with largest piece, turn cut end toward you and slice into ½-inch-thick pieces.

3. With knife almost parallel to cutting board, cut 2 smaller thirds into pieces.

Skillet Chicken and Rice with Carrots and Shallots

SERVES 4   **TOTAL TIME** 45 MINUTES **FAST**

✔ **WHY THIS RECIPE WORKS:** A traditional recipe for chicken and rice takes about 1½ hours, but we wanted to find a way to get this weeknight dinner on the table faster without sacrificing the texture of the chicken or the rice. Swapping boneless, skinless chicken breasts for a whole, cut-up chicken shaved off a lot of time, yet we still had trouble getting the rice to cook at the same rate as the chicken—until we spied the microwave. Also, we found that using a skillet helped to speed up the cooking time and develop a deeper flavor in the rice. Do not overcook the chicken in step 3 or it will taste dry.

2¾ cups chicken broth
1 cup long-grain white rice, rinsed
4 (6- to 8-ounce) boneless, skinless chicken breasts, trimmed
   Salt and pepper
2 tablespoons vegetable oil
3 shallots, sliced thin
3 garlic cloves, minced
3 carrots, peeled and sliced ¼ inch thick
2 tablespoons minced fresh parsley
2 tablespoons lemon juice

1. Combine 1¾ cups broth and rice in bowl, cover, and microwave until liquid is absorbed, about 10 minutes. Fluff rice with fork.

2. Pound thicker ends of breasts as needed, then pat dry with paper towels and season with salt and pepper. Heat 1 tablespoon oil in 12-inch nonstick skillet over medium-high heat until just smoking. Brown chicken lightly on both sides, about 5 minutes; transfer to plate.

3. Add remaining 1 tablespoon oil, shallots, and ½ teaspoon salt to now-empty skillet and cook over medium heat until softened, about 2 minutes. Stir in garlic and cook until fragrant, about 30 seconds. Stir in remaining 1 cup broth, microwaved rice, and carrots, scraping up any browned bits. Nestle browned chicken, with any accumulated juices, into rice, cover, and simmer gently until rice is tender and chicken registers 160 degrees, 10 to 15 minutes.

4. Transfer chicken to platter, brushing any rice that sticks to chicken back into skillet. Gently fold parsley and lemon juice into rice. Season with salt and pepper to taste and serve.

VARIATIONS
Skillet Chicken and Chipotle Rice with Tomatoes, Olives, and Scallions

Omit carrots. Add 2 teaspoons minced canned chipotle chile in adobo sauce to skillet with garlic. Add 1 (14.5-ounce) can diced tomatoes, drained, to skillet with broth. Substitute ⅓ cup pitted large green olives, chopped coarse, and 3 thinly sliced scallions for parsley and lemon juice.

Skillet Chicken and Curried Coconut Rice with Peas

Omit carrots. Substitute 1 (13.5-ounce) can light coconut milk for broth in step 1. Add 1 tablespoon green curry paste to skillet with garlic. Substitute 2 tablespoons minced fresh cilantro for parsley and 2 tablespoons lime juice for lemon juice. Add ⅔ cup thawed frozen peas to skillet with cilantro and lime juice.

Making Skillet Chicken and Rice

1. MICROWAVE RICE: Combine 1¾ cups broth and rice in bowl, cover, and microwave until liquid is absorbed, about 10 minutes. Fluff rice with fork.

2. BROWN CHICKEN: Heat 1 tablespoon oil in 12-inch nonstick skillet over medium-high heat until just smoking. Brown chicken lightly on both sides, about 5 minutes; transfer to plate.

3. NESTLE CHICKEN INTO RICE MIXTURE: Sauté shallots and garlic, then stir in remaining broth, microwaved rice, and carrots, scraping up any browned bits. Nestle browned chicken into rice.

4. COOK CHICKEN TO 160 DEGREES: Cover skillet and simmer gently until rice is tender and chicken registers 160 degrees, 10 to 15 minutes.

Toasted orzo and a generous amount of garlic and herbs add a lot of flavor to our one-skillet chicken meal.

Skillet Chicken and Orzo with Tomatoes and Parmesan

SERVES 4 **TOTAL TIME** 45 MINUTES **FAST**

✔ **WHY THIS RECIPE WORKS:** Our skillet chicken and orzo with tomatoes makes a great one-dish meal after a busy day. Lightly browning the chicken and then finishing it at a gentle simmer resulted in chicken that was both flavorful and tender. We liked the subtle nuttiness of orzo, and discovered that dry-toasting it before cooking intensified the flavor. A generous amount of aromatics and herbs provided deep flavor without the need for long simmering. Be careful not to overcook the chicken in step 4 or it will taste dry.

1½ cups orzo
4 (6- to 8-ounce) boneless, skinless chicken breasts, trimmed
   Salt and pepper
2 tablespoons extra-virgin olive oil
3 garlic cloves, minced
2 teaspoons minced fresh oregano or ½ teaspoon dried

Pinch red pepper flakes
1 (14.5-ounce) can diced tomatoes
2 cups chicken broth
¼ cup grated Parmesan cheese
3 tablespoons chopped fresh basil

1. Toast orzo in 12-inch nonstick skillet over medium-high heat until golden brown, 3 to 5 minutes; transfer to bowl.

2. Pound thicker ends of breasts as needed, then pat dry with paper towels and season with salt and pepper. Heat 1 tablespoon oil in now-empty skillet over medium-high heat until just smoking. Brown chicken lightly on both sides, about 5 minutes; transfer to plate.

3. Add remaining 1 tablespoon oil, garlic, oregano, and pepper flakes to now-empty skillet and cook until fragrant, about 30 seconds. Stir in tomatoes, broth, and toasted orzo.

4. Nestle browned chicken, with any accumulated juices, into orzo. Cover and simmer gently until chicken registers 160 degrees, about 10 minutes. Transfer chicken to platter, brushing any orzo that sticks to chicken back into skillet, and tent with aluminum foil.

5. Continue to cook orzo until al dente and creamy, about 5 minutes longer. Stir in Parmesan and basil and season with salt and pepper to taste. Serve with chicken.

VARIATION

Skillet Chicken and Orzo with Spinach and Feta

Omit tomatoes, Parmesan, and basil. Increase chicken broth to 2½ cups. After orzo has become creamy in step 5, stir in 10 cups baby spinach, 1 handful at a time, until wilted, about 2 minutes. Off heat, stir in 1 cup crumbled feta cheese and 1 tablespoon lemon juice.

Chicken and Couscous with Dried Fruit and Smoked Almonds

SERVES 4 **TOTAL TIME** 35 MINUTES **FAST**

✔ **WHY THIS RECIPE WORKS:** This easy yet elegant chicken and couscous dish relies on just one pan to cook the chicken and then sauté the aromatics and simmer the couscous. Preparing the chicken first meant we were able to capitalize on the flavorful browned bits, or fond, left behind to infuse the couscous with deep, savory flavor. Since the couscous cooks so quickly, it comes together in a flash while the chicken rests. Toasting the couscous in a small amount of oil helped to develop its nutty flavor. To make the most of our ingredients, we bypassed the typical onions and garlic in favor of scallions; the sautéed whites gave our couscous an aromatic foundation, and the greens made for a bright, fresh-tasting garnish. Dried mixed fruit not only contributed some texture, it also gave the dish a subtle sweetness that tasters found neither over the top nor cloying. For some crunch and more savory depth, we stirred in a handful of chopped smoked almonds. The smoky flavor contrasted nicely with the sweetness of the fruit and added an unexpected twist to this simple dinner.

4 **(6- to 8-ounce) boneless, skinless chicken breasts, trimmed**
Salt and pepper
2 **tablespoons vegetable oil**
3 **scallions, white and green parts separated, minced**
1 **cup couscous**
1½ **cups water**
½ **cup dried mixed fruit, coarsely chopped**
¼ **cup smoked almonds, chopped**

1. Adjust oven rack to lower-middle position and heat oven to 200 degrees. Pound thicker ends of breasts as needed, then pat dry with paper towels and season with salt and pepper. Heat 1 tablespoon oil in 12-inch skillet over medium-high heat until just smoking. Add chicken and cook, turning as needed, until chicken is golden brown on both sides and registers 160 degrees, about 10 minutes. Transfer chicken to plate and keep warm in oven.

2. Add remaining 1 tablespoon oil, scallion whites, and ½ teaspoon salt to now-empty skillet and cook over medium heat until softened, 3 to 5 minutes. Stir in couscous and cook for 30 seconds. Stir in water and dried fruit, scraping up any browned bits. Bring to brief simmer, then remove from heat, cover, and let sit until liquid is absorbed, about 3 minutes.

3. Gently fold almonds into couscous with half of scallion greens. Season with salt and pepper to taste. Sprinkle remaining scallion greens over top and serve with chicken.

Latin-Style Chicken and Rice

SERVES 4 TO 6   **TOTAL TIME** 1 HOUR 50 MINUTES

✓ **WHY THIS RECIPE WORKS:** When done right, *arroz con pollo* (literally, "rice with chicken") is satisfying Latino comfort food—tender chicken nestled in rice rich with peppers, onions, and herbs. But the traditional method for making it takes all day; we wanted to turn this one-dish dinner into a fast but flavorful weeknight meal. Using just thighs (rather than a combination of white and dark meat) ensured that all the chicken would cook through at the same rate, while removing the skin and bones after cooking made our dish

less greasy and easier to eat. Poaching the thighs in chicken broth gave our dish even more chicken flavor for minimal effort. A 15-minute marinade before cooking plus a quick toss with marinade after cooking contributed bold flavor to our chicken. To cut even more time, we added the rice to the pot before the chicken finished cooking—a few quick stirs guaranteed each component cooked quickly and evenly. To keep the dish from becoming greasy, it is important to remove excess fat and most of the skin from the chicken thighs, leaving just enough skin to protect the meat. To use long-grain rice instead of medium-grain, increase the amount of water added in step 3 from ¼ cup to ¾ cup, adding the additional ¼ cup water in step 4 as needed. When removing the chicken from the bones in step 5, we found it better to use two spoons rather than two forks; forks tended to shred the meat, while spoons pulled it apart in chunks.

6 **garlic cloves, minced**
5 **teaspoons distilled white vinegar**
Salt and pepper
½ **teaspoon dried oregano**
4 **pounds bone-in chicken thighs, trimmed**
2 **tablespoons vegetable oil**
1 **onion, chopped fine**
1 **small green bell pepper, stemmed, seeded, and chopped fine**
¼ **teaspoon red pepper flakes**
¼ **cup minced fresh cilantro**
1¾ **cups chicken broth**
1 **(8-ounce) can tomato sauce**
¼ **cup water, plus extra as needed**
3 **cups medium-grain white rice**
½ **cup Manzanilla olives, pitted and halved**
1 **tablespoon capers, rinsed**
½ **cup jarred whole pimentos, cut into 2 by ¼-inch strips**
Lemon wedges

1. Adjust oven rack to middle position and heat oven to 350 degrees. Combine garlic, 1 tablespoon vinegar, 1 teaspoon salt, ½ teaspoon pepper, and oregano in large bowl. Add chicken, coat evenly with marinade, and set aside for 15 minutes.

2. Heat 1 tablespoon oil in Dutch oven over medium heat until shimmering. Add onion, bell pepper, and pepper flakes and cook, stirring occasionally, until vegetables begin to soften, about 5 minutes. Stir in 2 tablespoons cilantro.

3. Clear center of pot and increase heat to medium-high. Add chicken to center of pot and cook lightly on both sides, 4 to 8 minutes. Stir in broth, tomato sauce, and water and bring to simmer. Cover, reduce heat to medium-low, and cook for 20 minutes.

4. Stir in rice, olives, capers, and ¾ teaspoon salt and return to simmer. Cover, transfer to oven, and cook, stirring every 10 minutes, until thighs register 175 degrees, about 30 minutes. If, after 20 minutes, rice appears dry and bottom of pot begins to scorch, stir in additional ¼ cup water.

5. Remove pot from oven. Transfer chicken to plate, let cool slightly, then gently pull meat from bones in large chunks using 2 spoons, discarding skin and bones. Toss pulled chicken with pimentos, remaining 2 teaspoons vinegar, remaining 1 tablespoon oil, and remaining 2 tablespoons cilantro in large bowl, and season with salt and pepper to taste. Place chicken on top of rice, cover, and let stand until warmed through, about 5 minutes. Serve with lemon wedges.

Unstuffed Chicken Cordon Bleu

SERVES 4   **TOTAL TIME** 35 MINUTES **FAST**

WHY THIS RECIPE WORKS: Most chicken cordon bleu recipes call for pounding the chicken breasts before stuffing them with ham and cheese, rolling them up, coating them with bread crumbs, and baking or frying the lot—not exactly weeknight-friendly dining. For an easier path to cordon bleu heaven, we arranged chicken breasts on a sheet pan and topped them with slices of ham and grated Gruyère for an inside-out approach that kept the work to a minimum. Brushing the chicken with mustard added a tangy sharpness and also provided the "glue" to help the ham and cheese stay in place. For the crunchy, golden bread-crumb topping, we tested a variety of candidates, eventually ditching panko and fresh bread crumbs in favor of crumbled Ritz crackers, which stayed crisp and offered a rich, buttery flavor. After 20 minutes in a hot oven, our streamlined chicken cordon bleu delivered all the rich flavors and appealing textures of the authentic versions. Swiss cheese can be substituted for the Gruyère.

  1 **tablespoon vegetable oil**
  4 **(6- to 8-ounce) boneless, skinless chicken breasts, trimmed**
      Pepper
  2 **tablespoons Dijon mustard**
  4 **slices (4 ounces) deli ham, folded in half**
  4 **ounces Gruyère cheese, shredded (1 cup)**
 15 **Ritz crackers (1¾ ounces), coarsely crushed**

1. Adjust oven rack to lower-middle position and heat oven to 475 degrees. Brush rimmed baking sheet with oil. Pound thicker ends of breasts as needed, then pat dry with paper towels and season with pepper. Arrange on prepared sheet.

We top boneless chicken breasts with ham and cheese and cracker crumbs for a streamlined cordon bleu.

2. Spread mustard over top of chicken, then top with ham and Gruyère. Sprinkle cracker crumbs over top, pressing on crumbs to adhere.

3. Bake until chicken registers 160 degrees, 20 to 25 minutes, rotating sheet halfway through baking. Serve.

Making Unstuffed Chicken Cordon Bleu

1. After seasoning chicken, spread with Dijon mustard. Top with 1 slice ham, folded in half, and ¼ cup shredded Gruyère.

2. Sprinkle crushed Ritz crackers over top of cheese, pressing on crumbs to adhere. Bake chicken for 20 to 25 minutes.

Chicken Tikka Masala

SERVES 4 TO 6   **TOTAL TIME** 55 MINUTES

✔ WHY THIS RECIPE WORKS: To create an approachable method for producing moist, tender chunks of chicken in a rich, lightly spiced tomato sauce, we began by coating the chicken in a yogurt mixture seasoned with cumin, coriander, and cayenne. Baking the chicken breasts was quick and worked well, but the additional char we achieved with the broiler was better and required no extra time. The basic combination of garam masala, fresh ginger, and fresh cilantro gave our masala sauce an authentic Indian taste. We prefer to use whole Greek yogurt here, but 2 percent Greek yogurt can be substituted; do not use 0 percent Greek yogurt. Serve with rice.

6 tablespoons vegetable oil
1 onion, chopped fine
1 tablespoon garam masala
1 tablespoon grated fresh ginger
2 garlic cloves, minced
1 (28-ounce) can crushed tomatoes
⅔ cup heavy cream
1 cup plain Greek yogurt
   Salt
1 teaspoon ground cumin
1 teaspoon ground coriander
½ teaspoon cayenne pepper
2 pounds boneless, skinless chicken breasts, trimmed
¼ cup minced fresh cilantro

1. Combine oil and onion in Dutch oven and cook over medium-high heat until softened, about 5 minutes. Stir in garam masala, ginger, and garlic and cook until fragrant, about 30 seconds. Stir in tomatoes, cover, and simmer gently, stirring occasionally, until flavors meld, about 15 minutes. Stir in cream, cover, and keep warm.

2. Meanwhile, adjust oven rack 6 inches from broiler element and heat broiler. Line broiler-pan bottom with aluminum foil and lay slotted broiler pan on top. Combine yogurt, 1 teaspoon salt, cumin, coriander, and cayenne in medium bowl. Pound thicker ends of breasts as needed, then pat dry with paper towels.

3. Using tongs, dip chicken into yogurt mixture (chicken should be coated with thick layer of yogurt) and arrange on prepared broiler-pan top. Discard excess yogurt mixture. Broil chicken until lightly charred in spots and chicken registers 160 degrees, 10 to 18 minutes, flipping halfway through cooking.

4. Transfer chicken to cutting board, let rest for 5 minutes, then cut into 1-inch chunks. Stir chicken into warm sauce and let heat through, about 2 minutes. Stir in cilantro and season with salt to taste. Serve.

After coating the chicken with a spicy yogurt mixture, we broil the breasts whole so they don't dry out.

NOTES FROM THE TEST KITCHEN

Shopping for Garam Masala

Garam masala, which means "hot mixture," is a northern Indian combination of up to 12 dry-roasted, ground spices and is used in a wide range of dishes. It is often the base to which other spices are added, and the exact composition of a from-scratch mixture varies with the tastes of the cook. The most common ingredients include black peppercorns, cinnamon, cloves, cardamom, coriander, cumin, dried chiles, fennel, mace, nutmeg, and bay leaves. Ginger and caraway seeds also make frequent appearances. While we've found that commercial mixtures tend to be less aromatic and more muted than batches we toast and grind fresh ourselves, grinding whole spices to concoct this blend can be both time-consuming and expensive. If you choose to purchase garam masala at the supermarket, we suggest you check the ingredients and buy a brand that sticks with mostly traditional ingredients. Avoid blends that include such ingredients as dehydrated onion and yeast extract. For the test kitchen's favorite brand, see page 811.

Chicken Baked in Foil with Zucchini and Tomatoes

SERVES 4   TOTAL TIME 1 HOUR 20 MINUTES

✓ **WHY THIS RECIPE WORKS:** Despite its reputation for delivering bland, boring food, steaming in a pouch (we use aluminum foil) is actually an excellent way to cook delicate boneless, skinless chicken breasts. Besides being healthy, this method is fast and convenient, and it keeps food moist. We solved the bland problem by adding vegetables and fruits that are first tossed with a little olive oil and bold seasonings like tarragon, oregano, and garlic. The result is moist, perfectly cooked chicken with highly flavorful vegetables. To prevent overcooking, open each packet promptly after baking.

- 2 **zucchini, sliced ¼ inch thick**
  Salt and pepper
- 2 **tablespoons extra-virgin olive oil**
- 2 **garlic cloves, minced**
- 1 **teaspoon minced fresh oregano or ¼ teaspoon dried**
- ⅛ **teaspoon red pepper flakes**
- 8 **ounces plum tomatoes, cored, seeded, and chopped**
- 4 **(6- to 8-ounce) boneless, skinless chicken breasts, trimmed**
- ¼ **cup chopped fresh basil**
  Lemon wedges

1. Toss zucchini with ¼ teaspoon salt in colander and let drain for 30 minutes. Spread zucchini out on several layers of paper towels and pat dry; transfer to bowl. Adjust oven rack to middle position and heat oven to 450 degrees. Cut eight 12-inch sheets of aluminum foil.

2. Combine oil, garlic, oregano, pepper flakes, and ⅛ teaspoon pepper in small bowl. Toss zucchini with half of oil mixture, and toss tomatoes with remaining oil mixture in separate bowl. Pound thicker ends of breasts as needed, then pat dry with paper towels and season with salt and pepper.

3. Arrange zucchini in center of 4 pieces of foil. Lay chicken on zucchini, then top with tomato mixture. Place remaining pieces of foil on top and fold edges over several times to seal. (Foil packets can be refrigerated for up to 3 hours; increase baking time to 30 minutes.)

4. Place packets on rimmed baking sheet and cook until chicken registers 160 degrees, about 25 minutes. (To test doneness of chicken, you will need to open one packet.)

5. Carefully open packets, allowing steam to escape away from you, and let cool briefly. Smooth out edges of foil. Using spatula, gently slide chicken and vegetables, with any accumulated juices, onto individual plates. Sprinkle with basil and serve with lemon wedges.

Making a Foil Pouch

1. Arrange vegetables in center of 12-inch sheet of aluminum foil.

2. Lay chicken on top of vegetables and spoon topping over chicken.

3. Place second piece of foil on top of chicken and fold edges of foil together several times to create well-sealed packet.

VARIATION

Chicken Baked in Foil with Fennel, Carrots, and Orange

SERVES 4   TOTAL TIME 1 HOUR

- 2 **tablespoons extra-virgin olive oil**
- 1 **shallot, sliced thin**
- 1 **teaspoon minced fresh tarragon**
  Salt and pepper
- 2 **oranges, peeled and cut into ¼-inch pieces**
- 2 **carrots, peeled and cut into matchsticks**
- 1 **fennel bulb (about 12 ounces), stalks discarded, bulb halved, cored, and sliced thin**
- 4 **(6- to 8-ounce) boneless, skinless chicken breasts, trimmed**
- 2 **scallions, sliced thin**

1. Adjust oven rack to middle position and heat oven to 450 degrees. Cut eight 12-inch sheets of aluminum foil.

2. Combine oil, shallot, tarragon, ¼ teaspoon salt, and ⅛ teaspoon pepper in small bowl. Toss oranges with half of oil mixture in separate bowl. Toss carrots and fennel with remaining oil mixture in third bowl. Pound thicker ends of breasts as needed, then pat dry with paper towels and season with salt and pepper

3. Arrange carrot-fennel mixture in center of 4 pieces of foil. Lay chicken on vegetables, then top with orange mixture. Place remaining pieces of foil on top and fold edges over several times to seal. (Foil packets can be refrigerated for up to 3 hours; increase baking time to 30 minutes.)

4. Place packets on rimmed baking sheet and cook until chicken registers 160 degrees, about 25 minutes. (To test doneness of chicken, you will need to open one packet.)

5. Carefully open packets, allowing steam to escape away from you, and let cool briefly. Smooth out edges of foil. Using spatula, gently slide chicken, vegetables, and fruit, with any accumulated juices, onto individual plates. Sprinkle with scallions and serve.

Simple Stuffed Chicken Breasts with Boursin

SERVES 4   **TOTAL TIME** 45 MINUTES   **FAST**

✔ WHY THIS RECIPE WORKS: For a simpler approach to stuffed bone-in chicken breasts, we started with a simple filling. And it didn't get much easier—or more delicious—than Boursin. Instead of cutting fussy pockets to hold the filling, we used the skin on the chicken as a natural pocket. We loosened the skin and fit about 1½ tablespoons of the cheese underneath. The skin held the filling in place, and when the chicken emerged from the oven it was moist and tender with a creamy, saucelike filling. It is important to buy chicken breasts with the skin still attached and intact, otherwise the stuffing will leak out. Also, try to buy chicken breasts of similar size so that they will cook at the same rate.

　　4　**(10- to 12-ounce) bone-in split chicken breasts, trimmed**
　　　　Salt and pepper
　　1　**(5.2-ounce) package Boursin Garlic and Fine Herbs cheese, softened**
　　1　**tablespoon unsalted butter, melted**

1. Adjust oven rack to middle position and heat oven to 450 degrees. Line rimmed baking sheet with aluminum foil.

2. Pat chicken dry with paper towels and season with salt and pepper. Use your fingers to gently loosen center portion of skin covering each breast. Spoon Boursin equally underneath skin of each breast. Gently press on skin to spread out cheese.

3. Arrange chicken, skin side up, on prepared baking sheet. Brush chicken with melted butter and bake until chicken registers 160 degrees, about 30 minutes, rotating sheet halfway through baking. Let chicken cool for 5 minutes. Serve.

VARIATION

Simple Stuffed Chicken Breasts with Gorgonzola and Walnuts

Substitute 4 ounces softened Gorgonzola, mixed with ¼ cup toasted and chopped walnuts, for Boursin.

Stuffing Bone-In Chicken Breasts

1. Use your fingers to gently loosen center portion of skin covering each breast, making pocket for filling.

2. Using spoon, place Boursin underneath loosened skin, over center of each chicken breast. Gently press on skin to spread out filling.

Teriyaki Glazed Chicken Drumsticks

SERVES 4   **TOTAL TIME** 40 MINUTES   **FAST**

✔ WHY THIS RECIPE WORKS: We generally recommend cooking chicken drumsticks to 175 degrees, at which point they become safe to eat. Depending on the cooking method, however, we found that giving them extra time to simmer until they reached 180 degrees produced meltingly tender drumsticks. This is because collagen, the tough connective tissue present in large amounts in dark chicken meat, softens over time when heated gently. To enable us to give the drumsticks this extra time, we created simple glazes that required little more than mixing pantry ingredients in the skillet. Since the chicken skin doesn't become crisp here, we removed it before cooking. Try to buy drumsticks of similar size so that they will cook at the same rate.

½ cup soy sauce

½ cup sugar

¼ cup water

2 tablespoons mirin

2 teaspoons grated fresh ginger

1 garlic clove, minced

⅛ teaspoon red pepper flakes

8 (5-ounce) chicken drumsticks, skin removed, trimmed

2 scallions, sliced thin

1. Combine soy sauce, sugar, water, mirin, ginger, garlic, and pepper flakes in 12-inch nonstick skillet. Add drumsticks, cover, and simmer gently until chicken is tender and registers 180 degrees, about 20 minutes, flipping drumsticks over half-way through cooking.

2. Uncover, increase heat to medium-high, and simmer rapidly until sauce is slightly thickened, 5 to 7 minutes, turning drumsticks occasionally to coat. Transfer chicken to platter, pour glaze over top, and sprinkle with scallions. Serve.

VARIATION

Mustard Glazed Chicken Drumsticks

½ cup sugar

¼ cup whole-grain mustard

¼ cup water

3 tablespoons soy sauce

1 tablespoon cider vinegar

1 tablespoon dry mustard

1 garlic clove, minced

8 (5-ounce) chicken drumsticks, skin removed, trimmed

2 scallions, sliced thin

1. Combine sugar, mustard, water, soy sauce, vinegar, mustard, and garlic in 12-inch nonstick skillet. Add drumsticks, cover, and simmer gently until chicken is tender and registers 180 degrees, about 20 minutes, flipping drumsticks over half-way through cooking.

Removing Skin from Chicken Drumsticks

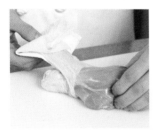

Chicken skin is often slippery, making it a challenge to remove by hand. To simplify, use paper towels to provide extra grip while pulling.

Chicken drumsticks turn tender and flavorful when simmered in a skillet with simple glaze ingredients.

2. Uncover, increase heat to medium-high, and simmer rapidly until sauce is slightly thickened, 5 to 7 minutes, turning drumsticks occasionally to coat. Transfer chicken to platter, pour glaze over top, and sprinkle with scallions. Serve.

Pan-Roasted Chicken Breasts with Shallot-Thyme Sauce

SERVES 4   **TOTAL TIME** 55 MINUTES

✔ **WHY THIS RECIPE WORKS:** Bone-in chicken breasts are more flavorful than boneless, skinless breasts, but getting the skin to crisp without overcooking the delicate meat can be a challenge. We turned to pan-roasting—browning in a skillet on the stovetop and then sliding the skillet into a hot oven to finish. Brining the chicken ensured the meat stayed moist and flavorful (see page 158 for brining instructions). Cooking the chicken at 450 degrees allowed the skin to crisp while the meat cooked through relatively quickly. We prefer to split whole chicken breasts ourselves because store-bought split chicken

PAN-ROASTING CHICKEN BREASTS AND MAKING A PAN SAUCE

Pan roasting is an easy way to cook bone-in chicken breasts. This technique delivers crisp skin, tender meat, and flavorful drippings. The chicken is first browned in a skillet on the stovetop, then slid into a hot oven to finish cooking. As a bonus, the browned bits left in the pan can be turned into a flavorful sauce. For more information about making a pan sauce, see page 184.

1. TRIM THE CHICKEN BREASTS: Using kitchen shears, trim off the rib section from each bone-in split chicken breast, following the vertical line of fat from the tapered end of the breast up to the socket where the wing was attached. **WHY?** Because there isn't a lot of meat on the rib section, we trim it off to allow more room in the pan for the chicken to brown properly. Removing the ribs also allows for more even cooking since the breasts can lay flat in the skillet.

2. GET THE SKILLET HOT: Heat the vegetable oil in a 12-inch ovensafe skillet over medium-high heat until just smoking. **WHY?** If the oil isn't hot enough, the chicken won't brown properly and will stick to the pan. Also, a very hot skillet helps to brown the chicken quickly.

3. BROWN THE CHICKEN: Carefully lay the chicken breasts skin side down in the skillet and cook until they are well browned on the first side, 6 to 8 minutes. Flip the chicken and brown lightly on the second side, about 3 minutes. **WHY?** Browning the chicken in a hot skillet renders all the fat and crisps the skin. It also builds fond in the skillet, and these browned bits can be used to add intense flavor to a pan sauce.

4. TRANSFER THE SKILLET TO THE OVEN: Flip the chicken breasts skin side down and transfer the skillet to a 450-degree oven. Roast the chicken until the thickest part of the breasts registers 160 degrees, 15 to 18 minutes. **WHY?** Once the chicken is browned on the stovetop, the skillet goes into a 450-degree oven to finish cooking. Cooking the chicken at 450 degrees allows the skin to crisp while the meat cooks through relatively quickly and remains moist.

5. REMOVE THE CHICKEN AND LET IT REST: Using a potholder (the skillet handle will be very hot), remove the skillet from the oven and transfer the chicken to a serving platter to rest while making the sauce. **WHY?** Allowing the chicken to rest lets it reabsorb its natural juices. This is the perfect time to make a quick pan sauce from the fond left in the skillet.

6. MAKE THE PAN SAUCE: Keeping the hot handle covered with a potholder, pour off all but 1 teaspoon of fat in the skillet. Add the shallot and cook; stir in the liquids, scrape up the browned bits, and simmer; finally, add the cold butter pieces to finish the sauce. **WHY?** The browned bits left in the skillet along with a little fat are the foundation for quickly building an easy pan sauce. Finishing the sauce with cold butter adds richness.

breasts are often sloppily butchered. However, if you prefer to purchase split chicken breasts, try to choose 10- to 12-ounce pieces with the skin intact. You will need a 12-inch ovensafe skillet for this recipe. For more information about making a pan sauce, see page 184. For other pan sauces, see page 128. If using kosher chicken, do not brine. If brining the chicken, do not season with salt in step 1.

CHICKEN

- 4 **(10- to 12-ounce) bone-in split chicken breasts, trimmed, brined if desired**
  Salt and pepper
- 1 **tablespoon vegetable oil**

SAUCE

- 1 **large shallot, minced**
- ¾ **cup chicken broth**
- ½ **cup dry vermouth or white wine**
- 2 **sprigs fresh thyme**
- 3 **tablespoons unsalted butter, cut into 3 pieces and chilled**
  Salt and pepper

1. FOR THE CHICKEN: Adjust oven rack to middle position and heat oven to 450 degrees. Pat chicken dry with paper towels and season with salt and pepper.

2. Heat oil in 12-inch ovensafe skillet over medium-high heat until just smoking. Cook chicken, skin side down, until well browned, 6 to 8 minutes, reducing heat if pan begins to scorch. Flip chicken and brown lightly on second side, about 3 minutes. Flip chicken skin side down, transfer skillet to oven, and roast until chicken registers 160 degrees, 15 to 18 minutes.

3. Using potholder (skillet handle will be hot), remove skillet from oven. Transfer chicken to serving platter and let rest while making sauce.

4. FOR THE SAUCE: Being careful of hot skillet handle, pour off all but 1 teaspoon fat left in skillet. Add shallot and cook over medium-high heat until softened, about 2 minutes. Stir in broth, vermouth, and thyme sprigs, scraping up any browned bits, and simmer until thickened and measures ⅔ cup, about 6 minutes.

5. Discard thyme sprigs and stir in any accumulated chicken juices. Turn heat to low and whisk in butter, one piece at a time. Off heat, season with salt and pepper to taste. Spoon sauce over chicken and serve.

Simple Baked Chicken

SERVES 4 TO 6   **TOTAL TIME** 1 HOUR

✅ **WHY THIS RECIPE WORKS:** We like the idea of a weeknight chicken dish that you can walk away from after putting it in the oven. But often some of the meat overcooks while the rest undercooks. We came up with a simple way to bake chicken that doesn't take a lot of time and is flavorful as is, yet this method also allows you to incorporate different seasoning arrangements into the basic recipe. Because different cuts of chicken cook at different rates, we recommend using only one cut of chicken (such as all breasts or all thighs); otherwise, be prepared to remove the various different cuts from the oven as soon as they reach their appropriate temperature for doneness.

- 4 **pounds bone-in chicken pieces (split breasts, whole legs, thighs, and/or drumsticks), trimmed**
- 2 **tablespoons unsalted butter, melted**
  Salt and pepper

1. Adjust oven rack to upper-middle position and heat oven to 450 degrees. Line broiler-pan bottom with aluminum foil and lay slotted broiler pan on top.

2. Pat chicken dry with paper towels and arrange skin side up on broiler-pan top. Brush chicken with melted butter and season with salt and pepper.

3. Roast until breasts register 160 degrees and legs, thighs, and/or drumsticks register 175 degrees, 30 to 50 minutes. Transfer chicken to cutting board and let rest for 5 minutes. Serve.

NOTES FROM THE TEST KITCHEN

Roasting Times for Chicken Parts

(450-DEGREE OVEN)

CUT OF CHICKEN	APPROXIMATE ROASTING TIME	TEMPERATURE OF THICKEST PORTION
Whole Breasts (24 ounces each)	50 minutes	160 degrees
Split Breasts (10 to 12 ounces each)	30 minutes	160 degrees
Whole Legs (10 to 12 ounces each)	45 minutes	175 degrees
Thighs (6 to 8 ounces each)	45 minutes	175 degrees
Drumsticks (3 to 4 ounces each)	30 minutes	175 degrees

Simple Baked Chicken with Honey and Mustard

Mix ¼ cup Dijon mustard, 2 tablespoons honey, and 1 teaspoon packed brown sugar together in bowl. Brush over chicken several times during last 5 minutes of cooking.

Simple Baked Chicken with Lemon and Herbs

Any strong-flavored fresh herb, such as rosemary, tarragon, or sage, can be substituted for the thyme.

Mix 3 tablespoons softened unsalted butter with 1 tablespoon minced fresh thyme, 1 teaspoon grated lemon zest, ¼ teaspoon salt, and ¼ teaspoon pepper in bowl. Rub butter mixture underneath skin of chicken. Proceed to brush skin with melted butter and season with salt and pepper before cooking.

Simple Baked Chicken with Five-Spice Powder and Ginger

Mix 3 tablespoons softened unsalted butter with 1 tablespoon grated fresh ginger, 1 teaspoon five-spice powder, ¼ teaspoon salt, and ¼ teaspoon pepper in bowl. Rub butter mixture underneath skin of chicken. Proceed to brush skin with melted butter and season with salt and pepper before cooking.

Simple Baked Chicken with Ginger and Soy

Mix 3 tablespoons softened unsalted butter with 1 tablespoon soy sauce, 1 tablespoon grated fresh ginger, 1 minced garlic clove, and ¼ teaspoon pepper in bowl. Rub butter mixture underneath skin of chicken. Proceed to brush skin with melted butter and season with salt and pepper before cooking. During last 10 minutes of cooking, brush chicken with 2 tablespoons honey, then sprinkle with 1 tablespoon sesame seeds.

Weeknight Roast Chicken

SERVES 3 TO 4   TOTAL TIME 1 HOUR 25 MINUTES

✔ WHY THIS RECIPE WORKS: When properly made, roast chicken has rich flavor and juicy meat that need little adornment. We discovered a simplified roasting method that skips both the V-rack and flipping the chicken and instead uses a preheated skillet. The hot skillet gave the thighs a jump start on cooking. Starting the chicken in a 450-degree oven, and then turning the oven off while the chicken finished, slowed the evaporation of juices, ensuring moist, tender meat. We prefer to use a 3½- to 4-pound chicken for this recipe. If roasting a larger bird, increase the time when the oven is on in step 2 to 35 to 40 minutes. You will need a 12-inch ovensafe skillet for this recipe. Serve with a pan sauce, if desired (see page 128). If making a sauce, be sure to save 1 tablespoon of the pan drippings.

1 (3½- to 4-pound) whole chicken, giblets discarded
1 tablespoon vegetable oil
   Salt and pepper

1. Adjust oven rack to middle position, place 12-inch ovensafe skillet on rack, and heat oven to 450 degrees. Pat chicken dry with paper towels. Rub entire surface with oil, season with salt and pepper, and rub in with hands to coat evenly. Tie legs together with twine and tuck wingtips behind back.

2. Transfer chicken, breast side up, to hot skillet in oven. Roast chicken until breast registers 120 degrees and thighs register 135 degrees, 25 to 35 minutes. Turn oven off and leave chicken in oven until breast registers 160 degrees and thighs register 175 degrees, 25 to 35 minutes.

3. Transfer chicken to carving board and let rest for 20 minutes. Carve and serve.

Making Weeknight Roast Chicken

1. HEAT SKILLET IN OVEN: Adjust oven rack to middle position, place 12-inch ovensafe skillet on rack, and heat oven to 450 degrees.

2. TIE AND TUCK: Rub chicken with oil and season with salt and pepper, tie legs together with twine, and tuck wingtips behind back.

3. ROAST BREAST SIDE UP: Transfer chicken, breast side up, to hot skillet in oven. Roast chicken until breast registers 120 degrees and thighs register 135 degrees, 25 to 35 minutes.

4. TURN OVEN OFF: Turn oven off and leave chicken in oven until breast registers 160 degrees and thighs register 175 degrees, 25 to 35 minutes.

Simple and satisfying, a roasted whole chicken is a classic must-have recipe for every cook, no matter their skill level. The biggest challenge is getting the white and dark meat to finish cooking at the same time since the breast meat dries out before the dark meat is done. Although many recipes resort to fussy methods, we found that a bit of simple prep, plus turning the chicken twice during cooking, was all that was needed to turn out a beautifully bronzed and perfectly cooked bird.

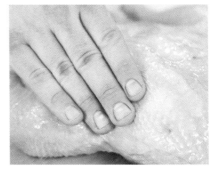

1. BRINE THE CHICKEN: Remove the gizzard packet and any excess fat from the cavity of the chicken. Stir ½ cup salt into 2 quarts of cold water in a large container. Submerge the chicken, cover, and refrigerate for 1 hour.
WHY? The process of brining the chicken dramatically improves its flavor and tenderness. As it soaks, the chicken absorbs the brine, and retains it during cooking. This results in tender, juicy meat, especially in the breast.

2. LOOSEN THE SKIN AND SPREAD BUTTER ON THE MEAT: Loosen the skin covering each breast. Place 1 tablespoon of butter under the skin directly on the meat and press on the skin to distribute the butter.
WHY? Loosening the skin makes it easier to spread the butter evenly and it allows for the fat in the skin to render. Be gentle so as not to tear the skin. Applying butter under the skin helps keep the lean breast meat moist.

3. RUB THE SKIN WITH OIL: Tuck the wing tips behind the back and rub the chicken's skin with oil and season with pepper.
WHY? Rubbing oil onto the skin of the chicken helps the skin crisp because the oil is 100 percent fat. Seasoning the chicken ensures that the meat remains flavorful. If you haven't brined the chicken, season with salt as well.

4. PLACE THE CHICKEN IN A V-RACK TO ROAST: Place the chicken wing side up in an oiled V-rack and set the rack in a preheated roasting pan. Roast for 15 minutes. Rotate the chicken so that the opposite wing side is facing up, and roast for another 15 minutes.
WHY? For even cooking, we roast the chicken with one wing facing up. Then we flip it and roast for another 15 minutes. Preheating the pan ensures the thighs and breast cook at the same rate.

5. FINISH COOKING THE CHICKEN BREAST SIDE UP: Using wads of paper towels, rotate the chicken so the breast side is facing up. Roast until the breast registers 160 degrees and the thighs register 175 degrees.
WHY? Cooking the chicken breast side up for the last 25 minutes ensures evenly cooked meat. If the pan starts to smoke, add 1 cup of water to the pan. For accuracy, take several readings in the thickest part of both the breast and thigh.

6. ALLOW THE CHICKEN TO REST BEFORE CARVING: Transfer the chicken to a carving board, and let it rest for 20 minutes. Carve the chicken and serve.
WHY? The heat of the oven forces the juices of the meat toward the center of the bird. Letting the chicken rest gives the juices time to redistribute, ensuring moist, flavorful chicken in every bite.

Classic Roast Chicken

SERVES 3 TO 4   **TOTAL TIME** 1 HOURS 25 MINUTES
(PLUS BRINING TIME)

✔ **WHY THIS RECIPE WORKS:** For the ultimate roast chicken boasting ultratender meat, we start by brining the chicken for an hour (see page 158 for instructions on brining). As for cooking method, roasting the chicken at 400 degrees for the duration of cooking (rather than adjusting the temperature partway through) worked best. Continuous basting didn't improve our roast chicken; we found that applying butter under the skin and rubbing the bird with oil before it went into the oven gave it great color and a crisp texture. Trussing also proved unnecessary; the dark meat cooked more quickly when left untrussed. The only extra step we found truly important was turning the bird twice for evenly cooked meat and crisp, browned skin. We recommend using a V-rack to roast the chicken. If you don't have a V-rack, set the bird on a regular roasting rack and use balls of aluminum foil to keep the chicken propped up on its side. If using kosher chicken, do not brine.

1   **(3½- to 4-pound) whole chicken, giblets discarded, brined**
2   **tablespoons unsalted butter, softened**
1   **tablespoon vegetable oil**
    Pepper

1. Adjust oven rack to lower-middle position, place roasting pan on rack, and heat oven to 400 degrees. Coat V-rack with vegetable oil spray.

2. Use your fingers to gently loosen center portion of skin covering each breast. Using spoon, place 1 tablespoon butter underneath skin over center of each chicken breast. Gently press on skin to spread out butter. Tuck wingtips behind back. Rub skin with oil and season with pepper. Place chicken, wing side up, on prepared V-rack. Place V-rack in preheated roasting pan and roast for 15 minutes.

3. Remove roasting pan from oven. Using 2 large wads of paper towels, rotate chicken so that opposite wing side is facing up. Return roasting pan to oven and roast for another 15 minutes.

4. Using 2 large wads of paper towels, rotate chicken again so that breast side is facing up, and continue to roast until breast registers 160 degrees and thighs register 175 degrees, 20 to 25 minutes longer. Transfer chicken to carving board and let rest for 20 minutes. Carve and serve.

To get chicken and root vegetables to roast at the same rate, we use chicken parts and arrange them carefully in the pan.

One-Pan Roast Chicken Parts with Root Vegetables

SERVES 4   **TOTAL TIME** 1 HOUR 10 MINUTES

✔ **WHY THIS RECIPE WORKS:** Cooking vegetables and chicken together in the same pan often leads to unevenly cooked chicken and greasy, soggy vegetables. To get the chicken and vegetables to cook at the same rate, we used chicken parts, which contain less overall fat than a whole chicken, and we were careful not to smother the vegetables underneath the chicken, which would cause them to steam. To ensure that the delicate white meat stayed moist while the darker meat cooked through, we placed the chicken breasts in the center of the pan, with the thighs and drumsticks around the perimeter. A similar treatment for the vegetables—leafy Brussels sprouts in the middle, hardier potatoes and carrots on the outside—also proved effective. We halve the chicken breasts crosswise for even cooking. Use Brussels sprouts no bigger than golf balls, as larger ones are often tough and woody.

ALL ABOUT **BRINING POULTRY AND PORK**

The process of brining (or soaking meat in a solution of water, salt, and sometimes sugar before cooking) can dramatically improve the flavor and tenderness of chicken, turkey, and pork. As it soaks, the meat absorbs the brine, and then retains it during cooking. The result? The juiciest and best-tasting poultry or pork you've ever eaten. Best of all, brining is easy; all you need is some refrigerator space, a little time, and a container big enough to submerge the meat fully in the brine. Brining isn't essential, but we highly recommend it in simple roasted or grilled recipes.

We prefer to use table salt for brining since it dissolves quickly in the water, but kosher salt can be substituted. It is important to note, however, that cup for cup table salt is stronger than kosher salt. To use Morton kosher salt in a brine, use one and a half times the amount of salt called for in the chart; double the amount of salt in the chart if using Diamond Crystal kosher salt.

Brining works faster than salting and can make lean cuts such as chicken breast or pork tenderloin juicier than salting since it adds, rather than merely helps retain, moisture. Do not brine kosher birds or enhanced pork.

BRINING DIRECTIONS: Dissolve the salt in the water in a container or bowl large enough to hold the brine and meat, following the amounts in the chart. Submerge the meat completely in the brine. Cover and refrigerate, following the times in the chart (do not brine for longer or else the meat will become overly salty). Remove the meat from the brine and pat dry with paper towels.

MEAT	COLD WATER	TABLE SALT	TIME
CHICKEN			
1 (3- to 8-pound) whole chicken	2 quarts	½ cup	1 hour
2 (3- to 8-pound) whole chickens	3 quarts	¾ cup	1 hour
4 pounds bone-in chicken pieces (whole breasts, split breasts, whole legs, thighs, and/or drumsticks)	2 quarts	½ cup	½ to 1 hour
Boneless, skinless chicken breasts (up to 6 breasts)	1½ quarts	3 tablespoons	½ to 1 hour
TURKEY			
1 (12- to 17-pound) whole turkey	2 gallons	1 cup	6 to 12 hours
1 (18- to 24-pound) whole turkey	3 gallons	1½ cups	6 to 12 hours
Bone-in turkey breast	1 gallon	½ cup	3 to 6 hours
PORK			
Bone-in pork chops (up to 6)	1½ quarts	3 tablespoons	½ to 1 hour
Boneless pork chops (up to 6)	1½ quarts	3 tablespoons	½ to 1 hour
1 (2½- to 6-pound) pork roast	2 quarts	¼ cup	1½ to 2 hours

12 ounces Brussels sprouts, trimmed and halved

12 ounces red potatoes, unpeeled, cut into 1-inch pieces

8 ounces shallots, peeled and halved

4 carrots, peeled and cut into 2-inch pieces, thick ends halved lengthwise

6 garlic cloves, peeled

4 teaspoons minced fresh thyme

2 teaspoons minced fresh rosemary

1 tablespoon vegetable oil

1 teaspoon sugar

Salt and pepper

2 tablespoons unsalted butter, melted

3½ pounds bone-in chicken pieces (2 split breasts cut in half crosswise, 2 drumsticks, and 2 thighs), trimmed

1. Adjust oven rack to upper-middle position and heat oven to 475 degrees. Toss Brussels sprouts, potatoes, shallots, carrots, garlic, 2 teaspoons thyme, 1 teaspoon rosemary, oil, sugar, ¾ teaspoon salt, and ¼ teaspoon pepper together in bowl. In separate bowl, combine melted butter, remaining 2 teaspoons thyme, remaining 1 teaspoon rosemary, ¼ teaspoon salt, and ⅛ teaspoon pepper.

2. Pat chicken dry with paper towels and season with salt and pepper. Place vegetables in single layer on rimmed baking sheet, arranging Brussels sprouts in center. Place chicken, skin side up, on top of vegetables, arranging breast pieces in center and leg and thigh pieces around perimeter of sheet.

3. Brush chicken with herb butter and roast until breasts register 160 degrees and drumsticks/thighs register 175 degrees, 35 to 40 minutes, rotating pan halfway through cooking.

4. Transfer chicken to serving platter, tent with aluminum foil, and let rest for 5 to 10 minutes. Toss vegetables in pan juices and transfer to platter with chicken. Serve.

Chicken with 40 Cloves of Garlic

SERVES 4   **TOTAL TIME** 1 HOUR

♥ **WHY THIS RECIPE WORKS:** To take the harshness out of this classic French dish while staying true to its name, we found that precooking the garlic cloves was key. Bone-in chicken thighs cooked quickly, meaning less time for the garlic to mellow, but a mere 4-minute head start in the microwave softened the cloves, and a pinch of sugar helped them brown in the rendered chicken fat in the pan. Fresh thyme, sherry, and cream made a luscious sauce, and mashing half of the garlic into the sauce ensured that there was sweet garlic flavor in every bite. Three or four heads of garlic should yield 40 cloves. You can substitute four bone-in, skin-on chicken

Precooking the 40 cloves in the microwave softens the garlic and tempers its harshness in this classic chicken dish.

breasts (halved crosswise) for the thighs, but bake the chicken in step 4 until it registers 160 degrees, 15 to 20 minutes. You will need a 12-inch ovensafe skillet for this recipe.

40 garlic cloves, peeled

2 teaspoons vegetable oil

½ teaspoon sugar

8 (5- to 7-ounce) bone-in chicken thighs, trimmed

Salt and pepper

½ cup dry sherry

¾ cup chicken broth

½ cup heavy cream

2 sprigs fresh thyme

1 bay leaf

2 teaspoons cornstarch mixed with 1 tablespoon water

1. Adjust oven rack to upper-middle position and heat oven to 450 degrees. Toss garlic, 1 teaspoon oil, and sugar together in bowl. Microwave garlic mixture until garlic is slightly softened and lightly spotted, about 4 minutes, stirring halfway through microwaving.

2. Pat chicken dry with paper towels and season with salt and pepper. Heat remaining 1 teaspoon oil in 12-inch ovensafe skillet over medium-high heat until just smoking. Brown chicken well on skin side only, 7 to 10 minutes; transfer to plate.

3. Pour off all but 1 tablespoon fat left in skillet. Add microwaved garlic mixture and cook over medium-low heat until evenly browned, about 1 minute. Stir in sherry, scraping up any browned bits. Increase heat to medium and simmer until sherry has nearly evaporated, about 4 minutes. Add broth, cream, thyme sprigs, and bay leaf. Whisk in cornstarch mixture and simmer until slightly thickened, about 3 minutes.

4. Return chicken to skillet, skin side up, with any accumulated juices. Transfer skillet to oven and bake until chicken registers 175 degrees, 18 to 22 minutes.

5. Transfer chicken and half of garlic to serving dish. Discard thyme sprigs and bay leaf. Using potato masher, mash remaining garlic into sauce. Season with salt and pepper to taste and pour some of sauce around chicken. Serve with remaining sauce.

Extra-Crunchy Fried Chicken

SERVES 4   **TOTAL TIME** 1 HOUR 45 MINUTES

WHY THIS RECIPE WORKS: For well-seasoned, extra-crunchy fried chicken we started by brining the chicken in heavily salted buttermilk. For the crunchy coating, we combined flour with a little baking powder and some seasonings, then added buttermilk to make a thick mixture that clung tightly to the meat. Frying the chicken with the lid on the pot for half the cooking time contained the splatter-prone oil and kept it hot. Keeping the oil at the correct temperature was essential for producing crunchy fried chicken that was neither too brown nor too greasy. Don't let the chicken soak in the buttermilk brine much longer than 1 hour or it will be too salty. You will need at least a 6-quart Dutch oven for this recipe. If you want to produce a slightly lighter version of this recipe, you can remove the skin from the chicken before soaking it in the buttermilk. The chicken will be slightly less crunchy.

  2 **tablespoons salt**
  2 **cups plus 6 tablespoons buttermilk**
  3½ **pounds bone-in chicken pieces (2 split breasts cut in half crosswise, 2 drumsticks, and 2 thighs), trimmed**
  3 **cups all-purpose flour**

Soaking the chicken in a salted buttermilk brine for just 1 hour ensures it will stay moist after frying.

  2 **teaspoons baking powder**
  ¾ **teaspoon dried thyme**
  ½ **teaspoon pepper**
  ¼ **teaspoon garlic powder**
  4–5 **cups peanut or vegetable oil**

1. Dissolve salt in 2 cups buttermilk in large bowl or container. Add chicken, cover, and refrigerate for 1 hour. Remove chicken from brine and pat dry with paper towels.

2. Whisk flour, baking powder, thyme, pepper, and garlic powder together in large bowl. Add remaining 6 tablespoons buttermilk and rub into flour mixture using your hands until evenly incorporated and flour mixture resembles coarse, wet sand.

3. Set wire rack inside rimmed baking sheet. Coat chicken thoroughly with flour mixture, pressing gently to adhere. Gently shake off excess flour and transfer chicken to prepared wire rack.

4. Line platter with triple layer of paper towels. Add oil to large Dutch oven to measure ¾ inch deep and heat over medium-high heat to 375 degrees. Place chicken pieces skin

Making even the simplest fried chicken is a kitchen production, one involving hot oil, thermometers, and a potential greasy mess. The problem with most fried chicken is that the meat is dry and flavorless, and the coating is soggy and often falls off. We found that soaking the chicken in a quick buttermilk brine seasons it and keeps it moist, and then a simple coating of buttermilk-moistened flour fries up to a deeply bronzed, crisp, and crunchy crust.

1. BRINE THE CHICKEN IN SALTED BUTTERMILK: Dissolve 2 tablespoons salt in 2 cups buttermilk in a large bowl. Add the chicken to the bowl and soak it in the seasoned buttermilk for just 1 hour before cooking.
WHY? Brining the chicken in salted buttermilk helps it to retain its moisture. Do not brine the chicken for longer than 1 hour. If you do the chicken will absorb too much salt and taste too salty.

2. MAKE THE FLOUR COATING: Whisk together the flour, baking powder, thyme, pepper, and garlic powder. Add the remaining buttermilk and rub it into the flour mixture with your fingers until it resembles coarse, wet sand.
WHY? Combining a small amount of buttermilk with the seasoned flour makes a wet dredging mixture. This method helps the coating stick to the chicken during frying and gives it a thicker, crunchier crust.

3. THOROUGHLY COAT THE CHICKEN: Remove the chicken from the brine and pat it dry. Coat the chicken evenly with the flour mixture, pressing on the flour. Gently shake off any excess flour and transfer the chicken to a wire rack set inside a rimmed baking sheet.
WHY? Gently pressing on the flour mixture helps it to adhere to the chicken. The thick, wet coating not only fries into a thick, supercrunchy crust, it also protects the chicken as it cooks.

4. HEAT THE OIL IN A LARGE DUTCH OVEN: Add the peanut oil to the Dutch oven until it measures ¾ inch deep. Heat the oil to 375 degrees and use a thermometer to check the temperature.
WHY? A pot with a capacity of at least 6 quarts allows all of the chicken to fry at once in a single layer. If the chicken is crowded, the pieces might stick together or to the bottom and will not brown properly, resulting in greasy fried chicken. We prefer the neutral flavor of peanut oil.

5. ADD THE CHICKEN AND FRY COVERED: Place the pieces skin side down in the hot oil, cover, and fry. Check and rearrange the pieces if some are browning faster. Maintain the oil at 315 degrees. Cover and continue frying until the chicken is deep golden brown on the first side.
WHY? Covering the pot traps the heat and steam to help the chicken cook through faster and stay moist. The cover also helps the oil to reheat and stay hot.

6. TURN THE CHICKEN PIECES AND FRY UNCOVERED: Once the chicken is golden brown on the first side, carefully turn the pieces over using tongs. Finish frying the chicken, uncovered, until the pieces are deep golden brown on the second side. Transfer chicken to a paper towel–lined platter and let it sit for 5 minutes.
WHY? Continuing to cook the chicken uncovered keeps the crust crisp. Letting the chicken sit allows any excess oil to drain away.

Fearless Frying

When done right, frying isn't difficult. It all comes down to the temperature of the oil. If the oil is too hot, the exterior of the food will burn before it cooks through. If it's not hot enough, the food won't release moisture and will fry up limp and soggy.

HAVE THE RIGHT THERMOMETER: A thermometer that can register high temperatures is essential. One that clips to the side of the pot, like a candy thermometer, saves you from dipping a thermometer in and out of a pot of hot oil.

USE A LARGE, HEAVY POT: A heavy pot or Dutch oven that is at least 6 quarts in capacity ensures plenty of room for the food to fry. You don't want the chicken pieces to stick to each other or to the bottom of the pot. A heavy-bottomed pot ensures even heating and helps to keep the oil hot.

USE PEANUT OIL: An oil with a high smoke point is a must for frying; we prefer the neutral flavor of peanut oil, but vegetable oil will also work. Fill the pot no more than halfway with oil. This will minimize any dangerous splattering once the food has been added.

KEEP THE OIL HOT: The temperature of the oil will drop a little when you first add the food to the pot, so we usually increase the heat right after adding the food to minimize the temperature change. If the oil splatters, wipe up as you go.

FRY IN BATCHES: Add food to the hot oil in small portions. Adding too much food at once will make the temperature drop too much and will turn out soggy—rather than crispy—fried food.

LET THE FRIED FOOD DRAIN: Let the finished food drain on paper towels to minimize greasiness.

REUSE THE OIL: Unless you have used it to fry fish, don't throw away your fry oil—you can use it three or four more times. To save oil for another use, let the oil cool to room temperature, then filter it through a strainer lined with two or three layers of cheesecloth or paper coffee filters to remove any bits of food. For short-term storage, store oils (leftover or new) in a cool, dark spot, since exposure to air and light makes oil turn rancid faster. But for long-term storage (beyond one month), the cooler the storage temperature, the better—we recommend the freezer.

side down in oil, cover, and fry for 4 minutes. Remove lid and lift chicken pieces to check for even browning; rearrange if browning is uneven. Adjust burner, if necessary, to maintain oil temperature of about 315 degrees. Cover and continue frying until deep golden brown on first side, 4 to 6 minutes.

5. Turn chicken pieces over using tongs. Continue to fry, uncovered, until chicken pieces are deep golden brown on second side, 6 to 8 minutes longer. Using tongs, transfer chicken to prepared platter; let sit for 5 minutes. Serve. (Fried chicken can be refrigerated for up to 1 day; reheat on wire rack in 400-degree oven for 10 to 15 minutes.)

Batter Fried Chicken

SERVES 4 TO 6   **TOTAL TIME** 1 HOUR 25 MINUTES

✔ **WHY THIS RECIPE WORKS:** The old-fashioned method of batter-fried chicken calls for dipping chicken parts in a batter not unlike pancake batter before frying. To keep the chicken moist, we brined it first. To ensure a crisp crust, we replaced the milk in our initial batters with plain old water. With milk, the sugars in the milk solids browned too fast and produced a soft crust. Using equal parts cornstarch and flour in the batter also helped ensure a crisp crust on the chicken. Adding baking powder to the batter added lift and lightness and prevented the coating from tasting doughy. You will need at least a 6-quart Dutch oven for this recipe.

	Salt
½	cup sugar
4	pounds bone-in chicken pieces (split breasts cut in half crosswise, drumsticks, and/or thighs), trimmed
1	cup all-purpose flour
1	cup cornstarch
5	teaspoons pepper
2	teaspoons baking powder
1	teaspoon paprika
½	teaspoon cayenne pepper
1¾	cups cold water
3	quarts peanut or vegetable oil

1. Dissolve ½ cup salt and sugar in 2 quarts cold water in large container. Add chicken, cover, and refrigerate for 30 minutes to 1 hour.

2. Whisk flour, cornstarch, pepper, baking powder, paprika, cayenne, and 1 teaspoon salt together in large bowl. Whisk in water until smooth; refrigerate until needed.

3. Add oil to large Dutch oven to measure 2 inches deep and heat over medium-high heat to 350 degrees. Remove chicken from brine and pat dry with paper towels. Remove batter from refrigerator and whisk to recombine. Set wire rack in rimmed baking sheet.

4. Add half of chicken to batter and coat thoroughly. Transfer chicken to hot oil, letting excess batter drip back into bowl. Fry chicken, adjusting burner as needed to maintain oil temperature between 300 and 325 degrees, until deep golden brown, breasts register 160 degrees, and thighs/drumsticks register 175 degrees, 12 to 15 minutes.

Making Batter Fried Chicken

1. BRINE CHICKEN: To prevent chicken meat from drying out while frying in hot oil, soak it in salt-sugar solution for 30 minutes to 1 hour.

2. MAKE BATTER: Make thin batter by whisking water, flour, baking powder, spices, and cornstarch together.

3. COAT CHICKEN: Dip chicken in batter to coat, then, to avoid doughy coating, let excess batter drip back into bowl before placing chicken in hot oil.

4. FRY IN BATCHES: To prevent chicken pieces from sticking together while they fry, don't crowd pot. Fry chicken in 2 batches.

5. Transfer fried chicken to prepared wire rack and let drain. Return oil to 350 degrees and repeat with remaining chicken. Serve. (Fried chicken can be refrigerated for up to 1 day; reheat on wire rack in 400-degree oven for 10 to 15 minutes.)

VARIATION

Honey Fried Chicken

If making this recipe ahead of time, be sure to toss the reheated chicken with the honey mixture just before serving.

Before serving, whisk 1 cup honey and 4 teaspoons hot sauce together in large bowl and microwave until hot, about 1½ minutes. Add fried chicken pieces to honey mixture, 1 at a time, and turn to coat.

Nashville Hot Fried Chicken

SERVES 4 TO 6   **TOTAL TIME** 1 HOUR 25 MINUTES

✔ **WHY THIS RECIPE WORKS:** Arriving at the correct heat level for our Nashville Hot Fried Chicken was harder than we anticipated. We created a spicy exterior to the chicken by "blooming" the spices (cooking them in oil for a short period) to create a complex yet still lip-burning spicy flavor. To make the spiciness more than skin deep, we added a healthy amount of hot sauce to our brine to inject flaming zest into the chicken. Most Nashville hot fried chicken recipes called for a bit of fiery cayenne pepper; we used a whole tablespoon. To ensure that the exterior doesn't burn before the inside cooks through, keep the oil between 300 and 325 degrees while the chicken is frying. Chicken quarters take longer to cook than smaller pieces. The pot is uncovered, so you can keep a close eye on things. You will need at least a 6-quart Dutch oven for this recipe. Serve on white bread with pickles.

½ cup hot sauce
Salt
½ cup plus ½ teaspoon sugar
1 (3½- to 4-pound) whole chicken, giblets discarded, quartered
3 quarts plus 3 tablespoons peanut or vegetable oil
1 tablespoon cayenne pepper
½ teaspoon paprika
¼ teaspoon garlic powder
2 cups all-purpose flour
½ teaspoon pepper

1. Whisk hot sauce, ½ cup salt, and ½ cup sugar into 2 quarts water in large bowl to dissolve. Add chicken, cover, and refrigerate for 30 minutes to 1 hour.

2. Meanwhile, heat 3 tablespoons oil in small saucepan over medium heat until shimmering. Add cayenne, paprika, garlic powder, ½ teaspoon salt, and remaining ½ teaspoon sugar and cook until fragrant, about 30 seconds; transfer to small bowl and set aside. In large bowl, combine flour, ½ teaspoon salt, and pepper.

3. Remove chicken from brine and leave wet. Working with 2 pieces chicken at a time, coat thoroughly with flour mixture, shaking off excess; transfer to wire rack. (Do not discard seasoned flour.)

4. Adjust oven rack to middle position and heat oven to 200 degrees. Heat remaining 3 quarts oil in large Dutch oven over medium-high heat to 350 degrees. Coat chicken with flour mixture again, pressing gently to adhere. Fry half of chicken, adjusting burner as necessary to maintain oil temperature between 300 and 325 degrees, until deep golden brown and white meat registers 160 degrees and dark meat registers 175 degrees, 20 to 25 minutes.

5. Transfer chicken to clean wire rack set inside rimmed baking sheet and keep warm in oven. Return oil to 350 degrees and repeat with remaining chicken. (Fried chicken can be refrigerated for up to 1 day; before continuing, reheat on wire rack in 400-degree oven for 10 to 15 minutes.)

6. Stir spicy oil mixture to recombine and brush evenly over fried chicken. Serve.

VARIATION

Nashville Extra-Hot Fried Chicken

Increase cayenne pepper to 3½ tablespoons and sugar to ¾ teaspoon in step 2.

Making Nashville Fried Chicken

For a superspicy kick, the fried chicken is brushed with a spiced oil mixture just before serving.

For lighter "fried" chicken, we remove the skin, coat the chicken with seasoned cornflakes, and bake it on a wire rack.

Oven-Fried Chicken

SERVES 4   **TOTAL TIME** 1 HOUR

WHY THIS RECIPE WORKS: The first thing that comes to mind when we think of fried chicken is the shatteringly crisp, ultracrunchy coating. But one serving of this American classic can weigh in at over 700 calories and 40 grams of fat. To lighten this dish, we ditched the deep-fryer and turned to the oven instead. But would we still be able to get that same crunchy, craggy, golden exterior? After removing the fatty skin from our chicken breasts, we tried a number of potential coatings, including everything from homemade bread crumbs and Melba toast crumbs to crushed potato and pita chips. Finally, we hit on cornflakes, which stayed crunchy and didn't become soggy the way some of the other coatings did. Garlic powder, cayenne pepper, and poultry seasoning (which adds several spices with just one ingredient) added flavor to the mild cereal, while buttermilk, whisked together with egg whites, gave our chicken that distinctive buttermilk tang without racking up the fat grams. After coating the sides and tops of the chicken breasts, we baked them in a superhot oven on a wire rack set inside a baking sheet—elevating the chicken allowed the hot air to circulate underneath so it cooked through evenly. Spraying the coated chicken with vegetable oil spray before baking helped the cornflakes become ultracrisp without adding much in the way of fat or calories. To crush the cornflakes, place them inside a zipper-lock bag and use a rolling pin or the bottom of a large skillet to break them into fine crumbs.

Vegetable oil spray
½ cup all-purpose flour
4 large egg whites
½ cup buttermilk
1½ teaspoons Dijon mustard
3 cups (3 ounces) cornflakes, finely crushed
1 tablespoon vegetable oil
¼ teaspoon garlic powder
Salt and pepper
⅛ teaspoon poultry seasoning
Pinch cayenne pepper
4 (10- to 12-ounce) bone-in split chicken breasts, skin removed, trimmed, and cut in half crosswise

1. Adjust oven rack to upper-middle position and heat oven to 425 degrees. Line rimmed baking sheet with aluminum foil, top with wire rack, and spray rack with oil spray. Spread flour into shallow dish. In second shallow dish, whisk egg whites until foamy, then whisk in buttermilk and mustard. In third shallow dish, combine cornflakes, oil, garlic powder, ½ teaspoon salt, ¼ teaspoon pepper, poultry seasoning, and cayenne.

2. Pat chicken dry with paper towels and season with salt and pepper. Working with 1 piece at a time and coating top and sides only, dredge chicken in flour, dip in egg white mixture, then coat with cornflake mixture, pressing gently to adhere; lay on prepared wire rack with uncoated side of chicken facing down.

3. Spray chicken with oil spray. Bake until crumbs are golden and chicken registers 160 degrees, about 35 minutes. Serve.

Weeknight Chicken Cacciatore

SERVES 4   **TOTAL TIME** 1 HOUR 10 MINUTES

✔ **WHY THIS RECIPE WORKS:** To turn a braised dish of bone-in chicken parts into a quick weeknight meal, we called on boneless, skinless chicken breasts. Browning them, along with meaty portobello mushrooms, created flavorful fond. Onions, red bell pepper, and plenty of garlic and fresh herbs came next, and deglazing the pan with red wine added even more depth. We finished cooking the chicken in the bubbling sauce (rounded out with chicken broth and diced tomatoes) to let all the flavors blend.

4 (6- to 8-ounce) boneless, skinless chicken breasts, trimmed and halved crosswise
Salt and pepper
3 tablespoons olive oil
1 pound portobello mushroom caps, gills removed, caps halved and sliced thin

Making Oven-Fried Chicken

1. CRUSH CORNFLAKES: To grind cornflakes into small pieces appropriate for coating chicken, place in zipper-lock bag and crush with rolling pin (or bottom of large skillet).

2. COAT TOP AND SIDES ONLY: Coat chicken only on top and sides to prevent bottom from getting soggy.

3. BAKE ON RACK: Bake chicken on wire rack to help it cook through more evenly. Spray wire rack with oil spray to prevent chicken from sticking.

4. TAKE TEMPERATURE: Do not overbake chicken or else it will taste very dry. Chicken is fully cooked when it registers 160 degrees.

1 pound onions, halved and sliced thin

1 red bell pepper, stemmed, seeded, and chopped

6 garlic cloves, minced

2 tablespoons tomato paste

2 teaspoons minced fresh rosemary

¼ teaspoon red pepper flakes

½ cup dry red wine

1 (14.5-ounce) can diced tomatoes

¾ cup chicken broth

1. Pat chicken dry with paper towels and season with salt and pepper. Heat 1 tablespoon oil in 12-inch nonstick skillet over medium-high heat until just smoking. Brown chicken lightly on all sides, about 5 minutes; transfer to plate.

2. Heat 1 tablespoon oil in now-empty skillet over medium-high heat until shimmering. Add mushrooms and ½ teaspoon salt and cook until well browned, 5 to 7 minutes; transfer to plate. Heat remaining 1 tablespoon oil in now-empty skillet over medium-high heat until shimmering. Add onions, bell pepper, and ½ teaspoon salt and cook until beginning to brown, 5 to 7 minutes.

3. Stir in garlic, tomato paste, rosemary, and pepper flakes and cook until fragrant, about 30 seconds. Stir in wine and any accumulated chicken juices, scraping up any browned bits, and simmer until reduced by half, about 1 minute. Add tomatoes and their juice. Stir in broth and bring to boil. Nestle chicken and mushrooms into skillet. Reduce heat to medium-low, cover, and simmer until chicken registers 160 degrees, about 10 minutes, flipping chicken halfway through cooking.

4. Transfer chicken to platter, tent loosely with aluminum foil, and let rest for 5 minutes. Continue to simmer sauce until slightly thickened, 3 to 5 minutes longer. Season sauce with salt and pepper to taste, spoon sauce over chicken, and serve.

Removing Portobello Gills

To remove gills from underside of portobello cap, scrape them off with spoon.

Our chicken Provençal starts with meaty bone-in chicken thighs, which are better suited to braising than chicken breasts.

Chicken Provençal

SERVES 4 TO 6   **TOTAL TIME** 2 HOURS 30 MINUTES

✔ **WHY THIS RECIPE WORKS:** Chicken Provençal represents the best of rustic peasant food—bone-in chicken simmered all day in a tomatoey, garlicky herb broth flavorful enough to mop up with crusty bread. We started with bone-in chicken thighs and browned them in oil to develop rich flavor and create fond. To keep the sauce from becoming greasy, we poured off most of the fat left behind before sautéing the mushrooms and onion. Diced tomatoes, white wine, and chicken broth also went into the sauce before we braised the browned chicken; minced anchovy made the dish taste richer and fuller. We used fresh parsley in addition to the traditional herbes de Provence, and we finished with grated lemon zest and pitted niçoise olives for a chicken Provençal with authentic, long-simmered flavor. This dish is often served with rice or slices of crusty bread, but soft polenta is also a good accompaniment.

12 (5- to 7-ounce) bone-in chicken thighs, trimmed
    Salt and pepper
 1 tablespoon vegetable oil
 1 pound white mushrooms, trimmed, halved if
    small or medium, quartered if large
 2 onions, chopped fine
 6 garlic cloves, minced
 1 anchovy fillet, rinsed and minced
 1 teaspoon herbes de Provence
 2 tablespoons all-purpose flour
 2 tablespoons tomato paste
 ⅓ cup dry white wine
2½ cups chicken broth
 1 (14.5-ounce) can diced tomatoes, drained
 2 bay leaves
 ½ cup niçoise olives, pitted and chopped
 ¼ cup minced fresh parsley
 ½ teaspoon grated lemon zest

1. Adjust oven rack to lower-middle position and heat oven to 300 degrees. Pat chicken dry with paper towels and season with salt and pepper. Heat oil in Dutch oven over medium-high heat until just smoking. Brown half of chicken well on both sides, about 10 minutes; transfer to plate. Pour off all but 1 tablespoon fat left in pot and repeat with remaining chicken; transfer to plate.

2. Pour off all but 1 tablespoon fat left in pot and stir in mushrooms, onions, and ¼ teaspoon salt. Cover and cook over medium heat, stirring often, until mushrooms have released their liquid, about 5 minutes. Uncover and cook, stirring often, until mushrooms are dry and browned, about 10 minutes.

3. Stir in garlic, anchovy, and herbes de Provence and cook until fragrant, about 30 seconds. Stir in flour and tomato paste and cook for 1 minute. Stir in wine, scraping up any browned bits. Gradually stir in broth, smoothing out any lumps. Stir in tomatoes and bay leaves.

4. Remove and discard skin from chicken. Nestle chicken, with any accumulated juices, into pot. Increase heat to high and bring to simmer. Cover, transfer pot to oven, and cook until chicken offers little resistance when poked with tip of paring knife but still clings to bones, about 1¼ hours.

5. Remove pot from oven and discard bay leaves. Stir in olives, cover, and let sit for 5 minutes. Stir in parsley and lemon zest. Season with salt and pepper to taste and serve. (Chicken can be refrigerated for up to 2 days; add water as needed when reheating to adjust consistency.)

Making Chicken Provençal

1. BROWN CHICKEN: Working in batches, brown chicken well on both sides, about 10 minutes.

2. STEAM THEN BROWN MUSHROOMS: Cook mushrooms, onions, and salt covered until mushrooms have released their liquid. Uncover and cook until mushrooms are dry and browned.

3. REMOVE SKIN: Remove and discard browned skin from chicken. Nestle chicken, with any accumulated juices, into pot.

4. COOK IN OVEN: Cover pot, transfer to oven, and cook until chicken offers little resistance when poked with tip of paring knife but still clings to bones, about 1¼ hours.

Quick Chicken Mole

SERVES 4   TOTAL TIME 30 MINUTES   **FAST**

✓ **WHY THIS RECIPE WORKS:** Mole in 30 minutes? Absolutely. Of course, we couldn't make a traditional mole using chocolate, dried fruits, nuts, and multiple types of chiles. But we found we could assemble a flavorful one in a few minutes thanks to chili powder, cocoa powder, and peanut butter—to name a few of our shortcut ingredients—and the help of the microwave and the blender. As for the chicken, there's no need to brown it—it's simply poached in this mixture and cooks in just 10 minutes. Toasted sesame seeds are also a nice garnish in this dish. Serve with rice.

Our quick chicken mole relies on chili powder, cocoa powder, peanut butter, and the speed of the microwave.

1 onion, chopped
1 tablespoon vegetable oil
⅓ cup raisins
2 tablespoons chili powder
2 tablespoons unsweetened cocoa powder
    Salt and pepper
1½ cups chicken broth
1 (14.5-ounce) can diced tomatoes, drained
2 tablespoons peanut butter
4 (6- to 8-ounce) boneless, skinless chicken breasts, trimmed
¼ cup minced fresh cilantro

1. Microwave onion, oil, raisins, chili powder, cocoa, and ½ teaspoon salt in bowl, stirring occasionally, until onion is softened, about 3 minutes. Process onion mixture, broth, tomatoes, and peanut butter in blender until smooth, about 1 minute. Transfer puree to 12-inch skillet.

2. Pound thicker ends of breasts as needed, then pat dry with paper towels and season with salt and pepper. Add chicken to skillet, cover, and simmer gently over medium

heat until chicken registers 160 degrees and sauce is slightly thickened, about 10 minutes. Season with salt and pepper to taste. Sprinkle with cilantro and serve.

Filipino Chicken Adobo

SERVES 4   **TOTAL TIME** 1 HOUR 40 MINUTES

WHY THIS RECIPE WORKS: Adobo is the national dish of the Philippines, and chicken adobo is among the most popular. The dish consists of chicken simmered in a mixture of vinegar, soy sauce, garlic, bay leaves, and black pepper. The problem with most recipes we found was that they were aggressively tart and salty. Our secret to taming both of these elements was coconut milk. The coconut milk's richness tempered the bracing acidity of the vinegar and subdued the briny soy sauce, bringing the sauce into balance. Light coconut milk can be substituted for regular coconut milk. Serve this dish over rice.

8 (5- to 7-ounce) bone-in chicken thighs, trimmed
⅓ cup soy sauce
1 (13.5-ounce) can coconut milk
¾ cup cider vinegar
8 garlic cloves, peeled
4 bay leaves
2 teaspoons pepper
1 scallion, sliced thin

1. Toss chicken with soy sauce in large bowl, cover, and refrigerate for 30 minutes to 1 hour.

2. Remove chicken from soy sauce, allowing excess to drip back into bowl. Transfer chicken, skin side down, to 12-inch nonstick skillet; set aside soy sauce. Place skillet over medium-high heat and cook until chicken skin is browned, 7 to 10 minutes. Meanwhile, whisk coconut milk, vinegar, garlic, bay leaves, and pepper into soy sauce.

3. Transfer chicken to plate and discard fat left in skillet. Return chicken to skillet, skin side down, add coconut milk mixture, and bring to boil. Reduce heat to medium-low and simmer, uncovered, for 20 minutes.

4. Flip chicken skin side up and continue to simmer, uncovered, until chicken registers 175 degrees, about 15 minutes. Transfer chicken to platter and tent with aluminum foil.

5. Discard bay leaves and skim fat from surface of sauce. Return skillet to medium-high heat and cook until sauce is thickened, 5 to 7 minutes. Pour sauce over chicken, sprinkle with scallion, and serve.

Moroccan Chicken with Green Olives

SERVES 4   **TOTAL TIME** 45 MINUTES **FAST**

✓ **WHY THIS RECIPE WORKS:** Traditional North African tagines (aromatic braises of meat, vegetables, and fruits) are labor-intensive and use hard-to-find ingredients. We came up with a few timesaving tricks for this version made with chicken, lemon, and olives. We swapped out bone-in chicken thighs (the standard choice) for quicker-cooking boneless thighs, and cut them in half to shorten their cooking time even more. Instead of calling for a laundry list of spices, we used garam masala, a prepared Indian spice mix, and gave it a boost with paprika. For more information on garam masala, see page 149. Look for large, pitted green olives at the olive bar in the supermarket. Pimento-stuffed olives can be substituted for the large green olives in a pinch. Serve with rice or couscous.

8   (3-ounce) boneless, skinless chicken thighs, trimmed and halved crosswise
    Salt and pepper
3   tablespoons olive oil
1   onion, halved and sliced thin
3   (4-inch) strips lemon zest plus 1 tablespoon juice
4   garlic cloves, minced
1½ teaspoons garam masala
1   teaspoon paprika
1   cup chicken broth
1   cup pitted large green olives, quartered
3   tablespoons minced fresh cilantro

1. Pat chicken dry with paper towels and season with salt and pepper. Heat 1 tablespoon oil in 12-inch skillet over medium-high heat until just smoking. Brown half of chicken lightly on one side, about 2 minutes; transfer to plate. Repeat with 1 tablespoon oil and remaining chicken; transfer to plate.

2. Add remaining 1 tablespoon oil and onion to now-empty skillet and cook over medium heat until softened, about 5 minutes. Stir in lemon zest, garlic, garam masala, and paprika and cook until fragrant, about 30 seconds. Stir in broth and olives, scraping up any browned bits.

3. Add browned chicken and any accumulated juices, cover, and simmer gently until chicken is very tender, about 15 minutes. Transfer chicken to platter and tent with aluminum foil.

4. Continue to simmer sauce until slightly thickened, about 5 minutes. Stir in cilantro and lemon juice and season with salt and pepper to taste. Pour sauce over chicken. Serve.

For fast and flavorful Morroccan chicken, we brown boneless thighs, use garam masala and paprika, and add green olives.

Chicken Pomodoro

SERVES 4   **TOTAL TIME** 45 MINUTES **FAST**

✓ **WHY THIS RECIPE WORKS:** Not every Italian dish requires hours of simmering and painstaking prep work. For a deeply flavored tomato sauce without the need for lengthy simmering, we started with a hefty dose of sautéed onion, garlic, and oregano, as well as a few red pepper flakes for spice. Heavy cream added a pleasant richness to the sauce, and fresh basil brought out the bright flavor of the tomatoes. Gently simmering the chicken in the creamy tomato sauce enriched the flavor of both the sauce and the chicken. While certain dried herbs like oregano work just as well as fresh, delicate herbs like basil are best used fresh. Be careful not to overcook the chicken in step 3 or it will taste dry. Serve over pasta, egg noodles, or rice.

4 (6- to 8-ounce) boneless, skinless chicken breasts, trimmed
 Salt and pepper
2 tablespoons olive oil
1 onion, chopped fine
4 garlic cloves, minced
1 tablespoon minced fresh oregano or 1 teaspoon dried
¼ teaspoon red pepper flakes
1 (14.5-ounce) can diced tomatoes
⅓ cup heavy cream
¼ cup chopped fresh basil

1. Pound thicker ends of breasts as needed, then pat dry with paper towels and season with salt and pepper. Heat 1 tablespoon oil in 12-inch skillet over medium-high heat until just smoking. Brown chicken lightly on both sides, about 5 minutes; transfer to plate.

2. Add remaining 1 tablespoon oil and onion to now-empty skillet and cook over medium heat until softened, about 5 minutes. Stir in garlic, oregano, and pepper flakes and cook until fragrant, about 30 seconds. Stir in tomatoes and their juice, cream, and ¼ teaspoon salt.

3. Add browned chicken and any accumulated juices, cover, and simmer gently until chicken registers 160 degrees, about 10 minutes. Transfer chicken to platter and tent with aluminum foil.

4. Continue to simmer sauce until slightly thickened, about 5 minutes. Stir in basil and season with salt and pepper to taste. Pour sauce over chicken and serve.

Lighter Chicken and Dumplings

SERVES 6   TOTAL TIME 2 HOURS

✔ **WHY THIS RECIPE WORKS:** The best chicken and dumplings boast dumplings as airy as drop biscuits in a broth full of clean, concentrated chicken flavor. We found that browning chicken thighs and then adding store-bought chicken broth produced the most flavorful stew base. To give our broth body, we added chicken wings to the pot—they readily gave up their collagen, giving the stew a velvety texture. For a light but sturdy dumpling recipe with good flavor, we came up with a formula that employed buttermilk for flavor and swapped in baking soda for baking powder. Wrapping the lid of the Dutch oven in a dish towel prevented moisture from saturating our light-as-air dumplings. We strongly recommend buttermilk for the dumplings, but it's acceptable to substitute ½ cup plain yogurt thinned with ¼ cup milk. If you want to include white meat (and don't mind losing a bit of flavor in the process), replace 2 chicken thighs with two 8-ounce boneless, skinless chicken breasts; brown the chicken breasts along with the thighs and remove them from the stew once they register 160 degrees, 20 to 30 minutes. The collagen in the wings helps thicken the stew; do not omit or substitute. Since the wings yield only about 1 cup of meat, using their meat is optional.

STEW
2½ pounds bone-in chicken thighs, trimmed
 Salt and pepper
2 teaspoons vegetable oil

Making Chicken and Dumplings

1. USE WINGS AND THIGHS: Add 2½ pounds browned chicken thighs and 1 pound chicken wings to stew. After stew simmers, remove and shred meat.

2. MAKE DUMPLINGS WITH EGG WHITE: Combine dry ingredients in bowl. Combine chilled buttermilk, melted butter, and egg white in separate bowl, then stir into dry ingredients.

3. BRING TO SIMMER: After adding shredded meat, return stew to simmer and then portion dumplings over top. If stew is not simmering, dumplings may break apart and not cook through evenly.

4. COVER AND COOK: Wrap lid of Dutch oven with clean dish towel and simmer gently until dumplings are cooked through. Towel will prevent condensation from making dumplings soggy.

2 small onions, chopped fine

2 carrots, peeled and cut into ¾-inch pieces

1 celery rib, chopped fine

¼ cup dry sherry

6 cups chicken broth

1 teaspoon minced fresh thyme

1 pound chicken wings

¼ cup minced fresh parsley

DUMPLINGS

2 cups (10 ounces) all-purpose flour

1 teaspoon sugar

1 teaspoon salt

½ teaspoon baking soda

¾ cup buttermilk, chilled

4 tablespoons unsalted butter, melted and hot

1 large egg white

1. FOR THE STEW: Pat chicken thighs dry with paper towels and season with salt and pepper. Heat oil in Dutch oven over medium-high heat until shimmering. Brown chicken thighs well on both sides, 10 to 14 minutes; transfer to plate.

2. Pour off all but 1 teaspoon fat left in pot and add onions, carrots, and celery. Cook vegetables, stirring often, until well browned, 7 to 9 minutes. Stir in sherry, scraping up any browned bits. Add broth, thyme, chicken wings, and chicken thighs and any accumulated juices. Bring to simmer, cover, and cook until thigh meat offers no resistance when poked with tip of paring knife but still clings to bones, 45 to 55 minutes.

3. Remove pot from heat. Transfer chicken to cutting board, let cool slightly, then shred into 1-inch pieces, discarding skin and bones. Meanwhile, let broth settle for 5 minutes, then skim fat from surface. Stir shredded meat into pot. (Stew can be refrigerated for up to 2 days.)

4. FOR THE DUMPLINGS: Whisk flour, sugar, salt, and baking soda together in large bowl. In separate bowl, stir chilled buttermilk and melted butter together until butter forms small clumps, then whisk in egg white. Stir buttermilk mixture into flour mixture with rubber spatula until just incorporated.

5. Return stew to simmer over medium-low heat, stir in parsley, and season with salt and pepper to taste. Using greased tablespoon measure, scoop level amount of dumpling batter over top of stew, spacing about ¼ inch apart (about 24 dumplings). Wrap lid of Dutch oven with clean dish towel (keep towel away from heat source), and cover pot. Simmer gently until dumplings have doubled in size and toothpick inserted into center comes out clean, 13 to 16 minutes. Serve.

Our easy technique for roasted turkey breast uses a dual oven temperature approach to deliver crisp skin and moist meat.

Easy Roast Turkey Breast

SERVES 8 TO 10   **TOTAL TIME** 2 HOURS 10 MINUTES

✔ **WHY THIS RECIPE WORKS:** Achieving crisp skin without drying out the delicate white meat is easier said than done when roasting a whole turkey breast. Brining was a good first step, flavoring the mild breast meat and helping it hold moisture (see page 158 for brining instructions). Loosening the skin and rubbing the meat underneath with softened butter promoted even browning and crispier skin. But the real challenge was determining the best roasting technique. After testing a range of oven temperatures, we determined that a dual-temperature approach was necessary: Starting the turkey breast in a 425-degree oven jump-started the browning process, while reducing the heat to 325 degrees for the remainder of the time allowed the meat to finish cooking gently. Many supermarkets are now selling "hotel-cut" turkey breasts, which still have the wings and rib cage attached. If this is the only type of breast you can find, you will need to remove the wings and cut away the rib cage with kitchen shears before proceeding with the recipe. If using a self-basting turkey (such as a frozen Butterball) or a kosher turkey, do not brine. If brining the turkey, do not season the butter in step 1, and do not season the turkey with salt in step 2.

- 4 **tablespoons unsalted butter, softened**
  Salt and pepper
- 1 **(6- to 7-pound) whole bone-in turkey breast, trimmed, brined if desired**

1. Adjust oven rack to middle position and heat oven to 425 degrees. Set V-rack inside roasting pan and spray with vegetable oil spray. Combine butter, 1 teaspoon salt, and ¼ teaspoon pepper in bowl.

2. Pat turkey dry with paper towels and season with salt and pepper. Use your fingers to gently loosen center portion of skin covering each breast. Using spoon, place butter mixture underneath skin over center of each chicken breast. Gently press on skin to spread out butter.

3. Place turkey, skin side up, on prepared V-rack and add 1 cup water to pan. Roast turkey for 30 minutes.

4. Reduce oven temperature to 325 degrees and continue to roast until turkey registers 160 degrees, about 1 hour longer.

5. Transfer turkey to carving board and let rest for 20 minutes. Carve turkey. Serve.

VARIATIONS

Easy Roast Turkey Breast with Lemon and Thyme

Add 3 minced garlic cloves, 2 tablespoons minced fresh thyme, and 1 teaspoon grated lemon zest to butter mixture.

Easy Roast Turkey Breast with Orange and Rosemary

Add 3 minced garlic cloves, 1 tablespoon minced fresh rosemary, 1 teaspoon grated orange zest, and ¼ teaspoon red pepper flakes to butter mixture.

Easy Roast Turkey Breast with Southwestern Flavors

Add 3 minced garlic cloves, 1 tablespoon minced fresh oregano, 2 teaspoons ground cumin, 2 teaspoons chili powder, ¾ teaspoon cocoa powder, and ½ teaspoon cayenne pepper to butter mixture.

Classic Roast Turkey

SERVES 10 TO 22   **TOTAL TIME** 3 TO 4½ HOURS (PLUS BRINING TIME)

✔ **WHY THIS RECIPE WORKS:** If you have time and can plan ahead, we recommend brining the turkey, as this further enhances the flavor and texture (see page 158 for instructions on brining). To ensure even cooking, we first roasted the bird breast side down, then flipped it breast side up to finish. Or you can skip this step and simply roast the turkey breast side up for the entire time and protect the breast with a piece of foil if it begins to overbrown. If using a disposable roasting pan, support it underneath with a rimmed baking sheet. Depending on the size of the turkey, total roasting time will vary from 2 to 3½ hours. If using a self-basting turkey (such as a frozen Butterball) or a kosher turkey, do not brine. If brining the turkey, do not season with salt in step 3. Consider saving the bones and a little of the meat to make Turkey Carcass Soup (page 94).

- 1 **(12- to 22-pound) turkey, fully thawed if frozen, brined if desired, neck, giblets, and tailpiece removed and reserved for gravy (optional)**
- 2 **onions, chopped coarse**
- 2 **carrots, peeled and chopped coarse**
- 2 **ribs celery, chopped coarse**
- 2 **tablespoons minced fresh thyme or 2 teaspoons dried**
- 4 **tablespoons unsalted butter, melted**
  Salt and pepper
- 1 **cup chicken broth, as needed**

NOTES FROM THE TEST KITCHEN

Thawing a Frozen Turkey

What's the best way to thaw a frozen turkey? Defrost the turkey in the refrigerator, calculating one day of defrosting for every 4 pounds of turkey. Say you're cooking a 12-pound turkey. The frozen bird should be placed in the refrigerator on Monday so that it's defrosted and ready to cook for Thanksgiving Day. If you plan on brining your bird the night before, start thawing that 12-pound bird on Sunday.

What if you forget to thaw your turkey ahead of time? Don't panic. You can still save the situation and quick-thaw the turkey in a large bucket with cold tap water. Place the turkey (still in its original wrapper) in the bucket and let it thaw for 30 minutes per pound; a 12-pound bird, for example, would take 6 to 8 hours. Change the cold water every half-hour to guard against bacteria growth.

Cooking a holiday turkey can strike fear into even the most seasoned cook. The challenge is the turkey itself. The white meat over-cooks easily and can turn out dry, but the dark meat has the opposite problem; it has a lot of fat and connective tissue and bene-fits from more cooking. Our foolproof go-to solution is to brine the turkey (soak it in salt water) to produce a moist, well-seasoned bird. Brining ensures that the white meat doesn't dry out in the oven while waiting for the dark meat to be done.

1. IF POSSIBLE, BRINE THE TURKEY: You'll need a container large enough to hold the turkey and the salted water. Submerge the turkey, cover, and refrigerate or store in a cool spot at least 6 hours. **WHY?** Brining adds moisture and flavor to the meat and helps it to hold on to more of its natural juices, even if the white meat is overcooked.

2. PAT THE TURKEY DRY AND TIE THE LEGS TOGETHER: Remove the turkey from the brine and pat it dry, inside and out, with paper towels. Trim the tailpiece, tie the legs together, and tuck the wings. **WHY?** Patting the turkey dry prevents soggy skin. Tying the legs prevents them from splaying open, which could make them cook unevenly.

3. SPREAD THE CHOPPED VEGETABLES IN THE ROASTING PAN: Spread the onions, carrots, celery, and thyme in the pan. **WHY?** The vegetables soak up the turkey drippings and prevent them from burning. The cooked vegetables can be used to make gravy.

4. LINE THE V-RACK WITH FOIL: Poke several holes in the foil. Set the rack in the roasting pan and spray the foil with vegetable oil spray. **WHY?** A V-rack elevates the bird, ensuring even cooking of the meat and crisping of the skin. Cutting holes in the foil lets the turkey juices drip down into the roasting pan where they can be used for gravy.

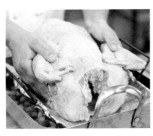

5. START THE TURKEY BREAST SIDE DOWN: Brush the turkey breast with half of the melted butter and season it with salt and pepper. Place the turkey, breast side down, on the V-rack. Brush the back of the turkey with the rest of the melted butter and season. **WHY?** Starting the turkey breast side down promotes browning and allows the dark meat to get a head start. Brushing the turkey with melted butter at the outset also contributes to browning.

6. ROAST, THEN TURN THE TURKEY OVER: After the turkey has roasted for 1 hour, gently tip the turkey so that any accumulated juices in the cavity run into the pan. Use clean dish towels or wads of paper towels to firmly grasp the turkey at each end and turn it breast side up on the rack. **WHY?** Turning the bird once during roasting gets the legs to cook faster. It also protects the delicate breast meat from overcooking.

7. LOWER THE OVEN TEMPERATURE AND CONTINUE ROASTING: Lower the oven temperature to 325 degrees. Continue to roast the turkey breast side up until the breast registers 160 degrees and the thighs register 175 degrees. **WHY?** The lower oven temperature allows the white meat to gently finish cooking without drying out. When taking the temperature, use the thickest part of the thigh and the breast.

8. LET THE TURKEY REST BEFORE CARVING: Transfer the turkey to a carving board and let it rest, uncovered, for 30 minutes before carving. You can use the turkey's resting time to make gravy. **WHY?** For a juicy turkey, be sure to let it rest for the full 30 minutes. Letting it rest allows the juices to redistrib-ute and reabsorb into the meat. The turkey stays plenty hot without foil; covering it will make the skin soggy.

Carving a turkey may happen only once or twice a year, but because the cut-up bird is usually on full display you want it to look good. Carving isn't difficult, but there is a definite way to approach it that will yield nicely portioned slices. Use a platter large enough to hold all the meat, and warm the platter prior to carving. If you like, you can line the platter with kale or another sturdy green for an attractive presentation. It is easiest to transfer the turkey to the platter as you carve; use the flat side of the knife. Keep the meat on the platter covered with foil as you work your way through the turkey. And be sure to let the roast turkey rest for 30 minutes before carving it. The resting time not only allows the juices to redistribute, it also makes carving easier. You can also use this technique for carving a whole roast chicken.

1. START WITH THE LEG QUARTERS:
Remove the kitchen twine used to hold the legs together. Start by slicing the turkey through the skin between the leg and the breast to expose the hip joint.
WHY? Removing the leg quarters first makes carving the breast much easier since this gets them out of the way.

2. REMOVE THE LEG QUARTERS: Pull the leg quarters away from the carcass. Separate the joint by gently pressing the leg out to the side and pushing up on the joint. Carefully cut through the joint.
WHY? After the initial cut, you'll run into bone. Rather than hacking through it, cut through the space created where you popped the joint out of the socket.

3. SEPARATE THE DRUMSTICKS FROM THE THIGHS: Cut through the joint that connects the drumstick to the thigh. Repeat on the second side. Slice the meat off of the drumsticks and thighs, leaving a bit of skin attached to each slice.
WHY? Leg quarters are rather large; smaller portions of dark meat (and white) mean everyone can enjoy some of each.

4. REMOVE THE WINGS: Pull the wings away from the carcass and carefully cut through the joint between the wing and the breast to remove the wings. Cut the wings in half for easier eating.
WHY? Removing the wings provides better access to the whole half of the breast meat. The wings can be added to the serving platter.

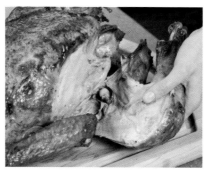

5. REMOVE THE BREAST MEAT: Cut down along 1 side following the curvature of the breastbone, pulling the breast meat away from the bone as you cut. Continue to cut and pry until the breast has been removed.
WHY? Carving the breast into serving pieces right off the carcass leaves the last few pieces looking ragged. It's tidier to carve the meat off in one piece first.

6. SLICE THE BREAST MEAT: Cut the breast meat crosswise into thin slices for serving.
WHY? Slicing the breast meat crosswise into smaller slices makes for attractive portions.

Roasting Times for an Unstuffed Turkey

The times below are guidelines, but you should gauge whether your turkey is done by checking when the breast registers 160 degrees and the thighs reach 175 degrees. It's true—a 22-pound bird takes only 3½ hours at the most.

RAW TURKEY WEIGHT	NUMBER OF SERVINGS	APPROXIMATE ROASTING TIME
12 to 14 pounds	10 to 12	2 to 2½ hours
15 to 17 pounds	14 to 16	2½ to 3 hours
18 to 22 pounds	20 to 22	3 to 3½ hours

1. Adjust oven rack to lowest position and heat oven to 425 degrees. Pat turkey dry with paper towels. Trim tailpiece, tie legs together, and tuck wings under bird. Chop neck and giblets into 1-inch pieces if using them for gravy.

2. Spread onions, carrots, celery, and thyme in large roasting pan. Line V-rack with heavy-duty aluminum foil and poke several holes in foil. Set rack inside roasting pan and spray foil with vegetable oil spray.

3. Brush breast side of turkey with half of butter and season with salt and pepper. Lay turkey in rack breast side down. Brush back of turkey with remaining butter and season with salt and pepper. Roast turkey for 1 hour.

4. Remove turkey from oven. Lower oven temperature to 325 degrees. Tip juice from cavity of turkey into pan. Flip turkey breast side up using clean dish towels or wads of paper towels. Continue to roast turkey until thickest portion of breast registers 160 degrees and thigh registers 175 degrees, about 1 to 2½ hours longer. (Add broth as needed to prevent drippings from burning.)

5. Tip turkey so that juice from cavity runs into roasting pan. Transfer turkey to carving board and let rest, uncovered, for 30 minutes. (Meanwhile, use roasted vegetables and drippings in pan to make gravy, if desired.) Carve and serve.

Classic Turkey Gravy

SERVES 12 TO 15   **TOTAL TIME** 2 HOURS 30 MINUTES

♥ **WHY THIS RECIPE WORKS:** We developed our turkey gravy to eliminate the rush once the turkey emerges from the oven. We simmered the neck, giblets, and tailpiece with onion, chicken broth, water, and herbs to build a rich and flavorful base for the gravy. We preferred the flavor and consistency of

Our turkey gravy can be made up to a day ahead of time then enriched with pan drippings while the bird rests.

a gravy made with a roux (flour and butter cooked to a rich brown) over a cornstarch-thickened gravy. In terms of timing, the broth is simmered with the roux while the bird is roasting, and then the roasted turkey drippings are stirred in just before serving. The reserved giblets can be added, if desired.

1 tablespoon vegetable oil
  Reserved turkey neck, giblets, and tailpiece
  (from Classic Roast Turkey, page 172)
1 onion, chopped
4 cups chicken broth
2 cups water
2 sprigs fresh thyme
8 sprigs fresh parsley
3 tablespoons unsalted butter
¼ cup all-purpose flour
1 cup dry white wine
  Salt and pepper

1. Heat oil in Dutch oven over medium heat until shimmering. Add neck, giblets, and tailpiece and cook until golden, about 5 minutes. Stir in onion and cook until softened, about

When you've taken the time to roast a whole turkey, you are going to want to make a flavorful gravy to go with it. The appeal of our turkey gravy recipe is that you can start it the day before and finish it with the pan drippings in the roasting pan on the stovetop while the bird is resting.

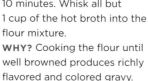

1. MAKE THE TURKEY BROTH: Brown the turkey parts, sauté the onion, then add chicken broth, water, and herbs and simmer for 30 minutes to make a flavorful broth.

WHY? The rich homemade turkey broth provides the base for the gravy. The broth can be prepared ahead of time, making it easier to finish the gravy once the turkey comes out of the oven.

2. STRAIN THE TURKEY BROTH: Strain the broth into a large container and reserve the giblets. The broth can be stored in the refrigerator for up to 1 day.

WHY? Straining the broth separates out the solids, allowing you to remove and discard the turkey neck and tailpiece. You can also remove and reserve the cooked giblets, if you plan to use them.

3. MAKE A DARK ROUX: Melt the butter in a large saucepan, add the flour, and cook, whisking constantly, until the flour is nutty brown and fragrant, about 10 minutes. Whisk all but 1 cup of the hot broth into the flour mixture.

WHY? Cooking the flour until well browned produces richly flavored and colored gravy. The roux is also the thickener.

4. SIMMER THE GRAVY UNTIL THICKENED: Bring the gravy to a boil, then continue to simmer the gravy until it is lightly thickened and very flavorful, about 30 minutes. Set it aside until the turkey is done.

WHY? Simmering the gravy deepens the flavor and thickens it. Simmering also takes away any floury taste.

5. PLACE THE ROASTING PAN ON THE STOVETOP: Once the turkey has been transferred to a carving board, discard the fat left in the pan, leaving the herbs and vegetables. Place pan over 2 burners of the stove set on medium-high heat.

WHY? The fond left behind in the roasting pan has important flavor that needs to be added to the gravy. Cooking this fond on the stovetop with some liquid makes it easy.

6. ADD THE WINE AND REDUCE AND ADD THE REMAINING BROTH: Add the wine to the pan of caramelized vegetables, scraping up any browned bits. Bring to a boil and cook until the wine is reduced by half. Add the remaining 1 cup broth and simmer for 15 minutes.

WHY? Adding the wine helps to loosen the fond in the pan. Reducing the liquid by boiling it briskly concentrates the flavors and drives off the raw alcohol flavor in the wine.

7. STRAIN THE PAN JUICES INTO THE GRAVY: Strain the pan juices into the saucepan of gravy, pressing on the vegetables.

WHY? Pressing on the vegetables extracts as much juice as possible as well as every last bit of flavor. Adding the defatted drippings from the pan further enriches the flavor of the gravy.

8. SEASON THE GRAVY TO TASTE: Add the reserved giblets to the gravy, if desired, and season the gravy with salt and pepper to taste.

WHY? Giblets add another layer of flavor to gravy, but not everyone likes them. Always taste for the final seasoning at the end because flavors become concentrated during cooking.

5 minutes. Reduce heat to low, cover, and cook until turkey parts and onion release their juices, about 15 minutes. Stir in broth, water, thyme, and parsley and bring to boil. Reduce heat to low and simmer, skimming as needed, until broth is rich and flavorful, about 30 minutes.

2. Strain broth into large container. If desired, reserve giblets; let cool slightly and chop fine. Refrigerate broth and giblets, separately, until needed, or for up to 1 day.

3. While turkey is roasting, bring broth to simmer in saucepan. In separate large saucepan, melt butter over medium-low heat. Add flour and cook, whisking constantly, until nutty brown and fragrant, 10 to 15 minutes. Vigorously whisk in all but 1 cup of hot broth. Bring to boil, then reduce to simmer and cook, stirring often, until gravy is lightly thickened and very flavorful, about 30 minutes; cover and set aside.

4. While roasted turkey rests on carving board, spoon out and discard as much fat as possible from roasting pan, leaving caramelized herbs and vegetables. Place pan over 2 burners set on medium-high heat. Add wine, scraping up any browned bits, and boil until reduced by half, about 5 minutes. Add remaining 1 cup broth and simmer for 15 minutes. Strain juices into saucepan of gravy, pressing to extract as much liquid as possible out of vegetables. Stir in reserved giblets, if using, and return to boil. Season with salt and pepper to taste and serve.

VARIATION

Classic Turkey Gravy for a Crowd
SERVES 16 TO 24

Using large Dutch oven to make gravy, increase chicken broth to 6 cups, water to 3 cups, butter to 5 tablespoons, flour to 6 tablespoons, and wine to 1½ cups.

Classic Bread Stuffing with Sage and Thyme
SERVES 12 TO 16   **TOTAL TIME** 2 HOURS 30 MINUTES

✔ **WHY THIS RECIPE WORKS:** Since a stuffed turkey takes longer to cook and often results in overcooked meat, we prefer to cook our stuffing outside the bird. Instead of oven drying in step 1, you can let bread stale overnight at room temperature. You can substitute three 14-ounce bags of plain dried bread cubes for the homemade cubes, but you'll need to increase the amount of chicken broth to 7 cups. This recipe can be halved and baked in a 13 by 9-inch baking dish for a smaller crowd.

3 **pounds hearty white sandwich bread, cut into ½-inch cubes**
12 **tablespoons unsalted butter**
4 **celery ribs, chopped fine**
2 **onions, chopped fine**
½ **cup minced fresh parsley**
3 **tablespoons minced fresh sage or 2 teaspoons dried**
3 **tablespoons minced fresh thyme or 1 teaspoon dried**
1 **tablespoon minced fresh marjoram or 1 teaspoon dried**
5 **cups chicken broth**
4 **large eggs, lightly beaten**
2 **teaspoons salt**
2 **teaspoons pepper**

1. Adjust oven racks to upper-middle and lower-middle positions and heat oven to 300 degrees. Grease 15 by 10-inch baking dish. Spread bread onto 2 rimmed baking sheets and bake, stirring occasionally, until bread is dry, 45 to 60 minutes. Let bread cool completely on sheets, about 30 minutes.

2. Adjust oven rack to middle position and heat oven to 400 degrees. Melt butter in 12-inch skillet over medium-high heat. Add celery and onions and cook until softened, about 10 minutes. Stir in parsley, sage, thyme, and marjoram and cook until fragrant, about 1 minute. Transfer to very large bowl.

3. Add dried, cooled bread, broth, eggs, salt, and pepper to vegetable mixture and toss to combine. Turn mixture into prepared baking dish. (Stuffing can be refrigerated for up to 2 days.)

4. Cover with aluminum foil and bake for 25 minutes. Remove foil and continue to bake until golden, about 30 minutes longer. Let cool for 10 minutes before serving.

Homemade Cornbread Dressing
SERVES 10 TO 12   **TOTAL TIME** 4 HOURS
(PLUS 2 HOURS COOLING TIME)

✔ **WHY THIS RECIPE WORKS:** Because our Homemade Cornbread Dressing is so flavorful, we could replace the butter with vegetable oil and eliminate buttermilk from the cornbread altogether. We found that if we forgot to stale our cornbread overnight, we could get the same results in less than an hour by baking it at a low temperature. A generous hand with the sausage and eggs, and adding half-and-half to the dressing, brought welcome flavor and richness to the dish. Instead of oven drying in step 3, you can let cut cornbread stale overnight at room temperature.

Making your own cornbread doesn't take long and is worth it for our rich-tasting cornbread and sausage dressing.

CORNBREAD

2⅔	cups milk
½	cup vegetable oil
4	large eggs
2	cups (10 ounces) cornmeal
2	cups (10 ounces) all-purpose flour
4	teaspoons baking powder
1	teaspoon salt

DRESSING

1½	pounds bulk pork sausage
2	onions, chopped fine
3	celery ribs, chopped fine
6	tablespoons unsalted butter
4	garlic cloves, minced
1	teaspoon ground sage
1	teaspoon dried thyme
3½	cups chicken broth
1	cup half-and-half
4	large eggs
½	teaspoon salt
⅛	teaspoon cayenne pepper

1. FOR THE CORNBREAD: Adjust oven racks to upper-middle and lower-middle positions and heat oven to 375 degrees. Grease and flour 13 by 9-inch baking pan. Whisk milk, oil, and eggs together in bowl.

2. In large bowl, combine cornmeal, flour, baking powder, and salt. Whisk in milk mixture until smooth. Pour batter into prepared pan and bake on lower-middle rack until golden and toothpick inserted in center comes out clean, about 30 minutes. Cool in pan on wire rack, about 2 hours. (Cornbread can be stored at room temperature for up to 2 days.)

3. Reduce oven to 250 degrees. Cut cornbread into 1-inch squares. Divide cornbread between 2 rimmed baking sheets and bake, stirring occasionally, until dry, 50 minutes to 1 hour. Let cornbread cool completely on sheets, about 30 minutes.

4. FOR THE DRESSING: Cook sausage in 12-inch nonstick skillet over medium-high heat until no longer pink, about 5 minutes; transfer to paper towel–lined plate. Pour off all but 2 tablespoons fat left in pan. Add onions, celery, and 2 tablespoons butter to fat in pan and cook over medium-high heat until vegetables soften, about 5 minutes. Stir in garlic, sage, and thyme and cook until fragrant, about 30 seconds. Stir in broth, remove from heat, and let cool 5 minutes.

5. In large bowl, whisk half-and-half, eggs, salt, and cayenne together. Slowly whisk in warm broth mixture until incorporated. Gently fold in dried cornbread and sausage. Let mixture sit, tossing occasionally, until cornbread is saturated, about 20 minutes.

6. Heat oven to 375 degrees. Grease 13 by 9-inch baking pan. Transfer cornbread mixture to prepared pan. Melt remaining 4 tablespoons butter and drizzle evenly over top. Bake on upper rack until top is golden brown and crisp, 30 to 40 minutes. Let cool for 15 minutes and serve.

Wild Rice Dressing

SERVES 10 TO 12   **TOTAL TIME** 2 HOURS 15 MINUTES

✔ **WHY THIS RECIPE WORKS:** While developing our Wild Rice Dressing recipe, we discovered the amount of liquid that a given variety of wild rice absorbed varied drastically. To allow for this, we boiled the rice in extra liquid and then drained the excess, reserving the liquid. Cream and eggs bound the dressing but on their own were far too rich. Adding some of the rice cooking liquid lightened the dish and enhanced the nutty, earthy flavor of the rice. We found that toasted bread added color and crunch and eliminated the need for staling bread. Covering the casserole kept the surface from getting too crunchy.

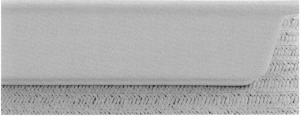

Small pieces of toasted bread add color and crunch and don't overwhelm the nutty flavor of the wild rice in this dressing.

2 cups chicken broth
2 cups water
1 bay leaf
2 cups wild rice
10 slices hearty white sandwich bread, torn into pieces
8 tablespoons unsalted butter
2 onions, chopped fine
3 celery ribs, chopped fine
4 garlic cloves, minced
1½ teaspoons dried sage
1½ teaspoons dried thyme
1½ cups heavy cream
2 large eggs
¾ teaspoon salt
½ teaspoon pepper

1. Bring broth, water, and bay leaf to boil in medium saucepan over medium-high heat. Stir in rice. Reduce heat to low, cover, and simmer until rice is tender, 35 to 45 minutes. Strain rice through fine-mesh strainer, reserving 1½ cups cooking liquid. Discard bay leaf.

FRESH CRANBERRY SAUCE

MAKES 2 CUPS   **TOTAL TIME** 20 MINUTES
(PLUS 1 HOUR COOLING TIME)

Whole-berry cranberry sauce is easy and fast, and it can be made well ahead of the bird. The taste far surpasses anything from a can. The cranberries cook for just 10 minutes. You can use frozen cranberries; do not defrost them, but add about 2 minutes to the simmering time.

1 cup sugar
¾ cup water
¼ teaspoon salt
1 (12-ounce) bag fresh cranberries, picked over

Bring sugar, water, and salt to boil in medium saucepan over medium heat, stirring occasionally. Stir in cranberries and simmer until slightly thickened and berries begin to pop, about 10 minutes. Cool to room temperature before serving, about 1 hour. (Sauce can be refrigerated for up to 1 week.)

CRANBERRY SAUCE WITH PEARS AND GINGER
Add 1 tablespoon grated fresh ginger and ¼ teaspoon cinnamon to pot with sugar, water, and salt. Peel, core, and cut 2 pears into ½-inch chunks and stir into sugar mixture with cranberries.

2. Adjust oven racks to upper-middle and lower-middle positions and heat oven to 325 degrees. Working in batches, pulse bread in food processor until coarsely ground. Spread crumbs onto 2 rimmed baking sheets and bake until golden, about 20 minutes, stirring occasionally. Let crumbs cool completely.

3. Melt 4 tablespoons butter in 12-inch skillet over medium heat. Add onions and celery and cook until golden, 8 to 10 minutes. Stir in garlic, sage, and thyme and cook until fragrant, about 30 seconds. Stir in reserved cooking liquid, remove from heat, and cool 5 minutes.

4. In large bowl, whisk cream, eggs, salt, and pepper together. Slowly whisk in warm broth mixture. Stir in rice and bread crumbs. Transfer mixture to 13 by 9-inch baking dish. (Dressing can be refrigerated for 1 day; increase baking time to 65 to 75 minutes.)

5. Melt remaining 4 tablespoons butter in now-empty skillet and drizzle evenly over dressing. Cover dish with aluminum foil and bake on lower-middle rack until set, 45 to 55 minutes. Remove foil and let cool for 15 minutes. Serve.

■ SIGNIFIES A **FAST** RECIPE (45 MINUTES OR LESS)

Pan-Seared Steaks with Red Wine Pan Sauce

SERVES 4   TOTAL TIME 30 MINUTES   **FAST**

☑ **WHY THIS RECIPE WORKS:** A well-caramelized exterior is the key to a great steak. But developing this flavorful crust indoors can be difficult. We've found the most important step is to get the pan really hot; cooking steaks in a pan that isn't properly preheated leads to steaks that overcook before they develop a good crust. Also, pat the steaks dry, otherwise their exterior will never brown properly. Finally, use a 12-inch traditional skillet to ensure the steaks have enough room to sear and to develop browned bits, the key to a flavorful sauce. Strip steaks and rib-eye steaks are our favorites to use in this recipe, but a boneless top sirloin will also work well. We prefer these steaks cooked to medium-rare, but if you prefer them more or less done, see our guidelines on page 15. To ensure that the steaks remain juicy after cooking, let them rest for 5 to 10 minutes even if you're not making the pan sauce. For more information on making a pan sauce, see page 184.

STEAKS

- 4   (8-ounce) boneless beef steaks, 1 to 1¼ inches thick, trimmed
    Kosher salt and pepper
- 1   tablespoon vegetable oil

RED WINE SAUCE

- 1   tablespoon vegetable oil
- 1   shallot, minced
- ¾   cup chicken broth
- ½   cup dry red wine
- 2   teaspoons packed brown sugar
- 3   tablespoons unsalted butter, cut into 3 pieces and chilled
- 1   teaspoon minced fresh thyme
    Salt and pepper

1. FOR THE STEAKS: Pat steaks dry with paper towels and season with salt and pepper. Heat oil in 12-inch skillet over medium-high heat until just smoking. Brown steaks on first side, about 4 minutes.

2. Flip steaks and continue to cook until meat registers 120 to 125 degrees (for medium-rare), 4 to 6 minutes. Transfer steaks to clean plate, tent with aluminum foil, and let rest while making sauce.

3. FOR THE SAUCE: Add oil to now-empty skillet and heat over medium-high heat until shimmering. Add shallot and cook until softened, about 2 minutes. Stir in broth, wine, and brown sugar, scraping up any browned bits, and simmer until thickened, about 5 minutes.

4. Stir in any accumulated meat juices. Turn heat to low and whisk in butter, 1 piece at a time. Off heat, stir in thyme and season with salt and pepper to taste. Spoon sauce over steaks and serve.

Teriyaki Flank Steak with Scallions

SERVES 4   TOTAL TIME 30 MINUTES   **FAST**

☑ **WHY THIS RECIPE WORKS:** This steak dish makes such an impressive presentation, no one would ever guess it's so easy. Salty, sweet, spicy, and acidic flavors gave the sauce a kick, while cornstarch produced a velvety texture. Grating the ginger allowed its flavor to disperse throughout the sauce. Drying the steak before searing it in a smoking-hot skillet ensured the meat browned properly; we used a nonstick skillet here because of the sticky sauce. Cooking the scallions and sauce in the same skillet that we used to cook the steak lent the meat's flavor to the sauce. Slice the cooked steak thinly against the grain; otherwise the meat will taste tough and rubbery. We prefer flank steak cooked to medium-rare, but if you prefer it more or less done, see our guidelines on page 15. Serve with rice.

- ½   cup soy sauce
- ⅓   cup sugar
- 2   tablespoons rice vinegar
- 1   tablespoon grated fresh ginger
- ¼   teaspoon red pepper flakes
- 1   teaspoon cornstarch
- 1   (1½- to 2-pound) flank steak, trimmed
- 2   tablespoons vegetable oil
- 12   scallions, cut into 1-inch lengths
- 2   teaspoons toasted sesame seeds

1. Whisk soy sauce, sugar, vinegar, ginger, pepper flakes, and cornstarch together in bowl.

2. Pat steak dry with paper towels. Heat 1 tablespoon oil in 12-inch nonstick skillet over medium-high heat until just smoking. Cook steak, turning as needed, until well browned on both sides and meat registers 120 to 125 degrees (for medium-rare), 8 to 12 minutes. Transfer to cutting board and tent with aluminum foil.

3. Add remaining 1 tablespoon oil and scallions to now-empty skillet and cook over medium heat until lightly browned, 2 to 3 minutes; transfer to bowl.

4. Add soy sauce mixture and any accumulated meat juices to now-empty skillet and simmer until thickened, 2 to 3 minutes. Slice steak thinly on bias against grain. Transfer to platter and top with sauce, scallions, and sesame seeds. Serve.

Steaks that are relatively thin, 1 to 1¼ inches thick, can be cooked in a hot pan on the stovetop. (Thicker steaks are best cooked at least partially in the oven; see recipe for Pepper-Crusted Filets Mignons on page 186.) And make sure to choose boneless steaks for indoor cooking. (The bone prevents direct contact between the meat and the pan, limiting browning; therefore, bone-in steaks are best grilled.) This method is ideal with both strip and rib-eye steaks.

1. TRIM THE FAT: Use a sharp paring or chef's knife to trim the hard, white fat from the perimeter of the steaks. Trim the fat so that it is no more than ⅛ inch thick.
WHY? Trimming the excess fat keeps splattering to a minimum. If you really want to keep down the mess, place a splatter screen covered with fine mesh over the skillet as the steaks cook.

2. PAT THE STEAKS DRY: Blot the steaks dry with paper towels.
WHY? Browning equals flavor, and browning occurs only once all the surface moisture has evaporated. Moisture collects in shrink-wrapped packages of meat, so if you don't dry the meat it will steam and not brown in the hot pan.

3. SEASON THE STEAKS LIBERALLY: Sprinkle the steaks with kosher salt and freshly ground black pepper. Make sure to coat both sides.
WHY? We prefer the large crystals of kosher salt because they are easier to distribute. For individual steaks, use ½ teaspoon kosher salt. Freshly ground pepper is a must; use as much as you like (a 4:1 salt-to-pepper ratio generally works well). To avoid contamination, premeasure the salt and pepper into a ramekin.

4. GET THE PAN VERY HOT: Heat 1 tablespoon vegetable oil in a large skillet. Wait until the oil just begins to smoke. Lay the steaks in the pan, making sure to leave room between them.
WHY? Many cooks fail to get the pan hot enough. When the oil begins to smoke, the pan is about 450 degrees, perfect for searing. A traditional skillet is key for maximum browning. If the meat is crowded into the pan, it will steam. A 12-inch skillet is the right size for cooking four 8-ounce steaks.

5. JUDGE DONENESS BY TEMPERATURE: Don't fuss with the steaks as they cook. Wait 3 or 4 minutes, or until well browned on the first side, and then flip them with tongs. Let the steaks cook another 3 to 5 minutes, and then test for doneness.
WHY? Leaving the meat in place helps build a better crust. Use tongs to lift a steak out of the pan and slide an instant-read thermometer through the side to test for doneness and ensure perfect results. See the chart on page 15 for doneness temperatures.

6. REST THE STEAKS BEFORE SERVING: Transfer the steaks to a large plate, loosely cover with aluminum foil, and let rest 5 to 10 minutes.
WHY? A short rest allows the muscle fibers in the meat to relax and reabsorb their natural juices. Use this time to make a quick sauce in the pan, turning those browned bits into a potent flavor source.

A flavorful pan sauce is a quick and easy way to dress up steak, pork, lamb chops, or chicken. The secret to a great-tasting pan sauce is the delicious browned bits, called fond, sticking to the bottom of the pan after the meat has been cooked. Pan sauces are usually made by adding liquid (broth, wine, or juice) to the pan once the meat has been removed. Although the ingredients and amounts change depending on the sauce, the basic steps for any pan sauce are the same.

1. BROWN THE MEAT: Heat the oil in a large skillet until just smoking. Add the meat and cook until well browned on both sides and it achieves the desired degree of doneness. Transfer the meat to a plate and keep it warm. Do not wash out the skillet.

WHY? Browning the meat creates the bits stuck to the skillet that add important flavor to the sauce. To brown properly, make sure to use a traditional skillet and to get the pan hot enough.

2. SAUTÉ THE AROMATICS: After removing the meat, add more oil, if necessary, to the now-empty skillet to equal 1 tablespoon, and heat until shimmering. Add the minced aromatics and cook until softened, 1 to 3 minutes.

WHY? A single shallot, a garlic clove or two, or a small onion will cook quickly, so don't let them burn and become unusable. The aromatics add to the flavor base.

3. ADD THE LIQUID: Stir in the liquid, usually broth or wine, and use a wooden spoon to loosen the bits on the bottom of the pan left from browning the meat.

WHY? By adding liquid to the pan, you'll be able to loosen the browned bits on the pan bottom and prevent the aromatics from browning further. The browned bits dissolve as the liquid simmers and enrich the sauce with meaty flavor.

4. SIMMER TO REDUCE THE LIQUID: Simmer the liquid until it is slightly thickened and reduced by about half. Stir in any accumulated juices from the resting meat.

WHY? Reducing the liquid by simmering it briskly both concentrates the flavors and thickens its consistency. The meat juices are potent and add even more flavor to the sauce.

5. WHISK IN THE COLD BUTTER: Reduce the heat to low and whisk in the cold butter, one piece at a time. Use a whisk to hold the butter while swirling it around in the skillet until it's melted.

WHY? The chilled butter pulls the sauce together and makes it thick and glossy. We generally add two to three pieces of butter, each about 1 tablespoon, to a pan sauce.

6. FINISH THE SAUCE AND SERVE: Off the heat, add any fresh herbs or potent ingredients to the sauce and season with salt and pepper. Spoon the sauce over the meat and serve immediately.

WHY? Waiting to add fresh herbs or other potent ingredients (mustard, lemon juice, vinegar) until the end preserves their flavor; they don't need any cooking time. Make sure to wait until the sauce is finished to adjust the seasonings.

PAN SAUCES FOR STEAKS, PORK, AND LAMB CHOPS

Here are some of our favorite pan sauces that taste great with beef steaks, pork tenderloins and chops, and lamb chops. Do not wash out the pan after searing the steaks or chops: Those browned bits, or fond, remaining on the bottom of the skillet add important flavor. For more information on making a pan sauce, see page 184. Each of these recipes serves 4.

Mushroom and Sherry Sauce
TOTAL TIME 25 MINUTES **FAST**

- 1 tablespoon vegetable oil
- 8 ounces white mushrooms, trimmed and sliced thin
- 1 garlic clove, minced
- 1 cup chicken broth
- ½ cup dry sherry
- 3 tablespoons unsalted butter, cut into 3 pieces and chilled
- 1 tablespoon minced fresh thyme
  Salt and pepper

Add oil to skillet and heat over medium-high heat until shimmering. Add mushrooms and cook until browned, about 10 minutes. Stir in garlic and cook until fragrant, about 15 seconds. Stir in broth and sherry, scraping up any browned bits, and simmer until thickened, about 5 minutes. Stir in any accumulated meat juices. Reduce heat to low and whisk in butter, 1 piece at a time. Off heat, stir in thyme and season with salt and pepper to taste.

Cognac and Mustard Sauce
TOTAL TIME 20 MINUTES **FAST**

- 1 tablespoon vegetable oil
- 2 shallots, minced
- 1 cup chicken broth
- ⅓ cup cognac or brandy
- 1 tablespoon whole-grain mustard
- 1 tablespoon lemon juice
- 3 tablespoons unsalted butter, cut into 3 pieces and chilled
- 2 teaspoons minced fresh tarragon
  Salt and pepper

Add oil to skillet and heat over medium-high heat until shimmering. Add shallots and cook until softened, about 2 minutes. Stir in broth and cognac, scraping up any browned bits, and simmer until thickened, about 5 minutes. Stir in mustard and lemon juice and any accumulated meat juices. Reduce heat to low and whisk in butter, 1 piece at a time. Off heat, stir in tarragon and season with salt and pepper to taste.

Bell Pepper and Vinegar Sauce
TOTAL TIME 25 MINUTES **FAST**

- 1 tablespoon vegetable oil
- 1 red bell pepper, stemmed, seeded, and sliced thin
- 1 red onion, halved and sliced thin
- 2 garlic cloves, minced
- 1 teaspoon minced fresh thyme
- 1 cup chicken or vegetable broth
- 1 tablespoon balsamic vinegar
  Salt and pepper

Add oil to skillet and heat over medium-high heat until shimmering. Add bell pepper and onion and cook until softened, about 6 minutes. Stir in garlic and thyme and cook until fragrant, about 30 seconds. Stir in broth, scraping up any browned bits, and simmer until thickened, about 6 minutes. Stir in vinegar and any accumulated meat juices. Season with salt and pepper to taste.

Chipotle Chile and Orange Sauce
TOTAL TIME 20 MINUTES **FAST**

- 1 tablespoon vegetable oil
- 1 shallot, minced
- 2 garlic cloves, minced
- 1 teaspoon minced canned chipotle chile in adobo sauce
- 1 cup orange juice
- 1 orange, peeled and chopped
- 1 tablespoon sugar
- 1 tablespoon minced fresh parsley or cilantro
  Salt and pepper

Add oil to skillet and heat over medium-high heat until shimmering. Add shallot and cook until softened, about 2 minutes. Stir in garlic and chipotle and cook until fragrant, about 15 seconds. Stir in orange juice, chopped orange, and sugar, scraping up any browned bits, and simmer until thickened, about 5 minutes. Stir in any accumulated meat juices. Off heat, stir in parsley and season with salt and pepper to taste.

Bourbon-Apricot Sauce
TOTAL TIME 25 MINUTES **FAST**

This sauce tastes particularly good with pork chops.

- 1 tablespoon vegetable oil
- 1 shallot, minced
- ½ cup bourbon
- ½ cup dried apricots, chopped
- 1 cup chicken broth
- 2 teaspoons minced fresh thyme
- 2 tablespoons red wine vinegar
  Salt and pepper

Add oil to skillet and heat over medium-high heat until shimmering. Add shallot and cook until softened, about 2 minutes. Stir in bourbon and apricots, scraping up any browned bits. Stir in broth and thyme and simmer until thickened, about 8 minutes. Stir in any accumulated pork juices and vinegar. Off heat, season with salt and pepper to taste.

Pepper-Crusted Filets Mignons with Blue Cheese–Chive Butter

SERVES 4   **TOTAL TIME** 40 MINUTES
(PLUS 1 HOUR SALTING TIME)

✔ **WHY THIS RECIPE WORKS:** Black peppercorns can give mild-tasting filet mignon a welcome flavor boost. But they can also create a punishing blast of heat. For a pepper-crusted filet mignon with a crust that wouldn't overwhelm the meat, we mellowed the peppercorns' heat by gently simmering them in oil. We then used a two-step process to create a well-browned and attractive pepper crust: First, we rubbed the raw steaks with a paste of the cooked cracked peppercorns, oil, and salt; then we pressed the paste into each steak using a sheet of plastic wrap to ensure it stayed put. The paste not only added flavor to the meat but also drew out the meat's own beefy flavor. To crush the peppercorns, spread half of them on a cutting board, place a skillet on top, and, pressing down firmly with both hands, use a rocking motion to crush the peppercorns beneath the "heel" of the skillet. Repeat with the remaining peppercorns. This recipe is pretty spicy; if you prefer a very mild pepper flavor, drain the cooled peppercorns in a fine-mesh strainer in step 1, toss them with 5 tablespoons of fresh oil, add the salt, and proceed. We prefer filets mignons cooked to medium-rare, but if you prefer them more or less done, see our guidelines on page 15.

STEAKS

- 5 tablespoons black peppercorns, crushed
- 5 tablespoons plus 2 teaspoons vegetable oil
- 1½ teaspoons salt
- 4 (7- to 8-ounce) center-cut filets mignons, 1½ to 2 inches thick, trimmed

BLUE CHEESE–CHIVE BUTTER

- 1½ ounces (¼ cup) mild blue cheese, room temperature
- 3 tablespoons unsalted butter, softened
- ⅛ teaspoon salt
- 2 tablespoons minced fresh chives

1. FOR THE STEAKS: Heat peppercorns and 5 tablespoons oil in small saucepan over low heat until faint bubbles appear. Continue to cook at bare simmer, swirling pan occasionally, until pepper is fragrant, 7 to 10 minutes; remove from heat and let cool.

2. Stir salt into pepper mixture, then rub thoroughly over steaks. Wrap steaks with plastic wrap, pressing gently to make sure peppercorns adhere. Let steaks stand at room temperature for 1 hour.

3. FOR THE BLUE CHEESE–CHIVE BUTTER: Mix blue cheese, butter, and salt together in bowl with rubber spatula until smooth. Fold in chives; set aside.

4. Adjust oven rack to middle position, place baking sheet on oven rack, and heat oven to 450 degrees. When oven reaches 450 degrees, heat remaining 2 teaspoons oil in 12-inch skillet over medium-high heat until just smoking. Place steaks in skillet and cook, without moving, until dark brown crust has formed on first side, 3 to 4 minutes. Using tongs, turn steaks and cook until well browned on second side, about 3 minutes.

5. Transfer steaks to hot baking sheet in oven and roast until meat registers 120 to 125 degrees (for medium-rare), 5 to 7 minutes. Transfer steaks to wire rack set in second rimmed baking sheet, top each with 1 to 2 tablespoons blue cheese butter, and tent with aluminum foil. Let steaks rest for 5 to 10 minutes and serve.

Making Pepper-Crusted Filets Mignons

1. COOK PEPPERCORNS: Heat peppercorns and oil over low heat until faint bubbles appear. Continue to cook at bare simmer until pepper is fragrant, 7 to 10 minutes.

2. RUB STEAKS: Rub steaks with oil-pepper mixture, wrap in plastic, and press gently to make sure peppercorns adhere. Let steaks stand at room temperature for 1 hour.

3. SEAR IN HOT SKILLET: Heat oil in skillet until just smoking. Sear steaks on both sides until well browned.

4. TRANSFER TO HOT OVEN: Transfer steaks to preheated baking sheet and roast until meat registers 120 to 125 degrees (for medium-rare).

Simmering the ground beef in tomato sauce and chicken broth until the mixture thickens makes a flavorful taco filling.

Classic Beef Tacos

SERVES 4　　**TOTAL TIME** 45 MINUTES **FAST**

✔ **WHY THIS RECIPE WORKS:** Most everyone in the test kitchen has fond childhood memories of enjoying ground beef tacos, but in reality the stale-tasting fillings (made with supermarket seasoning packets) and store-bought shells leave a lot to be desired. We set out to develop a ground beef taco with a boldly spiced beef mixture and fresh toppings. We like to fry corn tortillas to make superior homemade taco shells. For the filling, we sautéed onion, then added garlic and the spices to bring out their flavor. Using very lean ground beef prevented greasiness, and adding tomato sauce, chicken broth, brown sugar, and vinegar created roundness and depth. In our opinion, cheese, lettuce, and tomatoes are essential taco toppings, while diced avocado, minced onion, sour cream, minced jalapeños, and chopped cilantro are other worthy additions.

- 1　tablespoon vegetable oil
- 1　onion, chopped fine
- 3　garlic cloves, minced

- 2　tablespoons chili powder
- 1　teaspoon ground cumin
- 1　teaspoon ground coriander
- ½　teaspoon dried oregano
- ¼　teaspoon cayenne pepper
- 　　Salt
- 1　pound 90 percent lean ground beef
- ½　cup canned tomato sauce
- ½　cup chicken broth
- 2　teaspoons cider vinegar
- 1　teaspoon packed light brown sugar
- 8　taco shells

1. Heat oil in 10-inch skillet over medium heat until shimmering. Add onion and cook until softened, about 5 minutes. Stir in garlic, chili powder, cumin, coriander, oregano, cayenne, and 1 teaspoon salt and cook until fragrant, about 30 seconds.

2. Stir in ground beef and cook, breaking up meat with wooden spoon, until no longer pink, about 5 minutes. Stir in tomato sauce, broth, vinegar, and sugar and simmer until thickened, about 10 minutes. Season with salt to taste.

3. Divide filling evenly among taco shells and serve.

Making Your Own Taco Shells

1. In 8-inch skillet, heat ¾ cup vegetable oil to 350 degrees. Using tongs, slip half of tortilla into hot oil and submerge it using metal spatula. Fry until just set, but not brown, about 30 seconds.

2. Flip tortilla. Hold tortilla open about 2 inches while keeping bottom submerged in oil. Fry until golden brown, about 1½ minutes. Flip again and fry other side until golden brown.

3. Transfer shell, upside down, to paper towel–lined baking sheet to drain. Repeat with remaining tortillas, keeping oil between 350 and 375 degrees. For best results, use homemade taco shells immediately.

Indoor Steak Tacos

SERVES 4 TO 6 **TOTAL TIME** 1 HOUR

✔ **WHY THIS RECIPE WORKS:** To develop a steak taco recipe using an indoor cooking method that yielded steak taco meat as tender, juicy, and rich-tasting as the grilled method, we chose flank steak, which is beefy and tender when sliced thin across the grain. Pan searing gave us the browned exterior and crisp, brittle edges characteristic of grilled meat. A paste of oil, cilantro, scallions, garlic, and jalapeño, which we applied to the meat and then scraped off just before cooking, gave our steak taco recipe a flavor boost without sacrificing browning. For a less spicy dish, remove some or all of the ribs and seeds from the jalapeño before chopping it for the paste. We prefer the flank steak cooked to medium-rare, but if you prefer it more or less done, see our guidelines on page 15. To warm tortillas, brush both sides with oil, stack on a plate, wrap in a damp dish towel, and microwave until warm and pliable, about 1 minute. Serve with minced white or red onion, thinly sliced radishes or cucumber, salsa, and lime wedges.

½ cup fresh cilantro leaves, plus extra for serving
3 garlic cloves, peeled and coarsely chopped
3 scallions, coarsely chopped
1 jalapeño chile, stemmed and coarsely chopped
½ teaspoon ground cumin
¼ cup plus 2 tablespoons vegetable oil
1 tablespoon lime juice
1 (1½- to 1¾-pound) flank steak, trimmed and sliced with grain into 4 pieces
Salt and pepper
½ teaspoon sugar
12 (6-inch) corn tortillas, warmed

1. Pulse cilantro, garlic, scallions, jalapeño, and cumin in food processor until finely chopped, 10 to 12 pulses. Add ¼ cup oil and process until mixture is smooth and resembles pesto, about 15 seconds, scraping down bowl as needed. Transfer 2 tablespoons herb paste to medium bowl, stir in lime juice, and set aside.

2. Using dinner fork, poke each piece of steak 10 to 12 times on each side. Place steaks in large baking dish, rub thoroughly with 1½ teaspoons salt, then coat with remaining herb paste. Cover with plastic wrap and refrigerate 30 minutes to 1 hour.

3. Scrape herb paste off steaks and sprinkle with sugar and ½ teaspoon pepper. Heat remaining 2 tablespoons oil in 12-inch nonstick skillet over medium-high heat until just smoking. Cook steaks, turning as needed, until well browned on all sides and meat registers 120 to 125 degrees (for medium-rare), 4 to 6 minutes. Transfer steaks to cutting board and let rest for 5 minutes.

4. Slice steaks thinly against grain, add to bowl with reserved herb paste, and toss to coat. Season with salt and pepper to taste. Spoon small amount of sliced steak into center of each warmed tortilla and serve, passing extra cilantro separately.

Making Steak Tacos

1. CUT STEAK: Slice trimmed flank steak with grain into 4 strips.

2. POKE AND SEASON MEAT: Pierce steak pieces with fork, then season meat and coat with herb paste. Refrigerate at least 30 minutes.

3. SEAR STEAK: Cook steak in hot 12-inch nonstick skillet using generous 2 tablespoons oil to promote browning.

4. TOSS WITH HERB PASTE: Slice cooked steaks thinly against grain, then toss with additional herb paste and lime juice to brighten flavors.

Primal Cuts of Beef

Because the flavor and texture of steaks and roasts can vary widely depending on what part of the cow they come from, it's helpful to understand the primal cuts from which the retails cuts are butchered.

At the wholesale level, a cow is divided into eight different cuts, commonly referred to as primal cuts. From these primal cuts, butchers make the retail cuts that are available in the supermarket. For more information on the names used for different cuts of meat and their primal cuts, as well as on the test kitchen's favorite cuts and our flavor ratings, see the All About guides to beef steaks (see page 190) and beef roasts (see page 200).

CHUCK/SHOULDER: The chuck (or shoulder) runs from the neck down to the fifth rib. There are four major muscles in this region. Meat from the chuck tends to be flavorful and fairly fatty, which is why ground chuck makes the best hamburgers. Chuck also contains a fair amount of connective tissue, so when the meat is not ground it generally requires a long cooking time.

RIB: The rib section extends along the back of the animal from the sixth to the twelfth rib. Prime rib and rib-eye steaks come from this area. Rib cuts have great beefy flavor and are tender.

SHORT LOIN: The short loin (also called the loin) extends from the last rib back through the midsection of the animal to the hip area. It contains two major muscles: the tenderloin and the shell. The tenderloin is extremely tender (it is positioned right under the spine) and has a quite mild flavor. The shell is a much larger muscle and has a more robust beef flavor as well as more fat.

SIRLOIN: The sirloin contains relatively inexpensive cuts that are sold as both steaks and roasts. We find that sirloin cuts are fairly lean and tough. In general, we prefer other parts of the animal, although top sirloin makes a decent roast.

ROUND: Roasts and steaks cut from the back of the cow, called the round, are usually sold boneless; they are quite lean and can be tough. Again, we generally prefer cuts from other parts of the cow, although we have found that top round can be roasted with some success.

BRISKET, PLATE, AND FLANK: Moderately thick boneless cuts are removed from the three primal cuts that run along the underside of the animal. The brisket is rather tough and contains a lot of connective tissue. The plate is rarely sold at the retail level (it is used to make pastrami). The flank is a leaner cut that makes an excellent steak when grilled.

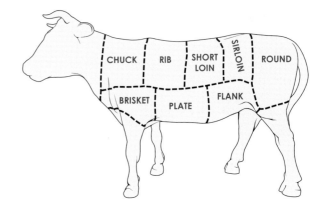

Beef Grades: Prime, Choice, and Select

Most meat available to consumers is confined to three of the quality grades assigned by the U.S. Department of Agriculture (USDA): prime, choice, and select. Grading is voluntary on the part of the meat-packer. If meat is graded, it should bear a USDA stamp indicating the grade, though it may not be visible to the consumer. To grade meat, inspectors evaluate color, grain, surface texture, and fat content and distribution.

Prime meat is heavily marbled with intramuscular fat, which makes for a tender, flavorful steak. About 2 percent of graded beef is considered prime. Prime meats are most often served in restaurants or sold in high-end butcher shops. The majority of graded beef found in supermarkets is choice. While the levels of marbling in choice beef can vary, it is generally moderately marbled. Select beef has little marbling.

Our advice: When you're willing to splurge, prime meat is worth the extra money, but choice meat is a fine, affordable option. Just stay clear of select-grade steak.

ALL ABOUT **BEEF STEAKS**

With the wide variety of steaks at the supermarket these days, it's tough to know which cut of meat to buy. And the cut you choose has everything to do with the flavor of the steak. Here are 12 of the test kitchen's favorite beef steaks. We've rated each steak on a scale from 1 to 4 stars for both tenderness and flavor and have indicated the best cooking method for each. We've also listed the primal cut from which the steak is cut. See page 189 for more information about primal cuts and beef grading.

	TYPE	TENDERNESS	FLAVOR
	Top Blade Steak (Chuck/Shoulder) Top blade (or simply blade) steak is a small shoulder cut. It is an all-purpose steak. While it is very tender and richly flavored, a line of gristle that runs through the center of the meat makes it a poor option for serving whole. Remove the gristle and slice the steak thin for stir-fries, or cut into cubes for kebabs or stews.	★★★	★★★
	Shoulder Steak (Chuck/Shoulder) Sometimes labeled as London broil or chuck steak, this 1½- to 2-pound boneless steak is a great value for cost-conscious cooks. Although cut from the shoulder, it is relatively lean, with a moderately beefy flavor. Since this steak can be a bit tough, it should be sliced thin on the bias after cooking. Grill or pan-roast.	★★	★★
	Rib-Eye Steak (Rib) Cut from the rib area just behind the shoulder, a rib-eye steak is essentially a boneless piece of prime rib. This pricey, fat-streaked steak is tender and juicy, with a pronounced beefiness. In the West, rib eyes are sometimes labeled Spencer steaks; in the East, they may be called Delmonico steaks. Grill, pan-sear, or broil.	★★★	★★★★
	Strip Steak (Short Loin) Available both boneless and bone-in, this moderately expensive steak is also called top loin, shell, sirloin strip, Kansas City strip, or New York strip. Cut from the shell muscle that runs along the middle of the steer's back, strip steaks are well marbled, with a tight grain, pleasantly chewy texture, and big, beefy flavor. Grill, pan-sear, or broil.	★★★	★★★★
	Tenderloin Steak (Short Loin) Cut from the center of the back, the tenderloin is the most tender (and most expensive) cut of the cow. Depending on their thickness, tenderloin steaks may be labeled (from thickest to thinnest) Châteaubriand, filet mignon, or tournedos. Tenderloin steaks are buttery smooth and very tender, but they have little flavor. Grill, pan-sear, or broil.	★★★★	★
	T-Bone Steak (Short Loin) A classic grilling steak, this cut is named for the T-shaped bone that runs through the meat. This bone separates two muscles, the flavorful strip (or shell, top of photo) and the buttery tenderloin (bottom of photo). Because the tenderloin is small and will cook more quickly than the strip, this side should be positioned over the cooler side of the fire when grilling. Grill.	★★★	★★★★

TYPE	TENDERNESS	FLAVOR
Porterhouse Steak (Short Loin) The porterhouse is really just a huge T-bone steak with a larger tenderloin section, which accounts for its higher price. It is cut farther back on the animal than the T-bone. Like the T-bone steak, the porterhouse steak, with both strip and tenderloin sections, has well-balanced flavor and texture. Most porterhouse steaks are big enough to serve two. Grill.	★★★	★★★★
Top Sirloin Steak (Sirloin) Cut from the hip, this steak (along with its bone-in version, round-bone steak) is sometimes called New York sirloin steak or sirloin butt. Top sirloin steak is a large, inexpensive steak with decent tenderness and flavor, but do not confuse it with the superior strip steak. Slice thin against the grain after cooking. Grill or pan-sear.	★★	★★
Flap Meat Sirloin Steak (Sirloin) Cut from the area just before the hip, this large (upward of 2½ pounds), rectangular steak is most often sold in strips or cubes. To ensure that you are buying the real thing, buy the whole steak and cut it yourself. Though not particularly tender, flap meat has a distinct grain and a robust beefiness. Slice thin against the grain after cooking. Grill, pan-roast (whole), or pan-sear (strips).	★★	★★★
Flank Steak (Flank) Flank steak, aka jiffy steak, is a large, flat cut from the underside of the cow, with a distinct longitudinal grain. Flank steak is thin and cooks quickly, making it ideal for the grill. Although very flavorful, flank is slightly chewy. It should not be cooked past medium and should always be sliced thin across the grain. Grill, pan-sear, or slice thinly and stir-fry.	★★	★★★
Skirt Steak (Plate) This long, thin steak is cut from the underside (or "plate") of the cow. Also known as fajita or Philadelphia steak, it has a distinct grain and an especially beefy taste. As its alias implies, sliced skirt is a good option for fajitas, but it can also be cooked as a whole steak. Grill, pan-sear, or slice thin and stir-fry.	★★	★★★
Top Round Steak (Round) This inexpensive steak is cut from the round. Also known as London broil, it has good beefy flavor, but does not possess a tender texture. To dramatically diminish chewiness, slice this steak ultrathin. Grill or broil.	★	★★★

Chicken-Fried Steak

SERVES 4 TO 6   TOTAL TIME 55 MINUTES

✔ WHY THIS RECIPE WORKS: Many recipes for chicken-fried steak call for using cube steaks, which are cut from the round and put through a tenderizing machine that makes small, cubelike indentations. Unfortunately, overzealous supermarket butchers often mangle the job, so we knew we needed a different cut of meat. In the end, we settled on inexpensive but flavorful sirloin steak tips. To tenderize the steaks, we borrowed an idea from the cubing process and scored the meat on both sides, then pounded the tips until they were thin. For an ultracrunchy coating that stayed put, pounding the seasoned flour into the steak with a meat pounder was key. We ditched the deep-fry method we'd been using in favor of a shallower fry, since submerging the coated meat in deep fat trapped moisture and prevented it from evaporating, resulting in sogginess. Sirloin tips or steak tips, also sold as flap meat, can be packaged variously as whole steaks, cubes, or strips. For this recipe, buy a whole 1-pound steak and cut it yourself. Serve with Cream Gravy.

- 3½ cups all-purpose flour
- ½ cup cornstarch
- 1 tablespoon garlic powder
- 1 tablespoon onion powder
- ½ teaspoon cayenne pepper
- 2 teaspoons baking powder
  Salt and pepper
- 4 large eggs
- ¼ cup whole milk
- 1 pound sirloin steak tips, cut into 4 pieces
- 1½ cups peanut or vegetable oil

1. Whisk flour, cornstarch, garlic powder, onion powder, cayenne, baking powder, 1 teaspoon salt, and 2 teaspoons pepper together in large bowl. Transfer 1 cup seasoned flour to shallow dish. Beat eggs in second shallow dish. Add milk to bowl with remaining flour mixture and rub with fingers until mixture resembles coarse meal.

2. Pat steaks dry with paper towels and season with salt and pepper. With sharp knife, cut 1/16-inch-deep slits on both sides of steaks, spaced ¼ inch apart, in crosshatch pattern. Dredge steaks in seasoned flour then pound steaks into 1/8- to ¼-inch-thick steaks using meat pounder or heavy small skillet.

3. Dredge pounded steaks in seasoned flour again, then dip in eggs, and transfer to bowl with milk-flour mixture, pressing to help crumbs adhere. Lay steaks on wire rack set over rimmed baking sheet. Refrigerate steaks for at least 15 minutes or up to 4 hours. (Do not discard milk-flour mixture.)

CREAM GRAVY

MAKES 3 CUPS   TOTAL TIME 15 MINUTES **FAST**
Do not use low-fat or skim milk in this recipe.

- 3 tablespoons unsalted butter
- 3 tablespoons all-purpose flour
- ½ teaspoon garlic powder
- 1½ cups chicken broth
- 1½ cups whole milk
- ¾ teaspoon salt
- ½ teaspoon pepper

Melt butter in 12-inch skillet over medium heat. Stir in flour and garlic powder and cook until golden, about 2 minutes. Slowly whisk in broth, milk, salt, and pepper and simmer until thickened, about 5 minutes. Serve. (Gravy can be refrigerated for up to 2 days.)

---

4. Adjust oven rack to middle position and heat oven to 200 degrees. Heat oil in large Dutch oven over medium-high heat until just smoking. Return 2 steaks to bowl with milk-flour mixture and coat thoroughly, then add to skillet and fry until deep golden brown and crisp on both sides, 4 to 6 minutes. Transfer fried steak to clean wire rack set over rimmed baking sheet and keep warm in oven. Repeat with remaining steaks. Serve.

Sloppy Joes

SERVES 4   TOTAL TIME 35 MINUTES **FAST**

✔ WHY THIS RECIPE WORKS: A cafeteria staple, Sloppy Joes are typically little more than a sweet, greasy dumping ground for third-rate burger meat. We wanted to develop a recipe with a more balanced, less sweet flavor and much less greasy meat. Combining tomato puree and ketchup, with just a touch of brown sugar, yielded a sufficiently sweet, rich tomato base. Using 85 percent lean ground beef to cut down on the slick factor, we cooked the meat until just pink—not browned—before adding the sauce, which ensured the meat stayed tender. Flavoring the filling with garlic, chili powder, and hot sauce gave it some heat to balance the sweetness. Be careful not to cook the meat beyond pink in step 1; if you let it brown at this point it will end up dry and crumbly. The meat will finish cooking once the liquid ingredients are added.

2 **tablespoons vegetable oil**
1 **onion, chopped fine**
   Salt and pepper
2 **garlic cloves, minced**
½ **teaspoon chili powder**
1 **pound 85 percent lean ground beef**
1 **teaspoon packed brown sugar**
1 **cup tomato puree**
½ **cup ketchup**
¼ **cup water**
¼ **teaspoon hot sauce**
4 **hamburger buns**

1. Heat oil in 12-inch skillet over medium heat until shimmering. Stir in onion and ½ teaspoon salt, cover, and cook, stirring often, until softened, about 10 minutes. Uncover, stir in garlic and chili powder and cook until fragrant, about 30 seconds. Add ground beef and cook, breaking up meat with wooden spoon, until just pink, about 3 minutes.

2. Stir in ¼ teaspoon pepper, sugar, tomato puree, ketchup, water, and hot sauce and simmer until sauce is slightly thicker than ketchup, 8 to 10 minutes. Season with salt and pepper to taste. Spoon meat mixture onto hamburger buns and serve.

VARIATIONS
Sloppy Janes
Substitute ground turkey for ground beef.

Sloppy Josés
Increase chili powder to 1 tablespoon. Add 2 teaspoons ground cumin and ¼ teaspoon cayenne pepper to pan with onions. Stir in ½ teaspoon minced canned chipotle chile in adobo sauce and 1 (15-ounce) can black beans, rinsed, with other ingredients in step 2.

Juicy Pub-Style Burgers with Special Sauce
SERVES 4   **TOTAL TIME** 1 HOUR 10 MINUTES

WHY THIS RECIPE WORKS: Few things are as satisfying as a thick, juicy, pub-style burger. But avoiding the usual gray band of overcooked meat is a challenge. We wanted a patty that was well seared, juicy, and evenly rosy from center to edge. Grinding our own meat in the food processor was a must, and sirloin steak tips were the right cut for the job. We cut the meat into ½-inch chunks before grinding and lightly packing the meat to form patties—a technique that gave the burgers

Hand-ground beef plus a homemade sauce give these thick, juicy, pub-style burgers deep flavor.

just enough structure to hold their shape in the skillet. A little melted butter improved their flavor and juiciness, but our biggest discovery came when we transferred the burgers from the stovetop to the oven to finish cooking—the stovetop provided intense heat for searing, while the oven's gentle ambient heat allowed for even cooking, thus eliminating the overcooked gray zone. A few premium (yet simple) toppings were all that was needed to vary our pub-style burger recipe. Sirloin steak tips are also sold as flap meat. When tossing the ground meat with butter and pepper and then shaping the patties, take care not to overwork the meat or the burgers will become dense. We prefer these burgers cooked to medium-rare, but if you prefer them more or less done, see our guidelines on page 15.

BURGERS
2 **pounds sirloin steak tips, trimmed and cut into ½-inch chunks**
4 **tablespoons unsalted butter, melted and cooled**
   Salt and pepper
1 **teaspoon vegetable oil**
4 **hamburger buns, toasted and buttered**

SPECIAL SAUCE

- ¾ **cup mayonnaise**
- 2 **tablespoons soy sauce**
- 1 **tablespoon packed dark brown sugar**
- 1 **tablespoon Worcestershire sauce**
- 1 **tablespoon minced fresh chives**
- 1 **garlic clove, minced**
- ¾ **teaspoon pepper**

1. FOR THE BURGERS: Spread beef chunks onto baking sheet and freeze until meat is very firm and hard at edges but still pliable, about 35 minutes.

2. Working with one-quarter of meat at a time, pulse in food processor until finely ground into ¹⁄₁₆-inch pieces, about 35 pulses, stopping to redistribute meat as needed. Transfer meat to clean baking sheet, discarding any long strands of gristle or large chunks of fat.

3. Adjust oven rack to middle position and heat oven to 300 degrees. Drizzle melted butter over ground meat and season with 1 teaspoon pepper. Gently toss with fork to combine. Divide meat into 4 lightly packed balls, then gently flatten into ¾-inch-thick patties. Refrigerate patties until ready to cook. (Patties can be covered and refrigerated for up to 1 day.)

4. FOR THE SAUCE: Whisk all ingredients together in bowl; set aside for serving.

5. Season 1 side of patties with salt and pepper. Using spatula, flip patties and season other side. Heat oil in 12-inch skillet over high heat until just smoking. Using spatula, transfer burgers to skillet and cook without moving for 2 minutes. Flip burgers and cook on second side for 2 minutes. Transfer to rimmed baking sheet and bake until burgers register 125 degrees (for medium-rare), 3 to 5 minutes.

6. Transfer burgers to platter and let rest for 5 to 10 minutes before serving with buns and special sauce.

VARIATIONS

Juicy Pub-Style Burgers with Crispy Shallots and Blue Cheese

Before cooking burgers, cook 3 thinly sliced shallots in ½ cup vegetable oil in medium saucepan over high heat, stirring often, until golden, about 8 minutes; transfer to paper towel–lined plate and season with salt. Before finishing burgers in oven, top each with 2 tablespoons crumbled blue cheese. Top burgers with crispy shallots before serving.

Juicy Pub-Style Burgers with Peppered Bacon and Aged Cheddar

Before cooking burgers, lay 6 slices bacon on rimmed baking sheet and sprinkle with 2 teaspoons coarsely ground pepper. Place second rimmed baking sheet on top of bacon and bake in 375-degree until bacon is crisp, 15 to 20 minutes; transfer to paper towel–lined plate and let cool. Cut bacon in half crosswise. Before finishing burgers in oven, top each with ¼ cup shredded aged cheddar cheese. Top burgers with bacon before serving.

Making Pub-Style Burgers

1. FREEZE, THEN GRIND: Spread steak chunks onto baking sheet and freeze until meat is very firm, about 35 minutes. Then, pulse meat in batches in food processor until finely ground.

2. ADD BUTTER: Spread ground meat out onto clean baking sheet and discard long strands of gristle or large chunks of hard meat or fat. Drizzle with melted butter, season with pepper, and shape meat into patties.

3. SEAR IN SKILLET: Using spatula, transfer burgers to hot, well-oiled skillet and cook without moving for 2 minutes. Flip burgers and cook on second side for 2 minutes.

4. FINISH IN OVEN: Transfer seared burgers to clean baking sheet and bake until burgers register 125 degrees (for medium-rare), 3 to 5 minutes.

This stir-fry mixes tender and beefy marinated flank steak, crisp green broccoli, and red bell pepper in a flavorful sauce.

Stir-Fried Beef and Broccoli with Oyster Sauce

SERVES 4   **TOTAL TIME** 50 MINUTES

✔ **WHY THIS RECIPE WORKS:** Order beef and broccoli in most Chinese restaurants and you are served a pile of tough meat with overcooked army-issue broccoli, all drenched in a thick-as-pudding brown sauce. We set out to rescue beef and broccoli. For the meat, we found that flank steak offered the biggest beefy taste, and slicing it thin made it tender. We cooked the beef in two batches over high heat to make sure it browned and didn't steam. Then we cooked the broccoli until crisp-tender using a combination of methods—sautéing and steaming—and added some red bell pepper for sweetness and color. For the sauce, a combination of oyster sauce, chicken broth, dry sherry, brown sugar, and toasted sesame oil, lightly thickened with cornstarch, clung to the beef and vegetables without being gloppy. To make slicing the flank steak easier, freeze it for 15 minutes. Serve with Sticky Rice (page 142).

SAUCE

- 5 tablespoons oyster sauce
- 2 tablespoons chicken broth
- 1 tablespoon dry sherry
- 1 tablespoon packed light brown sugar
- 1 teaspoon toasted sesame oil
- 1 teaspoon cornstarch

STIR-FRY

- 1 (1-pound) flank steak, trimmed and sliced thin against grain into 2-inch-long pieces
- 3 tablespoons soy sauce
- 6 garlic cloves, minced
- 1 tablespoon grated fresh ginger
- 3 tablespoons vegetable oil
- 1¼ pounds broccoli, florets cut into bite-size pieces, stalks peeled and cut ⅛ inch thick on bias
- ⅓ cup water
- 1 small red bell pepper, stemmed, seeded, and cut into ¼-inch pieces
- 3 scallions, sliced ½ inch thick on bias

1. FOR THE SAUCE: Whisk all ingredients together in bowl.

2. FOR THE STIR-FRY: Combine beef and soy sauce in bowl, cover, and let marinate for 10 minutes to 1 hour. Drain beef and discard liquid. In separate bowl, combine garlic, ginger, and 1½ teaspoons oil.

3. Heat 1½ teaspoons oil in 12-inch nonstick skillet over high heat until just smoking. Add half of beef, break up any clumps, and cook, without stirring, for 1 minute. Stir beef and continue to cook until browned, about 2 minutes; transfer to bowl. Repeat with 1½ teaspoons oil and remaining beef; transfer to bowl.

4. Heat 1 tablespoon oil in now-empty skillet over medium-high heat until just smoking. Add broccoli and cook for 30 seconds. Add water, cover, and reduce heat to medium. Steam broccoli until crisp-tender, about 2 minutes; transfer to paper towel–lined plate. Wipe out skillet with paper towels.

5. Heat remaining 1½ teaspoons oil in now-empty skillet over high heat until just smoking. Add bell pepper and cook, stirring often, until spotty brown, about 1½ minutes.

6. Clear center of skillet, add garlic mixture, and cook, mashing mixture into skillet, until fragrant, about 30 seconds. Return broccoli and beef, and any accumulated beef juices, to skillet and toss to combine. Whisk sauce to recombine, then add to skillet. Cook, stirring constantly, until sauce is thickened, about 30 seconds. Transfer to platter, sprinkle with scallions, and serve.

Korean-Style Steak and Rice Bowls

SERVES 4 TOTAL TIME 50 MINUTES

✔ WHY THIS RECIPE WORKS: Our inspiration for this dish came from a traditional Korean dish known as *bibimbap*, which comprises rice, a variety of vegetables, and a little meat, and is topped with a fried egg and served in a bowl. Our quick twist on this customary dish calls for prepared kimchi, a speedy alternative to chopping and cooking many separate vegetables. We found it best not to drain the kimchi before measuring it; the pickling liquid is quite flavorful and, when slightly warmed on top of the cooked rice, lends its robust flavor to the dish. Steak tips, also sold as flap meat, are sold as whole steaks, cubes, and strips; look for either a whole steak or strips that are easy to cut into small pieces for this recipe. To make the beef easier to slice, freeze it for 15 minutes. Kimchi comes in spicy and mild varieties, and can be found in the refrigerated section of Asian markets and in some well-stocked supermarkets. Handle the cooked rice very gently and do not stir it too much when adding the flavorings in step 1, or the rice will turn gluey. Serve with Sriracha or Asian chili-garlic sauce.

1½ cups short-grain white rice or sushi rice, rinsed
3 cups water
   Salt and pepper
2 tablespoons seasoned rice vinegar
2 tablespoons minced fresh cilantro
2 tablespoons soy sauce
1 tablespoon packed brown sugar
1 pound sirloin steak tips, trimmed, cut into strips (if necessary), and sliced thin against grain on bias
3 tablespoons vegetable oil
2 cups cabbage kimchi, cut into 1-inch pieces
4 large eggs, cracked into 2 small bowls (2 eggs per bowl)

1. Adjust oven rack to lower-middle position and heat oven to 200 degrees. Bring rice, water, and 1 teaspoon salt to boil in medium saucepan. Cover, reduce heat to low, and simmer for 6 minutes. Remove from heat and let sit until rice is tender and water is absorbed, about 15 minutes. Fluff rice with fork and fold in vinegar and cilantro; cover to keep warm.

2. Meanwhile, whisk soy sauce and sugar together in bowl, then stir in beef. Heat 1 tablespoon oil in 12-inch nonstick skillet over high heat until just smoking. Add half of beef, break up any clumps, and cook, without stirring, for 1 minute. Stir beef and continue to cook until browned, about 2 minutes; transfer to bowl. Repeat with 1 tablespoon oil and remaining beef; transfer to bowl.

3. Portion rice into 4 individual serving bowls. Top with kimchi and beef and any accumulated beef juices. Keep warm in oven.

4. Wipe out now-empty skillet with paper towels, add remaining 1 tablespoon oil, and heat over medium heat until shimmering. Add eggs and season with salt and pepper. Cover and cook until whites are set, 2 to 3 minutes. Remove rice bowls from oven, top with fried eggs, and serve.

VARIATION

Mexican-Style Steak Burrito Bowls

SERVES 4   TOTAL TIME 45 MINUTES **FAST**

We prefer the smoky heat of chipotle chile powder in this recipe, but traditional chili powder or ancho chile powder can be substituted. Serve with diced avocado, shredded Monterey Jack cheese, and lime wedges.

1½ cups long-grain white rice, rinsed
2¼ cups water
   Salt and pepper
2 tablespoons lime juice
12 ounces cherry tomatoes, quartered
5 scallions, sliced thin
¼ cup minced fresh cilantro
3 tablespoons vegetable oil
1 pound sirloin steak tips, trimmed, cut into strips (if necessary), and sliced thin against grain on bias
2 teaspoons chipotle chile powder

1. Bring rice, water, and 1 teaspoon salt to boil in medium saucepan. Cover, reduce heat to low, and simmer until rice is tender and water is absorbed, about 20 minutes. Fluff rice with fork and fold in 1 tablespoon lime juice; cover to keep warm.

2. Meanwhile, combine tomatoes, scallions, cilantro, 2 teaspoons oil, remaining 1 tablespoon lime juice, ½ teaspoon salt, and ¼ teaspoon pepper in bowl; set aside.

3. Toss beef with 1 teaspoon oil, chile powder, ½ teaspoon salt, and ¼ teaspoon pepper in bowl. Heat 1 tablespoon oil in 12-inch nonstick skillet over high heat until just smoking. Add half of beef, break up any clumps, and cook, without stirring, for 1 minute. Stir beef and continue to cook until browned, about 2 minutes; transfer to bowl. Repeat with remaining 1 tablespoon oil and remaining beef; transfer to bowl.

4. Portion rice into 4 individual serving bowls. Top with beef and any accumulated juices and tomato mixture. Serve.

Thai Red Beef Curry

SERVES 4   **TOTAL TIME** 30 MINUTES   **FAST**

✔ **WHY THIS RECIPE WORKS:** A simple curry dish can be a delightful meal on a busy day. Too often the takeout versions are greasy and flavorless. We sought a way to elevate curry and keep it a quick-to-make dinner. With almost all of our beef recipes, the first step is to brown the meat, to enhance and deepen the flavor of the dish. But in this curry, we found the big, distinct flavors of curry paste, coconut milk, and fish sauce made the browning of the meat unnecessary. Therefore, we saved some time and simply slipped the beef into the simmering broth and let it absorb the bold Thai flavors. Light coconut milk can be substituted for regular coconut milk, but the sauce will be slightly thinner. If you prefer your curry a little less spicy, reduce the amount of curry paste to 1 tablespoon. Serve this dish over aromatic jasmine rice or regular white rice.

- 1 tablespoon vegetable oil
- 1½ tablespoons red curry paste
- 1 (13.5-ounce) can coconut milk
- 2 tablespoons fish sauce
- 4 teaspoons packed light brown sugar
- 1 (1½-pound) flank steak, trimmed and sliced thin against grain into 2-inch-long pieces
- 1 red bell pepper, stemmed, seeded, and cut into ¼-inch-thick strips
- 8 ounces snap peas, strings removed
- ½ cup coarsely chopped fresh basil
- 1 tablespoon lime juice
  Salt

1. Heat oil in 12-inch skillet over medium heat until shimmering. Add curry paste and cook until fragrant, about 1 minute. Whisk in coconut milk, fish sauce, and sugar and simmer until slightly thickened, about 5 minutes.

2. Add beef and cook until pieces separate and turn firm, 3 to 5 minutes. Stir in bell pepper and peas and cook until peas are crisp-tender, about 5 minutes. Off heat, stir in basil and lime juice. Season with salt to taste. Serve.

Glazing the meatloaf twice ensures a crisp, flavorful crust.

All-American Meatloaf

SERVES 6 TO 8   **TOTAL TIME** 1 HOUR 45 MINUTES

✔ **WHY THIS RECIPE WORKS:** Meatloaf packed with bland, starchy fillers hardly deserves its name. Could we put the meatiness back in this American classic? We found a couple of small steps that can be taken to make meatloaf better. First, use a mix of meats. A mixture of beef, pork, and veal (labeled meatloaf mix at the supermarket) gave the loaf a rounded, meaty flavor. Second, select the right binders. Crushed saltines or bread crumbs added nice texture and did not mask the flavor of the meat. Lastly, bake the loaf free-form on a wire rack set in a rimmed baking sheet. This lets the juice drain away as the loaf cooks. The result is a loaf with a crusty, glazed exterior that is much different from the soggy masses that emerge from standard loaf pans. If you cannot find meatloaf mix, substitute 1 pound of 90 percent lean ground beef and 1 pound of ground pork.

1 tablespoon vegetable oil

1 onion, chopped fine

2 garlic cloves, minced

½ teaspoon dried thyme

½ cup ketchup

¼ cup packed light brown sugar

4 teaspoons cider vinegar

½ cup milk

2 large eggs

⅓ cup minced fresh parsley

2 teaspoons Dijon mustard

2 teaspoons Worcestershire sauce

1 teaspoon salt

½ teaspoon pepper

¼ teaspoon hot sauce

⅔ cup crushed saltines or 1⅓ cups fresh bread crumbs

2 pounds meatloaf mix

1. Adjust oven rack to middle position and heat oven to 350 degrees. Fold piece of heavy-duty aluminum foil into 10 by 6-inch rectangle. Place foil in center of wire rack and place rack in rimmed baking sheet. Grease foil, then poke holes in foil with skewer about every ½ inch.

2. Heat oil in 8-inch nonstick skillet over medium-high heat until shimmering. Add onion and cook until softened, about 5 minutes. Stir in garlic and thyme and cook until fragrant, about 15 seconds; let cool. In bowl, combine ketchup, sugar, and vinegar.

3. In large bowl, mix sautéed onion mixture, milk, eggs, parsley, mustard, Worcestershire, salt, pepper, and hot sauce together. Stir in crushed saltines. Add meatloaf mix and knead with hands until evenly blended.

4. Turn meat mixture onto foil-lined rack in baking sheet and shape into 9 by 5-inch loaf. Brush with half of ketchup mixture and bake for 45 minutes.

5. Brush loaf with remaining ketchup mixture and bake until loaf registers 160 degrees, 15 to 25 minutes. Let cool for 20 minutes before serving.

Cheesy Southwestern Meatloaf

SERVES 6 TO 8   **TOTAL TIME** 1 HOUR 45 MINUTES

✔ **WHY THIS RECIPE WORKS:** For this Southwestern take on meatloaf, we used meatloaf mix for its tender texture and slightly sweet flavor. A little sour cream in addition to the classic eggs kept the loaf moist. Ground corn tortillas, not bread crumbs, bound the meat mixture and added intense corn flavor. A classic palette of Southwestern spices and herbs flavored the meat. We covered the raw loaf with salsa, which turned into a sticky glaze as it baked. Halfway through baking, we covered the top of the loaf with pepper Jack cheese, which then melted into a smooth layer. Use either medium or hot salsa for the glaze. If you cannot find meatloaf mix, substitute 1 pound of 90 percent lean ground beef and 1 pound of ground pork.

Making All-American Meatloaf

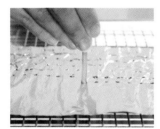

1. MAKE SPECIAL RACK: Fold piece of heavy-duty foil into 10 by 6-inch rectangle. Place foil in center of wire rack and place rack in rimmed baking sheet. Grease foil, then poke holes with skewer about ½ inch apart.

2. SAUTÉ AROMATICS: Heat oil in nonstick skillet until shimmering. Add onion and cook until softened, about 5 minutes. Stir in garlic and thyme and cook until fragrant, about 15 seconds; let cool.

3. MIX EVERYTHING THOROUGHLY: Mix onion mixture, milk, eggs, parsley, mustard, Worcestershire, salt, pepper, and hot sauce. Stir in crushed crackers. Add meatloaf mix and knead with hands until evenly blended.

4. COOK TO 160 DEGREES: Brush with half of ketchup mixture and bake for 45 minutes. Brush with remaining ketchup mixture and bake until loaf registers 160 degrees. Let cool before serving.

1 cup prepared salsa

3 tablespoons packed brown sugar

4 (6-inch) corn tortillas

½ cup sour cream

3 large eggs

1 (4-ounce) can green chiles, drained and finely chopped

¾ cup chopped scallions

¼ cup minced fresh cilantro

1 tablespoon chili powder

1 teaspoon ground cumin

1 teaspoon salt

½ teaspoon pepper

2 pounds meatloaf mix

4 ounces pepper Jack cheese, shredded (1 cup)

1. Adjust oven rack to middle position and heat oven to 350 degrees. Fold piece of heavy-duty aluminum foil into 10 by 6-inch rectangle. Place foil in center of wire rack and place rack in rimmed baking sheet. Grease foil, then poke holes in foil with skewer about every ½ inch.

2. Combine salsa and sugar in small saucepan; set aside. Tear tortillas into small pieces and process in food processor to consistency of cornmeal, about 30 seconds.

3. In large bowl, stir sour cream, eggs, chiles, scallions, cilantro, chili powder, cumin, salt, and pepper together. Stir in ground tortillas. Add meatloaf mix and knead with hands until evenly blended.

4. Turn meat mixture onto foil-lined rack in baking sheet and shape into 9 by 5-inch loaf. Brush with ¼ cup salsa mixture and bake for 40 minutes.

5. Sprinkle pepper Jack over top and bake until loaf registers 160 degrees, 20 to 30 minutes. Let meatloaf cool for 20 minutes. Simmer remaining salsa mixture over medium-high heat until thickened, 3 to 5 minutes. Serve with warm salsa mixture.

Roast Beef Top Round with Gravy

SERVES 6 TO 8   TOTAL TIME 3½ TO 4½ HOURS
(PLUS 1 HOUR SALTING TIME)

✓ **WHY THIS RECIPE WORKS:** This recipe uses a top round roast, an inexpensive cut from the rump of the steer that's most commonly roasted and sliced for deli sandwiches. Since this cut is irregular, we tied it with kitchen twine to create a uniform shape that cooked evenly. And because it's relatively lean, we seared the roast quickly on the stovetop to build flavor before roasting it slowly so that it didn't dry out. Many gravy recipes call for beef broth to be added to the drippings. In search of more potent flavor, we first cooked down the beef broth to half its original volume, and the gravy was much improved. But then we realized we could get the same concentrated beef flavor by turning to canned condensed beef consommé, to which we added only half of the water called for to reconstitute it. You can substitute a top sirloin roast for the top round roast. Look for an evenly shaped roast with at least a ¼-inch fat cap. We prefer this beef roast cooked to medium-rare, but if you prefer it more or less done, see our guidelines on page 15.

1 (4- to 5-pound) boneless top round roast, fat trimmed to ¼ inch
  Kosher salt and pepper

1 tablespoon vegetable oil

4 tablespoons unsalted butter

2 carrots, peeled and cut into 2-inch pieces

1 onion, cut into ½-inch rounds

1 celery rib, cut into 2-inch pieces

½ cup all-purpose flour

1 teaspoon tomato paste

2 (10.5-ounce) cans beef consommé

1½ cups water

1. Tie roast at 1-inch intervals with kitchen twine. Rub roast thoroughly with 4 teaspoons salt, wrap in plastic wrap, and refrigerate for 1 to 24 hours.

2. Adjust oven rack to middle position and heat oven to 225 degrees. Pat roast dry with paper towels and rub with 2 teaspoons pepper. Heat oil in 12-inch ovensafe skillet over medium-high heat until just smoking. Brown roast lightly on all sides, 8 to 12 minutes; transfer to plate.

3. Pour off all but 2 tablespoons fat left in pan. Add butter and melt over medium heat. Add carrots, onion, and celery and cook until lightly browned, 6 to 8 minutes. Stir in flour and tomato paste and cook until paste begins to darken, about 2 minutes.

4. Off heat, push vegetables to center of pan. Place roast on top of vegetables and transfer skillet to oven. Cook until meat registers 120 to 125 degrees (for medium-rare), 2½ to 3½ hours.

5. Remove skillet from oven. Transfer roast to carving board, tent with aluminum foil, and let rest for 20 minutes. Meanwhile, carefully return skillet with vegetables to stovetop (skillet handle will be hot), and cook over medium-high heat, stirring often, until deep golden brown, about 5 minutes. Slowly whisk in consommé and water, scraping up any browned bits, and bring to boil. Reduce heat to medium and simmer until thickened, 10 to 15 minutes.

6. Strain gravy through fine-mesh strainer into serving bowl and season with salt and pepper to taste. Remove twine and slice roast thinly against grain. Serve with gravy.

These eight beef roasts are the test kitchen's top picks. We've rated each roast on a scale from 1 to 4 stars for flavor. Given that even the toughest cut can make a great roast if cooked properly, we don't rate these cuts for tenderness. We've also listed the primal cut from which each roast is cut. See page 189 for more information on primal cuts and beef grading.

	TYPE	FLAVOR
	Chuck-Eye Roast (Chuck/Shoulder) This boneless roast is cut from the center of the first five ribs (the term "eye" refers to any center-cut piece of meat). It is very tender and juicy but also contains an excessive amount of fat. This cut should be trussed using kitchen twine, so if the butcher has not done it for you, do it yourself. It is also called boneless chuck roll and boneless chuck fillet. We like the chuck-eye roast for its compact, uniform shape, deep flavor, and tenderness in pot roast. This is our top choice for stewing and braising.	★★★
	**Top Blade Roast (Chuck/Shoulder)** This broad, flat cut is quite flavorful, and because it is boneless it's the best substitute for a chuck-eye roast. Even after cooking, this cut retains a distinctive strip of connective tissue, which is not unpleasant to eat. This roast is sometimes labeled as blade roast or top chuck roast.	★★★
	**Rib Roast, First Cut (Rib)** Butchers tend to cut a rib roast, which consists of ribs 6 through 12 if left whole, into two distinct cuts. The more desirable of the two cuts consists of ribs 10 through 12. Since this portion of the roast is closer to the loin end, it is sometimes called the "loin end." Other butchers call it the "small end" or the "first cut." Whatever it is called, it is more desirable because it contains the large, single rib-eye muscle and is less fatty. The less desirable second cut consists of ribs 6 through 9 and is fattier and more irregularly shaped but still an excellent roast.	★★★★
	Tenderloin Roast (Short Loin) The tenderloin (also called the whole filet) is the most tender piece of beef you can buy. Its flavor is pleasantly mild, almost nonbeefy. Unpeeled tenderloins come with an incredibly thick layer of exterior fat still attached, which should be removed. Peeled roasts have scattered patches of fat that need not be removed. This roast can be cut into individual steaks to make filets mignons.	★
	Top Sirloin Roast (Sirloin) This cut from the hip area tastes incredibly meaty and has plenty of marbling, which makes for a succulent roast. Aside from the vein of gristle that runs through it, and that we found slightly unpleasant to eat, the roast was tender and juicy, with big, beefy flavor. Other parts of the sirloin are lean and tough, but top sirloin roast is one of our favorite inexpensive roasts.	★★★
	Eye-Round Roast (Round) This boneless roast is quite inexpensive but not nearly as flavorful as the top cuts. However, it does have a nice shape that slices neatly, making it a better choice than other round or rump roasts. In order to make this lean cut as tender as possible, roast it in a very low oven.	★★
	Top Round Roast (Round) The round roast is cut from the cow's rump and it is a bargain. It has very good flavor, is relatively juicy, and, when sliced thin, isn't too chewy. Most deli roast beef is cut from the top round. This roast has an odd shape, which can make even cooking (and carving) a challenge. We cook all round roasts the same: salt, sear, and then roast in a very low oven.	★★★
	Brisket (Brisket) This large, rectangular cut weights 13 pounds, so it is often divided into two subcuts, the flat cut (pictured here) and the point cut. The flat cut is leaner, thinner, and more widely available. When shopping for flat-cut brisket, look for a roast with a decent fat cap on top. The point cut is well marbled and thicker, and if you can find it, you can use it in place of the flat-cut brisket in most recipes; however, the cooking time might need to be extended slightly.	★★★

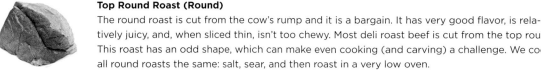

Slow-Roasted Beef

SERVES 6 TO 8 **TOTAL TIME** 2½ TO 3 HOURS
(PLUS 18 HOURS FOR SALTING)

✔ **WHY THIS RECIPE WORKS:** Roasting inexpensive beef usually yields tough meat best suited for sandwiches. We wanted to transform a bargain cut into a tender, juicy roast that could stand on its own at dinner. The eye-round roast has good flavor and relative tenderness, and it also has a uniform shape that guarantees even cooking. Searing the meat before roasting, as well as salting it as much as 24 hours before roasting, vastly improved its flavor. But the big surprise was the method that produced remarkably tender and juicy beef—roasting the meat at a very low 225 degrees and then turning off the oven toward the end of cooking. This approach allowed the meat's enzymes to act as natural tenderizers, breaking down the roast's tough connective tissue. Open the oven door as little as possible, and remove the roast from the oven while taking its temperature. If the roast has not reached the desired temperature in the time specified in step 4, reheat the oven to 225 degrees for 5 minutes, then shut it off and continue to cook the roast to the desired temperature. We don't recommend cooking this roast past medium. For a smaller (2½- to 3½-pound) roast, reduce the amount of kosher salt to 1 tablespoon and pepper to 1½ teaspoons. For a larger (4½- to 6-pound) roast, cut the meat in half crosswise before cooking to create two smaller roasts. Serve with any of the sauces on page 203 or compound butters on page 202.

> 1 **(3½- to 4½-pound) boneless eye-round roast, trimmed**
> 4 **teaspoons kosher salt**
> 2 **teaspoons plus 1 tablespoon vegetable oil**
> 2 **teaspoons pepper**

1. Rub roast thoroughly with salt, wrap in plastic wrap, and refrigerate for 18 to 24 hours.

2. Adjust oven rack to middle position and heat oven to 225 degrees. Pat roast dry with paper towels, rub with 2 teaspoons oil, and sprinkle with pepper.

3. Heat remaining 1 tablespoon oil in 12-inch skillet over medium-high heat until just smoking. Brown roast well on all sides, 12 to 16 minutes; reduce heat if pan begins to scorch. Transfer roast to wire rack set in rimmed baking sheet and roast until meat registers 115 degrees (for medium-rare), 1¼ to 1¾ hours, or 125 degrees (for medium), 1¾ to 2¼ hours.

4. Turn oven off and leave roast in oven, without opening door, until meat registers 130 degrees (for medium-rare) or 140 degrees (for medium), 30 to 50 minutes.

5. Transfer roast to carving board and let rest for 15 minutes. Slice meat crosswise as thinly as possible and serve.

Roast Beef Tenderloin

SERVES 10 TO 12 **TOTAL TIME** 2 HOURS 10 MINUTES

✔ **WHY THIS RECIPE WORKS:** When it comes to roasting beef, we prefer to cook the meat at a low oven temperature to ensure that the whole roast is evenly cooked throughout. But because of the tenderloin's long, thin shape, we found a hotter oven temperature was better. Cooking the roast at 425 degrees developed a flavorful crust, while the interior remained rosy and moist throughout. To flavor the meat, we salted it, wrapped it in plastic, and let it rest on the counter before roasting. Tucking the narrow tip end of the tenderloin under and tying it securely gave the tenderloin a more consistent thickness that allowed it to cook through more evenly. The

Making Slow-Roasted Beef

1. SALT MEAT: Rub roast with 4 teaspoons kosher salt, wrap in plastic wrap, and refrigerate 18 to 24 hours.

2. SEAR ROAST: Heat 1 tablespoon oil in 12-inch skillet over medium-high heat until starting to smoke. Sear roast until browned on all sides, 3 to 4 minutes per side.

3. ROAST BEEF: Roast beef in 225-degree oven for 1¼ to 2¼ hours (depending on desired doneness), then turn oven off and let roast sit in oven for 30 to 50 minutes.

4. SLICE THINLY: After removing roast from oven, let it rest for 15 minutes, then slice meat crosswise as thinly as possible.

great thing about a tenderloin is that the center of the roast will always be a degree more rare than the ends. For example, if the center is medium-rare, then the ends will be medium, which is ideal for a party where you want to give your guests some options. We prefer beef tenderloin when the center is cooked to medium-rare, but if you prefer it more or less done, see our guidelines on page 15. Serve with any of the sauces on page 203 or one of the compound butters.

1 **(6-pound) whole beef tenderloin, trimmed**
1½ **tablespoons kosher salt**
2 **tablespoons vegetable oil**
 Pepper

1. Tuck tail end of tenderloin and tie roast at 2-inch intervals with kitchen twine. Pat roast dry with paper towels and rub with salt. Cover loosely with plastic wrap and let sit at room temperature for 1 hour.

2. Adjust oven rack to upper-middle position and heat oven to 425 degrees. Pat tenderloin dry with paper towels, rub with oil, and season with pepper. Set tenderloin on wire rack set over aluminum foil–lined rimmed baking sheet.

3. Roast until center of meat registers 120 to 125 degrees (for medium-rare), 40 to 50 minutes. (Center of roast will remain a degree more rare than the ends.)

4. Transfer roast to carving board, tent with foil, and let rest for 15 to 20 minutes. Remove twine, slice roast into ½-inch-thick pieces, and serve.

Preparing a Beef Tenderloin for Roasting

1. Tuck tail end of tenderloin under to create roast with more even shape.

2. Using kitchen twine, tie roast at 2-inch intervals.

COMPOUND BUTTERS FOR MEAT

Compound butters—butter mixed with fresh herbs and other potent ingredients like mustard and lemon juice—are an easy way to add savory flavor to plain beef, pork, or lamb. Here in the test kitchen, we like to make a double or triple batch, roll it into a log, and store it in the freezer so that flavored butter is always just a slice away.

TO MAKE COMPOUND BUTTER: Whip 8 tablespoons softened unsalted butter with fork until light and fluffy. Mix in any of the ingredient combinations listed below and season with salt and pepper to taste. Wrap in plastic wrap and let rest to blend flavors, about 10 minutes, or roll into log and refrigerate. (Compound butter can be refrigerated in airtight container for up to 4 days or frozen, wrapped tightly in plastic, for up to 2 months.)

GARLIC-HERB COMPOUND BUTTER `FAST`
2 **tablespoons minced fresh sage or**
 1½ teaspoons dried
1 **tablespoon minced fresh parsley**
1 **tablespoon minced fresh thyme or**
 ¾ teaspoon dried
2 **garlic cloves, minced**

ROSEMARY-PARMESAN COMPOUND BUTTER `FAST`
6 **tablespoons grated Parmesan cheese**
4 **teaspoons minced fresh rosemary or**
 1 teaspoon dried
2 **garlic cloves, minced**
¼ **teaspoon red pepper flakes**

BLUE CHEESE COMPOUND BUTTER `FAST`
2 **ounces blue cheese, crumbled (½ cup)**
2 **teaspoons brandy**

MUSTARD-GARLIC COMPOUND BUTTER `FAST`
¼ **cup Dijon mustard**
4 **garlic cloves, minced**
4 **teaspoons minced fresh thyme or 1 teaspoon dried**

ANCHOVY-GARLIC COMPOUND BUTTER `FAST`
¼ **cup minced fresh parsley**
2 **anchovy fillets, rinsed and minced**
1 **tablespoon lemon juice**
2 **garlic cloves, minced**

SAUCES FOR BEEF ROASTS

These sauces offer a variety of flavors, all of which taste great with roast beef, including Slow-Roasted Beef (page 201), Roast Beef Tenderloin (page 201), and Best Prime Rib (page 204).

Persillade Relish

TOTAL TIME 20 MINUTES **FAST**

- ¾ cup minced fresh parsley
- ½ cup extra-virgin olive oil
- 6 tablespoons minced cornichons plus 1 teaspoon cornichon juice
- ¼ cup capers, rinsed and chopped coarse
- 2 scallions, minced
- 1 teaspoon sugar
  Salt and pepper

Combine all ingredients in bowl and season with salt and pepper to taste. Let sit at room temperature until flavors have blended, about 10 minutes. (Relish can be refrigerated for up to 1 day; bring to room temperature before serving.)

Horseradish Sauce

TOTAL TIME 15 MINUTES **FAST**

This sauce is a classic accompaniment with roast tenderloin, but it also tastes great with fresh salmon and a variety of smoked fish.

- 1 cup sour cream
- 3 tablespoons prepared horseradish
- 1 tablespoon mayonnaise
- 1 tablespoon lemon juice
- 1 garlic clove, minced
- ¼ teaspoon sugar
  Salt and pepper

Combine all ingredients in bowl and season with salt and pepper to taste. Let sit at room temperature until flavors have blended, about 10 minutes. (Sauce can be refrigerated for up to 4 days.)

Mustard-Cream Sauce

TOTAL TIME 15 MINUTES **FAST**

- ½ cup sour cream
- ½ cup heavy cream
- 2 large egg yolks
- 5 teaspoons Dijon mustard
- 1 tablespoon white wine vinegar
  Salt and pepper
- ⅛ teaspoon sugar
- 1 tablespoon minced fresh chives

Whisk sour cream, heavy cream, egg yolks, mustard, vinegar, ¼ teaspoon salt, and sugar together in small saucepan. Cook over medium heat, whisking constantly, until sauce thickens and coats back of spoon, 4 to 5 minutes. Transfer to serving bowl, stir in chives, and season with salt and pepper to taste. Serve warm or at room temperature.

Béarnaise Sauce

TOTAL TIME 20 MINUTES **FAST**

Be sure to add the melted butter to the blender very slowly and follow the specified blending times.

- ½ cup dry white wine
- 3 whole black peppercorns
- 2 sprigs fresh tarragon
- 3 large egg yolks
- 1 tablespoon lemon juice
- 16 tablespoons unsalted butter, melted
  Hot water
- 2 teaspoons minced fresh tarragon
- ⅛ teaspoon cayenne pepper
  Salt and pepper

1. Cook wine, peppercorns, and tarragon sprigs in 8-inch skillet over medium heat until liquid has reduced to 2 tablespoons, about 5 minutes. Strain wine and transfer to blender.

2. Add egg yolks and lemon juice to blender, and process until smooth and frothy, about 10 seconds. With blender running, very slowly drizzle in half of melted butter until mixture is quite thick, about 1½ minutes.

3. Blend in 2 teaspoons hot water, then continue to slowly blend in remaining melted butter, about 1 minute.

4. Blend in additional hot water, 1 teaspoon at a time, as needed until sauce coats back of spoon. Stir in tarragon and cayenne and season with salt and pepper to taste. (Sauce can be kept warm in covered bowl set over saucepan of barely simmering water for up to 1 hour; stir often and do not let sauce get too hot.)

Pomegranate-Port Sauce

TOTAL TIME 45 MINUTES **FAST**

- 2 cups pomegranate juice
- 1½ cups ruby port
- 1 shallot, minced
- 1 tablespoon sugar
- 1 teaspoon balsamic vinegar
- 1 sprig fresh thyme
  Salt and pepper
- 4 tablespoons unsalted butter, cut into 4 pieces and chilled

1. Simmer pomegranate juice, port, shallot, sugar, vinegar, thyme, and 1 teaspoon salt in saucepan over medium-high heat until reduced to 1 cup, 30 to 35 minutes. Strain sauce through fine-mesh strainer and return to saucepan. (Saucepan can be covered and set aside at room temperature for up to 2 hours; reheat gently and adjust consistency as needed with water before continuing.)

2. Return saucepan to medium heat and whisk in butter, 1 piece at a time. Season with salt and pepper to taste.

Best Prime Rib

SERVES 6 TO 8   **TOTAL TIME** 5 TO 6 HOURS
(PLUS 24 HOURS FOR SALTING)

✔ **WHY THIS RECIPE WORKS:** The perfect prime rib should have a dark and substantial crisp crust encasing a juicy, rosy center. To achieve this perfect roast, we started by salting the roast, then refrigerating it uncovered for at least 24 hours. This not only seasoned the meat but also dried out the exterior for better browning. Searing a superdry roast in a superhot skillet helped it develop a nice thick crust. To further enhance tenderness, we cooked the roast at a very low temperature, which allowed the meat's enzymes to act as natural tenderizers. A quick trip under the broiler restored the crispness the crust had lost while the meat was resting. Look for a roast with an untrimmed fat cap (ideally ½ inch thick). We prefer the flavor and texture of prime-grade beef, but choice grade will work as well. Monitoring the roast with a meat-probe thermometer is best. If you use an instant-read thermometer, open the oven door as little as possible and remove the roast from the oven while taking its temperature. If the roast has not reached the correct temperature in the time range specified in step 4, reheat the oven to 200 degrees for 5 minutes, then shut it off and continue to cook the roast until it reaches the desired temperature. Serve with any of the sauces on page 203 or compound butters on page 202.

> 1 **(7-pound) first-cut beef standing rib roast (3 bones)**
>   **Kosher salt and pepper**
> 2 **teaspoons vegetable oil**

1. Using sharp knife, cut roast from bones. Cut slits 1 inch apart in crosshatch pattern in fat cap of roast, being careful not to cut into meat. Rub 2 tablespoons salt thoroughly over roast and into slits. Place meat back on bones (to save space in refrigerator), transfer to large plate, and refrigerate, uncovered, for at least 1 day and up to 4 days.

2. Adjust oven rack to middle position and heat oven to 200 degrees. Heat oil in 12-inch skillet over high heat until just smoking. Remove roast from bones. Sear top and sides of roast until browned, 6 to 8 minutes; do not sear side of roast that was cut from bones.

NOTES FROM THE TEST KITCHEN

Salting Meat

No matter how well cooked your meat is, if it's not properly seasoned it won't taste very good. Meat should be seasoned with salt and pepper before cooking. You will also want to taste meat before serving to adjust the seasonings. Heat tames the punch of pepper, so use it sparingly after cooking.

As for salt, you can season the meat for flavor right before cooking, but you can also use salt (and time) in advance of cooking to improve the texture of many cuts. There are two ways to do this: salting or brining (for information on brining, see page 158). Salting is more convenient (no need to cram a large container of salt water in the fridge), and it won't thwart the goal of well-browned crust on steak, chops, and roasts since no moisture is added to their exteriors. However, salting is a slow process and takes more time than brining.

When salt is applied to raw meat, juices inside the meat are drawn to the surface. The salt then dissolves in the exuded liquid, forming a brine that is eventually reabsorbed by the meat. The salt changes the structure of the muscle proteins, allowing them to hold on to more of their own natural juices. Salting is the best choice for meats that are already relatively juicy and/or well marbled.

We prefer to use kosher salt for salting because it's easier to distribute the salt evenly. If using Morton Kosher Salt, reduce the amounts listed by one-third.

---

3. Fit roast back onto bones, let cool for 10 minutes, then tie together with kitchen twine between ribs. Transfer roast, fat side up, to wire rack set in rimmed baking sheet and season with pepper. Roast until meat registers 110 degrees, 3 to 4 hours.

4. Turn oven off and leave roast in oven, without opening door, until meat registers 120 degrees (for rare) or 125 degrees (for medium-rare), 30 to 75 minutes.

5. Remove roast from oven (leave roast on baking sheet), tent with aluminum foil, and let rest for at least 30 minutes and up to 75 minutes.

6. Adjust oven rack 8 inches from broiler element and heat broiler. Remove foil from roast, form into 3-inch ball, and place under ribs to elevate fat cap. Broil until top of roast is well browned and crisp, 2 to 8 minutes. Transfer roast to carving board, remove twine, and remove roast from ribs. Slice meat into ¾-inch-thick pieces, season with salt, and serve.

Top chefs say that 18 hours in a 120-degree oven is the route to prime rib perfection. So what's a home cook to do? To achieve a roast with a deep-colored crust encasing a tender, juicy, rosy-pink center, start by salting the roast overnight. To further enhance tenderness, cook the roast at a very low temperature. A brief stint under the broiler before serving ensures a crisp, flavorful crust.

1. REMOVE THE ROAST FROM THE BONES: Using a sharp knife, cut the meat from the bones in a single piece. **WHY?** Removing the roast from the bones facilitates browning of the meat in a skillet before the roast (tied back to the bones) goes into a low-temperature oven. This also makes it easy to season the meat all over and makes carving a snap.

2. CROSSHATCH THE FAT CAP: Cut slits 1 inch apart in a crosshatch pattern in the fat cap of the roast, being careful not to cut into the meat. **WHY?** The crosshatches help the salt penetrate into the meat and will speed up the rendering process in the oven.

3. SALT AND REFRIGERATE THE ROAST: Rub kosher salt thoroughly over the roast, working it into the slits. Place the meat back on the bones and refrigerate for 1 to 3 days. **WHY?** Curing the roast for at least a day improves its beefy flavor and makes the meat more tender. Because the exterior dries out in the refrigerator, the meat browns easily, too.

4. SEAR THE ROAST: Remove the roast from the bones and sear it in a hot skillet until browned. Do not sear the backside of the roast. **WHY?** Despite the long cooking time in the oven, the roast won't brown sufficiently unless it first spends some time in a skillet. Don't brown the side of the roast that will be attached to the bones.

5. TIE THE MEAT BACK ONTO THE BONES: Fit the browned roast back onto the bones, let cool for 10 minutes, then tie them together with kitchen twine between each rib. **WHY?** The bones make browning the roast in a skillet impossible, but they provide some insulation against the baking sheet in the oven and ensure more even cooking.

6. ROAST SLOWLY: Place the roast on a wire rack set in a rimmed baking sheet, season the meat with pepper, and roast in a 200-degree oven until it registers 110 degrees, 3 to 4 hours. **WHY?** A low-temperature oven ensures even cooking so that the roast is rosy throughout. Also, the enzymes in the meat have more time to tenderize the roast.

7. TURN OFF THE OVEN TO FINISH COOKING: Turn the oven off and leave the roast in the oven, without opening the door, until the meat registers 120 degrees for rare, or 125 degrees for medium-rare, 30 to 75 minutes. **WHY?** A gentle finish ensures that the roast doesn't overcook.

8. BROIL THE TOP: Let the roast rest on the counter for 30 to 75 minutes, then broil until the top is well browned and crisp, 2 to 8 minutes. **WHY?** The fat cap will lose some of its crispness as the roast rests. A quick stint under the broiler ensures a crisp, browned top. The roast is now ready to carve and serve.

The sauce for this pot roast gets its rich flavor from blending the cooked vegetables with the cooking liquid.

Classic Pot Roast

SERVES 6 TO 8   **TOTAL TIME** 4½ TO 5 HOURS
(PLUS 1 HOUR SALTING TIME)

✔ **WHY THIS RECIPE WORKS:** We started our pot roast by selecting a well-marbled chuck-eye roast. Splitting the roast along its natural seams meant we could trim off excess fat that would have made the finished dish greasy. Working with two smaller roasts instead of one large one also allowed us to cut back on the cooking time. To beef up the gravy, we used a combination of beef broth and red wine for the braising liquid. We also added a bit of glutamate-rich tomato paste. In the interest of streamlining, we determined that the initial sear called for in most pot roast recipes wasn't necessary—we found that the "dry" part of the meat that stays above the braising liquid eventually browns, even without searing. Blending the cooked vegetables with the defatted cooking liquid and extra beef broth gave us a full-bodied gravy, which we finished with a spoonful of balsamic vinegar and a bit more wine for brightness. Chilling the whole cooked pot roast overnight improves its flavor and makes it moister and easier to slice.

1   (3½- to 4-pound) boneless beef chuck-eye roast, pulled into 2 pieces at natural seam and trimmed of large knobs of fat
     Kosher salt and pepper
2   tablespoons unsalted butter
2   onions, halved and sliced thin
1   large carrot, peeled and chopped
1   celery rib, chopped
2   garlic cloves, minced
2–3 cups beef broth
¾   cup dry red wine
1   tablespoon tomato paste
1   bay leaf
1   sprig fresh thyme, plus ¼ teaspoon minced
1   tablespoon balsamic vinegar

1. Rub roasts thoroughly with 1 tablespoon salt, place on wire rack set in rimmed baking sheet, and let sit at room temperature for 1 hour. Pat beef dry with paper towels, season with pepper, and tie each with 3 pieces of kitchen twine.

2. Adjust oven rack to lower-middle position and heat oven to 300 degrees. Melt butter in Dutch oven over medium heat. Add onions and cook, stirring often, until softened and beginning to brown, 8 to 10 minutes. Stir in carrot and celery and cook until softened, about 5 minutes. Stir in garlic and cook until fragrant, about 30 seconds. Stir in 1 cup broth, ½ cup wine, tomato paste, bay leaf, and thyme sprig and bring to simmer.

3. Nestle meat on top of vegetables. Cover pot tightly with aluminum foil, then cover with lid and transfer to oven. Cook until beef is tender and fork slips easily in and out of meat, 3½ to 4 hours, turning meat halfway through cooking.

4. Transfer roasts to carving board and tent with foil. Strain liquid through fine-mesh strainer into 4-cup liquid measuring cup. Reserve strained vegetables, discarding bay leaf and thyme sprig. Let liquid settle for 5 minutes, then skim fat and add broth as needed until liquid measures 3 cups.

5. Process liquid and strained vegetables in blender until smooth, about 2 minutes. Transfer gravy to medium saucepan and bring to simmer over medium heat.

6. Remove twine, slice meat against grain into ½-inch-thick pieces, and transfer to serving platter. Stir remaining ¼ cup wine, minced thyme, and vinegar into gravy and season with salt and pepper to taste. Spoon half of gravy over meat and serve with remaining gravy.

TO MAKE AHEAD: Before separating out meat, broth, and vegetables in step 4, contents can be cooled and refrigerated together in large container for up to 2 days. To serve, slice meat ½ inch thick, lay in large baking dish, and cover with foil; reheat in 325-degree for 45 minutes. Finish gravy using broth and vegetables as directed.

Pot roasting takes a large, tough, fatty cut of meat and simmers it gently for hours, partially submerged in liquid in a covered pot, until its toughness gives way to a meltingly fork-tender texture. There is no shortage of ways to cook a pot roast, but this simple approach is our favorite. We took a chuck-eye roast and split it along its natural seams to remove the excess fat that usually mars a good pot roast. We left the pieces separate too, which cut back on cooking time. We also found the initial sear that is called for in most recipes unnecessary. The part of the meat that stays above the braising liquid browns with the extended cooking time.

1. DIVIDE THE ROAST INTO 2 PIECES: Pull apart the roast at its natural seams. Remove any excess fat. Season the roasts with kosher salt and place on a wire rack set in a rimmed baking sheet.
WHY? Opening the roast allows you to trim extra fat, and leaving the two lobes as separate roasts shaves about an hour off the cooking time.

2. TIE THE ROASTS: Pat the roasts dry with paper towels and season with pepper. Tie 3 pieces of kitchen twine around each piece of meat to form an even shape.
WHY? Tying the roasts gives them a neater, more even shape, which ensures they cook through evenly.

3. BUILD THE SAUCE BASE: Soften the onions, carrot, celery, and garlic in a large Dutch oven, then add the broth, wine, tomato paste, and herbs.
WHY? Sautéing the aromatics creates a savory base of flavor for the sauce. The tomato paste and beef broth boost the meaty flavor.

4. BRAISE THE ROASTS IN THE OVEN: Nestle the roasts on top of the vegetables. Cover the pot with foil and cover with the lid. Place the pot in the oven.
WHY? Braising in the oven provides a steady heat that allows for even cooking without the need to monitor the pot.

5. COOK THE BEEF UNTIL IT'S TENDER: Cook the beef until fully tender and a fork slips easily into the meat, 3½ to 4 hours, turning the meat halfway through cooking. Transfer the roasts to a carving board and tent loosely with foil to rest.
WHY? Gently simmering the meat for hours until it's well-done, reaching a temperature of about 210 degrees, fully melts the fat and connective tissue, creating tender meat.

6. STRAIN THE LIQUID AND RESERVE THE VEGETABLES: Strain the liquid into a 4-cup liquid measuring cup. Discard the bay leaf and thyme sprig. Transfer the vegetables to a blender. Let the liquid settle, then skim off the fat.
WHY? When the roast is tender, the vegetables will have broken down and thickened the sauce. Letting the liquid sit allows you to remove the excess fat easily. If you skip this step, the sauce will be greasy.

7. BLEND THE VEGETABLES AND MAKE THE SAUCE: Add enough beef broth to the defatted cooking liquid to reach 3 cups. Add the liquid to the vegetables and blend until smooth. Transfer to a saucepan and bring to a simmer.
WHY? Blending the vegetables with the cooking liquid and extra beef broth coaxes every bit of flavor out of them. Reducing the sauce on the stovetop concentrates its flavor and gives it substantial texture.

8. SLICE THE MEAT AND FINISH THE SAUCE: Remove the twine and slice the meat against the grain into ½-inch-thick slices. Stir the remaining wine, minced thyme, and vinegar into the sauce and season with salt and pepper. Spoon half of the sauce over the meat and pass the rest.
WHY? Slicing the meat against the grain ensures the slices are tender not stringy. Balsamic vinegar and red wine brighten the finished sauce.

Storing Meat Safely

Throwing away meat because it went bad before you had a chance to cook it is frustrating, particularly when you've spent a lot of money on a nice steak or cut of lamb. Proper storage is the best way to prolong its shelf life and prevent waste.

REFRIGERATING MEAT: Raw meat should be refrigerated well wrapped and never on shelves that are above other food. Check regularly to ensure your refrigerator's temperature is between 35 and 40 degrees. Most raw and cooked meat will keep for two to three days in the refrigerator. Raw ground meat and raw poultry will keep for two days, while smoked ham and bacon will keep for up to two weeks.

FREEZING MEAT: In general, meat tastes best when it hasn't been frozen. The slow process of freezing that occurs in a home freezer (as compared with a commercial freezer) causes large ice crystals to form. The crystals rupture the cell walls of the meat, permitting the release of juices during cooking, resulting in drier meat. If you're going to freeze meat, wrap it well in plastic wrap and then place the meat in a zipper-lock bag and squeeze out excess air. Label the bag and use the meat within a few months.

THAWING MEAT: All meat can be thawed safely on a plate or rimmed baking sheet in the refrigerator (and this is the only safe method for large cuts like whole chickens). Never thaw meat on the counter, where bacteria will rapidly multiply. According to the U.S. Department of Agriculture, frozen food that is properly thawed is safe to refreeze. However, a second freeze-thaw cycle aggravates moisture loss, reducing the quality of the meat, so we don't recommend it.

QUICK THAW FOR SMALL CUTS: Flat cuts like chicken breasts, pork chops, and steaks will thaw more quickly when left on a metal surface rather than on a wood or a plastic one, because metal can transfer ambient heat much more quickly. To thaw frozen wrapped steaks, chops, and ground meat (flattened to 1 inch thick before freezing), place in a skillet (heavy steel and cast-iron skillets work best) in a single layer. Flip the meat every half-hour until it's thawed. Small cuts can also be sealed in zipper-lock bags and submerged in hot (140-degree) water—this method will safely thaw chicken breasts, steaks, and chops in under 15 minutes.

Braised Boneless Beef Short Ribs

SERVES 6   **TOTAL TIME** 3½ TO 4 HOURS

✔ **WHY THIS RECIPE WORKS:** Short ribs have great flavor and a luscious texture, but they can release a lot of fat during cooking, necessitating an overnight rest so the fat can solidify into an easy-to-remove layer. We wanted a more convenient (and less time-consuming) approach, so we decided to make the most of boneless short ribs, which traditionally render less fat. To restore the body that the bones' connective tissue would have added, we sprinkled a bit of gelatin into the sauce. To ramp up the richness of the sauce, we reduced wine with browned aromatics (onions and garlic) before using the liquid to cook the meat. As for the excess fat, the level was low enough that we could strain and defat the liquid in a fat separator. Reducing the liquid concentrated the flavors and made for a rich, luxurious sauce for our fork-tender boneless short ribs. Make sure that the ribs are at least 4 inches long and 1 inch thick. We recommend a bold red wine such as a Cabernet Sauvignon. Serve with buttered egg noodles, mashed potatoes, or roasted potatoes.

3½ pounds boneless beef short ribs, trimmed
    Salt and pepper
2   tablespoons vegetable oil
2   large onions, sliced thin
1   tablespoon tomato paste
6   garlic cloves, peeled
2   cups red wine
1   cup beef broth
4   large carrots, peeled and cut into 2-inch pieces
4   sprigs fresh thyme
1   bay leaf
¼   cup cold water
½   teaspoon unflavored gelatin

1. Adjust oven rack to lower-middle position and heat oven to 300 degrees. Pat beef dry with paper towels and season with salt and pepper. Heat 1 tablespoon oil in Dutch oven over medium-high heat until just smoking. Cook half of beef until well browned on both sides, 8 to 12 minutes. Transfer browned beef to bowl and repeat with remaining 1 tablespoon oil and beef; transfer to bowl.

2. Add onions to fat left in pot and cook over medium heat, stirring often, until browned, 12 to 15 minutes; if onions brown too quickly, stir in 1 to 2 tablespoons water. Stir in tomato paste and cook, stirring constantly, until it browns on sides and bottom of pot, about 2 minutes. Stir in garlic and cook until fragrant, about 30 seconds.

3. Stir in wine, scraping up any browned bits, and simmer until reduced by half, 8 to 10 minutes. Stir in broth, carrots, thyme sprigs, and bay leaf. Add browned beef and any accumulated juices, and return to simmer. Cover pot, transfer to oven, and cook until beef is tender and fork slips easily in and out of meat, 2 to 2½ hours, turning meat twice during cooking.

4. Using tongs, transfer meat and carrots to serving platter and tent with aluminum foil. Strain cooking liquid through fine-mesh strainer into fat separator or bowl, pressing on solids to extract as much liquid as possible. Let liquid settle for 5 minutes, then skim fat. Meanwhile, add water to small bowl and sprinkle gelatin over top; let stand for 5 minutes.

5. Return defatted juices to now-empty pot and simmer over medium heat until reduced to 1 cup, 5 to 10 minutes. Off heat, stir in gelatin mixture and season with salt and pepper to taste. Pour sauce over meat and serve.

VARIATION

Braised Boneless Beef Short Ribs with Guinness and Prunes

Substitute 1 cup Guinness (or other full-flavored porter or stout) for red wine and omit wine reduction time in step 3. Add ⅓ cup pitted prunes to pot with broth.

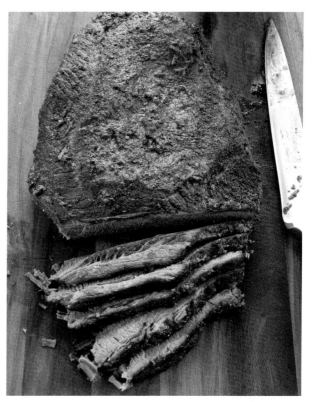

Cooking the roast wrapped tightly with aluminum foil for hours in a low oven results in rich, tender brisket.

Oven-Barbecued Beef Brisket

SERVES 8 TO 10   **TOTAL TIME** 6 HOURS

✓ **WHY THIS RECIPE WORKS:** We love the rich flavor and tender texture of barbecued brisket, but because grilling season is cruelly short in many regions of the country, we wanted to come up with a recipe that would deliver that same smoky flavor and velvety texture indoors. To begin, we liberally seasoned the meat with a spicy rub, poking it in with a fork so the spices' flavors could penetrate into the meat. We wrapped it in bacon, which bathed the brisket in smoky fat as it baked. We cooked the meat slow and low, sealed in aluminum foil, which retained any released moisture, helping the meat cook faster and become more tender—in essence, the brisket braised in its own juices. You can substitute 3½ cups of store-bought sauce. If you do use another sauce, skip steps 3 and 4 and go directly to step 5.

BRISKET
- 1 **pound bacon**
- 4 **teaspoons packed brown sugar**
- 4 **teaspoons paprika**
- 2 **teaspoons dry mustard**
- 2 **teaspoons salt**
- 2 **teaspoons pepper**
- 1 **teaspoon onion powder**
- 1 **teaspoon garlic powder**
- 1 **teaspoon ground cumin**
- ¼ **teaspoon cayenne pepper**
- 1 **(4- to 5-pound) beef brisket, fat trimmed to ¼ inch**

SMOKY BACON BBQ SAUCE
- 1–2 **cups chicken broth**
  Bacon from cooked brisket
- 1 **onion, chopped fine**
- ½ **cup cider vinegar**
- ⅓ **cup packed dark brown sugar**
- ½ **cup ketchup**
- 1½ **teaspoons minced canned chipotle chile in adobo sauce**

1. FOR THE BRISKET: Adjust oven rack to upper-middle position and heat oven to 275 degrees. Lay half of bacon crosswise over bottom of broiler-safe 13 by 9-inch baking dish, overlapping as needed. Combine sugar, paprika, dry mustard, salt, pepper, onion powder, garlic powder, cumin, and cayenne in bowl, breaking up any lumps. Massage spice mixture into meat and poke all over with fork. Place brisket, fat side down, in bacon-lined pan and top with remaining bacon, tucking ends underneath brisket. Cover pan with aluminum foil and roast until brisket is fully tender and fork slips easily in and out of meat, about 4 hours.

2. Remove pan from oven, carefully flip brisket fat side up, and replace foil. Return brisket to oven, turn oven off, and let brisket rest for 1 hour. (Bacon-wrapped meat and accumulated juices can be refrigerated separately for up to 3 days. To serve, remove bacon, rewrap brisket with foil, and reheat in 350-degree oven for 1 hour. Finish sauce using bacon and juices as directed.)

3. FOR THE SAUCE: Pour accumulated juices into 4-cup measuring cup and transfer bacon to cutting board; leave brisket in baking dish and set aside. Let juices settle for 5 minutes, then skim fat and add broth as needed until liquid measures 3 cups.

4. Finely chop bacon and cook in medium saucepan over medium heat until fat has rendered, about 5 minutes. Add onion and cook until softened, about 5 minutes. Off heat, stir in vinegar and sugar, then return to medium heat and reduce to syrupy consistency, about 5 minutes. Stir in reserved liquid and reduce to 3 cups, about 8 minutes. Off heat, stir in ketchup and chipotle.

5. Adjust oven rack 8 inches from broiler element and heat broiler. Brush brisket with 1 cup sauce and broil until top is lightly charred and fat is crisped, 5 to 7 minutes. Transfer brisket to carving board and slice against grain into ¼-inch-thick slices. Serve with remaining sauce.

Making Oven-Barbecued Beef Brisket

1. Combine brown sugar and spices in bowl, breaking up any lumps. Massage dry rub into meat and poke all over with fork.

2. Arrange half of bacon strips, overlapping slightly, crosswise on bottom of broiler-safe 13 by 9-inch baking dish. Place brisket, fat side down, in bacon-lined pan, and place remaining strips of bacon on top.

Corned beef gets a flavor boost by simmering it in the oven with bay leaves, whole peppercorns, and mustard seeds.

Corned Beef and Cabbage

SERVES 8   **TOTAL TIME** 2½ TO 3½ HOURS

✓ **WHY THIS RECIPE WORKS:** Corned beef and cabbage makes its way to the dinner table (in this country, anyway) but once a year in celebration of St. Patrick's Day, and maybe for good reason. The meat can be unbearably salty, dry, and rubbery. And when cooked with the stale spice packet that often gets packaged with the meat, it's flavorless at best. The accompanying vegetables are usually mushy, greasy, and monotone in flavor. To solve the problem of dry, stringy meat, we employed a stovetop simmer. To ensure that the cabbage, carrots, and potatoes typically served with the corned beef didn't overcook and get mushy, we cooked them after the meat was done, using the broth that remained. The salt and fat in the broth gave the vegetables a rich flavor, and the meat could rest in the oven during this time. When cutting the cabbage, make sure to leave the core intact, or the wedges will fall apart during cooking. Serve this renowned homey dish with horseradish, Horseradish Sauce (page 203), or grainy mustard.

CORNING YOUR OWN BEEF

Packaged corned beef is relatively easy to find in most supermarkets, but we found the flavor and texture of homemade corned beef far superior. If you have the time (5 to 7 days) and the refrigerator space, we highly recommend giving this a try.

½ cup kosher salt
1 tablespoon black peppercorns, crushed
1 tablespoon dried thyme
2 teaspoons allspice
2 teaspoons paprika
2 bay leaves, crumbled
1 (3½- to 4½-pound) beef brisket, trimmed

Combine salt, crushed peppercorns, thyme, allspice, paprika, and crumbled bay leaves in bowl. Spear brisket about 30 times per side with meat fork or metal skewer. Rub brisket thoroughly with salt mixture and place in zipper-lock bag, forcing out as much air as possible. Place on rimmed baking sheet, cover with similar-sized pan, and weight with 2 bricks or large cans. Refrigerate for 5 to 7 days, flipping meat daily. Rinse and pat meat dry before using.

1 (3- to 4-pound) corned beef, trimmed
3 bay leaves
1 tablespoon whole black peppercorns
1 tablespoon whole mustard seeds
Water
1½ pounds small red potatoes, unpeeled
1½ pounds carrots, peeled and cut into thirds
1 head green cabbage (2 pounds), cut into 8 wedges

1. Combine corned beef, bay leaves, peppercorns, and mustard seeds in large Dutch oven, and cover by ½ inch of water. Bring to simmer and cook, skimming as needed, until fork slides easily in and out of center of meat, 2 to 3 hours.

2. Adjust oven rack to lower-middle position and heat oven to 200 degrees. Transfer meat to large baking dish and ladle 1 cup of cooking liquid over top. Tent with aluminum foil and keep warm in oven.

3. Add potatoes and carrots to liquid left in pot and simmer until they begin to soften, about 10 minutes. Add cabbage and simmer until all vegetables are tender, 10 to 15 minutes.

4. When ready to serve, remove meat from oven, slice against grain into ¼-inch-thick slices, and arrange on platter. Transfer cooked vegetables to platter and moisten with additional cooking liquid as needed. Serve.

Sautéed Pork Cutlets with Mustard-Cider Sauce

SERVES 4   **TOTAL TIME** 55 MINUTES

✓ **WHY THIS RECIPE WORKS:** Pork loin cutlets seem to offer everything the time-pressed cook could want in a weeknight meal: thrift, almost no preparation, and dinner on the table in minutes. Sadly, the pork loin is often poorly butchered into ragged and uneven slabs, which result in dry cutlets that develop very little color. Instead of pork cutlets, we opted to start with flavorful boneless country-style pork ribs. Brining the pork with a little added sugar helped them retain moisture and encouraged browning. We then sautéed them in a combination of vegetable oil and butter, which further promoted browning. For the rich pan sauce, we reduced a flour-thickened mixture of cider, broth, and seasonings and swirled in coarse mustard and butter. Look for ribs that are 3 to 5 inches long. Cut ribs more than 5 inches long in half crosswise before slicing them lengthwise to make pounding more manageable. For brining directions, see page 158. If the pork is enhanced (see page 218), do not brine. If brining the pork, do not season with salt in step 2.

MUSTARD-CIDER SAUCE
1 tablespoon unsalted butter
1 small shallot, minced
1 teaspoon all-purpose flour
1 teaspoon dry mustard
½ cup beef or chicken broth
¼ cup apple cider
½ teaspoon minced fresh sage
2 teaspoons whole-grain mustard
Salt and pepper

PORK
1½ pounds boneless country-style pork ribs, trimmed, brined if desired
Salt and pepper
1 tablespoon vegetable oil
½ tablespoon unsalted butter, cut into 2 pieces

1. FOR THE SAUCE: Melt ½ tablespoon butter in small saucepan over medium heat. Add shallot and cook until softened, about 1½ minutes. Stir in flour and dry mustard and cook for 30 seconds. Slowly whisk in broth, smoothing out any lumps. Whisk in cider and sage and bring to boil. Reduce heat to low and simmer for 5 minutes. Remove pan from heat and cover; set aside.

2. FOR THE PORK: Adjust oven rack to middle position and heat oven to 200 degrees. Cut each rib lengthwise to create 2 or 3 cutlets about ⅜ inch wide. Place cutlets between 2 layers of plastic wrap and gently pound to ¼-inch thickness. Season with salt and pepper.

3. Heat oil in 12-inch skillet over medium-high heat until just smoking. Add 1 piece butter, let melt, and quickly add half of cutlets. Brown cutlets lightly on both sides, about 2 to 4 minutes; transfer to plate and keep warm in oven. Repeat with remaining butter and cutlets; transfer to plate.

4. Return now-empty skillet to medium heat, add reserved sauce, and bring to simmer. Cook, scraping up any browned bits, until sauce is slightly thickened and has reduced to ½ cup, about 2 minutes. Stir in any accumulated pork juices and simmer for 30 seconds. Off heat, whisk in whole-grain mustard and remaining ½ tablespoon butter. Season with salt and pepper to taste. Spoon sauce over pork and serve.

VARIATION

Sautéed Pork Cutlets with Lemon-Caper Sauce

Substitute ¼ cup white wine and 2 teaspoons lemon juice for apple cider and sage in step 1. Substitute 2 tablespoons rinsed capers, 1 teaspoon finely grated lemon zest, and 1 teaspoon minced fresh parsley for mustard in step 4.

Turning Pork Ribs into Cutlets

1. Start with 1 boneless country-style pork rib.

2. Cut the rib lengthwise into 2 or 3 cutlets about ⅜ inch wide.

3. Gently pound each cutlet to ¼-inch thickness between layers of plastic wrap.

Sautéed Pork Chops with Mustard and Tarragon Sauce

SERVES 4   **TOTAL TIME** 35 MINUTES `FAST`

✔ **WHY THIS RECIPE WORKS:** Pork chops are relatively fast to cook, making them an ideal easy weeknight meal. But all too often they turn out dry and tough, so we wanted to find a simple way to guarantee the elusive juicy, tender pork chop. Cooking the pork chops entirely over a medium-high flame resulted in meat that was dry on the outside and underdone in the center, while a cooler flame ensured a properly cooked center but left the exterior pale. In order to achieve a well-browned exterior and a properly cooked center, we cooked the chops over two levels of heat. First we seared the chops on one side over medium-high heat. Once they had browned, we flipped the chops, reduced the heat to medium, and let them reach the proper internal temperature. This recipe will work with any type of pork chop, but the rib chop is our favorite. For brining directions, see page 158. If the pork is enhanced (see page 218), do not brine. If brining the pork, do not season with salt in step 1. For more information on making a pan sauce, see page 184.

PORK CHOPS

4 (8- to 10-ounce) bone-in pork rib or center-cut chops, ¾ to 1 inch thick, trimmed, brined if desired
   Salt and pepper
2 teaspoons vegetable oil

MUSTARD AND TARRAGON SAUCE

1 tablespoon vegetable oil
1 shallot, minced
1 cup chicken broth
½ cup dry white wine
1 tablespoon Dijon mustard
3 tablespoons unsalted butter, cut into 3 pieces and chilled
2 teaspoons minced fresh tarragon
   Salt and pepper

1. FOR THE PORK CHOPS: Cut 2 slits about 2 inches apart through fat on edges of each pork chop. Pat pork dry with paper towels and season with salt and pepper. Heat oil in 12-inch skillet over medium-high heat until just smoking. Brown chops on first side, about 3 minutes.

2. Flip chops over, reduce heat to medium, and continue to cook until chops register 145 degrees, 5 to 10 minutes. Transfer chops to plate, tent with aluminum foil, and let rest for 5 to 10 minutes.

3. FOR THE SAUCE: Add oil to now-empty skillet and heat over medium-high heat until shimmering. Add shallot and cook until softened, about 2 minutes. Stir in broth and wine, scraping up any browned bits, and simmer until thickened, about 5 minutes.

4. Stir in mustard and any accumulated pork juices. Reduce heat to low and whisk in butter, 1 piece at a time. Off heat, stir in tarragon and season with salt and pepper to taste. Spoon sauce over pork and serve

Preventing Curled Pork Chops

Pork chops—especially thin-cut chops—have a tendency to buckle and curl as they cook. To prevent it, cut 2 small slits, about 2 inches apart, into the fat and connective tissue on edges of each chop.

Skillet Barbecued Pork Chops

SERVES 4   **TOTAL TIME** 30 MINUTES   **FAST**

✔ **WHY THIS RECIPE WORKS:** Think barbecued pork chops only come off a grill? Think again. We produced highly flavorful pork chops, paired with a tangy sauce, indoors with the help of a skillet. And we didn't have to brine or marinate the chops. Center-cut, bone-in pork chops worked best here. The bone added valuable flavor and prevented the chops from drying out. Adding brown sugar to the spice mixture encouraged a crust to form as did making sure the chops were patted dry. We found heating a nonstick skillet over medium-high heat with a little oil until the oil smoked was ideal for quickly browning the chops. Store-bought barbecue sauce works just fine to coat the chops.

- ¾ **cup barbecue sauce**
- 2 **tablespoons cider vinegar**
- 3 **tablespoons packed brown sugar**
- 1 **tablespoon paprika**
- ½ **teaspoon ground cumin**
- ½ **teaspoon salt**
- ½ **teaspoon pepper**
- ¼ **teaspoon cayenne pepper**
- 4 **(8- to 10-ounce) bone-in pork rib or center-cut chops, ¾ to 1 inch thick, trimmed**
- 1 **tablespoon vegetable oil**

1. Whisk barbecue sauce and vinegar together in bowl. Combine sugar, paprika, cumin, salt, pepper, and cayenne in separate bowl. Whisk 1 teaspoon spice mixture into barbecue sauce mixture.

2. Cut 2 slits about 2 inches apart through fat on edges of each pork chop. Pat chops dry with paper towels and rub with remaining spice mixture. Heat oil in 12-inch nonstick skillet over medium-high heat until just smoking. Cook chops until well browned on both sides, about 8 minutes.

3. Reduce heat to medium-low. Brush chops with barbecue sauce mixture, flip, and cook until sauce is caramelized, about 1 minute. Brush once more with sauce, flip, and cook until second side is caramelized and meat registers 145 degrees, about 1 minute. Serve with remaining sauce.

Maple-Glazed Pork Chops

SERVES 4   **TOTAL TIME** 25 MINUTES   **FAST**

✔ **WHY THIS RECIPE WORKS:** To prevent our skillet-browned pork chops from curling as they cooked, we made a few slashes through the fat and silverskin. We didn't want to spend extra time brining or marinating our chops, so we seared them over medium-high heat, then gently simmered in a glaze to keep them from drying out. Once the chops were done, we let them rest while we reduced the glaze until it was thick and glossy, but not overly syrupy, adding the juices from the rested meat. Be careful not to overreduce the glaze in step 4. If the glaze thickens to the correct consistency before the chops reach 145 degrees, add a few tablespoons of water to the pan.

GLAZE
- ½ **cup maple syrup**
- 2 **teaspoons Dijon mustard**
- ¼ **cup cider vinegar**
- 1 **teaspoon minced fresh thyme**

CHOPS
- 4 **boneless pork chops, ¾ to 1 inch thick, trimmed**
  Salt and pepper
- 1 **tablespoon vegetable oil**

1. FOR THE GLAZE: Combine all ingredients in bowl.

2. FOR THE CHOPS: Cut 2 slits about 2 inches apart through fat on edges of each pork chop. Pat chops dry with paper towels and season with salt and pepper. Heat oil in 12-inch skillet over medium-high heat until just smoking. Brown pork well on first side, about 5 minutes.

3. Flip chops and add glaze. Reduce heat to medium-low and cook until chops register 145 degrees, 5 to 8 minutes.

4. Transfer chops to plate and tent with aluminum foil. Increase heat to medium and continue to simmer glaze until thick and syrupy, 2 to 6 minutes, adding any accumulated pork juices. Pour glaze over chops and serve.

VARIATIONS

Orange–Chipotle-Glazed Pork Chops

Substitute following mixture for maple glaze: ⅔ cup orange juice, 1 teaspoon lime juice, 1 teaspoon minced canned chipotle chile in adobo sauce, and 1½ tablespoons sugar. Simmer glaze as directed, adding ½ teaspoon grated lime zest to glaze with accumulated pork juices.

Pineapple–Soy-Glazed Pork Chops

Substitute following mixture for maple glaze: ⅔ cup pineapple juice, 1 tablespoon soy sauce, ¼ cup rice vinegar, 1 teaspoon grated fresh ginger, and 2 tablespoons packed brown sugar. Simmer glaze as directed, adding ½ teaspoon toasted sesame oil with accumulated pork juices.

Crispy Pan-Fried Pork Chops

SERVES 4 **TOTAL TIME** 45 MINUTES **FAST**

✔ **WHY THIS RECIPE WORKS:** Using boneless center-cut loin chops kept our crispy pan-fried pork chops recipe fast and easy. Cornstarch formed a light, ultracrisp sheath, while buttermilk brought a lighter texture and tangy flavor to the coating; minced garlic and mustard perked up the coating's flavor. Ground cornflakes added texture to the coating, especially once we mixed them with cornstarch before dredging the meat. Finally, we found two ways to ensure our coating stayed put during frying: We lightly scored the pork chops before coating them, and then we gave them a short rest before putting them in the pan. We prefer natural to enhanced pork (pork that has been injected with a salt solution to increase moistness and flavor) for this recipe. You can substitute ¾ cup of store-bought cornflake crumbs for the whole cornflakes. If using crumbs, omit the processing step and mix the crumbs with the cornstarch, salt, and pepper in a shallow dish.

⅔ **cup cornstarch**
1 **cup buttermilk**
2 **tablespoons Dijon mustard**

1 **garlic clove, minced**
3 **cups cornflakes**
   Salt and pepper
8 **(3- to 4-ounce) boneless pork chops, ½ to ¾ inch thick, trimmed**
⅔ **cup vegetable oil**
   Lemon wedges

1. Spread ⅓ cup cornstarch in shallow dish. In second shallow dish, whisk buttermilk, mustard, and garlic together. Process cornflakes, ½ teaspoon salt, ½ teaspoon pepper, and remaining ⅓ cup cornstarch in food processor until finely ground, about 10 seconds; transfer to third shallow dish.

2. Adjust oven rack to middle position and heat oven to 200 degrees. Set wire rack in rimmed baking sheet. With sharp knife, cut 1/16-inch-deep slits on both sides of chops, spaced ½ inch apart, in crosshatch pattern. Season chops with salt and pepper. Working with 1 chop at a time, dredge in cornstarch, dip into buttermilk mixture, then coat with cornflake crumbs, pressing gently to adhere; transfer to prepared wire rack. Let coated chops sit for 10 minutes.

3. Heat ⅓ cup oil in 12-inch nonstick skillet over medium-high heat until shimmering. Cook 4 chops until golden brown on both sides and chops register 145 degrees, 4 to 10 minutes.

4. Transfer chops to paper towel–lined plate and let drain for 30 seconds on each side; do not drain chops longer than 30 seconds. Transfer drained chops to clean wire rack set in rimmed baking sheet, and keep warm in oven. Discard oil in skillet, wipe clean with paper towels, and repeat process with remaining oil and pork chops. Serve with lemon wedges.

Making Crispy Pan-Fried Pork Chops

1. With sharp knife, cut 1/16-inch-deep slits on both sides of chops, spaced ½ inch apart, in crosshatch pattern.

2. After coating chops, transfer to wire rack set over rimmed baking sheet and let sit for 10 minutes.

Cooking stuffed pork chops on a preheated baking sheet results in a crispy brown exterior.

Herb-Stuffed Pork Chops

SERVES 4   **TOTAL TIME** 45 MINUTES **FAST**

WHY THIS RECIPE WORKS: Rarely well executed, stuffed pork chops are typically crammed full of a soggy bread stuffing. We were after a perfectly cooked pork chop—thick and juicy, seared crusty brown on the outside—enhanced by a flavorful stuffing. We developed a stuffing mixture that incorporated enough moisture, fat, and assertive flavors to enhance the lean, mild pork. Baking the chops on a preheated baking sheet in a hot oven was an easy way to achieve a seared exterior and an evenly cooked interior. We found that tenting the chops with foil for a few minutes after they were done cooking helped them retain heat while they rested. Tasters preferred fontina cheese, but we found Monterey Jack or Gruyère cheese worked equally well.

¼ cup vegetable oil
3 garlic cloves, minced
1 slice hearty white sandwich bread, toasted and torn into pieces
½ cup chopped fresh parsley
1 tablespoon chopped fresh thyme
3 ounces fontina cheese, shredded (¾ cup)
   Salt and pepper
4 (6- to 8-ounce) boneless pork chops, about 1 inch thick, trimmed

1. Adjust oven rack to upper-middle position, place rimmed baking sheet on rack, and heat oven to 475 degrees. Combine oil and garlic in bowl. Pulse 2 tablespoons oil mixture, bread, parsley, thyme, fontina, ¼ teaspoon salt, and ¼ teaspoon pepper in food processor until coarsely ground, 5 to 10 pulses.

2. Pat pork dry with paper towels and season with salt and pepper. Using paring knife, cut 1-inch opening into side of each chop to make pocket for stuffing. Spoon herb mixture into pocket and seal by threading toothpick through pork about ½ inch from opening.

3. Coat chops with remaining oil mixture and transfer to preheated baking sheet. Bake until browned and meat registers 145 degrees, 12 to 15 minutes, flipping chops halfway through cooking. Transfer to platter, tent with aluminum foil, and let rest for 5 to 10 minutes. Serve.

Stuffing Pork Chops

1. Using paring knife, cut 1-inch opening into side of each chop to make pocket for stuffing.

2. Spoon herb mixture into pocket.

3. Thread toothpick through pork about ½ inch from opening to help seal in stuffing.

ALL ABOUT **PORK CUTS**

These 13 pork cuts are the test kitchen's top picks. We've rated each cut on a scale from 1 to 4 stars for flavor. Given that even the toughest cut can make a great dish if cooked properly, we haven't rated these cuts for tenderness. A pig is butchered into five different cuts: blade shoulder, arm shoulder, loin, leg, and side.

	TYPE	FLAVOR
	**Pork Butt (Blade Shoulder)** This large, flavorful cut (often labeled Boston butt or pork shoulder at markets) can weigh as much as 8 pounds when sold with the bone in. Many markets take out the bone and sell this cut in smaller chunks, often wrapped in netting to hold the roast together. This cut is ideal for slow roasting, barbecuing, stewing, or braising. Use it for pulled pork and other shredded pork dishes.	★★★★
	**Shoulder Arm Picnic (Arm Shoulder)** This affordable cut (often labeled "picnic roast" at markets) can be sold bone-in or boneless. It is rich in fat and connective tissue. Use it like pork butt for barbecuing, braising, or other slow-cooking methods.	★★★★
	Boneless Blade-End Roast (Loin) This is our favorite boneless roast for roasting. It is cut from the shoulder end of the loin and has more fat (and flavor) than the boneless center-cut loin roast. Unfortunately, this cut can be hard to find. This roast is also sold with the bone in, although this cut is even harder to locate.	★★★★
	**Center-Cut Loin Roast (Loin)** This boneless roast is widely available and a good choice for roasting. We prefer the more flavorful boneless blade roast, but the two cuts can be used interchangeably. Make sure to buy a center-cut roast with a decent fat cap on top.	★★
	**Center Rib Roast (Loin)** Often referred to as the pork equivalent of prime rib or rack of lamb, this mild, fairly lean roast consists of a single muscle with a protective fat cap. It may be cut with anywhere from five to eight ribs. Because the bones (and nearby fat) are still attached, we find this roast a better option than the center-cut loin roast, which is cut from the same muscle but is minus the bones and fat.	★★★
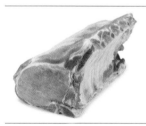 	**Tenderloin Roast (Loin)** This lean, delicate, boneless roast cooks very quickly because it's so small, usually weighing just about 1 pound. Since there is very little marbling, this roast (which is equivalent to beef tenderloin) cannot be overcooked without ruining its texture. Tenderloins are often sold two to a package. Many tenderloins sold in the supermarket are enhanced; look for one that has no ingredients other than pork on the label.	★

	TYPE	FLAVOR
	Blade Chop (Loin)	★★★
	Cut from the shoulder end of the loin, these chops can be difficult to find at the market. They are fatty and tough, despite good flavor and juiciness. These chops are best suited to low-and-slow cooking methods that break down their connective tissue, such as braising or barbecuing.	
	Rib Chop (Loin)	★★★
	Cut from the rib section of the loin, these chops have a relatively high fat content, rendering them flavorful and unlikely to dry out during cooking. They are a favorite in the test kitchen. These chops are easily identified by the bone that runs along one side and the one large eye of loin muscle. These tender chops are a good choice for grilling and pan searing.	
	Center-Cut Chop (Loin)	★★
	These chops can be identified by the bone that divides the loin meat from the tenderloin muscle. The lean tenderloin section cooks more quickly than the loin section, making these chops a challenge. They have good flavor, but since they contain less fat than the rib chops, they are not quite as moist. Because the loin and tenderloin muscles in these chops are bisected by bulky bone or cartilage, they don't lie flat, making these chops a poor choice for pan searing. Save them for the grill, but position the ultralean tenderloin away from the fire to keep it from drying out.	
	Baby Back Ribs (Loin)	★★★
	Baby back ribs (also referred to as loin back ribs) are cut from the section of the rib cage closest to the backbone. Loin center-cut roasts and chops come from the same part of the pig, which explains why baby back ribs can be expensive. This location also explains why baby back ribs are much leaner than spareribs—and why they need special attention to keep from drying out on the grill.	
	St. Louis Spareribs (Side)	★★★★
	Regular spareribs are cut close to the belly of the pig (which is also where bacon comes from). Because whole spareribs contain the brisket bone and surrounding meat, each rack can weigh upward of 5 pounds. Some racks of spareribs are so big they barely fit on the grill. We prefer this more manageable cut because the brisket bone and surrounding meat are trimmed off to produce a narrower, rectangular rack that usually weighs in at a relatively svelte 3 pounds.	
	Country-Style Ribs (Loin)	★★★
	These meaty, tender, boneless ribs are cut from the upper side of the rib cage from the fatty blade end of the loin. Butchers usually cut them into individual ribs and package several ribs together. These ribs can be braised and shredded for pasta sauce, or pounded flat and grilled or pan-seared as cutlets.	
	Fresh Ham, Shank End (Leg)	★★★
	The leg is divided into two cuts—the tapered shank end and the more rounded sirloin end. The sirloin end has a lot of bones that make carving tricky. We prefer the shank end. This cut is usually covered in a thick layer of fat and skin, which should be scored before roasting. This cut is not as fatty as you might think and benefits from brining.	

Jump-starting the dirty rice in the microwave helps to make this pork chop dinner a quick one-dish supper.

Pan-Seared Pork Chops with Dirty Rice

SERVES 4   TOTAL TIME 45 MINUTES   **FAST**

✔ **WHY THIS RECIPE WORKS:** Wanting an alternative to the typical pork chop dinner, we looked to the South for inspiration and paired our flavorful pork with dirty rice—a side dish of cooked rice, cured meats, vegetables, and seasonings. Utilizing a Cajun seasoning mix made easy work of adding several bold spices at once, and we reinforced it with some garlic and thyme. Since the side of the pork chop that was nestled into the rice during cooking lost its crispness anyway, we saved time by browning only one side of the chops, then nestling them browned side facing up. Buy chops of similar thickness so that they cook at the same rate. For brining directions, see page 158. If the pork is enhanced, do not brine. If brining the pork, do not season with salt in step 2. If you can't find chorizo sausage, use andouille or linguiça.

NOTES FROM THE TEST KITCHEN

Natural Versus Enhanced Pork

Because modern pork is so lean and therefore somewhat bland and prone to dryness if overcooked, many producers now inject their fresh pork products with a sodium solution. So-called enhanced pork is now the only option at many supermarkets, especially when buying lean cuts like the tenderloin. (To be sure, read the label; if the pork has been enhanced it will have an ingredient label.) Enhanced pork is injected with a solution of water, salt, sodium phosphates, sodium lactate, potassium lactate, sodium diacetate, and varying flavor agents, generally adding 7 to 15 percent extra weight. While enhanced pork does cook up juicier (it has been pumped full of water!), we find the texture almost spongy, and the flavor is often unpleasantly salty. We prefer the genuine pork flavor of natural pork and rely on brining to keep it juicy. Also, enhanced pork loses six times more moisture than natural pork when frozen and thawed—yet another reason to avoid enhanced pork. If you do buy enhanced pork, do not brine it.

2½ cups chicken broth
1   cup long-grain white rice, rinsed
4   (8- to 10-ounce) bone-in pork rib or center-cut chops, ¾ to 1 inch thick, trimmed, brined if desired
    Salt and pepper
1   tablespoon vegetable oil
4   ounces chorizo sausage, cut into ¼-inch pieces
1   red bell pepper, stemmed, seeded, and chopped fine
1   small onion, chopped fine
6   garlic cloves, minced
1   teaspoon minced fresh thyme or ¼ teaspoon dried
¾   teaspoon Cajun seasoning or chili powder
3   scallions, sliced thin

1. Combine 1¼ cups broth and rice in bowl, cover, and microwave until liquid is absorbed, about 10 minutes. Fluff rice with fork.

2. Meanwhile, cut 2 slits about 2 inches apart through fat on edges of each pork chop. Pat chops dry with paper towels and season with salt and pepper. Heat oil in 12-inch skillet over medium-high heat until just smoking. Cook chops until well browned on first side, about 5 minutes; transfer to plate.

3. Pour off all but 1 tablespoon fat left in skillet. Add chorizo, bell pepper, and onion and cook over medium heat until vegetables are softened, about 5 minutes. Stir in garlic, thyme, and Cajun seasoning and cook until fragrant, about 30 seconds. Stir in remaining 1¼ cups broth and microwaved rice, scraping up any browned bits.

4. Nestle pork chops, browned side up, into pan, adding any accumulated juices. Cover and simmer gently until pork registers 145 degrees, 8 to 10 minutes.

5. Transfer chops to clean plate, brushing any rice that sticks to chops back into skillet, tent with aluminum foil, and let rest for 5 to 10 minutes. Gently fold scallions into rice and season with salt and pepper to taste. Serve.

Stir-Fried Pork, Eggplant, and Onions

SERVES 4   TOTAL TIME 45 MINUTES   **FAST**

✓ **WHY THIS RECIPE WORKS:** A stir-fry might be quick, but it is not always easy to get right. We wanted a foolproof recipe that would produce flavorful, juicy meat and perfectly cooked vegetables. Our recipe is reminiscent of a classic Thai stir-fry, with its intense and slightly salty flavor. We cooked the eggplant and onions individually to allow even cooking and good browning. We felt that the mildness of the pork and eggplant demanded generous amounts of garlic and pepper, so we added a whopping 12 cloves of garlic and 2 teaspoons of pepper to make the dish more assertive. To make the pork easier to slice, freeze it for 15 minutes. Leaving the skin on the eggplant keeps pieces intact during cooking. Serve with Sticky Rice (page 142).

SAUCE
- ½ cup chicken broth
- ¼ cup water
- 4 teaspoons fish sauce
- 2½ tablespoons packed light brown sugar
- 4 teaspoons soy sauce
- 2 teaspoons lime juice
- 2 teaspoons cornstarch

STIR-FRY
- 5 tablespoons vegetable oil
- 1 tablespoon cornstarch
- 1 tablespoon all-purpose flour
- 1 teaspoon fish sauce
- 1 (1-pound) pork tenderloin, trimmed and sliced thin
- 12 garlic cloves, minced
- 2 teaspoons pepper
- 1 pound eggplant, cut into ¾-inch pieces
- 1 large onion, halved and sliced ¼ inch thick
- ¼ cup coarsely chopped fresh cilantro

1. FOR THE SAUCE: Whisk all ingredients together in bowl.

2. FOR THE STIR-FRY: Whisk 2 tablespoons oil, cornstarch, flour, and fish sauce together in bowl until smooth, then stir in pork. In separate bowl, combine garlic, pepper, and 1 tablespoon oil.

3. Heat 1 teaspoon oil in 12-inch nonstick skillet over high heat until just smoking. Add half of pork mixture, breaking up any clumps, and cook, without stirring, for 1 minute; transfer to clean large bowl. Repeat with 1 teaspoon oil and remaining pork; transfer to bowl.

4. Add 1 tablespoon oil to now-empty skillet and return to high heat until just smoking. Add eggplant and cook, stirring often, until browned and no longer spongy, 5 to 7 minutes; transfer to bowl with pork. Add remaining 1 teaspoon oil and onion to skillet and cook until onion is just softened and lightly browned, about 2 minutes.

5. Clear center of skillet, add garlic mixture, and cook, mashing mixture into skillet, until fragrant, about 1 minute. Stir garlic mixture into onion.

6. Return cooked pork and eggplant, and any accumulated juices, to skillet and toss to combine. Whisk sauce to recombine, then add to skillet. Cook, stirring constantly, until sauce is thickened, about 30 seconds. Sprinkle with cilantro. Serve.

Slicing Pork for Stir-Fries

1. Place pork tenderloin on clean, dry cutting board. Using sharp chef's knife, slice pork crosswise into ¼-inch-thick medallions.

2. Slice each medallion into ¼-inch-wide strips.

Thai Pork Lettuce Wraps

SERVES 6 AS APPETIZER OR 4 AS MAIN COURSE

TOTAL TIME 1 HOUR

✓ **WHY THIS RECIPE WORKS:** We wanted to replicate the light, delicious Thai salad of boldly flavored minced pork (or sometimes beef or chicken) known as *larb*. This pungent, light dish is incredibly simple to make, and it calls for ingredients that we either could find easily at the supermarket, or were confident we could replicate from the pantry. Right away we found that the texture and fat in preground pork was too inconsistent, so we chopped pork in the food processor and then marinated it in a little fish sauce so it would retain moisture during cooking. To balance our recipe's blend of tart (lime juice), salty (fish sauce), and hot (pepper flakes) flavors, we added a little sugar. We prefer natural pork in this recipe. If using enhanced pork, skip the marinating in step 1 and reduce the amount of fish sauce to 2 tablespoons, adding it all in step 4. Don't skip toasting the rice; it's integral to the texture and flavor of the dish. Any style of white rice can be used. Toasted rice powder (*kao kua*) can also be found in many Asian markets. This dish can be served with Sticky Rice (page 142) and steamed vegetables as an entrée. To save time, prepare the other ingredients while the pork is in the freezer.

- 1 **(1-pound) pork tenderloin, trimmed and cut into 1-inch chunks**
- 2½ **tablespoons fish sauce**
- 1 **tablespoon white rice**
- ¼ **cup chicken broth**
- 2 **shallots, peeled and sliced into thin rings**
- 3 **tablespoons lime juice (2 limes)**
- 2 **teaspoons sugar**
- ¼ **teaspoon red pepper flakes**
- 3 **tablespoons roughly chopped fresh mint**
- 3 **tablespoons roughly chopped fresh cilantro**
- 1 **head Bibb lettuce (8 ounces), leaves separated and left whole**

1. Place pork chunks on large plate in single layer. Freeze pork until firm and starting to harden around edges but still pliable, 15 to 20 minutes. Working with half of semifrozen meat at a time, pulse in food processor until coarsely chopped, about 5 pulses; transfer to bowl. Toss meat with 1 tablespoon fish sauce, cover, and refrigerate for 15 minutes.

2. Toast rice in 8-inch skillet over medium-high heat, stirring constantly, until deep golden brown, about 5 minutes. Transfer rice to small bowl, let cool for 5 minutes, then grind into fine meal using spice grinder (10 to 30 seconds) or mortar and pestle.

3. Bring broth to simmer in 12-inch nonstick skillet over medium-high heat. Add marinated pork and cook, stirring frequently, until pork is about half-pink, about 2 minutes. Sprinkle 1 teaspoon rice powder into skillet and cook, stirring constantly, until pork is no longer pink, 1 to 1½ minutes longer.

4. Transfer pork to large bowl and let cool for 10 minutes. Stir in remaining 1½ tablespoons fish sauce, remaining 2 teaspoons rice powder, shallots, lime juice, sugar, pepper flakes, mint, and cilantro and toss to combine. Serve with lettuce leaves.

Making Filling for Thai Pork Lettuce Wraps

1. GRIND PORK: After freezing pork chunks, pulse them in batches in food processor until coarsely chopped, about 5 pulses.

2. MARINATE MEAT: Toss freshly ground meat with 1 tablespoon fish sauce and let marinate for 15 minutes.

3. TOAST AND GRIND RICE: Toast rice in 8-inch skillet over medium-high heat, stirring constantly, until deep golden brown, about 5 minutes. Let rice cool, then grind into fine meal.

4. COOK PORK IN SIMMERING BROTH: Cook pork until it is half-pink, about 2 minutes. Sprinkle with 1 teaspoon rice powder and finish cooking pork. Transfer pork to bowl, cool, and add rest of filling ingredients.

Chinese Cilantro Pork

SERVES 4　　**TOTAL TIME** 30 MINUTES　**FAST**

✔ **WHY THIS RECIPE WORKS:** We used cilantro as a vegetable in this stir-fry, rather than as a garnish. To keep the cilantro's flavor distinct, we added a full bunch to the skillet—stems and all—near the end of cooking. A simple sauce brought a balance of sweet and sour flavors to this lighter, fresher stir-fry. To make the pork easier to slice, freeze it for 15 minutes. Be sure to dry the canned bamboo shoots thoroughly with paper towels after rinsing; otherwise the packing liquid will dilute the flavor of the sauce. Serve with Sticky Rice (page 142).

SAUCE
- ¾　cup chicken broth
- 4　teaspoons soy sauce
- 4　teaspoons rice vinegar
- 1　tablespoon sugar
- 2　teaspoons cornstarch
- ¼　teaspoon red pepper flakes

STIR-FRY
- 3　tablespoons vegetable oil
- 1　tablespoon cornstarch
- 1　tablespoon all-purpose flour
- 2　teaspoons soy sauce
- 1　(1-pound) pork tenderloin, trimmed and sliced thin
- 3　garlic cloves, minced
- 1　tablespoon grated fresh ginger
- 1　large bunch cilantro, stems trimmed, cut into 1-inch lengths
- 1　(8-ounce) can sliced bamboo shoots, rinsed and dried

1. FOR THE SAUCE: Whisk all ingredients together in bowl.

2. FOR THE STIR-FRY: Whisk 2 tablespoons oil, cornstarch, flour, and soy sauce together in medium bowl until smooth, then stir in pork. In separate bowl, combine garlic, ginger, and 1 teaspoon oil.

3. Heat 1 teaspoon oil in 12-inch nonstick skillet over high heat until just smoking. Add half of pork, breaking up any clumps, and cook, without stirring, for 1 minute. Stir pork and continue to cook until lightly browned, about 1 minute; transfer to clean bowl. Repeat with remaining oil and pork mixture; transfer to bowl.

4. Add garlic mixture to now-empty skillet and cook over medium heat, mashing mixture into skillet, until fragrant, about 30 seconds. Add cooked pork and any accumulated juices, cilantro, and bamboo shoots, and toss to combine.

5. Whisk sauce to recombine, then add to skillet. Cook, stirring constantly, until sauce is thickened and cilantro is slightly wilted, about 1 minute. Serve.

Roast Pork Tenderloin

SERVES 4 TO 6　　**TOTAL TIME** 30 MINUTES　**FAST**

✔ **WHY THIS RECIPE WORKS:** Pork tenderloin has a lot going for it—it is very tender with a buttery, fine-grained texture; it's easy to prepare; it cooks quickly; and its mild flavor is the perfect backdrop for a variety of sauces. But because pork tenderloin is so lean, it is usually dry and overcooked. We wanted a recipe that would produce flavorful and juicy pork tenderloin every time. After attempting to cook the tenderloin in the oven at a wide range of temperatures, we discovered that the best approach was to start it on the stovetop (for a good sear) and then finish it in the oven (for gentle, even cooking). A pan sauce is a good way to add flavor (see page 185) as is a glaze (see page 222). Pork tenderloins are often sold two to a package, weighing 1½ to 2 pounds. To ensure that the tenderloins don't curl during cooking, remove the silverskin from the meat. If you use an ovensafe skillet, it is not necessary to transfer the tenderloins to a baking dish. For brining directions, see page 158. If the pork is enhanced (see page 218), do not brine. If brining the pork, do not season with salt in step 1.

- 2　(12- to 16-ounce) pork tenderloins, trimmed, brined if desired
　　Salt and pepper
- 1　tablespoon vegetable oil

1. Adjust oven rack to lower-middle position and heat oven to 450 degrees. Pat tenderloins dry with paper towels and season with salt and pepper. Heat oil in 12-inch skillet over medium-high heat until just smoking. Brown tenderloins on all sides, about 10 minutes.

2. Transfer browned tenderloins to 13 by 9-inch baking dish and roast in oven until pork registers 145 degrees, 10 to 15 minutes, flipping meat halfway through roasting time.

3. Transfer tenderloins to carving board, tent with aluminum foil, and let rest for 5 to 10 minutes. Slice pork and serve.

Removing Pork Silverskin

Silverskin is a swath of connective tissue located between the meat and the fat that covers its surface. To remove silverskin, simply slip a knife under it, angle knife slightly upward, and use a gentle back-and-forth motion.

GLAZES FOR PORK ROASTS

Use these glazes to boost the flavor of roast pork, both pork tenderloin and boneless pork loin roasts. For tenderloin, the glaze should be brushed over the pork before roasting. For a boneless pork loin roast, the glaze should be brushed over the roast during the final 15 minutes of cooking (when the roast registers about 110 degrees). If the glaze begins to dry up and burn in the oven, stir about ¼ cup warm water into the pan.

MAPLE GLAZE FAST
- 1 **cup maple syrup**
- ½ **teaspoon ground cinnamon**
- ¼ **teaspoon cloves**
- ⅛ **teaspoon cayenne pepper**

Combine all ingredients in bowl. After browning pork, pour off fat left in skillet and add glaze, scraping up any browned bits. Simmer glaze briefly to thicken, about 30 seconds, then transfer to bowl.

SPICY HONEY GLAZE FAST
- ¾ **cup honey**
- ⅓ **cup lime juice (3 limes)**
- 1–2 **teaspoons minced canned chipotle chile in adobo sauce**
- 1½ **teaspoons ground cumin**

Combine all ingredients in bowl. After browning pork, pour off fat left in skillet and add glaze, scraping up any browned bits. Simmer glaze to thicken slightly, about 2 minutes, then transfer to bowl.

APRICOT-ORANGE GLAZE FAST
- 1 **cup apricot preserves**
- ½ **cup orange juice**
- ¼ **cup dried apricots, quartered**
- 3 **tablespoons lemon juice**

Combine all ingredients in bowl. After browning pork, pour off fat left in skillet and add glaze, scraping up any browned bits. Simmer glaze to thicken slightly, about 3 minutes, then transfer to bowl.

A sweet and spicy glaze applied toward the end of roasting adds flavor and moisture to this pork loin.

Roast Pork Loin

SERVES 4 TO 6   **TOTAL TIME** 1 HOUR 30 MINUTES

✔ **WHY THIS RECIPE WORKS:** Inexpensive and easy to find, a boneless pork loin roast seems nicely suited to roasting. Why, then, is it so often dry and flavorless? We found that searing before roasting allowed us to achieve a moist, flavorful roast. If your pork roast has a thick layer of fat on top, trim the fat until it measures just ⅛ inch thick. If you have time and can plan ahead, we recommend brining the pork, as this will further enhance its flavor and texture. This roast can be prepared using any of the glazes at left. If using a glaze, brush it over the pork during the final 15 to 20 minutes of roasting (when the center of the roast registers about 110 degrees). If you use an ovensafe skillet, it is not necessary to transfer the roast to a baking dish. The roast must be removed from the oven when it reaches 140 degrees or it will be dry and taste like cardboard. For brining directions, see page 158. If the pork is enhanced (see page 218), do not brine. If brining the pork, do not season with salt in step 1.

1 (2½- to 3-pound) boneless pork loin roast, trimmed, brined if desired
Salt and pepper
1 tablespoon vegetable oil

1. Adjust oven rack to lower-middle position and heat oven to 375 degrees. Pat roast dry with paper towels, season with salt and pepper, and tie at 1½-inch intervals with kitchen twine.

2. Heat oil in 12-inch skillet over medium-high heat until just smoking. Brown roast on all sides, about 10 minutes.

3. Transfer browned pork to 13 by 9-inch baking dish, and roast in oven until pork registers 140 degrees, 50 to 70 minutes, flipping meat halfway through roasting time.

4. Transfer roast to carving board, tent with aluminum foil, and let rest for 15 to 20 minutes. Remove twine, cut into ¼-inch-thick slices, and serve.

Tying a Roast

Wrap a piece of kitchen twine around roast and fasten it with a double knot, snip off excess, and repeat down length of roast, spacing each tie 1 to 1½ inches apart. Knots should be snug but not cut into the meat.

Wrapping pork loin with overlapping slices of bacon keeps the meat moist while cooking and provides a crispy crust.

Bacon-Wrapped Pork Loin with Roasted Red Potatoes

SERVES 4 TO 6   **TOTAL TIME** 1 HOUR 20 MINUTES

✔ **WHY THIS RECIPE WORKS:** Most pork roast recipes involve brining, tying with twine to promote even cooking, and searing in a skillet—all before transferring the meat to the oven for a long roast. Could we cook the pork plus a side dish from start to finish in the oven, and in one pan? Mimicking fattier cuts of pork, we added fat by wrapping our pork loin with bacon to provide moisture during cooking, and to give a crisp, brown shell in lieu of a crust. We rubbed salt, pepper, and ground fennel seed on the loin, then layered bacon slices crosswise over the entire roast. Precooking the bacon in the microwave allowed some of the bacon fat to render, and finishing the loin under the broiler at the end browned the bacon beautifully. Taking advantage of the large surface area of the baking sheet, we halved small red potatoes and arranged them cut side down around the pork. If your pork roast has a thick layer of fat on top, trim the fat until it measures just ⅛ inch thick. We prefer to use small red potatoes measuring about 1 inch in diameter in this recipe, but you can substitute larger red potatoes, cut into ¾-inch chunks.

12 ounces bacon
1 (2½- to 3-pound) boneless pork loin roast, trimmed
2 teaspoons ground fennel seed
   Salt and pepper
2½ pounds small red potatoes, unpeeled, halved
3 tablespoons vegetable oil

1. Adjust oven rack to upper-middle position and heat oven to 375 degrees. Lay bacon strips on large plate and weigh down with second plate. Microwave until slightly shriveled but still pliable, 1 to 3 minutes. Transfer bacon to paper towel–lined plate and let cool slightly.

2. Line rimmed baking sheet with aluminum foil. Pat pork dry with paper towels, rub with fennel, and season with salt and pepper. Place pork in center of prepared baking sheet. Lay bacon attractively over top of pork, slightly overlapping slices and tucking ends underneath roast.

3. Toss potatoes with 2 tablespoons oil in bowl and season with salt and pepper. Brush baking sheet around pork loin with remaining 1 tablespoon oil. Lay potatoes, cut side down, on oiled baking sheet around pork. Roast pork and potatoes until pork registers 130 degrees, 40 minutes to 1 hour, rotating baking sheet halfway through roasting.

4. Remove pork and potatoes from oven, position oven rack 6 inches from broiler element, and heat broiler. Broil pork and potatoes until bacon is crisp and browned and pork registers 140 degrees, 3 to 5 minutes.

5. Transfer pork to carving board and let rest for 15 to 20 minutes. Turn oven off and return potatoes to warm oven until serving time. Cut pork into ½-inch-thick slices and serve with potatoes.

Easy Stuffed Pork Loin

SERVES 8   **TOTAL TIME** 1 HOUR 40 MINUTES

✔ **WHY THIS RECIPE WORKS:** Roast stuffed pork loin could be an impressive centerpiece to a holiday meal, if only it didn't suffer from these problems: meat that is tough and dry; stuffing with a dull flavor; and a roast that looks sloppy, with stuffing oozing out. To ensure that our pork loin would be moist, we brined the roast. For a flavorful stuffing, we created a sweet and tangy apple and cranberry mixture, which we precooked. This step ensured that the meat didn't have to roast until it was overcooked and dry. We found that leaving a ⅛-inch-thick layer of fat on top of the roast is ideal; if your roast has a thicker fat cap, trim it to be ⅛ inch thick. For brining directions, see page 158. If the pork is enhanced (see page 218), do not brine. If brining the pork, do not season with salt in step 3.

1   **tablespoon unsalted butter**
1   **pound Granny Smith apples, peeled, cored, and cut into ¼-inch pieces**
2   **shallots, halved and sliced thin**
2   **teaspoons honey**
½   **cup chicken broth**
¼   **cup dried cranberries**
1   **tablespoon minced fresh thyme or 1 teaspoon dried**
     Pinch red pepper flakes
     Salt and pepper
1   **(3-pound) boneless pork loin roast, trimmed, brined if desired**
1   **teaspoon minced fresh rosemary or ¼ teaspoon dried**
1   **teaspoon ground coriander**

1. Adjust oven rack to lower-middle position and heat oven to 375 degrees. Melt butter in 12-inch skillet over medium heat. Add apples, shallots, and honey, cover, and cook until apples release their liquid, 3 to 5 minutes. Uncover and continue to cook, stirring often, until shallots and apples are well browned, 10 to 12 minutes.

2. Stir in broth, cranberries, 1 teaspoon thyme, and pepper flakes and cook until apples are soft and pan is almost dry, 1 to 2 minutes. Transfer filling to bowl and season with salt and pepper to taste.

3. Slice pork loin open. Season inside with salt and pepper, mound stuffing evenly down center, then tie pork around filling with kitchen twine into tidy roast. (Filled and tied pork loin can be wrapped tightly in plastic wrap and refrigerated for up to 1 day; roast as directed.)

4. Pat outside of roast dry with paper towels. Mix remaining 2 teaspoons thyme, rosemary, coriander, ¼ teaspoon salt, and ⅛ teaspoon pepper together in bowl, then rub herb mixture

Stuffing a Pork Loin

1. Slice pork roast open down middle, from end to end, cutting about two-thirds of way through meat. Open roast like a book.

2. Cut into halves of roast, being careful not to cut through completely, stopping ½ inch before edge. Press pork flat.

3. Season inside of pork with salt and pepper, then mound filling evenly down center of roast.

4. Wrap sides of pork around filling, then tie roast closed with butcher's twine at 1-inch intervals. Don't tie roast too tight or you may squeeze out filling.

evenly over outside of roast. Place pork in 13 by 9-inch baking dish and roast until pork registers 140 degrees, 50 to 70 minutes, rotating dish halfway through roasting.

5. Transfer pork to carving board, tent with aluminum foil, and let rest for 15 to 20 minutes. Remove twine, slice pork, and serve.

VARIATION

Easy Stuffed Pork Loin with Figs and Balsamic Vinegar

Substitute ⅓ cup coarsely chopped dried figs for cranberries, and add 1 tablespoon balsamic vinegar to skillet with broth.

Spicy Mexican Shredded Pork Tostadas

SERVES 4 TO 6   **TOTAL TIME** 1 HOUR 50 MINUTES

✓ **WHY THIS RECIPE WORKS:** We wanted our pork tostadas to have the crisp texture and smoky tomato flavor of traditional Mexican shredded pork (called *tinga*). To get smoky, fork-tender pork on the stovetop, we simmered cubed pork butt roast in water flavored with garlic, onion, and thyme, then fried the drained meat in a hot pan to make it crisp. Finally, we used canned tomato sauce and chipotle chile powder to build a deep and complex sauce. The trimmed pork should weigh about 1½ pounds. Pork butt roast is often labeled Boston butt in the supermarket. Tinga is traditionally served on tostadas (crisp fried corn tortillas; to make your own tostadas, see page 292), but you can also serve the meat in tacos and burritos or simply over rice. We prefer the complex flavor of chipotle chile powder, but two teaspoons minced canned chipotle chiles can be used in its place. Sour cream, minced scallions, and diced avocado also taste great on these tostadas.

 2   **pounds boneless pork butt roast, trimmed and**
     cut into 1-inch pieces
 2   **onions, 1 quartered and 1 chopped fine**
 5   **garlic cloves, 3 peeled and smashed and 2 minced**
 4   **sprigs fresh thyme**
     Salt
 2   **tablespoons vegetable oil**
 ½   **teaspoon dried oregano**
 1   **(15-ounce) can tomato sauce**
 1   **tablespoon chipotle chile powder**
 2   **bay leaves**
 12 **corn tostadas**
     Queso fresco or feta cheese
     Fresh cilantro leaves
     Lime wedges

A hefty dose of chipotle chile powder and tomato sauce give these pork tostadas their deep, smoky, spicy flavor.

1. Bring pork, quartered onion, smashed garlic cloves, thyme sprigs, 1 teaspoon salt, and 6 cups water to simmer in large saucepan over medium-high heat, skimming off any foam that rises to surface. Reduce heat to medium-low, partially cover, and cook until pork is tender, 75 to 90 minutes.

2. Drain pork, reserving 1 cup cooking liquid. Discard onion, garlic, and thyme sprigs and return pork to saucepan. Using potato masher, mash pork until shredded into rough ½-inch pieces. (Shredded pork can be refrigerated for up to 2 days.)

3. Heat oil in 12-inch nonstick skillet over medium-high heat until shimmering. Add shredded pork, chopped onion, and oregano and cook, stirring often, until pork is well browned and crisp, 7 to 10 minutes. Stir in minced garlic and cook until fragrant, about 30 seconds. Stir in tomato sauce, chile powder, reserved pork cooking liquid, and bay leaves; simmer until almost all liquid has evaporated, 5 to 7 minutes.

4. Discard bay leaves and season with salt to taste. Spoon shredded pork onto tostadas, sprinkle with queso fresco and cilantro, and serve with lime wedges.

Slow-Roasted Pork Shoulder with Peach Sauce

SERVES 8 TO 12   **TOTAL TIME** 7 TO 8 HOURS
(PLUS 12 HOURS FOR SALTING)

✓ **WHY THIS RECIPE WORKS:** When we think of a pork roast today, the first thing that comes to mind is pork loin. It may be lean, but it typically needs a serious flavor boost. We wanted to explore the glories of old-fashioned, more flavorful (read: less lean) pork. One such cut is the shoulder roast. It may take longer to cook, but it's also inexpensive and loaded with flavorful intramuscular fat, plus it boasts a thick fat cap that renders to a bronze, baconlike crust. We started by rubbing the roast's exterior with brown sugar and salt, then left it to rest in the refrigerator overnight. The sugar dried out the exterior and boosted browning. Elevating the pork shoulder on a V-rack and pouring water in the roasting pan kept the pork's drippings from burning as the meat roasted, and it also created a significant jus. Finally, a fruity sauce with sweet and tart elements cut the pork shoulder's richness. Pork butt roast is often labeled Boston butt in the supermarket. Add more water to the roasting pan as necessary to prevent the fond from burning.

PORK ROAST

- 1   (6- to 8-pound) bone-in pork butt roast
- ⅓   cup kosher salt
- ⅓   cup packed light brown sugar
-     Pepper

PEACH SAUCE

- 10   ounces frozen sliced peaches, cut into 1-inch chunks, or 2 fresh peaches, peeled, pitted, and cut into ½-inch wedges
- 2   cups dry white wine
- ½   cup granulated sugar
- ¼   cup plus 1 tablespoon rice vinegar
- 2   sprigs fresh thyme
- 1   tablespoon whole-grain mustard

1. FOR THE PORK ROAST: Using sharp knife, cut slits 1 inch apart in crosshatch pattern in fat cap of roast, being careful not to cut into meat. Combine salt and sugar in bowl. Rub salt mixture over entire pork shoulder and into slits. Wrap roast tightly in double layer of plastic wrap, place on rimmed baking sheet, and refrigerate for 12 to 24 hours.

2. Adjust oven rack to lowest position and heat oven to 325 degrees. Unwrap roast and brush any excess salt mixture from surface. Season roast with pepper. Spray V-rack with vegetable oil spray, set rack in large roasting pan, and place roast on rack. Add 1 quart water to roasting pan.

3. Roast pork, basting twice during cooking, until meat is extremely tender and meat near bone registers 190 degrees, 5 to 6 hours. Transfer roast to carving board, tent with aluminum foil, and let rest for 1 hour. Transfer liquid in roasting pan to fat separator and let sit for 5 minutes. Pour off ¼ cup jus and set aside for sauce; discard fat and remaining jus.

4. FOR THE SAUCE: Simmer peaches, wine, sugar, ¼ cup vinegar, ¼ cup defatted jus, and thyme sprigs in small saucepan, stirring occasionally, until reduced to 2 cups, about 30 minutes. Off heat, discard thyme sprigs and stir in remaining 1 tablespoon vinegar and mustard; cover to keep warm.

5. Using sharp paring knife, cut around inverted T-shaped bone until it can be pulled free from roast (use clean dish towel to grasp bone). Using slicing knife, slice roast. Serve with sauce.

Making Slow-Roasted Pork Shoulder

1. SCORE MEAT: Using sharp knife, cut slits 1 inch apart in crosshatch pattern in fat cap of pork butt, being careful not to cut into meat.

2. SALT AND REFRIGERATE: Combine kosher salt and brown sugar, then rub over pork and into slits. Wrap roast tightly in plastic, place on rimmed baking sheet, and refrigerate at least 12 hours.

3. ROAST 5 TO 6 HOURS: Place roast in greased V-rack in roasting pan. Add water to pan and roast until meat is extremely tender, 5 to 6 hours, basting meat twice during cooking.

4. REST MEAT: Transfer roast to carving board and let rest, tented loosely with aluminum foil, for 1 hour, before slicing and serving.

Oven-Barbecued Pulled Pork

SERVES 8   **TOTAL TIME** 5½ TO 6½ HOURS
(PLUS 8 HOURS FOR SPICE RUB)

✓ **WHY THIS RECIPE WORKS:** The barbecue season for much of the country is cruelly short, especially when the craving strikes for tender pulled pork in midwinter. Could we find a way to replicate outdoor barbecuing inside using the low, slow heat of the oven? We were able to create a smoky flavor using Chinese Lapsang Souchong tea leaves, which are cured over smoldering pine or cypress boughs. We cut a boneless pork butt in half, increasing the surface area of the meat and thereby allowing more smoke flavor to permeate the pork. After a 30-minute smoking period, we added apple juice to the pan and let the pork cook for several hours at 250 degrees, until it yielded moist, tender meat. Now all we needed to do was shred the pork and toss it with sauce. This indoor pulled pork was smoky-tasting, tender to a fault, and judiciously spicy. Some brands of tea are ground coarser than others, and loose tea is often not ground at all; if necessary, grind the tea to a fine powder in a spice grinder before measuring. Be careful when opening the crimped foil to add the juice, as hot steam and smoke will billow out. Store-bought barbecue sauce will work with this recipe. Pork butt roast is often labeled Boston butt in the supermarket. Serve the pulled pork on white bread with dill pickle chips.

Ground Lapsang Souchong tea leaves replicate the smoky flavor of the grill in this pulled pork barbecued in the oven.

3	tablespoons sweet paprika
2	tablespoons packed dark brown sugar
4	teaspoons chili powder
2	teaspoons ground cumin
	Salt and pepper
1	(5-pound) boneless pork butt roast, trimmed and cut in half widthwise
¼	cup finely ground Lapsang Souchong tea (12 tea bags)
½	cup apple juice
2½	cups barbecue sauce

1. Mix paprika, sugar, chili powder, cumin, 1 tablespoon salt, and 2 teaspoons pepper together in bowl, then rub mixture evenly over pork. Wrap pork in plastic wrap and refrigerate for 8 to 24 hours.

2. Transfer pork to freezer and freeze until well chilled, about 45 minutes. Adjust 1 oven rack to lowest position and second rack at least 5 inches from broiler element. Place baking stone on lower rack and heat oven to 500 degrees.

3. Line rimmed baking sheet with aluminum foil. Sprinkle tea evenly over prepared sheet and top with wire rack. Unwrap pork, transfer to prepared wire rack, and cover with foil, crimping edges tightly around sheet to seal. Place baking sheet on baking stone and roast pork for 30 minutes.

4. Reduce oven temperature to 250 degrees, leaving oven door open for 1 minute to cool. While oven is open, carefully open 1 corner of foil and pour apple juice into bottom of baking sheet; reseal foil. Continue to roast pork until meat is very tender and meets little resistance when poked with fork, 3 to 4 hours.

5. Remove foil and move baking sheet to higher rack. Heat broiler and broil pork until well browned and crisp in spots, 5 to 10 minutes. Flip meat over and continue to broil until well browned and crisp, 5 to 7 minutes longer.

6. Transfer pork to cutting board and let rest, uncovered, until just cool enough to handle, about 30 minutes. Shred meat into thin shreds, discarding large pieces of fat. Toss shredded meat with ½ cup of sauce in serving bowl and serve, passing remaining sauce separately.

To keep it moist, spiral-sliced ham gets glazed twice—toward the end of cooking and again once out of the oven.

Spiral-Sliced Ham with Maple-Orange Glaze

SERVES 12 TO 14   **TOTAL TIME** 3½ TO 4 HOURS

✔ **WHY THIS RECIPE WORKS:** We wanted to produce a moist and tender ham with a glaze that complemented but didn't overwhelm the meat. Bone-in hams that have been spiral-sliced offered the best flavor with the least amount of carving. We found it important to avoid labels that read "Ham with water added," as these hams simply didn't taste as good. Soaking the ham in hot water and then roasting it in an oven bag kept it moist and reduced its cooking time. Finally, we glazed the ham twice, once toward the end of cooking and then again when it came out of the oven. You can bypass the 90-minute soaking time, but the heating time will increase to 18 to 20 minutes per pound for a cold ham. If there is a tear in the ham's inner covering, wrap it in several layers of plastic wrap before soaking it. Instead of the plastic oven bag, the ham may be placed cut side down in the roasting pan and covered tightly with foil, but you will need to add 3 to 4 minutes per pound to the heating time. If using an oven bag, be sure to cut slits in the bag so it does not burst.

HAM

- 1 (7- to 10-pound) spiral-sliced bone-in half ham
- 1 large plastic oven bag

MAPLE-ORANGE GLAZE

- ¾ cup maple syrup
- ½ cup orange marmalade
- 2 tablespoons unsalted butter
- 1 tablespoon Dijon mustard
- 1 teaspoon pepper
- ¼ teaspoon ground cinnamon

1. FOR THE HAM: Leaving ham's inner plastic or foil covering intact, place ham in large container, cover with hot tap water, and let sit for 45 minutes. Drain, cover again with hot tap water, and let sit for another 45 minutes.

2. Adjust oven rack to lowest position and heat oven to 250 degrees. Drain and unwrap ham, and remove plastic disk covering bone. Place ham in oven bag. Gather top of bag tightly so bag fits snugly around ham, tie bag, and trim excess plastic. Set ham, cut side down, in large roasting pan and cut 4 slits in top of bag with paring knife.

3. Bake ham until center registers 100 degrees, 1 to 1½ hours (about 10 minutes per pound).

4. FOR THE GLAZE: Meanwhile, combine all ingredients in small saucepan and cook over medium heat, stirring occasionally, until mixture is thickened and has reduced to 1 cup, 5 to 10 minutes; set aside.

5. Remove ham from oven and increase oven temperature to 350 degrees. Cut open oven bag and roll back sides to expose ham. Brush ham with one-third of glaze and return to oven until glaze becomes sticky, about 10 minutes (if glaze is too thick to brush, return to heat to loosen).

6. Remove ham from oven, transfer to carving board, and brush entire ham with half of remaining glaze. Tent with aluminum foil and let rest for 15 to 20 minutes. While ham rests, heat remaining glaze with 4 to 6 tablespoons of ham juices until it forms thick but fluid sauce. Carve ham and serve with sauce.

VARIATION

Spiral-Sliced Ham with Cherry-Port Glaze

Substitute following mixture for maple-orange glaze: Simmer ½ cup ruby port in small saucepan over medium heat until reduced to 2 tablespoons, about 5 minutes. Stir in 1 cup packed dark brown sugar, ½ cup cherry preserves, and 1 teaspoon pepper and cook, stirring occasionally, until mixture is thickened and has reduced to 1 cup, 5 to 10 minutes.

Glazed ham is appealingly simple but often comes out dry and jerkylike. We found that heating the ham to an internal temperature of no higher than 120 degrees was enough to take the chill off without drying it out. Soaking the ham in hot water before heating it and placing it in an oven bag kept it moist and also reduced the cooking time. Finally, we determined that it was best to apply the glaze toward the end of cooking and then again once it came out of the oven.

1. SOAK THE HAM IN HOT WATER:
Leaving the ham's inner plastic or foil covering intact, place the ham in a large container and cover with hot tap water. Let it sit for 45 minutes. Drain, cover the ham again with hot tap water, and let it sit for another 45 minutes.
WHY? Placing the wrapped ham in hot water raises its internal temperature and decreases the cooking time by 1 hour, which prevents the meat from drying out in the oven.

2. USE AN OVEN BAG: Drain and unwrap the ham, removing the plastic disk covering the bone. Place the ham in an oven bag. Gather the top of the bag tightly so that the bag fits snugly around the ham. Tie the bag and trim any excess plastic.
WHY? Cooking the ham in an oven bag reduces the oven time by another half-hour or so.

3. CUT SLITS IN THE BAG: Set the ham, cut side down, in a large roasting pan and cut 4 slits in the bag with a paring knife.
WHY? The slits will allow excess steam to escape from the bag as the ham cooks. Skip this step and the pressure from the steam will cause the bag to burst.

4. ROAST THE HAM IN A LOW-TEMPERATURE OVEN: Bake the ham in a 250-degree oven until the center of the ham registers 100 degrees, 1 to 1½ hours (about 10 minutes per pound).
WHY? A low-temperature oven ensures that the exterior of the ham doesn't race ahead of the center and dry out. Remember, the ham is already cooked; you are simply warming it.

5. RAISE THE HEAT AND GLAZE THE HAM: Remove the ham from the oven and raise the oven to 350 degrees. Cut open the bag, brush the ham with one-third of the glaze, and return to the oven.
WHY? Once the ham is nearly cooked, apply the glaze. If applied too early, the glaze just runs off. Raising the oven temperature helps the glaze to brown. Once the glaze is sticky, transfer the ham to a carving board and brush it with half of the remaining glaze, then let the ham rest.

6. CARVE AND SLICE: Once the ham has rested for 15 to 20 minutes, carve along one side of the bone to remove the meat. Separate the spiral cuts and slice any unsliced sections. Rotate the ham and repeat on the other side of the bone. Serve with the remaining glaze.
WHY? Some spiral cuts will require finishing with a knife to separate the individual pieces. Also, a portion of the ham (likely near the top) will be unsliced. You should cut this part into thin slices.

Pan-Seared Lamb Chops with Red Wine–Rosemary Sauce

SERVES 4   TOTAL TIME 30 MINUTES   FAST

✓ **WHY THIS RECIPE WORKS:** Lamb chops make a quick and flavorful meal, but because they are a premium cut of meat—particularly when using loin or rib chops—they are an expensive undertaking, so there can be no mistakes. Our goal was to develop a way to pan-sear them that would guarantee perfectly cooked lamb every time, juicy and tender and with a good crust. A really hot skillet is the most important step to perfect pan-seared lamb chops. If the pan isn't properly pre-heated, the chops will overcook before a good crust forms. A red wine pan sauce makes good use of the browned bits left in the skillet and is a nice complement to the rich lamb. For more information on making a pan sauce, see page 184. We prefer these chops cooked to medium-rare, but if you prefer them more or less done, see our guidelines on page 15. To ensure that the chops remain juicy after cooking, let them rest for 5 to 10 minutes even if you're not making the pan sauce. For information about buying lamb chops, see page 324. You can also serve these chops with any of the sauces on page 185.

CHOPS
- 8 (4-ounce) lamb loin or rib chops, ¾ to 1 inch thick, trimmed
  Salt and pepper
- 1 tablespoon vegetable oil

RED WINE SAUCE
- 1 tablespoon vegetable oil
- 1 shallot, minced
- ¾ cup chicken broth
- ½ cup dry red wine
- 2 teaspoons packed brown sugar
- 3 tablespoons unsalted butter, cut into 3 pieces and chilled
- 1 teaspoon minced fresh rosemary or ¼ teaspoon dried
  Salt and pepper

1. FOR THE CHOPS: Pat chops dry with paper towels and season with salt and pepper. Heat oil in 12-inch skillet over medium-high heat until just smoking. Brown chops on first side, about 4 minutes.

2. Flip chops and continue to cook until meat registers 120 to 125 degrees (for medium-rare), 4 to 6 minutes. Transfer chops to clean plate, tent with aluminum foil, and let rest while making sauce.

3. FOR THE SAUCE: Add oil to now-empty skillet and heat over medium-high heat until shimmering. Add shallot and cook until softened, about 2 minutes. Stir in broth, wine, and brown sugar, scraping up any browned bits, and simmer until thickened, about 5 minutes.

4. Stir in any accumulated meat juices. Reduce heat to low and whisk in butter, 1 piece at a time. Off heat, stir in rosemary and season with salt and pepper to taste. Spoon sauce over chops and serve.

Roast Boneless Leg of Lamb

SERVES 4 TO 6   TOTAL TIME 1 HOUR 40 MINUTES

✓ **WHY THIS RECIPE WORKS:** Boneless leg of lamb would seem to be an easy supper. But it's not so simple as season-ing the lamb, throwing it in the oven, and then checking it occasionally. We wanted a foolproof method for achieving a crisp crust and a perfectly cooked interior every time. We first settled on a half leg as the right amount to serve four to six people. Next we found that pan-searing the roast and then finishing it in the oven produced a great crust and a tender, juicy interior. For this recipe we prefer to use the sirloin end of the leg, although the shank end can be used. These two roasts are usually sold in elastic netting that must be removed before cooking. We prefer leg of lamb cooked to medium-rare, but if you prefer it more or less done, see our guidelines on page 15. Serve the lamb with Sweet and Sour Mint Sauce (page 231).

Preparing a Boneless Leg of Lamb

1. Place the rough side of the meat (the side that was closest to the bone) facing up on a counter or cutting board. Pound the meat to 1-inch thickness to ensure even cooking.

2. Rub the meat with oil and then season it with salt and pepper. Roll the meat into a tidy roast and tie it with twine at 2-inch intervals.

1 (3½- to 4-pound) boneless half leg of lamb, trimmed
2 tablespoons vegetable oil
   Salt and pepper

1. Adjust oven rack to lower-middle position and heat oven to 375 degrees. Lay lamb on clean counter, with interior (which was against bone) facing up. Pound meat to even 1-inch thickness, then rub with 1 tablespoon oil and season with salt and pepper. Roll meat into tidy roast and tie at 2-inch intervals with kitchen twine. Pat roast dry with paper towels and season with salt and pepper.

2. Heat remaining 1 tablespoon oil in 12-inch skillet over medium-high heat until just smoking. Brown roast on all sides, about 10 minutes. Transfer roast to wire rack set over rimmed baking sheet. Roast lamb until meat registers 120 to 125 degrees (for medium-rare), 45 to 55 minutes.

3. Transfer lamb to carving board, tent with aluminum foil, and let rest for 15 to 20 minutes. Slice into ½-inch-thick slices and serve.

Roast Rack of Lamb

SERVES 4 TO 6   TOTAL TIME 40 MINUTES   FAST

✔ **WHY THIS RECIPE WORKS:** If you're going to spend the money on rack of lamb, you want to be sure you cook it right—as with other simple dishes, there's no disguising imperfection. We wanted to develop a foolproof recipe that produced perfectly pink and juicy meat encased in an intensely brown, crisp shell. To prepare the racks, we frenched them (cleaned the rib bones of meat and fat), and also discovered that we needed to remove a second layer of internal fat (along with a thin strip of meat) to avoid a greasy finished dish. After testing various oven temperatures, we discovered that it was best to sear the racks first on the stovetop and then finish them in a 425-degree oven. Have the butcher french the racks for you if possible. We prefer rack of lamb cooked to medium-rare, but if you prefer it more or less done, see our guidelines on page 15. Serve the lamb with Sweet and Sour Mint Sauce.

2 (1- to 1¼-pound) racks of lamb, trimmed and frenched
   Salt and pepper
2 tablespoons vegetable oil

1. Adjust oven rack to lower-middle position, place rimmed baking sheet on oven rack, and heat oven to 425 degrees.

2. Pat lamb dry with paper towels and season with salt and pepper. Heat oil in 12-inch skillet over medium-high heat until just smoking. Brown racks on both sides, about 10 minutes. Transfer lamb to preheated baking sheet and roast until meat registers 120 to 125 degrees (for medium-rare), 10 to 15 minutes.

3. Transfer lamb to carving board, tent with aluminum foil, and let rest for 5 to 10 minutes. To serve, use chef's knife to slice between ribs.

Preparing a Rack of Lamb

1. Using boning knife, scrape ribs clean of any scraps of meat or fat.

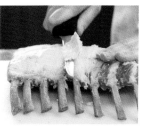

2. Trim off outer layer of fat, then trim flap of meat underneath it and fat underneath that flap.

3. Remove silverskin by sliding boning knife between silverskin and flesh.

SWEET AND SOUR MINT SAUCE

MAKES ¾ CUP   TOTAL TIME 25 MINUTES   FAST

This bracing sauce is traditionally served with lamb.

½ cup minced fresh mint
¼ cup red wine vinegar
1 tablespoon sugar
½ teaspoon salt

Combine all ingredients in bowl and let sit until sugar dissolves, about 20 minutes.

Seafood

■ SIGNIFIES A **FAST** RECIPE (45 MINUTES OR LESS)

Oven-Roasted Salmon

SERVES 4   **TOTAL TIME** 30 MINUTES **FAST**

✅ **WHY THIS RECIPE WORKS:** Roasting a salmon fillet can create a brown exterior, but often the price is an overcooked interior. We developed a hybrid roasting method, preheating the oven and baking sheet to 500 degrees then turning down the heat just before placing the fish in the oven. The initial blast of high heat firmed the exterior and rendered some excess fat. The fish gently cooked and stayed moist as the temperature slowly dropped. To ensure uniform pieces of fish that cooked at the same rate, we found it best to buy a whole center-cut fillet and cut it into four pieces ourselves. If your knife is not sharp enough to cut through the skin easily, try a serrated knife. It is important to keep the skin on during cooking; remove it afterward if you choose not to serve it. Serve with lemon wedges or any of the relishes on page 235.

1 (1¾- to 2-pound) skin-on salmon fillet, 1½ inches thick
2 teaspoons vegetable oil
   Salt and pepper

1. Adjust oven rack to lowest position, place rimmed baking sheet on rack, and heat oven to 500 degrees. Cut salmon crosswise into 4 fillets. Make 4 or 5 shallow slashes, about 1 inch apart, on skin side of each fillet, being careful not to cut into flesh. Pat salmon dry with paper towels, rub with oil, and season with salt and pepper.

2. Reduce oven temperature to 275 degrees and remove baking sheet. Carefully place salmon, skin side down, on baking sheet. Roast until center is still translucent when checked with tip of paring knife and registers 125 degrees (for medium-rare), 9 to 13 minutes. Transfer salmon to plates and serve.

Honey-Lime Glazed Salmon

SERVES 4   **TOTAL TIME** 30 MINUTES **FAST**

✅ **WHY THIS RECIPE WORKS:** Rich, meaty salmon and a sweet glaze are a fantastic pairing, but most recipes fall short by cooking the glazed fish under the broiler, which results in unevenly cooked salmon and a burnt glaze. For flawless results, we began on the stovetop, coating the salmon fillets with brown sugar and cornstarch and browning them in a nonstick skillet. We flipped the fillets, spooned the already-thickened glaze over them, and transferred the skillet to the oven. Our salmon hit its target temperature in less than 10 minutes, and the brown sugar–cornstarch mixture not only aided in browning, it also created a surface on the fish that gave the glaze something to cling to. To ensure uniform pieces of fish, buy a whole center-cut fillet and cut it into four pieces yourself. You will need a 12-inch ovensafe nonstick skillet for this recipe.

HONEY-LIME GLAZE
¼ cup honey
1 teaspoon grated lime zest plus 2 tablespoons juice
1 teaspoon chili powder
½ teaspoon cornstarch
⅛ teaspoon cayenne pepper

SALMON
1 teaspoon packed light brown sugar
¼ teaspoon salt
¼ teaspoon cornstarch
⅛ teaspoon pepper
1 (1¾- to 2-pound) skin-on salmon fillet, 1½ inches thick
1 teaspoon vegetable oil

Making Oven-Roasted Salmon

1. PREHEAT BAKING SHEET: Adjust oven rack to lowest position, place rimmed baking sheet on rack, and heat oven to 500 degrees.

2. SCORE FISH: Cut salmon into 4 equal pieces, then cut 4 or 5 shallow slashes, about 1 inch apart, through skin on each piece. Be careful not to cut into flesh.

3. PLACE ON HOT SHEET: Pat salmon dry, rub fillets with vegetable oil, and season with salt and pepper. Place skin side down on preheated baking sheet.

4. ROAST AT LOWER HEAT: Roast salmon in 275-degree oven until center is still translucent and registers 125 degrees in thickest part.

RELISHES FOR FISH

These brightly flavored relishes are sure to dress up any type of simple seafood dish, from sautéed fish fillets to crab cakes. They can be served with our Oven-Roasted Salmon (page 234), Oven-Poached Side of Salmon (page 238), Easy Salmon Cakes (page 240), Pan-Roasted Fish Fillets (page 242), Pan-Seared Sesame-Crusted Tuna Steaks (page 244), Crunchy Oven-Fried Fish (page 252), Pan-Fried Fish Sticks (page 253), Fried Catfish (page 255), or Classic Pan-Fried Crab Cakes (page 257).

Fresh Tomato Relish

MAKES ABOUT 1 CUP

TOTAL TIME 25 MINUTES **FAST**

Be sure to use super-ripe tomatoes in this simple relish.

- 2 tomatoes, cored, seeded, and cut into ¼-inch pieces
- 1 small shallot, minced
- 1 small garlic clove, minced
- 2 tablespoons chopped fresh basil
- 1 tablespoon extra-virgin olive oil
- 1 teaspoon red wine vinegar
  Salt and pepper

Combine all ingredients in bowl, let sit for 15 minutes, and season with salt and pepper to taste.

Avocado-Orange Relish

MAKES ABOUT 1½ CUPS

TOTAL TIME 25 MINUTES **FAST**

For a spicier relish, add some of the jalapeño chile seeds. To keep the avocado from discoloring, prepare this salsa close to the serving time.

- 1 large orange, peeled and cut into ½-inch pieces
- 1 avocado, halved, pitted, and cut into ½-inch pieces
- 2 tablespoons finely chopped red onion
- 4 teaspoons lime juice
- 1 small jalapeño chile, stemmed, seeded, and minced
- 2 tablespoons minced fresh cilantro
  Salt and pepper

Combine all ingredients in bowl, let sit for 15 minutes, and season with salt and pepper to taste.

Spicy Cucumber Relish

MAKES ABOUT 1 CUP

TOTAL TIME 25 MINUTES **FAST**

For a spicier relish, add some of the serrano chile seeds.

- 1 cucumber, peeled, halved lengthwise, seeded, and cut into ¼-inch pieces
- 1 small shallot, minced
- 1 serrano chile, stemmed, seeded, and minced
- 2 tablespoons minced fresh mint
- 1 tablespoon lime juice, plus extra to taste
  Salt

Combine all ingredients in bowl, let sit for 15 minutes, and season with salt and extra lime juice to taste.

Tangerine and Ginger Relish

MAKES ABOUT 1 CUP

TOTAL TIME 35 MINUTES **FAST**

Fresh ginger is crucial to the flavor of this relish; do not substitute dried ground ginger.

- 4 tangerines, peeled and cut into ½-inch pieces
- 2 teaspoons lemon juice
- 2 teaspoons extra-virgin olive oil
- 1 scallion, sliced thin
- 1½ teaspoons grated fresh ginger
  Salt and pepper

Place tangerines in strainer set over bowl and let drain for 15 minutes; reserve 1 tablespoon drained juice. Combine reserved juice, lemon juice, oil, scallion, and ginger in bowl. Stir in drained tangerines and let sit for 15 minutes. Season with salt and pepper to taste.

Grapefruit and Basil Relish

MAKES ABOUT 1 CUP

TOTAL TIME 35 MINUTES **FAST**

The sweetness of this relish depends on the sweetness of the grapefruits. If the grapefruits are sour, add a pinch of sugar to the relish.

- 2 Ruby Red grapefruits, peeled, segmented, and cut into ½-inch pieces
- 2 tablespoons chopped fresh basil
- 1 small shallot, minced
- 2 teaspoons lemon juice
- 2 teaspoons extra-virgin olive oil
  Salt and pepper

Place grapefruits in strainer set over bowl and let drain for 15 minutes; reserve 1 tablespoon drained juice. Combine reserved juice, basil, shallot, lemon juice, and oil in bowl. Stir in drained grapefruits and let sit for 15 minutes. Season with salt and pepper to taste.

Mango and Mint Relish

MAKES ABOUT 1½ CUPS

TOTAL TIME 25 MINUTES **FAST**

For a spicier relish, add some of the jalapeño chile seeds.

- 2 mangos, peeled, pitted, and cut into ½-inch pieces
- 1 jalapeño chile, stemmed, seeded, and minced
- 3 tablespoons lime juice (2 limes)
- 3 tablespoons extra-virgin olive oil
- 2 tablespoons minced fresh mint
  Salt and pepper

Combine all ingredients in bowl, let sit for 15 minutes, and season with salt and pepper to taste.

1. FOR THE GLAZE: Whisk all ingredients together in small saucepan and simmer over medium-high heat until thickened, about 1 minute; remove from heat and cover to keep warm.

2. FOR THE SALMON: Adjust oven rack to middle position and heat oven to 300 degrees. Combine sugar, salt, cornstarch, and pepper in bowl. Cut salmon crosswise into 4 fillets, pat dry with paper towels, and rub sugar mixture evenly over flesh side.

3. Heat oil in 12-inch ovensafe nonstick skillet over medium-high heat until just smoking. Lay salmon, flesh side down, in skillet and cook until well browned, about 1 minute. Using tongs, carefully flip salmon and cook on skin side for 1 minute.

4. Off heat, spoon glaze over salmon fillets. Transfer skillet to oven and roast until center is still translucent when checked with tip of paring knife and registers 125 degrees (for medium-rare), 7 to 10 minutes.

5. Using potholders (skillet handle will be hot), remove skillet from oven. Transfer fish to plates and serve.

VARIATIONS

Soy-Mustard Glazed Salmon

Substitute following ingredients for glaze and cook as directed: 3 tablespoons packed light brown sugar, 2 tablespoons soy sauce, 2 tablespoons mirin, 1 tablespoon sherry vinegar, 1 tablespoon whole-grain mustard, 1 tablespoon water, 1 teaspoon cornstarch, and ⅛ teaspoon red pepper flakes.

Pomegranate-Balsamic Glazed Salmon

Substitute following ingredients for glaze and cook as directed: 3 tablespoons packed light brown sugar, 3 tablespoons pomegranate juice, 2 tablespoons balsamic vinegar, 1 tablespoon whole-grain mustard, 1 teaspoon cornstarch, and pinch cayenne pepper.

Poached Salmon with Herb and Caper Vinaigrette

SERVES 4   **TOTAL TIME** 45 MINUTES   **FAST**

✔ **WHY THIS RECIPE WORKS:** Incorrectly poached salmon is dry, and the flavor is so washed out that not even the richest sauce can redeem it. We wanted irresistibly supple salmon, accented by the delicate flavor of the poaching liquid and accompanied by a simple pan sauce. Poaching the salmon in just enough liquid to come half an inch up its sides meant we didn't need much to boost the flavor of the liquid. However, the part of the salmon that wasn't submerged in liquid needed to be steamed for thorough cooking, and the low cooking temperature required to poach the salmon evenly didn't create

We poach the salmon on a bed of lemon slices and herbs and use the poaching liquid as the base for a vinaigrette.

enough steam. By increasing the ratio of wine to water the additional alcohol lowered the liquid's boiling point, producing more vapor even at the lower temperature. To keep the bottoms of the fillets from overcooking, we placed them on top of lemon slices. We reduced the poaching liquid and added some olive oil for an easy vinaigrette-style sauce. To ensure uniform pieces of fish that cooked at the same rate, we found it best to buy a whole center-cut fillet and cut it into four pieces ourselves.

2 lemons, 1 cut into ¼-inch-thick slices and 1 cut into wedges
2 tablespoons minced fresh parsley, stems reserved
2 tablespoons minced fresh tarragon, stems reserved
1 large shallot, minced
½ cup dry white wine
½ cup water
1 (1¾- to 2-pound) skinless salmon fillet, about 1½ inches thick
2 tablespoons capers, rinsed and minced
2 tablespoons extra-virgin olive oil
1 tablespoon honey
    Salt and pepper

Poaching rarely lives up to its promise to produce silken, delicately flavored fish. It typically requires prepping a slew of ingredients for the poaching broth, only to dump them down the drain at the end. And much of the salmon flavor leaches out of the fish and into the liquid. We solve both these problems by using a shallow poaching technique: Less poaching liquid means less ingredient prep (and waste), as well as less salmon flavor lost to the liquid. We finish our recipe by reducing the poaching liquid to add to our vinaigrette-style sauce, giving our salmon a serious flavor boost.

1. LINE THE PAN WITH LEMON SLICES: Arrange the lemon slices in a single layer over the bottom of a 12-inch skillet and scatter the herb stems and shallot over the top.

WHY? The lemons help keep the salmon elevated off the surface of the skillet so that the fillets poach evenly. The herb stems and shallot add more flavor to the cooking liquid.

2. ADD WATER AND WINE: Add ½ cup each white wine and water to the skillet. **WHY?** This small amount of liquid may seem meager compared with a classic poaching method (which submerges the fish in cups of simmering liquid), but using less liquid actually helps the fish cook more gently because the fish is steamed rather than simmered.

3. LAY THE SALMON FILLETS IN THE SKILLET: Pat the salmon dry and season with salt and pepper. Lay the fillets, skinned side down, on top of the lemons. **WHY?** Placing the salmon skinned side down will leave the nonskinned side above the liquid, preserving the fillets' appearance and making them more presentable. Be sure to use skinless salmon here or else the finished sauce will have a very strong flavor and an oily texture.

4. BRING THE LIQUID TO A SIMMER, REDUCE THE HEAT, AND COVER: Once the poaching liquid is simmering, turn down the heat, and cover the pan. Cook until the sides are opaque but the centers of the fillets are still translucent. **WHY?** Turning down the heat allows the salmon to cook gently; covering the pan provides a consistent but gentle steaming environment, protecting the delicate fish.

5. LET THE SALMON DRAIN: Once the salmon is cooked through, transfer the fish and lemon slices to a paper towel–lined plate, cover with foil, and let the fillets drain while finishing the sauce. **WHY?** If you skip this step, the fish will leak poaching liquid onto the plate, which makes a mess and waters down the sauce.

6. REDUCE, THEN STRAIN THE POACHING LIQUID: Return the pan with the poaching liquid to high heat and simmer until reduced to 2 tablespoons. Strain the reduced liquid, then add minced herbs, shallot, capers, oil, and honey to create a vinaigrette-style sauce. **WHY?** The reduced poaching liquid is used as the "vinegar" in the sauce. Using the same liquid, the sauce is easy to make.

1. Arrange lemon slices in single layer in 12-inch skillet. Top with parsley and tarragon stems and 2 tablespoons shallot. Add wine and water. Cut salmon crosswise into 4 fillets and lay, skinned side down, on lemon slices.

2. Set pan over high heat and bring liquid to simmer. Reduce heat to low, cover, and cook until center of salmon is still translucent when checked with tip of paring knife and registers 125 degrees (for medium-rare), 11 to 16 minutes.

3. Remove pan from heat. Using spatula, carefully transfer salmon and lemon slices to paper towel–lined plate. Tent salmon with aluminum foil.

4. Return pan with poaching liquid to high heat and simmer until liquid has reduced to 2 tablespoons, 4 to 5 minutes. Strain liquid through fine-mesh strainer into bowl. Whisk in minced parsley, minced tarragon, remaining shallot, capers, oil, and honey. Season with salt and pepper to taste.

NOTES FROM THE TEST KITCHEN

Buying Salmon

FRESH VERSUS FARMED: In season, we prefer the more pronounced flavor of wild-caught salmon to farmed Atlantic salmon (traditionally the main farm-raised variety in the Unites States). If you're going to spend the extra money for wild salmon, make sure it looks and smells fresh, and realize that high-quality salmon is available only from late spring through the end of summer.

CUTS OF SALMON: There are many ways to buy salmon. Our preference is for thick, center-cut fillets, which can be poached, steamed, pan-seared, roasted, or grilled. Cut from the head end or center, these fillets are the prime cut of the fish. They are thick enough to sear nicely without overcooking and are easy to skin (if desired). Buy the total amount you need in one piece and cut the individual fillets yourself. You will also see thin fillets at the market. Stay away from these. These are cut from the tail end, and they cook so fast that it is impossible to get a nice sear before the fish is overcooked—plus one end is very, very thin while the other is always much thicker.

SKIN-ON OR BONE-IN: For some recipes you will want to buy the salmon skin-on; for recipes that call for skinless salmon, you can easily remove it yourself or ask your fishmonger to do it. Bone-in steaks are an excellent choice for pan searing, grilling, or roasting, but they should not be poached. You may see boneless steaks rolled and tied into a circular shape; these are as versatile as the bone-in steaks.

5. Season salmon with salt and pepper. Using spatula, carefully transfer salmon, without lemon slices, to plates. Serve with sauce and lemon wedges.

VARIATION

Poached Salmon with Dill and Sour Cream Sauce

Substitute 2 tablespoons minced fresh dill plus 8 to 12 dill stems for parsley and tarragon. Omit capers, olive oil, and honey. After straining reduced poaching liquid, return it to skillet and whisk in remaining shallot and 1 tablespoon Dijon mustard; simmer until slightly thickened, about 4 minutes. Whisk in 2 tablespoons sour cream, season with lemon juice to taste, and simmer until thickened, about 1 minute. Off heat, whisk in 2 tablespoons unsalted butter and minced dill.

Skinning Salmon Fillets

1. Using tip of boning knife (or sharp chef's knife), begin to cut skin away from fish at corner of fillet.

2. When enough skin is exposed, grasp skin firmly with piece of paper towel, hold taut, and carefully slice flesh off skin.

Oven-Poached Side of Salmon

SERVES 8 TO 10   **TOTAL TIME** 1 HOUR 30 MINUTES (PLUS CHILLING TIME)

 **WHY THIS RECIPE WORKS:** A side of salmon is an elegant choice when entertaining. We wanted a method for cooking a side of salmon that didn't require a poacher. To do this, we decided to get rid of the water and steam the salmon in its own moisture. We wrapped the seasoned fish in heavy-duty foil and placed it directly on the oven rack, which offered more even cooking than using a baking sheet. Cooking the salmon low and slow gave the best results—moist, rich fish. If serving a big crowd, you can oven-poach two individually wrapped sides of salmon in the same oven (on the upper- and lower-middle racks) without altering the cooking time. White wine vinegar can be substituted for the cider vinegar. Serve with any of the relishes on page 235.

1 (4-pound) skin-on side of salmon, pinbones removed
Salt

2 tablespoons cider vinegar

6 sprigs fresh tarragon or dill, plus 2 tablespoons minced

2 lemons, sliced thin, plus lemon wedges

1. Adjust oven rack to middle position and heat oven to 250 degrees. Cut 3 pieces of heavy-duty aluminum foil to be 1 foot longer than side of salmon. Working with 2 pieces of foil, fold up 1 long side of each by 3 inches. Lay sheets side by side with folded sides touching, fold edges together to create secure seam, and press seam flat. Center third sheet of foil over seam. Spray foil with vegetable oil spray.

Making Oven-Poached Side of Salmon

1. MAKE LEAK-PROOF FOIL PACKAGE: Working with 2 foil pieces, fold up 1 long side of each by 3 inches. Lay with folded sides touching, fold edges together, and press flat. Center third sheet over seam.

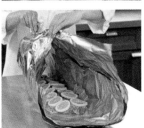

2. ADD AROMATICS AND SEAL PACKAGE: Lay salmon down center of foil. Sprinkle with vinegar, then top with herb sprigs and lemon slices. Fold edges up over salmon and together; do not crimp tightly.

3. PLACE DIRECTLY ON RACK: Lay foil-wrapped fish directly on oven rack (without baking sheet), and cook for 45 minutes to 1 hour.

4. CHILL AND SERVE: Let salmon cool for 30 minutes, then refrigerate until cold, at least 1 hour or up to 2 days. Before serving, unwrap salmon, brush away aromatics, and gently transfer to platter.

2. Pat salmon dry with paper towels and season with salt. Lay salmon, skin side down, in center of foil. Sprinkle with vinegar, then top with tarragon sprigs and lemon slices. Fold foil up over salmon to create seam on top and gently fold foil edges together to secure; do not crimp too tightly.

3. Lay foil-wrapped fish directly on oven rack (without baking sheet). Cook until color of salmon has turned from pink to orange and thickest part registers 135 to 140 degrees, 45 minutes to 1 hour.

4. Remove fish from oven and open foil. Let salmon cool at room temperature for 30 minutes. Pour off any accumulated liquid, then reseal salmon in foil and refrigerate until cold, at least 1 hour or up to 2 days. (If salmon is very cold, let sit at room temperature for 30 minutes before serving.)

5. To serve, unwrap salmon and brush away lemon slices, tarragon sprigs, and any solidified poaching liquid. Transfer fish to serving platter, sprinkle with minced tarragon, and serve with lemon wedges.

Broiled Salmon with Mustard and Crisp Dilled Crust

SERVES 8 TO 10   **TOTAL TIME** 45 MINUTES   **FAST**

✓ **WHY THIS RECIPE WORKS:** We wanted to pull off a crowd-pleasing side of salmon that was moist and firm, with a golden brown crumb crust for a textural contrast. We toasted plain bread crumbs and mixed in crushed potato chips and minced dill for a crisp and flavorful coating. A thin layer of mustard boosted the flavor and helped the crumb mixture adhere. One problem: the crust burned by the time the fish was cooked. So we switched gears and broiled the fish until it was nearly done, then spread on the mustard and crumbs for a second run under the broiler. Heavy-duty aluminum foil measuring 18 inches wide is essential for creating a sling that aids in transferring the cooked side to a carving board. Use a large baking sheet so that the salmon will lie flat. If you can't get the fish to lie flat, even when positioning it diagonally on the baking sheet, trim the tail end. If you prefer to cook a smaller (2-pound) fillet, ask to have it cut from the thick center of the fillet, not the thin tail end, and begin checking doneness a minute earlier. We prefer thick-cut and kettle-cooked potato chips in this recipe; ridged chips will work in a pinch.

3 slices hearty white sandwich bread, crusts removed

4 ounces high-quality potato chips, finely crushed (1 cup)

6 tablespoons minced fresh dill

1 (3½-pound) skin-on side of salmon, pinbones removed

1   teaspoon olive oil
    Salt and pepper
3   tablespoons Dijon mustard
    Lemon wedges

1. Adjust oven rack to middle position and heat oven to 400 degrees. Pulse bread in food processor to even ¼-inch pieces, about 10 pulses. Spread crumbs evenly on rimmed baking sheet and toast, stirring occasionally, until golden brown and crisp, 4 to 5 minutes. Combine toasted crumbs, crushed potato chips, and dill in bowl.

2. Adjust oven racks 3 inches and 6 inches from broiler element and heat broiler. Cut piece of heavy-duty aluminum foil to be 1 foot longer than side of salmon, then fold lengthwise in thirds. Lay foil diagonally across rimmed baking sheet. Lay salmon, skin side down, on foil, rub with oil, and season with salt and pepper. Broil salmon on upper rack until surface is spotty brown and center is still translucent when checked with tip of paring knife and registers 125 degrees (for medium-rare), 9 to 11 minutes.

3. Remove fish from oven. Working quickly, spread evenly with mustard, then press bread-crumb mixture onto fish. Return salmon to lower rack and broil until crust is deep golden brown, about 1 minute.

4. Using foil sling, transfer salmon to cutting board (or serving platter). Run spatula underneath salmon to loosen it from foil. Using spatula to hold salmon in place on cutting board, gently pull foil out from underneath salmon. Serve with lemon wedges.

Removing Pinbones

Pinbones are small white bones that run through the center of a side of fish or a fish fillet. Most salmon is sold with the pinbones removed, but it never hurts to check one more time.

1. For large side of salmon, drape fish over inverted bowl. Grasp protruding pinbones with needle-nose pliers or tweezers and pull to remove.

2. For fillets, run fingers over surface to locate pinbones. (They will feel like tiny bumps.) Remove and discard.

For a new take on classic fish cakes we coat fresh chopped salmon in coarse panko bread crumbs.

Easy Salmon Cakes

SERVES 4   **TOTAL TIME** 40 MINUTES   **FAST**

✔ **WHY THIS RECIPE WORKS:** We wanted to create a spinoff of classic New England fish cakes, using salmon instead of haddock or cod. We were after pure salmon flavor, combined with a few choice complementary ingredients and just enough binder to hold the cakes together. We opted to use mayonnaise and bread crumbs instead of the typical fish cake's potato binder. For cakes that held together but weren't pasty, we pulsed 1-inch pieces of fresh salmon in the food processor. Coating the cakes with ultracrisp panko bread crumbs ensured just the right crisped exterior. A few additions—parsley, lemon juice, scallion, shallot, and Dijon mustard—took our cakes to the next level. After a few minutes in the skillet, our fresh salmon cakes were ready. If buying a skin-on salmon fillet, purchase 1⅓ pounds of fish in order to yield 1¼ pounds after the skin is removed. When processing the salmon it is okay to have some pieces that are larger than ¼ inch. It is important to avoid overprocessing the fish. Serve with lemon wedges or with any of the relishes on page 235 or creamy sauces on page 254.

3 tablespoons plus ¾ cup panko bread crumbs
2 tablespoons minced fresh parsley
2 tablespoons mayonnaise
4 teaspoons lemon juice
1 scallion, sliced thin
1 small shallot, minced
1 teaspoon Dijon mustard
¾ teaspoon salt
¼ teaspoon pepper
  Pinch cayenne pepper
1¼ pounds skinless salmon fillet, cut into 1-inch pieces
½ cup vegetable oil

Making Salmon Cakes

1. CHOP FISH: Hand-chop fish into 1-inch pieces, then add to food processor.

2. PULSE FISH: Pulse chopped fish in 3 batches into ¼-inch bits, being careful not to overprocess. Mix with bread-crumb binder and flavorings.

3. COAT CAKES WITH CRUMBS: Gently coat shaped cakes in coarse panko bread crumbs.

4. COOK CAKES: Heat oil in nonstick skillet until shimmering. Cook salmon cakes until golden brown. Transfer to paper towel–lined plate and let drain for 1 minute.

1. Combine 3 tablespoons panko, parsley, mayonnaise, lemon juice, scallion, shallot, mustard, salt, pepper, and cayenne in large bowl. Working in 3 batches, pulse salmon in food processor until coarsely chopped into ¼-inch pieces, about 2 pulses; transfer each batch to bowl with panko mixture. Gently mix until uniformly combined.

2. Spread remaining ¾ cup panko into shallow dish. Using ⅓-cup measure, scoop level amounts of salmon mixture onto baking sheet to make 8 cakes. Carefully coat each cake with bread crumbs, gently pressing into 1-inch-thick patties, and return to baking sheet.

3. Heat oil in 12-inch nonstick skillet over medium-high heat until shimmering. Cook salmon cakes until golden brown on both sides, 4 to 5 minutes. Transfer cakes to paper towel–lined plate, let drain for 1 minute, and serve.

VARIATION

Easy Salmon Cakes with Smoked Salmon, Capers, and Dill

Reduce amount of fresh salmon to 1 pound and salt to ½ teaspoon. Substitute 1 tablespoon minced fresh dill for parsley. Add 4 ounces finely chopped smoked salmon and 1 tablespoon rinsed and minced capers to bowl with salmon mixture.

Sole Meunière with Browned Butter and Lemon

SERVES 4   **TOTAL TIME** 35 MINUTES **FAST**

✔ **WHY THIS RECIPE WORKS:** The best fish meunière recipes produce perfectly cooked fillets—delicately crisp and golden brown on the outside and moist and flavorful on the inside—that are napped in a buttery yet light sauce. Whole Dover sole is the most authentic choice, but it's also prohibitively expensive; both sole and flounder fillets proved to be good stand-ins, and we found that the fillets needed to be at least ⅜ inch thick to prevent overcooking. For the coating, we produced the perfect crust without eggs or bread crumbs. Instead, we simply dried the fillets, seasoned them with salt and pepper, let them sit for 5 minutes, then dredged them in flour. A nonstick skillet coated with a mixture of oil and butter prevented sticking. For the sauce, we browned additional butter and brightened it with lemon juice. Haddock is also a good substitute for sole. Try to purchase fillets that are of similar size. If using smaller fillets (3 ounces each), serve two fillets per person and reduce the cooking time on the second side by 1 to 2 minutes. You will need to cook smaller fillets in three or four batches and wipe out the skillet with paper towels after the second and third batches to prevent any browned bits from scorching.

FISH

4 (6-ounce) skinless sole fillets
Salt and pepper
½ cup all-purpose flour
2 tablespoons vegetable oil
2 tablespoons unsalted butter

BROWNED BUTTER AND LEMON SAUCE

4 tablespoons unsalted butter, cut into 4 pieces
2 tablespoons capers, rinsed and minced
1 tablespoon lemon juice
1 tablespoon minced fresh parsley
Salt and pepper

Making Sole Meunière

1. PAT SOLE DRY, SEASON, AND FLOUR: Pat sole dry, season, and let sit until fish glistens, about 5 minutes. Coat fillets with flour, shake off excess, and transfer to clean plate.

2. COOK SOLE: Heat oil in nonstick skillet until shimmering and add butter, swirling to coat pan bottom. Place 2 fillets in skillet and cook until bottom is golden brown, about 3 minutes.

3. FLIP SOLE: To gently flip fillets, use 1 spatula to lift long side of sole and second one to catch fish and lower back into pan. Cook until thickest part of fish separates into flakes. Repeat with remaining fillets.

4. MAKE SAUCE: Melt butter for sauce in traditional skillet. Swirl pan constantly until butter is golden brown and has nutty aroma. Off heat, add capers, lemon juice, and parsley and season with salt and pepper.

1. FOR THE FISH: Adjust oven rack to middle position, set large ovensafe platter on rack, and heat oven to 200 degrees. Pat sole dry with paper towels, season with salt and pepper, and let sit until fish glistens with moisture, about 5 minutes.

2. Spread flour in shallow dish. Dredge sole through flour, shake off excess, and transfer to clean plate. Heat 1 tablespoon oil in 12-inch nonstick skillet over medium-high heat until shimmering. Add 1 tablespoon butter and swirl to melt.

3. Gently lay 2 sole fillets in pan and cook until golden, about 3 minutes. Turn sole over using 2 spatulas and cook until second side is golden and fish flakes apart when gently prodded with paring knife, about 2 minutes. Transfer to platter in oven. Wipe out skillet with paper towels and repeat with remaining 1 tablespoon oil, 1 tablespoon butter, and sole fillets; transfer to oven.

4. FOR THE SAUCE: Add butter to 10-inch skillet and melt over medium-high heat. Continue to cook butter, swirling pan constantly, until golden brown with nutty aroma, about 1½ minutes. Off heat, stir in capers, lemon juice, and parsley. Season with salt and pepper to taste. Spoon sauce over sole and serve.

VARIATION
Sole Amandine

Thin trout fillets are also delicious with this sauce.

Omit capers. Add ½ cup slivered or sliced almonds to skillet after butter has melted in step 4; almonds will turn golden brown and fragrant.

Pan-Roasted Fish Fillets

SERVES 4　　**TOTAL TIME** 30 MINUTES　**FAST**

✓ **WHY THIS RECIPE WORKS:** Pan-roasted fish seems like a simple dish, but in reality it is usually well executed only by practiced chefs. Attempts made by home cooks often result in dry, overbaked fillets. We set out to develop a foolproof recipe for producing succulent, well-browned fillets. We quickly learned we needed thick fillets; skinnier pieces overcooked by the time they achieved a serious sear. We then turned to a common restaurant method to cook the fish: We seared the fillets in a hot pan, flipped them, then transferred the pan to a hot oven to finish cooking. Sprinkling the fillets with sugar accelerated browning on the stovetop, shortening the cooking time and thus ensuring the fish didn't dry out. After a short stay in the oven to finish cooking through, the fish emerged well browned, tender, and moist, and best of all not one taster detected any out-of-place sweetness. Thick white fish fillets with a meaty texture, like halibut, cod, sea bass, or

Pan roasting is a great way to cook thicker white fish fillets like cod, halibut, sea bass, and red snapper. Starting these white fish in a hot skillet on the stovetop and then transferring the skillet to the oven ensures that the crust is well browned and the interior is cooked but still moist. In addition, the mess is minimal because the cooking time on the stovetop is reduced to just a few minutes. A sprinkle of sugar accelerates the browning, giving the fish a rich color and deep flavor.

1. PAT THE FISH DRY: Thoroughly pat dry 4 skinless white fish fillets, 1 to 1½ inches thick (6 to 8 ounces each), with paper towels and season with salt and pepper. **WHY?** For a good sear, the fish must be dry. Damp fish will just steam, not brown. We use thicker white fish fillets with a meaty texture that won't cook through too quickly.

2. SPRINKLE THE FISH WITH SUGAR: Sprinkle a very light dusting of sugar (about ⅛ teaspoon) evenly over 1 side of each fillet. **WHY?** Just a small amount of sugar helps caramelize the exterior of the fish, giving it an attractively browned crust after just a few minutes in a smoking hot skillet, without affecting the flavor.

3. SEAR THE FISH IN A HOT PAN: Heat oil in an ovensafe nonstick skillet over high heat until just smoking. Place the fillets sugared side down and press lightly to ensure even contact with the pan. **WHY?** The stovetop jump-starts the browning process. The oil should be smoking and the burner set to high while cooking the fish. There is no risk of burning it since the cooking time is very short. An ovensafe pan is essential.

4. FLIP THE FISH CAREFULLY: Cook until the fillets are just browned, 1 to 1½ minutes. Using 2 spatulas, flip the fillets. **WHY?** Using 2 spatulas makes flipping the delicate fish much easier. Slide 1 spatula under the piece of fish and use the second spatula to guide the fish as you flip it. Use plastic nonstick spatulas, or you can use thin metal fish spatulas if you take care not to scratch the surface of the pan.

5. TRANSFER THE SKILLET TO A HOT OVEN: Transfer the skillet to the middle rack in a 425-degree oven. **WHY?** After the fish is seared and turned, a short cooking time in a very hot oven ensures the fillets are properly cooked through. Cooking them through on the stovetop is not as foolproof and creates a splattery mess. There's plenty of residual heat in the pan to brown the second side in the oven.

6. ROAST THE FISH: Roast the fillets until their centers are just opaque and register 135 degrees. Use a potholder to remove the skillet from the oven and immediately transfer the fish to plates. **WHY?** For the best results, use an instant-read thermometer to check the fish. White fish will be very dry if it is overcooked, and mushy and unappealing if undercooked. Remove the fish from the hot pan or it will continue to cook.

COMPOUND BUTTERS

Compound butters are a great accompaniment to simple roasted white fish. Here in the test kitchen, we like to make a double or triple batch, roll it into a log, and store it in the freezer so that flavored butter is always just a slice away.

TO MAKE COMPOUND BUTTER: Whip 8 tablespoons softened unsalted butter with fork until light and fluffy. Mix in any of the ingredient combinations listed below and season with salt and pepper to taste. Wrap in plastic wrap and let rest to blend flavors, about 10 minutes, or roll into log and refrigerate. (Butter can be refrigerated in airtight container for up to 4 days or frozen, wrapped tightly in plastic wrap, for up to 2 months.)

PARSLEY-CAPER COMPOUND BUTTER `FAST`

- ¼ cup minced fresh parsley
- 4 teaspoons capers, rinsed and minced

PARSLEY-LEMON COMPOUND BUTTER `FAST`

- ¼ cup minced fresh parsley
- 4 teaspoons grated lemon zest

TARRAGON-LIME COMPOUND BUTTER `FAST`

- ¼ cup minced scallion
- 2 tablespoons minced fresh tarragon
- 4 teaspoons lime juice

TAPENADE COMPOUND BUTTER `FAST`

- 10 oil-cured black olives, pitted and chopped fine
- 1 anchovy fillet, rinsed and minced
- 1 tablespoon brandy
- 2 teaspoons minced fresh thyme
- 2 garlic cloves, minced
- ¼ teaspoon grated orange zest

CHIPOTLE-CILANTRO COMPOUND BUTTER `FAST`

- 2 teaspoons minced canned chipotle chile in adobo sauce, plus 2 teaspoons adobo sauce
- 4 teaspoons minced fresh cilantro
- 2 garlic cloves, minced
- 2 teaspoons honey
- 2 teaspoons grated lime zest

red snapper, work best in this recipe. Because most fish fillets differ in thickness, some pieces may finish cooking before others—be sure to immediately remove any fillet that reaches 135 degrees. You will need an ovensafe 12-inch nonstick skillet for this recipe. Serve with lemon wedges, a compound butter, or with any of the relishes on page 235.

- 4 (6- to 8-ounce) skinless white fish fillets, 1 to 1½ inches thick
  Salt and pepper
- ½ teaspoon sugar
- 1 tablespoon vegetable oil

1. Adjust oven rack to middle position and heat oven to 425 degrees. Pat fish dry with paper towels, season with salt and pepper, and sprinkle sugar lightly over 1 side of each fillet.

2. Heat oil in 12-inch ovensafe nonstick skillet over high heat until just smoking. Lay fillets, sugared side down, in skillet and press lightly to ensure even contact with pan. Cook until browned, 1 to 1½ minutes.

3. Turn fish over using 2 spatulas and transfer skillet to oven. Roast fish until centers are just opaque and register 135 degrees, 7 to 10 minutes.

4. Using potholders (skillet handle will be hot), remove skillet from oven. Transfer fish to plates and serve.

Pan-Seared Sesame-Crusted Tuna Steaks

SERVES 4   **TOTAL TIME** 25 MINUTES   `FAST`

✔ **WHY THIS RECIPE WORKS:** Moist and rare in the middle, and with a nice exterior crust, pan-seared tuna is a popular entrée in restaurants. To make this dish at home, we found starting with high-quality tuna—sushi grade if possible—was critical. A thickness of at least 1 inch was necessary for the tuna to remain rare at the center and at the same time achieve a good sear on the exterior. Before searing the tuna in a nonstick skillet, we rubbed the steaks with oil and coated them with sesame seeds. The sesame seeds browned during cooking and formed a beautiful, nutty-tasting crust. The cooking times given in the recipe are for steaks cooked to rare and medium-rare. For tuna steaks cooked medium, observe the timing for medium-rare, then tent the steaks with aluminum foil for 5 minutes before slicing. If you prefer tuna steaks cooked so rare that they are still cold in the center, try to purchase steaks that are 1½ inches thick and cook them according to the timing for rare steaks. Bear in mind, though, that the cooking

Coating tuna steaks with sesame seeds before searing them creates a toasted, nutty-tasting crust.

times are estimates and the best way to check for doneness is by using an instant-read thermometer. Serve with lemon or lime wedges or any of the relishes on page 235.

¾ cup sesame seeds
4 (8-ounce) tuna steaks, 1 inch thick
2 tablespoons vegetable oil
Salt and pepper

1. Spread sesame seeds in shallow dish. Pat tuna dry with paper towels, rub thoroughly with 1 tablespoon oil, and season with salt and pepper. Press both sides of each steak into sesame seeds to coat.

2. Heat remaining 1 tablespoon oil in 12-inch nonstick skillet over medium-high heat until just smoking. Gently lay tuna in pan and cook until seeds are golden brown, 1½ to 2 minutes.

3. Carefully flip tuna and cook until golden brown on second side and tuna registers 110 degrees (for rare) or 125 degrees (for medium-rare), 1½ to 3 minutes. Transfer tuna to cutting board and immediately slice into ⅓-inch-thick pieces. Serve.

VARIATION
Pan-Seared Pepper-Crusted Tuna Steaks
Omit sesame seeds and press ½ teaspoon cracked black peppercorns onto each side of oiled tuna steaks before cooking.

Prosciutto-Wrapped Cod with Lemon-Caper Butter

SERVES 4   TOTAL TIME 40 MINUTES   FAST

✔ **WHY THIS RECIPE WORKS:** For a simple yet elegant cod dish, we found prosciutto to be just the ticket. We wrapped cod fillets in two thin sheets of prosciutto before arranging them in a skillet, then we browned and crisped the prosciutto on the stovetop before transferring the skillet to the oven to cook the fish through. The prosciutto infused the fish with its salty pork flavor and provided a layer of insulation to the fish during cooking. A warm butter sauce, enlivened by capers, parsley, lemon zest and juice, and garlic, brought the dish together. Do not season the cod with salt before wrapping with the prosciutto; the briny capers and salty prosciutto add plenty of salt to the dish. Halibut and haddock are good substitutes for the cod. You will need a 12-inch ovensafe nonstick skillet for this recipe.

4 (6- to 8-ounce) skinless cod fillets,
   1 to 1½ inches thick
   Pepper
8 thin slices prosciutto (3 ounces)
1 tablespoon vegetable oil
4 tablespoons unsalted butter, softened
2 tablespoons capers, rinsed and minced
2 tablespoons minced fresh parsley
1 teaspoon grated lemon zest plus 1 tablespoon juice
1 garlic clove, minced

1. Adjust oven rack to upper-middle position and heat oven to 450 degrees. Pat cod dry with paper towels and season with pepper. Wrap each fillet widthwise with 2 overlapping pieces of prosciutto.

2. Heat oil in 12-inch ovensafe nonstick skillet over medium-high heat until just smoking. Brown prosciutto lightly on both sides, 2 to 4 minutes. Transfer skillet to oven and bake until cod flakes apart when gently prodded with paring knife and registers 140 degrees, about 8 minutes.

3. Using potholders (skillet handle will be hot), remove skillet from oven. Transfer fish to serving platter. Add butter, capers, parsley, lemon zest and juice, and garlic to now-empty skillet. Cook over medium heat, swirling pan, until butter has melted. Spoon butter sauce over fish and serve.

We know that buying fish can be confusing and that markets don't always stock the type of fish (or cut) you desire. This chart will help you sort out your options and explain what you'll generally find at the market. And since we believe that some fish are suitable for sautéing, baking, or poaching, and some are not, we've listed what we think are the best cooking methods for all the fish below.

TYPE OF FISH	WHAT YOU'LL FIND AT THE MARKET	TEXTURE	FLAVOR	BEST COOKING METHODS
Bluefish	Whole fish and fillets	Medium firm, dark-fleshed fish	Pronounced, well suited to robust sauces and accompaniments	Stuffing and roasting or grilling (whole fish); steaming, braising, broiling, baking (fillets)
Catfish	Whole fish and fillets	Medium firm, flaky white fish	Mild to slightly earthy	Pan-searing, sautéing, baking, pan-frying, deep-frying
Cod	Whole and portioned fillets (both with and without skin)	Medium firm, meaty white fish	Clean, mild flavor; suited to most any preparation and flavor combination	Steaming, braising, baking, oven-frying, deep-frying, grilling; also great for soups and stews
Flounder	Whole fish and very thin fillets, interchangeable with sole	Delicate and flaky white fish	Sweet and mild, identical to sole	Stuffing and baking (whole fish); steaming, sautéing, pan-frying (fillets)
Grouper	Whole fish and fillets	Medium firm, meaty white fish	Mild to bland	Stuffing and baking (whole fish); steaming, pan-searing, sautéing, baking, pan-frying (fillets)
Haddock	Fillets, usually with skin on; ask fishmonger to remove skin	Medium firm white fish; similar in texture to cod, but slightly thinner	Very mild, well suited to robust flavors	Steaming, poaching, braising, sautéing, baking, oven-frying, pan-frying
Halibut	Whole steaks, belly steaks, fillets	Very firm, lean white fish; steaks similar to swordfish	Mild but rich, well suited to robust flavors	Steaming, pan-searing, roasting, grilling (steaks); steaming, pan-searing, sautéing, baking, roasting, deep-frying, grilling (fillets)
Mahi-Mahi	Steaks, fillets, whole fish; usually without skin	Medium firm, off-white flaky fish	Sweet and mild; well suited to robust flavors	Baking (fillets), braising, pan-frying, grilling (small whole fish, fillets with skin), soups and stews
Mako Shark	Steaks, fillets, chunks; usually without skin	Firm and meaty texture similar to swordfish, pinkish-white fish	Mild, clean, and slightly sweet; similar to swordfish	Braising, pan-frying, pan-searing, deep-frying, grilling (steaks or kebabs), soups and stews; avoid overcooking

TYPE OF FISH	WHAT YOU'LL FIND AT THE MARKET	TEXTURE	FLAVOR	BEST COOKING METHODS
Monkfish	Skinless, boneless loin-shaped pieces cut from tail; ask fishmonger to remove gray membrane	Very meaty, firm, pinkish-white fish, texture somewhat akin to lobster meat	Hearty and rich, slightly muskier than lobster	Steaming, poaching, braising, sautéing, baking, oven-frying, pan-frying
Red Snapper	Whole fish (with colorful skin and many bones), fillets, occasionally steaks	Medium firm, flaky white fish	Mild to moderate, stands up well to bold flavors	Baking, deep-frying, grilling, stuffing and roasting (whole fish); steaming, poaching, braising, pan-searing, sautéing, broiling, baking, pan-frying, grilling (fillets)
Salmon	Available wild and farm raised; whole fish, whole sides, bone-in and boneless steaks, fillets	Medium firm, deep pink to orange in color; wild salmon is larger and leaner; farm-raised salmon is smaller and fattier	Mild (farm raised), moderate to pronounced (wild)	Poaching, roasting (whole fish and sides); steaming, poaching, pan-searing, broiling, baking, roasting, grilling (steaks and fillets)
Sea Bass	Whole fish and fillets	Medium firm white fish with translucent quality	Sweet and mild	Steaming, deep-frying, grilling, stuffing and roasting (whole fish); steaming, poaching, braising, pan-searing, sautéing (fillets)
Sole	Fillets, interchangeable with flounder	Very delicate, flaky white fish	Sweet and mild, best suited to simple preparations	Steaming, sautéing, stuffing and baking
Spanish Mackerel	Steaks, fillets, whole fish; best for practicing filleting, as bones are easily removed	Medium firm, off-white, flaky, oily fish	Full, rich, pronounced flavor	Braising, poaching, pan-frying (small whole fish, fillets, steaks), pan-searing, broiling, grilling, smoking
Swordfish	Steaks	Very firm and meaty	Mild to moderate, well suited to robust flavors	Pan-searing, broiling, grilling
Tilapia	Mostly fillets (with and without skin)	Medium firm, pale-pink flesh	Moderate	Braising, sautéing, baking, oven-frying, pan-frying
Trout	Whole fish and fillets	Delicate and flaky, ranges in color from pale golden to pink	Rich and flavorful	Pan-frying, grilling, stuffing and roasting (whole fish); sautéing, pan-frying (fillets)
Tuna	Steaks	Very firm, meaty fish that ranges in color from pink to deep ruby red	Mild to moderate	Braising, pan-searing, grilling; best cooked rare to medium, not beyond

Buying and Storing Fish

WHAT TO LOOK FOR: The most important factor when buying fish is making sure the fish you buy is fresh. Always buy fish from a trusted source (preferably one with high volume to help ensure freshness). The store, and the fish in it, should smell like the sea, not fishy or sour. And all the fish should be on ice or properly refrigerated. Fillets and steaks should look bright, shiny, and firm, not dull or mushy. Whole fish should have moist, taut skin, clear eyes, and bright red gills.

WHAT TO ASK FOR: It is always better to have your fishmonger slice steaks and fillets to order rather than buying precut pieces that may have been sitting around. Don't be afraid to be picky at the seafood counter; a ragged piece of cod or a tail end of salmon will be difficult to cook properly. It is important to keep your fish cold, so if you have a long ride home, ask your fishmonger for a bag of ice.

BUYING FROZEN FISH: Thin fish fillets like flounder and sole are the best choice if you have to buy your fish frozen, because thin fillets freeze quickly, minimizing moisture loss. Firm fillets like halibut, snapper, tilapia, and salmon are acceptable to buy frozen if cooked beyond medium-rare, but at lower degrees of doneness they will have a dry, stringy texture. When buying frozen fish, make sure it is frozen solid, with no signs of freezer burn or excessive crystallization around the edges and no blood in the packaging. The ingredients should include only the name of the fish you are buying.

DEFROSTING FISH: To defrost fish in the refrigerator overnight, remove the fish from its packaging, place it in a single layer on a rimmed plate or dish (to catch any water), and cover it with plastic wrap. You can also do a "quick thaw" by leaving the vacuum-sealed bags under cool running tap water for 30 minutes. Do not use a microwave to defrost fish; it will alter the texture of the fish or, worse, partially cook it. Dry the fish thoroughly with paper towels before seasoning and cooking it.

HOW TO STORE IT: Because fish is so perishable, it's best to buy it the day it will be cooked. If that's not possible, it's important to store it properly. When you get home, unwrap the fish, pat it dry, put it in a zipper-lock bag, press out the air, and seal the bag. Then set the fish on a bed of ice in a bowl or other container (that can hold the water once the ice melts), and place it in the back of the fridge, where it is coldest. If the ice melts before you use the fish, replenish it. The fish should keep for one day.

Braised Cod with Leeks and Cherry Tomatoes

SERVES 4   **TOTAL TIME** 40 MINUTES   **FAST**

✔ **WHY THIS RECIPE WORKS:** Braising is a great way to add flavor to mild-tasting fish, plus it's mess-free (no oil splattering on the stovetop). Cherry tomatoes and a white wine sauce added brightness and freshness, and leeks provided a subtle, sweet flavor. After the leeks were tender, we stirred in a good amount of minced garlic and halved cherry tomatoes, plus a big splash of wine, and nestled the cod into the pan. To ensure the cod cooked through gently and evenly, we turned down the heat and covered the skillet with a tight-fitting lid so that the fish partially simmered and partially steamed. A pat of butter contributed richness. Haddock, snapper, tilapia, bluefish, monkfish, and sea bass fillets are all good substitutions for the cod.

> 3 **tablespoons unsalted butter**
> 1 **pound leeks, white and light green parts only, halved lengthwise, sliced thin, and washed thoroughly**
>   **Salt and pepper**
> 4 **garlic cloves, minced**
> 12 **ounces cherry tomatoes, halved**
> ½ **cup dry white wine or dry vermouth**
> 4 **(6- to 8-ounce) skinless cod fillets, 1 to 1½ inches thick**

1. Melt 2 tablespoons butter in 12-inch nonstick skillet over medium-high heat. Add leeks and ¼ teaspoon salt and cook until softened, about 5 minutes. Stir in garlic and cook until fragrant, about 30 seconds. Stir in tomatoes, wine, and ¼ teaspoon pepper and bring to simmer.

2. Pat cod dry with paper towels and season with salt and pepper. Nestle cod into skillet and spoon some vegetables and sauce over top. Cover and reduce heat to medium-low. Cook until cod flakes apart when gently prodded with paring knife and registers 140 degrees, 10 to 12 minutes.

3. Carefully transfer fish to platter. Stir remaining 1 tablespoon butter into vegetables, season with salt and pepper to taste, and spoon vegetables and sauce over fish. Serve.

Tucking the Tail

If you end up with a piece of fish with a thinner tail end, simply tuck the thinner end under itself before cooking so that it will cook at the same rate as the other pieces.

We add flavor to the artichokes in this baked cod dish by tossing them with the oil from sun-dried tomatoes and roasting them.

Baked Cod with Artichokes, Olives, and Sun-Dried Tomatoes

SERVES 4   **TOTAL TIME** 50 MINUTES

✓ **WHY THIS RECIPE WORKS:** Wanting to infuse baked cod with the zesty flavors of the Mediterranean, we turned to artichoke hearts, kalamata olives, and chopped tomatoes. The dish was good, but needed a flavor boost. Switching from regular tomatoes to sun-dried solved the problem, plus the flavorful packing oil provided brightness and aromatic notes to our artichokes, which we roasted to ensure that they were nicely browned and deeply flavored. Lemon zest and juice added brightness, and fresh basil brought color. You can substitute haddock or halibut for the cod. To thaw the frozen artichokes quickly, microwave them in a covered bowl for 3 to 5 minutes.

- 1 pound frozen artichoke hearts, thawed and patted dry
- ¾ cup oil-packed sun-dried tomatoes, drained, ¼ cup oil reserved
  Salt and pepper
- 1 teaspoon grated lemon zest plus 1 tablespoon juice
- ½ cup pitted kalamata olives, chopped coarse
- 4 (6- to 8-ounce) skinless cod fillets, 1 to 1½ inches thick
- 2 tablespoons chopped fresh basil

1. Adjust oven rack to middle position and heat oven to 450 degrees. Toss artichokes with 2 tablespoons tomato oil in bowl, season with salt and pepper, and spread into 13 by 9-inch baking dish. Roast artichokes until lightly browned, about 15 minutes.

2. Remove baking dish from oven and stir in lemon zest, olives, sun-dried tomatoes, and 1 tablespoon tomato oil. Pat cod dry with paper towels and nestle into vegetables. Brush cod with remaining 1 tablespoon tomato oil and season with salt and pepper.

3. Bake until cod flakes apart when gently prodded with paring knife and registers 140 degrees, 15 to 18 minutes. Drizzle with lemon juice, sprinkle with basil, and serve.

Cod Baked in Foil with Leeks and Carrots

SERVES 4   **TOTAL TIME** 50 MINUTES

✓ **WHY THIS RECIPE WORKS:** Cooking mild fish like cod *en papillote*—in a tightly sealed parchment package so it can steam in its own juices—is an easy, mess-free way to enhance its delicate flavor. However, without the right blend of flavorings, the fish can taste lean and bland, and not all vegetables pair well with cod. We found that foil was easier to work with than parchment. Placing the packets on the oven's lower-middle rack concentrated the exuded liquid and deepened the flavor. Haddock, red snapper, halibut, and sea bass also work well in this recipe as long as the fillets are 1 to 1¼ inches thick. Open each packet promptly after baking to prevent overcooking. Zest the lemon before cutting it into wedges.

- 4 tablespoons unsalted butter, softened
- 1 teaspoon minced fresh thyme
- 2 garlic cloves, minced
- 1¼ teaspoons grated lemon zest
  Salt and pepper
- 2 tablespoons minced fresh parsley
- 2 carrots, peeled and cut into matchsticks
- 1 pound leeks, white and light green parts only, halved lengthwise, washed thoroughly, and cut into matchsticks
- ¼ cup dry vermouth or dry white wine
- 4 (6- to 8-ounce) skinless cod fillets, 1 to 1¼ inches thick
  Lemon wedges

1. Adjust oven rack to lower-middle position and heat oven to 450 degrees. Mash butter, thyme, half of garlic, ¼ teaspoon lemon zest, ¼ teaspoon salt, and ⅛ teaspoon pepper in bowl. In separate bowl, combine parsley, remaining 1 teaspoon zest, and remaining garlic. In third bowl, combine carrots and leeks and season with salt and pepper.

2. Cut eight 12-inch sheets of aluminum foil; arrange 4 flat on counter. Divide vegetable mixture among foil sheets, mounding it in center, and sprinkle with vermouth. Pat cod dry with paper towels, season with salt and pepper, and place on top of vegetables. Spread butter mixture over fish.

3. Place second square of foil on top of fish. Press edges of foil together and fold over several times until packet is well sealed and measures about 7 inches. Place packets on rimmed baking sheet, overlapping as needed. (Packets can be refrigerated for up to 3 hours before cooking; if refrigerated for longer than 30 minutes, increase cooking time by 2 minutes.)

4. Bake packets for 15 minutes. Carefully open foil, allowing steam to escape away from you. Using thin metal spatula, gently slide cod and vegetables, and any accumulated juices, onto plate. Sprinkle with parsley mixture and serve with lemon wedges.

VARIATION
Cod Baked in Foil with Zucchini and Tomatoes
SERVES 4   TOTAL TIME 60 MINUTES
Haddock, red snapper, halibut, and sea bass also work well in this recipe as long as the fillets are 1 to 1¼ inches thick. Open each packet promptly after baking to prevent overcooking.

  1 **pound zucchini, sliced ¼ inch thick**
     Salt and pepper
  2 **plum tomatoes, cored, seeded, and chopped**
  2 **tablespoons extra-virgin olive oil**
  2 **garlic cloves, minced**
  1 **teaspoon minced fresh oregano**
  ⅛ **teaspoon red pepper flakes**
  ¼ **cup dry vermouth or dry white wine**
  4 **(6- to 8-ounce) skinless cod fillets, 1 to 1¼ inches thick**
  ¼ **cup chopped fresh basil**
     Lemon wedges

1. Toss zucchini with ½ teaspoon salt in bowl, transfer to colander, and let sit for 30 minutes. Pat zucchini dry thoroughly with paper towels, pressing firmly on each slice to remove as much liquid as possible. Meanwhile, combine tomatoes, oil, garlic, oregano, pepper flakes, ¼ teaspoon salt, and ⅛ teaspoon pepper in bowl.

2. Adjust oven rack to lower-middle position and heat oven to 450 degrees. Cut eight 12-inch sheets of aluminum foil; arrange 4 flat on counter. Shingle zucchini in center of foil sheets and sprinkle with vermouth. Pat cod dry with paper towels, season with salt and pepper, and place on top of zucchini. Spread tomato mixture over fish.

3. Place second square of foil on top of fish. Press edges of foil together and fold over several times until packet is well sealed and measures about 7 inches. Place packets on rimmed baking sheet, overlapping as needed. (Packets can be refrigerated for up to 3 hours before cooking; if refrigerated for longer than 30 minutes, increase cooking time by 2 minutes.)

4. Bake packets for 15 minutes. Carefully open foil, allowing steam to escape away from you. Using thin metal spatula, gently slide cod and vegetables, and any accumulated juices, onto plate. Sprinkle with basil and serve with lemon wedges.

Assembling Foil Packets

1. Cut eight 12-inch sheets of foil; arrange 4 flat on counter. Place vegetables in center of foil sheets and sprinkle with vermouth.

2. Pat cod dry with paper towels, season with salt and pepper, and place on top of vegetables. Spread butter mixture on top of fish.

3. Place second square of foil on top of fish. Press edges of foil together and fold over several times until packet is well sealed and measures about 7 inches.

Lemon-Herb Cod Fillets with Crispy Garlic Potatoes

SERVES 4   **TOTAL TIME** 50 MINUTES

☑ **WHY THIS RECIPE WORKS:** We wanted a fuss-free fish fillet dinner that was suitable for a weeknight meal yet impressive enough to serve guests. For an oven-to-table cod and potato recipe, we gave the sliced potatoes a head start by microwaving them with oil and garlic until just tender. We then nestled the cod fillets on top of the potatoes in a casserole dish. In the oven, the potatoes got nicely crisped and infused with flavor while the fish cooked through gently and evenly. Best of all, the side dish and entrée were ready at the same time. Halibut and haddock are good substitutes for the cod.

1½ **pounds russet potatoes, unpeeled, sliced into ¼-inch-thick rounds**
2 **tablespoons extra-virgin olive oil**
3 **garlic cloves, minced**
  Salt and pepper
4 **(6- to 8-ounce) skinless cod fillets, 1 to 1½ inches thick**
3 **tablespoons unsalted butter, cut into ¼-inch pieces**
4 **sprigs fresh thyme**
1 **lemon, sliced thin**

1. Adjust oven rack to lower-middle position and heat oven to 425 degrees. Combine potatoes, oil, and garlic in bowl and season with salt and pepper. Microwave, uncovered, until potatoes are just tender, 12 to 14 minutes.

2. Transfer hot potatoes to 13 by 9-inch baking dish and press lightly into even layer. Pat cod dry with paper towels, season with salt and pepper, and lay on top of potatoes. Place butter, thyme sprigs, and lemon slices on top of cod. Bake until fish flakes apart when gently prodded with paring knife and registers 140 degrees, 15 to 18 minutes.

3. Slide spatula underneath potatoes and fish, gently transfer to plates, and serve.

Sole Florentine

SERVES 4 TO 6   **TOTAL TIME** 45 MINUTES **FAST**

☑ **WHY THIS RECIPE WORKS:** A classic dish, sole Florentine features sweet fillets of sole wrapped around a rich spinach filling. Add a creamy sauce and a topping of buttery cracker crumbs and it is easy to understand why this dish has long been a restaurant favorite. We built the base of the sauce by sautéing shallot, thyme, and garlic, and then whisking in

Roasting cod fillets on top of a bed of thinly sliced potatoes makes an easy and elegant dish for this classic duo.

cream. To thicken it, a simple slurry made with cream and cornstarch worked perfectly. For the filling we turned to frozen spinach, adding Parmesan to bind it and a little of the sauce for richness. After assembling the stuffed fillets, we simply added the sauce and sprinkled crushed Ritz crackers on top for crunch before baking. Try to buy fish fillets of equal size to ensure even cooking. Be sure to squeeze out as much moisture as possible from the thawed spinach or it will water down the sauce. To check the doneness of the fish, use the tip of a paring knife to prod the fish gently—the flesh should be opaque and flaky, but still juicy.

2 **tablespoons unsalted butter**
1 **shallot, minced**
2 **teaspoons minced fresh thyme**
1 **small garlic clove, minced**
2 **cups heavy cream**
4 **teaspoons cornstarch**
  Salt and pepper
2 **(10-ounce) packages frozen spinach, thawed and squeezed dry**

1 ounce Parmesan cheese, grated (½ cup)
8 (6-ounce) skinless sole fillets, ¼ to ½ inch thick
15 Ritz crackers, crushed fine
Lemon wedges

1. Melt 1 tablespoon butter in medium saucepan over medium-high heat. Add shallot and cook until softened, about 2 minutes. Stir in thyme and garlic and cook until fragrant, about 30 seconds. Stir in 1¾ cups cream and bring to simmer. Whisk remaining ¼ cup cream and cornstarch together in bowl, then whisk mixture into saucepan and simmer until sauce is thickened, about 2 minutes. Season with salt and pepper to taste. Set aside to cool.

2. Adjust oven rack to middle position and heat oven to 475 degrees. Combine 1 cup sauce, spinach, and Parmesan in bowl and season with salt and pepper to taste. Pat sole dry with paper towels and season with salt and pepper. Grease 13 by 9-inch baking dish with remaining 1 tablespoon butter.

3. Place sole on clean counter or cutting board, smooth side down. Divide spinach filling equally among sole fillets, mounding it in middle of each fillet. Fold tapered end of sole tightly over filling and then fold thicker end of fish over top to make tidy bundle.

4. Arrange sole bundles in baking dish, seam side down, leaving small space between bundles, and press lightly to flatten. Pour remaining sauce over top. (Filled sole can be refrigerated for up to 1 day.) Sprinkle cracker crumbs over fish and bake until all but very center of sole turns from translucent to opaque and filling is hot, 12 to 15 minutes. Serve with lemon wedges.

Making Fish Bundles

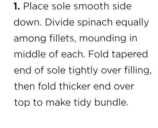

1. Place sole smooth side down. Divide spinach equally among fillets, mounding in middle of each. Fold tapered end of sole tightly over filling, then fold thicker end over top to make tidy bundle.

2. Arrange sole bundles in baking dish, seam side down and evenly spaced apart, and press lightly to flatten. Pour remaining sauce over top and sprinkle with Ritz crumbs.

We bake our oven-fried fish on a wire rack to ensure a crunchy crust.

Crunchy Oven-Fried Fish

SERVES 4   **TOTAL TIME** 1 HOUR

✔ **WHY THIS RECIPE WORKS:** Batter-fried is the gold standard for fish with a flavorful coating, but frying can be a messy operation. We wanted moist, flavorful oven-baked fillets coated in a crunchy crust. Meaty, dense varieties of fish, like swordfish and tuna, didn't provide contrast between crust and interior. Cod and haddock proved the best bet, and fresh bread crumbs, crisped in the oven, created the best coating. We dipped the fillets first in flour and then in a wash of eggs and mayonnaise before applying the browned crumbs. Placing the coated fish on a wire rack for baking allowed air to circulate, crisping all sides. We boosted flavor by adding shallot and parsley to the breading and horseradish and paprika to the egg wash. To prevent overcooking, buy fish fillets at least 1 inch thick. Serve with lemon wedges or with any of the relishes on page 235 or creamy sauces on page 254.

4 slices hearty white sandwich bread,
   torn into 1-inch pieces
2 tablespoons unsalted butter, melted

Salt and pepper

¼ cup plus 5 tablespoons all-purpose flour

2 large eggs

3 tablespoons mayonnaise

½ teaspoon paprika

2 teaspoons prepared horseradish (optional)

2 tablespoons minced fresh parsley

1 small shallot, minced

1¼ pounds cod, haddock, or other thick white fish fillet, 1 to 1½ inches thick, cut into 4 pieces

1. Adjust oven rack to middle position and heat oven to 350 degrees. Pulse bread, melted butter, ¼ teaspoon salt, and ¼ teaspoon pepper in food processor until bread is coarsely ground, about 8 pulses. Transfer crumbs to rimmed baking sheet and bake, stirring occasionally, until deep golden brown, about 15 minutes. Let crumbs cool. (Crumbs can be stored at room temperature for up to 3 days.)

2. Spread ¼ cup flour into shallow dish. In second shallow dish, whisk eggs, mayonnaise, paprika, ¼ teaspoon pepper, and horseradish, if using, together; whisk in remaining 5 tablespoons flour until smooth. In third shallow dish, combine cooled bread-crumb mixture, parsley, and shallot.

3. Increase oven temperature to 425 degrees. Grease wire rack and place in rimmed baking sheet. Pat cod dry with paper towels and season with salt and pepper. Working with 1 fillet at a time, dredge in flour, dip in egg mixture, then coat with thick layer of bread-crumb mixture, pressing gently to adhere; transfer to prepared wire rack.

4. Bake until fish registers 140 degrees, 18 to 25 minutes. Using thin spatula, transfer fillets to plates and serve.

Pan-Fried Fish Sticks

SERVES 4   **TOTAL TIME** 45 MINUTES   FAST

☑ **WHY THIS RECIPE WORKS:** We wanted an easy and delicious alternative to frozen fish sticks that the entire family would enjoy. The key was to create a flavorful breading that would both adhere to the fish and provide a supercrispy crust. The solution was simple: a mixture of ground sandwich bread and saltines. Following our traditional bound breading procedure, we dredged the fish in flour, then in a mixture of beaten eggs and mayonnaise, which added acidity, and finally in the bread crumb–saltine mixture. We avoided mess and grease by pan-frying instead of deep-frying. Halibut, haddock, and catfish can be substituted for the cod. Serve with lemon wedges or with any of the relishes on page 235 or creamy sauces on page 254.

4 slices hearty white sandwich bread, torn into large pieces

16 saltines

½ cup all-purpose flour

2 large eggs

¼ cup mayonnaise

2 pounds skinless cod fillets, cut into 1-inch-thick strips
Salt and pepper

1 cup vegetable oil

1. Adjust oven rack to middle position and heat oven to 200 degrees. Pulse bread and saltines in food processor to fine crumbs; transfer to shallow dish. Spread flour into second shallow dish. Whisk eggs and mayonnaise together in third shallow dish.

Making Oven-Fried Fish

1. MAKE CRUMBS: Pulse bread, butter, salt, and pepper in food processor until coarsely ground. Bake until deep golden brown. Cool and combine with parsley and shallot in shallow dish.

2. MAKE BATTER: In second shallow dish, whisk eggs, mayonnaise, paprika, pepper, and horseradish (if using); whisk in 5 tablespoons flour until smooth.

3. FLOUR IT, BATTER IT, BREAD IT: Pat fish dry with paper towels and season with salt and pepper. Dredge fillets in flour, dip in egg mixture, then coat with bread-crumb mixture, pressing to adhere.

4. BAKE ON RACK: Place fish on greased wire rack set in rimmed baking sheet, and bake in 425-degree oven until fish registers 140 degrees, 18 to 25 minutes.

CREAMY SAUCES FOR FISH

These easy homemade sauces taste great with many of our fish dishes. Try them with any of the following recipes: Easy Salmon Cakes (page 240), Crunchy Oven-Fried Fish (page 252), Pan-Fried Fish Sticks (page 253), Fried Catfish (page 255), Classic Pan-Fried Crab Cakes (page 257), Popcorn Shrimp (page 259), and Shrimp Burgers (page 262).

Sweet and Tangy Tartar Sauce

MAKES ABOUT 1 CUP

TOTAL TIME 25 MINUTES FAST

Be sure to rinse the capers before mincing them or else the sauce will have a strong, briny flavor.

- ¾ cup mayonnaise
- ½ small shallot, minced
- 2 tablespoons capers, rinsed and minced
- 2 tablespoons sweet pickle relish
- 1½ teaspoons white vinegar
- ½ teaspoon Worcestershire sauce
  Salt and pepper

Combine all ingredients in bowl, let sit for 15 minutes, and season with salt and pepper to taste. (Sauce can be refrigerated for up to 5 days.)

Creamy Chipotle Chile Sauce

MAKES ABOUT ½ CUP

TOTAL TIME 25 MINUTES FAST

You can vary the spiciness of this sauce by adjusting the amount of chipotle.

- ¼ cup mayonnaise
- ¼ cup sour cream
- 2 teaspoons minced canned chipotle chile in adobo sauce
- 2 teaspoons minced fresh cilantro
- 1 small garlic clove, minced
- 1 teaspoon lime juice, plus extra as needed
  Salt and pepper

Combine all ingredients in bowl, let sit for 15 minutes, and season with salt, pepper, and extra lime juice to taste. (Sauce can be refrigerated for up to 5 days.)

Old Bay Dipping Sauce

MAKES ABOUT ¾ CUP

TOTAL TIME 20 MINUTES FAST

Old Bay seasoning can be found in the spice aisle of most supermarkets.

- ½ cup plain Greek yogurt
- ¼ cup mayonnaise
- 1 tablespoon Dijon mustard
- 1 tablespoon Old Bay seasoning
  Salt and pepper

Combine all ingredients in bowl, let sit for 15 minutes, and season with salt and pepper to taste. (Sauce can be refrigerated for up to 5 days.)

Pickled Jalapeño Mayonnaise

MAKES ABOUT ¾ CUP

TOTAL TIME 25 MINUTES FAST

Pickled jalapeño chiles are sold in both jars and cans and can usually be found next to the taco and enchilada ingredients at the supermarket.

- ½ cup mayonnaise
- 2 tablespoons chopped pickled jalapeño chiles
- 1 scallion, chopped fine
- 2 teaspoons lime juice, plus extra as needed
  Salt and pepper

Combine all ingredients in bowl, let sit for 15 minutes, and season with salt, pepper, and extra lime juice to taste. (Sauce can be refrigerated for up to 5 days.)

Comeback Sauce

MAKES ABOUT 1 CUP

TOTAL TIME 20 MINUTES FAST

Comeback Sauce is a Mississippi-born condiment often served with fried foods. It can also be used as a dipping sauce for crackers, or as a mayonnaise substitute on sandwiches. Chili sauce, a condiment similar to ketchup, has a sweet flavor and a subtle, spicy kick; do not substitute Asian chili-garlic sauce.

- ½ cup mayonnaise
- ⅓ cup chopped onion
- 2 tablespoons vegetable oil
- 2 tablespoons chili sauce
- 1 tablespoon ketchup
- 2½ teaspoons Worcestershire sauce
- 2½ teaspoons hot sauce
- 1 teaspoon yellow mustard
- 1 teaspoon lemon juice
- 1 garlic clove, minced
- ¾ teaspoon pepper
- ⅛ teaspoon paprika

Process all ingredients in blender until smooth, about 30 seconds. (Sauce can be refrigerated for up to 5 days.)

2. Pat cod dry with paper towels and season with salt and pepper. Working with 1 piece at a time, dredge cod in flour, dip in egg, then coat with thick layer of bread-crumb mixture, pressing gently to adhere; transfer to clean plate.

3. Heat ½ cup oil in 12-inch nonstick skillet over medium heat until just smoking. Fry half of fish strips until deep golden and crisp on all sides, about 4 minutes. Transfer fish to paper towel–lined plate and keep warm in oven. Discard oil left in skillet, wipe out skillet with paper towels, and repeat with remaining oil and fish. Serve.

Fried Catfish

SERVES 4 TO 6　　**TOTAL TIME** 40 MINUTES　**FAST**

✔ **WHY THIS RECIPE WORKS:** The best fried catfish can be found in the Mississippi Delta, but replicating that recipe turned out to be harder than we thought. We tried lots of tricks to re-create the perfectly cooked sweet catfish encased in a crisp, thin cornmeal crust with just the right amount of spice. We discovered that mixing cornmeal ground in a spice grinder with regular cornmeal resulted in a perfectly textured crust. Buttermilk's thickness and tangy flavor also worked better than a standard egg wash, especially when we added a little hot sauce. We decided to cut the catfish in half to increase the surface area so that we would get even more of our delicious crust. Depending on the size of your spice grinder, you may have to grind the cornmeal in several batches. If you don't have a spice grinder, process the cornmeal in a blender until finely ground, 60 to 90 seconds. Use a Dutch oven that holds 6 quarts or more. Serve with lemon wedges or with any of the relishes on page 235 or creamy sauces on page 254.

- 2 **cups buttermilk**
- 1 **teaspoon hot sauce**
- 2 **cups cornmeal**
- 4 **teaspoons salt**
- 2 **teaspoons pepper**
- 2 **teaspoons granulated garlic**
- 1 **teaspoon cayenne pepper**
- 2 **quarts peanut or vegetable oil**
- 4 **(6- to 8-ounce) skinless catfish fillets, halved lengthwise along natural seam**

A mixture of regular and finely ground cornmeal makes the coating on our fried catfish incredibly crunchy.

1. Set wire rack inside rimmed baking sheet and line half of rack with triple layer of paper towels. Whisk buttermilk and hot sauce together in shallow dish. Process 1 cup cornmeal in spice grinder to fine powder, 30 to 45 seconds. Transfer ground cornmeal to second shallow dish and stir in salt, pepper, granulated garlic, cayenne, and remaining 1 cup cornmeal.

2. Add oil to large Dutch oven until it measures about 1½ inches deep, and heat over medium-high heat to 350 degrees. Meanwhile, pat catfish dry with paper towels. Dip fillets in buttermilk mixture, letting excess drip back into dish. Dredge fish in cornmeal mixture, shaking off excess, and transfer to large plate.

3. Working with 4 pieces of catfish at a time, add to hot oil and cook until golden brown and crisp, about 5 minutes; adjust burner, if necessary, to maintain oil temperature between 325 and 350 degrees.

4. Transfer fried catfish to paper towel–lined side of rack, let drain for 1 minute, then transfer fish to unlined side of rack. Return oil to 350 degrees and repeat with remaining catfish. Serve.

California-Style Fish Tacos

SERVES 6   **TOTAL TIME** 1 HOUR 10 MINUTES

✓ **WHY THIS RECIPE WORKS:** It's easy to see the appeal of the fish taco: Crispy fried white fish, crunchy cabbage, and creamy white sauce come together on a corn tortilla to deliver an irresistible combination of flavors and textures. But how often have you bitten into a taco only to find overly battered fish hiding underneath a bevy of toppings? We were determined to come up with a tasty version that was easy enough to make for a weeknight dinner. We chose mild but sturdy white fish and coated it with an ultrathin beer batter to avoid a thick, bready coating. Cornstarch and baking powder in the batter ensured that the fish fried up golden brown and crisp. A quick pickle of red onions and jalapeños added color and spice, and we used a portion of the vinegary pickling liquid to dress the shredded cabbage. Our creamy white sauce got its tang from lime juice and sour cream, and a sprinkle of fresh cilantro provided the finishing touch. Although this recipe looks involved, all the components are easy to execute, and most can be prepared in advance. Light-bodied American lagers, such as Budweiser, work best here. Cut the fish on a slight bias if your fillets aren't quite 4 inches wide. You should end up with about 24 pieces of fish. Use a Dutch oven that holds 6 quarts or more.

WHITE SAUCE
- ½ cup mayonnaise
- ½ cup sour cream
- 2 tablespoons lime juice
- 2 tablespoons milk

PICKLED ONIONS AND CABBAGE SLAW
- 1 small red onion, halved and sliced thin
- 2 jalapeño chiles, stemmed and sliced into thin rings
- 1 cup white wine vinegar
- 2 tablespoons lime juice
- 1 tablespoon sugar
-    Salt and pepper
- 3 cups shredded green cabbage

FISH
- ¾ cup all-purpose flour
- ¼ cup cornstarch
- 1 teaspoon baking powder
-    Salt and pepper
- 1 cup beer
- 1 quart peanut or vegetable oil
- 2 pounds skinless white fish fillets, such as cod, haddock, or halibut, cut crosswise into 4 by 1-inch strips
- 24 (6-inch) corn tortillas, warmed
- 1 cup fresh cilantro leaves

1. FOR THE SAUCE: Whisk all ingredients together in bowl and refrigerate until needed. (Sauce can be refrigerated for up to 2 days.)

2. FOR THE ONIONS AND SLAW: Combine onion and jalapeños in medium bowl. Bring vinegar, lime juice, sugar, and 1 teaspoon salt to boil in small saucepan. Pour vinegar mixture over onion mixture and let sit for 30 minutes. (Mixture can be refrigerated for up to 2 days.) Measure out ¼ cup pickling liquid and toss with cabbage, ½ teaspoon salt, and ½ teaspoon pepper in separate bowl.

3. FOR THE FISH: Adjust oven rack to middle position and heat oven to 200 degrees. Set wire rack inside rimmed baking sheet. Whisk flour, cornstarch, baking powder, and 1 teaspoon salt together in large bowl. Whisk in beer until smooth.

4. Add oil to large Dutch oven until it measures ¾ inch deep and heat over medium-high heat to 350 degrees. Meanwhile, pat fish dry with paper towels, season with salt and pepper, and gently stir into batter.

5. Working with 5 or 6 pieces of fish at a time, remove from batter, allowing excess to drip back into bowl, and add to hot oil, briefly dragging fish along surface of oil to prevent sticking. Fry fish, stirring gently, until golden brown on both sides, about 4 minutes; adjust burner, if necessary, to maintain oil temperature between 325 and 350 degrees.

6. Transfer fish to prepared wire rack and keep warm in oven. Return oil to 350 degrees and repeat with remaining fish. Divide fish evenly among tortillas. Top with pickled onions, cabbage slaw, white sauce, and cilantro leaves. Serve.

NOTES FROM THE TEST KITCHEN

Buying Crabmeat

Check the fish counter for containers of fresh or pasteurized crabmeat. It does cost more than the small cans you'll find near the tuna, but it's well worth the additional cost. Depending upon the season, pasteurized crabmeat can cost significantly less than fresh, and it has a long shelf life. You should always use fresh crabmeat for crab cakes where the texture and flavor of the crab takes center stage, but pasteurized crabmeat is fine for dips and casseroles. Jumbo lump is the highest-quality crabmeat (and the most expensive, too) and, as the name suggests, consists of large lumps of meat.

Classic Pan-Fried Crab Cakes

SERVES 4   TOTAL TIME 1 HOUR

✔ **WHY THIS RECIPE WORKS:** We wanted cakes with a crisp brown exterior and a creamy, well-seasoned filling that tasted of sweet crab, not filler. Fresh crabmeat provided the best taste and texture and was worth its high price tag. After experimenting with different binders, we settled on fine dry bread crumbs; their mild flavor kept the crabmeat front and center, they held the cakes together well, and they mixed easily with the crab. An egg and some mayonnaise bound the cakes together. Old Bay is the traditional seasoning for crab, and there was no reason to leave it out; some herbs and pepper were the only other additions we found necessary. Carefully folding the ingredients together rather than stirring them kept the texture chunky rather than pasty, and a short stint in the refrigerator ensured that the cakes wouldn't fall apart during their cooking time in the skillet. The amount of bread crumbs you need to add will depend on the crabmeat's juiciness. Start with the smallest amount, and add more after adding the egg only if the cakes won't hold together. Use fresh or pasteurized crabmeat (usually sold next to the fresh seafood) rather than the canned crabmeat (packed in tuna fish–like cans) found in the supermarket aisles. Serve with lemon wedges or with any of the relishes on page 235 or creamy sauces on page 254.

- 1 **pound jumbo lump crabmeat, picked over for shells and pressed dry between paper towels**
- 4 **scallions, green parts only, minced**
- 1 **tablespoon chopped fresh parsley, cilantro, dill, or basil**
- ¼ **cup mayonnaise**
- 2–4 **tablespoons plain dry bread crumbs**
- 1½ **teaspoons Old Bay seasoning**
  Salt and pepper
- 1 **large egg, lightly beaten**
- ¼ **cup all-purpose flour**
- ¼ **cup vegetable oil**

1. Gently mix crabmeat, scallions, parsley, mayonnaise, 2 tablespoons bread crumbs, and Old Bay in bowl, being careful not to break up crab lumps. Season with salt and pepper to taste. Carefully fold in egg with rubber spatula until mixture just clings together. If cakes don't bind, add more bread crumbs, 1 tablespoon at a time, until they do.

2. Divide crab mixture into 4 portions and shape into ½-inch-thick round cakes. Transfer cakes to large plate, cover, and refrigerate until firm, at least 30 minutes. (Cakes can be refrigerated for up to 1 day.)

3. Spread flour into shallow dish. Lightly dredge crab cakes in flour. Heat oil in 12-inch nonstick skillet over medium-high heat until shimmering. Add crab cakes and cook until crisp and well browned on both sides, 8 to 10 minutes. Serve.

Pan-Seared Shrimp

SERVES 4   TOTAL TIME 30 MINUTES FAST

✔ **WHY THIS RECIPE WORKS:** A good recipe for pan-seared shrimp is hard to find. Of the handful of recipes we uncovered, the majority resulted in shrimp that were either dry and flavorless or pale, tough, and gummy. We wanted shrimp that were well caramelized but still moist, briny, and tender. Brining peeled shrimp inhibited browning, so instead we seasoned the shrimp with salt, pepper, and sugar, which brought out their natural sweetness and aided in browning. We cooked the shrimp in batches in a large, piping-hot skillet and then tossed them with butter, lemon juice, and fresh parsley; we also like pairing these shrimp with a thick, glazelike sauce with assertive ingredients and plenty of acidity as a foil for their richness. The cooking time is for extra-large shrimp (about 21 to 25 shrimp per pound). If using smaller or larger shrimp, be sure to adjust the cooking time as needed.

- 2 **pounds extra-large shrimp (21 to 25 per pound), peeled and deveined**
- ⅛ **teaspoon sugar**
  Salt and pepper
- 2 **tablespoons vegetable oil**
- 2 **tablespoons unsalted butter**
- 1 **tablespoon lemon juice**
- 1 **tablespoon minced fresh parsley**
  Lemon wedges

1. Pat shrimp dry with paper towels and season with sugar, salt, and pepper. Heat 1 tablespoon oil in 12-inch nonstick skillet over high heat until just smoking. Add half of shrimp to skillet in single layer and cook, without stirring, until spotty brown and edges turn pink, about 1 minute.

2. Remove skillet from heat, flip shrimp, and let sit until opaque in very center, about 30 seconds; transfer to bowl. Repeat with remaining 1 tablespoon oil and shrimp; transfer to bowl.

Shrimp Basics

BUYING SHRIMP: Virtually all of the shrimp sold in supermarkets today have been previously frozen, either in large blocks of ice or by a method called "individually quick-frozen," or IQF for short. Supermarkets simply defrost the shrimp before displaying them on ice at the fish counter. We highly recommend purchasing bags of still-frozen shrimp and defrosting them as needed at home, since there is no telling how long "fresh" shrimp may have been kept on ice at the market. IQF shrimp have a better flavor and texture than shrimp frozen in blocks, and they are convenient for two because it's easy to defrost just the amount you need. Shrimp are sold both with and without their shells, but we find shell-on shrimp to be firmer and sweeter. Also, shrimp should be the only ingredient listed on the bag; some packagers add preservatives, but we find treated shrimp to have an unpleasant, rubbery texture.

SORTING OUT SHRIMP SIZES: Shrimp are sold both by size (small, medium, etc.) and by the number needed to make 1 pound, usually given in a range. Choosing shrimp by the numerical rating is more accurate, because the size label varies from store to store. Here's how the two sizing systems generally compare:

Small	51 to 60 per pound
Medium	41 to 50 per pound
Medium-Large	31 to 40 per pound
Large	26 to 30 per pound
Extra-Large	21 to 25 per pound
Jumbo	16 to 20 per pound

DEFROSTING SHRIMP: You can thaw frozen shrimp overnight in the refrigerator in a covered bowl. For a quicker thaw, place them in a colander under cold running water; they will be ready in a few minutes. Thoroughly dry the shrimp before cooking.

3. Off heat, return all shrimp and any accumulated juices to skillet. Add butter, lemon juice, and parsley and toss to coat until butter melts. Cover and let sit until shrimp are cooked through, 1 to 2 minutes. Season with salt and pepper to taste. Serve with lemon wedges.

VARIATION

Pan-Seared Shrimp with Chipotle-Lime Glaze
Substitute following mixture for butter, lemon juice, and parsley in step 3: 2 tablespoons lime juice, 2 tablespoons chopped fresh cilantro, 1 teaspoon minced canned chipotle chile in adobo sauce, 4 teaspoons packed brown sugar, and 2 teaspoons adobo sauce.

Peeling and Deveining Shrimp

 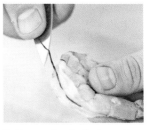

1. Break shell under swimming legs, which will come off as shell is removed. Leave tail intact if desired, or tug tail to remove shell.

2. Use paring knife to make shallow cut along back of shrimp to expose vein. Use tip of knife to lift out vein. Discard vein by wiping blade against paper towel.

Simple Shrimp Scampi
SERVES 4   **TOTAL TIME** 30 MINUTES   **FAST**

☑ **WHY THIS RECIPE WORKS:** Restaurant versions of shrimp scampi run the gamut from batter-dipped, deep-fried shrimp drenched in bad oil to boiled shrimp and tomato sauce on a bed of pasta. We wanted shrimp in a light sauce smacking of garlic and lemon and garnished with parsley. Cooking the shrimp and garlic quickly was the key to avoiding overcooked, tough shellfish and bitter-tasting garlic. We first cooked the shrimp in a large skillet in batches and set them aside, then used the same skillet to cook the garlic in butter. White wine and lemon juice gave the sauce just the right punch. Adding parsley at the end of cooking ensured it kept its fresh flavor. Serve with plenty of chewy bread to sop up the garlicky sauce. This dish is also nice served over a bed of simple white rice.

2 pounds extra-large shrimp (21 to 25 per pound), peeled and deveined
⅛ teaspoon sugar
Salt and pepper
2 tablespoons vegetable oil
3 tablespoons unsalted butter
4 garlic cloves, minced
2 tablespoons lemon juice
2 tablespoons minced fresh parsley
1 tablespoon dry white wine or dry vermouth
Pinch cayenne pepper

1. Pat shrimp dry with paper towels and season with sugar, salt, and pepper. Heat 1 tablespoon oil in 12-inch nonstick skillet over high heat until just smoking. Add half of shrimp to skillet in single layer and cook, without stirring, until spotty brown and edges turn pink, about 1 minute.

2. Remove skillet from heat, flip shrimp, and let sit until opaque in very center, about 30 seconds; transfer to bowl. Repeat with remaining 1 tablespoon oil and shrimp; transfer to bowl.

3. Melt 1 tablespoon butter in now-empty skillet over low heat. Add garlic and cook until fragrant, about 15 seconds. Stir in lemon juice, parsley, wine, and cayenne, then whisk in remaining 2 tablespoons butter. Off heat, return all shrimp and any accumulated juices to skillet. Cover and let sit until shrimp are cooked through, 1 to 2 minutes. Season with salt and pepper to taste and serve.

Cornstarch and baking powder help create a light and crunchy crust for popcorn shrimp.

Popcorn Shrimp

SERVES 4   **TOTAL TIME** 1 HOUR

✔ **WHY THIS RECIPE WORKS:** When properly fried, popcorn shrimp are just as crunchy, salty, and addictive as their namesake. Sadly, most recipes produce greasy, gummy shrimp, often coated in too much batter. We wanted shrimp coated in a light batter and fried until just golden brown. To increase the flavor of the shrimp, we marinated them in a little oil, lemon zest, garlic, and Old Bay. For a crisp coating, we replaced some of the flour with cornstarch. A little baking powder increased browning and added a bit of lift to the batter. To impart a brininess that complemented the shrimp, we replaced the water in the batter with clam juice but reduced the liquid amount so that the batter clung to the shrimp. After some testing, we settled on medium-large shrimp as the optimal size. Leave plenty of space between the frying shrimp to prevent them from sticking and use a Dutch oven that holds 6 quarts or more. Serve with lemon wedges or with any of the creamy sauces on page 254.

1½ pounds medium-large shrimp (31 to 40 per pound), peeled, deveined, and tails removed
2 quarts peanut or vegetable oil
1 teaspoon grated lemon zest
1 garlic clove, minced
4½ teaspoons Old Bay seasoning
1½ cups all-purpose flour
½ cup cornstarch
2 teaspoons pepper
1 teaspoon baking powder
1½ cups bottled clam juice

1. Toss shrimp, 1 tablespoon oil, lemon zest, garlic, and ½ teaspoon Old Bay together in bowl, cover, and refrigerate for 30 to 60 minutes.

2. Adjust oven rack to middle position and heat oven to 200 degrees. Set wire rack inside rimmed baking sheet. Add remaining oil to large Dutch oven until it measures 1½ inches deep and heat over medium-high heat to 375 degrees.

3. Combine flour, cornstarch, remaining 4 teaspoons Old Bay, pepper, and baking powder in large bowl. Stir in clam juice until smooth. Fold shrimp into batter until evenly coated.

4. Working with one-quarter of shrimp at a time, remove each shrimp from batter, allowing excess to drip back into bowl, and add to hot oil. Fry shrimp, stirring often, until golden brown, about 2 minutes; adjust burner, if necessary, to maintain oil temperature between 350 and 375 degrees. Transfer fried shrimp to paper towel–lined plate, let drain briefly, then transfer to prepared wire rack; keep warm in oven. Return oil to 375 degrees and repeat with remaining shrimp. Serve.

USING COOKED SHRIMP IN A PINCH

Although we generally reach for uncooked frozen shrimp for most recipes, there are times when the convenience of already cooked shrimp cannot be beat.

LAST-MINUTE CEVICHE `FAST`

Combine 1 pound coarsely chopped cooked and peeled shrimp, 1 finely chopped red bell pepper, 4 thinly sliced scallions, 1 minced jalapeño pepper, ¼ cup extra-virgin olive oil, 1 teaspoon lime zest plus ¼ cup juice, ¼ cup lemon juice, 3 tablespoons minced fresh cilantro, 1 minced garlic clove, ½ teaspoon sugar, and ½ teaspoon salt in bowl. Cover and refrigerate for 10 minutes. Season with salt and pepper to taste. (Serves 6 as an appetizer)

SHRIMP FRIED RICE `FAST`

Heat 1½ teaspoons vegetable oil in 12-inch nonstick skillet over medium heat until shimmering. Add 2 beaten large eggs and cook, stirring often, until scrambled, about 2 minutes; transfer to bowl. Heat 2 tablespoons vegetable oil in now-empty skillet over high heat until just smoking. Add 4 cups cooked rice, 1 pound cooked and peeled shrimp, 3 tablespoons soy sauce, 3 tablespoons oyster sauce, and 2 minced garlic cloves; cook, stirring constantly, until heated through, about 3 minutes. Off heat, stir in 1 cup thawed frozen peas, 5 thinly sliced scallions, and cooked eggs; let sit, covered, until heated through, about 2 minutes. (Serves 4 to 6)

MEDITERRANEAN PASTA SALAD WITH SHRIMP `FAST`

In large bowl, whisk 6 tablespoons olive oil, 3 tablespoons red wine vinegar, 3 tablespoons lemon juice, 1 minced shallot, ¼ teaspoon dried oregano, ¼ teaspoon garlic powder, and ¼ teaspoon pepper together. Toss with 1 pound freshly cooked farfalle, 1 pound cooked and peeled shrimp, 12 ounces quartered cherry tomatoes, 1 cup chopped pitted kalamata olives, ½ cup crumbled feta cheese, and 2 tablespoons minced fresh parsley. Cover and refrigerate for 10 minutes. Season with salt and pepper. (Serves 8 to 10)

Greek-Style Shrimp with Orzo and Feta

SERVES 4   **TOTAL TIME** 1 HOUR

✓ **WHY THIS RECIPE WORKS:** To pay homage to the classic Greek duo of shrimp and orzo, we toasted our orzo, then cooked it in shrimp broth (made in the microwave with the shrimp shells) and tomato juice from canned tomatoes. Though it is not traditional, we also added saffron, which gave the dish a sunny hue. After we took the orzo off the heat, we stirred in the shrimp and diced tomatoes, sprinkled salty, tangy feta cheese on top, and finished the dish in the oven. Make sure that the orzo is cooked just until al dente, or slightly firm to the bite; otherwise it may overcook in the oven. If your shrimp are larger or smaller, be sure to alter the cooking time in step 4 accordingly. The small amount of saffron makes a big difference to the flavor and look of the dish; do not omit it. You can find marinated feta at the supermarket or you can make your own (see page 285). You will need a 12-inch ovensafe nonstick skillet for this recipe.

 1 **pound medium-large shrimp (31 to 40 per pound), peeled and deveined, shells reserved**
    Salt and pepper
3½ **cups water**
 12 **ounces (2 cups) orzo**
 1 **(14.5-ounce) can diced tomatoes with garlic and onion, drained with juice reserved**
 1 **pinch saffron threads, crumbled**
 2 **cups (8 ounces) crumbled marinated feta**
 3 **scallions, sliced thin**

1. Adjust oven rack to middle position and heat oven to 400 degrees. Pat shrimp dry with paper towels, season with salt and pepper, and transfer to bowl; cover and refrigerate.

2. Combine shrimp shells, water, ¼ teaspoon salt, and ¼ teaspoon pepper in bowl, cover, and microwave until liquid is hot and shells are pink, about 6 minutes. Strain broth, discarding shells.

3. Toast orzo in 12-inch ovensafe nonstick skillet over medium heat until lightly browned, about 4 minutes. Stir in strained shrimp broth, reserved tomato juice, and saffron. Bring to simmer and cook, stirring often, until orzo is al dente, 10 to 12 minutes.

4. Off heat, stir in shrimp and tomatoes. Sprinkle feta over top. Transfer skillet to oven and bake until shrimp are cooked through and cheese is lightly browned, about 20 minutes.

5. Using potholders (skillet handle will be hot), remove skillet from oven. Sprinkle with scallions and serve.

A quick brine keeps these shrimp moist and flavorful while they broil in the oven.

Garlicky Roasted Shrimp with Parsley and Anise

SERVES 4 TO 6   **TOTAL TIME** 45 MINUTES   **FAST**

✓ **WHY THIS RECIPE WORKS:** Roasting quick-cooking shrimp until they develop deep, flavorful browning seemed like an easy route to a weeknight recipe. We were surprised, then, when we ended up with pale shrimp without even a hint of flavor. We knew we could do better. Quickly brining the shrimp kept them plump and moist, and added seasoning throughout. To further protect them as they cooked, and to produce a more roasted flavor, we left their shells on. For tons of flavor, we tossed the shrimp with a savory mixture of spices and herbs and then broiled them in a single layer on a wire rack. When we saw how quickly the tasters gobbled up the shrimp, we knew we had something good, so we developed two equally tasty variations. Don't be tempted to use smaller shrimp with this cooking technique; they will be overseasoned and prone to overcooking.

¼ cup salt
2 pounds shell-on jumbo shrimp (16 to 20 per pound)
4 tablespoons unsalted butter, melted
¼ cup vegetable oil
6 garlic cloves, minced
1 teaspoon anise seeds
½ teaspoon red pepper flakes
¼ teaspoon pepper
2 tablespoons minced fresh parsley
Lemon wedges

1. Dissolve salt in 1 quart cold water in large container. Using kitchen shears or sharp paring knife, cut through shell of shrimp and devein but do not remove shell. Using paring knife, continue to cut shrimp ½ inch deep, taking care not to cut in half completely. Submerge shrimp in brine, cover, and refrigerate for 15 minutes.

2. Adjust oven rack 4 inches from broiler element and heat broiler. Combine melted butter, oil, garlic, anise seeds, pepper flakes, and pepper in large bowl. Remove shrimp from brine and pat dry with paper towels. Add shrimp and parsley to butter mixture and toss well, making sure butter mixture gets into interior of shrimp. Arrange shrimp in single layer on wire rack set in rimmed baking sheet.

3. Broil shrimp until opaque and shells are beginning to brown, 2 to 4 minutes, rotating sheet halfway through broiling. Flip shrimp and continue to broil until second side is opaque and shells are beginning to brown, 2 to 4 minutes, rotating sheet halfway through broiling. Transfer shrimp to serving platter and serve with lemon wedges.

VARIATIONS
Garlicky Roasted Shrimp with Cilantro and Lime

Annatto powder, also called achiote, can be found with the Latin American foods at your supermarket. An equal amount of paprika can be substituted.

Omit butter and increase vegetable oil to ½ cup. Omit anise seeds and pepper. Add 2 teaspoons lightly crushed coriander seeds, 2 teaspoons grated lime zest, and 1 teaspoon annatto powder to oil mixture in step 2. Substitute ¼ cup minced fresh cilantro for parsley, and lime wedges for lemon wedges.

Garlicky Roasted Shrimp with Cumin, Ginger, and Sesame

Omit butter and increase vegetable oil to ½ cup. Reduce garlic to 2 cloves and omit anise seeds and pepper. Add 2 teaspoons toasted sesame oil, 1½ teaspoons grated fresh ginger, and 1 teaspoon cumin seeds to oil mixture in step 2. Substitute 2 thinly sliced scallion greens for parsley and omit lemon wedges.

Toasted sesame oil and sesame seeds pull together the flavors in this fast shrimp stir-fry.

Sesame-Ginger Shrimp

SERVES 4 **TOTAL TIME** 45 MINUTES **FAST**

✓ **WHY THIS RECIPE WORKS:** Stir-fries are perfect for shrimp, but it's all too easy to overcook the shrimp or bury its flavor. To make the perfect stir-fry with moist shrimp and tender vegetables, all coated with a light sesame-ginger sauce, we chose extra-large shrimp to minimize the risk of overcooking. Red bell pepper and scallions provided flavor and a nice textural contrast to the sweet shrimp. A simple sauce made with sesame oil, oyster and soy sauces, and lemon juice, plus a little cornstarch, perfectly coated the ingredients at the end and sprinkling on sesame seeds added a nice crunchiness. Serve with Sticky Rice (page 142).

SAUCE

- ½ cup water
- 1 tablespoon toasted sesame oil
- 1 tablespoon oyster sauce
- 2 teaspoons soy sauce
- 1 teaspoon lemon juice
- 1 teaspoon cornstarch

STIR-FRY

- 1 pound extra-large shrimp (21 to 25 per pound), peeled and deveined
- 2 teaspoons soy sauce
- 2 garlic cloves, minced
- 1 teaspoon grated fresh ginger
- ¼ teaspoon red pepper flakes
- 2 tablespoons plus 1 teaspoon vegetable oil
- 1 red bell pepper, stemmed, seeded, and cut into ¼-inch-thick strips
- 5 scallions, white and light green parts only, cut into 2-inch pieces
- 1 tablespoon sesame seeds, toasted

1. FOR THE SAUCE: Whisk all ingredients together in bowl.

2. FOR THE STIR-FRY: Toss shrimp with soy sauce in bowl. In separate bowl, combine garlic, ginger, pepper flakes, and 1 teaspoon vegetable oil.

3. Heat 1 tablespoon oil in 12-inch nonstick skillet over high heat until just smoking. Add bell pepper and scallions and cook until spotty brown, about 5 minutes; transfer to bowl.

4. Add remaining 1 tablespoon vegetable oil and shrimp mixture to now-empty skillet and cook, stirring often, until just opaque, about 30 seconds. Clear center of skillet, add garlic mixture, and cook, mashing mixture into skillet, until fragrant, about 30 seconds. Stir garlic mixture into shrimp.

5. Stir in cooked vegetables. Whisk sauce to recombine, then add to skillet. Cook, stirring constantly, until sauce is thickened, about 30 seconds. Transfer stir-fry to platter, sprinkle with sesame seeds, and serve.

Shrimp Burgers

SERVES 4 **TOTAL TIME** 1 HOUR 10 MINUTES

✓ **WHY THIS RECIPE WORKS:** Shrimp burgers have a tendency to be dry, mushy, and/or rubbery. But with just a few key steps we avoided these textural problems. First, we used a food processor to obtain a combination of textures—finely chopped pieces to help bind the burgers, as well as some larger, bite-size chunks. Second, a minimal amount of bread was necessary to bind the burgers. Third, since overpacking the burgers made them dense and rubbery, we handled them gently when shaping. And finally, we put the uncooked burgers in the refrigerator to firm up—this helped prevent them from falling apart during cooking. It is best to buy shell-on shrimp and peel them yourself. Serve with any of the creamy sauces on page 254.

3. Scrape shrimp mixture onto small baking sheet, divide into 4 equal portions, and loosely pack each into 1-inch-thick patty. Cover with plastic wrap and refrigerate for 30 minutes. (Burgers can be refrigerated for up to 1 day.)

4. Heat oil in 12-inch nonstick skillet over medium-high heat until shimmering. Gently lay shrimp burgers in skillet and cook until crisp and browned on both sides, 8 to 10 minutes. Gently transfer burgers to platter and serve with lemon wedges.

To keep our shrimp burgers from falling apart during cooking, we refrigerate the patties briefly beforehand.

1 slice high-quality white sandwich bread, torn into 1-inch pieces
1 pound extra-large shrimp (21 to 25 per pound), peeled, deveined, and tails removed
3 tablespoons mayonnaise
2 scallions, sliced thin
2 tablespoons minced fresh parsley
1 teaspoon grated lemon zest
⅛ teaspoon salt
⅛ teaspoon pepper
 Pinch cayenne pepper
1 tablespoon canola oil
 Lemon wedges

1. Pulse bread in food processor to coarse crumbs, about 4 pulses; transfer to bowl. Wipe out food processor with paper towels, add shrimp, and pulse until there is even mix of finely minced and coarsely chopped pieces, about 7 pulses.

2. Whisk mayonnaise, scallions, parsley, lemon zest, salt, pepper, and cayenne together in large bowl. Gently fold in processed shrimp and bread crumbs until just combined.

South Carolina Shrimp Boil

SERVES 8   **TOTAL TIME** 1 HOUR

✓ **WHY THIS RECIPE WORKS:** While New England has its clambakes and New Orleans its crawfish boils, South Carolina has its own unique seafood boil that features shell-on shrimp, smoked sausage, corn on the cob, and potatoes simmered in a broth seasoned with Old Bay. While its simple, one-pot aspect is a big part of its charm, it can also be its biggest downfall. Cooks often throw everything into the pot at once, resulting in mushy potatoes, mealy corn, and rubbery shrimp. We started out with less liquid, knowing that the flavor of our broth would be more intense if we used less water to dilute the seasonings. After reinforcing the broth with 2 bottles of clam juice, we added diced tomatoes, which infused the broth with tomato flavor faster than if we used whole tomatoes. Keeping the sausage in the pot for the entire cooking process imparted extra flavor to the corn and potatoes. To ensure the shrimp achieved maximum flavor without overcooking, we cooked them in a metal steamer basket nestled on top of the sausage and vegetables, which produced juicy and robustly flavored shrimp. This recipe uses shell-on shrimp; if you substitute peeled shrimp, reduce the amount of Old Bay seasoning to ¼ teaspoon.

2 teaspoons vegetable oil
1½ pounds andouille sausage, cut into 2-inch lengths
2 garlic cloves, peeled and crushed
5 teaspoons Old Bay seasoning
3 cups water
2 (8-ounce) bottles clam juice
1 (14.5-ounce) can diced tomatoes
4 ears fresh corn, husks and silk removed, cut into 2-inch rounds
1½ pounds red potatoes, unpeeled, cut into 1-inch pieces
1 bay leaf
2 pounds shell-on extra-large shrimp (21 to 25 per pound)
1 tablespoon minced fresh parsley

1. Heat oil in large Dutch oven over medium-high heat until just smoking. Add sausage and cook until well browned, about 5 minutes. Stir in garlic and 1 tablespoon Old Bay and cook until fragrant, about 30 seconds. Stir in water, clam juice, tomatoes and their juice, corn, potatoes, and bay leaf and bring to boil. Reduce heat to simmer, cover, and cook until potatoes are barely tender, 15 to 20 minutes.

2. Toss shrimp with remaining 2 teaspoons Old Bay and place in collapsible steamer basket. Nestle steamer basket into pot, cover, and continue to simmer, stirring occasionally, until shrimp are just cooked through, 10 to 12 minutes.

3. Remove steamer basket and transfer shrimp to large serving bowl. Strain vegetables and sausage, discarding liquid, garlic cloves, and bay leaf; transfer to serving bowl with shrimp. Sprinkle with parsley and serve.

NOTES FROM THE TEST KITCHEN

Buying Scallops

In general, most recipes use only one type of scallop—sea scallops. The other scallop varieties, bay and Calico (the latter often mislabeled as bay), are much smaller and often too rare and expensive or very cheap and rubbery.

DRY VERSUS WET SCALLOPS: Wet scallops are dipped in preservatives (a solution of water and sodium tripolyphosphate, known as STP) to extend their shelf life. Unfortunately, these watery preservatives dull the scallops' flavor and ruin their texture. Unprocessed, or dry, scallops have much more flavor and a creamy, smooth texture, plus they brown very nicely. Dry scallops look ivory or pinkish; wet scallops are bright white.

DISTINGUISHING DRY FROM WET: If your scallops are not labeled, you can find out if they are wet or dry with this quick microwave test: Place one scallop on a paper towel–lined plate and microwave for 15 seconds. A dry scallop will exude very little water, while a wet scallop will leave a sizable ring of moisture on the paper towel. (The microwaved scallop can be cooked as is.)

TREATING WET SCALLOPS: When you can find only wet scallops, you can hide the off-putting taste of the preservative by soaking the scallops in a solution of 1 quart cold water, ¼ cup lemon juice, and 2 tablespoons salt for 30 minutes. Be sure to pat the scallops very dry after soaking them. Even with this treatment, these scallops will be harder to brown than untreated dry scallops.

After searing and flipping the scallops, we baste them with butter to keep the interiors moist and tender.

Pan-Seared Scallops

SERVES 4   **TOTAL TIME** 30 MINUTES   **FAST**

✓ **WHY THIS RECIPE WORKS:** Producing crisp-crusted restaurant-style scallops at home means overcoming a major obstacle: a weak stovetop. We wanted pan-seared scallops with perfectly brown crusts and moist, tender centers. Blotting the scallops dry, waiting until the oil was just smoking to add them to the skillet, and switching to a nonstick skillet were all steps in the right direction. But it wasn't until we tried a common restaurant technique—butter basting—that our scallops really improved. We seared the scallops in oil on one side and added butter to the skillet before flipping them. We then used a large spoon to ladle the foaming butter over the scallops. Adding the butter midway through ensured that it had just enough time to work its browning magic on the scallops, but not enough time to burn. Be sure to purchase dry scallops for this recipe. If you can find only "wet" scallops, or if your scallops are not labeled, see "Buying Scallops" for more information. Serve with any of the sauces on page 265 or relishes on page 235. For the best results, prepare the sauce or relish while the scallops dry in step 1.

1½ **pounds large sea scallops,**
  tendons removed
  Salt and pepper
2 **tablespoons vegetable oil**
2 **tablespoons unsalted butter**
  Lemon wedges

1. Place scallops on rimmed baking sheet lined with clean kitchen towel. Top with another clean kitchen towel and press gently on scallops to dry. Let scallops sit between towels at room temperature for 10 minutes.

2. Season both sides of scallops with salt and pepper. Heat 1 tablespoon oil in 12-inch nonstick skillet over high heat until just smoking. Add half of scallops in single layer, flat side down, and cook until well browned, 1½ to 2 minutes.

3. Add 1 tablespoon butter to skillet. Using tongs, flip scallops. Continue to cook, using large spoon to baste scallops with melted butter (tilt skillet so butter runs to one side) until sides of scallops are firm and centers are opaque, 30 to 90 seconds longer (remove smaller scallops as they finish cooking).

4. Transfer scallops to large plate and tent with aluminum foil. Wipe out skillet with paper towels and repeat with remaining oil, scallops, and butter. Serve with lemon wedges.

Prepping Scallops

Use your fingers to peel away the small, crescent-shaped muscle that is sometimes attached to scallops, as this tendon becomes incredibly tough when cooked.

Clams with Israeli Couscous, Chorizo, and Leeks

SERVES 4   **TOTAL TIME** 30 MINUTES   **FAST**

✓ **WHY THIS RECIPE WORKS:** To infuse this simple clam dish with big flavor, we added chorizo, thyme, and dry vermouth for a potent broth to steam our shellfish. We added larger-grained Israeli couscous instead of traditional small-grain couscous, as it is the perfect vehicle for soaking up flavors and also adds textural appeal. Israeli couscous, also known as pearl couscous, is about the size of a caper and is not precooked, unlike the smaller grains. It has a unique, nutty flavor that gives this dish just the right boost.

SAUCES FOR PAN-SEARED SCALLOPS

LEMON BROWNED BUTTER **FAST**

MAKES ABOUT ¼ CUP

4 **tablespoons unsalted butter, cut into 4 pieces**
1 **small shallot, minced**
1 **tablespoon minced fresh parsley**
½ **teaspoon minced fresh thyme**
2 **teaspoons lemon juice**
  Salt and pepper

Heat butter in small heavy-bottomed saucepan over medium heat, swirling pan constantly, until butter turns dark golden brown and has nutty aroma, 4 to 5 minutes. Add shallot and cook until fragrant, about 30 seconds. Off heat, stir in parsley, thyme, and lemon juice. Season with salt and pepper to taste.

TOMATO-GINGER SAUCE **FAST**

MAKES ABOUT ½ CUP

6 **tablespoons unsalted butter, cut into 6 pieces**
1 **plum tomato, cored, seeded, and chopped fine**
1 **tablespoon grated fresh ginger**
1 **tablespoon lemon juice**
¼ **teaspoon red pepper flakes**
  Salt

Heat butter in small heavy-bottomed saucepan over medium heat, swirling pan constantly, until butter turns dark golden brown and has nutty aroma, 4 to 5 minutes. Add tomato, ginger, lemon juice, and pepper flakes and cook, stirring constantly, until fragrant, about 1 minute. Season with salt to taste.

ORANGE-LIME VINAIGRETTE **FAST**

MAKES ABOUT ½ CUP

2 **tablespoons orange juice**
2 **tablespoons lime juice**
1 **small shallot, minced**
1 **tablespoon minced fresh cilantro**
⅛ **teaspoon red pepper flakes**
2 **tablespoons vegetable oil**
2 **tablespoons extra-virgin olive oil**
  Salt

Combine orange juice, lime juice, shallot, cilantro, and pepper flakes in bowl. Slowly whisk in vegetable oil and olive oil. Season with salt to taste.

For this one-dish supper, clams are steamed in a fragrant mixture of sautéed leeks and chorizo, vermouth, and fresh tomatoes.

Small quahogs or cherrystones are good alternatives to the littleneck clams. We like the punch that dry vermouth adds to this dish, but dry white wine will also work. Be sure to use Israeli couscous; regular (or fine-grain) couscous won't work here.

2 cups Israeli couscous
  Salt and pepper
2 tablespoons unsalted butter
1½ pounds leeks, white and light green parts only, halved lengthwise, sliced thin, and washed thoroughly
6 ounces chorizo sausage, halved lengthwise and sliced thin
3 garlic cloves, minced
1 tablespoon minced fresh thyme
1 cup dry vermouth or dry white wine
3 tomatoes, cored, seeded, and chopped
4 pounds littleneck clams, scrubbed
½ cup minced fresh parsley

1. Bring 2 quarts water to boil in medium saucepan. Stir in couscous and 2 teaspoons salt and cook until al dente, about 8 minutes; drain.

2. Meanwhile, melt butter in Dutch oven over medium heat. Add leeks and chorizo and cook until leeks are tender, about 4 minutes. Stir in garlic and thyme and cook until fragrant, about 30 seconds. Stir in vermouth and cook until slightly reduced, about 1 minute. Stir in tomatoes and clams, cover, and cook until clams open, 8 to 12 minutes.

3. Use slotted spoon to transfer clams to large serving bowl, discarding any that refuse to open. Stir drained couscous and parsley into pot and season with salt and pepper to taste. Portion couscous mixture into bowls, top with clams, and serve.

Oven-Steamed Mussels

SERVES 2 TO 4   **TOTAL TIME** 40 MINUTES **FAST**

WHY THIS RECIPE WORKS: Steamed mussels should be quick and easy, as they come with their own built-in, briny-sweet broth. But they come in all different sizes so they cook at different rates, especially when piled on top of each other in the pot. To get them to cook at the same rate, we realized we needed to expand the surface area for cooking. We found that cooking the mussels in a wide roasting pan in the oven meant that the heat surrounded the mussels on all sides, leading to more even (and gentle) cooking than was possible on the stove. Even in a 500-degree oven, the mussels took a few minutes longer, and only a few didn't open—the rest were plump and moist. With wine, thyme, and bay leaves as a base, the mussels' liquid made a tasty broth. Discard any mussel with an unpleasant odor or with a cracked shell or a shell that won't close. Serve with crusty bread.

1 tablespoon extra-virgin olive oil
3 garlic cloves, minced
  Pinch red pepper flakes
1 cup dry white wine
3 sprigs fresh thyme
2 bay leaves
4 pounds mussels, scrubbed and debearded
¼ teaspoon salt
2 tablespoons unsalted butter, cut into 4 pieces
2 tablespoons minced fresh parsley

1. Adjust oven rack to lowest position and heat oven to 500 degrees. Heat oil, garlic, and pepper flakes in large roasting pan over medium heat and cook, stirring constantly, until fragrant, about 30 seconds. Stir in wine, thyme sprigs, and bay leaves and boil until wine is slightly reduced, about 1 minute.

2. Stir in mussels and salt. Cover pan tightly with aluminum foil and transfer to oven. Cook until most mussels have opened (a few may remain closed), 15 to 18 minutes.

3. Remove pan from oven. Push mussels to sides of pan. Add butter to center and whisk until melted. Discard thyme sprigs and bay leaves. Stir in parsley and serve.

VARIATIONS

Oven-Steamed Mussels with Hard Cider and Bacon

Substitute 4 slices thick-cut bacon, cut into ½-inch pieces, for garlic and pepper flakes; cook until bacon has rendered and is starting to crisp, about 5 minutes. Substitute dry hard cider for wine and ¼ cup heavy cream for butter.

Oven-Steamed Mussels with Leeks and Pernod

Increase oil to 3 tablespoons and omit pepper flakes and thyme sprigs. Add 1 pound leeks, white and light green parts only, halved lengthwise, sliced thin, and washed thoroughly, to pan with garlic and cook until leeks are wilted, about 3 minutes. Substitute ½ cup Pernod and ¼ cup water for wine, ¼ cup crème fraîche for butter, and chives for parsley.

Debearding Mussels

Occasionally, mussels will have a weedy but harmless piece, called a beard, protruding from its shell. Grasp it between your thumb and the flat side of a paring knife and tug it off before cooking.

NOTES FROM THE TEST KITCHEN

Buying Mussels and Clams

For the best flavor and texture, mussels and clams should be as fresh as possible. They should smell clean, not sour or sulfurous, and the shells should look moist. Look for tightly closed mussels and clams—avoid any that are broken or sitting in a puddle of water. Some shells may gape slightly, but they should close when they are tapped. Discard any that won't close; they may be dead and should not be eaten. Most mussels and clams today are farmed and free of grit. Soft-shell clams, however, almost always contain a lot of sand and should be submerged in a large bowl of cold water and drained several times before cooking. Both clams and mussels need to be scrubbed and rinsed before cooking; simply use a brush to scrub away any sand trapped in the outer shell. Some mussels may also need to be debearded. The best way to store mussels and clams is in the refrigerator in a colander of ice set over a bowl; discard any water that accumulates so that the shellfish are never submerged.

Making Oven-Steamed Mussels

1. COOK AROMATICS AND ADD WINE: Cook oil, garlic, and red pepper flakes in roasting pan until fragrant. Add wine, thyme sprigs, and bay leaves and cook until wine is slightly reduced.

2. ADD MUSSELS AND COVER: Add mussels and salt. Cover tightly with aluminum foil and transfer to oven.

3. COOK UNTIL MUSSELS OPEN: Cook until mussels have opened (a few may remain closed), about 15 to 18 minutes. Remove pan from oven.

4. FINISH BROTH: Push mussels to sides of pan, and add butter. Whisk until melted. Discard thyme sprigs and bay leaves. Sprinkle with parsley.

Steamed Whole Lobsters

SERVES 4   TOTAL TIME 25 MINUTES   **FAST**

✔ **WHY THIS RECIPE WORKS:** The secret to tender lobster is not so much in the preparation and cooking as it is in the selection of the creature itself. After some research into the life cycle of the lobster, we discovered that the variations in the texture of lobster meat depend a great deal on what part of the molting cycle a lobster is in. You will find both hard-shell and soft-shell lobsters available; lobsters are in their prime when their shells are fully hardened. Soft-shell lobsters have less meat and tail meat that is underdeveloped. We prefer hard-shell lobsters to soft-shell though they are generally only available in late spring and early summer. Steaming is far tidier than boiling, as you avoid dealing with waterlogged crustaceans at the dinner table. Neither beer nor wine improved the flavor, so we simply relied on water.

4 **live lobsters**
8 **tablespoons salted butter, melted**
 Lemon wedges

1. Fit stockpot or Dutch oven with steamer basket or pasta insert. Add water, keeping level below basket. Bring water to boil over high heat.

2. Add lobsters, cover, and return water to boil. Reduce heat to medium-high and steam until lobsters are done, following cooking times in chart on page 269. Serve immediately with melted butter and lemon wedges.

> ### HARD-SHELL VERSUS SOFT-SHELL LOBSTERS
>
> At various times throughout the year, lobsters go through a molting stage in order to grow into a larger shell. If caught during this molting stage, the lobsters are called soft-shell. You can, in fact, tell that they are soft-shell lobsters just by squeezing their soft sides. Does this matter? Yes and no. Soft-shell lobsters have less meat and are considered to be less flavorful by true connoisseurs. For most of us, though, soft-shell lobsters taste just fine. The only thing to keep in mind when cooking soft-shell lobsters is that they cook faster than hard-shell ones do (see the chart on page 269).
>
> To determine whether a lobster has a hard shell or a soft shell, squeeze the side of the body. A soft-shell lobster will yield to pressure, while a hard-shell lobster will feel hard and tightly packed.

Removing Lobster Meat from the Shell

There's a lot more meat in a lobster than just the tail and claws—if you know how to get it. Here's our tried-and-true approach to extracting every last bit, no special tools needed. The method works for both hard- and soft-shell lobsters.

1. SEPARATE TAIL: Once cooked lobster is cool enough to handle, set it on cutting board. Grasp tail with one hand and body with other hand and twist to separate.

2. FLATTEN TAIL: Lay tail on its side on counter and use both hands to press down on tail until shell cracks.

3. TAKE OUT TAIL MEAT: Hold tail, shell facing down. Pull back on sides to crack open shell, and remove meat. Rinse meat under water to remove green tomalley if you wish; pat meat dry with paper towels and remove dark vein.

4. MOVE TO KNUCKLES: Twist "arms" to remove claws and attached "knuckles." Twist knuckles to remove from claws. Break knuckles at joint and use handle of teaspoon to push out meat.

5. REMOVE CLAW MEAT: Wiggle hinged portion of each claw to separate. If meat is stuck inside small part, remove it with skewer. Break open claws, cracking each side, and remove meat.

6. FINISH WITH LEGS: Twist legs to remove and lay flat on counter. Using rolling pin, roll toward open end, pushing out meat. Stop rolling before reaching end of leg; otherwise, open tip can crack and release pieces of shell.

We keep our lobster rolls simple, flavoring the mayonnaise with celery, lemon juice, chives, and a small pinch of cayenne.

New England Lobster Rolls

SERVES 6   TOTAL TIME 25 MINUTES   **FAST**

✔ **WHY THIS RECIPE WORKS:** Found at roadside stands along the Northeast coast, these summertime sandwiches highlight the delicate flavor of lobster. Though traditionalists like to leave the lobster meat in large hunks, we found these pieces challenging to eat, so we cut the tougher tail into smaller pieces. To keep it simple and highlight the lobster, we opted for a single soft lettuce leaf to line each roll, and a couple of tablespoons of minced celery for unobtrusive crunch. Onions and shallots proved too overwhelming, but a teaspoon of chives gave the salad a bright herb flavor. A splash of lemon juice and a pinch of cayenne provided a counterbalance to the rich lobster meat and buttery bun. This recipe is best when made with lobster you've cooked yourself. Use a very small pinch of cayenne pepper, as it should not make the dressing spicy. We prefer New England–style top-loading hot dog buns,

Lobster Steaming Times and Yields

	TIME (IN MINUTES)	MEAT YIELD (IN OUNCES)
SOFT-SHELL		
1 lb	8 to 9	about 3
1¼ lbs	11 to 12	3½ to 4
1½ lbs	13 to 14	5½ to 6
1¾ lbs–2 lbs	17 to 18	6¼ to 6½
HARD-SHELL		
1 lb	10 to 11	4 to 4½
1¼ lbs	13 to 14	5½ to 6
1½ lbs	15 to 16	7½ to 8
1¾ lbs–2 lbs	about 19	8½ to 9

as they provide maximum surface on the sides for toasting. If using other buns, butter, salt, and toast the interior of each bun instead of the exterior.

- 2 tablespoons mayonnaise
- 2 tablespoons minced celery
- 1½ teaspoons lemon juice
- 1 teaspoon minced fresh chives
- Salt
- Pinch cayenne pepper
- 1 pound cooked lobster meat, tail meat cut into ½-inch pieces and claw meat cut into 1-inch pieces
- 2 tablespoons unsalted butter, softened
- 6 New England–style hot dog buns
- 6 leaves Boston lettuce

1. Whisk mayonnaise, celery, lemon juice, chives, ⅛ teaspoon salt, and cayenne together in large bowl. Add lobster and gently toss to combine.

2. Place 12-inch nonstick skillet over low heat. Butter both sides of hot dog buns and sprinkle lightly with salt. Place buns in skillet, with 1 buttered side down; increase heat to medium-low and cook until crisp and brown, 2 to 3 minutes. Flip and cook second side until crisp and brown, 2 to 3 minutes longer.

3. Transfer buns to large platter. Line each bun with lettuce leaf. Spoon lobster salad into buns and serve immediately.

Seafood Risotto with Shrimp and Scallops

SERVES 4 TO 6   **TOTAL TIME** 1 HOUR 45 MINUTES

✔ **WHY THIS RECIPE WORKS:** Seafood risotto is a special-occasion dish—a glamorous mix of flavors, shapes, and textures against a lush backdrop of creamy Arborio rice. With a wide array of seafood to choose from, the preparation can easily become complicated, so we decided to set some limits. We chose universally appealing shrimp and sweet, meaty bay scallops, perfect for their smaller size. We made a quick broth by simmering the shrimp shells in a base of bottled clam juice and chicken broth with bay leaves and canned tomatoes. As for the seafood, we stirred the shrimp and scallops into the fully cooked risotto, covered the pot, and allowed them to steam, resulting in flawlessly tender seafood. Do not buy peeled shrimp; you will need the shrimp shells to make the broth. You can substitute ½ pound sea scallops, quartered, for the bay scallops. We recommend "dry" scallops, which don't have chemical additives and taste better than "wet" (see page 264).

A quick-to-make seafood broth infuses this risotto dish with flavor without overwhelming the shrimp and scallops.

12 ounces large shrimp (26 to 30 per pound), peeled and deveined, shells reserved
4½ cups chicken broth
4 (8-ounce) bottles clam juice
1 (14.5-ounce) can diced tomatoes, drained
2 bay leaves
5 tablespoons unsalted butter
1 onion, chopped fine
5 garlic cloves, minced
1 teaspoon minced fresh thyme or ¼ teaspoon dried
⅛ teaspoon saffron threads, crumbled
2 cups Arborio rice
1 cup dry white wine
12 ounces small bay scallops
1 tablespoon lemon juice
2 tablespoons minced fresh parsley
Salt and pepper

1. Combine shrimp shells, broth, clam juice, tomatoes, and bay leaves in large saucepan and bring to boil. Reduce heat to simmer and cook, stirring often, for 20 minutes. Strain broth through fine-mesh strainer into large measuring cup, pressing on solids to extract as much liquid as possible. Return broth to saucepan, cover, and keep warm over low heat.

2. Melt 2 tablespoons butter in large Dutch oven over medium heat. Add onion and cook until softened, 5 to 7 minutes. Stir in garlic, thyme, and saffron and cook until fragrant, about 30 seconds. Stir in rice and cook, stirring frequently, until grains are translucent around edges, about 3 minutes.

3. Stir in wine and cook, stirring frequently, until fully absorbed, 2 to 3 minutes. Stir in 3½ cups of warm broth. Bring to simmer and cook, stirring about every 3 minutes, until broth is absorbed and bottom of pot is dry, 13 to 17 minutes.

4. Continue to cook rice, stirring often and adding hot broth, 1 cup at a time, every few minutes as pan bottom turns dry, until rice is cooked through but still somewhat firm in center, 13 to 17 minutes.

5. Stir in shrimp and scallops and cook, stirring often, until seafood is just cooked through, about 3 minutes. Remove pot from heat, cover, and let stand for 5 minutes. Stir in remaining 3 tablespoons butter, lemon juice, and parsley, and season with salt and pepper to taste. Add remaining broth as needed to adjust risotto consistency before serving.

VARIATION

Seafood Risotto with Shrimp, Scallops, and Squid
Reduce amount of shrimp and scallops to 8 ounces each. Add 8 ounces squid, bodies cut crosswise into ½-inch rings and tentacles left whole, to risotto with shrimp and scallops.

Quick Skillet Paella

SERVES 4 TO 6   **TOTAL TIME** 1 HOUR

✔**WHY THIS RECIPE WORKS:** Paella, Spain's famous rice and seafood dish, can be a big hit at restaurants but an unwieldy and time-consuming production at home. The key to re-creating this recipe was replacing the paella pan with a 12-inch skillet with a tight-fitting lid, and paring down both the prep work and the ingredients while keeping the dish's signature flavors. We focused on fast-cooking proteins: shrimp, chorizo, and either clams or mussels. Because the shrimp, rice, sausage, and clams all cook at different rates, we cooked them in stages, first sautéing the shrimp, followed by the sausage, and then setting them aside. We used the sausage's fat to cook the aromatics and herbs before toasting the rice, which then soaked up the flavors of clam juice, tomatoes, and saffron. We steamed the clams toward the end, letting them release their liquid into the rice. Now we had a tasty paella recipe that could be cooked in about an hour. If you can't find chorizo, use tasso, andouille, or linguiça.

We simplify paella by cooking it in a skillet and paring down the ingredient list while keeping its signature flavors.

1 pound extra-large shrimp (21 to 25 per pound), peeled and deveined
½ teaspoon chili powder
¼ teaspoon pepper
2 tablespoons vegetable oil
8 ounces chorizo sausage, sliced ½ inch thick
1 onion, chopped fine
½ teaspoon minced fresh thyme or ¼ teaspoon dried
3 garlic cloves, minced
1 cup long-grain white rice
2 (8-ounce) bottles clam juice
1 (14.5-ounce) can diced tomatoes, drained
¼ teaspoon saffron threads, crumbled
1 dozen clams or mussels, scrubbed, mussels debearded
½ cup frozen peas
2 tablespoons minced fresh parsley
  Lemon wedges

1. Pat shrimp dry with paper towels and season with chili powder and pepper. Heat 1 tablespoon oil in 12-inch nonstick skillet over medium-high heat until just smoking. Add shrimp and cook until curled and pink on both sides, about 2 minutes. Transfer to bowl and cover with aluminum foil.

2. Add remaining 1 tablespoon oil to skillet and heat until shimmering. Add chorizo and cook until lightly browned, about 3 minutes. Transfer chorizo to bowl with shrimp.

3. Add onion and thyme to fat left in skillet and cook over medium heat until softened, about 5 minutes. Stir in garlic and cook until fragrant, about 15 seconds. Stir in rice and cook until grains are sizzling and lightly toasted, about 1 minute.

4. Stir in clam juice, tomatoes, and saffron, scraping up any browned bits. Bring to boil, then cover, reduce heat to low, and cook until rice is tender and liquid is absorbed, about 15 minutes.

5. Off heat, stir in cooked shrimp and chorizo. Arrange clams over top and sprinkle with peas. Cover and cook over medium heat until shellfish have opened, about 7 minutes, discarding any that don't open.

6. Remove skillet from heat and let stand, covered, for 5 minutes. Sprinkle with parsley. Serve with lemon wedges.

VARIATION

Paella for a Crowd

This scaled-up version of paella will serve 8 to 10.

Substitute large Dutch oven for skillet. Increase amount of shrimp to 1½ pounds and rice to 1½ cups, and double all remaining ingredients. Cooking times will remain same.

Vegetarian Entrées

■ SIGNIFIES A **FAST** RECIPE (45 MINUTES OR LESS)

Spinach Strudel

SERVES 4 TOTAL TIME 45 MINUTES **FAST**

✔ **WHY THIS RECIPE WORKS:** Sweet strudels might be better known, but savory strudels have a long and delicious history. Our starting point for this recipe was a filling of spinach with ricotta and feta cheeses. We added golden raisins and pine nuts for their contrasting textures. Next we turned to simplifying the strudel assembly. We found that we could simply stack the greased phyllo sheets, mound the filling into a long rectangle, then roll up the strudel into a log. We also left the sides open to guard against leaking filling. A few vents to allow steam to escape kept the top crisp during baking and cooling. Squeeze the spinach thoroughly until it's dry, or else the filling will be wet and may leak. Be sure to use phyllo that is fully thawed or it will crack and flake apart when handled. Phyllo dough is also available in larger 18 by 14-inch sheets; if using, cut them in half to make 14 by 9-inch sheets. Don't thaw the phyllo in the microwave; let it sit in the refrigerator overnight or on the counter for 4 to 5 hours.

- 10 ounces frozen spinach, thawed, squeezed dry, and chopped coarse
- 6 ounces (¾ cup) whole-milk ricotta cheese
- 3 ounces feta cheese, crumbled (¾ cup)
- 6 scallions, sliced thin
- ½ cup golden raisins
- 2 tablespoons pine nuts, toasted
- 2 tablespoons lemon juice
- 1 tablespoon minced fresh oregano
- 2 garlic cloves, minced
- ½ teaspoon ground nutmeg
  Salt and pepper
- 10 (14 by 9-inch) phyllo sheets, thawed
  Olive oil spray

1. Adjust oven rack to middle position and heat oven to 400 degrees. Line baking sheet with parchment paper. Mix spinach, ricotta, feta, scallions, raisins, pine nuts, lemon juice, oregano, garlic, and nutmeg together in bowl and season with salt and pepper to taste.

2. On clean counter, layer phyllo sheets on top of one another, coating each sheet thoroughly with olive oil spray. Mound spinach mixture into narrow log along bottom edge of phyllo, leaving 2-inch border at bottom and ½-inch border on sides. Fold bottom edge of dough over filling, then continue to roll dough around filling into tight log, leaving ends open.

3. Gently transfer strudel, seam side down, to prepared baking sheet. Lightly spray strudel with oil spray and cut four 1½-inch vents at diagonal across top.

4. Bake strudel until golden, about 20 minutes, rotating baking sheet halfway through baking. Let strudel cool on baking sheet for 5 minutes, then slice and serve.

VARIATION

Spinach Strudel with Olives and Goat Cheese
Substitute ½ cup pitted and chopped kalamata olives for raisins and 3 ounces crumbled goat cheese for feta.

Making Spinach Strudel

1. LAYER PHYLLO: On clean counter, layer phyllo sheets on top of one another, coating each sheet thoroughly with olive oil spray (about 3 seconds per sheet).

2. MOUND FILLING: Mound spinach mixture into narrow log along bottom edge of phyllo, leaving 2-inch border at bottom and ½-inch border on sides.

3. LEAVE ENDS OPEN: Fold bottom edge of dough over filling, then continue to roll dough around filling into tight log, leaving ends open.

4. CUT VENTS: Gently transfer strudel, seam side down, to prepared baking sheet. Lightly spray strudel with olive oil spray and cut four 1½-inch vents at diagonal across top.

Store-bought puff pastry makes an easy base for a savory tart that highlights fennel.

Fennel, Olive, and Goat Cheese Tarts

SERVES 4   **TOTAL TIME** 45 MINUTES   **FAST**

✓ **WHY THIS RECIPE WORKS:** We enjoy savory tarts and wanted a simple recipe for one that would highlight the flavor of fennel. Taking advantage of store-bought puff pastry, we parbaked it, then cut through some of the layers to create a smaller inner rectangle that would serve as a bed for the filling. A layer of tangy goat cheese thinned out with olive oil and mixed with chopped fresh basil and lemon zest made the perfect creamy base for a topping of sautéed fennel mixed with oil-cured black olives. To thaw frozen puff pastry, let it sit either in the refrigerator for 1 day or on the counter for 30 minutes to 1 hour.

- 1 (9½ by 9-inch) sheet puff pastry, thawed and cut in half
- 3 tablespoons extra-virgin olive oil
- 1 large fennel bulb, stalks discarded, bulb halved, cored, and sliced thin
- 3 garlic cloves, minced
- ½ cup dry white wine
- ½ cup pitted oil-cured black olives, chopped
- 1 teaspoon grated lemon zest plus 1 tablespoon juice
  Salt and pepper
- 8 ounces goat cheese, softened
- 5 tablespoons chopped fresh basil

1. Adjust oven rack to middle position and heat oven to 425 degrees. Lay puff pastry on parchment-lined baking sheet and poke all over with fork. Bake pastry until puffed and golden brown, about 15 minutes, rotating baking sheet halfway through baking. Using tip of paring knife, cut ½-inch-wide border around top edge of each pastry, then press centers down with fingertips.

2. Meanwhile, heat 1 tablespoon oil in 12-inch skillet over medium-high heat until shimmering. Add fennel and cook until softened and browned, about 10 minutes. Stir in garlic and cook until fragrant, 30 seconds. Add wine, cover, and cook for 5 minutes. Uncover and cook until liquid has evaporated and fennel is very soft, 3 to 5 minutes. Off heat, stir in olives and lemon juice and season with salt and pepper to taste.

3. Mix goat cheese, ¼ cup basil, remaining 2 tablespoons oil, lemon zest, and ¼ teaspoon pepper together in bowl, then spread evenly over center of pastry shells. Spoon fennel mixture over top. (Tarts can be held at room temperature for 2 hours before baking.)

4. Bake tarts until cheese is heated through and crust is deep golden, 5 to 7 minutes. Sprinkle with remaining 1 tablespoon basil. Serve.

Making a Puff Pastry Tart Shell

1. Lay pastry rectangles on parchment-lined baking sheet and poke all over with fork. Bake pastry until puffed and golden, about 15 minutes.

2. Using tip of paring knife, cut ½-inch border around top edge of each baked pastry and press center down with your fingertips to create bed for filling.

Tomato Tart

SERVES 4 TO 6   **TOTAL TIME** 1 HOUR 15 MINUTES

♥ **WHY THIS RECIPE WORKS:** Tomato tarts sound promising, but often recipes yield tarts with soggy crusts and fillings with very little flavor. We set out to develop a simple recipe with a flavorful and foolproof crust, a creamy base, and a topping of fragrant sliced tomatoes. To ensure that the tomatoes didn't leach moisture into the tart, we salted them and let them rest for half an hour. We combined a trio of cheeses—Parmesan, ricotta, and mozzarella—with olive oil into a base layer to go under the tomatoes. Now all we had to do was spread the cheese mixture over the bottom of the baked tart shell, shingle the tomatoes on top, and bake until the tomatoes were slightly wilted. Drizzling the tomatoes with a mixture of olive oil and minced garlic before baking kept them from drying out and infused them with flavor. We prefer the light flavor of part-skim ricotta here, but whole-milk ricotta can be substituted; do not use fat-free ricotta.

- 3 **plum tomatoes, cored and sliced ¼ inch thick**
  Salt and pepper
- 3 **tablespoons extra-virgin olive oil**
- 1 **garlic clove, minced**
- 1 **ounce Parmesan cheese, grated (½ cup)**
- ½ **cup part-skim ricotta cheese**
- 1 **ounce mozzarella, shredded (¼ cup)**
- 1 **recipe Olive Oil and Parmesan Tart Shell (page 277), baked and cooled**
- 2 **tablespoons chopped fresh basil**

1. Spread tomatoes out over several layers of paper towels, sprinkle with ½ teaspoon salt, and let drain for 30 minutes. Combine 2 tablespoons oil and garlic in small bowl. In separate bowl, combine Parmesan, ricotta, mozzarella, and remaining 1 tablespoon oil and season with salt and pepper to taste.

2. Adjust oven rack to middle position and heat oven to 425 degrees. Spread ricotta mixture evenly over bottom of

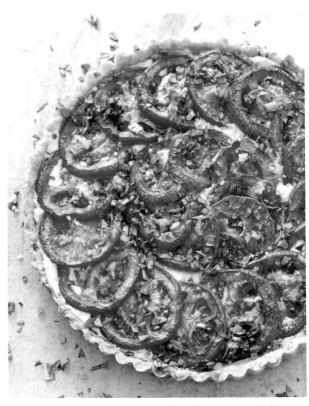

Removing some of the moisture from the tomatoes is key to ensuring that the crust bakes up crisp and flaky.

tart shell. Blot tomatoes dry with paper towels, and shingle attractively on top of ricotta in concentric circles. Drizzle with garlic-oil mixture. (Tart can be held at room temperature for up to 2 hours before baking.)

3. Bake tart until bubbling and tomatoes are slightly wilted, 20 to 25 minutes, rotating baking sheet halfway through baking.

4. Let tart cool on baking sheet for at least 10 minutes or up to 2 hours. To serve, remove outer metal ring of tart pan, slide thin metal spatula between tart and tart pan bottom, and carefully slide tart onto serving platter or cutting board. Sprinkle with basil before serving.

Making a Tomato Tart

Shingle tomatoes in concentric circles, starting at outside edge and working in.

VARIATIONS
Mushroom Tart

Omit tomatoes and garlic-oil mixture. Heat 1 tablespoon extra-virgin olive oil in 12-inch nonstick skillet over medium-high heat until shimmering. Add 1 pound white button mushrooms, sliced thin, and ½ teaspoon salt and cook until lightly browned, about 15 minutes. Stir in 1 minced garlic clove and 2 teaspoons minced fresh thyme and cook until fragrant, about 1 minute longer. Spoon mushroom mixture over ricotta mixture and bake tart as directed.

Zucchini Tart

Substitute 1 large zucchini, sliced into ¼-inch-thick rounds, for tomatoes. Salt zucchini as directed in step 1.

OLIVE OIL AND PARMESAN TART SHELL

MAKES ONE 9-INCH TART

TOTAL TIME 1 HOUR 30 MINUTES

This dough does not need to be chilled before using; if it becomes too mushy to work with, however, let it firm up in the refrigerator for a few minutes.

- 1¼ cups (6¼ ounces) all-purpose flour
- 1 tablespoon sugar
- ½ teaspoon salt
- 6 tablespoons extra-virgin olive oil
- 3 tablespoons ice water
- 1 ounce Parmesan cheese, grated (½ cup)

1. Process flour, sugar, and salt together in food processor until combined. Drizzle oil over flour mixture and pulse until mixture resembles coarse sand, about 12 pulses. Add 2 tablespoons ice water and continue to process until large clumps of dough form and no powdery bits remain, about 5 seconds. If dough doesn't clump, add remaining 1 tablespoon water and pulse to incorporate, about 4 pulses; dough should feel quite sticky. (Dough can be wrapped well and refrigerated for up to 2 days or frozen for up to 1 month; let dough sit at room temperature until very soft before using.)

2. Tear dough into walnut-size pieces and pat into 9-inch tart pan with removable bottom, pressing it ¾ inch up sides of pan. Cover with plastic wrap and smooth out any bumps using your palm. Leaving plastic in place, place tart pan on large plate and freeze until dough is firm, about 30 minutes.

3. Adjust rack to middle position and heat oven to 375 degrees. Set frozen tart pan on baking sheet. Remove plastic and press double layer of aluminum foil into frozen shell and over edges of pan and fill with pie weights. Bake until tart shell is golden brown and set, about 30 minutes, rotating baking sheet halfway through baking.

4. Carefully remove weights and foil and sprinkle Parmesan evenly over bottom of tart shell. Continue to bake until cheese is golden, 5 to 10 minutes. Let tart shell cool completely on baking sheet.

Whole-wheat couscous combined with zucchini and fennel turns our stuffed tomatoes into a hearty vegetarian entrée.

Stuffed Tomatoes with Couscous and Zucchini

SERVES 4   **TOTAL TIME** 50 MINUTES

WHY THIS RECIPE WORKS: To turn stuffed tomatoes into a filling and flavorful vegetarian entrée, we knew we'd need to find a solution to the problem that plagues most recipes: drab and soggy fillings. So our first step was to core and seed the tomatoes, salt their interiors, and let them drain, thereby drawing out excess liquid. After 30 minutes, the tomatoes had given up most of their liquid, ensuring that we could pack them with the filling without risk of sogginess. For the stuffing, we turned to nutty-tasting whole-wheat couscous instead of bread crumbs and paired it with sautéed zucchini and fennel. It was easy to build the entire filling in one saucepan, adding broth toward the end then letting the couscous finish cooking off the heat. Goat cheese and Parmesan added heartiness and richness. We stuffed our tomatoes and sprinkled them with a bit more Parmesan on top before baking them. Try to buy tomatoes of equal size with flat, sturdy bottoms that can sit upright on their own.

8 large tomatoes (8 ounces each)
   Salt and pepper
3 tablespoons extra-virgin olive oil
1 fennel bulb, stalks discarded, halved, cored,
   and minced
2 shallots, minced
1 zucchini (8 ounces), cut into ¼-inch pieces
4 garlic cloves, minced
⅔ cup whole-wheat couscous
¾ cup vegetable broth
2 ounces Parmesan cheese, grated (1 cup)
2 ounces goat cheese, crumbled (½ cup)
¼ cup chopped fresh basil

1. Slice top ⅛ inch off each tomato and carefully remove core and seeds. Sprinkle inside of each tomato with ⅛ teaspoon salt. Place upside down on several layers of paper towels and let drain for 30 minutes.

2. Meanwhile, adjust oven rack to upper-middle position and heat oven to 375 degrees. Heat 2 tablespoons oil in large saucepan over medium heat until shimmering. Add fennel and shallots and cook until softened and lightly browned, 10 to 12 minutes.

Preparing Tomatoes for Stuffing

1. Using sharp knife, slice top ⅛ inch off each tomato.

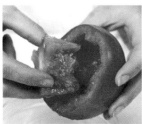

2. Using fingers (or a paring knife) remove and discard core and any seeds inside tomato.

3. Sprinkle inside of each tomato with ⅛ teaspoon salt, place upside down on paper towels, and let drain for 30 minutes.

3. Stir in zucchini and cook until tender, about 5 minutes. Stir in garlic and cook until fragrant, about 30 seconds. Stir in couscous and cook until lightly toasted, 1 to 2 minutes. Stir in broth and bring to brief simmer. Remove pan from heat, cover, and let sit for 5 minutes. Using fork, gently fluff couscous and stir in ½ cup Parmesan, goat cheese, and basil. Season with salt and pepper to taste.

4. Pat inside of each tomato dry with paper towels. Arrange tomatoes, cut side up, in 13 by 9-inch baking dish lined with aluminum foil. Brush cut edges of tomatoes with remaining 1 tablespoon oil. Mound couscous filling into tomatoes, pack lightly with back of spoon, and sprinkle with remaining ½ cup Parmesan. (Stuffed tomatoes can be held at room temperature for 1 hour before baking.)

5. Bake until cheese is lightly browned and tomatoes are tender, about 15 minutes. Serve.

Stuffed Acorn Squash

SERVES 4   **TOTAL TIME** 45 MINUTES   **FAST**

✔ **WHY THIS RECIPE WORKS:** Stuffing and roasting an acorn squash the traditional way can take hours, but we found a few shortcuts that didn't compromise either the flavor or texture. Our solution was to cook the squash in the microwave, which takes about 15 minutes, and make an easy filling in the meantime. For the filling, we used quick-cooking couscous. While the couscous cooked off the heat, we sautéed garlic and onion, then cooked baby spinach until it wilted, folding this mixture into the couscous along with pine nuts and Pecorino Romano cheese. To finish the dish, we just needed a sprinkle of additional cheese and a few minutes under the broiler. Be sure to look for similar-size squash (1½ pounds each) to ensure even cooking. For an accurate measurement of boiling water, bring a full kettle of water to a boil, then measure out the desired amount.

2 acorn squashes (1½ pounds each),
   halved pole to pole and seeded
3 tablespoons vegetable oil
1 cup couscous
½ cup golden raisins
   Salt and pepper
1 cup boiling water
1 onion, chopped fine
4 garlic cloves, minced
6 ounces (6 cups) baby spinach
½ cup pine nuts, toasted
1½ ounces Pecorino Romano cheese, grated (¾ cup)

1. Brush cut side of squash with 1 tablespoon oil and place, cut side down, on large plate. Cover and microwave until soft, 12 to 16 minutes.

2. Meanwhile, combine couscous, raisins, 1 tablespoon oil, and 1 teaspoon salt in medium bowl. Stir in boiling water, cover tightly with plastic wrap, and let sit until liquid is absorbed and couscous is tender, about 5 minutes. Fluff couscous with fork.

3. Heat remaining 1 tablespoon oil in 12-inch skillet over medium-high heat until shimmering. Add onion and cook until softened, about 5 minutes. Stir in garlic and cook until fragrant, about 30 seconds. Stir in spinach and cook until wilted and most of liquid has evaporated, about 2 minutes. Off heat, stir in couscous mixture, pine nuts, and ½ cup Pecorino. Season with salt and pepper to taste.

Making Stuffed Acorn Squash

1. MICROWAVE SQUASH: Brush cut side of squash with oil and place, cut side down, on large plate. Cover and microwave until soft, 12 to 16 minutes.

2. MAKE COUSCOUS: Combine couscous, raisins, oil, and salt. Stir in boiling water, cover tightly with plastic, and let sit until liquid is absorbed and couscous is tender, about 5 minutes.

3. SAUTÉ SPINACH: Heat oil, add onion, and cook until softened. Stir in garlic and cook until fragrant, then add spinach and cook until wilted and most of liquid has evaporated.

4. FINISH UNDER BROILER: Mound couscous mixture into seasoned squash, pack lightly with back of spoon, then sprinkle with Pecorino. Broil until lightly browned, 4 to 5 minutes.

4. Adjust oven rack 8 inches from broiler element and heat broiler. Transfer squash, cut side up, to rimmed baking sheet and season with salt and pepper. Mound couscous mixture into squash, pack lightly with back of spoon, and sprinkle with remaining ¼ cup Pecorino. (Stuffed squash can be held at room temperature for 2 hours before baking.)

5. Broil until lightly browned, 4 to 5 minutes. Serve.

Stuffed Portobello Mushrooms

SERVES 4   **TOTAL TIME** 45 MINUTES   **FAST**

✓ **WHY THIS RECIPE WORKS:** Meaty portobello mushrooms make a great vehicle for stuffing given their large size and broad and rather flat shape. As with all stuffed mushrooms, ridding the mushrooms of excess moisture was a key step. We roasted the portobellos to both deepen their earthy flavor and eliminate excess moisture. For the filling, we sautéed two chopped mushroom caps which gave us a good base along with a hefty amount of microwaved and chopped baby spinach. Pungent Gorgonzola (rather than bread crumbs) kept the stuffing intact. Panko bread crumbs sprinkled on top of the stuffed mushrooms provided appealing crunch. After a few minutes under the broiler, the mushrooms emerged sizzling with a filling that was fresh-tasting and flavorful. Sherry is available in three forms: dry, cream (or sweet), and cooking. You can substitute cream sherry with a squeeze of fresh lemon juice for the dry sherry here, but do not substitute cooking sherry.

  5 **tablespoons extra-virgin olive oil**
10 **large portobello mushroom caps,**
      8 whole, 2 chopped fine
      Salt and pepper
12 **ounces (12 cups) baby spinach**
  2 **tablespoons water**
  1 **onion, chopped fine**
  4 **garlic cloves, minced**
  ½ **cup dry sherry**
  4 **ounces Gorgonzola cheese, crumbled (1 cup)**
  1 **cup walnuts, toasted and chopped**
  ¾ **cup panko bread crumbs**

1. Adjust oven rack to upper-middle position and heat oven to 500 degrees. Brush rimmed baking sheet with 1 tablespoon oil. Lay 8 mushroom caps, gill side down, on baking sheet and brush tops with 2 tablespoons oil. Roast until tender, 10 to 12 minutes. Remove baking sheet from oven, flip mushrooms gill side up, and season with salt and pepper.

2. Meanwhile, microwave spinach, water, and ¼ teaspoon salt in covered bowl until wilted, about 2 minutes. Drain spinach, let cool slightly, then wrap in clean dish towel and squeeze out excess liquid. Transfer spinach to cutting board and chop coarse.

3. Heat remaining 2 tablespoons oil in 12-inch skillet over medium-high heat until shimmering. Add onion and cook until softened, 5 to 7 minutes. Stir in chopped mushrooms and cook until they begin to release liquid, about 4 minutes.

4. Stir in garlic and cook until fragrant, about 30 seconds. Stir in sherry and cook until evaporated, about 2 minutes. Stir in chopped spinach, Gorgonzola, and walnuts and let heat through, about 1 minute. Season with salt and pepper to taste.

5. Spoon filling into roasted mushroom caps, press filling flat with back of spoon, and sprinkle with panko. (Stuffed mushrooms can be held at room temperature for 2 hours before baking.)

6. Bake until panko is golden and filling is hot, 2 to 4 minutes. Serve.

NOTES FROM THE TEST KITCHEN

Getting to Know Eggplant

Though it's commonly thought of as a vegetable, eggplant is actually a fruit. When shopping, look for eggplants that are firm, with smooth skin and no soft or brown spots. They should feel heavy for their size. Eggplants are very perishable and will get bitter if they overripen, so aim to use them within a day or two. They can be stored in a cool, dry place short-term, but for more than one or two days, refrigeration is best.

There are many varieties of eggplant. They can be anywhere from 2 to 12 inches long, round or oblong, ranging in color from dark purple to white. Here are a few of the most common varieties:

GLOBE: The most common variety in the United States, globe eggplant has a mild flavor and tender texture that works well in most applications. It is extremely watery, however, so often it's best to salt and drain it before cooking.

ITALIAN: Also called baby eggplant, Italian eggplant looks like a smaller version of a globe eggplant. It has moderately moist flesh and a distinct spicy flavor.

CHINESE: Chinese eggplant has firm, somewhat dry flesh with an intense, slightly sweet taste. It is best for sautéing, stewing, and stir-frying.

THAI: With crisp flesh and a grassy flavor with a hint of spiciness, Thai eggplant can be eaten raw or sautéed or stir-fried.

Bulgur mixed with Pecorino cheese and tomatoes makes the perfect filling for our stuffed eggplants.

Stuffed Eggplants with Bulgur

SERVES 4   **TOTAL TIME** 1 HOUR

✔ **WHY THIS RECIPE WORKS:** When baked, eggplants turn rich and creamy, losing the bitterness they have when raw. Italian eggplants, which are slightly smaller than the ubiquitous globe eggplants, are a perfect size and shape for stuffing when halved. We found that roasting them prior to stuffing was key to preventing the eggplant from turning watery and tasteless. The slight caramelizing effect of roasting them added a bit of depth, too. We then let the eggplant drain briefly (which got rid of excess liquid) before stuffing them. Bulgur, which requires only soaking before it's ready to eat, made a perfect filling base with its good texture and nutty flavor. Pecorino cheese added richness while tomatoes lent a nice bright flavor and a bit of moisture. Using fine- or medium-grind bulgur is important to the success of this recipe; do not use coarse-grind or cracked-wheat bulgur or skip the step of rinsing the bulgur before cooking. The time it takes for the bulgur to become tender and fluffy in step 3 will depend on the age and type of bulgur used. For more information on scoring eggplants, see page 22.

Bulgur

Bulgur is made from parboiled or steamed wheat kernels/berries that are then dried, partially stripped of their outer bran layer, and coarsely ground. Don't confuse it with cracked wheat, which is not parcooked. Most recipes using bulgur call for medium grind, which we rinse to remove any detritus and simply soak in water or another liquid until tender.

Bulgur is sold in four numbered grind sizes, but bulk bins and many U.S. brands often don't identify the grind by number or provide a description of the size—and when they do, they're inconsistent. This guide should help.

#1	Fine	The smallest grind, similar to couscous in appearance.
#2	Medium	The most widely available size in bulk bins and supermarket brands, with grains about the size of sesame seeds or kosher salt.
#3	Coarse	Slightly coarser than medium grind but sometimes interchangeable with it in recipes.
#4	Extra-Coarse	Nearly whole kernels that closely resemble steel-cut oats.

4 (10-ounce) Italian eggplants, halved lengthwise and scored
2 tablespoons extra-virgin olive oil
Salt and pepper
½ cup fine- or medium-grind bulgur wheat, rinsed and drained
¼ cup water
1 onion, chopped fine
3 garlic cloves, minced
2 teaspoons minced fresh oregano or ½ teaspoon dried
¼ teaspoon ground cinnamon
Pinch cayenne pepper
1 pound plum tomatoes, cored, seeded, and chopped
2 ounces Pecorino Romano cheese, grated (1 cup)
2 tablespoons pine nuts, toasted
2 teaspoons red wine vinegar
2 tablespoons minced fresh parsley

1. Adjust oven racks to upper-middle and lowest positions, place rimmed baking sheet lined with parchment paper on lowest rack, and heat oven to 400 degrees.

2. Brush scored sides of eggplant with 1 tablespoon oil and season with salt and pepper. Lay eggplant, cut side down, on hot baking sheet and roast until flesh is tender, 40 to 50 minutes. Transfer eggplant, cut side down, to paper towel–lined baking sheet and let drain.

3. Meanwhile, toss bulgur with water in large bowl and let sit until grains are tender and fluffy, 20 to 40 minutes.

4. Heat remaining 1 tablespoon oil in 12-inch skillet over medium heat until shimmering. Add onion and cook until softened, 5 to 7 minutes. Stir in garlic, oregano, cinnamon, cayenne, and ½ teaspoon salt and cook until fragrant, about 30 seconds. Stir in soaked bulgur, tomatoes, ¾ cup Pecorino, pine nuts, and vinegar and let warm through, about 1 minute. Season with salt and pepper to taste.

5. Return eggplant, cut side up, to parchment-lined baking sheet. Using two forks, gently push eggplant flesh to sides to make room for filling. Mound bulgur mixture into eggplant shells, pack lightly with back of spoon, and sprinkle with remaining ¼ cup Pecorino. (Stuffed eggplant can be held at room temperature for 2 hours before baking.)

6. Bake on upper-middle rack until cheese is melted, 5 to 10 minutes. Sprinkle with parsley and serve.

Easy Stuffed Zucchini

SERVES 4　　**TOTAL TIME** 45 MINUTES　**FAST**

✔ **WHY THIS RECIPE WORKS:** For vegetarian stuffed zucchini, we nixed the usual ground beef and swapped in soy crumbles. To give the flavor of the crumbles a lift, we combined them with some sautéed onion, garlic, and red pepper flakes. Marinara sauce worked well to bind the crumbles while preshredded Italian cheese blend added good depth of flavor. To ensure that the zucchini cooked up tender, we hollowed them out and roasted them on a preheated baking sheet before mounding them with the filling. Topped with more cheese, our stuffed zucchini went back into the oven for a final warmthrough. For more information on soy crumbles, see page 298.

4 (8-ounce) zucchini, halved lengthwise and seeded
2 tablespoons vegetable oil
Salt and pepper
1 onion, chopped fine
3 garlic cloves, minced
Pinch red pepper flakes
12 ounces soy crumbles
1½ cups (6 ounces) shredded Italian cheese blend
1 cup marinara sauce
¼ cup chopped fresh basil

Soy crumbles mixed with sautéed onion and garlic and cheese give our stuffed zucchini a meaty texture.

1. Adjust oven rack to middle position, place rimmed baking sheet lined with parchment paper on rack, and heat oven to 400 degrees. Brush cut sides of zucchini with 1 tablespoon oil and season with salt and pepper. Lay zucchini, cut side down, on hot baking sheet and roast until slightly softened and skins are wrinkled, 10 to 12 minutes. Remove from oven and flip zucchini cut side up.

2. Meanwhile, heat remaining 1 tablespoon oil in 12-inch nonstick skillet over medium-high heat until shimmering. Add onion and cook until softened, 5 to 7 minutes. Stir

Seeding Zucchini

To make room for filling, use a soupspoon to scrape out seeds and flesh until walls of each zucchini half are ¼ inch thick.

in garlic and pepper flakes and cook until fragrant, about 30 seconds. Stir in soy crumbles and let heat through, about 2 minutes. Off heat, stir in 1 cup cheese, ½ cup marinara, and 3 tablespoons basil.

3. Mound filling evenly into zucchini and pack lightly with back of spoon. Spoon remaining ½ cup marinara sauce over top and sprinkle with remaining ½ cup cheese. (Stuffed zucchini can be held at room temperature for 2 hours before baking.)

4. Bake until filling is heated through and cheese is melted, 8 to 10 minutes. Sprinkle with remaining 1 tablespoon basil and serve.

Zucchini Fritters with Cucumber-Yogurt Sauce

SERVES 4 TO 6   **TOTAL TIME** 45 MINUTES   `FAST`

✔ **WHY THIS RECIPE WORKS:** These zucchini fritters, packed with feta cheese and dill and served with a yogurt sauce, make an appealing vegetarian entrée or side dish. The key was to prevent the zucchini, which has a high moisture content, from turning the fritters soggy. Simply salting the shredded zucchini, letting it drain, and then squeezing it out in a clean dish towel solved this issue. To allow the delicate flavor of the zucchini to shine through we avoided heavy batters and bound the zucchini with just a few eggs and a little flour. Use the large holes of a box grater or the shredding disk of a food processor to shred the zucchini and cucumber. Do not let the squeeze-dried zucchini sit on its own for too long or it will turn brown. Make sure to squeeze the zucchini until it is completely dry or the fritters will fall apart in the skillet. Serve with lemon wedges.

1 **pound zucchini, shredded**
  Salt and pepper
1 **cup plain Greek yogurt**
½ **cup extra-virgin olive oil**
¼ **cup minced fresh dill**
2 **garlic cloves, minced**
1 **cucumber, peeled, halved lengthwise, seeded, and shredded**
8 **ounces feta cheese, crumbled (2 cups)**
2 **scallions, minced**
2 **large eggs, lightly beaten**
¼ **cup all-purpose flour**

Cucumber-yogurt sauce is the perfect accompaniment to these feta cheese and dill-packed zucchini fritters.

1. Adjust oven rack to middle position and heat oven to 200 degrees. Toss shredded zucchini with 1 teaspoon salt and let drain in fine-mesh strainer for 10 minutes.

2. Meanwhile, whisk yogurt, 2 tablespoons oil, 2 tablespoons dill, and half of garlic together in medium bowl. Stir in cucumber and season with salt and pepper to taste. Cover and refrigerate until needed.

3. Wrap zucchini in clean dish towel, squeeze out excess liquid, and transfer to large bowl. Stir in feta, scallions, eggs, remaining 2 tablespoons dill, remaining garlic, and ¼ teaspoon pepper. Sprinkle flour over mixture and stir to incorporate.

4. Heat 3 tablespoons oil in 12-inch nonstick skillet over medium heat until shimmering. Drop 2-tablespoon-size portions of batter into skillet and use back of spoon to press batter into 2-inch-wide fritters (you should fit about 6 fritters in pan at a time). Fry until golden brown on both sides, 4 to 6 minutes.

5. Transfer fritters to paper towel–lined baking sheet and keep warm in oven. Wipe skillet clean with paper towels and repeat with remaining 3 tablespoons oil and remaining batter. Serve fritters warm or at room temperature with cucumber sauce.

Barley Risotto with Roasted Butternut Squash

SERVES 4 TO 6   **TOTAL TIME** 1 HOUR 45 MINUTES

✔ **WHY THIS RECIPE WORKS:** Most people think of barley as a staple used to make beer and whiskey, or as an addition to soup. We found that preparing barley using a risotto-style cooking method was a great way to make a simple vegetarian dinner. We used pearl barley in this dish for two reasons—it is widely available in supermarkets and, because the bran has been removed from the outside of the grain, the starchy interior is exposed, which helps to create a supple, velvety sauce when simmered (much the same as risotto made with Arborio rice). We used our well-tested risotto cooking method with one minor change; we added more liquid, because barley takes a bit longer to cook. Serve with grated Parmesan cheese.

- 2 **pounds butternut squash, peeled, seeded, and cut into ½-inch cubes (6 cups)**
- 2 **tablespoons olive oil**
-   **Salt and pepper**
- 4 **cups chicken broth**
- 4 **cups water**
- 1 **onion, minced**
- 2 **garlic cloves, minced**
- 1½ **cups pearl barley, rinsed**
- 1 **cup dry white wine**
- 2 **ounces Parmesan cheese, grated (1 cup)**
- 1 **tablespoon unsalted butter**
- 1 **teaspoon minced fresh sage**
- ⅛ **teaspoon ground nutmeg**

1. Adjust oven rack to upper-middle position and heat oven to 450 degrees. Toss squash with 1 tablespoon oil and season with salt and pepper. Spread squash out onto parchment paper–lined rimmed baking sheet and roast until tender and golden brown, about 30 minutes.

2. Meanwhile, bring broth and water to simmer in medium saucepan. Reduce heat to lowest possible setting and cover to keep warm.

3. Heat remaining 1 tablespoon oil in large saucepan over medium heat until shimmering. Add onion and cook until onion is softened, 5 to 7 minutes. Stir in garlic and cook until fragrant, about 30 seconds. Stir in barley and cook, stirring often, until lightly toasted and aromatic, about 4 minutes. Stir in wine and cook until it has been completely absorbed, about 2 minutes.

4. Stir in 3 cups warm broth and half of roasted squash. Simmer, stirring occasionally, until liquid is absorbed and bottom of pan is dry, 22 to 25 minutes.

5. Stir in 2 cups more warm broth and simmer, stirring occasionally, until liquid is absorbed and bottom of pan is dry, 15 to 18 minutes.

6. Continue to cook risotto, stirring often and adding remaining broth as needed to prevent pan bottom from becoming dry, until barley is cooked through but still somewhat firm in center, 15 to 20 minutes. Off heat, stir in remaining roasted squash, Parmesan, butter, sage, and nutmeg. Season with salt and pepper to taste and serve.

Cheesy Polenta with Eggplant and Tomato Ragu

SERVES 4   TOTAL TIME 40 MINUTES   **FAST**

✔ **WHY THIS RECIPE WORKS:** A rich and hearty ragu spooned over cheesy polenta is a vegetarian comfort classic. But cooking traditional polenta from scratch requires constant attention, so here we turned to quick-cooking instant polenta, which takes just a few minutes to whip together. For the ragu we paired eggplant and tomatoes. To concentrate the flavor of the eggplant, we first browned it in a skillet, adding garlic and then deglazing the pan with the tomatoes and their juice. Letting this mixture simmer for just a few minutes thickened it and gave us a rich-tasting ragu. Be aware that shopping for polenta can be confusing—instant polenta can look just like traditional polenta and is often identifiable only by the word "instant" in its title, which in our experience can be slightly hidden. Be sure to use instant polenta here; traditional polenta requires a slightly different cooking method. Leaving the skin on the eggplant helps keep the pieces intact during cooking.

Polenta, a classic comfort food, makes a meal when topped with a rich ragu of eggplant and tomato.

    1   **(28-ounce) can whole peeled tomatoes**
    ¼   **cup extra-virgin olive oil**
    1   **pound eggplant, cut into ¾-inch chunks**
        Salt and pepper
    3   **garlic cloves, minced**
    4   **cups water**
    1   **cup instant polenta**
    1½ **ounces Parmesan cheese, grated (¾ cups),**
        plus extra for serving
    ⅓   **cup chopped fresh basil**

1. Pour tomatoes and their juice into bowl and crush with hands into 1-inch pieces; set aside.

2. Heat oil in 12-inch nonstick skillet over medium-high heat until shimmering. Add eggplant and ¼ teaspoon salt and cook until beginning to brown, 5 to 7 minutes. Reduce heat to medium and continue to cook, stirring occasionally, until

eggplant is tender, about 5 minutes. Stir in garlic and cook until fragrant, about 30 seconds. Stir in tomatoes and simmer until slightly thickened, about 2 minutes. Season with salt and pepper to taste; cover and keep warm.

3. Meanwhile, bring water to boil in large saucepan. Gradually whisk in polenta and ½ teaspoon salt. Cook over medium heat, whisking constantly, until very thick, about 5 minutes. Off heat, stir in Parmesan and season with salt and pepper to taste.

4. Portion polenta into 4 individual serving bowls, top with eggplant mixture, and sprinkle with basil. Serve with extra Parmesan.

VARIATION

Cheesy Polenta with Zucchini, Tomatoes, and Fresh Mozzarella

SERVES 4   TOTAL TIME 30 MINUTES   **FAST**

Be sure to use instant polenta here; traditional polenta requires a slightly different cooking method. Don't skip the step of freezing the mozzarella or the cheese will become chewy in the finished dish. Either store-bought or homemade pesto will work fine here; see page 410 for our pesto recipe.

    4   ounces fresh mozzarella cheese, cut into ½-inch cubes
    2   tablespoons olive oil
    1   pound zucchini, halved lengthwise and sliced
        ¼ inch thick
        Salt and pepper
   12   ounces cherry tomatoes, halved if small or
        quartered if large
    ½   cup basil pesto
    4   cups water
    1   cup instant polenta
   1½   ounces Parmesan cheese, grated (¾ cup),
        plus extra for serving

1. Place mozzarella on plate and freeze until slightly firm, about 10 minutes.

2. Heat oil in 12-inch nonstick skillet over medium-high heat until shimmering. Add zucchini and ¼ teaspoon salt and cook until beginning to brown, about 5 minutes. Stir in tomatoes and cook until zucchini is tender, about 3 minutes. Off heat, stir in pesto and season with salt and pepper to taste; cover and keep warm.

3. Meanwhile, bring water to boil in large saucepan. Gradually whisk in polenta and ½ teaspoon salt. Cook over medium heat, whisking constantly, until very thick, about 5 minutes. Off heat, stir in Parmesan and season with salt and pepper to taste.

4. Stir chilled mozzarella into zucchini mixture. Portion polenta into 4 individual serving bowls and top with zucchini mixture. Serve with extra Parmesan.

MARINATED FETA CHEESE

Marinated feta combines several ingredients—feta cheese, olive oil, herbs, spices, and peppercorns—in one. This multitasker comes in handy when we need not just tangy bites of cheese, but also an aromatic backbone and a flavorful fat (the marinade) for cooking. You can find marinated feta at supermarket olive bars or packed in jars near the olives. You can also make it at home with this simple recipe.

MARINATED FETA CHEESE

Combine 1 cup extra-virgin olive oil, 4 thinly sliced garlic cloves, 1½ teaspoons grated lemon zest, ½ teaspoon red pepper flakes, ½ teaspoon salt, and ¼ teaspoon dried thyme in small saucepan. Cook over low heat until garlic is softened, about 10 minutes. Off heat, stir in 12 ounces feta, cut into ½-inch cubes, and let sit at room temperature for 1 hour. Serve. (Marinated feta can be refrigerated for up to 1 week.)

Orzo Primavera with Feta

SERVES 4   **TOTAL TIME** 40 MINUTES   **FAST**

✔ **WHY THIS RECIPE WORKS:** We wanted to make the most of a handful of spring vegetables that didn't require excessive peeling, chopping, and blanching for a creamy orzo dish that rivaled pasta primavera. We bypassed store-bought broth and made our own by simmering the tough leek greens and asparagus ends in salted water. Following our standard method for making risotto, we toasted the orzo, sautéed the leek whites in the savory oil from marinated feta for an aromatic backbone, and then added our homemade broth to cook the orzo. Adding the asparagus to the skillet partway through cooking and stirring in the peas at the end ensured they were perfectly done and retained their color.

    1   pound leeks, white and light green parts halved
        lengthwise, sliced thin, and washed thoroughly; dark
        green parts chopped coarse and washed thoroughly
    1   pound asparagus, trimmed and cut on bias into ½-inch
        lengths; ends reserved
    4   cups water, plus extra as needed
        Salt and pepper
   1½   cups orzo
   1½   cups (6 ounces) crumbled marinated feta cheese,
        plus 2 tablespoons marinade
    ½   cup frozen peas
    2   teaspoons lemon juice

1. Bring leek greens, asparagus ends, water, and ¼ teaspoon salt to simmer in medium saucepan, then lower heat to medium-low and simmer gently for 10 minutes. Strain through fine-mesh strainer into 4-cup measuring cup, pressing on solids to extract as much liquid as possible. Add water as needed until liquid measures 3½ cups.

2. Toast orzo in 12-inch nonstick skillet over medium-high heat until golden, 3 to 5 minutes; transfer to bowl. Add feta marinade, leek whites, and ½ teaspoon salt to now-empty skillet and cook over medium heat until softened, about 5 minutes.

3. Stir in toasted orzo and 3 cups strained broth, cover, and simmer gently for 5 minutes. Stir in asparagus spears, cover, and continue to cook, stirring often, until asparagus is nearly tender, about 7 minutes. Stir in peas, cover, and cook until heated through, about 1 minute.

4. Off heat, stir in lemon juice and season with salt and pepper to taste. Loosen consistency of orzo with remaining ½ cup broth as needed. Sprinkle with feta and serve.

Farro's slightly sweet and nutty flavor pairs well with a wild mushroom ragout.

Wild Mushroom Ragout with Farro

SERVES 4   TOTAL TIME 45 MINUTES   **FAST**

✔ **WHY THIS RECIPE WORKS:** Farro is a whole grain popular in Italy and we love it for its slightly sweet, nutty flavor and chewy texture. We decided to give this dish a simple Italian profile and pair it with a mushroom ragout. Chunks of portobellos and other mushrooms add texture while dried porcini add flavor and depth. For the best flavor, we prefer to use a combination of white, shiitake, and oyster mushrooms; however, you can choose just one or two varieties if you like. The woody stems of shiitakes are unpleasant to eat so be sure to remove them. Drizzle individual portions with good balsamic vinegar before serving if desired. For more information on farro, see page 509.

1½ cups farro
3½ cups vegetable broth
    Salt and pepper
1 pound portobello mushroom caps, halved and sliced ½ inch wide

18 ounces assorted mushrooms, trimmed and halved if small or quartered if large
2 tablespoons extra-virgin olive oil
1 onion, chopped fine
½ ounce dried porcini mushrooms, rinsed and minced
3 garlic cloves, minced
1 teaspoon minced fresh thyme or ¼ teaspoon dried
¼ cup dry Madeira
1 (14.5-ounce) can diced tomatoes, drained and chopped
2 tablespoons minced fresh parsley

1. Simmer farro and broth in large saucepan over medium heat until farro is tender and creamy, 20 to 25 minutes. Season with salt and pepper to taste; cover and keep warm.

2. Meanwhile, microwave portobello and assorted mushrooms in covered bowl until tender, 6 to 8 minutes. Drain, reserving mushroom juices.

3. Heat oil in Dutch oven over medium-high heat until shimmering. Add onion and porcini and cook until softened and lightly browned, 5 to 7 minutes. Stir in drained mushrooms and cook, stirring often, until mushrooms are dry and lightly browned, about 5 minutes.

4. Stir in garlic and thyme and cook until fragrant, about 30 seconds. Stir in Madeira and reserved mushroom juices, scraping up any browned bits. Stir in tomatoes and simmer gently until sauce is slightly thickened, about 8 minutes. Off heat, stir in parsley and season with salt and pepper to taste. Portion farro into 4 individual serving bowls and top with mushroom mixture. Serve.

Quinoa Patties with Spinach and Sun-Dried Tomatoes

SERVES 4   TOTAL TIME 2 HOURS

✔ **WHY THIS RECIPE WORKS:** For these appealing quinoa patties we used classic white quinoa, which softened enough for us to shape, and skipped the usual toasting step as it causes the grains to separate. One whole egg plus one yolk and cheese bound the grains together perfectly while chilling the patties for 30 minutes further ensured that they stayed together. Cooking the patties on the stovetop over medium heat created a crust on the outside while allowing the interiors to remain moist. We like the convenience of prewashed quinoa. If you buy unwashed quinoa (or if you are unsure if it's washed), rinse it before cooking to remove its bitter protective coating (called saponin). For more information on quinoa, see page 509.

½ cup oil-packed sun-dried tomatoes, chopped coarse, plus 1 tablespoon oil

4 scallions, chopped fine

4 garlic cloves, minced

2 cups water

1 cup prewashed white quinoa

1 teaspoon salt

1 large egg plus one large yolk, lightly beaten

2 ounces (2 cups) baby spinach, chopped

2 ounces Monterey Jack cheese, shredded (½ cup)

½ teaspoon grated lemon zest plus 2 teaspoons juice

2 tablespoons vegetable oil

1. Heat tomato oil in large saucepan over medium heat until shimmering. Add scallions and cook until softened, 3 to 5 minutes. Stir in garlic and cook until fragrant, about 30 seconds. Stir in water, quinoa, and salt and bring to simmer. Reduce heat to medium-low, cover, and continue to simmer until quinoa is tender, 16 to 18 minutes.

2. Remove pan from heat and let sit, covered, until liquid is fully absorbed, about 10 minutes. Transfer quinoa to large bowl and let cool for 15 minutes. Stir in sun-dried tomatoes, egg and yolk, spinach, Monterey Jack, and lemon zest and juice.

3. Line rimmed baking sheet with parchment paper. Divide quinoa mixture into 8 equal portions, pack firmly into ½-inch-thick patties, and place on prepared sheet. Refrigerate, uncovered, until patties are chilled and firm, about 30 minutes.

4. Heat 1 tablespoon vegetable oil in 12-inch nonstick skillet over medium heat until shimmering. Carefully lay 4 chilled patties in hot skillet. Cook until set up and well browned on first side, 8 to 10 minutes. Gently flip patties. Cook until golden on second side, 8 to 10 minutes.

5. Transfer patties to plate and tent with aluminum foil. Return now-empty skillet to medium heat and repeat with remaining 1 tablespoon vegetable oil and remaining patties. Serve.

Cooking Quinoa Patties

Carefully lay 4 chilled patties in hot skillet. Cook until set up and well browned on first side, 8 to 10 minutes. Gently flip patties. Cook until golden on second side, 8 to 10 minutes.

Kale roasted in the oil from marinated feta adds texture and flavor to this baked quinoa dish.

Baked Quinoa with Roasted Kale and Chickpeas

SERVES 4   **TOTAL TIME** 50 MINUTES

☑ **WHY THIS RECIPE WORKS:** Quinoa makes a stellar side dish, but we wanted this grain to be at the center of a robust, flavorful vegetarian casserole with layers of flavor and a cheesy topping. At first, we baked a simple mixture of quinoa, chickpeas, lemon zest, and scallions. Tasters liked the flavors, but wanted more texture and volume. Kale proved to be the perfect solution, and by roasting it briefly with oil from the marinated feta before baking it with the quinoa, we boosted its earthy flavor and eliminated some excess moisture. Fresh tomatoes and a squirt of lemon juice, folded in toward the end of baking, ensured our dish was bright-tasting. Topped with a sprinkling of marinated feta cheese, this baked quinoa was ready to take center stage. We like the convenience of prewashed quinoa. If you buy unwashed quinoa (or if you are unsure if it's washed), rinse it before cooking to remove its bitter protective coating (called saponin). For more information on quinoa, see page 509.

    6 ounces kale, stemmed and chopped
1½ cups (6 ounces) crumbled marinated feta cheese,
    plus 3 tablespoons marinade
    1 (15-ounce) can chickpeas, rinsed
    1 cup prewashed white quinoa
    Salt and pepper
    1 teaspoon grated lemon zest plus 2 teaspoons juice
1½ cups water
    2 plum tomatoes, cored and chopped fine

1. Adjust oven rack to middle position and heat oven to 450 degrees. Toss kale with 1 tablespoon feta marinade, spread in even layer on aluminum foil–lined baking sheet, and roast until crisp and lightly browned at edges, 6 to 8 minutes.

2. Toss roasted kale with chickpeas, quinoa, remaining 2 tablespoons marinade, ½ teaspoon salt, and ¼ teaspoon pepper and transfer to 8-inch square baking dish.

3. Microwave lemon zest and water in covered bowl until just boiling, about 2 minutes. Pour hot water over quinoa mixture and cover dish tightly with foil. Bake until quinoa is tender and no liquid remains, 20 to 25 minutes.

4. Remove dish from oven and fluff quinoa with fork. Gently fold in tomatoes and lemon juice and sprinkle with feta. Continue to bake casserole, uncovered, until feta is heated through, 6 to 8 minutes. Serve.

A combination of finely chopped chickpeas along with larger pieces gives these chickpea cakes just the right texture.

Chickpea Cakes with Cucumber-Yogurt Sauce

SERVES 6   TOTAL TIME 50 MINUTES

✔ **WHY THIS RECIPE WORKS:** Like black beans, chickpeas make great veggie burgers. We found that unlike beans, however, chickpeas needed to go into the food processor to help them break down, though getting the right texture took a bit of trial and error. If underprocessed, the beans were too coarse and didn't hold together; if overprocessed, we ended up with hummus. We wanted a combination of two textures: some finely chopped chickpeas to help bind the patties, along with some larger pieces for texture. To bind the patties, two eggs did the trick, and for richness we added yogurt and olive oil. A combination of garam masala and cayenne pepper ensured these patties were anything but bland. Serving the patties with a fresh and cooling raita, a cucumber and yogurt sauce, helped brighten the dish. Avoid overmixing the chickpea mixture in step 2 or the cakes will have a mealy texture. Use the large holes of a box grater or the shredding disk of a food processor to shred the cucumber. Serve with lime wedges.

    1 cucumber, peeled, halved lengthwise,
      seeded, and shredded
      Salt and pepper
1¼ cups plain Greek yogurt
    6 scallions, sliced thin
    ¼ cup minced fresh cilantro
    2 (15-ounce) cans chickpeas, rinsed
    2 large eggs
    6 tablespoons extra-virgin olive oil
    1 teaspoon garam masala
    ⅛ teaspoon cayenne pepper
    1 cup panko bread crumbs
    1 shallot, minced

1. Toss cucumber with ½ teaspoon salt and let drain in fine-mesh strainer for 15 minutes. Combine drained cucumber, ¾ cup yogurt, 2 tablespoons scallions, and 1 tablespoon cilantro in bowl and season with salt and pepper to taste.

2. Meanwhile, pulse chickpeas in food processor to coarse puree with few large pieces remaining, about 8 pulses. Whisk eggs, 2 tablespoons oil, garam masala, cayenne, and

⅛ teaspoon salt together in medium bowl. Gently stir in processed chickpeas, panko, shallot, remaining ½ cup yogurt, remaining scallions, and remaining 3 tablespoons cilantro until just combined. Divide chickpea mixture into 6 equal portions and lightly pack into 1-inch-thick patties.

3. Heat 2 tablespoons oil in 12-inch nonstick skillet over medium heat until shimmering. Carefully lay 3 patties in hot skillet. Cook until set up and well browned on first side, 4 to 5 minutes. Gently flip patties. Cook until golden on second side, 4 to 5 minutes.

4. Transfer cakes to plate and tent with aluminum foil. Return now-empty skillet to medium heat and repeat with remaining 2 tablespoons oil and remaining patties. Serve with cucumber-yogurt sauce.

Vegetable Tagine with Chickpeas and Olives

SERVES 4   **TOTAL TIME** 45 MINUTES   **FAST**

☑ **WHY THIS RECIPE WORKS:** Traditional North African tagines—fragrant, spiced stews of vegetables, beans, dried fruits, and slowly braised meats—are long-simmered affairs with myriad ingredients. Making this recipe vegetarian meant we didn't need to slowly braise a tough cut of meat. Microwaving the potatoes and carrots before adding them to the pot further streamlined the process, making this dish perfect for a last-minute or weeknight supper. Some tagines call for a laundry list of spices; we use garam masala, a blend of several spices, plus paprika. Olives and lemon round out the Moroccan flavors. Look for Greek green olives in the supermarket's refrigerated section (packed in brine) or salad bar. Often, fresh green olives are not sold pitted but rather are cracked or whole, so you may need to remove the pits yourself. Serve with couscous or rice.

1   **pound red potatoes, cut into ½-inch chunks**
1   **pound carrots, peeled and cut into ½-inch pieces**
¼   **cup extra-virgin olive oil**
     Salt and pepper
1   **onion, halved and sliced thin**
4   **(3-inch) strips lemon zest, sliced into matchsticks, plus 2 tablespoons juice**
5   **garlic cloves, minced**
4   **teaspoons paprika**
2   **teaspoons garam masala**

We use garam masala and paprika to spice our Moroccan-style vegetable tagine.

3   **cups vegetable broth**
2   **(15-ounce) cans chickpeas, rinsed**
½   **cup pitted Greek green olives, halved**
½   **cup golden raisins**
¼   **cup minced fresh cilantro**

1. Combine potatoes, carrots, 2 tablespoons oil, 1 teaspoon salt, and ½ teaspoon pepper in bowl, cover, and microwave until vegetables begin to soften, about 10 minutes.

2. Meanwhile, cook remaining 2 tablespoons oil, onion, and lemon zest in Dutch oven over medium-high heat until onion begins to brown, about 8 minutes. Stir in garlic, paprika, and garam masala and cook until fragrant, about 30 seconds.

3. Stir in microwaved potatoes and carrots and coat with spices. Stir in broth, chickpeas, olives, and raisins. Cover and simmer gently until flavors blend, about 10 minutes. Uncover and simmer until vegetables are tender and sauce is slightly thickened, about 7 minutes. Stir in lemon juice and cilantro and season with salt and pepper to taste. Serve.

Skillet Rice and Beans with Corn and Fresh Tomatoes

SERVES 6   **TOTAL TIME** 50 MINUTES

✓ **WHY THIS RECIPE WORKS:** Rice and beans are a familiar combination the world over, but often the recipes require lots of work only to produce a dull, overcooked dish. We wanted a recipe for a delicious weeknight meal with fresh-tasting vegetables, plump beans, and soft rice and began by sautéing onions and corn. Garlic, cumin, and cayenne contributed their potent flavors. Toasting the rice briefly before stirring in broth and black beans ensured that it would soak up all of the flavors and become tender and plump. We finished by sprinkling tomatoes, scallions, cilantro, and lime juice over the dish before serving. A few variations gave us enough recipes to never get tired of this traditional pairing. We prefer the flavor of fresh corn; however, 1½ cups frozen corn, thawed and patted dry, can be substituted.

2	tablespoons extra-virgin olive oil
12	ounces grape tomatoes, quartered
5	scallions, sliced thin
¼	cup minced fresh cilantro
1	tablespoon lime juice
	Salt and pepper
1	onion, chopped fine
2	ears corn, kernels cut from cobs
4	garlic cloves, minced
1	teaspoon ground cumin
	Pinch cayenne pepper
1	cup long-grain white rice, rinsed
3	cups vegetable broth
2	(15-ounce) cans black beans, rinsed

1. Combine 1 tablespoon oil, tomatoes, scallions, cilantro, and lime juice in bowl and season with salt and pepper to taste; set aside for serving.

2. Heat remaining 1 tablespoon oil in 12-inch nonstick skillet over medium-high heat until shimmering. Add onion and cook until softened and lightly browned, 5 to 7 minutes. Stir in corn and cook until lightly browned, about 4 minutes.

3. Stir in garlic, cumin, and cayenne and cook until fragrant, about 30 seconds. Stir in rice and coat with spices, about 1 minute. Stir in broth and beans and bring to simmer. Cover and simmer gently, stirring occasionally, until rice is tender and liquid is absorbed, about 20 minutes.

4. Season with salt and pepper to taste, sprinkle tomato mixture over top, and serve.

NOTES FROM THE TEST KITCHEN

Rinsing Canned Beans

Canned beans are made by pressure-cooking dried beans directly in the can with water, salt, and preservatives. As the beans cook, starches and proteins leach into the liquid, thickening it. In dishes that feature many bold flavors and contrasting textures, such as black bean burgers, rinsing the beans didn't affect the taste.

However, in bean-only recipes, such as hummus, we found that rinsed beans were brighter in flavor and less pasty than versions made with unrinsed beans. So while rinsing the beans may not be necessary for a robust dish like chili, a thick, salty bean liquid does have the potential to throw a simpler recipe off-kilter. As rinsing canned beans only takes a few seconds, we recommend doing so.

VARIATIONS

Skillet Rice and Chickpeas with Coconut Milk

Substitute 2 finely chopped yellow bell peppers for corn, 1½ teaspoons garam masala for cumin, and canned chickpeas for black beans. Substitute 1 cup coconut milk for 1 cup broth.

Spanish-Style Skillet Rice and Chickpeas

Substitute 2 finely chopped red bell peppers for corn, pinch crumbled saffron threads for cumin, and canned chickpeas for black beans.

Black Bean Burgers

SERVES 6   **TOTAL TIME** 40 MINUTES   **FAST**

✓ **WHY THIS RECIPE WORKS:** A reliable staple for any vegetarian cook, black beans often appear in recipes as the primary source of protein. Recently, black beans have emerged as the chief component of vegetarian burgers—a healthy, satisfying meal. When freshly made, these burgers are a far cry from the heavy, dry, frozen varieties of veggie burgers. We found that a 3:1 ratio of mashed beans to whole beans made a burger that was not too soft, nor too dense and pasty. To ensure that the burgers held together once cooked, we added two eggs and also incorporated bread crumbs—binding ingredients often used in meatloaf and meatball recipes. It worked like a charm and the eggs provided more protein and added richness. Avoid overmixing the bean mixture in step 1 or the burgers will have a mealy texture. Serve with a salad and your favorite burger toppings.

Mashed and whole black beans give these tasty and easy-to-make burgers the perfect texture.

2 (15-ounce) cans black beans, rinsed
2 large eggs
5 tablespoons olive oil
1 teaspoon ground cumin
½ teaspoon salt
⅛ teaspoon cayenne pepper
1 cup panko bread crumbs
1 red bell pepper, stemmed, seeded, and chopped fine
¼ cup minced fresh cilantro
1 shallot, minced

1. Place 2½ cups beans in large bowl and mash them with potato masher until mostly smooth. In separate bowl, whisk eggs, 1 tablespoon oil, cumin, salt, and cayenne together. Stir egg mixture, remaining beans, panko, bell pepper, cilantro, and shallot into mashed beans until just combined. Divide mixture into 6 equal portions and lightly pack into 1-inch-thick burgers.

2. Heat 2 tablespoons oil in 12-inch nonstick skillet over medium heat until shimmering. Carefully lay 3 burgers in skillet and cook until well browned on both sides, 4 to 5 minutes per side.

3. Transfer burgers to plate and tent loosely with aluminum foil. Return now-empty skillet to medium heat and repeat with remaining 2 tablespoons oil and remaining burgers. Serve.

VARIATION

Black Bean Burgers with Corn and Chipotle Chiles

Substitute 1 tablespoon minced canned chipotle chile in adobo sauce for cayenne. Reduce amount of red bell pepper to ¼ cup and add ¾ cup frozen corn, thawed and patted dry, to bean mixture.

Indian-Spiced Red Lentils

SERVES 6   **TOTAL TIME** 50 MINUTES

✔ WHY THIS RECIPE WORKS: A blend of aromatic spices along with earthy lentils makes dal, or spiced stewed lentils, a satisfying vegetarian meal as well as a side for any Indian main dish. To cut down on ingredients, we turned to garam masala to add the best flavoring. It took some trial and error to get the consistency just right—too much water and coconut milk made it thin and soupy; too little and it was thick and pasty. The lentils were tender and starting to disintegrate after only about 20 minutes of simmering. Then we stirred in chopped fresh tomatoes and minced cilantro to finish the dish. For more information on garam masala, see page 149. Serve with rice.

2 tablespoons vegetable oil
1 onion, chopped fine
   Salt and pepper
4 garlic cloves, minced
1 tablespoon grated fresh ginger
1 teaspoon garam masala
3 cups water
1¼ cups red lentils, picked over and rinsed
1 cup coconut milk
3 plum tomatoes, cored, seeded, and chopped
¼ cup minced fresh cilantro

1. Heat oil in large saucepan over medium heat until shimmering. Add onion and 1 teaspoon salt and cook until softened, about 5 minutes. Stir in garlic, ginger, and garam masala and cook until fragrant, about 15 seconds.

2. Stir in water, lentils, and coconut milk and bring to boil. Reduce to simmer, partially cover, and cook until lentils break down to form thick puree, 20 to 30 minutes.

3. Stir in tomatoes and cilantro and season with salt and pepper to taste. Serve.

A drizzle of *crema* made from sour cream and lime juice complements the rest of the ingredients in our tostadas.

THREE WAYS TO MAKE TOSTADAS

The Mexican tostada is a close relative of the tortilla chip—only bigger, flatter, and less salty. Traditionally, tostadas are made from stale corn tortillas that are toasted or deep-fried to make them more flavorful as well as sturdy enough to support a thick layer of refried beans or forkfuls of shredded meat. And although you can buy tostadas, it is easy enough to make your own. Below are three ways to do so (listed in order of the test kitchen's preference).

FRY: Heat ¾ cup vegetable oil in 8-inch heavy-bottomed skillet over medium heat to 350 degrees. Poke center of each 6-inch tortilla 3 or 4 times with fork. Fry tortillas one at a time, keeping them flat and submerged with potato masher, until crisp and lightly browned, 45 to 60 seconds. Drain on paper towel–lined plate and season with salt to taste.

BAKE: Spray 6-inch tortillas lightly with vegetable oil spray and spread out over rimmed baking sheet(s). Bake in 450-degree oven until lightly browned and crisp, about 10 minutes.

MICROWAVE: Place 6-inch tortillas in single layer on large plate and microwave, flipping every 30 seconds, until lightly browned and crisp, about 1 to 1½ minutes.

Vegetable and Bean Tostadas

SERVES 4 TO 6   **TOTAL TIME** 35 MINUTES **FAST**

WHY THIS RECIPE WORKS: These vegetarian-friendly tostadas boast big flavor and appealing textures, combining refried beans, sautéed onions and peppers, a crunchy coleslaw topping spiced with jalapeños, and a drizzle of a cool *crema* (sour cream mixed with lime juice). We used coleslaw mix tossed with the brine from jarred jalapeños to make an easy slaw. Canned refried beans saved time, only needing to be warmed in the oven on top of the tostadas, while we sautéed the onions and peppers. We then topped the tostadas with the cooked vegetables, slaw, and some tangy queso fresco. A spoonful of crema and a sprinkle of cilantro complemented the rest of the ingredients. Both store-bought and homemade tostadas will work well here.

- 1 **(14-ounce) bag green coleslaw mix**
- 1 **tablespoon finely chopped jarred jalapeños, plus**
  ¼ cup brine
  Salt and pepper
- ½ **cup sour cream**
- 3 **tablespoons lime juice (2 limes)**
- 1 **(15-ounce) can vegetarian refried pinto beans**
- 12 **(6-inch) corn tostadas**
- 2 **tablespoons vegetable oil**
- 2 **onions, halved and sliced thin**
- 3 **green bell peppers, stemmed, seeded,**
  and cut into 2-inch-long matchsticks
- 3 **garlic cloves, minced**
- 4 **ounces queso fresco or feta cheese, crumbled (1 cup)**
- ¼ **cup fresh cilantro leaves**

1. Toss coleslaw mix with 3 tablespoons jalapeño brine in bowl and season with salt and pepper to taste. In separate bowl, whisk sour cream and 2 tablespoons lime juice together.

2. Adjust oven racks to upper-middle and lower-middle positions and heat oven to 450 degrees. Combine refried beans, jalapeños, and remaining 1 tablespoon jalapeño brine together in bowl and season with salt and pepper to taste. Spread bean mixture evenly over tostadas and arrange on 2 rimmed baking sheets. Bake tostadas until beans are warm, 5 to 10 minutes.

3. Meanwhile, heat oil in 12-inch skillet over medium-high heat until just smoking. Add onions and peppers and cook until softened and lightly browned, 5 to 7 minutes. Stir in garlic and cook until fragrant, about 30 seconds. Off heat, stir in remaining 1 tablespoon lime juice and season with salt and pepper to taste.

4. Top warm tostadas with cooked vegetables, slaw, and queso fresco. Drizzle with sour cream–lime juice mixture, sprinkle with cilantro leaves, and serve.

VARIATION

Roasted Tomato and Corn Tostadas

Substitute refried black beans for refried pinto beans. Substitute 2 ears corn, kernels cut from cobs, for peppers; cook with onions as directed. Before adding garlic to skillet, stir in 1 pound halved cherry tomatoes and let wilt slightly, about 3 minutes.

Warm Cabbage Salad with Crispy Fried Tofu

SERVES 4   **TOTAL TIME** 45 MINUTES   **FAST**

✓ **WHY THIS RECIPE WORKS:** When paired with crispy pan-fried tofu and a zesty dressing, ordinary bagged coleslaw mix is transformed into an impressive vegetarian entrée. For the cabbage salad, we developed a dressing with extra punch, mixing together oil, vinegar, soy sauce, sugar, and Asian chili-garlic sauce, and heating it in the microwave first. We tossed this warm dressing over the coleslaw mix, to which we added peanuts, scallions, cilantro, and mint. For the tofu, we found that dredging it in a mixture of cornmeal and cornstarch before pan frying created the perfect crust—textured and golden without being gritty—a nice contrast to its creamy interior. We prefer the texture of soft or medium-firm tofu here. Firm or extra-firm tofu will also work, but they will taste drier. Be sure to handle the tofu gently and pat it dry thoroughly before seasoning and coating. Bags of coleslaw mix can vary in size, but a few ounces more or less won't make a difference here.

28   ounces soft tofu
 1   (14-ounce) bag green coleslaw mix
 ¾   cup unsalted peanuts, toasted and crushed
 4   scallions, sliced thin
 ½   cup fresh cilantro leaves
 ½   cup chopped fresh mint
 3   tablespoons plus ¾ cup vegetable oil

Golden fried tofu contrasts with a warm cabbage salad that we tossed with a tangy dressing.

 5   tablespoons rice vinegar
 2   tablespoons soy sauce
 2   tablespoons sugar
1–2   teaspoons Asian chili-garlic sauce
 ¾   cup cornstarch
 ¼   cup cornmeal
      Salt and pepper

1. Cut tofu in half lengthwise, then cut each half crosswise into 6 slices. Spread tofu out over paper towel–lined baking sheet and let drain for 20 minutes.

2. Meanwhile, combine coleslaw mix, peanuts, scallions, cilantro, and mint in large bowl. In separate bowl, whisk 3 tablespoons oil, vinegar, soy sauce, sugar, and chili-garlic sauce together. Cover and microwave dressing until simmering, 1 to 2 minutes. Measure out and reserve 2 tablespoons dressing for serving. Pour remaining warm dressing over cabbage mixture and toss to combine.

3. Combine cornstarch and cornmeal in shallow dish. Gently pat tofu dry with paper towels and season with salt and pepper. Working with several tofu pieces at a time, coat thoroughly with cornstarch mixture, pressing gently to adhere; transfer to wire rack set over baking sheet.

4. Heat remaining ¾ cup oil in 12-inch nonstick skillet over medium-high heat until shimmering. Working in 2 batches, fry tofu until crisp and golden on all sides, about 4 minutes. Gently lift tofu from oil, letting excess oil drip back into skillet, and transfer to paper towel–lined plate. Drizzle tofu with reserved dressing and serve with cabbage.

Glazed Caribbean Tofu with Rice and Pigeon Peas

SERVES 4   **TOTAL TIME** 45 MINUTES   `FAST`

✓ **WHY THIS RECIPE WORKS:** A glaze made with curry and pineapple preserves and brightened with a little lime juice ensures this tofu is anything but mild mannered, and it takes just minutes to cook on the stovetop. While the tofu drained, we started our side dish in a saucepan. Enriching the rice's cooking liquid with coconut milk makes it a creamy, rich companion for the spicy-sweet tofu, and adding onion, jalapeño, and pigeon peas lends complementary flavor, texture, and heartiness. Canned pigeon peas (popular in West Indian cooking) can be found in most supermarkets; however, black-eyed peas or kidney beans can be substituted if necessary. To make this dish spicier, include the chile seeds and ribs when mincing the chiles. Garnish with sliced scallions, if desired.

28 **ounces firm tofu**
    Salt and pepper
 1 **tablespoon curry powder**
 1 **onion, diced**
 2 **jalapeño chiles, stemmed, seeded, and minced**
 ¼ **cup vegetable oil**
1½ **cups long-grain rice**
 1 **(15-ounce) can pigeon peas, rinsed**
 1 **(13.5-ounce) can coconut milk**
 1 **cup plus 3 tablespoons water**
 ½ **cup pineapple preserves**
 2 **tablespoons lime juice**
 ¼ **teaspoon red pepper flakes**

1. Cut tofu in half lengthwise, then cut each half crosswise into 6 slices. Spread tofu out over paper towel–lined baking sheet and let drain for 20 minutes. Gently pat tofu dry with paper towels, season with salt and pepper, and sprinkle with curry powder.

A sweet-and-spicy pineapple glaze lends bold flavor to the crisp, pan-fried tofu in this Caribbean-inspired dish.

2. Meanwhile, cook onion, jalapeño, and 2 tablespoons oil in large saucepan over medium-high heat until softened, about 3 minutes. Stir in rice and cook until opaque, about 1 minute. Stir in peas, coconut milk, 1 cup water, and 1 teaspoon salt. Bring to boil, then reduce heat to low, cover, and cook until rice is tender, about 20 minutes. Season with salt and pepper to taste.

3. Microwave pineapple preserves until bubbling, about 1 minute, then whisk in remaining 3 tablespoons water, lime juice, and pepper flakes.

4. Heat remaining 2 tablespoons oil in 12-inch nonstick skillet over medium-high heat until just smoking. Add half of tofu and cook until golden and crisp on all sides, about 5 minutes; transfer to paper towel–lined plate. Repeat with remaining tofu, then return first batch of tofu to skillet. Add pineapple mixture and simmer, turning tofu to coat, until glaze thickens, about 1 minute. Serve with rice.

Buying and Storing Tofu

Tofu is made from the curds of soy milk, which are pressed into blocks and sold either fresh or vacuum-packed in water. We love it in the test kitchen because it is an ideal canvas for bold or aromatic sauces, such as those used in curries and stir-fries. Tofu takes to a wide variety of preparations from stir-frying and sautéing to roasting, braising, grilling, and scrambling.

You can find tofu in a variety of textures, such as silken, soft, medium-firm, firm, and extra-firm. We prefer the latter two in stir-frying because firmer tofu holds its shape well while being moved around a hot pan. In recipes where the contrast of a crunchy crust to a creamy interior is desired, such as our Warm Cabbage Salad with Crispy Fried Tofu (page 293), medium or soft tofu is best. Light tofu is also available in silken and firm varieties. Light firm tofu can be substituted in recipes; however, it isn't as flavorful and will taste drier than regular tofu.

Before cooking with tofu, we like to drain it for best texture as well as to prevent excess liquid from diluting the dish's flavor. Spread cut tofu out over a paper towel–lined baking sheet and let drain for 20 minutes, then gently pat it dry.

Keep in mind that tofu is perishable and should be kept well chilled to maximize its shelf life. We prefer to use it within a few days of opening. If you want to keep an open package of tofu fresh for several days, cover the tofu with fresh water and store it in the refrigerator in an airtight container, changing the water daily. Any hint of sourness means the tofu is past its prime.

Asian Braised Tofu with Winter Squash and Coconut Milk

SERVES 4   **TOTAL TIME** 1 HOUR

✔ **WHY THIS RECIPE WORKS:** Nothing is better in the colder months than a hearty braised dish with layers of flavor, but most recipes involve meat. We wanted a braise with satisfying and rich Asian flavors using only vegetarian ingredients. We turned to tofu plus a combination of butternut squash and eggplant, which we browned first in a skillet. To build a flavorful base for our braise, we sautéed onion, garlic, ginger, and lemon grass until softened and fragrant. For the braising liquid, we combined vegetable broth plus coconut milk, which added richness and a creamy texture. The drained tofu and vegetables needed only 20 minutes to cook through and lend their flavors to our vegetarian braise, which we finished with some cilantro, lime juice, and soy sauce. Serve with rice.

Smashing Lemon Grass

1. Trim dry top (this part is usually green) and tough bottom of each stalk.

2. Peel and discard dry outer layer until moist, tender inner stalk is exposed.

3. Smash peeled stalk with bottom of heavy saucepan to release maximum flavor.

14 **ounces extra-firm tofu, cut into ¾-inch pieces**
   Salt and pepper
3 **tablespoons vegetable oil**
1½ **pounds butternut squash, peeled, seeded, and cut into ½-inch cubes (3½ cups)**
1 **pound eggplant, cut into ½-inch chunks**
1 **onion, chopped fine**
8 **garlic cloves, minced**
2 **tablespoons grated fresh ginger**
1 **lemon grass stalk, trimmed and smashed**
1 **(13.5-ounce) can coconut milk**
½ **cup vegetable broth**
½ **cup minced fresh cilantro**
4 **teaspoons lime juice**
   Soy sauce
2 **scallions, sliced thin**

1. Spread tofu out over paper towel–lined baking sheet and let drain for 20 minutes. Gently pat tofu dry with paper towels and season with salt and pepper to taste.

2. Meanwhile, heat 1 tablespoon oil in 12-inch nonstick skillet over medium-high heat until shimmering. Add squash and cook until golden brown, 8 to 10 minutes; transfer to large bowl.

3. Add 1 tablespoon oil to now-empty skillet and heat over medium-high heat until shimmering. Add eggplant and cook until golden brown, 5 to 7 minutes; transfer to bowl with squash.

4. Add remaining 1 tablespoon oil to skillet and heat over medium heat until shimmering. Add onion and cook until softened and lightly browned, 5 to 7 minutes. Stir in garlic, ginger, and lemon grass and cook until fragrant, about 30 seconds. Stir in coconut milk, broth, browned squash-eggplant mixture, and drained tofu. Bring to simmer, reduce heat to medium-low, and cook until vegetables are softened and sauce is slightly thickened, 15 to 20 minutes.

5. Off heat, remove lemon grass. Stir in cilantro and lime juice. Season with soy sauce and pepper to taste. Sprinkle with scallions and serve.

Stir-Fried Tofu and Bok Choy

SERVES 4   **TOTAL TIME** 45 MINUTES   **FAST**

✔ **WHY THIS RECIPE WORKS:** Tofu stir-fries make a quick and tasty vegetarian meal, but many recipes result in lackluster tofu and vegetables in a gummy sauce. We found several key techniques to achieve creamy tofu with a browned crust and crisp-tender vegetables, all lightly coated in a flavorful sauce. Removing as much of the tofu's moisture as possible by letting it drain on a paper towel–lined baking sheet helped it brown in its relatively short cooking time. Coating the pieces in cornstarch further helped in creating a crispy crust while keeping the interior creamy, and also made a craggy surface that held the sauce nicely. We stir-fried the tofu in a skillet over high heat before adding the slower-cooking vegetables, which ensured that the bok choy and carrots didn't get soggy. We then sautéed the aromatics, added back the tofu with bok choy greens, and poured in a sauce lightly thickened with cornstarch that clung to the tofu and vegetables without being gloppy.

SAUCE

- ½ cup vegetable broth
- ¼ cup soy sauce
- 2 tablespoons Chinese rice wine or dry sherry
- 1 tablespoon sugar
- 2 teaspoons cornstarch
- 1 teaspoon toasted sesame oil

A sauce thickened with cornstarch coats the tofu and vegetables in this stir-fry without becoming gloppy.

STIR-FRY

- 14 ounces extra-firm tofu, cut into 1-inch cubes
- ⅓ cup cornstarch
- 3 scallions, minced
- 3 garlic cloves, minced
- 1 tablespoon grated fresh ginger
- 3 tablespoons vegetable oil
- 1 small head bok choy (1 pound), stalks and greens separated, stalks sliced thin and greens cut into 1-inch pieces
- 2 carrots, peeled and cut into matchsticks

1. FOR THE SAUCE: Whisk all ingredients together in bowl.

2. FOR THE STIR-FRY: Spread tofu out over paper towel–lined baking sheet and let drain for 20 minutes. Gently pat tofu dry with paper towels then toss with cornstarch in bowl. Transfer coated tofu to strainer and shake gently over bowl to remove excess cornstarch.

Vegetarian stir-fries often yield soggy tofu with limp vegetables and a gloppy sauce. For perfectly cooked tofu, draining it first then coating it with cornstarch proved to be key. We then followed our tried-and-true stir-fry method using a hot skillet and staggering the cooking of the tofu and vegetables which are united at the end with the sauce. As with all stir-fries, it is important to prep all the ingredients before you start cooking.

1. SLICE AND DRAIN THE TOFU: Slice the tofu into 1-inch cubes and spread out over a paper towel–lined baking sheet. Let them sit for 20 minutes. Gently pat the tofu dry with paper towels.
WHY? Cutting up the tofu allows for more surface area for the coating. Simply letting the tofu drain on paper towels and then patting it dry removed enough excess water to ensure that it would turn crispy when stir-fried.

2. COAT THE TOFU WITH CORNSTARCH: Toss the tofu in batches with ⅓ cup cornstarch. Place the coated tofu in a fine-mesh strainer and shake off any excess cornstarch.
WHY? The tofu needs to be very dry in order to brown and turn crisp; a cornstarch coating helps it brown more easily and also helps the sauce cling to the tofu.

3. GET THE SKILLET HOT AND STIR-FRY THE TOFU: Heat 2 tablespoons oil in a large nonstick skillet over high heat until just smoking. Add the tofu and cook until it's well browned on all sides, 10 to 15 minutes; transfer the tofu to a bowl.
WHY? It's crucial to heat the oil until it's just smoking before adding the tofu or it won't brown properly. Using a 12-inch skillet provides enough room to brown the tofu properly.

4. STAGGER COOKING THE VEGETABLES: Add 2 teaspoons oil to the skillet and heat until it's shimmering. Add the bok choy stalks and carrots and cook until the vegetables are crisp-tender, about 4 minutes.
WHY? The bok choy stalks take longer to cook than its thinner leaves. The stalks and carrots are cooked first to ensure they cook through properly.

5. CLEAR THE CENTER OF THE PAN AND ADD THE AROMATICS: Clear the center of the skillet, add the garlic-ginger mixture and cook, mashing it into the skillet, until fragrant. Stir the mixture into the vegetables.
WHY? Mashing the aromatics into the center of the pan before mixing them into the vegetables ensures they cook through and won't taste harsh in the finished dish.

6. RETURN THE TOFU TO THE PAN AND ADD THE SAUCE: Return the tofu to the pan and add the bok choy greens. Whisk the sauce to recombine, then add it to the skillet. Cook, stirring constantly, until the sauce has thickened, 1 to 2 minutes.
WHY? In order for the sauce to coat the ingredients, everything must be back in the pan. Whisking helps reincorporate the cornstarch that has settled on the bottom of the sauce.

PUTTING SOY CRUMBLES TO WORK

Made of seasoned, textured soy protein, soy crumbles make a great stand-in for ground beef and require no prep at all. You may see several brands at the supermarket; any of them will work in our recipes, but be sure to select plain, not flavored, soy crumbles. In general you will find them in the refrigerated section with other meatless products. They can be a bit salty, so season with a light hand when cooking with them. Here are three fast everyday recipes using soy crumbles. Each serves 4 to 6.

HEARTY VEGETABLE CHILI FAST

Cook 1 minced onion, 1 chopped red bell pepper, and 2 tablespoons vegetable oil in Dutch oven over medium-high heat until softened, about 3 minutes. Add 1 zucchini and 1 yellow squash, chopped; cook until browned, 5 to 7 minutes. Add 2 minced garlic cloves and 1½ tablespoons chili powder; cook until fragrant, about 30 seconds. Add 1 (15-ounce) can tomato sauce, 1 can rinsed kidney beans, 1 cup vegetable broth, and 12 ounces soy crumbles; simmer for 10 minutes. Add 2 tablespoons minced cilantro; season with salt and pepper to taste.

VEGETARIAN SHEPHERD'S PIE FAST

Cook 1 minced onion, 8 ounces sliced cremini, and 1 tablespoon vegetable oil in 12-inch nonstick skillet over high heat until softened, about 3 minutes. Add ¼ cup flour and 1 tablespoon tomato paste; cook for 1 minute. Whisk in 2½ cups vegetable broth and 2 teaspoons soy sauce; simmer until thickened, about 3 minutes. Transfer to 2-quart broiler-safe dish. Stir in 12 ounces soy crumbles and 2 cups thawed frozen pea-carrot mix. Spread 4 cups warm mashed potatoes over top. Broil 6 inches from element until hot and golden, about 5 minutes.

SPAGHETTI WITH MEATLESS MEATY SAUCE FAST

Cook 4 ounces minced cremini, 1 minced onion, and 1 tablespoon olive oil in large saucepan over medium-high heat until browned, 5 to 7 minutes. Add 4 minced garlic cloves and 1 teaspoon dried oregano; cook until fragrant, about 1 minute. Add 12 ounces soy crumbles and 2 (28-ounce) cans crushed tomatoes; simmer 15 minutes. Toss with 1 pound cooked spaghetti. Add pasta cooking water as needed; season with salt and pepper to taste.

3. Combine scallions, garlic, ginger, and 1 teaspoon oil in bowl; set aside. Heat 2 tablespoons oil in 12-inch nonstick skillet over high heat until just smoking. Add tofu and cook until crisp and well browned on all sides, 10 to 15 minutes; transfer to bowl.

4. Add remaining 2 teaspoons oil to skillet and return to high heat until shimmering. Add bok choy stalks and carrots and cook until vegetables are crisp-tender, about 4 minutes. Clear center of skillet, add garlic mixture, and cook, mashing mixture into skillet, until fragrant, about 30 seconds. Stir garlic mixture into vegetables.

5. Return tofu to skillet. Stir in bok choy greens. Whisk sauce to recombine, then add to skillet. Cook, stirring constantly, until sauce is thickened, 1 to 2 minutes. Serve.

Spicy Asian Lettuce Wraps
SERVES 4   TOTAL TIME 45 MINUTES **FAST**

✔ **WHY THIS RECIPE WORKS:** Making bold-flavored Thai lettuce wraps often requires rounding up a lot of exotic ingredients. We wanted to make an easy vegetarian version that kept all of the flavors, but used common pantry items. We used soy crumbles and added sautéed bell pepper for a contrasting sweet flavor and texture. Cooking the rice with vegetable broth deepened the flavors of the dish. After adding the soy crumbles, we stirred in Asian chili-garlic sauce, soy sauce, and brown sugar, and cooked until it thickened slightly. Soy crumbles can be a bit salty, so be sure to taste before adding any additional salt.

  2   **tablespoons vegetable oil**
  1   **red bell pepper, chopped**
  2   **teaspoons grated fresh ginger**
  1   **cup long-grain white rice**
1½   **cups vegetable broth**
 12   **ounces soy crumbles**
  1   **tablespoon Asian chili-garlic sauce**
  1   **tablespoon soy sauce**
  1   **tablespoon packed brown sugar**
  3   **scallions, thinly sliced**
  2   **tablespoons minced fresh cilantro**
      Salt and pepper
  1   **head Bibb lettuce, leaves separated**

1. Heat oil in 12-inch nonstick skillet and cook over medium-high heat until shimmering. Add bell pepper and cook until softened, about 5 minutes. Stir in ginger and cook until fragrant, about 30 seconds. Stir in rice and cook for 1 minute. Stir in broth and bring to boil. Reduce heat to low, cover, and cook until rice is tender, about 20 minutes.

2. Stir in soy crumbles and let heat through, about 2 minutes. Stir in chili-garlic sauce, soy sauce, and sugar and cook until sauce has thickened slightly, about 1 minute. Off heat, stir in scallions and cilantro. Season with salt and pepper to taste and transfer to serving bowl. Serve with lettuce leaves.

Tempeh Tacos

SERVES 4 TO 6   **TOTAL TIME** 30 MINUTES   `FAST`

✓**WHY THIS RECIPE WORKS:** Although there are plenty of recipes for homemade beef or chicken tacos, vegetarian versions are harder to come by. For a recipe that had a filling with great savory flavor and texture that was 100 percent vegetarian friendly, we chose to use tempeh, which came across as mildly nutty when mixed with the bold taco seasonings, and provided a meaty texture. Vegetable broth mixed with canned tomato sauce formed the perfect base for the tempeh filling. Any type of tempeh will work well in these tacos, but we preferred the flavor of five-grain tempeh. Serve with your favorite taco toppings, such as shredded cheddar cheese, shredded lettuce, diced tomatoes, diced avocado, minced onion, sour cream, and hot sauce. For how to make your own taco shells, see page 187.

Tempeh seasoned with chili powder, garlic, and oregano makes a great filling for vegetarian tacos.

2	tablespoons vegetable oil
1	onion, chopped fine
3	tablespoons chili powder
4	garlic cloves, minced
1	teaspoon dried oregano
2	(8-ounce) packages 5-grain tempeh, crumbled into ¼-inch pieces
1	(8-ounce) can tomato sauce
1	cup vegetable broth
1	teaspoon packed light brown sugar
2	tablespoons minced fresh cilantro
1	tablespoon lime juice
	Salt and pepper
12	taco shells

1. Heat oil in 12-inch nonstick skillet over medium-high heat until shimmering. Add onion and cook until softened, about 3 minutes. Stir in chili powder, garlic, and oregano and cook until fragrant, about 30 seconds. Stir in tempeh and cook until lightly browned, about 5 minutes.

2. Stir in tomato sauce, broth, and sugar and simmer until thickened, about 2 minutes. Off heat, stir in cilantro and lime juice and season with salt and pepper to taste. Divide filling evenly among taco shells. Serve.

NOTES FROM THE TEST KITCHEN

Tempeh

While tofu has hit the mainstream, its relative tempeh might not be as familiar. Tempeh is made by fermenting cooked soybeans and forming a firm, dense cake. (Some versions of tempeh also contain beans, grains, and flavorings.) Because it holds its shape better than tofu when cooked, it serves as a good meat substitute and is a mainstay of many vegetarian diets (and is particularly popular in Southeast Asia). Although it has a strong, almost nutty flavor, it tends to absorb the flavors of any foods or sauces to which it is added, making it a versatile choice for many sorts of dishes from chilis to tacos. Tempeh is sold in most supermarkets and can be found with different grain combinations and flavorings. We prefer to use five-grain tempeh in our recipes, but any tempeh variety will work.

Grilling

■ SIGNIFIES A **FAST** RECIPE (45 MINUTES OR LESS)

Perfect Grilled Hamburgers

SERVES 4   **TOTAL TIME** 40 MINUTES   **FAST**

✓ **WHY THIS RECIPE WORKS:** Burgers often come off the grill tough, dry, and bulging in the middle. We wanted a moist and juicy burger, with a texture that was tender and cohesive, not dense and heavy. Just as important, we wanted a flavorful, deeply caramelized reddish brown crust that would stick to the meat, and we wanted a nice flat surface capable of holding as many condiments as we could pile on. For juicy, robustly fla-vored meat, we opted for chuck, ground to order, with a ratio of 20 percent fat to 80 percent lean. We formed the meat into 6-ounce patties that were fairly thick, with a depression in the middle. Testing had taught us that indenting the center of each burger ensured that the patties would come off the grill with an even thickness instead of puffed up like a tennis ball. For our cheeseburgers, we took an unconventional approach and mixed the cheese in with the meat for an even distribution of cheese flavor. Weighing the meat on a kitchen scale is the most accurate way to portion it. If you don't own a scale, do your best to divide the meat evenly into quarters. Eighty percent lean ground chuck is our favorite for flavor, but 85 percent lean works, too.

Making a depression in the ungrilled patties yields burgers with a uniform thickness.

1½   **pounds 80 percent lean ground chuck**
1   **teaspoon salt**
½   **teaspoon pepper**
4   **hamburger buns**

1. Break meat into small pieces in bowl, sprinkle with salt and pepper, and toss lightly to mix. Divide meat into 4 por-tions. Working with 1 portion at a time, lightly toss from hand to hand to form ball, then gently flatten into ¾-inch-thick patty. Press center of patties down with fingertips to create ¼-inch-deep depression.

2A. FOR A CHARCOAL GRILL: Open bottom vent com-pletely. Light large chimney starter filled with charcoal bri-quettes (6 quarts). When top coals are partially covered with ash, pour evenly over half of grill. Set cooking grate in place, cover, and open lid vent completely. Heat grill until hot, about 5 minutes.

2B. FOR A GAS GRILL: Turn all burners to high, cover, and heat grill until hot, about 15 minutes. Leave all burners on high.

3. Clean and oil cooking grate. Place burgers on grill (on hotter side if using charcoal) and cook, without pressing on them, until well browned on first side, 2 to 3 minutes. Flip burgers and continue to grill, 2 to 3 minutes for rare, 2½ to 3½ minutes for medium-rare, and 3 to 4 minutes for medium.

4. Transfer burgers to platter, tent with aluminum foil, and let rest for 5 minutes. Serve with buns.

VARIATIONS

Perfect Grilled Cheeseburgers

Since the cheese is evenly distributed in these burgers, just a little goes a long way.

Mix ¾ cup shredded cheddar, Swiss, or Monterey Jack cheese or ¾ cup crumbled blue cheese into meat with salt and pepper.

Perfect Grilled Hamburgers with Garlic and Chipotles

Toast 3 unpeeled garlic cloves in 8-inch skillet over medium heat until fragrant, about 8 minutes. When cool enough to handle, peel and mince. Mix garlic, 2 tablespoons minced scallion, and 1 tablespoon minced canned chipotle chile in adobo sauce into meat with salt and pepper.

Perfect Grilled Hamburgers with Cognac and Mustard

Mix 1½ tablespoons cognac, 1 tablespoon minced fresh chives, and 2 teaspoons Dijon mustard into meat with salt and pepper.

Grilled Well-Done Hamburgers

SERVES 4   TOTAL TIME 45 MINUTES   **FAST**

✓ **WHY THIS RECIPE WORKS:** These days, many backyard cooks prefer grilling burgers to medium-well and beyond. The problem is that the meat comes off the grill dry and tough. We wanted a well-done burger that was as tender and as moist as can be. Taste tests proved that well-done burgers made with 80 percent lean chuck were noticeably moister than burgers made from leaner beef, but they still weren't juicy enough. Because we couldn't force the meat to retain moisture, we opted to pack the patties with a panade, a paste made from bread and milk that's often used to keep meatloaf and meatballs moist. Mixing the panade into the beef created burgers that were juicy and tender even when well-done. To punch up the flavor, we also added minced garlic and tangy steak sauce.

 1 slice hearty white sandwich bread, crust removed, bread chopped
 2 tablespoons whole milk
 2 teaspoons steak sauce
 1 garlic clove, minced
 ¾ teaspoon salt
 ¾ teaspoon pepper
1½ pounds 80 percent lean ground chuck
 4 hamburger buns

1. Mash bread and milk in large bowl into paste with fork. Stir in steak sauce, garlic, salt, and pepper. Break meat into small pieces, add to bowl, and toss lightly to mix. Divide meat into 4 portions. Working with 1 portion at a time, lightly toss from hand to hand to form ball, then gently flatten into ¾-inch-thick patty. Press center of patties down with fingertips to create ¼-inch-deep depression.

2A. FOR A CHARCOAL GRILL: Open bottom vent completely. Light large chimney starter filled with charcoal briquettes (6 quarts). When top coals are partially covered with ash, pour evenly over half of grill. Set cooking grate in place, cover, and open lid vent completely. Heat grill until hot, about 5 minutes.

2B. FOR A GAS GRILL: Turn all burners to high, cover, and heat grill until hot, about 15 minutes. Leave all burners on high.

3. Clean and oil cooking grate. Place burgers on grill (on hotter side if using charcoal) and cook, without pressing on them, until well browned on first side, 2 to 4 minutes. Flip burgers and continue to grill 3 to 4 minutes for medium-well or 4 to 5 minutes for well-done.

4. Transfer burgers to platter, tent with aluminum foil, and let rest for 5 minutes. Serve with buns.

VARIATION
Well-Done Bacon-Cheeseburgers

Most bacon burgers simply top the burgers with bacon. We also mixed some bacon fat into the ground beef, which added juiciness and unmistakable bacon flavor throughout the burger.

Cook 8 slices bacon in 12-inch nonstick skillet over medium heat until crisp, 7 to 9 minutes; transfer to paper towel–lined plate. Refrigerate 2 tablespoons rendered bacon fat until just warm, then mix into meat with salt and pepper. Top burgers with sliced cheese of choice during final 2 minutes of grilling. Top burgers with bacon before serving.

Turkey Burgers

SERVES 4   TOTAL TIME 45 MINUTES   **FAST**

✓ **WHY THIS RECIPE WORKS:** A lean, fully cooked turkey burger, simply seasoned with salt and pepper, is a poor stand-in for an all-beef burger. We wanted a turkey burger that grilled up juicy and full of flavor. We took a close look at the ground turkey sold and found several kinds: ground white meat, ground dark meat, and generically labeled 93 percent lean ground turkey. After trying burgers made from all three, tasters preferred the deeper flavor and juicier texture of the ground dark meat, followed by the 93 percent lean meat. Since ground dark meat can be hard to find, we went with the 93 percent lean turkey and added mild ricotta cheese, which kept the burgers moist. To keep our burgers from being bland, we found Worcestershire and Dijon mustard gave them a pleasant tang. Be sure to use ground turkey, not ground turkey breast (also labeled 99 percent fat-free). We prefer the richer flavor and softer texture of whole-milk ricotta here, but part-skim or fat-free will also work. Because these burgers are made of ground poultry, be sure to cook them through completely in step 4.

1¼ pounds 93 percent lean ground turkey
 ½ cup whole-milk ricotta cheese
 2 teaspoons Worcestershire sauce
 2 teaspoons Dijon mustard
 ½ teaspoon salt
 ¼ teaspoon pepper
 4 hamburger buns

1. Break turkey into small pieces in bowl and add ricotta, Worcestershire, mustard, salt, and pepper. Using your hands, lightly knead the mixture until thoroughly combined. Divide meat into 4 portions. Working with 1 portion at a time, lightly toss from hand to hand to form ball, then gently flatten into 1-inch-thick patty. Press center of patties down with fingertips to create ¼-inch-deep depression.

2A. FOR A CHARCOAL GRILL: Open bottom vent completely. Light large chimney starter three-quarters filled with charcoal briquettes (4½ quarts). When top coals are partially covered with ash, pour two-thirds evenly over half of grill, then pour remaining coals over other half of grill. Set cooking grate in place, cover, and open lid vent completely. Heat grill until hot, about 5 minutes.

2B. FOR A GAS GRILL: Turn all burners to high, cover, and heat grill until hot, about 15 minutes. Leave all burners on high.

3. Clean and oil cooking grate. Place burgers on grill (on hotter side if using charcoal) and cook, without pressing on them, until well seared on both sides, 5 to 7 minutes, turning as needed.

4. Slide burgers to cooler part of grill if using charcoal, or turn all burners to medium if using gas. Cover and continue to cook burgers until cooked through, 5 to 7 minutes, flipping them halfway through cooking. Transfer burgers to platter, tent with aluminum foil, and let rest for 5 minutes. Serve with buns.

VARIATION
Chicken Burgers
Ground chicken tends to be much more moist than ground turkey and therefore requires less ricotta.

Substitute ground chicken for ground turkey and reduce amount of ricotta to ¼ cup.

CUSTOMIZING BURGERS

A simple plain beef, turkey, or portobello burger has its merits, but it can also be the perfect base for a variety of toppings. Here are some of our favorite combinations.

TEX-MEX BURGER
Guacamole, sour cream, spicy tomato salsa, and pickled jalapeños

BISTRO BURGER
Blue cheese, sautéed mushrooms, and caramelized onions

ITALIAN BURGER
Basil pesto, sliced mozzarella cheese, and roasted garlic cloves on focaccia

CALIFORNIA BURGER
Avocado, sprouts, and sliced cucumbers on a whole-wheat bun

Scoring the top of the portobello caps releases moisture from the mushrooms which then evaporates on the grill.

Grilled Portobello Burgers
SERVES 4   **TOTAL TIME** 50 MINUTES

✔ **WHY THIS RECIPE WORKS:** To avoid mushroom burgers with soggy buns, we knew we had to find a way to rid the mushrooms of a lot of their excess moisture. We decided to try a technique that had worked for us in the past with oven-roasted mushrooms—scoring—and it worked like a charm on the grill. Before cooking, we lightly scored the mushrooms on the smooth, non-gill side in a crosshatch pattern. This helped expedite the release of moisture from the mushrooms, which dripped out and evaporated on the grill, ensuring intense mushroom flavor and dry and toasty buns. If your mushrooms are larger or smaller than 4 to 5 inches, you may need to adjust the cooking time accordingly.

4 (4- to 5-inch) portobello mushroom caps
1 large red onion, sliced into ½-inch-thick rounds (do not separate rings)
3 tablespoons plus 1 teaspoon olive oil
   Salt and pepper

2 garlic cloves, minced

2 teaspoons minced fresh thyme

2 ounces goat cheese, crumbled (½ cup)

4 hamburger buns

1 ounce (1 cup) baby arugula

¼ teaspoon balsamic vinegar

1 tomato, cored and sliced thin

1. Using tip of sharp knife, lightly score top of each mushroom cap in crosshatch pattern. Brush onion rounds with 1 tablespoon oil and season with salt and pepper. Combine 2 tablespoons oil, garlic, thyme, ¼ teaspoon salt, and ¼ teaspoon pepper in bowl.

2A. FOR A CHARCOAL GRILL: Open bottom vent completely. Light large chimney starter three-quarters filled with charcoal briquettes (4½ quarts). When top coals are partially covered with ash, pour evenly over grill. Set cooking grate in place, cover, and open lid vent completely. Heat grill until hot, about 5 minutes.

2B. FOR A GAS GRILL: Turn all burners to high, cover, and heat grill until hot, about 15 minutes. Turn all burners to medium-high.

3. Clean and oil cooking grate. Place mushrooms, gill side down, and onion rounds on grill. Cook portobellos until lightly charred and beginning to soften on gill side, 4 to 6 minutes. Flip mushrooms, brush with garlic-oil mixture, and cook until tender and browned on second side, 4 to 6 minutes. Sprinkle with cheese and let melt, about 2 minutes.

4. Meanwhile, cook onions, turning as needed, until spottily charred on both sides, 8 to 12 minutes. As they finish cooking, transfer mushrooms and onions to platter and tent with aluminum foil. Split hamburger buns open and grill until warm and lightly charred, about 30 seconds. Transfer to platter.

5. Toss arugula with balsamic vinegar and remaining 1 teaspoon oil in bowl and season with salt and pepper to taste. Separate onion rings. Assemble mushroom caps, arugula, tomato, and onion on buns and serve.

Scoring Portobello Mushrooms for Grilling

Using tip of sharp knife, lightly score top of each mushroom cap in crosshatch pattern.

Wisconsin Brats and Beer

SERVES 6 TO 8   **TOTAL TIME** 1 HOUR

WHY THIS RECIPE WORKS: Recipes for the Midwest's favorite tailgating dish sound foolproof, but our first attempts resulted in gray, soggy sausages and bland onions floating in hot beer. To perfect our recipe, we braised the sausages first with grilled onions to start flavoring them. Braising after grilling made the brats soggy, so we threw them directly on the grill for a final crisping after braising. Searing the onions before stirring them into the beer gave the mixture serious flavor, and the addition of Dijon mustard lent brightness and body to the sauce. Light-bodied lagers work best here. Depending on the size of your grill, you may need to cook the onions in two batches in step 3.

2 pounds onions, sliced into ½-inch-thick rounds (do not separate rings)

3 tablespoons vegetable oil

Pepper

2 (12-ounce) cans/bottles beer

⅔ cup Dijon mustard

1 teaspoon sugar

1 teaspoon caraway seeds

1 (13 by 9-inch) disposable aluminum roasting pan

2 pounds bratwurst (8 to 12 sausages)

8–12 (6-inch) sub rolls

1. Brush onion rounds with oil and season with pepper; set aside. Combine beer, mustard, sugar, caraway seeds, and 1 teaspoon pepper in disposable pan, then add sausages in single layer.

2A. FOR A CHARCOAL GRILL: Open bottom vent completely. Light large chimney starter filled with charcoal briquettes (6 quarts). When top coals are partially covered with ash, pour evenly over grill. Set cooking grate in place, cover, and open lid vent completely. Heat grill until hot, about 5 minutes.

2B. FOR A GAS GRILL: Turn all burners to high, cover, and heat grill until hot, about 15 minutes. Leave all burners on high.

3. Clean and oil cooking grate. Place onions on grill and cook, turning as needed, until lightly charred on both sides, 6 to 10 minutes. Transfer onions to pan. Place pan in center of grill, cover grill, and cook for 15 minutes.

4. Move pan to 1 side of grill. Transfer sausages directly to grill and brown on all sides, about 5 minutes. Transfer sausages to platter and tent with aluminum foil. Continue to cook onion mixture in pan until sauce is slightly thickened, about 5 minutes. Serve sausages and onions with rolls.

To many die-hard grillers, nothing beats cooking over a live charcoal fire. We've found that even the best gas grills don't brown and sear as well as charcoal. A charcoal grill offers some other advantages over gas, including more options for creating custom fires (see page 308) and a better capability for imparting smoke and wood flavor. That said, using a charcoal grill does require some extra effort. Setting up the grill and properly heating and cleaning it before cooking are as important to successful grilling as getting the food just right.

1. USE A CHIMNEY STARTER: Remove the cooking grate and open the bottom vent. Fill the bottom of the chimney starter with crumpled newspaper, set it on the charcoal grate, and fill the top with charcoal.
WHY? We strongly recommend using a chimney starter. Lighter fluid imparts an off-flavor to grilled foods. A large starter holds about 6 quarts of charcoal. This simple device gets all of the charcoal ready at once.

2. GET THE COALS HOT: Ignite the newspaper and allow the charcoal to burn until the briquettes on top are partly covered with a thin layer of gray ash.
WHY? Fine gray ash is a sign that the coals are fully lit and hot and are ready to be turned out into the grill. Don't pour out the coals prematurely; you will be left with both unlit coals at the bottom of the pile that may never ignite as well as a cooler fire.

3. POUR OUT THE COALS: Once the coals are covered with gray ash, empty the briquettes onto the grill and distribute them in one of the custom grill setups.
WHY? Different types of food require different types of fire, so arrange the coals as called for in the recipe.

4. GET THE COOKING GRATE HOT: Set the cooking grate in place, cover, and heat the grate until hot, about 5 minutes.
WHY? A hot cooking grate jump-starts the cooking process and reduces sticking once you place food on the grill. Also, a blast of heat will make it easier to clean the grate.

5. SCRUB THE COOKING GRATE CLEAN: Use a grill brush to scrape the cooking grate clean.
WHY? Some cooks think a dirty cooking grate "seasons" the food. This makes no sense as you wouldn't cook in a dirty pan. If you skip the cleaning step, food is more likely to stick and to pick up off-flavors.

6. OIL THE COOKING GRATE: Using tongs, dip a wad of paper towels in vegetable oil and wipe the cooking grate several times.
WHY? The oil offers another layer of protection against sticking. But the oil burns off and so needs to be reapplied every time you grill. Pouring the oil into a small bowl makes it easy to dip the paper towels to apply multiple coats.

Texas Smoked Sausages

SERVES 6 TO 8 **TOTAL TIME** 1 HOUR 10 MINUTES

✓ **WHY THIS RECIPE WORKS:** Spicy smoked sausages are a staple of Texas barbecue, a vestige of German butchers who settled in the area. These pork sausages are seasoned with cayenne pepper and garlic and smoked until the casing is wrinkled. At home, most people don't want to make their own sausages, nor do they have a smoker. Could we get some of the deep smoky Texas flavor on a grill with store-bought sausages? After examining our sausage options at the grocery store, hot Italian sausage stood out as the best choice. We set up soaked wood chips on the hotter side of the grill, and we put the sausages on the cooler side and covered them until cooked through. After 20 minutes though, tasters found the smoke flavor too mild. Neither searing on the hot side nor scoring seemed to help. What if we left the sausages on the grill longer? After 45 minutes, they had great smoke flavor and despite the longer cooking time, they were extremely moist and juicy. Best of all, their skin had deepened to a dark, slightly wrinkled red, like the sausages from the real Texas barbecue joints. If you'd like to use wood chunks instead of wood chips when using a charcoal grill, substitute 3 medium wood chunks, soaked in water for 1 hour, for the wood chip packet. Although hot Italian sausage is more similar to what you'd get in Texas, sweet Italian sausages can be substituted.

> 3 cups wood chips, soaked in water for 15 minutes and drained
> 2 pounds hot Italian sausage links (8 to 12 links)
> 8–12 (6-inch) sub rolls

1. Using large piece of heavy-duty aluminum foil, wrap soaked chips in foil packet and cut several vent holes in top.

2A. FOR A CHARCOAL GRILL: Open bottom vent halfway. Light large chimney starter filled with charcoal briquettes (6 quarts). When top coals are partially covered with ash, pour evenly over half of grill. Place wood chip packet on coals. Set cooking grate in place, cover, and open lid vent halfway. Heat grill until hot and wood chips are smoking, about 5 minutes.

2B. FOR A GAS GRILL: Remove cooking grate and place wood chip packet directly on primary burner. Set cooking grate in place, turn all burners to high, cover, and heat grill until hot and wood chips are smoking, about 15 minutes. Leave primary burner on high and turn off other burner(s).

3. Clean and oil cooking grate. Lay sausages on cooler part of grill, away from coals and flames. Cover (position lid vent over sausages if using charcoal) and cook until sausages are well browned and cooked through, about 45 minutes, turning every 15 minutes. Serve with rolls.

NOTES FROM THE TEST KITCHEN

Better Gas Grilling

In the test kitchen, we use both charcoal and gas grills. A gas grill is convenient and easy to use, but doesn't impart nearly as much smoke flavor to barbecued foods.

CHOOSING A GRILL: When choosing a grill, even heat distribution and good fat drainage are two important factors. We also like our gas grills to have a generous cooking surface area—at least 350 square inches—and three independently operating burners.

READ THE MANUAL ON HOW TO LIGHT: First and foremost, read all the instructions in your owner's manual thoroughly, and follow the directions regarding the order in which the burners must be lit. On most gas grills, an electric lighter lights the burner, though we have found that electric igniters can fail occasionally, especially in windy conditions. For these situations, most models have a hole for lighting the burners with a match. Be sure to wait several minutes (or as directed) between attempts at lighting the grill. This waiting time allows excess gas to dissipate and is an important safety measure.

CHECK THE PROPANE LEVEL: Running out of fuel is an easy way to ruin dinner. If your grill doesn't have a gas gauge or propane level indicator, don't worry. You can use this technique to estimate how much gas is left in the tank: Bring a cup or so of water to boil in a teakettle or saucepan, then pour the boiling water over the side of the tank. Place your hand on the tank. Where the water has warmed the metal, the tank is empty; where the tank remains cool to the touch, there is propane inside.

LIGHT WITH THE LID UP: Don't attempt to light a gas grill with the lid down; this can trap gas and cause a dangerous explosion of fire.

HEAT THE GRILL UNTIL HOT: Heat the grill with all the burners turned to high (even if you plan on cooking over low heat) and keep the lid down for at least 15 minutes. Once the grill is hot, scrape the cooking grate clean with a grill brush and then adjust the burners as desired.

KEEP THE LID DOWN: Whether cooking by direct or indirect heat we often keep the lid down. Keeping the lid down concentrates the heat when searing and keeps the temperature steady when slow-cooking.

Two of the biggest mistakes outdoor grillers make happen before the food even hits the grill: creating too much fire and setting up the fire incorrectly. The first problem is easy to avoid—add the amount of charcoal called for in recipes or, if cooking on a gas grill, adjust the burner temperatures as directed. The second problem is more complicated. Depending on the food being cooked, we use one of the five grill setups outlined below. You might have to adapt these setups based on the shape, depth, and/or circumference of your grill.

	TYPE/DESCRIPTION	CHARCOAL	GAS
	Single-Level Fire A single-level fire delivers a uniform level of heat across the entire cooking surface and is often used for small, quick-cooking pieces of food, such as sausages, some fish, and some vegetables.	Distribute the lit coals in an even layer across the bottom of the grill.	After preheating the grill, turn all the burners to the heat setting as directed in the recipe.
	Two-Level Fire This setup creates two cooking zones: a hotter area for searing and a slightly cooler area to cook food more gently. It is often used for thick chops and bone-in chicken pieces.	Evenly distribute two-thirds of the lit coals over half of the grill, then distribute the remainder of the coals in an even layer over the other half of the grill.	After preheating the grill, leave the primary burner on high and turn the other(s) to medium. The primary burner is the one that must be left on; see your owner's manual if in doubt.
	Modified Two-Level (Half-Grill) Fire Like a two-level fire, this fire has two cooking zones, but the difference in heat level is more dramatic. One side is intensely hot, and the other side is comparatively cool. It's great for cooking fatty foods because the coal- or flame-free zone provides a place to set food while flare-ups die down. For foods that require long cooking times, you can brown the food on the hotter side, then set it on the cooler side to finish with indirect heat. It's also good for cooking chicken breasts over the cooler side gently, then giving them a quick sear on the hotter side.	Distribute the lit coals over half of the grill, piling them in an even layer. Leave the other half of the grill free of coals.	After preheating the grill, adjust the primary burner as directed in the recipe, and turn off the other burner(s).
	Banked Fire A banked fire is similar to a modified two-level fire, except the heat is concentrated in an even smaller part of the grill. The large coal- or flame-free area can accommodate a pan of water and large cuts of meat. This setup is often used for large foods that require hours on the grill, such as brisket or pulled pork.	Bank all the lit coals steeply against one side of the grill, leaving the rest of the grill free of coals.	After preheating the grill, adjust the primary burner as directed in the recipe, and turn off the other burner(s).
	Double-Banked Fire This fire sets up a cool area in the middle so that the food cooks evenly without having to rotate it. Since the flame-free area is narrow and the heat output is not steady over an extended time, this type of fire is good for relatively small, quick-cooking foods such as a whole chicken. We sometimes place a disposable pan in the empty center area to catch drips and prevent flareups. The pan also keeps the coals banked against the sides. This type of fire can be created in a gas grill only if the grill has at least three burners—and burners that ideally run from front to back on the grill.	Divide the lit coals into two steeply banked piles on opposite sides of the grill, leaving the center free of coals.	After preheating the grill, leave the primary burner and burner at the opposite end of the grill on medium-high, medium, or as directed in the recipe, and turn off the center burner(s).

Grilled Beef Kebabs with Lemon-Rosemary Marinade

SERVES 4 TO 6   **TOTAL TIME** 1 HOUR 15 MINUTES
(PLUS 1 HOUR MARINATING TIME)

✓ **WHY THIS RECIPE WORKS:** Most beef kebabs are disappointing, with overcooked meat and raw or mushy vegetables. We wanted foolproof kebabs: chunks of beef with a thick char and a juicy interior, all thoroughly seasoned and paired with browned, tender-firm vegetables. For the meat, we chose well-marbled steak tips for their beefy flavor and tender texture. For the marinade, we used salt for moisture, oil for flavor, and sugar for browning. For depth, we added tomato paste, seasonings and herbs, and beef broth. We chose three grill favorites for the vegetables: peppers, onions, and zucchini. Grilling the beef and vegetables on separate skewers over our tweaked version of a two-level fire allowed the vegetables to cook at a lower temperature while the beef seared over the hotter center area. If you can't find sirloin steak tips, sometimes labeled flap meat, substitute 2½ pounds blade steak (if using, cut each steak in half to remove the gristle). If you have long, thin pieces of meat, roll or fold them into approximate 2-inch cubes. You will need four 12-inch metal skewers for this recipe. We prefer these steak kebabs cooked to medium-rare, but if you prefer them more or less done, see the chart on page 15. For more information on how to cut up onions for kebabs, see page 326.

MARINADE

- 1 onion, chopped
- ⅓ cup beef broth
- ⅓ cup vegetable oil
- 3 tablespoons tomato paste
- 6 garlic cloves, chopped
- 2 tablespoons chopped fresh rosemary
- 2 teaspoons grated lemon zest
- 2 teaspoons salt
- 1½ teaspoons sugar
- ¾ teaspoon pepper

BEEF AND VEGETABLES

- 2 pounds sirloin steak tips, trimmed and cut into 2-inch chunks
- 1 large zucchini, halved lengthwise and sliced 1 inch thick
- 1 large red bell pepper, stemmed, seeded, and cut into 1½-inch pieces
- 1 large red onion, cut into 1-inch pieces, 3 layers thick

1. FOR THE MARINADE: Process all ingredients in blender until smooth, about 45 seconds. Reserve ¾ cup marinade separately for vegetables.

Skewering the beef and vegetables separately for kebabs ensures that each of the components cooks perfectly.

2. FOR THE BEEF AND VEGETABLES: Combine remaining marinade and beef in 1-gallon zipper-lock bag and toss to coat; press out as much air as possible and seal bag. Refrigerate for 1 to 2 hours, flipping bag every 30 minutes. Gently combine zucchini, bell pepper, and onion with reserved marinade in bowl. Cover and let sit at room temperature for 30 minutes.

3. Remove beef from bag, pat dry with paper towels, and thread tightly onto two 12-inch metal skewers. Thread vegetables onto two 12-inch metal skewers, in alternating pattern of zucchini, bell pepper, and onion.

4A. FOR A CHARCOAL GRILL: Open bottom vent completely. Light large chimney starter mounded with charcoal briquettes (7 quarts). When top coals are partially covered with ash, pour evenly over center of grill, leaving 2-inch gap between grill wall and charcoal. Set cooking grate in place, cover, and open lid vent completely. Heat grill until hot, about 5 minutes.

4B. FOR A GAS GRILL: Turn all burners to high, cover, and heat grill until hot, about 15 minutes. Leave primary burner on high and turn other burner(s) to medium-low.

5. Clean and oil cooking grate. Place beef skewers on grill (directly over coals if using charcoal or over hotter side if grilling using gas). Place vegetable skewers on cooler part(s) of grill (near edge of coals if using charcoal). Cook (covered if using gas), turning skewers every 3 to 4 minutes, until beef is well browned and registers 120 to 125 degrees (for medium-rare), 12 to 16 minutes.

6. Transfer beef skewers to platter and tent with aluminum foil. Continue cooking vegetable skewers until tender and lightly charred, about 5 minutes longer. Serve.

VARIATION

Grilled Beef Kebabs with North African Marinade

Substitute 20 cilantro sprigs, 2 teaspoons sweet paprika, 1½ teaspoons ground cumin, and ½ teaspoon cayenne pepper for lemon zest and rosemary in marinade.

Making Grilled Beef Kebabs

1. MARINATE STEAK TIPS: Combine meat chunks with some of marinade in zipper-lock bag and toss to coat; press out air and seal bag. Refrigerate, flipping bag every 30 minutes.

2. MARINATE VEGETABLES: Gently combine zucchini, bell pepper, and onion with reserved marinade in bowl, cover, and let sit at room temperature for 30 minutes.

3. SKEWER MEAT AND VEGETABLES: Remove beef from bag, pat dry, and thread tightly onto metal skewers. Thread vegetables, in alternating pattern of zucchini, pepper, and onion.

4. USE TWO-LEVEL FIRE: Place beef kebabs on hotter part of grill and vegetable skewers on cooler part(s) of grill. Cook (covered if using gas), turning skewers occasionally, for 12 to 16 minutes.

Grilled Boneless Steaks

SERVES 4 **TOTAL TIME** 45 MINUTES (PLUS 1 HOUR SALTING TIME)

✓ **WHY THIS RECIPE WORKS:** Turning out a perfectly grilled steak with a flavorful charred exterior and a rosy, medium-rare interior requires a few tricks. The first trick is to buy a decent steak. There are only a few types of steak that don't require a marinade to help the meat stay tender and juicy (see list below). Second, to bring out its flavor, season the meat with salt and let it sit before cooking. Third, brush the steaks with oil (and season with pepper) in order to get a good sear; the oil is especially helpful for thin or lean steaks like flank and filet mignon. Next, build a fire with two heat zones—a hotter side for searing and a cooler side for cooking the steaks through. Depending on the size and thickness of the steaks and the desired doneness, the cooking time can vary dramatically. Finally, use a thermometer to determine the doneness. We prefer these steaks cooked to medium-rare, but if you prefer them more or less done, see the chart on page 15. This recipe works best with strip steaks, rib-eye steaks, filets mignons, sirloin steak, and flank steak; try to buy steaks of even thickness so they cook at the same rate. If cooking filet mignon, look for steaks that are a bit thicker, about 2 inches.

2–2½ **pounds boneless beef steaks, 1 to 2 inches thick, trimmed**
Kosher salt and pepper
Vegetable oil

1. Season steaks thoroughly with 1 teaspoon salt and let sit at room temperature for 1 hour. Pat steaks dry with paper towels, brush lightly with oil, and season with pepper.

2A. FOR A CHARCOAL GRILL: Open bottom vent completely. Light large chimney starter filled with charcoal briquettes (6 quarts). When top coals are partially covered with ash, pour two-thirds evenly over half of grill, then pour remaining coals over other half of grill. Set cooking grate in place, cover, and open lid vent completely. Heat grill until hot, about 5 minutes.

2B. FOR A GAS GRILL: Turn all burners to high, cover, and heat grill until hot, about 15 minutes. Leave primary burner on high and turn other burner(s) to medium.

3. Clean and oil cooking grate. Place steaks on hotter side of grill. Cook (covered if using gas), turning as needed, until nicely charred on both sides, 4 to 6 minutes. Slide steaks to cooler side of grill and continue to cook until they register 120 to 125 degrees (for medium-rare), 4 to 8 minutes.

4. Transfer steaks to platter, tent with aluminum foil, and let rest for 5 to 10 minutes before serving.

Grilling a perfect boneless steak with a flavorful charred exterior and a rosy interior isn't hard to do, but it does require using a foolproof cooking technique and following a few key steps.

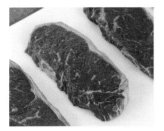

1. BUY DECENT STEAKS: Strip, rib-eye, sirloin, and flank steaks and filets mignons work best on the grill. **WHY?** Not all steaks are created equal. Only a few types of steak don't require a marinade to help the meat stay tender and juicy.

2. SALT THE STEAKS: Season the steaks thoroughly with kosher salt and let them sit at room temperature for 1 hour. **WHY?** Using salt (and time) in advance of cooking improves the texture of many cuts. Salting the meat also brings out its flavor.

3. BRUSH THE STEAKS WITH OIL: Brush the steaks lightly with oil and season with pepper. **WHY?** Brushing the meat with oil before grilling promotes a good sear. The oil also helps protect thin or lean steaks like flank and filet mignon.

4. BUILD THE RIGHT FIRE: Build a two-level charcoal fire (see page 308) or leave the primary burner of a gas grill on high and turn the other burner(s) to medium. **WHY?** A two-level setup provides a fire with two cooking zones.

5. SEAR THE STEAKS: Cook the steaks on the hotter side of the grill until nicely charred on both sides, 4 to 6 minutes. **WHY?** The hotter side of the grill is used to sear the exterior of the steaks to develop color and flavor.

6. COOK THE STEAKS THROUGH: Move the steaks to the cooler side of the grill to finish cooking. **WHY?** The slightly cooler area of the grill allows the steaks to finish cooking through more gently.

7. USE A THERMOMETER TO TEST FOR DONENESS: Cook the steaks until they register 120 to 125 degrees (for medium-rare), 4 to 8 minutes. **WHY?** Using a thermometer to check the temperature of the steaks eliminates any guesswork and ensures they are cooked to the desired doneness.

8. LET THE STEAKS REST: Tent the steaks with aluminum foil and let them rest for 5 to 10 minutes before serving. **WHY?** A short rest gives the muscle fibers in the meat time to relax and reabsorb their natural juices.

Finishing bone-in steaks over indirect heat helps to prevent charring and produces deep grilled flavor.

Grilled Porterhouse or T-Bone Steaks Serves

SERVES 4 TO 6   **TOTAL TIME** 45 MINUTES
(PLUS 1 HOUR SALTING TIME)

✔ **WHY THIS RECIPE WORKS:** Porterhouse and T-bone steaks are really two steaks in one—a tender New York strip steak on one side of the bone and a buttery, quicker-cooking tenderloin on the other. The trick is to cook both cuts of meat to the perfect doneness at the same time. As with boneless steaks, we make a two-level fire and sear the steak over the hotter side first, then slide it to the cooler side to cook through. The key is to position the tenderloin so it always faces the cooler side of the grill—this prevents it from overcooking. Also, when you move the steak to the cooler side, position it so that the big bone along the bottom of the steak faces the hotter side of the grill. This protects the narrow top of the steak from drying out. Salting the meat for 1 hour before grilling boosted flavor from crust to bone. Be sure to buy steaks that are at least 1 inch thick. We prefer these steaks cooked to medium-rare, but if you prefer them more or less done, see the chart on page 15.

2   (1¾-pound) porterhouse or T-bone steaks,
    1 to 1½ inches thick, trimmed
    Salt and pepper

1. Season each steak thoroughly with 1 teaspoon salt and let sit at room temperature for 1 hour. Pat steaks dry with paper towels and season with pepper.

2A. FOR A CHARCOAL GRILL: Open bottom vent completely. Light large chimney starter three-quarters filled with charcoal briquettes (4½ quarts). When top coals are partially covered with ash, pour evenly over half of grill. Set cooking grate in place, cover, and open lid vent completely. Heat grill until hot, about 5 minutes.

2B. FOR A GAS GRILL: Turn all burners to high, cover, and heat grill until hot, about 15 minutes. Leave primary burner on high and turn other burner(s) to low.

3. Clean and oil cooking grate. Place steaks on hotter side of grill with tenderloin sides facing cooler side of grill. Cook (covered if using gas) until dark crust forms, 6 to 8 minutes. Flip and turn steaks so that tenderloin sides are still facing cooler side of grill. Continue to cook until dark brown crust forms on second side, 6 to 8 minutes.

4. Slide steaks to cooler side of grill and turn so that bone side is facing hotter side of grill. Cover grill and cook, turning as needed, until meat registers 120 to 125 degrees (for medium-rare), 2 to 4 minutes.

5. Transfer steaks to carving board, tent with aluminum foil, and let rest for 5 to 10 minutes. Cut strip and tenderloin pieces off bones, then slice each piece ¼ inch thick. Serve.

Carving Porterhouse and T-Bone Steaks

1. After meat has rested, cut along bone to remove large top loin, or strip, section.

2. Cut smaller tenderloin section off bone. Cut each large piece crosswise into ¼-inch-thick slices for serving.

Light rum, ginger, garlic, and scallion give our drunken flank steak marinade a lively kick.

Drunken Steak

SERVES 4   **TOTAL TIME** 55 MINUTES
(PLUS 1 HOUR MARINATING TIME)

✔ **WHY THIS RECIPE WORKS:** We tried several drunken steak recipes, but the flavor was all over the place—some steaks were barely tipsy while others had us picking a designated driver. We wanted our recipe to fall somewhere in the middle of these two extremes. Loose-grained steaks, like the flank steak in this recipe, absorbed more marinade, and thus more flavor, than tight-grained steaks. Scoring the surface of the meat allowed the marinade to penetrate into the steak without compromising the interior color or texture. Tasters preferred the cleaner flavor of light rum. The soy sauce in the marinade not only added intense flavor, but also kept the meat moist during cooking due to its salt. The marinade's sugar content (from the alcohol and the brown sugar) encouraged a crust to form on the steak on the grill. Since the flavor of the marinade dulled a little during cooking, we refreshed it by drizzling a bit of reserved marinade over the rested and sliced cooked steak just before serving. Other thin steaks with a loose grain, such as skirt or

steak tips, can be substituted for the flank steak. If using a gas grill, grill the steak covered for maximum heat output. Don't marinate the steak for longer than 4 hours or it will turn gray and mushy. We prefer flank steak cooked to medium-rare, but if you prefer it more or less done, see the chart on page 15.

> 1 **cup light rum**
> ½ **cup soy sauce**
> 1 **tablespoon packed brown sugar**
> 1 **tablespoon grated fresh ginger**
> 1 **garlic clove, minced**
> 1 **scallion, minced**
> 1 **(1½-pound) flank steak, trimmed**

1. Whisk rum, soy sauce, sugar, ginger, and garlic together in bowl to dissolve sugar. Transfer ¼ cup of marinade to separate bowl, stir in scallion, and reserve for serving.

2. Using sharp knife, lightly score both sides of steak at 1½-inch intervals in crosshatch pattern. Combine remaining marinade and steak in 1-gallon zipper-lock bag and toss to coat; press out as much air as possible and seal bag. Refrigerate for 1 to 4 hours, flipping bag every 30 minutes. Before grilling, remove steak from bag and pat dry with paper towels.

3A. FOR A CHARCOAL GRILL: Open bottom vent completely. Light large chimney starter filled with charcoal briquettes (6 quarts). When top coals are partially covered with ash, pour evenly over half of grill. Set cooking grate in place, cover, and open lid vent completely. Heat grill until hot, about 5 minutes.

3B. FOR A GAS GRILL: Turn all burners to high, cover, and heat grill until hot, about 15 minutes. Leave primary burner on high and turn other burner(s) to medium.

4. Clean and oil cooking grate. Place steak on hotter side of grill. Cook (covered if using gas), turning as needed, until lightly charred on both sides and meat registers 120 to 125 degrees (for medium-rare), 8 to 12 minutes.

5. Transfer steak to carving board, tent with aluminum foil, and let rest for 5 to 10 minutes. Slice steak thinly against grain, drizzle with reserved marinade, and serve.

Scoring Flank Steak

Using sharp knife, lightly score both sides of steak at 1½-inch intervals in crosshatch pattern.

Grilled Southwestern Steak Tips

SERVES 4 TO 6   **TOTAL TIME** 1 HOUR
(PLUS 1 HOUR MARINATING TIME)

✔ **WHY THIS RECIPE WORKS:** Steak tips, even when cooked correctly, can be really chewy. We wanted steak tips with deep flavor and tender texture. For our recipe, we chose sirloin steak tips, also known as flap meat, an affordable cut that stayed tender and moist during a brief stint on the grill. To further tenderize and keep the meat juicy, we created soy sauce–based marinades, which not only tenderized and flavored the steak, but also promoted browning during grilling. For grilling, we seared the steaks over high heat (finishing them over cooler heat if needed), which helped cook this often unevenly shaped cut thoroughly. Letting the steak tips rest for 5 to 10 minutes after grilling also helped to ensure juicy meat. When grilling, bear in mind that steak tips cooked medium-rare to medium are firmer and not quite so chewy as steaks cooked rare.

MARINADE

- ⅓ cup soy sauce
- ⅓ cup vegetable oil
- 3 garlic cloves, minced
- 1 tablespoon packed dark brown sugar
- 1 tablespoon tomato paste
- 1 tablespoon chili powder
- 2 teaspoons ground cumin
- ¼ teaspoon cayenne pepper

STEAK

- 2 pounds sirloin steak tips, trimmed
  Lime wedges

1. FOR THE MARINADE: Whisk all ingredients together in bowl to dissolve sugar.

2. FOR THE STEAK: Combine marinade and steak in 1-gallon zipper-lock bag and toss to coat; press out as much air as possible and seal bag. Refrigerate for 1 hour, flipping bag once halfway through marinating. Before grilling, remove steak from bag and pat dry with paper towels.

3A. FOR A CHARCOAL GRILL: Open bottom vent completely. Light large chimney starter filled with charcoal briquettes (6 quarts). When top coals are partially covered with ash, pour two-thirds evenly over half of grill, then pour remaining coals over other half of grill. Set cooking grate in place, cover, and open lid vent completely. Heat grill until hot, about 5 minutes.

3B. FOR A GAS GRILL: Turn all burners to high, cover, and heat grill until hot, about 15 minutes. Leave primary burner on high and turn other burner(s) to medium.

4. Clean and oil cooking grate. Place steak on hotter side of grill. Cook (covered if using gas), turning as needed, until well browned on both sides and meat registers 120 to 125 degrees (for medium-rare) or 130 to 135 degrees (for medium), 10 to 14 minutes. (If steaks begin to burn, slide to cooler side of grill to finish cooking.)

5. Transfer steak to carving board, tent with aluminum foil, and let rest for 5 to 10 minutes. Slice steak very thinly and serve with lime wedges.

VARIATION

Grilled Steak Tips with Asian Flavors

Substitute following mixture for marinade: Whisk ⅓ cup soy sauce, 3 tablespoons vegetable oil, 3 tablespoons toasted sesame oil, 2 tablespoons packed dark brown sugar, 1 tablespoon grated fresh ginger, 2 teaspoons grated orange zest, 1 thinly sliced scallion, 3 minced garlic cloves, and ½ teaspoon red pepper flakes together in bowl to dissolve sugar.

Grilled Marinated Skirt Steak

SERVES 4 TO 6   **TOTAL TIME** 1 HOUR

✔ **WHY THIS RECIPE WORKS:** Intensely beefy skirt steak is a popular cut because its loose grain makes it an ideal candidate for soaking up a flavorful marinade. But while a marinade might add flavor, sometimes the wet meat can simply steam on the grill instead of browning and forming a crust. To achieve a charred crust, we first seared our steaks after seasoning them with salt, pepper, and sugar, and then we marinated them once they came off the grill. Poking the grilled steaks with a fork let the bold, savory flavors penetrate into the meat and, since the marinade never touched raw meat, we could also serve the marinade on the side as a sauce. Keep the marinade at room temperature or it will cool down the steaks. We prefer skirt steak cooked to medium-rare, but if you prefer it more or less done, see the chart on page 15.

MARINADE

- ½ cup soy sauce
- ¼ cup Worcestershire sauce
- 2 scallions, sliced thin
- 4 garlic cloves, minced
- 1 tablespoon Dijon mustard
- 2 teaspoons balsamic vinegar
- 2 tablespoons sugar
- 1½ teaspoons pepper
- ¼ cup vegetable oil

We pour the marinade over our seared skirt steaks after, not before, grilling.

STEAK
- 2 (12-ounce) skirt steaks, trimmed and cut crosswise into 4-inch pieces
- 2 teaspoons sugar
- ½ teaspoon salt
- ½ teaspoon pepper

1. FOR THE MARINADE: Combine all ingredients except oil in bowl. Slowly whisk in oil until incorporated and sugar has dissolved; set aside.

2. FOR THE STEAK: Pat meat dry with paper towels and sprinkle thoroughly with sugar, salt, and pepper.

3A. FOR A CHARCOAL GRILL: Open bottom vent completely. Light large chimney starter mounded with charcoal briquettes (7 quarts). When top coals are partially covered with ash, pour evenly over half of grill. Set cooking grate in place, cover, and open lid vent completely. Heat grill until hot, about 5 minutes.

3B. FOR A GAS GRILL: Turn all burners to high, cover, and heat grill until hot, about 15 minutes. Leave all burners on high.

4. Clean and oil cooking grate. Place steaks on hotter side of grill. Cook (covered if using gas), turning as needed, until well browned on both sides and meat registers 120 to 125 degrees (for medium-rare), 4 to 8 minutes.

5. Transfer steaks to 13 by 9-inch pan and poke all over with fork. Pour marinade over top, tent with aluminum foil, and let rest for 5 to 10 minutes. Transfer meat to carving board and slice thin against grain. Pour marinade into serving bowl. Serve.

VARIATIONS

Grilled Hoisin-Scallion Marinated Skirt Steak

Substitute following mixture for marinade: Combine ½ cup soy sauce, ¼ cup hoisin sauce, 2 thinly sliced scallions, 2 tablespoons sugar, 1–2 teaspoons Asian chili-garlic sauce, and 1 teaspoon grated fresh ginger in bowl. Slowly whisk in ¼ cup vegetable oil and 1 teaspoon toasted sesame oil until incorporated and sugar has dissolved.

Grilled Black Pepper–Honey Marinated Skirt Steak

Substitute following mixture for marinade: Combine ½ cup soy sauce, 3 tablespoons honey, 2 tablespoons Dijon mustard, 2 teaspoons pepper, and ½ teaspoon minced fresh thyme in bowl. Slowly whisk in ¼ cup vegetable oil until incorporated

Skirt Steak Fajitas

SERVES 4   **TOTAL TIME** 1 HOUR
(PLUS 30 MINUTES MARINATING TIME)

✔ **WHY THIS RECIPE WORKS:** Skirt steak makes great fajitas, but it can cook up tough if not handled properly. For foolproof skirt steak fajitas that packed meaty flavor and wouldn't overcook, we started with a marinade that included soy sauce. This helped brine the steak, keeping the meat moist. Pricking the steak with a fork helped the marinade penetrate the meat and cut the marinating time to only 30 minutes. After the steak was cooked, we drizzled it with a second marinade and sliced the meat against the grain to make it more tender. We prefer the beefier flavor of skirt steak, but you can use flank steak, which is wider. Don't marinate the steak for longer than 2 hours or it will begin to turn mushy. We prefer skirt steak cooked to medium-rare, but if you prefer it more or less done, see the chart on page 15. To make this dish spicier, add the chile seeds to the marinade in step 1. Serve the fajitas as is or with salsa, shredded cheese, and/or sour cream.

½ cup lime juice (4 limes)
¼ cup vegetable oil
2 tablespoons soy sauce
3 garlic cloves, minced
2 teaspoons ground cumin
2 teaspoons packed brown sugar
1 jalapeño chile, stemmed, seeded, and minced
1 tablespoon chopped fresh cilantro
2 (12-ounce) skirt steaks, trimmed and halved crosswise
2 bell peppers, stemmed, seeded, and quartered
1 onion, sliced into ½-inch-thick rounds
   (do not separate rings)
   Salt and pepper
8–12 (6-inch) flour tortillas

1. Combine lime juice, 2 tablespoons oil, soy sauce, garlic, cumin, sugar, and jalapeño in bowl. Transfer ¼ cup of marinade to separate bowl, stir in cilantro, and set aside. Cut steaks in half widthwise and poke each side about 25 times with fork. Combine steaks and remaining marinade in 1-gallon zipper-lock bag and toss to coat; press out as much air as possible and seal bag. Refrigerate for 30 minutes to 2 hours.

2. Before grilling, remove steak from bag and pat dry with paper towels. Brush peppers and onion rounds with remaining 2 tablespoons oil and season with salt and pepper.

3A. FOR A CHARCOAL GRILL: Open bottom vent completely. Light large chimney starter filled with charcoal briquettes (6 quarts). When top coals are partially covered with ash, pour two-thirds evenly over half of grill, then pour remaining coals over other half of grill. Set cooking grate in place, cover, and open lid vent completely. Heat grill until hot, about 5 minutes.

3B. FOR A GAS GRILL: Turn all burners to high, cover, and heat grill until hot, about 15 minutes. Leave primary burner on high and turn other burner(s) to medium.

4. Clean and oil cooking grate. Place steaks on hotter side of grill and place bell peppers and onion rounds on cooler side of grill. Cook (covered if using gas), turning as needed, until steak and vegetables are nicely charred and meat registers 120 to 125 degrees (for medium-rare), 8 to 12 minutes. As they finish cooking, transfer steak and vegetables to carving board and tent with aluminum foil. Let steak rest for 5 to 10 minutes.

5. Working in batches, grill tortillas over cooler part of grill, turning as needed, until warmed and lightly browned, about 40 seconds. As tortillas finish cooking, wrap in dish towel or large sheet of foil.

6. Separate onion rings and slice bell peppers into ¼-inch-wide strips; toss together in bowl with half of reserved marinade. Slice meat thinly against grain and toss with remaining reserved marinade in separate bowl. Arrange steak and vegetables on platter and serve with tortillas.

Grill-Roasted Beef Tenderloin

SERVES 10 TO 12 **TOTAL TIME** 1 HOUR 20 MINUTES (PLUS 1 HOUR SALTING TIME)

✓ **WHY THIS RECIPE WORKS:** Grilled tenderloin sounds appealing, but with a whole tenderloin going for as much as $100, uneven cooking, bland flavor, and a tough outer crust just don't cut it. To flavor the meat, we salted it, covered it loosely in plastic, and let it rest on the counter before hitting the hot grill. Tucking the narrow tip end of the tenderloin under and tying it securely gave the tenderloin a more consistent thickness that allowed it to cook through more evenly on the grill. Direct heat was too hot for the roast to endure throughout the entire cooking time, so after briefly searing the meat over the coals and flames, we moved it away from the heat for grill roasting via indirect heat. As a variation, we liked adding wood chips to the grill as it gently boosted the meat's smoky flavor. To prevent the meat from tasting too smoky, we held off on adding the wood chips to the grill until after we'd seared the meat. Beef tenderloins purchased from wholesale clubs require a good amount of trimming before cooking; for information on how to tie a beef tenderloin roast, see page 202. We prefer beef tenderloin when the center is cooked to medium-rare, but if you prefer it more or less done, see the chart on page 15.

1 (6-pound) whole unpeeled beef tenderloin, trimmed
1½ tablespoons kosher salt
2 tablespoons vegetable oil
1 tablespoon pepper

1. Tuck tail end of tenderloin and tie roast at 2-inch intervals with kitchen twine. Pat roast dry with paper towels and rub with salt. Cover loosely with plastic wrap and let sit at room temperature for 1 hour. Pat tenderloin dry with paper towels, rub with oil, and season with pepper.

2A. FOR A CHARCOAL GRILL: Open bottom vent halfway. Light large chimney starter filled with charcoal briquettes

Making a Foil Packet for Wood Chips

After soaking wood chips in water for 15 minutes, spread drained chips in center of 15 by 12-inch piece of heavy-duty aluminum foil. Fold to seal edges, then cut several slits to allow smoke to escape.

(6 quarts). When top coals are partially covered with ash, pour evenly over half of grill. Set cooking grate in place, cover, and open lid vent halfway. Heat grill until hot, about 5 minutes.

2B. FOR A GAS GRILL: Turn all burners to high, cover, and heat grill until hot, about 15 minutes. Leave all burners on high.

3. Clean and oil cooking grate. Place roast on hotter side of grill. Cook (covered if using gas), turning as needed, until well browned on all sides, 8 to 10 minutes. If using gas, leave primary burner on high and turn off other burner(s).

4. Slide beef to cooler side of grill. Cover (position lid vent over meat if using charcoal) and cook until center of meat registers 120 to 125 degrees (for medium-rare), 15 to 30 minutes. (Center of roast will remain a degree more rare than ends.)

5. Transfer roast to carving board, tent with aluminum foil, and let rest for 15 to 20 minutes. Remove twine, cut into ½-inch-thick slices, and serve.

VARIATION
Smoked, Grill-Roasted Beef Tenderloin

If you'd like to use wood chunks instead of wood chips when using a charcoal grill, substitute two medium wood chunks, soaked in water for 1 hour, for the wood chip packet.

Before grilling, soak 2 cups wood chips in water for 15 minutes, then drain. Using large piece of heavy-duty aluminum foil, wrap soaked chips in foil packet and cut several vent holes in top. After browning meat in step 3, transfer to large platter. Remove cooking grate, place wood chip packet directly on coals or primary burner, set cooking grate back in place, and cover. Let chips begin to smoke, about 5 minutes, before returning meat to grill and cooking as directed in step 4.

California Barbecued Tri-Tip

SERVES 4 TO 6   TOTAL TIME 1 HOUR 40 MINUTES
(PLUS 1 HOUR SALTING TIME)

✔ **WHY THIS RECIPE WORKS:** Unlike other barbecue recipes, California barbecued tri-tip recipes call for cooking the meat (bottom sirloin roast) over high heat and seasoning it with only salt, pepper, garlic, and the sweet smoke of the grill. This consistently produces a charred exterior and very rare center—but we wanted the outside cooked less and the inside cooked more. To achieve this, we pushed all the coals in our grill to one side, which created a hot zone for searing and a cooler one for finishing the meat slowly. To prevent the meat from tasting like ashes, we held off on adding the wood chips until after we'd seared the meat. If you'd like to use wood

We grill a beef roast over two heat zones to allow the outside to develop a browned crust and the center to cook slowly.

chunks instead of wood chips on a charcoal grill, substitute two medium wood chunks, soaked in water for 1 hour, for the wood chip packet. We prefer tri-tip when the center is cooked to medium-rare, but if you prefer it more or less done, see the chart on page 15. Serve with Santa Maria Salsa (page 318).

2 tablespoons vegetable oil
6 garlic cloves, minced
¾ teaspoon salt
1 (2-pound) beef tri-tip roast, trimmed
1 teaspoon pepper
¾ teaspoon garlic salt
2 cups wood chips, soaked in water for 15 minutes and drained

1. Combine oil, garlic, and salt in bowl. Pat meat dry with paper towels, poke each side about 20 times with fork, then rub evenly with oil-garlic mixture. Wrap meat in plastic wrap and let sit at room temperature for 1 hour, or refrigerate for up to 1 day.

2. Unwrap meat, wipe off garlic paste using paper towels, and season with pepper and garlic salt. Using large piece of heavy-duty aluminum foil, wrap soaked chips in foil packet and cut several vent holes in top.

3A. FOR A CHARCOAL GRILL: Open bottom vent halfway. Light large chimney starter filled with charcoal briquettes (6 quarts). When top coals are partially covered with ash, pour evenly over half of grill. Set cooking grate in place, cover, and open lid vent halfway. Heat grill until hot, about 5 minutes.

3B. FOR A GAS GRILL: Turn all burners to high, cover, and heat grill until hot, about 15 minutes. Leave all burners on high.

4. Clean and oil cooking grate. Place roast on hotter side of grill. Cook (covered if using gas), turning as needed, until well browned on all sides, 8 to 10 minutes. Transfer meat to plate.

5. Remove cooking grate and place wood chip packet directly on coals or primary burner; cover grill and let chips begin to smoke, about 5 minutes. If using gas, leave primary burner on high and turn off other burner(s).

6. Place meat on cooler side of grill. Cover (position lid vent over meat if using charcoal) and cook until meat registers 120 to 125 degrees (for medium-rare), about 20 minutes. (Center of roast will remain a degree more rare than ends.)

7. Transfer meat to carving board, tent with foil, and let rest for 15 to 20 minutes. Slice meat thinly and serve.

SANTA MARIA SALSA

MAKES 4 CUPS   **TOTAL TIME** 1 HOUR 40 MINUTES
The distinct texture of each ingredient is part of this salsa's appeal, so we don't recommend using a food processor.

- 2 **pounds tomatoes, cored and chopped fine**
- 2 **teaspoons salt**
- 2 **jalapeño chiles, stemmed, seeded, and chopped fine**
- 1 **small red onion, chopped fine**
- 1 **celery rib, chopped fine**
- ¼ **cup lime juice (2 limes)**
- ¼ **cup chopped fresh cilantro**
- 1 **garlic clove, minced**
- ⅛ **teaspoon dried oregano**
- ⅛ **teaspoon Worcestershire sauce**

Toss tomatoes with salt in strainer and let drain for 30 minutes. Toss drained tomatoes with remaining ingredients in bowl, cover, and let stand at room temperature until flavors have melded, about 1 hour. (Salsa can be refrigerated for up to 2 days.)

Grilled Honey-Glazed Pork Chops

SERVES 4   **TOTAL TIME** 1 HOUR

✔ **WHY THIS RECIPE WORKS:** Pork chops and honey are a natural pairing, and grilling should enhance the combination, with the honey glaze complementing the smoky char. But we battled glazes that slid right off the chops, while chops appearing slightly lacquered required such lengthy grilling and basting times that the meat was as dry as a bone. Painting the chops with glaze partway through cooking showed the most promise. We rubbed our chops with a sugar mixture that caramelized on the grill, creating a rough surface for our super-reduced glaze to stick to. We cooked the chops over indirect heat until almost done, then brushed them with the glaze and finished with a fast sear. The glaze never had time to melt off. And the meat was perfectly cooked too. For more information on cutting slits in the sides of the chops, see page 213.

- 4 **(10-ounce) bone-in pork rib or center-cut chops, 1 inch thick, trimmed**
- ¼ **cup sugar**
- 1 **teaspoon salt**
- 1 **teaspoon pepper**
- 2 **tablespoons cider vinegar**
- ½ **teaspoon cornstarch**
- ¼ **cup honey**
- 1½ **tablespoons Dijon mustard**
- ½ **teaspoon minced fresh thyme**
- ⅛ **teaspoon cayenne pepper**

1. Pat chops dry with paper towels and cut 2 slits about 2 inches apart through fat on edges of each chop. Combine sugar, salt, and pepper in bowl, then rub thoroughly over chops.

2. Whisk vinegar and cornstarch together in small saucepan until smooth, then stir in honey, mustard, thyme, and cayenne. Bring mixture to boil, then reduce heat to medium-low and simmer until thickened and measures ¼ cup, 5 to 7 minutes.

3A. FOR A CHARCOAL GRILL: Open bottom vent completely. Light large chimney starter filled with charcoal briquettes (6 quarts). When top coals are partially covered with ash, pour two-thirds evenly over half of grill, then pour remaining coals over other half of grill. Set cooking grate in place, cover, and open lid vent completely. Heat grill until hot, about 5 minutes.

3B. FOR A GAS GRILL: Turn all burners to high, cover, and heat grill until hot, about 15 minutes. Leave primary burner on high and turn other burner(s) to medium-low.

4. Clean and oil cooking grate. Place chops on cooler side of grill. Cook (covered if using gas), turning as needed, until meat registers 145 degrees, 6 to 10 minutes.

5. Brush tops of chops with glaze, flip glazed side down, and grill over hotter part of grill until caramelized, about 1 minute. Repeat with second side of chops. Transfer chops to platter, tent with aluminum foil, and let rest for 5 to 10 minutes. Brush chops with remaining glaze before serving.

Smoked Double-Thick Pork Chops

SERVES 6 TO 8   **TOTAL TIME** 1 HOUR 45 MINUTES
(PLUS 1 HOUR SALTING TIME)

✔ **WHY THIS RECIPE WORKS:** Most grilled double-thick pork chop recipes result in a charred exterior and raw meat, or gray meat that tastes steamed. We wanted ours to have great taste and tenderness. Starting the chops over indirect heat made for juicy and tender meat and wood chips infused the pork with a nice smoky flavor. Coating the pork chops with a rub of brown sugar and herbs and spices helped produce a flavorful crust, and a quick stint over hot coals at the end of cooking gave the crust a crisp texture and rich color. We prefer blade chops, which have more fat to prevent them from drying out, but leaner loin chops will also work. If you'd like to use wood chunks instead of wood chips when using a charcoal grill, substitute two medium wood chunks, soaked in water for 1 hour, for the wood chip packet. These chops are huge; you may want to slice the meat off the bone before serving.

¼ cup packed dark brown sugar
1 tablespoon ground fennel
1 tablespoon ground cumin
1 tablespoon ground coriander
1 tablespoon paprika
1 teaspoon salt
1 teaspoon pepper
4 (1¼- to 1½-pound) bone-in blade-cut pork chops, about 2 inches thick, trimmed
2 cups wood chips, soaked in water for 15 minutes and drained

1. Combine sugar, fennel, cumin, coriander, paprika, salt, and pepper in bowl. Pat pork chops dry with paper towels and rub them evenly with spice mixture. Wrap chops in plastic wrap and refrigerate for 1 hour or up to 1 day. Using large piece of heavy-duty aluminum foil, wrap soaked chips in foil packet and cut several vent holes in top.

NOTES FROM THE TEST KITCHEN

Cutting Your Own Double-Thick Pork Chops

We like juicy blade-end chops that are at least 2 inches thick for our Smoked Double-Thick Pork Chops recipe. If you can't find them prepackaged at your grocery store, just buy a 4½- to 5-pound bone-in blade roast and cut it into 2-inch portions yourself. If cutting your own chops, ask your butcher or meat department manager if the chine bone (a part of the backbone) has been removed from the base of the roast—this thick bone can make carving difficult. If the chine bone has not been removed, ask the butcher to cut the chops for you.

2A. FOR A CHARCOAL GRILL: Open bottom vent halfway. Light large chimney starter filled with charcoal briquettes (6 quarts). When top coals are partially covered with ash, pour into steeply banked pile against side of grill. Place wood chip packet on coals. Set cooking grate in place, cover, and open lid vent halfway. Heat grill until hot and wood chips are smoking, about 5 minutes.

2B. FOR A GAS GRILL: Remove cooking grate and place wood chip packet directly on primary burner. Set cooking grate in place, turn all burners to high, cover, and heat grill until hot and wood chips are smoking, about 15 minutes. Leave primary burner on high and turn off other burner(s).

3. Clean and oil cooking grate. Place pork chops on cooler side of grill with bone sides facing hotter side of grill. Cover (position lid vent over pork if using charcoal) and cook until meat registers 145 degrees, 50 minutes to 1 hour.

4. Slide chops to hotter side of grill and cook, turning as needed, until well browned, about 4 minutes. Transfer to platter and let rest for 15 to 20 minutes before serving.

Chipotle-Grilled Pork Tacos

SERVES 4   **TOTAL TIME** 1 HOUR

✔ **WHY THIS RECIPE WORKS:** Pork tenderloin can become bland and dry when cooked. We wanted a grilled pork taco recipe that kept this lean cut tender and juicy. One of the ways we did this was by halving the pork tenderloins lengthwise to create more surface area for the smoky wet rub, which developed into a flavorful crust. Chipotle chiles, which are smoked jalapeños, added rich flavor. They are packed in a tomato-based adobo sauce and can be found in the Mexican foods section of most supermarkets. We allowed the pork to rest for at least 5 minutes before slicing so the juices could redistribute. Toasting the tortillas over the fire until they were lightly charred—about 30 seconds—added an extra layer of flavor.

¼ cup mayonnaise
 1 (8-ounce) can pineapple chunks in juice, drained and chopped, ¼ cup juice reserved
 3 tablespoons minced fresh cilantro
 3 garlic cloves, minced
1½ tablespoons minced canned chipotle chiles in adobo sauce
 1 (8-ounce) bag coleslaw mix
 3 scallions, sliced thin
   Salt
 2 (12- to 16-ounce) pork tenderloins, trimmed and sliced in half lengthwise
12 (6-inch) corn tortillas
   Lime wedges

1. Whisk mayonnaise, pineapple juice, cilantro, garlic, and chipotle together in large bowl. Transfer ¼ cup of mayonnaise mixture to separate bowl and reserve for pork. Stir chopped pineapple chunks, coleslaw mix, scallions, and ½ teaspoon salt into remaining mayonnaise mixture and toss to combine. Pat pork dry with paper towels, season with salt, and rub with reserved mayonnaise mixture.

2A. FOR A CHARCOAL GRILL: Open bottom vent completely. Light large chimney starter filled with charcoal briquettes (6 quarts). When top coals are partially covered with ash, pour evenly over grill. Set cooking grate in place, cover, and open lid vent completely. Heat grill until hot, about 5 minutes.

2B. FOR A GAS GRILL: Turn all burners to high, cover, and heat grill until hot, about 15 minutes. Leave all burners on high.

3. Clean and oil cooking grate. Place pork on grill. Cook (covered if using gas), turning as needed, until well browned and meat registers 145 degrees, about 6 minutes. Transfer pork to carving board, tent with aluminum foil, and let rest for 5 to 10 minutes.

4. Working in batches, grill tortillas, turning as needed, until warmed and lightly charred, about 30 seconds. As tortillas finish cooking, wrap in dish towel or large sheet of foil. Slice pork thinly and serve with tortillas, coleslaw mixture, and lime wedges.

We roll pork tenderloin in cornstarch and dip it in beaten egg whites to help keep its crunchy crust in place on the grill.

Spice-Crusted Grilled Pork Tenderloin

SERVES 4 TO 6   **TOTAL TIME** 1 HOUR

✓ **WHY THIS RECIPE WORKS:** To avoid a sandy exterior for spice-crusted grilled pork tenderloin, we used cracked mustard seeds, coriander seeds, black peppercorns, sugar, salt, and cornmeal. To help the crust stay put, we first rolled the tenderloin in cornstarch, then dipped it in lightly beaten egg whites before adding the spices to the exterior. Gently pressing the spices onto the pork also helped the crust stay in place. A spritz of oil spray right before grilling further ensured the crust stuck to the pork instead of the grill. To crack the spices, place them in two zipper-lock bags, one inside the other, and press or gently pound with a skillet, rolling pin, or meat pounder. We prefer Demerara or turbinado sugar for their crunch, but plain brown sugar works too.

SPICE MIXTURE

1½ tablespoons mustard seeds, cracked

1 tablespoon coriander seeds, cracked

1 tablespoon cornmeal

1 teaspoon black peppercorns, cracked

1 teaspoon Demerara or turbinado sugar

1 teaspoon kosher salt

PORK

½ cup cornstarch

2 large egg whites

2 (12- to 16-ounce) pork tenderloins, trimmed

Vegetable oil spray

1. FOR THE SPICE MIXTURE: Combine all ingredients on rimmed baking sheet.

2. FOR THE PORK: Place cornstarch in large bowl. Beat egg whites in second large bowl until foamy. Pat pork dry with paper towels. Working with 1 tenderloin at a time, coat lightly with cornstarch, dip in egg whites, then coat with spice mixture, pressing gently to adhere. Transfer tenderloins to clean baking sheet and spray all sides with oil spray.

3A. FOR A CHARCOAL GRILL: Open bottom vent completely. Light large chimney starter filled with charcoal briquettes (6 quarts). When top coals are partially covered with ash, pour evenly over half of grill. Set cooking grate in place, cover, and open lid vent completely. Heat grill until hot, about 5 minutes.

3B. FOR A GAS GRILL: Turn all burners to high, cover, and heat grill until hot, about 15 minutes. Leave primary burner on high and turn off other burner(s).

4. Clean and oil cooking grate. Place tenderloins on hotter side of grill. Cook (covered if using gas), turning as needed, until browned on all sides, 6 to 8 minutes. Slide pork to cooler side of grill, cover, and cook until meat registers 145 degrees, 6 to 12 minutes.

5. Transfer pork to carving board, tent with aluminum foil, and let rest for 5 to 10 minutes. Slice pork thinly and serve.

VARIATIONS

Everything Bagel–Crusted Grilled Pork Tenderloin

Substitute following mixture for spice mixture: Combine 1 tablespoon cornmeal, 1 tablespoon sesame seeds, 1 tablespoon minced garlic, 1 teaspoon cracked black peppercorns, 1 teaspoon kosher salt, 1 teaspoon poppy seeds, and ½ teaspoon caraway seeds on rimmed baking sheet.

Coffee-and-Fennel-Crusted Grilled Pork Tenderloin

Substitute following mixture for spice mixture: Combine 1 tablespoon cornmeal, 2 teaspoons fennel seeds, 1 teaspoon instant espresso powder, 1 teaspoon cracked black peppercorns, 1 teaspoon kosher salt, 1 teaspoon Demerara or turbinado sugar, and ¼ teaspoon red pepper flakes on rimmed baking sheet.

Grilled Rosemary Pork Loin

SERVES 6 TO 8 **TOTAL TIME** 2 HOURS

✔ **WHY THIS RECIPE WORKS:** In theory, rosemary, garlic, and pork make a perfect trio. Turning theory into dinner is another matter. For our pork loin recipe we found it better to score, rather than trim, the thin layer of fat on the top of the pork loin, as scoring encouraged the fat to melt and baste the meat during cooking. To flavor every bite with our garlic, rosemary, parsley, and oil paste, we butterflied the meat to allow us to spread the interior of the loin with the herb paste. Mincing the parsley, rosemary, and garlic makes for a homogeneous filling. We then rolled up the roast, tied it with kitchen twine, and brushed it with olive oil to help it brown and to reduce sticking on the grill. On the grill, we browned the roast directly over high heat, then finished cooking it on the cooler side of the grill.

⅓ cup minced fresh parsley

1½ tablespoons minced fresh rosemary

2 garlic cloves, minced

Salt and pepper

3 tablespoons extra-virgin olive oil

1 (2½- to 3-pound) boneless pork loin roast

1. Combine parsley, rosemary, garlic, ¾ teaspoon salt, ¾ teaspoon pepper, and 2 tablespoons oil in bowl. Using sharp knife, lightly score fat on top of roast in crosshatch pattern. With roast fat side up, cut horizontally through meat, one-third above bottom, stopping ½ inch from edge. Open roast and press flat; 1 side will be twice as thick. Continue cutting thicker side of roast in half, stopping ½ inch from edge; open roast and press flat.

2. Spread herb mixture over cut side of pork, leaving ½-inch border on sides. Roll pork up tightly and tie at 1-inch intervals with kitchen twine. (Roast can be refrigerated for 1 day.) Rub roast with remaining 1 tablespoon oil and season with salt and pepper.

3A. FOR A CHARCOAL GRILL: Open bottom vent completely. Light large chimney starter filled with charcoal briquettes (6 quarts). When top coals are partially covered with ash, pour evenly over half of grill. Set cooking grate in place, cover, and open lid vent completely. Heat grill until hot, about 5 minutes.

3B. FOR A GAS GRILL: Turn all burners to high, cover, and heat grill until hot, about 15 minutes. Leave primary burner on high and turn off other burner(s).

4. Clean and oil cooking grate. Place roast on hotter side of grill. Cook (covered if using gas), turning as needed until well browned on all sides, about 12 minutes. Slide roast to cooler side of grill and turn fat side up. Cover and cook until meat registers 140 degrees, 35 to 45 minutes.

5. Transfer pork to carving board, tent with aluminum foil, and let rest 15 to 20 minutes. Remove twine, cut into ½-inch-thick slices, and serve.

Scoring and Butterflying a Pork Loin

1. Using sharp knife, lightly score fat on top of roast in crosshatch pattern.

2. With roast fat side up, cut horizontally through meat, one-third above bottom, stopping ½ inch from edge.

3. Open roast and press flat; 1 side will be twice as thick.

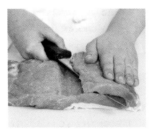

4. Repeat, cutting thicker side of roast in half horizontally, stopping ½ inch from edge.

Cuban-Style Grill-Roasted Pork

SERVES 8 TO 10   **TOTAL TIME** 5 TO 6 HOURS
(PLUS BRINING, SALTING, AND RESTING TIME)

✓ **WHY THIS RECIPE WORKS:** We wanted a boldly flavored Cuban-style roast pork with crackling-crisp skin and tender meat infused with flavor. To speed up cooking, we abandoned cooking the pork entirely on the grill (which required constant refueling and rotating over several hours) in favor of a combination cooking method: cooking the pork on the grill until our initial supply of coals died down, and then finishing it in the oven. To give the pork added flavor, we again combined methods, first brining the pork in a powerful solution that included two heads of garlic and orange juice, then rubbing a similarly flavored paste into slits cut all over the pork. Let the meat rest for a full hour before serving or it will not be as tender. This roast has a crisp skin that should be served along with the meat. Top the meat with Mojo Sauce (page 323). Traditional accompaniments include black beans, rice, and fried plantains.

PORK
1 (7- to 8-pound) bone-in, skin-on pork picnic shoulder
3 cups sugar
2 cups salt
2 garlic heads, unpeeled cloves separated and crushed
4 cups orange juice

PASTE
12 garlic cloves, chopped coarse
2 tablespoons ground cumin
2 tablespoons dried oregano
1 tablespoon salt
1½ teaspoons pepper
6 tablespoons orange juice
2 tablespoons distilled white vinegar
2 tablespoons vegetable oil

1. FOR THE PORK: Cut 1-inch-deep slits (1 inch long) all over roast, spaced about 2 inches apart. Dissolve sugar and salt in 6 quarts cold water in large container. Stir in garlic and orange juice. Submerge pork in brine, cover, and refrigerate for 18 to 24 hours. Remove pork from brine and pat dry with paper towels.

2. FOR THE PASTE: Pulse garlic, cumin, oregano, salt, and pepper in food processor to coarse paste, about 10 pulses. With processor running, add orange juice, vinegar, and oil and process until smooth, about 20 seconds. Rub paste all over pork and into slits. Wrap meat in plastic wrap and let sit at room temperature for 1 hour.

```
MOJO SAUCE
```

MOJO SAUCE

MAKES ABOUT 1 CUP   TOTAL TIME 25 MINUTES **FAST**

    4 garlic cloves, minced
    2 teaspoons kosher salt
    ½ cup extra-virgin olive oil
    ½ teaspoon ground cumin
    ¼ cup distilled white vinegar
    ¼ cup orange juice
    ¼ teaspoon dried oregano
    ⅛ teaspoon pepper

1. Place minced garlic on cutting board and sprinkle with salt. Using flat side of chef's knife, drag garlic and salt back and forth across cutting board in small circular motions until garlic is ground into smooth paste.

2. Heat oil in medium saucepan over medium heat until shimmering. Add garlic paste and cumin and cook, stirring, until fragrant, about 30 seconds. Off heat, whisk in vinegar, orange juice, oregano, and pepper. Transfer to bowl and let cool to room temperature. Whisk sauce to recombine before serving. (Sauce can be refrigerated for up to 1 day; bring to room temperature before serving.)

3A. FOR A CHARCOAL GRILL: Open bottom vent halfway. Light large chimney starter two-thirds filled with charcoal briquettes (4½ quarts). When top coals are partially covered with ash, pour into steeply banked pile against side of grill. Set cooking grate in place, cover, and open lid vent halfway. Heat grill until hot, about 5 minutes.

3B. FOR A GAS GRILL: Turn all burners to high, cover, and heat grill until hot, about 15 minutes. Turn primary burner to medium-high and turn off other burner(s). (Adjust primary burner as needed to maintain grill temperature around 325 degrees.)

4. Clean and oil cooking grate. Place roast, skin side up, on cooler side of grill. Cover (position lid vent over meat if using charcoal) and cook for 2 hours. During final 20 minutes of cooking, adjust oven rack to lower-middle position and heat oven to 325 degrees.

5. Transfer pork to wire rack set in rimmed baking sheet and transfer to oven. Roast pork until skin is browned and crisp and meat registers 190 degrees, 3 to 4 hours.

6. Transfer roast to carving board and let rest for 1 hour. Remove skin in 1 large piece. Scrape off and discard fat from top of roast and from underside of skin. Cut meat away from bone in 3 or 4 large pieces, then slice into ¼-inch-thick slices. Cut skin into strips. Serve with Mojo sauce.

Grilled Lamb Kofte

SERVES 4 TO 6   TOTAL TIME 1 HOUR
(PLUS 1 HOUR CHILLING TIME)

✓ **WHY THIS RECIPE WORKS:** In the Middle East, kebabs called *kofte* feature ground meat, not chunks, mixed with lots of spices and fresh herbs. Our challenge was to get their sausagelike texture just right. We skipped the traditional bread panade in favor of a little gelatin to keep our kofte moist after grilling. And we added ground pine nuts for richness and texture. You will need eight 12-inch metal skewers for this recipe. Serve with rice pilaf or make sandwiches with warm pita bread, sliced red onion, and chopped fresh mint.

YOGURT-GARLIC SAUCE
    1 cup plain whole-milk yogurt
    2 tablespoons lemon juice
    2 tablespoons tahini
    1 garlic clove, minced
    ½ teaspoon salt

KOFTE
    ½ cup pine nuts
    4 garlic cloves, peeled
 1½ teaspoons hot smoked paprika
    1 teaspoon salt
    1 teaspoon ground cumin
    ½ teaspoon pepper
    ¼ teaspoon ground coriander
    ¼ teaspoon ground cloves
    ⅛ teaspoon ground nutmeg
    ⅛ teaspoon ground cinnamon
 1½ pounds ground lamb
    ½ cup grated onion, drained
    ⅓ cup minced fresh parsley
    ⅓ cup minced fresh mint
 1½ teaspoons unflavored gelatin
    1 (13 by 9-inch) disposable aluminum roasting pan
       (if using charcoal)

1. FOR THE YOGURT-GARLIC SAUCE: Whisk all ingredients together in bowl.

2. FOR THE KOFTE: Process pine nuts, garlic, paprika, salt, cumin, pepper, coriander, cloves, nutmeg, and cinnamon into coarse paste in food processor, 30 to 45 seconds; transfer to large bowl. Add lamb, onion, parsley, mint, and gelatin to bowl and knead with your hands until thoroughly combined and mixture feels slightly sticky, about 2 minutes.

3. Divide mixture into 8 equal portions. Shape each portion into 5-inch-long cylinder about 1 inch in diameter. Using eight

12-inch metal skewers, thread 1 cylinder onto each skewer, pressing gently to adhere. Transfer skewers to lightly greased baking sheet, cover with plastic wrap, and refrigerate for 1 hour or up to 1 day.

4A. FOR A CHARCOAL GRILL: Using skewer, poke 12 holes in bottom of disposable pan. Open bottom vent completely and place disposable pan in center of grill. Light large chimney starter two-thirds filled with charcoal briquettes (4 quarts). When top coals are partially covered with ash, pour into disposable pan. Set cooking grate in place, cover, and open lid vent completely. Heat grill until hot, about 5 minutes.

4B. FOR A GAS GRILL: Turn all burners to high, cover, and heat grill until hot, about 15 minutes. Leave all burners on high.

5. Clean and oil cooking grate. Place skewers on grill (directly over coals if using charcoal) at 45-degree angle to grate. Cook (covered if using gas) until browned and meat easily releases from grill, 4 to 7 minutes. Flip skewers and continue to cook until browned on second side and meat registers 160 degrees, about 6 minutes. Transfer skewers to platter and serve, passing yogurt-garlic sauce separately.

VARIATION
Grilled Beef Kofte

Substitute 80 percent lean ground beef for lamb. Increase garlic to 5 cloves, paprika to 2 teaspoons, and cumin to 2 teaspoons.

Grilling Kofte

Place skewers of kofte on grill at 45-degree angle to cooking grate.

Grilled Loin or Rib Lamb Chops

SERVES 4   **TOTAL TIME** 45 MINUTES   `FAST`

✔ **WHY THIS RECIPE WORKS:** Lamb loin and rib chops are often cut quite thick—about 1½ inches in our experience—so the challenge in our grilled lamb chops recipe was to cook them through without overbrowning the exterior. We found that using a two-level fire was best—the chops could be seared on the hotter side of the grill, then moved to the cooler side to cook through. This method also reduced potential flare-ups (which

NOTES FROM THE TEST KITCHEN

Choosing Lamb Chops

Grilling lamb chops is straightforward, but shopping for them can be confusing. Look for chops that come from the rib area and the loin, but avoid shoulder chops—they can be tough and are best braised or cut off the bone and used in stews.

A loin chop looks like a smaller T-bone steak, with the bone running down the center and meat on either side. It contains a portion of both the loin and the tenderloin, which are the leanest, most tender cuts. The smaller piece on one side of the bone is very tender and fine-grained. The larger piece of meat on the other side of the bone is chewier.

Rib chops, one of the most popular cuts, are juicier and more flavorful than loin chops. The bone runs along the edge of the rib chop, with all the meat on one side. Rib chops can range in size from small and dainty to larger and meaty. Each chop has a tender eye of lean, pink meat and a thick layer of fat.

Both cuts, though tender, tend to dry out if cooked past medium because they have less intramuscular fat than shoulder chops.

often occur with lamb). To make these chops worth their high price, keep an eye on the grill to make sure the meat does not overcook. We prefer these chops cooked to medium-rare, but if you prefer them more or less done, see the chart on page 15.

8   loin or rib lamb chops, 1¼ to 1½ inches thick, trimmed
2   tablespoons extra-virgin olive oil
    Salt and pepper

1. Rub chops with oil and season with salt and pepper.

2A. FOR A CHARCOAL GRILL: Open bottom vent completely. Light large chimney starter filled with charcoal briquettes (6 quarts). When top coals are partially covered with ash, pour two-thirds evenly over half of grill, then pour remaining coals over other half of grill. Set cooking grate in place, cover, and open lid vent completely. Heat grill until hot, about 5 minutes.

2B. FOR A GAS GRILL: Turn all burners to high, cover, and heat grill until hot, about 15 minutes. Leave primary burner on high and turn other burner(s) to medium.

3. Clean and oil cooking grate. Place chops on hotter side of grill. Cook (covered if using gas), turning as needed, until nicely charred on both sides, 2 to 4 minutes. Slide chops to cooler part of grill and cook, turning as needed, until meat registers 120 to 125 degrees (for medium-rare), 6 to 9 minutes.

4. Transfer chops to platter, tent with aluminum foil, and let rest for 5 to 10 minutes. Serve.

Grilled Rack of Lamb

SERVES 4 TO 6   **TOTAL TIME** 1 HOUR 15 MINUTES

✓ **WHY THIS RECIPE WORKS:** Lamb and the grill have great chemistry. The intense heat of the coals produces a great crust and melts away the meat's abundance of fat, distributing flavor throughout, while imparting a smokiness that's the perfect complement to lamb's rich, gamy flavor. But the rendering fat can cause flare-ups that scorch the meat and impart sooty flavors, ruining this pricey cut. To solve this problem, we trimmed the excess fat from the racks of lamb and stacked the coals to the sides of the grill, creating a cooler center where the fat could safely render before we moved the lamb over direct heat to brown the exterior. A simple wet rub of robust herbs and a little oil enhanced the meat's flavor without overwhelming it. Our method gave us a rack of lamb that was pink and juicy, with a well-browned crust that contrasted nicely with the lush, ultratender interior. We prefer the milder taste and bigger size of domestic lamb, but you may substitute lamb from New Zealand or Australia. Since imported racks are generally smaller, follow the shorter cooking times given in the recipe. While most lamb is sold frenched (meaning part of each rib bone is exposed), chances are there will still be some extra fat between the bones. Remove the majority of this fat, leaving an inch at the top of the small eye of meat. For more information on preparing a rack of lamb, see page 231.

    4 teaspoons vegetable oil
    4 teaspoons minced fresh rosemary
    2 teaspoons minced fresh thyme
    2 garlic cloves, minced
    2 (1½- to 1¾-pound) racks of lamb (8 ribs each),
       trimmed and frenched
       Salt and pepper
    1 (13 by 9-inch) disposable aluminum roasting pan
       (if using charcoal)

1. Combine 1 tablespoon oil, rosemary, thyme, and garlic in bowl; set aside. Pat lamb dry with paper towels, rub with remaining 1 teaspoon oil, and season with salt and pepper.

2A. FOR A CHARCOAL GRILL: Open bottom vent completely and place disposable pan in center of grill. Light large chimney starter filled with charcoal briquettes (6 quarts). When top coals are partially covered with ash, pour into 2 even piles on either side of disposable pan. Set cooking grate in place, cover, and open lid vent completely. Heat grill until hot, about 5 minutes.

2B. FOR A GAS GRILL: Turn all burners to high, cover, and heat grill until hot, about 15 minutes. Leave primary burner on high and turn off other burner(s).

3. Clean and oil cooking grate. Place lamb, bone side up, on cooler part of grill with meaty side of racks very close to, but not quite over, hot coals or lit burner. Cover and cook until meat is lightly browned, faint grill marks appear, and fat has begun to render, 8 to 10 minutes.

4. Flip racks bone side down and slide to hotter part of grill. Cook until well browned, 3 to 4 minutes. Brush racks with herb mixture, flip bone side up, and cook until well browned, 3 to 4 minutes. Stand racks up, leaning them against each other for support, and cook until bottom is well browned and meat registers 120 to 125 degrees (for medium-rare) or 130 to 135 degrees (for medium), 3 to 8 minutes.

5. Transfer lamb to carving board, tent with aluminum foil, and let rest for 15 to 20 minutes. Cut between ribs to separate chops and serve.

VARIATION

Grilled Rack of Lamb with Sweet Mustard Glaze
Omit rosemary and add 3 tablespoons Dijon mustard, 2 tablespoons honey, and ½ teaspoon grated lemon zest to oil, thyme, and garlic. Reserve 2 tablespoons of glaze to brush over lamb before serving.

Grilling Rack of Lamb

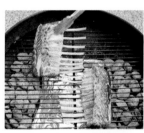

1. Place lamb, bone side up, on cooler part of grill with meaty side of racks very close to, but not quite over, hot coals or lit burner. Cover and cook until meat is lightly browned.

2. Flip racks bone side down and slide to hotter part of grill. Cook until well browned, then brush with herb mixture, flip racks, and brown well on second side.

3. Stand racks up, leaning them against each other for support, and cook until bottom is well browned.

Grilled Chicken Kebabs

SERVES 4   **TOTAL TIME** 1 HOUR
(PLUS 3 HOURS MARINATING TIME)

WHY THIS RECIPE WORKS: To keep the chicken in our grilled chicken kebabs from drying out, we marinated it in a blend of yogurt, olive oil, garlic, and herbs. The tangy, mildly acidic yogurt tenderized the chicken and added valuable flavor—as long as the chicken marinated for between 3 and 6 hours. For the vegetable component, we preferred firm vegetables like red onion and bell pepper. When cut into pieces of similar size they cooked evenly and became soft—but not mushy—by the time the chicken was cooked through. Don't skimp on the marinating time; any less than 3 hours and the chicken won't be as flavorful or as tender. Conversely, marinating for more than 6 hours will make the chicken mushy. You will need four 12-inch metal skewers for this recipe. For more information on how to cut onions for kebabs, see below.

½ **cup plain whole-milk yogurt**
½ **cup extra-virgin olive oil**
4 **garlic cloves, minced**
2 **teaspoons dried thyme**
2 **teaspoons dried oregano**
1 **teaspoon salt**
1 **teaspoon pepper**
¼ **teaspoon cayenne pepper**
1½ **pounds boneless, skinless chicken breasts, trimmed and cut into 1-inch cubes**
2 **tablespoons chopped fresh basil**
3 **tablespoons lemon juice**
2 **red bell peppers, stemmed, seeded, and cut into 1-inch pieces**
1 **large red onion, cut into 1-inch pieces, 3 layers thick**

1. Whisk yogurt, ¼ cup oil, 1 tablespoon garlic, thyme, oregano, salt, pepper, and cayenne together in large bowl. Stir in chicken, cover, and refrigerate for 3 to 6 hours. Whisk remaining ¼ cup oil, remaining garlic, basil, and lemon juice together in bowl; set aside for serving.

2. Remove chicken from marinade. Thread each of four 12-inch skewers with 2 pieces pepper, 1 section onion, 2 pieces chicken, and 1 section onion. Repeat twice more, ending with 2 additional pieces of pepper.

3A. FOR A CHARCOAL GRILL: Open bottom vent completely. Light large chimney starter filled with charcoal briquettes (6 quarts). When top coals are partially covered with ash, pour evenly over grill. Set cooking grate in place, cover, and open lid vent completely. Heat grill until hot, about 5 minutes.

3B. FOR A GAS GRILL: Turn all burners to high, cover, and heat grill until hot, about 15 minutes. Leave all burners on high.

4. Clean and oil cooking grate. Place kebabs on grill. Cook (covered if using gas), turning as needed, until vegetables and chicken are charred around edges and chicken is cooked through, about 12 minutes. Transfer kebabs to platter and brush with lemon dressing. Serve.

Preparing Onions for Kebabs

1. Peel onion, trim off stem and root ends, then quarter onion.

2. Pull onion apart into sections that are 3 layers thick; discard core.

3. Cut each 3-layer section into 1-inch pieces.

4. Skewer onion through center of each piece.

Grilled Chicken Fajitas

SERVES 4 TO 6   **TOTAL TIME** 1 HOUR 15 MINUTES

WHY THIS RECIPE WORKS: Too often, chicken fajitas need to be slathered with sour cream and salsa to mask their bland flavor and soggy ingredients. We wanted to go back to the basics, creating a simple combination of smoky grilled vegetables and strips of chicken wrapped up in warm flour tortillas. Marinating the chicken in a high-acid mixture created a bright tang. We created two levels of heat on the grill, which allowed us to grill the chicken, peppers, and onions simultaneously. We gave the chicken and vegetables a final burst of fresh flavor by tossing them with a small amount of reserved marinade. Six-inch tortillas made the perfect wrappers, and we heated them briefly on the cooler side of the grill until they puffed up and lost their raw, gummy texture. You can use red, yellow, orange, or green bell peppers in this recipe. Although these fajitas are plenty flavorful on their own, you can serve them with guacamole, salsa, shredded cheese, and lime wedges.

We cook chicken and vegetables for fajitas over two heat levels and toss them again with marinade when off the grill.

  6 tablespoons vegetable oil
  ⅓ cup lime juice (3 limes)
  1 jalapeño chile, stemmed, seeded, and minced
  1½ tablespoons minced fresh cilantro
  3 garlic cloves, minced
  1 tablespoon Worcestershire sauce
  1½ teaspoons packed brown sugar
     Salt and pepper
  1½ pounds boneless, skinless chicken breasts, trimmed and pounded ½-inch thick
  2 large bell peppers, stemmed, seeded, and quartered
  1 large red onion, sliced into ½-inch-thick rounds (do not separate rings)
8–12 (6-inch) flour tortillas

1. Whisk ¼ cup oil, lime juice, jalapeño, cilantro, garlic, Worcestershire, sugar, 1 teaspoon salt, and ¾ teaspoon pepper together in bowl. Transfer ¼ cup of marinade to separate bowl and set aside. Add 1 teaspoon salt to remaining marinade and combine with chicken in 1-gallon zipper-lock bag. Toss chicken to coat, press out as much air as possible, and seal bag. Refrigerate for 15 minutes, flipping bag once halfway through marinating.

2. Brush peppers and onion rounds with remaining 2 tablespoons oil and season with salt and pepper. Remove chicken from bag and let excess marinade drip off but do not pat dry.

3A. FOR A CHARCOAL GRILL: Open bottom vent completely. Light large chimney starter filled with charcoal briquettes (6 quarts). When top coals are partially covered with ash, pour two-thirds evenly over half of grill, then pour remaining coals over other half of grill. Set cooking grate in place, cover, and open lid vent completely. Heat grill until hot, about 5 minutes.

3B. FOR A GAS GRILL: Turn all burners to high, cover, and heat grill until hot, about 15 minutes. Leave primary burner on high and turn other burner(s) to medium.

4. Clean and oil cooking grate. Place chicken on hotter side of grill and place bell peppers and onion rounds on cooler side of grill. Cook (covered if using gas), turning as needed, until chicken and vegetables are nicely charred and chicken registers 160 degrees, 8 to 12 minutes. As they finish cooking, transfer chicken and vegetables to carving board and tent with aluminum foil. Let chicken rest for 5 to 10 minutes.

5. Working in batches, grill tortillas over cooler part of grill, turning as needed, until warmed and lightly browned, about 40 seconds. As tortillas finish cooking, wrap in dish towel or large sheet of foil.

6. Separate onion rings and slice bell peppers into ¼-inch-wide strips; toss together in bowl with half of reserved marinade. Slice chicken on bias into ¼-inch-thick slices and toss with remaining reserved marinade in separate bowl. Arrange chicken and vegetables on platter and serve with tortillas.

A charred jalapeño and onion bring complex flavor to a simple tomatillo salsa for chicken tacos.

Grilled Chicken Tacos with Salsa Verde

SERVES 4   **TOTAL TIME** 55 MINUTES

✔ **WHY THIS RECIPE WORKS:** A Mexican dinner in a hurry doesn't have to mean lackluster tacos and flavorless salsa. We quickly grilled boneless chicken breasts until they were nicely charred, and then let them rest before slicing them for serving in our grilled chicken tacos. Instead of husking and boiling fresh tomatillos for salsa verde, we enhanced canned tomatillos with grilled onions and a jalapeño for a quick, flavor-packed salsa. For a hotter salsa, leave in the ribs and seeds of the jalapeño. Tasters preferred the tacos served with sliced avocados, lime wedges, and sour cream.

- 1½ **pounds boneless, skinless chicken breasts, trimmed and pounded ½ inch thick**
      Salt and pepper
- 1   **onion, sliced into ½-inch-thick rounds (do not separate rings)**

- 1   **jalapeño chile, stemmed, halved lengthwise, and seeded**
- 1   **tablespoon vegetable oil**
- 8   **(6-inch) corn tortillas**
- 1   **(11-ounce) can tomatillos, drained**
- ½   **cup chopped fresh cilantro**
- 1   **tablespoon lime juice**
- 2   **garlic cloves, minced**

1. Pat chicken dry with paper towels and season with salt and pepper. Brush onion and jalapeño with oil and season with salt.

2A. FOR A CHARCOAL GRILL: Open bottom vent completely. Light large chimney starter filled with charcoal briquettes (6 quarts). When top coals are partially covered with ash, pour evenly over grill. Set cooking grate in place, cover, and open lid vent completely. Heat grill until hot, about 5 minutes.

2B. FOR A GAS GRILL: Turn all burners to high, cover, and heat grill until hot, about 15 minutes. Leave all burners on high.

3. Clean and oil cooking grate. Place chicken, onion, and jalapeño on grill. Cook (covered if using gas), turning as needed, until chicken and vegetables are nicely charred and chicken registers 160 degrees, 8 to 12 minutes. As they finish cooking, transfer chicken and vegetables to carving board and tent with aluminum foil. Let chicken rest for 5 to 10 minutes.

4. Working in batches, grill tortillas, turning as needed, until warmed and lightly browned, about 30 seconds. As tortillas finish cooking, wrap in dish towel or large sheet of foil.

5. Coarsely chop grilled onion and jalapeño. Pulse onion, jalapeño, tomatillos, cilantro, lime juice, garlic, and ½ teaspoon salt in food processor until coarsely ground, about 10 pulses. Slice chicken on bias into ¼-inch-thick slices, and serve with salsa and tortillas.

Grilled Lemon-Parsley Chicken Breasts

SERVES 4   **TOTAL TIME** 1 HOUR
(PLUS 30 MINUTES MARINATING TIME)

✔ **WHY THIS RECIPE WORKS:** Because they have no skin and little fat, boneless chicken breasts invariably turn out dry and leathery when grilled. A common solution—marinating them in bottled salad dressings laden with sweeteners and stabilizers—often imparts off-flavors. We wanted grilled chicken breasts that would come off the grill juicy and flavorful and we wanted to look beyond bottled salad dressing to get there. To start, we made a simple marinade with olive oil, lemon juice, garlic, parsley, sugar, and mustard—and we made a separate vinaigrette to serve with the grilled chicken for extra moisture and flavor. We slowly cooked the chicken breasts on the cooler side of the grill. We then gave the breasts a quick sear on the hotter side of the grill to finishing cooking and absorb grill flavor. Don't skimp on the marinating time; any less than 30 minutes and the chicken won't be as flavorful or as tender. Conversely, marinating for more than 1 hour will make the chicken mushy.

    6 tablespoons extra-virgin olive oil
    2 tablespoons lemon juice
    1 tablespoon minced fresh parsley
 1¼ teaspoons sugar
    1 teaspoon Dijon mustard
      Salt and pepper
    2 tablespoons water
    3 garlic cloves, minced
    4 (6- to 8-ounce) boneless, skinless chicken breasts,
      trimmed

1. Whisk 3 tablespoons oil, 1 tablespoon lemon juice, parsley, ¼ teaspoon sugar, mustard, ¼ teaspoon salt, and ¼ teaspoon pepper together in bowl and set aside for serving.

2. Whisk remaining 3 tablespoons oil, remaining 1 tablespoon lemon juice, remaining 1 teaspoon sugar, 1½ teaspoons salt, ½ teaspoon pepper, water, and garlic together in bowl. Combine oil mixture and chicken in 1-gallon zipper-lock bag and toss to coat; press out as much air as possible and seal bag. Refrigerate 30 minutes to 1 hour, flipping bag occasionally. Remove chicken from marinade and let excess marinade drip off but do not pat dry.

3A. FOR A CHARCOAL GRILL: Open bottom vent completely. Light large chimney starter filled with charcoal briquettes (6 quarts). When top coals are partially covered with ash, pour evenly over half of grill. Set cooking grate in place, cover, and open lid vent completely. Heat grill until hot, about 5 minutes.

3B. FOR A GAS GRILL: Turn all burners to high, cover, and heat grill until hot, about 15 minutes. Leave primary burner on high and turn off other burner(s).

4. Clean and oil cooking grate. Place chicken on cooler side of grill, smooth side down, with thicker sides facing coals or flame. Cover and cook until bottom of chicken just begins to develop light grill marks and is no longer translucent, 6 to 9 minutes.

5. Flip chicken and rotate so that thinner sides face coals or flame. Cover and cook until chicken is opaque and firm to touch and registers 140 degrees, 6 to 9 minutes.

6. Slide chicken to hotter side of grill and cook, flipping as needed, until well browned on both sides and chicken registers 160 degrees, 2 to 6 minutes. Transfer chicken to carving board, tent with aluminum foil, and let rest for 5 to 10 minutes. Slice chicken on bias into ¼-inch-thick slices and transfer to plates. Drizzle with reserved sauce and serve.

VARIATION
Grilled Chipotle-Lime Chicken Breasts
Substitute lime juice for lemon juice and increase juice in sauce for serving to 4 teaspoons. Substitute minced canned chipotle chile in adobo sauce for mustard and cilantro for parsley.

Grilled Bone-In Chicken
SERVES 4 TO 6   **TOTAL TIME** 1 HOUR

✓ **WHY THIS RECIPE WORKS:** Flare-ups can turn chicken into a charred mess if you're not paying attention. The method we developed for bone-in chicken avoids this pitfall by starting the chicken over a relatively cool area of the grill. This allows the fat in the chicken skin to render slowly, thereby avoiding flare-ups and encouraging ultracrisp skin. In addition to the quality of the finished product, we like this approach because it is effectively hands-off: You don't have to constantly flip and switch the chicken pieces. This recipe works with breasts, legs, thighs, or a combination of parts. Because of the skin, there is no need to coat the chicken with oil. For extra flavor, rub the chicken with one of the Spice Rubs (page 332) before cooking, or brush with any of the Barbecue Sauces (page 351) during the final few minutes of grilling. If using kosher chicken, do not brine. If brining the chicken, do not season with salt in step 1.

    4 pounds bone-in chicken pieces (split breasts cut
      in half, drumsticks, and/or thighs), trimmed and
      brined if desired
      Salt and pepper
    1 (13 by 9-inch) disposable aluminum roasting pan
      (if using charcoal)

1. Pat chicken dry with paper towels and season with salt and pepper.

2A. FOR A CHARCOAL GRILL: Open bottom vent completely and place disposable pan in center of grill. Light large chimney starter filled with charcoal briquettes (6 quarts). When top coals are partially covered with ash, pour into 2 even piles on either side of disposable pan. Set cooking grate in place, cover, and open lid vent completely. Heat grill until hot, about 5 minutes.

2B. FOR A GAS GRILL: Turn all burners to high, cover, and heat grill until hot, about 15 minutes. Turn all burners to medium-low.

3. Clean and oil cooking grate. Place chicken, skin side down, on grill (over disposable pan if using charcoal). Cover and cook until skin is crisp and golden, about 20 minutes.

4. Slide chicken to hotter side of grill if using charcoal, or turn all burners to medium-high if using gas. Cook (covered if using gas), turning as needed, until well browned on both sides and breasts register 160 degrees and drumsticks and/or thighs register 175 degrees, 5 to 15 minutes.

5. Transfer chicken to platter, tent with aluminum foil, and let rest for 5 to 10 minutes before serving.

Grilling Bone-In Chicken on Charcoal Grill

1. Bank coals on either side of grill, leaving center of grill clear. Heat grill, then lay chicken, skin side down, in single layer in center of grill. Cover and cook for 20 minutes.

2. Slide chicken to hotter side of grill and cook, turning as needed, until well browned and cooked through, 5 to 15 minutes longer.

NOTES FROM THE TEST KITCHEN

Grilling Chicken for a Crowd

Grilling bone-in, skin-on chicken pieces for a crowd can be a frustrating proposition. An overloaded grill tends to cook slowly and unevenly, and all that dripping fat just invites flare-ups. We found that our recipe for Grilled Bone-In Chicken (page 329) alleviated many of these problems, but no matter how great a griller you are, when the grill is filled, hot spots (on a gas grill) and proximity to the coals (on a charcoal grill) will cause the chicken pieces to brown at different rates. The trick, then, is to move the chicken around as needed to even out the hot spots and avoid flare-ups. Expect a 5- to 15-minute-longer grilling time and remove the chicken pieces from the grill as soon as they are done to make room for the others.

Classic Barbecued Chicken

SERVES 4 TO 6   **TOTAL TIME** 1 HOUR 30 MINUTES

✔ **WHY THIS RECIPE WORKS:** We found that starting barbecued chicken over low heat slowly rendered the fat without flare-ups. Using homemade barbecue sauce makes a big difference, but you can substitute 3 cups of store-bought sauce. We created a complex layer of barbecue flavor by applying the sauce in coats and turning the chicken as it cooked over moderate heat and then finishing it over higher heat. Don't try to grill more than 10 pieces of chicken at a time; you won't be able to line them up as directed in step 4.

- 1 **teaspoon salt**
- 1 **teaspoon pepper**
- ¼ **teaspoon cayenne pepper**
- 3 **pounds bone-in chicken pieces (split breasts cut in half, drumsticks, and/or thighs), trimmed**
- 1 **(13 by 9-inch) disposable aluminum roasting pan (if using charcoal)**
- 1 **recipe Kansas City Barbecue Sauce for Chicken (page 351)**

1. Combine salt, pepper, and cayenne in bowl. Pat chicken dry with paper towels and rub with spices. Reserve 2 cups barbecue sauce for cooking; set aside remaining 1 cup sauce for serving.

2A. FOR A CHARCOAL GRILL: Open bottom vent completely and place disposable pan on 1 side of grill. Light large chimney starter filled with charcoal briquettes (6 quarts). When top coals are partially covered with ash, pour evenly over other half of grill (opposite disposable pan). Set cooking grate in place, cover, and open lid vent completely. Heat grill until hot, about 5 minutes.

2B. FOR A GAS GRILL: Turn all burners to high, cover, and heat grill until hot, about 15 minutes. Leave primary burner on high and turn other burner(s) off. (Adjust primary burner as needed to maintain grill temperature around 350 degrees.)

3. Clean and oil cooking grate. Place chicken, skin side down, on cooler side of grill. Cover and cook until chicken begins to brown, 30 to 35 minutes.

4. Slide chicken into single line between hotter and cooler sides of grill. Cook uncovered, flipping chicken and brushing every 5 minutes with some of sauce reserved for cooking, until sticky, about 20 minutes.

5. Slide chicken to hotter side of grill and cook, uncovered, flipping and brushing with remaining sauce for cooking, until well glazed, breasts register 160 degrees, and/or thighs/drumsticks register 175 degrees, about 5 minutes. Transfer chicken to platter, tent with aluminum foil, and let rest for 5 to 10 minutes. Serve with remaining sauce.

Classic barbecued chicken is one of America's favorite summertime meals. Our foolproof recipe for barbecue chicken produces meat that is perfectly cooked through. The chicken boasts intense flavor from the grill and a thick crust made from layers of tangy-sweet barbecue sauce. Cook only your favorite chicken parts or use a mix of breasts, drumsticks, and/or thighs.

1. MAKE THE SAUCE: For a quick barbecue sauce, whisk all of the ingredients together in a saucepan and bring to a simmer; cook until the sauce is thickened. The sauce can be made up to 4 days ahead.
WHY? Homemade barbecue sauce is easy to make and tastes the best. You can, however, substitute store-bought barbecue sauce.

2. BUILD A HALF-GRILL FIRE: For both charcoal and gas grills, concentrate all of the heat on just one side of the grill.
WHY? A half-grill fire creates two cooking zones with dramatically different heat levels. One side is intensely hot, and the other side is cooler.

3. START THE CHICKEN ON THE COOLER SIDE: Place the chicken skin side down on the cooler side of the grill. Cover and cook until the chicken begins to brown, 30 to 35 minutes.
WHY? Cooking on the cooler side first allows the chicken to stay on the grill longer and cook through without burning. Starting over lower heat slowly renders the fat and prevents flare-ups.

4. MOVE THE CHICKEN AND BASTE: Slide the chicken to the middle into a single line between the hotter and cooler sides of the grill. Cook the chicken, flipping the pieces and brushing them with some sauce every 5 minutes, for about 20 minutes.
WHY? Basting and turning the pieces will cook the chicken through evenly, while building up a thick, multilayered "skin" of barbecue flavor.

5. MOVE THE CHICKEN TO THE HOTTER SIDE AND GLAZE: Slide the chicken to the hotter side of the grill and cook, flipping the pieces and brushing them with sauce, until they are well glazed and cooked through, about 5 minutes.
WHY? The heat of the hotter part of the grill allows the sauce to caramelize. This high-heat finish gives the chicken a robust, crusty char.

6. LET THE CHICKEN REST: Transfer the chicken to a platter, tent it loosely with aluminum foil, and let it rest for 5 to 10 minutes before serving.
WHY? Resting allows the chicken's juices to redistribute before cutting into it.

SPICE RUBS

Spice rubs can be used to add flavor to grilled meats, poultry, and seafood. They are fast and easy to make. To prepare a spice rub, simply mix together the spices. To use, measure out what you will need and, to prevent cross-contamination, put away any remaining rub before your hands touch the meat. (Spice rubs can be stored at room temperature for up to 1 month.) Lightly brush the poultry, meat, or fish with oil, sprinkle with the spice rub, and gently rub in the seasonings to make sure they adhere. Unless otherwise directed, spice rubs should be applied just before cooking. For meat and poultry, plan on using about 1 tablespoon of rub per portion; for fish you will need only about 1 teaspoon per portion. Each recipe makes ¾ cup.

BASIC BARBECUE SPICE RUB `FAST`

This classic rub works well on any poultry, meat, or seafood.

- 3 tablespoons packed light or dark brown sugar
- 3 tablespoons paprika
- 2 tablespoons dry mustard
- 2 tablespoons pepper
- 1 tablespoon onion powder
- 1 tablespoon garlic powder
- 1 tablespoon ground cumin
- 2 teaspoons salt
- ¾ teaspoon cayenne pepper

CAJUN SPICE RUB `FAST`

This extra spicy rub works on poultry, meat, or seafood.

- ½ cup paprika
- 2 tablespoons garlic powder
- 1 tablespoon dried thyme
- 2 teaspoons ground celery seeds
- 2 teaspoons salt
- 2 teaspoons pepper
- 2 teaspoons cayenne pepper

HERB SPICE RUB `FAST`

This rub works well with lamb, pork, or chicken.

- ¼ cup dried thyme
- ¼ cup dried rosemary
- ¼ cup pepper
- 12 bay leaves, ground in a food processor or finely crumbled
- 1 teaspoon ground cloves or ground allspice

Jerk Chicken

SERVES 4 TO 6   **TOTAL TIME** 1 HOUR 15 MINUTES
(PLUS 2 HOURS MARINATING TIME)

✔ WHY THIS RECIPE WORKS: Smoky, spicy Jamaican jerk is the marriage of hot chiles, warm spices, and grilled meat—one we wanted to bring into our own backyard. We began by making a paste of habanero chiles, allspice (a traditional jerk ingredient), garlic, scallions, and thyme for an herbal touch. To temper the heat and spice, we added vegetable oil and molasses, both of which made the paste smoother and more cohesive. We rubbed the paste under the skin and then marinated the chicken in the rest. This method produced dramatic results in only 2 hours. A double-banked fire allowed the chicken to cook through and the skin to brown. This dish is very spicy; to tone down the spice level, remove the habanero seeds and ribs before processing the chiles. The oil of the habaneros can cause your skin to burn; be sure to use gloves when handling the mixture in step 2. If you cannot find habaneros, substitute 4 to 6 jalapeño chiles.

- 1 bunch scallions, chopped
- 2–3 habanero chiles, stemmed
- ¼ cup vegetable oil
- 2 tablespoons molasses
- 1 tablespoon dried thyme
- 3 garlic cloves, peeled
- 2 teaspoons ground allspice
- 2 teaspoons salt
- 3 pounds bone-in chicken pieces (split breasts cut in half, drumsticks and/or thighs), trimmed
- 1 (13 by 9-inch) disposable aluminum roasting pan (if using charcoal)
  Lime wedges

1. Process scallions, chiles, oil, molasses, thyme, garlic, allspice, and salt in food processor until pureed, about 1 minute, scraping down bowl as needed. Gently loosen skin covering chicken pieces.

2. Wearing gloves, rub 1 tablespoon pureed scallion mixture underneath skin of each piece chicken, and transfer to 1-gallon zipper-lock bag. Add remaining pureed scallion mixture to bag and toss chicken to coat; press out as much air as possible and seal bag. Refrigerate for 2 to 36 hours.

3A. FOR A CHARCOAL GRILL: Open bottom vent completely and place disposable pan in center of grill. Light large chimney starter filled with charcoal briquettes (6 quarts). When top coals are partially covered with ash, pour into 2 even piles on either side of disposable pan. Set cooking grate in place, cover, and open lid vent completely. Heat grill until hot, about 5 minutes.

3B. FOR A GAS GRILL: Turn all burners to high, cover, and heat grill until hot, about 15 minutes. Turn all burners to medium-low. (Adjust burners as needed to maintain grill temperature around 350 degrees.)

4. Clean and oil cooking grate. Place chicken, skin side down, in center of grill (over disposable pan if using charcoal). Cover and cook until skin is well browned and breasts register 155 degrees, 20 to 30 minutes.

5. Slide chicken to hotter side of grill. Cook (covered if using gas), flipping as needed, until nicely charred, breasts register 160 degrees, and drumsticks and/or thighs register 175 degrees, 5 to 15 minutes.

6. Transfer chicken to platter, tent with aluminum foil, and let rest for 5 to 10 minutes. Serve with lime wedges.

VARIATION
Sweet 'n' Smoky Jerk Chicken

Although not a traditional Jamaican ingredient, chipotle chiles create a variation with an appealing smokiness, which is balanced nicely by the sweetness from additional molasses. Increase molasses to ¼ cup and substitute 2 tablespoons minced canned chipotle chile in adobo sauce for habanero chiles.

Grilled Pesto Chicken

SERVES 4   **TOTAL TIME** 1 HOUR 20 MINUTES
(PLUS 1 HOUR MARINATING TIME)

✔ **WHY THIS RECIPE WORKS:** Basil pesto isn't just for pasta. We found a way to imbue chicken with basil and garlic that would hold up on the grill. How did we get enough flavor into the chicken? We used homemade pesto which tastes stronger and fresher than store-bought. We used the pesto base in separate mixtures for marinating, stuffing, and saucing the chicken. We found that bone-in chicken breasts had the most flavor. We cut pockets in them to fill with pesto, then marinated them in more pesto. We added a third dose of pesto in a sauce to serve with the chicken after it was grilled. We had grilled pesto chicken with a capital P.

  4 **cups fresh basil leaves**
  ¾ **cup extra-virgin olive oil**
  5 **garlic cloves, peeled**
1½ **tablespoons lemon juice**
     Salt and pepper
  2 **ounces Parmesan cheese, grated (1 cup)**
  4 **(12-ounce) bone-in split chicken breasts, trimmed**

1. Process basil, ½ cup oil, garlic, lemon juice, and ¾ teaspoon salt in food processor until smooth, about 1 minute,

scraping down bowl as needed. Remove ¼ cup pesto from processor and reserve as marinade. Add Parmesan to pesto left in processor and pulse to incorporate, about 3 pulses; remove ¼ cup pesto and reserve as stuffing. Add remaining ¼ cup oil to pesto left in processor and pulse to incorporate, about 3 pulses; set aside for serving.

2. Starting on thick side of breast, closest to breastbone, cut horizontal pocket into each breast, stopping ½ inch from edge so halves remain attached. Season chicken, inside and out, with salt and pepper. Place 1 tablespoon pesto reserved for stuffing in each pocket. Tie each chicken breast with 2 pieces kitchen twine to secure. In large bowl, rub chicken with pesto reserved for marinade, cover, and refrigerate for 1 hour.

3A. FOR A CHARCOAL GRILL: Open bottom vent completely. Light large chimney starter filled with charcoal briquettes (6 quarts). When top coals are partially covered with ash, pour evenly over half of grill. Set cooking grate in place, cover, and open lid vent completely. Heat grill until hot, about 5 minutes.

3B. FOR A GAS GRILL: Turn all burners to high, cover, and heat grill until hot, about 15 minutes. Turn all burners to medium-low. (Adjust burners as needed to maintain grill temperature of 350 degrees.)

4. Clean and oil cooking grate. Place chicken, skin side up, on cooler side of grill if using charcoal. Cover and cook until chicken registers 155 degrees, 25 to 35 minutes.

5. Slide chicken to hotter side of grill if using charcoal or turn all burners to high if using gas, and flip skin side down. Cover and cook until well browned and chicken registers 160 degrees, 5 to 10 minutes.

6. Transfer chicken to platter, tent with aluminum foil, and let rest for 5 to 10 minutes. Remove twine, carve chicken, and serve with remaining sauce.

Stuffing Chicken with Pesto

1. Starting on thick side of breast, closest to breast-bone, cut horizontal pocket into each breast, stopping ½ inch from edge so halves remain attached.

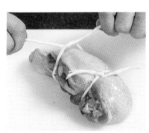

2. Season chicken, inside and out, with salt and pepper. Place 1 tablespoon pesto reserved for stuffing in each pocket. Tie each chicken breast with 2 pieces kitchen twine to secure.

A yogurt marinade keeps chicken moist and tender on the grill and yogurt also makes a cool herbed sauce for serving.

Grilled Indian-Spiced Chicken with Raita

SERVES 4   **TOTAL TIME** 1 HOUR 10 MINUTES
(PLUS 1 HOUR MARINATING TIME)

WHY THIS RECIPE WORKS: Inspired by yogurt-marinated chicken cooked in an Indian tandoor oven, this dish packs in surprising flavor in spite of its short ingredient list. As with authentic tandoori recipes, we marinated the chicken in yogurt. For the spice rub, curry powder alone tasted harsh and one-dimensional. Garam masala added complexity, but the raw taste remained. Adding the spices to the yogurt marinade solved the problem—the yogurt kept the chicken moist and tender, plus it helped to deepen the spices once they hit the grill. To prevent the marinade from burning, we started the chicken on the cooler side of the grill, then finished it on the hotter side so it would brown. More yogurt, plus garlic and cilantro, provided a cool, creamy counterpoint to the grilled meat. See page 149 for more information on garam masala.

1½ cups plain whole-milk yogurt
1 tablespoon curry powder
1 tablespoon garam masala
   Salt and pepper
4 (10- to 12-ounce) bone-in split chicken breasts, trimmed
2 tablespoons minced fresh cilantro
1 small garlic clove, minced

1. Whisk ¾ cup yogurt, curry powder, garam masala, 1 teaspoon salt, and ¼ teaspoon pepper together in bowl. Combine marinade and chicken in 1-gallon zipper-lock bag and toss to coat; press out as much air as possible and seal bag. Refrigerate for 1 to 6 hours, flipping bag occasionally.

2. Combine remaining ¾ cup yogurt, cilantro, and garlic in bowl and season with salt and pepper to taste. Cover and refrigerate until ready to serve. Remove chicken from bag and let excess marinade drip off but do not pat dry.

3A. FOR A CHARCOAL GRILL: Open bottom vent completely. Light large chimney starter filled with charcoal briquettes (6 quarts). When top coals are partially covered with ash, pour evenly over half of grill. Set cooking grate in place, cover, and open lid vent completely. Heat grill until hot, about 5 minutes.

3B. FOR A GAS GRILL: Turn all burners to high, cover, and heat grill until hot, about 15 minutes. Leave primary burner on high and turn other burner(s) to medium-low.

4. Clean and oil cooking grate. Place chicken on cooler side of grill, skin side down with thicker ends facing hotter side of grill. Cover and grill until chicken begins to brown and registers 155 degrees, 25 to 35 minutes.

5. Slide chicken to hotter side of grill, or turn all burners to high if using gas, and cook, turning as needed, until well browned and registers 160 degrees, 3 to 5 minutes. Transfer chicken to platter and let rest for 5 to 10 minutes. Serve with yogurt-cilantro sauce.

Grilled Chicken alla Diavola

SERVES 3 TO 4   **TOTAL TIME** 1 HOUR 30 MINUTES
(PLUS 2 HOURS BRINING TIME)

WHY THIS RECIPE WORKS: Butterflying a chicken is a win-win when it comes to grilling. It allows the chicken to cook through more quickly and evenly and also exposes more skin to the grill so it can brown and become ultracrisp. But crisp skin and tender meat are only half the battle—the chicken has to be flavorful, too. To that end, we set out to infuse our bird with bold heat and garlicky flavor. Adding two heads of garlic to a brine was our first move. Next, we created a potent garlic-pepper oil and rubbed some under the skin of the chicken before grilling. For one last punch of flavor, we reserved some of the garlicky oil to serve with the chicken. If using a kosher chicken, do not brine in step 1. This dish is very spicy; for milder heat, reduce the amount of red pepper flakes.

2 **garlic heads, plus 4 cloves minced**
3 **bay leaves**
    Salt and pepper
1 **(3- to 4-pound) whole chicken, giblets discarded**
¼ **cup extra-virgin olive oil**
2 **teaspoons red pepper flakes**
1 **(13 by 9-inch) disposable aluminum roasting pan (if using charcoal)**
    Lemon wedges

1. Combine 2 garlic heads, bay leaves, and ½ cup salt in zipper-lock bag, crush gently with meat pounder, and transfer to large container. Stir in 2 quarts water to dissolve salt. Trim chicken, butterfly, immerse in brine, and refrigerate for 2 hours.

2. Cook oil, minced garlic, pepper flakes, and 2 teaspoons pepper in small saucepan over medium heat until fragrant, about 3 minutes. Let oil cool, then measure out 2 tablespoons for serving.

3. Remove chicken from brine and pat dry with paper towels. Gently loosen skin covering breast and thighs and rub remaining garlic-pepper oil underneath skin. Tuck wingtips behind back.

4A. FOR A CHARCOAL GRILL: Open bottom vent completely and place disposable pan in center of grill. Light large chimney starter filled with charcoal briquettes (6 quarts). When top coals are partially covered with ash, pour into 2 even piles on either side of disposable pan. Set cooking grate in place, cover, and open lid vent completely. Heat grill until hot, about 5 minutes.

4B. FOR A GAS GRILL: Turn all burners to high, cover, and heat grill until hot, about 15 minutes. Turn all burners to medium-low. (Adjust burners as needed to maintain grill temperature of 350 degrees.)

5. Clean and oil cooking grate. Place chicken, skin side down, in center of grill (over disposable pan if using charcoal). Cover and cook until skin is crisp, breast registers 160 degrees, and thighs register 175 degrees, 30 to 45 minutes.

6. Transfer chicken to carving board and let rest for 5 to 10 minutes. Carve chicken and serve with reserved garlic oil and lemon wedges.

Butterflying a Chicken

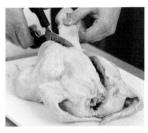

1. Cut through bones on either side of backbone and trim any excess fat or skin around neck.

2. Flip chicken over and use heel of your hand to flatten breastbone.

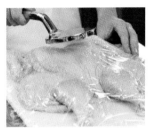

3. Cover chicken with plastic wrap and pound breast to be same thickness as leg and thigh.

Beer-Can Chicken

SERVES 4 TO 6   **TOTAL TIME** 2 HOURS 10 MINUTES

✔ **WHY THIS RECIPE WORKS:** Beer-can chicken involves resting a whole chicken upright on a can of beer and grill-roasting it. But after testing some recipes, we found several common problems: flavorless chicken, flabby skin coated in a weak glaze, and lots of grill flare-ups. We started by rubbing the chicken with a spice rub for maximum flavor. Piercing the skin with a skewer allowed the fat to escape, further crisping the skin. We also punched extra holes in the top of the beer can to allow the greatest amount of steam to escape. A disposable pan caught the dripping fat, preventing any flare-ups. Finally, we coated the chicken with a sweet-tart glaze toward the end of cooking. Look for chickens that weigh 3 to 3½ pounds; if they are significantly larger, you may have trouble fitting the lid on the grill. If you'd like to use wood chunks instead of wood chips when using a charcoal grill, substitute four medium wood chunks, soaked in water for 1 hour, for the wood chip packet.

RUB AND CHICKEN

- 2 tablespoons packed brown sugar
- 2 tablespoons paprika
- 1 tablespoon salt
- 1 tablespoon pepper
- 1 teaspoon cayenne pepper
- 2 (3- to 3½-pound) whole chickens, giblets discarded

GLAZE AND BEER

- 2 tablespoons packed brown sugar
- 2 tablespoons ketchup
- 2 tablespoons white vinegar
- 1 teaspoon hot sauce
- 2 (12-ounce) cans beer
- 4 bay leaves
- 1 (13 by 9-inch) disposable aluminum roasting pan (if using charcoal)
- 4 cups wood chips, soaked in water for 15 minutes and drained

1. FOR THE RUB AND CHICKEN: Combine sugar, paprika, salt, pepper, and cayenne in bowl. Measure out 1 tablespoon spice rub and reserve for glaze. Pat chickens dry with paper towels and gently loosen skin covering breasts and thighs. Massage remaining spice rub over and under skin and inside cavities of both chickens. Poke skin all over with skewer and tuck wingtips behind back.

2. FOR THE GLAZE AND BEER: Combine sugar, ketchup, vinegar, hot sauce, 2 tablespoons beer, and reserved 1 tablespoon spice rub in bowl. Remove 1 cup beer from each can, then crumble 2 bay leaves into each can. Punch additional holes in top of each can. Using 2 large pieces of heavy-duty aluminum foil, wrap soaked chips in 2 foil packets and cut several vent holes in tops.

3A. FOR A CHARCOAL GRILL: Open bottom vent halfway and place disposable pan in center of grill. Light large chimney starter filled with charcoal briquettes (6 quarts). When top coals are partially covered with ash, pour into 2 even piles on either side of disposable pan. Place wood chip packet on each pile of coals. Set cooking grate in place, cover, and open lid vent halfway. Heat grill until hot and wood chips are smoking, about 5 minutes.

3B. FOR A GAS GRILL: Remove cooking grate and place wood chip packets directly on primary burner. Set cooking grate in place, turn all burners to high, cover, and heat grill until hot and wood chips are smoking, about 15 minutes. Turn all burners to medium-low. (Adjust burners as needed to maintain grill temperature around 350 degrees.)

4. Clean and oil cooking grate. Place chickens, upright on cans, in center of grill (over disposable pan if using charcoal). Cover and cook until skin is well browned and very crisp, 40 to 60 minutes.

5. Brush chickens with glaze and continue to cook, covered, until breasts register 160 degrees and thighs register 175 degrees, about 20 minutes.

6. Wearing oven mitts, transfer chickens (still on their cans) to carving board. Tent chicken with foil and let rest for 5 to 10 minutes. Working with 1 chicken at a time, hold base of can with oven mitt, insert tongs into chicken's neck cavity, and pull chicken off can. Carve chickens and serve.

Making Beer-Can Chicken

1. SPICE AND POKE CHICKEN: Massage spice mixture over and under chicken skin and inside cavities, then poke skin all over with skewer.

2. PUNCH EXTRA HOLES IN CAN: Remove 1 cup beer from each can, then crumble 2 bay leaves into each can. Punch additional holes in top of each can.

3. STEADY BIRD ON CAN: Place chickens, upright on cans, in center of grill (over disposable pan if using charcoal), cover, and cook until skin is well browned and very crisp, 40 to 60 minutes.

4. FINISH WITH GLAZE: Brush chickens with glaze and continue to cook for another 20 minutes.

Smoked Turkey Breast

SERVES 6 TO 8   **TOTAL TIME** 2 HOURS 20 MINUTES
(PLUS 8 HOURS SALTING TIME)

✔ WHY THIS RECIPE WORKS: For smoked turkey with plump, juicy meat lightly perfumed with smoke, we chose a turkey breast, which cooked relatively quickly on the grill. Rubbing salt and brown sugar under and over the skin and resting in the refrigerator overnight allowed the seasonings to penetrate the meat. Before grilling, we dried the skin and applied a second round of rub, replacing the salt with pepper for kick. Piercing the skin before grilling allowed some of the fat to drain away, which helped crisp the skin. Two cups of wood chips added enough smokiness without overwhelming the mild meat. After grilling the bird for an hour and a half, we had smoky, well-seasoned, juicy meat with golden, crisp skin. Much like whole turkeys, turkey breasts come in a wide range of sizes. If your turkey breast is larger or smaller than 5 pounds, you will need to adjust the grilling time accordingly. If you'd like to use wood chunks instead of wood chips when using a charcoal grill, substitute two medium wood chunks, soaked in water for 1 hour, for the wood chip packet.

- 3 tablespoons packed brown sugar
- 1 tablespoon salt
- 1 (5-pound) whole bone-in turkey breast, trimmed
- 2 teaspoons pepper
- 2 cups wood chips
- 1 (13 by 9-inch) disposable aluminum roasting pan (if using charcoal)

1. Combine 2 tablespoons sugar and salt in bowl. Pat turkey dry with paper towels, gently loosen skin covering breast, and rub sugar-salt mixture evenly over and under skin. Tightly wrap turkey with plastic wrap and refrigerate for 8 to 24 hours.

2. Just before grilling, soak wood chips in water for 15 minutes, then drain. Using large piece of heavy-duty aluminum foil, wrap soaked chips in foil packet and cut several vent holes in top. Combine remaining 1 tablespoon sugar and pepper in bowl. Unwrap turkey, pat dry with paper towels, and rub sugar-pepper mixture under and over skin. Poke skin all over with skewer.

3A. FOR A CHARCOAL GRILL: Open bottom vent halfway and place disposable pan in center of grill. Light large chimney starter filled with charcoal briquettes (6 quarts). When top coals are partially covered with ash, pour into 2 even piles on either side of disposable pan. Place wood chip packet on coals. Set cooking grate in place, cover, and open lid vent halfway. Heat grill until hot and wood chips are smoking, about 5 minutes.

3B. FOR A GAS GRILL: Remove cooking grate and place wood chip packet directly on primary burner. Set cooking grate in place, turn all burners to high, cover, and heat grill until hot and wood chips are smoking, about 15 minutes. Turn all burners to medium-low. (Adjust burners as needed to maintain grill temperature around 350 degrees.)

4. Clean and oil cooking grate. Place turkey breast, skin side up, in center of grill (over disposable pan if using charcoal). Cover (position lid vent over turkey if using charcoal) and cook until skin is well browned and breast registers 160 degrees, about 1½ hours.

5. Transfer turkey to carving board, tent with foil, and let rest for 15 to 20 minutes. Carve turkey and serve.

Preparing a Turkey Breast for Grilling

1. Pat turkey dry with paper towels and gently loosen skin covering breast.

2. Rub sugar mixture evenly over and under skin, wrap turkey with plastic wrap, and refrigerate for 8 to 24 hours.

3. Before grilling, rub sugar-pepper mixture evenly over and under skin, then poke skin all over with skewer.

Grilled Salmon Steaks with Lemon-Caper Sauce

SERVES 4　　**TOTAL TIME** 1 HOUR

✓ **WHY THIS RECIPE WORKS:** Hearty salmon steaks are a common choice for grilling, but in spite of their thick cut they often end up with a burnt exterior and a dry, flavorless interior. To make the process foolproof, we first turned the oblong steaks into sturdy medallions. By carefully removing a bit of skin from the tail of the steak, tightly wrapping the skin of another tail around the skinned portion, and then tying with kitchen twine, we had neat steaks that cooked evenly and could be easily moved around the grill. We used a two-level cooking approach, beginning with an initial sear over the hotter part of the grill. While the steaks seared, we made a simple bright lemon and caper sauce directly in a disposable aluminum pan over the cooler side of the grill. When the steaks were browned, we transferred them to the pan, coating them with the sauce, and finished cooking over the lower heat, which ensured they remained moist and tender. Before eating, lift out the small circular bone from the center of each steak.

LEMON-CAPER SAUCE

- 3 tablespoons unsalted butter, cut into 3 pieces
- 1 teaspoon grated lemon zest plus 6 tablespoons juice (2 lemons)
- 1 shallot, minced
- 1 tablespoon capers, rinsed
- ⅛ teaspoon salt
- 1 (13 by 9-inch) disposable aluminum roasting pan
- 2 tablespoons minced fresh parsley

SALMON

- 4 (10-ounce) salmon steaks, 1 to 1½ inches thick
  Salt and pepper
- 2 tablespoons vegetable oil

1. FOR THE SAUCE: Combine butter, lemon zest and juice, shallot, capers, and salt in disposable pan.

2. FOR THE SALMON: Pat salmon dry with paper towels. Working with 1 steak at a time, carefully trim 1½ inches of skin from 1 tail. Tightly wrap other tail around skinned portion and tie steak with kitchen twine. Season salmon with salt and pepper and brush both sides with oil.

3A. FOR A CHARCOAL GRILL: Open bottom vent completely. Light large chimney starter filled with charcoal briquettes (6 quarts). When top coals are partially covered with ash, pour evenly over half of grill. Set cooking grate in place, cover, and open lid vent completely. Heat grill until hot, about 5 minutes.

3B. FOR A GAS GRILL: Turn all burners to high, cover, and heat grill until hot, about 15 minutes. Leave primary burner on high and turn off other burner(s).

4. Clean cooking grate, then repeatedly brush grate with well-oiled paper towels until black and glossy, 5 to 10 times. Place salmon on hotter side of grill. Cook, turning once, until browned on both sides, 4 to 6 minutes. Meanwhile, set disposable pan with butter mixture on cooler part of grill and cook until butter has melted, about 2 minutes.

5. Transfer salmon to pan and gently turn to coat with butter mixture. Cook (covered if using gas) until center of salmon is still translucent when checked with tip of paring knife and registers 125 degrees (for medium-rare), 6 to 14 minutes, flipping salmon and rotating pan halfway through grilling. Remove twine and transfer salmon to platter. Off heat, whisk parsley into sauce. Drizzle sauce over steaks. Serve.

Making Grilled Salmon Steaks

1. TRIM 1 TAIL: Working with 1 steak at a time, carefully trim 1½ inches of skin from 1 tail.

2. WRAP AND TIE: Tightly wrap other tail around skinned portion and tie steak with kitchen twine.

3. GRILL BRIEFLY ON HOTTER SIDE: Place salmon on hotter side of grill and brown both sides, 4 to 6 minutes.

4. FINISH COOKING WITH SAUCE: Transfer salmon to pan, coat with butter mixture, and cook for 6 to 14 minutes longer.

Portioning a whole fillet into pieces and placing them on a foil rectangle makes this silky, delicate fish easy to get off the grill.

Grill-Smoked Salmon

SERVES 6   **TOTAL TIME** 50 MINUTES
(PLUS 1 HOUR SALTING TIME)

✓ **WHY THIS RECIPE WORKS:** There's more to smoked salmon than the thin, glossy slices stacked on bagels. With a little time—and a sweet touch—we produced silky, smoky dinnertime fillets. The two most common methods for smoking fish are cold and hot smoking. Both approaches require special equipment and a serious time investment and result in a product that is more ingredient than main dish. Our unique hybrid recipe produced an entrée that captures both the uniquely smooth and lush texture of cold-smoked salmon and the forward smokiness of hot-smoked salmon. The best part? It cooked in only 30 to 40 minutes on a regular charcoal or gas grill. To ensure uniform pieces of fish that cook at the same rate, we found it best to buy a whole center-cut fillet and cut it into 6 pieces ourselves. Do not use mesquite wood in this recipe. If you'd like to use wood chunks instead of wood chips when using a charcoal grill, substitute two medium

---

"SMOKED SALMON PLATTER" SAUCE

MAKES 1½ CUPS   **TOTAL TIME** 10 MINUTES **FAST**

- 1 large egg yolk
- 2 teaspoons Dijon mustard
- 2 teaspoons sherry vinegar
- ½ cup vegetable oil
- 2 tablespoons capers, rinsed, plus 1 teaspoon caper brine
- 1 large hard-cooked egg, chopped fine
- 2 tablespoons minced shallot
- 2 tablespoons minced fresh dill

Whisk egg yolk, mustard, and vinegar together in medium bowl. Whisking constantly, slowly drizzle in oil until emulsified, about 1 minute. Gently fold in capers and brine, hard-cooked egg, shallot, and dill.

---

wood chunks, soaked in water for 15 minutes, for the wood chip packet. Serve the salmon with lemon wedges or "Smoked Salmon Platter" Sauce.

- 2 tablespoons sugar
- 1 tablespoon kosher salt
- 6 (6- to 8-ounce) center-cut skin-on salmon fillets
- 2 cups wood chips, 1 cup soaked in water for 15 minutes and drained

1. Combine sugar and salt in bowl. Set salmon, skin side down, on wire rack set in rimmed baking sheet and sprinkle flesh side evenly with sugar mixture. Refrigerate, uncovered, for 1 hour. Meanwhile, using large piece of heavy-duty aluminum foil, wrap both soaked wood chips and remaining 1 cup unsoaked chips in foil packet and cut several vent holes in top.

2. Brush any excess salt and sugar from salmon using paper towels and blot salmon dry. Return fish to wire rack and refrigerate, uncovered, until ready to cook. Fold piece of heavy-duty foil into 18 by 6-inch rectangle.

3A. FOR A CHARCOAL GRILL: Open bottom vent halfway. Light large chimney starter one-third filled with charcoal briquettes (2 quarts). When top coals are partially covered with ash, pour into steeply banked pile against side of grill. Place wood chip packet on coals. Set cooking grate in place, cover, and open lid vent halfway. Heat grill until hot and wood chips are smoking, about 5 minutes.

3B. FOR A GAS GRILL: Remove cooking grate and place wood chip packet directly on primary burner. Set cooking grate in place and turn primary burner to high (leave other burner[s] off). Cover and heat grill until hot and wood chips begin to smoke, 15 to 25 minutes. Turn primary burner to medium. (Adjust primary burner as needed to maintain grill temperature between 275 to 300 degrees.)

4. Clean and oil cooking grate. Place foil rectangle on cooler side of grill and place salmon fillets on foil, spaced at least ½ inch apart. Cover (position lid vent over fish if using charcoal) and cook until center of salmon is still translucent when checked with tip of paring knife and registers 125 degrees (for medium-rare), 30 to 40 minutes. Transfer to platter. Serve warm or at room temperature.

Grilled Red Curry Mahi-Mahi with Pineapple Salsa

SERVES 4   **TOTAL TIME** 40 MINUTES **FAST**

Our sweet pineapple salsa accents the curried flavor and char of grilled mahi-mahi.

✔ **WHY THIS RECIPE WORKS:** Mahi-mahi boasts a hearty, meaty texture that makes it a great candidate for the grill, plus the flavorful char contributes rich, smoky notes to this mild-tasting fish. To give ours even more flavor, we added a layer of red curry paste before tossing it on the grill. Now all we needed was a fruit salsa to sweeten things up. Pineapple, cut into small pieces and combined with scallion and cilantro, gave us a sweet but bright and zingy salsa. We prefer the flavor of red curry paste here, but you can substitute green curry paste if you prefer.

- **12** ounces pineapple, cut into ¼-inch pieces
- **1** scallion, sliced thin
- **4** tablespoon minced fresh cilantro
- **2** tablespoons vegetable oil
  Salt and pepper
- **4** (6-ounce) skin-on mahi-mahi fillets, 1 to 1½ inches thick
- **1** tablespoon red curry paste

NOTES FROM THE TEST KITCHEN

Buying Pineapple

When it comes to pineapple, we prefer Costa Rican–grown pineapples, also labeled "extra-sweet" or "gold." We find this fruit to be consistently "honey-sweet" in comparison to the "acidic" Hawaiian pineapples with greenish, not yellow, skin. Pineapples will not ripen further once picked, so be sure to purchase golden, fragrant fruit that gives slightly when pressed. Unpeeled pineapples should be stored at room temperature.

1. Combine pineapple, scallion, cilantro, and 1 tablespoon oil in bowl, and season with salt and pepper to taste. Pat fish dry with paper towels. Combine curry paste with remaining 1 tablespoon oil in bowl and brush over flesh of fish.

2A. FOR A CHARCOAL GRILL: Open bottom vent completely. Light large chimney starter filled with charcoal briquettes (6 quarts). When top coals are partially covered with ash, pour evenly over grill. Set cooking grate in place, cover, and open lid vent completely. Heat grill until hot, about 5 minutes.

2B. FOR A GAS GRILL: Turn all burners to high, cover, and heat grill until hot, about 15 minutes. Leave all burners on high.

3. Clean cooking grate, then repeatedly brush grate with well-oiled paper towels until black and glossy, 5 to 10 times. Place fish, skin side up, on grill. Cook (covered if using gas) until well browned on first side, about 3 minutes. Gently flip fish and continue to cook until flesh flakes apart when gently prodded with paring knife and registers 140 degrees, 3 to 8 minutes. Transfer fish to platter and serve with pineapple salsa.

Grilled Swordfish Skewers with Basil Oil

SERVES 4   **TOTAL TIME** 1 HOUR

✓ **WHY THIS RECIPE WORKS:** Swordfish has a robust taste all its own and needs co-starring ingredients with just as much oomph. For these skewers, we paired swordfish with pieces of red onion and lemon. Once grilled, the onion pieces softened slightly yet retained some texture, and the lemon went from tart and acidic to sweet and rich. A simple basil oil, brushed over our skewers once they came off the grill, complemented the bright lemon flavor. Rubbing the swordfish with a bit of ground coriander added complexity and provided flavor that popped with the lemon and basil. We like the flavor of swordfish here but you can substitute other firm-fleshed fish such as mahi-mahi or halibut. You will need four 12-inch metal skewers for this recipe. For more information on how to cut onions for kebabs, see page 326.

1   (1½-pound) skinless swordfish steak, cut into
    1¼-inch pieces
4   teaspoons ground coriander
    Salt and pepper
3   lemons, quartered lengthwise and halved crosswise
1   large red onion, cut into 1-inch pieces, 3 layers thick
¼   cup extra-virgin olive oil
2   tablespoons chopped fresh basil

1. Pat swordfish dry with paper towels, rub with coriander, and season with salt and pepper. Thread fish, lemons, and onion evenly in alternating pattern onto four 12-inch metal skewers. Brush skewers with 1 tablespoon oil. Combine remaining 3 tablespoons oil and basil in bowl and season with salt and pepper to taste.

2A. FOR A CHARCOAL GRILL: Open bottom vent completely. Light large chimney starter three-quarters filled with charcoal briquettes (4½ quarts). When top coals are partially covered with ash, pour evenly over grill. Set cooking grate in place, cover, and open lid vent completely. Heat grill until hot, about 5 minutes.

2B. FOR A GAS GRILL: Turn all burners to high, cover, and heat grill until hot, about 15 minutes. Turn all burners to medium-high.

3. Clean cooking grate, then repeatedly brush grate with well-oiled paper towels until black and glossy, 5 to 10 times. Place skewers on grill. Cook (covered if using gas), turning as needed, until fish is opaque and flakes apart when gently prodded with paring knife, 5 to 8 minutes.

4. Transfer skewers to platter, tent with aluminum foil, and let rest for 5 to 10 minutes. Brush skewers with basil oil before serving.

Heating the spices in butter and coating snapper fillets with them before grilling makes a rich and smoky crust.

Grilled Blackened Red Snapper

SERVES 4   **TOTAL TIME** 1 HOUR

✓ **WHY THIS RECIPE WORKS:** Blackened fish is usually prepared in a cast-iron skillet, but it can lead to a relentlessly smoky kitchen. We thought we'd solve this issue by throwing our fish on the grill, but this introduced a host of new challenges—curled fillets that stuck to the grill, and spices that tasted raw and harsh. To prevent curling fillets, we simply needed to score the skin. We solved the sticking problem by oiling the grate with a heavy hand. Finally, to give the fish its flavorful "blackened but not burned" coating, we bloomed our spice mixture in melted butter, allowed it to cool, and then applied the coating to the fish. Once on the grill, the spice crust acquired the proper depth and richness while the fish cooked through. Striped bass, halibut, or grouper can be substituted for the snapper; if the fillets are thicker or thinner, they will have slightly different cooking times. Serve the fish with lemon wedges, Rémoulade Sauce (page 342), or Pineapple and Cucumber Salsa with Mint (page 342).

2 tablespoons paprika
2 teaspoons onion powder
2 teaspoons garlic powder
¾ teaspoon ground coriander
¾ teaspoon salt
¼ teaspoon cayenne pepper
¼ teaspoon black pepper
¼ teaspoon white pepper
3 tablespoons unsalted butter
4 (6- to 8-ounce) red snapper fillets, ¾ inch thick

1. Combine paprika, onion powder, garlic powder, coriander, salt, cayenne, black pepper, and white pepper in bowl. Melt butter in 10-inch skillet over medium heat. Stir in spice mixture and cook, stirring often, until fragrant and spices turn dark rust color, 2 to 3 minutes. Transfer mixture to pie plate and let cool to room temperature. Use a fork to break up any large clumps.

2. Pat snapper dry with paper towels. Using sharp knife, make shallow diagonal slashes every inch along skin side of fish, being careful not to cut into flesh. Using your fingers, rub spice mixture evenly over top, bottom, and sides of fish (you should use all of spice mixture).

3A. FOR A CHARCOAL GRILL: Open bottom vent completely. Light large chimney starter two-thirds filled with charcoal briquettes (4 quarts). When top coals are partially covered with ash, pour evenly over half of grill. Set cooking grate in place, cover, and open lid vent completely. Heat grill until hot, about 5 minutes.

3B. FOR A GAS GRILL: Turn all burners to high, cover, and heat grill until hot, about 15 minutes. Leave all burners on high.

4. Clean cooking grate, then repeatedly brush grate with well-oiled paper towels until black and glossy, 5 to 10 times.

5. Place fish skin side down on grill (hot side if using charcoal) with fillets diagonal to grate. Cook until skin is very dark brown and crisp, 3 to 5 minutes. Carefully flip fish and continue to cook until dark brown and beginning to flake when prodded with paring knife and center is opaque but still moist, about 5 minutes longer. Serve.

SAUCES FOR GRILLED FISH

PINEAPPLE AND CUCUMBER SALSA WITH MINT

MAKES ABOUT 3 CUPS   **TOTAL TIME** 30 MINUTES   **FAST**

To make this dish spicier, reserve and add the chile seeds.

½ large pineapple, peeled, cored, and cut into ¼-inch pieces
½ cucumber, peeled, halved lengthwise, seeded, and cut into ¼-inch pieces
1 small shallot, minced
1 serrano chile, stemmed, seeded, and minced
2 tablespoons chopped fresh mint
1 tablespoon lime juice, plus extra as needed
½ teaspoon grated fresh ginger
Salt
Sugar

Combine pineapple, cucumber, shallot, chile, mint, lime juice, ginger, and ½ teaspoon salt in bowl and let sit at room temperature for 15 to 30 minutes. Season with extra lime juice, salt, and sugar to taste before serving.

RÉMOULADE SAUCE

MAKES ABOUT ½ CUP   **TOTAL TIME** 10 MINUTES   **FAST**

½ cup mayonnaise
1½ teaspoons sweet pickle relish
1 teaspoon hot sauce
1 teaspoon lemon juice
1 teaspoon minced fresh parsley
½ teaspoon capers, rinsed
½ teaspoon Dijon mustard
1 small garlic clove, minced
Salt and pepper

Pulse all ingredients in food processor until well combined but not smooth, about 10 pulses. Season with salt and pepper to taste and serve. (Sauce can be refrigerated for up to 3 days.)

Grilled Whole Fish

SERVES 4   **TOTAL TIME** 1 HOUR

✔ **WHY THIS RECIPE WORKS:** A grilled whole fish possesses a deeper flavor than fillets or steaks. Knowing there was more to it than simply placing the fish on the grill, we set out to create a recipe for a whole fish that had crispy skin and moist meat. Making shallow diagonal slashes on the skin on both sides helped ensure even cooking and, as a bonus, enabled us to gauge the doneness more easily. To prevent the skin from sticking, we greased the cooking grate and coated the fish with a film of oil. Tongs tore the delicate skin, so we used two thin metal spatulas to roll the fish over once the first side was done. They also made it easier to remove the cooked fish from the grill. After a rest under foil, the fish needed only a few cuts for us to use one of our spatulas to lift away the meat from the bones on each side in a single piece. Snapper, bass, trout, mackerel, and bluefish all work well here. For added flavor, season the fish inside and out with a spice rub (page 332).

> 2 (1½-pound) whole fish, scaled and gutted
> 3 tablespoons vegetable oil
>   Salt and pepper
>   Lemon wedges

1. Using sharp knife, make shallow diagonal slashes every 2 inches along both sides of fish, beginning just behind dorsal fin. Pat fish dry with paper towels, rub thoroughly with oil, and season inside and out with salt and pepper.

2A. FOR A CHARCOAL GRILL: Open bottom vent completely. Light large chimney starter filled with charcoal briquettes (6 quarts). When top coals are partially covered with ash, pour evenly over grill. Set cooking grate in place, cover, and open lid vent completely. Heat grill until hot, about 5 minutes.

2B. FOR A GAS GRILL: Turn all burners to high, cover, and heat grill until hot, about 15 minutes. Leave all burners on high.

3. Clean and oil cooking grate. Place fish on grill, perpendicular to grate. Cook (covered if using gas) until first side is browned and crisp, 6 to 9 minutes. Using 2 spatulas, gently flip fish and cook until second side is browned and crisp, 6 to 9 minutes.

4. Using 2 spatulas, gently transfer fish to platter. Tent with aluminum foil and let rest for 5 to 10 minutes. To serve, use sharp knife to make vertical cut just behind head from top to belly, then make another cut along top of fish from head to tail. Use metal spatula to lift meat away from bones in single piece, starting at head end and running spatula over bones to lift out fillet. Repeat on second side of fish, discarding head and skeleton. Serve with lemon wedges.

Grilling Whole Fish

1. SLASH SKIN: Using sharp knife, make shallow diagonal slashes every 2 inches along both sides of fish, beginning just behind dorsal fin.

2. USE 2 SPATULAS TO FLIP: Cook until first side is browned and crisp, 6 to 9 minutes, then flip fish over using 2 spatulas and continue to cook on second side.

3. DON'T OVERCOOK: When both sides are browned and crisp, gently transfer fish to platter using 2 spatulas.

4. REMOVE MEAT CAREFULLY: Make vertical cut behind head from top to belly; make another cut along top of fish from head to tail. Use spatula to lift meat from bones in single piece, starting at head and lifting out fillet.

Grilled Shrimp with Spicy Lemon-Garlic Sauce

SERVES 4   **TOTAL TIME** 55 MINUTES

✔ **WHY THIS RECIPE WORKS:** Shrimp can turn from moist and juicy to rubbery and dry in the blink of an eye—especially when grilled. While grilling shrimp in their shells can shield them from the coals' scorching heat, any seasonings are stripped off along with the shells when it's time to eat. For tender, juicy, boldly seasoned grilled shrimp we decided to go with peeled shrimp and find a way to prevent them from drying out. We seasoned the shrimp with salt, pepper, and sugar (to help browning) and set them over a very hot fire.

This worked well with jumbo shrimp, but smaller shrimp overcooked before charring. Because jumbo shrimp cost as much as $25 per pound, we wanted a less expensive solution. We created faux jumbo shrimp by cramming a skewer with several normal-size shrimp pressed tightly together. Our final step was to take the shrimp off the fire before they were completely cooked (but after they had picked up attractive grill marks). We finished cooking them in a heated sauce waiting on the cooler side of the grill; this final simmer infused them with bold flavor. To fit all of the shrimp on the cooking grate at once, you will need three 14-inch metal skewers. Serve with grilled bread.

LEMON-GARLIC SAUCE

- **4** tablespoons unsalted butter, cut into 4 pieces
- ¼ cup lemon juice (2 lemons)
- **3** garlic cloves, minced
- ½ teaspoon red pepper flakes
- ⅛ teaspoon salt
- **1** (10-inch) disposable aluminum pie pan
- ⅓ cup minced fresh parsley

SHRIMP

- 1½ pounds extra-large shrimp (21 to 25 per pound), peeled and deveined
- 2–3 tablespoons vegetable oil
  Salt and pepper
- ¼ teaspoon sugar
  Lemon wedges

1. FOR THE SAUCE: Combine butter, lemon juice, garlic, pepper flakes, and salt in disposable pan.

2. FOR THE SHRIMP: Pat shrimp dry with paper towels. Thread shrimp tightly onto three 14-inch skewers, alternating direction of heads and tails. Brush shrimp with oil and season with salt and pepper. Sprinkle 1 side of each skewer evenly with sugar.

3A. FOR A CHARCOAL GRILL: Open bottom vent completely. Light large chimney starter filled with charcoal briquettes (6 quarts). When top coals are partially covered with ash, pour evenly over half of grill. Set cooking grate in place, cover, and open lid vent completely. Heat grill until hot, about 5 minutes.

3B. FOR A GAS GRILL: Turn all burners to high, cover, and heat grill until hot, about 15 minutes. Leave primary burner on high and turn other burner(s) to medium-low.

4. Clean cooking grate, then repeatedly brush grate with well-oiled paper towels until black and glossy, 5 to 10 times. Place disposable pan with sauce ingredients on hotter side of grill and cook until hot, 1 to 3 minutes; slide pan to cooler side of grill.

5. Place shrimp skewers, sugared side down, on hotter side of grill; use tongs to push shrimp together on skewers if they have separated. Cook shrimp until lightly charred on first side, 4 to 5 minutes. Flip skewers and cook until second side is pink and slightly translucent, 1 to 2 minutes.

6. Using potholder, carefully lift each skewer from grill and use tongs to slide shrimp off skewers and into pan with sauce. Toss shrimp and sauce to combine. Slide pan to hotter side of grill and cook, stirring, until shrimp are opaque throughout, about 30 seconds.

7. Stir in parsley. Transfer shrimp to platter and serve with lemon wedges.

Making Grilled Shrimp with Spicy Lemon-Garlic Sauce

1. MAKE SAUCE IN DISPOSABLE PAN: Combine butter, lemon juice, garlic, red pepper flakes, and salt in disposable pan.

2. PACK SHRIMP ONTO SKEWERS: Pat shrimp dry with paper towels. Thread shrimp onto 3 skewers, alternating direction of heads and tails.

3. SPRINKLE WITH SUGAR: Sprinkle 1 side of each skewer evenly with sugar.

4. GRILL SHRIMP, THEN TOSS WITH SAUCE: Grill sugared side of shrimp for 4 minutes, then grill second side for 1 minute. Slide shrimp into pan with sauce and finish cooking on hotter side of grill.

Grilled Shrimp with Fresh Tomatoes, Feta, and Olives

Substitute following mixture for lemon-garlic sauce: Combine ¼ cup extra-virgin olive oil, 1 finely chopped large tomato, 1 tablespoon minced fresh oregano, and ⅛ teaspoon salt in disposable pan; cook as directed. Stir 1 cup crumbled feta cheese, ⅓ cup chopped kalamata olives, 3 thinly sliced scallions, and 2 tablespoons lemon juice into shrimp before serving.

Grilled Vegetable and Bread Salad

SERVES 4   **TOTAL TIME** 45 MINUTES   **FAST**

✔ **WHY THIS RECIPE WORKS:** Pair grilled vegetable chunks with cubes of rustic bread, fresh herbs, and a bright vinaigrette, and you have a Mediterranean-style salad that needs little else. We began by choosing the vegetables. Mindful of complementary cooking times, we matched zucchini with red onion and red bell pepper, and grilled them over a single-level medium-heat fire until they were perfectly browned, tender, and full of smoky flavor. The sturdy texture and strong wheat flavor of a rustic loaf of Italian-style bread paired well with the bolder grilled flavor of the vegetables. Grilling the bread slices (we put them alongside the vegetables) made the pieces sturdier and added an appealing texture. Once the bread and vegetables were grilled, we simply cut them into 1-inch pieces and tossed them with a lemon-based vinaigrette. A few ounces of goat cheese crumbled on top added a creamy finishing touch. Be sure to use a hearty Italian bread—it is important for both the flavor and the texture of this salad. Thick slices of a French baguette, cut on an extreme bias, also work well here.

2   **zucchini, halved lengthwise**
2   **red bell peppers, stemmed, seeded, and flattened**
1   **red onion, sliced into ½-inch-thick rounds (do not separate rings)**
6   **ounces crusty, rustic Italian-style bread, sliced 1 inch thick**
5   **tablespoons extra-virgin olive oil**
    Salt and pepper
2   **tablespoons chopped fresh basil**
1   **teaspoon grated lemon zest plus 4 teaspoons juice**
1   **teaspoon Dijon mustard**
1   **garlic clove, minced**
2   **ounces goat cheese, crumbled (½ cup)**

Thick slices of grilled rustic bread add a pleasant texture to a salad of flavorful grilled vegetables.

1. Lightly coat zucchini, bell peppers, onion rounds, and bread with 2 tablespoons oil and season with salt and pepper.

2A. FOR A CHARCOAL GRILL: Open bottom vent completely. Light large chimney starter half filled with charcoal briquettes (3 quarts). When top coals are partially covered with ash, pour evenly over grill. Set cooking grate in place, cover, and open lid vent completely. Heat grill until hot, about 5 minutes.

2B. FOR A GAS GRILL: Turn all burners to high, cover, and heat grill until hot, about 15 minutes. Turn all burners to medium.

3. Clean and oil cooking grate. Place bread and vegetables on grill. Cook (covered if using gas), turning as needed, until bread is golden, about 4 minutes, and vegetables are spottily charred, 8 to 12 minutes. Transfer bread and vegetables to platter as they finish.

4. Cut vegetables and bread into 1-inch pieces. Whisk remaining 3 tablespoons oil, basil, lemon zest and juice, mustard, and garlic together in large bowl. Add vegetables and bread and toss to coat. Season with salt and pepper to taste, sprinkle with goat cheese, and serve.

Grilling Vegetables at a Glance

To easily grill a vegetable to serve alongside dinner, use this chart as a guide. Brush or toss the vegetables with oil before grilling. Grill vegetables over a single-level fire (see page 308).

VEGETABLE	PREPARATION	GRILLING DIRECTIONS
Asparagus	Snap off tough ends.	Grill, turning once, until tender and streaked with light grill marks, 5 to 7 minutes.
Bell Pepper	Core, seed, and cut into large wedges.	Grill, turning every 2 minutes, until streaked with dark grill marks, 8 to 10 minutes.
Corn	Remove all but last layer of husk.	Grill, turning every 2 minutes, until husk chars and peels away at tip, 8 to 10 minutes.
Endive	Cut in half lengthwise through stem end.	Grill flat side down until streaked with dark grill marks, 5 to 7 minutes.
Eggplant	Remove ends. Cut into ¼-inch-thick rounds.	Grill, turning once, until flesh is browned, 8 to 10 minutes.
Fennel	Slice bulb through base into ¼-inch-thick pieces.	Grill, turning once, until streaked with dark grill marks and quite soft, 7 to 9 minutes.
White or Cremini Mushrooms	Trim thin slice from stems, then thread onto skewers.	Grill, turning several times, until golden brown, 6 to 7 minutes.
Onions	Peel and cut into ½-inch-thick rings.	Grill, turning occasionally, until lightly charred, 10 to 12 minutes.
Cherry Tomatoes	Remove stems, then thread onto skewers.	Grill, turning several times, until streaked with dark grill marks, 3 to 6 minutes.
Plum Tomatoes	Cut in half lengthwise and seed.	Grill, turning once, until streaked with dark grill marks, about 6 minutes.
Zucchini or Yellow Summer Squash	Remove ends. Slice lengthwise into ½-inch-thick strips.	Grill, turning once, until streaked with dark grill marks, 8 to 10 minutes.

Grilled Eggplant with Yogurt Sauce

SERVES 6 TO 8   **TOTAL TIME** 1 HOUR

✓ **WHY THIS RECIPE WORKS:** To get grilled eggplant that isn't leathery or spongy, the size of the slice is crucial; ¼ inch is just the right thickness to produce a charred exterior and tender flesh. For flavor, we quickly infused olive oil with garlic and red pepper flakes in the microwave and brushed it on the eggplant slices before grilling. We saved a tablespoon of the oil and mixed it with yogurt, lemon, and fresh herbs for a Mediterranean-inspired sauce to drizzle on at the end. For spicier eggplant, increase the amount of red pepper flakes to ¼ teaspoon.

  6   **tablespoons extra-virgin olive oil**
  5   **garlic cloves, minced**
  ⅛   **teaspoon red pepper flakes**
  ½   **cup plain whole-milk yogurt**
  3   **tablespoons minced fresh mint**
  1   **teaspoon grated lemon zest plus 2 teaspoons juice**
  1   **teaspoon ground cumin**
     Salt and pepper
  2   **pounds eggplant, sliced into ¼-inch-thick rounds**

1. Microwave oil, garlic, and pepper flakes in bowl until garlic is golden and crisp, about 2 minutes. Strain oil through fine-mesh strainer into clean bowl; reserve oil and crispy garlic mixture separately.

2. Combine 1 tablespoon strained garlic oil, yogurt, mint, lemon zest and juice, cumin, and ¼ teaspoon salt in bowl; set aside. Brush eggplant thoroughly with remaining garlic oil and season with salt and pepper.

3A. FOR A CHARCOAL GRILL: Open bottom vent completely. Light large chimney starter filled with charcoal briquettes (6 quarts). When top coals are partially covered with ash, pour evenly over grill. Set cooking grate in place, cover, and open lid vent completely. Heat grill until hot, about 5 minutes.

3B. FOR A GAS GRILL: Turn all burners to high, cover, and heat grill until hot, about 15 minutes. Turn all burners to medium-high.

4. Clean and oil cooking grate. Place half of eggplant on grill. Cook (covered if using gas), turning as needed, until browned and tender, 8 to 10 minutes. Transfer to platter and repeat with remaining eggplant. Before serving, drizzle with yogurt sauce and sprinkle with crispy garlic mixture.

We found that one-inch-thick slabs of tofu provide the best surface for grilling and glazing.

Grilled Soy-Ginger Glazed Tofu

SERVES 4 TO 6   **TOTAL TIME** 1 HOUR

✔ **WHY THIS RECIPE WORKS:** The key to successfully grilled tofu lies not only in how it's cut but also in how it's turned. We tried grilling tofu that had been cut into planks, strips, and cubes, and found in the end that tofu cut lengthwise into 1-inch slabs fared best on the grill. This shape maximized surface contact with the grill and the larger pieces were easier to manage and turn. Using two spatulas provided the best leverage for flipping the delicate tofu. Dry sherry or white wine can be substituted for the mirin in this recipe. Light firm tofu can be substituted here; however, it has a drier texture and much less flavor. Be sure to handle the tofu gently or it may break apart.

TOFU
- **28** ounces firm tofu, cut lengthwise into 1-inch-thick slabs
- **2** tablespoons vegetable oil
- Salt and pepper

SOY-GINGER GLAZE
- ⅓ cup soy sauce
- ⅓ cup water
- ⅓ cup sugar
- ¼ cup mirin
- 1 tablespoon grated fresh ginger
- 2 garlic cloves, minced
- 2 teaspoons cornstarch
- 1 teaspoon Asian chili-garlic sauce
- ¼ cup minced fresh cilantro

1. FOR THE TOFU: Spread tofu out over paper towel–lined baking sheet and let drain for 20 minutes. Gently pat tofu dry with paper towels, brush with oil, and season with salt and pepper.

2. FOR THE GLAZE: Meanwhile, simmer soy sauce, water, sugar, mirin, ginger, garlic, cornstarch, and chili-garlic sauce in small saucepan over medium-high heat until thickened and reduced to ¾ cup, 5 to 7 minutes.

3A. FOR A CHARCOAL GRILL: Open bottom vent completely. Light large chimney starter filled with charcoal briquettes (6 quarts). When top coals are partially covered with ash, pour two-thirds evenly over half of grill, then pour remaining coals over other half of grill. Set cooking grate in place, cover, and open lid vent completely. Heat grill until hot, about 5 minutes.

3B. FOR A GAS GRILL: Turn all burners to high, cover, and heat grill until hot, about 15 minutes. Leave primary burner on high and turn other burner(s) to medium.

4. Clean and oil cooking grate. Gently place tofu on hotter side of grill, perpendicular to grate. Cook (covered if using gas) until lightly browned on both sides, 6 to 10 minutes, gently turning tofu halfway through cooking with 2 spatulas.

5. Slide tofu to cooler part of grill, brush with ¼ cup glaze, and cook until well browned on first side, 1 to 2 minutes. Turn tofu, using 2 spatulas. Brush with ¼ cup glaze and cook until well browned on second side, 1 to 2 minutes.

6. Transfer tofu to platter and brush with remaining ¼ cup glaze. Sprinkle with cilantro and serve.

VARIATION

Grilled Asian Barbecue Glazed Tofu

Substitute following mixture for soy-ginger glaze: Simmer ⅓ cup ketchup, ⅓ cup hoisin sauce, 2 tablespoons rice vinegar, 1½ tablespoons soy sauce, 1½ tablespoons toasted sesame oil, and 1 tablespoon grated fresh ginger in small saucepan over medium-high heat until thickened and reduced to ¾ cup, 5 to 7 minutes. Substitute 1 minced scallion for cilantro before serving.

Barbecued Pulled Chicken

SERVES 8 **TOTAL TIME** 2 HOURS 30 MINUTES
(PLUS 1 HOUR BRINING TIME)

✓ **WHY THIS RECIPE WORKS:** Barbecuing is the perfect method for cooking fatty cuts of pork or beef, but relatively lean chicken is another story. For barbecued pulled chicken with smoky flavor and moist, tender meat, we'd have to come up with some tricks. Brining the birds kept the white meat moist and juicy, and arranging the chickens on the grill with the breast meat farther from the heat source than the dark meat evened out the cooking times. We prefer to halve the chickens ourselves, but you may be able to buy halved chickens from your butcher. If you'd like to use wood chunks instead of wood chips when using a charcoal grill, substitute two medium wood chunks, soaked in water for 1 hour, for the wood chip packet.

Salt and pepper
2 (4-pound) whole chickens, giblets discarded
2 cups wood chips, soaked in water for 15 minutes and drained
1 recipe Kansas City Barbecue Sauce for Chicken (page 351)
8 hamburger buns

1. Dissolve 1 cup salt in 4 quarts cold water in large container. Remove backbones from chickens and split chickens in half lengthwise through center of breastbone. Using metal skewer, poke 20 holes all over each chicken half. Submerge chicken in brine, cover, and refrigerate for 1 hour.

2. Remove chicken from brine, pat dry with paper towels, and season with pepper. Using large piece of heavy-duty aluminum foil, wrap soaked wood chips in foil packet and cut several vent holes in top.

3A. FOR A CHARCOAL GRILL: Open bottom vent halfway. Light large chimney starter filled with charcoal briquettes (6 quarts). When top coals are partially covered with ash, pour into steeply banked pile against side of grill. Place wood chip packet on coals. Set cooking grate in place, cover, and open lid vent halfway. Heat grill until hot and wood chips are smoking, about 5 minutes.

3B. FOR A GAS GRILL: Remove cooking grate and place wood chip packet directly on primary burner. Set cooking grate in place, turn all burners to high, cover, and heat grill until hot and wood chips are smoking, about 15 minutes. Leave primary burner on high and turn off other burner(s). (Adjust primary burner as needed to maintain grill temperature around 350 degrees.)

4. Clean and oil cooking grate. Place chicken, skin side up, on cooler side of grill with legs facing hotter side of grill. Cover (position lid vent over chicken if using charcoal) and cook until breasts register 160 degrees and thighs register 175 degrees, 75 to 85 minutes.

5. Transfer chicken to carving board, tent with foil, and let rest for 15 minutes. Remove meat from bones, separating dark and light meat; discard skin and bones. Roughly chop dark meat into ½-inch pieces. Using 2 forks, shred white meat into thin strands. Combine chicken and sauce in large saucepan and cook over medium-low heat until warmed through, about 5 minutes. Serve on hamburger buns.

Splitting Chickens

1. Place chicken, breast side down, on cutting board. Use kitchen shears to cut along either side of backbone; remove backbone.

2. Flip chicken and use your hand to flatten. Using chef's knife, cut lengthwise through breastbone to separate chicken into halves.

Shredded Barbecued Beef

SERVES 8 TO 10 **TOTAL TIME** 4½ TO 5½ HOURS
(PLUS SALTING AND RESTING TIME)

✓ **WHY THIS RECIPE WORKS:** For our shredded barbecued beef, we cut a chuck roast into quarters. The smaller pieces of beef absorbed more smoke flavor and cooked much faster. After cooking the meat in a disposable roasting pan on the cooler side of the grill for a few hours, we flipped all four pieces, wrapped the pan in foil, and placed the roast in the oven to finish cooking. If you prefer a smooth barbecue sauce, strain the sauce before tossing it with the beef in step 5. We like to serve this beef on white bread with plenty of pickle chips. If you'd like to use wood chunks instead of wood chips when using a charcoal grill, substitute three medium wood chunks, soaked in water for 1 hour, for the wood chip packets.

1 tablespoon salt

1 tablespoon pepper

1 teaspoon cayenne pepper

1 (5- to 6-pound) boneless beef chuck-eye roast, trimmed and quartered

1 (13 by 9-inch) disposable aluminum roasting pan

3 cups wood chips, soaked in water for 15 minutes and drained

1 recipe Basic Barbecue Sauce (page 351), warmed

1. Combine salt, pepper, and cayenne in bowl. Pat beef dry with paper towels and rub with spice mixture. Wrap meat in plastic wrap and let sit at room temperature for at least 1 hour or refrigerate up to 24 hours; unwrap and transfer to disposable pan. Using large piece of heavy-duty aluminum foil, wrap soaked wood chips in foil packet and cut several vent holes in top.

2A. FOR A CHARCOAL GRILL: Open bottom vent halfway. Light large chimney starter half filled with charcoal briquettes (3 quarts). When top coals are partially covered with ash, pour into steeply banked pile against side of grill. Place wood chip packet on coals. Set cooking grate in place, cover, and open lid vent halfway. Heat grill until hot and wood chips are smoking, about 5 minutes.

2B. FOR A GAS GRILL: Remove cooking grate and place wood chip packet directly on primary burner. Set cooking grate in place, turn all burners to high, cover, and heat grill until hot and wood chips are smoking, about 15 minutes. Turn primary burner to medium and turn off other burner(s). (Adjust primary burner as needed to maintain grill temperature between 250 and 300 degrees.)

3. Place pan with meat on cooler side of grill. Cover (position lid vent over meat if using charcoal) and cook until meat is deep red, about 2 hours. During final 20 minutes of grilling, adjust oven rack to lower-middle position and heat oven to 300 degrees.

4. Flip meat over in pan, cover pan tightly with foil, and transfer to oven. Roast beef until fork slips easily in and out of meat, 2 to 3 hours.

5. Transfer meat to large bowl, tent loosely with foil, and let rest for 30 minutes. Using 2 forks, pull meat into shreds, discarding any excess fat or gristle. Toss meat with ½ cup barbecue sauce and serve with remaining sauce.

Our flavorful barbecued and shredded boneless pork roast spends two hours on the grill and two hours in the oven.

Lexington-Style Pulled Pork

SERVES 8   **TOTAL TIME** 4½ TO 5½ HOURS

(PLUS SALTING AND RESTING TIME)

WHY THIS RECIPE WORKS: Pulled pork recipes take hours to prepare, and our goal was to simplify the recipe without sacrificing flavor. To do so, we used a combination of grilling and oven roasting to reduce the cooking time from all day to just 4 or 5 hours. To infuse the pulled pork with ample smoke flavor despite the abbreviated cooking time, we doubled the amount of wood chips. We opted to use flavorful pork butt, since it has enough fat to stay moist and succulent during long, slow cooking. To bump up the flavor, we coated the pork with a basic barbecue rub and let it sit for at least an hour before placing it on the grill. Boneless pork butt (also labeled Boston butt) is often wrapped in elastic netting; be sure to remove the netting before rubbing the meat with the spices in step 1. The cooked meat can be shredded or chopped. If you'd like to use wood chunks instead of wood chips when using a charcoal grill, substitute four medium wood chunks, soaked in water for 1 hour, for the wood chip packets.

2 tablespoons paprika

2 tablespoons pepper

2 tablespoons packed brown sugar

1 tablespoon salt

1 (4- to 5-pound) boneless pork butt roast, trimmed

4 cups wood chips, soaked in water for 15 minutes and drained

1 recipe Lexington Barbecue Sauce (page 351), warmed

1. Combine paprika, pepper, sugar, and salt in bowl. Pat meat dry with paper towels and rub evenly with spice mixture. Wrap meat in plastic wrap and let sit at room temperature for at least 1 hour or refrigerate for up to 1 day. Using 2 large pieces of heavy-duty aluminum foil, wrap soaked chips in 2 foil packets and cut several vent holes in tops.

2A. FOR A CHARCOAL GRILL: Open bottom vent halfway. Light large chimney starter half filled with charcoal briquettes (3 quarts). When top coals are partially covered with ash, pour into steeply banked pile against side of grill. Place wood chip packets on coals. Set cooking grate in place, cover, and open lid vent halfway. Heat grill until hot and wood chips are smoking, about 5 minutes.

2B. FOR A GAS GRILL: Remove cooking grate and place wood chip packets directly on primary burner. Set cooking grate in place, turn all burners to high, cover, and heat grill until hot and wood chips are smoking, about 15 minutes. Turn primary burner to medium and turn off other burner(s). (Adjust primary burner as needed to maintain grill temperature around 275 degrees.)

SOUTH CAROLINA PULLED PORK

This regional recipe, nicknamed "Carolina Gold," has a distinctive mustard-based sauce.

Substitute following mixture for spice mixture in step 1 of Lexington-Style Pulled Pork: 3 tablespoons dry mustard, 2 tablespoons salt, 1½ tablespoons packed light brown sugar, 2 teaspoons pepper, 2 teaspoons paprika, and ¼ teaspoon cayenne pepper.

Substitute following South Carolina mustard barbecue sauce for Lexington sauce: Whisk together ½ cup yellow mustard, ½ cup packed light brown sugar, ¼ cup distilled white vinegar, 2 tablespoons Worcestershire sauce, 1 tablespoon hot sauce, 1 teaspoon salt, and 1 teaspoon pepper. Brush pork with ½ cup sauce before finishing in the oven. (Sauce can be refrigerated for up to 4 days.)

---

3. Clean and oil cooking grate. Unwrap meat and place on cooler side of grill. Cover (position lid vent over meat if using charcoal) and cook until pork has dark, rosy crust, about 2 hours. During final 20 minutes of grilling, adjust oven rack to lower-middle position and heat oven to 325 degrees.

4. Transfer pork to large roasting pan, cover pan tightly with foil, and transfer to oven. Roast pork until fork slips easily in and out of meat, 2 to 3 hours. Remove pork from oven and let rest, still covered with foil, for 30 minutes. When cool enough to handle, unwrap pork and pull meat into thin shreds using 2 forks, discarding excess fat and gristle. Toss pork with ½ cup barbecue sauce and serve with remaining sauce.

Making Pulled Pork

1. ADD SPICE: Pat meat dry with paper towels and rub evenly with spice mixture. Wrap meat in plastic wrap and let sit at room temperature for at least 1 hour, or refrigerate for up to 1 day.

2. SMOKE FOR 2 HOURS: Place meat on cooler side of grill. Cover (position lid vent over meat if using charcoal) and cook until pork has dark, rosy crust, about 2 hours.

3. FINISH IN OVEN UNTIL FORK-TENDER: Transfer pork to large roasting pan, cover pan tightly with aluminum foil, and roast pork in oven until fork slips easily in and out of meat, 2 to 3 hours.

4. SHRED AND TOSS WITH SAUCE: Remove from oven, let rest for 30 minutes, then pull meat into thin shreds, discarding fat and gristle. Toss pork with ½ cup barbecue sauce before serving.

BARBECUE SAUCES

Barbecue sauce is often as important as the meat. Ranging from thin, vinegary mops to thick, sweet glazes, barbecue sauces vary vastly from region to region. These recipes are some of our favorites. (The sauces can be refrigerated for up to 4 days.)

Basic Barbecue Sauce

MAKES ABOUT 2 CUPS

For a thinner, smoother texture, strain the sauce after it has finished cooking. This recipe can be doubled or tripled.

- 1 tablespoon vegetable oil
- 1 onion, chopped fine
  Salt and pepper
- 1 garlic clove, minced
- 1 teaspoon chili powder
- ¼ teaspoon cayenne pepper
- 1¼ cups ketchup
- 6 tablespoons molasses
- 3 tablespoons cider vinegar
- 2 tablespoons Worcestershire sauce
- 2 tablespoons Dijon mustard
- 1 teaspoon hot sauce

1. Heat oil in medium saucepan over medium heat until shimmering. Add onion and pinch salt and cook until softened, 5 to 7 minutes. Stir in garlic, chili powder, and cayenne and cook until fragrant, about 30 seconds.

2. Whisk in ketchup, molasses, vinegar, Worcestershire, mustard, and hot sauce. Bring sauce to simmer and cook, stirring occasionally, until thickened and measures 2 cups, about 25 minutes.

3. Let sauce cool to room temperature. Season with salt and pepper to taste and serve.

Kansas City Barbecue Sauce for Beef and Pork

MAKES ABOUT 4 CUPS

For a thinner, smoother texture, strain this thick, sweet, and smoky tomato-based sauce after it has finished cooking.

- 1 tablespoon vegetable oil
- 1 onion, chopped fine
  Salt and pepper
- 4 cups chicken broth
- 1 cup root beer
- 1 cup cider vinegar
- 1 cup dark corn syrup
- ½ cup molasses
- ½ cup tomato paste
- ½ cup ketchup
- 2 tablespoons brown mustard
- 1 tablespoon hot sauce
- ½ teaspoon garlic powder
- ¼ teaspoon liquid smoke

1. Heat oil in large saucepan over medium heat until shimmering. Add onion and pinch salt and cook until softened, 5 to 7 minutes. Whisk in broth, root beer, vinegar, corn syrup, molasses, tomato paste, ketchup, mustard, hot sauce, and garlic powder.

2. Bring sauce to simmer and cook, stirring occasionally, until thickened and measures 4 cups, about 1 hour.

3. Off heat, stir in liquid smoke. Let sauce cool to room temperature. Season with salt and pepper to taste and serve.

VARIATION

KANSAS CITY BARBECUE SAUCE FOR CHICKEN

Increasing the vinegar balances the sauce's sweetness and swapping coffee for the root beer boosts the smoky flavor.

Substitute 1 cup brewed coffee for root beer, and omit corn syrup. Increase vinegar to 1¼ cups and increase molasses to ¾ cup.

Texas Barbecue Sauce

MAKES ABOUT 2 CUPS

In Texas, lots of barbecued meats are served with this vinegary dipping sauce.

- 2 tablespoons unsalted butter
- ¼ cup finely chopped onion

  Salt and pepper
- 1½ teaspoons chili powder
- 1 garlic clove, minced
- 2¼ cups tomato juice
- ¾ cup distilled white vinegar
- 2 tablespoons Worcestershire sauce
- 2 tablespoons molasses
- ½ teaspoon dry mustard mixed with 1 tablespoon water
- 1 teaspoon minced canned chipotle chile in adobo sauce

1. Melt butter in medium saucepan over medium heat. Add onion and pinch salt and cook until softened, 2 to 3 minutes. Stir in chili powder and garlic and cook until fragrant, about 30 seconds. Whisk in tomato juice, ½ cup vinegar, Worcestershire, molasses, mustard mixture, and chipotle.

2. Bring sauce to simmer and cook, stirring occasionally, until thickened and measures 1¾ cups, 30 to 40 minutes.

3. Off heat, stir in remaining ¼ cup vinegar. Let sauce cool to room temperature. Season with salt and pepper to taste and serve.

Lexington Barbecue Sauce

MAKES ABOUT 2½ CUPS

This vinegary sauce is a standard in North Carolina. It has just enough ketchup and sugar to take the edge off the acidity.

- 1 cup water
- 1 cup cider vinegar
- ½ cup ketchup
- 1 tablespoon sugar
- ¾ teaspoon salt
- ½ teaspoon pepper
- ½ teaspoon red pepper flakes

Whisk all ingredients together in bowl until sugar and salt are dissolved. Serve.

Pork Ribs

We love pork ribs, but not all are created equal, and we call for different types of ribs for different recipes, depending on which style works best. Here are the key differences between the varieties available.

SPARERIBS: Ribs from near the pig's fatty belly. They need a fair amount of home trimming.

ST. LOUIS-STYLE: Spareribs that have been trimmed of skirt meat and excess cartilage. Minimal fuss.

BABY BACK: Smaller, leaner ribs from the (adult) pig's back. Tender, though the meat dries out too quickly for some recipes.

Kansas City Sticky Ribs

SERVES 4 TO 6   **TOTAL TIME** 4 TO 5 HOURS
(PLUS SALTING AND RESTING TIME)

✓ **WHY THIS RECIPE WORKS:** Kansas City ribs are slow-smoked pork ribs slathered in a sauce so thick, sweet, and sticky that you need a case of wet naps to get your hands clean. But authentic ribs can take all day to prepare. We knew we could come up with a faster method for Kansas City ribs—one that would produce the same fall-off-the-bone, tender, smoky meat of the long-cooked original recipe. We quickly learned that spareribs, which are well marbled with fat, produced moist tender ribs, but some racks were so big they barely fit on the grill. We turned to a more manageable cut, referred to as "St. Louis" ribs, which is a narrower, rectangular rack that offers all the taste of whole spareribs without any of the trouble. A spice rub added flavor and encouraged a savory crust on the meat. We barbecued the ribs, covered with foil, over indirect heat for 2 hours—the foil trapped some of the steam over the meat, so that it cooked up super moist and tender. Using wood chips on the grill imparted great smoky flavor. For sticky, saucy ribs, we brushed the ribs all over with barbecue sauce, wrapped them in foil, and finished them in the oven until they were tender and falling off the bone. If you can't find St. Louis–style racks, baby back ribs will work fine; just reduce the oven cooking time to 1 to 2 hours. If you'd like to use wood chunks instead of wood chips when using a charcoal grill, substitute two medium wood chunks, soaked in water for 1 hour, for the wood chip packet.

3 tablespoons paprika
2 tablespoons packed brown sugar
1 tablespoon salt
1 tablespoon pepper
¼ teaspoon cayenne pepper
2 (2½- to 3-pound) racks St. Louis–style spareribs, trimmed and membrane removed
2 cups wood chips, soaked in water for 15 minutes and drained
1 recipe Kansas City Barbecue Sauce for Beef and Pork (page 351)

1. Combine paprika, sugar, salt, pepper, and cayenne in bowl. Pat ribs dry with paper towels and rub evenly with spice mixture. Wrap ribs in plastic wrap and let sit at room temperature for at least 1 hour, or refrigerate for up to 24 hours. Using large piece of heavy-duty aluminum foil, wrap soaked chips in foil packet and cut several vent holes in top.

2A. FOR A CHARCOAL GRILL: Open bottom vent halfway. Light large chimney starter three-quarters filled with charcoal briquettes (4½ quarts). When top coals are partially covered with ash, pour into steeply banked pile against side of grill. Place wood chip packet on coals. Set cooking grate in place, cover, and open lid vent halfway. Heat grill until hot and wood chips are smoking, about 5 minutes.

2B. FOR A GAS GRILL: Remove cooking grate and place wood chip packet directly on primary burner. Set cooking grate in place, turn all burners to high, cover, and heat grill until hot and wood chips are smoking, about 15 minutes. Turn primary burner to medium-high and turn off other burner(s). (Adjust primary burner as needed to maintain grill temperature around 325 degrees.)

3. Clean and oil cooking grate. Unwrap ribs and place, meat side down, on cooler side of grill; ribs may overlap slightly. Place sheet of foil directly on top of ribs. Cover (position lid vent over meat if using charcoal) and cook until ribs are deep red and smoky, about 2 hours, flipping and rotating racks halfway through cooking. During final 20 minutes of grilling, adjust oven rack to middle position and heat oven to 250 degrees.

4. Remove ribs from grill, brush evenly with 1 cup sauce, and wrap tightly with foil. Lay foil-wrapped ribs on rimmed baking sheet and continue to cook in oven until tender and fork inserted into ribs meets no resistance, 1½ to 2½ hours.

5. Remove ribs from oven and let rest, still wrapped, for 30 minutes. Unwrap ribs and brush thickly with 1 cup sauce. Slice ribs between bones and serve with remaining sauce.

It's hard to choose a best-loved style of ribs, but we'd be willing to bet that Kansas City sticky ribs are a top contender. These meaty ribs are smoky and unbelievably tender, covered with a thick and sweet tomato-based sauce. And they don't take all day to make—they start on the grill but then finish cooking in the oven.

1. CHOOSE THE RIGHT RIBS:
Purchase 2 racks of St. Louis–style spareribs and remove the membrane.
WHY? Ribs must be trimmed before cooking. St. Louis–style ribs are already trimmed of both belly meat and excess cartilage, so they are minimal fuss. The membrane would keep smoke from getting in.

2. RUB THE RIBS WITH THE SPICE MIXTURE: Pat the ribs dry. Rub both sides of the ribs evenly with the spice rub, wrap the meat in plastic wrap, and let it sit at room temperature for at least 1 hour.
WHY? The spice rub adds a layer of flavor to the meat and helps the ribs develop a crust.

3. MAKE THE BARBECUE SAUCE: Cook the barbecue sauce until thickened and let cool to room temperature.
WHY? Homemade barbecue sauce is easy to make and tastes the best. Kansas City sauce is sweet, smoky, tangy, and tomatoey.

4. MAKE A STEEPLY BANKED FIRE: Pour all of the lit coals steeply against one side of the grill. Preheat and adjust a gas grill as directed in the recipe.
WHY? Banking the coals turns the grill into an oven. Placing the ribs over the coal-free area lets them cook slowly without burning.

5. COVER THE RIBS WITH FOIL ON THE COOLER SIDE OF THE GRILL: Place the ribs on the cooler side of the grill and place a sheet of aluminum foil directly on top of the ribs. Cover and cook until deep red and smoky, 2 hours.
WHY? The foil holds in some of the steam to make the ribs tender and moist. Because they are still exposed to the fire, the ribs also develop a nice crusty exterior.

6. REMOVE THE RIBS FROM THE GRILL AND SLATHER ON THE SAUCE: Remove the ribs from the grill and brush with the sauce.
WHY? Slathering a layer of sauce on the ribs both before and after they cook in the oven helps make the ribs sticky and finger-licking good.

7. MOVE THE RIBS TO THE OVEN: Wrap the ribs tightly with foil and bake in a low oven (250 degrees) until tender, 1½ to 2½ hours.
WHY? The slow heat of the oven and the foil prevent the ribs from drying out, resulting in moister ribs.

8. LET THE RIBS REST:
Remove the ribs from the oven and let them rest, still wrapped, for 30 minutes. Unwrap and brush them thickly with sauce.
WHY? Letting the ribs rest in the foil traps the steam and makes the meat moist and tender. Slice the ribs between the bones to serve.

Memphis Spareribs

SERVES 4 TO 6   **TOTAL TIME** 4½ TO 5½ HOURS
(PLUS SALTING AND RESTING TIME)

WHY THIS RECIPE WORKS: Every Southern city seems to put its own spin on ribs. In Memphis, cooks season the ribs with a spicy dry rub both before grilling and just before the ribs come off the grill. For an easy barbecue recipe that captured the flavor and spirit of Memphis, spareribs worked fine, but St. Louis–style spareribs were even better because they had much of the excess fat and cartilage already trimmed. Using more sugar than salt balanced the spiciness of the rub; brown sugar lent an earthiness that emphasized the pork flavor. Rubbing the ribs at least 1 hour before grilling gave the spices a chance to penetrate the meat. Finally, we simmered the remaining "mop" (the liquid used to baste the ribs as they cook) to concentrate it, then used it tableside as a sauce. If you can't find St. Louis–style racks, baby back ribs will work fine; just reduce the cooking time in the oven in step 5 to 1 to 2 hours. These ribs are moderately spicy, but you can adjust the amounts of cayenne and hot sauce. If you'd like to use wood chunks instead of wood chips when using a charcoal grill, substitute two medium wood chunks, soaked in water for 1 hour, for the wood chip packet.

We use St. Louis–style ribs and a unique outdoor-indoor technique for crusty and savory Memphis spareribs.

¼   **cup paprika**
3   **tablespoons packed brown sugar**
2   **tablespoons chili powder**
2   **teaspoons garlic powder**
2   **teaspoons onion powder**
1   **teaspoon cayenne pepper**
     Salt and pepper
2   **(2½- to 3-pound) racks St. Louis–style spareribs, trimmed and membrane removed**
3   **cups apple cider**
1   **cup cider vinegar**
2   **cups wood chips, soaked in water for 15 minutes and drained**
2   **teaspoons hot sauce**

1. Combine paprika, sugar, chili powder, garlic powder, onion powder, cayenne, 2 tablespoons pepper, and 1 tablespoon salt in bowl. Reserve 7 teaspoons of spice mixture separately for finishing ribs and sauce. Pat ribs dry with paper towels and rub evenly with remaining spice mixture. Wrap ribs in plastic wrap and let sit at room temperature for at least 1 hour, or refrigerate for up to 24 hours.

2. Bring cider and vinegar to simmer in small saucepan; remove from heat and cover to keep warm. Using large piece of heavy-duty aluminum foil, wrap soaked chips in foil packet and cut several vent holes in top

3A. FOR A CHARCOAL GRILL: Open bottom vent halfway. Light large chimney starter three-quarters filled with charcoal briquettes (4½ quarts). When top coals are partially covered with ash, pour into steeply banked pile against side of grill. Place wood chip packet on coals. Set cooking grate in place, cover, and open lid vent halfway. Heat grill until hot and wood chips are smoking, about 5 minutes.

3B. FOR A GAS GRILL: Remove cooking grate and place wood chip packet directly on primary burner. Set cooking grate in place, turn all burners to high, cover, and heat grill until hot and wood chips are smoking, about 15 minutes. Turn primary burner to medium-high and turn off other burner(s). (Adjust primary burner as needed to maintain grill temperature around 325 degrees.)

4. Clean and oil cooking grate. Unwrap ribs and place, meat side down, on cooler side of grill; ribs may overlap slightly. Cover (position lid vent over meat if using charcoal) and cook until ribs are deep red and smoky, about 2 hours, flipping, rotating, and switching ribs and basting with warm mop every

30 minutes. During final 20 minutes of grilling, adjust oven rack to middle position and heat oven to 250 degrees.

5. Transfer ribs, meat side up, to rimmed baking sheet and cover tightly with foil. Continue to cook ribs in oven until tender and fork inserted into ribs meets no resistance, 1½ to 2½ hours, basting with warm mop every 30 minutes.

6. Remove ribs from oven and unwrap. Adjust oven rack 6 inches from broiler element and heat broiler. Sprinkle ribs with 2 tablespoons reserved spice mixture and broil until browned and dry on surface and spices are fragrant, about 2 minutes, flipping ribs over halfway through broiling.

7. Remove ribs from oven, tent with foil, and let rest for 30 minutes. While ribs rest, add remaining 1 teaspoon spice mixture to remaining mop and simmer, uncovered, until thickened and saucy, 10 to 15 minutes. Stir in hot sauce and season with salt and pepper to taste. Slice ribs between bones and serve with sauce.

NOTES FROM THE TEST KITCHEN

Using Wood Chips and Chunks

Wood chips and chunks add great smoky flavor to grilled foods, and they are essential for providing the deep, smoky flavor that is the hallmark of good barbecue. Wood chips will work on either a charcoal or a gas grill, but chunks are suited only to charcoal fires since they must rest in a pile of lit coals to smoke. Soaked wood chunks can be added directly to lit charcoal, but wood chips typically require a little more prep before putting them on the fire (although occasionally we put chips directly on lit coals). Wood chips and chunks are made from hardwoods because they burn more slowly than softer woods. Hickory and mesquite are most common, though some stores may also carry apple, cherry, or oak. Resinous wood like pine is not used for grilling because it gives foods an off-flavor.

On a charcoal grill you have the choice of using wood chips that have been soaked in water and wrapped in an aluminum foil packet (see page 316), or wood chunks. Both the packet of wood chips and the wood chunks (which need to be soaked for an hour or so) should be placed directly on top of the hot coals.

For gas grills, wood chips are soaked in water for 15 minutes before draining and placing them in a foil packet. This packet should sit underneath the cooking grate directly on top of the primary burner. As the packet heats, the chips will smolder and lend a smoky flavor to the food.

Whether you choose chips or chunks, charcoal or gas, you're guaranteed to add more than flavor: Foods exposed to smoke also develop a rich mahogany color on the grill.

Texas-Style Barbecued Beef Ribs

SERVES 4   **TOTAL TIME** 3 TO 3½ HOURS
(PLUS SALTING TIME)

WHY THIS RECIPE WORKS: In Texas, good beef ribs are all about intense meat flavor—not just smoke and spice. We found that the juiciest meat with the most flavor was accomplished by leaving the fat and membrane on the back of the ribs in place. The fat not only basted the ribs as they cooked but also rendered to a crisp, baconlike texture. A simple mixture of salt, pepper, cayenne, and chili powder rubbed into each rack was all that it took to bring out the flavor of the meat. To turn our grill into a backyard smoker, we made a slow, even fire with a temperature in the range of 250 to 300 degrees. A couple hours of slow cooking were enough to render some of the fat and make the ribs juicy, tender, and slightly chewy. For a real Texas-style barbecue sauce to pair with our ribs, we pulled together the usual ingredients—vinegar, onion, and molasses, to name a few—with dry mustard and chipotle chiles for spiciness. Savory Worcestershire sauce added depth while tomato juice (in place of ketchup) provided tangy flavor and helped thin the sauce out. It is important to use beef ribs with a decent amount of meat, not bony scraps; otherwise, the rewards of making this recipe are few. If you'd like to use wood chunks instead of wood chips when using a charcoal grill, substitute two medium wood chunks, soaked in water for 1 hour, for the wood chip packet.

4   teaspoons chili powder
2   teaspoons salt
1½   teaspoons pepper
½   teaspoon cayenne pepper
4   (1¼-pound) beef rib slabs, trimmed
2   cups wood chips, soaked in water for
     15 minutes and drained
1   recipe Texas Barbecue Sauce (page 351)

1. Combine chili powder, salt, pepper, and cayenne in bowl. Pat ribs dry with paper towels and rub evenly with spice mixture. Wrap ribs in plastic wrap and let sit at room temperature for 1 hour. Using large piece of heavy-duty aluminum foil, wrap soaked chips in foil packet and cut several vent holes in top.

2A. FOR A CHARCOAL GRILL: Open bottom vent halfway. Light large chimney starter half filled with charcoal briquettes (3 quarts). When top coals are partially covered with ash, pour into steeply banked pile against side of grill. Place wood chip packet on coals. Set cooking grate in place, cover, and open lid vent halfway. Heat grill until hot and wood chips are smoking, about 5 minutes.

To achieve juicy, meaty beef ribs on the grill we leave the fat and membrane on the ribs.

2B. FOR A GAS GRILL: Remove cooking grate and place wood chip packet directly on primary burner. Set cooking grate in place, turn all burners to high, cover, and heat grill until hot and wood chips are smoking, about 15 minutes. Turn primary burner to medium and turn off other burner(s). (Adjust primary burner as needed to maintain grill temperature between 250 and 300 degrees.)

3. Clean and oil cooking grate. Unwrap ribs and place, meat side down, on cooler side of grill; ribs may overlap slightly. Cover (position lid vent over meat if using charcoal) and cook for 1 hour.

4. If using charcoal, remove cooking grate and add 20 new briquettes; set cooking grate in place. Flip and rotate ribs. Cover and cook until meat begins to pull away from bone, 1¼ to 1¾ hours.

5. Transfer ribs to carving board, tent with foil, and let rest for 5 to 10 minutes. Cut ribs between bones and serve with sauce.

Kansas City Barbecued Brisket

SERVES 8 TO 10   **TOTAL TIME** 5½ TO 6 HOURS
(PLUS SALTING AND RESTING TIME)

✓ **WHY THIS RECIPE WORKS:** In researching recipes for barbecued brisket, we found cooks could agree on one thing: cooking low and slow (for up to 12 hours) for the purpose of tenderizing. That seemed like a lot of time. We wanted to figure out a way to make cooking this potentially delicious cut of meat less daunting and less time-consuming and we wanted to trade in a specialized smoker for a backyard grill. Scoring the fat cap on the brisket helped it render and let the potent spice rub penetrate the meat. (We rubbed it the day before for deep seasoning.) We put the brisket on the cooler side of the grill for gentle cooking, having set it in a disposable aluminum pan to catch the flavorful juices. After a couple of hours of letting it smoke on the grill, we added our homemade barbecue sauce to the pan, covered it, and moved it to the oven, where the steamy environment fully tenderized the meat. Finally, we let the brisket rest in the turned-off oven so that it could reabsorb some of the juices that it had lost, ensuring moist, tender meat. If you'd like to use wood chunks instead of wood chips when using a charcoal grill, substitute two medium wood chunks, soaked in water for 1 hour, for the wood chip packet.

1½ tablespoons paprika
1½ tablespoons packed brown sugar
1 tablespoon chili powder
1 tablespoon pepper
2 teaspoons salt
1 teaspoon granulated garlic
1 teaspoon onion powder
1 (5- to 6-pound) beef brisket, flat cut,
   fat trimmed to ¼ inch
2 cups wood chips
1 (13 by 9-inch) disposable aluminum roasting pan
1 cup ketchup
1 cup water
3 tablespoons molasses
1 tablespoon hot sauce

1. Combine paprika, sugar, chili powder, pepper, salt, granulated garlic, and onion powder in bowl. Cut ½-inch crosshatch pattern through brisket fat cap, ¼ inch deep. Rub brisket with spice mixture. Wrap brisket in plastic wrap and refrigerate for 6 to 24 hours.

We score the fat on brisket to help it render on the grill and so the spice rub can deeply season the meat.

2. Just before grilling, soak wood chips in water for 15 minutes, then drain. Using large piece of heavy-duty aluminum foil, wrap soaked chips in foil packet and cut several vent holes in top. Unwrap brisket, pat dry with paper towels, and transfer to disposable pan.

3A. FOR A CHARCOAL GRILL: Open bottom vent halfway. Light large chimney starter filled with charcoal briquettes (6 quarts). When top coals are partially covered with ash, pour evenly over half of grill. Place wood chip packet on coals. Set cooking grate in place, cover, and open lid vent halfway. Heat grill until hot and wood chips are smoking, about 5 minutes.

3B. FOR A GAS GRILL: Remove cooking grate and place wood chip packet directly on primary burner. Set cooking grate in place, turn all burners to high, cover, and heat grill until hot and wood chips are smoking, about 15 minutes. Leave primary burner on high and turn off other burner(s). (Adjust primary burner as needed to maintain grill temperature around 350 degrees.)

4. Place pan with brisket on cooler side of grill. Cover (position lid vent over meat if using charcoal) and cook for 2 hours. During final 20 minutes of grilling, adjust oven rack to lower-middle position and heat oven to 300 degrees.

5. Whisk ketchup, water, molasses, and hot sauce together in bowl, then pour over brisket. Cover pan tightly with foil and transfer to oven. Cook until brisket registers 195 degrees, 2½ to 3 hours. Turn off heat and let brisket rest in oven for 1 hour.

6. Transfer brisket to carving board. Skim fat from sauce. Cut brisket against grain into ¼-inch-thick slices. Serve with sauce.

Making Kansas City Barbecued Brisket

1. SCORE AND SEASON MEAT: Cut ½-inch crosshatch pattern through brisket fat cap, ¼ inch deep. Rub brisket with spice mixture. Wrap brisket in plastic and refrigerate for 6 to 24 hours.

2. SMOKE FOR 2 HOURS: Place pan with brisket on cooler side of grill. Cover (position lid vent over meat if using charcoal) and cook for 2 hours.

3. ADD SAUCE AND FINISH IN OVEN: Whisk sauce ingredients together, then pour over brisket. Cover pan tightly and transfer to oven. Cook until brisket registers 195 degrees, 2½ hours.

4. LET REST IN TURNED-OFF OVEN: Turn off heat and let brisket rest in oven for 1 hour before serving.

Casseroles

Classic Baked Pasta Casseroles

Chicken Casseroles and More

Beef and Pork Casseroles

■ SIGNIFIES A **FAST** RECIPE (45 MINUTES OR LESS)

Simple Cheese Lasagna

SERVES 6 TO 8   **TOTAL TIME** 1 HOUR 10 MINUTES

✔ **WHY THIS RECIPE WORKS:** Lasagna is the ultimate in Italian comfort food, and while you could spend hours in the kitchen making the noodles and sauce, a simple cheese lasagna can be made in a fraction of the time using no-boil noodles and a homemade sauce that takes just 25 minutes. For the cheese layer, we stuck with tradition and combined ricotta, Parmesan, fresh basil, and an egg to help thicken and bind the mixture. No-boil lasagna noodles eliminated the process of boiling and draining conventional lasagna noodles. After layering the ingredients, we covered the pan for the first part of the baking time, and then uncovered it to create a bubbling lasagna with a crowning layer of beautifully browned cheese. Do not use nonfat ricotta or fat-free mozzarella here. You can substitute 4 cups jarred tomato sauce combined with 1 (28-ounce) can diced tomatoes, drained, for the Chunky Tomato Sauce, if desired.

- 1 pound (2 cups) whole-milk ricotta cheese
- 2½ ounces Parmesan cheese, grated (1¼ cups)
- ½ cup chopped fresh basil
- 1 large egg, lightly beaten
- ½ teaspoon salt
- ½ teaspoon pepper
- 1 recipe (6 cups) Chunky Tomato Sauce
- 12 no-boil lasagna noodles
- 1 pound whole-milk mozzarella cheese, shredded (4 cups)

1. Adjust oven rack to middle position and heat oven to 375 degrees. Mix ricotta, 1 cup Parmesan, basil, egg, salt, and pepper together in bowl.

2. Spread ¼ cup sauce over bottom of 13 by 9-inch baking dish. Lay 3 noodles in dish, spread generous 3 tablespoons ricotta mixture over each noodle, then top with 1 cup mozzarella and 1½ cups sauce (in that order). Repeat layering process 2 more times. Top with remaining 3 noodles, remaining sauce, remaining mozzarella, and remaining Parmesan.

3. Cover dish tightly with greased aluminum foil and bake for 15 minutes. Uncover and continue to bake until cheese is browned and sauce is bubbling, about 25 minutes. Let casserole cool for 10 minutes. Serve.

CHUNKY TOMATO SAUCE

MAKES 6 CUPS   **TOTAL TIME** 25 MINUTES   **FAST**

Although this sauce was created specifically for lasagna and other pasta casseroles, it also tastes great over regular pasta.

- 1 tablespoon extra-virgin olive oil
- 1 onion, chopped fine
  Salt and pepper
- 6 garlic cloves, minced
- ¼ teaspoon dried oregano
- ⅛ teaspoon red pepper flakes
- 1 (28-ounce) can crushed tomatoes
- 1 (28-ounce) can diced tomatoes

Cook oil, onion, and 1 teaspoon salt in large saucepan over medium heat until onion is softened, 5 to 7 minutes. Stir in garlic, oregano, and pepper flakes and cook until fragrant, about 30 seconds. Stir in crushed tomatoes and diced tomatoes with their juice and simmer until sauce is slightly thickened and measures 6 cups, about 15 minutes. Season with salt and pepper to taste.

VARIATION

SMALL-BATCH CHUNKY TOMATO SAUCE
This version yields 4 cups and works well in the Eggplant Parmesan recipe on page 379.

Reduce garlic to 3 cloves and substitute 14.5-ounce can diced tomatoes for 28-ounce can; cook as directed.

VARIATIONS

Simple Sausage Lasagna
Either pork or turkey sausage can be used here.

Cook 1½ pounds sweet or hot Italian sausage, casings removed, in 12-inch nonstick skillet over medium heat, breaking up meat with wooden spoon, until well browned, about 10 minutes; drain sausage through fine-mesh strainer. When assembling lasagna, sprinkle sausage evenly among first three layers, on top of ricotta.

Simple Mushroom Lasagna
Either white or cremini mushrooms can be used here.

Combine 1½ pounds thinly sliced mushrooms, 2 tablespoons extra-virgin olive oil, 2 minced garlic cloves, ½ teaspoon dried oregano, and pinch salt in 12-inch nonstick skillet. Cover and cook over medium-high heat, stirring often, until

It's easy to understand the enduring appeal of lasagna. This dish is endlessly variable, but even the most basic lasagna tastes rich and is satisfying. An easy layering process and a baking method in which the lasagna is first covered, and then uncovered, yield a bubbling lasagna with a beautiful layer of browned cheese.

1. ADD SOME SAUCE TO THE BAKING DISH: Spread ¼ cup tomato sauce over the bottom of a 13 by 9-inch baking dish. **WHY?** Adding a little sauce to the bottom of the pan keeps the noodles from sticking to the pan. Also, the moisture from the sauce helps to hydrate the noodles on the bottom layer. There's no need to grease the baking dish.

2. START LAYERING: Arrange 3 no-boil lasagna noodles crosswise on top of the sauce, leaving space between the noodles. Spoon 3 tablespoons of filling onto each noodle and spread it to an even thickness. **WHY?** The noodles will expand when baking and so should not be touching in the dish. Holding the edge of the noodle makes it easier to spread the ricotta.

3. ADD MOZZARELLA AND SAUCE: Sprinkle the layer evenly with 1 cup shredded mozzarella cheese, then pour 1½ cups tomato sauce evenly over the mozzarella. Repeat the layering process two more times (noodles, filling, mozzarella, sauce) before the final layer. **WHY?** Careful layering and precise portioning of cheese and sauce ensure a well-constructed lasagna.

4. MAKE THE FINAL LAYER: Place 3 noodles on top. Spread the remaining 1¼ cups sauce over the noodles. Sprinkle with 1 cup mozzarella and ¼ cup Parmesan. **WHY?** Finishing with sauce and two types of cheese makes for a browned and appealingly cheesy casserole. Just a little grated Parmesan adds a hit of flavor to the top of the lasagna.

5. COVER THE DISH AND START BAKING: Spray a large sheet of aluminum foil lightly with vegetable oil spray and cover the lasagna. Bake on the middle rack of a 375-degree oven for 15 minutes. **WHY?** Covering the lasagna helps it cook through without drying out and facilitates a moist environment in which the no-boil noodles can soften and expand. We spray the foil with oil to keep it from sticking to the cheesy top.

6. FINISH BAKING IT UNCOVERED: Remove the foil and continue to bake until the cheese is browned and the sauce is bubbling, about 25 minutes longer. Let the lasagna cool for 10 minutes before serving. **WHY?** Baking the lasagna uncovered for the last 25 minutes allows excess moisture to cook off and gives the top of the lasagna a chance to brown. It is important to let the lasagna sit for at least 10 minutes before serving; it needs to firm up a little before you cut it.

mushrooms have released their liquid, about 10 minutes. Uncover and cook until liquid has evaporated and mushrooms are well browned, about 10 minutes. When assembling lasagna, sprinkle mushrooms evenly among first three layers, on top of ricotta.

TO MAKE AHEAD: Assembled, unbaked lasagna can be refrigerated for up to 1 day. To serve, cover dish tightly with greased aluminum foil and bake in 375-degree oven for 25 minutes. Uncover and continue to bake until cheese is browned and sauce is bubbling, about 25 minutes.

Hearty Vegetable Lasagna

SERVES 12   **TOTAL TIME** 2 HOURS 30 MINUTES

✔ **WHY THIS RECIPE WORKS:** For a hearty vegetable lasagna with bold flavor, we started with a summery mix of eggplant, zucchini, and yellow squash. Salting and microwaving the eggplant and sautéing the vegetables cut down on excess moisture and deepened their flavor. Spinach and olives added textural contrast and flavor. We dialed up the usual cheese filling by switching out mild ricotta for tangy cottage cheese mixed with heavy cream (for richness) and Parmesan and garlic (for added flavor). Our quick no-cook tomato sauce brought enough moisture to ensure that the no-boil noodles softened properly. Do not use fat-free mozzarella cheese here. Garnish the baked lasagna with chopped fresh basil, if desired.

NO-COOK TOMATO SAUCE

- 1 (28-ounce) can crushed tomatoes
- ¼ cup chopped fresh basil
- 2 tablespoons extra-virgin olive oil
- 2 garlic cloves, minced
- ½ teaspoon salt
- ¼ teaspoon red pepper flakes

NO-COOK CREAM SAUCE

- 4 ounces Parmesan cheese, grated (2 cups)
- 1 cup whole-milk cottage cheese
- 1 cup heavy cream
- 2 garlic cloves, minced
- 1 teaspoon cornstarch
- ¼ teaspoon salt
- ½ teaspoon pepper

LASAGNA

- 1½ pounds eggplant, peeled and cut into ½-inch pieces (7 cups)
  - Salt and pepper
- 1 pound zucchini, cut into ½-inch pieces (4 cups)
- 1 pound yellow squash, cut into ½-inch pieces (4 cups)
- 5 tablespoons plus 1 teaspoon extra-virgin olive oil
- 4 garlic cloves, minced
- 1 tablespoon minced fresh thyme
- 12 ounces (12 cups) baby spinach
- 12 no-boil lasagna noodles
- ½ cup pitted kalamata olives, minced
- 12 ounces whole-milk mozzarella cheese, shredded (3 cups)

Preparing Vegetables for Lasagna

1. Toss eggplant with salt, then spread evenly over plate lined with coffee filters. Microwave, uncovered, 10 minutes, tossing halfway through cooking.

2. Combine microwaved eggplant, zucchini, and squash, and sauté in batches in hot nonstick skillet until lightly browned, about 7 minutes for each batch.

3. Clear center of skillet, add half of garlic mixture, and mash mixture into pan until fragrant, about 30 seconds. Repeat with remaining vegetables and garlic mixture.

No-cook tomato and cream sauces allow the flavors of the vegetables to shine through in our fresh-tasting lasagna.

1. FOR THE TOMATO SAUCE: Whisk all ingredients together in bowl.

2. FOR THE CREAM SAUCE: Whisk all ingredients together in bowl.

3. FOR THE LASAGNA: Line large plate with double layer of coffee filters and coat lightly with vegetable oil spray. Toss eggplant with ½ teaspoon salt in bowl, then spread evenly over prepared plate. Microwave, uncovered, until eggplant is dry to touch and slightly shriveled, about 10 minutes, tossing halfway through cooking.

4. Let eggplant cool slightly, then toss with zucchini and squash, ½ teaspoon salt, and ½ teaspoon pepper in bowl. In separate bowl, combine 1 tablespoon oil, garlic, and thyme.

5. Heat 2 tablespoons oil in 12-inch nonstick skillet over medium-high heat until shimmering. Add half of vegetables and cook until lightly browned, about 7 minutes. Clear center of skillet, add half of garlic mixture, and mash mixture into pan until fragrant, about 30 seconds. Stir garlic mixture into vegetables and transfer vegetables to large bowl. Repeat with 2 tablespoons oil, remaining vegetables, and remaining garlic mixture; transfer to bowl.

NOTES FROM THE TEST KITCHEN

No-Boil Noodles

No-boil (also called oven-ready) lasagna noodles are pre-cooked at the factory; during baking, the moisture from the sauce softens, or rehydrates, them. The most common no-boil noodle measures 7 inches long and 3½ inches wide; 3 noodles fit perfectly in a 13 by 9-inch dish, and 2 noodles fit nicely in an 8-inch square dish. Note that some no-boil lasagna noodle packages contain only 12 noodles; be sure to check the recipe for how many noodles are required. Our favorite brand is Barilla No-Boil Lasagne; we found these delicate, flat noodles closely resembled fresh pasta in texture.

6. Heat remaining 1 teaspoon oil in now-empty skillet over medium-high heat until shimmering. Add spinach, 1 handful at a time, and cook, stirring frequently, until wilted, about 3 minutes. Transfer spinach to paper towel–lined plate, let drain for 2 minutes, then stir into cooked vegetables.

7. Adjust oven rack to middle position and heat oven to 375 degrees. Grease 13 by 9-inch baking dish, then spread 1 cup tomato sauce over bottom of dish. Lay 4 noodles into dish (noodles will overlap), and top with half of vegetable mixture, half of olives, half of cream sauce, and 1 cup mozzarella (in that order). Repeat layering process 1 more time. Top with remaining 4 noodles, remaining tomato sauce, and remaining mozzarella.

8. Cover dish tightly with greased aluminum foil and place on foil-lined rimmed baking sheet. Bake until edges are bubbling, about 35 minutes. Let casserole cool for 25 minutes. Serve.

TO MAKE AHEAD: Lasagna cannot be assembled ahead of time; however, both sauces and cooked vegetables can be refrigerated separately for up to 1 day.

Baked Manicotti

SERVES 6 TO 8   **TOTAL TIME** 1 HOUR 40 MINUTES

✔ **WHY THIS RECIPE WORKS:** Manicotti may look homey, but blanching and stuffing pasta tubes is a tedious chore, and the ricotta filling can be uninspired and watery. We wanted a simpler, better recipe that had all of the comforting, cheesy flavor but none of the fuss. We did away with the slippery pasta tubes and instead spread the filling onto no-boil lasagna noodles that we had briefly soaked in hot water to make them pliable enough to roll up easily. After baking the manicotti, we sprinkled the dish with Parmesan and broiled it for a few minutes to give it a nicely bronzed crown. Do not use nonfat ricotta or fat-free mozzarella here. Some brands of no-boil noodles contain only 12 noodles per package; note that this recipe requires 16 noodles.

 2 tablespoons extra-virgin olive oil
 3 garlic cloves, minced
 ½ teaspoon red pepper flakes (optional)
 2 (28-ounce) cans crushed tomatoes
 ¼ cup chopped fresh basil
   Salt and pepper
 1½ pounds (3 cups) part-skim ricotta cheese
 4 ounces Parmesan cheese, grated (2 cups)
 8 ounces whole-milk mozzarella cheese, shredded (2 cups)
 2 large eggs, lightly beaten
 2 tablespoons minced fresh parsley
 16 no-boil lasagna noodles

1. Cook oil, garlic, and pepper flakes, if using, in large saucepan over medium heat until fragrant but not brown, 1 to 2 minutes. Stir in tomatoes and simmer until slightly thickened, about 15 minutes. Off heat, stir in 2 tablespoons basil and season with salt and pepper to taste. Cover to keep warm; set aside.

2. Mix ricotta, 1 cup Parmesan, mozzarella, eggs, parsley, remaining 2 tablespoons basil, ¾ teaspoon salt, and ½ teaspoon pepper together in bowl.

3. Pour 1 inch of boiling water into 13 by 9-inch broiler-safe baking dish. Slip noodles into water, 1 at a time. Let noodles soak, separating them with tip of knife to prevent sticking, until pliable, about 5 minutes. Remove noodles from water and place in single layer on clean dish towels. Discard water and dry baking dish.

4. Adjust oven rack to middle position and heat oven to 375 degrees. Spread 1½ cups sauce into now-empty baking dish. Working with several noodles at a time, spread ¼ cup ricotta mixture evenly over bottom three-quarters of each noodle. Roll noodles up around filling, then lay, seam side down, in baking dish. Spoon remaining sauce evenly over top to cover pasta completely.

5. Cover dish tightly with greased aluminum foil. Bake until bubbling, about 40 minutes. Remove baking dish from oven. Position oven rack 6 inches from broiler element and heat broiler. Uncover dish, sprinkle with remaining 1 cup Parmesan, and broil until cheese is spotty brown, 4 to 6 minutes. Let casserole cool for 10 minutes. Serve.

TO MAKE AHEAD: Assembled, unbaked manicotti can be refrigerated for up to 1 day. To serve, cover dish tightly with greased aluminum foil and bake in 375-degree oven for 1 hour. Remove baking dish from oven. Position oven rack 6 inches from broiler element and heat broiler. Uncover dish, sprinkle with remaining 1 cup Parmesan, and broil until cheese is spotty brown, 4 to 6 minutes.

VARIATION
Baked Manicotti Puttanesca
Add 3 rinsed and minced anchovy fillets to pot with garlic in step 1. Add ¼ cup pitted and quartered kalamata olives and 2 tablespoons rinsed and minced capers to ricotta mixture in step 2.

Assembling Manicotti

1. Pour boiling water into 13 by 9-inch baking dish. Slip noodles into water, 1 at a time. Let noodles soak, separating with tip of knife to prevent sticking, until pliable, about 5 minutes.

2. Remove noodles from water and place in single layer on clean dish towels.

3. Working with several noodles at a time, spread ¼ cup ricotta mixture evenly over bottom three-quarters of each noodle.

4. Roll noodles up around filling then lay, seam side down, in baking dish.

Easy Baked Ziti with Ricotta Cheese

SERVES 6 TO 8   **TOTAL TIME** 1 HOUR 20 MINUTES

✓ **WHY THIS RECIPE WORKS:** For an inspired—not tired—baked ziti, we kept things simple and focused on perfecting every element of this family favorite. Cooking the pasta al dente ensured that it was tender, but not overcooked, in the finished dish. Sautéed garlic and red pepper flakes provided a savory foundation to our easy sauce, and two big cans of crushed tomatoes added rich, long-simmered flavor in short order while keeping the casserole moist. Stirring some of the pasta cooking water into the briefly simmered sauce provided further insurance against dryness. A middle layer of ricotta promised creamy as well as tomatoey forkfuls of pasta, while a topping of shredded mozzarella and grated Parmesan gave the ziti a nicely browned crust. Finishing with chopped basil kept our perfect baked ziti fresh-looking and bright-tasting. Do not use nonfat ricotta or fat-free mozzarella here. You can use any short tubular pasta in place of the ziti. Don't forget to reserve 1½ cups of the pasta cooking water in step 2; the water is used to thin out the sauce in step 3.

A middle layer of ricotta cheese adds creaminess and richness to baked ziti.

12 ounces (1½ cups) whole-milk or part-skim ricotta cheese
¼ cup extra-virgin olive oil
   Salt and pepper
12 ounces whole-milk mozzarella cheese, shredded (3 cups)
3 ounces Parmesan cheese, grated (1½ cups)
1½ pounds (7½ cups) ziti
3 garlic cloves, minced
½ teaspoon red pepper flakes
2 (28-ounce) cans crushed tomatoes
¼ cup chopped fresh basil

1. Adjust oven rack to middle position and heat oven to 400 degrees. Mix ricotta, 2 tablespoons oil, ½ teaspoon salt, and ½ teaspoon pepper together in bowl. In separate bowl, combine mozzarella and Parmesan.

2. Meanwhile, bring 6 quarts water to boil in Dutch oven. Add pasta and 1½ tablespoons salt and cook, stirring often, until al dente. Reserve 1½ cups pasta cooking water, drain pasta, and set aside.

3. Dry now-empty pot, add remaining 2 tablespoons oil, garlic, and pepper flakes, and cook over medium heat until fragrant but not brown, 1 to 2 minutes. Stir in tomatoes and simmer until slightly thickened, about 15 minutes. Off heat, season with salt and pepper to taste, then stir in cooked pasta and reserved cooking water.

4. Pour half of pasta-sauce mixture into 13 by 9-inch baking dish. Dollop large spoonfuls of ricotta mixture evenly over pasta, then pour remaining pasta-sauce mixture over ricotta. Sprinkle with mozzarella mixture. Bake until filling is bubbling and cheese is spotty brown, 25 to 35 minutes. Let casserole cool for 10 minutes. Sprinkle with basil and serve.

TO MAKE AHEAD: Assembled, unbaked casserole can be refrigerated for up to 1 day. To serve, cover dish tightly with greased aluminum foil and bake in 400-degree oven until hot throughout, 25 to 30 minutes. Uncover and continue to bake until cheese is lightly browned, 25 to 30 minutes. Sprinkle with basil before serving.

VARIATION

Easy Baked Ziti with Italian Sausage

Add 1 pound sweet or hot Italian sausage, casings removed, to pot before adding oil, garlic, and pepper flakes in step 3; cook sausage, breaking up meat with wooden spoon, until no longer pink, about 5 minutes. Stir in oil, garlic, and pepper flakes, and cook until fragrant, about 30 seconds, before adding tomatoes.

Our gnocchi casserole starts with boiled, store-bought gnocchi.

Baked Gnocchi with Tomato and Basil

SERVES 4   **TOTAL TIME** 50 MINUTES

✔ **WHY THIS RECIPE WORKS:** Gnocchi is the pillow-soft pasta, typically made from potatoes, that has a luxurious appeal especially when bathed in a flavorful tomato and basil sauce. To make the most of our time, we boiled the gnocchi while making a simple sauce. Then we simmered the gnocchi in the sauce to boost the pasta's flavor. Topped with shredded mozzarella and then baked, this simple gnocchi casserole is sure to please. The partially cooked, vacuum-packed gnocchi found in the pasta aisle works best here, but frozen gnocchi can also be used. If your skillet is not ovensafe, transfer the gnocchi and sauce to a shallow 2-quart casserole dish before sprinkling with the cheese and baking.

1 pound vacuum-packed gnocchi
  Salt and pepper
1 onion, chopped fine
1 tablespoon extra-virgin olive oil
6 garlic cloves, minced
⅛ teaspoon red pepper flakes
1 (28-ounce) can crushed tomatoes
1 cup water
½ cup chopped fresh basil
8 ounces mozzarella cheese, shredded (2 cups)

1. Adjust oven rack to upper-middle position and heat oven to 475 degrees. Bring 4 quarts water to boil in large pot. Add gnocchi and 1 tablespoon salt and cook, stirring often, until tender and floating. Drain gnocchi and set aside.

2. Meanwhile, combine onion and oil in 12-inch ovensafe skillet and cook until onion is softened, about 3 minutes. Stir in garlic and pepper flakes and cook until fragrant, about 30 seconds. Stir in tomatoes and water and cook until slightly thickened, about 5 minutes. Season with salt and pepper to taste.

3. Stir in boiled gnocchi and cook, stirring occasionally, until sauce is thickened, 5 to 7 minutes. Stir in basil and sprinkle with mozzarella. Bake until cheese is well browned, about 8 minutes. Let cool slightly and serve.

Cheesy Ravioli Bake with Sausage

SERVES 4 TO 6   **TOTAL TIME** 50 MINUTES

✔ **WHY THIS RECIPE WORKS:** For a lasagna-like casserole that's also a snap to prepare, we started with store-bought ravioli. Sautéed Italian sausage gave our speedy sauce deep flavor. Cooking a spoonful of tomato paste with the sausage provided further depth, and a can of crushed tomatoes made for a smooth sauce with real clinginess. A small amount of heavy cream provided some underlying richness. Tossing the cooked ravioli in the sauce, then pouring the mixture into a baking dish and sprinkling it with mozzarella, made for a casserole that practically assembled itself. After five minutes in the oven, the cheese had perfectly melted into a lightly browned, gooey layer. We prefer fresh ravioli here; however, 1 pound of frozen cheese ravioli can be substituted.

2 (9-ounce) packages fresh cheese ravioli
  Salt and pepper
1 pound sweet or hot Italian sausage, casings removed
3 garlic cloves, minced
1 tablespoon tomato paste
1 (28-ounce) can crushed tomatoes
3 tablespoons chopped fresh basil
¼ cup heavy cream
4 ounces mozzarella cheese, shredded (1 cup)

1. Adjust oven rack to middle position and heat oven to 475 degrees. Bring 4 quarts water to boil in large pot. Add ravioli and 1 tablespoon salt and cook, stirring often, until tender. Drain ravioli and return it to pot.

2. Meanwhile, cook sausage in 12-inch nonstick skillet over medium-high heat, breaking meat up with wooden spoon, until no longer pink, about 5 minutes. Stir in garlic and tomato paste and cook until fragrant, about 1 minute. Stir in tomatoes and cook until slightly thickened, 8 to 10 minutes. Stir in basil and cream and simmer until slightly thickened, about 2 minutes.

3. Stir sauce into ravioli and season with salt and pepper to taste. Spread mixture into 13 by 9-inch baking dish and sprinkle with mozzarella. Bake until cheese is melted and lightly browned, about 5 minutes. Let cool slightly and serve.

VARIATION

Cheesy Ravioli Bake with Fennel, Olives, and Feta

Omit tomato paste. Substitute 1 fennel bulb, trimmed and sliced thin, for sausage; cook as directed until fennel is softened, about 6 minutes. Add ½ cup pitted and chopped kalamata olives with basil and cream in step 2. Substitute 1 cup crumbled feta cheese for mozzarella.

Shredding Semisoft Cheese

To prevent grater from becoming clogged when shredding mozzarella and other semisoft cheeses, use vegetable oil spray to lightly coat holes, then shred away.

Removing Sausage from Its Casing

Italian sausage is sold in several forms, including links (most common), bulk-style tubes, and patties. To remove sausage from its casing, hold sausage firmly on one end, and squeeze sausage out of opposite end.

American Chop Suey

SERVES 4   **TOTAL TIME** 45 MINUTES   **FAST**

WHY THIS RECIPE WORKS: Despite its Chinese name, chop suey is not a Chinese dish. In fact, it's probably the furthest thing from it. It is a combination of ground beef, vegetables, and macaroni all cooked in a tomato sauce and topped with a good layer of melted cheese. To prevent the filling from tasting overly greasy, we used 90 percent lean ground beef. A basic mixture of onions, red pepper, and celery helped make the dish taste fresh and added some much needed texture. Using a combination of diced tomatoes, tomato sauce, and chicken broth gave the sauce a hearty flavor without having a heavy texture. To streamline the method for this weeknight workhorse dinner, we cooked everything right in the same skillet (including the pasta) then slid it into a hot oven to melt the cheese on top. We like to use Colby cheese here because it melts well and has good flavor, but cheddar or Monterey Jack are good substitutes. An equal amount of small shells can be substituted for the macaroni if desired.

> 2 tablespoons vegetable oil
> 1 onion, chopped fine
> 1 red bell pepper, stemmed, seeded, and cut into ½-inch pieces
> 1 celery rib, chopped
>   Salt and pepper
> 2 garlic cloves, minced
> 1 pound 90 percent lean ground beef
> 1 (15-ounce) can tomato sauce
> 1 (14.5-ounce) can diced tomatoes
> 1½ cups chicken broth
> 8 ounces (2 cups) elbow macaroni
> 4 ounces Colby cheese, shredded (1 cup)

1. Adjust oven rack to middle position and heat oven to 450 degrees. Heat oil in 12-inch ovensafe skillet over medium heat until shimmering. Add onion, bell pepper, celery, and ½ teaspoon salt and cook, stirring often, until softened, 5 to 7 minutes. Stir in garlic and cook until fragrant, about 30 seconds. Stir in beef, breaking up meat with wooden spoon, and cook until lightly browned and no longer pink, 3 to 5 minutes.

2. Stir in tomato sauce, diced tomatoes with their juice, and chicken broth. Stir in pasta. Cover, increase heat to medium-high, and cook at vigorous simmer, stirring often, until pasta is nearly tender, 9 to 12 minutes.

3. Stir pasta thoroughly and season with salt and pepper to taste. Sprinkle evenly with cheese. Transfer skillet to oven and bake until cheese is melted and lightly browned, about 5 minutes. Serve.

Baked Macaroni and Cheese

SERVES 6   **TOTAL TIME** 1 HOUR 35 MINUTES

WHY THIS RECIPE WORKS: For a classic, home-style macaroni and cheese that would appeal to adults and kids alike, we kept things simple, staying away from pungent cheeses and an overly rich sauce made with eggs and cream. Instead, we started with a béchamel sauce—butter, flour, and milk—adding chicken broth both for a savory flavor and to keep the sauce from becoming too thick in the oven, and added the cheese. Using a combination of sharp cheddar and Colby gave us both ultracheesy flavor and an incredibly creamy texture. Once the cheese was incorporated, we stirred in our macaroni (cooked until nearly tender) and moved it all to a baking dish. For a crunchy topping, we tossed some panko bread crumbs with melted butter, sprinkled them over the casserole, and baked the dish until it was bubbling and golden on top.

- 8 tablespoons unsalted butter
- 1 cup panko bread crumbs
- Salt and pepper
- 1 pound (4 cups) elbow macaroni or small shells
- 1 garlic clove, minced
- 1 teaspoon dry mustard
- ¼ teaspoon cayenne pepper
- 6 tablespoons all-purpose flour
- 3½ cups whole milk
- 2¼ cups chicken broth
- 1 pound Colby cheese, shredded (4 cups)
- 8 ounces extra-sharp cheddar cheese, shredded (2 cups)

1. Adjust oven rack to middle position and heat oven to 350 degrees. Melt 2 tablespoons butter in microwave, then toss with panko in bowl, and season with salt and pepper. Spread panko onto rimmed baking sheet and bake until golden, about 10 minutes. Increase oven temperature to 400 degrees.

2. Meanwhile, bring 4 quarts water to boil in Dutch oven. Add pasta and 1 tablespoon salt and cook, stirring often, until nearly al dente. Drain pasta and set aside.

3. Dry now-empty pot, add remaining 6 tablespoons butter, and melt over medium heat. Stir in garlic, mustard, and cayenne and cook until fragrant, about 30 seconds. Stir in flour and cook for 1 minute. Slowly whisk in milk and broth until smooth. Simmer, whisking often, until thickened, about 15 minutes.

4. Off heat, gradually whisk in Colby and cheddar until melted. Season with salt and pepper to taste. Stir in cooked pasta, breaking up any clumps. Pour into 13 by 9-inch baking dish and sprinkle with toasted bread-crumb mixture. Bake until golden and bubbling around edges, 25 to 35 minutes. Let casserole cool for 10 minutes. Serve.

TO MAKE AHEAD: Assembled, unbaked casserole can be refrigerated for up to 1 day. To serve, cover with greased aluminum foil and bake in 400-degree oven until hot throughout, 20 to 25 minutes. Uncover and continue to bake until crumbs are crisp, 10 to 20 minutes.

Making Baked Macaroni and Cheese

1. UNDERCOOK MACARONI: Bring 4 quarts water to boil in large Dutch oven. Add pasta and 1 tablespoon salt and cook, stirring often, until nearly al dente.

2. MAKE A SAUCE: Melt butter and stir in garlic, mustard, and cayenne; cook until fragrant. Stir in flour and cook for 1 minute. Slowly whisk in milk and broth and simmer until thickened.

3. USE TWO KINDS OF CHEESE: Off heat, gradually whisk shredded Colby and cheddar into sauce until melted.

4. BAKE UNCOVERED: Pour macaroni mixture into 13 by 9-inch baking dish, sprinkle with toasted bread-crumb mixture, and bake until golden and bubbling around edges, 25 to 35 minutes.

Ultimate Chili Mac

SERVES 6   **TOTAL TIME** 1 HOUR 40 MINUTES

🗸 **WHY THIS RECIPE WORKS:** Sure, it's a kid favorite, but chili mac is a dish with a huge adult following, too. For the ultimate chili mac, we started by sautéing onion, bell pepper, and garlic, then adding and browning ground beef. In lieu of fresh chiles (jalapeños added too much heat for this family-friendly supper), we added chili powder and cumin. A mix of tomato products—puree and diced—created a thick sauce to ensure that the pasta stayed tender in the oven. Stirring some of the shredded cheese into the chili mac also helped. Colby Jack cheese, also known as CoJack, is a creamy blend of Colby and Monterey Jack cheeses. If unavailable, substitute Monterey Jack cheese. Ground turkey can be substituted for the ground beef. Don't forget to reserve ¾ cup of the pasta cooking water in step 1; the water is used to thin out the chili base of the casserole.

- 8 ounces (2 cups) elbow macaroni
   Salt and pepper
- 2 tablespoons vegetable oil
- 2 onions, chopped fine
- 1 red bell pepper, stemmed, seeded, and chopped fine
- 6 garlic cloves, minced
- 2 tablespoons chili powder
- 1 tablespoon ground cumin
- 1½ pounds 85 percent lean ground beef
- 1 (28-ounce) can tomato puree
- 1 (14.5-ounce) can diced tomatoes
- 1 tablespoon packed brown sugar
- 10 ounces Colby Jack cheese, shredded (2½ cups)

1. Adjust oven rack to middle position and heat oven to 400 degrees. Bring 4 quarts water to boil in Dutch oven. Add pasta and 1 tablespoon salt and cook, stirring often, until nearly al dente. Reserve ¾ cup cooking water. Drain pasta and set aside.

2. Dry now-empty pot, add oil, and heat over medium heat until shimmering. Add onions, bell pepper, and ¾ teaspoon salt and cook until softened, 8 to 10 minutes. Stir in garlic, chili powder, and cumin and cook until fragrant, about 1 minute. Stir in beef and cook, breaking up meat with wooden spoon, until no longer pink, 5 to 8 minutes.

3. Stir in tomato puree, diced tomatoes and their juice, sugar, and ¾ cup reserved cooking water. Cover pot partially (leaving about 1 inch of pot open) and simmer, stirring occasionally, until flavors have blended, about 20 minutes.

4. Off heat, season with salt and pepper to taste. Stir in cooked pasta, breaking up any clumps, then stir in 1 cup cheese. Pour into 13 by 9-inch baking dish. Sprinkle remaining 1½ cups cheese over top.

5. Bake until bubbling around edges and cheese is spotty brown, about 15 minutes. Let casserole cool for 10 minutes. Serve.

TO MAKE AHEAD: Let filling cool in baking dish before topping with cheese in step 4; assembled, unbaked casserole can be refrigerated for up to 1 day. To serve, cover dish tightly with greased aluminum foil and bake in 400-degree oven until hot throughout, 40 to 45 minutes. Uncover and bake until cheese is lightly browned, 5 to 10 minutes.

Spicy Spaghetti Pie

SERVES 4   **TOTAL TIME** 1 HOUR

🗸 **WHY THIS RECIPE WORKS:** This pasta dish takes the classic flavors of spaghetti and tomato sauce and turns them into a family-friendly, sliceable pie. Thinner versions of spaghetti (vermicelli or thin spaghetti) proved a better choice than spaghetti itself, which didn't stick together well when we cut into the pie. For bold flavor, we used an easy-to-find shredded Mexican cheese blend (a combination of Monterey Jack, cheddar, and asadero cheeses) and spicy pepperoni. Heavy cream added an underlying richness that countered the acidity of the tomatoes. Using a spatula to press the pasta into the pie plate ensured that the finished pie sliced neatly. In order to make the pie sliceable, we folded in just a portion of the sauce with the pasta and then served the pie topped with a little extra sauce, passing the remainder at the table.

- 12 ounces vermicelli or thin spaghetti
   Salt and pepper
- 4 ounces sliced deli pepperoni, chopped fine
- 1 onion, chopped fine
- ½ teaspoon red pepper flakes
- 3 (14.5-ounce) cans diced tomatoes
- 8 ounces shredded Mexican cheese blend (2 cups)
- ¾ cup heavy cream
- ½ cup chopped fresh basil
- 1½ cups water, plus extra as needed

This family-friendly spaghetti pie has crisp pieces of pepperoni and plenty of shredded Mexican cheese blend.

1. Adjust oven rack to upper-middle position and heat oven to 475 degrees. Grease 9-inch pie plate with vegetable oil spray. Bring 4 quarts water to boil in large pot. Add pasta and 1 tablespoon salt and cook, stirring often, until nearly al dente. Drain pasta and return it to pot.

2. Meanwhile, cook pepperoni in 12-inch skillet over medium-high heat until crisp, about 2 minutes. Stir in onion and cook until softened, about 5 minutes. Stir in pepper flakes and cook for 30 seconds. Stir in tomatoes and their juice and simmer until sauce is thickened and reduced to 4 cups, about 10 minutes. Season with salt and pepper to taste.

3. Add 2 cups tomato sauce, cheese, cream, and basil to pasta and toss to combine. Transfer pasta mixture to prepared pie plate and press with spatula to flatten surface. Bake until golden and bubbling around edges, about 15 minutes. Let pie cool for 10 minutes.

4. While casserole bakes and cools, add water to remaining sauce in skillet and simmer, mashing tomatoes with back of spoon, until sauce is smooth and thickened, about 25 minutes. Add extra water as needed to adjust sauce consistency. Slice pie into wedges and serve with remaining sauce.

TO MAKE AHEAD: Assembled, unbaked casserole and extra tomato sauce can be refrigerated for up to 1 day. To serve, cover dish tightly with greased aluminum foil and bake in 450-degree oven until hot throughout, about 45 minutes. Remove foil and continue to bake until golden on top, 10 to 15 minutes. Let pie cool for 10 minutes. While casserole bakes and cools, reheat sauce as directed in step 4.

Pressing Pasta into a Pie Plate

Transfer pasta mixture to prepared pie plate and press with spatula to flatten surface so it can be sliced into tidy pieces for serving.

Tuna Noodle Casserole

SERVES 8 TO 10   **TOTAL TIME** 1 HOUR 50 MINUTES

WHY THIS RECIPE WORKS: Most tuna noodle casseroles suffer from overcooked noodles, a reliance on canned soup, and a soggy, bland topping. Marinating the tuna in warmed, seasoned oil for just 10 minutes allowed the flavors to penetrate, turning the fish flaky and moist. We found that rinsing the egg noodles after boiling removes any residual starch that would otherwise make the casserole pasty and also halts the cooking process, preventing the noodles from overcooking within the casserole. We ditched the condensed soup, opting to make a homemade version, and browned the mushrooms thoroughly to develop flavor. Finally, adding potato chips to the topping lent a satisfying crunch and great flavor to every bite.

4	ounces Monterey Jack cheese, shredded (1 cup)
4	ounces sharp cheddar cheese, shredded (1 cup)
2	cups potato chips, crushed
2	slices hearty white sandwich bread, torn into 1-inch pieces
6	tablespoons unsalted butter
	Salt and pepper
3	(6-ounce) cans solid white tuna in water
2	tablespoons vegetable oil
2	teaspoons lemon juice
12	ounces (7¾ cups) wide egg noodles
10	ounces white mushrooms, trimmed and sliced ¼ inch thick

1 **onion, chopped fine**

1 **red bell pepper, stemmed, seeded, and chopped fine**

3 **tablespoons all-purpose flour**

3½ **cups half-and-half**

1½ **cups chicken broth**

1½ **cups frozen peas**

1. Adjust oven rack to middle position and heat oven to 425 degrees. Combine Monterey Jack and cheddar in bowl. Pulse potato chips, bread, ¼ cup cheese mixture, 2 tablespoons butter, ¼ teaspoon salt, and ¼ teaspoon pepper in food processor until coarsely ground, about 8 pulses; set aside.

2. Place tuna in fine-mesh strainer and press dry with paper towels. Transfer to large bowl and flake into coarse pieces with fork. Microwave oil, lemon juice, ½ teaspoon salt, and ½ teaspoon pepper in bowl until bubbling around edges, about 30 seconds. Stir oil mixture into tuna and let sit for 10 minutes.

3. Bring 4 quarts water to boil in Dutch oven. Add pasta and 1 tablespoon salt and cook until just al dente. Drain pasta, rinse under cold water for 2 minutes, and drain again; set aside.

4. Dry now-empty pot, add 1 tablespoon butter, and melt over medium-high heat. Add mushrooms and ¼ teaspoon salt and cook until liquid evaporates and mushrooms are browned, 6 to 8 minutes; transfer to bowl with tuna.

5. Add 1 tablespoon butter, onion, and bell pepper to now-empty pot and cook over medium-high heat until softened, 5 to 7 minutes; transfer to bowl with tuna and mushrooms.

6. Add remaining 2 tablespoons butter to now-empty pot and melt over medium heat. Add flour and cook, whisking constantly, until golden, about 1 minute. Slowly whisk in half-and-half and broth and bring to boil. Reduce heat to medium-low and simmer until slightly thickened, 5 to 7 minutes.

7. Off heat, whisk in remaining cheese mixture until smooth. Stir in pasta, tuna-vegetable mixture, peas, ½ teaspoon salt, and ½ teaspoon pepper. Scrape mixture into 13 by 9-inch baking dish and top with bread-crumb mixture. Bake until golden brown, 12 to 14 minutes. Let casserole cool for 10 minutes. Serve.

Marinating Tuna

Marinating tuna makes it moist and flavorful. Microwave oil, lemon juice, salt, and pepper in bowl until bubbling around edges, about 30 seconds. Stir oil mixture into tuna and let sit for 10 minutes.

TO MAKE AHEAD: Do not add peas to filling or top casserole with bread-crumb mixture. Casserole and bread-crumb mixture can be refrigerated separately for up to 1 day. To serve, cover casserole dish tightly with greased aluminum foil and bake in 400-degree oven until hot throughout, about 45 minutes. Uncover, stir in peas, and top with bread-crumb mixture; bake until topping is crisp and golden, about 10 minutes.

Chicken Noodle Casserole

SERVES 8 TO 10   **TOTAL TIME** 1 HOUR 45 MINUTES

✔ WHY THIS RECIPE WORKS: To update this retro dish, we started by ditching the condensed soup and other canned ingredients. We cooked the egg noodles until just al dente and then shocked them in cold water to prevent them from overcooking in the oven. A flour-thickened sauce made up of half-and-half and chicken broth created a rich, savory base, and a combination of cheeses—cheddar for flavor, American for smooth melting—was key. Precooked chicken turned rubbery after being baked into the casserole, so we simmered boneless, skinless chicken breasts in the sauce until they were nearly cooked through before shredding them and tossing them in with the noodles. Crushed buttery Ritz Crackers became a quick, crunchy topping for the casserole. Our updated recipe needed only 15 minutes in the oven before it came out bubbling and golden brown.

12 **ounces (7¾ cups) wide egg noodles**

Salt and pepper

3 **tablespoons unsalted butter**

1 **onion, chopped fine**

1 **red bell pepper, stemmed, seeded, and chopped fine**

3 **tablespoons all-purpose flour**

2½ **cups half-and-half**

2½ **cups chicken broth**

1 **pound boneless, skinless chicken breasts, trimmed and halved lengthwise**

4 **slices deli American cheese (4 ounces), chopped**

4 **ounces sharp cheddar cheese, shredded (1 cup)**

1½ **cups frozen peas**

25 **Ritz Crackers, crushed coarse**

1. Adjust oven rack to upper-middle position and heat oven to 425 degrees. Bring 4 quarts water to boil in Dutch oven. Add noodles and 1 tablespoon salt and cook, stirring often, until just al dente, about 3 minutes. Drain pasta, rinse under cold water for 2 minutes, and drain again; set aside.

EASY RICE CASSEROLES

If you keep a few packages of precooked rice in your pantry, it's a snap to assemble one of these comforting rice casseroles. Our favorite brand of precooked rice is Minute Ready to Serve White Rice. Each of these recipes serves 4.

CHICKEN DIVAN RICE CASSEROLE `FAST`

Whisk 1 cup chicken broth, ½ cup heavy cream, 2 tablespoons cornstarch, 2 minced garlic cloves, and ½ teaspoon dry mustard together in large saucepan. Cook over medium heat, whisking constantly, until thickened, 2 to 3 minutes. Off heat, stir in 2 cups shredded cheddar cheese, 2 cups shredded rotisserie chicken, 8 ounces thawed frozen broccoli florets (chopped if large), and 2 cups cooked rice. Season with salt and pepper to taste. Pour into 2-quart casserole dish. Sprinkle with 1 cup crushed Ritz crackers (24 crackers). Bake in 375-degree oven until bubbling and browned, about 20 minutes.

CREOLE SHRIMP AND RICE CASSEROLE `FAST`

Whisk 1 cup chicken broth, ¼ cup chopped andouille sausage, 2 tablespoons cornstarch, 2 minced garlic cloves, and 2 teaspoons Cajun seasoning together in large saucepan. Cook over medium heat, whisking constantly, until thickened, 2 to 3 minutes. Off heat, stir in 1 pound peeled and deveined large shrimp, 1 cup thawed frozen mixed bell peppers, and 2 cups cooked rice. Season with salt and pepper to taste. Pour into 2-quart casserole dish. Sprinkle with 2 cups crushed Fritos. Bake in 375-degree oven until bubbling, about 20 minutes.

ASIAN-INSPIRED CHICKEN RICE CASSEROLE `FAST`

Whisk 1 cup chicken broth, 1 cup coconut milk, 2 tablespoons cornstarch, 1 tablespoon grated fresh ginger, and 2 minced garlic cloves together in large saucepan. Cook over medium heat, whisking constantly, until thickened, 2 to 3 minutes. Off heat, stir in 2 cups shredded rotisserie chicken, 1 cup thawed frozen edamame, 1 cup thawed frozen carrot coins, 2 cups cooked rice, ½ cup chopped canned baby corn, and 2 tablespoons chopped fresh basil. Season with salt and pepper to taste. Pour into 2-quart casserole dish. Toss 2 cups panko bread crumbs with 2 tablespoons vegetable oil in bowl and sprinkle over top. Bake in 375-degree oven until bubbling, about 20 minutes.

Our updated version of chicken noodle casserole features a homemade sauce and boneless, skinless chicken breasts.

2. Dry now-empty pot, add 1 tablespoon butter, and melt over medium-high heat. Add onion and bell pepper and cook until softened, 5 to 7 minutes; transfer to bowl.

3. Add remaining 2 tablespoons butter to now-empty pot and melt over medium heat. Add flour and cook, whisking constantly, for 1 minute. Slowly whisk in half-and-half and broth and bring to boil. Reduce heat to medium-low and simmer until slightly thickened, about 5 minutes. Add chicken and cook until no longer pink, 8 to 10 minutes; chicken should be slightly underdone.

4. Remove pot from heat. Transfer chicken to cutting board, let cool slightly, and shred into bite-size pieces. Whisk American and cheddar cheeses into sauce until smooth. Stir shredded chicken, noodles, onion mixture, peas, 1½ teaspoons salt, and 1¼ teaspoons pepper into cheese sauce.

5. Transfer mixture to 13 by 9-inch baking dish and top with crushed crackers. Bake until golden brown and bubbling, about 15 minutes. Let casserole cool for 10 minutes. Serve.

TO MAKE AHEAD: Do not add peas to filling or top casserole with crushed crackers. Casserole can be refrigerated for up to 1 day. To serve, cover casserole dish tightly with greased aluminum foil and bake in 400-degree oven until hot throughout, about 45 minutes. Uncover, stir in peas, and top with crushed crackers; bake until topping is crisp and golden, about 10 minutes.

Chicken Pot Pie with Pie Dough Topping

SERVES 6 TO 8   **TOTAL TIME** 1 HOUR 25 MINUTES

✓ **WHY THIS RECIPE WORKS:** For a streamlined chicken pot pie recipe, we began by sautéing aromatics and vegetables before adding flour to make a roux. Then we added sherry, broth, and cream to build a sauce before folding in cubed boneless, skinless chicken breasts. Undercooking the chicken slightly when making the filling ensured that the breasts didn't overcook during baking. You can substitute a store-bought pie dough for homemade pie dough; overlap two pie dough rounds by a half, brushing water between them to help them seal, then roll them together to make a rectangle roughly 15 by 11 inches. You can also uses biscuits instead of pie dough; see variation page 374. The filling must be hot when you top it with the pie dough, or the crust will be gummy.

- 4 **tablespoons unsalted butter**
- 3 **carrots, peeled and sliced ¼ inch thick**
- 2 **celery ribs, sliced ¼ inch thick**
- 1 **onion, chopped fine**
  Salt and pepper
- 2 **garlic cloves, minced**
- 2 **teaspoons minced fresh thyme or ½ teaspoon dried**
- ½ **cup all-purpose flour**
- ¼ **cup dry sherry**
- 3 **cups chicken broth**
- ¼ **cup heavy cream**
- 2 **bay leaves**
- 3 **pounds boneless, skinless chicken breasts, trimmed and cut into 1-inch pieces**
- 1 **cup frozen peas**
- 1 **recipe Foolproof Double-Crust Pie Dough (page 698) or All-Butter Double Crust Pie Dough (page 701)**

1. Adjust oven rack to lower-middle position and heat oven to 425 degrees. Melt butter in Dutch oven over medium heat. Add carrots, celery, onion, and ¼ teaspoon salt and cook until softened, 5 to 7 minutes. Stir in garlic and thyme and cook until fragrant, about 15 seconds. Stir in flour and cook for 1 minute.

2. Slowly whisk in sherry, scraping up any browned bits. Stir in broth, cream, and bay leaves. Simmer until mixture is thickened, about 10 minutes.

3. Season sauce with salt and pepper to taste. Stir in chicken and simmer gently until no longer pink, about 5 minutes; chicken should be slightly underdone.

4. Discard bay leaves and stir in peas. Pour mixture into 13 by 9-inch baking dish; filling should be hot.

Topping Chicken Pot Pie

1. After rolling pie dough out into 15 by 11-inch rectangle, gently roll dough around rolling pin, then unroll over baking dish.

2. Trim dough, allowing it to overhang dish by ½ inch, then fold edge of dough under itself so that edge is flush with lip of dish.

3a. Using your fingers, flute edge of dough attractively all around edge of dish.

3b. If using biscuits, cut into 3-inch rounds, then place evenly over hot pot-pie filling, spacing about ¼ inch apart.

You can top our rich chicken pot pie filling with either pie dough or easy-to-make cream biscuits.

5. Roll pie dough out into 15 by 11-inch rectangle and drape it over dish. Trim and crimp edges. Bake until topping is golden brown and filling is bubbly, about 20 minutes. Let casserole cool for 10 minutes. Serve.

TO MAKE AHEAD: Pot pie cannot be assembled ahead of time; however, filling can be prepared through step 3 and refrigerated for up to 2 days. Reheat filling gently in large saucepan on stovetop, adding additional broth as needed to loosen its consistency, before assembling and baking casserole.

VARIATION

Chicken Pot Pie with Biscuit Topping

When making pot pie, we prefer to cut the biscuits into 3-inch rounds (which is slightly thinner and wider than the Cream Biscuits recipe on page 560) so that they cover the filling better and bake through more quickly. In terms of timing, make the biscuits just before baking the casserole.

Substitute 1 recipe Cream Biscuits (page 560) for pie dough; stamp biscuit dough into eight 3-inch-round biscuits. Lay unbaked biscuits evenly on top of filling in baking dish, about ¼ inch apart; bake as directed.

King Ranch Casserole

SERVES 6 TO 8   **TOTAL TIME** 1 HOUR 30 MINUTES

✓ **WHY THIS RECIPE WORKS:** King Ranch Casserole is the ultimate comfort food in Texas: layers of tender chicken, corn tortillas, and spicy tomatoes, all bound together in a rich, cheesy sauce. We wanted a recipe that captured the dish's mildly spicy flavor but didn't include the canned soup relied on by most recipes. To achieve this, we started our recipe's sauce with onions, chiles, cumin, and canned Ro-tel tomatoes. Instead of discarding the tomatoes' juice, we reduced the liquid to intensify the tomato flavor. Flour added thickness, cream added richness, and chicken broth gave the sauce even more flavor. We crisped the tortillas in the oven and broke them into bite-size pieces, which kept them from turning to mush in the casserole. If you can't find Ro-tel tomatoes, substitute one 14.5-ounce can diced tomatoes and one 4-ounce can chopped green chiles. Colby Jack cheese, also known as CoJack, is a creamy blend of Colby and Monterey Jack cheeses. If unavailable, substitute Monterey Jack cheese.

- 12 **(6-inch) corn tortillas**
  Vegetable oil spray
- 1 **tablespoon unsalted butter**
- 2 **onions, chopped fine**
- 2 **jalapeño chiles, stemmed, seeded, and minced**
- 2 **teaspoons ground cumin**
- 2 **(10-ounce) cans Ro-tel Diced Tomatoes & Green Chilies**
- 5 **tablespoons all-purpose flour**
- 1 **cup heavy cream**
- 3 **cups chicken broth**
  Salt and pepper

NOTES FROM THE TEST KITCHEN

Ro-tel Tomatoes

This blend of tomatoes, green chiles, and spices was created by Carl Roettele in Elsa, Texas, in the early 1940s. By the 1950s, Ro-tel tomatoes had become popular in the Lone Star State and beyond. The spicy, tangy tomatoes add just the right flavor to countless local recipes, like King Ranch Casserole. We call on Ro-tel tomatoes when we need an extra flavor boost, often in Southwest- and Texas-inspired recipes. If you can't find them, substitute one 14.5-ounce can diced tomatoes and one 4-ounce can chopped green chiles.

Canned Ro-tel tomatoes plus jalapeño chiles and cumin are key to our zesty King Ranch Casserole.

1½   **pounds boneless, skinless chicken breasts, trimmed, halved lengthwise, and cut crosswise into ½-inch slices**
1   **pound Colby Jack cheese, shredded (4 cups)**
2   **tablespoons minced fresh cilantro**
2¼   **cups Fritos, crushed**

1. Adjust oven racks to upper-middle and lower-middle positions and heat oven to 450 degrees. Lay tortillas on 2 baking sheets, lightly coat both sides with oil spray, and bake until slightly crisp and browned, about 12 minutes. Cool slightly, then break into bite-size pieces.

2. Meanwhile, melt butter in Dutch oven over medium-high heat. Add onions, chiles, and cumin and cook until lightly browned, about 8 minutes. Stir in tomatoes and their juice and cook until most of liquid has evaporated, about 10 minutes.

3. Stir in flour and cook for 1 minute. Stir in cream and broth, bring to simmer, and cook until thickened, 2 to 3 minutes. Season with salt and pepper to taste. Stir in chicken and cook until no longer pink, about 4 minutes; chicken should be slightly underdone. Off heat, stir in cheese and cilantro until cheese is melted.

4. Scatter half of tortilla pieces in 13 by 9-inch baking dish set over rimmed baking sheet. Spoon half of filling evenly over tortillas. Scatter remaining tortillas over filling, then top with remaining filling.

5. Bake casserole on lower rack until filling is bubbling, about 15 minutes. Sprinkle Fritos evenly over top and bake until Fritos are lightly browned, about 10 minutes. Let casserole cool for 10 minutes. Serve.

TO MAKE AHEAD: Do not top casserole with Fritos; casserole can be refrigerated for up to 1 day. To serve, cover casserole dish tightly with greased aluminum foil and bake in 450-degree oven until hot throughout, about 30 minutes. Uncover, top with Fritos, and bake until Fritos are lightly browned, about 10 minutes.

Chicken Enchiladas with Red Chili Sauce

SERVES 4   **TOTAL TIME** 1 HOUR 30 MINUTES

✅ **WHY THIS RECIPE WORKS:** Chicken enchiladas are a labor of love—requiring an entire day in the kitchen. We wanted to make enchiladas in 90 minutes. For the sauce, we ditched the dried chiles, instead using a blend of chili powder, coriander, and cumin, and sautéed the spices with the aromatics for fuller flavor. To keep things simple, we cooked boneless, skinless thighs right in the sauce. Pickled jalapeño and fresh cilantro added complexity to the filling. We saved time by brushing the tortillas with oil and reheating them in the microwave rather than frying them in hot oil. Placed seam side down in two columns in a baking dish, between layers of sauce, the enchiladas cooked quickly in the oven. Be sure to cool the chicken filling before filling the tortillas; otherwise, the hot filling will make the enchiladas soggy. Serve with sour cream, diced avocado, shredded lettuce, and lime wedges.

¼   **cup vegetable oil**
1   **onion, chopped fine**
3   **garlic cloves, minced**
3   **tablespoons chili powder**
2   **teaspoons ground coriander**
2   **teaspoons ground cumin**
½   **teaspoon salt**
2   **teaspoons sugar**
1   **pound boneless, skinless chicken thighs, trimmed and cut into ¼-inch-wide strips**
2   **(8-ounce) cans tomato sauce**
1   **cup water**

½ cup minced fresh cilantro

¼ cup jarred jalapeños, chopped

12 ounces sharp cheddar cheese, shredded (3 cups)

12 (6-inch) corn tortillas

1. Heat 2 tablespoons oil in medium saucepan over medium-high heat until shimmering. Add onion and cook until softened, 5 to 7 minutes. Stir in garlic, chili powder, coriander, cumin, salt, and sugar and cook until fragrant, about 30 seconds. Stir in chicken and coat thoroughly with spices. Stir in tomato sauce and water, bring to simmer, and cook until chicken is cooked through, about 8 minutes.

2. Strain mixture through fine-mesh strainer into bowl, pressing on chicken and onion to extract as much sauce as possible; set sauce aside. Transfer chicken mixture to bowl, refrigerate for 20 minutes to chill, then stir in cilantro, jalapeños, and 2½ cups cheese.

3. Adjust oven rack to middle position and heat oven to 450 degrees. Spread ¾ cup sauce over bottom of 13 by 9-inch baking dish. Brush both sides of tortillas with remaining 2 tablespoons oil. Stack tortillas, wrap in damp dish towel, and place on plate; microwave until warm and pliable, about 1 minute.

4. Working with 1 warm tortilla at a time, spread ⅓ cup chicken filling across center of tortilla. Roll tortilla tightly around filling and place seam side down in baking dish; arrange enchiladas in 2 columns across width of dish.

5. Pour remaining sauce over top to cover completely and sprinkle with remaining ½ cup cheese. Cover dish tightly with greased aluminum foil and bake until enchiladas are heated through and cheese is melted, 15 to 20 minutes. Serve.

TO MAKE AHEAD: Do not pour sauce over top of enchiladas as directed in step 5; enchiladas, sauce, and cheese can be refrigerated separately for up to 1 day. To serve, spray enchiladas with vegetable oil spray and bake uncovered in 400-degree oven until hot throughout, 10 to 15 minutes. Top with remaining sauce and cheese, cover tightly with greased aluminum foil, and bake until sauce is bubbling and cheese is melted, 15 to 20 minutes.

Enchiladas Verdes

SERVES 4 TO 6   **TOTAL TIME** 1 HOUR 45 MINUTES

✔ WHY THIS RECIPE WORKS: To re-create the enchiladas verdes found in good Mexican restaurants, we needed a recipe for moist, tender chicken infused with fresh, citrusy flavors and wrapped in soft corn tortillas that are topped with just the right amount of cheese. We broiled dark green poblano chiles and fresh (as opposed to canned) tomatillos to concentrate the flavors and promote charring. A few pulses in the food processor kept our sauce pleasantly chunky, while a little of the poaching broth thinned it just enough. You can substitute three 11-ounce cans tomatillos, drained and rinsed, for the fresh ones in this recipe. If you can't find poblanos, substitute 4 large jalapeño chiles (with seeds and ribs removed). Be sure to cool the chicken filling before filling the tortillas; otherwise, the hot filling will make the enchiladas soggy. Serve with thinly sliced radishes and sour cream.

Making Chicken Enchiladas with Red Chili Sauce

1. SIMMER CHICKEN IN SAUCE: Cook aromatics and spices in saucepan, then stir in raw chicken. Add tomato sauce and water, bring to simmer, and cook until chicken is cooked through, about 8 minutes.

2. MICROWAVE TORTILLAS: Brush both sides of tortillas with oil. Stack tortillas, wrap in damp dish towel, and place on plate; microwave until warm and pliable, about 1 minute.

3. ASSEMBLE ENCHILADAS: Spread ⅓ cup chicken filling across center of each tortilla. Roll tortilla tightly around filling and place seam side down in baking dish; arrange enchiladas in 2 columns across width of dish.

4. BAKE COVERED: Cover dish tightly with greased aluminum foil and bake until enchiladas are heated through and cheese is melted, 15 to 20 minutes.

3 tablespoons vegetable oil

1 onion, chopped fine

3 garlic cloves, minced

½ teaspoon ground cumin

1½ cups chicken broth

1 pound boneless, skinless chicken breasts, trimmed

½ cup minced fresh cilantro

8 ounces pepper Jack or Monterey Jack cheese, shredded (2 cups)

Salt and pepper

1½ pounds tomatillos, husks and stems removed, rinsed well and dried, halved if larger than 2 inches in diameter

3 poblano chiles, halved lengthwise, stemmed, and seeded

1 teaspoon sugar, plus extra as needed

12 (6-inch) corn tortillas

2 scallions, sliced thin

1. Heat 2 teaspoons oil in medium saucepan over medium heat until shimmering. Add onion and cook until golden, 6 to 8 minutes. Stir in two-thirds of garlic and cumin and cook until fragrant, about 30 seconds. Reduce heat to low and stir in broth and chicken. Cover and simmer until chicken registers 160 degrees, 15 to 20 minutes, flipping chicken halfway through cooking.

2. Transfer chicken to plate, let cool slightly, then shred into bite-size pieces; refrigerate shredded chicken for 20 minutes. Combine chilled chicken, cilantro, and 1½ cups cheese in bowl and season with salt and pepper to taste. Reserve ¼ cup cooking liquid for sauce; discard extra liquid.

3. Adjust oven rack 6 inches from broiler element and heat broiler. Toss tomatillos and poblanos with 1 teaspoon oil. Arrange tomatillos cut side down and poblanos skin side up on aluminum foil–lined rimmed baking sheet. Broil until vegetables are blackened and beginning to soften, 5 to 10 minutes. Let vegetables cool slightly, then remove skins from poblanos (leave tomatillo skins intact).

4. Pulse broiled vegetables and any accumulated juices, reserved cooking liquid, remaining garlic, sugar, and 1 teaspoon salt in food processor until sauce is somewhat chunky, about 8 pulses. Season with salt, pepper, and extra sugar to taste.

5. Adjust oven racks to upper-middle and lower-middle positions and heat oven to 450 degrees. Spread ¾ cup sauce over bottom of 13 by 9-inch baking dish. Brush both sides of tortillas

with remaining 2 tablespoons oil. Stack tortillas, wrap in damp dish towel, and place on plate; microwave until warm and pliable, about 1 minute.

6. Working with 1 warm tortilla at a time, spread ⅓ cup chicken filling across center of tortilla. Roll tortilla tightly around filling and place seam side down in baking dish; arrange enchiladas in 2 columns across width of dish.

7. Pour remaining sauce over top to cover completely and sprinkle with remaining ½ cup cheese. Cover dish tightly with greased aluminum foil and bake until enchiladas are heated through and cheese is melted, 15 to 20 minutes. Sprinkle with scallions and serve.

TO MAKE AHEAD: Do not top enchiladas with sauce or cheese as directed in step 7; enchiladas, sauce, and cheese can be refrigerated separately for up to 1 day. To serve, spray enchiladas with vegetable oil spray and bake uncovered in 400-degree oven until hot throughout, 10 to 15 minutes. Top with sauce and cheese, cover tightly with greased aluminum foil, and bake until sauce is bubbling and cheese is melted, 15 to 20 minutes.

Roasting Poblanos and Tomatillos

To concentrate flavor and add smokiness, broil tomatillos and chiles in oven.

NOTES FROM THE TEST KITCHEN

Tomatillos

Called *tomates verdes* (green tomatoes) in much of Mexico, small green tomatillos have a tangier, more citrusy flavor than true green tomatoes. When choosing tomatillos, look for pale-green orbs with firm flesh that fills and splits open the fruit's outer papery husk, which must be removed before cooking. Avoid tomatillos that are too yellow and soft, as these specimens are past their prime and will taste sour and muted. Canned tomatillos are a reasonable substitute for fresh, though they won't contribute the same depth of flavor.

Making eggplant Parmesan at home is a major undertaking, involving salting, breading, and frying eggplant just for starters. Our recipe not only renders the dish doable in less than 2 hours, but it also delivers spectacular results. Gone are the soggy, slick eggplant slices and heavy, lifeless flavors—we bake our breaded eggplant, make a quick-cooked tomato sauce, and assemble with care to make the easiest and best-tasting eggplant Parmesan. This recipe requires salting eggplant slices, and although it takes some time, it's a simple step that has a big impact on the finished dish.

1. SALT AND DRY THE EGGPLANT: Toss the eggplant with kosher salt and let the slices drain in a colander for 30 to 45 minutes. Wipe off the excess salt, then pat dry thoroughly.
WHY? Salting draws moisture from the eggplant and ensures a crisp, not soggy, coating.

2. MAKE FRESH BREAD CRUMBS: Pulse hearty white sandwich bread in a food processor to fine, even crumbs. Transfer to a shallow dish and stir in Parmesan, salt, and pepper.
WHY? Store-bought bread crumbs taste stale, but freshly made bread crumbs have a superior flavor and crunch.

3. PREHEAT THE BAKING SHEETS: Adjust the oven racks and place 1 rimmed baking sheet on each rack; heat the oven to 425 degrees.
WHY? Preheating the sheets allows them to heat thoroughly so that the eggplant slices immediately begin to brown and crisp once they're placed on them.

4. PREPARE A SIMPLE TOMATO SAUCE: Sauté the aromatics, then add the crushed and diced tomatoes and simmer until thickened.
WHY? Prepare this easy-to-make homemade sauce (page 360); it tastes fresher than store-bought.

5. BREAD THE EGGPLANT: Whisk together eggs in a shallow dish. Place 8 to 10 eggplant slices in a zipper-lock bag containing flour and pepper, seal, and shake to coat. Dip the eggplant into the egg, then coat with bread crumbs, pressing gently to adhere. Repeat with the rest of the eggplant.
WHY? Dipping the eggplant in flour, then egg, then bread crumbs creates a substantial but not heavy coating that crisps up nicely in the oven.

6. BAKE THE EGGPLANT: Spread the eggplant out onto the preheated and well-oiled baking sheets in a single layer. Bake until the eggplant is well browned and crisp, about 30 minutes, flipping the eggplant and switching and rotating the sheets halfway through baking.
WHY? Baking the eggplant on preheated sheets results in crisp, golden-brown slices. It also is easier and less messy than frying eggplant on the stovetop in multiple batches.

7. ASSEMBLE THE FIRST LAYER: Spread 1 cup tomato sauce in the bottom of a 13 by 9-inch baking dish. Layer half of the eggplant, overlapping the slices to fit. Spoon 1 cup sauce over the top and sprinkle with 1 cup of mozzarella.
WHY? Adding sauce to the bottom keeps everything from sticking. Precise portioning ensures even layers and a well-balanced eggplant Parmesan.

8. FINISH LAYERING AND BAKE: Lay the remaining eggplant in the dish, dot with 1 cup sauce, and sprinkle with Parmesan and more mozzarella. Bake until the cheese is browned, 13 to 15 minutes.
WHY? Completely covering the casserole with sauce and cheese makes the eggplant soggy. Because the eggplant is already cooked, the dish is ready as soon as it is hot throughout and the cheese is melted and browned.

Eggplant Parmesan

SERVES 6 TO 8   **TOTAL TIME** 1 HOUR 40 MINUTES

✔ **WHY THIS RECIPE WORKS:** Frying the eggplant for this classic Italian dish not only is time-consuming, but it can also make the dish heavy and dull. In the hope of eliminating the grease as well as some of the prep time, we opted to cook the breaded eggplant in the oven after salting and draining the slices (which removed bitterness and improved texture). Baking the eggplant on preheated and oiled baking sheets resulted in crisp, golden brown slices, and a traditional bound breading of flour, egg, and fresh bread crumbs mixed with Parmesan cheese worked best for giving the eggplant a crisp coating. After the eggplant was cooked through, we layered it into a baking dish with tomato sauce and some mozzarella. Leaving the top layer of eggplant mostly unsauced helped ensure that it would crisp up nicely in the oven. Use kosher salt when salting the eggplant; the coarse grains don't dissolve as readily as the fine grains of regular table salt, so any excess can be easily wiped away. You can substitute 4 cups jarred tomato sauce if desired.

  2 pounds eggplant, sliced into ¼-inch-thick rounds
     Kosher salt and pepper
  8 slices hearty white sandwich bread,
     torn into quarters
  3 ounces Parmesan cheese, grated (1½ cups)
  1 cup all-purpose flour
  4 large eggs
  6 tablespoons vegetable oil
  1 recipe Small-Batch Chunky Tomato Sauce (page 360)
  8 ounces whole-milk or part-skim mozzarella cheese,
     shredded (2 cups)
 10 fresh basil leaves, roughly torn

1. Toss eggplant with 1½ teaspoons salt and let drain in colander until it releases about 2 tablespoons liquid, 30 to 45 minutes; wipe excess salt from eggplant. Line baking sheet with triple layer of paper towels, spread eggplant over top, and cover with more paper towels. Press firmly on eggplant to remove as much liquid as possible.

2. Meanwhile, pulse bread in food processor to fine, even crumbs, about 15 pulses. Transfer crumbs to large, shallow dish and stir in 1 cup Parmesan, ¼ teaspoon salt, and ½ teaspoon pepper. Combine flour and 1 teaspoon pepper in large zipper-lock bag. Whisk eggs together in separate shallow dish.

3. Adjust oven racks to upper-middle and lower-middle positions, place rimmed baking sheet on each rack, and heat oven to 425 degrees. Working with 8 to 10 eggplant slices at a time, toss eggplant with flour mixture in bag to coat, dip in egg, then coat with bread-crumb mixture, pressing gently to adhere; set breaded slices on wire rack set in rimmed baking sheet. Repeat with remaining eggplant.

4. Remove preheated baking sheets from oven, brush each with 3 tablespoons oil, then lay eggplant on sheets in single layer. Bake until eggplant is well browned and crisp, about 30 minutes, flipping eggplant and switching and rotating baking sheets halfway through cooking.

5. Spread 1 cup tomato sauce over bottom of 13 by 9-inch baking dish. Lay half of baked eggplant slices in dish, overlapping them as needed to fit. Spoon 1 cup sauce over top and sprinkle with 1 cup mozzarella. Lay remaining eggplant in dish, dot with 1 cup sauce (leaving most of eggplant exposed so it will remain crisp), and sprinkle with remaining Parmesan and remaining 1 cup mozzarella. Bake until cheese is browned, 13 to 15 minutes. Let casserole cool for 10 minutes. Sprinkle with basil leaves and serve with remaining sauce.

Tex-Mex Cheese Enchiladas

SERVES 4 TO 6   **TOTAL TIME** 1 HOUR 15 MINUTES

✔ **WHY THIS RECIPE WORKS:** Unlike their Mexican kin, Tex-Mex enchiladas have no meat and no tomatoey sauce. Instead, a smoky chile gravy provides the bulk of flavor in the dish. Dried ancho chiles, along with cumin, garlic, and oregano, were the perfect backbone for our roux-based sauce, and a splash of vinegar brightened it up. Instead of going with the processed cheese typical of the dish, we opted for a mixture of cheddar for flavor and Monterey Jack for smooth meltability. Finally, although traditional recipes call for frying the corn tortillas one at a time, we found that brushing them with oil and microwaving them for a mere minute made them more pliable and easier to fill with the cheese mixture. Dried chiles vary in size and weight. You'll get a more accurate measure if you seed and tear them first; you need about ½ cup of prepped chiles. You can substitute 2 tablespoons of ancho chile powder and 1 tablespoon of ground cumin for the whole ancho chiles and cumin seeds, decreasing the toasting time to 1 minute, but you'll lose some flavor.

  2 dried ancho chiles, stemmed, seeded,
     and torn into ½-inch pieces (½ cup)
  1 tablespoon cumin seeds
  1 tablespoon garlic powder
  2 teaspoons dried oregano
  5 tablespoons vegetable oil
  3 tablespoons all-purpose flour
     Salt and pepper

A smoky chile gravy provides the bold flavor that is the hallmark of these Tex-Mex enchiladas.

3. Adjust oven rack to middle position and heat oven to 450 degrees. Spread ½ cup sauce over bottom of 13 by 9-inch baking dish. Combine cheeses in bowl; set ½ cup cheese mixture aside for topping. Brush both sides of tortillas with remaining 2 tablespoons oil. Stack tortillas, wrap in damp dish towel, and place on plate; microwave until warm and pliable, about 1 minute.

4. Working with 1 warm tortilla at a time, spread ¼ cup cheese mixture across center of tortilla and sprinkle with 1 tablespoon onion. Roll tortilla tightly around filling and place seam side down in baking dish; arrange enchiladas in 2 columns across width of dish.

5. Pour remaining sauce over top to cover completely and sprinkle with reserved cheeses. Cover dish tightly with greased aluminum foil. Bake until sauce is bubbling and cheese is melted, about 15 minutes. Sprinkle with remaining onion and serve.

TO MAKE AHEAD: Do not top enchiladas with sauce or cheese as directed in step 5; enchiladas, sauce, and cheese can be refrigerated separately for up to 1 day. To serve, spray enchiladas with vegetable oil spray and bake uncovered in 400-degree oven until hot throughout, 10 to 15 minutes. Stir ¼ cup warm water into sauce. Top enchiladas with sauce and cheese, cover tightly with greased aluminum foil, and bake until sauce is bubbling, 15 to 20 minutes.

Arranging Enchiladas

In order to fit 12 enchiladas into a 13 by 9-inch casserole dish, you need to arrange them widthwise in the pan, in two rows of six enchiladas.

NOTES FROM THE TEST KITCHEN

Dried Ancho Chiles

The sauce in our Tex-Mex Cheese Enchiladas, often called "gravy," gets its hallmark flavor and red color from toasted and ground ancho chiles. When fresh, these broad, blackish-green chiles are called poblanos. Because anchos are naturally smoky and fruity, their complex flavor and mild heat make them an excellent option for grinding into powder for use in spice rubs or chili. Look for dried chiles that are pliable and brightly colored.

- 2 **cups chicken broth**
- 2 **teaspoons distilled white vinegar**
- 8 **ounces Monterey Jack cheese, shredded (2 cups)**
- 6 **ounces sharp cheddar cheese, shredded (1½ cups)**
- 12 **(6-inch) corn tortillas**
- 1 **onion, chopped fine**

1. Toast anchos and cumin seeds in 12-inch skillet over medium-low heat, stirring often, until fragrant, about 2 minutes. Transfer to spice grinder and let cool for 5 minutes. Add garlic powder and oregano and grind to fine powder.

2. Heat 3 tablespoons oil in now-empty skillet over medium-high heat until shimmering. Whisk in ground chile mixture, flour, ½ teaspoon salt, and ½ teaspoon pepper and cook until fragrant and slightly deepened in color, about 1 minute. Slowly whisk in broth and bring to simmer. Reduce heat to medium-low and cook, whisking often, until sauce has thickened and measures 1½ cups, about 5 minutes. Whisk in vinegar and season with salt and pepper to taste. Remove from heat, cover, and keep warm.

Beef Pot Pie

SERVES 6 TO 8   **TOTAL TIME** 2 HOURS 10 MINUTES

✔ WHY THIS RECIPE WORKS: Beef pot pie usually requires some time because the filling takes about as much time as beef stew to make. To speed up the process, we hastened the cooking time of the beef by cutting it into ½-inch pieces, which worked perfectly in a pot pie filling. For the vegetables, we sautéed carrots, onions, and garlic after browning the beef, and added frozen peas just before baking to preserve their color. A bit of flour, red wine, broth, and tomato paste created a deeply flavored sauce in which we simmered the browned beef. Within 45 minutes we had a tender, flavorful stew—the perfect foundation for our pot pie. We transferred the stew to a casserole dish, draped homemade pie dough over it, and finished the pot pie in the oven. For the best flavor, buy a chuck-eye roast and trim and cut it yourself rather than purchasing prepackaged stew meat. Be sure to make the pie dough first and let it chill while making the filling. You can substitute a store-bought pie dough for homemade pie dough; overlap two pie dough rounds by a half, brushing water between them to help them seal, then roll them together to make a rectangle roughly 15 by 11 inches. The filling must be hot when you top it with the pie dough, or the crust will be gummy.

- 1 **(3-pound) boneless beef chuck-eye roast, pulled apart at seams, trimmed, and cut into ½-inch pieces**
  Salt and pepper
- 1 **tablespoon vegetable oil**
- 2 **carrots, peeled and cut into ½-inch pieces**
- 1 **onion, chopped fine**
- 4 **garlic cloves, minced**
- 5 **tablespoons all-purpose flour**
- ¾ **cup dry red wine**
- 1½ **cups chicken broth**
- 1½ **cups beef broth**
- 1 **tablespoon tomato paste**
- 2 **teaspoons minced fresh thyme or 1 teaspoon dried**
- 1 **cup frozen peas**
- 1 **recipe Foolproof Double-Crust Pie Dough (page 698) or All-Butter Double-Crust Pie Dough (page 701)**

1. Adjust oven rack to middle position and heat oven to 400 degrees. Pat beef dry with paper towels and season with salt and pepper. Heat oil in Dutch oven over medium-high heat until just smoking. Brown half of beef on all sides, about 10 minutes; transfer to bowl. Repeat with remaining beef using fat left in pot; transfer to bowl.

2. Add carrots, onion, and ½ teaspoon salt to fat left in pot and cook over medium heat until onion has softened, about 5 minutes. Stir in garlic and cook until fragrant, about 30 seconds. Stir in flour and cook for 1 minute. Whisk in wine, scraping up any browned bits. Whisk in chicken broth, beef broth, tomato paste, and thyme. Add browned beef and any accumulated juices and simmer until meat is tender, about 45 minutes.

3. Stir in peas. Pour mixture into 13 by 9-inch baking dish; filling should be hot.

4. Roll pie dough out into 15 by 11-inch rectangle and drape it over dish. Trim and crimp edges. Bake until topping is golden brown and filling is bubbly, about 20 minutes. Let casserole cool for 10 minutes. Serve.

TO MAKE AHEAD: Pot pie cannot be assembled ahead of time; however, filling can be prepared through step 2 and refrigerated for up to 2 days. Reheat filling gently in large saucepan on stovetop, adding additional broth as needed to loosen its consistency, before assembling and baking casserole.

Beef Enchiladas

SERVES 4 TO 6   **TOTAL TIME** 2 HOURS 45 MINUTES

✔ WHY THIS RECIPE WORKS: Traditional beef enchiladas recipes require simmering steak for hours. Common shortcuts call for hamburger and canned sauce, which result in enchiladas with none of the richness of the original. Sticking with the steak and using a few shortcuts gave us a recipe that cut the cooking time considerably without sacrificing flavor. Instead of using ground chiles and tomatoes, we used chili powder and canned tomato sauce, along with onions, garlic, and spices to make a quick sauce with authentic flavor. Inexpensive blade steak lent our recipe the soft chew and beefy flavor we were after. Authentic beef enchiladas recipes fry the corn tortillas and then dip them in sauce to soften and season them. Instead, we brushed the tortillas with oil and warmed them quickly in the microwave. We then assembled the enchiladas, topped them with sauce and cheese, and baked them until heated through. Cut back on the pickled jalapeños if you like your enchiladas on the mild side. Serve with sour cream, diced avocado, shredded lettuce, and lime wedges.

Inexpensive but tender blade steaks give these enchiladas big beefy flavor.

1¼ pounds beef blade steaks, trimmed
   Salt and pepper
3 tablespoons vegetable oil
2 onions, chopped
3 garlic cloves, minced
3 tablespoons chili powder
2 teaspoons ground coriander
2 teaspoons ground cumin
1 teaspoon sugar
1 (15-ounce) can tomato sauce
½ cup water
8 ounces Monterey Jack cheese, shredded (2 cups)
⅓ cup minced fresh cilantro
¼ cup jarred jalapeños, chopped
12 (6-inch) corn tortillas

1. Pat beef dry with paper towels and season with salt and pepper. Heat 1 tablespoon oil in Dutch oven over medium-high heat until just smoking. Brown meat on both sides, about 6 minutes; transfer to plate.

2. Add onions to fat left in pot and cook over medium heat until golden, about 5 minutes. Stir in garlic, chili powder, coriander, cumin, sugar, and 1 teaspoon salt and cook until fragrant, about 30 seconds. Stir in tomato sauce, water, and browned meat and any accumulated juices. Bring to simmer, then cover, reduce heat to low, and simmer gently until beef is tender and can be broken apart with wooden spoon, about 1½ hours.

3. Strain mixture through fine-mesh strainer into bowl, pressing on beef mixture to break meat into small pieces; set sauce aside. Transfer beef mixture to bowl, refrigerate for 20 minutes to chill, then stir in 1 cup cheese, cilantro, and jalapeños.

4. Adjust oven rack to middle position and heat oven to 450 degrees. Spread ¾ cup sauce over bottom of 13 by 9-inch baking dish. Brush both sides of tortillas with remaining 2 tablespoons oil. Stack tortillas, wrap in damp dish towel, and place on plate; microwave until warm and pliable, about 1 minute.

5. Working with 1 warm tortilla at a time, spread ⅓ cup beef filling across center of tortilla. Roll tortilla tightly around filling and place seam side down in baking dish; arrange enchiladas in 2 columns across width of dish.

6. Pour remaining sauce over top to cover completely and sprinkle with remaining 1 cup cheese. Cover dish tightly with greased aluminum foil and bake until enchiladas are heated through and cheese is melted, 15 to 20 minutes. Serve.

TO MAKE AHEAD: Do not top enchiladas with sauce or cheese as directed in step 6; enchiladas, sauce, and cheese can be refrigerated separately for up to 1 day. To serve, spray enchiladas with vegetable oil spray and bake uncovered in 400-degree oven until hot throughout, 10 to 15 minutes. Top with sauce and cheese, cover tightly with greased aluminum foil, and bake until sauce is bubbling and cheese is melted, 15 to 20 minutes.

Trimming Blade Steaks

1. Halve each steak lengthwise to expose gristle in center.

2. Slice away gristle and discard.

Beef Taco Bake

SERVES 6   **TOTAL TIME** 40 MINUTES   **FAST**

✔ **WHY THIS RECIPE WORKS:** This easy, family-friendly casserole incorporates all the fun of taco night but without the mess. We made our own highly flavored filling, starting with ground beef that we sautéed with onions and then adding garlic, chili powder, and oregano. We stirred in Ro-tel tomatoes, cider vinegar, and brown sugar and let everything simmer until it thickened nicely. Refried beans mixed with tomatoes and cilantro made a rich base for our casserole. Store-bought taco shells crumbled over the top added the right crunch to resemble the Tex-Mex favorite without getting our hands all messy. If you can't find Ro-tel tomatoes, substitute one 14.5-ounce can diced tomatoes and one 4-ounce can chopped green chiles, reserving 6 tablespoons of the tomato juice and 2 tablespoons of the chile juice. Colby Jack cheese, also known as CoJack, is a creamy blend of Colby and Monterey Jack cheeses. If unavailable, substitute Monterey Jack cheese. Serve with your favorite taco toppings, such as shredded lettuce, sour cream, and salsa.

Our beef taco bake is an easy casserole made with layers of refried beans, cheese, spicy beef, and taco shell pieces.

1	tablespoon vegetable oil
1½	pounds 90 percent lean ground beef
1	onion, chopped fine
	Salt and pepper
4	garlic cloves, minced
3	tablespoons chili powder
½	teaspoon dried oregano
2	(10-ounce) cans Ro-tel Diced Tomatoes & Green Chilies, drained with ½ cup juice reserved
2	teaspoons cider vinegar
1	teaspoon packed brown sugar
1	(16-ounce) can refried beans
¼	cup minced fresh cilantro
8	ounces Colby Jack cheese, shredded (2 cups)
12	taco shells, broken into 1-inch pieces
2	scallions, sliced thin

1. Adjust oven rack to middle position and heat oven to 475 degrees. Heat oil in 12-inch skillet over medium heat until shimmering. Add beef, onion, and ½ teaspoon salt and cook, breaking up meat with wooden spoon, until meat is no longer pink, about 5 minutes. Stir in garlic, chili powder, and oregano and cook until fragrant, about 1 minute.

2. Stir in half of tomatoes, reserved tomato juice, vinegar, and brown sugar and simmer until mixture is very thick, about 5 minutes. Season with salt and pepper to taste.

3. Meanwhile, mix remaining tomatoes, beans, and cilantro together in bowl. Spread mixture evenly into 13 by 9-inch baking dish. Sprinkle 1 cup cheese over top.

4. Spread beef mixture in baking dish and sprinkle with ½ cup cheese. Scatter taco shell pieces over top, then sprinkle with remaining ½ cup cheese. Bake until filling is bubbling and top is spotty brown, about 10 minutes. Let casserole cool slightly, sprinkle with scallions, and serve.

Chiles Rellenos Casserole

SERVES 6 TO 8   **TOTAL TIME** 1 HOUR 30 MINUTES

✔ **WHY THIS RECIPE WORKS:** Too often, this Tex-Mex casserole is a gloppy mess. We wanted to replicate the roasted chile flavor, hearty filling, and crisp fried shell of the original—without all the work. To prevent greasiness, we used 90 percent lean ground beef and drained it after sautéing. Fresh poblano peppers added smokiness and browned nicely in the skillet after the beef. We added the classic combo of garlic, cumin, oregano, and cayenne, along with Ro-tel tomatoes and

Monterey Jack cheese. For the topping, whipped egg whites folded into a milk and flour mixture and spread over the top turned golden brown in the oven. If you can't find Ro-tel tomatoes, substitute one 14.5-ounce can diced tomatoes and one 4-ounce can chopped green chiles.

    1 tablespoon vegetable oil
    1 onion, chopped fine
    2 pounds 90 percent lean ground beef
    4 poblano chiles (or 6 Anaheim), stemmed, seeded, and chopped
    2 garlic cloves, minced
    2 teaspoons ground cumin
    1 teaspoon dried oregano
    ¼ teaspoon cayenne pepper
       Salt and pepper
    1 (10-ounce) can Ro-tel Diced Tomatoes & Green Chilies, drained
   10 ounces Monterey Jack cheese, shredded (2½ cups)
    ½ cup all-purpose flour
    ¾ cup skim milk
    2 large egg whites

1. Adjust oven rack to upper-middle position and heat oven to 450 degrees. Heat oil in 12-inch nonstick skillet over medium heat until shimmering. Add onion and cook until softened, about 5 minutes. Add beef and cook, breaking up meat with wooden spoon, until no longer pink, 8 to 10 minutes. Using slotted spoon, transfer beef mixture to paper towel–lined plate.

2. Pour off all but 2 tablespoons fat left in skillet, add poblanos, and cook over medium-high heat until browned, 8 to 10 minutes. Stir in beef mixture, garlic, cumin, oregano, cayenne, ¾ teaspoon salt, and ½ teaspoon pepper and cook until fragrant, about 30 seconds. Stir in tomatoes and cook until beef mixture is dry, about 1 minute. Off heat, stir in 2 cups cheese. Scrape mixture into 13 by 9-inch baking dish and press into even layer.

3. Combine flour, ½ teaspoon salt, and ¼ teaspoon pepper in large bowl. Slowly whisk in milk until smooth; set aside. Using stand mixer fitted with whisk, whip egg whites on medium-low speed until foamy, about 1 minute. Increase speed to medium-high and whip until stiff peaks form, about 3 minutes. Whisk one-third whipped egg whites into batter to loosen, then gently fold in remaining whites until combined.

4. Pour batter over beef mixture. Bake until topping is light golden and puffed, about 15 minutes. Sprinkle with remaining ½ cup cheese and continue to bake until golden brown, about 10 minutes. Let casserole cool for 10 minutes. Serve.

Mild-tasting ground pork is the perfect partner for all the bold ingredients in this south-of-the-border take on lasagna.

Mexican Lasagna with Pork, Corn, and Pinto Beans

SERVES 6 TO 8   **TOTAL TIME** 1 HOUR 30 MINUTES

WHY THIS RECIPE WORKS: At some point, time-pressed cooks came up with a recipe with the flavor profile of enchiladas but with easier assembly, layering the enchilada ingredients rather than rolling them into a tortilla, and including add-ins such as tomatoes, bell peppers, and beans. We found countless recipes, most of which call for using canned soups and other jarred ingredients and gobs of cheese, then baking the whole mess until the flavors are lifeless. Our goal was to breathe some life and spice into this typically heavy dish, with a spicy filling spread between layers of corn tortillas. We chose pork for its natural sweetness that would pair well with earthy corn tortillas, and sautéed it with onions, spices, and canned chipotle chile. Pinto beans and frozen corn contributed contrasting sweet flavor to the spicy filling. Brushing the tortillas with oil and heating them briefly in the oven prevented them from becoming soggy during baking, even under layers of melted cheese. And to make cutting and serving the casserole easier, we quartered the tortillas that made up the top layer so there would be no need to cut through a whole one. Ground turkey can be substituted for the ground pork. Colby Jack cheese, also known as CoJack, is a creamy blend of Colby and Monterey Jack cheeses. If unavailable, substitute Monterey Jack cheese. Serve with salsa, diced avocado, sour cream, and/or scallions.

3 tablespoons vegetable oil
1 onion, chopped fine
2 red bell peppers, stemmed, seeded, and cut into ½-inch pieces
   Salt and pepper
3 garlic cloves, minced
1 tablespoon minced canned chipotle chile in adobo sauce
2 teaspoons chili powder
1½ pounds ground pork
2 tablespoons all-purpose flour
2 cups chicken broth
1 (15-ounce) can pinto beans, rinsed
1 (14.5-ounce) can diced tomatoes, drained
2 cups frozen corn, thawed
¼ cup plus 2 tablespoons minced fresh cilantro
2 tablespoons lime juice
18 (6-inch) corn tortillas
12 ounces Colby Jack cheese, shredded (3 cups)

1. Heat 1 tablespoon oil in Dutch oven over medium heat until shimmering. Add onion, bell peppers, and ½ teaspoon salt and cook until softened, 8 to 10 minutes. Stir in garlic, chipotle, chili powder, and ¼ teaspoon pepper and cook until fragrant, about 30 seconds. Stir in pork and cook, breaking up meat with wooden spoon, until no longer pink, 5 to 8 minutes.

2. Stir in flour and cook for 1 minute. Gradually stir in chicken broth and bring to simmer. Stir in beans, tomatoes, and corn and simmer until mixture is slightly thickened and flavors have blended, about 10 minutes. Off heat, stir in ¼ cup cilantro and lime juice. Season with salt and pepper to taste.

3. Meanwhile, adjust oven rack to upper-middle and lower-middle positions and heat oven to 450 degrees. Brush both sides of tortillas with remaining 2 tablespoons oil. Spread tortillas over 2 baking sheets (some overlapping is fine) and bake until soft and pliable, 2 to 4 minutes.

4. Spread one-third of pork mixture over bottom of 13 by 9-inch baking dish. Top with 6 warmed tortillas, overlapping as needed, and sprinkle with 1 cup cheese. Repeat with half of remaining pork mixture, 6 tortillas, and 1 cup cheese. Top

NOTES FROM THE TEST KITCHEN

Chili Powder

Chili powder is a seasoning blend made from ground dried chiles and an assortment of other ingredients. Much like curry powder, there is no single recipe, but cumin, garlic, and oregano are traditional additions. Chili powder is not to be confused with the lesser-known chile powder (also often spelled chili powder), made solely from chiles without additional seasonings. Besides its obvious use—to add spicy depth and heat to chili and sauces—we also use it in spice rubs and marinades. Our favorite brand has a deep, roasty, and complex flavor, subtle sweetness, and just the right amount of heat.

with remaining pork filling. Cut remaining 6 tortillas into quarters and scatter over top. Sprinkle with remaining 1 cup cheese.

5. Bake on upper-middle rack until filling is bubbling and topping is golden brown, about 15 minutes. Let casserole cool for 10 minutes. Sprinkle with remaining 2 tablespoons cilantro and serve.

TO MAKE AHEAD: Assembled, unbaked casserole can be refrigerated for up to 1 day. To serve, cover dish tightly with greased aluminum foil and bake in 450-degree oven until hot throughout, about 30 minutes. Uncover and continue to bake until topping is golden brown, about 10 minutes. Sprinkle with cilantro before serving.

Shepherd's Pie

SERVES 6 TO 8   **TOTAL TIME** 1 HOUR 35 MINUTES

✓ **WHY THIS RECIPE WORKS:** Shepherd's pie, a meaty beef or lamb, carrot, and pea filling topped with rich mashed potatoes, can be pub grub at its very best, though it rarely is. For a full-flavored, firm-topped shepherd's pie, we thoroughly softened the vegetables and browned the beef in butter for the richest flavor. We jazzed up the filling's flavor with soy sauce, broth, and beer. The soy sauce lent depth and meatiness; its distinctive flavor disappeared behind the other ingredients. Finally, we made the mashed potatoes for the topping extra stiff and very rich for the best texture and flavor. Spreading the potatoes firmly to the edges sealed the baking dish and prevented any filling from bubbling out during baking, and brushing the mashed potato topping with an egg ensured that the potatoes turned stiff and firm once baked. Although just about any mild beer will work in this recipe, we particularly enjoyed the sweet flavor of O'Doul's nonalcoholic amber.

We brushed a beaten egg on the mashed potatoes for a shepherd's pie topping that remained stiff and firm once baked.

FILLING

- 2 tablespoons unsalted butter
- 1 large onion, chopped fine
- 2 carrots, peeled and chopped fine
- 2 pounds 85 percent lean ground beef
  Salt and pepper
- 5 tablespoons all-purpose flour
- 1 tablespoon tomato paste
- ¼ cup heavy cream
- 1¾ cups chicken broth
- ¾ cup beer
- 2 tablespoons soy sauce
- 2 teaspoons minced fresh thyme
- 1 cup frozen peas

TOPPING

- 2½ pounds russet potatoes, peeled and cut into 2-inch pieces
  Salt and pepper
- 2 tablespoons unsalted butter, melted
- ⅓ cup heavy cream, warmed
- 1 large egg, beaten

1. FOR THE FILLING: Melt butter in 12-inch skillet over medium-high heat. Add onion and carrots and cook until soft, about 8 minutes. Stir in meat, ½ teaspoon salt, and ½ teaspoon pepper and cook, breaking up meat with wooden spoon, until browned, about 12 minutes. Stir in flour and tomato paste and cook for 1 minute.

2. Stir in cream and cook for 1 minute. Stir in broth, beer, soy sauce, and thyme and simmer, stirring often, until mixture has thickened slightly, 15 to 20 minutes. Off heat, stir in peas and season with salt and pepper to taste. Transfer mixture to 3-quart broiler-safe casserole dish.

3. FOR THE TOPPING: Adjust oven rack to upper-middle position and heat oven to 375 degrees. Cover potatoes with water in large saucepan. Add ½ teaspoon salt and bring to boil. Reduce heat to simmer and cook until potatoes are tender, 15 to 20 minutes. Drain potatoes, return to saucepan, and mash with butter and cream until smooth. Season with salt and pepper to taste.

4. Using rubber spatula, spread potatoes over filling along edges of dish, then fill in center. Smooth top, then brush with egg and drag fork across top to make ridges. Bake until filling is bubbling, about 15 minutes. Adjust oven rack 8 inches from broiler element and heat broiler. Broil casserole until top is golden, 3 to 5 minutes. Let casserole cool for 10 minutes. Serve.

TO MAKE AHEAD: Casserole cannot be assembled ahead of time; however, filling can be refrigerated for up to 2 days. Do not add peas to filling until ready to assemble casserole. Reheat filling gently in saucepan on stovetop, adding additional broth as needed to loosen its consistency. Stir in peas, then assemble and bake casserole.

Spreading Potatoes onto Shepherd's Pie

Using rubber spatula, spread potatoes around edges of dish, then fill in center.

Our tamale pie features a rich ground beef, black bean, and corn filling enriched with shredded cheese.

Tamale Pie with Cornmeal Topping

SERVES 6 TO 8 **TOTAL TIME** 1 HOUR 35 MINUTES

WHY THIS RECIPE WORKS: Tamale pie—lightly seasoned, tomatoey ground beef with a cornbread topping—is easy to prepare and makes a satisfying supper. But in many recipes, the filling either tastes bland and one-dimensional or turns heavy. As for the cornbread topping, it's usually from a mix and tastes like it. We wanted a tamale pie with a rich, well-seasoned filling and a cornmeal topping with real corn flavor. We found 90 percent lean ground beef gave us a good balance of richness and flavor. We started by browning the beef then adding onion and jalapeño. For seasoning, we used a generous amount of chili powder, which we added to the aromatics in the skillet to "bloom," or intensify, its flavor. The addition of canned black beans made our pie heartier, and canned diced tomatoes contributed additional flavor

and texture. Monterey Jack cheese stirred into the mixture enriched the filling and also helped thicken it. And to finish our pie, we made a simple cornmeal batter, which we spread over the filling and baked. Thirty minutes later, we pulled out a rich, hearty pie with a crunchy, corny topping that perfectly complemented the spicy tamale filling. We liked coarse cornmeal for the crust on this pie and had the best results using Goya Coarse Yellow Cornmeal. Ground pork or turkey can be substituted for the beef.

3 tablespoons vegetable oil
1 pound 90 percent lean ground beef
1 onion, chopped fine
1 jalapeño chile, stemmed, seeded, and minced
  Salt and pepper
2 tablespoons chili powder
1 tablespoon minced fresh oregano or 1 teaspoon dried
2 garlic cloves, minced
1 (15-ounce) can black beans, rinsed
1 (14.5-ounce) can diced tomatoes
1 cup fresh or frozen corn
2½ cups water
¾ cup coarse cornmeal
4 ounces Monterey Jack cheese, shredded (1 cup)

1. Adjust oven rack to lower-middle position and heat oven to 375 degrees. Heat 1 tablespoon oil in 12-inch skillet over medium-high heat until just smoking. Add ground beef and cook, breaking up meat with wooden spoon, until just beginning to brown, about 5 minutes.

2. Stir in onion, jalapeño, and ¼ teaspoon salt and cook until vegetables are softened, about 5 minutes. Stir in chili powder, oregano, and garlic and cook until fragrant, about 30 seconds. Stir in beans, tomatoes with their juice, and corn and simmer until most of liquid has evaporated, about 3 minutes. Off heat, season with salt and pepper to taste.

3. Bring water to boil in large saucepan. Add ¼ teaspoon salt and then slowly pour in cornmeal while whisking vigorously to prevent clumping. Reduce heat to medium and cook, whisking constantly, until cornmeal thickens, about 3 minutes. Stir in remaining 2 tablespoons oil.

4. Stir cheese into beef mixture, then scrape into deep-dish pie plate (or other 2-quart baking dish). Spread cornmeal mixture over top and seal against edge of dish. Cover with aluminum foil and bake until crust has set and filling is hot throughout, about 30 minutes. Let casserole cool for 10 minutes. Serve.

Pasta

■ SIGNIFIES A **FAST** RECIPE (45 MINUTES OR LESS)

Spaghetti with Garlic and Olive Oil

SERVES 4 TO 6   **TOTAL TIME** 30 MINUTES **FAST**

✓ **WHY THIS RECIPE WORKS:** Called *aglio e olio* in the old country, spaghetti with garlic and olive oil relies on a hefty hand with the garlic—we used a whopping 12 cloves. Cooking the garlic slowly over low heat turned it golden, nutty-tasting, and subtly sweet. Stirring a bit of raw garlic into the sauce, along with more olive oil, before tossing it with the cooked pasta ensured a hit of potent garlic flavor in each bite. Don't forget to reserve some of the pasta cooking water before draining the pasta; the water is used to loosen the texture of the sauce.

- 6 **tablespoons extra-virgin olive oil**
- 12 **garlic cloves, minced (4 tablespoons)**
-    **Salt and pepper**
- 3 **tablespoons minced fresh parsley**
- 2 **teaspoons lemon juice**
- ¾ **teaspoon red pepper flakes**
- 1 **pound spaghetti**
-    **Grated Parmesan cheese**

1. Cook 3 tablespoons oil, 3 tablespoons garlic, and ½ teaspoon salt in 10-inch nonstick skillet over low heat, stirring often, until garlic foams and is sticky and straw-colored, about 10 minutes. Off heat, stir in parsley, lemon juice, pepper flakes, remaining 3 tablespoons oil, and remaining 1 tablespoon garlic.

2. Meanwhile, bring 4 quarts water to boil in large pot. Add pasta and 1 tablespoon salt and cook, stirring often, until al dente. Reserve ½ cup cooking water, then drain pasta and return it to pot.

3. Stir 2 tablespoons reserved cooking water into garlic sauce to loosen, then add sauce to pasta and toss to combine. Season with salt and pepper to taste and add remaining reserved cooking water as needed to adjust consistency. Serve with Parmesan.

Slow-Cooking Garlic

Garlic can easily overbrown and turn bitter. Cooking it slowly over low heat for about 10 minutes gives garlic time to release its flavor and turn nutty-tasting and subtly sweet.

Spaghetti with Garlic, Olive Oil, and Marinated Artichokes

Heat 1 tablespoon extra-virgin olive oil in 12-inch nonstick skillet over high heat until shimmering. Add 3 cups marinated artichokes, drained and patted dry, and cook until edges are crisp and browned, about 6 minutes. Add artichokes to cooked pasta with garlic sauce.

Spaghetti with Pecorino Romano and Black Pepper

SERVES 4 TO 6   **TOTAL TIME** 30 MINUTES **FAST**

✓ **WHY THIS RECIPE WORKS:** With just three main ingredients, this Roman dish is as delicious as it is easy. But our attempts ended up with cheese that formed clumps. For a cheesy sauce that stayed creamy, we whisked some of the pasta water with the grated Pecorino; the cooking water provided starch that kept the cheese's proteins from fusing together. Cutting the amount of cooking water in half upped the starch level even more. Do not adjust the amount of water for cooking the pasta, as the amount is critical for success. Heavy cream further ensured a smooth sauce (half-and-half can be substituted). Use high-quality imported Pecorino Romano—not the bland domestic cheese labeled "Romano."

- 6 **ounces Pecorino Romano cheese, 4 ounces grated fine (2 cups) and 2 ounces grated coarse (1 cup)**
- 1 **pound spaghetti**
-    **Salt**
- 2 **tablespoons heavy cream**
- 2 **teaspoons extra-virgin olive oil**
- 1½ **teaspoons pepper**

1. Place finely grated Pecorino in medium bowl. Set colander in large bowl.

2. Bring 2 quarts water to boil in large pot. Add pasta and 1½ teaspoons salt and cook, stirring often, until al dente. Drain pasta into prepared colander, reserving cooking water. Measure 1½ cups cooking water into liquid measuring cup; discard extra water.

3. Transfer drained pasta to now-empty large bowl. Slowly whisk 1 cup reserved cooking water into finely grated Pecorino until smooth, then whisk in cream, oil, and pepper. Gradually pour cheese mixture over pasta and toss to combine. Let pasta rest for 1 to 2 minutes, tossing frequently and adding remaining cooking water as needed to adjust consistency. Serve with coarsely grated Pecorino.

We use salt pork to create rich and meaty flavor in the sauce of this classic pasta dish.

Pasta All'Amatriciana

SERVES 4 TO 6   **TOTAL TIME** 30 MINUTES   `FAST`

✔ **WHY THIS RECIPE WORKS:** To create an authentic-tasting version of *pasta all'amatriciana*, we needed an alternative to hard-to-find *guanciale*, or cured pork jowl. Humble salt pork, though an unlikely solution, provided the rich, clean meatiness we were after. To ensure tender bites of pork throughout, we first simmered it in water to cook it gently and render fat, a step that allowed the meat to turn golden quickly once the water evaporated. Finally, to ensure the grated Pecorino Romano didn't clump in the hot sauce, we first mixed it with a little cooled pork fat before tossing it with the pasta. Now the flavor of pork, tomato, red pepper flakes, and Pecorino shone through. Look for salt pork that is roughly 70 percent fat and 30 percent lean meat; leaner salt pork may not render enough fat. If it is difficult to slice, put the salt pork in the freezer for 15 minutes to firm up. Use high-quality imported Pecorino Romano—not the bland domestic cheese labeled "Romano." Don't forget to reserve some of the pasta cooking water before draining the pasta; the water is used to loosen the texture of the sauce when tossed with the pasta.

All About Parmesan Cheese

Parmesan is a hard, grainy cheese made from cow's milk. It has a rich, sharp flavor and a melt-in-your-mouth texture. We frequently reach for it to sprinkle on top of pasta dishes or to add a rich, salty flavor to sauces, soups, and stews.

BUYING PARMESAN: We recommend authentic Italian Parmigiano-Reggiano. Most of the other Parmesan-type cheeses are too salty and one-dimensional. When shopping, make sure some portion of the words "Parmigiano-Reggiano" is stenciled on the golden rind. To ensure that you're buying a properly aged cheese, examine the condition of the rind. It should be a few shades darker than the straw-colored interior and penetrate about ½ inch deep. And closely scrutinize the center of the cheese. Those small white spots found on many samples are actually good things—they signify the presence of calcium phosphate crystals, which are formed only after the cheese has been aged for the proper amount of time.

STORING PARMESAN: We have found that the best way to preserve the flavor and texture of Parmesan is to wrap it in parchment paper, then aluminum foil. However, if you have just a small piece of cheese, tossing it in a zipper-lock bag works almost as well; just be sure to squeeze out as much air as possible before sealing the bag. Note that these methods also work for Pecorino Romano.

PARMESAN VERSUS PECORINO ROMANO: While Parmesan is a cow's-milk cheese, Pecorino Romano is made from sheep's milk, but the two do have a similar texture and flavor. We have found that Parmesan and Pecorino Romano generally can be used interchangeably, especially when the amount called for is moderate. However, when Parmesan is called for in larger quantities, it is best to stick with the Parmesan, as Pecorino Romano can be fairly pungent.

CAN YOU PREGRATE YOUR OWN PARMESAN?: We've never been tempted by tasteless, shelf-stable powdered Parmesan cheese, and even the higher-quality grated Parmesan in the refrigerated section of the supermarket is uneven in quality. But what about grating your own Parmesan to have at the ready? Do you sacrifice any flavor for convenience? Tasters were hard-pressed to detect any difference between freshly grated Parmesan and cheese that had been grated and stored for up to three weeks. To grind Parmesan, cut a block into 1-inch chunks. Place the chunks in a food processor and process until ground into coarse particles, about 20 seconds. Refrigerate in an airtight container until ready to use.

8 ounces salt pork, rind removed, rinsed thoroughly, and patted dry
½ cup water
½ teaspoon red pepper flakes
2 tablespoons tomato paste
¼ cup dry red wine
1 (28-ounce) can diced tomatoes
2 ounces Pecorino Romano cheese, finely grated (1 cup)
1 pound spaghetti
Salt

1. Slice pork into ¼-inch-thick strips, then cut each strip crosswise into ¼-inch pieces. Bring pork and water to simmer in 10-inch nonstick skillet over medium heat, and cook until water evaporates and pork begins to sizzle, 5 to 8 minutes.

2. Reduce heat to medium-low and continue to cook, stirring frequently, until fat renders and pork turns golden, 5 to 8 minutes. Using slotted spoon, transfer pork to bowl. Pour off all but 1 tablespoon fat left in skillet; reserve drained fat.

3. Add pepper flakes and tomato paste to fat left in skillet and cook over medium heat for 20 seconds. Stir in wine and cook for 30 seconds. Stir in tomatoes and their juice and rendered pork and bring to simmer. Cook, stirring frequently, until thickened, 12 to 16 minutes. While sauce simmers, smear 2 tablespoons reserved fat and ½ cup Pecorino Romano together in bowl to form paste.

4. Meanwhile, bring 4 quarts water to boil in large pot. Add pasta and 1 tablespoon salt and cook, stirring often, until al dente. Reserve ½ cup cooking water, then drain pasta and return it to pot. Add sauce, ⅓ cup reserved cooking water, and Pecorino mixture and toss to combine. Add remaining reserved cooking water as needed to adjust consistency. Serve with remaining ½ cup Pecorino Romano.

Pasta Caprese

SERVES 4 TO 6   **TOTAL TIME** 40 MINUTES   **FAST**

 WHY THIS RECIPE WORKS: Adding the popular Caprese trio of ripe tomatoes, fresh mozzarella, and fragrant basil to hot pasta ought to result in a satisfying, summery pasta dish. But usually the heat from the pasta makes the cheese clump. Our solution: Freeze the cheese. Dicing the cheese and chilling it before adding it to the hot pasta allowed the cheese to soften but kept it from fully melting (and turning chewy). Basil and lemon juice gave a bright finish. The success of this recipe depends on high-quality ingredients, including ripe in-season tomatoes and a fruity olive oil. Don't skip the step of freezing the mozzarella, or it will become chewy in the finished dish.

Our light Caprese pasta is packed full of flavor from ripe tomatoes, fresh mozzarella, and summery basil.

¼ cup extra-virgin olive oil
2 teaspoons lemon juice, plus extra as needed
1 small shallot, minced
1 small garlic clove, minced
Salt and pepper
1½ pounds vine-ripened tomatoes, cored, seeded, and cut into ½-inch pieces
12 ounces fresh mozzarella cheese, cut into ½-inch pieces
1 pound penne
¼ cup chopped fresh basil
Sugar

1. Whisk oil, lemon juice, shallot, garlic, ½ teaspoon salt, and ¼ teaspoon pepper together in large serving bowl. Add tomatoes, toss gently to combine, and let marinate for 10 to 45 minutes (do not overmarinate). Pat mozzarella dry with paper towels, place on plate, and freeze until slightly firm, about 10 minutes.

2. Meanwhile, bring 4 quarts water to boil in large pot. Add pasta and 1 tablespoon salt and cook, stirring often, until al dente. Drain pasta, then add to bowl of marinated tomatoes.

Add frozen mozzarella, toss gently to combine, and let sit for 5 minutes. Stir in basil and season with salt, pepper, sugar, and extra lemon juice to taste. Serve.

Freezing Mozzarella

Cut mozzarella into ½-inch pieces, pat dry with paper towels, and place on plate. Freeze mozzarella until slightly firm, about 10 minutes, before tossing with hot pasta.

Fusilli with Fresh Tomato Sauce

SERVES 4 TO 6   **TOTAL TIME** 1 HOUR

✓ **WHY THIS RECIPE WORKS:** Full, juicy, in-season tomatoes are a perfect match for pasta—if you know how to prepare them. For a sauce that made the most of their bright, fresh flavor and meaty texture, we cooked the chopped tomatoes briefly in extra-virgin olive oil with a few cloves of garlic and a pinch of red pepper flakes. Peeling and seeding the tomatoes first gave us a more refined sauce, perfect for an elegant yet easy summer supper. Using a skillet promoted quick evaporation, and thinning out the sauce with a small amount of pasta cooking water brought it to just the right consistency to cling to the pasta. Chopped basil, saved for the end, contributed additional freshness and color, and a bit more olive oil enriched the sauce. The success of this dish depends on using ripe, flavorful tomatoes. Don't forget to reserve some of the pasta cooking water before draining the pasta; the water is used to loosen the texture of the sauce when tossed with the pasta.

> 2 **pounds very ripe, in-season tomatoes**
> ¼ **cup extra-virgin olive oil**
> 3 **garlic cloves, minced**
>   **Pinch red pepper flakes**
>   **Salt and pepper**
> 1 **pound fusilli**
> 2 **tablespoons chopped fresh basil**
>   **Grated Parmesan cheese**

1. Bring 4 quarts water to boil in large pot. Using paring knife, cut out stem and core and make small X in bottom of each tomato. Working with several tomatoes at a time, add to boiling water and cook until skins begin to loosen, 15 to 45 seconds. Remove tomatoes from water (do not drain pot), let cool slightly, then remove loosened tomato skins with paring knife. Seed tomatoes and cut into ½-inch pieces.

2. Heat 2 tablespoons oil, garlic, and pepper flakes in 12-inch skillet over medium heat until garlic is fragrant but not browned, about 2 minutes. Stir in tomatoes and ¼ teaspoon salt, increase heat to medium-high, and cook until tomatoes lose their shape and form chunky sauce, about 10 minutes. (Sauce can be refrigerated for up to 2 days.)

3. Meanwhile, return pot of water to boil. Add pasta and 1 tablespoon salt and cook, stirring often, until al dente. Reserve ½ cup cooking water, then drain pasta and return it to pot. Add sauce, basil, ¼ cup reserved cooking water, and remaining 2 tablespoons oil and toss to combine. Season with salt and pepper to taste and add remaining reserved cooking water as needed to adjust consistency. Serve with Parmesan.

Peeling Fresh Tomatoes

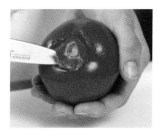

1. Using paring knife, cut out stem and core.

2. Make small X in bottom of each tomato.

3. Add several tomatoes at a time to boiling water and cook until skins begin to loosen, 15 to 45 seconds.

4. Remove loosened tomato skins with paring knife.

Pairing Pasta Shapes and Sauces

Pairing a pasta shape with the right sauce might be an art form in Italy, but we think there's only one basic rule to follow: Thick, chunky sauces go with short pastas, and thin, smooth, or light sauces with strand pasta. (Of course, there are a few exceptions—but that's where the art comes in.) Although we specify pasta shapes for every recipe in this book, you should feel free to substitute other pasta shapes as long as you're following this one basic rule. Here are the most common pastas we use, along with what their names really mean, plus some measuring tips.

SHORT PASTAS

Short tubular or molded pasta shapes do an excellent job of trapping and holding on to chunky sauces in dishes such as our Long-Cooked Meat Ragu (page 403) and Pasta alla Norma with Olives and Capers (page 398). Sauces with very large chunks are best with rigatoni or other large tubes. Sauces with small chunks pair better with fusilli or penne.

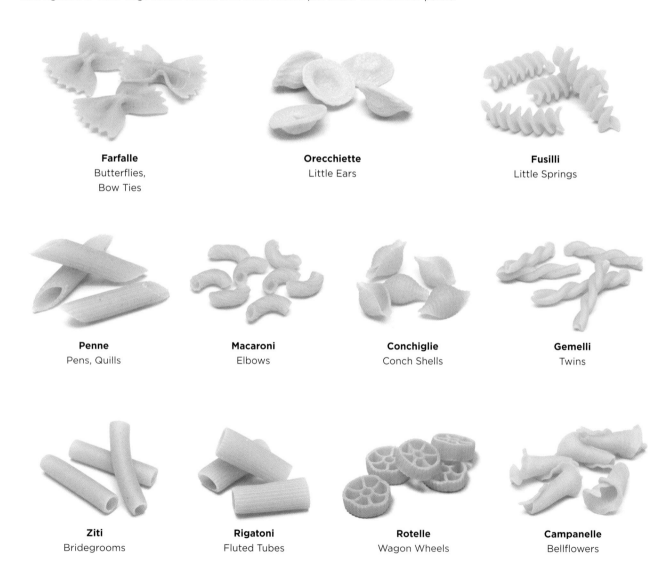

Farfalle
Butterflies,
Bow Ties

Orecchiette
Little Ears

Fusilli
Little Springs

Penne
Pens, Quills

Macaroni
Elbows

Conchiglie
Conch Shells

Gemelli
Twins

Ziti
Bridegrooms

Rigatoni
Fluted Tubes

Rotelle
Wagon Wheels

Campanelle
Bellflowers

STRAND PASTAS

Long strands are best with smooth sauces or sauces with very small chunks. In general, wider noodles, such as pappardelle and fettuccine, can support slightly chunkier sauces, like our Pasta with Classic Bolognese Sauce (page 404).

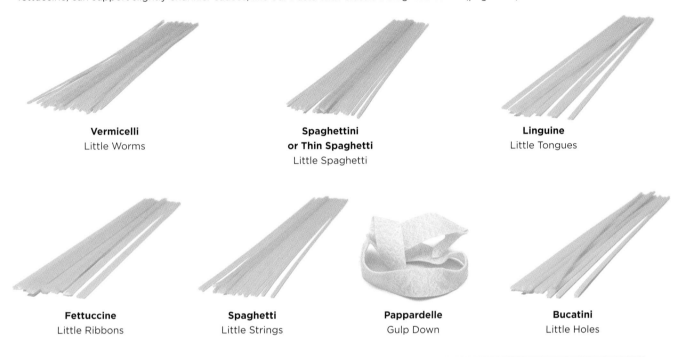

Vermicelli
Little Worms

**Spaghettini
or Thin Spaghetti**
Little Spaghetti

Linguine
Little Tongues

Fettuccine
Little Ribbons

Spaghetti
Little Strings

Pappardelle
Gulp Down

Bucatini
Little Holes

Measuring Less Than a Pound of Pasta

It's easy enough to measure out a pound of pasta, as most packages are sold in this quantity. But we've included some recipes, most notably "Skillet Pastas," that call for less than 1 pound of pasta. Obviously, you can weigh out partial pounds of pasta using a scale, or you can judge by how full the box is, but we think it's easier to measure shaped pasta using a dry measuring cup, and strand pasta by determining the diameter.

MEASURING SHORT PASTA

PASTA TYPE*	8 OUNCES	12 OUNCES
Elbow Macaroni and Small Shells	2 cups	3 cups
Orecchiette	2¼ cups	3⅓ cups
Penne, Ziti, and Campanelle	2½ cups	3¾ cups
Rigatoni, Fusilli, Medium Shells, Wagon Wheels, Wide Egg Noodles	3 cups	4½ cups
Farfalle	3¼ cups	4¾ cups

* These amounts do not apply to whole-wheat pasta.

MEASURING LONG PASTA

When 8 ounces of uncooked strand pasta are bunched together into a tight circle, the diameter measures about 1¼ inches. When 12 ounces of uncooked strand pasta are bunched together, the diameter measures about 1¾ inches.

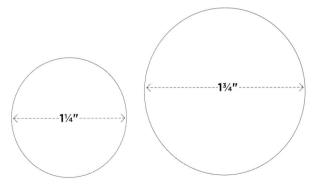

Classic Spaghetti Marinara

SERVES 4 TO 6   **TOTAL TIME** 1 HOUR

✔ **WHY THIS RECIPE WORKS:** For the best, most robustly flavored marinara sauce, we started by picking the right tomatoes. Canned whole tomatoes provide great flavor and texture year-round; using our hands to remove the hard core and seeds was easy. For a sauce with intense tomato flavor, we sautéed the tomatoes until they glazed the bottom of the pan, then we added the reserved juice. Using a skillet provided more surface area and encouraged faster evaporation and flavor concentration, while red wine added depth. Adding a portion of uncooked tomatoes, along with chopped basil and a drizzle of olive oil, just before serving gave our sauce a bright, fresh finish. If you prefer a chunkier sauce, give it just 3 or 4 pulses in the food processor in step 4.

- 2 (28-ounce) cans whole peeled tomatoes
- 3 tablespoons extra-virgin olive oil
- 1 onion, chopped fine
- 2 garlic cloves, minced
- 2 teaspoons minced fresh oregano or ½ teaspoon dried
- ⅓ cup dry red wine
- 3 tablespoons chopped fresh basil
  Salt and pepper
  Sugar
- 1 pound spaghetti
  Grated Parmesan cheese

CUSTOMIZING TOMATO SAUCE

To dress up our basic marinara sauce, here are some ideas to use singly or in combination.

TO INCORPORATE	DO THIS
Red Pepper Flakes	Cook 1 teaspoon with garlic and oil
Parsley	Replace basil with ¼ cup minced fresh
Heavy Cream	Add ¾ cup to finished sauce and simmer until thickened, about 3 minutes
Anchovies	Cook 8 rinsed and minced fillets with garlic and oil
Olives	Add ½ cup, pitted and chopped, with basil
Capers	Add 3 tablespoons, rinsed, with basil

---

1. Drain tomatoes in fine-mesh strainer set over large bowl. Open tomatoes with hands and remove and discard seeds and fibrous cores; let tomatoes drain, about 5 minutes. Measure out and reserve ¾ cup tomatoes separately. Reserve 2½ cups drained tomato juice; discard extra juice.

2. Heat 2 tablespoons oil in 12-inch skillet over medium heat until shimmering. Add onion and cook until softened and lightly browned, 5 to 7 minutes. Stir in garlic and oregano and cook until fragrant, about 30 seconds. Stir in remaining drained tomatoes and increase heat to medium-high. Cook, stirring often, until liquid has evaporated and tomatoes begin to brown and stick to pan, 10 to 12 minutes.

3. Stir in wine and cook until thick and syrupy, about 1 minute. Stir in reserved tomato juice, scraping up any browned bits. Bring to simmer and cook, stirring occasionally, until sauce is thickened, 8 to 10 minutes.

4. Transfer sauce to food processor, add reserved ¾ cup tomatoes, and pulse until slightly chunky, about 8 pulses. Return sauce to now-empty skillet, stir in basil and remaining 1 tablespoon oil, and season with salt, pepper, and sugar to taste. (Sauce can be refrigerated for up to 3 days or frozen for up to 1 month.)

5. Meanwhile, bring 4 quarts water to boil in large pot. Add pasta and 1 tablespoon salt and cook, stirring often, until al dente. Reserve ½ cup cooking water, then drain pasta and return it to pot. Add sauce and toss to combine. Season with salt and pepper to taste and add reserved cooking water as needed to adjust consistency. Serve with Parmesan.

Spaghetti Puttanesca

SERVES 4 TO 6   **TOTAL TIME** 30 MINUTES **FAST**

✔ **WHY THIS RECIPE WORKS:** Many puttanesca recipes produce a dish that is too fishy or too salty and acidic, while others are timidly flavored and dull. We wanted to bring out as much flavor as we could from each ingredient, while not letting any one prevail. We bloomed the garlic, anchovies, and red pepper flakes in hot olive oil to develop and blend their flavors. Then we added tomatoes and simmered for only 15 minutes to preserve their sweetness and meaty texture. We like kalamata or niçoise olives in this sauce because they have a nice briny flavor, but nearly any black olive will work here (avoid canned California black olives). The deep flavor of good-quality, oil-packed anchovy fillets is a must in this recipe. The fishier, flatter taste of commercial anchovy paste won't do here. Since anchovy fillets vary in size, more than 8 fillets may be necessary to yield 4 teaspoons of minced anchovies. If you like the fruitiness of extra-virgin olive oil, stir a tablespoon or two into the sauced pasta before serving.

3   tablespoons extra-virgin olive oil

4   garlic cloves, minced

4   teaspoons minced anchovy fillets (about 8 fillets)

1   teaspoon red pepper flakes

3   (14.5-ounce) cans diced tomatoes

½   cup kalamata olives, pitted and chopped

¼   cup minced fresh parsley

3   tablespoons capers, rinsed

   Salt and pepper

1   pound spaghetti

   Grated Parmesan cheese

1. Cook oil, garlic, anchovies, and pepper flakes in medium saucepan over medium heat, stirring often, until garlic is fragrant but not browned, about 2 minutes.

2. Stir in tomatoes and their juice and simmer until thickened slightly, 15 to 20 minutes. Stir in olives, parsley, and capers. Season with salt and pepper to taste. (Sauce can be refrigerated for up to 3 days or frozen for up to 1 month.)

3. Meanwhile, bring 4 quarts water to boil in large pot. Add pasta and 1 tablespoon salt and cook, stirring often, until al dente. Reserve ½ cup cooking water, then drain pasta and return it to pot. Add sauce and toss to combine. Season with salt and pepper to taste and add reserved cooking water as needed to adjust consistency. Serve with Parmesan.

Both hand-chopped and processed canned tomatoes, along with heavy cream, make this vodka sauce rich and smooth.

Penne alla Vodka

SERVES 4 TO 6   TOTAL TIME 45 MINUTES **FAST**

✔ **WHY THIS RECIPE WORKS:** In *penne alla vodka*, splashes of vodka and cream turn a simple tomato sauce luxurious. For a sauce that was not too thin or too chunky and that would cling to the penne, we combined both processed and hand-chopped tomatoes. A heavy hand with the vodka added zing, but to prevent the finished dish from tasting overly boozy, we added the vodka early on to allow the alcohol to mostly cook off. Just half a cup of heavy cream kept the brightness of the tomatoes intact and gave us a velvety but not over-the-top sauce. Allowing the penne to finish cooking in the sauce encouraged cohesiveness. Red pepper flakes give this dish some kick; for more heat, increase the amount.

1   (28-ounce) can whole peeled tomatoes,
     drained with juice reserved

2   tablespoons extra-virgin olive oil

¼   cup finely chopped onion

1   tablespoon tomato paste

2   garlic cloves, minced

¼   teaspoon red pepper flakes

   Salt and pepper

⅓   cup vodka

½   cup heavy cream

1   pound penne

2   tablespoons chopped fresh basil

   Grated Parmesan cheese

1. Pulse half of tomatoes in food processor until smooth, about 12 pulses. Cut remaining tomatoes into ½-inch pieces, discarding cores. Combine pureed and diced tomatoes in liquid measuring cup and add reserved juice until mixture measures 2 cups; discard extra juice.

2. Heat oil in large saucepan over medium heat until shimmering. Add onion and tomato paste and cook, stirring occasionally, until onion is softened and lightly browned, 5 to 7 minutes. Stir in garlic and pepper flakes and cook until fragrant, about 30 seconds.

3. Stir in tomato mixture and ½ teaspoon salt. Off heat, add vodka. Return sauce to medium-high heat and simmer, stirring often, until alcohol flavor is cooked off, 8 to 10 minutes.

Stir in cream and cook until heated through, about 1 minute. (Sauce can be refrigerated for up to 3 days or frozen for up to 1 month.)

4. Meanwhile, bring 4 quarts water to boil in large pot. Add pasta and 1 tablespoon salt and cook, stirring often, until al dente. Reserve ½ cup cooking water, then drain pasta and return it to pot. Add sauce and cook over medium heat, tossing to combine, until pasta absorbs some sauce, 1 to 2 minutes. Stir in basil, season with salt and pepper to taste, and add reserved cooking water as needed to adjust consistency. Serve with Parmesan.

Ziti with Roasted Tomato Sauce and Goat Cheese

SERVES 4 TO 6   **TOTAL TIME** 1 HOUR

WHY THIS RECIPE WORKS: Oven-roasted, charred tomatoes make a great base for a vibrant, slightly smoky pasta sauce in this dish. To expose their juicy flesh, we halved our tomatoes and then roasted them on a wire rack placed in a baking sheet. Cooking them elevated allowed for maximum air circulation and promoted better charring, leading to a more concentrated roasted tomato flavor. Tossing the tomatoes with tomato paste prior to cooking gave the sauce a deep red color and another layer of tomato flavor. For some aromatic backbone, we used the open space on the rack to roast an onion and garlic cloves; setting them on a piece of aluminum foil in the center of the rack prevented them from falling through the wires or off the edge. A few crumbles of goat cheese provided a tangy richness, while woodsy fresh rosemary paired nicely with the roasted, smoky notes of the sauce. Don't forget to reserve some of the cooking water before draining the pasta; the water is used to loosen the texture of the sauce before tossing it with the pasta.

- 2 **tablespoons tomato paste**
- 2 **tablespoons extra-virgin olive oil**
- 1 **teaspoon minced fresh rosemary or ¼ teaspoon dried**
  Salt and pepper
- ⅛ **teaspoon red pepper flakes**
- 3 **pounds vine-ripened tomatoes, cored and halved pole to pole**
- 1 **small onion, sliced into ½-inch-thick rings**
- 6 **garlic cloves, peeled**
- 1 **teaspoon red wine vinegar**
  Sugar
- 1 **pound ziti**
- 2 **ounces goat cheese, crumbled (½ cup)**

1. Adjust oven rack to middle position and heat oven to 475 degrees. Line rimmed baking sheet with aluminum foil, top with wire rack, and place 4-inch square of foil in center of rack. Combine tomato paste, 1 tablespoon oil, rosemary, ¾ teaspoon salt, ¼ teaspoon pepper, and pepper flakes in large bowl. Add tomatoes, onion, and garlic, and toss to coat. Place onion rounds and garlic on foil square. Arrange tomatoes, cut side down, on rack around garlic and onions. Roast until vegetables are soft and tomato skins are well charred, 45 to 55 minutes.

2. Let roasted vegetables cool for 5 minutes. Pulse garlic and onion in food processor until finely chopped, about 5 pulses. Add tomatoes, vinegar, and remaining 1 tablespoon oil to processor and pulse until tomatoes are broken down but still chunky, about 5 pulses, scraping down bowl as needed. Season mixture with salt, pepper, and sugar to taste. (Sauce can be refrigerated for up to 3 days or frozen for up to 1 month.)

3. Meanwhile, bring 4 quarts water to boil in large pot. Add pasta and 1 tablespoon salt and cook, stirring often, until al dente. Reserve ½ cup cooking water, then drain pasta and return it to pot. Add sauce and toss to combine. Season with salt and pepper to taste and add reserved cooking water as needed to adjust consistency. Sprinkle individual portions with goat cheese before serving.

Roasting Tomatoes

Line rimmed baking sheet with foil, top with wire rack, and place 4-inch square of foil in center of rack. After coating, place onion rounds and garlic on foil square. Arrange tomatoes, cut side down, around edges of rack.

Pasta alla Norma with Olives and Capers

SERVES 4 TO 6   **TOTAL TIME** 40 MINUTES **FAST**

WHY THIS RECIPE WORKS: With its lively combination of tender eggplant, robust tomato sauce, al dente pasta, and salty, milky ricotta salata, *pasta alla norma* sings with each bite—appropriate, given that it was named for the title character of an opera. For our version, we microwaved salted eggplant on coffee filters to draw out its moisture. A secret ingredient, anchovies, gave our tomato sauce a deep, savory flavor without any fishiness; capers and chopped kalamatas

Salting and microwaving eggplant before sautéing it ensures it's nicely browned and tender in this savory pasta sauce.

provided potency. Finally, shards of ricotta salata, a slightly aged ricotta, added a salty tang. If you can't find ricotta salata you can substitute French feta, Pecorino Romano, or Cotija (a firm, crumbly Mexican cheese). We prefer to use kosher salt in this recipe because it clings best to the eggplant in step 1; if using table salt, reduce salt amounts by half. To prevent the eggplant from breaking up into small pieces, be sure not to peel away the skin, and do not stir it frequently when sautéing in step 2. To give this dish a little extra kick, add additional pepper flakes.

1½ pounds eggplant, cut into ½-inch pieces
    Kosher salt and pepper
3½ tablespoons extra-virgin olive oil,
    plus extra for serving
4   garlic cloves, minced
2   anchovy fillets, rinsed and minced
¼   teaspoon red pepper flakes
1   (28-ounce) can crushed tomatoes
½   cup pitted kalamata olives, chopped coarse
6   tablespoons minced fresh parsley
2   tablespoons capers, rinsed
1   pound rigatoni
    Shredded ricotta salata

1. Line large plate with double layer of coffee filters and coat lightly with vegetable oil spray. Toss eggplant with 1 teaspoon salt in bowl, then spread evenly over prepared plate. Microwave, uncovered, until eggplant is dry to touch and slightly shriveled, about 10 minutes, tossing halfway through cooking. Let eggplant cool slightly, then return to bowl and toss gently with 1 tablespoon oil.

2. Heat 1 tablespoon oil in 12-inch nonstick skillet over medium-high heat until shimmering. Add eggplant and cook, stirring occasionally, until well browned and fully tender, about 10 minutes; transfer to clean plate.

3. Let now-empty skillet cool slightly, about 3 minutes. Add 1 tablespoon oil, garlic, anchovies, and pepper flakes to cooled skillet and cook over medium heat until fragrant, about 1 minute. Stir in tomatoes, increase heat to medium-high, and simmer, stirring occasionally, until slightly thickened, 8 to 10 minutes.

4. Stir in eggplant and cook until eggplant is heated through and flavors meld, 3 to 5 minutes. Stir in olives, parsley, capers, and remaining ½ tablespoon oil, and season with salt to taste.

5. Meanwhile, bring 4 quarts water to boil in large pot. Add pasta and 2 tablespoons salt and cook, stirring often, until al dente. Reserve ½ cup cooking water, then drain pasta and return it to pot. Add sauce and toss to combine. Season with salt and pepper to taste, and add reserved cooking water as needed to adjust consistency. Serve with ricotta salata and extra olive oil.

NOTES FROM THE TEST KITCHEN

Capers

Capers are sun-dried pickled flower buds from the spiny shrub *Capparis spinosa*, and their unique flavor is most commonly found in Mediterranean cooking. The ideal caper packs an acidic punch with a lingering sweetness that is both floral and pungent, and a crunchy texture that matches its flavorful bite. Capers range in size from tiny nonpareils to large caperberries, and they develop their flavor from being cured, either in a salty brine (sometimes with vinegar) or packed in salt. Brined capers are the most commonly available, and we've found that we prefer the smaller nonpareil capers for their compact size and slight crunch.

Pasta is one of those things that is easy to cook, but hard to cook just right. For perfect pasta, you must pay attention to everything from the water-to-pasta ratio to the time between draining and saucing. We've been cooking pasta for a long time and have come up with a few simple steps that deliver perfectly cooked al dente pasta every time.

1. USE PLENTY OF WATER: To cook 1 pound pasta, bring 4 quarts of water to a rolling boil in a Dutch oven or large pot.
WHY? Pasta leaches starch as it cooks; without plenty of water to dilute the starch the noodles stick together. Fill a pot of at least 6 quarts with cold tap water; warm water can pick up off-flavors from your water heater. Make sure the water is at a rolling boil. Pasta cooks best (and fastest) in boiling, rather than simmering, water.

2. SALT THE WATER, DON'T OIL IT: Add 1 tablespoon salt to the boiling water.
WHY? Salt is crucial because it adds flavor to the pasta (most of the salt will go down the drain with the cooking water). Adding oil to the cooking water just creates a slick on the surface of the water, doing nothing for the pasta. Oil also prevents the sauce from adhering to the pasta.

3. ADD THE PASTA AND STIR: Add the pasta to the boiling salted water and stir constantly for 1 to 2 minutes.
WHY? Stirring the pasta when you first add it to the water, and again occasionally as it cooks, will prevent it from sticking together or to the pot.

4. CHECK OFTEN FOR DONENESS: Several minutes before the pasta should be done, begin tasting it. When the pasta is almost al dente, remove the pot from the heat.
WHY? Tasting for doneness is really the only way to know when to stop cooking pasta. The timing given on the packaging is almost always too long and results in overcooked pasta. Because pasta continues to cook after it is drained, you need to drain it when it is a little underdone.

5. RESERVE SOME COOKING WATER, THEN DRAIN: Reserve ½ cup cooking water (the amount can vary per recipe), then drain the pasta. Shake the drained pasta in the colander once or twice to remove any excess liquid.
WHY? The cooking water is flavorful and can help loosen a thick sauce. Don't rinse the pasta or shake the colander too vigorously; the small amount of cooking water that remains on the pasta helps to spread the sauce when tossing with the pasta.

6. SAUCE IN THE POT: Return the drained pasta to the now-empty pot, add the sauce, and toss using tongs or a pasta fork. Add pasta cooking water as needed until the sauce reaches the proper consistency.
WHY? You can never coat the pasta evenly with sauce if you serve up the cooked pasta and then top it with sauce. Saucing pasta in the pot ensures evenly coated, hot pasta. You usually need 3 to 4 cups of sauce per pound of pasta.

Three whole eggs and two types of cheese result in a creamy and tangy carbonara sauce.

Spaghetti alla Carbonara

SERVES 4 TO 6   **TOTAL TIME** 50 MINUTES

✔ **WHY THIS RECIPE WORKS:** Spaghetti draped in a velvety sauce of cheese and eggs with bits of crispy bacon—is there anything more indulgent than carbonara? Though the method is pretty straightforward—make an egg and cheese sauce, cook the bacon, cook the pasta, then toss until all is creamy and combined—we had to nail down the details. First up, determining the right number of eggs: Three whole eggs gave our carbonara superior texture and richness. Next, the cheese: Opting for two kinds—Pecorino Romano and Parmesan—gave us creaminess with a sharp, tangy bite. For the bacon, we liked the standard domestic variety, which contributed crunch, a little sweetness, and some smoky flavor. Pouring the egg-and-cheese mixture (which also included raw garlic so our dish would retain some of its bite) over the hot pasta ensured evenly covered strands.

- ¼ **cup extra-virgin olive oil**
- 8 **slices bacon, cut into ¼-inch pieces**
- ½ **cup dry white wine**
- 3 **large eggs**
- 1½ **ounces Parmesan cheese, grated (¾ cup)**
- ¼ **cup finely grated Pecorino Romano cheese**
- 2 **garlic cloves, minced**
- 1 **pound spaghetti**
   Salt and pepper

1. Adjust oven rack to lower-middle position, set large ovensafe serving bowl on rack, and heat oven to 200 degrees.

2. Heat oil in 12-inch skillet over medium heat until shimmering. Add bacon and cook until crisp, about 8 minutes. Stir in wine, bring to simmer, and cook until slightly reduced, 6 to 8 minutes. Remove from heat and cover to keep warm. In separate bowl, whisk eggs, Parmesan, Pecorino, and garlic together.

3. Meanwhile, bring 4 quarts water to boil in large pot. Add pasta and 1 tablespoon salt and cook, stirring often, until al dente. Reserve ⅓ cup cooking water, then drain pasta and transfer to warmed serving bowl.

4. Immediately pour bacon mixture and egg mixture over hot pasta and toss to combine. Season with salt and pepper to taste, and add reserved cooking water as needed to adjust consistency. Serve immediately.

Fettuccine Alfredo

SERVES 4   **TOTAL TIME** 50 MINUTES

✔ **WHY THIS RECIPE WORKS:** Classic Alfredo sauce should be transcendent, boasting fresh cream flavor and a silky, elegant texture. Using a light hand with two of the richer ingredients—Parmesan and butter—was a good starting point, giving our sauce distinctive flavor without being overwhelming; restraint with the requisite ground nutmeg was important, too. The real challenge was managing the heavy cream, which is usually reduced by half, making for an overly thick sauce. We found it better to reduce only a portion of the cream, then add a splash of fresh cream at the end for clean flavor and silky texture. Also, fresh fettuccine was essential, as dried noodles didn't hold on to the sauce. Undercooking the pasta, then letting it finish cooking in the sauce, ensured that the finished sauce had the perfect consistency—neither too thick nor too thin. Finally, we found that serving Alfredo immediately in freshly warmed bowls is crucial; otherwise the dish congeals within a minute or so. Not only is it easy to use the boiling water for the pasta to warm the bowls, but the extra drips of water left inside the bowls help to keep the sauce fluid. Note that this dish is very rich, and therefore the portion size is quite small; serve it with a substantial salad or simply prepared fish or chicken.

1½ cups heavy cream
2 tablespoons unsalted butter
  Salt and pepper
1 (9-ounce) package fresh fettuccine
1½ ounces Parmesan cheese, grated (¾ cup)
⅛ teaspoon ground nutmeg

1. Bring 1 cup cream and butter to simmer in large saucepan. Reduce heat to low and simmer gently until mixture measures ⅔ cup, 12 to 15 minutes. Off heat, stir in remaining ½ cup cream, ½ teaspoon salt, and ½ teaspoon pepper. Cover and set aside.

2. Meanwhile, bring 4½ quarts water to boil in large pot. Ladle ½ cup boiling water into each individual serving bowl; set aside to warm. Return pot of water to boil, add pasta and 1 tablespoon salt, and cook, stirring often, until just shy of al dente. Reserve ¼ cup cooking water, then drain pasta.

3. Return cream mixture to simmer. Reduce heat to low and add drained pasta, Parmesan, and nutmeg. Cook, tossing gently, until cheese is melted, sauce coats pasta, and pasta is al dente, 1 to 2 minutes. Add reserved cooking water as needed to adjust consistency (sauce may look thin but will gradually thicken as pasta is served). Drain water from warmed serving bowls, portion pasta into bowls, and serve immediately.

NOTES FROM THE TEST KITCHEN

Buying and Cooking Fresh Pasta

Good-quality fresh pasta is readily available in supermarkets and offers a convenient option for home cooks. The taste of store-bought fresh pasta compares favorably with both fresh pasta from a local Italian market and fresh homemade pasta. It is usually sold in 9-ounce containers in the refrigerated section of the store. Fresh pasta is the best choice for many dishes, including fettuccine Alfredo, because the rough surface of fresh noodles is porous and so absorbs sauces better than the smooth surface of dried pasta.

Cooking fresh pasta is very different from cooking dried pasta. Fresh pasta cooks much faster than dried and might be done in as little as 2 or 3 minutes, so taste early and often to avoid overcooking it.

Pasta with Weeknight Meat Sauce
SERVES 4 TO 6   **TOTAL TIME** 45 MINUTES   **FAST**

✔ **WHY THIS RECIPE WORKS:** For a quick yet richly flavored meat sauce that tasted like it had simmered all day, we discovered a few tricks that maintained flavor but brought this dish to the table in just 45 minutes. Incorporating mushrooms (for a deeper flavor) and including a panade (to keep the meat moist) helped keep the long-simmered flavor. Except for ground round (which tasters found spongy and bland), this recipe will work with most any type of ground beef, as long as it is 85 percent lean. If using dried oregano, add the entire amount with the reserved tomato juice in step 2. Just about any pasta shape complements this simple meat sauce.

2 ounces white mushrooms, trimmed and halved
1 slice hearty white sandwich bread, torn into quarters
2 tablespoons whole milk
  Salt and pepper
½ pound 85 percent lean ground beef
1 tablespoon extra-virgin olive oil
½ onion, chopped fine
3 garlic cloves, minced
⅛ teaspoon red pepper flakes
1 tablespoon tomato paste
1 (14.5-ounce) can diced tomatoes, drained with ¼ cup juice reserved
1½ teaspoons minced fresh oregano or ½ teaspoon dried
1 (15-ounce) can tomato sauce
¼ cup grated Parmesan cheese, plus extra for serving
1 pound spaghetti

1. Pulse mushrooms in food processor until finely chopped, about 4 pulses; transfer to bowl. Pulse bread, milk, ½ teaspoon salt, and ½ teaspoon pepper in now-empty food processor until paste forms, about 4 pulses. Add ground beef and pulse until well combined, about 3 pulses.

2. Heat oil in large saucepan over medium-high heat until just smoking. Add onion and processed mushrooms and cook until softened and lightly browned, about 5 minutes. Stir in garlic, pepper flakes, and tomato paste and cook until fragrant, about 30 seconds. Stir in ¼ cup reserved tomato juice and 1 teaspoon fresh oregano (if using dried, add full amount), scraping up any browned bits. Stir in meat mixture and cook, breaking up meat with wooden spoon, until no longer pink, about 3 minutes.

3. Stir in diced tomatoes and tomato sauce, bring to gentle simmer, and cook until sauce has thickened and flavors meld, about 10 minutes. Stir in Parmesan and remaining ½ teaspoon fresh oregano, and season with salt and pepper to taste.

4. Meanwhile, bring 4 quarts water to boil in large pot. Add pasta and 1 tablespoon salt and cook, stirring often, until al dente. Reserve ½ cup cooking water, then drain pasta and return it to pot. Add sauce and toss to combine. Season with salt and pepper to taste and add reserved cooking water as needed to adjust consistency. Serve with extra Parmesan.

Long-Cooked Meat Ragu

SERVES 4 TO 6   **TOTAL TIME** 2½ TO 3 HOURS

✓ **WHY THIS RECIPE WORKS:** Rustic Italian-style ragu is all about low-and-slow simmering—it relies on lots of time but minimal heat to turn the meat, cooked with tomatoes and red wine, fall-apart tender. For this recipe, we liked beef short ribs, which turned tender and moist during braising; they gave the sauce a truly meaty flavor. Processing whole and diced canned tomatoes made a sauce that was too smooth, while pulsing them briefly gave us a sauce that was too even in texture. Chopping whole canned tomatoes by hand was an easy fix—our sauce now had the perfect rustic texture and appearance. To prevent the sauce from becoming greasy, trim as much fat as possible from the ribs. Pork spareribs or country-style ribs can be substituted for the beef short ribs. This thick, robust sauce is best with tubular pasta, such as rigatoni, ziti, or penne, or with egg noodles.

This rustic ragu gets its texture from slowly simmering beef short ribs with finely chopped tomatoes.

1½	**pounds beef short ribs, trimmed**
	Salt and pepper
1	**tablespoon extra-virgin olive oil**
1	**onion, chopped fine**
½	**cup dry red wine**
1	**(28-ounce) can whole peeled tomatoes, drained with juice reserved, tomatoes chopped fine**
1	**pound rigatoni**
	Grated Parmesan or Pecorino Romano cheese

1. Pat ribs dry with paper towels and season with salt and pepper. Heat oil in 12-inch skillet over medium-high heat until just smoking. Brown ribs well on all sides, about 10 minutes; transfer to plate.

2. Pour off all but 1 teaspoon fat left in skillet, add onion, and cook over medium heat until softened, about 5 minutes. Stir in wine and simmer, scraping up any browned bits, until wine has reduced to glaze, about 2 minutes.

3. Return browned ribs and any accumulated juices to skillet. Stir in tomatoes and reserved juice and bring to boil. Reduce heat to low, cover, and simmer gently, turning ribs several times, until meat is very tender and falling off bones, 1½ to 2 hours.

4. Transfer ribs to cutting board, let cool slightly, then shred meat, discarding fat and bones. Return shredded meat to sauce and simmer gently over medium heat until meat is heated through and sauce is slightly thickened, about 5 minutes. Season with salt and pepper to taste. (Sauce can be refrigerated for up to 3 days or frozen for up to 1 month.)

5. Meanwhile, bring 4 quarts water to boil in large pot. Add pasta and 1 tablespoon salt and cook, stirring often, until al dente. Reserve ½ cup cooking water, then drain pasta and return it to pot. Add sauce and toss to combine. Season with salt and pepper to taste and add reserved cooking water as needed to adjust consistency. Serve with Parmesan.

VARIATION

Long-Cooked Meat Ragu with Warm Spices

Before adding wine to skillet, add 2 tablespoons minced fresh parsley, ½ teaspoon ground cinnamon, and pinch ground cloves and cook until fragrant, about 30 seconds.

Pasta with Classic Bolognese Sauce

SERVES 4 TO 6   **TOTAL TIME** 4 HOURS

WHY THIS RECIPE WORKS: A good Bolognese sauce should be thick and smooth with rich, complex flavor. The meat should be first and foremost, but there should be sweet, salty, and acidic flavors in the background. To get this complexity, we built our Bolognese in layers, starting with just onion, carrot, and celery, sautéed in butter. Then we added meatloaf mix (a combination of ground beef, veal, and pork). For dairy, we used milk, which complemented the meat flavor without adding too much richness. Once the milk was reduced, we added white wine to the pot for a more robust sauce, followed by chopped whole canned tomatoes. A long, slow simmer produced a luxuriously rich sauce with layers of flavor and tender meat. If you would like to double this recipe, increase the simmering times for the milk and the wine to 30 minutes each, and the simmering time to 4 hours once the tomatoes are added. Just about any pasta shape complements this meaty sauce, but fettuccine and linguine are the test kitchen favorites. If you can't find meatloaf mix, use 6 ounces (85 percent lean) ground beef and 6 ounces ground pork.

For thick and tender classic Bolognese, we simmer the meat with milk, white wine, and canned tomatoes.

5   tablespoons unsalted butter
2   tablespoons finely chopped onion
2   tablespoons minced carrot
2   tablespoons minced celery
12 ounces meatloaf mix
    Salt and pepper
1   cup whole milk
1   cup dry white wine
1   (28-ounce) can whole peeled tomatoes, drained with juice reserved, tomatoes chopped fine
1   pound fettuccine or linguine
    Grated Parmesan cheese

1. Melt 3 tablespoons butter in Dutch oven over medium heat. Add onion, carrot, and celery and cook until softened, 5 to 7 minutes. Stir in meatloaf mix and ½ teaspoon salt and cook, breaking up meat with wooden spoon, until no longer pink, about 3 minutes.

2. Stir in milk, bring to simmer, and cook until milk evaporates and only rendered fat remains, 10 to 15 minutes. Stir in wine, bring to simmer, and cook until wine evaporates, 10 to 15 minutes.

3. Stir in tomatoes and reserved tomato juice and bring to simmer. Reduce heat to low so that sauce continues to simmer just barely, with occasional bubble or two at surface, until liquid has evaporated, about 3 hours. Season with salt to taste. (Sauce can be refrigerated for up to 2 days or frozen for up to 1 month.)

4. Meanwhile, bring 4 quarts water to boil in large pot. Add pasta and 1 tablespoon salt and cook, stirring often, until al dente. Reserve ½ cup cooking water, then drain pasta and return it to pot. Add sauce and remaining 2 tablespoons butter and toss to combine. Season with salt and pepper to taste and add reserved cooking water as needed to adjust consistency. Serve with Parmesan.

VARIATION

Pasta with Beef Bolognese Sauce
Substitute 12 ounces 85 percent lean ground beef for meatloaf mix.

A rich and silky Bolognese sauce is the king of pasta sauces. Making one with complex flavors takes some time, but most of it is hands-off. Technique and time are important to success here, so don't be tempted to take shortcuts to speed up the process.

1. SAUTÉ THE AROMATICS IN BUTTER:
Melt 3 tablespoons unsalted butter in a Dutch oven and cook the finely chopped onion and minced carrot and celery until softened.
WHY? Sautéing the aromatics is the first step in developing layers of flavor for this sauce. Cooking them in butter rather than oil adds rich flavor.

2. ADD THE MEATLOAF MIX: Stir in 12 ounces meatloaf mix and salt and cook, breaking up the meat until it is no longer pink, about 3 minutes.
WHY? A combination of ground beef, veal, and pork makes this sauce especially complex; the veal adds delicacy while the pork makes it sweet.

3. STIR IN THE MILK AND SIMMER: Add 1 cup whole milk and simmer until it evaporates and only the rendered fat remains, about 10 minutes.
WHY? Adding whole milk provides just enough dairy flavor to complement the meat, and adding it ahead of the wine is best because the meat is more tender and can absorb it better.

4. STIR IN THE WINE AND SIMMER: Add 1 cup dry white wine and simmer until it evaporates, about 10 minutes.
WHY? The acidity of the wine balances the richness of the meat and adds further depth to the sauce.

5. ADD THE TOMATOES AND COOK 3 HOURS: Drain 1 can of whole tomatoes, then chop the tomatoes and add them and the reserved juice to the pot. Simmer the mixture over low heat until the liquid has evaporated, about 3 hours.
WHY? Canned whole tomatoes taste far better in this sauce than crushed and have the added benefit of the tomato liquid, which helps keep the sauce from scorching. The long simmering time tenderizes the meat and builds flavor.

6. FINISH WITH BUTTER AND PASTA COOKING WATER: Add 2 tablespoons butter to the cooked pasta along with the sauce, and toss to combine. Season with salt and pepper to taste and add pasta cooking water as needed to adjust the consistency.
WHY? At the end of the cooking time we enrich the sauce by swirling in a couple tablespoons of butter. The starchy pasta water makes it easy to adjust the consistency of the sauce so it combines perfectly with the pasta.

Making tender, flavorful meatballs is a time-consuming endeavor, one that is often disappointing in the end. Our method eliminates the need to brown the meatballs in a skillet, turning to the oven instead.

1. COOK THE ONIONS AND THE AROMATICS: Cook the onions. Add the garlic, oregano, and red pepper flakes and cook until fragrant. Reserve half of mixture for the meatballs.
WHY? The fond from the browned onions adds depth to the sauce and the meatballs. It saves time to cook one large batch of aromatics.

2. MAKE THE SAUCE: Add the tomato paste to the onion mixture in the pot and cook, then add the red wine and cook. Add the tomatoes and water and simmer.
WHY? Cooking the tomato paste brings out its flavor and the wine needs to cook off some of the alcohol. The sauce must cook for at least 45 minutes to develop flavor. The water keeps the sauce from becoming too thick.

3. MAKE A PANADE: Mash 4 slices of white sandwich bread and ¾ cup milk together in a large bowl until smooth, then mix in the reserved onion mixture until thoroughly combined.
WHY? This paste binds the meatballs and adds moisture and richness.

4. ADD THE SAUSAGE AND FLAVORINGS: Crumble the sausage into the bowl with the onion mixture and add the Parmesan, parsley, eggs, garlic, and salt and mash with a fork.
WHY? These ingredients season and help bind the meatballs, so it's important that they're thoroughly incorporated.

5. ADD THE GROUND CHUCK LAST: Using your hands, gently work 2½ pounds of 80 percent lean ground chuck into the sausage mixture.
WHY? Overworked ground beef makes for dense, rubbery meatballs. Adding it last helps prevent overkneading.

6. FORM INTO BALLS: Gently roll the mixture into thirty 2½-inch meatballs and place them on two rimmed baking sheets.
WHY? Even sizing means even cooking. Use a kitchen ruler to measure the first meatball and use that as your guide when forming the rest.

7. BROWN THE MEATBALLS IN THE OVEN: Bake the meatballs on the lower-middle and upper-middle racks of a 475-degree oven until well browned, about 20 minutes.
WHY? The hot oven will give the meatballs a tasty seared crust, and baking is easier and neater than browning on the stovetop.

8. FINISH THE MEATBALLS IN THE SAUCE: Transfer the browned meatballs to the pot with the marinara and simmer for 15 minutes.
WHY? The meatballs will finish cooking evenly in the sauce (and will flavor the sauce in the process).

Meatballs and Marinara

SERVES 8 TO 10   TOTAL TIME 2 HOURS

✓ WHY THIS RECIPE WORKS: Most meatball recipes call for equal amounts of pork and beef, but ours has more beef than pork—the resulting drier, leaner mixture held its shape well. For extra flavor, we chose sweet Italian sausage for the pork portion of the mix. Browning the meatballs in the oven was easier than cooking them on the stovetop, and finishing them in the tomato sauce flavored both components.

SAUCE

- ¼ cup extra-virgin olive oil
- 3 onions, chopped fine
- 8 garlic cloves, minced
- 1 tablespoon dried oregano
- ½ teaspoon red pepper flakes
- 1 (6-ounce) can tomato paste
- 1 cup dry red wine
- 1 cup water
- 4 (28-ounce) cans crushed tomatoes
- ½ cup grated Parmesan cheese
- ¼ cup chopped fresh basil
  Salt and pepper

MEATBALLS AND PASTA

- 4 slices hearty white sandwich bread, torn into pieces
- ¾ cup milk
- ½ pound sweet Italian sausage, casings removed
- 2 ounces Parmesan cheese, grated (1 cup)
- ½ cup minced fresh parsley
- 2 large eggs
- 2 garlic cloves, minced
- 1½ teaspoons salt
- 2½ pounds 80 percent lean ground chuck
- 2 pounds spaghetti

1. FOR THE SAUCE: Heat oil in Dutch oven over medium-high heat until shimmering. Add onions and cook until golden, 10 to 15 minutes. Stir in garlic, oregano, and pepper flakes and cook until fragrant, about 30 seconds. Transfer half of onion mixture to bowl; set aside for meatballs.

2. Stir tomato paste into onion mixture left in pot and cook over medium-high heat until fragrant, about 1 minute. Stir in wine and cook until slightly thickened, about 2 minutes. Stir in water and tomatoes and simmer over low heat until sauce is no longer watery, 45 to 60 minutes. Stir in Parmesan and basil, and season with salt and pepper to taste.

3. FOR THE MEATBALLS AND PASTA: Meanwhile, line 2 rimmed baking sheets with aluminum foil and spray with vegetable oil spray. Adjust oven racks to lower-middle and upper-middle positions and heat oven to 475 degrees. Mash bread and milk together in large bowl until smooth. Mix in reserved onion mixture, sausage, Parmesan, parsley, eggs, garlic, and salt. Add beef and knead with hands until well combined.

4. Shape meat mixture into 30 meatballs (about ¼ cup each) and place on prepared sheets, spaced evenly apart. Roast meatballs until well browned, about 20 minutes. Transfer meatballs to pot with sauce and simmer for 15 minutes. (Meatballs and marinara can be refrigerated for up to 3 days or frozen for up to 1 month.)

5. Meanwhile, bring 8 quarts water to boil in 12-quart pot. Add pasta and 2 tablespoons salt and cook, stirring often, until al dente. Reserve ½ cup cooking water, then drain pasta and return it to pot. Add several spoonfuls of sauce (without meatballs) and toss to combine. Add reserved cooking water as needed to adjust consistency. Serve pasta with remaining sauce and meatballs.

Spaghetti with Turkey-Pesto Meatballs

SERVES 4 TO 6   TOTAL TIME 1 HOUR

✓ WHY THIS RECIPE WORKS: For an easy, family-friendly spin on the typical spaghetti-and-meatballs dinner, we replaced the beef with ground turkey and added fresh pesto to the meatballs for big flavor. The pesto replaces the need for garlic, cheese, and even egg called for in standard meatball recipes, making these meatballs nearly prep-free—all they need is a sprinkling of salt, pepper, and bread crumbs (we like panko). Processing a portion of the canned diced tomatoes in a food processor gave us a mostly smooth sauce with a few bigger bites of tomato. You can make your own pesto (see page 410) or use your favorite store-bought brand from the refrigerated section of the supermarket—refrigerated pesto has a fresher flavor than the jarred pesto sold in the grocery aisles. Do not use ground turkey breast meat (sometimes labeled 99 percent fat-free); it will make meatballs that are dry and grainy. You can substitute ground chicken or pork or 90 percent lean ground beef for the ground turkey if desired. You will need a 12-inch skillet with at least 2-inch sides to accommodate both the meatballs and the sauce; the skillet will be quite full.

1½ pounds 93 percent lean ground turkey
1 (7-ounce) container basil pesto (⅔ cup)
⅔ cup panko bread crumbs
Salt and pepper
3 (14.5-ounce) cans diced tomatoes
1 tablespoon extra-virgin olive oil
1 onion, chopped fine
4 garlic cloves, minced
Pinch red pepper flakes
1 pound spaghetti
3 tablespoons chopped fresh basil

1. Gently mix turkey, pesto, panko, ½ teaspoon salt, and ¼ teaspoon pepper in bowl using hands until uniform. Shape mixture into eighteen 1½-inch meatballs.

2. Pulse 2 cans diced tomatoes in food processor until mostly smooth, about 12 pulses; set aside. Heat oil in 12-inch nonstick skillet over medium heat until just smoking. Brown meatballs well on all sides, about 10 minutes; transfer to paper towel–lined plate.

3. Add onion and ⅛ teaspoon salt to fat left in skillet and cook over medium heat until softened, 5 to 7 minutes. Stir in garlic and pepper flakes and cook until fragrant, about 30 seconds. Stir in processed tomatoes and remaining 1 can diced tomatoes and their juice. Bring to simmer and cook for 10 minutes. Return meatballs to skillet, cover, and simmer gently until meatballs are cooked through, about 10 minutes. (Sauce and meatballs can be refrigerated for up to 3 days or frozen for up to 1 month.)

4. Meanwhile, bring 4 quarts water to boil in large pot. Add pasta and 1 tablespoon salt and cook, stirring often, until al dente. Reserve 1 cup cooking water, then drain pasta and return it to pot. Add several large spoonfuls of tomato sauce (without meatballs) to pasta and toss to combine. Season with salt and pepper to taste and add reserved cooking water as needed to adjust consistency. Divide pasta among individual bowls. Top each bowl with remaining sauce and meatballs, sprinkle with basil, and serve.

Stovetop Macaroni and Cheese

SERVES 4   **TOTAL TIME** 35 MINUTES   **FAST**

✔ **WHY THIS RECIPE WORKS:** Just about the only thing boxed macaroni and cheese has going for it is its fast prep. We wanted a quick stovetop macaroni and cheese with an ultracreamy texture and authentic cheese flavor—so good that it would satisfy everyone at the table. We cooked the macaroni al dente, then drained and combined it with butter and an egg custard. For the cheese we chose cheddar, American, or Monterey Jack—and plenty of it. We stirred the cheese into the macaroni mixture until the sauce turned thick and creamy. It is important to cook the mixture over low heat in step 3. The sauce will be loose as you add the rest of the evaporated milk but will thicken up as it gently cooks.

2 large eggs
1 (12-ounce) can evaporated milk
1 teaspoon dry mustard
Salt and pepper
¼ teaspoon hot sauce
8 ounces (2 cups) elbow macaroni
4 tablespoons unsalted butter
12 ounces sharp cheddar, American, or Monterey Jack cheese, shredded (3 cups)

1. Whisk eggs, 1 cup evaporated milk, mustard, ½ teaspoon salt, ¼ teaspoon pepper, and hot sauce together in bowl.

2. Meanwhile, bring 2 quarts water to boil in Dutch oven. Add pasta and 1½ teaspoons salt and cook, stirring often, until al dente. Drain pasta and return it to pot.

3. Add butter to pasta and cook over low heat, stirring constantly, until melted. Add egg mixture and 2 cups shredded cheese and cook, stirring constantly, until well combined and cheese starts to melt, 1 to 2 minutes. Gradually add remaining evaporated milk and remaining cheese, stirring constantly, until mixture is hot and creamy, about 5 minutes. Remove from heat and serve.

VARIATIONS

Stovetop Macaroni and Cheese with Tomato

Stir 1 (14.5-ounce) can drained diced tomatoes into pasta after all evaporated milk and cheese have been added.

Stovetop Macaroni and Cheese with Carrots and Peas

Before cooking pasta, cook 2 carrots, peeled and cut into ½-inch pieces, in boiling water until tender, about 5 minutes; transfer to paper towel–lined plate. Stir cooked carrots and ½ cup thawed frozen peas into pasta after all evaporated milk and cheese have been added.

Stovetop Macaroni and Cheese with Broccoli and Ham

Before cooking pasta, cook 1½ cups bite-size broccoli florets in boiling water until crisp-tender, about 3 minutes; transfer to paper towel–lined plate. Stir cooked broccoli and 3 ounces diced deli ham into pasta after all evaporated milk and cheese have been added.

Eggs and evaporated milk help to make our stovetop mac and cheese thick and creamy.

Spicy Macaroni and Cheese with Chipotle

Stir 1 tablespoon minced canned chipotle chile in adobo sauce and ¼ cup canned chopped green chiles into pasta after all evaporated milk and cheese have been added.

Pasta with Garlicky Tuscan Chicken

SERVES 4 TO 6   **TOTAL TIME** 1 HOUR

✓ **WHY THIS RECIPE WORKS:** Traditionally, Tuscan chicken combines mild, tender chicken with lots of garlic and lemon to create an intensely flavored dish. We decided to add penne to the mix for an easy weeknight supper. We started by coating boneless, skinless chicken breasts with flour, then we pan-fried them to golden perfection before setting them aside to build the garlic sauce. To infuse the sauce with intense garlic flavor that wasn't harsh, we sliced a whopping 12 cloves thin and sautéed them over moderate heat for a few minutes. This slow-and-low approach mellowed the garlic's harshness and drew out its sweet, nutty notes. Adding sliced shallot to the mix enhanced the overall sweetness and provided further insulation against burnt garlic. Red pepper flakes, white wine, and chicken broth served as the base of the sauce, and a hefty amount of peppery arugula added another flavor dimension and color.

3	(6- to 8-ounce) boneless, skinless chicken breasts, trimmed
	Salt and pepper
½	cup plus 1 tablespoon all-purpose flour
3	tablespoons extra-virgin olive oil
12	garlic cloves, sliced thin
3	shallots, sliced thin
	Pinch red pepper flakes
¾	cup dry white wine
3	cups chicken broth
1	pound penne
5	ounces (5 cups) baby arugula
1½	ounces Parmesan cheese, grated (¾ cup), plus extra for serving
1	tablespoon lemon juice

1. Pat chicken dry with paper towels and season with salt and pepper. Place ½ cup flour in shallow dish. Working with 1 piece of chicken at a time, dredge in flour, shaking off excess.

2. Heat 2 tablespoons oil in 12-inch skillet over medium-high heat until just smoking. Carefully lay chicken in skillet and cook until well browned on first side, 6 to 8 minutes. Flip chicken over, reduce heat to medium, and continue to cook until chicken registers 160 degrees, 6 to 8 minutes longer; transfer to plate and tent with aluminum foil.

3. Add remaining 1 tablespoon oil, garlic, and shallots to now-empty skillet and cook over medium-low heat until softened and beginning to brown, about 3 minutes. Stir in pepper flakes and remaining 1 tablespoon flour and cook for 30 seconds. Whisk in wine, then broth, until smooth. Increase heat to medium-high, bring to simmer, and cook until sauce is slightly thickened and measures 2½ cups, about 15 minutes; transfer to liquid measuring cup and cover to keep warm.

4. Meanwhile, bring 4 quarts water to boil in large pot. Add pasta and 1 tablespoon salt and cook, stirring often, until al dente. Reserve ½ cup cooking water, then drain pasta and return it to pot. Add 2 cups sauce, arugula, Parmesan, and lemon juice and toss until arugula is slightly wilted. Add reserved cooking water as needed to adjust consistency and season with salt and pepper to taste.

5. Slice chicken thinly on bias. Portion pasta into individual bowls, top with chicken, and drizzle with remaining ½ cup sauce. Serve with extra Parmesan.

Flavorful pestos can be made with lots of different ingredients—from parsley and arugula to sun-dried tomatoes, cherry tomatoes, roasted red peppers, and more. Regardless of the type, a good pesto has two basic requirements: You should use a high-quality extra-virgin olive oil (because its flavor will really shine through), and you should toast the garlic (to help tame its fiery, raw flavor). Note that the flavor and texture of these pestos varies quite a bit which means that the amount you need to adequately coat your pasta will vary. All the recipes here provide enough pesto to sauce at least 1 pound of pasta.

TO MAKE PESTO: Process all ingredients except oil and cheese in food processor until smooth, scraping down bowl as needed. With processor running, slowly add oil until incorporated. Transfer pesto to bowl, stir in cheese(s), and season with salt and pepper to taste. When tossing pesto with cooked pasta, add some of pasta cooking water as needed (up to ½ cup) to loosen consistency of pesto.

TO MAKE AHEAD: Pesto can be refrigerated for up to 3 days or frozen for up to 3 months. To prevent browning, press plastic wrap flush to surface or top with thin layer of olive oil.

Classic Basil Pesto

MAKES ¾ CUP

TOTAL TIME 15 MINUTES `FAST`

Pounding the basil briefly before processing the pesto helps bring out its flavorful oils. To bruise the basil, place it in a large zipper-lock bag and pound lightly with a rolling pin or meat pounder. The optional parsley helps give the pesto a vibrant green hue. For sharper flavor, substitute Pecorino Romano for the Parmesan.

- **2 cups fresh basil leaves, lightly bruised**
- **2 tablespoons fresh parsley leaves (optional)**
- **¼ cup pine nuts, toasted**
- **3 garlic cloves, toasted and minced**
- **7 tablespoons extra-virgin olive oil**
- **¼ cup grated Parmesan cheese**

Parsley and Toasted Nut Pesto

MAKES 1½ CUPS

TOTAL TIME 20 MINUTES `FAST`

Though basil is the go-to herb when making a green pesto, parsley makes a surprisingly delicious substitute. To stand up to the grassy, heartier flavor of parsley, we found it necessary to ramp up the nut flavor. Pecans have a more pronounced flavor than pine nuts. You can substitute walnuts, blanched almonds, skinned hazelnuts, or any combination thereof for the pecans.

- **1 cup pecans, toasted**
- **¼ cup fresh parsley leaves**
- **3 garlic cloves, toasted and minced**
- **7 tablespoons extra-virgin olive oil**
- **¼ cup grated Parmesan cheese**

Roasted Red Pepper Pesto

MAKES 1½ CUPS

TOTAL TIME 20 MINUTES `FAST`

This pesto tastes great when made with homemade roasted red peppers but jarred roasted red peppers work fine in this recipe. The pesto made with jarred peppers will have a more acidic flavor, so be sure to rinse and dry the jarred peppers well before using.

- **2 roasted red bell peppers, peeled and chopped (1 cup)**
- **¼ cup fresh parsley leaves**
- **3 garlic cloves, toasted and minced**
- **1 shallot, chopped**
- **1 tablespoon fresh thyme leaves**
- **½ cup extra-virgin olive oil**
- **¼ cup grated Parmesan cheese**

Tomato and Almond Pesto

MAKES 1½ CUPS

TOTAL TIME 20 MINUTES `FAST`

This is a traditional Sicilian pesto known as *Trapanese*. A single pepperoncini adds a nice, spicy kick; however, you can substitute ½ teaspoon red wine vinegar and ¼ teaspoon red pepper flakes for the pepperoncini if necessary.

- **12 ounces cherry or grape tomatoes**
- **½ cup fresh basil leaves**
- **¼ cup slivered almonds, toasted**
- **1 small pepperoncini (hot pepper in vinegar), stemmed, seeded, and minced**
- **1 garlic clove, toasted and minced Pinch red pepper flakes (optional)**
- **⅓ cup extra-virgin olive oil**
- **1 ounce Parmesan cheese, grated (½ cup)**

Sun-Dried Tomato Pesto

MAKES 1½ CUPS

TOTAL TIME 15 MINUTES **FAST**

We prefer sun-dried tomatoes packed in oil over those that are packaged dried.

- 1 cup oil-packed sun-dried tomatoes, patted dry and chopped
- ¼ cup walnuts, toasted
- 3 garlic cloves, toasted and minced
- ½ cup extra-virgin olive oil
- 1 ounce Parmesan cheese, grated (½ cup)

Parsley, Arugula, and Ricotta Pesto

MAKES 1½ CUPS

TOTAL TIME 15 MINUTES **FAST**

Part-skim ricotta can be substituted here; do not use nonfat ricotta or the pesto will be dry and gummy.

- 1 cup fresh parsley leaves
- 1 cup baby arugula
- ¼ cup pine nuts, toasted
- 3 garlic cloves, toasted and minced
- 7 tablespoons extra-virgin olive oil
- ⅓ cup whole-milk ricotta cheese
- 2 tablespoons grated Parmesan cheese

Kale and Sunflower Seed Pesto

MAKES 1½ CUPS

TOTAL TIME 20 MINUTES **FAST**

Kale, with its earthy, slightly bitter flavor, and sunflower seeds, with their strong flavor, are well matched here.

- 2 cups packed chopped kale leaves
- 1 cup fresh basil leaves
- ½ cup raw sunflower seeds, toasted
- 2 garlic cloves, toasted and minced
- 1 teaspoon red pepper flakes (optional)
- ½ cup extra-virgin olive oil
- 1½ ounces Parmesan cheese, grated (¾ cup)

Green Olive and Orange Pesto

MAKES 1½ CUPS

TOTAL TIME 20 MINUTES **FAST**

Using high-quality green olives is crucial to the success of this pesto. Look for fresh green olives (packed in brine) in the supermarket's refrigerated section or at the salad bar.

- 1½ cups packed fresh parsley leaves
- 1½ ounces Parmesan cheese, grated (¾ cup)
- ½ cup pitted green olives
- ½ cup slivered almonds, toasted
- 2 garlic cloves, toasted and minced
- ½ teaspoon grated orange zest plus 2 tablespoons juice
- ½ cup extra-virgin olive oil

Toasting Garlic

Toast unpeeled cloves in small skillet over medium heat, shaking pan occasionally, until color of cloves deepens slightly, about 7 minutes. Let toasted garlic cool slightly, then peel and mince.

MAKING THE MOST OF PESTO

Sure, pesto tastes terrific on pasta, but don't sell it short; its robust, concentrated flavor can jazz up just about anything, from sandwiches and omelets to soups and salads. Because a few tablespoons can transform a dish from boring to best in show, it's always nice to have some pesto on hand. Here are some of our favorite ways to use pesto.

- Stir pesto into mashed potatoes for a simple twist on this classic comfort food.
- Dollop pesto onto soups for a heady, herbal aroma.
- Brush pesto on fish or chicken after roasting or grilling for a quick and flavorful glaze.
- Toss warm steamed veggies with pesto for an interesting riff on the weeknight side dish.
- Use pesto in place of mayonnaise or mustard on deli sandwiches.

- Thin pesto with lemon juice to make a quick vinaigrette.
- Drizzle pesto over slices of pizza or calzones.
- Use pesto to flavor fresh cheeses such as mozzarella or ricotta.
- Use a few tablespoons of pesto as an easy marinade for chicken or fish.
- Stir a couple of tablespoons of pesto into equal parts mayonnaise and sour cream for a quick dipping sauce. Serve with veggies or chips.

Buying Canned Tomatoes

Since canned tomatoes are processed at the height of fresh-ness, they deliver more flavor than off-season fresh tomatoes. But with all the options lining supermarket shelves, it's not always clear what you should buy. We tested a variety of canned tomato products to determine the best uses for each and our favorite brands (see page 819).

WHOLE TOMATOES: Whole tomatoes are peeled tomatoes packed in their own juice or puree. They are best when fresh tomato flavor is a must. Whole tomatoes are quite soft and break down quickly when cooked. We found that those packed in juice had a livelier, fresher flavor than those packed in puree.

DICED TOMATOES: Diced tomatoes are peeled, machine-diced, and packed in their own juice or puree. Many brands contain calcium chloride, a firming agent that helps the chunks maintain their shape. Diced tomatoes are best for rustic tomato sauces with a chunky texture, and in long-cooked stews and soups where you want the tomatoes to hold their shape. We favor diced tomatoes packed in juice because they have a fresher flavor than those packed in puree.

CRUSHED TOMATOES: Crushed tomatoes are whole tomatoes ground very finely, then enriched with tomato puree. They work well in smoother sauces, and their thicker consistency makes them ideal when you want to make a sauce quickly. You can also crush your own canned diced tomatoes in a food processor.

TOMATO PUREE: Tomato puree is made from cooked tomatoes that have been strained to remove their seeds and skins. Tomato puree works well in long-simmered, smooth, thick sauces with a deep, hearty flavor.

TOMATO PASTE: Tomato paste is tomato puree that has been cooked to remove almost all moisture. Because it's naturally full of glutamates, tomato paste brings out subtle depths and savory notes. We use it in a variety of recipes, including both long-simmered sauces and quicker-cooking dishes, to lend a deeper, well-rounded tomato flavor and color.

Pasta with Chicken Cacciatore Sauce

SERVES 4 TO 6   **TOTAL TIME** 1 HOUR

WHY THIS RECIPE WORKS: This dish simplifies an Italian favorite: chicken cacciatore, which is rustic braised chicken simmered in a rich tomato-mushroom sauce and served over pasta. For this easier version, we turned to quick-cooking boneless, skinless chicken breasts instead of the usual chicken thighs (which require a fair amount of cooking time to turn tender), and we sliced them thinly. After sautéing them in a skillet, we set them aside and built a rich-tasting tomato sauce. Fresh mushrooms plus dried porcini added the classic mushroomy depth to the sauce. Woodsy herbs provide complexity in traditional recipes, but we found a shortcut by using herbes de Provence. After building the sauce and letting it simmer for 15 minutes, we stirred in the browned chicken, letting the flavors of the chicken and the sauce combine before adding Parmesan and parsley and tossing it all together with freshly cooked pasta for a satisfying one-dish meal. For more information on slicing chicken thinly, see page 138.

- 1 **pound boneless, skinless chicken breasts, trimmed and sliced thin**
   Salt and pepper
- 3 **tablespoons extra-virgin olive oil**
- 1 **onion, chopped fine**
- 10 **ounces white mushrooms, trimmed and quartered**
- ½ **ounce dried porcini mushrooms, rinsed and minced**
- 4 **garlic cloves, minced**
- ¾ **teaspoon herbes de Provence**
- 2 **teaspoons all-purpose flour**
- ½ **cup dry red wine**
- 1 **cup chicken broth**
- 1 **(28-ounce) can diced tomatoes**
- ½ **teaspoon sugar**
- 1 **pound penne**
- 2 **ounces Parmesan cheese, grated (1 cup), plus extra for serving**
- ¼ **cup minced fresh parsley**

1. Pat chicken dry with paper towels and season with salt and pepper. Heat 1 tablespoon oil in 12-inch nonstick skillet over high heat until just smoking. Add chicken in single layer and cook, without stirring, until beginning to brown, about 1 minute. Stir chicken and continue to cook until nearly cooked through, about 2 minutes; transfer to bowl and cover to keep warm.

2. Add onion, white mushrooms, porcini, remaining 2 tablespoons oil, and ½ teaspoon salt to now-empty skillet. Cover and cook over medium heat until mushrooms have released their liquid, about 5 minutes. Uncover and continue to cook until mushrooms are dry and browned, about 5 minutes.

3. Stir in garlic and herbes de Provence and cook until fragrant, about 30 seconds. Stir in flour and cook for 1 minute. Whisk in wine, then broth, until smooth. Stir in tomatoes and sugar, bring to simmer, and cook until sauce is thick, about 15 minutes.

4. Meanwhile, bring 4 quarts water to boil in large pot. Add pasta and 1 tablespoon salt and cook, stirring often, until al dente. Reserve ½ cup cooking water, then drain pasta and return it to pot.

5. Add chicken and any accumulated juices to sauce, return to simmer, and cook until chicken is cooked through, about 1 minute. Add chicken-sauce mixture, Parmesan, and parsley to pasta and toss to combine. Season with salt and pepper to taste and add reserved cooking water as needed to adjust consistency. Serve with extra Parmesan.

Shrimp Fra Diavolo with Linguine

SERVES 4 TO 6   **TOTAL TIME** 45 MINUTES   **FAST**

WHY THIS RECIPE WORKS: Most shrimp fra diavolo recipes lack depth of flavor, with the star ingredients, shrimp and garlic, contributing little to an acidic, unbalanced tomato sauce. We wanted a shrimp fra diavolo with a seriously garlicky, spicy tomato sauce studded with sweet, firm shrimp. Adding raw shrimp to the finished sauce doesn't infuse the shrimp with any flavor whatsoever. We began by searing the shrimp briefly to help them caramelize and enrich their sweetness, adding red pepper flakes, which took on a toasty, earthy note. Then we flambéed the shrimp with cognac—the combined forces of cognac and flame brought out the shrimp's sweet, tender notes and imbued our fra diavolo with the cognac's richness and complexity. We sautéed the garlic slowly for mellow, nutty flavor, and reserved some raw garlic for a last-minute punch of heat and spice. Simmered diced tomatoes and some white wine (balanced by a bit of sugar) completed our perfect fra diavolo in less than an hour. Before flambéing, roll up long sleeves, tie back long hair, and turn off the exhaust fan and lit burners. This dish is fairly spicy; to make it milder, reduce the amount of pepper flakes.

Searing the shrimp and flambéing it in cognac brings out its natural sweetness and adds depth of flavor to fra diavolo.

1 pound medium-large shrimp (31 to 40 per pound), peeled and deveined
6 tablespoons extra-virgin olive oil
  Salt
1 teaspoon red pepper flakes
¼ cup cognac or brandy
12 garlic cloves, minced
1 (28-ounce) can diced tomatoes, drained
1 cup dry white wine
½ teaspoon sugar
1 pound linguine
¼ cup minced fresh parsley

1. Toss shrimp with 1 tablespoon oil, ¾ teaspoon salt, and ½ teaspoon pepper flakes in bowl. Heat 1 tablespoon oil in 12-inch skillet over high heat until just smoking. Add shrimp mixture in even layer and cook, without stirring, until bottoms of shrimp turn spotty brown, about 30 seconds. Off heat, flip shrimp, add cognac, and let warm through, about 5 seconds. Wave lit match over pan until cognac ignites, then shake pan to distribute flames. When flames subside, transfer shrimp mixture to clean bowl.

2. Let now-empty skillet cool slightly, about 3 minutes. Add 3 tablespoons oil and three-quarters of garlic to cooled skillet and cook over low heat, stirring constantly, until garlic foams and is sticky and straw-colored, about 10 minutes. Stir in tomatoes, wine, sugar, ¾ teaspoon salt, and remaining ½ teaspoon pepper flakes. Increase heat to medium-high and simmer until thickened, about 8 minutes.

3. Meanwhile, bring 4 quarts water to boil in large pot. Add pasta and 1 tablespoon salt and cook, stirring often, until al dente. Reserve ½ cup cooking water, then drain pasta and return it to pot.

4. Stir shrimp and any accumulated juices, remaining garlic, and parsley into sauce and bring to quick simmer to heat shrimp through, about 1 minute. Off heat, stir in remaining 1 tablespoon oil. Add several large spoonfuls of sauce (without shrimp) to pasta and toss to combine. Season with salt to taste and add reserved cooking water as needed to adjust consistency. Divide pasta among individual bowls. Top each bowl with remaining sauce and shrimp and serve.

Flambéing Shrimp

Off heat, add cognac and let warm through, about 5 seconds. Wave lit match over pan until cognac ignites, then gently shake pan back and forth until flames subside and finally extinguish themselves.

Spaghetti with Lemon, Basil, and Shrimp

SERVES 4 TO 6   **TOTAL TIME** 30 MINUTES   **FAST**

✔ **WHY THIS RECIPE WORKS:** For a recipe with a handful of ingredients, pasta with shellfish is awfully hard to get right. We love the combination of tender pasta and succulent shrimp or bite-size bay scallops, but all too often the shellfish is overcooked and tough and the pasta is boring and flavorless. For an extraordinary but simple spaghetti dinner, we created a creamy vinaigrette packed with bright, lemony flavor and tossed it with tender shrimp, hot pasta, butter, and chopped basil. Grated Parmesan ensured that our vinaigrette was perfectly clingy and hung on to the pasta and shellfish. Because this recipe is so simple, it is important to use high-quality extra-virgin olive oil, fresh-squeezed lemon juice, and fresh basil.

½   **cup extra-virgin olive oil**
2   **teaspoons grated lemon zest plus ⅓ cup juice (2 lemons)**
1   **small garlic clove, minced to a paste**
    Salt and pepper
2   **ounces Parmesan cheese, grated (1 cup)**
1   **pound small shrimp (51 to 60 per pound), peeled, deveined, and tails removed**
4   **tablespoons unsalted butter, softened**
1   **pound spaghetti**
¼   **cup chopped fresh basil**

1. Whisk olive oil, lemon zest and juice, garlic, and ½ teaspoon salt together in bowl, then stir in Parmesan until thick and creamy.

2. Pat shrimp dry with paper towels and season with salt and pepper. Melt 2 tablespoons butter in 12-inch nonstick skillet over medium heat. Add shrimp in single layer and cook until shrimp are curled and pink on both sides, about 2 minutes; transfer to separate bowl and cover.

3. Meanwhile, bring 4 quarts water to boil in large pot. Add pasta and 1 tablespoon salt and cook, stirring often, until al dente. Reserve ½ cup cooking water, then drain pasta and return it to pot. Add olive oil mixture, shrimp and any accumulated juices, remaining 2 tablespoons butter, and basil and toss to combine. Season with salt and pepper to taste and add reserved cooking water as needed to adjust consistency. Serve.

VARIATION

Spaghetti with Lemon, Basil, and Bay Scallops
Substitute 1 pound small bay scallops for shrimp; cook as directed in step 2, increasing cooking time to 3 minutes.

Mincing Garlic to a Paste

Mince garlic, then sprinkle with pinch salt. Scrape side of chef's knife blade across garlic, mashing it into cutting board to make sticky garlic paste.

For a simple one-dish meal, we cook mussels in the same pot as the pasta and sauce.

Mussels Marinara with Spaghetti

SERVES 4 TO 6   **TOTAL TIME** 1 HOUR

✔ **WHY THIS RECIPE WORKS:** The hardest part about making mussels marinara is the timing. Nailing perfectly cooked mussels and al dente pasta simultaneously can be tricky—and the mussel flavor often gets lost. Our simple solution was to cook everything together in the same pot and stagger the ingredients. This simplified the timing and ensured that all of the mussel flavor stayed right in the pot. To start, we built a tomato sauce with just the right texture by chopping canned whole tomatoes, which we simmered with some basic aromatics. We also added an anchovy and some bottled clam juice to reinforce the salty ocean flavor of the mussels. We cooked the pasta right in the sauce, added the mussels, and continued to cook the dish until they opened. More olive oil and some parsley finished off this perfectly cooked one-dish meal. When adding the spaghetti in step 3, stir gently to avoid breaking the noodles until they soften enough to be stirred more easily. If necessary, add hot water, 1 tablespoon at a time, to adjust the consistency of the sauce before serving. If desired, drizzle with additional extra-virgin olive oil before serving.

2 (28-ounce) cans whole peeled tomatoes
3 tablespoons extra-virgin olive oil
1 onion, chopped fine
6 garlic cloves, minced
1 anchovy fillet, rinsed and minced
½ teaspoon red pepper flakes
2 cups water
1 (8-ounce) bottle clam juice
1 pound spaghetti
2 pounds mussels, scrubbed and debearded
¼ cup minced fresh parsley
   Salt and pepper

1. Pulse tomatoes and their juice, 1 can at a time, in food processor until coarsely chopped and no large pieces remain, 6 to 8 pulses; transfer to bowl.

2. Heat 2 tablespoons oil in Dutch oven over medium-high heat until shimmering. Add onion and cook until softened, about 3 minutes. Stir in garlic, anchovy, and pepper flakes and cook until fragrant, about 30 seconds. Stir in processed tomatoes and simmer gently until tomatoes no longer taste raw, about 10 minutes.

3. Stir in water, clam juice, and pasta. Cover, increase heat to medium-high, and cook at vigorous simmer, stirring often, until pasta is nearly tender, about 12 minutes. Stir in mussels, cover, and continue to simmer vigorously until pasta is tender and mussels have opened, about 2 minutes.

4. Uncover, reduce heat to low, and stir in remaining 1 tablespoon oil and parsley. Cook, tossing pasta gently, until well coated with sauce, about 1 minute. Season with salt and pepper to taste and serve.

Campanelle with Sautéed Mushrooms and Thyme

SERVES 4 TO 6   **TOTAL TIME** 45 MINUTES   **FAST**

✔ **WHY THIS RECIPE WORKS:** For an effortless pasta and mushroom dish with bold, earthy flavor, we doubled up on the mushrooms—cremini for their rich, meaty nature, and shiitakes for their hearty flavor and chewy texture—and simply sautéed them with butter and oil. Because shiitakes contain more moisture, we gave them a head start in the pan. Minced thyme deepened the woodsy notes of the dish. Once the mushrooms had browned, we set them aside and built our sauce, scraping up the browned bits left in the pan to ensure that none of that meaty mushroom flavor went to waste. Chicken broth provided the backbone of the sauce, while heavy cream added a silky richness.

Two kinds of mushrooms—shiitake and cremini—are combined in this earthy pasta dish.

2 tablespoons unsalted butter

2 tablespoons extra-virgin olive oil

3 large shallots, minced

  Salt and pepper

3 garlic cloves, minced

10 ounces shiitake mushrooms, stemmed and sliced ¼ inch thick

10 ounces cremini mushrooms, trimmed and sliced ¼ inch thick

4 teaspoons minced fresh thyme

1¼ cups chicken broth or vegetable broth

½ cup heavy cream

1 tablespoon lemon juice

1 pound campanelle

2 ounces Parmesan cheese, grated (1 cup)

2 tablespoons minced fresh parsley

1. Heat butter and oil in 12-inch skillet over medium heat until butter has melted. Add shallots and ½ teaspoon salt and cook until softened, about 4 minutes. Stir in garlic and cook until fragrant, about 30 seconds. Stir in shiitakes, increase heat to medium-high, and cook for 2 minutes. Stir in cremini mushrooms and cook, stirring occasionally, until golden brown, about 8 minutes. Stir in thyme and cook 30 seconds. Transfer mixture to bowl and cover to keep warm.

2. Add broth to now-empty skillet and bring to boil over high heat, scraping up any browned bits. Off heat, stir in cream and lemon juice. Season with salt and pepper to taste. (Sauce and mushrooms can be refrigerated separately for up to 2 days.)

3. Meanwhile, bring 4 quarts water to boil in large pot. Add pasta and 1 tablespoon salt and cook, stirring often, until al dente. Reserve ½ cup cooking water, then drain pasta and return it to pot. Add mushroom mixture, cream sauce, Parmesan, and parsley and cook over medium heat, tossing to combine, until pasta absorbs some sauce, 1 to 2 minutes. Season with salt and pepper to taste and add reserved cooking water as needed to adjust consistency. Serve.

Pasta with Roasted Cauliflower, Garlic, and Walnuts

SERVES 4 TO 6   **TOTAL TIME** 1 HOUR

✔ **WHY THIS RECIPE WORKS:** Roasting transforms mild-mannered cauliflower into an intensely flavored, sweet, nutty foil for pasta. To achieve a golden exterior, we sliced the cauliflower into wedges for maximum surface area while leaving the core and florets intact. Tossing the cauliflower with sugar jump-started the browning; preheating the baking sheet also helped. Cream-based sauces muted the nutty cauliflower flavor, and pestos overwhelmed it, so we focused on a simple lemony vinaigrette with roasted garlic. For more information on squeezing roasted garlic from their skins, see page 56. Don't forget to reserve some of the pasta cooking water before draining the pasta; the water is used to loosen the texture of the sauce when tossed with the pasta.

2 garlic heads, top quarter cut off to expose garlic cloves

6 tablespoons plus 1 teaspoon extra-virgin olive oil

1 head cauliflower (2 pounds), trimmed and cut into 8 wedges

  Salt and pepper

¼ teaspoon sugar

2 tablespoons lemon juice, plus extra as needed

¼ teaspoon red pepper flakes

1 pound campanelle

1 ounce Parmesan cheese, grated (½ cup), plus extra for serving

1 tablespoon minced fresh parsley

¼ cup walnuts, toasted and chopped coarse

1. Adjust oven rack to middle position, place large rimmed baking sheet on rack, and heat oven to 500 degrees. Place garlic heads, cut side up, in center of 12-inch square of aluminum foil. Drizzle each with ½ teaspoon oil and wrap securely. Place packet on oven rack next to baking sheet and roast until garlic is very tender, about 40 minutes.

2. Meanwhile, toss cauliflower with 2 tablespoons oil, 1 teaspoon salt, ¼ teaspoon pepper, and sugar in bowl. Remove baking sheet from oven. Carefully lay cauliflower, either cut side down, on hot baking sheet in even layer. Roast cauliflower until well browned and tender, 20 to 25 minutes.

3. Transfer roasted cauliflower to cutting board, let cool slightly, then cut into ½-inch pieces. Transfer garlic packet to cutting board, let cool for 10 minutes, then unwrap and squeeze to remove garlic cloves from skins. Mash garlic cloves smooth with fork in bowl, then stir in lemon juice and pepper flakes and slowly whisk in remaining ¼ cup oil.

4. Bring 4 quarts water to boil in large pot. Add pasta and 1 tablespoon salt and cook, stirring often, until al dente. Reserve 1 cup cooking water, then drain pasta and return it to pot. Add chopped cauliflower, garlic sauce, Parmesan, parsley, and ¼ cup reserved cooking water and toss to combine. Season with salt, pepper, and extra lemon juice to taste and add reserved cooking water as needed to adjust consistency. Sprinkle individual portions with walnuts and serve with extra Parmesan.

Cutting Cauliflower into Wedges

1. Remove outer leaves from cauliflower and cut stalk flush with bottom. Place head upside down and cut cauliflower crown in half through stalk.

2. Cut each half of crown in half to make 4 wedges, and cut each of those in half again to make 8 equal wedges.

VARIATION

Pasta with Roasted Broccoli, Garlic, and Almonds

Substitute 1½ pounds broccoli for cauliflower, Manchego cheese for Parmesan, and toasted slivered almonds for walnuts. Cut broccoli crowns from large stems. Peel stems and cut into 2- to 3-inch lengths about ½ inch thick. Cut smaller crowns (3 to 4 inches in diameter) into 4 wedges, and cut larger crowns (4 to 5 inches in diameter) into 6 wedges. Roast broccoli on preheated baking sheet as directed until well browned and tender, 10 to 15 minutes.

Farfalle with Artichokes, Pancetta, and Spinach

SERVES 4 TO 6   **TOTAL TIME** 45 MINUTES   **FAST**

✔ **WHY THIS RECIPE WORKS:** Artichokes boast a sweet, earthy, nutty flavor that pairs incredibly well with pasta, but fresh artichokes can be a pain to prep and cook. Enter frozen artichoke hearts—they simply need to be thawed and patted dry to remove excess moisture prior to cooking. For a bright, creamy sauce, shallots, garlic, lemon zest and lemon juice, plus cream and white wine, did the trick. Pancetta, cooked at the outset and then set aside, provided crispy bites, and fresh tarragon contributed a hint of anise. This dish cried out for something green, so we tossed in a hefty dose of baby spinach at the end of cooking. Farfalle, with its flat, wide surface, made the perfect cradle for the creamy sauce and wilted spinach. Though we prefer pancetta here, you can substitute prosciutto or bacon.

2 tablespoons unsalted butter
6 ounces thinly sliced pancetta, cut into
   ¼-inch-wide strips
2 shallots, minced
18 ounces frozen artichoke hearts, thawed and
   patted dry
3 garlic cloves, minced
2 teaspoons all-purpose flour
1 cup dry white wine
1 cup chicken broth
1 cup heavy cream
1 teaspoon grated lemon zest plus 1 tablespoon juice
2 tablespoons minced fresh tarragon
1 pound farfalle
   Salt and pepper
1 ounce Parmesan cheese, grated (½ cup)
4 ounces (4 cups) baby spinach

1. Cook 1 tablespoon butter and pancetta in 12-inch skillet over medium heat until pancetta is well browned and crisp, about 8 minutes; transfer to paper towel–lined plate.

2. Add remaining 1 tablespoon butter and shallots to fat left in pan and cook over medium heat until shallots are softened, about 3 minutes. Stir in artichoke hearts and cook until tender and beginning to brown, about 6 minutes. Stir in garlic and cook until fragrant, about 30 seconds. Stir in flour and cook for 1 minute. Stir in wine, then broth and cream, until smooth. Bring to simmer and cook until sauce is slightly thickened, 15 to 20 minutes. Off heat, stir in lemon zest and juice and tarragon.

3. Meanwhile, bring 4 quarts water to boil in large pot. Add pasta and 1 tablespoon salt and cook, stirring often, until al dente. Reserve ½ cup cooking water, then drain pasta and return it to pot. Add sauce, pancetta, Parmesan, and spinach, and toss until spinach is slightly wilted. Season with salt and pepper to taste and add reserved cooking water as needed to adjust consistency. Serve.

Skillet Pasta with Fresh Tomato Sauce

SERVES 4   TOTAL TIME 50 MINUTES

✓ WHY THIS RECIPE WORKS: For an effortless but delicious and bright fresh tomato sauce, we minimized tomato prep and cooked the pasta right in the sauce. We simply cored and chopped our tomatoes, then simmered them briefly, just until they started to break down and exude their juice. With the addition of a few cups of water, there was enough liquid in the pan to cook the pasta; by covering the pan, we ensured that the sauce didn't dry out. Starch released from the pasta helped thicken the sauce, making it nicely clingy. Although not traditional for tomato sauce, white wine enhanced the sauce's bright acidity. The curves of bell-shaped campanelle cradled the sauce perfectly and gave this rustic dish an elegant touch. Other pasta shapes can be substituted for the campanelle; however, their cup measurements may vary (see page 395).

2 tablespoons extra-virgin olive oil
1 onion, chopped fine
4 garlic cloves, minced
1 tablespoon tomato paste
2 pounds tomatoes, cored and cut into ½-inch pieces
  Salt and pepper
½ cup dry white wine

3½ cups water, plus extra as needed
12 ounces (3¾ cups) campanelle
¼ cup chopped fresh basil
  Grated Parmesan cheese

1. Heat oil in 12-inch nonstick skillet over medium heat until shimmering. Add onion and cook until softened, 5 to 7 minutes. Stir in garlic and tomato paste and cook until fragrant, about 1 minute. Stir in tomatoes, 1 teaspoon salt, and ½ teaspoon pepper and cook until tomato pieces lose their shape, 5 to 7 minutes. Stir in wine and simmer for 2 minutes.

2. Stir in water and pasta. Cover, increase heat to medium-high, and cook at vigorous simmer, stirring often, until pasta is nearly tender, about 12 minutes.

3. Uncover and continue to simmer, tossing pasta gently, until pasta is tender and sauce has thickened, 3 to 5 minutes; if sauce becomes too thick, add extra water as needed. Off heat, stir in basil and season with salt and pepper to taste. Serve with Parmesan.

Coring and Dicing Fresh Tomatoes

1. Using paring knife, cut out stem and core.

2. Using chef's knife or serrated knife, cut tomato into round slices.

3. Cut slices into strips, then cut strips into dice.

Skillet Penne with Chicken and Broccoli

SERVES 4　　TOTAL TIME 45 MINUTES　**FAST**

✔ **WHY THIS RECIPE WORKS:** To move this multiple-pot recipe to a single skillet, we browned the chicken, then set it aside while we built the sauce. Chicken broth and water, with minced garlic, red pepper flakes, and white wine, formed the base of the sauce and provided liquid to cook the pasta. Leaving the pan uncovered intensified the flavors as the sauce reduced. For bright-green, tender broccoli, we added it to the pan when the pasta was almost ready. Parmesan added creaminess and rich, savory flavor. For more information on slicing chicken thinly, see page 138.

1　**pound boneless, skinless chicken breasts, trimmed and sliced thin**
　　Salt and pepper
¼　**cup extra-virgin olive oil**
1　**onion, chopped fine**
6　**garlic cloves, minced**
¼　**teaspoon red pepper flakes**
¼　**teaspoon dried oregano**
½　**cup dry white wine**
2½　**cups water**
2　**cups chicken broth**
8　**ounces (2½ cups) penne**
8　**ounces broccoli florets, cut into 1-inch pieces**
2　**ounces Parmesan cheese, grated (1 cup), plus extra for serving**

1. Pat chicken dry with paper towels and season with salt and pepper. Heat 1 tablespoon oil in 12-inch nonstick skillet over medium-high heat until just smoking. Add chicken in single layer and cook without stirring for 1 minute. Stir chicken and continue to cook until nearly cooked through, about 2 minutes; transfer to bowl and cover to keep warm.

2. Add onion, 1 tablespoon oil, and ½ teaspoon salt to now-empty skillet and cook over medium heat until onion is softened, 5 to 7 minutes. Stir in garlic, pepper flakes, and oregano and cook until fragrant, about 30 seconds. Stir in wine and simmer until nearly evaporated, 1 to 2 minutes. Stir in water, broth, and pasta. Increase heat to medium-high and cook at vigorous simmer, stirring often, until pasta is nearly tender, about 12 minutes.

3. Stir in broccoli and cook until pasta and broccoli are tender and sauce has thickened, 3 to 5 minutes. Stir in chicken and any accumulated juices and let warm through, about 1 minute. Off heat, stir in remaining 2 tablespoons oil and Parmesan. Season with salt and pepper to taste. Serve with extra Parmesan.

Bachelor Spaghetti with Sausage, Peppers, and Onions

SERVES 4　　TOTAL TIME 45 MINUTES　**FAST**

✔ **WHY THIS RECIPE WORKS:** You won't need to dirty even a knife to make this superstreamlined but surprisingly flavorful spaghetti dinner featuring the classic combination of sausage, peppers, and onions. We kept things simple by starting with frozen chopped onions and frozen sliced bell peppers, and then relying on garlic powder, dried oregano, and red pepper flakes for seasoning. To draw out flavor from the dried herbs and spices, we sautéed them with the sausage and onions, which worked to deepen their flavor. Using canned tomato sauce and simmering everything covered provided rich, intense flavor in short order. For the pasta, we opted for thin spaghetti; we preferred its texture to that of traditional spaghetti for our one-pan pasta cooking method that cooks the pasta right in the sauce. We broke the spaghettini in half so that it would fit in the skillet, ensuring that the pasta cooked evenly. To make this dish even easier, you can use bulk Italian sausage or sausage patties, which can go directly into the skillet, saving the step of removing the sausage from its casings. You can substitute 2 finely chopped onions for the frozen onions, 4 minced garlic cloves for the garlic powder, and 2 thinly sliced red bell peppers for the frozen peppers if desired.

1　**tablespoon extra-virgin olive oil**
2　**cups frozen chopped onions, thawed**
　　Salt and pepper
1　**pound hot or sweet Italian sausage, casings removed**
1　**teaspoon garlic powder**
¼　**teaspoon dried oregano**
¼　**teaspoon red pepper flakes**
3　**cups water**
1　**(15-ounce) can tomato sauce**
2½　**cups (8 ounces) frozen sliced bell peppers**
8　**ounces thin spaghetti or spaghettini, broken in half**
　　Grated Parmesan cheese

1. Heat oil in 12-inch nonstick skillet over medium heat until shimmering. Add onions and ¼ teaspoon salt and cook until onions are softened and golden, about 12 minutes. Stir in sausage, garlic powder, oregano, and pepper flakes. Increase heat to medium-high and cook, breaking up meat with wooden spoon, until sausage is no longer pink, 7 to 10 minutes.

2. Stir in water, tomato sauce, bell peppers, and pasta. Cover and cook at vigorous simmer, stirring often, until pasta is tender, 12 to 15 minutes. Season with salt and pepper to taste. Serve with Parmesan.

We move chili mac to the skillet where the macaroni cooks in beef chili and a thick tomatoey and cheesy sauce.

1 tablespoon vegetable oil
1 onion, chopped fine
1 tablespoon chili powder
1 tablespoon ground cumin
  Salt and pepper
3 garlic cloves, minced
1 tablespoon packed brown sugar
1 pound 90 percent lean ground beef
2 cups water
1 (15-ounce) can tomato sauce
8 ounces (2 cups) elbow macaroni
1 cup frozen corn, thawed
1 (4.5-ounce) can chopped green chiles, drained
2 tablespoons minced fresh cilantro
8 ounces shredded Mexican cheese blend (2 cups)

1. Heat oil in 12-inch nonstick skillet over medium heat until shimmering. Add onion, chili powder, cumin, and ½ teaspoon salt and cook, stirring often, until onion is softened, 5 to 7 minutes. Stir in garlic and brown sugar and cook until fragrant, about 30 seconds. Stir in beef, breaking up meat with wooden spoon, and cook until lightly browned and no longer pink, 3 to 5 minutes.

2. Stir in water, tomato sauce, and macaroni. Cover, increase heat to medium-high, and cook at vigorous simmer, stirring often, until macaroni is nearly tender, 9 to 12 minutes.

3. Off heat, stir in corn, green chiles, cilantro, and 1 cup cheese. Season with salt and pepper to taste. Sprinkle remaining 1 cup cheese over top, cover, and let stand off heat until cheese melts, 2 to 4 minutes. Serve.

Skillet Tex-Mex Chili Mac

SERVES 4   TOTAL TIME 45 MINUTES   FAST

✔ **WHY THIS RECIPE WORKS:** Chili mac is a favorite childhood comfort food whose appeal extends well into adulthood. Many recipes we found were a sorry mixture of canned chili and jarred salsa stirred into packaged macaroni and cheese. Our goal was to create a quick skillet version combining the best spicy beef chili, real cheese, and perfectly cooked macaroni. Starting with the chili, we sautéed onion and garlic with chili powder and cumin before adding some lean ground beef. We added some water and a can of tomato sauce before sprinkling in the macaroni, which thickened and bound the dish together as the pasta cooked. Brown sugar helped tame the acidity of the tomato sauce. At the end, we stirred in green chiles, sweet corn, and cilantro. A shredded Mexican cheese blend helped bind the mixture together and infuse the dish with cheesy flavor. If you can't find shredded Mexican cheese blend, substitute 1 cup each shredded Monterey Jack cheese and shredded cheddar cheese. To make the dish spicier, add ½ teaspoon red pepper flakes along with the chili powder. You can substitute small shells for the macaroni.

Skillet Wagon Wheel Pasta with Turkey Sausage

SERVES 4   TOTAL TIME 45 MINUTES   FAST

✔ **WHY THIS RECIPE WORKS:** For a family-friendly pasta supper that would appeal to diners of all ages, we picked a fun pasta shape—wagon wheels—and added sausage for heartiness. Turkey sausage won us over for its meaty but not overpowering flavor. For the backbone of our sauce, we sautéed an onion and garlic with the sausage; a small amount of flour worked well as the thickener, and adding it before the cooking liquid (a mix of chicken broth and water) and pasta enabled its raw flavor to cook off. We simmered the pasta uncovered so the sauce could reduce and thicken; grated Parmesan gave it a velvety sheen. Baby spinach and peas, stirred in at the end, lightened the dish, while a handful of minced tarragon added a bit of interest for the adults in the crowd. The spinach may look like too much at first, but it wilts down substantially as it cooks. Italian chicken sausage can be substituted for the turkey sausage. Other pasta shapes can be substituted for the wagon wheels; however, their cup measurements may vary (see page 395).

- 1 tablespoon extra-virgin olive oil
- 1 onion, chopped fine
- 8 ounces sweet or hot Italian turkey sausage, casings removed
- 3 garlic cloves, minced
- 2 teaspoons all-purpose flour
- 2½ cups chicken broth
- 2 cups water
- 8 ounces (3 cups) wagon wheel (or rotelle) pasta
- 5 ounces (5 cups) baby spinach
- 2 ounces Parmesan cheese, grated (1 cup), plus extra for serving
- ½ cup frozen peas, thawed
- 1 tablespoon minced fresh tarragon (optional)
  Salt and pepper

1. Heat oil in 12-inch nonstick skillet over medium heat until shimmering. Add onion and cook until softened, about 5 minutes. Stir in sausage and cook, breaking up meat with wooden spoon, until no longer pink, about 4 minutes. Stir in garlic and cook until fragrant, about 30 seconds. Stir in flour and cook for 1 minute.

2. Stir in broth, water, and pasta. Increase heat to medium-high and cook at vigorous simmer, stirring often, until pasta is tender and sauce has thickened, 15 to 18 minutes.

3. Stir in spinach, 1 handful at a time, until wilted, about 2 minutes. Off heat, stir in Parmesan, peas, and tarragon, if using. Season with salt and pepper to taste, and serve with extra Parmesan.

Skillet Ravioli with Meat Sauce

SERVES 4 **TOTAL TIME** 45 MINUTES **FAST**

✔ **WHY THIS RECIPE WORKS:** For an effortless take on the classic duo of cheese ravioli and meat sauce, we cooked fresh ravioli in a quick sauce that we enhanced with a couple of key ingredients. Instead of using ground beef, we turned to meatloaf mix, which is a combination of ground beef, pork, and veal; it didn't need a long simmering time before it was both tender and flavorful. To further bump up the flavor of our sauce, we called upon a powerhouse ingredient, dried porcini mushrooms, for savory depth. For the tomatoes, we liked the

Cooking the ravioli right in the meat sauce ensures that it absorbs meaty flavor.

canned crushed variety—they thickened to the perfect consistency. Because we cooked the ravioli right in the sauce, it absorbed the rich, meaty flavors as it simmered—and there's just one pot to clean. This recipe works with two 9-ounce packages or one 20-ounce package of fresh cheese ravioli. Do not substitute frozen ravioli. If necessary, add hot water, 1 tablespoon at a time, to adjust the consistency of the sauce before serving. If you can't find meatloaf mix, use 8 ounces (85 percent lean) ground beef and 8 ounces ground pork.

- 2 tablespoons extra-virgin olive oil
- 1 onion, chopped fine
- 3 garlic cloves, minced
- ⅛ ounce dried porcini mushrooms, rinsed and minced
- 1 pound meatloaf mix
- 1 (28-ounce) can crushed tomatoes
  Salt and pepper
- 1½ cups water
- 18–20 ounces fresh cheese ravioli
- ¼ cup chopped fresh basil
  Grated Parmesan cheese

1. Heat oil in Dutch oven over medium heat until shimmering. Add onion and cook until softened and lightly browned, 8 to 10 minutes. Stir in garlic and porcini and cook until fragrant, about 1 minute.

2. Stir in meatloaf mix and cook, breaking up meat with wooden spoon, for 1 minute. Stir in tomatoes, ¼ teaspoon salt, and ¼ teaspoon pepper and simmer until sauce is slightly thickened, 8 to 10 minutes.

3. Stir in water and pasta. Increase heat to medium-high and cook at vigorous simmer, stirring often, until pasta is tender and sauce is thickened, 6 to 9 minutes. Off heat, stir in basil and season with salt and pepper to taste. Serve with Parmesan.

Skillet Lasagna

SERVES 4 TO 6 **TOTAL TIME** 1 HOUR

✔ **WHY THIS RECIPE WORKS:** Lasagna is a crowd-pleaser that never goes out of style, but even with no-boil noodles it can be a time-consuming affair. We wondered if it would be possible to get the same flavors and textures in less time in a skillet on the stovetop. Sautéing onion and garlic added depth, while red pepper flakes brought heat. Meatloaf mix contributed deep meaty flavor but kept our shopping list short. We simply sprinkled broken lasagna noodles over the meat, then poured canned diced tomatoes and tomato sauce over them, instilling a slightly chunky and substantial texture and providing liquid in which to cook the noodles. Once the noodles were soft, we stirred in Parmesan, placed dollops of ricotta on top, and covered the pan, allowing the ricotta to heat through but still remain a distinct element. Any brand of curly-edged lasagna noodles will work here. Do not use no-boil lasagna noodles. If the pasta is especially dry and prone to shattering, you may need to add extra water to the skillet while the pasta cooks. If you can't find meatloaf mix, use 8 ounces (85 percent lean) ground beef and 8 ounces ground pork. To make the dish spicy, increase the amount of red pepper flakes to 1 teaspoon.

> 1 **(28-ounce) can diced tomatoes**
> **Water as needed**
> 1 **tablespoon extra-virgin olive oil**
> 1 **onion, chopped fine**
> **Salt and pepper**
> 3 **garlic cloves, minced**
> ⅛ **teaspoon red pepper flakes**
> 1 **pound meatloaf mix**
> 10 **curly-edged lasagna noodles, broken into 2-inch lengths**
> 1 **(8-ounce) can tomato sauce**
> 1 **ounce Parmesan cheese, grated (½ cup), plus extra for serving**
> 8 **ounces whole-milk ricotta cheese (1 cup)**
> ¼ **cup chopped fresh basil**

1. Pour tomatoes with their juice into quart measuring cup and add water until mixture measures 4 cups.

2. Heat oil in 12-inch nonstick skillet over medium heat until shimmering. Add onion and ½ teaspoon salt and cook until onion is softened, about 5 minutes. Stir in garlic and pepper flakes and cook until fragrant, about 15 seconds. Add meatloaf mix and cook, breaking up meat into small pieces with wooden spoon, until no longer pink, about 5 minutes.

Making Skillet Lasagna

1. ADD WATER TO TOMATOES: Pour tomatoes with their juice into quart measuring cup and add water until mixture measures 4 cups.

2. COOK AROMATICS AND MEAT: After sautéing onions, garlic, and pepper flakes, add meatloaf mix to skillet and cook, breaking up meat into small pieces, until no longer pink, about 5 minutes.

3. ADD BROKEN NOODLES AND TOMATOES AND COOK: Sprinkle noodle pieces over meat, then pour diced tomato mixture and tomato sauce over top. Cover and simmer about 20 minutes.

4. ADD RICOTTA OFF HEAT: Before serving, dot heaping tablespoons of ricotta over noodles. Cover skillet and let stand off heat to warm ricotta through, about 5 minutes.

3. Sprinkle noodle pieces evenly over meat. Pour diced tomato mixture and tomato sauce over noodles. Cover and bring to simmer. Reduce heat to medium-low and continue to simmer, stirring occasionally, until noodles are tender, about 20 minutes. (The sauce should still look watery after 15 minutes of cooking. If dry, add up to ¼ cup additional water to loosen sauce.)

4. Off heat, stir in Parmesan. Season with salt and pepper to taste. Dot heaping tablespoons of ricotta over noodles. Cover skillet and let stand off heat for 5 minutes. Sprinkle with basil and serve with extra Parmesan.

VARIATION
Skillet Lasagna with Italian Sausage and Red Bell Pepper

Add 1 large chopped red bell pepper to skillet with onion. Substitute 1 pound hot or sweet Italian sausage, casings removed, for meatloaf mix.

Beef Lo Mein with Broccoli and Bell Pepper

SERVES 4   TOTAL TIME 1 HOUR

✓ **WHY THIS RECIPE WORKS:** For a better-than-takeout beef lo mein, we started with the sauce—oyster sauce, soy sauce, hoisin sauce, sesame oil, and five-spice powder infused our dish with bold, complex flavor. Marinating the meat in a portion of this mixture briefly, prior to stir-frying it, ensured well-seasoned beef. To guarantee crisp-tender broccoli, we steamed it first, then cooked it uncovered so it could brown. Red bell pepper strips simply needed to be sautéed for a couple of minutes until they were the perfect texture. A generous amount of scallions added a sweet, grassy pungency, ginger and garlic contributed some punch, and sweet-and-spicy chili-garlic sauce completed the dish. Fresh Chinese noodles provided the perfect chewy texture, although we found that dried linguine worked well as a substitute.

Our boldly flavored lo mein sauce complements crisp broccoli and tender red bell pepper.

- 3 **tablespoons soy sauce**
- 2 **tablespoons oyster sauce**
- 2 **tablespoons hoisin sauce**
- 1 **tablespoon toasted sesame oil**
- ¼ **teaspoon five-spice powder**
- 1 **pound flank steak, trimmed and sliced thin against grain on bias**
- ½ **cup chicken broth**
- 1 **teaspoon cornstarch**
- 2 **garlic cloves, minced**

- 2 **teaspoons grated fresh ginger**
- 4½ **teaspoons vegetable oil**
- 12 **ounces broccoli florets, cut into 1-inch pieces**
- ⅓ **cup water**
- 1 **red bell pepper, stemmed, seeded, sliced into ½-inch-wide strips, and halved crosswise**
- 2 **bunches scallions, white parts sliced thin, green parts cut into 1-inch pieces**
- 12 **ounces fresh Chinese noodles or 8 ounces dried linguine**
- 1 **tablespoon Asian chili-garlic sauce**

1. Whisk soy sauce, oyster sauce, hoisin sauce, sesame oil, and five-spice powder together in medium bowl. Combine 3 tablespoons sauce mixture and beef in separate bowl, cover, and refrigerate for at least 15 minutes or up to 1 hour. Whisk broth and cornstarch into remaining sauce mixture. In small bowl, combine garlic, ginger, and ½ teaspoon vegetable oil.

2. Heat 1 teaspoon vegetable oil in 12-inch nonstick skillet over high heat until just smoking. Add half of marinated beef in single layer and cook without stirring for 1 minute. Stir beef and continue to cook until browned, about 1 minute;

transfer to large bowl. Repeat with 1 teaspoon vegetable oil and remaining marinated beef; transfer to bowl.

3. Wipe out skillet with paper towels, add 1 teaspoon vegetable oil, and heat over high heat until just smoking. Add broccoli and cook for 30 seconds. Add water, cover, and steam until broccoli is bright green and begins to soften, about 2 minutes. Uncover and continue to cook until water has evaporated and broccoli begins to brown, about 2 minutes; transfer to bowl with beef.

4. Add remaining 1 teaspoon vegetable oil and bell pepper to now-empty skillet and cook over high heat until crisp-tender and spotty brown, about 2 minutes. Add scallions and cook until wilted, 2 to 3 minutes. Clear center of skillet, add garlic-ginger mixture, and cook, mashing mixture into skillet, until fragrant, about 30 seconds; stir into peppers. Stir in beef and broccoli and any accumulated juices. Stir in broth mixture and simmer until sauce has thickened, 1 to 2 minutes. Remove from heat and cover to keep warm.

5. Meanwhile, bring 4 quarts water to boil in large pot. Add noodles and cook, stirring often, until tender. Drain noodles and return them to pot. Add beef mixture and chili-garlic sauce, and toss to combine. Serve.

Pork Lo Mein with Shiitakes and Napa Cabbage

SERVES 4   **TOTAL TIME** 1 HOUR

✓ **WHY THIS RECIPE WORKS:** For a satisfying lo mein starring tender pork, meaty mushrooms, and still-crisp cabbage, we started by searing strips of meat from country-style pork ribs (which we liked for their tenderness and rich flavor) over high heat. We used our meat marinade as a sauce base—adding chicken broth and a spoonful of cornstarch gave it some body. Shiitakes contributed rich, meaty flavor, and strips of napa cabbage added textural intrigue. Fresh Chinese noodles provided the perfect chewy texture, although we found that dried linguine worked well as a substitute.

3   tablespoons soy sauce
2   tablespoons oyster sauce
2   tablespoons hoisin sauce
1   tablespoon toasted sesame oil
¼   teaspoon five-spice powder
1   pound boneless country-style pork ribs, trimmed and sliced crosswise into ⅛-inch-thick pieces
½   cup chicken broth

1   teaspoon cornstarch
2   garlic cloves, minced
2   teaspoons grated fresh ginger
4½   teaspoons vegetable oil
¼   cup Chinese rice wine or dry sherry
8   ounces shiitake mushrooms, stemmed and halved if small or quartered if large
2   bunches scallions, white parts sliced thin, green parts cut into 1-inch pieces
½   small head napa cabbage, cored and sliced crosswise into ½-inch-thick pieces (4 cups)
12   ounces fresh Chinese noodles or 8 ounces dried linguine
1   tablespoon Asian chili-garlic sauce

1. Whisk soy sauce, oyster sauce, hoisin sauce, sesame oil, and five-spice powder together in medium bowl. Combine 3 tablespoons sauce mixture and pork in separate bowl, cover, and refrigerate for at least 15 minutes or up to 1 hour. Whisk broth and cornstarch into remaining sauce mixture. In separate bowl, combine garlic, ginger, and ½ teaspoon vegetable oil.

2. Heat 1 teaspoon vegetable oil in 12-inch nonstick skillet over high heat until just smoking. Add half of marinated pork in single layer and cook without stirring for 1 minute. Stir pork and continue to cook until browned, about 2 minutes. Stir in 2 tablespoons wine and cook until nearly evaporated, 30 to 60 seconds; transfer to large bowl. Repeat with 1 teaspoon vegetable oil, remaining marinated pork, and remaining 2 tablespoons wine; transfer to bowl.

3. Wipe out skillet with paper towels, add 1 teaspoon vegetable oil, and heat over high heat until just smoking. Add mushrooms and cook until browned, 4 to 6 minutes. Stir in scallions and cook until wilted, 2 to 3 minutes; transfer to bowl with pork.

4. Add remaining 1 teaspoon vegetable oil and cabbage to now-empty skillet and cook over high heat until spotty brown, 3 to 5 minutes. Clear center of skillet, add garlic-ginger mixture, and cook, mashing mixture into skillet, until fragrant, about 30 seconds; stir into cabbage. Stir in pork and vegetables and any accumulated juices. Stir in broth mixture and simmer until sauce has thickened, 1 to 2 minutes. Remove from heat and cover to keep warm.

5. Meanwhile, bring 4 quarts water to boil in large pot. Add noodles and cook, stirring often, until tender. Drain noodles and return them to pot. Add pork mixture and chili-garlic sauce, and toss to combine. Serve.

Ramen with Crispy Chicken and Kimchi

SERVES 4　　TOTAL TIME 1 HOUR

✔ WHY THIS RECIPE WORKS: Crispy, golden chicken is served with tender ramen simmered in a kimchi-spiked broth in this lively dish that combines elements of Japanese and Korean cuisine. To ensure chicken thighs with ultracrisp skin, we placed a heavy weight on top as they cooked (a Dutch oven worked well)—this guaranteed that more of the skin came in contact with the hot pan. Seasoning the chicken first with five-spice powder delivered warm spice notes in every bite. To infuse our dish with spicy-hot flavor, we added kimchi (spicy Korean pickled vegetables). When that wasn't quite enough, we added its pickling liquid, too. Look for kimchi in the refrigerated section of the market. Do not substitute other types of noodles for the ramen noodles here.

½　teaspoon five-spice powder
¼　teaspoon salt
8　(5- to 7-ounce) bone-in chicken thighs, trimmed
2　teaspoons vegetable oil
2　cups cabbage kimchi, drained with ⅓ cup pickling liquid reserved
3　garlic cloves, minced
2　cups chicken broth
1½　cups water
4　(3-ounce) packages ramen noodles, seasoning packets discarded
3　tablespoons Chinese rice wine or dry sherry
1　tablespoon soy sauce
2　teaspoons sugar
⅓　cup minced fresh cilantro

Making Crispy Chicken

1. Place chicken, skin side down, in hot pan and weight with heavy pot.

2. Cook until skin is deep mahogany brown and very crisp, 15 to 20 minutes.

1. Combine five-spice powder and salt in bowl. Pat chicken dry with paper towels and season with spice mixture. Heat oil in 12-inch nonstick skillet over medium-high heat until just smoking. Add chicken, skin side down, and weight with heavy pot. Cook until skin is deep mahogany brown and very crisp, 15 to 20 minutes. (Chicken should be moderately brown after 10 minutes; adjust heat as necessary.)

2. Remove pot, flip chicken over, and reduce heat to medium. Continue to cook chicken, without weight, until it registers 175 degrees, about 10 minutes; transfer to plate.

3. Discard all but 1 tablespoon fat left in skillet. Add drained kimchi and garlic and cook over medium heat until fragrant, about 1 minute. Stir in broth, water, and reserved kimchi liquid. Break ramen into chunks and add to skillet. Bring to simmer and cook, tossing ramen constantly with tongs to separate, until it is just tender but there is still liquid in pan, about 2 minutes.

4. Stir in wine, soy sauce, and sugar until incorporated. Off heat, stir in cilantro. Serve with chicken.

Ramen with Beef, Shiitakes, and Spinach

SERVES 4　　TOTAL TIME 45 MINUTES **FAST**

✔ WHY THIS RECIPE WORKS: In Japan, ramen shops line the streets, offering piping-hot bowls of noodles paired with meat and vegetables for a rich, hearty pick-me-up any time of day. For our own flavorful take on this Japanese staple, we started with instant ramen noodles but ditched the übersalty seasoning packet in favor of building our own sauce. After stir-frying flank steak strips, which we'd marinated in soy sauce, and shiitake mushrooms, we added garlic, ginger, and chicken broth to the pan. Next, we stirred in the ramen and simmered it just until tender and the sauce was nicely thickened. Soy sauce, rice wine, and a bit of sugar added savory, sweet flavor to the velvety sauce, and spinach, stirred in at the end, added freshness and color. Do not substitute other types of noodles for the ramen noodles here. The sauce in this dish will seem a bit brothy when finished, but the liquid will be absorbed quickly by the noodles when serving. Freezing the beef for 15 minutes before slicing makes it easier to slice thin.

1　pound flank steak, trimmed and sliced thin against grain on bias
8　teaspoons soy sauce
2　tablespoons vegetable oil
8　ounces shiitake mushrooms, stemmed and sliced thin
3　garlic cloves, minced

1 tablespoon grated fresh ginger

3½ cups chicken broth

4 (3-ounce) packages ramen noodles, seasoning packets discarded

3 tablespoons Chinese rice wine or dry sherry

2 teaspoons sugar

6 ounces (6 cups) baby spinach

1. Toss beef with 2 teaspoons soy sauce in bowl. Heat 1 tablespoon oil in 12-inch nonstick skillet over high heat until just smoking. Add beef in single layer and cook without stirring for 1 minute. Stir beef and continue to cook until browned, about 1 minute; transfer to clean bowl.

2. Wipe out skillet with paper towels, add remaining 1 tablespoon oil, and heat over medium-high heat until shimmering. Add mushrooms and cook until browned, about 4 minutes. Stir in garlic and ginger and cook until fragrant, about 30 seconds. Stir in broth.

3. Break ramen into chunks and add to skillet. Bring to simmer and cook, tossing ramen constantly with tongs to separate, until it is just tender but there is still liquid in pan, about 2 minutes.

4. Stir in remaining 2 tablespoons soy sauce, wine, and sugar. Stir in spinach, 1 handful at a time, until it is wilted and sauce is thickened. Add cooked beef and any accumulated juices and heat until warmed through, about 30 seconds. Serve.

Pork, shiitakes, and bok choy pair nicely with nutty, chewy soba noodles in this Asian-inspired dish.

Soba Noodles with Pork, Shiitakes, and Bok Choy

SERVES 4   **TOTAL TIME** 55 MINUTES

WHY THIS RECIPE WORKS: Mild pork, crunchy baby bok choy, and meaty shiitake mushrooms are the perfect pairing for the rich, nutty flavor of soba noodles. Soba noodles are cooked just like Italian pasta—boiled in hot water, but without salt, then drained and tossed with the other ingredients. For the sauce, we started with a base of soy sauce, then added oyster sauce, sugar, chili-garlic sauce, and sesame oil for a nice balance of sweet and spicy flavors. Sake contributed clean, rice-like notes that bolstered the complexity of the sauce. Vermouth can be substituted for the sake if necessary. A large head of bok choy (stems and leaves separated and sliced crosswise into ½-inch-thick pieces) can be substituted for the baby bok choy; add the stems with the mushrooms and the leaves with the cooked pork. Do not substitute other types of noodles for the soba noodles here.

¼ cup soy sauce

3 tablespoons sugar

2 tablespoons oyster sauce

1 tablespoon Asian chili-garlic sauce

4 teaspoons sake (Japanese rice wine)

1 tablespoon toasted sesame oil

1 pound boneless country-style pork ribs, trimmed and sliced crosswise into ⅛-inch-thick pieces

6 garlic cloves, minced

1 tablespoon grated fresh ginger

4 teaspoons vegetable oil

6 heads baby bok choy (4 ounces each), sliced crosswise into ½-inch-thick pieces

10 ounces shiitake mushrooms, stemmed and quartered

8 ounces dried soba noodles

2 scallions, sliced thin on bias

1. Whisk soy sauce, sugar, oyster sauce, chili-garlic sauce, sake, and sesame oil together in medium bowl. Combine 3 tablespoons sauce mixture and pork in separate bowl, cover, and refrigerate for at least 15 minutes or up to 1 hour. In small bowl, combine garlic, ginger, and 1 teaspoon vegetable oil.

2. Heat 1 teaspoon vegetable oil in 12-inch nonstick skillet over high heat until just smoking. Add half of marinated pork in single layer and cook without stirring for 1 minute. Stir and continue to cook until browned, about 2 minutes; transfer to clean bowl. Repeat with 1 teaspoon vegetable oil and remaining marinated pork; transfer to bowl.

3. Wipe out skillet with paper towels, add remaining 1 teaspoon vegetable oil, and heat over high heat until just smoking. Add bok choy and mushrooms and cook, stirring often, until vegetables are browned, 5 to 7 minutes.

4. Clear center of skillet, add garlic-ginger mixture, and mash it into pan until fragrant, about 30 seconds; stir into vegetables. Stir in cooked pork and any accumulated juices. Stir in soy sauce mixture and simmer until sauce has thickened, about 1 minute. Remove from heat and cover to keep warm.

5. Meanwhile, bring 4 quarts water to boil in large pot. Add noodles and cook, stirring often, until tender. Reserve ½ cup cooking water, then drain noodles and return them to pot. Add pork mixture and toss to combine. Add reserved cooking water as needed to adjust consistency. Sprinkle individual portions with scallions and serve.

Udon Noodles with Pork, Shiitakes, and Miso

SERVES 4   **TOTAL TIME** 1 HOUR 30 MINUTES

WHY THIS RECIPE WORKS: Udon noodles in a miso-flavored broth is a tempting noodle bar dish—the thick, chewy noodles, matched with the potent miso, make for an otherworldly experience. For a sweet yet savory backbone, we wanted a richly flavored pork broth—but we didn't want to spend all day making it. Browned country-style pork ribs (coarsely chopped in the food processor to create more flavor-releasing surface area), combined with water and chicken broth, gave us deep, savory flavor in record time. Ginger, garlic, onion, mirin, soy sauce, and, of course, miso (we prefer bolder red miso, although milder white miso can be substituted) amped up our broth quickly; adding the miso at the last minute prevented its flavor from becoming dulled over the heat. Cooking sliced shiitake mushrooms, fresh udon noodles, and more pork (thin slices of the country-style ribs) right in our strained broth infused them with flavor—and kept this easy dish contained to just one pot. Do not trim the excess fat from the ribs, as the fat contributes flavor and moisture. Do not substitute other types of noodles for the udon noodles here.

1½   **pounds boneless country-style pork ribs**
1   **tablespoon vegetable oil**

1   **onion, chopped**
6   **garlic cloves, peeled and smashed**
1   **(1-inch) piece ginger, peeled, sliced thin, and smashed**
3   **cups chicken broth**
2   **cups water**
¼   **cup red miso**
8   **ounces shiitake mushrooms, stemmed and sliced thin**
1   **pound fresh udon noodles**
2   **tablespoons mirin**
1   **tablespoon soy sauce**
½   **teaspoon toasted sesame oil**
2   **scallions, sliced thin on bias**
1   **tablespoon sesame seeds, toasted**

1. Slice 8 ounces of pork crosswise into ⅛-inch-thick pieces; refrigerate until needed. Cut remaining 1 pound pork into 1-inch chunks, then pulse in food processor to coarsely chopped texture, 10 to 12 pulses.

2. Heat vegetable oil in Dutch oven over medium heat until shimmering. Add processed pork and cook, breaking up meat with wooden spoon, until well browned, about 10 minutes. Stir in onion, garlic, and ginger and cook until onion begins to soften, about 2 minutes. Stir in broth and water and bring to boil. Reduce to gentle simmer, cover partially (leaving about 1 inch of pot open), and cook until broth is flavorful, about 40 minutes.

3. Strain broth through fine-mesh strainer, gently pressing on solids to extract as much liquid as possible. Return strained broth to clean Dutch oven and bring to simmer. Whisk miso with ½ cup hot broth in bowl until dissolved and smooth; set aside.

4. Stir mushrooms into simmering broth and cook until nearly tender, about 2 minutes. Add noodles and cook, stirring often, until noodles and mushrooms are tender, about 3 minutes. Stir in miso mixture and return to brief simmer.

5. Stir in sliced pork, mirin, soy sauce, and sesame oil, then immediately remove pot from heat. Cover and let stand off heat until pork is cooked through, 2 to 3 minutes. Sprinkle individual portions with scallions and sesame seeds, and serve.

Slicing Country-Style Pork Ribs Thinly

Using sharp chef's knife, slice pork crosswise into ⅛-inch-thick pieces.

Pad Thai with Shrimp

SERVES 4   **TOTAL TIME** 45 MINUTES   **FAST**

✔ **WHY THIS RECIPE WORKS:** With its sweet-and-sour, salty-spicy sauce, plump, sweet shrimp, and tender rice noodles, pad thai is Thailand's most well-known noodle dish. But making it at home can be a chore, thanks to lengthy ingredient lists with hard-to-find items. We found we could achieve just the right balance of flavors in the sauce using a simple combination of fish sauce, lime juice, rice vinegar, and brown sugar. With such a flavorful base at the ready, we didn't even need to season the shrimp—we merely sautéed them in the pan until barely pink at the edges, then stirred them in later to finish cooking. To get the texture of the rice noodles just right, we first soaked them in hot water so they'd start to soften, then stir-fried them in the pan. Scrambled eggs, chopped peanuts, bean sprouts, and thinly sliced scallions completed our easy and authentic-tasting pad thai. Do not substitute other types of noodles for the rice noodles here.

8 ounces (¼-inch-wide) rice noodles
⅓ cup water
¼ cup lime juice (2 limes)
3 tablespoons fish sauce
3 tablespoons packed brown sugar
1 tablespoon rice vinegar
¼ cup vegetable oil
12 ounces medium shrimp (41 to 50 per pound), peeled, deveined, and tails removed
3 garlic cloves, minced
2 large eggs, lightly beaten
¼ teaspoon salt
6 tablespoons chopped unsalted roasted peanuts
6 ounces (3 cups) bean sprouts
5 scallions, sliced thin on bias
Lime wedges
Fresh cilantro leaves
Sriracha sauce

1. Cover noodles with very hot tap water in large bowl and stir to separate. Let noodles soak until softened, pliable, and limp but not fully tender, about 20 minutes; drain. In separate bowl, whisk water, lime juice, fish sauce, brown sugar, rice vinegar, and 2 tablespoons oil together.

2. Pat shrimp dry with paper towels. Heat 1 tablespoon oil in 12-inch nonstick skillet over high heat until just smoking. Add shrimp in single layer and cook, without stirring, until beginning to brown, about 1 minute. Stir shrimp and continue to cook until spotty brown and just pink around edges, about 30 seconds; transfer to bowl.

3. Add remaining 1 tablespoon oil and garlic to now-empty skillet and cook over medium heat until fragrant, about 30 seconds. Stir in eggs and salt and cook, stirring vigorously, until eggs are scrambled, about 20 seconds.

4. Add drained noodles and fish sauce mixture. Increase heat to high and cook, tossing gently, until noodles are evenly coated. Add cooked shrimp, ¼ cup peanuts, bean sprouts, and three-quarters of scallions. Cook, tossing constantly, until noodles are tender, about 2 minutes. (If necessary, add 2 tablespoons water to skillet and continue to cook until noodles are tender.)

5. Transfer noodles to serving platter and sprinkle with remaining peanuts and remaining scallions. Serve with lime wedges, cilantro leaves, and Sriracha.

Soaking Rice Noodles

UNDERSOAKED: These noodles are undersoaked and are still too hard. They will take too long to stir-fry.

OVERSOAKED: These noodles are oversoaked and are too soft and gummy. They will overcook when stir-fried and stay tangled.

PERFECTLY SOAKED: These noodles are perfectly soaked and are just softened. They will turn tender when stir-fried and remain separated.

This dish features wide rice noodles and chicken in an intensely flavored sauce with lots of Thai basil.

Drunken Noodles with Chicken

SERVES 4　**TOTAL TIME** 1 HOUR

✔ **WHY THIS RECIPE WORKS:** This renowned dish features wide rice noodles in a spicy, potent sauce flavored with lots of basil. For our version, we selected the widest noodles we could find and soaked them in hot water until they were pliable but not fully limp. Then we added them to our hot skillet with a combination of soy sauce (for savory depth), lime juice (for its sweet-tart notes), dark brown sugar (preferred over light brown sugar for its richer flavor), and chili-garlic sauce (which contributed both heat and spicy flavor). Tossing the noodles in the sauce over the heat ensured that they would absorb its flavors and finish cooking as the sauce thickened. Thin slices of chicken, which we quickly stir-fried, made our noodle dish hearty and filling. Do not substitute other types of noodles for the rice noodles here; however, you can substitute (¼-inch-wide) dried flat rice noodles and reduce their soaking time to 20 minutes. For more information on slicing chicken thinly, see page 138.

Understanding Asian Noodles

Here are some of the most common types of Asian noodles.

FRESH CHINESE NOODLES: You can find fresh Chinese noodles in many supermarkets as well as Asian markets. Some noodles are cut thin, and others are cut slightly wider. Their texture is a bit more starchy and chewy than that of dried noodles, and their flavor is cleaner (less wheaty) than Italian pasta, making them an excellent match with well-seasoned sauces and soups. Fresh Chinese noodles cook quickly.

RICE NOODLES: Rice noodles are made from rice powder and water. They come in several widths: ¼ inch wide, which is similar to linguine; ⅜ inch wide; and thin vermicelli. Since they can overcook quickly, we often soften them off the heat in hot water before adding them to a dish toward the end of cooking. We've also had some success boiling the noodles as long as we carefully watch the time, and we usually rinse them after draining to ensure they cool quickly and don't overcook.

SOBA NOODLES: Soba noodles have a nutty flavor and delicate texture. They get their unusual flavor from buckwheat flour. Buckwheat flour contains no gluten, so a binder, usually wheat, is added to give the noodles structure and hold them together during cooking. Soba noodles must contain a minimum of 30 percent buckwheat flour, the higher the percentage, the higher the price. Soba noodles are traditionally served cold, but we also like them warm.

UDON NOODLES: These Japanese noodles, which are made from wheat, are available in varying thicknesses and can be round or squared. They are typically used in soups and have an appealing chewy texture. You can find them alongside the tofu in most grocery stores as well as Asian markets. They can contain quite a bit of salt (up to 4,000 milligrams of sodium per 12 ounces); because of that, we don't add salt to the cooking water when boiling them.

RAMEN NOODLES: Typically fried in oil and then dried and packaged, ramen noodles take only a few minutes to cook, making them a more convenient, quicker-cooking choice than other dried noodles. We sometimes use plain ramen noodles as the pasta in Asian-inspired recipes; we just get rid of the salty, stale-tasting seasoning packet and add our own mix of fresh herbs and spices.

- 12 ounces (⅜-inch-wide) rice noodles
- 12 ounces boneless, skinless chicken breasts, trimmed and sliced thin
- 1 tablespoon plus ½ cup soy sauce
- ¾ cup packed dark brown sugar
- ⅓ cup lime juice (3 limes), plus lime wedges for serving
- ¼ cup Asian chili-garlic sauce
- ¼ cup vegetable oil
- ½ head napa cabbage, cored and cut into 1-inch pieces (6 cups)
- 1½ cups coarsely chopped fresh Thai basil or cilantro
- 4 scallions, sliced thin on bias

1. Cover noodles with very hot tap water in large bowl and stir to separate. Let noodles soak until softened, pliable, and limp but not fully tender, 35 to 40 minutes; drain.

2. Meanwhile, toss chicken with 1 tablespoon soy sauce in bowl, cover, and refrigerate for at least 10 minutes or up to 1 hour. In separate bowl, whisk remaining ½ cup soy sauce, brown sugar, lime juice, and chili-garlic sauce together.

3. Heat 2 teaspoons oil in 12-inch nonstick skillet over high heat until just smoking. Add marinated chicken in single layer and cook without stirring for 1 minute. Stir and continue to cook until nearly cooked through, about 2 minutes; transfer to large bowl.

4. Add 1 teaspoon oil to now-empty skillet and heat over high heat until just smoking. Add cabbage and cook, stirring often, until spotty brown, 3 to 5 minutes; transfer to bowl with chicken.

5. Wipe out skillet with paper towels, add remaining 3 tablespoons oil, and heat over medium-high heat until shimmering. Add drained rice noodles and soy sauce mixture and cook, tossing gently, until sauce has thickened and noodles are well coated and tender, 5 to 10 minutes.

6. Stir in chicken and cabbage and any accumulated juices, and basil. Cook until chicken is cooked through, about 1 minute. Sprinkle with scallions and serve with lime wedges.

Cold Sesame Noodles

SERVES 4 TO 6   **TOTAL TIME** 30 MINUTES   **FAST**

✔ **WHY THIS RECIPE WORKS:** For easy, authentic-tasting sesame noodles, we turned to everyday pantry staples to deliver the same sweet, nutty, addictive flavor. Grinding chunky peanut butter and toasted sesame seeds together made the perfect stand-in for hard-to-find Asian sesame paste. Garlic and ginger, soy sauce, rice vinegar, hot sauce, and brown sugar rounded out the sauce. After tossing cooked Chinese noodles with the sauce, scallions, and carrot, we sprinkled on

another spoonful of sesame seeds for more crunch and nutty flavor. Adding shredded chicken makes for a nice variation. We prefer the flavor and texture of chunky peanut butter here; however, creamy peanut butter can be used. If you cannot find fresh Chinese egg noodles, substitute 12 ounces dried spaghetti or linguine.

- 5 tablespoons sesame seeds
- 5 tablespoons soy sauce
- ¼ cup chunky peanut butter
- 2 tablespoons rice vinegar
- 2 tablespoons packed light brown sugar
- 1 tablespoon grated fresh ginger
- 2 garlic cloves, minced
- 1 teaspoon hot sauce
- ½ cup hot water
- 1 pound fresh Chinese noodles or 12 ounces dried spaghetti or linguine
- 2 tablespoons toasted sesame oil
- 4 scallions, sliced thin on bias
- 1 carrot, peeled and grated

1. Toast sesame seeds in 8-inch skillet over medium heat, stirring often, until golden and fragrant, about 10 minutes. Reserve 1 tablespoon seeds for garnish.

2. Process remaining 4 tablespoons sesame seeds, soy sauce, peanut butter, vinegar, sugar, ginger, garlic, and hot sauce in blender until smooth, about 30 seconds. With blender running, add hot water, 1 tablespoon at a time, until sauce has consistency of heavy cream (you may not need all water). (Sauce can be refrigerated for up to 3 days; add warm water as needed to loosen consistency before using.)

3. Meanwhile, bring 4 quarts water to boil in large pot. Add noodles and cook, stirring often, until tender. Drain noodles, rinse with cold water, and drain again, leaving noodles slightly wet. Transfer noodles to large bowl and toss with oil.

4. Add scallions, carrot, and sauce and toss to combine. Sprinkle individual portions with reserved 1 tablespoon sesame seeds, and serve.

Toasting Sesame Seeds

Toast sesame seeds in 8-inch skillet over medium heat, stirring, until golden and fragrant, about 10 minutes.

We use two cups of basil leaves in this spicy noodle dish to keep it fresh and bright.

Spicy Basil Noodles with Crispy Tofu, Snap Peas, and Bell Pepper

SERVES 4   **TOTAL TIME** 1 HOUR 15 MINUTES

⚓ **WHY THIS RECIPE WORKS:** Spicy basil noodles are like a wake-up call for the sleepy palate. This brightly flavored Thai dish combines tender rice noodles with fragrant fresh basil and a spicy, aromatic sauce. We infused our dish with subtle heat by creating a paste of hot chiles, garlic, and shallots in the food processor. Cooking the mixture briefly deepened its flavor and mellowed the harshness of the raw aromatics. Fish sauce, brown sugar, lime juice, and chicken broth added sweet and savory flavors and gave our sauce a bit of body. A generous amount of basil gives this dish its trademark fresh flavor and color—we used a whopping 2 cups and stirred it in at the end to keep its freshness intact. Pan-fried tofu offered both creamy and crispy textures that paired well with the tender rice noodles, and stir-fried snap peas and red bell pepper strips added some crunch. To make this dish spicier, add the chile seeds. Do not substitute other types of noodles for the rice noodles here; however, you can substitute (¼-inch-wide) dried flat rice noodles and reduce their soaking time to 20 minutes.

12 ounces (⅜-inch-wide) rice noodles
14 ounces extra-firm tofu, cut into 1-inch cubes
 8 Thai, serrano, or jalapeño chiles, stemmed and seeded
 6 garlic cloves, peeled
 4 shallots, peeled
 2 cups chicken broth
 ¼ cup fish sauce
 ¼ cup packed brown sugar
 3 tablespoons lime juice (2 limes)
   Salt and pepper
 ½ cup cornstarch
 7 tablespoons vegetable oil
 6 ounces snap peas, strings removed
 1 red bell pepper, stemmed, seeded, sliced into ¼-inch-wide strips, and halved crosswise
 2 cups fresh Thai basil leaves or sweet basil leaves

1. Cover noodles with very hot tap water in large bowl and stir to separate. Let noodles soak until softened, pliable, and limp but not fully tender, 35 to 40 minutes; drain. Spread tofu out over paper towel–lined baking sheet and let drain for 20 minutes.

2. Meanwhile, pulse chiles, garlic, and shallots in food processor into smooth paste, about 30 pulses, scraping down bowl as needed; set aside. In bowl, whisk broth, fish sauce, sugar, and lime juice together.

3. Adjust oven rack to upper-middle position and heat oven to 200 degrees. Gently pat tofu dry with paper towels, season with salt and pepper, then toss with cornstarch in bowl. Transfer coated tofu to strainer and shake gently over bowl to remove excess cornstarch. Heat 3 tablespoons oil in 12-inch nonstick skillet over medium-high heat until just smoking. Add tofu and cook, turning as needed, until all sides are crisp and browned, about 8 minutes; transfer to paper towel–lined plate and keep warm in oven.

4. Wipe out skillet with paper towels, add 1 tablespoon oil, and heat over high heat until just smoking. Add snap peas and bell pepper and cook, stirring often, until vegetables are crisp-tender and beginning to brown, 3 to 5 minutes; transfer to separate bowl.

5. Add remaining 3 tablespoons oil to now-empty skillet and heat over medium-high heat until shimmering. Add processed chile mixture and cook until moisture evaporates and color deepens, 3 to 5 minutes. Add drained noodles and broth mixture and cook, tossing gently, until sauce has thickened and noodles are well coated and tender, 5 to 10 minutes.

6. Stir in cooked vegetables and basil and cook until basil wilts slightly, about 1 minute. Top individual portions with crispy tofu and serve.

Pizza and Calzones

Sandwiches

■ SIGNIFIES A **FAST** RECIPE (45 MINUTES OR LESS)

Classic Pizza Dough

MAKES 2 POUNDS **TOTAL TIME** 1 HOUR 10 MINUTES TO 1 HOUR 40 MINUTES

✔ **WHY THIS RECIPE WORKS:** With a homemade pizza dough waiting in the refrigerator, you're already halfway to an easy dinner. Great pizza crust doesn't require the amount of kneading that other types of dough require, and while you can certainly use a stand mixer to make it, a food processor does a great job in a matter of minutes. Once the dough comes together, it needs only an hour or so to rise before you can assemble the pizzas. All-purpose flour can be substituted for the bread flour, but the resulting crust will be a little less chewy.

4¼   cups (23⅓ ounces) bread flour
2¼   teaspoons instant or rapid-rise yeast
1½   teaspoons salt
 2   tablespoons olive oil
1½   cups warm water (110 degrees)

1. Pulse flour, yeast, and salt together in food processor to combine, about 5 pulses. With processor running, add oil, then water, and process until rough ball forms, 30 to 40 seconds. Let dough rest for 2 minutes, then process for 30 seconds longer. (If after 30 seconds dough is very sticky and clings to blade, add extra flour as needed.)

2. Transfer dough to lightly floured counter and knead until smooth, about 1 minute. Shape dough into tight ball, place in large lightly oiled bowl, and cover tightly with plastic wrap. (Bowl of dough can be refrigerated for up to 16 hours; let sit at room temperature for 30 minutes before using.)

3. Place in warm spot and let dough rise until doubled in size, 1 to 1½ hours.

VARIATION

One-Pound Classic Pizza Dough

Reduce amounts of all ingredients by half; mix, knead, and let rise as directed.

Classic Cheese Pizza

MAKES TWO 14-INCH PIZZAS **SERVES** 4 TO 6
TOTAL TIME 1 HOUR

✔ **WHY THIS RECIPE WORKS:** Homemade pizza really is far better than frozen or delivery and our recipe results in a pie as good as any you could get at a pizzeria. Leaving the outer edge of the pizza slightly thicker than the center ensured a chewy yet crisp

Bread flour and a hot baking stone are the secrets to making pizzeria-style pizza at home.

crust. We transferred the rolled-out dough to a parchment-lined baking sheet, and, after spreading on a light layer of sauce and sprinkling it with two cheeses, we slid the parchment sheet onto a preheated baking stone. We like to use our Classic Pizza Dough and Easy Pizza Sauce (page 435); however, you can substitute premade dough and sauce from the supermarket or local pizzeria. For the crispiest crust we use a baking stone. If you do not have a baking stone, bake the pizza on a rimless (or inverted) baking sheet that has been preheated just like a baking stone.

 2   pounds pizza dough
 1   tablespoon extra-virgin olive oil
 2   cups pizza sauce
 ¼   cup grated Parmesan cheese
12   ounces mozzarella cheese, shredded (3 cups)

1. Adjust oven rack to lower-middle position, place baking stone on rack, and heat oven to 500 degrees. Let baking stone heat for at least 30 minutes or up to 1 hour. Line rimless (or inverted) baking sheet with parchment paper.

2. Transfer dough to lightly floured counter, divide in half, and cover with greased plastic wrap. Working with 1 piece of dough at a time (keep other piece covered), use fingertips to gently flatten into 8-inch disk, leaving 1 inch of outer edge slightly thicker than center. Using hands, gently stretch dough into 14-inch round, working along edges and giving dough quarter turns as you stretch. Transfer dough to parchment-lined baking sheet and reshape as needed.

3. Lightly brush outer ½-inch edge of dough with ½ tablespoon oil. Using back of spoon, spread 1 cup pizza sauce evenly over dough, leaving ½-inch border. Sprinkle 2 tablespoons Parmesan and 1½ cups mozzarella evenly over sauce.

4. Slide parchment paper and pizza onto hot baking stone. Bake pizza until edges are brown and cheese is golden in spots, 8 to 13 minutes, rotating pizza halfway through baking. (Prepare second pizza while first bakes.)

5. Remove pizza from oven by sliding parchment paper back onto baking sheet. Transfer pizza to wire rack, discarding parchment. Let pizza cool for 5 minutes, then slice and serve. Let stone reheat for 5 minutes before baking second pizza.

VARIATIONS

Classic Pepperoni Pizza

Working in 2 batches, microwave 3½ ounces sliced pepperoni between triple layers of coffee filters on plate for 30 seconds to render some fat; use fresh coffee filters for each batch. Top pizzas with microwaved pepperoni before baking.

Classic Sausage, Pepper, and Onion Pizza

Cook 1 thinly sliced bell pepper, 1 thinly sliced onion, 1 tablespoon vegetable oil, and ¼ teaspoon salt in 12-inch nonstick skillet over medium-high heat until slightly softened, about 5 minutes; transfer to paper towel–lined plate. Pinch 12 ounces Italian sausage, casings removed, into small pieces. Top pizzas with cooked vegetables and raw sausage before baking.

EASY PIZZA SAUCE

MAKES 2 CUPS   **TOTAL TIME** 10 MINUTES   **FAST**

While it is convenient to use jarred pizza sauce, we think it is almost as easy, and a lot tastier, to whip up your own.

- 1 **(28-ounce) can whole peeled tomatoes, drained with juice reserved**
- 1 **tablespoon extra-virgin olive oil**
- 1 **teaspoon red wine vinegar**
- 2 **garlic cloves, minced**
- 1 **teaspoon dried oregano**
- ½ **teaspoon salt**
- ¼ **teaspoon pepper**

Process drained tomatoes with oil, vinegar, garlic, oregano, salt, and pepper in food processor until smooth, about 30 seconds. Transfer mixture to liquid measuring cup and add reserved tomato juice until sauce measures 2 cups. (Sauce can be refrigerated for up to 1 week or frozen for up to 1 month.)

Classic Pizza Margherita

Substitute following mixture for pizza sauce: Pulse 1 (28-ounce) can diced tomatoes with their juice in food processor until crushed, about 3 pulses; transfer to fine-mesh strainer and let drain for 30 minutes. Combine drained tomatoes with 1 tablespoon chopped fresh basil, 1 small minced garlic clove, ½ teaspoon sugar, and ¼ teaspoon salt in bowl. Substitute 12 ounces fresh mozzarella cheese, cut into 1-inch chunks, for shredded mozzarella and Parmesan. Sprinkle pizza with chopped fresh basil and sea salt to taste before serving.

Baking Classic Cheese Pizza

1. After stretching dough out with your hands, transfer it to parchment-lined baking sheet using a rolling pin and reshape as needed.

2. Brush edges with oil, then top with pizza sauce, Parmesan, and mozzarella, leaving ½-inch border.

3. Slide parchment paper and pizza onto hot baking stone. Bake pizza for 8 to 13 minutes, leaving parchment paper in place during entire baking time.

4. To remove pizza from oven, gently slide parchment paper and pizza back onto baking sheet.

A parlor-quality thin-crust pizza with a crisp and chewy crust can be made at home using a few of our tricks, including the break-through technique of placing the baking stone near the top of the oven. Letting the dough proof for 24 hours in the refrigerator allows its flavor to develop and prevents it from puffing up in the oven.

1. MAKE THE DOUGH: Process the flour, sugar, and yeast. Slowly add the ice water. Let the dough sit for 10 minutes. Add the oil and salt and process until the dough forms a ball.
WHY? High-protein bread flour produces a chewy crust. We use enough water to create a wet dough that stretches without tearing and stays tender. Sugar promotes browning.

2. LET THE DOUGH RISE: Knead the dough briefly. Shape it into a tight ball and place it in a lightly oiled bowl. Cover the bowl tightly with plastic and refrigerate for at least 24 hours.
WHY? Letting the dough rise in the refrigerator for 24 hours allows for a long, slow fermentation, which builds flavor. It also slows gluten development so the dough stays looser and easier to stretch and shape.

3. PREPARE THE SAUCE: Process drained whole peeled tomatoes with oil, vinegar, garlic, oregano, salt, and pepper until smooth. Transfer to a liquid measuring cup and add reserved juice until the sauce measures 2 cups.
WHY? We like the taste of a fresh, uncooked sauce on our thin-crust pizza. Our quick-to-make Easy Pizza Sauce comes together in just 10 minutes.

4. PREHEAT THE BAKING STONE: Adjust an oven rack to the second highest position, set a baking stone on the rack, and heat the oven to 500 degrees.
WHY? Placing the baking stone near the top of the oven creates a smaller oven space. Heat reflected from the stone browns both the top and bottom of the pizza.

5. BRING THE DOUGH TO ROOM TEMPERATURE: Remove the dough from the refrigerator, divide in half, and then shape each half into a smooth, tight ball. Place on a lightly oiled baking sheet, cover loosely with plastic wrap, and let stand for 1 hour.
WHY? Dividing the dough in half and allowing it to come to room temperature will make the pizzas easier to stretch and roll out.

6. HEAT THE BROILER AND SHAPE THE PIZZA: While the broiler heats, coat the first dough ball with flour. Gently flatten into an 8-inch disk, leaving the outer edge slightly thicker than the center. Stretch the dough into a 12-inch round, working along the edges and giving the dough quarter turns.
WHY? Because of the long cold fermentation, the dough is very easy to work with and easily shaped using your hands, no rolling pin required.

7. TOP THE PIZZA WITH SAUCE AND CHEESE: Transfer the dough to a floured pizza peel and stretch into a 13-inch round. Spread the sauce evenly over the dough. Sprinkle ¼ cup Parmesan and 1 cup mozzarella over the sauce.
WHY? A pizza peel is the best way to transfer the pizza to the hot baking stone and flouring it well ensures the pie slides off easily. We keep toppings to a minimum as an overloaded pizza bakes up soggy.

8. BAKE THE PIZZA THEN LET IT REST: Slide the pizza carefully onto the hot baking stone and return the oven to 500 degrees. Bake until the crust is well browned and the cheese is bubbly. Transfer to a wire rack and let cool.
WHY? The preheated baking stone quickly bakes and crisps the pizza's crust. The pizza will be extremely hot when removed from the oven, so allow it to rest for a few minutes for easier slicing.

Ultimate New York–Style Pizza

MAKES TWO 13-INCH PIZZAS **SERVES** 4 TO 6
TOTAL TIME 2 HOURS 25 MINUTES
(PLUS 24 HOURS TO REFRIGERATE DOUGH)

✔ **WHY THIS RECIPE WORKS:** With home ovens that reach only 500 degrees and dough that's impossible to stretch thin, even the savviest cooks can struggle to produce New York–style pizza—a thin, crisp, and spottily charred pizza with a tender yet chewy crust. High-protein bread flour resulted in a chewy, nicely tanned pizza crust, and the right ratio of flour, water, and yeast gave us dough that would stretch and would retain moisture as it baked. We kneaded the dough quickly in a food processor, then let it proof in the refrigerator for at least 1 day to develop its flavors. After we shaped and topped the pizza, it went onto a blazing hot baking stone to cook. Placing the stone near the top of the oven was a surprising improvement, allowing the top as well as the bottom of the pizza to brown. Many baking stones, especially thinner ones, can crack under the intense heat of the broiler; be sure to check the manufacturer's website. Our recommended stone, by Old Stone Oven, can handle the heat of the broiler (see page 798). It is important to use ice water in the dough to prevent it from overheating in the food processor. We like to use our Easy Pizza Sauce (page 435); however, you can substitute store-bought sauce. You will need a pizza peel for this recipe. Shape the second dough ball while the first pizza bakes, but don't top the pizza until right before you bake it.

DOUGH

- 3 cups (16½ ounces) bread flour
- 2 teaspoons sugar
- ½ teaspoon instant or rapid-rise yeast
- 1⅓ cups ice water
- 1 tablespoon vegetable oil
- 1½ teaspoons salt

PIZZA

- 1 cup pizza sauce
- 1 ounce Parmesan cheese, grated (½ cup)
- 8 ounces whole-milk mozzarella cheese, shredded (2 cups)

1. FOR THE DOUGH: Pulse flour, sugar, and yeast in food processor to combine, about 5 pulses. With processor running, slowly add ice water and process until dough is just combined and no dry flour remains, about 10 seconds. Let dough rest for 10 minutes.

2. Add oil and salt to dough and process until it forms satiny, sticky ball that clears sides of workbowl, 30 to 60 seconds. Transfer dough to lightly oiled counter and knead until smooth, about 1 minute. Shape dough into tight ball and place in large lightly oiled bowl. Cover bowl tightly with plastic wrap and refrigerate for at least 1 day or up to 3 days.

3. FOR THE PIZZA: One hour before baking pizza, adjust oven rack 4½ inches from broiler element, set baking stone on rack, and heat oven to 500 degrees. Remove dough from refrigerator and divide in half. Shape each half into smooth, tight ball. Place on lightly oiled baking sheet, spaced at least 3 inches apart, cover loosely with greased plastic wrap, and let stand for 1 hour.

4. Heat broiler for 10 minutes. Meanwhile, coat 1 ball of dough generously with flour and place on well-floured counter. Using fingertips, gently flatten dough into 8-inch disk, leaving 1 inch of outer edge slightly thicker than center. Using hands, gently stretch dough into 12-inch round, working along edges and giving dough quarter turns as you stretch. Transfer dough to well-floured peel and stretch into 13-inch round. Using back of spoon, spread ½ cup sauce evenly over dough, leaving ¼-inch border. Sprinkle ¼ cup Parmesan and 1 cup mozzarella evenly over sauce.

5. Slide pizza carefully onto stone and return oven to 500 degrees. Bake until crust is well browned and cheese is bubbly and partially browned, 8 to 10 minutes, rotating pizza halfway through baking. Transfer pizza to wire rack, let cool for 5 minutes, then slice and serve.

6. Heat broiler for 10 minutes. Repeat steps 4 and 5 with remaining ingredients to make second pizza, returning oven to 500 degrees when pizza is placed on stone.

Whole-Wheat Pizza with Garlic Oil, Three Cheeses, and Basil

MAKES TWO 13-INCH PIZZAS **SERVES** 4 TO 6
TOTAL TIME 2 HOURS 30 MINUTES
(PLUS 18 HOURS TO REFRIGERATE DOUGH)

✔ **WHY THIS RECIPE WORKS:** For a thin-crust pizza with balanced whole-wheat flavor, we used a combination of 60 percent whole-wheat flour and 40 percent bread flour. To ensure that this higher-than-normal ratio of whole-wheat to bread flour still produced a great crust, we increased the amount of water, resulting in a stretchier dough and better chew. A traditional tomato-based pizza sauce clashed with the whole-wheat flavor, so we opted instead for an oil-based sauce. Like our Ultimate New York–Style Pizza, this uses a blazing hot baking stone. Many baking stones, especially thinner ones, can crack under the intense heat of the broiler; be sure to check the manufacturer's website. Our recommended stone, by Old Stone Oven, can handle the heat of the broiler (see page 798). It is important to use ice water in the

Making Pizza at Home

Making your own pizza is fun. Here are some of our favorite tips for easy, parlor-worthy pizza.

EASY CHEESE SHREDDING: Use a clean plastic bag (a large zipper-lock bag works best) to hold the grater and the cheese. By placing the bag around both, you can grate without getting your hands dirty, or worrying about rogue pieces flying off into your kitchen. The best part? Leftover shredded cheese is ready for storage, no transfer needed.

KEEP TOPPINGS ON HAND: Homemade pizza is a blank canvas that can be creatively covered with myriad toppings. To have topping options on hand, try this simple solution: Whenever cooking something such as roasted red peppers, caramelized onions, or sausage, reserve some in a plastic container, label it, and freeze it. The next time you're making pizza, simply defrost and top away.

NO PEEL? NO STONE? NO PROBLEM: A baking stone is a terrific investment if you enjoy making bread and pizza, and a peel makes the process easier. But you can make do with rimless or inverted baking sheets for both the stone and the peel. To improvise a baking stone, preheat a baking sheet for 30 minutes. As for an improvised peel, cover a rimless or an inverted rimmed baking sheet with parchment paper, shape and top the pizza on the parchment, and slide parchment and pizza directly onto the preheated stone.

CLEAN CUTTING GUARANTEED: If you use a knife to cut pizza, you risk pulling cheese in every direction. A pizza wheel negates this risk. Look for one that is large and sharp enough to glide through thick and thin crusts without dislodging toppings.

TWO WAYS TO REHEAT: Reheating pizza in the microwave turns it soggy, and just throwing it into a hot oven can dry it out. Here's a reheating method that really works: Place the cold slices on a rimmed baking sheet, cover the sheet tightly with aluminum foil, and place it on the lowest rack of a cold oven. Then set the oven temperature to 275 degrees and let the pizza warm for 25 to 30 minutes. This approach leaves the interior of the crust soft, the cheese melty, and the toppings and bottom crust hot and crisp. For just a slice or two, place a nonstick skillet over medium heat and add dried oregano. Place the pizza in the skillet and reheat, covered, for about 5 minutes. The pizza will come out hot and crisp, and with an irresistible aroma.

dough to prevent it from overheating in the food processor. We recommend King Arthur brand bread flour. You will need a pizza peel for this recipe. Shape the second dough ball while the first pizza bakes, but don't top the pizza until right before you bake it.

DOUGH

- 1½ cups (8¼ ounces) whole-wheat flour
- 1 cup (5½ ounces) bread flour
- 2 teaspoons honey
- ¾ teaspoon instant or rapid-rise yeast
- 1¼ cups ice water
- 2 tablespoons extra-virgin olive oil
- 1¾ teaspoons salt

PIZZA

- ¼ cup extra-virgin olive oil
- 2 garlic cloves, minced
- ½ teaspoon pepper
- ½ teaspoon dried oregano
- ⅛ teaspoon red pepper flakes
- ⅛ teaspoon salt
- 1 cup fresh basil leaves
- 1 ounce Pecorino Romano cheese, grated (½ cup)
- 8 ounces whole-milk mozzarella cheese, shredded (2 cups)
- 6 ounces (¾ cup) whole-milk ricotta cheese

1. FOR THE DOUGH: Pulse whole-wheat flour, bread flour, honey, and yeast in food processor to combine, about 5 pulses. With processor running, slowly add ice water and process until dough is just combined and no dry flour remains, about 10 seconds. Let dough rest for 10 minutes.

2. Add oil and salt to dough and process until it forms satiny, sticky ball that clears sides of workbowl, 45 to 60 seconds. Transfer dough to lightly oiled counter and knead until smooth, about 1 minute. Shape dough into tight ball and place in large lightly oiled bowl. Cover bowl tightly with plastic wrap and refrigerate for at least 18 hours or up to 2 days.

3. FOR THE PIZZA: One hour before baking pizza, adjust oven rack 4½ inches from broiler element, set baking stone on rack, and heat oven to 500 degrees. Remove dough from refrigerator and divide in half. Shape each half into smooth, tight ball. Place on lightly oiled baking sheet, spaced at least 3 inches apart, cover loosely with greased plastic wrap, and let stand for 1 hour.

4. Meanwhile, heat oil in 8-inch skillet over medium-low heat until shimmering. Add garlic, pepper, oregano, pepper flakes, and salt. Cook, stirring constantly, until fragrant, about 30 seconds. Transfer to bowl and let cool.

To keep the whole-wheat flavor front and center, we use 60 percent whole-wheat flour and 40 percent bread flour.

5. Heat broiler for 10 minutes. Meanwhile, coat 1 ball of dough generously with flour and place on well-floured counter. Using fingertips, gently flatten dough into 8-inch disk, leaving 1 inch of outer edge slightly thicker than center. Using hands, gently stretch dough into 12-inch round, working along edges and giving dough quarter turns as you stretch. Transfer dough to well-floured peel and stretch into 13-inch round.

6. Using back of spoon, spread half of garlic oil evenly over dough, leaving ¼-inch border. Layer ½ cup basil leaves evenly over sauce, then sprinkle with ¼ cup Pecorino and 1 cup mozzarella.

7. Slide pizza carefully onto stone and return oven to 500 degrees. Bake until crust is well browned and cheese is bubbly and partially browned, 8 to 10 minutes, rotating pizza halfway through baking. Transfer pizza to wire rack and dollop half of ricotta evenly over top. Let cool for 5 minutes, then slice and serve.

8. Heat broiler for 10 minutes. Repeat steps 5 through 7 with remaining ingredients to make second pizza, returning oven to 500 degrees when pizza is placed on stone.

Pepperoni

Pepperoni dates back to ancient Rome, where it was a convenient food for soldiers on the march. It reached America with the Italian immigrants who arrived around 1900. Pepperoni started being used as a pizza topping in New York City, and its production underwent a total transformation from artisanal to commercial. Today pepperoni is the most-ordered pizza topping in the United States.

More than just a pizza topping, pepperoni provides meaty, savory depth in a few of our dishes, from pastas to casseroles. Pepperoni is made from cured and fermented pork along with just a little beef, and it is seasoned with black pepper, sugar, anise, cayenne, paprika (the source of its orange color), and lots of salt. It should have spice, heat, and chew, and the flavors shouldn't get lost once baked.

Pepperoni Pan Pizza

MAKES TWO 9-INCH PIZZAS **SERVES** 4 TO 6
TOTAL TIME 1 HOUR 30 MINUTES
(PLUS 1 TO 1½ HOURS RISING TIME)

WHY THIS RECIPE WORKS: Pan pizza (often called deep-dish pizza) is known for a buttery crust that's crispy on the bottom and chewy in the middle. To make our dough, we used a few tricks we learned from baking. Many tender yeast breads are made with milk, and we decided to give it a try, using skim milk to make a dough, which rose better and baked up especially soft and light with just the right chew. All-purpose flour yielded a softer crust than bread flour. Kneading the dough in a stand mixer also helped the dough attain a chewy, bready texture. Because this dough was very prone to tearing and snapping back when overworked, we used a rolling pin for the first part of shaping the dough, and then gently stretched it over the tops of our knuckles. The final step was to microwave the pepperoni between layers of coffee filters, which kept the grease off of the pizza and gave us crisp pepperoni worthy of our perfect pan crust. We like to use our Easy Pizza Sauce (page 435); however, you can substitute store-bought sauce.

DOUGH
- ¾ **cup plus 2 tablespoons skim milk, warmed to 110 degrees**
- 2 **teaspoons sugar**
- 2 **tablespoons extra-virgin olive oil**

2⅓ cups (11⅔ ounces) all-purpose flour
2¼ teaspoons instant or rapid-rise yeast
½ teaspoon salt

PIZZA
6 tablespoons extra-virgin olive oil
3½ ounces sliced pepperoni
1⅓ cups plzza sauce
12 ounces part-skim mozzarella cheese,
    shredded (3 cups)

1. FOR THE DOUGH: Combine warm milk, sugar, and oil in liquid measuring cup. Using stand mixer fitted with dough hook, combine flour, yeast, and salt. With mixer on low speed, slowly add milk mixture to flour mixture. After dough comes together, increase speed to medium-low and knead until dough is shiny and smooth, about 5 minutes.

2. Transfer dough to lightly oiled counter and knead until smooth, about 1 minute. Shape dough into tight ball, place in large lightly oiled bowl, and cover tightly with plastic wrap. (Bowl of dough can be refrigerated for up to 16 hours; let sit at room temperature for 30 minutes before using.) Place bowl in warm spot and let dough rise until doubled in size, 1 to 1½ hours.

3. FOR THE PIZZA: Coat two 9-inch cake pans with oil. Transfer dough to lightly floured counter, divide in half, and cover with greased plastic wrap. Working with 1 piece of dough at a time (keep other piece covered), use rolling pin to flatten dough into 7-inch round. Drape dough over your knuckles and gently stretch into 9½-inch circle that is slightly thinner in center. Place dough in oiled pan and gently push it to edges.

Shaping Dough for Pan Pizza

1. Use rolling pin to flatten dough into 7-inch round. Drape dough over knuckles and, using its weight, gently stretch into a circle that is slightly thinner in center.

2. Place dough in oiled pan and gently push to edges, taking care not to let too much oil spill over top.

Cover with plastic wrap and place in warm spot until dough is puffy and slightly risen, 20 to 30 minutes.

4. While dough rises, adjust oven rack to middle position and heat oven to 400 degrees. Working in 2 batches, microwave pepperoni between triple layers of coffee filters on plate for 30 seconds to render some fat; use fresh coffee filters for each batch.

5. Using back of spoon, spread ⅔ cup pizza sauce evenly over each dough round, leaving ½-inch border. Sprinkle mozzarella evenly over sauce and top with pepperoni. Bake until cheese is melted and pepperoni is browned around edges, about 20 minutes, rotating pans halfway through baking. Let pizzas cool in pans for 1 minute, then transfer to cutting board using spatula. Cut each pizza into 8 wedges and serve.

Simple Skillet Pizza

MAKES TWO 11-INCH PIZZAS **SERVES** 4
TOTAL TIME 45 MINUTES **FAST**

WHY THIS RECIPE WORKS: If you want to make home-made pizza but don't want to wait for a baking stone to heat up in the oven, you can simply use a skillet. The trick is to assemble the pizza in the skillet and start cooking it on the stovetop. This both heats up the skillet and starts to cook the bottom crust. Once the bottom crust began to brown, we simply slid the skillet into a very hot oven to finish cooking the pizza through and melt the cheese. Be sure to let the dough sit out at room temperature while preparing the remaining ingredients and heating the oven, otherwise it will be difficult to stretch. We like to use our One-Pound Classic Pizza Dough (page 434) and Easy Pizza Sauce (page 435); however, you can substitute premade dough and sauce from the supermarket or your local pizzeria. Feel free to sprinkle simple toppings over the pizza before baking, such as pepperoni, sautéed mushrooms, or browned sausage, but keep the toppings light or they may weigh down the thin crust and make it soggy.

¼ cup extra-virgin olive oil
1 pound pizza dough, room temperature
1 cup pizza sauce
¼ cup grated Parmesan cheese
6 ounces mozzarella cheese, shredded (1½ cups)

1. Adjust oven rack to upper-middle position and heat oven to 500 degrees. Grease 12-inch ovensafe skillet with 2 tablespoons oil.

2. Place dough on lightly floured counter, divide in half, and cover with greased plastic wrap. Working with 1 piece of dough at a time (keep other piece covered), use rolling pin to flatten dough into 11-inch round. Transfer dough to prepared skillet and reshape as needed. Using back of spoon, spread ½ cup pizza sauce evenly over dough, leaving ½-inch border. Sprinkle 2 tablespoons Parmesan and ¾ cup mozzarella over sauce.

3. Set skillet over high heat and cook until outside edge of dough is set, pizza is lightly puffed, and bottom crust is spotty brown when gently lifted with spatula, about 3 minutes.

4. Transfer skillet to oven and bake pizza until edges are brown and cheese is melted and spotty brown, 7 to 10 minutes. Using potholders (skillet handle will be hot), remove skillet from oven and slide pizza onto wire rack. Let pizza cool for 5 minutes, then slice and serve. Wipe out skillet with paper towels and let cool slightly, then repeat with remaining ingredients to make second pizza.

Making Skillet Pizza

1. Place dough on lightly floured counter, divide in half, and cover with greased plastic wrap. Roll 1 piece of dough into 11-inch round.

2. Grease ovensafe skillet with oil. Transfer dough to prepared skillet and reshape as needed. Spread pizza sauce evenly, leaving ½-inch border at edge, and sprinkle with cheese.

3. Set skillet over high heat and cook pizza until outside edge is set and bottom crust is spotty brown, about 3 minutes. Transfer skillet to oven and bake until edges are brown and cheese is melted and spotty brown.

FAVORITE PIZZA TOPPINGS

When you want a break from standard toppings, try one of the combinations listed below, or get creative with your own ideas. Utilize leftovers like barbecued chicken or roasted potatoes. Try different types of cheeses, deli meats, vegetables, and herbs. The pantry is another source of inspiration; pickled chile peppers, olives, and marinated artichoke hearts are all tasty toppings. And don't overlook fruit; fresh or canned pineapple, thinly sliced pear (with blue cheese), and dried figs (with goat cheese) are all excellent options.

FOUR-CHEESE PIZZA: Omit pizza sauce and sprinkle oiled dough with shredded mozzarella, shredded provolone, grated Parmesan, and crumbled blue cheese.

WHITE PIZZA: Omit pizza sauce and dollop ricotta cheese over oiled dough, then sprinkle with grated Parmesan cheese. Sprinkle leaves of baby spinach or arugula over pizza during final 2 minutes of baking.

PESTO PIZZA: Substitute ⅓ cup Basil Pesto (page 410) for pizza sauce and top with thin slices of tomato (patted dry), crumbled goat cheese, and grated Parmesan cheese.

NOTES FROM THE TEST KITCHEN

Store-Bought Pizza Dough

While pizza dough is nothing more than bread dough with oil added for softness and suppleness, we have found that minor changes can yield dramatically different results. We think homemade dough is worth the modest effort, but we have to admit that prepared dough can be a great time-saving option for a weeknight pizza made at home. Many supermarkets and pizzerias sell dough for just a few dollars a pound, and the dough can be easily frozen. We found that store-bought dough worked well and tasted fine, but we recommend buying dough from a pizzeria, where it is more likely to be fresh. Supermarket pizza dough is frequently unlabeled, so there's no way to know how long the dough has been sitting in the refrigerated case, or how much dough is in the bag. Be sure to bring the dough up to room temperature for about 2 hours before proceeding. If frozen, let the dough thaw on the counter for 3 hours or overnight in the refrigerator before use.

Fresh versus Supermarket Mozzarella

For such a mild-mannered cheese, mozzarella sure is popular. In 2006, it passed cheddar to become the leading cheese in the United States in per-capita consumption, with most supermarkets stocking two main varieties: fresh (usually packed in brine) and supermarket, or low-moisture (available either as a block or preshredded).

WHAT'S THE DIFFERENCE?: Both varieties are made by stretching and pulling the curds by hand or machine, which aligns the proteins into long chains and gives the cheese its trademark elasticity. However, the final products differ considerably, particularly when it comes to water weight. According to federal standards, fresh mozzarella must have a moisture content between 52 percent and 60 percent by weight, which makes it highly perishable. Drier, firmer low-moisture mozzarella hovers between 45 percent and 52 percent and is remarkably shelf-stable—it can last in the fridge for weeks.

WHEN TO USE FRESH: We prefer the sweet richness and tender bite of the fresh stuff for snacking, sandwiches, and Caprese salad but tend not to use it in cooked applications, since heat can destroy its delicate flavor and texture.

WHEN TO USE SUPERMARKET: For most baked dishes, we turn to the low-moisture kind. It offers mellow flavor that blends seamlessly with bolder ingredients and melts nicely in everything from lasagna to pizza. It's a staple in the test kitchen and in many of our home refrigerators. We prefer supermarket mozzarella that, when baked, is creamy and clean-tasting and has a bit of soft (not rubbery) chew, plenty of gooey stretch, and just a touch of flavorful browning.

HOW TO STORE MOZZARELLA: Storing supermarket mozzarella presents a conundrum: as it sits, it releases moisture. If this moisture evaporates too quickly, the cheese dries out. But if the moisture stays on the cheese's surface, it encourages mold. To find the best storage method, we tried wrapping mozzarella in various materials, refrigerated the samples for six weeks, and monitored them for mold and dryness. Those wrapped in plastic—whether cling wrap or zipper-lock bags—were the first to show mold. Those in waxed or parchment paper alone lost too much moisture and dried out. The best method: waxed or parchment paper loosely wrapped with aluminum foil. The paper wicks moisture away, while the foil cover traps enough water to keep the cheese from drying out. Fresh mozzarella does not store well and is best eaten within a day or two.

French Bread Pizzas

SERVES 4 TO 6   **TOTAL TIME** 30 MINUTES   **FAST**

✔ **WHY THIS RECIPE WORKS:** Skip the freezer aisle offerings—you can easily prepare our French Bread Pizzas at home using ingredients that you probably have on hand. We made a flavored olive oil in the microwave with garlic, basil, and red pepper flakes, and then brushed it on slices of soft supermarket French bread. Sprinkling the slices with Parmesan and baking them for just a few minutes kept the bread from becoming soggy when we added sauce and mozzarella. Once we topped the pizzas, they needed only a few minutes in the oven for the cheese to melt and begin to brown. We like to use our Easy Pizza Sauce (page 435); however, you can substitute premade sauce from the supermarket.

1   (24-inch) loaf French bread
6   tablespoons extra-virgin olive oil
4   garlic cloves, minced
¼   cup finely chopped fresh basil
⅛   teaspoon red pepper flakes
1   ounce Parmesan cheese, grated (½ cup)
1   cup pizza sauce
8   ounces mozzarella cheese, shredded (2 cups)

1. Adjust oven rack to upper-middle position and heat oven to 475 degrees. Cut bread crosswise into four 6-inch pieces, then split each piece in half lengthwise. Microwave oil, garlic, 2 tablespoons basil, and pepper flakes in bowl until fragrant, 30 to 60 seconds.

2. Brush half of oil mixture over crust and edges of bread. Arrange bread, cut side up, on aluminum foil–lined baking sheet. Sprinkle Parmesan evenly over bread and bake until cheese begins to brown, about 3 minutes.

3. Whisk pizza sauce, remaining 2 tablespoons basil, and remaining oil mixture together in bowl. Spread sauce evenly over bread, then top with mozzarella. Bake until cheese is melted and spotty brown, 5 to 7 minutes. Serve.

VARIATION
French Bread Pepperoni Pizzas
Microwave 2 ounces sliced pepperoni between triple layers of coffee filters on plate for 30 seconds to render some fat. Top mozzarella with pepperoni before baking in step 3.

Lavash Pizzas with Chicken and Spinach

SERVES 4   **TOTAL TIME** 30 MINUTES   FAST

✓ **WHY THIS RECIPE WORKS:** Using lavash, a Middle Eastern flatbread, instead of traditional pizza dough gave this crust a crisp, crackerlike texture. We first brushed the lavash with oil and toasted them quickly in the oven, then spread them with a mixture of sautéed ground chicken, spinach, and shredded fontina. Topped with goat cheese and returned to the oven for a few minutes until the cheese begins to brown, these lavash pizzas make a simple yet sophisticated dinner. You can substitute ground turkey for the chicken. Lavash can often be found near the tortillas in the supermarket. If you cannot fit both lavash on a single baking sheet, use two baking sheets and bake on the upper-middle and lower-middle racks, switching and rotating the baking sheets halfway through baking.

    3 tablespoons extra-virgin olive oil
    2 pieces lavash bread
    1 pound ground chicken
   10 ounces frozen chopped spinach,
       thawed and squeezed dry
    4 ounces fontina cheese, shredded (1 cup)
    3 garlic cloves, minced
    ½ teaspoon red pepper flakes
    ¼ teaspoon salt
    ¼ teaspoon pepper
    4 ounces goat cheese, crumbled (1 cup)

1. Adjust oven rack to middle position and heat oven to 475 degrees. Brush 2 tablespoons oil over both sides of lavash and lay on baking sheet. Bake lavash until golden brown, about 5 minutes, flipping halfway through baking.

2. Meanwhile, heat remaining 1 tablespoon oil in 12-inch skillet over medium heat until shimmering. Add chicken and cook, breaking up any large pieces with wooden spoon, until no longer pink, about 5 minutes.

3. Combine cooked chicken, spinach, fontina, garlic, pepper flakes, salt, and pepper in bowl. Spread mixture evenly over each lavash and top with goat cheese. Bake until cheese is melted and spotty brown, 6 to 8 minutes. Serve.

VARIATIONS

Lavash Pizzas with Lamb, Tomatoes, and Feta

Omit spinach. Substitute 1 pound ground lamb for chicken. Add 1 tomato, cored and cut into ½-inch pieces, and ½ teaspoon ground cinnamon to meat mixture. Substitute 1 cup crumbled feta cheese for goat cheese. Sprinkle with 2 tablespoons minced fresh parsley before serving.

Adding rich toppings to toasted lavash bread, such as lamb, tomatoes, and feta, makes an instant dinner.

Lavash Pizzas with Spinach, Tomatoes, and Olives

Omit chicken and 1 tablespoon oil; skip step 2. Reduce pepper flakes to ¼ teaspoon. Add 1 tomato, cored and cut into ½-inch pieces, and ½ cup pitted large green olives, chopped, to spinach mixture. Substitute ½ cup grated Parmesan cheese for goat cheese.

Lavash Pizzas with Curried Cauliflower and Fennel

Omit chicken, spinach, and 1 tablespoon oil; skip step 2. Melt 2 tablespoons unsalted butter in 12-inch skillet over medium-high heat. Add 2 cups chopped cauliflower, 1 chopped head fennel, 3 tablespoons water, ½ teaspoon salt, and ½ teaspoon curry powder. Cover and cook, stirring occasionally, until vegetables are tender, 6 to 8 minutes; let cool slightly. Combine cauliflower mixture with fontina and spices before topping lavash. Sprinkle with 2 thinly sliced scallions before serving.

Greek Pita Pizzas with Hummus

SERVES 4 **TOTAL TIME** 30 MINUTES **FAST**

WHY THIS RECIPE WORKS: These simple personal pizzas, which rely on toasted pita rounds for the crusts, make an easy-to-assemble weeknight meal. Topping the pizzas with prepared hummus in lieu of tomato sauce, along with feta, onion, and kalamata olives, gave them a Greek-inspired flavor in little time, while lightly dressed arugula, added just before serving, made them appealingly fresh. We found both plain and roasted red pepper hummus worked well here. If you cannot fit all four pitas on a single baking sheet, use two baking sheets and bake on the upper-middle and lower-middle racks, switching and rotating the baking sheets halfway through baking.

¼ cup extra-virgin olive oil

4 (8-inch) pita breads

2 tablespoons red wine vinegar

¼ teaspoon pepper

⅛ teaspoon salt

1 small red onion, halved and sliced thin

½ cup pitted kalamata olives, chopped

½ cup hummus

4 ounces shredded Italian cheese blend (1 cup)

4 ounces feta cheese, crumbled (1 cup)

2 ounces (2 cups) baby arugula

1. Adjust oven rack to middle position and heat oven to 475 degrees. Brush 2 tablespoons oil over both sides of pitas and lay on baking sheet. Bake pitas until golden brown, about 5 minutes, flipping halfway through baking.

2. Meanwhile, whisk remaining 2 tablespoons oil, vinegar, pepper, and salt together in bowl. In separate bowl, toss onion and olives with 2 tablespoons of vinaigrette.

3. Spread 2 tablespoons hummus evenly over each pita. Sprinkle with Italian cheese blend and feta, then top with onion mixture. Bake pitas until onions soften and cheese is melted and spotty brown, 6 to 8 minutes, rotating baking sheet halfway through baking.

4. Before serving, whisk remaining vinaigrette to recombine. Toss arugula with vinaigrette in bowl, pile on top of pizzas, and serve.

Our perfectly sealed calzones have easy-to-make rich fillings that won't ooze or leak during baking.

Ricotta and Spinach Calzones

SERVES 4 **TOTAL TIME** 50 MINUTES

WHY THIS RECIPE WORKS: With soggy fillings and bready crusts, bad calzones are found everywhere. The best recipe should result in a balance of crisp crust with plenty of chew and a healthy proportion of rich and flavorful filling. We spread an easy-to-make filling featuring ricotta and spinach onto the bottom half of a rolled-out pizza round, and brushed egg wash over the edges before folding the top half over the bottom half. We cut vents in the tops to allow steam to escape while baking. The calzones needed only 15 minutes in the oven and a few minutes to cool before serving. We like to use our One-Pound Classic Pizza Dough (page 434); however, you can substitute premade dough from the supermarket or your local pizzeria. Be sure to let the dough sit out at room temperature while preparing the remaining ingredients and heating the oven, or it will be difficult to stretch. Serve with your favorite marinara or tomato pasta sauce.

10 ounces frozen chopped spinach,
     thawed and squeezed dry
8 ounces (1 cup) whole-milk ricotta cheese
4 ounces mozzarella cheese, shredded (1 cup)
1 ounce Parmesan cheese, grated (½ cup)
1 tablespoon extra-virgin olive oil
1 large egg, lightly beaten with 2 tablespoons water,
     plus 1 large yolk
2 garlic cloves, minced
1½ teaspoons minced fresh oregano
⅛ teaspoon red pepper flakes
1 pound pizza dough, room temperature

1. Adjust oven rack to lower-middle position and heat oven to 500 degrees. Cut two 9-inch square pieces of parchment paper. Combine spinach, ricotta, mozzarella, Parmesan, oil, egg yolk, garlic, oregano, and pepper flakes in bowl.

2. Place dough on lightly floured counter, divide in half, and cover with greased plastic wrap. Working with 1 piece of dough at a time (keep other piece covered), use rolling pin to flatten dough into 9-inch round. Transfer each piece of dough to parchment square and reshape as needed.

3. Spread half of spinach filling evenly over half of each dough round, leaving 1-inch border at edge. Brush edge with egg wash. Fold other half of dough over filling, leaving ½-inch border of bottom half uncovered. Press edges of dough together and crimp to seal.

4. With sharp knife, cut 5 steam vents, about 1½ inches long, in top of calzone. Brush with remaining egg wash. Transfer calzones (still on parchment) onto baking sheet, trimming parchment as needed to fit. Bake until golden brown, about 15 minutes, rotating baking sheet halfway through baking. Transfer calzones to wire rack and let cool for 5 minutes before serving.

VARIATIONS
Sausage and Broccoli Rabe Calzones
Omit spinach. Microwave 6 ounces chopped broccoli rabe, 4 ounces Italian sausage, pinched into small pieces, and 1 tablespoon water in covered bowl until sausage is no longer pink and broccoli rabe is crisp-tender, about 4 minutes; drain mixture well, let cool, and add to ricotta mixture.

Meat Lovers' Calzones
Omit spinach, oregano, and pepper flakes. Toss 4 ounces sliced salami, 4 ounces sliced capicola, and 2 ounces sliced

pepperoni, all quartered, together in bowl. Working in 3 batches, microwave meats between triple layers of coffee filters on plate for 30 seconds to render some fat; use fresh coffee filters for each batch. Let meats cool, then add to ricotta mixture.

Cheesy Broccoli Calzones
Omit spinach. Reduce ricotta to ½ cup and increase shredded mozzarella to 1½ cups. Add ½ cup crumbled feta cheese and 10 ounces frozen broccoli florets, thawed and chopped, to ricotta mixture.

Assembling a Calzone

1. Spread half of spinach filling evenly over half of each dough round, leaving 1-inch border at edge.

2. Brush edge of dough with egg wash. Fold other half of dough over filling, leaving ½-inch border of bottom half uncovered.

3. Press edges of dough together, pressing out any air pockets. To crimp, start at 1 end and place index finger diagonally across edge; pull bottom layer of dough over tip of finger and press to seal.

4. Cut 5 steam vents, about 1½ inches long, across top of each calzone. Cut through only top layer of dough.

Classic Grilled Cheese Sandwiches

SERVES 4   **TOTAL TIME** 25 MINUTES **FAST**

✔ **WHY THIS RECIPE WORKS:** In our grilled cheese recipe, the right ingredients—coupled with the proper technique—gave us perfect sandwiches. Buttering the bread—not the pan—gave our sandwiches the most even browning. Cooking the sandwiches over medium-low heat allowed the cheese to melt evenly and the bread to brown deeply. Sharp cheddar cheese tempered by smooth-melting Monterey Jack provided the best combination of flavor and texture for the sandwiches. For a crisp crust, we pressed the grilled cheese sandwiches with a cake pan to mimic a panini press.

5½ **ounces sharp cheddar cheese, shredded (1⅓ cups)**
2½ **ounces Monterey Jack cheese, shredded (⅔ cup)**
 4 **tablespoons unsalted butter, melted**
 8 **slices hearty white sandwich bread**

1. Adjust oven rack to middle position and heat oven to 200 degrees. Combine cheeses in bowl.

2. Brush melted butter evenly over 1 side of each slice of bread. Flip 4 slices over, top evenly with ½ cup cheese mixture, and compact cheese lightly. Top with remaining 4 slices bread, buttered side up, and press down gently.

3. Heat 12-inch nonstick skillet over medium-low heat for 1 minute. Place 2 sandwiches in pan and place round cake pan on top, pressing lightly. Leave cake pan on top and cook until first side is golden brown, 3 to 5 minutes. Flip sandwiches, press again with cake pan, and cook until golden on second side, about 2 minutes.

4. Transfer sandwiches to wire rack set in rimmed baking sheet and keep warm in oven. Wipe out skillet with paper towels and cook remaining 2 sandwiches. Serve.

Making Grilled Cheese Sandwiches

Place 2 sandwiches in skillet and place 9-inch round cake pan on top. Press lightly for several seconds to compact filling and help bread make even contact with pan.

Grown-Up Grilled Cheese Sandwiches

SERVES 4   **TOTAL TIME** 30 MINUTES **FAST**

✔ **WHY THIS RECIPE WORKS:** In an attempt to liven up grilled cheese, some add so many ingredients that the cheese is an afterthought. Our recipe began by mixing flavorful aged cheddar with a small amount of wine and Brie in a food processor. These two ingredients helped the aged cheddar melt evenly without becoming greasy. A little bit of shallot increased the sandwiches' complexity without detracting from the cheese, and a smear of mustard-butter on the bread added a sharp bite. Look for a cheddar aged for about one year (avoid cheddar aged for longer; it won't melt well). To bring the cheddar to room temperature quickly, microwave the pieces until warm, about 30 seconds.

 7 **ounces aged cheddar cheese, cut into 24 equal pieces, room temperature**
 2 **ounces Brie cheese, rind removed**
 2 **tablespoons dry white wine or dry vermouth**
 4 **teaspoons minced shallot**
 3 **tablespoons unsalted butter, softened**
 1 **teaspoon Dijon mustard**
 8 **slices hearty white sandwich bread**

1. Adjust oven rack to middle position and heat oven to 200 degrees. Process cheddar, Brie, and wine in food processor until smooth paste forms, 20 to 30 seconds. Add shallot and pulse to combine, 3 to 5 pulses; transfer to bowl. In separate bowl, combine butter and mustard.

2. Brush butter-mustard mixture evenly over 1 side of each slice of bread. Flip 4 slices over and spread processed cheese mixture evenly over second side. Top with remaining 4 slices bread, buttered side up, and press down gently.

3. Heat 12-inch nonstick skillet over medium heat for 2 minutes. Place 2 sandwiches in skillet, reduce heat to medium-low, and cook until both sides are crisp and golden brown, 6 to 9 minutes per side.

4. Transfer sandwiches to wire rack set in rimmed baking sheet and keep warm in oven. Wipe out skillet with paper towels and cook remaining 2 sandwiches. Serve.

VARIATIONS
Grown-Up Grilled Cheese Sandwiches with Gruyère and Chives

Substitute room-temperature Gruyère cheese, cut into 24 equal pieces, for cheddar, hearty rye sandwich bread for white bread, and 4 teaspoons minced fresh chives for shallot.

Our grown-up grilled cheese sandwiches pair flavorful cheeses with complementary shallots, chives, or dates.

Grown-Up Grilled Cheese Sandwiches with Asiago and Dates

Substitute room-temperature Asiago cheese, cut into 24 equal pieces, for cheddar, hearty oatmeal sandwich bread for white bread, and 4 teaspoons finely chopped dates for shallot.

Oven "Grilled" Cheese Sandwiches for a Crowd

SERVES 8   TOTAL TIME 25 MINUTES **FAST**

✔ **WHY THIS RECIPE WORKS:** Grilled cheese sandwiches can be made two at a time in a skillet, but what if you're cooking for a crowd of hungry people? Since a skillet couldn't begin to handle eight sandwiches at once, we turned to a baking sheet and the oven. We used our classic method of brushing sandwich bread slices with melted butter and then filling them with shredded cheddar and Monterey Jack cheeses. To jump-start cooking and crisping our sandwiches, we preheated the baking sheet in the oven before cooking. To mimic an Italian panini press, we preheated a second sheet pan and placed it on top of the sandwiches

in the oven. In about 6 minutes, we had eight "grilled" sandwiches that required no flipping or making sandwiches two by two. You'll need two rimmed baking sheets for this recipe.

11 **ounces sharp cheddar cheese, shredded (2⅔ cups)**
5 **ounces Monterey Jack cheese, shredded (1⅓ cups)**
8 **tablespoons unsalted butter, melted**
16 **slices hearty white sandwich bread**

1. Adjust oven racks to middle and lower-middle positions. Place 1 rimmed baking sheet on each rack and heat oven to 450 degrees. Combine cheeses in bowl.

2. Brush melted butter evenly over 1 side of each slice of bread. Flip 8 slices over, top evenly with ½ cup cheese mixture, and compact cheese lightly. Top with remaining 8 slices bread, buttered side up, and press down gently.

3. Remove hot baking sheets from oven. Arrange sandwiches on 1 sheet, then return to middle rack of oven. Carefully place second sheet over sandwiches, rim side up, and press lightly. Bake sandwiches, with second pan resting on top, until golden, 5 to 6 minutes. Serve.

VARIATIONS

Smoked Turkey and Chutney Oven "Grilled" Cheese Sandwiches for a Crowd

When assembling sandwiches, layer ingredients as follows between slices of buttered bread: 1 tablespoon chutney, ¼ cup cheese mixture, several slices red onion, 1 slice smoked turkey, and ¼ cup cheese mixture. (You will need ½ cup chutney, ½ red onion, and 8 slices smoked turkey total.)

Pesto and Capicola Oven "Grilled" Cheese Sandwiches for a Crowd

Salami can be substituted for the capicola here.

Substitute shredded provolone for cheddar. When assembling sandwiches, layer ingredients as follows between slices of buttered bread: 1 tablespoon pesto, ¼ cup cheese mixture, 2 slices capicola, and ¼ cup cheese mixture. (You will need ½ cup pesto and 16 slices capicola total.)

Making Oven "Grilled" Cheese Sandwiches

Arrange sandwiches on preheated baking sheet and return to oven. Carefully place second preheated baking sheet on top of sandwiches, rim side up, and press lightly. Sandwiches "grill" in oven without flipping.

WINNING SANDWICH COMBINATIONS

It's easy to get into a sandwich rut using the same ingredients again and again. Here are a few of the test kitchen's favorite sandwich combinations.

Condiments and spreads, about 2 tablespoons per sandwich, should be put on both slices of bread; this will help prevent the bread from becoming soggy. To keep a sandwich from becoming too big and unwieldy, use 3 to 4 ounces of meat and an ounce of cheese per sandwich. As to vegetables and other garnishes, be judicious.

ROAST BEEF WITH BOURSIN AND ARUGULA `FAST`
Roast Beef
Boursin Cheese
Thinly Sliced Red Onion
Arugula
Sourdough Bread

PROSCIUTTO WITH GOAT CHEESE AND RADICCHIO `FAST`
Prosciutto
Goat Cheese
Shredded Radicchio
Oil and Red Wine Vinegar
Olive Bread

MOZZARELLA WITH ROASTED PEPPERS AND PESTO `FAST`
Fresh Mozzarella
Roasted Red Peppers
Classic Basil Pesto (page 410)
Focaccia

SPINACH AND FETA WITH SUN-DRIED TOMATOES `FAST`
Baby Spinach
Feta Cheese
Sun-Dried Tomatoes
Mayonnaise
Pita Bread

EGG SALAD WITH BACON AND RADISHES `FAST`
Classic Egg Salad (page 73)
Crumbled Bacon
Thinly Sliced Radishes
Bibb Lettuce
Toasted Challah

To keep the bread in our Reubens from becoming soggy, we quickly cook the sauerkraut to remove excess moisture.

Best Reuben Sandwiches

SERVES 4   **TOTAL TIME** 35 MINUTES   `FAST`

✔ **WHY THIS RECIPE WORKS:** The traditional Reuben is the epitome of a deli sandwich. But most recipes produce sandwiches with chilly centers, unmelted cheese, soggy rye, and watery sauerkraut. Instead of the usual Thousand Island or Russian, we made a homemade dressing with mayonnaise and prepared cocktail sauce, which we mixed with hand-chopped fresh, crunchy pickles and pickle juice. To combat sogginess, we drained and rinsed the sauerkraut and quickly cooked it in a skillet with some cider vinegar and brown sugar; this extra step not only added flavor, it also allowed the sauerkraut's excess moisture to evaporate. We chose shredded Swiss for our sandwich, and, to fully melt the cheese, we covered the skillet for part of the cooking time. Corned beef is typically made from either the brisket or the round. We prefer the corned beef brisket. We prefer pouched sauerkraut, sold near the pickles in most supermarkets, to jarred or canned varieties.

- ¼ cup mayonnaise
- ¼ cup finely chopped sweet pickles plus 1 teaspoon pickle brine
- 2 tablespoons cocktail sauce
- 1 cup sauerkraut, drained and rinsed
- 2 tablespoons cider vinegar
- 1 teaspoon packed brown sugar
- 4 tablespoons unsalted butter, melted
- 8 slices hearty rye bread
- 4 ounces Swiss cheese, shredded (1 cup)
- 12 ounces thinly sliced corned beef

1. Adjust oven rack to middle position and heat oven to 200 degrees. Whisk mayonnaise, pickles, pickle brine, and cocktail sauce together in bowl; set aside.

2. Cook sauerkraut, vinegar, and sugar in 12-inch nonstick skillet over medium-high heat, stirring occasionally, until liquid evaporates, about 3 minutes; transfer to bowl. Wipe out skillet with paper towels.

3. Brush melted butter evenly over 1 side of each slice of bread. Flip bread over and spread mayonnaise mixture evenly over second side. Assemble 4 sandwiches by layering ingredients as follows between prepared bread (with mayonnaise mixture inside sandwich): half of Swiss, half of corned beef, sauerkraut, remaining corned beef, and remaining Swiss. Press gently on sandwiches to set.

4. Heat now-empty skillet over medium-low heat for 2 minutes. Place 2 sandwiches in pan and cook until golden brown on first side, about 4 minutes. Flip sandwiches, cover skillet, and cook until second side is golden brown and cheese is melted, about 4 minutes.

5. Transfer sandwiches to wire rack set in rimmed baking sheet and keep warm in oven. Wipe out skillet with paper towels and cook remaining 2 sandwiches. Serve.

Cooking Sauerkraut

Cook sauerkraut, vinegar, and sugar in 12-inch skillet over medium-high heat, stirring occasionally, until liquid evaporates, about 3 minutes.

Roast Beef and Blue Cheese Panini

SERVES 4   TOTAL TIME 35 MINUTES   FAST

✔ **WHY THIS RECIPE WORKS:** Italians have it right when it comes to sandwiches: They load meat, cheese, and flavorful condiments between slices of crusty bread and then compact the sandwich in a heated, ridged press. We wanted a panini recipe that we could make without using either a panini press or an indoor grill. To achieve the signature ridged grill marks, we used a nonstick grill pan as the base, and the weight of a Dutch oven on top. For this panini, we paired roast beef and mayonnaise spiked with blue cheese and horseradish. Spinach and thin slices of red onion provided a crunchy bite. We like to use rustic, artisanal bread for this recipe; do not use a baguette, but rather look for a wide loaf that will yield big slices. We like the attractive grill marks that a grill pan gives the panini, but you can substitute a 12-inch nonstick skillet. Buy refrigerated prepared horseradish, not the shelf-stable kind, which contains preservatives and additives.

- 4 ounces blue cheese, crumbled (1 cup)
- ⅓ cup mayonnaise
- 2 tablespoons prepared horseradish, drained
- ½ teaspoon pepper
- 2 tablespoons olive oil
- 8 (½-inch-thick) slices crusty bread
- 8 ounces thinly sliced deli roast beef
- 2 ounces (2 cups) baby spinach
- ½ cup thinly sliced red onion

1. Adjust oven rack to middle position and heat oven to 200 degrees. Combine blue cheese, mayonnaise, horseradish, and pepper in bowl.

2. Brush oil evenly over 1 side of each slice of bread. Flip bread over and spread blue cheese mixture evenly over second side. Assemble 4 sandwiches by layering roast beef, spinach, and onion between prepared bread (with blue cheese mixture inside sandwich). Press gently on sandwiches to set.

Cooking Panini

Place 2 sandwiches in grill pan, place Dutch oven on top, and cook until golden brown. Flip sandwiches, replace Dutch oven, and cook until second side is crisp.

3. Heat 12-inch nonstick grill pan over medium heat for 1 minute. Place 2 sandwiches in pan, place Dutch oven on top, and cook until bread is golden and crisp, about 4 minutes. Flip sandwiches, replace Dutch oven, and cook until second side is crisp and cheese is melted, about 4 minutes.

4. Transfer sandwiches to wire rack set in rimmed baking sheet and keep warm in oven. Wipe out skillet with paper towels and cook remaining 2 sandwiches. Serve.

Portobello Panini

SERVES 4   **TOTAL TIME** 45 MINUTES   **FAST**

✔ **WHY THIS RECIPE WORKS:** The meaty texture of portobello mushrooms makes them excellent for sandwiches. Add fontina cheese, roasted red peppers, and an herbed mayonnaise, and you are guaranteed an irresistible panini. To ensure the mushrooms are tender in the final sandwich, we precooked them in the grill pan before assembling and toasting the sandwiches. Using shredded fontina helped speed the melting process and guaranteed an even layer of gooey cheese. A nonstick grill pan and a Dutch oven mimicked the signature marks of a panini press. We like to use rustic, artisanal bread for this recipe; do not use a baguette, but rather look for a wide loaf that will yield big slices. We like the attractive grill marks that a grill pan gives the panini, but you can substitute a 12-inch nonstick skillet.

½   cup mayonnaise
4   garlic cloves, minced
1   teaspoon minced fresh rosemary or ¼ teaspoon dried
6   large portobello mushroom caps, halved
6   tablespoons extra-virgin olive oil
¼   teaspoon salt
¼   teaspoon pepper
8   (½-inch-thick) slices crusty bread
8   ounces fontina cheese, shredded (2 cups)
½   cup jarred roasted red peppers, patted dry and sliced ½ inch thick

1. Adjust oven rack to middle position and heat oven to 200 degrees. Combine mayonnaise, garlic, and rosemary in bowl. In separate bowl, toss mushrooms with ¼ cup oil, salt, and pepper.

2. Heat 12-inch nonstick grill pan over medium heat for 1 minute. Place mushrooms, gill side up, in pan and place Dutch oven on top. Cook until mushrooms are well browned on both sides, about 5 minutes per side. Transfer mushrooms to plate and wipe out pan with paper towels.

3. Brush remaining 2 tablespoons oil evenly over 1 side of each slice of bread. Flip bread over and spread mayonnaise mixture evenly over second side. Assemble 4 sandwiches by layering ingredients as follows between prepared bread (with mayonnaise mixture inside sandwich): half of fontina, cooked mushrooms, red peppers, and remaining fontina. Press gently on sandwiches to set.

4. Return grill pan to medium heat for 1 minute. Place 2 sandwiches in pan, place Dutch oven on top, and cook until bread is golden and crisp, about 4 minutes. Flip sandwiches, replace Dutch oven, and cook until second side is crisp and cheese is melted, about 4 minutes.

5. Transfer sandwiches to wire rack set in rimmed baking sheet and keep warm in oven. Wipe out skillet with paper towels and cook remaining 2 sandwiches. Serve.

NOTES FROM THE TEST KITCHEN

Using Portobello Mushrooms

Portobellos are the giants of the mushroom family, ranging from 4 to 6 inches in diameter. They are the mature form of cremini mushrooms, and as a result of the extra growing time they have a particularly intense, meaty flavor. Available year-round, they have a steak-like texture and robust flavor that make them ideal for being sautéed, stir-fried, roasted, grilled, or stuffed.

BUYING PORTOBELLOS: If possible, buy loose mushrooms rather than prepackaged so you can inspect their quality. Look for mushrooms with fully intact caps and dry gills. Wet, damaged gills are a sign of spoilage. The stems are woody and are often discarded, so buy mushrooms with stems only if you plan to use them (such as in soup, stock, or stuffing).

STORING PORTOBELLOS: Because they release moisture, which can encourage spoilage, portobellos need some air circulation to stay fresh. They are best stored in a partially open zipper-lock bag, which maximizes air circulation without drying out the mushrooms.

PREPARING PORTOBELLOS: To clean portobellos, simply wipe them with a damp towel. Remove the woody stems before cooking and either discard or reserve them. If you are using the portobellos in a sauce, we recommend gently scraping out the black gills with a spoon before cooking to prevent a muddy-looking sauce.

Sun-dried tomatoes, bacon, and arugula elevate this sandwich to an above-average turkey panini.

Smoked Turkey Club Panini

SERVES 4   **TOTAL TIME** 35 MINUTES   **FAST**

✔ **WHY THIS RECIPE WORKS:** We used bold, flavorful sun-dried tomatoes and their oil both on the sandwich and mixed into the mayonnaise for a new twist on our panini recipe. Bacon microwaved until crisp gave the sandwich smokiness, while Swiss cheese and arugula added additional flavor. Grilling the sandwiches under a heavy Dutch oven created a perfectly pressed panini. We like to use rustic, artisanal bread for this recipe; do not use a baguette, but rather look for a wide loaf that will yield big slices. We like the attractive grill marks that a grill pan gives the panini, but you can substitute a 12-inch nonstick skillet.

8 slices bacon
⅓ cup oil-packed sun-dried tomatoes, patted dry and minced, plus 2 tablespoons tomato packing oil
⅓ cup mayonnaise
8 (½-inch-thick) slices crusty bread

8 ounces deli Swiss cheese
8 ounces thinly sliced deli smoked turkey
2 ounces (2 cups) baby arugula

1. Adjust oven rack to middle position and heat oven to 200 degrees. Arrange bacon between double layers of coffee filters on plate and microwave until crisp, about 5 minutes. Combine sun-dried tomatoes and mayonnaise in bowl.

2. Brush tomato oil evenly over 1 side of each slice of bread. Flip bread over and spread mayonnaise mixture evenly over second side. Assemble 4 sandwiches by layering ingredients as follows between prepared bread (with mayonnaise mixture inside sandwich): half of Swiss, turkey, crisp bacon, arugula, and remaining Swiss. Press gently on sandwiches to set.

3. Heat 12-inch nonstick grill pan over medium heat for 1 minute. Place 2 sandwiches in pan, set Dutch oven on top, and cook until bread is golden and crisp, about 4 minutes. Flip sandwiches, replace Dutch oven, and cook until second side is crisp and cheese is melted, about 4 minutes.

4. Transfer sandwiches to wire rack set in rimmed baking sheet and keep warm in oven. Wipe out skillet with paper towels and cook remaining 2 sandwiches. Serve.

Texas-Size BBQ Chicken and Cheddar Sandwiches

SERVES 4   **TOTAL TIME** 35 MINUTES   **FAST**

✔ **WHY THIS RECIPE WORKS:** The combination of bacon, cheddar, chicken, chile, and barbecue sauce ensures that these big, hot, toasty, oven-baked sandwiches also pack Texas-size flavor. We fried bacon until crisp, then browned boneless chicken breasts in some of the rendered fat and finished them in barbecue sauce mixed with minced chipotle chile in adobo and a splash of water. Once the chicken had cooled, we cut the breasts into pieces and arranged them on rolls. After topping each sandwich with the barbecue sauce mixture, bacon, and shredded cheddar, we baked them open-faced in the oven until the cheese melted. With the roll tops back on, the sandwiches were ready to eat. Using a homemade or high-quality barbecue sauce makes a difference here; see our recipes for homemade barbecue sauce on page 351.

4 slices bacon, halved crosswise
4 boneless, skinless chicken breasts, trimmed
    Salt and pepper
1 cup barbecue sauce
1 teaspoon minced canned chipotle chile in adobo sauce

¼ cup water

4 deli-style onion rolls, split open completely

6 ounces cheddar cheese, shredded (1½ cups)

1. Adjust oven rack to upper-middle position and heat oven to 400 degrees. Cook bacon in 12-inch nonstick skillet over medium-high heat until crisp, about 4 minutes. Transfer to paper towel–lined plate and pour off all but 1 tablespoon fat left in pan.

2. Pat chicken dry with paper towels and season with salt and pepper. Add chicken to fat left in skillet and cook over medium-high heat until lightly browned on first side, about 4 minutes. Flip chicken and add barbecue sauce, chipotle, and water. Cover, reduce heat to medium, and simmer until sauce is slightly thickened and chicken is cooked through and registers 160 degrees, about 8 minutes. Transfer chicken to cutting board, let cool slightly, then cut crosswise into ¼-inch-thick slices.

3. Arrange rolls cut side up on rimmed baking sheet. Divide chicken among bottom halves of rolls and top with sauce, cheddar, and bacon. Bake open-faced sandwiches in oven until cheese is melted and rolls are lightly toasted, about 4 minutes. Place toasted roll tops on top of sandwiches, and serve.

Muffuletta

SERVES 6 TO 8   **TOTAL TIME** 1 HOUR
(PLUS 8 HOURS CHILLING TIME)

✓ **WHY THIS RECIPE WORKS:** What makes this New Orleans–style sandwich special is the olive salad. While the original recipe for this salad seems to be a closely guarded secret, we created a tasty version by combining olives with roasted red peppers, sun-dried tomatoes, olive oil, and herbs. The salad needed at least 8 hours to marinate, and then we drained it before making the sandwich, making sure to reserve some of the marinade to spread on the bread. Creating a hollow in the bread for the savory salad made the sandwich easier to assemble and kept it from becoming soggy. Before serving, we wrapped the sandwich, placed it between two plates, and weighted it down with heavy cans in the refrigerator to allow all of the flavors to meld. Be sure to use good-quality brine-cured olives in this recipe—do not use canned olives. Brine-cured olives are sold either in plastic deli containers in the refrigerated section or in jars in the pickle aisle. If you wish, you can cut this sandwich into small wedges and serve as a party appetizer.

We created our own version of olive salad for this sandwich inspired by the New Orleans original.

OLIVE SALAD

1 cup pitted green olives, chopped coarse

1 cup pitted black olives, chopped coarse

¾ cup extra-virgin olive oil

½ cup jarred roasted red peppers, drained and chopped fine

½ cup oil-packed sun-dried tomatoes, drained and chopped

¼ cup minced fresh parsley

2 tablespoons lemon juice

1 teaspoon dried oregano

1 garlic clove, minced

SANDWICH

1 large (9-inch) round Italian or French bread

8 ounces thinly sliced mortadella

8 ounces thinly sliced provolone

8 ounces thinly sliced hard salami

1. FOR THE OLIVE SALAD: Combine all ingredients in bowl, cover, and refrigerate for at least 8 hours or up to 1 day. Before making sandwich, transfer olive salad to fine-mesh strainer set over bowl and let drain for at least 10 minutes, reserving drained marinade.

2. FOR THE SANDWICH: Cut bread in half horizontally and remove most of interior crumb. Brush inside of both bread halves with drained olive salad marinade. Spread half of olive salad inside bottom half of bread, then cover evenly with layers of mortadella, provolone, salami, and remaining olive salad (in that order). Place top half of bread on top.

3. Wrap sandwich tightly in plastic wrap, place between 2 plates, and weight with several heavy cans. Refrigerate weighted sandwich for at least 30 minutes or up to 1 day. To serve, unwrap sandwich and cut into wedges.

Making Muffuletta

1. HOLLOW OUT ROUND LOAF: Cut bread in half horizontally and remove most of interior crumb.

2. SPREAD OLIVE SALAD OVER BOTTOM: Brush bottom of bread with drained olive marinade and spread half of olive salad inside.

3. LAYER MEATS AND CHEESE: Layer mortadella, provolone, salami, and remaining olive salad (in that order) into sandwich, then place top half of bread on top.

4. WEIGHT AND REFRIGERATE: Wrap sandwich tightly, place between 2 plates, and weight with several heavy cans. Refrigerate weighted sandwich for at least 30 minutes or up to 1 day.

Thinly sliced skirt steak is topped with melted American cheese and chopped peppers to re-create a classic Philly cheesesteak.

Philly Cheesesteaks

SERVES 4   **TOTAL TIME** 30 MINUTES
(PLUS 1 HOUR FREEZING TIME)

✓ WHY THIS RECIPE WORKS: Bringing cheesesteaks home required coming up with a simple and economical way to mimic the thinly shaved slivers of rib eye usually obtained with a meat slicer. We found that when skirt steak was partially frozen, its thin profile and open-grained texture made for easy slicing, and its flavor was nearest to rib eye but without the sticker shock. To best approximate the wide griddle typically used in Philadelphia, we cooked the meat in two batches, letting any excess moisture drain off before giving it a final warm-up. Finally, to bind it all together, we let slices of American cheese melt into the meat, along with a bit of grated Parmesan to boost its flavor. If skirt steak is unavailable, substitute sirloin steak tips (also called flap meat). Top these sandwiches with chopped pickled hot peppers, sautéed onions or bell peppers, sweet relish, or hot sauce.

2 **pounds skirt steak, trimmed and sliced with grain into 3-inch-wide pieces**

4 **(8-inch) Italian sub rolls, split lengthwise**

2 **tablespoons vegetable oil**

   Salt and pepper

¼ **cup grated Parmesan cheese**

8 **slices white American cheese**

1. Freeze steak on large plate until very firm, about 1 hour.

2. Adjust oven rack to middle position and heat oven to 400 degrees. Spread split rolls on baking sheet and toast until lightly browned, 5 to 10 minutes.

3. Using sharp knife, shave steak pieces as thinly as possible against grain. Mound meat on cutting board and chop coarsely with knife 10 to 20 times.

4. Heat 1 tablespoon oil in 12-inch nonstick skillet over high heat until just smoking. Add half of meat in even layer and cook without stirring until well browned on first side, 4 to 5 minutes. Stir and continue to cook until meat is no longer pink, 1 to 2 minutes; transfer to colander. Wipe out skillet with paper towels and repeat with remaining 1 tablespoon oil and meat; transfer to colander.

5. Return now-empty skillet to medium heat. Add drained meat, season with salt and pepper, and cook, stirring constantly, until heated through, 1 to 2 minutes. Reduce heat to low, sprinkle with Parmesan, and shingle cheese slices over top. Let cheese melt, about 2 minutes. Fold melted cheese thoroughly into meat, divide mixture evenly among toasted rolls, and serve.

Shaving Meat for Philly Cheesesteaks

1. Cut trimmed meat into 3-inch-wide strips. Spread meat out over large plate and freeze.

2. Using sharp knife, shave partially frozen meat as thinly as possible against grain.

We brown our homemade corn cakes in a skillet, finish baking them in the oven, then stuff them with black beans or chicken.

Black Bean and Cheese Arepas

SERVES 8   **TOTAL TIME** 1 HOUR

✓ **WHY THIS RECIPE WORKS:** *Arepas* are a type of corn cake popular in Venezuela and Colombia, though iterations exist in other Latin countries. The Venezuelan variety is served as sandwiches that are split open and stuffed with anything from meat and cheese to corn, beans, or even fish. The arepa itself is made using *masarepa* (precooked corn flour) along with water and salt, but getting the consistency right proved to be a challenge. In the end, we found that using just a half cup more water than masarepa produced a dough that was easy to shape, and a small amount of baking powder lightened the texture just enough. The dough is shaped into rounds, browned in a skillet with some oil, and finished in the oven. We made a filling of mashed black beans mixed with Monterey Jack cheese. Cilantro added freshness, lime juice injected a bit of acidity, and chili powder brought a hint of heat.

AREPAS

- 10 ounces (2 cups) masarepa blanca
- 1 teaspoon salt
- 1 teaspoon baking powder
- 2½ cups warm water
- ¼ cup vegetable oil

BLACK BEAN FILLING

- 1 (15-ounce) can black beans, rinsed
- 4 ounces Monterey Jack cheese, shredded (1 cup)
- 2 tablespoons minced fresh cilantro
- 2 scallions, sliced thin
- 1 tablespoon lime juice
- ¼ teaspoon chili powder

  Salt and pepper

1. FOR THE AREPAS: Adjust oven rack to middle position and heat oven to 400 degrees. Whisk masarepa, salt, and baking powder together in large bowl. Gradually add water and stir until combined. Using generous ⅓ cup dough, form eight 3-inch rounds, each about ½ inch thick.

2. Heat 2 tablespoons oil in 12-inch nonstick skillet over medium-high heat until shimmering. Add 4 arepas and cook until golden on both sides, about 4 minutes per side. Transfer arepas to wire rack set in rimmed baking sheet. Wipe out skillet with paper towels and repeat with remaining 2 tablespoons oil and remaining 4 arepas; transfer to baking sheet. (Fried arepas can be refrigerated for up to 3 days or frozen for up to 1 month. Increase baking time as needed in step 3; if frozen, do not thaw before baking.)

Masarepa

This precooked corn flour, also called *harina precocida* and *masa al instante,* is prepared from starchier large-kernel white corn (as opposed to the small-kernel yellow corn familiar to most Americans). The germ is removed from the kernels during processing, and the kernels are then dried and ground to a fine flour. Both white and yellow masarepa can be found at many large supermarkets in the U.S.; the white variety, or *masarepa blanca*, is most often used in Colombia and Venezuela, so we chose to use it in our arepas recipe. Masarepa shouldn't be confused with masa harina, which has been treated with lime and is used for making tortillas.

3. Bake arepas on wire rack until they sound hollow when tapped on bottom, about 10 minutes.

4. FOR THE FILLING: Meanwhile, using potato masher or fork, mash beans in bowl until most are broken. Stir in remaining ingredients and season with salt and pepper to taste.

5. Using a fork, gently split hot, baked arepas open and stuff each with generous 3 tablespoons filling. Serve.

VARIATION

Chicken and Avocado Arepas

Omit black beans and cheese, and add 1 cup finely shredded cooked chicken and 1 chopped avocado to filling.

Making Arepas

1. BROWN AREPAS: Cook arepas, 4 at a time, in hot, well-oiled skillet until golden on both sides, about 4 minutes per side.

2. BAKE AREPAS: Bake arepas on wire rack until they sound hollow when tapped on bottom, about 10 minutes.

3. SPLIT AREPAS: Using fork, gently split hot arepas open.

4. STUFF AREPAS: Stuff each arepa with generous 3 tablespoons filling.

■ SIGNIFIES A **FAST** RECIPE (45 MINUTES OR LESS)

To complement the delicate flavor of the artichokes, we toss them in a simple dressing of garlic, lemon, basil, and oil.

18 ounces frozen artichokes, thawed and patted dry
2 garlic cloves, peeled
3 tablespoons extra-virgin olive oil
   Salt and pepper
1 tablespoon lemon juice
1 tablespoon chopped fresh basil

1. Adjust oven rack to middle position, place aluminum foil–lined rimmed baking sheet on rack, and heat oven to 450 degrees. Toss artichokes and garlic with 2 tablespoons oil, ½ teaspoon salt, and ⅛ teaspoon pepper in bowl. Spread vegetables evenly over hot baking sheet and roast until browned around edges, 15 to 20 minutes.

2. Remove vegetables from oven and let cool slightly. Mince roasted garlic, then combine with lemon juice, basil, and remaining 1 tablespoon oil in large bowl. Add roasted artichokes and toss to coat. Season with salt and pepper to taste. Serve.

VARIATIONS

Roasted Artichokes with Fennel, Mustard, and Tarragon

Roast 1 small fennel bulb, trimmed and sliced thin, along with artichokes and garlic. Reduce lemon juice to 1 teaspoon, substitute 1 tablespoon minced fresh tarragon for basil, and add 1 tablespoon whole-grain mustard to dressing.

Roasted Artichokes with Olives, Bell Pepper, and Lemon

Roast ½ cup coarsely chopped kalamata olives and 1 coarsely chopped red bell pepper along with artichokes and garlic. Substitute 1 tablespoon minced fresh parsley for basil.

Roasted Artichokes with Lemon and Basil

SERVES 4   TOTAL TIME 40 MINUTES   FAST

✓ **WHY THIS RECIPE WORKS:** Roasting artichokes brings out their delicate, vegetal flavor and makes for an easy and quick side dish, especially if you use frozen ones. But frozen artichokes contain a considerable amount of water, which can prevent browning and dilute flavor. To solve this problem, we preheated a baking sheet in a 450-degree oven, tossed the artichokes and a couple of garlic cloves with oil, salt, and pepper, and then spread everything out on the sizzling-hot sheet. The excess water quickly evaporated during roasting, giving us golden-brown, deeply flavored artichokes. Lining the baking sheet with foil made cleanup a snap. After the garlic cooled slightly, we minced it and tossed it in a simple dressing with just lemon juice, olive oil, and basil, which highlighted the artichokes' flavor without overpowering them. To thaw frozen artichokes quickly, microwave them in a covered bowl for 3 to 5 minutes; drain and pat dry before using.

Broiled Asparagus

SERVES 4   TOTAL TIME 15 MINUTES   FAST

✓ **WHY THIS RECIPE WORKS:** Broiling asparagus concentrates its flavor, helps to lightly caramelize its exterior, and, perhaps best of all, can be done in just minutes. And while we enjoyed the spears as is—with a little oil, salt and pepper, and lemon juice—we also came up with a simple balsamic glaze and an Asian vinaigrette, which we could prepare while the asparagus cooked. All we had to do was drizzle these dressings over the hot asparagus before serving for a perfect quick side dish worthy of a special-occasion meal. To ensure even cooking, choose asparagus that is roughly ½ inch thick. This asparagus can be served warm, at room temperature, or even chilled if desired.

1 pound asparagus, trimmed
1 tablespoon extra-virgin olive oil
  Salt and pepper
1 teaspoon lemon juice (optional)

Adjust oven rack 6 inches from broiler element and heat broiler. Toss asparagus with oil in bowl and season with salt and pepper. Lay asparagus in single layer on rimmed baking sheet. Broil, shaking pan occasionally, until asparagus is tender and lightly browned, about 10 minutes. Transfer asparagus to serving dish and sprinkle with lemon juice, if using. Serve.

VARIATIONS

Broiled Asparagus with Balsamic Glaze
Simmer ¾ cup balsamic vinegar in 8-inch skillet over medium heat until reduced to ¼ cup, 15 to 20 minutes. Off heat, stir in ¼ cup extra-virgin olive oil; drizzle over broiled asparagus before serving.

Broiled Asparagus with Soy-Ginger Vinaigrette
Substitute vegetable oil for olive oil. Whisk ¼ cup lime juice, 3 tablespoons toasted sesame oil, 3 tablespoons soy sauce, 2 thinly sliced scallions, 2 minced garlic cloves, 1 tablespoon grated fresh ginger, and 1 tablespoon honey together in bowl; drizzle over broiled asparagus before serving.

Trimming Asparagus

1. Remove 1 stalk of asparagus from bunch and bend at thicker end until it snaps.

2. With broken asparagus as guide, trim tough ends from remaining asparagus bunch using chef's knife.

Pan-Roasted Asparagus
SERVES 4 TO 6   **TOTAL TIME** 20 MINUTES   FAST

✓ **WHY THIS RECIPE WORKS:** Pan roasting is a simple stovetop cooking method that delivers crisp, evenly browned spears without the fuss of having to rotate each spear individually. We started with thicker spears (thin ones overcooked before browning) and arranged them in the pan with half pointed in one direction and half in the other. To help the asparagus release moisture for better caramelization and flavor, we parcooked it, covered, with butter and oil before browning it. The water evaporating from the butter helped to steam the asparagus, producing bright green, crisp-tender spears. At this point, we removed the lid, cranked up the heat, and cooked the spears until they were evenly browned on the bottom. Tasters preferred the flavor of spears browned on only one side, so there was no need to brown the asparagus all over; and, as a bonus, the half-browned spears never had a chance to go limp. We then came up with a couple of variations that included accent ingredients like cherry tomatoes, olives, red onion, and bacon. We simply cooked any garnish ingredients first, then set them aside while we prepared the asparagus. This recipe works best with asparagus that is at least ½ inch thick near the base. If using thinner spears, reduce the covered cooking time to 3 minutes and the uncovered cooking time to 5 minutes. Do not use pencil-thin asparagus; it cannot withstand the heat and overcooks too easily. You will need a 12-inch skillet with a tight-fitting lid for this recipe.

1 tablespoon extra-virgin olive oil
1 tablespoon unsalted butter
2 pounds thick asparagus, trimmed
  Salt and pepper
1 tablespoon lemon juice (optional)

1. Heat oil and butter in 12-inch skillet over medium-high heat. When butter has melted, add half of asparagus with tips pointed in one direction and remaining asparagus with tips pointed in opposite direction. Shake pan gently to help distribute spears evenly (they will not quite fit in single layer). Cover and cook until asparagus is bright green and still crisp, about 5 minutes.

2. Uncover, increase heat to high, and season with salt and pepper. Cook, moving spears around with tongs as needed, until asparagus is tender and well browned on 1 side, 5 to 7 minutes. Transfer asparagus to serving dish and sprinkle with lemon juice, if using. Serve.

Pan-Roasted Asparagus with Cherry Tomatoes and Kalamata Olives

Before cooking asparagus, cook 2 minced garlic cloves with 1 tablespoon extra-virgin olive oil in 12-inch nonstick skillet over medium heat until just golden, 2 to 3 minutes. Stir in 2 cups halved cherry tomatoes and ½ cup pitted, chopped kalamata olives and cook until tomatoes begin to break down, 1 to 2 minutes; transfer mixture to bowl. Rinse and dry skillet, then cook asparagus as directed. Before serving, top asparagus with tomato mixture, ¼ cup chopped fresh basil, and ½ cup grated Parmesan cheese.

Pan-Roasted Asparagus with Red Onion and Bacon

Before cooking asparagus, cook 4 chopped bacon slices in 12-inch nonstick skillet over medium heat until crisp, 7 to 10 minutes; transfer to paper towel–lined plate. Pour off all but 1 tablespoon fat left in pan, add 1 thinly sliced red onion, and cook over medium-high heat until slightly softened, about 3 minutes. Add 2 tablespoons balsamic vinegar and 1 tablespoon maple syrup and cook until onions are well glazed, about 2 minutes; transfer to bowl. Rinse and dry skillet, then cook asparagus as directed. Before serving, top asparagus with onions and bacon.

Stir-Fried Bok Choy with Soy Sauce and Ginger

SERVES 4   **TOTAL TIME** 20 MINUTES   **FAST**

✔ **WHY THIS RECIPE WORKS:** Cooking bok choy, like many hearty greens, requires that the tender leaves and the tough stems be handled separately. For this simple stir-fry, we cooked the thinly sliced stalks until tender, cleared the center of the skillet following our standard stir-fry method, and mashed a mixture of grated ginger and oil into the center of the skillet until fragrant. After combining the ginger with the stalks, we added the greens and a simple sauce made with soy sauce and sugar, tossing everything together until the greens wilted.

- **2 tablespoons soy sauce**
- **1 teaspoon sugar**
- **2 tablespoons vegetable oil**
- **1 tablespoon grated fresh ginger**
- **1½ pounds bok choy, stalks and greens separated, stalks sliced ¼ inch thick and leaves cut into 1-inch pieces**

1. Combine soy sauce and sugar in bowl. In separate bowl, combine 1 tablespoon oil and ginger. Heat remaining 1 tablespoon oil in 12-inch nonstick skillet over medium-high heat until just smoking. Add bok choy stalks and cook, stirring often, until lightly browned, 5 to 7 minutes.

2. Clear center of pan, add ginger mixture, and cook, mashing ginger into skillet, until fragrant, about 30 seconds. Stir ginger mixture into bok choy stems. Stir in bok choy greens and soy sauce mixture. Cook, tossing constantly, until greens are wilted and tender, about 1 minute. Transfer bok choy to serving dish. Serve.

Roasted Broccoli

SERVES 4   **TOTAL TIME** 25 MINUTES   **FAST**

✔ **WHY THIS RECIPE WORKS:** Roasting is a great way to deepen the flavor of vegetables, but broccoli can be tricky to roast given its awkward shape, woody stalks, and shrubby florets. We wanted a roasted broccoli recipe that would give us evenly cooked broccoli—stalks and florets—and add concentrated flavor and dappled browning. The key was the way we prepared the broccoli. We sliced the crown in half, then cut each half into uniform wedges. The stalks were cut into rectangular pieces slightly smaller than the more delicate florets. Cutting the broccoli this way promoted even cooking and great browning by maximizing the vegetable's contact with the baking sheet. Tossing the broccoli with a scant ½ teaspoon of sugar along with salt, pepper, and a splash of olive oil gave us blistered, bubbled, and browned stalks that were sweet and full-flavored, along with crisp-tipped florets. Trim away the outer peel from the broccoli stalk, otherwise it will turn tough when cooked.

- **1¾ pounds broccoli**
- **3 tablespoons extra-virgin olive oil**
- **½ teaspoon sugar**
- **Salt and pepper**
- **Lemon wedges**

1. Adjust oven rack to lowest position, place rimmed baking sheet on rack, and heat oven to 500 degrees. Cut broccoli at juncture of crowns and stalks. Cut crowns into 4 wedges if 3 to 4 inches in diameter, or 6 wedges if 4 to 5 inches in diameter. Trim tough outer peel from stalks, then cut into ½-inch thick planks about 2 to 3 inches long.

We prepare broccoli for roasting by cutting the florets and the stalks into pieces that will cook at the same rate.

2. Toss broccoli with oil, sugar, ½ teaspoon salt, and pinch pepper in bowl. Working quickly, lay broccoli in single layer on hot baking sheet, placing flat sides down. Roast until stalks are well browned and tender and florets are lightly browned, 9 to 11 minutes. Transfer broccoli to serving dish and serve with lemon wedges.

VARIATION
Roasted Broccoli with Garlic
Stir 1 tablespoon minced garlic into oil before tossing with raw broccoli.

Cutting Broccoli Crowns into Wedges

Cut broccoli crowns that measure 3 to 4 inches in diameter into 4 wedges, and broccoli crowns that measure 4 to 5 inches in diameter into 6 wedges.

Skillet Broccoli with Olive Oil and Garlic
SERVES 4   **TOTAL TIME** 20 MINUTES   **FAST**

✓ **WHY THIS RECIPE WORKS:** The problem with sautéing broccoli florets is getting the toothsome core to cook through before the delicate outer buds overcook and begin to fall apart. A quick solution is to use a stir-fry method. The broccoli first is browned for color, then quickly steamed to cook through, and finally sautéed with some aromatics for a boost in flavor. The best thing about the stir-fry method is that you can do all three steps in quick succession when you use a 12-inch skillet with a tight-fitting lid. Either a traditional or a nonstick 12-inch skillet will work for this recipe. Using broccoli florets, rather than a bunch of broccoli, can save valuable prep time for this side dish. If buying broccoli in a bunch instead, you will need about 1½ pounds of broccoli in order to yield 1 pound of florets.

3 tablespoons extra-virgin olive oil
2 garlic cloves, minced
½ teaspoon minced fresh thyme
1 pound broccoli florets, cut into 1-inch pieces
   Salt and pepper
3 tablespoons water

1. Combine 1 tablespoon oil, garlic, and thyme in bowl. Heat remaining 2 tablespoons oil in 12-inch skillet over medium-high heat until just smoking. Add broccoli and ¼ teaspoon salt and cook, without stirring, until beginning to brown, about 2 minutes.

2. Add water, cover, and cook until broccoli is bright green but still crisp, about 2 minutes. Uncover and continue to cook until water has evaporated and broccoli is crisp-tender, about 2 minutes.

3. Clear center of pan, add garlic mixture, and cook, mashing mixture into skillet, until fragrant, about 30 seconds. Stir garlic mixture into broccoli. Transfer broccoli to serving dish and season with salt and pepper to taste. Serve.

VARIATION
Skillet Broccoli with Sesame Oil and Ginger
Omit thyme. In garlic mixture, substitute 1 tablespoon toasted sesame oil for olive oil, and add 1 tablespoon grated fresh ginger. Substitute 2 tablespoons vegetable oil for olive oil when cooking broccoli.

For a smooth and cheesy sauce for broccoli, we use Monterey Jack, cheddar, and a bit of Parmesan.

2 pounds broccoli, florets cut into 1-inch pieces, stems peeled and cut into ½-inch pieces
2 tablespoons vegetable oil
  Salt and pepper
1 tablespoon unsalted butter
4 teaspoons all-purpose flour
¼ teaspoon dry mustard
⅛ teaspoon cayenne pepper
1 cup half-and-half
½ cup water
2 ounces Monterey Jack cheese, shredded (½ cup)
2 ounces sharp cheddar cheese, shredded (½ cup)
¼ cup grated Parmesan cheese

1. Adjust oven rack to lower-middle position, place rimmed baking sheet on rack, and heat oven to 450 degrees. Toss broccoli with oil, ¾ teaspoon salt, and ¼ teaspoon pepper in bowl. Lay broccoli in single layer on hot baking sheet and roast until spotty brown, 15 to 18 minutes, stirring halfway through cooking.

2. Meanwhile, melt butter in medium saucepan over medium heat. Add flour, mustard, and cayenne and cook, stirring constantly, until golden and fragrant, about 1 minute. Slowly whisk in half-and-half and water and bring to boil. Reduce heat to medium-low and simmer until slightly thickened, 8 to 10 minutes.

3. Off heat, whisk in cheeses until smooth. Season with salt and pepper to taste. Transfer roasted broccoli to serving dish and pour cheese sauce over top. Serve.

Broccoli with Cheese Sauce

SERVES 4 TO 6   **TOTAL TIME** 35 MINUTES   FAST

✓ **WHY THIS RECIPE WORKS:** Our initial attempts at constructing a recipe for broccoli with cheese sauce fell flat, as the sauce kept separating. Because fat helps prevent this problem, we switched from milk to half-and-half thinned with a little water. We found cheddar cheese to be extremely flavorful, but when used alone it left the sauce gritty. Switching to equal parts Monterey Jack and cheddar solved the problem, while a little Parmesan added nuttiness. We tried several methods to prepare the broccoli and settled on roasting, which resulted in a more distinct, nutty flavor that perfectly complemented the cheese sauce. It also produced drier broccoli, which prevented the sauce from sliding off. For a silky smooth sauce, wait until the Monterey Jack and cheddar are thoroughly integrated before adding the Parmesan. If the sauce gets too thick, whisk in 1 to 2 tablespoons of hot water.

Garlicky Broccolini

SERVES 4   **TOTAL TIME** 25 MINUTES   FAST

✓ **WHY THIS RECIPE WORKS:** Broccolini is a bit more delicate than its cousin, so we had to adjust our tried-and-true broccoli pan-steaming method for our broccolini recipe. We found that sautéing the broccolini before steaming it left us with scorched tips, so we reversed the order. Also, we split the thicker stalks in half at the base to ensure they cooked evenly. Although it has a more intense flavor than broccoli, broccolini still pairs well with the familiar ingredients we use in broccoli recipes—olive oil, garlic, and red pepper flakes. You will need a 12-inch nonstick skillet with a tight-fitting lid for this recipe.

2 garlic cloves, minced
2 tablespoons extra-virgin olive oil
⅛ teaspoon red pepper flakes
⅓ cup water

Salt and pepper
1   pound broccolini, trimmed
2   tablespoons grated Parmesan cheese

1. Combine garlic, oil, and pepper flakes in bowl. Bring water and ½ teaspoon salt to boil in 12-inch nonstick skillet over high heat. Add broccolini, cover, and reduce heat to medium-low. Cook until broccolini is bright green and tender, about 5 minutes. Uncover and cook until liquid evaporates, about 30 seconds.

2. Clear center of pan, add garlic mixture, and cook, mashing mixture into skillet, until fragrant, about 30 seconds. Stir garlic mixture into broccolini and season with salt and pepper to taste. Transfer broccolini to serving dish and sprinkle with Parmesan. Serve.

Trimming Broccolini

1. Trim only tough, dry ends from broccolini.

2. Split thicker stalks in half at base.

Braised Brussels Sprouts

SERVES 4   TOTAL TIME 25 MINUTES   FAST

✔ **WHY THIS RECIPE WORKS:** Brussels sprouts probably have the worst reputation of any vegetable—kids and adults alike flee at the sight of them. They are almost always poorly prepared. When done right, Brussels sprouts are crisp, tender, and nutty-tasting. Braising Brussels sprouts is the quickest method to cook these little cabbages, and we've found that using a skillet on the stovetop works best. A combination of chicken broth with a quickly sautéed shallot for the braising liquid was easy and also added depth. We began in a covered

skillet to quickly steam the sprouts, then removed the lid to let the broth reduce to a flavorful glaze during the final few minutes of cooking. When trimming the Brussels sprouts, be careful not to cut too much off the stem end or the leaves will fall away from the core. You will need a 12-inch nonstick skillet with a tight-fitting lid for this recipe.

2   tablespoons unsalted butter
1   shallot, minced
    Salt and pepper
1   pound Brussels sprouts, trimmed and halved
1   cup chicken broth

1. Melt butter in 12-inch nonstick skillet over medium heat. Add shallot and ¼ teaspoon salt and cook until softened, about 2 minutes. Add Brussels sprouts, broth, and ⅛ teaspoon pepper and bring to simmer. Cover and cook until sprouts are bright green, about 9 minutes.

2. Uncover and continue to cook until sprouts are tender and liquid is slightly thickened, about 2 minutes. Season with salt and pepper to taste. Transfer sprouts to serving dish. Serve.

VARIATIONS
Brussels Sprouts with Bacon
Before cooking sprouts, cook 3 slices chopped bacon in 12-inch nonstick skillet over medium heat until crisp, 7 to 10 minutes; transfer to paper towel–lined plate. Cook sprouts as directed, substituting bacon fat left in pan for butter. Sprinkle sprouts with bacon before serving.

Curried Brussels Sprouts with Currants
Add 1½ teaspoons curry powder to pan with shallot. Add 3 tablespoons currants to pan with sprouts.

Cream-Braised Brussels Sprouts
Substitute heavy cream for broth. Add pinch nutmeg to pan with sprouts. Sprinkle with 2 tablespoons minced fresh parsley or chives before serving.

Halving Brussels Sprouts

Cut sprouts in half through stem end so that leaves stay intact.

ALL ABOUT **VEGETABLE COOKING TIMES**

Sometimes you want to prepare vegetables in the simplest (and quickest) way by steaming, boiling, or microwaving them. Just follow the times in the chart for perfectly cooked vegetables every time. For ways to dress up plain veggies, see page 472.

TYPE OF VEGETABLE	AMOUNT/ YIELD	PREPARATION	BOILING TIME (AMOUNT OF WATER AND SALT)	STEAMING TIME	MICROWAVING TIME (AMOUNT OF WATER)
Asparagus	1 bunch (1 pound)/ serves 3	tough ends trimmed	2 to 4 minutes (4 quarts water plus 1 tablespoon salt)	3 to 5 minutes	3 to 6 minutes (3 tablespoons water)
Beets	1½ pounds (6 medium)/ serves 4	greens discarded and beets scrubbed well	X	35 to 55 minutes	18 to 24 minutes (¾ cup water)
Broccoli	1 bunch (1½ pounds)/ serves 4	florets cut into 1- to 1½-inch pieces and stalks peeled and cut into ¼-inch-thick pieces	2 to 4 minutes (4 quarts water plus 1 tablespoon salt)	4 to 6 minutes	4 to 6 minutes (3 tablespoons water)
Brussels Sprouts	1 pound/ serves 4	stem ends trimmed, discolored leaves removed, and halved through the stem	6 to 8 minutes (4 quarts water plus 1 tablespoon salt)	7 to 9 minutes	X
Carrots	1 pound/ serves 4	peeled and sliced ¼ inch thick on the bias	3 to 4 minutes (4 quarts water plus 1 tablespoon salt)	5 to 6 minutes	4 to 7 minutes (2 tablespoons water)
Cauliflower	1 head (2 pounds)/ serves 4 to 6	cored and florets cut into 1-inch pieces	5 to 7 minutes (4 quarts water plus 1 tablespoon salt)	7 to 9 minutes	4 to 7 minutes (¼ cup water)
Green Beans	1 pound/ serves 4	stem ends trimmed	3 to 5 minutes (4 quarts water plus 1 tablespoon salt)	6 to 8 minutes	4 to 6 minutes (3 tablespoons water)
Red Potatoes	2 pounds (6 medium)/ serves 4	scrubbed and poked several times with a fork	16 to 22 minutes (4 quarts water plus 1 tablespoon salt)	18 to 24 minutes	6 to 10 minutes (no water and uncovered)
Russet Potatoes	2 pounds (4 medium)/ serves 4	scrubbed and poked several times with a fork	X	X	8 to 12 minutes (no water and uncovered)
Snap Peas	1 pound/ serves 4	stems trimmed and strings removed	2 to 4 minutes (4 quarts water plus 1 tablespoon salt)	4 to 6 minutes	3 to 6 minutes (3 tablespoons water)
Snow Peas	1 pound/ serves 4	stems trimmed and strings removed	2 to 3 minutes (4 quarts water plus 1 tablespoon salt)	4 to 6 minutes	3 to 6 minutes (3 tablespoons water)
Squash (Winter)	2 pounds/ serves 4	peeled, seeded, and cut into 1-inch chunks	X	12 to 14 minutes	8 to 11 minutes (¼ cup water)
Sweet Potatoes	2 pounds/ (3 medium) serves 4	peeled and cut into 1-inch chunks	X	12 to 14 minutes	8 to 10 minutes (¼ cup water)

X=Not Recommended

Roasted Brussels Sprouts

SERVES 6 TO 8 **TOTAL TIME** 40 MINUTES **FAST**

✔ **WHY THIS RECIPE WORKS:** Roasting is a simple and quick way to produce Brussels sprouts that are caramelized on the outside and tender on the inside. To ensure we achieved this balance, we started by roasting them covered with foil, tossing in a little bit of water to create a steamy environment, which cooked them through. We then removed the foil and roasted them for another 10 minutes to allow the exterior to dry out and caramelize. If you are buying loose Brussels sprouts, select those that are about 1½ inches long. Quarter Brussels sprouts longer than 2½ inches; don't cut sprouts that are shorter than 1 inch.

2¼ pounds Brussels sprouts, trimmed and halved
 3 tablespoons extra-virgin olive oil
 1 tablespoon water
    Salt and pepper

1. Adjust oven rack to upper-middle position and heat oven to 500 degrees. Toss Brussels sprouts with oil, water, ¾ teaspoon salt, and ¼ teaspoon pepper in bowl. Transfer sprouts to rimmed baking sheet and arrange cut side down.

2. Cover sheet tightly with aluminum foil and roast for 10 minutes. Remove foil and continue to cook until sprouts are well browned and tender, 10 to 12 minutes. Transfer Brussels sprouts to serving dish and season with salt and pepper to taste. Serve.

VARIATIONS

Roasted Brussels Sprouts with Garlic, Red Pepper Flakes, and Parmesan

While Brussels sprouts roast, cook 3 tablespoons extra-virgin olive oil, 2 minced garlic cloves, and ½ teaspoon red pepper flakes in 8-inch skillet over medium heat until fragrant, 1 to 2 minutes; remove from heat. Toss roasted Brussels sprouts with garlic mixture and sprinkle with ¼ cup grated Parmesan cheese before serving.

Roasted Brussels Sprouts with Bacon and Pecans

While Brussels sprouts roast, cook 4 slices bacon in 12-inch nonstick skillet over medium heat until crisp, 7 to 10 minutes. Transfer bacon to paper towel–lined plate and crumble into small pieces; reserve 1 tablespoon bacon fat. Toss roasted Brussels sprouts with 2 tablespoons extra-virgin olive oil, reserved bacon fat, crumbled bacon, and ½ cup finely chopped toasted pecans before serving.

Simple Cream-Braised Cabbage

SERVES 4 **TOTAL TIME** 20 MINUTES **FAST**

✔ **WHY THIS RECIPE WORKS:** The French have been cooking cabbage in cream for ages, and when we tried it, tasters loved the subtle mix of flavors, complemented by a slight residual crunch. We cut the richness of the cream with lemon juice (for its acidity) and shallot (for its subtle, sweet onion flavor). The cabbage needed only minutes to braise in a 12-inch skillet with a tight-fitting lid before it was ready to serve.

¼ cup heavy cream
 1 teaspoon lemon juice
 1 shallot, minced
 ½ head green cabbage, cored and shredded (4 cups)
    Salt and pepper

Heat cream, lemon juice, and shallot in 12-inch skillet over medium heat. Add cabbage and toss to coat. Cover and simmer, stirring occasionally, until cabbage is wilted but still bright green, 7 to 9 minutes. Season with salt and pepper to taste. Transfer cabbage to serving dish. Serve.

Sweet and Sour Red Cabbage

SERVES 6 TO 8 **TOTAL TIME** 1 HOUR

✔ **WHY THIS RECIPE WORKS:** Slowly cooking cabbage transforms it into something entirely new, bringing out a sweet and silky richness that can come only with time. Though our recipe for a German-style cabbage slowly braised with sweet and sour flavors appeared simple, it required a delicate balancing act between the sweet and sour elements. To add some smoky depth and richness, we began by cooking finely chopped bacon, and then sautéed onion with cinnamon, caraway seed, and allspice in the rendered fat. For the sweetener we used brown sugar, which we then balanced with fruity cider vinegar, which complemented the cabbage. Cooking the cabbage in apple cider, covered, for 30 to 40 minutes was key to softening it without losing all its crunch. A splash of cider vinegar before serving helped perk up the flavors and balance the sweetness. This cabbage tastes even better the next day. You can substitute ¼ teaspoon ground cinnamon for the cinnamon stick if necessary.

4 slices bacon, chopped fine
1 onion, chopped fine
1 cinnamon stick
½ teaspoon caraway seeds

¼ teaspoon ground allspice

Salt and pepper

1 head red cabbage (2 pounds), cored and shredded

1½ cups apple cider

3 bay leaves

3 tablespoons packed light brown sugar

1 teaspoon minced fresh thyme or ½ teaspoon dried

3 tablespoons cider vinegar

1. Cook bacon in Dutch oven over medium heat until fat begins to render, about 2 minutes. Stir in onion, cinnamon stick, caraway seeds, allspice, and ¼ teaspoon salt and cook until onion is softened and lightly browned, about 10 minutes.

2. Stir in cabbage, cider, bay leaves, 1 tablespoon sugar, thyme, and ½ teaspoon salt. Cover and cook, stirring often, until cabbage is wilted and tender, 30 to 40 minutes.

3. Discard cinnamon stick and bay leaves. Stir in vinegar and remaining 2 tablespoons sugar. Season with salt and pepper to taste and transfer to serving dish. Serve. (Cabbage can be refrigerated for up to 3 days; reheat in microwave, stirring often, until hot.)

Glazed Carrots

SERVES 4   **TOTAL TIME** 25 MINUTES   **FAST**

✔ **WHY THIS RECIPE WORKS:** For well-seasoned carrots with a glossy and clingy yet modest glaze, we started by slicing the carrots on the bias, which lent visual appeal without requiring much work. Most glazed carrot recipes start by steaming, parboiling, or blanching the carrots prior to glazing. To make our glazed carrots a one-pot operation, we steamed them directly in the skillet, and we used chicken broth (along with some salt and sugar) rather than water for fuller flavor. When the carrots were almost tender, we removed the lid and turned up the heat to reduce the cooking liquid. Then we added butter and a bit more sugar, finishing with a sprinkling of lemon juice. You will need a 12-inch nonstick skillet with a tight-fitting lid for this recipe.

1 pound carrots, peeled and sliced ½ inch thick on bias

½ cup chicken broth

3 tablespoons sugar

Salt and pepper

1 tablespoon unsalted butter, cut into 4 pieces

2 teaspoons lemon juice

Carrots cut on the bias are steamed and then glazed right in the skillet and dressed up with orange and dried cranberries.

1. Bring carrots, broth, 1 tablespoon sugar, and ½ teaspoon salt to boil in 12-inch nonstick skillet. Reduce to simmer, cover, and cook, stirring occasionally, until carrots are almost tender, about 5 minutes.

2. Uncover, return to boil, and cook until liquid has thickened and reduced to about 2 tablespoons, about 2 minutes.

3. Stir in butter and remaining 2 tablespoons sugar. Continue to cook, stirring frequently, until carrots are completely tender and glaze is lightly golden, about 3 minutes. Off heat, stir in lemon juice and season with salt and pepper to taste. Transfer carrots to serving dish. Serve.

VARIATIONS

Glazed Carrots with Orange and Cranberries

Dried cherries can be used in place of the cranberries if you prefer.

Substitute ¼ cup orange juice for ¼ cup of broth. Add ¼ cup dried cranberries and ½ teaspoon grated orange zest to skillet with carrots. Omit 2 tablespoons sugar in step 3.

Glazed Curried Carrots with Currants and Almonds

Add 1½ teaspoons curry powder to skillet with carrots. Add ¼ cup currants to skillet with butter. Sprinkle with ¼ cup toasted sliced or slivered almonds before serving.

Honey-Glazed Carrots with Lemon and Thyme

Substitute honey for sugar. Add ½ teaspoon minced fresh thyme and ½ teaspoon grated lemon zest to skillet with butter.

Slicing Carrots on Bias

Cut carrots on bias into pieces about ½ inch thick and 2 inches long.

Skillet-Roasted Carrots and Parsnips

SERVES 6 TO 8   **TOTAL TIME** 40 MINUTES   **FAST**

✔ **WHY THIS RECIPE WORKS:** Offering earthy sweetness and satisfying texture, carrots and parsnips are a great pairing. But cooking these two vegetables together wasn't quite as straightforward as we had thought. Our initial attempts at skillet-roasting them resulted in either crunchy carrots and perfectly cooked parsnips or tender carrots sitting in a pool of parsnip mash. After numerous trials, we found a foolproof method that browns first and steams second, which allowed the vegetables to cook through evenly. This technique guaranteed perfectly cooked carrots and parsnips every time, coaxing the best flavor and texture out of both. Parsnips wider than 1 inch may have tough, fibrous cores that are best trimmed and discarded. Any combination of carrots and parsnips with a total weight of 3 pounds can be used in this recipe. You will need a 12-inch skillet with a tight-fitting lid.

   ¾ **cup warm water**
1½ **teaspoons sugar**
      Salt and pepper
   3 **tablespoons vegetable oil**
1½ **pounds carrots, peeled and sliced ½ inch thick on bias**
1½ **pounds parsnips, peeled and sliced ½ inch thick on bias**
   1 **tablespoon minced fresh parsley**

1. Whisk water, sugar, and 1 teaspoon salt together in bowl to dissolve sugar. Heat oil in 12-inch skillet over medium-high heat until shimmering. Add carrots and parsnips and cook, stirring occasionally, until golden brown, 12 to 14 minutes.

2. Add water mixture, cover, and reduce heat to medium-low. Cook, stirring occasionally, until vegetables are tender and liquid has evaporated, 12 to 14 minutes. Off heat, stir in parsley and season with salt and pepper to taste. Transfer vegetables to serving dish. Serve.

VARIATIONS

Maple-Rosemary Skillet-Roasted Carrots and Parsnips

Substitute apple cider for water, 1 tablespoon maple syrup for sugar, and ½ teaspoon minced fresh rosemary for parsley.

Honey-Orange Skillet-Roasted Carrots and Parsnips

Substitute orange juice for water, 1 tablespoon honey for sugar, and ½ teaspoon minced fresh thyme (or rosemary or tarragon) for parsley.

Slicing Parsnips

1. Cut peeled parsnip in half, separating thin, tapered end from large, bulbous end.

2. Slice thin end on diagonal into ½-inch pieces.

3. Quarter bulbous end lengthwise, then slice each piece on diagonal into ½-inch pieces.

Roasted Cauliflower

SERVES 4 TO 6 **TOTAL TIME** 1 HOUR

✔ **WHY THIS RECIPE WORKS:** Roasting vegetables is all about caramelizing sugars to produce big flavor. Since browning happens best when the vegetables are in contact with the hot pan, we sliced a head of cauliflower into eight wedges, creating more flat surface area than you'd get with florets. To keep the cauliflower from drying out, we started it covered with aluminum foil in a hot oven, letting it steam for 10 minutes until barely soft, and then we removed the foil so it could brown. Flipping each slice halfway through roasting ensured even cooking and color. This dish stands well on its own, drizzled with extra-virgin olive oil, or try the variations we created.

1   head cauliflower (2 pounds)
¼   cup extra-virgin olive oil
    Salt and pepper

1. Adjust oven rack to lowest position and heat oven to 475 degrees. Trim outer leaves of cauliflower and cut stem flush with bottom of head. Cut head into 8 equal wedges, keeping core and florets intact. Place wedges cut side down on parchment paper–lined rimmed baking sheet. Drizzle with 2 tablespoons oil, season with salt and pepper, and rub gently to distribute oil and seasonings over cauliflower.

2. Cover sheet tightly with aluminum foil and roast for 10 minutes. Remove foil and continue to roast until bottoms of cauliflower wedges are golden, about 15 minutes.

3. Remove sheet from oven and carefully flip wedges using spatula. Continue to roast cauliflower until golden all over, about 15 minutes longer. Season with salt and pepper to taste. Transfer cauliflower to serving dish and drizzle with remaining 2 tablespoons oil. Serve.

VARIATIONS
Chili Roasted Cauliflower
Add 2 teaspoons chili powder to oil before drizzling over raw cauliflower.

Cutting Cauliflower for Roasting

After trimming away any leaves and cutting stem flush with bottom of head, carefully slice head into 8 equal wedges, keeping core and florets intact.

Roasted Cauliflower with Bacon and Scallions
Arrange 6 slices chopped bacon around cauliflower on baking sheet before roasting. Stir 2 teaspoons cider vinegar into oil before drizzling over roasted cauliflower. Sprinkle with 2 thinly sliced scallions before serving.

Southern-Style Collard Greens

SERVES 6 **TOTAL TIME** 1 HOUR 10 MINUTES

✔ **WHY THIS RECIPE WORKS:** Any Southerner will tell you that collard greens require long cooking and the smokiness of cured pork to be edible. We tend to agree—slowly cooking the greens in a sweet, smoky broth goes far in tempering the assertive bitterness of collards. After a lot of testing, we found that 6 cups of chicken broth was the perfect amount to cook 2 pounds of collards. Using less liquid didn't cover the collards completely in the pot, while using more liquid washed out their flavor. We found that 45 minutes was enough to make sure the collards became tender but not mushy. Cooking the greens in the oven helped maintain a constant temperature and made this dish relatively hands-off. The leftover cooking liquid, traditionally called pot "liquor" (or "likker"), can be sopped up with cornbread or biscuits, or used to cook a second batch of collard greens, as is traditionally done in the South. Serve with hot sauce or vinegar, if desired. For more information on how to cut up collard greens, see page 471.

4   slices bacon, chopped
1   onion, chopped fine
    Salt and pepper
3   garlic cloves, minced
6   cups chicken broth
2   pounds collard greens, stemmed and chopped coarse

1. Adjust oven rack to lower-middle position and heat oven to 350 degrees. Cook bacon in Dutch oven over medium heat until fat begins to render, about 2 minutes. Stir in onion and ¼ teaspoon salt and cook until onion is softened, 5 to 7 minutes. Stir in garlic and cook until fragrant, about 30 seconds. Add broth, increase heat to medium-high, and bring to simmer.

2. Stir in greens, 1 handful at a time, until wilted. Cover, place pot in oven, and cook until greens are tender and broth is flavorful, about 45 minutes. Remove pot from oven and season with salt and pepper to taste. Serve.

Corn on the Cob

SERVES 8   **TOTAL TIME** 15 MINUTES   FAST

✓ **WHY THIS RECIPE WORKS:** After experimenting with grilling, steaming, roasting, and microwaving, our tasters unanimously agreed: Nothing beats the ease and flavor of freshly boiled corn on the cob. When boiling the corn, we found it best to hold the salt—salted cooking water makes the corn kernels tough. While omitting the salt was a clear departure from our technique for boiling vegetables, we found that a few teaspoons of granulated sugar was a welcome addition. The slightly sweetened water helped accentuate the natural sweetness of the corn. If you know that you have supersweet corn, however, omit the sugar. Don't cook more than eight ears of corn at a time in the pot.

- 8 **ears corn, husks and silk removed**
- 4 **teaspoons sugar (optional)**
  Salted butter (optional)

Bring 4 quarts water to boil in large pot. Add corn and sugar, if using. Return water to boil and cook until corn is tender, about 6 minutes. Remove corn from water using tongs, allowing excess water to drip back into pot, and transfer to serving dish. Serve with butter, if desired.

A few teaspoons of sugar added to the cooking water help to highlight the natural sweetness of corn on the cob.

FLAVORED BUTTERS FOR CORN ON THE COB

Quick and easy to make, a flavored butter adds another dimension to corn on the cob. Each recipe uses one stick of butter and is enough for eight ears of corn.

CHESAPEAKE BAY BUTTER   FAST
Using fork, beat 8 tablespoons softened, unsalted butter with 1 tablespoon hot sauce, 1 teaspoon Old Bay seasoning, and 1 minced garlic clove.

LATIN-SPICED BUTTER   FAST
Using fork, beat 8 tablespoons softened, unsalted butter with 1 teaspoon chili powder, ½ teaspoon ground cumin, ½ teaspoon grated lime zest, and 1 minced garlic clove. (Sprinkle cobs with ½ cup grated Parmesan cheese, if desired.)

BASIL PESTO BUTTER   FAST
Using fork, beat 8 tablespoons softened, unsalted butter with 1 tablespoon basil pesto and 1 teaspoon lemon juice.

BARBECUE-SCALLION BUTTER   FAST
Using fork, beat 8 tablespoons softened, unsalted butter with 2 tablespoons barbecue sauce and 1 minced scallion.

Easy Creamed Corn

SERVES 4 TO 6   **TOTAL TIME** 20 MINUTES   FAST

✓ **WHY THIS RECIPE WORKS:** Oftentimes, creamed corn recipes call for an extensive cooking time and a laundry list of ingredients, including an overabundant amount of cream and butter. In fact, some recipes we found cooked the corn for almost an hour and used a whole stick of butter along with several cups of heavy cream. We dialed back on the fat so we could actually taste the corn—2 tablespoons butter and just 3 to 5 minutes of simmering time was all the corn required. Using fresh corn is key to the success of this recipe; do not substitute frozen corn.

- 8 **ears corn, husks and silk removed**
- 2 **tablespoons unsalted butter**
- 1 **cup heavy cream**
  Salt and pepper
  Pinch sugar

LAST-MINUTE VEGETABLE SIDES

When you're short on time, it's good to have a few easy side dish recipes at your fingertips. These sides are quick, require little prep work, and go with almost anything.

ROASTED BABY CARROTS WITH BROWNED BUTTER `FAST`

Adjust oven rack to middle position and heat oven to 475 degrees. Toss 1 pound baby carrots, thoroughly dried, with 1 tablespoon olive oil and ¼ teaspoon salt in bowl and spread into single layer over broiler-pan bottom. Roast carrots for 12 minutes. Shake pan and continue to roast carrots, shaking pan occasionally, until carrots are lightly browned and tender, about 8 minutes longer. Meanwhile, cook 1½ tablespoons unsalted butter in small saucepan over medium heat, swirling occasionally, until browned, 1 to 2 minutes. Toss carrots with browned butter and serve. (Serves 4)

STIR-FRIED EDAMAME WITH GINGER `FAST`

Cook 2 cups shelled, frozen edamame and ½ cup water in covered 12-inch nonstick skillet over high heat until edamame are fully thawed, 7 minutes. Uncover and cook until water evaporates and edamame are tender, 2 minutes. Clear center of pan. Add 1 tablespoon sesame oil, 1 minced scallion, and 1 tablespoon grated fresh ginger and cook until fragrant, 1 minute. Stir in 1 tablespoon soy sauce and serve. (Serves 4)

SKILLET-STEAMED GREEN BEANS `FAST`

Cook 1 pound trimmed green beans, ¼ cup water, and pinch salt in covered 12-inch nonstick skillet over high heat until beans begin to soften, 5 minutes. Uncover and cook until water evaporates and beans are tender, 2 minutes. Stir in 1 tablespoon unsalted butter and serve. (Serves 4)

BOILED RED POTATOES WITH BUTTER AND HERBS `FAST`

We prefer to use small red potatoes, measuring 1 to 2 inches in diameter, in this recipe. If using larger potatoes, halve or quarter the potatoes and adjust the cooking time as needed.

Cover 2 pounds unpeeled small red potatoes (about 12 potatoes) by 1 inch water in large pot and bring to boil over high heat. Reduce to simmer and cook until potatoes are tender, 20 to 25 minutes. Drain potatoes well, then toss gently with 2 tablespoons unsalted butter in large bowl until butter melts. Season with salt and pepper to taste, sprinkle with 1 tablespoon minced fresh chives, tarragon, or parsley, and serve. (Serves 4)

1. Using paring knife, cut kernels off cobs into large bowl, then use back of knife to scrape pulp from cob into bowl.

2. Melt butter in large saucepan over medium-high heat. Stir in corn kernels and pulp and cook until fragrant, about 1 minute. Stir in cream, ½ teaspoon salt, and sugar and simmer until corn is tender and mixture has thickened, 3 to 5 minutes. Season with salt and pepper to taste and serve.

VARIATIONS

Easy Creamed Corn with Tarragon

Add 3 tablespoons minced fresh tarragon to saucepan with butter.

Easy Creamed Corn with Bacon and Scallions

Omit butter. Cook 2 slices chopped bacon in large saucepan over medium-high heat until crisp, about 3 minutes; transfer to paper towel–lined plate. Add corn and 2 minced scallions to fat left in pot and cook as directed. Sprinkle with crisp bacon before serving.

Easy Creamed Corn with Chipotle and Cilantro

Add 2 teaspoons minced canned chipotle chile in adobo sauce to saucepan with corn. Stir in 2 tablespoons minced fresh cilantro before serving.

Braised Hearty Greens

SERVES 4 TO 6   **TOTAL TIME** 1 HOUR

☑ **WHY THIS RECIPE WORKS:** For a one-pot hearty greens recipe with no parcooking, we cooked half of the greens with a little bit of liquid before adding the rest, which prevented the pot from overflowing, then covered the pot. When the greens had almost the tender-firm texture we wanted, we removed the lid to allow the liquid to cook off. The result: a winter greens recipe that highlighted the greens' cabbagelike flavor and firm texture. Don't be alarmed by the giant mound of greens—they wilt significantly when cooked. Collards may need a few extra minutes of covered cooking in step 1.

4	tablespoons unsalted butter
½	cup thinly sliced red onion
2½	pounds hearty greens (kale, mustard, turnip, or collards), stemmed and chopped coarse
1	cup chicken broth
1	tablespoon packed brown sugar
	Salt and pepper
⅛	teaspoon cayenne pepper
2	tablespoons cider vinegar

1. Melt 2 tablespoons butter in Dutch oven over medium heat. Add onion and cook until softened, about 5 minutes. Stir in half of greens, broth, sugar, ½ teaspoon salt, and cayenne. Cover and cook until greens begin to wilt, about 1 minute. Stir in remaining greens. Turn heat to medium-low, cover, and cook, stirring occasionally, until greens are completely tender, about 30 minutes.

2. Uncover and increase heat to medium-high. Cook, stirring occasionally, until liquid is nearly evaporated, about 10 minutes. Stir in remaining 2 tablespoons butter and vinegar and cook until butter is melted, about 30 seconds. Transfer greens to serving dish and season with salt and pepper to taste. Serve.

VARIATIONS

Braised Hearty Greens with Pancetta and Pine Nuts

Omit butter. Before cooking onion, cook 6 ounces chopped pancetta in Dutch oven until crisp and browned, 6 to 8 minutes; transfer to paper towel–lined plate. Cook onions as directed, substituting pancetta fat left in pot for butter. Substitute red wine vinegar for cider vinegar. Sprinkle with ⅓ cup toasted pine nuts before serving.

Braised Hearty Greens with White Beans

Add 1 (15-ounce) can rinsed small white beans to pot after uncovering in step 2. Substitute red wine vinegar for cider vinegar.

Prepping Hearty Greens

1. Lay leaf flat on cutting board and cut out stem running through center of leaf. Discard stem.

2. Chop (or slice) leaves as directed in recipe, then wash prepped leaves thoroughly using salad spinner.

A two-step cooking method of sautéing and then steaming results in evenly cooked, tender green beans.

Simple Sautéed Green Beans with Garlic

SERVES 4   **TOTAL TIME** 20 MINUTES   **FAST**

✔ **WHY THIS RECIPE WORKS:** For tender, lightly browned, fresh-tasting beans using just one pan, we turned to sautéing. But simply sautéing raw beans in oil resulted in blackened exteriors and undercooked interiors. For the best results, we sautéed the beans until spotty brown, then added water to the pan and covered it so the beans could cook through. Once the beans were softened we lifted the lid to vaporize whatever water remained in the pan and promote additional browning. A little butter added to the pan at this stage lent richness and promoted even more browning. Adding a little garlic to the pan with the butter added a nice hit of flavor without overcomplicating the recipe. This recipe yields crisp-tender beans. If you prefer a slightly more tender texture (or if you are using large, tough beans), increase the water by 1 tablespoon and increase the covered cooking time by 1 minute. You will need a 12-inch nonstick skillet with a tight-fitting lid for this recipe.

1 tablespoon unsalted butter, softened
3 garlic cloves, minced
1 teaspoon extra-virgin olive oil
1 pound green beans, trimmed and cut into
    2-inch lengths
    Salt and pepper
¼ cup water

1. Mash butter and garlic together in bowl. Heat oil in 12-inch nonstick skillet over medium heat until just smoking. Add beans and pinch salt, and cook, stirring occasionally, until spotty brown, 4 to 6 minutes.

2. Add water, cover, and cook until beans are bright green but still crisp, about 2 minutes. Uncover, increase heat to high, and cook until water evaporates, 30 to 60 seconds.

3. Stir in butter-garlic mixture and cook until beans are crisp-tender, lightly browned, and beginning to wrinkle, 1 to 3 minutes. Transfer beans to serving dish and season with salt and pepper to taste. Serve.

VARIATIONS

Sautéed Green Beans with Smoked Paprika and Almonds

Add ¼ teaspoon smoked paprika to butter-garlic mixture. Sprinkle beans with ¼ cup toasted slivered almonds before serving.

Spicy Sautéed Green Beans with Ginger

Substitute vegetable oil for olive oil and following mixture for butter-garlic mixture: Combine 1 teaspoon toasted sesame oil, 1 teaspoon grated fresh ginger, and 1 teaspoon Asian chili-garlic sauce in bowl.

NOTES FROM THE TEST KITCHEN

Dressing Up Vegetables

Here are a few easy ways to add more flavor to simply cooked vegetables before serving.

• Cook butter in a small skillet over medium heat until it browns, then drizzle over the vegetables and sprinkle with toasted nuts.
• Dot with a flavored butter (see page 469).
• Sprinkle with fruity extra-virgin olive oil and grated Parmesan cheese, fresh herbs, or red pepper flakes.
• Sprinkle with toasted sesame seeds, soy sauce, and toasted sesame oil.
• Toss with a pesto (see pages 410–411).
• Toss with butter, salt, pepper, and lemon juice.
• Toss with a vinaigrette (see pages 52–53).

Mediterranean Braised Green Beans

SERVES 4 TO 6   **TOTAL TIME** 1 HOUR 20 MINUTES

WHY THIS RECIPE WORKS: Braising green beans takes more time than sautéing or steaming them, but you can simultaneously cook and flavor the beans with this slower method, which works especially well for older, tougher beans. We created a recipe for braising green beans that rendered them meltingly tender and flavorful in about an hour. We first cooked the beans in baking soda and water, which softened their fibrous skins. We then added tomatoes, whose acidity neutralized the soda. We moved the pot to let it simmer in a low oven, where the gentle heat prevented the beans' interiors from collapsing. A sprinkle of parsley and red wine vinegar added bright notes to the finished dish. A dollop of yogurt can be spooned over the beans to add a nice tang. To make a light entrée, serve the beans with rice or crusty bread. These beans taste great both warm and at room temperature.

5 tablespoons extra-virgin olive oil
1 onion, chopped fine
4 garlic cloves, minced
    Pinch cayenne pepper
1½ cups water
½ teaspoon baking soda
1½ pounds green beans, trimmed and cut into 2- to
    3-inch lengths
1 tablespoon tomato paste
1 (14.5-ounce) can diced tomatoes
1 teaspoon salt
¼ teaspoon pepper
¼ cup chopped fresh parsley
    Red wine vinegar

1. Adjust oven rack to lower-middle position and heat oven to 275 degrees. Heat 3 tablespoons oil in Dutch oven over medium heat until shimmering. Add onion and cook, stirring occasionally, until softened, 3 to 5 minutes. Stir in garlic and cayenne and cook until fragrant, about 30 seconds. Add water, baking soda, and green beans and bring to simmer. Reduce heat to medium-low and cook, stirring occasionally, for 10 minutes.

2. Stir in tomato paste, tomatoes and their juice, salt, and pepper. Cover pot, transfer to oven, and cook until sauce is slightly thickened and green beans can be easily cut with side of fork, 40 to 50 minutes.

3. Stir in parsley and season with vinegar to taste. Transfer beans to serving dish and drizzle with remaining 2 tablespoons oil. Serve.

VARIATION

Mediterranean Braised Green Beans with Mint and Feta

Add ¾ teaspoon ground allspice with garlic and cayenne. Substitute 2 tablespoons chopped fresh mint for parsley. Substitute ½ cup crumbled feta cheese for drizzling oil before serving.

Sautéed Mushrooms with Marsala

SERVES 4   **TOTAL TIME** 40 MINUTES **FAST**

✓ **WHY THIS RECIPE WORKS:** Supermarket mushrooms tend to shrink and shrivel when sautéed. We wanted to develop a quick sauté method that delivered enough white mushrooms to make a delicious, ample side dish. To get more flavor and less shriveling, we discovered that overloading the skillet and extending the cooking time allowed the mushrooms to give up just enough liquid to eventually fit in a single layer without shrinking to nothing. They browned nicely after we added a little butter, and from there it was easy to enhance the dish with shallot, thyme, and Marsala, a classic combination for complementing the earthy flavor of mushrooms.

  1 **tablespoon vegetable oil**
1½ **pounds white mushrooms, trimmed and halved if small or quartered if large**
  1 **tablespoon unsalted butter**
  1 **shallot, minced**
  1 **tablespoon minced fresh thyme**
 ¼ **cup dry Marsala**
     Salt and pepper

1. Heat oil in 12-inch skillet over medium-high heat until shimmering. Add mushrooms and cook, stirring occasionally, until they release their liquid, about 5 minutes. Increase heat to high and cook, stirring occasionally, until liquid has evaporated, about 8 minutes.

2. Reduce heat to medium and add butter. Cook, stirring often, until mushrooms are dark brown, about 8 minutes. Add shallot and thyme and cook until softened, about 3 minutes. Add Marsala and cook until it has evaporated, about 2 minutes. Season with salt and pepper to taste. Transfer mushrooms to serving dish. Serve.

We soak onion rings in beer and malt vinegar to soften them before battering and frying.

Beer-Battered Onion Rings

SERVES 4 TO 6   **TOTAL TIME** 1 HOUR 10 MINUTES

✓ **WHY THIS RECIPE WORKS:** Recipes for beer-battered onion rings often result in soggy, heavy, and raw rings. To create a better onion ring with maximum crunch and tender onions, we soaked the onion slices in a mixture of beer, malt vinegar, salt, and pepper to soften them and build flavor. For the batter, we settled on one that combined flour, salt and pepper, cornstarch, and baking powder with more beer. The beer gave the coating flavor, and the carbonation provided lift to the batter. Baking powder yielded a coating that was thick and substantial yet light, while cornstarch added crunch. In step 1, do not soak the onion rounds longer than 2 hours or they will turn soft and become too saturated to crisp properly. Cider vinegar can be used in place of malt vinegar. Use a candy thermometer to make sure the oil gets to 350 degrees. Tasters preferred the gentle flavor of sweet onions, but ordinary yellow onions can be substituted for the sweet onions if necessary.

2 **sweet onions, peeled and sliced into ½-inch-thick rounds**
3 **cups beer**
2 **teaspoons malt vinegar**
 Salt and pepper
2 **quarts peanut or vegetable oil**
¾ **cup all-purpose flour**
¾ **cup cornstarch**
1 **teaspoon baking powder**

1. Combine onion rounds, 2 cups beer, vinegar, ½ teaspoon salt, and ½ teaspoon pepper in large zipper-lock bag; press out as much air as possible and seal bag. Refrigerate for at least 30 minutes or up to 2 hours.

Making Onion Rings

1. SLICE ONIONS ½ INCH THICK: Using chef's knife, slice sweet onions into ½-inch-thick rounds.

2. BRINE ONIONS: Combine onion rounds, beer, vinegar, salt, and pepper in large zipper-lock bag; press out as much air as possible and seal bag. Refrigerate for at least 30 minutes.

3. MAKE THIN BATTER: Combine flour, cornstarch, baking powder, salt, and pepper in large bowl. Slowly whisk in ¾ cup beer until just combined. Whisk in remaining beer, 1 tablespoon at a time.

4. FRY IN BATCHES: Stir one-third of rings into batter to coat. Carefully transfer onions to oil, 1 ring at a time. Fry until rings are golden brown and crisp, about 5 minutes, flipping halfway through frying.

2. Heat oil in large Dutch oven over medium-high heat to 350 degrees. While oil is heating, combine flour, cornstarch, baking powder, ½ teaspoon salt, and ¼ teaspoon pepper in large bowl. Slowly whisk in ¾ cup beer until just combined (some lumps will remain). Whisk in remaining ¼ cup beer, 1 tablespoon at a time, as needed until batter falls from whisk in steady stream and leaves faint trail across surface of batter in bowl.

3. Adjust oven rack to middle position and heat oven to 200 degrees. Remove onions from refrigerator, drain, and thoroughly pat dry with paper towels. Separate onions into rings.

4. Transfer one-third of onion rings to batter and stir to coat. Working with 1 ring at a time, carefully transfer onions to oil. Fry until rings are golden brown and crisp, about 5 minutes, flipping halfway through frying. Drain rings on paper towel–lined baking sheet and season with salt and pepper to taste; keep warm in oven. Return oil to 350 degrees and repeat with remaining onion rings in 2 batches. Serve.

Fast Buttery Peas

SERVES 4   **TOTAL TIME** 15 MINUTES   **FAST**

✔ **WHY THIS RECIPE WORKS:** Frozen peas have already been blanched, so the keys to making a good and simple side dish with them are to avoid overcooking and to pair the peas with ingredients that don't require much preparation. We found that after sautéing a shallot, thyme, and garlic in butter, we could simply add the frozen peas and let them cook through for a few minutes for a fresh and bright side dish. Using a skillet instead of a saucepan allowed the peas to heat more quickly and evenly over the larger surface, and covering the skillet sped up the cooking time. Adding 2 teaspoons of sugar to the skillet helped to highlight their sweet, refreshing flavor. Do not thaw the peas before adding them to the skillet. You will need a 12-inch nonstick skillet with a tight-fitting lid for this recipe.

2 **tablespoons unsalted butter**
1 **shallot, minced**
1 **teaspoon minced fresh thyme**
1 **garlic clove, minced**
1 **pound frozen peas (3 cups)**
2 **teaspoons sugar**
 Salt and pepper

Melt butter in 12-inch nonstick skillet over medium-high heat. Add shallot, thyme, and garlic and cook until softened, about 2 minutes. Stir in peas and sugar, cover, and cook until peas are heated through, about 4 minutes. Transfer peas to serving dish and season with salt and pepper to taste. Serve.

VARIATIONS

Sautéed Buttery Peas with Mint and Feta
Substitute 1 tablespoon minced fresh mint for thyme and sprinkle with ¾ cup crumbled feta cheese before serving.

Creamy Peas with Tarragon
Substitute 1 tablespoon minced fresh tarragon for thyme. Before adding peas to skillet, add ½ cup heavy cream and simmer until thickened, about 2 minutes.

Roasted Red Potatoes

SERVES 4 **TOTAL TIME** 1 HOUR

✔ **WHY THIS RECIPE WORKS:** The most crucial characteristic for roasted potatoes is texture. After roasting several varieties, we found that low-starch, high-moisture red potatoes, such as Red Bliss, yielded a crisp yet delicate crust and a moist, dense interior. As for the cooking method, many recipes call for partially boiling the potatoes before roasting them. Although this technique works well, it is time-consuming. Instead, we covered the potatoes with foil for the first 20 minutes of cooking so that they would steam in their own moisture. Then we removed the foil and roasted the potatoes until they became crusty and golden on the outside and creamy on the inside. These potatoes were great served either simply plain or varied with simple additions of aromatics, fresh herbs, or even cheese and olives. If using very small potatoes, cut them in half instead of into wedges and flip them cut side up during the final 10 minutes of roasting.

2 **pounds red potatoes, unpeeled and cut into ¾-inch wedges**
3 **tablespoons extra-virgin olive oil**
   Salt and pepper

1. Adjust oven rack to middle position and heat oven to 425 degrees. Toss potatoes with oil in bowl and season with salt and pepper. Arrange potatoes in single layer on rimmed baking sheet, with either cut side facing down. Cover with aluminum foil and roast for 20 minutes.

Covering the potatoes for part of their roasting time allows them to steam in their own moisture.

2. Remove foil and continue to roast until sides of potatoes touching pan are crusty and golden, about 15 minutes. Flip potatoes over using metal spatula and continue to roast until crusty and golden on second side, about 8 minutes. Season potatoes with salt and pepper to taste and transfer to serving dish. Serve.

VARIATIONS

Roasted Red Potatoes with Garlic and Rosemary
During final 3 minutes of roasting, sprinkle 2 tablespoons minced fresh rosemary over potatoes. Toss roasted potatoes with 1 garlic clove, mashed to a paste, before serving.

Roasted Red Potatoes with Feta, Olives, and Oregano
During final 3 minutes of roasting, sprinkle 1 tablespoon minced fresh oregano over potatoes. Combine ½ cup crumbled feta cheese, 12 pitted and chopped kalamata olives, 1 tablespoon lemon juice, and 1 garlic clove, mashed to a paste, in bowl. Toss roasted potatoes with feta mixture before serving.

All About Potatoes

Potatoes have varying textures (determined by starch level) and fall into three main categories—baking, all-purpose, or boiling.

BAKING POTATOES: These dry, floury potatoes contain more total starch than other categories, giving them a dry, mealy texture. They are the best choice when baking and frying. In our opinion, they are also the best potatoes for mashing because they can drink up butter and cream. They work well when you want to thicken a stew or soup, but not when you want distinct chunks of potatoes. Common varieties: Russet, Russet Burbank, and Idaho.

ALL-PURPOSE POTATOES: These potatoes contain less total starch than dry, floury potatoes but more than firm, waxy potatoes. They are considered "in-between" potatoes; their texture is more mealy than that of waxy potatoes, putting them closer to dry, floury potatoes. All-purpose potatoes can be mashed or baked but won't be as fluffy as dry, floury potatoes. They can be used in salads and soups but won't be quite as firm as waxy potatoes. Common varieties: Yukon Gold, Yellow Finn, Purple Peruvian, Kennebec, and Katahdin.

BOILING POTATOES: These potatoes contain a relatively low amount of total starch, which means they have a firm, smooth, and waxy texture. Often they are called "new" potatoes because they are less-mature potatoes harvested in the late spring and summer. They are less starchy than "old" potatoes because they haven't had time to convert their sugar to starch. They also have thinner skins. Firm, waxy potatoes are perfect when you want the potatoes to hold their shape, as with potato salad. They are also a good choice when roasting or boiling. Common varieties: Red Bliss, French Fingerling, Red Creamer, and White Rose.

BUYING POTATOES: Look for potatoes that are firm and free of green spots, sprouts, and cracks. Potatoes with a greenish tinge have had too much exposure to light and should also be avoided. Try to buy loose potatoes rather than those sold in plastic bags, which cause potatoes to sprout, soften, and rot.

STORING POTATOES: If stored under unsuitable heat and light conditions, potatoes will germinate and grow. To avoid this, keep them in a cool, dark place. Store potatoes in a paper (not plastic) bag and keep them away from onions, which give off gases that will hasten sprouting. Most varieties should keep for several months. The exception is new potatoes—because of their thinner skins, they will keep for no more than one month.

For the best baked potatoes with evenly cooked skin, we bake them directly on the oven rack.

Best Baked Potatoes

SERVES 4   **TOTAL TIME** 1 HOUR 35 MINUTES

✓ **WHY THIS RECIPE WORKS:** The best baked potatoes have a thick, chewy skin and a light, fluffy interior, and we wanted to find the best way to make them. After baking all-purpose, Yukon Gold, and russet potatoes, we determined only russets produced the fluffy, dry texture we were looking for. We also discovered that traditional slow baking was the best method mainly because of the effect it has on the potato's skin. A substantial brown layer developed just under the skin when the potato was baked at 350 degrees for 1 hour and 15 minutes, and it added incredible flavor. In addition, we found that cooking the potatoes right on the oven rack was the best way to promote even browning and skin that was perfectly cooked all the way around, not just on top. The most important step to a fluffy potato is opening it wide while it is still steaming-hot; if the steam stays trapped inside, it will make the interior soggy. You can bake as many potatoes as you like without altering the cooking time.

4 russet potatoes (8 ounces each), unpeeled and rubbed lightly with vegetable oil

Adjust oven rack to middle position and heat oven to 350 degrees. Place potatoes directly on rack and bake until paring knife easily pierces flesh, about 1¼ hours. Remove potatoes from oven and make dotted X on top of each potato with tines of fork. Press in at ends of each potato to release steam and push flesh up and out. Serve.

Releasing Steam from Baked Potatoes

Remove potatoes from oven and make dotted X on top of each potato with tines of fork. Press in at ends of each potato to release steam and push flesh up and out.

Fastest-Ever Baked Potatoes

SERVES 4 **TOTAL TIME** 35 MINUTES **FAST**

✔ **WHY THIS RECIPE WORKS:** When you don't have time to bake a potato through completely in the oven, you can jump-start it in the microwave. Cooking the potatoes in the microwave for just a few minutes until they began to soften, then transferring them to a very hot oven, worked well and shaved over half an hour off the traditional baked potato cooking time. For this recipe, look for evenly sized russet potatoes with firm, unblemished skin.

4 russet potatoes (8 ounces each), unpeeled

1. Adjust oven rack to middle position and heat oven to 450 degrees. Poke several holes in each potato with fork. Microwave potatoes until slightly softened, 6 to 12 minutes, turning potatoes over halfway through cooking.

2. Carefully transfer potatoes to oven and cook directly on hot oven rack until paring knife easily pierces flesh, about 20 minutes. Remove potatoes from oven and make dotted X on top of each potato with tines of fork. Press in at ends of each potato to release steam and push flesh up and out. Serve.

Twice-Baked Potatoes

SERVES 6 TO 8 **TOTAL TIME** 2 HOURS

✔ **WHY THIS RECIPE WORKS:** Twice-baked potatoes are not difficult to make, but the process can be time-consuming, and too many versions feature rubbery skins filled with pasty, bland fillings. We wanted to perfect the process to achieve twice-baked potatoes with slightly crisp skins and a rich, creamy filling. We oiled the potatoes before baking for a crisp skin, and we let the baked potatoes cool slightly before slicing them open and removing the flesh. We found that we could prevent the hollowed-out shells from turning soggy by keeping them in the oven while making the filling. And for the filling, we found it best to combine the potato with tangy dairy ingredients—sour cream and buttermilk were ideal—plus a small amount of butter and, for its bold flavor, sharp cheddar cheese. For a perfect finish, we placed the filled potatoes under the broiler for a browned, crisp topping. You can substitute other types of cheese, such as Gruyère, fontina, or feta, for the cheddar. Yukon Gold potatoes, though slightly more moist than our ideal, can be substituted for the russets.

4 russet potatoes (7 to 8 ounces each), unpeeled and rubbed lightly with vegetable oil
4 ounces sharp cheddar cheese, shredded (1 cup)
½ cup sour cream
½ cup buttermilk
2 tablespoons unsalted butter, room temperature
3 scallions, sliced thin
Salt and pepper

1. Adjust oven rack to upper-middle position and heat oven to 400 degrees. Bake potatoes on aluminum foil–lined baking sheet until skin is crisp and deep brown and paring knife easily pierces flesh, about 1 hour. Transfer potatoes to wire rack and let cool for 10 minutes; set baking sheet aside.

2. Using oven mitt to handle hot potatoes, cut each potato in half lengthwise. Using soupspoon, scoop flesh from each half into medium bowl, leaving ⅛- to ¼-inch thickness of flesh in each shell. Return potato shells, cut side up, to foil-lined baking sheet. Return shells to oven and bake until dry and slightly crisped, about 10 minutes.

3. Meanwhile, mash potato flesh with fork until smooth. Stir in cheese, sour cream, buttermilk, butter, and scallions. Season filling with salt and pepper to taste.

4. Remove shells from oven and heat broiler. Carefully spoon filling into warm shells. Return filled potatoes to oven and broil until crisp on top, 10 to 15 minutes. Let potatoes cool for 5 to 10 minutes before serving.

VARIATIONS

Twice-Baked Potatoes with Pepper Jack and Bacon

Cook 8 slices chopped bacon in 10-inch skillet over medium heat until crisp, 7 to 10 minutes; transfer to paper towel–lined plate. Substitute pepper Jack cheese for cheddar and add crisp bacon to filling.

Twice-Baked Potatoes with Chipotle Chile and Onion

Melt 2 tablespoons unsalted butter in 10-inch skillet over medium heat. Add 1 finely chopped onion and cook until softened, 5 to 7 minutes. Omit butter in step 3 and add cooked onions, 1 tablespoon minced canned chipotle chile in adobo sauce, and 2 tablespoons minced fresh cilantro to filling.

Twice-Baked Potatoes with Monterey Jack and Pesto

Substitute Monterey Jack cheese for cheddar, reduce butter-milk to ¼ cup, omit butter, and add ¼ cup basil pesto to filling.

Twice-Baked Potatoes with Indian Spices and Peas

Melt 2 tablespoons butter in 10-inch skillet over medium heat. Add 1 finely chopped onion and cook until softened, 5 to 7 minutes. Stir in 3 minced garlic cloves, 1 teaspoon grated fresh ginger, 1 teaspoon ground cumin, 1 teaspoon ground coriander, ¼ teaspoon ground cinnamon, ¼ teaspoon ground turmeric, and ¼ teaspoon ground cloves; cook until fragrant, about 30 seconds. Off heat, stir in 1 cup thawed frozen peas. Substitute spiced pea mixture for cheddar and butter in filling.

Classic Mashed Potatoes

SERVES 4   **TOTAL TIME** 55 MINUTES

WHY THIS RECIPE WORKS: Many people would never consider consulting a recipe when making mashed potatoes; instead they just add chunks of butter and spurts of cream until their conscience tells them to stop. Little wonder, then, that mashed potatoes made this way are consistent only in their mediocrity. We wanted mashed potatoes that were perfectly smooth and creamy, with great potato flavor and plenty of buttery richness every time. We began by selecting russet potatoes for their high starch content. Boiling them whole and unpeeled yielded mashed potatoes that were rich, earthy, and sweet. We used a food mill or ricer for the smoothest texture (a potato masher can be used if you prefer your potatoes a little chunky). For smooth, velvety potatoes, we added melted butter first and then half-and-half. Melting, rather than merely softening, the butter enabled it to coat the starch molecules quickly and easily, so the potatoes turned out creamy and light. From there, it was easy to come up with a number of flavorful variations. Russet potatoes make fluffier mashed potatoes, but Yukon Golds have an appealing buttery flavor and can be used instead.

2 pounds russet potatoes, unpeeled
8 tablespoons unsalted butter, melted
1 cup half-and-half, warmed
   Salt and pepper

1. Place potatoes in large saucepan and cover with 1 inch cold water. Bring to boil over high heat, reduce heat to medium-low,

Making Mashed Potatoes

 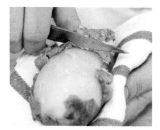  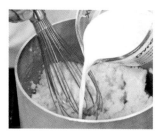

1. SIMMER POTATOES: Cover unpeeled russet potatoes with 1 inch cold water and simmer until potatoes are tender, 30 to 45 minutes. Drain.

2. PEEL POTATOES: Using folded dish towel to hold potatoes, peel just-boiled potatoes with paring knife.

3. MASH POTATOES: For slightly chunky texture, mash potatoes in pot with potato masher. For creamy texture, use ricer or food mill set over pot.

4. ADD BUTTER, THEN HALF-AND-HALF: Stir in melted butter until incorporated, then gently whisk in warm half-and-half and season with salt and pepper to taste.

and simmer until potatoes are just tender (paring knife can be slipped in and out of potatoes with little resistance), 30 to 45 minutes. Drain.

2. Using potholder or folded dish towel to hold potatoes, peel skins from potatoes with paring knife. For slightly chunky texture, return peeled potatoes to now-empty pot and mash smooth using potato masher. For creamy texture, set ricer or food mill over now-empty pot; cut peeled potatoes into large chunks and press or mill into saucepan in batches.

3. Stir in melted butter until incorporated. Gently whisk in warm half-and-half and season with salt and pepper to taste. Serve.

VARIATIONS

Mashed Potatoes with Scallions and Horseradish

Stir ¼ cup prepared horseradish and 3 minced scallions, green parts only, into warm half-and-half before adding to mashed potatoes.

Garlic Mashed Potatoes

Toasting the garlic is essential for mellowing its harsh flavor. Avoid using unusually large garlic cloves, as they will not soften adequately during toasting.

Toast 20 unpeeled garlic cloves in covered 8-inch skillet over lowest heat possible until spotty dark brown and slightly softened, about 22 minutes. Off heat, let sit, covered, until fully softened, 15 to 20 minutes. Peel and mince garlic, then stir into mashed potatoes with half-and-half. (If using ricer or food mill, softened garlic cloves can be processed along with potatoes.)

Buttermilk Mashed Potatoes

SERVES 4   TOTAL TIME 45 MINUTES   **FAST**

✔ **WHY THIS RECIPE WORKS:** Buttermilk mashed potatoes should be both rich and tart, like a baked potato drenched in butter and sour cream. But simply stirring buttermilk into boiled and mashed potatoes didn't yield any of its flavor. The key to soaking up the buttermilk flavor turned out to be cooking the potatoes directly in the buttermilk, which we thinned with a little water. Buttermilk is acidic, which slows cooking, but a pinch of baking soda balanced the acid so that the potatoes cooked through in a reasonable amount of time. Because simmering the buttermilk dulled its flavor slightly, we added a little reserved buttermilk at the end to bring back the missing tang. Don't be alarmed if the buttermilk looks separated. Once you mash the potatoes into it, the puree comes together.

- 2 **pounds Yukon Gold potatoes, peeled, quartered, and cut into ½-inch pieces**
- 1 **cup buttermilk**
- 6 **tablespoons water**
- 6 **tablespoons unsalted butter, cut into 6 pieces**
- ⅛ **teaspoon baking soda**
  Salt and pepper

1. Combine potatoes, ¾ cup buttermilk, water, 2 tablespoons butter, baking soda, and ½ teaspoon salt in Dutch oven. Bring to boil, then cover and reduce heat to low. Simmer, stirring occasionally, until potatoes are just tender (paring knife can be slipped in and out of potatoes with little resistance), 20 to 25 minutes.

2. Uncover and cook over medium heat until liquid has nearly evaporated, about 3 minutes. Off heat, add remaining 4 tablespoons butter and mash potatoes smooth with potato masher. Using rubber spatula, fold in remaining ¼ cup buttermilk until absorbed. Season with salt and pepper to taste and serve.

Mashed Potato Casserole

SERVES 6 TO 8   TOTAL TIME 1 HOUR 40 MINUTES

✔ **WHY THIS RECIPE WORKS:** The appeal of mashed potato casserole is considerable, with the promise of fluffy, buttery, creamy potatoes nestled under a savory golden crust. And with all the mashing and mixing done beforehand, it's the perfect convenience dish during the holiday season. But the recipes we tried gave us bland, gluey, dense potatoes. We wanted our casserole to be worth the effort. Using half-and-half instead of heavy cream lightened the recipe, and cutting it with chicken broth kept the potatoes moist and provided an even lighter texture. Beating eggs into the potato mixture helped it achieve a fluffy, airy texture and allowed us to use a hand-held mixer to mash the potatoes without them turning gluey. Fresh garlic and Dijon mustard gave our casserole a flavorful bite. We like to use a shallow 2-quart gratin dish, which allows for the most surface area (and browned crust), but a 13 by 9-inch baking dish also works.

- 4 **pounds russet potatoes, peeled and cut into 1-inch chunks**
- ½ **cup half-and-half**
- ½ **cup chicken broth**
- 12 **tablespoons unsalted butter, cut into pieces**
- 1 **garlic clove, minced**
- 2 **teaspoons Dijon mustard**

2 teaspoons salt
4 large eggs
¼ cup minced fresh chives

1. Place potatoes in Dutch oven and add water to cover by 1 inch. Bring to boil over high heat. Reduce heat to medium and simmer until potatoes are just tender (paring knife can be slipped in and out of potatoes with little resistance), about 20 minutes.

2. Meanwhile, adjust oven rack to upper-middle position and heat oven to 375 degrees. Grease 2-quart casserole dish. Heat half-and-half, broth, butter, garlic, mustard, and salt in saucepan over medium-low heat until butter is melted, about 5 minutes; cover to keep warm.

3. Drain potatoes and transfer to large bowl. Using hand-held mixer set at medium-low speed, beat potatoes while slowly adding half-and-half mixture until smooth and creamy, about 1 minute. Scrape down bowl, then beat in eggs, 1 at a time, until incorporated, about 1 minute. Using rubber spatula, gently fold in chives.

4. Transfer potato mixture to prepared baking dish and smooth top with rubber spatula. (Casserole can be refrigerated for up to 1 day; let sit at room temperature for 1 hour before baking.)

5. Bake until potatoes rise and begin to brown, 35 to 45 minutes. Let casserole cool for 10 minutes. Serve.

Scalloped Potatoes

SERVES 4 TO 6   **TOTAL TIME** 1 HOUR 10 MINUTES

✓ **WHY THIS RECIPE WORKS:** Rich and creamy scalloped potatoes are a holiday favorite, but they typically require labor-intensive preparation. We wanted a lighter, quicker version that we could make for weeknight dinners. We used traditional russet potatoes to form tight, cohesive layers, and mixed heavy cream with an equal amount of chicken broth to offset the typical heaviness of the dish. We parboiled the sliced potatoes in the broth-cream mixture on top of the stove, then poured the whole mixture into a casserole dish and finished it in the oven. Prep and assemble all of the other ingredients before slicing the potatoes or they will begin to brown (do not store them in water; this will make the gratin bland and watery). If the potato slices do start to discolor, put them in a bowl and cover with the cream and chicken broth. Slicing the potatoes ⅛ inch thick is crucial for the success of this dish; use a mandoline, a V-slicer, or a food processor fitted with a ⅛-inch-thick slicing blade. You can substitute Parmesan for the cheddar if desired.

2 tablespoons unsalted butter
1 onion, chopped fine
1 tablespoon minced fresh thyme or 1 teaspoon dried
2 garlic cloves, minced
1¼ teaspoons salt
¼ teaspoon pepper
2½ pounds russet potatoes, peeled and sliced ⅛ inch thick
1 cup chicken broth
1 cup heavy cream
2 bay leaves
4 ounces cheddar cheese, shredded (1 cup)

1. Adjust oven rack to middle position and heat oven to 425 degrees. Melt butter in Dutch oven over medium-high heat. Add onion and cook until softened, 5 to 7 minutes. Stir in thyme, garlic, salt, and pepper and cook until fragrant, about 30 seconds. Add potatoes, chicken broth, cream, and bay leaves and bring to simmer.

2. Cover, reduce heat to medium-low, and simmer until potatoes are almost tender (paring knife can be slipped in and out of potato slice with some resistance), about 10 minutes.

3. Discard bay leaves. Transfer mixture to 8-inch square baking dish and press into even layer. Sprinkle evenly with cheddar. Bake until bubbling around edges and top is golden brown, about 15 minutes. Let casserole cool 10 minutes before serving.

TO MAKE AHEAD: Do not top casserole with cheddar; casserole can be refrigerated for up to 1 day. To serve, cover dish tightly with greased aluminum foil and bake in 400-degree oven until hot throughout, about 45 minutes. Uncover, top with cheddar, and continue to bake until cheddar is lightly browned, about 30 minutes. Let casserole cool for 10 minutes before serving.

VARIATIONS

Scalloped Potatoes with Chipotle Chile and Smoked Cheddar Cheese

Add 2 teaspoons minced canned chipotle chile in adobo sauce to pot with potatoes. Substitute smoked cheddar for cheddar.

Scalloped Potatoes with Wild Mushrooms

Add 8 ounces cremini mushrooms, trimmed and sliced ¼ inch thick, and 4 ounces shiitake mushrooms, stemmed and sliced ¼ inch thick, to pot with onion; cook as directed.

Traditional scalloped potato recipes involve layering thinly sliced potatoes, making a flour-thickened sauce, and baking the whole thing for well over an hour. Our recipe is faster and easier to make, and it requires no fussy layering. We parcook thinly sliced russet potatoes on the stovetop and then finish them in a casserole dish in the oven, cutting the cooking time in half.

1. THINLY SLICE RUSSET POTATOES: Peel and slice the potatoes ⅛ inch thick using a mandoline, V-slicer, or food processor.
WHY? Russet potatoes have a high starch content, so they form tight, cohesive layers that are the hallmark of the dish. Slicing them ⅛ inch thick is also crucial. If cut thicker, the potatoes won't hold together. If too thin, the potatoes will melt together entirely.

2. SAUTÉ THE AROMATICS: Melt the butter in a Dutch oven over medium-high heat. Add the onion and cook until softened. Stir in the thyme, garlic, salt, and pepper.
WHY? Sautéing the onion and garlic helps build the base for the sauce. Thyme adds an herbaceous flavor that complements the earthy potatoes.

3. SIMMER THE POTATOES IN BROTH AND CREAM: Add the potatoes, chicken broth, cream, and bay leaves and bring to a simmer. Cover, reduce the heat, and simmer until the potatoes are almost tender, about 10 minutes.
WHY? Parcooking the potatoes in broth and cream infuses them with flavor, while the starch that releases thickens the sauce.

4. PRESS THE POTATOES INTO A BAKING DISH: Transfer the potatoes to a baking dish and press them into an even layer.
WHY? Cooking the potatoes on the stovetop creates the sauce, so there is no need for fussy layering, saving time.

5. TOP WITH SHREDDED CHEESE AND BAKE: Sprinkle the casserole evenly with the cheddar cheese. Bake in a 425-degree oven until the cream is bubbling around the edges and the top is golden brown, about 15 minutes.
WHY? Because the potatoes are already partially cooked, they need only a short time in the oven to finish cooking and to allow the cheese to brown and form a crust.

6. LET THE CASSEROLE COOL FOR 10 MINUTES: Remove the casserole from the oven and let it cool for 10 minutes before serving.
WHY? Cooling the casserole gives it time to set up, ensuring you get attractive portions.

Easier French Fries

SERVES 3 TO 4   **TOTAL TIME** 45 MINUTES   **FAST**

✓ **WHY THIS RECIPE WORKS:** Traditional methods of making French fries involve rinsing, soaking, double frying, and then draining and salting them—not an easy process. We wanted a recipe for crispy fries with a tender interior and lots of potato flavor, but without all of the fuss. The key was to submerge the potatoes in room-temperature oil before frying them over high heat until browned. This gave the potatoes' interiors an opportunity to soften and cook through before the exteriors started to crisp. Starchy russets turned leathery with the longer cooking time. With lower-starch Yukon Golds, however, the result was a crisp exterior and a creamy interior. The fries stuck to the bottom of the pot at first, but letting the potatoes cook in the oil for 20 minutes before stirring gave them enough time to form a crust that would protect them. Thinner fries were also less likely to stick. We prefer peanut oil for frying, but vegetable or canola oil can be substituted. This recipe will not work with sweet potatoes or russets.

2½ **pounds Yukon Gold potatoes, unpeeled**
6   **cups peanut or vegetable oil**
    Kosher salt

1. Using chef's knife, square off sides of potatoes. Cut potatoes lengthwise into ¼-inch planks, then slice each plank into ¼-inch-thick fries. Combine potatoes and oil in large Dutch oven. Cook over high heat until oil has reached rolling boil, about 5 minutes.

2. Once boiling, continue to cook, without stirring, until potatoes are limp but exteriors are beginning to firm, about 15 minutes.

3. Using tongs, stir potatoes, gently scraping up any that stick, and continue to cook, stirring occasionally, until golden and crisp, 5 to 10 minutes. Using skimmer, transfer fries to paper towel–lined baking sheet. Season with salt and serve.

Oven Fries

SERVES 4   **TOTAL TIME** 1 HOUR

✓ **WHY THIS RECIPE WORKS:** The ease and neatness of oven frying—as opposed to deep frying in a pot of hot oil—make this technique such an engaging proposition that we decided to try to make oven fries that were worth eating on their own terms. We were after fries with a golden, crisp crust and a richly creamy interior. We started by soaking russet potatoes, cut into wedges, in hot water for 10 minutes to remove excess starch. Then, to prevent them from sticking to the baking sheet, we poured oil and sprinkled salt and pepper directly on the pan to elevate the spuds just enough. To get the right combination of creamy interior and crisp crust, we covered the potatoes with aluminum foil to steam them for the first 5 minutes of cooking, and then uncovered them and continued to bake until they were golden and crisp. Use a heavy-duty rimmed baking sheet for this recipe because the intense heat of the oven may cause lightweight pans to warp. Nonstick baking sheets work great with this recipe. Peeling or not peeling the potatoes is a personal choice; both will work well in this recipe.

Cutting French Fries

1. Using chef's knife, square off sides of scrubbed, unpeeled potatoes.

2. Cut potatoes lengthwise into ¼-inch-thick planks.

3. Slice each plank into ¼-inch-thick fries.

3 large russet potatoes, each quartered lengthwise and cut into 10 to 12 evenly sized wedges
5 tablespoons vegetable oil
Salt and pepper

1. Adjust oven rack to lowest position and heat oven to 475 degrees. Place potatoes in large bowl, cover with hot tap water, and let soak for 10 minutes. Meanwhile, coat heavy-duty rimmed baking sheet with ¼ cup oil. Sprinkle baking sheet evenly with ¾ teaspoon salt and ¼ teaspoon pepper.

2. Drain potatoes, spread over paper towels, and thoroughly pat dry. Toss dried potatoes with remaining 1 tablespoon oil. Arrange potatoes with either cut side facing down in single layer on prepared baking sheet. Cover sheet tightly with aluminum foil and bake for 5 minutes.

3. Remove foil and continue to bake until sides of potatoes touching pan are crusty and golden, 15 to 20 minutes, rotating baking sheet after 10 minutes.

4. Using metal spatula, scrape potato wedges loose from pan and flip over. Continue to bake until fries are golden and crisp on both sides, 10 to 15 minutes, rotating pan as needed for even browning. Transfer fries to paper towel–lined baking sheet. Season with salt to taste and serve.

Cutting Oven Fries

Quarter potato lengthwise, then cut each quarter into evenly sized wedges. One large potato should make 10 to 12 wedges.

Crispy Potato Latkes

SERVES 4 TO 6   **TOTAL TIME** 55 MINUTES

☑ **WHY THIS RECIPE WORKS:** Most latke recipes consist of combining shredded raw potato, onions, and eggs, forming them into disks, and shallow-frying them until crisp and brown. Sadly, they tend to be greasy throughout or undercooked and tough. We wanted our latkes to be somewhat thick, golden, and very crisp on the outside, and very creamy in the center. To achieve all of these goals, we needed to remove as much water as possible from the potato shreds by wringing them in a dish towel. We minimized the release

Removing as much water as possible from the shredded potatoes results in crispy yet tender latkes.

of any remaining water by microwaving the shreds briefly to cause the starches in the potatoes to form a gel. With the water taken care of, the latkes crisped up quickly and absorbed minimal oil. We prefer shredding the potatoes on the large holes of a box grater, but you can also use the large shredding disk of a food processor; cut the potatoes into 2-inch lengths first so you are left with short shreds. Serve with applesauce and sour cream.

2 pounds russet potatoes, unpeeled and shredded
½ cup grated onion
Salt and pepper
2 large eggs, lightly beaten
2 teaspoons minced fresh parsley
Vegetable oil

1. Adjust oven rack to middle position and heat oven to 200 degrees. Toss potatoes with onion and 1 teaspoon salt in bowl. Working in 2 batches, wring potato mixture of excess moisture using clean dish towel over bowl; reserve drained liquid and transfer dried potatoes to clean bowl.

2. Cover potatoes and microwave until just warmed through but not hot, 1 to 2 minutes, stirring with fork every 30 seconds. Spread potatoes over baking sheet and let cool for 10 minutes; return to bowl.

3. Meanwhile, let bowl of drained potato liquid sit for 5 minutes so that starch can settle to bottom. Pour off liquid, leaving starch in bowl. Whisk eggs into starch until smooth. Add starch-egg mixture, parsley, and ¼ teaspoon pepper to cooled potatoes and toss gently to combine.

4. Add oil to 12-inch skillet until it measures ¼ inch deep. Heat oil over medium-high heat until shimmering but not smoking (about 350 degrees). Set wire rack in rimmed baking sheet and line with triple layer of paper towels.

5. Using ¼ cup potato mixture per latke, measure 5 latkes into hot skillet, pressing each into ⅓-inch-thick pancake. Cook until golden brown on both sides, about 6 minutes, adjusting heat as needed so that oil bubbles around edges of pancakes.

6. Transfer latkes to prepared baking sheet and keep warm in oven. Repeat with remaining potato mixture, adding oil as needed to maintain ¼-inch depth and returning oil to 350 degrees between batches. Season latkes with salt and pepper to taste and serve.

TO MAKE AHEAD: Cooked latkes can be held at room temperature for up to 4 hours or frozen for up to 1 month. Reheat latkes on baking sheet in 375-degree oven until crisp and hot, flipping them over halfway through reheating, 3 minutes per side for room-temperature latkes and 6 minutes per side for frozen latkes.

Root Vegetable Gratin

SERVES 6 TO 8   **TOTAL TIME** 2 HOURS 35 MINUTES

✔ **WHY THIS RECIPE WORKS:** This hearty gratin, a cousin to classic scalloped potatoes, swaps out some of the potatoes for carrots and parsnips. Bathed in a rich béchamel sauce, this satisfying dish is topped with nutty Gruyère cheese. To make sure the different vegetables cooked at the same rate, we cut each one to the same thinness and baked them together in a casserole tightly wrapped in aluminum foil at a moderate temperature for an hour and a half. Then we removed the foil, sprinkled Gruyère over the top, and baked it uncovered for another 20 minutes, allowing the cheese to brown. We like to use a shallow 2-quart gratin dish, which allows for the most

surface area (and browned crust), but a 13 by 9-inch baking dish also works. Prep and assemble all of the other ingredients before slicing the potatoes and parsnips or they will begin to brown (do not store them in water; this will make the gratin bland and watery). Slicing the potatoes, carrots, and parsnips ⅛ inch thick is crucial for the success of this dish; use a mandoline, a V-slicer, or a food processor fitted with a ⅛-inch-thick slicing blade. Parmesan cheese can be substituted for the Gruyère, if desired.

  1 **pound russet potatoes, peeled and sliced ⅛ inch thick**
  1 **pound carrots, peeled and sliced ⅛ inch thick**
  1 **pound parsnips, peeled and sliced ⅛ inch thick**
  2 **tablespoons unsalted butter**
  2 **shallots, minced**
1½ **teaspoons salt**
  3 **garlic cloves, minced**
  2 **teaspoons minced fresh thyme**
  ¼ **teaspoon pepper**
  ⅛ **teaspoon ground nutmeg**
  ⅛ **teaspoon cayenne pepper**
  1 **tablespoon all-purpose flour**
1½ **cups heavy cream**
  3 **ounces Gruyère cheese, shredded (¾ cup)**

1. Adjust oven rack to middle position and heat oven to 350 degrees. Grease 2-quart casserole dish. Place potatoes, carrots, and parsnips in large bowl; set aside.

2. Melt butter in small saucepan over medium heat. Add shallots and salt and cook until softened, about 2 minutes. Stir in garlic, thyme, pepper, nutmeg, and cayenne and cook until fragrant, about 30 seconds. Stir in flour and cook until incorporated, about 1 minute. Whisk in cream, bring to simmer, and cook until thickened, about 2 minutes.

3. Pour sauce over vegetable mixture and toss to coat thoroughly. Transfer mixture to prepared dish and gently pack vegetables into even layer, removing any air pockets. Cover dish with aluminum foil and bake until vegetables are almost tender (paring knife can be slipped in and out of potato slice with some resistance), about 1½ hours.

4. Remove foil, sprinkle with Gruyère, and continue to bake, uncovered, until vegetables are lightly browned on top and fork inserted into center meets little resistance, 20 to 30 minutes. Let gratin cool for 10 minutes. Serve.

Spinach with Garlic and Lemon

SERVES 4   **TOTAL TIME** 20 MINUTES   **FAST**

✓ **WHY THIS RECIPE WORKS:** Overcooked spinach, bitter burnt garlic, and pallid lemon flavor are all too often the hallmarks of this simple side dish. Instead, we sought tender sautéed spinach, seasoned with a perfect balance of garlic and lemon. For the spinach, we found that we greatly preferred the hearty flavor and texture of curly-leaf spinach over delicate baby spinach, which wilted down into mush. We cooked the spinach in extra-virgin olive oil and, once cooked, used tongs to squeeze the spinach in a colander over the sink to get rid of all the excess moisture. Minced garlic, cooked after the spinach, added a sweet nuttiness. As for seasoning, all the spinach needed was salt and a squeeze of lemon juice. Leave some water clinging to the spinach leaves after rinsing to help encourage steam when cooking. Two pounds of flat-leaf spinach (about 3 bunches) can be substituted for the curly-leaf spinach.

> 3 tablespoons extra-virgin olive oil
> 20 ounces curly-leaf spinach, stemmed
> 2 garlic cloves, minced
>   Salt
>   Lemon juice

1. Heat 1 tablespoon oil in Dutch oven over high heat until shimmering. Add spinach in handfuls, stirring and tossing each handful to wilt slightly before adding more. Cook spinach, stirring constantly, until uniformly wilted, about 1 minute. Transfer spinach to colander and squeeze between tongs to release excess liquid.

2. Wipe now-empty pot dry with paper towels. Add garlic and remaining 2 tablespoons oil to pot and cook over medium heat until fragrant, about 30 seconds. Add squeezed spinach and toss to coat. Off heat, season with salt and lemon juice to taste. Transfer spinach to serving dish. Serve.

VARIATIONS

Spinach with Shallots and Goat Cheese

Substitute 2 thinly sliced shallots for garlic, cooking shallots until softened, about 2 minutes. Sprinkle spinach with ⅓ cup crumbled goat cheese before serving.

Spinach with Bacon and Balsamic Vinegar

Omit lemon juice. Before cooking spinach, cook 4 slices finely chopped bacon in Dutch oven over medium heat until crisp, 7 to 10 minutes. Transfer bacon to paper towel–lined plate and pour off all but 1 tablespoon bacon fat. Cook spinach as directed, substituting bacon fat left in pot for 1 tablespoon oil. Sprinkle spinach with 1 tablespoon balsamic vinegar before serving.

Flavorful herbed cheese turns a small amount of heavy cream into super-easy one-pot creamed spinach.

Easy Creamed Spinach

SERVES 4   **TOTAL TIME** 20 MINUTES   **FAST**

✓ **WHY THIS RECIPE WORKS:** Most creamed spinach recipes produce stringy spinach in a stodgy, heavy sauce. Wanting to reinvigorate this staple, we reduced the amount of cream to ¼ cup and combined it with Boursin, a flavorful herbed cheese, which turned into a simple sauce. To avoid a watery sauce, we drained and pressed excess liquid from the cooked spinach before adding it to the creamy sauce. Leave some water clinging to the spinach leaves after rinsing to help encourage steam when cooking. Two pounds of flat-leaf spinach (about 3 bunches) can be substituted for the curly-leaf spinach, but do not use delicate baby spinach.

> 1 tablespoon extra-virgin olive oil
> 20 ounces curly-leaf spinach, stemmed and chopped coarse
> 1 (5.2-ounce) package Boursin Garlic & Fine Herbs cheese
> ¼ cup heavy cream
>   Salt and pepper

1. Heat oil in Dutch oven over high heat until shimmering. Add spinach in handfuls, stirring and tossing each handful to wilt slightly before adding more. Cook spinach, stirring constantly, until uniformly wilted, about 1 minute. Transfer spinach to colander and squeeze between tongs to release excess liquid.

2. Wipe now-empty pot dry with paper towels. Whisk Boursin and cream together in pot and simmer over medium-high heat until thickened, about 2 minutes. Add squeezed spinach and toss to coat. Off heat, season with salt and pepper to taste. Transfer spinach to serving dish. Serve.

Roasted Winter Squash Halves

SERVES 4 **TOTAL TIME** 45 MINUTES **FAST**

☑ **WHY THIS RECIPE WORKS:** Winter squashes, with their tough skin and dense interior, are ideal for slow cooking and are best roasted until well done, which helps develop the sweetest flavor and smoothest texture. Though varieties of winter squash vary significantly in size and texture, we hoped to develop a one-recipe-fits-all approach. We found that roasting the unpeeled and seeded halves cut side down gave a slightly better texture than roasting them cut side up. We used a foil-lined baking sheet that had been oiled. The oil promoted better browning and reduced the risk of sticking, and the foil made cleanup easy. This recipe can be made with butternut, acorn, buttercup, kabocha, or delicata squash. The cooking time will vary depending on the kind of squash you use. Start checking for doneness after the first 30 minutes.

> 2 **tablespoons extra-virgin olive oil**
> 2 **pounds winter squash, halved lengthwise and seeded**
>   **Salt and pepper**

1. Adjust oven rack to middle position and heat oven to 400 degrees. Line rimmed baking sheet with aluminum foil and grease foil with 1 tablespoon oil. Brush cut sides of squash with remaining 1 tablespoon oil and place cut side down on

Halving Winter Squash

To keep fingers safe when cutting open squash, pound very lightly on back of knife with rubber mallet to drive blade slowly through squash.

For the best texture and flavor, we roast winter squash halves cut side down on an oiled baking sheet until they're tender.

prepared baking sheet. Roast until fork inserted into center meets little resistance, 30 to 50 minutes.

2. Remove squash from oven and flip cut side up. If necessary, cut large pieces in half to yield 4 pieces. Season with salt and pepper to taste. Transfer squash to serving dish. Serve.

VARIATIONS

Roasted Winter Squash Halves with Soy Sauce and Maple Syrup

Substitute vegetable oil for olive oil. While squash roasts, combine 3 tablespoons maple syrup, 2 tablespoons soy sauce, and ½ teaspoon grated fresh ginger in bowl. After flipping cooked squash cut side up in step 2, brush with maple mixture and return to oven until well caramelized, 5 to 10 minutes.

Roasted Winter Squash Halves with Browned Butter and Sage

While squash roasts, melt 6 tablespoons unsalted butter in 8-inch skillet over medium heat. Add 6 thinly sliced fresh sage leaves and cook, swirling pan often, until butter is golden and sage is crisp, 4 to 5 minutes. Drizzle sage butter over roasted squash before serving.

Pureed Butternut Squash

SERVES 4 TO 6   **TOTAL TIME** 30 MINUTES **FAST**

✔ **WHY THIS RECIPE WORKS:** With its silky-smooth texture and earthy, lightly sweetened flavor, pureed butternut squash is a serious crowd-pleaser, but what's the best way to cook it? Most recipes for pureed squash are similar in that they cook the squash until tender, then puree it with some butter and/or heavy cream in a food processor. We tested a variety of squash cooking methods, including roasting, steaming, braising, and microwaving, and found that the microwave worked best. Not only was it one of the easiest cooking methods, but tasters far preferred the clean, sweet squash flavor that the microwave produced. The surprising thing about microwaving the squash was the amount of liquid released while cooking—we drained nearly ½ cup of squash liquid out of the bowl before pureeing. (We tasted the liquid and found it had a slightly bitter flavor, which is why we did not opt to include it in the puree.) The squash puree needed only 2 tablespoons of half-and-half and 2 tablespoons of butter to help round out its flavor and add some complexity.

- 2 **pounds butternut squash, peeled, seeded, and cut into 1½-inch pieces (5 cups)**
- 2 **tablespoons half-and-half**
- 2 **tablespoons unsalted butter**
- 1 **tablespoon packed brown sugar**
   Salt and pepper

1. Microwave squash in covered bowl until tender and easily pierced with fork, 15 to 20 minutes, stirring halfway through cooking time.

2. Drain squash in colander, then transfer to food processor. Add half-and-half, butter, sugar, and 1 teaspoon salt and process until squash is smooth, about 20 seconds, stopping to scrape down bowl as needed.

3. Transfer pureed squash to serving dish and season with salt and pepper to taste. Serve. (Squash puree can be refrigerated for up to 2 days; reheat in microwave, stirring often, until hot.)

VARIATIONS

Pureed Butternut Squash with Sage and Toasted Almonds

While squash microwaves, cook 1 tablespoon unsalted butter with ½ teaspoon minced fresh sage in 8-inch skillet over medium-low heat until fragrant, about 2 minutes. Substitute sage butter for butter added to food processor. Sprinkle with ¼ cup toasted sliced almonds before serving.

Pureed Butternut Squash with Orange

Add 2 tablespoons orange marmalade to food processor with butter.

Pureed Butternut Squash with Honey and Chipotle Chiles

Substitute honey for sugar. Add 1½ teaspoons minced canned chipotle chile in adobo sauce to food processor with butter.

Cutting Up Butternut Squash

1. After peeling squash, trim off top and bottom and cut squash in half where narrow neck and wide curved bottom meet.

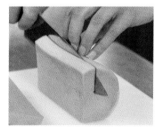

2. Cut neck of squash into evenly sized planks. Cut planks into evenly sized pieces, according to recipe.

3. Cut squash base in half lengthwise, then scoop out and discard seeds and fibers.

4. Slice each base half into evenly sized lengths, then cut lengths into evenly sized pieces, according to recipe.

Spaghetti Squash with Garlic and Parmesan

SERVES 4   **TOTAL TIME** 50 MINUTES

✔ **WHY THIS RECIPE WORKS:** The delicate flavor and creamy flesh of spaghetti squash make it a great addition to any meal, but many recipes bury the squash's flavor underneath too many competing flavors. We kept our recipe simple so the delicate and earthy flavor of the squash would shine through. Roasting the squash halves cut side down after brushing them with oil and seasoning with salt and pepper brought out the sweetness of the flesh. Once the squash was cooked, shredding it was as simple as holding the halves over a bowl and scraping them with a fork. After draining excess liquid, we dressed the squash with Parmesan, fresh basil, lemon juice, and garlic for an easy, flavorful side dish that tasted like summer. Choose a firm squash with an even pale-yellow color. Avoid greenish-tinged squashes, which are immature, or those that yield to gentle pressure, which are old.

- 1 (2½-pound) spaghetti squash, halved lengthwise and seeded
- 2 tablespoons extra-virgin olive oil
  Salt and pepper
- ¼ cup grated Parmesan cheese
- 1 tablespoon chopped fresh basil
- 1 teaspoon lemon juice
- 1 garlic clove, minced

1. Adjust oven rack to middle position and heat oven to 450 degrees. Brush cut sides of squash with 1 tablespoon oil and season with salt and pepper. Lay squash cut side down in 13 by 9-inch baking dish. Roast squash until just tender and tip of paring knife can be slipped into flesh with slight resistance, 25 to 30 minutes.

2. Flip squash over and let cool slightly. Holding squash with clean dish towel over large bowl, use fork to scrape squash flesh from skin while shredding it into fine pieces.

3. Drain excess liquid from bowl of shredded squash, then gently stir in Parmesan, basil, lemon juice, garlic, and remaining 1 tablespoon oil. Season with salt and pepper to taste and serve.

NOTES FROM THE TEST KITCHEN

Keeping Side Dishes Warm

MAKE USE OF YOUR SLOW COOKER: Mashed potatoes seem to cool off faster than anything else you serve. Simply transfer the potatoes to a slow cooker set to low; adjust the consistency with hot cream or milk as needed before serving.

USE YOUR FONDUE POT: Keep sauces and gravy hot by transferring them to a fondue pot set to low. Other creamy dishes you can keep hot using this method include creamed onions, candied sweet potatoes, and macaroni and cheese.

USE KITCHEN APPLIANCES TO YOUR ADVANTAGE: If your stovetop has an oven located just underneath, the oven's vents are typically located just behind the back burners. You can make use of the hot air coming out of the oven vent to warm up serving dishes and dinner plates by stacking them on top of one of the back burners. Make sure that the burner itself is cold and clean and that the stack of plates is stable.

PREWARM SERVING DISHES: Prewarming serving dishes can keep sides warm for an extra 10 to 20 minutes. Briefly heat your empty serving dishes in a warm oven or the microwave, or you can even use the drying cycle of the dishwasher.

VARIATION

Spaghetti Squash with Asian Flavors

Omit Parmesan, basil, lemon juice, garlic, and remaining 1 tablespoon oil in step 3. Toss shredded squash with 1 tablespoon soy sauce, 2½ teaspoons vegetable oil, ½ teaspoon toasted sesame oil, 1 teaspoon rice vinegar, 2 thinly sliced scallions, and ½ teaspoon toasted sesame seeds before serving.

Preparing Spaghetti Squash

Holding roasted squash half with clean dish towel over large bowl, use fork to scrape squash flesh from skin, shredding flesh into fine pieces.

Roasted Sweet Potatoes

SERVES 4 TO 6   **TOTAL TIME** 1 HOUR 25 MINUTES

✔ **WHY THIS RECIPE WORKS:** Too often, roasted sweet potatoes turn out starchy and bland. We wanted a recipe that gave us potatoes with a nicely caramelized exterior, a smooth, creamy interior, and an earthy sweetness. We started the sliced potatoes in a cold (versus preheated) oven and covered them with foil to allow plenty of time for their starches to convert to sugars. We removed the foil after 30 minutes and continued to roast the potatoes until crisp. We had our perfect roasted sweet potato recipe: supersweet and tender potatoes with a slightly crisp, caramelized exterior. Choose potatoes that are as even in width as possible; trimming the small ends prevents them from burning. If you prefer not to peel the potatoes, just scrub them well before cutting. Note that the size of the rimmed baking sheet matters here; if your sheet is too small, there will not be enough room for the potatoes to roast in a single layer.

- **3 pounds sweet potatoes, ends trimmed, peeled, rinsed, and cut into ¾-inch-thick rounds**
- **2 tablespoons vegetable oil**
- **Salt and pepper**

1. Line 18 by 13-inch heavy-duty rimmed baking sheet with aluminum foil and coat with vegetable oil spray. Toss potatoes with oil, 1 teaspoon salt, and pepper to taste in large bowl. Lay potatoes in single layer on prepared baking sheet and cover tightly with foil.

2. Adjust oven rack to middle position and place potatoes in cold oven. Turn oven to 425 degrees and cook potatoes for 30 minutes.

3. Remove baking sheet from oven and remove top layer of foil. Return potatoes to oven and cook until bottom edges of potatoes are golden brown, 15 to 25 minutes.

4. Remove baking sheet from oven and, using thin metal spatula, flip slices over. Continue to roast until bottom edges of potatoes are golden brown, 18 to 22 minutes. Let roasted potatoes cool for 5 to 10 minutes, then transfer to serving dish. Serve.

VARIATIONS

Roasted Sweet Potatoes with Maple-Thyme Glaze

Whisk ¼ cup maple syrup, 2 tablespoons melted unsalted butter, and 2 teaspoons minced fresh thyme together in bowl. Brush mixture over both sides of partially cooked potatoes when flipping in step 4; continue to roast potatoes as directed.

Roasted Sweet Potatoes with Spiced Brown Sugar Glaze

Cook ¼ cup packed light brown sugar, 2 tablespoons apple juice, 2 tablespoons unsalted butter, ¼ teaspoon ground cinnamon, ¼ teaspoon ground ginger, and ⅛ teaspoon ground nutmeg in small saucepan over medium heat until butter has melted and sugar is dissolved, 2 to 4 minutes. Brush mixture over both sides of partially cooked potatoes when flipping in step 4; continue to roast potatoes as directed.

Making Roasted Sweet Potatoes

1. CUT POTATOES INTO ROUNDS: Rinse peeled sweet potatoes and cut into ¾-inch-thick rounds.

2. START COVERED IN COLD OVEN: Cover baking sheet tightly with foil and place in cold oven. Turn oven to 425 degrees.

3. UNCOVER: Remove top layer of foil and return potatoes to oven to continue roasting until bottom edges are golden brown.

4. FLIP AND FINISH ROASTING: Flip slices over with thin spatula and continue to roast until bottom edges are golden brown. Let cool before serving.

Simmering the sweet potatoes directly in the butter and cream before mashing preserves their delicate flavor.

Mashed Sweet Potatoes

SERVES 4 **TOTAL TIME** 50 MINUTES

✔ **WHY THIS RECIPE WORKS:** When developing this recipe, we initially used our traditional mashed potato recipe as a guide. Unfortunately, every time we boiled the sweet potatoes in water before mashing them, they tasted too bland. To preserve as much of the sweet potato flavor as possible, we simmered them in a covered pot over low heat in a combination of butter and heavy cream. When they were prepared in this way, we didn't boil away any of their flavor. Adding salt brought out the potatoes' delicate flavor, and just a teaspoon of sugar bolstered their sweetness. Once the potatoes were tender, we mashed them in the saucepan. We skipped the typical pumpkin pie seasoning and instead let the simple sweet potato flavor shine through. This recipe can be easily doubled, but be sure to use a large Dutch oven and double the cooking time.

2 pounds sweet potatoes, peeled, quartered lengthwise, and cut crosswise into ¼-inch-thick slices
4 tablespoons unsalted butter, cut into 4 pieces

2 tablespoons heavy cream
1 teaspoon sugar
   Salt and pepper

Combine all ingredients and ½ teaspoon salt in large saucepan. Cover and cook over low heat, stirring occasionally, until potatoes fall apart when poked with fork, about 40 minutes. Off heat, mash potatoes with potato masher until smooth. Season with salt and pepper to taste. Transfer to serving dish. Serve.

VARIATIONS

Maple-Orange Mashed Sweet Potatoes

Stir 2 tablespoons maple syrup and ½ teaspoon grated orange zest into potatoes before mashing.

Garlic-Scented Mashed Sweet Potatoes with Coconut Milk and Cilantro

Substitute ½ cup coconut milk for butter and cream. Add ¼ teaspoon red pepper flakes and 1 minced garlic clove to saucepan with potatoes. Stir 1 tablespoon minced fresh cilantro into mashed potatoes before serving.

Sweet Potato Casserole

SERVES 8 TO 10 **TOTAL TIME** 1 HOUR 10 MINUTES

✔ **WHY THIS RECIPE WORKS:** Boiling the sweet potatoes for our casserole washed out the flavor and made for a watery casserole. But roasting took too long. Remembering the trick we learned when making mashed sweet potatoes, we simmered the potatoes in butter and cream, which preserved their flavor. Spices like ginger, nutmeg, and cinnamon made our casserole taste more like dessert than a side dish, so we stuck with just salt and pepper. A small dose of cream cheese made the casserole richer, and it helped ensure the dish wasn't too sweet. If you prefer silky-smooth potatoes, use a hand-held mixer to beat the potatoes in step 3. Use sharp, clean scissors sprayed with cooking spray (to prevent sticking and make cleanup easier) to snip the marshmallows in half through the equator.

5 pounds sweet potatoes, peeled and cut into 1-inch chunks
6 tablespoons heavy cream
6 tablespoons unsalted butter, cut into 6 pieces
2 teaspoons sugar
1 teaspoon salt
½ teaspoon pepper
2 ounces cream cheese
1 (10-ounce) bag marshmallows, halved crosswise

1. Combine potatoes, cream, butter, sugar, salt, and pepper in Dutch oven. Cover and cook over medium heat, stirring often, until potatoes begin to break down, 20 to 25 minutes.

2. Reduce heat to medium-low and continue to cook, covered, until liquid has been absorbed and potatoes are completely tender, 15 to 20 minutes. Meanwhile, adjust oven rack to upper-middle position and heat oven to 450 degrees.

3. Add cream cheese to potatoes. Using potato masher, mash until potatoes are smooth and cream cheese is fully incorporated. Continue to cook, stirring constantly, until potatoes are thickened, about 5 minutes.

4. Transfer potato mixture to 2-quart baking dish and smooth top with rubber spatula.

5. Top casserole with single layer marshmallows. Bake until marshmallows are browned, about 5 minutes. Serve.

Making Sweet Potato Casserole

1. OMIT WATER: Simmer sweet potatoes in butter and cream to infuse them with flavor and keep them from becoming watery.

2. COOK POTATOES UNTIL TENDER: Cover and cook until liquid has been absorbed and potatoes are completely tender.

3. MASH POTATOES: Add cream cheese and mash until fully incorporated and potatoes are smooth and thickened.

4. TOAST MARSHMALLOWS: Transfer potatoes to baking dish, top with single layer of marshmallows, and bake until marshmallows are browned.

TO MAKE AHEAD: After transferring sweet potato mixture to baking dish, mixture can be refrigerated, covered, up to 2 days. Microwave until warm, 4 to 7 minutes, before topping with marshmallows and baking as directed.

Sautéed Zucchini or Yellow Summer Squash

SERVES 4   **TOTAL TIME** 55 MINUTES

WHY THIS RECIPE WORKS: Because zucchini and yellow summer squash are so watery, they often cook up soggy and bland. We wanted to find a way to make sautéed summer squash with concentrated flavor and an appealing texture. The key was to remove water by salting and draining for 30 minutes and then patting the squash dry. We sautéed an onion first for some depth, then we added the squash, along with lemon zest, to the hot skillet, where the squash became tender and lightly browned. A little lemon juice and parsley stirred in off the heat lent bright flavors. Do not add more salt when cooking, or the dish will be too salty. Basil, mint, tarragon, or chives can be substituted for the parsley.

1½   **pounds zucchini or yellow summer squash, sliced ¼ inch thick**
     Kosher salt and pepper
3   **tablespoons extra-virgin olive oil**
1   **small onion, chopped fine**
1   **teaspoon grated lemon zest plus 1 tablespoon juice**
1   **tablespoon minced fresh parsley**

1. Toss zucchini with 1 tablespoon salt and let drain in colander set over bowl until roughly ⅓ cup water drains from zucchini, about 30 minutes. Pat zucchini dry with paper towels and carefully wipe away any residual salt.

2. Heat oil in 12-inch nonstick skillet over medium heat until shimmering. Add onion and cook until almost softened, about 3 minutes. Increase heat to medium-high, add zucchini and lemon zest, and cook until zucchini is golden brown, about 10 minutes.

3. Off heat, stir in lemon juice and parsley and season with pepper to taste. Transfer zucchini to serving dish. Serve.

VARIATION

Sautéed Zucchini or Yellow Summer Squash with Olives and Oregano

Substitute 1 teaspoon minced fresh oregano for parsley. Add ¼ cup pitted chopped kalamata olives to zucchini with lemon juice.

Rice, Grains, and Beans

■ SIGNIFIES A **FAST** RECIPE (45 MINUTES OR LESS)

Basmati Rice Pilaf

SERVES 4 TO 6   **TOTAL TIME** 50 MINUTES

✓ **WHY THIS RECIPE WORKS:** Many rice pilaf recipes call for soaking the rice overnight, but we found this wasn't necessary; simply rinsing the rice before cooking removed excess starch and ensured the fluffy, rather than clumpy, grains that we were after. We sautéed an onion in a saucepan first for an easy flavor boost, then we added the rice. Toasting the rice for a few minutes in the pan deepened its flavor. Instead of following the traditional ratio of 1 cup of rice to 2 cups of water, we found using a little less liquid delivered better results. Placing a dish towel under the lid while the rice finished steaming off the heat absorbed excess moisture in the pan and guaranteed our rice was perfectly fluffy. Long-grain white, jasmine, or Texmati rice can be substituted for the basmati. A nonstick saucepan works best here, although a traditional saucepan will also work.

1 tablespoon extra-virgin olive oil
1 small onion, chopped fine
  Salt and pepper
1½ cups basmati rice, rinsed
2¼ cups water

1. Heat oil in large saucepan over medium heat until shimmering. Add onion and ¼ teaspoon salt and cook until onion is softened, about 5 minutes. Stir in rice and cook, stirring often, until grain edges begin to turn translucent, about 3 minutes.

2. Stir in water and bring to simmer. Reduce heat to low, cover, and continue to simmer until rice is tender and water is absorbed, 16 to 18 minutes.

3. Remove pot from heat and lay clean folded dish towel underneath lid. Let sit for 10 minutes. Fluff rice with fork, season with salt and pepper to taste, and serve.

VARIATIONS
Herbed Basmati Rice Pilaf

Add 2 minced garlic cloves and 1 teaspoon minced fresh thyme to pot with rice. When fluffing cooked rice, stir in ¼ cup minced fresh parsley and 2 tablespoons minced fresh chives.

Basmati Rice Pilaf with Peas, Scallions, and Lemon

Add 2 minced garlic cloves, 1 teaspoon grated lemon zest, and ⅛ teaspoon red pepper flakes to pot with rice. Before covering rice with dish towel in step 3, sprinkle ½ cup thawed frozen peas over top. When fluffing cooked rice, stir in 2 thinly sliced scallions and 1 tablespoon lemon juice.

Basmati Rice Pilaf with Currants and Toasted Almonds

Add 2 minced garlic cloves, ½ teaspoon ground turmeric, and ¼ teaspoon ground cinnamon to pot with rice. Before covering rice with dish towel in step 3, sprinkle ¼ cup currants over top. When fluffing cooked rice, stir in ¼ cup toasted sliced almonds.

Simple White Rice

SERVES 6   **TOTAL TIME** 45 MINUTES   **FAST**

✓ **WHY THIS RECIPE WORKS:** White rice seems like an easy enough dish to make, but it can be deceptively temperamental, quickly dissolving into unpleasant, gummy grains. For really great long-grain rice with distinct, separate grains that didn't clump together, we rinsed the rice of excess starch first. Then, to add a rich dimension, we sautéed the grains in butter before covering them with water. After simmering the rice until all of the liquid was absorbed, we placed a dish towel between the lid and pot to absorb excess moisture and ensure dry, fluffy grains. A nonstick saucepan works best here, although a traditional saucepan will also work.

1 tablespoon unsalted butter or vegetable oil
2 cups long-grain white rice, rinsed
3 cups water
  Salt and pepper

1. Melt butter in large saucepan over medium heat. Add rice and cook, stirring constantly, until grains become chalky and opaque, 1 to 3 minutes. Add water and 1 teaspoon salt, increase heat to high, and bring to boil, swirling pot to blend ingredients. Reduce heat to low, cover, and simmer until all liquid is absorbed, 18 to 20 minutes.

2. Remove pot from heat and lay clean folded dish towel underneath lid. Let sit for 10 minutes. Fluff rice with fork, season with salt and pepper to taste, and serve.

JAZZING UP PLAIN RICE

To gussy up plain rice, try tossing in some butter, minced fresh herbs, and/or citrus zest. Or use a compound butter (see page 202). Dried fruits, toasted nuts, olives, and cheese are also good additions. On a hot day, let the rice cool, then toss with a vinaigrette (see pages 52–53) to make rice salad.

Rice pilaf should be fragrant, fluffy, and tender. Unfortunately, many recipes don't agree on the method for guaranteeing these results. Our recipe relies on a few simple steps and just the right ratio of water to rice for perfect pilaf every time. We also found that cooking the pilaf over the lowest heat possible reduces the risk of scorching.

1. RINSE THE RICE: Place 1½ cups rice in a fine-mesh strainer and rinse under cold water until the water runs clear, occasionally stirring the rice with your hand. Drain the rice over a bowl.
WHY? Rinsing the rice washes away excess starch that otherwise will make the pilaf sticky and gummy.

2. SAUTÉ THE ONION: Heat the oil in a large saucepan over medium heat until shimmering. Add a small, finely chopped onion and ¼ teaspoon salt and cook, stirring occasionally, until the onion is soft.
WHY? The sautéed onion adds depth to this simple dish. The salt helps the onion release its juices and soften more quickly.

3. TOAST THE RICE: Stir in the drained rice and cook, stirring often, until the edges of the grains start to turn translucent, about 3 minutes.
WHY? Toasting the rice highlights its nutty flavor and helps it to cook up fluffy and light. The rice should smell fragrant but not change color.

4. ADD WATER AND SIMMER: Stir in 2¼ cups water and bring to a simmer. Reduce the heat to the lowest possible setting, cover, and continue to simmer until the rice is tender, 16 to 18 minutes.
WHY? After much testing, we found that a ratio of 3 parts water to 2 parts rice yields perfect fluffy rice. The gentle low heat will prevent the rice from scorching. Once the lid is in place, don't stir the pot or the rice will become gummy.

5. STEAM THE RICE OFF THE HEAT: Remove the pot from the heat and lay a folded dish towel underneath the lid. Let the pot sit for 10 minutes.
WHY? Allowing the rice to sit off the heat lets the heat and moisture trapped in the pot finish steaming the rice, ensuring tender grains. A dish towel under the lid absorbs any extra moisture in the pot and keeps the rice from becoming gummy.

6. FLUFF THE RICE: With a fork, fluff the rice and season it with salt and pepper.
WHY? A fork does the best job of separating the individual grains, producing a light, fluffy pilaf. Sprinkling the salt and pepper over the rice as you fluff will distribute them evenly. Be sure not to stir the rice too much, or you can break up the grains and make the pilaf starchy.

ALL ABOUT **COOKING RICE**

Here are three simple methods for basic rice cooking: boiling, pilaf-style (which we think yields the best results), and microwaving. Boiling, or simmering the rice in ample amounts of water (like pasta) on the stovetop, is easy. While some may argue it doesn't produce the best rice, we think it is a great (and foolproof) method when you want rice to round out a meal or fill a burrito. The best thing about simmering rice on the stovetop is that rinsing and measuring aren't even necessary. And microwaving rice? Well, after working on it for a while in the test kitchen, we can honestly say that not only does the microwave work, it works really well. Plus you can cook the rice right in the serving bowl.

If you want to make rice for a crowd, use the boiling method and double the amount of rice (there's no need to add more water or salt). We don't recommend cooking more than 1 cup of rice in the microwave.

BOILING DIRECTIONS: Bring the water to a boil in a large saucepan. Stir in the rice and 2½ teaspoons salt. Return to a boil, then reduce to a simmer and cook until the rice is tender, following the cooking times given in the chart below. Drain.

PILAF-STYLE DIRECTIONS: Rinse the rice (see page 510). Heat 1 tablespoon vegetable or olive oil in a medium saucepan (preferably nonstick) over medium-high heat until shimmering. Stir in the rice and cook until the edges of the grains begin to turn translucent, about 3 minutes. Stir in the water and ¼ teaspoon salt. Bring the mixture to a simmer, then reduce the heat to low, cover, and continue to simmer until the rice is tender and has absorbed all the water, following the cooking times given in the chart below. Off the heat, place a clean folded dish towel under the lid and let the rice sit for 10 minutes. Fluff the rice with a fork.

MICROWAVE DIRECTIONS: Rinse the rice (see page 510). Combine the water, the rice, 1 tablespoon oil, and ¼ teaspoon salt in a bowl. Cover and microwave on high (full power) until the water begins to boil, 5 to 10 minutes. Reduce the microwave heat to medium (50 percent power) and continue to cook until the rice is just tender, following the cooking times given in the chart below. Remove from the microwave and fluff with a fork. Cover the bowl with plastic wrap, poke several vent holes in the plastic with the tip of a knife, and let sit until completely tender, about 5 minutes.

TYPE OF RICE	COOKING METHOD	AMOUNT OF RICE	AMOUNT OF WATER	COOKING TIME
Short- and Medium-Grain White Rice	Boiled	1 cup	4 quarts	10 to 15 minutes
	Pilaf-Style	1 cup	1¾ cups	10 to 15 minutes
	Microwave	X	X	X
Long-Grain White Rice	Boiled	1 cup	4 quarts	12 to 17 minutes
	Pilaf-Style	1 cup	1¾ cups	16 to 18 minutes
	Microwave	1 cup	2 cups	10 to 15 minutes
Short- and Medium-Grain Brown Rice	Boiled	1 cup	4 quarts	22 to 27 minutes
	Pilaf-Style	1 cup	1¾ cups	40 to 50 minutes
	Microwave	1 cup	2 cups	25 to 30 minutes
Long-Grain Brown Rice	Boiled	1 cup	4 quarts	25 to 30 minutes
	Pilaf-Style	1 cup	1¾ cups	40 to 50 minutes
	Microwave	1 cup	2 cups	25 to 30 minutes
Wild Rice	Boiled	1 cup	4 quarts	35 to 40 minutes
	Pilaf-Style	X	X	X
	Microwave	X	X	X
Basmati, Jasmine, or Texmati Rice	Boiled	1 cup	4 quarts	12 to 17 minutes
	Pilaf-Style	1 cup	1¾ cups	16 to 18 minutes
	Microwave	1 cup	2 cups	10 to 15 minutes

X = Not recommended

We turn to the oven for hands-off and perfectly cooked white rice.

1. Adjust oven rack to middle position and heat oven to 450 degrees. Combine boiling water, rice, oil, and ½ teaspoon salt in 8-inch square baking dish. Cover dish tightly with double layer of aluminum foil. Bake rice until tender and no water remains, about 20 minutes.

2. Remove dish from oven, uncover, and fluff rice with fork, scraping up any rice that has stuck to bottom. Re-cover dish with foil and let stand for 10 minutes. Season with salt and pepper to taste and serve.

VARIATIONS
Hands-Off Baked Saffron Rice
Stir pinch saffron threads into boiling water before adding to baking dish.

Hands-Off Baked Coconut Rice
Substitute following mixture for boiling water: Combine 2 cups water, ¾ cup coconut milk, and ⅛ teaspoon ground cardamom in bowl, cover, and microwave until hot, about 2 minutes. When fluffing cooked rice, stir in 1 tablespoon minced fresh cilantro.

Hands-Off Baked Curried Rice
Stir 1 teaspoon curry powder into boiling water before adding to baking dish. When fluffing cooked rice, stir in ¼ cup raisins.

Hands-Off Baked White Rice
SERVES 4   TOTAL TIME 45 MINUTES   **FAST**

✓ **WHY THIS RECIPE WORKS:** Wanting an easy and hands-off version of everyday rice, we found our answer by using the oven. After a few tests, we uncovered some tricks that ensured perfect rice every time. First, be sure to rinse the rice before combining it with the water for cooking, or else the excess starch clinging to the rice will make everything taste gluey. Second, use boiling water, or else the rice will take forever to cook through in the oven. For an accurate measurement of boiling water, bring a full kettle of water to a boil, then measure out the desired amount.

2¾ cups boiling water
1⅓ cups long-grain white rice, rinsed
1 tablespoon extra-virgin olive oil
   Salt and pepper

Easy Baked Brown Rice
SERVES 4 TO 6   TOTAL TIME 1 HOUR 45 MINUTES

✓ **WHY THIS RECIPE WORKS:** Brown rice should be ultimately satisfying, with a nutty, gutsy flavor and more textural personality—slightly sticky and just a bit chewy—than white rice. We found moving the recipe to the oven ensured more even cooking and guarded against scorching. For evenly cooked grains, we had to tweak the liquid-to-rice ratio established in our Simple White Rice (page 494), settling on 3¼ cups liquid to 1½ cups brown rice. Rice made with chicken broth only was too salty, so we used a combination of water and broth. The steady, even heat of the oven eliminated the risk of scorching and produced light and fluffy grains every time. Short-grain brown rice can be substituted for the long-grain rice. A Dutch oven with a tight-fitting lid is essential for this recipe; if the lid fits loosely, wrap aluminum foil tightly over the mouth of the pot, underneath the lid. To make this dish vegetarian, substitute vegetable broth for the chicken broth.

1 tablespoon extra-virgin olive oil
1 small onion, chopped fine
  Salt and pepper
2¼ cups water
1 cup chicken broth
1½ cups long-grain brown rice

1. Adjust oven rack to middle position and heat oven to 375 degrees. Heat oil in Dutch oven over medium heat until shimmering. Add onion and ¼ teaspoon salt and cook, stirring occasionally, until well browned, 12 to 14 minutes.

2. Add water and broth, cover, and bring to boil. Off heat, stir in rice. Cover, transfer pot to oven, and bake rice until tender, 65 to 70 minutes.

3. Remove pot from oven and uncover. Fluff rice with fork, scraping up any rice that has stuck to bottom. Lay clean folded dish towel underneath lid. Let sit for 10 minutes. Season with salt and pepper to taste and serve.

Making Brown Rice

1. SAUTÉ ONION: Heat oil in Dutch oven until shimmering. Add onion and salt. Cook, stirring occasionally, until well browned.

2. ADD WATER AND BROTH, THEN RICE: Add water and broth, cover, and bring to boil. Stir in rice off heat.

3. BAKE UNTIL TENDER: Cover pot and transfer to preheated oven. Bake until rice is tender, 65 to 70 minutes.

4. STEAM OFF HEAT: Remove pot from oven and fluff rice with fork. Lay dish towel underneath lid and let sit for 10 minutes.

VARIATION

Easy Baked Brown Rice with Parmesan, Lemon, and Herbs

When fluffing cooked rice, stir in ½ cup grated Parmesan, ¼ cup minced fresh parsley, ¼ cup chopped fresh basil, 1 teaspoon grated lemon zest, and ½ teaspoon lemon juice.

Wild Rice Pilaf with Pecans and Cranberries

SERVES 6 TO 8   **TOTAL TIME** 1 HOUR

✔ **WHY THIS RECIPE WORKS:** Properly cooked wild rice is chewy yet tender and pleasingly rustic—not crunchy or gluey, like the wild rice so many recipes produce. We wanted to figure out how to produce properly cooked wild rice with fluffy pilaf-style results every time. We found that simmering the wild rice in plenty of liquid and then draining off any excess was the most reliable method. Cooking times from batch to batch varied, so we started checking for doneness after 35 minutes. A combination of water and chicken broth performed much better than water alone. Mild yet rich, the broth tempered the rice's muddiness and brought out its earthy, nutty flavors. We also added some white rice to balance the wild rice's strong flavor profile. To make this dish vegetarian, substitute vegetable broth for the chicken broth. For an accurate measurement of boiling water, bring a full kettle of water to a boil, then measure out the desired amount.

1¾ cups chicken broth
¼ cup water plus 2¼ cups boiling water
2 bay leaves
8 sprigs fresh thyme, divided into 2 bundles, each tied together with kitchen twine
1 cup wild rice, picked over and rinsed
3 tablespoons unsalted butter
1 onion, chopped fine
1 large carrot, peeled and chopped fine
  Salt and pepper
1½ cups long-grain white rice, rinsed
¾ cup dried cranberries
¾ cup pecans, toasted and chopped coarse
2 tablespoons minced fresh parsley

1. Bring broth, ¼ cup water, bay leaves, and 1 bundle thyme to boil in medium saucepan over medium-high heat. Add wild rice, cover, and reduce heat to low. Simmer until rice is plump and tender and most of liquid has been absorbed, 35 to 45 minutes. Drain rice through fine-mesh strainer, discarding

The key to perfectly tender and flavorful wild rice is to simmer it in a combination of broth and water.

liquid. Discard bay leaves and thyme. Return rice to now-empty saucepan; cover and set aside.

2. Meanwhile, melt butter in medium saucepan over medium-high heat. Add onion, carrot, and 1 teaspoon salt and cook until vegetables are softened, about 4 minutes. Stir in white rice and cook, stirring often, until grain edges begin to turn translucent, about 3 minutes.

3. Stir in 2¼ cups boiling water and second thyme bundle and bring to simmer. Reduce heat to low, cover, and continue to simmer until white rice is tender and water is absorbed, 16 to 18 minutes. Off heat, discard thyme, fluff rice with fork, and stir in cranberries.

4. Gently toss wild rice, white rice mixture, pecans, and parsley together in bowl. Season with salt and pepper to taste and serve.

VARIATION

Wild Rice Pilaf with Scallions, Cilantro, and Almonds

Omit dried cranberries. Substitute toasted sliced almonds for pecans and cilantro for parsley. Add 2 thinly sliced scallions and 1 teaspoon lime juice to pilaf before serving.

Getting to Know Rice

All rice (except wild rice) starts out as brown rice. A grain of rice is made up of endosperm, germ, bran, and a hull or husk. Brown rice is simply husked and cleaned. White rice has the germ and bran removed. This makes the rice cook up faster and softer, and it's more shelf-stable, but this process also removes much of the fiber, protein, and other nutrients, as well as flavor.

LONG-GRAIN WHITE RICE: This broad category includes generic long-grain rice as well as aromatic varieties such as basmati, Texmati, and jasmine. The grains are slender and elongated and measure four to five times longer than they are wide. The rice cooks up light and fluffy with firm, distinct grains, making it good for pilafs and salads. Avoid converted rice, which is par-boiled during processing. In our opinion, this tan-colored rice cooks up too separate, and the flavor is a bit off.

MEDIUM-GRAIN WHITE RICE: This category includes a variety of specialty rices used to make risotto (Arborio) and paella (Valencia), as well as many Japanese and Chinese brands. The grains are fat, measuring two to three times longer than they are wide. This rice cooks up a bit sticky (the starch is what makes risotto creamy), and when simmered, the grains clump together, making this rice a common choice in Chinese restaurants.

SHORT-GRAIN WHITE RICE: The grains of short-grain white rice are almost round, and the texture is quite sticky and soft when cooked. This rice is used in sushi.

BROWN RICE: As with white rice, brown rice comes in a variety of grain sizes: short, medium, and long. Long-grain brown rice, the best choice for pilafs, cooks up fluffy, with separate grains. Medium-grain brown rice is a bit more sticky, perfect for risotto, paella, and similar dishes. Short-grain brown rice is the most sticky, ideal for sushi and other Asian dishes.

BASMATI RICE: Prized for its nutty flavor and sweet aroma, basmati rice is eaten in pilafs and biryanis and with curries. Indian basmati is aged for a minimum of one year. Aging dehydrates the rice, which translates into grains that, once cooked, expand greatly. We don't recommend American-grown basmati.

WILD RICE: Wild rice is not in the same family as other rices; it's actually an aquatic grass. Wild rice is North America's only native grain. It grows naturally in lakes and also is cultivated in man-made paddies in Minnesota, California, and Canada. We prefer brands that parboil the grains during processing.

Fresh tomatoes, tomato paste, jalapeños, and cilantro make our baked Mexican rice both flavorful and colorful.

Mexican Rice

SERVES 6 TO 8   **TOTAL TIME** 1 HOUR

✔ **WHY THIS RECIPE WORKS:** Rice cooked the Mexican way is a flavorful pilaf-style dish, but we've had our share of soupy or greasy versions. We wanted tender rice infused with fresh flavor. To keep the grains distinct, we rinsed the rice before cooking it. Sautéing the rice in vegetable oil before adding the liquid produced superior grains. We found that equal parts chicken broth and fresh tomatoes that had been pureed along with an onion (all combined in a 2:1 ratio with the rice) were ideal for a flavorful base. For flavor and color, we added a little tomato paste. Baking the rice ensured even cooking, as did stirring the rice at the halfway mark. Cilantro, jalapeño, and lime juice complemented the richer tones of the cooked tomatoes, garlic, and onion. Because the spiciness of jalapeños varies, we tried to control the heat by removing the ribs and seeds from those chiles that were cooked in the rice. A Dutch oven with a tight-fitting lid is essential for this recipe; if the lid fits loosely, wrap aluminum foil tightly over mouth of pot, underneath the lid. To make this dish vegetarian, substitute vegetable broth for the chicken broth.

2 tomatoes, cored and quartered
1 onion, chopped coarse
⅓ cup vegetable oil
2 cups long-grain white rice, rinsed
4 garlic cloves, minced
3 jalapeño chiles, 2 chiles seeded and minced, 1 chile minced with seeds and ribs
2 cups chicken broth
1 tablespoon tomato paste
1½ teaspoons salt
½ cup minced fresh cilantro
   Lime wedges

1. Adjust oven rack to middle position and heat oven to 350 degrees. Process tomatoes and onion in food processor until smooth, about 15 seconds. Transfer puree to liquid measuring cup and spoon off excess as needed until mixture measures 2 cups.

2. Heat oil in Dutch oven over medium-high heat for 1 to 2 minutes. Drop 3 or 4 grains rice in oil; if grains sizzle, oil is ready. Add rice and cook, stirring frequently, until rice is light golden and translucent, 6 to 8 minutes.

3. Stir in garlic and seeded minced jalapeños and cook until fragrant, about 30 seconds. Stir in tomato-onion puree, broth, tomato paste, and salt and bring to boil. Cover pot, transfer to oven, and bake until liquid is absorbed and rice is tender, 30 to 35 minutes, stirring well halfway through cooking.

4. Stir in cilantro and, to taste, minced jalapeño with seeds. Serve with lime wedges.

Rice Pilaf with Vermicelli

SERVES 4 TO 6   **TOTAL TIME** 55 MINUTES

✔ **WHY THIS RECIPE WORKS:** This take on our simple rice pilaf marries long-grain white rice with tender vermicelli and infuses them with garlic and warm spices for a side dish that is anything but ordinary. We followed our traditional rice pilaf method, building flavor by first browning the vermicelli in butter, then sautéing aromatics and blooming the spices. Sautéing the rice and vermicelli next, until the grains of rice began to turn translucent, gave our pilaf great flavor and texture. Adding boiling water kept the cooking time under 20 minutes, at which point we removed the pot from the heat and let it sit for 10 more minutes before serving. For an accurate measurement of boiling water, bring a full kettle of water to a boil, then measure out the desired amount.

3 tablespoons unsalted butter

4 ounces vermicelli, broken into 1-inch pieces (1 cup)

1 small onion, chopped fine

Salt and pepper

2 garlic cloves, minced

½ teaspoon ground cumin

½ teaspoon ground coriander

Pinch allspice

1½ cups long-grain white rice, rinsed

3¼ cups boiling water

1. Melt 1½ tablespoons butter in Dutch oven over medium heat. Add vermicelli and cook, stirring occasionally, until browned, about 3 minutes; transfer to bowl.

2. Melt remaining 1½ tablespoons butter in now-empty pot over medium heat. Add onion and 1½ teaspoons salt and cook until onion is softened and lightly browned, 5 to 7 minutes. Stir in garlic, cumin, coriander, allspice, and pinch pepper and cook until fragrant, about 30 seconds. Stir in toasted vermicelli and rice and cook until edges of rice grains begin to turn translucent, about 3 minutes.

3. Stir in boiling water. Cover, reduce heat to low, and cook until liquid is absorbed and rice and pasta are tender, 16 to 20 minutes. Remove pot from heat and let stand, covered, for 10 minutes. Fluff with fork, season with salt and pepper to taste, and serve.

Dirty Rice

SERVES 4 TO 6　　**TOTAL TIME** 1 HOUR

WHY THIS RECIPE WORKS: Dirty rice gets its name from the chicken giblets—the gizzard, heart, kidneys, and liver—that were used to flavor the rice, at the same time turning it brown, or "dirty." We wanted to streamline this classic Cajun dish and keep its richness but skip most of the giblets. We used ground pork to replace the giblets and heart, but kept the chicken livers for an irreplaceable flavor. For our rice, we preferred the sweet flavor of red bell pepper, with a bit of cayenne pepper for spice. Cooking the meat and vegetables separately from the rice, and combining everything once the rice was cooked through, ensured the rice cooked evenly and kept the dirty rice from tasting muddy. Serve with hot sauce.

1 tablespoon vegetable oil

8 ounces ground pork

1 onion, chopped fine

1 celery rib, chopped fine

1 red bell pepper, stemmed, seeded, and chopped fine

3 garlic cloves, minced

4 ounces chicken livers, rinsed, trimmed, and chopped fine

¼ teaspoon dried thyme

¼ teaspoon cayenne pepper

Salt

2¼ cups chicken broth

2 bay leaves

1½ cups long-grain white rice, rinsed

3 scallions, sliced thin

1. Heat oil in Dutch oven over medium heat until shimmering. Add pork and cook until browned, about 5 minutes. Stir in onion, celery, and bell pepper and cook until softened, about 10 minutes. Add garlic, chicken livers, thyme, cayenne, and 1 teaspoon salt and cook until browned, 3 to 5 minutes. Transfer to fine-mesh strainer set over bowl; cover with aluminum foil to keep warm.

2. Add chicken broth, bay leaves, and rice to now-empty pot and bring to boil over high heat, scraping up any browned bits. Reduce heat to low, cover, and cook until rice is tender, 15 to 17 minutes.

3. Off heat, discard bay leaves. Fluff rice with fork, and gently stir in drained chicken liver mixture. Sprinkle with scallions and serve.

Almost Hands-Free Risotto with Parmesan

SERVES 6　　**TOTAL TIME** 55 MINUTES

WHY THIS RECIPE WORKS: Classic risotto can demand half an hour of stovetop tedium for the best creamy results. Our goal was 5 minutes of stirring, tops. First, we swapped out the saucepan for a Dutch oven, which has a thick, heavy bottom, deep sides, and a tight-fitting lid—perfect for trapping and distributing heat evenly. Typical recipes dictate adding the broth in small increments after the wine has been absorbed and stirring constantly after each addition, but we added most of the broth at once and covered the pan, allowing the rice to simmer until almost all the broth had been absorbed, stirring just twice. After adding the second and final addition of broth, we stirred the pot and then turned off the heat. Without sitting over a direct flame, the sauce turned out perfectly creamy and the rice was thickened, velvety, and just barely chewy. To finish, we simply stirred in butter and a squeeze of lemon juice. This more hands-off method requires precise timing, so we strongly recommend using a timer. To make this dish vegetarian, substitute vegetable broth for the chicken broth.

5 cups chicken broth
1½ cups water
4 tablespoons unsalted butter
1 large onion, chopped fine
  Salt and pepper
1 garlic clove, minced
2 cups Arborio rice
1 cup dry white wine
2 ounces Parmesan cheese, grated (1 cup)
1 teaspoon lemon juice

1. Bring broth and water to boil in large saucepan over high heat. Cover and reduce heat to medium-low to maintain bare simmer.

Making Almost Hands-Free Risotto

1. SIMMER BROTH AND WATER: Bring broth and water to boil. Cover and reduce heat to medium-low to maintain simmer.

2. MELT BUTTER IN DUTCH OVEN, ADD ONION: Add onion to melted butter and cook until softened. Stir in garlic. Add rice, stirring often until grains are translucent on edges.

3. STIR IN BROTH, THEN COVER: Stir in wine and cook until absorbed. Stir in 5 cups hot broth. Reduce heat to medium-low, cover, and simmer until rice is al dente, stirring twice.

4. LET STAND 5 MINUTES: Add ¾ cup broth and stir until risotto becomes creamy. Stir in Parmesan. Remove from heat, cover, and let stand for 5 minutes. Stir in remaining butter and lemon juice.

2. Melt 2 tablespoons butter in Dutch oven over medium heat. Add onion and ¾ teaspoon salt and cook until onion is softened, 4 to 5 minutes. Stir in garlic and cook until fragrant, about 30 seconds. Stir in rice and cook, stirring often, until grain edges begin to turn translucent, about 3 minutes.

3. Stir in wine and cook, stirring constantly, until fully absorbed, 2 to 3 minutes. Stir in 5 cups hot broth mixture. Reduce heat to medium-low, cover, and simmer until almost all liquid has been absorbed and rice is just al dente, 18 to 19 minutes, stirring twice during cooking.

4. Add ¾ cup hot broth mixture and stir gently and constantly until risotto becomes creamy, about 3 minutes. Stir in Parmesan. Remove pot from heat, cover, and let stand for 5 minutes. Stir in remaining 2 tablespoons butter and lemon juice. Season with salt and pepper to taste. Before serving, stir in remaining broth mixture as needed to loosen texture of risotto.

VARIATIONS
Almost Hands-Free Risotto with Herbs
Stir in 2 tablespoons minced fresh parsley and 2 tablespoons minced fresh chives before serving.

Almost Hands-Free Risotto with Porcini
Add ¼ ounce rinsed and minced porcini mushrooms to pot with garlic. Substitute soy sauce for lemon juice.

Almost Hands-Free Risotto with Fennel and Saffron
Add 1 fennel bulb, cored and chopped fine, to pot with onion and cook until softened, about 12 minutes. Add ¼ teaspoon ground coriander and large pinch saffron threads to pot with garlic.

NOTES FROM THE TEST KITCHEN

Saffron

Sometimes known as "red gold," saffron is the world's most expensive spice. It's made from the dried stigmas of *Crocus sativus* flowers; the stigmas are so delicate they must be harvested by hand in a painstaking process.

Luckily, a little saffron goes a long way, adding a distinct reddish-gold color, notes of honey and grass, and a slight hint of bitterness to dishes like bouillabaisse, paella, and risotto. The saffron you find in the supermarket is usually Spanish. When shopping for saffron, what should you look for? We held a small tasting of broths infused with different saffron samples. The reddest threads yielded intensely flavorful, heady, perfumed broths. So, when shopping, go for the red, that is, with no spots of yellow or orange. Or, to save money, a good-quality powdered saffron would be just as flavorful and fragrant as the threads.

A broth made with the reserved squash seeds and fibers infuses this risotto with even more flavor.

Butternut Squash Risotto

SERVES 6   **TOTAL TIME** 1 HOUR 30 MINUTES

✔ **WHY THIS RECIPE WORKS:** Butternut squash and risotto should make a perfect culinary couple, but too often the squash and rice never become properly intertwined. We wanted a creamy, orange-tinted rice fully infused with deep (but not overly sweet) squash flavor. To perfect our risotto, we concentrated on developing the flavor of the squash and keeping it tender. First, we sautéed the squash to intensify its flavor. Next, we found that adding the squash in two stages, half with the toasted rice and half just before serving, gave us great squash flavor and preserved its delicate texture. Finally, we sautéed the squash seeds and fibers, steeped them in the chicken broth before straining the liquid, and used it to cook the rice—this infused the dish with sweet, earthy, butternut squash flavor. Parmesan cheese added richness, and fresh sage and nutmeg lent woodsy, warm notes. We found that a 1½-pound squash consistently yielded a cup or so more than the 3½ cups needed in step 1; the extra squash is added to the skillet along with the fibers and seeds in step 2. To make this dish vegetarian, substitute vegetable broth for the chicken broth.

2   tablespoons extra-virgin olive oil
1½ pounds butternut squash, peeled, seeded with fibers and seeds reserved, and cut into ½-inch cubes (4½ cups)
    Salt and pepper
4   cups chicken broth
1   cup water
4   tablespoons unsalted butter
2   small onions, chopped fine
2   garlic cloves, minced
2   cups Arborio rice
1½ cups dry white wine
1½ ounces Parmesan cheese, grated (¾ cup)
2   tablespoons minced fresh sage
¼   teaspoon ground nutmeg

1. Heat oil in 12-inch nonstick skillet over medium-high heat until shimmering. Add 3½ cups squash, spread in even layer, and cook without stirring until golden brown, about 5 minutes. Season with ¼ teaspoon salt and ¼ teaspoon pepper and continue to cook, stirring occasionally, until squash is tender and browned, about 5 minutes; transfer to bowl.

2. Add remaining cubed squash and reserved squash fibers and seeds to now-empty skillet and cook over medium heat, stirring often, until lightly browned, about 4 minutes. Transfer to large saucepan and add broth and water. Cover pot, bring to boil over high heat, then reduce heat to medium-low and simmer gently for 10 minutes. Strain broth through fine-mesh strainer, pressing on solids to extract as much liquid as possible; return strained broth to saucepan, cover, and keep warm over low heat.

3. Melt 3 tablespoons butter in now-empty skillet over medium heat. Add onions, garlic, ½ teaspoon salt, and ½ teaspoon pepper and cook until onions are softened, 5 to 7 minutes. Stir in rice and cook, stirring often, until grain edges begin to turn translucent, about 3 minutes. Add wine and cook, stirring frequently, until fully absorbed, 4 to 5 minutes.

4. Stir in 3 cups hot broth mixture and half of browned squash cubes. Simmer, stirring every 3 to 4 minutes, until liquid is absorbed and bottom of pan is almost dry, about 12 minutes.

5. Stir in ½ cup hot broth mixture and cook, stirring constantly, until absorbed, about 3 minutes; repeat with additional broth mixture 2 or 3 times, until rice is al dente. Off heat, stir in remaining 1 tablespoon butter, Parmesan, sage, and nutmeg. Gently fold in remaining browned squash cubes. Before serving, stir in remaining broth mixture as needed to loosen texture of risotto.

Toasting couscous grains in butter deepens their flavor, as does cooking them in chicken broth and water.

Classic Couscous

SERVES 4 TO 6   **TOTAL TIME** 20 MINUTES   **FAST**

✔ **WHY THIS RECIPE WORKS:** At its best, couscous is light and fluffy, with the ability to absorb flavors. But it often falls flat, with a bland flavor and a heavy, clumpy texture. We wanted to develop a classic version to accompany saucy dishes, as well as a few flavor-packed versions that were as convenient as the box kind but much fresher-tasting. Toasting the couscous grains in butter deepened their flavor and helped them cook up fluffy and separate. To bump up the flavor even further, we replaced half of the cooking liquid with chicken broth. Do not substitute large-grain couscous (also known as Israeli couscous) here; it requires a much different cooking method. To make this dish vegetarian, substitute vegetable broth for the chicken broth.

2 tablespoons unsalted butter
2 cups couscous
1 cup water
1 cup chicken broth
  Salt and pepper

Melt butter in medium saucepan over medium-high heat. Add couscous and cook, stirring frequently, until grains are just beginning to brown, about 5 minutes. Add water, broth, and ½ teaspoon salt and stir briefly to combine. Cover, remove pan from heat, and let stand until grains are tender, about 7 minutes. Uncover, fluff grains with fork, and season with salt and pepper to taste. Serve.

VARIATIONS

Couscous with Garlic, Lemon, and Herbs

Stir 2 minced garlic cloves and 1 teaspoon grated lemon zest into toasted couscous and cook until fragrant, about 15 seconds, before adding liquids and salt. Gently fold 2 tablespoons minced fresh parsley (or tarragon, chives, or cilantro) and 1 tablespoon lemon juice into couscous before serving.

Couscous with Curry with Mint

Stir 1½ teaspoons curry powder and 2 minced garlic cloves into toasted couscous and cook until fragrant, about 15 seconds, before adding liquids and salt. Gently fold 2 tablespoons minced fresh mint into couscous before serving.

Old-Fashioned Stovetop Grits

SERVES 4   **TOTAL TIME** 30 MINUTES   **FAST**

✔ **WHY THIS RECIPE WORKS:** A staple of the Southern table, grits can be a substantial start to the day, or a good addition to the dinner plate. But often grits cook up bland and watery or too thick and gluey. In the search for the best recipe, we began by looking at the variety of grits available and found two forms: quick-cooking, which cook in 5 minutes, and old-fashioned, which cook in 10 to 15 minutes. Initially, we were excited about the possibility of cooking grits for only 5 minutes, but these instant grits were too creamy and tasted overprocessed. The old-fashioned grits were creamy, but at the same time they retained a slightly coarse texture. We kept the recipe simple by bringing milk, water, and a pinch of salt to a boil, then slowly pouring the grits into the pot, whisking the entire time to prevent clumping. The grits finished cooking, covered, over low heat, which prevented them from burning, and we made to sure to stir them often to ensure they cooked evenly. If you're serving these grits for breakfast, they can be drizzled with maple syrup, honey, or molasses. If serving them with dinner, sprinkle with grated Parmesan or shredded cheddar cheese and season with minced fresh herbs. These grits taste best made with whole milk; you can substitute low-fat milk but do not use nonfat milk.

4 cups whole milk
1 cup water
  Salt and pepper
1 cup old-fashioned grits
2 tablespoons unsalted butter

1. Bring milk, water, and ¼ teaspoon salt to boil in medium saucepan. Pour grits into pot in very slow stream while whisking constantly in circular motion to prevent clumping.

2. Cover and reduce heat to low. Cook, stirring often and vigorously (make sure to scrape corners of pot), until grits are thick and creamy, 10 to 15 minutes. Stir in butter and season with salt and pepper to taste. Serve.

Cheesy Baked Grits

SERVES 6 TO 8   **TOTAL TIME** 1 HOUR 30 MINUTES

✔ **WHY THIS RECIPE WORKS:** Grits are a simple but satisfying side dish. We wanted a rich and cheesy version, baked until it was brown on the top and creamy in the middle. We began building flavor by sautéing some chopped onion in butter. Then we brought water—enriched with cream and spiked with a dash of hot sauce—to a boil and whisked in the grits. Once they were thickened, we stirred in plenty of tangy cheddar cheese along with beaten eggs, which gave the dish an airy texture, and moved the grits to the oven to develop a nicely browned crust. Smoked cheddar or gouda can be substituted for the cheddar.

  2 tablespoons unsalted butter
  1 onion, chopped fine
  1 teaspoon salt
4½ cups water
1½ cups heavy cream
  ¾ teaspoon hot sauce
1½ cups old-fashioned grits
  8 ounces extra-sharp cheddar cheese, shredded (2 cups)
  4 large eggs, lightly beaten
  ¼ teaspoon pepper

1. Adjust oven rack to lower-middle position and heat oven to 350 degrees. Grease 13 by 9-inch baking dish. Melt butter in large saucepan over medium heat. Add onion and salt and cook until softened, about 5 minutes. Stir in water, cream, and hot sauce and bring to boil.

2. Pour grits into pot in very slow stream while whisking constantly in circular motion to prevent clumping. Cover and

These cheesy baked grits feature a hefty dose of tangy cheddar and a dash of hot sauce for extra kick.

reduce heat to low. Cook, stirring often and vigorously (make sure to scrape corners of pot), until grits are thick and creamy, 10 to 15 minutes.

3. Off heat, whisk in 1 cup cheddar, eggs, and pepper. Pour mixture into prepared baking dish and smooth top with rubber spatula. Sprinkle remaining 1 cup cheddar over top. Bake until top is browned and grits are hot, 35 to 45 minutes. Let casserole cool for 10 minutes. Serve.

VARIATIONS

Cheesy Baked Grits with Sausage and Bell Pepper

Add 1 pound crumbled breakfast sausage and 1 finely chopped red bell pepper to pot with onion; increase cooking time to 8 to 10 minutes.

Cheesy Baked Grits with Pepper Jack Cheese and Bell Pepper

Add 1 finely chopped red bell pepper to pot with onion; increase cooking time to 8 to 10 minutes. Substitute pepper Jack cheese for cheddar.

Creamy Parmesan Polenta

SERVES 4   **TOTAL TIME** 55 MINUTES

✓ WHY THIS RECIPE WORKS: If you don't stir polenta almost constantly, it forms intractable lumps. Is there a way to get creamy, smooth polenta with rich corn flavor, but without the fussy process? From the outset, we knew that the right type of cornmeal was essential. Coarse-ground degerminated cornmeal gave us the soft but hearty texture and nutty flavor we were looking for. Adding a pinch of baking soda to the pot helped soften the cornmeal's hard, gritty texture, which cut the cooking time in half. Simmering over the lowest setting and covering the pot during the entire cooking time eliminated the need for stirring. Parmesan cheese and butter, stirred in at the last minute, ensured a satisfying, rich dish. Coarse-ground degerminated cornmeal such as yellow grits (with grains the size of couscous) works best in this recipe. Avoid instant and quick-cooking products, as well as whole-grain, stone-ground, and regular cornmeal. Do not omit the baking soda—it reduces the cooking time and makes for a creamier polenta. If the polenta bubbles or sputters even slightly after the first 10 minutes, the heat is too high and you may need a flame tamer (see below).

7½ cups water
    Salt and pepper
    Pinch baking soda
1½ cups coarse-ground cornmeal
 4 ounces Parmesan cheese, grated (2 cups),
    plus extra for serving
 2 tablespoons unsalted butter

1. Bring water to boil in large, heavy-bottomed saucepan over medium-high heat. Stir in 1½ teaspoons salt and baking soda. Slowly pour cornmeal into water in steady stream while stirring back and forth with wooden spoon. Bring mixture to boil, stirring constantly, about 1 minute. Reduce heat to lowest setting and cover.

2. After 5 minutes, whisk polenta to smooth out any lumps that may have formed, about 15 seconds. (Make sure to scrape down sides and bottom of pan.) Cover and continue to cook, without stirring, until grains of polenta are tender but slightly al dente, about 25 minutes longer. (Polenta should be loose and should barely hold its shape but will continue to thicken as it cools.)

3. Off heat, stir in Parmesan and butter, and season with salt and pepper to taste. Let stand, covered, for 5 minutes. Serve with extra Parmesan.

Making Creamy Polenta

1. BOIL WATER AND ADD BAKING SODA: Bring water to boil over medium-high heat. Stir in salt and pinch baking soda.

2. SLOWLY STIR IN CORNMEAL: Slowly pour in cornmeal, stirring constantly. Bring to boil, continuing to stir. Reduce heat to lowest setting and cover.

3. WHISK, THEN COOK COVERED: After 5 minutes, whisk until smooth. Cover and continue to cook until grains are tender.

4. STIR IN CHEESE, THEN LET STAND: Remove pot from heat. Stir in cheese, butter, and salt and pepper to taste. Cover and let stand for 5 minutes.

Making a Flame Tamer

A flame tamer keeps polenta and sauces from simmering too briskly. You can buy one or easily make one. Shape a sheet of heavy-duty foil into a 1-inch-thick ring that fits on your burner, making sure the ring is of even thickness.

Oven-Baked Barley

SERVES 4 TO 6   **TOTAL TIME** 1 HOUR 35 MINUTES

✓ **WHY THIS RECIPE WORKS:** Nutty tasting and substantial, barley offers a great alternative to rice, and it can be similarly flavored, with herbs, toasted nuts, or additional vegetables. For our recipe, we turned to the method we created for simple baked white rice, which started with boiling water to shorten the cooking time, covering the baking dish with foil, and baking the rice in the oven. We used easy-to-find pearl barley, but settling on the right ratio of water to barley required some testing. Barley can absorb two to three times its volume in cooking liquid, and when we tried our standard ratio the water disappeared before the barley was fully cooked. We increased the water, finally landing on 3½ cups to 1½ cups of barley. After covering the dish with a double layer of foil and giving it 70 minutes in the oven followed by a 10-minute rest, we peeled back the foil to reveal perfectly cooked barley, with grains that were separate and fully cooked without being soggy. Don't substitute hulled barley for the pearl barley. Be sure to cover the pot when bringing the water to a boil in step 1; any water loss due to evaporation will affect how the barley cooks.

1½ cups pearl barley, rinsed
3½ cups water
 1 tablespoon unsalted butter
    Salt and pepper

1. Adjust oven rack to middle position and heat oven to 375 degrees. Spread barley in 8-inch square baking dish. Bring water, butter, and ½ teaspoon salt to boil in covered medium saucepan over high heat.

2. Pour hot water mixture immediately over barley. Cover baking dish tightly with double layer of aluminum foil. Bake barley until tender and no liquid remains, 70 to 80 minutes.

3. Remove baking dish from oven, uncover, and fluff barley with fork. Re-cover dish with foil and let barley stand for 10 minutes. Season with salt and pepper to taste and serve.

VARIATION

Oven-Baked Barley with Porcini Mushrooms

Before adding water and salt to pot, melt 2 tablespoons unsalted butter in saucepan over medium heat. Add 1 finely chopped onion and cook until softened, 5 to 7 minutes. Stir in 1 teaspoon minced fresh thyme and ¼ ounce dried porcini mushrooms, rinsed and minced; cook until fragrant, about 30 seconds. Add water and salt to pan and bring to boil; pour hot water mixture over barley and bake as directed.

Barley Risotto

SERVES 4 TO 6   **TOTAL TIME** 1 HOUR 30 MINUTES

✓ **WHY THIS RECIPE WORKS:** For a great alternative to rice, we found that preparing barley with a risotto-style cooking method was a good way to use this healthy grain. We used pearl barley in this dish because the bran has been removed from the outside of the grain, leaving the starchy interior exposed, which helped to create a supple, velvety sauce when simmered (much the same as risotto made with Arborio rice). We used the classic risotto cooking method with one minor change: We added more liquid, because barley takes a bit longer to cook. You may not need to use all of the broth when cooking the risotto. To make this dish vegetarian, substitute vegetable broth for the chicken broth. Serve with lemon wedges and extra grated Parmesan cheese.

 4 cups chicken broth
 4 cups water
 1 tablespoon vegetable oil
 1 onion, chopped fine
 1 carrot, peeled and chopped fine
1½ cups pearl barley, rinsed
 1 cup dry white wine
 1 teaspoon minced fresh thyme
 2 ounces Parmesan cheese, grated (1 cup)
 1 tablespoon unsalted butter
    Salt and pepper

1. Bring broth and water to simmer in medium saucepan. Reduce heat to lowest possible setting and cover to keep warm.

2. Heat oil in large saucepan over medium heat until shimmering. Add onion and carrot and cook until vegetables are softened, 5 to 7 minutes. Stir in barley and cook, stirring often, until lightly toasted and aromatic, about 4 minutes. Stir in wine and cook until it has been completely absorbed, about 2 minutes.

3. Stir in thyme and 3 cups warm broth. Simmer, stirring occasionally, until liquid is absorbed and bottom of pan is dry, 22 to 25 minutes.

4. Stir in 2 cups warm broth and simmer, stirring occasionally, until liquid is absorbed and bottom of pan is dry, 15 to 18 minutes.

5. Continue to cook risotto, stirring often and adding remaining broth as needed to prevent pan bottom from becoming dry, until barley is cooked through but still somewhat firm in center, 15 to 20 minutes. Off heat, stir in Parmesan and butter. Season with salt and pepper to taste and serve.

Your typical natural foods store sells more than a dozen types of grain, and the supermarket sells almost as many. The following are our favorites. The list includes cornmeal and couscous, which aren't technically grains, but we include them here since they are prepared and served like grains.

Amaranth

Amaranth, a staple of the Incas and Aztecs, is second only to quinoa for protein content among grains. The tiny gold, black-flecked seeds are also high in vitamins and minerals. Amaranth has a complex flavor that's very nutty and earthy. It is often dry-toasted before being cooked and can be prepared like porridge or rice. The whole seeds can also be popped like popcorn.

Barley

While barley might be most familiar as a key ingredient in beer, it is a nutritious high-fiber, high-protein, and low-fat cereal grain with a nutty flavor that is similar to that of brown rice. It is great in soups and in salads, as risotto, and as a simple side dish. Barley is available in multiple forms. Hulled barley, which is sold with the hull removed and the fiber-rich bran intact, is considered a whole grain and is higher in nutrients compared to pearl (or pearled) barley, which is hulled barley that has been polished to remove the bran. There is a quick-cooking barley, which is available as kernels or flakes. Hulled barley takes a long time to cook and should be soaked prior to cooking. Pearl barley cooks much more quickly, making it a more versatile choice when you are adding it to soups or making risotto or a simple pilaf. Use it as a stand-in for dishes where you might ordinarily use rice, such as stir-fries or curry.

Buckwheat Groats and Kasha

Buckwheat, despite its name, is not related to wheat but is in fact an herb that is related to sorrel and rhubarb. Native to Russia, buckwheat appears in cuisines all over the globe, particularly in Eastern Europe and Japan (think soba noodles). Buckwheat has an assertive flavor and can be found in several forms. Hulled, crushed buckwheat seeds are known as buckwheat groats, and because of their high carbohydrate content they are generally treated like a grain. Grayish green in color, groats have a mildly earthy flavor. They are often eaten as a staple like rice and are baked into puddings and porridges.

   Kasha is buckwheat groats that have been roasted. This process gives kasha a darker color and a noticeably earthier and roasty flavor that some people love, and others don't. Kasha is often served pilaf-style and as a hot cereal, and it also is traditionally used in blintzes, combined with pasta to make a traditional Eastern European Jewish dish called *kasha varnishkas*, and included as part of a filling for pastries known as knishes.

Bulgur

Bulgur is made from parboiled or steamed wheat kernels/berries that are then dried, partially stripped of their outer bran layer, and coarsely ground. The result of this process is a relatively fast-cooking, highly nutritious grain that can be used in a variety of applications. Bulgur is perfect for tabbouleh or salads because it requires little more than a soak to become tender and flavorful. We especially like soaking it in flavorful liquids, such as lemon or lime juice, to imbue the whole grain with bright flavor. Coarse-grind bulgur, which requires simmering, is our top choice for making pilaf. Note that medium-grind bulgur can work in either application if you make adjustments to soaking or cooking times. Cracked wheat, on the other hand, often sold alongside bulgur, is not precooked and cannot be substituted for bulgur. Be sure to rinse bulgur, regardless of grain size, to remove excess starches that can turn the grain gluey. For more information on grind size, see page 281.

Cornmeal

For many consumers, buying cornmeal used to mean picking up a container of Quaker, or perhaps (especially if you lived in the South) a stone-ground local variety. But at most supermarkets today, you've got a lot more options to sort through: fine-, medium-, and coarse-ground; instant and quick-cooking; whole-grain, stone-ground, and regular. What do they all mean, which should you buy, and does it even matter? Yes, it definitely does matter. Whether you are making Southern-style cornbread, pancakes, polenta, or a rustic Italian-style cake, different recipes require different grinds and types of cornmeal. What you use can make a big difference. Make sure to read—and buy—carefully.

Couscous

Couscous is a starch made from durum semolina, the high-protein wheat flour that is also used to make Italian pasta. Traditional Moroccan couscous is made by rubbing coarse-ground durum semolina and water between the hands to form small granules. The couscous is then dried and cooked over a simmering stew in a steamer called a *couscoussier*. About the size of bread crumbs, the boxed couscous found in most supermarkets is a precooked version that needs only a few minutes of steeping in hot liquid in order to be fully cooked. Israeli couscous, also known as pearl couscous, is larger than traditional couscous (about the size of a caper) and is not precooked. It has a unique, nutty flavor.

Farro

A favorite ingredient in Tuscan cuisine, these hulled whole-wheat kernels boast a sweet, nutty flavor and a chewy bite. In Italy, the grain is available in three sizes—*farro piccolo*, *farro medio*, and *farro grande*—but the midsize type is most common in the United States. Although we usually turn to the absorption method for quicker-cooking grains, farro takes better to the pasta method because the abundance of water cooks the grains more evenly. When cooked, the grains will be tender but have a slight chew, similar to al dente pasta.

Millet

Believed to be the first domesticated cereal grain, this tiny cereal grass seed has a long history and is still a staple in a large part of the world, particularly in Asia and Africa. The seeds can be ground into flour or used whole. Millet has a mellow corn flavor that works well in both savory and sweet applications, including flatbreads, puddings, and pan-fried cakes. It can be cooked pilaf-style, or it can be turned into a creamy breakfast porridge or polenta-like dish by slightly overcooking the seeds, which causes them to burst and release starch. To add texture to baked goods, try incorporating a small amount of millet into the batter.

Oat Berries (Oat Groats)

Labeled either oat berries or oat groats, this whole grain is simply whole oats that have been hulled and cleaned. They are the least processed oat product (other forms are processed further, such as rolled flat, cut, or ground). Because they have hardly been processed, they retain a high nutritional value. They have an appealing chewy texture and a mildly nutty flavor. Oats are usually thought of as a breakfast cereal, but oat berries make a great savory side dish cooked pilaf-style.

Oats

From breakfast table to cookie jar, this nutritious cereal grass is a versatile grain. Rolled (or old-fashioned) oats are made by hulling, cleaning, steaming, and rolling whole oats. We love oats for their toasty flavor and hearty chew in cookies and in toppings for crisps and cobblers. Steel-cut oats are dense and chewy (too chewy for most baked goods), with a strong buttery flavor. These whole-grain oats are partially cooked and then cut into pieces with steel blades. Steel-cut oats take about 25 minutes longer to cook than rolled oats.

Quinoa

Quinoa originated in the Andes Mountains of South America, and while it is generally treated as a grain, it is actually the seed of the goosefoot plant. Sometimes referred to as a "super grain," quinoa is high in protein, and its protein is complete, which means it possesses all of the amino acids in the balanced amounts that our bodies require. Beyond its nutritional prowess, we love quinoa for its addictive crunchy texture, nutty taste, and ease of preparation. Cooked as a pilaf or for a salad, it can be ready in about 20 minutes. Unless labeled "prewashed," quinoa should always be rinsed before cooking to remove its protective layer (called saponin), which is unpleasantly bitter.

Wheat Berries

Wheat berries, often erroneously referred to as "whole wheat," are whole, unprocessed kernels of wheat. Since none of the grain has been removed, wheat berries are an excellent source of nutrition. Compared to more refined forms of wheat (cracked wheat, bulgur, and flour), wheat berries require a relatively long cooking time. In the test kitchen, we like to toast the dry wheat berries until they are fragrant, and then simmer them for about an hour until they are tender but still retain a good bite.

Farro with Mushrooms and Thyme

SERVES 4   **TOTAL TIME** 50 MINUTES

✔ **WHY THIS RECIPE WORKS:** Since farro is a popular ingredient in Tuscan cuisine, we decided to give this dish a simple and fresh Italian profile. Mushrooms sautéed with shallot and thyme lent the dish some meatiness, and using sherry to deglaze the pan after the mushrooms browned was a natural complement and added some complexity to the dish. Finishing with a couple tablespoons of fresh parsley and sherry vinegar added brightness and freshness that balanced the hearty, savory flavors. White mushrooms can be substituted for the cremini.

- 1   **cup farro, rinsed**
     Salt and pepper
- 2   **tablespoons vegetable oil**
- 8   **ounces cremini mushrooms, trimmed and chopped coarse**
- 1   **shallot, minced**
- 1   **teaspoon minced fresh thyme**
- 2   **tablespoons dry sherry**
- 2   **tablespoons minced fresh parsley**
- 1   **teaspoon sherry vinegar**

1. Bring 4 quarts water to boil in Dutch oven. Stir in farro and 1 tablespoon salt. Return to boil, reduce heat, and simmer until tender, 15 to 20 minutes. Drain well and set aside.

2. Heat oil in 12-inch skillet over medium-high heat until shimmering. Add mushrooms, shallot, thyme, and ¼ teaspoon salt and cook, stirring often, until moisture has evaporated and vegetables start to brown, 5 to 8 minutes.

3. Add sherry and cook, scraping up any browned bits, until pan is almost dry, 1 to 2 minutes. Add boiled farro and cook, stirring constantly, until heated through, about 1 minute. Off heat, stir in parsley and vinegar, and season with salt and pepper to taste. Serve.

Rinsing Rice and Grains

Place rice or grains in fine-mesh strainer and rinse under cool water until water runs clear, occasionally stirring rice/grains around lightly with your hand. Let drain briefly.

Farro Risotto

SERVES 4 TO 6   **TOTAL TIME** 50 MINUTES

✔ **WHY THIS RECIPE WORKS:** Italians often prepare farro in much the same way that they cook Arborio rice for risotto, by cooking the farro slowly into a creamy dish called *farotto*. We set out to come up with our own version, one that cooked for half an hour or less, yet still produced a dish that was creamy and rich while highlighting farro's nutty flavor and chewy texture. To do so, we adapted the method we developed for Almost Hands-Free Risotto with Parmesan (page 501), which adds the bulk of the liquid at the beginning of cooking, keeps the pot covered, and requires less stirring throughout. A few modifications were in order, however. Farro, it turns out, did require frequent stirring to ensure that the grains cooked evenly. And instead of keeping the lid on, we removed it—which made sense if we were stirring. We also found that we didn't need to warm the liquid before adding it to the pot—the farro cooked through just fine. As for flavorings, onion was a good start, and garlic, thyme, and sweet, earthy carrots made our farro even better. In early tests, we followed risotto-making tradition by finishing the farro with butter and Parmesan, but these additions masked the nutty grain. Instead, we opted for a fresher finish, substituting fresh minced parsley and lemon juice, which delivered a light, bright version of this rich and creamy grain dish. To make this dish vegetarian, substitute vegetable broth for the chicken broth.

- 1   **tablespoon extra-virgin olive oil**
- 1   **onion, chopped fine**
- 1   **carrot, peeled and chopped fine**
     Salt and pepper
- 3   **garlic cloves, minced**
- 1   **teaspoon minced fresh thyme**
- 1½   **cups farro, rinsed**
- 2   **cups chicken broth**
- 1½   **cups water**
- 2   **tablespoons minced fresh parsley**
- 1   **teaspoon lemon juice**

1. Heat oil in large saucepan over medium heat until shimmering. Add onion, carrot, and ¼ teaspoon salt and cook until vegetables are softened, 5 to 7 minutes. Stir in garlic and thyme and cook until fragrant, about 30 seconds.

2. Stir in farro and cook until lightly toasted, about 2 minutes. Stir in broth and water and bring to simmer. Reduce heat to low and continue to simmer, stirring often, until farro is tender, 20 to 25 minutes.

3. Stir in parsley and lemon juice. Season with salt and pepper to taste and serve.

ALL ABOUT **COOKING GRAINS**

From amaranth to wheat berries, the types of grains and the best methods for cooking them can vary tremendously. Some grains, such as bulgur, cook in minutes, while others, such as barley or oat berries, take much longer. Here in the test kitchen we have homed in on three basic methods for cooking grains. We then determined which are best for each type of grain. Of the three cooking methods for grains, pilaf-style is our favorite because it produces grains with a light and fluffy texture and a slightly toasted flavor.

BOILING DIRECTIONS: Bring the water to a boil in a large saucepan. Stir in the grain and ½ teaspoon salt. Return to a boil, then reduce to a simmer and cook until the grain is tender, following the cooking times given in the chart below. Drain.

PILAF-STYLE DIRECTIONS: Rinse and then dry the grains on a towel (see page 513). Heat 1 tablespoon oil in a medium saucepan (preferably nonstick) over medium-high heat until shimmering. Stir in the grain and toast until lightly golden and fragrant, 2 to 3 minutes. Stir in the water and ¼ teaspoon salt. Bring the mixture to a simmer, then reduce the heat to low, cover, and continue to simmer until the grain is tender and has absorbed all of the water, following the cooking times given below. Off the heat, let the grain stand for 10 minutes, then fluff with a fork.

MICROWAVE DIRECTIONS: Rinse the grain (see page 510). Combine the water, the grain, 1 tablespoon oil, and ¼ teaspoon salt in a bowl. Cover and cook following the times and temperatures given below. Remove from the microwave and fluff with a fork. Cover the bowl with plastic wrap, poke several vent holes with the tip of a knife, and let sit until completely tender, about 5 minutes.

TYPE OF GRAIN	COOKING METHOD	AMOUNT OF GRAIN	AMOUNT OF WATER	COOKING TIME
Amaranth *	Pilaf-Style	1 cup	1½ cups	20 to 25 minutes
	Boiled	X	X	X
	Microwave	1 cup	2 cups	5 to 10 minutes on high, then 15 to 20 minutes on medium
Pearl Barley	Pilaf-Style	X	X	X
	Boiled	1 cup	4 quarts	20 to 25 minutes
	Microwave	X	X	X
Buckwheat (Kasha)	Pilaf-Style	1 cup	2 cups	10 to 15 minutes
	Boiled	1 cup	2 quarts	10 to 12 minutes
	Microwave	X	X	X
Bulgur (Medium- to Coarse-Grind)	Pilaf-Style **	1 cup	1 cup	16 to 18 minutes
	Boiled	1 cup	4 quarts	5 minutes
	Microwave	1 cup	1 cup	5 to 10 minutes on high
Farro	Pilaf-Style	X	X	X
	Boiled	1 cup	4 quarts	15 to 20 minutes
	Microwave	X	X	X
Millet	Pilaf-Style ***	1 cup	2 cups	15 to 20 minutes
	Boiled	X	X	X
	Microwave	X	X	X
Oat Berries	Pilaf-Style	1 cup	1⅓ cups	30 to 40 minutes
	Boiled	1 cup	4 quarts	30 to 40 minutes
	Microwave	X	X	X
Quinoa (any color)	Pilaf-Style	1 cup	1 cup + 3 tablespoons	18 to 20 minutes
	Boiled	X	X	X
	Microwave	1 cup	2 cups	5 minutes on medium, then 5 minutes on high
Wheat Berries	Pilaf-Style	X	X	X
	Boiled	1 cup	4 quarts	1 hour
	Microwave	X	X	X

* Do not rinse.
** For pilaf, do not rinse, and skip the toasting step, adding the grain to the pot with the liquid.

*** For pilaf, increase the toasting time until the grains begin to pop, about 12 minutes.
X = Not recommended

We pair naturally nutty oat berries with Gorgonzola, tart cherries, and toasted walnuts for a great side dish.

Oat Berry Pilaf with Walnuts and Gorgonzola

SERVES 4 TO 6　　**TOTAL TIME** 1 HOUR 10 MINUTES

✓ **WHY THIS RECIPE WORKS:** While we think of oats mostly as part of a wholesome breakfast, oat berries—whole oats that have been hulled and cleaned—have a pleasant chew. For a great side dish, we created a satisfying oat berry pilaf with hearty add-ins. To cook the oat berries, we opted not to toast them since they naturally have a nutty flavor, and instead added the water and oat berries to the pan after sautéing some shallot. After testing various ratios of water to oat berries, we settled on 2 cups water to 1½ cups oat berries. Creamy, pungent Gorgonzola provided a nice balance to the earthy oat berries' nutty flavor. First we tried stirring the Gorgonzola into the oat berries once they were cooked, but the result was a thick, gluey mixture. It was better to wait and simply sprinkle the cheese over the oat berries just before serving. The addition of tart cherries and tangy balsamic vinegar cut through the richness and strong flavors, while parsley gave our pilaf the freshness it needed.

1　tablespoon extra-virgin olive oil
1　shallot, minced
2　cups water
1½　cups oat berries (groats), rinsed
　　Salt and pepper
¾　cup walnuts, toasted and chopped
½　cup dried cherries
2　tablespoons minced fresh parsley
1　tablespoon balsamic vinegar
2　ounces Gorgonzola cheese, crumbled (½ cup)

1. Heat oil in large saucepan over medium heat until shimmering. Add shallot and cook until softened, about 2 minutes. Stir in water, oat berries, and ¼ teaspoon salt and bring to simmer. Reduce heat to low, cover, and continue to simmer until oat berries are tender but still slightly chewy, 30 to 40 minutes.

2. Remove pot from heat and lay clean folded dish towel underneath lid. Let sit for 10 minutes. Fluff oat berries with fork and fold in walnuts, cherries, and parsley. Season with salt and pepper to taste and drizzle with vinegar. Serve, sprinkling individual portions with Gorgonzola.

Curried Millet Pilaf

SERVES 4 TO 6　　**TOTAL TIME** 45 MINUTES　**FAST**

✓ **WHY THIS RECIPE WORKS:** Since millet is a staple in Middle Eastern and Indian cuisines, we turned to that part of the world to inspire the flavor profile of this pilaf, adding basil, mint, raisins, almonds, and curry powder. Toasting the millet before simmering the seeds in water gave them some nutty depth; we first dried the tiny soggy seeds so they would toast properly. After some testing, we landed on a 2:1 ratio of liquid to millet, which ensured evenly cooked, fluffy seeds. To finish, we served it with a dollop of yogurt for richness and an appealing cooling counterpoint to the heat of the curry. We prefer whole-milk yogurt in this recipe, but low-fat yogurt can be substituted if desired. Unlike other grains, we have found that millet can become gluey if allowed to steam off the heat. Once all the liquid has been absorbed, use a gentle hand to stir in the basil, raisins, almonds, and scallion greens, and then immediately serve this pilaf.

1　tablespoon extra-virgin olive oil
3　scallions, white and green parts separated, sliced thin
1　teaspoon curry powder
1½　cups millet, rinsed and dried on a towel
3　cups water
　　Salt and pepper
½　cup chopped fresh basil and/or mint

¼ cup raisins
¼ cup sliced almonds, toasted
½ cup plain yogurt

1. Heat oil in large saucepan over medium heat until shimmering. Add scallion whites and curry and cook until fragrant, about 1 minute. Stir in millet and cook, stirring often, until lightly browned, about 2 minutes.

2. Stir in water and ¾ teaspoon salt and bring to boil. Reduce heat to low, cover, and simmer until liquid is absorbed, 15 to 20 minutes.

3. Off heat, fluff millet with fork and gently stir in basil, raisins, almonds, and scallion greens. Season with salt and pepper to taste. Serve, dolloping individual portions with yogurt.

Drying Grains

1. After rinsing grains, spread out over rimmed baking sheet lined with clean dish towel and let dry for 15 minutes.

2. When grains are dry, pick up towel by corners and gently shake grains into bowl.

Easy Baked Quinoa with Lemon, Garlic, and Parsley

SERVES 4   TOTAL TIME 50 MINUTES

❤ **WHY THIS RECIPE WORKS:** There are many ways to prepare quinoa, but this hands-off method delivers perfectly cooked quinoa—plus, it's simple to incorporate flavorful add-ins. For the cooking liquid we turned to chicken broth, which we microwaved with lemon zest until just boiling; we poured the hot liquid over the quinoa, which we had combined with olive oil and garlic in a baking dish, then covered the dish with foil and placed it in the oven. Lemon juice and parsley stirred in before serving lent bright notes to this side dish. We like the convenience of prewashed quinoa. If you buy unwashed quinoa (or if you are unsure whether it's washed), rinse it before cooking to remove its bitter protective coating (called saponin). To make this dish vegetarian, substitute vegetable broth for the chicken broth.

1½ cups prewashed white quinoa
2 tablespoons olive oil
2 garlic cloves, minced
1½ cups chicken broth
1 teaspoon grated lemon zest plus 1 teaspoon juice
  Salt and pepper
2 tablespoons minced fresh parsley

1. Adjust oven rack to middle position and heat oven to 450 degrees. Combine quinoa, olive oil, and garlic in 8-inch square baking dish.

2. Microwave broth, lemon zest, and ¼ teaspoon salt in covered bowl until just boiling, about 5 minutes. Pour hot broth over quinoa mixture and cover dish tightly with double layer of aluminum foil. Bake quinoa until tender and no liquid remains, about 25 minutes.

3. Remove dish from oven, uncover, and fluff quinoa with fork, scraping up any quinoa that has stuck to bottom. Re-cover dish with foil and let stand for 10 minutes. Fold in lemon juice and parsley, and season with salt and pepper to taste. Serve.

VARIATIONS
Easy Baked Quinoa with Scallions and Feta
Substitute 4 thinly sliced scallions for parsley. Fold ½ cup crumbled feta into quinoa before serving.

Easy Baked Quinoa with Tomatoes, Parmesan, and Basil
Omit lemon zest, lemon juice, and parsley. Fold 1 finely chopped tomato, ½ cup grated Parmesan, and 2 tablespoons chopped fresh basil into quinoa before serving.

Easy Baked Quinoa with Curry, Cauliflower, and Cilantro
Substitute 2 teaspoons curry powder for lemon zest, and fresh cilantro for parsley. Sprinkle 2 cups small cauliflower florets evenly into dish before baking.

NOTES FROM THE TEST KITCHEN

Storing Rice, Grains, and Beans

To prevent open boxes and bags of rice, grains, and beans from spoiling in the pantry, store them in airtight containers, and, if you have space, keep rice and grains in the freezer. This is especially important for whole grains that turn rancid with oxidation. Use rice and grains within six months. Though beans are less susceptible to pests and spoilage than rice and grains, and can be kept up to a year, it's best to use beans within the first month or two of purchase.

Toasting the grains brings out the nutty flavor of the quinoa in this salad.

Quinoa Salad with Red Bell Pepper and Cilantro

SERVES 4   **TOTAL TIME** 1 HOUR

✓ **WHY THIS RECIPE WORKS:** Easy to prepare in advance, quinoa salad makes a great fresh-tasting weekday lunch or picnic food. But too often the grains are overcooked or unevenly cooked, and the resulting salad is clumpy or gritty. Toasting the quinoa helped to deepen its flavor. The quinoa was then simmered until it was nearly tender and spread over a rimmed baking sheet to cool. This ensured the grains (quinoa is actually a seed, but is treated as a grain) didn't overcook and stayed fluffy and separate. Inspired by quinoa's Peruvian roots, we decided on a Latin flavor profile. Red bell pepper, jalapeño, and cilantro provided fresh flavors as well as color, sweetness, and some heat; adding lime juice and cumin to the dressing brought it all together. After the simmering in step 1, there will still be a bit of water in the pan; it will be absorbed as the quinoa cools. To make this dish spicier, add the chile seeds. We like the convenience of prewashed quinoa. If you buy unwashed quinoa (or

if you are unsure whether it's washed), rinse it before cooking to remove its bitter protective coating (called saponin).

> 1 cup prewashed white quinoa
> 1½ cups water
> Salt and pepper
> ½ red bell pepper, stemmed, seeded, and chopped fine
> ½ jalapeño chile, stemmed, seeded, and minced
> 2 tablespoons finely chopped red onion
> 1 tablespoon minced fresh cilantro
> 2 tablespoons lime juice
> 1 tablespoon extra-virgin olive oil
> 2 teaspoons Dijon mustard
> 1 garlic clove, minced
> ½ teaspoon ground cumin

1. Toast quinoa in medium saucepan over medium-high heat, stirring frequently, until quinoa is lightly toasted and aromatic, about 5 minutes. Stir in water and ¼ teaspoon salt and bring to simmer. Reduce heat to low, cover, and continue to simmer until quinoa has absorbed most of water and is nearly tender, about 12 minutes. Spread quinoa out over rimmed baking sheet and set aside until tender and cool, about 20 minutes.

2. When quinoa is cool, toss with bell pepper, jalapeño, onion, and cilantro in large bowl. In separate bowl, whisk lime juice, oil, mustard, garlic, and cumin together, then pour over quinoa mixture and toss to coat. Season with salt and pepper to taste and serve. (Quinoa salad can be refrigerated for up to 1 day.)

Bulgur Pilaf with Mushrooms

SERVES 6   **TOTAL TIME** 55 MINUTES

✓ **WHY THIS RECIPE WORKS:** The nuttiness of coarse bulgur makes it the perfect grain for a pilaf, especially when paired with earthy mushrooms. For big flavor, we found that widely available cremini mushrooms gave the pilaf some heft and paired well with the bulgur. A quarter-ounce of dried porcini added nice earthiness and depth. But our real breakthrough came when we added a dash of soy sauce. An odd choice for a Mediterranean dish, the soy sauce deepened the mushroom flavor and gave the finished dish a rich mahogany color. Once the bulgur became tender, we removed the pot from the heat, placed a dish towel underneath the lid, and let it steam, which resulted in tender grains. Do not use fine-grind bulgur or cracked wheat in this recipe. To make this dish vegetarian, substitute vegetable broth for the chicken broth.

2 tablespoons extra-virgin olive oil
1 onion, chopped fine
¼ ounce dried porcini mushrooms, rinsed and minced
  Salt and pepper
8 ounces cremini or white mushrooms, trimmed and quartered
2 garlic cloves, minced
1 cup coarse-grain or extra coarse–grind bulgur, rinsed
¾ cup chicken broth
¾ cup water
1 teaspoon soy sauce
¼ cup minced fresh parsley

1. Heat 1 tablespoon oil in large saucepan over medium heat until shimmering. Add onion, porcini mushrooms, and ¼ teaspoon salt and cook until onion is softened, 5 to 7 minutes.

2. Stir in cremini mushrooms, increase heat to medium-high, and cook until cremini begin to brown, about 4 minutes. Stir in garlic and cook until fragrant, about 30 seconds.

3. Stir in bulgur, broth, water, and soy sauce and bring to simmer. Reduce heat to low, cover, and simmer gently until bulgur is tender, 16 to 18 minutes.

4. Remove pot from heat and lay clean folded dish towel underneath lid. Let sit for 10 minutes. Fluff bulgur with fork and gently stir in remaining 1 tablespoon oil and parsley. Season with salt and pepper to taste. Serve.

VARIATION

Bulgur Pilaf with Shiitake Mushrooms and Asian Flavors

Substitute 8 ounces thinly sliced shiitake mushrooms for cremini, and 2 thinly sliced scallions for parsley. Add 1 tablespoon grated fresh ginger to pot with garlic.

Bulgur with Red Grapes and Feta

SERVES 4   TOTAL TIME 1 HOUR

✔ **WHY THIS RECIPE WORKS:** Since bulgur is made from wheat berries that have been steamed or boiled and then ground into fine, medium, coarse, or very coarse grains, we knew a gentle cooking method would work best. While it was a candidate for the absorption cooking method, we found that if we used medium-grind grains, we could reconstitute it by soaking it for an hour and thus ensure grains that stayed intact—ideal for a salad. Adding a little lemon juice to the soaking water boosted the flavor, as did a dressing spiked with cumin and cayenne. Grapes, almonds, and feta gave the salad a Mediterranean profile, while scallions and mint lent a touch of freshness and color.

1½ cups medium-grind bulgur, rinsed
¾ cup water
¼ cup plus 1 tablespoon lemon juice (2 lemons)
  Salt
¼ cup extra-virgin olive oil
¼ teaspoon ground cumin
  Pinch cayenne pepper
6 ounces seedless red grapes, quartered (1 cup)
½ cup slivered almonds, toasted
2 ounces feta cheese, crumbled (½ cup)
2 scallions, sliced thin
¼ cup minced fresh mint

1. Combine bulgur, water, ¼ cup lemon juice, and ¼ teaspoon salt in bowl. Let stand until grains are softened, about 1 hour.

2. Whisk oil, remaining 1 tablespoon lemon juice, cumin, cayenne, and ¼ teaspoon salt together in large bowl. Add soaked bulgur, grapes, ⅓ cup almonds, ⅓ cup feta, scallions, and mint and toss to combine. Season with salt to taste. Sprinkle with remaining almonds and feta before serving.

Tabbouleh

SERVES 4   TOTAL TIME 1 HOUR 30 MINUTES

✔ **WHY THIS RECIPE WORKS:** Tabbouleh is a traditional Middle Eastern salad made of bulgur, parsley, tomato, and onion steeped in a penetrating mint and lemon dressing. For our recipe, we started by salting the tomatoes to rid them of excess moisture that otherwise made our salad soggy. Soaking the bulgur in lemon juice and some of the drained tomato liquid, rather than in water, allowed it to soak up lots of flavor. A whole chopped onion overwhelmed the salad, but scallions added just the right amount of oniony flavor. Bright parsley, mint, and a bit of cayenne pepper rounded out the dish. We added the herbs and vegetables while the bulgur was still soaking, so the components had time to mingle, resulting in a cohesive, balanced dish.

3 tomatoes, cored and cut into ½-inch pieces
  Salt and pepper
½ cup medium-grind bulgur, rinsed
¼ cup lemon juice (2 lemons)
6 tablespoons extra-virgin olive oil
⅛ teaspoon cayenne pepper
1½ cups minced fresh parsley
½ cup minced fresh mint
2 scallions, sliced thin

1. Toss tomatoes with ¼ teaspoon salt in fine-mesh strainer set over bowl and let drain for 30 minutes, tossing occasionally. Toss bulgur with 2 tablespoons lemon juice and 2 tablespoons drained tomato juice in bowl. Let stand until grains begin to soften, 30 to 40 minutes.

2. In large bowl, whisk remaining 2 tablespoons lemon juice, oil, cayenne, and ¼ teaspoon salt together. Add drained tomatoes, soaked bulgur, parsley, mint, and scallions and toss gently to combine. Cover and let stand at room temperature until flavors have blended and bulgur is tender, about 1 hour.

3. Before serving, toss to recombine and season with salt and pepper to taste.

VARIATION

Spiced Tabbouleh

Add ¼ teaspoon ground cinnamon and ¼ teaspoon ground allspice to dressing with cayenne.

Boston Baked Beans

SERVES 4 TO 6   **TOTAL TIME** 5½ TO 6 HOURS

✔ **WHY THIS RECIPE WORKS:** Heady with smoky pork and bittersweet molasses, authentic Boston baked beans are both sweet and savory, a combination of flavors brought together by a long simmer. We wanted to create a recipe for beans packed with multiple levels of intense flavor, yet traditional enough to make a New Englander proud. We started with a combination of salt pork and bacon and browned them in a Dutch oven before sautéing an onion in the rendered fat. After adding dried white beans and water, along with molasses and mustard, we finished cooking the dish in the oven, ensuring the beans cooked through evenly and preventing scorching on the bottom of the pot. We removed the lid for the last hour of cooking to reduce the sauce to a syrupy, intensified state. A teaspoon of cider vinegar, stirred in at the end, gave our sauce tanginess, while another tablespoon of molasses boosted its flavor. Be sure to use mild molasses; dark molasses will taste too strong. You will need a Dutch oven with a tight-fitting lid for this recipe.

- 4 **ounces salt pork, rind removed, cut into ½-inch pieces**
- 2 **slices bacon, chopped fine**
- 1 **onion, chopped fine**
- 9 **cups water**
- 1 **pound (2½ cups) dried small white beans, picked over and rinsed**

We pack baked beans with multiple layers of flavor by browning salt pork, bacon, and onion in a Dutch oven.

- ½ **cup plus 1 tablespoon molasses**
- 1½ **tablespoons brown mustard**
  Salt and pepper
- 1 **teaspoon cider vinegar**

1. Adjust oven rack to lower-middle position and heat oven to 300 degrees. Cook salt pork and bacon in Dutch oven over medium heat until lightly browned and most fat has rendered, about 7 minutes. Stir in onion and cook until softened, 5 to 7 minutes. Stir in water, beans, ½ cup molasses, mustard, and 1¼ teaspoons salt. Increase heat to medium-high and bring to boil.

2. Cover pot and transfer to oven. Bake until beans are tender, about 4 hours, stirring every hour.

3. Remove lid and continue to bake until liquid has thickened to syrupy consistency, 1 to 1½ hours.

4. Remove pot from oven. Stir in remaining 1 tablespoon molasses and vinegar and season with salt and pepper to taste. Serve. (Beans can be refrigerated for up to 4 days; reheat gently on stovetop, adding additional water as needed to adjust consistency.)

Barbecue Baked Beans

SERVES 4 TO 6   **TOTAL TIME** 5½ TO 6 HOURS

✓ **WHY THIS RECIPE WORKS:** Most barbecue joints serve ladlefuls of smoky, deep-flavored beans alongside the slabs of ribs and mounds of pulled pork. We wanted to make those creamy textured, saucy beans at home to accompany our own barbecue. To get there, we used dried pinto or navy beans. Bacon was a convenient substitute for smoky barbecued meat, and we blended barbecue sauce, brown sugar, and mustard for a sweet but spicy, deep flavor—a fair amount of garlic and onion helped, too. The secret ingredient in our recipe was coffee. Its roasted, slightly bitter flavor tied all the ingredients together. We found that the oven provided steady, uniform heat, guaranteeing that the beans cooked through evenly and preventing the thick, sweet sauce from scorching on the bottom of the pot. To finish, we stirred in more barbecue sauce, then seasoned the beans with an extra splash of hot sauce to complement the sweet and tangy flavors. If you don't have time to make freshly brewed coffee, instant will do just fine. You will need a Dutch oven with a tight-fitting lid for this recipe.

4   slices bacon, chopped fine
1   onion, chopped fine
4   garlic cloves, minced
1   pound (2½ cups) dried pinto or navy beans, picked over and rinsed
8   cups water
1   cup strong brewed coffee
½   cup plus 2 tablespoons barbecue sauce
¼   cup packed dark brown sugar
1½ tablespoons brown mustard
1   tablespoon molasses
½   teaspoon hot sauce, plus extra to taste
    Salt and pepper

1. Adjust oven rack to lower-middle position and heat oven to 300 degrees. Cook bacon in Dutch oven over medium heat until beginning to crisp, about 5 minutes. Stir in onion and cook until softened, about 5 minutes. Stir in garlic and cook until fragrant, about 30 seconds. Stir in beans, water, coffee, ½ cup barbecue sauce, brown sugar, mustard, molasses, hot sauce, and 1¼ teaspoons salt. Increase heat to medium-high and bring to boil.

2. Cover pot and transfer to oven. Bake until beans are tender, about 4 hours, stirring every hour.

3. Remove lid and continue to bake until liquid has thickened to syrupy consistency, 1 to 1½ hours.

4. Remove pot from oven. Stir in remaining 2 tablespoons barbecue sauce and season with hot sauce, salt, and pepper to taste. Serve. (Beans can be refrigerated for up to 4 days; reheat gently on stovetop, adding additional water as needed to adjust consistency.)

Cajun Red Beans

SERVES 6 TO 8   **TOTAL TIME** 3 TO 3½ HOURS

✓ **WHY THIS RECIPE WORKS:** A Cajun classic, red beans is a highly flavored stewed kidney bean dish most often served over a bed of simple white rice. The best versions balance the sweetness of the beans with a smoky, spicy flavor built on a base of vegetables and herbs. Unfortunately, too many versions of this dish that we have tested have been either bland and boring or fiery hot. We began our recipe with dried kidney beans, as canned beans broke apart and turned mushy long before the broth was fully seasoned. We flavored the broth with the trinity of Cajun cooking: onion, bell pepper, and celery. Softening the vegetables in rendered bacon fat lent the cooking liquid a deep, meaty flavor. Cayenne and hot sauce added heat without overwhelming the dish. After cooking the beans covered in the oven until tender, we removed the lid, stirred in andouille sausage, and continued to bake uncovered until the liquid thickened. After giving everything a short rest, we had perfectly cooked, tender red beans with plenty of Cajun flavor. Andouille is the traditional sausage for this dish, but we also had good results with kielbasa. You will need a Dutch oven with a tight-fitting lid for this recipe.

4   slices bacon, chopped fine
1   onion, chopped fine
1   red bell pepper, stemmed, seeded, and chopped fine
1   celery rib, chopped fine
    Salt and pepper
4   garlic cloves, minced
1   teaspoon dried oregano
1   teaspoon dried thyme
6   cups water
1   pound (2½ cups) dried small red kidney beans, picked over and rinsed
4   bay leaves
½   teaspoon cayenne pepper
½   teaspoon hot sauce, plus extra to taste
8   ounces andouille or kielbasa sausage, quartered and sliced ½ inch thick

1. Adjust oven rack to lower-middle position and heat oven to 300 degrees. Cook bacon in Dutch oven over medium heat until crisp, about 8 minutes. Stir in onion, bell pepper, celery, and 1 teaspoon salt and cook until vegetables are softened, about 8 minutes.

2. Stir in garlic, oregano, and thyme and cook until fragrant, about 30 seconds. Stir in water, scraping up any browned bits. Stir in beans, bay leaves, cayenne, hot sauce, and 1 teaspoon pepper. Increase heat to medium-high and bring to boil.

3. Cover pot and transfer to oven. Bake until beans are tender, 1½ to 2 hours, stirring every 30 minutes.

4. Remove lid and stir in andouille. Continue to bake, uncovered, until liquid has thickened, about 30 minutes. Discard bay leaves and let beans sit for 10 minutes. Season with salt, pepper, and hot sauce to taste. Serve.

Cuban Black Beans and Rice

SERVES 6 TO 8   **TOTAL TIME** 1 HOUR 45 MINUTES
(PLUS 8 HOURS SOAKING TIME)

WHY THIS RECIPE WORKS: Beans and rice is a familiar combination the world over, but Cuban black beans and rice is unique in that the rice is cooked in the inky concentrated liquid left over from cooking the beans, which renders the grains just as flavorful as the beans. An important factor for this recipe was to use beans that were as pliable as possible and less likely to burst open while cooking, so we brined them in a saltwater solution overnight and then made sure to cook them with salt to soften their skins. We simmered a portion of the *sofrito* (the traditional combination of bell pepper, onion, and garlic) with our beans to infuse them with flavor. Lightly browning the remaining sofrito vegetables and spices with salt pork added complex, meaty flavor, and baking the dish in the oven eliminated the crusty bottom that can form when cooked on the stove. It is important to use lean—not fatty—salt pork. If you can't find it, substitute six slices of bacon and reduce its cooking time to 8 minutes. You will need a Dutch oven with a tight-fitting lid for this recipe.

    Salt
1   cup dried black beans, picked over and rinsed
2   cups chicken broth
2   cups water
2   large green bell peppers, halved, stemmed, and seeded

1   large onion, halved crosswise
1   garlic head, 5 cloves minced, rest of head halved crosswise with skin left intact
2   bay leaves
6   ounces lean salt pork, rind removed, cut into ¼-inch pieces
2   tablespoons vegetable oil
4   teaspoons ground cumin
1   tablespoon minced fresh oregano
1½ cups long-grain white rice, rinsed
2   tablespoons red wine vinegar
2   scallions, sliced thin
    Lime wedges

1. Dissolve 1½ tablespoons salt in 2 quarts cold water in large container. Add beans and soak at room temperature for at least 8 hours or up to 1 day. Drain and rinse well.

2. Combine drained beans, broth, water, 1 green bell pepper half, root end of onion half, garlic head halves, bay leaves, and 1 teaspoon salt in Dutch oven. Bring to simmer over medium-high heat. Cover, reduce heat to low, and cook until beans are just soft, 30 to 40 minutes. Discard bell pepper, onion, garlic, and bay leaves, then drain beans in colander set over bowl; reserve 2½ cups bean cooking liquid.

3. Meanwhile, adjust oven rack to middle position and heat oven to 350 degrees. Cook salt pork and 1 tablespoon oil in now-empty pot over medium-low heat, stirring often, until lightly browned and fat is rendered, 15 to 20 minutes. Coarsely chop remaining bell pepper halves and onion half, then pulse in food processor into ¼-inch pieces, about 8 pulses; set aside.

4. Add remaining 1 tablespoon oil, processed vegetables, cumin, and oregano to salt pork. Increase heat to medium and cook, stirring often, until vegetables begin to brown, 10 to 15 minutes. Stir in minced garlic and cook until fragrant, about 30 seconds. Stir in rice until evenly combined.

5. Stir in drained beans, 2½ cups reserved cooking liquid, vinegar, and ½ teaspoon salt. Increase heat to medium-high and bring to simmer. Cover pot and transfer to oven. Bake until liquid is absorbed and rice is tender, about 30 minutes.

6. Fluff rice and beans with fork. Let rest, uncovered, for 5 minutes. Serve with scallions and lime wedges.

VARIATION
Vegetarian Cuban Black Beans and Rice
Substitute water for chicken broth, and omit salt pork. Add 1 tablespoon tomato paste to pot with processed vegetables in step 4. Increase salt to 1½ teaspoons in step 5.

A humble comfort food, beans and rice sounds simple, but all too often the dish ends up mushy and bland. If you follow these steps, from salt-soaking the beans to fully cooking the bean-rice mixture in the oven, the result will be perfectly tender and flavorful beans and fluffy rice to serve as a main course or as a great accompaniment to just about any kind of meat, poultry, or fish.

1. SALT-SOAK THE BEANS:
Dissolve salt in cold water in a large container. Add the beans and soak at room temperature for at least 8 hours. Drain the beans and rinse well.
WHY? Salt-soaking the beans softens the skins, which shortens the cooking time, and results in a creamier texture with fewer burst beans.

2. SIMMER THE BEANS:
Combine the beans, broth, water, bell pepper half, onion half, halved garlic head, bay leaves, and salt in a Dutch oven. Simmer, cover, and cook until the beans are just soft.
WHY? Aromatic vegetables and chicken broth infuse the beans with extra flavor. Gentle simmering prevents the beans from blowing out.

3. DRAIN THE BEANS, RESERVING THE LIQUID:
Discard the bell pepper, onion, garlic, and bay leaves. Drain the beans in a colander set over a bowl, reserving 2½ cups cooking liquid.
WHY? We cook the rice and beans in some of the bean cooking liquid, which adds even more flavor.

4. RINSE THE RICE AND PROCESS THE PEPPER AND ONION: Rinse the rice. Process the remaining bell pepper and onion into rough ¼-inch pieces.
WHY? Rinsing the rice removes excess starch, preventing gumminess. The vegetables are processed into pieces large enough to brown but small enough to blend in.

5. COOK THE PEPPER AND ONION AND PREHEAT THE OVEN: Cook the salt pork until it is lightly browned and the fat has rendered. Add more oil, along with the chopped peppers and onion, cumin, and oregano. Cook until the vegetables begin to brown. Add the minced garlic and cook until fragrant. Preheat the oven to 350 degrees.
WHY? Salt pork adds meatiness. Browning the peppers, onion, and garlic along with the spices in the pork fat creates the flavor base for the dish.

6. ADD THE RICE, BEANS, AND RESERVED COOKING LIQUID: Add the rice and stir to coat. Stir in the beans, reserved bean cooking liquid, vinegar, and salt. Bring the mixture to a simmer.
WHY? We use a modified rice pilaf technique, adding the rice first to coat, before adding the softened beans and the liquids. The red wine vinegar adds brightness.

7. COVER THE POT AND MOVE TO THE OVEN: Cover the pot and transfer it to the oven. Cook until the liquid is absorbed and the rice is tender, about 30 minutes.
WHY? With so much food in the pot, the rice will cook unevenly on the stovetop. The indirect heat of the oven cooks the rice gently and evenly. Plus it is far easier than monitoring a pot on the stovetop and adjusting the burner so the rice doesn't scorch.

8. FLUFF THE RICE AND BEANS AND LET THEM REST: Fluff the rice and beans with a fork and let them rest, uncovered, for 5 minutes. Serve with the scallions and lime wedges.
WHY? Fluffing the rice separates the grains without crushing them, giving the rice a light and fluffy texture. Letting the dish rest uncovered allows the rice and beans to absorb any excess moisture.

Hoppin' John

SERVES 6 TO 8 **TOTAL TIME** 1 HOUR 35 MINUTES

✓ **WHY THIS RECIPE WORKS:** Fresh black-eyed peas—a staple in a traditional Hoppin' John—are hard to come by, so many recipes rely on the dried variety. The dried route added hours, so we tested both canned and frozen black-eyed peas and discovered frozen worked just as well. Cooking the rice and black-eyed peas together made for deep flavor, but it also made the dish overly starchy. We fixed this by first rinsing the rice. We steered clear of ham hocks, which took too long to give up their flavor, and used boneless ham. To ensure that the rice cooked evenly, we covered the surface with foil. Small boneless hams are available but an equal weight of ham steak can be used. You will need a Dutch oven with a tight-fitting lid for this recipe. Serve with hot sauce.

- 6 slices bacon, chopped
- 1 (1- to 1½-pound) boneless ham, cut into ¾-inch-thick planks
- 1 onion, chopped fine
- 2 celery ribs, chopped fine
- 4 garlic cloves, minced
- ½ teaspoon dried thyme
- 4 cups chicken broth
- 2 pounds frozen black-eyed peas
- 2 bay leaves
- 1½ cups long-grain white rice, rinsed
- 3 scallions, sliced thin

1. Cook bacon in Dutch oven over medium heat until crisp, about 8 minutes; transfer to paper towel–lined plate. Pour off all but 1 tablespoon fat left in pot. Add ham and cook over medium heat, stirring occasionally, until lightly browned, about 6 minutes; transfer to plate with bacon.

2. Add onion and celery to fat left in pot and cook over medium heat until softened, about 5 minutes. Stir in garlic and thyme and cook until fragrant, about 30 seconds. Stir in broth, peas, bay leaves, and browned ham, scraping up any browned bits with wooden spoon, and bring to boil. Cover, reduce heat to low, and simmer gently until peas are just tender, about 20 minutes.

3. Transfer ham to cutting board and cut into ½-inch pieces; set aside. Stir rice into pot. Place square of aluminum foil directly on surface of simmering liquid. Cover pot and cook until liquid is absorbed and rice is tender, about 20 minutes, stirring and repositioning foil twice during cooking.

4. Remove pot from heat and let stand, covered, for 10 minutes. Fluff rice with fork. Stir in scallions, bacon, and ham. Serve.

Skillet Chickpeas

SERVES 4 **TOTAL TIME** 30 MINUTES **FAST**

✓ **WHY THIS RECIPE WORKS:** For many people, chickpeas are synonymous with hummus, but with their buttery, nutty flavor, these beans also make a great side dish. Convenient canned chickpeas needed only a few minutes of cooking to warm through, keeping our dish quick and simple. To develop a rich foundation of flavor, we first toasted garlic and red pepper flakes in oil, then added a minced onion and cooked it until all was lightly browned and aromatic. We added the chickpeas and some chicken broth to this mixture and simmered it covered until the flavors blended, then turned up the heat and reduced the liquid to a light, flavorful glaze. A little parsley and lemon juice brightened and balanced the flavors. Make sure you rinse the chickpeas thoroughly before cooking to get rid of excess salt.

- 3 tablespoons extra-virgin olive oil
- 4 garlic cloves, sliced thin
- ⅛ teaspoon red pepper flakes
- 1 onion, chopped fine
- 2 (15-ounce) cans chickpeas, rinsed
- 1 cup chicken broth
- 2 tablespoons minced fresh parsley
- 2 teaspoons lemon juice
  Salt and pepper

1. Cook oil, garlic, and pepper flakes in 12-inch nonstick skillet over medium heat, stirring often, until garlic is lightly golden, about 2 minutes. Stir in onion and cook until softened and lightly browned, 5 to 7 minutes.

2. Stir in chickpeas and broth, cover, and simmer until chickpeas are heated through, about 7 minutes. Uncover, increase heat to high, and simmer until liquid has reduced to light glaze, about 3 minutes. Off heat, stir in parsley and lemon juice. Season with salt and pepper to taste and serve.

White Bean Gratin

SERVES 4 **TOTAL TIME** 30 MINUTES **FAST**

✓ **WHY THIS RECIPE WORKS:** A Tuscan-inspired white bean gratin should boast a rustic, rich texture and a light seasoning of garlic and rosemary. In traditional versions of this dish, dried beans are gently cooked for hours over low heat, allowing the beans to break down and bind together. To make it more practical as a side dish, we wanted to re-create this dish with convenient, timesaving canned beans. It took several

For a creamy texture we mash a portion of the white beans before simmering them in chicken broth in this savory gratin.

failed attempts before we found the solution: Mashing some of the beans before adding them to the pot gave the finished dish a creamy, saucy texture in just 10 minutes. Simmering the beans in chicken broth allowed them to absorb rich, savory flavor. We limited supporting ingredients to the classics: onion, garlic, rosemary, and Parmesan, and finished the dish under the broiler until the cheese became golden. Make sure to rinse the beans thoroughly before cooking to get rid of excess salt. You will need a 10-inch ovensafe skillet for this recipe.

2 (15-ounce) cans white or cannellini beans, rinsed
2 tablespoons extra-virgin olive oil
1 onion, chopped fine
3 garlic cloves, minced
1 teaspoon minced fresh rosemary or ¼ teaspoon dried
2 cups chicken broth
2 ounces Parmesan cheese, grated (1 cup)

1. Adjust oven rack 6 inches from broiler element and heat broiler. Place ⅔ cup beans in bowl and mash smooth with potato masher.

2. Heat oil in 10-inch ovensafe skillet over medium-high heat until shimmering. Add onion and cook until softened and lightly browned, 7 to 10 minutes. Stir in garlic and rosemary and cook until fragrant, about 30 seconds.

3. Stir in broth and simmer until slightly thickened, 3 to 5 minutes. Stir in mashed beans and remaining whole beans and bring to brief simmer. Off heat, sprinkle with Parmesan. Transfer skillet to broiler and broil until cheese is golden and edges are bubbling, 3 to 5 minutes. Let cool slightly before serving.

French Lentils

SERVES 4 TO 6   **TOTAL TIME** 1 HOUR 10 MINUTES

✓ **WHY THIS RECIPE WORKS:** For a side dish that highlights smaller French lentils, we began by slowly cooking carrots, onions, and celery to bring out their sweet flavors. Garlic and thyme added earthy and herbal flavors that complemented the lentils, and cooking them in chicken broth made the dish more rich and complex than using just water. We cooked the lentils until they became completely tender, and finished the dish with a splash of olive oil along with some parsley and lemon juice. French green lentils, or *lentilles du Puy*, are our preferred choice for this recipe, but it works with any type of lentil except red or yellow; note that cooking times may vary depending on the type of lentils used. To make this dish vegetarian, substitute vegetable broth for the chicken broth.

2 carrots, peeled and chopped fine
1 onion, chopped fine
1 celery rib, chopped fine
2 tablespoons extra-virgin olive oil
  Salt and pepper
2 garlic cloves, minced
1 teaspoon minced fresh thyme or ¼ teaspoon dried
1¾ cups chicken broth
1 cup lentils, picked over and rinsed
2 tablespoons minced fresh parsley
2 teaspoons lemon juice

1. Combine carrots, onion, celery, 1 tablespoon oil, and ¼ teaspoon salt in large saucepan. Cover and cook over medium-low heat, stirring occasionally, until vegetables are softened, 8 to 10 minutes. Stir in garlic and thyme and cook until fragrant, about 30 seconds.

2. Stir in broth and lentils and bring to simmer. Reduce heat to low, cover, and simmer gently, stirring occasionally, until lentils are mostly tender but still slightly crunchy, about 35 minutes.

3. Uncover and continue to cook, stirring occasionally, until lentils are completely tender, about 8 minutes. Stir in remaining 1 tablespoon oil, parsley, and lemon juice. Season with salt and pepper to taste and serve.

VARIATION

French Lentils with Chard

Omit parsley. Stir 8 ounces Swiss chard leaves, cut into 1-inch pieces, into pot after uncovering in step 3.

NOTES FROM THE TEST KITCHEN

Getting to Know Lentils

Lentils come in dozens of sizes and colors (and from many parts of the world), and the differences in flavor and color are considerable. Because they are thin-skinned, they require no soaking, which makes them a most versatile legume. In the test kitchen, we evaluated the most commonly available types of lentils in terms of taste, texture, and appearance. Here's what we found.

BROWN AND GREEN LENTILS: These larger lentils are what you'll find in every supermarket. They are a uniform drab brown or green. Tasters commented on their "mild yet light and earthy flavor"; some found their texture "creamy," while others complained that they were "chalky." But everyone agreed that they held their shape and were tender inside. This is an all-purpose lentil, great in soups and salads or simmered, then tossed with olive oil and herbs.

LENTILLES DU PUY: These dark green French lentils from the city of Le Puy are smaller than the more common brown and green varieties. They are a dark olive-green, almost black. Tasters praised these for their "rich, earthy, complex flavor" and "firm yet tender texture." This is the kind to use if you are looking for a lentil that will keep its shape (and look beautiful on the plate) when cooked, so it's perfect for salads and dishes where the lentils take center stage, like our French Lentils (page 521) or Hearty Lentil Soup (page 110).

RED AND YELLOW LENTILS: Split, very colorful, and skinless, these small orange-red or golden-yellow lentils completely disintegrate when cooked. If you are looking for a lentil that will quickly break down into a thick puree, this is the one to use (see Indian-Spiced Red Lentils page 291).

Soaking the lentils in salt water for an hour ensures that they cook up tender but still intact.

Lentil Salad with Olives, Mint, and Feta

SERVES 4 TO 6   **TOTAL TIME** 1 HOUR 55 MINUTES

WHY THIS RECIPE WORKS: The main requirement in making a lentil salad is cooking the lentils so that they maintain their shape and firm-tender bite. This involves two key steps. The first is to salt-soak the lentils in warm salt water, which softens the lentils' skin, leading to fewer blowouts. The second step is to cook the lentils in the oven, which heats them gently and uniformly. Once we had perfectly cooked lentils, all we had left to do was to pair the earthy beans with a tart vinaigrette and boldly flavored mix-ins. French green lentils, or *lentilles du Puy*, are our preferred choice for this recipe, but it works with any type of lentil except red or yellow. Salt-soaking helps keep the lentils intact, but if you don't have time, they'll still taste good. The salad can be served warm or at room temperature.

1 cup lentils, picked over and rinsed

Salt and pepper

2 cups chicken broth

5 garlic cloves, lightly crushed and peeled

1 bay leaf

5 tablespoons extra-virgin olive oil

3 tablespoons white wine vinegar

½ cup coarsely chopped pitted kalamata olives

½ cup minced fresh mint

1 large shallot, minced

1 ounce feta cheese, crumbled (¼ cup)

1. Combine lentils and 1 teaspoon salt in bowl. Cover with 4 cups warm water (about 110 degrees) and soak for 1 hour. Drain well. (Drained lentils can be refrigerated for up to 2 days before cooking.)

2. Adjust oven rack to middle position and heat oven to 325 degrees. Combine drained lentils, 2 cups water, broth, garlic, bay leaf, and ½ teaspoon salt in medium saucepan. Cover pot and transfer to oven. Bake until lentils are tender but still intact, 40 to 60 minutes.

3. Drain lentils well, discarding garlic and bay leaf. Whisk oil and vinegar together in large bowl. Add drained lentils, olives, mint, and shallot, and toss to combine. Season with salt and pepper to taste. Transfer to serving dish, sprinkle with feta, and serve.

VARIATIONS

Lentil Salad with Carrots and Cilantro

While lentils bake, combine 2 carrots, peeled and cut into 2-inch-long matchsticks, 1 teaspoon ground cumin, ½ teaspoon ground cinnamon, and ⅛ teaspoon cayenne pepper in bowl. Cover and microwave until carrots are crisp-tender, 2 to 4 minutes. Substitute lemon juice for vinegar, cooked carrot mixture for olives, and ¼ cup minced fresh cilantro for mint. Omit shallot and feta.

Lentil Salad with Hazelnuts and Goat Cheese

Substitute red wine vinegar for white wine vinegar, and add 2 teaspoons Dijon mustard to dressing. Omit olives and substitute ¼ cup minced fresh parsley for mint. Substitute ½ cup crumbled goat cheese for feta, and sprinkle salad with ½ cup coarsely chopped toasted hazelnuts before serving.

Refried Beans

SERVES 4 TO 6 **TOTAL TIME** 40 MINUTES **FAST**

✔ WHY THIS RECIPE WORKS: Refried beans are all too often mealy, dry, and flavorless. We wanted deeply flavored refried beans that boasted a rich, creamy texture. In traditional *frijoles refritos*, dried pinto beans are cooked in lard and mashed. To start, we found that dried beans aren't essential—rinsed canned pinto beans worked just fine. For authentic flavor, we reached for salt pork, which we sautéed to render its fat. Using the fat to cook the onion and chiles deepened the flavor of the beans exponentially. Processing a portion of the beans with broth created the creamy texture we were after, while pulsing the remaining beans ensured some chunky bites. Onion, garlic, two types of chiles, and cumin gave the dish complexity, and cilantro and lime juice added at the end gave our refried beans brightness. Make sure you rinse the beans thoroughly before cooking to get rid of excess salt.

½ cup chicken broth

2 (15-ounce) cans pinto beans, rinsed

1 tablespoon vegetable oil

3 ounces salt pork, rind removed, chopped fine

1 small onion, chopped fine

1 jalapeño chile, stemmed, seeded, and minced

1 poblano chile, stemmed, seeded, and minced

¼ teaspoon salt

3 small garlic cloves, minced

½ teaspoon ground cumin

1 tablespoon minced fresh cilantro

2 teaspoons lime juice (optional)

1. Process broth and all but 1 cup beans in food processor until smooth, about 15 seconds, scraping down bowl if necessary. Add remaining beans and pulse until slightly chunky, about 10 pulses.

2. Heat oil in 12-inch nonstick skillet over medium heat until shimmering. Add salt pork and cook, stirring occasionally, until fat has rendered and pork is well browned, about 10 to 15 minutes; discard pork, leaving fat behind in pan.

3. Add onion, jalapeño, poblano, and salt to fat left in pan and cook over medium-high heat, stirring occasionally, until softened and beginning to brown, about 5 minutes. Stir in garlic and cumin and cook until fragrant, about 30 seconds. Stir in processed beans, reduce heat to medium, and cook, stirring often, until beans are thick and creamy, about 5 minutes. Stir in cilantro and lime juice, if using. Serve.

Eggs and Breakfast

■ SIGNIFIES A **FAST** RECIPE (45 MINUTES OR LESS)

Soft-Cooked Eggs

MAKES 4   TOTAL TIME 15 MINUTES   FAST

✔ **WHY THIS RECIPE WORKS:** Traditional methods for making soft-cooked eggs are hit-or-miss. We wanted a recipe that delivered a set white and a fluid yolk every time. Calling for fridge-cold eggs and boiling water reduced temperature variables and provided the steepest temperature gradient, ensuring that the yolk at the center stayed fluid while the white cooked through. Using only ½ inch of boiling water to cook the eggs meant the recipe took less time and energy. And because of the eggs' curved shape, they had very little contact with the water so they did not lower the temperature when they went into the saucepan. This means the same timing for anywhere from one to six eggs. Be sure to use large eggs that have no cracks and that are taken cold right from the refrigerator. Because precise timing is vital to the success of this recipe, we strongly recommend using a digital timer. If you have one, a steamer basket makes lowering the eggs into the boiling water easier. We recommend serving these eggs in eggcups and with buttered toast for dipping, or you may simply use the dull side of a butter knife to crack the egg along the equator, break the egg in half, and scoop out the insides with a teaspoon.

4 large eggs, cold

1. Bring ½ inch water to boil in medium saucepan over medium-high heat. Using tongs, gently place eggs in boiling water (eggs will not be submerged). Cover saucepan and cook eggs for 6½ minutes.

2. Remove cover, transfer saucepan to sink, and place under cold running water for 30 seconds. Remove eggs from pan and serve.

Fried Eggs

SERVES 2   TOTAL TIME 15 MINUTES   FAST

✔ **WHY THIS RECIPE WORKS:** Anyone can make fried eggs, but few and far between are the cooks who can make them perfectly every time. Eggs can stick to the skillet, yolks can break, and over- or undercooked eggs seem to be the norm. We decided to eliminate the guesswork and figure out the best and easiest way to fry the perfect egg every time. For us, this meant a firm white and a yolk that was thick yet still runny. A nonstick skillet proved key. The initial heat setting was also important; preheating the skillet over low heat helped to put it at just the right temperature to receive the eggs, which were added all at once with the help of small bowls. Covering the skillet as soon as the eggs were added and cooking them just 2 or 3 minutes delivered perfect fried eggs every time. When checking the eggs for doneness, lift the lid just a crack to prevent loss of steam should they need further cooking. When cooked, the thin layer of white surrounding the yolk will turn opaque, but the yolk should remain runny. To cook two eggs, use an 8- or 9-inch nonstick skillet and halve the amounts of oil and butter. You can use this method with extra-large or jumbo eggs without altering the timing. You will need a 12- or 14-inch nonstick skillet with a tight-fitting lid for this recipe.

2 teaspoons vegetable oil
4 large eggs
   Salt and pepper
2 teaspoons unsalted butter, cut into 4 pieces and chilled

1. Heat oil in 12- or 14-inch nonstick skillet over low heat for 5 minutes. Meanwhile, crack 2 eggs into small bowl and

Making Fried Eggs

1. HEAT SKILLET: Heat oil in nonstick skillet over low heat for 5 minutes.

2. CRACK EGGS INTO SMALL BOWLS: While skillet heats, crack 2 eggs into small bowl. Repeat with remaining eggs.

3. ADD EGGS ALL AT ONCE: Increase heat. Add butter and swirl to coat pan. Working quickly, position bowls on either side of skillet and add eggs simultaneously.

4. COVER PAN, THEN FINISH OFF HEAT: Cover and cook 1 minute. Remove skillet from burner and let stand, covered, until eggs achieve desired doneness.

season with salt and pepper. Repeat with remaining 2 eggs and second small bowl.

2. Increase heat to medium-high and heat until oil is shimmering. Add butter to skillet and quickly swirl to coat pan. Working quickly, pour 1 bowl of eggs in 1 side of pan and second bowl of eggs in other side. Cover and cook for 1 minute.

3. Remove skillet from heat and let stand, covered, 15 to 45 seconds for runny yolks (white around edge of yolk will be barely opaque), 45 to 60 seconds for soft but set yolks, and about 2 minutes for medium-set yolks. Slide eggs onto plates and serve immediately.

NOTES FROM THE TEST KITCHEN

Storing Eggs

In the test kitchen, we've tasted two- and three-month-old eggs and found them perfectly palatable. However, at four months, the white was very loose and the yolk had off-flavors, though it was still edible. Our advice is to use your discretion; if eggs smell odd or are discolored, pitch them. Older eggs also lack the structure-lending properties of fresh eggs, so beware when baking.

IN THE REFRIGERATOR: Eggs often suffer more from improper storage than from age. If your refrigerator has an egg tray in the door, don't use it—eggs should be stored on a shelf, where the temperature is below 40 degrees (the average refrigerator door temperature in our kitchen is closer to 45 degrees). Eggs are best stored in their cardboard or plastic carton, which protects them from absorbing flavors from other foods. The carton also helps maintain humidity, which slows down the evaporation of the eggs' moisture.

IN THE FREEZER: Extra whites can be frozen for later use, but we have found their rising properties compromised. Frozen whites are best in recipes that call for small amounts (like an egg wash) or that don't depend on whipping (an omelet). Yolks can't be frozen as is, but adding sugar syrup (microwave 2 parts sugar to 1 part water, stirring occasionally, until sugar is dissolved) to the yolks allows them to be frozen. Stir a scant ¼ teaspoon sugar syrup per yolk into the yolks before freezing. Defrosted yolks treated this way will behave just like fresh yolks in custards and other recipes.

To prevent scrambled eggs from getting tough when they cook, we beat them gently with a fork instead of a whisk.

Best Scrambled Eggs

SERVES 4   **TOTAL TIME** 10 MINUTES   **FAST**

✔ **WHY THIS RECIPE WORKS:** Scrambled eggs often end up tough and dry, or runny. We wanted foolproof scrambled eggs with fluffy, moist curds that were creamy and light. The first step was to add salt to the uncooked eggs; salt dissolves some of the egg proteins so they are unable to bond when cooked, creating more tender curds. Beating the eggs gently with a fork until thoroughly combined ensured our scramble didn't turn tough. Half-and-half was preferred over milk, producing clean-tasting curds that were both fluffy and stable. To replicate the richer flavor of farm-fresh eggs, we added extra yolks. We started the eggs on medium-high heat to create puffy curds, then finished them over low heat to ensure that they wouldn't overcook. It's important to follow visual cues, as skillet thickness will have an effect on cooking times. If you don't have half-and-half, you can substitute 2 tablespoons plus 2 teaspoons whole milk and 4 teaspoons heavy cream. To dress up the eggs, add 2 tablespoons minced fresh parsley, chives, basil, or cilantro, or 1 tablespoon minced fresh dill or tarragon after reducing the heat to low.

8 large eggs plus 2 large yolks
¼ cup half-and-half
Salt and pepper
1 tablespoon unsalted butter, chilled

1. Beat eggs and yolks, half-and-half, ¼ teaspoon salt, and ¼ teaspoon pepper together with fork in bowl until thoroughly combined and mixture is pure yellow; do not overbeat.

2. Melt butter in 10-inch nonstick skillet over medium-high heat, swirling to coat pan. Add egg mixture and, using heat-resistant rubber spatula, constantly and firmly scrape along bottom and sides of skillet until eggs begin to clump and spatula leaves trail on bottom of skillet, 1½ to 2½ minutes.

3. Reduce heat to low and gently but constantly fold eggs until clumped and slightly wet, 30 to 60 seconds. Immediately transfer eggs to warmed plates and season with salt to taste. Serve immediately.

VARIATIONS

Best Scrambled Eggs for Two
Reduce eggs to 4, egg yolks to 1, half-and-half to 2 tablespoons, salt and pepper to ⅛ teaspoon each, and butter to ½ tablespoon. Cook eggs in 8-inch nonstick skillet for 45 to 75 seconds over medium-high heat, and then 30 to 60 seconds over low heat.

Best Scrambled Eggs for One
Reduce eggs to 2, egg yolks to 1, half-and-half to 1 tablespoon, salt and pepper to pinch each, and butter to ¼ tablespoon. Cook eggs in 8-inch nonstick skillet for 30 to 60 seconds over medium-high heat, and then 30 to 60 seconds over low heat.

Scrambling Eggs

1. Add egg mixture and, using heat-resistant rubber spatula, constantly and firmly scrape along bottom and sides of skillet until eggs begin to clump and spatula leaves trail.

2. Reduce heat to low and gently but constantly fold eggs until clumped and slightly wet, 30 to 60 seconds.

Poached Eggs

MAKES 6   TOTAL TIME 20 MINUTES FAST

✔ **WHY THIS RECIPE WORKS:** A poached egg should be tender and evenly cooked, with a white like baked custard and a yolk that runs just a little. But a poached egg is very delicate; it can be hard to get it in and out of the water without breaking it, and the boiling water or the bottom of the pot can damage it as well. There's also the problem of those unappealing wandering strands of egg white. To address these difficulties, we traded in the usual saucepan for a shallow nonstick skillet, which gave us much easier access to the eggs. We cracked the eggs into teacups and tipped them simultaneously into the boiling water. The addition of vinegar to the cooking water helped to set the eggs quickly, and salting the water seasoned the eggs nicely. Removing the skillet from the heat limited the eggs' exposure to rapidly boiling water, which can cause them to disintegrate. These simple tricks gave us perfectly cooked eggs with no feathering of whites. You will need a 12-inch nonstick skillet with a tight-fitting lid for this recipe.

Salt and pepper
2 tablespoons distilled white vinegar
6 large eggs

1. Fill 12-inch nonstick skillet nearly to rim with water, add 1 teaspoon salt and vinegar, and bring to boil over high heat. Meanwhile, crack eggs into 3 teacups with handles (2 eggs per cup).

2. Lower lips of cups into water and tip eggs into skillet. Cover, remove from heat, and let sit until whites are set, about 4½ minutes (yolks will be slightly runny; for firmer yolks, cook an additional 30 to 60 seconds).

3. Using slotted spoon, carefully remove each egg, letting water drain back into skillet, and transfer to paper towel–lined plate. Season with salt and pepper to taste and serve immediately.

NOTES FROM THE TEST KITCHEN

Cooking Times for Poached Eggs

NUMBER OF EGGS	COOKING TIME
2 large	3½ minutes
4 large	4 minutes
8 large	5 minutes
12 large	6 minutes

Poaching Eggs

1. HEAT WATER: Fill 12-inch nonstick skillet nearly to rim with water, add 1 teaspoon salt and 2 tablespoons vinegar and bring to boil over high heat.

2. CRACK EGGS INTO TEACUPS: Crack eggs into 3 teacups (2 eggs per cup).

3. ADD EGGS TO WATER: Lower lips of cups into water and tip eggs into skillet.

4. COOK COVERED OFF HEAT: Cover, remove from heat, and let sit until whites are set. (Cooking time will vary based on number of eggs being cooked; see Cooking Times for Poached Eggs chart on page 528.)

Eggs Benedict

SERVES 6   **TOTAL TIME** 40 MINUTES   **FAST**

✔ **WHY THIS RECIPE WORKS:** Eggs Benedict is easy enough for a restaurant to pull off, but even seasoned cooks grow anxious at the idea of tackling this multicomponent dish at home. Wanting to streamline the recipe, we began with the hollandaise. Many newer recipes call for making it in a blender or food processor to ensure an emulsified sauce. These methods work, but only if the sauce is served immediately. Our unconventional technique began with whisking softened butter and egg yolks together on the stovetop in a double boiler, then adding a lot of water, followed by lemon juice off the heat. It was foamier than a classic hollandaise, but it held without breaking while we prepared the other components. As for the eggs, we simply used our favorite egg poaching technique, cracking the eggs into teacups and then gently sliding them into a large covered skillet filled with boiling water. Seasoning the water with salt helped flavor the eggs, and adding a little vinegar helped to set the egg whites. You will need an instant-read thermometer and a 12-inch nonstick skillet with a tight-fitting lid for this recipe. For an accurate measurement of boiling water, bring a full kettle of water to a boil, then measure out the desired amount.

12   tablespoons unsalted butter, softened
12   large eggs plus 6 large yolks
½   cup boiling water
2   teaspoons lemon juice
⅛   teaspoon cayenne pepper
Salt
12   slices Canadian bacon
6   English muffins, split and toasted
2   tablespoons distilled white vinegar

1. Whisk butter and 6 egg yolks together in large heatproof bowl set over medium saucepan filled with ½ inch of barely simmering water (don't let bowl touch water). Slowly add boiling water and cook, whisking constantly, until thickened and sauce registers 160 degrees, 7 to 10 minutes. Off heat, stir in lemon juice and cayenne. Season with salt to taste. (Hollandaise can be held at room temperature for up to 1 hour or refrigerated for up to 3 days; before serving, microwave on 50 percent power for 1 minute, stirring every 10 seconds, until heated through.)

2. Adjust oven rack to middle position and heat oven to 300 degrees. Place 1 slice Canadian bacon on each toasted English muffin half and arrange on baking sheet; keep warm in oven. Fill 12-inch nonstick skillet nearly to rim with water. Add vinegar and 1 teaspoon salt, and bring to boil over high heat. Meanwhile, crack eggs into 4 teacups with handles (3 eggs per cup).

3. Lower lips of teacups into water and tip eggs into skillet. Cover, remove from heat, and let sit until whites are set, about 6 minutes (yolks will be slightly runny; for firmer yolks, cook an additional 30 to 60 seconds).

4. Using slotted spoon, carefully remove each egg, letting water drain back into skillet, and transfer to paper towel–lined plate. Arrange 1 poached egg on top of each English muffin. Spoon 1 to 2 tablespoons hollandaise over each egg, and serve immediately with remaining hollandaise.

Eggs Florentine

SERVES 4   **TOTAL TIME** 35 MINUTES   **FAST**

✓ **WHY THIS RECIPE WORKS:** This simple open-faced egg sandwich pairs spinach, goat cheese, and tomato, along with a poached egg, on top of a toasted English muffin. We began by spreading goat cheese mixed with lemon juice and pepper on the muffins and topping them with thin slices of fresh tomato. The spinach was sautéed quickly in a skillet with shallot and garlic, squeezed of excess water, and added to the sandwiches. We used the same skillet to poach our eggs, filling it with water and some vinegar and bringing it to a boil. Cracking the eggs into teacups allowed us to slip them into the water simultaneously, and cooking them covered, off the heat, ensured perfectly cooked eggs to top our tasty sandwiches. You will need a 12-inch nonstick skillet with a tight-fitting lid for this recipe.

- 4 **ounces goat cheese, crumbled (1 cup)**
- 1 **teaspoon lemon juice**
  Salt and pepper
- 4 **English muffins, split, toasted, and still warm**
- 2 **tomatoes, cored, seeded, and sliced thin (about 16 slices)**
- 1 **tablespoon olive oil**
- 1 **large shallot, minced**
- 1 **garlic clove, minced**
- 8 **ounces (8 cups) baby spinach**
- 2 **tablespoons distilled white vinegar**
- 8 **large eggs**

1. Adjust oven rack to middle position and heat oven to 300 degrees. Combine goat cheese, lemon juice, and ⅛ teaspoon pepper in bowl until smooth. Spread goat cheese mixture evenly over toasted English muffins, top with tomato, and arrange on baking sheet; keep warm in oven.

2. Heat oil in 12-inch nonstick skillet over medium heat until shimmering. Add shallot and cook until softened, about 2 minutes. Stir in garlic and cook until fragrant, about 30 seconds. Stir in spinach and ⅛ teaspoon salt and cook until wilted, about 1 minute. Using tongs, squeeze out any excess moisture from spinach and divide evenly among English muffins.

3. Wipe out now-empty skillet with paper towels and fill nearly to rim with water. Add vinegar and 1 teaspoon salt and bring to boil over high heat. Meanwhile, crack eggs into 4 teacups with handles (2 eggs per cup).

4. Lower lips of teacups into water and tip eggs into skillet. Cover, remove from heat, and let sit until whites are set, about 5 minutes (yolks will be slightly runny; for firmer yolks, cook an additional 30 to 60 seconds).

5. Using slotted spoon, carefully remove each egg, letting water drain back into skillet, and transfer to paper towel–lined plate. Arrange 1 poached egg on top of each English muffin. Season with salt and pepper to taste and serve immediately

Fluffy Diner-Style Cheese Omelet

SERVES 2   **TOTAL TIME** 25 MINUTES   **FAST**

✓ **WHY THIS RECIPE WORKS:** For a tall, fluffy omelet, we ditched the whisk for an electric mixer, which helped us incorporate air into the eggs. Cream added richness, but when we added it to the whipped eggs, the omelet lost its fluffiness. Combining the cream and eggs before whipping didn't work either; the fat in the cream made it impossible to whip air into the eggs. So we whipped the dairy first, then folded it into the whipped eggs. After letting the bottom of the omelet set on the stovetop, we popped the skillet into the oven, and 6 minutes later we had a perfectly puffy, fluffy omelet. A hand-held mixer makes quick work of whipping such a small amount of cream, but you can also use a stand mixer fitted with the whisk attachment. To make two omelets, double this recipe and cook the omelets simultaneously in two skillets, or set half of the ingredients aside to make the second omelet; be sure to wipe out the skillet before making the second omelet. You will need a 10-inch ovensafe nonstick skillet with a tight-fitting lid for this recipe.

- 3 **tablespoons heavy cream, chilled**
- 5 **large eggs, room temperature**
- ¼ **teaspoon salt**
- 2 **tablespoons unsalted butter**
- 2 **ounces sharp cheddar cheese, shredded (½ cup)**

1. Adjust oven rack to middle position and heat oven to 400 degrees. Using hand-held mixer, whip cream on medium-low speed in bowl until foamy, about 1 minute. Increase speed to high and whip until soft peaks form, 1 to 3 minutes. Set whipped cream aside.

2. Using dry, clean whisk attachment, whip eggs and salt in large bowl on high speed until frothy and eggs have at least doubled in volume, about 2 minutes. Using rubber spatula, gently fold whipped cream into eggs.

3. Melt butter in 10-inch ovensafe nonstick skillet over medium-low heat, swirling to coat pan. Add egg mixture and cook until edges are nearly set, 2 to 3 minutes. Sprinkle with ¼ cup cheddar and transfer to oven. Bake until eggs are set and edges are beginning to brown, 6 to 8 minutes.

Omelets often end up tough, rubbery, and overcooked. We discovered a few tricks to produce a tall, fluffy omelet like the ones you find at a diner. Using a hand-held mixer and a surprising ingredient, whipped cream, keeps these omelets light and airy, perfect for a meal at any time of the day.

1. WHIP THE CREAM: With a hand-held mixer, whip the chilled cream on medium-low speed until foamy. Increase the speed to high and whip until soft peaks form. Preheat the oven to 400 degrees.
WHY? Cream makes the omelets richer. Whipping it gives these omelets extra lift, and the colder the cream the more easily it will whip up.

2. WHIP THE EGGS: Whip the room-temperature eggs and salt in a large bowl on high speed until frothy and the eggs have doubled in volume.
WHY? Eggs whip up more easily and quickly at room temperature, so we remove them from the refrigerator an hour before cooking. We make sure the eggs double in volume for high, fluffy omelets.

3. FOLD THE CREAM INTO THE EGGS: Gently fold the whipped cream into the whipped eggs.
WHY? If you stir vigorously or overmix, you risk deflating the eggs and cream. Folding the cream into the eggs gently ensures that everything stays light and airy.

4. MELT THE BUTTER, THEN ADD THE EGG MIXTURE: Melt the butter in an ovensafe nonstick skillet, swirling to coat the pan. Add the egg mixture and cook until the edges are nearly set.
WHY? A nonstick skillet ensures that the omelet will be easy to remove. Heating the pan helps set the bottom and edges of the omelet without overcooking.

5. ADD HALF OF THE CHEESE: Sprinkle half of the cheese (and half of the filling, if using) over the eggs.
WHY? If you add all of the cheese at this point, it will weigh down the eggs, preventing them from puffing up in the oven. But adding half now ensures that the cheese melts in the oven.

6. TRANSFER THE SKILLET TO THE OVEN: Place the skillet in the preheated oven and bake until the eggs are set and the edges begin to brown, 6 to 8 minutes.
WHY? The even heat of the oven is the best way to set the top and cook the interior of the omelet.

7. REMOVE THE SKILLET FROM THE OVEN, ADD CHEESE, AND COVER: Remove the skillet from the oven and sprinkle with the remaining cheese (and remaining filling, if using). Cover with the lid and let sit, off the heat, until the cheese melts.
WHY? Once the omelet is almost set, the rest of the cheese is added, contributing more flavor without weighing it down. The lid traps just enough heat to finish setting up the omelet and to melt the cheese.

8. SLIDE, THEN FOLD THE OMELET ONTO A CUTTING BOARD: Tilt the skillet and, with a spatula, push half of the omelet onto a cutting board. Then tilt the skillet so that the omelet folds over itself to form a half-moon shape.
WHY? To prevent tearing when removing the omelet, we let the pan do most of the work. With the help of a rubber spatula, we push it out of the skillet and onto a board, and then let the skillet do the work of flipping the omelet.

4. Carefully remove skillet from oven (handle will be hot), then sprinkle eggs with remaining ¼ cup cheddar. Let sit, covered, until cheese melts, about 1 minute. Tilt skillet and, using rubber spatula, push half of omelet onto cutting board, then fold omelet over itself on cutting board to form half-moon shape. Cut omelet in half and serve.

VARIATION

Fluffy Diner-Style Cheese Omelet with Sausage and Bell Pepper

Before cooking eggs, cook 4 ounces crumbled sweet Italian sausage in 10-inch nonstick skillet over medium heat until browned, about 6 minutes; transfer to paper towel–lined plate. Add 1 tablespoon unsalted butter, 1 small finely chopped onion, and ½ finely chopped bell pepper to now-empty skillet and cook over medium heat until softened, about 10 minutes; transfer to plate with sausage. Clean skillet and cook omelet as directed, sprinkling half of sausage mixture over omelet with cheese in step 3 and remaining filling with remaining cheese in step 4.

Family-Size Cheese Omelet

SERVES 4   **TOTAL TIME** 20 MINUTES   **FAST**

✔ **WHY THIS RECIPE WORKS:** An omelet is a great breakfast or brunch dish, but cooking omelets one at a time for more than a couple of people is just not practical. We wanted to find a way to make an omelet that was big enough to serve four people and that would feature tender eggs and a rich, cheesy filling. Flipping a huge eight-egg omelet was clearly not going to work, so we had to find a way to cook the top of the omelet as well as the bottom. Cooking the eggs longer over lower heat resulted in an unpleasant texture. Cooking the top of the eggs under the broiler worked, but it dried out the omelet. Then we had the idea of covering the pan after the bottom of the eggs was set but the top was still runny, which worked like a charm. The lid trapped the heat and moisture to steam the top of the omelet, and it partially melted the cheese as well. Now we had a perfectly cooked omelet for four, with tender eggs and bits of melted cheese in every bite. Monterey Jack, Colby, or any other good melting cheese can be substituted for the cheddar. Finish with minced fresh herbs if desired. You will need a 12-inch nonstick skillet with a tight-fitting lid for this recipe.

 8 **large eggs**
 ½ **teaspoon salt**

To finish cooking our family-size omelet and keep it moist, we cover the pan once the bottom is set.

 ¼ **teaspoon pepper**
 2 **tablespoons unsalted butter**
 3 **ounces sharp cheddar cheese, shredded (¾ cup)**

1. Whisk eggs, salt, and pepper together in bowl. Melt butter in 12-inch nonstick skillet over medium heat, swirling to coat pan. Add eggs and cook, stirring gently in circular motion, until mixture is slightly thickened, about 1 minute.

2. Using heatproof rubber spatula, gently pull cooked eggs back from edge of skillet and tilt pan, allowing any uncooked egg to run to cleared edge of skillet. Repeat this process, working your way around skillet, until bottom of omelet is just set but top is still runny, about 1 minute. Cover skillet, reduce heat to low, and cook until top of omelet begins to set but is still moist, about 5 minutes.

3. Off heat, sprinkle with cheddar, cover, and let sit until cheese partially melts, about 1 minute. Using rubber spatula, slide half of omelet onto serving platter, then tilt skillet so remaining omelet flips over onto itself. Cut into wedges and serve immediately.

VARIATIONS

Family-Size Omelet with Tomato, Bacon, and Garlic

Omit butter. Before cooking eggs, cook 8 slices finely chopped bacon in 12-inch nonstick skillet over medium-high heat until brown and crisp, 5 to 7 minutes; transfer to paper towel–lined plate. Pour off all but 2 tablespoons fat left in pan, add 1 finely chopped tomato and ½ finely chopped bell pepper and cook over medium-high heat until softened, about 6 minutes. Stir in 4 minced garlic cloves and cook until fragrant, about 30 seconds. Reduce heat to medium, add eggs and bacon to vegetables in pan, and cook omelet as directed.

Family-Size Omelet with Arugula, Sun-Dried Tomatoes, and Provolone

Substitute provolone cheese for cheddar. Before cooking eggs, cook 1 finely chopped onion, 1 tablespoon olive oil, and ⅛ teaspoon red pepper flakes in 12-inch nonstick skillet over medium-high heat until onion is softened, about 5 minutes. Stir in ¼ cup oil-packed sun-dried tomatoes, patted dry and chopped fine. Add 5 cups baby arugula, a handful at a time, until wilted, about 1 minute. Reduce heat to medium, add butter and eggs to vegetables in pan, and cook omelet as directed.

Family-Size Denver Omelet

Before cooking eggs, melt 1 tablespoon unsalted butter in 12-inch nonstick skillet over medium-high heat. Add 4 ounces finely chopped ham steak and cook until lightly browned, about 3 minutes. Stir in 1 small onion, ½ red bell pepper, and ½ green bell pepper, all finely chopped, and cook until browned around edges, 6 to 7 minutes. Reduce heat to medium, add butter and eggs to ham and vegetables in pan, and cook omelet as directed.

Frittata with Parmesan and Herbs

SERVES 4   **TOTAL TIME** 20 MINUTES   **FAST**

✔ **WHY THIS RECIPE WORKS:** Since few cookbooks agree on a method for making frittatas, we had to test a number of techniques to determine which would consistently yield the best frittata, an Italian version of the filled omelet. Whereas an omelet should be soft, delicate, and slightly runny, a frittata should be tender but firm. And whereas an omelet usually encases its filling, a frittata incorporates it evenly throughout. It should also be easy to make. Our testing found that starting the frittata on the stovetop and finishing it in the oven set it evenly so it didn't burn or dry out. Conventional skillets

For a perfectly cooked, tender but firm frittata, we start it on the stove and finish cooking it in the oven.

required so much oil to prevent sticking that frittatas cooked in them were likely to be greasy, so we used an ovensafe nonstick pan for a clean release. You will need a 10-inch ovensafe nonstick skillet for this recipe.

- 6 **large eggs, lightly beaten**
- 1 **ounce Parmesan cheese, grated (½ cup)**
- ¼ **teaspoon salt**
- ¼ **teaspoon pepper**
- 1 **tablespoon olive oil**
- ½ **onion, chopped fine**
- 2 **tablespoons minced fresh parsley, basil, dill, tarragon, and/or mint**

1. Adjust oven rack to upper-middle position and heat oven to 350 degrees. Whisk eggs, Parmesan, salt, and pepper together in bowl.

2. Heat oil in 10-inch ovensafe nonstick skillet over medium heat until shimmering. Add onion and cook until softened, about 4 minutes. Add parsley and egg mixture and stir gently until eggs on bottom are set and firm, about 30 seconds.

3. Using heatproof rubber spatula, gently pull cooked eggs back from edge of skillet and tilt pan, allowing any uncooked egg to run to cleared edge of skillet. Repeat this process, working your way around skillet, until egg on top is mostly set but still moist, 1 to 2 minutes.

4. Transfer skillet to oven and bake until frittata top is set and dry to touch, about 3 minutes. Run spatula around skillet edge to loosen frittata, then carefully slide it out onto serving plate. Serve warm or at room temperature.

VARIATIONS
Frittata with Sun-Dried Tomatoes, Mozzarella, and Basil
Substitute basil for parsley and ½ cup shredded mozzarella for Parmesan. Add ¼ cup oil-packed sun-dried tomatoes, patted dry and chopped fine, to skillet with eggs.

Frittata with Asparagus, Ham, and Gruyère
Substitute ½ cup shredded Gruyère for Parmesan. Add 8 ounces asparagus, trimmed and cut on bias into ¼-inch pieces, and 2 ounces ¼-inch-thick deli ham, cut into ½-inch pieces, to skillet with onion.

Removing Frittata from the Pan

Run spatula around skillet edge to loosen frittata, then carefully slide it out onto serving plate.

Eggs in a Hole
MAKES 6   **TOTAL TIME** 30 MINUTES   FAST

✓ **WHY THIS RECIPE WORKS:** An egg fried in the cut-out center of a piece of toast makes a delicious breakfast. But without a griddle, you can't make more than two at a time. We tried making them in batches, keeping the first ones warm, but those overcooked. So we decided to move entirely to the oven, toasting the bread on both sides there. A preheated buttered baking sheet ensured that the bread browned without sticking, and cracking the eggs onto the hot pan helped them set up right away. Adding a second baking pan to the setup acted as insulation so the eggs cooked quickly but gently. If you don't have a biscuit cutter, cut the toast holes with a drinking glass.

6 **slices hearty white sandwich bread**
5 **tablespoons unsalted butter, softened**
6 **large eggs**
   Salt and pepper

1. Adjust oven racks to lowest and top positions, place rimmed baking sheet on lowest rack, and heat oven to 500 degrees. Spread 1 side of bread slices evenly with 2½ tablespoons butter. Using 2½-inch biscuit cutter, cut out and remove circle from center of each piece of buttered bread.

2. Remove hot sheet from oven, add remaining 2½ tablespoons butter, and let melt, tilting sheet to cover pan evenly. Place bread circles down center of sheet and bread slices on either side of circles, buttered side up. Return sheet to lowest oven rack and bake until bread is golden, 3 to 5 minutes, flipping bread and rotating sheet halfway through baking.

3. Remove sheet from oven and set inside second (room-temperature) rimmed baking sheet. Crack 1 egg into each bread hole. Season with salt and pepper. Bake on top oven rack until whites are barely set, 4 to 6 minutes, rotating sheet halfway through baking.

4. Transfer sheets to wire rack and let eggs sit until whites are completely set, about 2 minutes. Serve.

VARIATIONS
Eggs in a Hole with Ham and Gruyère
Mix butter with 1 tablespoon Dijon mustard before spreading over bread. Sprinkle ⅓ cup shredded Gruyère cheese and 2 ounces minced ham over eggs before baking.

Spicy Eggs in a Hole
Mix butter with 2 teaspoons hot sauce before spreading over bread. Sprinkle ½ cup shredded pepper Jack cheese over eggs before baking.

Scrambled Egg Muffins with Sausage
SERVES 6   **TOTAL TIME** 25 MINUTES   FAST

✓ **WHY THIS RECIPE WORKS:** Hearty scrambled eggs and sausage combined into a convenient muffin sounds like a great idea, but many recipes rely on packaged mixes or self-rising flour, which make the muffins taste bready and leaden. Looking for a recipe for an egg muffin that was fluffy, flavorful, and easy, we found that Ritz crackers, which are easy to crush and have a sweet and buttery flavor, gave the muffin enough structure without ruining the delicate structure of the eggs. We microwaved sausage quickly to render some of the fat before adding it to the quick-to-make batter. Once mixed and poured into a prepared muffin tin, they had to bake for only about 8 minutes before we had satisfying and savory breakfast muffins. These muffins will soufflé nicely during baking but will begin to fall as they sit for several minutes after being removed from the oven. You can substitute whole milk for the half-and-half in this recipe, but the eggs will be less rich and less tender. Using baking spray to grease the muffin tin, rather than vegetable oil spray, will make it easier to remove the muffins from the tin.

4	ounces bulk breakfast sausage, broken into ½-inch pieces
24	Ritz crackers, coarsely crushed
10	large eggs
⅓	cup half-and-half
4	ounces sharp cheddar cheese, shredded (1 cup)
4	scallions, sliced thin

1. Adjust oven rack to lower-middle position and heat oven to 450 degrees. Grease 12-cup muffin tin with baking spray.

2. Microwave sausage in uncovered bowl until fat begins to render, about 1 minute; drain. In separate bowl, whisk crackers, eggs, and half-and-half together until fully incorporated. Stir in cheddar, scallions, and drained sausage.

3. Slowly pour egg mixture into prepared muffin tin. Bake until tops are set and lightly golden, 8 to 10 minutes, rotating tin halfway through baking. Let muffins cool slightly, then run small knife around each muffin to loosen and remove from tin. Serve.

VARIATIONS
Scrambled Egg Muffins with Sun-Dried Tomatoes, Boursin, and Basil
Substitute 3 tablespoons oil-packed sun-dried tomatoes, patted dry and chopped fine, for sausage; do not microwave tomatoes. Substitute 1 (5.2-ounce) package crumbled Boursin Garlic and Fine Herbs cheese for cheddar, and ½ cup chopped fresh basil for scallions.

Scrambled Egg Muffins with Kielbasa, Pepper Jack, and Scallions
Substitute 4 ounces kielbasa sausage, cut into ⅓-inch pieces, for breakfast sausage; microwave as directed. Substitute 1 cup shredded pepper Jack cheese for cheddar.

NOTES FROM THE TEST KITCHEN

Buying Eggs

There are numerous—and often confusing—options when buying eggs at the supermarket. And when eggs are the focal point of a dish, the quality of the eggs makes a big difference. Here's what we've learned in the test kitchen about buying eggs.

CHOOSING EGGS: According to the U.S. Department of Agriculture (USDA), the average American eats upward of 250 eggs every year. Theoretically, these eggs come in three grades (AA, A, and B), six sizes (from peewee to jumbo), and a rainbow of colors. But the only grade we could find in the market was grade A, the only colors were brown and white, and the only sizes were jumbo, extra-large, large, and medium. So how do we choose? After extensive tasting, we could not discern any consistent flavor differences. The size (and volume) of the egg, however, is important, particularly when baking. In all of our recipes, we use large eggs.

HOW OLD ARE MY EGGS?: Egg cartons are marked with both a sell-by date and a pack date. The pack date is the day the eggs were graded and packed, which is generally within a week of when they were laid but may be as much as 30 days later. The sell-by date is within 30 days of the pack date, which is the legal limit set by the USDA. In short, a carton of eggs may be up to two months old by the end of the sell-by date. Even so, according to the USDA, eggs are still fit for consumption for an additional three to five weeks past the sell-by date.

EGG SIZES: If you do not have large eggs on hand, substitutions are possible. See the chart below for help in making accurate calculations. For half of an egg, whisk the yolk and white together, measure, and then divide in half.

LARGE		JUMBO	EXTRA-LARGE	MEDIUM
1	=	1	1	1
2	=	1½	2	2
3	=	2½	2½	3½
4	=	3	3½	4½
5	=	4	4	6
6	=	5	5	7

Simple Cheese Quiche

SERVES 6 TO 8   **TOTAL TIME** 55 MINUTES
(PLUS 1 HOUR COOLING TIME)

✔ **WHY THIS RECIPE WORKS:** Our ideal quiche has a tender, buttery pastry case embracing a velvety smooth custard that is neither too rich nor too lean. We tested numerous combinations of dairy and eggs to find the perfect combination. The baking temperature was equally important; 350 degrees was low enough to set the custard gently, and hot enough to brown the top before the filling dried out and became rubbery. To keep the crust from becoming soggy, we parbaked it before adding the filling. To avoid spilling the custard, we set the parbaked crust in the oven before pouring the custard into the pastry shell. For perfectly baked quiche every time, we pulled it out of the oven when it was still slightly soft and allowed it to set up as it cooled. Be sure to add the custard to the pie shell while the crust is still warm so that the quiche will bake evenly. You can substitute other fresh herbs for the chives, like thyme, parsley, or marjoram. You can use the Foolproof Single-Crust Pie Dough (page 698), the All-Butter Single-Crust Pie Dough (page 700), or store-bought pie dough in this recipe.

- 5 **large eggs**
- 2 **cups half-and-half**
- ¼ **teaspoon salt**
- ¼ **teaspoon pepper**
- 4 **ounces cheddar cheese, shredded (1 cup)**
- 1 **tablespoon minced fresh chives**
- 1 **recipe single-crust pie dough, partially baked and still warm**

1. Adjust oven rack to lower-middle position and heat oven to 350 degrees. Whisk eggs, half-and-half, salt, and pepper together in large bowl. Stir in cheddar and chives. Transfer filling to 4-cup liquid measuring cup.

2. Place warm pie shell on rimmed baking sheet and place in oven. Carefully pour egg mixture into warm shell until it reaches about ½ inch from top edge of crust (you may have extra egg mixture).

3. Bake quiche until top is lightly browned, center is set but soft, and knife inserted about 1 inch from edge comes out clean, 40 to 50 minutes. Let quiche cool for at least 1 hour or up to 3 hours. Serve slightly warm or at room temperature.

TO MAKE AHEAD: Let baked quiche cool completely, then cover with plastic wrap and refrigerate for up to 6 hours. (Crust of refrigerated quiche will be less crisp.) Quiche can be served slightly chilled, at room temperature, or warm; to serve warm, reheat in 350-degree oven for 10 to 15 minutes.

VARIATIONS

Quiche Lorraine

Cook 4 slices finely chopped bacon in 10-inch skillet over medium heat until crisp, 5 to 7 minutes; transfer to paper towel–lined plate. Discard all but 2 teaspoons fat left in skillet, add 1 small finely chopped onion, and cook over medium heat until lightly browned, about 5 minutes; transfer to plate with bacon. Substitute Gruyère cheese for cheddar, and stir bacon mixture into eggs with cheese and chives.

Leek and Goat Cheese Quiche

Melt 2 tablespoons unsalted butter in 10-inch skillet over medium-high heat. Add 2 finely chopped leeks, white and light green parts only, and cook until softened, about 6 minutes; transfer to plate. Substitute 1 cup crumbled goat cheese for cheddar, and stir leeks into eggs with cheese and chives.

Spinach and Feta Quiche

Removing the excess moisture from the spinach is crucial here.

Omit chives and substitute 1 cup crumbled feta cheese for cheddar. Stir 1 (10-ounce) package frozen chopped spinach, thawed and squeezed dry, into eggs with cheese.

Asparagus and Gruyère Quiche

Do not substitute precooked or frozen asparagus here.

Substitute Gruyère cheese for cheddar, and stir 1 bunch asparagus, sliced on bias into ¼-inch-thick pieces, into eggs with cheese and chives.

Broccoli and Cheddar Quiche

Do not substitute frozen broccoli here.

Bring 4 cups chopped broccoli florets, ½ cup water, and ¼ teaspoon salt to boil in covered 12-inch skillet and cook until broccoli is bright green, about 3 minutes. Uncover and continue to cook until broccoli is tender and water has evaporated, about 3 minutes; transfer to paper towel–lined plate. Distribute broccoli over warm pie shell before adding egg mixture.

Once you master the basic quiche recipe, it's easy to vary it, and since it can be served for breakfast, lunch, or dinner, it's handy to have in your repertoire. The keys to a great quiche are just the right proportion of dairy to eggs, and parbaking the crust. For more information on making a single-crust pie shell, see page 701.

1. MAKE AND CHILL THE PIE SHELL: Make the pie dough, fit it into a pie plate, and flute the edges. Line the pie shell with plastic wrap and place in the refrigerator or freezer (depending on the dough recipe used) until firm. Meanwhile, preheat the oven according to the dough recipe.
WHY? Refrigerating or freezing the pie shell reduces the risk of shrinking in the oven and enables the crust to hold all of the filling.

2. PARTIALLY BAKE THE CRUST: Line the chilled crust with a double layer of foil and fill it with pie weights. Bake until the pie dough looks dry and is light in color, 25 to 30 minutes.
WHY? Parbaking the crust prevents it from becoming soggy from the moisture in the custard. Pie weights keep the crust from shrinking and puffing as it bakes, and we use foil to make them easier to remove and to protect the edges from burning.

3. MAKE THE CUSTARD, THEN ADD REMAINING INGREDIENTS: In a large bowl, whisk together 5 eggs, 2 cups half-and-half, salt, and pepper. Whisk in the cheese and the chives.
WHY? A ratio of 5 eggs to 2 cups half-and-half delivered a rich, creamy custard. The trick to making it is to get the ingredients well combined, with no streaks of eggs, which will ensure a smooth texture in the finished quiche.

4. FILL THE WARM PIE SHELL IN THE OVEN: Lower the oven temperature to 350 degrees. Place the pie shell on a rimmed baking sheet and transfer it to the oven. Pour the custard into a large measuring cup and then fill the pie shell, stopping ½ inch from the top edge.
WHY? It is tricky to transfer a filled quiche to the oven without spilling; filling the pie shell in the oven is easier and safer. We avoid filling it all the way to the top so the custard won't bubble over while baking.

5. BAKE THE QUICHE: Bake until the top of the quiche is lightly browned, the center is set but soft, and a knife inserted about 1 inch from the edge comes out clean, 40 to 50 minutes.
WHY? Pulling the quiche from the oven before it has entirely set prevents it from overbaking. The center will still jiggle when the quiche is ready to come out of the oven, but it will continue to cook and set as it cools.

6. LET THE QUICHE REST: Let the quiche cool for at least an hour or up to 3 hours before serving.
WHY? It's important to let the quiche set up before slicing into it, or you'll have a mess on your hands. This will take at least an hour, perhaps a bit longer. The quiche can be kept at room temperature for up to 3 hours.

Huevos Rancheros

SERVES 2 TO 4 **TOTAL TIME** 1 HOUR

🗸 **WHY THIS RECIPE WORKS:** The huevos rancheros found on American brunch menus resemble heaping plates of nachos more often than they do the simple, satisfying Mexican meal of tortillas, eggs, and salsa. We wanted to use supermarket staples to produce the most authentic version possible. Starting at the top, with the salsa, we enhanced the flavor of the tomatoes, chiles, and onions by adding tomato paste and then roasting them. Garlic, cumin, cayenne, lime juice, and cilantro gave the salsa a zesty, clean flavor. The fried eggs presented a challenge: even if we didn't break the yolks when we placed the eggs on top of the tortillas, they ended up looking ragged. Poaching the eggs in the heated salsa left them looking perfect and gave them a boost of flavor. Finally, we brushed supermarket tortillas with oil, sprinkled a little salt on top, and toasted them so they'd be crisp and dry enough to provide a sturdy and flavorful base for the eggs and salsa. Serve with Refried Beans (page 523). You will need a 12-inch nonstick skillet with a tight-fitting lid for this recipe.

SALSA

- 3 jalapeño chiles, stemmed, halved, and seeded
- 1½ pounds plum tomatoes, cored and halved
- ½ onion, cut into ½-inch wedges
- 2 garlic cloves, peeled
- 2 tablespoons vegetable oil
- 1 tablespoon tomato paste
- Salt and pepper
- ½ teaspoon ground cumin
- ⅛ teaspoon cayenne pepper
- 3 tablespoons minced fresh cilantro
- 1–2 tablespoons lime juice plus lime wedges

TORTILLAS AND EGGS

- 4 (6-inch) corn tortillas
- 1 tablespoon vegetable oil
- Salt and pepper
- 4 large eggs

1. FOR THE SALSA: Adjust oven rack to middle position and heat oven to 375 degrees. Mince 1 jalapeño; set aside. Toss remaining 2 jalapeños, tomatoes, onion, garlic, oil, tomato paste, 1 teaspoon salt, cumin, and cayenne together in bowl. Arrange vegetables cut side down on rimmed baking sheet. Roast until tomatoes are tender and skins begin to shrivel and brown, 35 to 45 minutes.

2. Let roasted vegetables cool on baking sheet for 10 minutes. Process onion, garlic, and jalapeños in food processor until almost completely broken down, about 10 seconds. Add

For super-flavorful huevos rancheros, we poach the eggs directly in the heated salsa.

tomatoes and process until salsa is slightly chunky, about 10 seconds. Stir in minced jalapeño and 2 tablespoons cilantro. Season with salt, pepper, and lime juice to taste. (Salsa can be refrigerated for up to 1 day.)

3. FOR THE TORTILLAS AND EGGS: Increase oven temperature to 450 degrees. Brush both sides of each tortilla lightly with oil, sprinkle with salt, and place on clean baking sheet. Bake until tops just begin to color, 5 to 7 minutes. Flip tortillas and continue to bake until golden, 2 to 3 minutes. Remove tortillas from oven and cover baking sheet with aluminum foil to keep tortillas warm.

4. Meanwhile, bring salsa to gentle simmer in 12-inch nonstick skillet over medium heat. Off heat, make 4 shallow indentations (about 2 inches wide) in salsa using back of spoon. Crack 1 egg into each indentation and season eggs with salt and pepper. Cover and cook over medium-low heat until eggs are cooked through, 4 to 5 minutes for runny yolks or 6 to 7 minutes for set yolks.

5. Place tortillas on individual serving plates and gently top with cooked eggs. Spoon salsa around eggs to cover tortillas. Sprinkle with remaining 1 tablespoon cilantro. Serve with lime wedges.

Corned Beef Hash with Poached Eggs

SERVES 4   **TOTAL TIME** 40 MINUTES   **FAST**

✔ **WHY THIS RECIPE WORKS:** Many versions of this classic meat and potato breakfast require lots of prep but still end up soggy and greasy. We wanted to create a version that was flavorful and easy to prepare and that didn't take all morning to make. The key turned out to be getting some good browning on the potatoes, which made the difference between a hash with deep, hearty flavor and a hash that tasted mushy and bland. We started with frozen potatoes to save on prep time and gave them a head start by cooking them in the microwave before adding them to the skillet. Once the potatoes were in the skillet with the aromatics, we found that the trick to "hashing" was to pack them down so that they could brown on the bottom. We then used a spoon to flip browned portions of the mixture, packing everything down again and continuing to let the potatoes brown. This resulted in a hearty browned potato flavor throughout the entire dish. For the eggs, we poached them by simply nestling them into indentations we had made in the hash, covering the pan, and cooking them over low heat. Frozen hash browns come in several styles; we had the best results using cubed hash browns here (they are sometimes labeled "Southern" style). If you notice that the potatoes aren't getting brown in step 3, turn up the heat (but don't let them burn). Given the richness of this dish, we prefer to serve just one egg per person; however, you can nestle two eggs into each indentation and cook as directed. You will need a 12-inch nonstick skillet with a tight-fitting lid for this recipe.

    20 ounces (4 cups) frozen diced potatoes
     1 tablespoon vegetable oil
        Salt and pepper
     4 slices bacon, chopped
     1 onion, chopped fine
     2 garlic cloves, minced
    ½ teaspoon minced fresh thyme or ¼ teaspoon dried
    ⅓ cup heavy cream
    ¼ teaspoon hot sauce
    12 ounces thinly sliced corned beef, cut into
        ½-inch pieces
     4 large eggs

1. Microwave potatoes, oil, ½ teaspoon salt, and ¼ teaspoon pepper in covered bowl until hot, about 5 minutes.

2. Meanwhile, cook bacon in 12-inch nonstick skillet over medium-high heat until fat begins to render, about 2 minutes. Stir in onion and cook until softened and lightly browned, about 8 minutes.

3. Stir garlic and thyme into skillet and cook until fragrant, about 30 seconds. Stir in hot microwaved potatoes, cream, and hot sauce. Using back of spatula, gently pack potatoes into pan and cook undisturbed for 2 minutes. Flip hash, 1 portion at a time, and lightly repack into pan. Repeat flipping process every few minutes until potatoes are nicely browned, 6 to 8 minutes.

4. Stir in corned beef and lightly repack hash into pan. Off heat, make 4 shallow indentations (about 2 inches wide) in hash using back of spoon. Crack 1 egg into each indentation and season eggs with salt and pepper. Cover and cook over medium-low heat until eggs are cooked through, 4 to 5 minutes for runny yolks or 6 to 7 minutes for set yolks. Serve.

VARIATION

Sweet Potato Hash with Poached Eggs

Be sure to substitute sweet potatoes for just half of the potatoes here. If you try to replace all of the potatoes with sweet potatoes, the hash will have a very soft, mushy consistency.

Substitute 10 ounces frozen sweet potato fries, thawed and chopped coarse, for half of frozen diced potatoes. Substitute 12 ounces thinly sliced deli ham, cut into ½-inch pieces, for corned beef.

Adding Eggs to Hash

Off heat, make 4 shallow indentations (about 2 inches wide) in hash using back of spoon. Crack 1 egg into each indentation and season eggs with salt and pepper. Cover skillet and cook until eggs are cooked through.

NOTES FROM THE TEST KITCHEN

Freezing Bacon

Bacon is often sold by the pound or half-pound, but since many recipes call for just a few slices, you're bound to have some leftovers. And if you're not planning on cooking the rest soon, you may want to freeze it. But how can you freeze bacon so that you can use each slice as needed? We have found that the best way is simply to roll up each slice (or two slices together) tightly, put the rolled bacon in a zipper-lock bag, and freeze it. Then you can pull out the desired number of slices as you need them.

We kept the flavor but lost the grease by reducing the amount of oil in this Spanish suppertime omelet.

Spanish Tortilla with Roasted Red Peppers and Peas

SERVES 4 TO 6   **TOTAL TIME** 45 MINUTES   FAST

✓ **WHY THIS RECIPE WORKS:** This tapas bar favorite boasts meltingly tender potatoes in a dense, creamy omelet. But the typical recipe for Spanish tortilla calls for simmering the potatoes in up to 4 cups of extra-virgin olive oil. Using so much oil for this somewhat humble dish is just plain excessive. We found that cutting the amount of oil down to 6 tablespoons worked just as well. You still get all the flavor of the oil but none of the greasiness. Also, we found that firmer, less starchy Yukon Gold potatoes worked much better than the standard russets. Traditional recipes call for flipping the tortilla with the help of a single plate, but when we tried this the result was an egg-splattered floor. Sliding the omelet onto the plate and then using a second plate to flip it made a once-messy task foolproof. You will need a 10-inch nonstick skillet with a tight-fitting lid for this recipe.

6 tablespoons plus 1 teaspoon extra-virgin olive oil
1½ pounds Yukon Gold potatoes, peeled, quartered, and cut into ⅛-inch-thick slices
1 small onion, halved and sliced thin
  Salt and pepper
8 large eggs
½ cup jarred roasted red peppers, rinsed, patted dry, and cut into ½-inch pieces
½ cup frozen peas, thawed

1. Toss ¼ cup oil, potatoes, onion, ½ teaspoon salt, and ¼ teaspoon pepper together in bowl. Heat 2 tablespoons oil in 10-inch nonstick skillet over medium-high heat until shimmering. Add potato mixture to pan and reduce heat to medium-low. Cover and cook, stirring every 5 minutes, until potatoes are tender, about 25 minutes.

2. Whisk eggs and ½ teaspoon salt together in now-empty bowl, then gently fold in cooked potato mixture, red peppers, and peas. Make sure to scrape all of potato mixture out of skillet.

Flipping a Spanish Tortilla

1. After browning first side, loosen tortilla with heatproof rubber spatula and slide onto large plate.

2. Place second plate face down over tortilla. Invert tortilla onto second plate so that browned side faces up.

3. Slide tortilla back into pan, browned side up, then tuck edges into pan with rubber spatula.

3. Heat remaining 1 teaspoon oil in now-empty skillet over medium-high heat until just smoking. Add egg mixture and cook, shaking pan and folding mixture constantly for 15 seconds. Smooth top of egg mixture, reduce heat to medium, cover, and cook, gently shaking pan every 30 seconds, until bottom is golden brown and top is lightly set, about 2 minutes.

4. Off heat, run heatproof rubber spatula around edge of pan and shake pan gently to loosen tortilla; it should slide around freely in pan. Slide tortilla onto large plate, then invert onto second large plate and slide back into skillet browned side up. Tuck edges of tortilla into skillet with rubber spatula. Continue to cook over medium heat, gently shaking pan every 30 seconds, until second side is golden brown, about 2 minutes. Slide tortilla onto cutting board and let cool slightly. Serve warm or at room temperature.

Breakfast Strata with Spinach and Gruyère

SERVES 4 TO 6   **TOTAL TIME** 2 HOURS 15 MINUTES (PLUS 1 HOUR CHILLING TIME)

✔ **WHY THIS RECIPE WORKS:** Many recipes for this savory bread pudding are soggy and laden with excessive custard and ingredients, rendering this simple casserole an overindulgence in both preparation and consumption. Looking for a breakfast or brunch casserole that was simple, with just enough richness to satisfy, we started with the bread. Whole dried bread slices had the best texture and appearance, and buttering them added richness. We carefully selected a few complementary ingredients for the filling, then sautéed them to remove excess moisture and prevent the casserole from becoming waterlogged. Weighting the strata down overnight improved its texture, and we could bake it the following morning for a perfect make-ahead breakfast. The recipe can be doubled and assembled in a greased 13 by 9-inch baking dish; increase the baking time to 1 hour and 20 minutes. Substitute any semisoft melting cheese, such as Havarti, sharp cheddar, or Colby, for the Gruyère.

8–10 (½-inch-thick) slices French or Italian bread
   4 tablespoons unsalted butter, softened
   4 shallots, minced
      Salt and pepper
  10 ounces frozen chopped spinach, thawed and
      squeezed dry
   ½ cup dry white wine
   6 ounces Gruyère cheese, shredded (1½ cups)
   6 large eggs
  1¾ cups half-and-half

We sauté spinach with shallot and white wine then layer it with crisp bread slices and Gruyère for a simple breakfast casserole.

1. Adjust oven rack to middle position and heat oven to 225 degrees. Arrange bread in single layer on baking sheet and bake until dry and crisp, about 40 minutes, turning slices over halfway through baking. Let bread cool slightly, then butter 1 side of slices with 2 tablespoons butter.

2. Meanwhile, melt remaining 2 tablespoons butter in 10-inch nonstick skillet over medium heat. Add shallots and pinch salt and cook until softened, about 3 minutes. Stir in spinach and cook until warmed through, about 2 minutes; transfer to plate. Add wine to now-empty skillet and simmer over medium-high heat until it has reduced to ¼ cup, about 3 minutes; set aside to cool.

3. Grease 8-inch square baking dish. Arrange half of bread slices, buttered side up, in single layer in dish. Sprinkle half of spinach mixture and ½ cup Gruyère over top. Repeat with remaining bread, remaining spinach mixture, and ½ cup Gruyère to make second layer.

4. Whisk eggs, reduced wine, half-and-half, 1 teaspoon salt, and pinch pepper together in bowl, then pour evenly into dish. Cover dish tightly with plastic wrap, pressing it flush to surface of strata. Weight strata down and refrigerate for at least 1 hour or up to 1 day.

5. Remove strata from refrigerator and let sit at room temperature for 20 minutes. Meanwhile, adjust oven rack to middle position and heat oven to 325 degrees. Uncover strata and top with remaining ½ cup Gruyère. Bake until both edges and center are puffed and edges have pulled away slightly from sides of dish, 50 to 55 minutes. Let casserole cool for 5 minutes before serving.

VARIATION

Breakfast Strata with Sausage, Mushrooms, and Monterey Jack

Chorizo, kielbasa, or hot or sweet Italian sausage can be substituted for the breakfast sausage.

Omit spinach, and substitute Monterey Jack cheese for Gruyère. Before cooking shallots, add 8 ounces crumbled bulk breakfast sausage to skillet and cook until no longer pink, about 2 minutes. Stir in 8 ounces sliced white mushrooms and cook until they have released their moisture and are lightly browned, 5 to 10 minutes. Stir in shallots and continue to cook as directed.

Skillet Strata with Cheddar and Thyme

SERVES 4 TO 6   TOTAL TIME 35 MINUTES **FAST**

✓ **WHY THIS RECIPE WORKS:** Unlike a classic strata, which requires overnight time in the refrigerator, our fast strata recipe delivered the same cheesy richness in a fraction of the time. After numerous tests, we discovered the key was using fresh bread, not stale, and toasting it in the skillet. After the filling ingredients were sautéed, the fresh bread was added and cooked until lightly toasted so that it wouldn't turn to mush by the end of cooking. Then we added the custard mixture off the heat and finished the strata in the oven, producing a delicate souffléed texture, perfect for any meal. Do not trim the crusts from the bread or else the strata will be dense and eggy. You will need a 10-inch ovensafe nonstick skillet for this recipe.

6	**large eggs**
1½	**cups whole milk**
1	**teaspoon minced fresh thyme or ¼ teaspoon dried**
	Salt and pepper
4	**ounces sharp cheddar cheese, shredded (1 cup)**
4	**tablespoons unsalted butter**
1	**onion, chopped fine**
5	**slices hearty white sandwich bread, cut into 1-inch squares**

1. Adjust oven rack to middle position and heat oven to 425 degrees. Whisk eggs, milk, thyme, and ¼ teaspoon pepper together in bowl, then stir in cheddar.

2. Melt butter in 10-inch ovensafe nonstick skillet over medium-high heat. Add onion and ½ teaspoon salt and cook until onion is softened and lightly browned, about 6 minutes. Stir in bread until evenly coated and cook, stirring occasionally, until bread is lightly toasted, about 3 minutes.

3. Off heat, fold in egg mixture until slightly thickened and well combined with bread. Gently press on top of strata to help it soak up egg mixture. Transfer skillet to oven and cook until center of strata is puffed and edges have browned and pulled away slightly from sides of pan, about 12 minutes. Serve.

Making a Skillet Strata

1. COOK ONION: Melt butter in 10-inch ovensafe nonstick skillet over medium-high heat. Add onion and salt and cook until onion is softened and lightly browned, about 6 minutes.

2. TOAST BREAD: Stir in bread until evenly coated, and cook, stirring occasionally, until lightly toasted, about 3 minutes.

3. ADD EGG MIXTURE: Off heat, fold in egg mixture until slightly thickened and well combined with bread. Gently press on top of strata to help it soak up egg mixture.

4. FINISH IN OVEN: Transfer skillet to oven and cook until center of strata is puffed and edges have browned and pulled away slightly from sides of pan.

Skillet Strata with Spinach and Smoked Gouda

Removing the excess moisture from the spinach is important here.

Whisk 10 ounces frozen chopped spinach, thawed and squeezed dry, into egg mixture. After toasting bread in step 2, stir in 2 minced garlic cloves and cook until fragrant, about 30 seconds. Substitute shredded smoked gouda cheese for cheddar.

Skillet Strata with Sausage and Gruyère

Reduce butter to 1 tablespoon and add 8 ounces crumbled bulk breakfast sausage to skillet with onion in step 2. Substitute shredded Gruyère or Swiss cheese for cheddar.

Skillet Strata with Bacon, Scallions, and Pepper Jack

Omit thyme. Substitute 4 slices bacon, chopped fine, for butter. Cook bacon in skillet over medium-high heat until fat begins to render, about 2 minutes, before adding onion. Substitute pepper Jack cheese for cheddar. Before serving, sprinkle with 2 thinly sliced scallions.

Tofu Scramble with Shallot and Herbs

SERVES 4   TOTAL TIME 20 MINUTES   FAST

✔ **WHY THIS RECIPE WORKS:** Recipes for tofu scrambles are numerous, but most result in nothing but bland and boring imitations of scrambled eggs. We wanted a recipe that offered a creamy, egglike texture and a subtle, satisfying flavor. Soft tofu proved to have a texture closest to eggs, yielding pieces that, when crumbled, were smoother than crumbled firm tofu. A small amount of curry powder was key, contributing depth of flavor and a nice touch of color, without overwhelming the dish with actual curry flavor. We also found that the tofu could be crumbled into smaller or larger pieces to resemble egg curds of different sizes. Once we had perfected scrambled tofu, we came up with a few hearty variations. Do not substitute firm tofu for the soft tofu in this recipe. Be sure to press the tofu dry thoroughly before cooking.

1½ teaspoons vegetable oil
1 shallot, minced
14 ounces soft tofu, pressed dry with paper towels and crumbled into ¼- to ½-inch pieces
¼ teaspoon curry powder
¾ teaspoon salt

⅛ teaspoon pepper
2 tablespoons minced fresh basil, parsley, tarragon, or marjoram

Heat oil in 10-inch nonstick skillet over medium heat until shimmering. Add shallot and cook until softened, about 2 minutes. Stir in crumbled tofu, curry powder, salt, and pepper, and cook until tofu is hot, about 2 minutes. Off heat, stir in basil and serve.

Tofu Scramble with Spinach and Feta

Before adding tofu to skillet, add 4 cups baby spinach and cook until wilted, about 1 minute. Add ½ cup crumbled feta cheese to pan with tofu.

Tofu Scramble with Tomato, Scallions, and Parmesan

Add 1 seeded and finely chopped tomato and 1 minced garlic clove to pan with shallot; cook until tomato is no longer wet, 3 to 5 minutes. Add ¼ cup grated Parmesan cheese and 2 tablespoons minced scallions to pan with tofu.

Tofu Scramble with Shiitakes, Red Bell Pepper, and Goat Cheese

Before adding shallot to pan, cook 4 ounces stemmed and thinly sliced shiitake mushrooms, 1 finely chopped small red bell pepper, and pinch red pepper flakes, covered, until mushrooms have released their liquid, about 5 minutes. Uncover, add shallot, and continue to cook until mushrooms are dry and shallot is softened, about 2 minutes. Add ¼ cup crumbled goat cheese to pan with tofu.

Classic Buttermilk Pancakes

SERVES 4 TO 6   TOTAL TIME 25 MINUTES   FAST

✔ **WHY THIS RECIPE WORKS:** No one wants to ruin a Saturday morning pancake breakfast with tough, rubbery, bland pancakes. We set out to deliver perfectly light and fluffy pancakes with good flavor. Buttermilk was a must in our recipe—it not only lent flavor but also created pancakes with better texture, especially since we opted to use both baking powder and baking soda. To keep our pancakes as light and fluffy as possible, we made sure to avoid overmixing the batter, which would overdevelop the gluten and make the pancakes tough. We stopped stirring when the batter was lumpy and a few streaks of flour were still visible. A well-heated skillet also proved critical for avoiding dense, pale pancakes. Since using too much oil in the skillet would turn our delicate pancakes greasy and dense, we used a heatproof pastry brush or paper towels to distribute a small amount of oil over the cooking surface. We knew the first side was cooked as soon as bubbles appeared on the surface of the batter; the second side likewise needed just a short stint until the pancakes were golden brown. Getting the skillet hot enough before making the pancakes is key.

FRUIT PANCAKE TOPPINGS

To dress up pancakes, it's easy to throw together a few quick fruit toppings by softening the fruits in the microwave with a little sugar while the pancakes cook. All these toppings make 2½ to 3 cups.

DIRECTIONS: Combine all ingredients in bowl and microwave until fruits are softened but not mushy and juices are slightly thickened, 4 to 6 minutes, stirring once halfway through microwaving. Remove from microwave and stir, adding any fresh berries if called for. Serve.

APPLE-CRANBERRY PANCAKE TOPPING `FAST`

- 3   golden delicious apples, peeled, halved, cored, and cut into ¼-inch pieces
- ¼   cup dried cranberries
- 1   tablespoon sugar
- 1   teaspoon cornstarch
  - Pinch salt
  - Pinch ground nutmeg

PEAR-BLACKBERRY PANCAKE TOPPING `FAST`

- 3   ripe pears, peeled, halved, cored, and cut into ¼-inch pieces
- 1   tablespoon sugar
- 1   teaspoon cornstarch
  - Pinch salt
  - Pinch ground cardamom
- 5   ounces (1 cup) blackberries, berries more than 1 inch long cut in half crosswise

PLUM-APRICOT PANCAKE TOPPING `FAST`

- 1½   pounds plums, halved, pitted, and cut into ¼-inch pieces
- ¼   cup dried apricots, chopped coarse
- 1   tablespoon sugar
- 1   teaspoon cornstarch
  - Pinch salt
  - Pinch ground cinnamon

- 2   cups (10 ounces) all-purpose flour
- 2   tablespoons sugar
- 2   teaspoons baking powder
- ½   teaspoon baking soda
- ½   teaspoon salt
- 2   cups buttermilk
- 3   tablespoons unsalted butter, melted and cooled
- 1   large egg
- 1–2   teaspoons vegetable oil

1. Adjust oven rack to middle position and heat oven to 200 degrees. Spray wire rack with vegetable oil spray, set in rimmed baking sheet, and place in oven.

2. Whisk flour, sugar, baking powder, baking soda, and salt together in large bowl. Whisk buttermilk, melted butter, and egg together in large measuring cup. Make well in center of dry ingredients, add wet ingredients to well, and gently stir until just combined. Do not overmix; batter should be lumpy with few streaks of flour.

3. Heat 1 teaspoon oil in 12-inch nonstick skillet over medium heat until shimmering. Using paper towels, carefully wipe out oil, leaving thin film of oil on bottom and sides of pan. Using ¼-cup measure, portion batter into pan in 3 places. Cook until edges are set, first side is golden, and bubbles on surface are just beginning to break, 2 to 3 minutes.

4. Flip pancakes and continue to cook until second side is golden, 1 to 2 minutes. Serve immediately or transfer to wire rack in oven. Repeat with remaining batter, using remaining oil as necessary.

VARIATIONS

Blueberry Buttermilk Pancakes
Frozen blueberries can be substituted for fresh; thaw and rinse the berries gently to remove excess juice, then spread out on paper towels to absorb excess moisture before using.

After adding batter to skillet in step 3, sprinkle 1 tablespoon fresh blueberries over each pancake; cook pancakes as directed. (You will need 1 cup blueberries.)

Cornmeal Buttermilk Pancakes
Substitute 1½ cups cornmeal for 1 cup flour.

Buttermilk Grahamcakes
Process 5 ounces graham crackers (9 crackers) and 2 tablespoons cornmeal in food processor to fine crumbs, about 10 to 15 seconds. Substitute graham crumbs for 1 cup all-purpose flour.

Muesli ground into flour is the secret ingredient in these apple-cranberry-topped multigrain pancakes.

Multigrain Pancakes

SERVES 4 TO 6   **TOTAL TIME** 30 MINUTES   `FAST`

✔ **WHY THIS RECIPE WORKS:** Bland, dense, and gummy, most multigrain pancakes are more about appeasing your diet than pleasing your palate. We wanted flavorful, fluffy, and healthful flapjacks. After testing lots of grains, we found that muesli had all the ingredients and flavor we wanted in one convenient package—raw whole oats, wheat germ, rye, barley, toasted nuts, and dried fruit. But pancakes made with whole muesli were too chewy and gummy. We converted the muesli into a flour in the food processor and then found the perfect combination of muesli "flour," all-purpose flour, whole-wheat flour, and leavening to achieve the lightness we wanted. The pancakes were perfect after we tweaked the flavor with a little butter, vanilla, and brown sugar, and cut the acidity by replacing the buttermilk with a blend of milk and lemon juice. The pancakes can be cooked on an electric griddle. Set the griddle temperature to 350 degrees and cook as directed. Familia brand no-sugar-added muesli is the best choice for this recipe. If you can't find Familia, look for Alpen or any

Making Better Pancakes

Here are our tips for getting perfectly fluffy, golden-brown pancakes every time.

MAKE A WELL WHEN MIXING: Make a well in the center of the dry ingredients, pour the liquid ingredients into the well, and gently whisk together until just incorporated. We like this method when making liquidy batters, because it helps incorporate the wet ingredients into the dry without overmixing.

LEAVE SOME LUMPS: When stirring the batter, be careful not to overmix it—the batter should actually have a few lumps. Overmixed batter makes for dense pancakes.

GET THE SKILLET HOT BUT NOT SCORCHING: Heat the oil in a 12-inch nonstick skillet over medium heat for 3 to 5 minutes. If the skillet is not hot enough, the pancakes will be pale and dense. Knowing when the skillet is hot enough can take some practice; if you're not sure if the skillet is ready, try cooking just one small pancake to check.

WIPE OUT EXCESS OIL: Before adding the batter, use a wad of paper towels to carefully wipe out the excess oil, leaving a thin film of oil in the pan. If you use too much oil, the delicate cakes will taste greasy and dense.

USE A ¼-CUP MEASURE: Add the batter to the skillet in ¼-cup increments (two or three pancakes will fit at a time). Using a measuring cup ensures that the pancakes are the same size and that they cook at the same rate. Don't crowd the pan or the pancakes will run together and be difficult to flip.

FLIP WHEN YOU SEE BUBBLES: Cook the pancakes on the first side until large bubbles begin to appear, about 2 minutes. The bubbles indicate that the pancakes are ready to be flipped. If the pancakes are not browned when flipped, the skillet needs to be hotter; if the pancakes are too brown, turn down the heat.

no-sugar-added muesli. (If you can't find muesli without sugar, muesli with sugar added will work; reduce the brown sugar in the recipe to 1 tablespoon.) Mix the batter first and then heat the pan. Letting the batter sit while the pan heats will give the dry ingredients time to absorb the wet ingredients; otherwise, the batter will be runny.

2 cups whole milk

4 teaspoons lemon juice

1¼ cups (6 ounces) plus 3 tablespoons no-sugar-added muesli

¾ cup (3¾ ounces) all-purpose flour

½ cup (2¾ ounces) whole-wheat flour

2 tablespoons packed brown sugar

2¼ teaspoons baking powder

½ teaspoon baking soda

½ teaspoon salt

2 large eggs

3 tablespoons unsalted butter, melted and cooled

¾ teaspoon vanilla extract

1–2 teaspoons vegetable oil

1. Adjust oven rack to middle position and heat oven to 200 degrees. Spray wire rack with vegetable oil spray, set in rimmed baking sheet, and place in oven. Whisk milk and lemon juice together in large measuring cup; set aside to thicken while preparing other ingredients.

2. Process 1¼ cups muesli in food processor until finely ground, 2 to 2½ minutes. In large bowl, whisk processed muesli, remaining 3 tablespoons unground muesli, all-purpose flour, whole-wheat flour, sugar, baking powder, baking soda, and salt together.

3. Whisk eggs, melted butter, and vanilla into thickened milk mixture. Make well in center of dry ingredients, add wet ingredients to well, and gently stir until just combined. Do not overmix; batter should be lumpy with few streaks of flour.

4. Heat 1 teaspoon oil in 12-inch nonstick skillet over medium heat until shimmering. Using paper towels, carefully wipe out oil, leaving thin film of oil on bottom and sides of pan. Using ¼-cup measure, portion batter into pan in 4 places. Cook until small bubbles begin to appear evenly over surface, 2 to 3 minutes.

5. Flip pancakes and cook until second side is golden, 1½ to 2 minutes. Serve pancakes immediately or transfer to wire rack in oven. Repeat with remaining batter, using remaining oil as necessary.

Buttermilk Waffles

SERVES 4   **TOTAL TIME** 30 MINUTES   FAST

❤ **WHY THIS RECIPE WORKS:** Most waffle recipes are merely repurposed pancake recipes that rely on butter and maple syrup to mask the mediocre results. Our waffles had to have a crisp, golden-brown crust with a moist, fluffy interior. We started by trying to adapt our Classic Buttermilk Pancakes

Seltzer water gives our crunchy waffles lift, while baking soda helps them brown.

recipe (page 543). The result: the terrific flavor we expected, but a gummy, wet interior and not much crust. We needed a drier batter with much more leavening oomph. In tempura batters, seltzer is often used because the tiny bubbles inflate the batter the same way that a chemical leavener does. We tried replacing the buttermilk with a mixture of seltzer and powdered buttermilk, plus baking soda for browning. The resulting waffles were light and perfectly browned, but they lost their crispness after only a few moments off the heat. After some experimentation, we found that waffles made with oil stayed significantly crispier than those made with melted butter, which is partly water. While the waffles can be eaten as soon as they are removed from the waffle iron, they will have a crispier exterior if rested in a warm oven for 10 minutes. (This method also makes it possible to serve everyone at the same time.) Buttermilk powder is available in most supermarkets and is generally located near the dried-milk products or in the baking aisle. Leftover powdered buttermilk can be kept in the refrigerator for up to a year. Seltzer or club soda gives these waffles a light texture that would otherwise be provided by whipped egg whites. (Avoid sparkling water such as Perrier—it's not bubbly enough.) Use a freshly opened bottle of seltzer for maximum lift.

2 cups (10 ounces) all-purpose flour
½ cup powdered buttermilk
1 tablespoon sugar
¾ teaspoon salt
½ teaspoon baking soda
½ cup sour cream
2 large eggs
¼ teaspoon vanilla extract
¼ cup vegetable oil
1¼ cups unflavored seltzer water

1. Adjust oven rack to middle position and heat oven to 200 degrees. Set wire rack in rimmed baking sheet and place in oven.

2. Whisk flour, buttermilk powder, sugar, salt, and baking soda together in large bowl. In separate bowl, whisk sour cream, eggs, vanilla, and oil together, then gently stir in seltzer. Make well in center of dry ingredients, add wet ingredients to well, and gently stir until just combined. Do not overmix; batter should be lumpy with few streaks of flour.

3. Heat waffle iron and cook waffles according to manufacturer's instructions (use about ⅓ cup batter for 7-inch round iron). Serve immediately or transfer to wire rack in oven to keep warm while cooking remaining waffles.

Yeasted Waffles

SERVES 4   **TOTAL TIME** 45 MINUTES
(PLUS 12 HOURS TO REFRIGERATE BATTER)

✔ **WHY THIS RECIPE WORKS:** Raised waffles are barely on the current culinary radar, and that's a shame. They sound old-fashioned and require advance planning, but they are crisp, tasty, and easy to prepare. We wanted to revive this breakfast treat with yeasted waffles that were creamy and airy, tangy, and refined and complex. We settled on all-purpose flour, found the right amount of yeast to provide a pleasant tang, and added a full stick of melted butter for rich flavor. Refrigerating the batter overnight kept the growth of the yeast under control and produced waffles with superior flavor. Now all we had to do in the morning was heat up the waffle iron. While the waffles can be eaten as soon as they are removed from the iron, they will have a crispier exterior if rested in a warm oven for 10 minutes. (This method also makes it possible to serve everyone at the same time.) This batter must be made 12 to 24 hours in advance.

1¾ cups milk
8 tablespoons unsalted butter, cut into 8 pieces
2 cups (10 ounces) all-purpose flour

1 tablespoon sugar
1½ teaspoons instant or rapid-rise yeast
1 teaspoon salt
2 large eggs
1 teaspoon vanilla extract

1. Heat milk and butter in small saucepan over medium-low heat until butter is melted, 3 to 5 minutes. Let mixture cool until warm to touch.

2. Whisk flour, sugar, yeast, and salt together in large bowl. In small bowl, whisk eggs and vanilla together. Gradually whisk warm milk mixture into flour mixture until smooth, then whisk in egg mixture. Scrape down bowl with rubber spatula, cover tightly with plastic wrap, and refrigerate for at least 12 hours or up to 1 day.

3. Adjust oven rack to middle position and heat oven to 200 degrees. Set wire rack in rimmed baking sheet and place in oven. Heat waffle iron according to manufacturer's instructions. Remove batter from refrigerator when waffle iron is hot (batter will be foamy and doubled in size). Whisk batter to recombine (batter will deflate).

4. Cook waffles according to manufacturer's instructions (use about ½ cup batter for 7-inch round iron and about 1 cup batter for 9-inch square iron). Serve immediately or transfer to wire rack in oven to keep warm while cooking remaining waffles.

VARIATION
Blueberry Yeasted Waffles
We found that frozen wild blueberries—which are smaller—work best here. Larger blueberries release too much juice.

After removing waffle batter from refrigerator in step 3, gently fold 1½ cups frozen blueberries into batter.

NOTES FROM THE TEST KITCHEN

Shopping for Maple Syrup

All pure maple syrup is simply reduced sap from the sugar maple tree, but the supermarket still presents a variety of options. Syrup is separated into grades based on color, although individual states and countries employ different labeling standards. Two common categories are grade A and grade B. Grade A is the purest and most mild syrup from early in the season. It comes in light, medium, and dark varieties. Grade B is noticeably darker with a more assertive flavor, which makes it great for baking, but the two grades are interchangeable in our recipes. Our favorite syrup is a dark grade A that is good for cooking and the breakfast table. Note that we do not recommend so-called pancake syrup, which is artificially flavored corn syrup that often contains no real maple syrup at all.

French Toast

SERVES 4   **TOTAL TIME** 55 MINUTES

☑ **WHY THIS RECIPE WORKS:** French toast just isn't worth the trouble if the result is soggy, too eggy, or just plain bland. Our first task was to find out which type of bread fared best in a typical batter. Hearty white sandwich bread, dried in a low oven, produced French toast that was crisp on the outside and velvety on the inside, with no trace of sogginess. However, the toast still tasted more like scrambled eggs. Cutting out the egg whites and adding melted butter to the soaking liquid made a huge difference, turning the toast rich and custardlike. For a final touch, we flavored the toast with cinnamon, vanilla, and brown sugar. To prevent the butter from clumping during mixing, warm the milk in the microwave or a small saucepan until warm to the touch (about 80 degrees). The French toast can be cooked all at once on an electric griddle, but it may take an extra 2 to 3 minutes per side. Set the griddle temperature to 350 degrees and use the entire amount of butter (4 tablespoons) for cooking.

- 8 large slices hearty white sandwich bread or challah
- 1½ cups whole milk, warmed
- 3 large egg yolks
- 3 tablespoons packed light brown sugar
- 2 tablespoons unsalted butter plus 2 tablespoons melted
- 1 tablespoon vanilla extract
- ½ teaspoon ground cinnamon
- ¼ teaspoon salt

1. Adjust oven rack to middle position and heat oven to 300 degrees. Place bread on wire rack set in rimmed baking sheet. Bake bread until almost dry throughout (center should remain slightly moist), about 15 minutes, flipping slices halfway through baking. Remove bread from rack and let cool for 5 minutes. Return baking sheet with wire rack to oven and reduce temperature to 200 degrees.

2. Whisk milk, egg yolks, sugar, 2 tablespoons melted butter, vanilla, cinnamon, and salt together in bowl. Transfer mixture to 13 by 9-inch baking pan.

3. Soak bread in milk mixture until saturated but not falling apart, 20 seconds per side. Using firm slotted spatula, remove bread from milk mixture, 1 piece at a time, allowing excess milk mixture to drip back into pan, and transfer to clean rimmed baking sheet in single layer.

4. Melt ½ tablespoon butter in 12-inch skillet over medium-low heat. Using slotted spatula, transfer 2 slices soaked bread to skillet and cook until golden on first side, 3 to 4 minutes. Flip and continue to cook until second side is golden, 3 to 4 minutes. Transfer toast to wire rack in oven. Wipe out skillet with paper towels and repeat with remaining bread, 2 pieces at a time, adding ½ tablespoon butter to skillet for each batch. Serve.

VARIATIONS

Extra-Crisp French Toast
Pulse 1 slice hearty white sandwich bread or challah, torn into 1-inch pieces, 1 tablespoon packed light brown sugar, and ¼ teaspoon ground cinnamon in food processor until finely ground, 8 to 12 pulses (you should have about ½ cup). Sprinkle 1 tablespoon processed crumb mixture over 1 side of each slice of soaked bread. Cook as directed, starting with crumb mixture side down.

Almond-Crusted French Toast
Pulse ½ cup slivered almonds and 1 tablespoon packed light brown sugar in food processor until coarsely ground, 12 to 15 pulses (you should have about ½ cup). Add 1 tablespoon triple sec and 1 teaspoon grated orange zest to milk mixture in step 2. Sprinkle 1 tablespoon processed nut mixture over 1 side of each slice of soaked bread. Cook as directed, starting with nut mixture side down.

Pecan-Rum French Toast
Substitute 8 large slices cinnamon-raisin bread for hearty white sandwich bread. Pulse ½ cup pecans, 1 tablespoon packed light brown sugar, and ¼ teaspoon ground cinnamon in food processor until coarsely ground, 12 to 15 pulses (you should have about ½ cup). Add 2 teaspoons dark rum to milk mixture in step 2. Sprinkle 1 tablespoon processed nut mixture over 1 side of each slice of soaked bread. Cook as directed, starting with nut mixture side down.

Soaking French Toast

Soak bread in milk mixture until saturated but not falling apart, 20 seconds per side, using slotted spatula to help flip bread.

French Toast Casserole

SERVES 6 TO 8   **TOTAL TIME** 2 HOURS 10 MINUTES
(PLUS 8 HOURS TO REFRIGERATE CASSEROLE)

✔ **WHY THIS RECIPE WORKS:** The ideal French toast casserole has layers of rich, creamy custard and soft pieces of bread, all covered by a sweet topping of brown sugar, butter, and pecans. With this clear goal, we began our recipe testing with the bread. We found that French and Italian loaves, with their dense texture and thin, chewy crust, worked best. We also found that the casserole recipe was best when we "staled" the bread in a moderately hot oven, allowing it to toast slightly before assembling the dish. For the custard, we settled on eight whole eggs and a little less than twice as much whole milk as heavy cream, which gave us a rich and custardy but not cloying result. This was breakfast, after all, not dessert. Do not substitute low-fat or skim milk for the whole milk in this recipe. Walnuts can be substituted for the pecans. Be sure to use supermarket-style loaf bread with a thin crust and fluffy crumb; artisan loaves with a thick crust and a chewy crumb don't work well here. The casserole needs to sit in the refrigerator, well covered, for at least 8 hours in order to achieve the desired consistency.

For this rich, sweet breakfast casserole, we dry out the bread slices in the oven before adding the custard.

1	(16-ounce) loaf supermarket French or Italian bread, torn into 1-inch pieces
8	large eggs
2½	cups whole milk
1½	cups heavy cream
1	tablespoon granulated sugar
2	teaspoons vanilla extract
½	teaspoon ground cinnamon
½	teaspoon ground nutmeg
8	tablespoons unsalted butter, softened
1⅓	cups packed (9⅓ ounces) light brown sugar
3	tablespoons light corn syrup
2	cups pecans, chopped coarse

1. Adjust oven racks to upper-middle and lower-middle positions and heat oven to 325 degrees. Spread bread out over 2 baking sheets and bake until dry and light golden, about 25 minutes, switching and rotating baking sheets halfway through baking time. Let bread cool completely.

2. Grease 13 by 9-inch baking dish, then pack dried bread into dish. Whisk eggs in large bowl until combined, then whisk in milk, cream, granulated sugar, vanilla, cinnamon, and nutmeg. Pour egg mixture evenly over bread and press on bread lightly to submerge. Wrap dish tightly with plastic wrap and refrigerate for at least 8 hours or up to 1 day.

3. Stir butter, brown sugar, and corn syrup together in bowl until smooth, then stir in pecans. (Topping can be refrigerated for up to 1 day.)

4. Adjust oven rack to middle position and heat oven to 350 degrees. Unwrap casserole and sprinkle evenly with topping, breaking apart any large clumps. Place casserole on rimmed baking sheet and bake until puffed and golden, about 1 hour. Let casserole cool for 10 minutes before serving.

VARIATION

Rum-Raisin French Toast Casserole

While bread dries, microwave 1½ cups raisins and 1 cup rum in covered bowl until boiling, 1 to 2 minutes. Let sit, covered, until raisins are plump, about 15 minutes. Drain raisins thoroughly, discarding excess rum. Sprinkle raisins between bread pieces when assembling casserole in step 2.

Oven-Fried Bacon

SERVES 4 TO 6   **TOTAL TIME** 25 MINUTES **FAST**

👍 **WHY THIS RECIPE WORKS:** Most of us cook bacon by frying it in a pan, but controlling the temperature of a pan on the stovetop takes patience and constant attention, and even then it sometimes seems impossible to avoid getting raw and burnt spots. We'd heard that oven-fried bacon is just as good as fried bacon on the stovetop but without the constant tending and the splattering fat, so we thought it was worth a try. The result? Cooking bacon in the oven was in fact just as good, and it even had a couple of advantages. The oven offered a larger margin of error than the frying pan for perfectly cooked bacon. It also cooked the bacon strips more consistently, without raw or burnt spots. And the only tending needed was rotating the pan halfway through cooking. Oven-frying does take a couple of minutes longer than pan-frying (10 to 12 minutes for 12 strips), but you get perfectly crisp, evenly cooked bacon with no hassle. A large rimmed baking sheet is important here to contain the rendered bacon fat. If cooking more than one tray of bacon, switch their oven positions when you rotate them about halfway through cooking. You can use thin- or thick-cut bacon here, though the cooking times will vary.

12   slices bacon

Adjust oven rack to middle position and heat oven to 400 degrees. Arrange bacon slices in single layer in rimmed baking sheet. Bake bacon until fat begins to render, 5 to 6 minutes. Rotate pan and continue to bake until bacon is crisp and brown, 5 to 6 minutes for thin-cut bacon, 8 to 10 minutes for thick-cut bacon. Transfer bacon to paper towel–lined plate, let drain, and serve.

Classic Hash Browns

SERVES 4   **TOTAL TIME** 25 MINUTES **FAST**

👍 **WHY THIS RECIPE WORKS:** A side of freshly made hash browns seems to be a rare breakfast treat these days. We wanted to bring these thin, crisply sautéed potato cakes back to the breakfast table with a great recipe. High-starch russet potatoes worked best; they adhered well, browned beautifully, and had the most pronounced potato flavor. And we found there was no need to precook the potatoes—raw grated potatoes (squeezed of their moisture) held together while cooking and had a tender interior as well as plenty of potato flavor and an attractive, deeply browned crust. Cooked in a sizzling hot pan

We use russet potatoes, shredded and squeezed of excess moisture, to make these classic hash browns.

with melted butter, these were the very best that hash browns have to offer. We prefer hash browns prepared with potatoes that have been cut with the large shredding disk of a food processor, but a box grater can also be used. To prevent potatoes from turning brown, grate them just before cooking. Flipping the hash browns in step 3 is a lot like flipping our Spanish Tortilla; see page 540.

1   pound russet potatoes, peeled and shredded
¼   teaspoon salt
    Pinch pepper
2   tablespoons unsalted butter

1. Wrap shredded potatoes in clean dish towel and squeeze thoroughly of excess moisture. Toss potatoes with salt and pepper in bowl.

2. Meanwhile, melt 1 tablespoon butter in 10-inch skillet over medium-high heat until it begins to brown, swirling to coat pan. Scatter potatoes evenly into pan and press to flatten. Reduce heat to medium and cook until dark golden and crisp, 7 to 8 minutes.

3. Slide hash browns onto large plate. Add remaining 1 tablespoon butter to skillet and melt, swirling to coat pan. Invert hash browns onto second plate and slide, browned side up, back into skillet. Continue to cook over medium heat until bottom is dark golden and crisp, 5 to 6 minutes.

4. Fold hash brown cake in half and cook for 1 minute longer. Slide onto serving platter or cutting board, cut into wedges, and serve immediately.

VARIATION

Hash Brown "Omelet" with Cheddar, Tomato, and Basil

After melting butter in step 3 and sliding potatoes back into skillet, top hash browns with 1 seeded and finely chopped tomato, ¼ cup shredded cheddar cheese, and 1 tablespoon chopped fresh basil. Proceed with recipe, folding potato cake in half and cooking until cheese melts.

Home Fries

SERVES 6 TO 8   **TOTAL TIME** 1 HOUR

✔ **WHY THIS RECIPE WORKS:** Making home fries the traditional way means standing over a hot skillet, after which you get only three servings at most. We wanted a quicker, more hands-off method for making a larger amount. To speed things up, we developed a hybrid cooking technique: First, we parboiled diced russet potatoes, and then we coated them in butter and cooked them in a very hot oven. We discovered that boiling the potatoes with baking soda quickly breaks down their exterior while leaving their insides nearly raw, ensuring home fries with a crisp, brown crust and a moist, fluffy interior. We finished the home fries with diced onions, and then chives to reinforce the onion flavor. Don't skip the baking soda in this recipe. It's critical for home fries with just the right crisp texture.

3½ **pounds russet potatoes, peeled and cut into**
    ¾-inch dice
½   **teaspoon baking soda**
3   **tablespoons unsalted butter, cut into 12 pieces**
    Kosher salt and pepper
    Pinch cayenne pepper
3   **tablespoons vegetable oil**
2   **onions, cut into ½-inch dice**
3   **tablespoons minced fresh chives**

1. Adjust oven rack to lowest position, place rimmed baking sheet on rack, and heat oven to 500 degrees.

We discovered the secret to crisp home fries is to first parboil the potatoes with baking soda.

2. Bring 10 cups water to boil in Dutch oven over high heat. Add potatoes and baking soda. Return to boil and cook for 1 minute. Drain potatoes. Return potatoes to Dutch oven and place over low heat. Cook, shaking pot occasionally, until any surface moisture has evaporated, about 2 minutes. Remove from heat. Add butter, 1½ teaspoons salt, and cayenne; mix with rubber spatula until potatoes are coated with thick, starchy paste, about 30 seconds.

3. Remove baking sheet from oven and drizzle with 2 tablespoons oil. Transfer potatoes to baking sheet and spread into even layer. Roast for 15 minutes. While potatoes roast, combine onions, remaining 1 tablespoon oil, and ½ teaspoon salt in bowl.

4. Remove baking sheet from oven. Using thin, sharp metal spatula, scrape and turn potatoes. Clear about 8 by 5-inch space in center of baking sheet and add onion mixture. Roast for 15 minutes.

5. Scrape and turn again, mixing onions into potatoes. Continue to roast until potatoes are well browned and onions are softened and beginning to brown, 5 to 10 minutes. Stir in chives and season with salt and pepper to taste. Serve immediately.

MICROWAVED BACON

SERVES 4 TO 6   **TOTAL TIME** 20 MINUTES **FAST**

1 pound bacon (16 slices), thin or thick-cut

Place at least 4 layers of paper towels on microwave floor or turntable, or on plate. Arrange half of bacon in single layer on paper towels and cover with at least 2 more layers of paper towels. Cook at 70 percent power for 5 minutes. Check bacon for doneness and continue to cook in 30-second increments, as needed, until bacon is crisp and browned, about 3 minutes. Replace the paper towels and repeat with remaining bacon.

NOTES FROM THE TEST KITCHEN

Understanding Oats

We found only one type of oat that was just right for our ideal bowl of oatmeal. Also called Scottish or Irish oats, steel-cut oats are simply whole oats that have been cut into smaller pieces. They take longer to cook than regular rolled oats, but the outcome is worth the wait—and with our easy recipe, most of the time is hands-off. The hot cereal made with steel-cut oats had a faint nutty flavor, and while its consistency was surprisingly creamy, it also had a pleasing chewy quality. Rolled oats, on the other hand, resulted in bland, gummy oatmeal.

	UNCOOKED	COOKED
Oat Groats	Whole oats hulled and cleaned	These have a flavor reminiscent of brown rice and a very coarse texture.
Steel-Cut Oats	Groats cut crosswise into a few pieces	These make a creamy yet chewy hot cereal with a nutty flavor.
Rolled Oats	Groats steamed and pressed into flat flakes; also known as old-fashioned or regular	These American-style oats make a drab, gummy bowl of oatmeal.
Quick Oats	Groats rolled extra-thin	Cooked, these are flavorless and quick to cool into a flabby, pastelike consistency.
Instant Oats	Precooked rolled oats	These make a gummy, gelatinous cereal.

We soak steel-cut oats overnight to soften the grains and reduce their cooking time the next morning.

Overnight Steel-Cut Oatmeal

SERVES 4   **TOTAL TIME** 30 MINUTES (PLUS OVERNIGHT SOAKING)

✔ **WHY THIS RECIPE WORKS:** Most oatmeal fans agree that the steel-cut version of the grain offers the best flavor and texture, but many balk at the 40-minute cooking time. In this recipe, we considerably decrease the cooking time by stirring steel-cut oats into boiling water the night before. This enables the grains to hydrate and soften overnight. In the morning, more water (or fruit juice or milk) is added and the mixture is simmered for 4 to 6 minutes, until thick and creamy. A brief resting period off the heat ensures that the porridge achieves the perfect consistency. The oatmeal will continue to thicken as it cools. If you prefer a looser consistency, thin the oatmeal with boiling water.

4 cups water
1 cup steel-cut oats
¼ teaspoon salt

1. Bring 3 cups water to boil in large saucepan over high heat. Remove pan from heat; stir in oats and salt. Cover pan and let stand overnight.

2. Stir remaining 1 cup water into oats and bring to boil over medium-high heat. Reduce heat to medium and cook, stirring occasionally, until oats are softened but still retain some chew and mixture thickens and resembles warm pudding, 4 to 6 minutes. Remove pan from heat and let stand for 5 minutes before serving.

VARIATIONS

Apple-Cinnamon Overnight Steel-Cut Oatmeal

Substitute ½ cup apple cider and ½ cup whole milk for water in step 2. Stir ½ cup peeled and grated sweet apple, 2 tablespoons packed dark brown sugar, and ½ teaspoon ground cinnamon into oatmeal with cider and milk. Sprinkle each serving with 2 tablespoons coarsely chopped toasted walnuts.

Carrot Spice Overnight Steel-Cut Oatmeal

Substitute ½ cup carrot juice and ½ cup whole milk for water in step 2. Stir ½ cup finely grated carrot, ¼ cup packed dark brown sugar, ⅓ cup dried currants, and ½ teaspoon ground cinnamon into oatmeal with carrot juice and milk. Sprinkle each serving with 2 tablespoons coarsely chopped toasted pecans.

Almond Granola with Dried Fruit

MAKES ABOUT 9 CUPS   **TOTAL TIME** 1 HOUR 55 MINUTES

✓ **WHY THIS RECIPE WORKS:** Store-bought granola suffers from many shortcomings. It's often loose and gravelly and/or infuriatingly expensive. We wanted to make our own granola at home, with big clusters and a crisp texture. The secret was to firmly pack the granola mixture into a rimmed baking sheet before baking. Once it was baked, we could break it into crunchy clumps of any size. Chopping the almonds by hand is the first choice for superior texture and crunch. (A food processor does a lousy job of chopping whole nuts evenly.) You can substitute an equal quantity of slivered or sliced almonds. Use either a single type of dried fruit or a combination. Do not use quick oats.

⅓ **cup maple syrup**

⅓ **cup packed (2⅓ ounces) light brown sugar**

4 **teaspoons vanilla extract**

½ **teaspoon salt**

½ **cup vegetable oil**

5 **cups old-fashioned rolled oats**

2 **cups (10 ounces) raw almonds, chopped coarse**

2 **cups raisins or other dried fruit, chopped**

A combination of maple syrup, brown sugar, and vegetable oil binds together our crisp granola.

1. Adjust oven rack to upper-middle position and heat oven to 325 degrees. Whisk maple syrup, brown sugar, vanilla, and salt in large bowl. Whisk in oil. Fold in oats and almonds until thoroughly coated.

2. Transfer oat mixture to parchment paper–lined rimmed baking sheet and spread across sheet into thin, even layer (about ⅜ inch thick). Using stiff metal spatula, compress oat mixture until very compact. Bake until lightly browned, 40 to 45 minutes, rotating pan halfway through baking.

Pressing Granola into the Pan

Transfer oat mixture to parchment-lined baking sheet and spread across sheet into thin, even layer (about ⅜ inch thick). Using stiff metal spatula, compress oat mixture until very compact.

3. Remove granola from oven and let cool on baking sheet to room temperature, about 1 hour. Break cooled granola into pieces of desired size. Stir in dried fruit. (Granola can be stored at room temperature for up to 2 weeks.) Serve.

VARIATIONS

Pecan-Orange Granola with Dried Cranberries
Add 2 tablespoons finely grated orange zest and 2½ teaspoons ground cinnamon to maple syrup mixture in step 1. Substitute coarsely chopped pecans for almonds and dried cranberries for raisins.

Spiced Walnut Granola with Dried Apple
Add 2 teaspoons ground cinnamon, 1½ teaspoons ground ginger, ¾ teaspoon ground allspice, ½ teaspoon freshly grated nutmeg, and ½ teaspoon pepper to maple syrup mixture in step 1. Substitute coarsely chopped walnuts for almonds and chopped dried apples for raisins.

Tropical Granola with Dried Mango
Reduce vanilla extract to 2 teaspoons and add 1½ teaspoons ground ginger and ¾ teaspoon freshly grated nutmeg to maple syrup mixture in step 1. Substitute coarsely chopped macadamias for almonds, 1½ cups unsweetened shredded coconut for 1 cup oats, and chopped dried mango for raisins.

Layers of Greek yogurt, fresh fruit, and granola make these parfaits a winning breakfast.

Berry Yogurt Parfaits

SERVES 4   **TOTAL TIME** 15 MINUTES   `FAST`

WHY THIS RECIPE WORKS: Creamy Greek yogurt, fresh fruit, and crunchy granola make a delicious and wholesome start to the day—and layering them in a tall glass makes a simple breakfast feel like a special occasion. We used plain 2 percent Greek yogurt for its thick texture, then sweetened it with honey. The flavors and textures of fresh fruit and crispy granola complement the yogurt's natural tanginess. You can substitute lower-fat Greek yogurt here if desired; however, the parfaits will taste less rich. Do not substitute frozen fruit here. Serve the parfaits within 15 minutes after assembling or the granola will begin to turn soggy.

3   **cups 2 percent Greek yogurt**
¼   **cup honey**
4   **cups (20 ounces) raspberries, blueberries, blackberries, and/or sliced strawberries**
1½   **cups granola**

Whisk yogurt and honey together thoroughly in bowl. Using four 16-ounce glasses, spoon ¼ cup yogurt-honey mixture into each glass, then top with ⅓ cup berries, followed by 2 tablespoons granola. Repeat layering process 2 more times with remaining yogurt, berries, and granola. Serve.

VARIATIONS

Raspberry and Nectarine Yogurt Parfaits with Ginger
Add 1 teaspoon ground ginger to yogurt with honey. Substitute 2 cups raspberries and 2 peeled and chopped nectarines for mixed berries.

Winter Yogurt Parfaits with Dates, Bananas, and Oranges
Microwave 1 cup chopped dried dates with 1 cup water in bowl for 30 seconds; drain and let cool. Add 1 teaspoon ground cinnamon and ½ teaspoon ground nutmeg to yogurt with honey. Substitute softened dates, 3 thinly sliced bananas, and 2 segmented and chopped oranges for mixed berries.

SMOOTHIES

Making smoothies at home is fast and easy; they make a perfect snack or breakfast on the go. We set out to create creamy smoothies that deliver a healthy blast of fruit flavor. After lots of testing, we found frozen fruit to be ideal for smoothies—not only is it already prepped for you, but oftentimes it tastes sweeter and more ripe. (Frozen fruit is picked at the peak of ripeness and immediately chilled, preserving both its flavor and all of the vitamins.) Frozen fruit also makes the smoothie good and cold. Of course, you can substitute the same amount of fresh fruit in any of the recipes below if you prefer; simply add 10 ice cubes to the blender with the fruit.

TO MAKE A SMOOTHIE: Combine all the ingredients in a blender, with the liquids on the bottom. Blend on low speed until the mixture is combined but still coarse in texture, about 10 seconds. Increase the speed to high and puree until it is completely smooth, 20 to 40 seconds longer. Smoothies do not hold; serve immediately. All these smoothies serve two.

CLASSIC STRAWBERRY-BANANA SMOOTHIE `FAST`

- 1½ cups plain yogurt
- 1½ cups frozen strawberries
- 1 banana, broken into chunks
- 1 tablespoon sugar, plus extra to taste
- Pinch salt

VERY BERRY SMOOTHIE `FAST`

- 1 cup frozen mixed berries
- 1 banana, broken into chunks
- ¾ cup plain yogurt
- ¼ cup apple juice
- 1 tablespoon sugar, plus extra to taste

VITAMIN C SMOOTHIE `FAST`

- 1½ cups orange juice
- 1 cup frozen mango
- ½ cup frozen strawberries
- 1 tablespoon sugar, plus extra to taste
- Pinch salt

CHERRY SMOOTHIE `FAST`

- 1 cup milk
- 1½ cups frozen cherries
- ½ cup frozen strawberries
- 1 tablespoon sugar, plus extra to taste
- Pinch salt

MANGO SMOOTHIE `FAST`

- 1 cup frozen mango
- 1 banana, broken into chunks
- ¾ cup plain yogurt
- ⅜ cup pineapple juice
- 1 tablespoon sugar, plus extra to taste

CREAMSICLE SMOOTHIE `FAST`

- 1¼ cups vanilla frozen yogurt
- 1 cup orange juice
- 1 cup frozen strawberries
- 1 tablespoon sugar, plus extra to taste
- Pinch salt

ALOHA SMOOTHIE `FAST`

- 1½ cups plain yogurt
- ¾ cup frozen pineapple chunks
- ¾ cup frozen mango chunks
- 1 tablespoon sugar, plus extra to taste
- Pinch salt

ANTIOXIDANT SMOOTHIE `FAST`

- 1½ cups plain yogurt
- ½ cup pomegranate juice
- 1½ cups frozen blueberries
- 1 tablespoon sugar, plus extra to taste
- Pinch salt

RASPBERRY LIME RICKEY SMOOTHIE `FAST`

- 1¼ cups milk
- ½ cup vanilla frozen yogurt
- 1¼ cups frozen raspberries
- ¾ teaspoon grated lime zest plus ¼ cup lime juice (2 limes)
- 1 tablespoon sugar, plus extra to taste
- Pinch salt

GOING GREEN SMOOTHIE `FAST`

Use a sweet apple such as Fuji, Jonagold, Pink Lady, Jonathan, or Macoun. For added fiber, consider not peeling the apple.

- ¾ cup orange juice
- ¼ cup milk
- 1½ cups kale leaves, chopped coarse
- 1 sweet apple, peeled, cored, and quartered
- ½ banana, broken into chunks
- 10 ice cubes
- Pinch salt
- Sugar, to taste

■ SIGNIFIES A **FAST** RECIPE (45 MINUTES OR LESS)

Drop Biscuits

MAKES 12 BISCUITS   **TOTAL TIME** 35 MINUTES   **FAST**

✓ **WHY THIS RECIPE WORKS:** Too many drop biscuits are dense, gummy, and doughy, or lean and dry; we wanted a biscuit that could be easily broken apart and eaten piece by buttery piece. While oil-based biscuits are easy to work with, they lack flavor; butter was a must. Buttermilk instead of milk gave the biscuits a rich, buttery tang and made them more crisp on the exterior and fluffier on the interior. In terms of leavener, we needed a substantial amount, but too much baking powder left a metallic taste. Replacing some of the baking powder with baking soda gave the biscuits the rise they needed without the metallic bitterness. Now we were left with only one problem. Properly combining the butter and buttermilk required that both ingredients be at just the right temperature; if they weren't, the melted butter clumped in the buttermilk. Since this was supposed to be an easy recipe, we tried making a batch with the lumpy buttermilk. The result was a surprisingly better biscuit, slightly higher and with better texture. The water in the lumps of butter turned to steam in the oven, helping create additional height. For information on buttermilk substitutions, see page 577.

- 2 **cups (10 ounces) all-purpose flour**
- 2 **teaspoons baking powder**
- ½ **teaspoon baking soda**
- 1 **teaspoon sugar**
- ¾ **teaspoon salt**
- 1 **cup buttermilk, chilled**
- 8 **tablespoons unsalted butter, melted and cooled slightly, plus 2 tablespoons melted**

1. Adjust oven rack to middle position and heat oven to 475 degrees. Line rimmed baking sheet with parchment paper.

2. Whisk flour, baking powder, baking soda, sugar, and salt together in large bowl. In separate bowl, stir chilled buttermilk and 8 tablespoons warm melted butter together until butter forms small clumps. Stir buttermilk mixture into flour mixture until just incorporated and dough pulls away from sides of bowl.

3. Using greased ¼-cup measure, scoop out and drop 12 mounds of dough onto prepared sheet, spaced about 1½ inches apart (scant ¼ cup per mound). Bake until tops are golden brown and crisp, 12 to 14 minutes, rotating sheet halfway through baking.

4. Brush baked biscuits with remaining 2 tablespoons melted butter, transfer to wire rack, and let cool slightly before serving.

VARIATIONS

Cheddar and Scallion Drop Biscuits
Stir ½ cup shredded cheddar cheese and 2 thinly sliced scallions into flour mixture before adding buttermilk mixture.

Rosemary and Parmesan Drop Biscuits
Stir ¾ cup grated Parmesan cheese and ½ teaspoon minced fresh rosemary into flour mixture before adding buttermilk mixture.

Light and Fluffy Buttermilk Biscuits

MAKES 12 BISCUITS   **TOTAL TIME** 45 MINUTES   **FAST**

✓ **WHY THIS RECIPE WORKS:** A seemingly simple batch of biscuits can end up with any number of problems. For perfectly shaped biscuits that were light and fluffy as well as tender and flavorful, we began by chilling a combination of butter and shortening. This ensured the fat melted in the oven, not in the mixing bowl—and thus created pockets of steam that delivered flaky biscuits. Combining the fat and dry ingredients using the food processor rather than our hands, as many recipes prescribe, also helped keep the fats from getting too warm and melting prematurely. Since overprocessing can lead to crumbly biscuits, we stirred in the buttermilk by hand and stopped as soon as the dough had a uniform texture. Kneading a few times activated the gluten in the flour and helped the biscuits rise, but we were careful not to overdo it to avoid ending up with tough biscuits. After rolling and stamping the dough, we placed our biscuits upside down on the baking sheet. With the flat underside on top, the biscuits rose evenly. A hot oven jump-started the rising process; we then turned the heat down to finish baking without burning the biscuits.

- 3 **cups (15 ounces) all-purpose flour**
- 1 **tablespoon sugar**
- 1 **tablespoon baking powder**
- ½ **teaspoon baking soda**
- 1 **teaspoon salt**
- 8 **tablespoons unsalted butter, cut into ½-inch pieces and chilled**
- 4 **tablespoons vegetable shortening, cut into ½-inch pieces and chilled**
- 1¼ **cups buttermilk**

1. Adjust oven rack to middle position and heat oven to 450 degrees. Line rimmed baking sheet with parchment paper. Pulse flour, sugar, baking powder, baking soda, and salt in food

Nobody wants to make biscuits that are leaden or doughy, but many people do. What's the secret to making light and fluffy biscuits that rise high every time? We found a few techniques, including using a mix of butter and shortening, that deliver the best combination of flavor and texture. With our recipe, you'll be turning out perfectly shaped biscuits that are light and tender.

1. CHILL THE FAT: Cut 8 tablespoons unsalted butter and 4 tablespoons vegetable shortening into ½-inch pieces and refrigerate them until chilled, about 30 minutes. Meanwhile, heat the oven to 450 degrees.
WHY? Cutting the fat into small pieces ensures they will chill faster and be easier to cut into the dry ingredients. The cold fat will melt in the oven, not in the mixing bowl, creating flaky biscuits.

2. CUT THE FAT INTO THE FLOUR: Pulse the flour, sugar, baking powder, baking soda, and salt in a food processor until combined. Scatter the chilled fat over the dry ingredients and pulse until the mixture resembles coarse meal, about 15 pulses.
WHY? Pulsing the dry ingredients distributes them evenly. The food processor cuts the fat into the dry ingredients quickly, without warming the butter (unlike using your hands).

3. TRANSFER THE FLOUR MIXTURE TO A BOWL AND ADD THE BUTTERMILK: Transfer the flour mixture to a large bowl. Gently stir in the buttermilk until dough forms.
WHY? Stirring in the buttermilk by hand ensures that the dough is uniformly combined without overmixing, which can happen in the food processor.

4. KNEAD THE DOUGH, THEN ROLL IT OUT: Turn the dough out onto a lightly floured surface and knead it briefly, 8 to 10 times, to form a smooth, cohesive ball. Using a rolling pin, roll the dough into a 9-inch circle, about ¾ inch thick.
WHY? Kneading the dough develops the gluten, which helps to produce tall biscuits, but don't overdo it or the biscuits will be tough. Using a rolling pin ensures that the dough has a uniform height.

5. CUT OUT THE BISCUITS: Dip a 2½-inch round biscuit cutter in flour and, with a stamping motion, cut out the biscuits, dipping the cutter in flour again as needed. Gather the scraps, pat them into a ¾-inch-thick circle, and stamp out the remaining biscuits.
WHY? Flouring the cutter ensures that it won't stick. For tall, even biscuits, we push straight down and don't twist. Using our hands to gather and pat the scraps prevents the dough from being overworked.

6. FLIP THE BISCUITS, THEN BAKE THEM: Place the biscuits upside down on a parchment-lined baking sheet. Bake for 5 minutes, rotate the sheet, then lower the oven temperature to 400 degrees. Bake until the biscuits are golden brown, 10 to 12 minutes, then let them cool on a wire rack for 5 minutes.
WHY? With the flat underside on top, the biscuits will rise more evenly. The extra-hot oven jump-starts the rising process; lowering the heat allows the biscuits to cook through without burning.

processor until combined, about 5 pulses. Sprinkle chilled butter and shortening over top and pulse until mixture resembles coarse meal, about 15 pulses.

2. Transfer flour mixture to large bowl. Stir in buttermilk until combined. Turn dough out onto lightly floured counter and knead briefly, 8 to 10 times, to form smooth, cohesive ball. Roll dough into 9-inch circle, about ¾ inch thick.

3. Cut biscuits into rounds using 2½-inch biscuit cutter, dipping cutter in flour as needed. Gather dough scraps together, pat gently into ¾-inch-thick circle, and cut out additional rounds. Place biscuits upside down on prepared baking sheet. (Raw biscuits can be refrigerated for up to 1 day; bake as directed.)

4. Bake until biscuits begin to rise, about 5 minutes. Rotate sheet, reduce oven temperature to 400 degrees, and continue to bake until golden brown, 10 to 12 minutes. Transfer biscuits to wire rack, let cool for 5 minutes, and serve.

VARIATIONS

Light and Fluffy Buttermilk Biscuits with Cheddar and Scallions
Stir ½ cup shredded cheddar cheese and 2 thinly sliced scallions into flour mixture before adding buttermilk.

Light and Fluffy Buttermilk Biscuits with Parmesan and Black Pepper
Stir ¾ cup grated Parmesan cheese and 1 teaspoon coarsely ground black pepper into flour mixture before adding buttermilk.

Light and Fluffy Buttermilk Biscuits with Fontina and Rosemary
Stir ½ cup shredded fontina cheese and ½ teaspoon minced fresh rosemary into flour mixture before adding buttermilk.

Cream Biscuits

MAKES 8 BISCUITS   **TOTAL TIME** 45 MINUTES   **FAST**

✓ **WHY THIS RECIPE WORKS:** We were after a biscuit recipe that would be simpler than the traditional versions that require cutting butter or shortening into flour, rolling out dough, and stamping biscuits. Cream biscuits, which rely on plain heavy cream in lieu of butter or shortening, were our answer for easy-to-make light and tender biscuits. While most biscuit dough should be handled lightly, we found this dough benefited from 30 seconds of kneading. Although it was easy enough to quickly shape the dough with our hands and then stamp out rounds, alternatively we found we could shape the dough using an 8-inch cake pan, then turn the dough out

onto the counter and cut it into wedges. Popping the shaped biscuits into the oven immediately kept them from spreading.

> 2 **cups (10 ounces) all-purpose flour**
> 2 **teaspoons sugar**
> 2 **teaspoons baking powder**
> ½ **teaspoon salt**
> 1½ **cups heavy cream**

1. Adjust oven rack to upper-middle position and heat oven to 450 degrees. Line baking sheet with parchment paper. Whisk flour, sugar, baking powder, and salt together in large bowl. Stir in cream with wooden spoon until dough forms, about 30 seconds.

2. Turn dough out onto lightly floured counter and gather into ball. Knead dough briefly until smooth, about 30 seconds. Pat dough into ¾-inch-thick circle.

3. Cut biscuits into rounds using 2½-inch biscuit cutter, dipping cutter in flour as needed. (Alternatively, press dough evenly into 8-inch round cake pan, unmold onto counter, and cut into 8 wedges with bench scraper.) Gather dough scraps together, pat gently into ¾-inch-thick circle, and cut out additional biscuits.

4. Place biscuits on prepared baking sheet. Bake until golden brown, about 15 minutes, rotating sheet halfway through baking. Transfer biscuits to wire rack, let cool for 5 minutes, and serve.

TO MAKE AHEAD: Unbaked biscuits can be refrigerated for up 2 hours; bake as directed. They can also be frozen for up to 1 month; bake frozen biscuits (do not thaw) as directed, increasing baking time to 20 to 25 minutes.

VARIATIONS

Cream Biscuits with Fresh Herbs
Stir 2 tablespoons minced fresh parsley, cilantro, chives, tarragon, dill, or basil into flour mixture before adding cream.

Cream Biscuits with Cheddar Cheese
Stir ½ cup cheddar cheese, cut into ¼-inch cubes, into flour mixture before adding cream.

Flouring Your Biscuit Cutter

When stamping out biscuits, dip cutter in flour as needed to prevent dough from sticking.

Plenty of leavener and kneading, and a start in a hot oven, give these scones their impressive height.

British-Style Currant Scones

MAKES 12 SCONES   **TOTAL TIME** 45 MINUTES   `FAST`

✓ **WHY THIS RECIPE WORKS:** British scones are not as sweet or as rich as American scones, and that makes them more suitable for serving with butter and jam. To make the lightest, fluffiest scones, we added more than the usual amount of leavener: 2 teaspoons of baking powder per cup of flour. Rather than leaving pieces of cold butter in the dry ingredients as we do for flaky biscuits, we thoroughly worked in softened butter until it was fully integrated. This protected some of the flour granules from moisture, which in turn limited gluten development and kept the crumb tender and cakey. We added currants for tiny bursts of fruit flavor and brushed some reserved milk and egg on top for enhanced browning. We prefer whole milk in this recipe, but low-fat milk can be used. The dough will be quite soft and wet; dust your work surface and your hands liberally with flour. For a tall, even rise, use a sharp-edged biscuit cutter and push straight down; do not twist the cutter. Serve with jam, salted butter, or clotted cream.

Baking Soda and Baking Powder

BAKING SODA: Baking soda is a leavener that provides lift to cakes, muffins, biscuits, and other baked goods, and that also promotes browning. When baking soda, which is alkaline, encounters an acidic ingredient such as sour cream, buttermilk, lemon juice, vinegar, or brown sugar, carbon and oxygen combine to form carbon dioxide. The tiny bubbles of carbon dioxide gas then lift the dough. The leavening action happens as soon as the baking soda is mixed with the acidic ingredient, so you should be ready to bake soon after mixing.

BAKING POWDER: Baking powder also creates carbon dioxide to provide lift to a wide range of baked goods. The active ingredients in baking powder are baking soda and a dry acid, such as cream of tartar. It also contains cornstarch to absorb moisture and keep the powder dry. Cooks use baking powder rather than baking soda to achieve leavening when there is no natural acidity in the batter.

There are two kinds of baking powder. A single-acting baking powder has only one acid combined with the baking soda: a quick-acting acid that begins to work when liquid is added to the batter. A double-acting baking powder (like most supermarket brands) has two acids added to the baking soda: The second acid (often sodium aluminum sulfate) begins to work only when the dish is put in the oven, after the temperature has climbed above 120 degrees.

We recommend using double-acting baking powder in all recipes—baked goods rise higher with double-acting baking powder because most of the rise occurs at oven temperatures. Double-acting baking powder also provides sufficient lift in the oven to allow you to bake frozen dough. In addition, we have found that single-acting baking powder doesn't provide sufficient leavening for doughs with little liquid, such as scones and muffins. To replace 1 teaspoon of baking powder, mix ¼ teaspoon of baking soda with ½ teaspoon of cream of tartar and use immediately.

In many of our recipes, we use both baking soda and baking powder because the combination gives better control over how fast carbon dioxide is released as well as the alkalinity of the dough. More alkaline doughs brown faster and have weaker gluten, producing a more tender, porous crumb.

STORING CHEMICAL LEAVENERS: Keep baking powder and baking soda in a cool, dark, dry place in the pantry. Despite most manufacturer claims of one year, our tests have proven that baking powder loses its potency after six months.

- 3 cups (15 ounces) all-purpose flour
- ⅓ cup (2⅓ ounces) sugar
- 2 tablespoons baking powder
- ½ teaspoon salt
- 8 tablespoons unsalted butter, cut into ½-inch pieces and softened
- ¾ cup dried currants
- 1 cup whole milk
- 2 large eggs

1. Adjust oven rack to upper-middle position and heat oven to 500 degrees. Line rimmed baking sheet with parchment paper. Pulse flour, sugar, baking powder, and salt in food processor until combined, about 5 pulses. Add butter and pulse until fully incorporated and mixture looks like very fine crumbs with no visible butter, about 20 pulses. Transfer mixture to large bowl and stir in currants.

2. In separate bowl, whisk milk and eggs together. Reserve 2 tablespoons milk mixture for brushing. Add remaining milk mixture to flour mixture and gently fold together until almost no dry bits of flour remain.

3. Transfer dough to well-floured counter and gather into ball. With floured hands, knead until dough is smooth and free of cracks, 25 to 30 times. Press gently to form disk. Using floured rolling pin, roll disk into 9-inch round, about 1 inch thick.

4. Cut scones into rounds using 2½-inch biscuit cutter, dipping cutter in flour as needed. Place scones on prepared sheet. Gather dough scraps, form into ball, and knead gently until surface is smooth. Roll dough to 1-inch thickness and cut out 4 additional scones. Discard remaining dough.

5. Brush tops of scones with reserved milk mixture. Reduce oven temperature to 425 degrees and bake until risen and golden brown, 10 to 12 minutes, rotating sheet halfway through baking. Transfer scones to wire rack and let cool for at least 10 minutes. Serve warm or at room temperature.

Toasting the oats intensifies their flavor in these tender, crumbly scones.

of milk and heavy cream added richness without making these scones too heavy. An egg proved to be the ultimate touch of richness. Cutting the cold butter into the flour, instead of using melted butter, resulted in a lighter texture. A very hot oven made the scones rise spectacularly, gave them a craggy appearance, and meant they spent less time baking and therefore had less time to dry out. Rolled oats give the scones a deeper oat flavor, but quick-cooking oats create a softer texture; either type will work here. Half-and-half can be substituted for the milk and cream combination.

Oatmeal Scones

MAKES 8 SCONES   **TOTAL TIME** 1 HOUR 20 MINUTES

✔ **WHY THIS RECIPE WORKS:** The oatmeal scones served in a typical coffeehouse are so dry and leaden that they seem like a ploy to get people to buy more coffee to wash them down. We wanted rich toasted oat flavor in a tender, flaky, not-too-sweet scone. Whole rolled oats and quick oats performed better than instant or steel-cut oats, and toasting the oats brought out their nutty flavor. We used a minimal amount of sugar and baking powder, but plenty of cold butter. A mixture

- 1½ cups (4½ ounces) old-fashioned rolled oats or quick oats
- ¼ cup whole milk
- ¼ cup heavy cream
- 1 large egg
- 1½ cups (7½ ounces) all-purpose flour
- ⅓ cup (2⅓ ounces) plus 1 tablespoon sugar
- 2 teaspoons baking powder
- ½ teaspoon salt
- 10 tablespoons unsalted butter, cut into ½-inch pieces and chilled

1. Adjust oven rack to middle position and heat oven to 375 degrees. Spread oats evenly on baking sheet and bake until fragrant and lightly browned, 7 to 9 minutes; let cool on sheet, then reserve 2 tablespoons for dusting counter. Increase oven temperature to 450 degrees. Line second baking sheet with parchment paper.

2. Whisk milk, cream, and egg together in large measuring cup. Reserve 1 tablespoon in separate bowl for glazing.

3. Pulse flour, ⅓ cup sugar, baking powder, and salt in food processor until combined, about 4 pulses. Scatter chilled butter evenly over top and continue to pulse until mixture resembles coarse cornmeal, 12 to 14 pulses. Transfer mixture to medium bowl and stir in cooled oats. Gently fold in milk mixture until large clumps form. Mix dough by hand in bowl until dough forms cohesive mass.

4. Dust counter with 1 tablespoon reserved oats, turn dough out onto counter, and dust dough with remaining 1 tablespoon reserved oats. Gently pat dough into 7-inch circle about 1 inch thick. Using bench scraper, cut dough into 8 wedges. Place scones on prepared baking sheet, spaced about 2 inches apart.

5. Brush tops with reserved egg mixture and sprinkle with remaining 1 tablespoon sugar. Bake until golden brown, 12 to 14 minutes, rotating sheet halfway through baking. Let scones cool on baking sheet for 5 minutes, then transfer to wire rack and let cool to room temperature, about 30 minutes. Serve.

VARIATIONS
Cinnamon-Raisin Oatmeal Scones
Add ¼ teaspoon cinnamon to food processor with flour, and ½ cup raisins to flour mixture with toasted oats.

Apricot-Almond Oatmeal Scones
Reduce oats to 1 cup, and toast ½ cup slivered almonds with oats in step 1. Add ½ cup chopped dried apricots to flour mixture with toasted oats and almonds.

Cutting Oatmeal Scones

After shaping scone dough into evenly thick round, use bench scraper to cut dough into 8 equal wedges.

Blueberry Scones
MAKES 8 SCONES   **TOTAL TIME** 1 HOUR

✔ **WHY THIS RECIPE WORKS:** Blueberry scones should be sweet and bursting with juicy berries, but too often the berries weigh down the scones and impart little flavor. We began with traditional recipes, increasing the amounts of sugar and butter to add sweetness and richness; a combination of whole milk and sour cream lent even more richness plus some tang. For lightness, we borrowed a technique from puff pastry, where the dough is turned, rolled, and folded multiple times to create layers that are forced apart by steam when baked. To ensure that the butter would stay as cold and as solid as possible while baking, we froze it and then grated it into the dry ingredients using a coarse grater. Figuring out when to add the blueberries was a challenge; when we mixed them in with the dry ingredients they got mashed when we mixed the dough, but when we added them to the already-mixed dough, we ruined our pockets of butter. The solution was pressing the berries into the dough, rolling the dough into a log, then pressing the log into a rectangle and cutting the scones. If fresh blueberries are unavailable, you can substitute 1½ cups frozen blueberries (unthawed). Also, 1½ cups of fresh raspberries, blackberries, or chopped strawberries can be substituted for the blueberries. Consider freezing two sticks of butter in step 1 and grating just half of each stick for a total of 8 tablespoons; this will help keep your fingertips safely away from the grater.

8   **tablespoons unsalted butter plus**
    2 tablespoons melted
7½ **ounces (1½ cups) blueberries**
½   **cup whole milk**
½   **cup sour cream**
2   **cups (10 ounces) all-purpose flour**
½   **cup (3½ ounces) plus 1 tablespoon sugar**
2   **teaspoons baking powder**
¼   **teaspoon baking soda**
1   **teaspoon grated lemon zest**
½   **teaspoon salt**

1. Adjust oven rack to middle position and heat oven to 425 degrees. Line baking sheet with parchment paper. Freeze, then grate 8 tablespoons butter over large holes of box grater; keep frozen until needed. Place berries in freezer until needed. Whisk milk and sour cream together in medium bowl, and refrigerate until needed.

2. Whisk flour, ½ cup sugar, baking powder, baking soda, lemon zest, and salt together in medium bowl. Add frozen grated butter and toss with your fingers until thoroughly coated. Gently fold in chilled milk mixture until just combined.

3. Turn dough and any floury bits out onto well-floured counter. With lightly floured hands, knead dough gently 6 to 8 times until it just holds together in ragged ball, adding flour as needed to prevent sticking.

4. Roll dough out into 12-inch square. Gently fold top, bottom, then sides of dough over center to form 4-inch square, loosening dough from counter with bench scraper if necessary. Transfer to lightly floured plate and chill in freezer for 5 minutes; do not overchill.

5. Transfer dough to floured counter and roll again into 12-inch square. Sprinkle blueberries evenly over dough, and press them lightly into dough. Loosen dough from counter with bench scraper, roll into tight log, and pinch seam closed. Turn dough seam side down and press flat into 12 by 4-inch rectangle. Using floured bench scraper, cut dough crosswise into 4 equal rectangles, then cut each rectangle on diagonal into 2 triangles. (Raw scones can be refrigerated for up to 1 day; bake as directed.)

6. Place scones on prepared baking sheet, brush tops with melted butter, and sprinkle with remaining 1 tablespoon sugar. Bake until tops and bottoms are golden brown, 18 to 25 minutes, rotating sheet halfway through baking. Transfer scones to wire rack and let cool for at least 10 minutes. Serve warm or at room temperature.

NOTES FROM THE TEST KITCHEN

Using Frozen Blueberries

You can use either fresh or frozen blueberries in our muffins and scones. When blueberries are ripe during the summer, it's a no-brainer what you'd choose. But these days, you can find fresh berries in your supermarket almost year-round.

Last winter, the test kitchen tried fresh berries from Chile as well as five frozen brands in a cobbler. The frozen wild berries easily beat the fresh imported berries as well as the other frozen contenders. (Compared with cultivated berries, wild berries are smaller, more intense in color, firmer in texture, and more sweet and tangy in flavor.) While frozen cultivated berries trailed in the tasting, all but one brand received decent scores.

Why did frozen wild berries beat fresh berries? To help them survive the long trip north, the imported berries are picked before they have a chance to fully ripen. As a result, they are often tart and not so flavorful. Frozen berries have been picked at their peak—when perfectly ripe—and are then individually quick frozen (IQF) at −20 degrees. The quick freezing preserves their sweetness, letting us enjoy them all year round.

Making Blueberry Scones

1. GRATE BUTTER: Freeze, then grate 8 tablespoons unsalted butter over large holes of box grater; keep frozen until needed.

2. FOLD DOUGH: After rolling dough into 12-inch square, fold top, bottom, then sides of dough over center to form 4-inch square. Chill on plate in freezer for 5 minutes.

3. ROLL INTO LOG: Roll chilled dough again into 12-inch square, lightly press blueberries into dough, then loosen dough from counter with bench scraper and roll into tight log.

4. CUT INTO SCONES: After pressing dough log flat into 12 by 4-inch rectangle, use floured bench scraper to cut dough crosswise into 4 rectangles, then cut each on diagonal into 2 triangles.

Popovers

MAKES 6 POPOVERS   **TOTAL TIME** 1 HOUR 30 MINUTES
(PLUS 1 HOUR RESTING TIME)

✔ **WHY THIS RECIPE WORKS:** The perfect popover soars to towering heights, but only if you get the baking magic just right. For a foolproof recipe that would produce tall popovers with a crisp exterior and a custardy interior, our first move was to double the ingredient amounts found in most recipes to fill the cups of the popover pan almost completely. When choosing flour, we found that bread flour yielded popovers with the crispiest crust. The downside was that the bread flour's high protein content sometimes caused the batter to set up too

To allow steam to escape and maintain the popovers' height, poke a small hole in the top when almost done.

quickly, which impeded rise. Resting the batter for an hour before baking gave the proteins in the flour time to relax and prevented the popovers from setting up too quickly. Whole milk is traditional, but the fat weighed down our popovers; low-fat milk fixed the problem. Popovers can collapse as they cool, so we poked a hole in the top of the popovers toward the end of baking and then again once out of the oven. This slowly released the steam and kept the crisp structure intact. Bread flour makes for the highest and sturdiest popovers, but an equal amount of all-purpose flour may be substituted. We found that greasing the popover pan with shortening ensures the best release, but vegetable oil spray may be substituted; do not use butter. To gauge the popovers' progress without opening the oven door, use the oven light during baking.

> **Vegetable shortening, for greasing pan**
> 3 **large eggs**
> 2 **cups low-fat milk, heated to 110 degrees**
> 3 **tablespoons unsalted butter, melted and cooled**
> 2 **cups (11 ounces) bread flour**
> 1 **teaspoon salt**
> 1 **teaspoon sugar**

1. Adjust oven rack to lower-middle position and heat oven to 450 degrees. Grease 6-cup popover pan with vegetable shortening, then dust lightly with flour. Whisk eggs in medium bowl until light and foamy, then slowly whisk in milk and melted butter.

2. Combine flour, salt, and sugar in large bowl. Whisk three-quarters of milk mixture into flour mixture until no lumps remain, then whisk in remaining milk mixture. Transfer batter to large measuring cup, cover with plastic wrap, and let rest at room temperature for 1 hour. (Batter can be refrigerated for up to 1 day; bring to room temperature before baking.)

3. Whisk batter to recombine, then pour into prepared pan (batter will not quite reach top of cups). Bake until just beginning to brown, about 20 minutes.

4. Without opening oven door, reduce oven temperature to 300 degrees and continue to bake until golden brown all over, 35 to 40 minutes.

5. Poke small hole in top of each popover with skewer, and continue to bake until deep golden brown, about 10 minutes. Transfer popover pan to wire rack, poke popovers again with skewer, and let cool for 2 minutes. Remove popovers from pan and serve.

TO MAKE AHEAD: Baked, cooled popovers can be stored at room temperature for 2 days. Before serving, reheat on baking sheet in 400-degree oven until crisp and heated through, 5 to 8 minutes.

Bakery-Style Muffins

MAKES 12 MUFFINS   **TOTAL TIME** 50 MINUTES

✔ **WHY THIS RECIPE WORKS:** Jumbo bakery-style muffins should boast a rich, full flavor and a thick, crisp crust protecting their fragile, tender crumb. We wanted to develop a recipe for generously sized muffins that tasted great plain or with add-ins like dried fruit, citrus zest, nuts, and even chocolate chips. Cake flour made for a loose batter and squat, greasy muffins with no distinct crust. We switched to all-purpose flour for shapely, tender muffins with a nice contrast between crust and crumb. We tested all manner of dairy in our muffins and liked yogurt the best; it kept our batter thick and produced muffins with rounded, textured tops. For jumbo-size muffins, we increased the amount of all the ingredients to ensure there was enough batter to fill the muffin cups to the brim. This recipe is a simple muffin base into which flavorings should be added; see the variations for our favorite flavors.

Our basic muffin recipe can be endlessly varied depending on what you have in your pantry.

Portioning Muffin Batter

For neat, evenly portioned muffins it's important to have a strategy for filling the tins—especially because every recipe has a slightly different yield. If you don't you'll end up with muffins of different sizes and/or batter that overflows the cups, making it nearly impossible to get the muffins out without breaking them. Our foolproof way for filling muffin tins is to portion ⅓ cup of the batter into each cup, and then circle back and evenly add the remaining batter using a spoon. A spring-loaded #12 ice cream scoop (which holds ⅓ cup batter) makes it easy to portion batter into the cups without making a mess around the edges of the pan. Whether you are using an ice cream scoop or a measuring cup, spray it first with vegetable oil spray so that all the batter slides off easily.

3 cups (15 ounces) all-purpose flour
1 cup (7 ounces) sugar
1 tablespoon baking powder
½ teaspoon baking soda
½ teaspoon salt
1½ cups plain whole-milk or low-fat yogurt
2 large eggs
8 tablespoons unsalted butter, melted and cooled

1. Adjust oven rack to middle position and heat oven to 375 degrees. Grease 12-cup muffin tin.

2. Whisk flour, sugar, baking powder, baking soda, and salt together in large bowl. In separate bowl, whisk yogurt and eggs together until smooth. Gently fold yogurt mixture into flour mixture until just combined. Fold in melted butter; do not overmix.

3. Divide batter evenly among prepared muffin cups. Bake until golden brown and toothpick inserted in center comes out clean, 20 to 25 minutes, rotating muffin tin halfway through baking.

4. Let muffins cool in muffin tin for 5 minutes, then transfer to wire rack and let cool for 10 minutes before serving.

VARIATIONS
Lemon-Blueberry Muffins
Frozen blueberries can be substituted for the fresh blueberries; rinse and dry the frozen berries (do not thaw) before tossing with the flour.

Add 1 teaspoon grated lemon zest to yogurt mixture. Add 1½ cups fresh blueberries to flour mixture and gently toss before combining with yogurt mixture.

Lemon–Poppy Seed Muffins
Add 3 tablespoons poppy seeds to flour mixture and 1 tablespoon grated lemon zest to yogurt mixture. While muffins bake, simmer ¼ cup sugar and ¼ cup lemon juice together in small saucepan over medium heat until it turns into light syrup, 3 to 5 minutes. Brush warm syrup over warm baked muffins before serving.

Mocha Chip Muffins
Add 3 tablespoons instant espresso powder to yogurt mixture, and gently fold 1 cup semisweet chocolate chips into batter.

Apricot-Almond Muffins
Add ½ teaspoon almond extract to yogurt mixture. Gently fold 1 cup finely chopped dried apricots into batter. Sprinkle with ¼ cup sliced almonds before baking.

Muffins are quick to make and the batter is easy to prepare, yet there are some challenges. How do you mix the wet and dry ingredients together for big, beautiful muffins? What is the best way to get the batter into the tin and the baked muffins out? Our tips will help you to avoid the problems and make successful bakery-style muffins at home.

1. GREASE THE MUFFIN TIN WELL: Adjust the oven rack to the middle position and heat the oven to 375 degrees. Grease a 12-cup nonstick muffin tin.

WHY? Using a good nonstick muffin tin makes a big difference—muffins will brown better and come out of the pan far more easily. Greasing the pan with vegetable oil spray rather than using paper liners enables the exterior of the muffins to brown, adding flavor and textural interest.

2. GENTLY MIX THE MUFFIN BATTER: Whisk the dry ingredients together. In a separate bowl whisk together yogurt and eggs. Use a rubber spatula to gently fold the wet ingredients into the dry ingredients, then fold in melted butter.

WHY? Overmixing makes for tough muffins, so we blend the wet and dry ingredients separately and then combine them gently. Perfectly mixed batter will have a few streaks of flour. Using yogurt delivers a fine crumb and rounded and crusty tops.

3. PORTION THE BATTER CAREFULLY: Using either a greased ⅓-cup measure or a spring-loaded portion scoop, portion the batter into each muffin cup.

WHY? Greasing a measuring cup makes it easy to portion the batter. Careful portioning is critical or you will end up with some overfilled and some underfilled muffin cups, and muffins that won't bake at the same rate.

4. BAKE THE MUFFINS AND TEST FOR DONENESS: Bake the muffins until golden brown and a toothpick inserted into the center comes out clean, 25 to 30 minutes, rotating the pan halfway through baking.

WHY? These muffins are especially rich and take longer than other muffins to bake through properly. Rotating the pan ensures that all the muffins are evenly cooked.

5. LET THE MUFFINS COOL BRIEFLY IN THE PAN: Transfer the muffin tin to a cooling rack and let cool for 5 to 10 minutes.

WHY? Cooling the muffins in the tin will give them time to set and make them easier to remove from the pan without breaking. Trying to remove hot muffins from a hot tin never works—they are too delicate to be handled and will break apart.

6. FLIP THE MUFFINS OUT OF THE PAN: Turn the muffin tin over so that the muffins fall out onto the wire rack. Use the edge of a knife to gently loosen any muffins that stick to the edge of the pan. Cool the muffins for 10 minutes before serving.

WHY? If you have properly greased the pan and have not overfilled the muffin cups, the muffins should pop out easily once cooled.

A crunchy streusel topping makes tart berry muffins even nuttier-tasting.

Cranberry-Pecan Muffins

MAKES 12 MUFFINS   **TOTAL TIME** 1 HOUR 30 MINUTES

✅ **WHY THIS RECIPE WORKS:** To tame the harsh bite of the cranberries found in most cranberry-nut muffins, we chopped the cranberries in a food processor and added confectioners' sugar and a little salt (which we often use to tame the bitterness in eggplant). As for the nuts, we took a cue from cakes made with nut flour and augmented some of the all-purpose flour with pecan flour (made by grinding pecans in a food processor). These muffins boasted a rich, hearty crumb. But because we were working with less flour, our muffins spread rather than baking up tall and self-contained. We fixed the problem by letting the batter rest for 30 minutes. This allowed what flour there was to become more hydrated, resulting in a properly thickened batter that baked up perfectly domed. To replace the missing crunch of the nuts, we simply topped the muffins with a pecan streusel. If fresh cranberries aren't available, substitute frozen cranberries and microwave until they are partially thawed, 30 to 45 seconds.

STREUSEL
- 3 tablespoons all-purpose flour
- 1 tablespoon packed light brown sugar
- 4 teaspoons granulated sugar
- 2 tablespoons unsalted butter, cut into ½-inch pieces and softened
- Pinch salt
- ½ cup pecans

MUFFINS
- 1⅓ cups (6⅔ ounces) all-purpose flour
- 1½ teaspoons baking powder
- Salt
- 1¼ cups pecans, toasted and cooled
- 1 cup (7 ounces) plus 1 tablespoon granulated sugar
- 2 large eggs
- 6 tablespoons unsalted butter, melted and cooled
- ½ cup whole milk
- 8 ounces (2 cups) cranberries
- 1 tablespoon confectioners' sugar

1. FOR THE STREUSEL: Pulse flour, brown sugar, granulated sugar, softened butter, and salt in food processor until mixture resembles coarse sand, 4 to 5 pulses. Add pecans and pulse until coarsely chopped, about 4 pulses; transfer to bowl.

2. FOR THE MUFFINS: Whisk flour, baking powder, and ¾ teaspoon salt together in bowl. Process toasted pecans and granulated sugar until mixture resembles coarse sand, 10 to 15 seconds. Transfer pecan-sugar mixture to large bowl and whisk in eggs, melted butter, and milk until combined. Whisk flour mixture into egg mixture until just moistened and no streaks of flour remain. Set batter aside for 30 minutes to thicken.

3. Adjust oven rack to upper-middle position and heat oven to 425 degrees. Grease 12-cup muffin tin. Pulse cranberries, confectioners' sugar, and ¼ teaspoon salt in food processor until cranberries are very coarsely chopped, 4 to 5 pulses. Gently fold cranberries into rested batter.

4. Divide batter equally among prepared muffin cups (batter should completely fill cups and mound slightly). Sprinkle streusel over top and press lightly to adhere.

5. Bake until golden and toothpick inserted in center comes out clean, 17 to 18 minutes, rotating muffin tin halfway through baking. Let muffins cool in muffin tin for 10 minutes, then transfer to wire rack and let cool for 10 minutes before serving.

Better Bran Muffins

MAKES 12 MUFFINS   **TOTAL TIME** 1 HOUR

✔ **WHY THIS RECIPE WORKS:** Classic bran muffins rely on unprocessed wheat bran, but few stores carry this specialized ingredient. We tested bran cereal from the supermarket and found that twig-style cereal worked better than flakes, but soaking the twigs in milk, as most recipes recommend, left our muffins dense and heavy. Instead, we stirred together the wet ingredients and then added the cereal. Grinding half of the twigs in the food processor and leaving the rest whole kept the muffins light and airy. Whole-milk yogurt and melted butter added needed moisture to the batter. Molasses and brown sugar reinforced the earthy bran flavor. To address the texture of the muffins, we switched to baking soda instead of baking powder and used one egg plus a yolk—two eggs made the muffins too springy. To ensure that the raisins would soften fully, we plumped them in water in the microwave before adding them to the batter. We prefer Kellogg's All-Bran Original cereal in this recipe. Dried cranberries or dried cherries may be substituted for the raisins.

    1   cup raisins
    1   teaspoon water
    2¼ cups (5 ounces) All-Bran Original cereal
    1   large egg plus 1 large yolk
    ⅔   cup packed (4⅔ ounces) light brown sugar
    3   tablespoons molasses
    1   teaspoon vanilla extract
    6   tablespoons unsalted butter, melted and cooled
    1¾ cups plain whole-milk yogurt
    1¼ cups (6¼ ounces) all-purpose flour
    ½   cup (2¾ ounces) whole-wheat flour
    2   teaspoons baking soda
    ½   teaspoon salt

1. Adjust oven rack to middle position and heat oven to 400 degrees. Grease 12-cup muffin tin. Microwave raisins and water in covered bowl for 30 seconds. Let stand until raisins are softened, about 5 minutes; transfer to paper towel–lined plate to cool.

2. Process half of cereal in food processor until finely ground, about 1 minute. Whisk egg and yolk together in medium bowl until well combined and light-colored, about 20 seconds. Whisk in sugar, molasses, and vanilla until mixture is thick, about 30 seconds. Whisk in melted butter, then yogurt. Stir in processed cereal and remaining unprocessed cereal. Let sit until cereal is evenly moistened (there will still be some small lumps), about 5 minutes.

Greasing a Muffin Tin

To make sure your muffins slide effortlessly out of the muffin tin, it's important to grease the tin thoroughly; we like to use vegetable oil spray. We get this pan prep out of the way first, before we start making the batter. To prevent the spray from getting all over the counter or floor, we suggest spraying the muffin tin over the sink, a garbage can, or even an open dishwasher door.

3. Whisk all-purpose flour, whole-wheat flour, baking soda, and salt together in large bowl. Gently fold in cereal mixture until batter is just combined and evenly moistened; do not overmix. Gently fold in raisins.

4. Divide batter evenly among prepared muffin cups. Bake until dark golden and toothpick inserted in center comes out clean, 16 to 20 minutes, rotating muffin tin halfway through baking. Let muffins cool in muffin tin for 5 minutes, then transfer to wire rack and let cool for 10 minutes before serving.

Power Muffins

MAKES 12 MUFFINS   **TOTAL TIME** 1 HOUR

✔ **WHY THIS RECIPE WORKS:** For muffins packed with whole-grain goodness, we found our solution in a single bag of hot cereal mix, which already had a combination of seven grains. Hydrating the cereal mix with water in the microwave before incorporating it into the batter ensured that the grains were tender once the muffins were fully cooked. Our favorite brand of seven-grain mix is Bob's Red Mill. These muffins are very moist, so it is best to err on the side of overdone when testing for doneness.

    1   cup (5 ounces) seven-grain hot cereal mix
    1   cup dried cherries
    1   cup water
    1¾ cups (8¾ ounces) all-purpose flour
    2   teaspoons baking soda
    ½   teaspoon salt
    ½   cup plain whole-milk or low-fat yogurt
    6   tablespoons unsalted butter, melted and cooled
    ¼   cup packed (1¾ ounces) light brown sugar
    2   large eggs
    3   tablespoons molasses
    1   teaspoon vanilla extract
    ¼   cup sunflower seeds

1. Adjust oven rack to middle position and heat oven to 375 degrees. Grease 12-cup muffin tin. Microwave cereal mix, cherries, and water in covered bowl until most of liquid has been absorbed, about 3 minutes, stirring halfway through cooking.

2. Whisk flour, baking soda, and salt together in large bowl. In separate bowl, whisk yogurt, melted butter, sugar, eggs, molasses, and vanilla together until smooth, then whisk in microwaved cereal mixture. Gently fold yogurt mixture into flour mixture until just combined; do not overmix.

3. Divide batter evenly among prepared muffin cups and sprinkle with sunflower seeds. Bake until golden and toothpick inserted in center comes out clean, 16 to 18 minutes, rotating muffin tin halfway through baking. Let muffins cool in muffin tin for 5 minutes, then transfer to wire rack and let cool for 10 minutes before serving.

Applesauce Muffins

MAKES 12 MUFFINS   **TOTAL TIME** 50 MINUTES

✓ **WHY THIS RECIPE WORKS:** Applesauce is a great way to add moisture and flavor to a muffin. And because it does double duty, it also saves time by consolidating ingredients. To pack our applesauce muffins with big apple flavor, we added 1¼ cups applesauce, then enhanced it with cinnamon and a little vanilla. Sprinkling some chopped walnuts and sugar on top of the muffins before they went into the oven was an easy way to create a crunchy topping. You can substitute almonds or pecans for the walnuts. These muffins are very moist, so it is best to err on the side of overdone when testing for doneness.

2½ **cups (12½ ounces) all-purpose flour**
1½ **teaspoons baking soda**
 1 **teaspoon ground cinnamon**
 ½ **teaspoon salt**
1¼ **cups applesauce**
 1 **cup (7 ounces) plus 1½ teaspoons sugar**
10 **tablespoons unsalted butter, melted and cooled**
 2 **large eggs**
 1 **teaspoon vanilla extract**
 ½ **cup walnuts, chopped**

1. Adjust oven rack to middle position and heat oven to 375 degrees. Grease 12-cup muffin tin.

2. Whisk flour, baking soda, cinnamon, and salt together in large bowl. In separate bowl, whisk applesauce, 1 cup sugar,

Making Mini Muffins

Mini muffins are great for children, parties, bake sales, and just plain snacking. A recipe that yields 12 muffins can easily be converted to yield 36 mini muffins. Simply fill the mini muffin tins with a scant 2 tablespoons of batter and bake as directed, reducing the baking time to 10 to 15 minutes.

melted butter, eggs, and vanilla until smooth. Gently fold applesauce mixture into flour mixture until just combined; do not overmix.

3. Divide batter evenly among prepared muffin cups and sprinkle with walnuts and remaining 1½ teaspoons sugar. Bake until golden brown and toothpick inserted in center comes out clean, 16 to 18 minutes, rotating muffin tin halfway through baking. Let muffins cool in muffin tin for 5 minutes, then transfer to wire rack and let cool for 10 minutes before serving.

Corn Muffins

MAKES 12 MUFFINS   **TOTAL TIME** 50 MINUTES

✓ **WHY THIS RECIPE WORKS:** A good corn muffin has true corn flavor without being as dense and as "corny" as cornbread. To produce the right texture in our muffins, we chose three types of dairy—butter, milk, and sour cream—which gave us richness, moisture, and a bit of acidity for a tenderizing effect. We used a 2:1 ratio of flour to cornmeal for both structure and a real corn presence. Mixing the wet and dry ingredients separately, then folding them together, prevented the muffins from being too cakey. For baking, we cranked the oven to 400 degrees, which gave each muffin a crunchy golden crust. If stone-ground cornmeal is unavailable, any fine- or medium-ground cornmeal will work; do not use coarse-ground cornmeal.

 2 **cups (10 ounces) all-purpose flour**
 1 **cup (5 ounces) stone-ground cornmeal**
1½ **teaspoons baking powder**
 1 **teaspoon baking soda**
 ½ **teaspoon salt**
 2 **large eggs**
 ¾ **cup (5¼ ounces) sugar**
 8 **tablespoons unsalted butter, melted and cooled**
 ¾ **cup sour cream**
 ½ **cup whole milk**

1. Adjust oven rack to middle position and heat oven to 400 degrees. Grease 12-cup muffin tin.

2. Whisk flour, cornmeal, baking powder, baking soda, and salt together in large bowl. In separate bowl, whisk eggs and sugar together until well combined, then whisk in melted butter, sour cream, and milk. Gently fold egg mixture into flour mixture until just combined; do not overmix.

3. Divide batter evenly among muffin cups. Bake until light golden and toothpick inserted in center comes out clean, about 18 minutes, rotating muffin tin halfway through baking. Let muffins cool in muffin tin for 5 minutes, then transfer to wire rack and let cool for 10 minutes before serving.

VARIATION

Corn Muffins with Bacon, Cheddar, and Scallions

Reduce sugar to ½ cup. Cook 3 slices chopped bacon in 8-inch skillet over medium-high heat until crisp, about 5 minutes. Stir in 10 thinly sliced scallions, ¼ teaspoon salt, and ⅛ teaspoon pepper, and cook until scallions are heated through, about 1 minute; transfer to plate and let cool. Gently fold bacon mixture and 1¼ cups shredded cheddar cheese into batter. Sprinkle muffins with ¾ cup shredded cheddar before baking.

Savory Cheddar and Herb Muffins

MAKES 12 MUFFINS   TOTAL TIME 50 MINUTES

☑ WHY THIS RECIPE WORKS: To create great savory muffins that boasted big flavor, we began with a basic quick-bread batter, then incorporated a full cup of shredded cheddar cheese, along with sliced scallions and minced tarragon. Adding sour cream to the wet ingredients brought richness and tang to the muffins and helped to produce a tender crumb. Before baking them, we also made sure to give the muffins a sprinkling of Parmesan to ensure there would be plenty of cheese flavor. Shredded Parmesan adds a nice texture to these muffins and helps prevent the cheese from burning; use the large holes of a box grater to shred the Parmesan. Do not substitute finely grated or pregrated Parmesan.

- 3 cups (15 ounces) all-purpose flour
- 1 tablespoon baking powder
- 1 teaspoon salt
- ⅛ teaspoon pepper
- 4 ounces sharp cheddar cheese, shredded (1 cup)
- 2 scallions, sliced thin
- 1 tablespoon minced fresh tarragon
- 1¼ cups whole milk

NOTES FROM THE TEST KITCHEN

Storing Quick Breads and Muffins

Most leftover biscuits, scones, and muffins can be stored in a zipper-lock bag at room temperature for up to three days. If the leftover quick breads include perishable flavorings like bacon, it is best to refrigerate them, but in general the refrigerator causes baked goods to dry out and so is not our first choice for storage. When ready to serve, refresh most quick breads by placing them on a baking sheet and warming them in a 300-degree oven for about 10 minutes.

- ¾ cup sour cream
- 3 tablespoons unsalted butter, melted and cooled
- 1 large egg
- 1½ ounces Parmesan cheese, shredded (½ cup)

1. Adjust oven rack to middle position and heat oven to 375 degrees. Grease 12-cup muffin tin.

2. Whisk flour, baking powder, salt, and pepper together in large bowl. Stir in cheddar, scallions, and tarragon, breaking up any clumps, until coated with flour mixture. In separate bowl, whisk milk, sour cream, melted butter, and egg together until smooth. Gently fold milk mixture into flour mixture until just combined. Batter will be heavy and thick; do not overmix.

3. Divide batter evenly among muffin cups. Sprinkle Parmesan over top. Bake until golden brown and toothpick inserted in center comes out clean, 16 to 18 minutes, rotating muffin tin halfway through baking. Let muffins cool in muffin tin for 5 minutes, then transfer to wire rack and let cool for 10 minutes before serving.

VARIATIONS

Savory Cheddar Muffins with Jalapeño and Cilantro

Substitute ¼ cup chopped jarred jalapeños for scallions and 2 tablespoons minced fresh cilantro for tarragon.

Savory Feta and Spinach Muffins

Substitute 1 cup crumbled feta cheese for cheddar and 5 ounces frozen chopped spinach, thawed and squeezed dry, for scallions and tarragon.

Savory Boursin and Sun-Dried Tomato Muffins

Substitute 1 (5.2-ounce) package Boursin Garlic and Fine Herbs cheese, crumbled, for cheddar and ¼ cup oil-packed sun-dried tomatoes, patted dry and chopped, for scallions and tarragon.

Coffee Cake Muffins

MAKES 12 MUFFINS   **TOTAL TIME** 1 HOUR 20 MINUTES

✔ **WHY THIS RECIPE WORKS:** Compacting all the goodness of a rich coffee cake into a muffin recipe seemed like a great idea, but most of the coffee cake muffin recipes we tried resembled dry, cottony, yellow cupcakes with little or no cinnamon filling, while other recipes simply packed mounds of dry, gritty streusel on top. We set out to make a coffee cake muffin as good as a regular coffee cake—with the option of taking it to go. For muffins that were rich but not too dense, we cut back on the amount of butter and eggs most coffee cake recipes require, but kept the typical amount of sour cream—it gave the muffins a moist, velvety appeal. For the streusel topping, we cut a little butter and flour into our mixture of nuts, sugar, and cinnamon; these additions allowed the topping to clump and stay put on top of the muffins. Be sure to use muffin-tin liners for this recipe, or the cinnamon filling will stick to the pan.

STREUSEL

- ½ cup (3½ ounces) granulated sugar
- ⅓ cup packed (2⅓ ounces) light brown sugar
- ⅓ cup (1⅔ ounces) all-purpose flour
- 1 tablespoon ground cinnamon
- 4 tablespoons unsalted butter, cut into ½-inch pieces and chilled
- ½ cup pecans

MUFFINS

- 2 large eggs
- 1 cup sour cream
- 1½ teaspoons vanilla extract
- 1¾ cups (8¾ ounces) all-purpose flour
- ½ cup (3½ ounces) granulated sugar
- 1 tablespoon baking powder
- ¼ teaspoon salt
- 5 tablespoons unsalted butter, cut into pieces and softened

Keeping Streusel Topping in Place

To keep streusel topping in place, position 2¾-inch cookie cutter over muffin tin cup, then sprinkle streusel topping inside cookie cutter. Lift off cookie cutter and gently pat streusel into batter.

Our muffins use the same base mixture for both the rich cinnamon filling and the nutty streusel topping.

1. FOR THE STREUSEL: Pulse 5 tablespoons granulated sugar, brown sugar, flour, cinnamon, and butter in food processor until just combined. Transfer ¾ cup mixture to bowl for filling. Add pecans and remaining 3 tablespoons granulated sugar to mixture left in processor, and pulse until nuts are coarsely ground for topping, about 5 to 10 pulses; transfer to separate bowl. (Do not wash food processor.)

2. FOR THE MUFFINS: Adjust oven rack to middle position and heat oven to 375 degrees. Grease muffin tin and line with paper liners. Whisk eggs, sour cream, and vanilla together in bowl. Pulse flour, sugar, baking powder, salt, and butter in now-empty food processor until mixture resembles wet sand, about 10 to 15 pulses; transfer to large bowl. Using rubber spatula, gradually fold in egg mixture until just combined.

3. Place 1 tablespoon batter in each muffin cup and top with 1 tablespoon filling. Using back of spoon, press cinnamon filling lightly into batter, then top with remaining batter. Sprinkle topping evenly over top.

4. Bake until muffins are light golden brown and toothpick inserted into center comes out clean, 22 to 28 minutes, rotating muffin tin halfway through baking. Let muffins cool in muffin tin for 30 minutes, then transfer to wire rack. Serve warm or at room temperature.

Muffin Tin Doughnuts

MAKES 12 DOUGHNUTS   **TOTAL TIME** 1 HOUR

☑ **WHY THIS RECIPE WORKS:** After encountering lackluster "doughnut muffins" on bakery shelves, we were determined to make a baked good with the sugary, fried deliciousness of a classic cake doughnut. Initial recipes we tried had a bubbly, uneven crumb or were a bit tough and dry. Changing the mixing method helped; instead of creaming the butter and sugar in a mixer, we simply melted the butter and then whisked the wet ingredients (butter, eggs, and buttermilk) into the dry (flour, sugar, baking powder, salt, and nutmeg). To make the interior more compact and tender, we added an extra egg yolk and cut the all-purpose flour with a generous amount of cornstarch, which reduced gluten formation. After scooping the batter into a greased muffin tin, we baked the doughnuts in a hot (400-degree) oven so they would develop a crisp crust. While the doughnuts were still hot from the oven, we used a pastry brush to coat them generously with melted butter and then rolled them in a blanket of cinnamon sugar. The butter and spiced sugar fused to the surface, replicating the crisp, crunchy crust of a real fried doughnut. For information on buttermilk substitutions, see page 577.

DOUGHNUTS

- 2¾ cups (13¾ ounces) all-purpose flour
- 1 cup (7 ounces) sugar
- ¼ cup cornstarch
- 1 tablespoon baking powder
- 1 teaspoon salt
- ½ teaspoon ground nutmeg
- 1 cup buttermilk
- 8 tablespoons unsalted butter, melted
- 2 large eggs plus 1 large yolk

COATING

- 1 cup (7 ounces) sugar
- 2 teaspoons ground cinnamon
- 8 tablespoons unsalted butter, melted

NOTES FROM THE TEST KITCHEN

Do Muffin Papers Help?

We've found that muffins baked in paper liners usually bake up shorter and are paler in color than those baked in a greased muffin tin. So although we vote for greasing the tin whenever possible, some recipes, such as Coffee Cake Muffins (page 572), require paper liners to keep a sticky filling in the muffin instead of stuck to the pan.

Finishing Muffin Tin Doughnuts

1. After removing doughnuts from muffin tin, brush completely with melted butter.

2. Quickly drop buttered doughnut in cinnamon sugar and roll to coat evenly, pressing on sugar to adhere.

1. FOR THE DOUGHNUTS: Adjust oven rack to middle position and heat oven to 400 degrees. Grease 12-cup muffin tin. Whisk flour, sugar, cornstarch, baking powder, salt, and nutmeg together in large bowl. In separate bowl, whisk buttermilk, melted butter, and eggs and yolk together. Add buttermilk mixture to flour mixture and stir with rubber spatula until just combined.

2. Divide batter evenly among muffin cups. Bake until lightly browned and toothpick inserted in center comes out clean, 19 to 22 minutes, rotating muffin tin halfway through baking. Let doughnuts cool in tin for 5 minutes.

3. FOR THE COATING: Whisk sugar and cinnamon together in bowl. Remove doughnuts from tin. Working with 1 doughnut at a time, brush completely with melted butter, then roll in cinnamon sugar, pressing lightly to adhere. Transfer to wire rack and let cool for 15 minutes. Serve.

Simple Drop Doughnuts

MAKES 24 DOUGHNUTS   **TOTAL TIME** 45 MINUTES   **FAST**

☑ **WHY THIS RECIPE WORKS:** When coming up with a quick and simple recipe for homey, tender cake-style doughnuts, we first did away with rolling and stamping out the dough into rings. Instead, we merely dropped generous spoonfuls of batter into the hot fat, creating round doughnut "holes." All-purpose flour gave these doughnuts the right amount of structure, and just 2 tablespoons of butter added richness and tenderness without weighing the batter down. The most important factor in preventing greasy doughnuts was making sure we fried them at the right temperature; we were careful to keep the oil at 350 degrees while we cooked each batch of doughnuts until golden brown.

- 2 cups (10 ounces) all-purpose flour
- 2 teaspoons baking powder
- ¼ teaspoon salt
- ½ cup (3½ ounces) granulated sugar
- 2 large eggs
- 1 teaspoon ground nutmeg
- ½ cup whole milk
- 2 tablespoons unsalted butter, melted and cooled
- ½ teaspoon vanilla extract
- 2 quarts vegetable oil
    Confectioners' sugar, for dusting

1. Whisk flour, baking powder, and salt together in medium bowl. In separate bowl, whisk sugar, eggs, and nutmeg together until smooth, then whisk in milk, melted butter, and vanilla. Stir egg mixture into flour mixture with wooden spoon until evenly combined. (Batter can be refrigerated for up to 12 hours.)

2. Add oil to Dutch oven to measure 3 inches deep and heat over medium-high heat to 350 degrees. Line baking sheet with paper towels. Using 2 spoons, scoop out 6 Ping-Pong-ball-size portions of batter and carefully add to hot oil. Fry doughnuts until crisp and deeply browned on all sides, 3 to 6 minutes, adjusting heat as necessary to maintain oil at 350 degrees.

3. Using slotted spoon, transfer doughnuts to prepared sheet and let drain. Repeat with remaining batter. Dust with confectioners' sugar and serve warm.

VARIATIONS

Spice Drop Doughnuts

Add 1½ teaspoons ground cinnamon and ¼ teaspoon ground allspice to batter. In medium bowl, combine ½ cup sugar, 1 tablespoon ground cinnamon, ¾ teaspoon ground nutmeg, and ½ teaspoon ground allspice; set aside. Let fried doughnuts drain for 2 minutes, then roll in spiced sugar to coat.

Frying Doughnuts

Scoop out Ping-Pong-ball-size portions of batter with spoon. Using second spoon, gently scrape batter into hot oil, frying until deeply brown, 3 to 6 minutes.

Banana Drop Doughnuts

Add 1 mashed ripe banana to batter and substitute cinnamon for nutmeg. In medium bowl, combine ½ cup sugar and 1 tablespoon ground cinnamon; set aside. Let fried doughnuts drain for 2 minutes, then roll in cinnamon sugar to coat.

Orange Drop Doughnuts

Substitute 1 tablespoon grated orange zest for nutmeg and ½ cup orange juice for milk. Process ½ cup sugar and 1 teaspoon grated orange zest in food processor until fragrant, about 20 seconds; transfer to medium bowl and set aside. Let fried doughnuts drain for 2 minutes, then roll in orange sugar to coat.

Ultimate Banana Bread

MAKES 1 LOAF   **TOTAL TIME** 2 HOURS

✔ **WHY THIS RECIPE WORKS:** Our ideal banana bread is a moist, tender loaf that really tastes like bananas. We discovered that doubling the bananas in our favorite recipe was both a blessing and a curse. The abundance of fruit made for intense flavor, but the weight and moisture sank the loaf. Looking to add banana flavor without moisture, we placed our bananas in a bowl and microwaved them for a few minutes, then transferred the fruit to a strainer to drain. We simmered the exuded banana liquid in a saucepan until it was reduced, then incorporated it into the batter. Brown sugar complemented the bananas better than granulated sugar, and vanilla worked well with the bananas' faintly boozy, rumlike flavor, as did swapping out the oil for the nutty richness of butter. As a final embellishment, we sliced a sixth banana and shingled it on top of the loaf. A final sprinkle of granulated sugar helped the slices caramelize and gave the loaf an enticingly crunchy top. Be sure to use very ripe, heavily speckled (or even black) bananas in this recipe. The test kitchen's preferred loaf pan measures 8½ by 4½ inches; if you use a 9 by 5-inch loaf pan, start checking for doneness 5 minutes early.

- 1¾ cups (8¾ ounces) all-purpose flour
- 1 teaspoon baking soda
- ½ teaspoon salt
- 6 very ripe large bananas (2¼ pounds), peeled
- 8 tablespoons unsalted butter, melted and cooled
- 2 large eggs
- ¾ cup packed (5¼ ounces) light brown sugar
- 1 teaspoon vanilla extract
- ½ cup walnuts, toasted and chopped coarse (optional)
- 2 teaspoons granulated sugar

Making Banana Bread

1. MICROWAVE BANANAS:
Place 5 bananas in bowl, cover, and microwave until bananas are soft and have released liquid. Transfer to fine-mesh strainer set over bowl and let drain.

2. COOK BANANA LIQUID:
Transfer drained liquid to medium saucepan and cook over medium-high heat until reduced to ¼ cup, about 5 minutes.

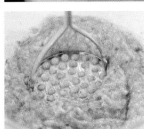

3. MASH BANANAS AND LIQUID: Stir reduced liquid into bananas and mash with potato masher until mostly smooth.

4. TOP WITH RAW BANANA AND SUGAR: Slice 1 banana on bias into ¼-inch-thick slices, and shingle slices on loaf down both sides, leaving center clear to ensure even rise. Sprinkle with granulated sugar.

1. Adjust oven rack to middle position and heat oven to 350 degrees. Grease 8½ by 4½-inch loaf pan. Whisk flour, baking soda, and salt together in large bowl.

2. Place 5 bananas in separate bowl, cover, and microwave until bananas are soft and have released liquid, about 5 minutes. Drain bananas in fine-mesh strainer set over medium bowl, stirring occasionally, for 15 minutes; you should have ½ to ¾ cup liquid.

3. Transfer drained liquid to medium saucepan and cook over medium-high heat until reduced to ¼ cup, about 5 minutes. Return drained bananas to bowl. Stir reduced liquid into bananas and mash with potato masher until mostly smooth. Whisk in butter, eggs, brown sugar, and vanilla.

NOTES FROM THE TEST KITCHEN

Ripening Bananas

The abundance of natural sugars in overripe bananas is the secret to big flavor and serious moisture in baked goods. Strategies for speeding ripening in bananas abound, but as we worked our way through over eight cases of fruit while developing our Ultimate Banana Bread, we found most of them ineffective. One theory, for example, holds that freezing or roasting underripe bananas in their skins will quickly render them sweet and soft enough for baking. While these methods do turn the bananas black—giving them the appearance of their supersweet, overripe brethren—they actually do little to encourage the necessary conversion of starch to sugar.

The best way to ripen bananas is to enclose them in a paper bag for a few days. Fruit produces ethylene gas, which hastens ripening, and the bag will trap the gas while still allowing some moisture to escape. Since fully ripe fruit emits the most ethylene, placing a ripe banana or other ripe fruit in the bag will speed the process along by a day or two.

4. Pour banana mixture into flour mixture and stir until just combined, with some streaks of flour remaining. Gently fold in walnuts, if using. Scrape batter into prepared loaf pan and smooth top. Slice remaining banana on bias into ¼-inch-thick slices and shingle down both sides of loaf pan, leaving center clear to ensure even rise. Sprinkle granulated sugar over top.

5. Bake until skewer inserted in center comes out clean, 55 minutes to 1¼ hours, rotating pan halfway through baking. Let loaf cool in pan for 15 minutes, then turn out onto wire rack and continue to cool. Serve warm or at room temperature.

Zucchini Bread

MAKES 1 LOAF   **TOTAL TIME** 2 HOURS
(PLUS 1½ HOURS COOLING TIME)

✔ **WHY THIS RECIPE WORKS:** Zucchini bread is great for using up unwanted vegetables, but most recipes call for only minimal amounts of zucchini and result in a loaf with a dense, underbaked texture. We wanted a recipe that increased the amount of zucchini while avoiding a gummy crumb. The first step was removing the excess moisture from the zucchini. After shredding 1½ pounds of zucchini, we wrapped it in a dish towel and twisted it tightly, squeezing out as much liquid as possible. Reducing the amount of sugar, which holds on to moisture, allowed more water to be driven off during baking and also resulted in a more savory flavor that tasters

We increase the amount of zucchini and reduce the sugar for a rich and savory quick bread.

preferred. Instead of butter, we used oil, which kept the bread moist and increased its shelf life. To help further reduce wetness and add a bit of texture, we substituted one-quarter of the all-purpose flour with water-absorbing whole-wheat flour. Baking the loaf at a slightly lower temperature than we use for other quick breads gave it time to bake through without scorching the exterior. With a sprinkle of sugar on top for crunch, our zucchini loaf was rich and moist, and without a hint of gumminess. Use the large holes of a box grater or the shredding disk of a food processor to shred the zucchini. The test kitchen's preferred loaf pan measures 8½ by 4½ inches; if using a 9 by 5-inch loaf pan, start checking for doneness 5 minutes early.

1½ **pounds zucchini, shredded (5 cups)**
1¼ **cups packed (8¾ ounces) brown sugar**
¼ **cup vegetable oil**
2 **large eggs**
1 **teaspoon vanilla extract**

1½ **cups (7½ ounces) all-purpose flour**
½ **cup (2¾ ounces) whole-wheat flour**
1 **tablespoon ground cinnamon**
1½ **teaspoons salt**
1 **teaspoon baking soda**
1 **teaspoon baking powder**
½ **teaspoon ground nutmeg**
¾ **cup walnuts, toasted and chopped coarse (optional)**
1 **tablespoon granulated sugar**

1. Adjust oven rack to middle position and heat oven to 325 degrees. Grease 8½ by 4½-inch loaf pan. Place shredded zucchini in center of dish towel, gather ends together, and twist tightly to remove as much liquid as possible.

2. Whisk brown sugar, oil, eggs, and vanilla together in medium bowl, then fold in dried zucchini. In large bowl, whisk all-purpose flour, whole-wheat flour, cinnamon, salt, baking soda, baking powder, and nutmeg together. Fold in zucchini mixture until just incorporated. Fold in walnuts, if using.

3. Scrape batter into prepared loaf pan, smooth top, and sprinkle with granulated sugar. Bake until top bounces back when gently pressed and skewer inserted in center comes out clean, 65 to 75 minutes, rotating pan halfway through baking.

4. Let bread cool in pan for 30 minutes, then turn out onto wire rack and let cool for 1½ hours before serving.

VARIATIONS

Zucchini Bread with Pistachios and Orange
Add 1 teaspoon grated orange zest to brown sugar mixture in step 2. Substitute ½ teaspoon ground cardamom for cinnamon and shelled pistachios for walnuts.

Zucchini Bread with Walnuts and Dried Cherries
Substitute 1 tablespoon cocoa powder for cinnamon and ground cloves for nutmeg. Prepare bread with walnuts and add ¾ cup chopped dried cherries to batter with walnuts.

Removing Moisture from Shredded Zucchini

Place shredded zucchini in center of dish towel, gather ends together, and twist tightly to remove as much liquid as possible.

Cranberry-Nut Bread

MAKES 1 LOAF   **TOTAL TIME** 1 HOUR 30 MINUTES
(PLUS 1 HOUR COOLING TIME)

✔ **WHY THIS RECIPE WORKS:** We were looking for cranberry bread with a thin, golden-brown crust and an interior texture somewhere between dense breakfast bread and light, airy cake. The standard quick-bread method of mixing—in which liquid and dry ingredients are mixed separately and then stirred together—helped us avoid a cakelike texture in the finished bread, We chose a combination of leaveners; baking soda supported the structure and promoted browning, while baking powder enhanced the flavor. Many recipes overcompensate for the cranberries with a surfeit of sugar in the batter. We used just 1 cup sugar to 1½ cups cranberries to give us a sweet, but not too sweet, loaf. A handful of toasted pecans added textural interest (walnuts work, too). As a final touch, we stirred orange juice and zest in with the liquid ingredients; the bright, citrusy flavor offset the tang of the cranberries, and the flecks of zest added a hint of color. Fresh or frozen cranberries (not thawed) will work here. The test kitchen's preferred loaf pan measures 8½ by 4½ inches; if you use a 9 by 5-inch loaf pan, start checking for doneness 5 minutes early. See the box at right for information on buttermilk substitutions.

    ⅔ cup buttermilk
    6 tablespoons unsalted butter, melted and cooled
    1 tablespoon grated orange zest plus ⅓ cup juice
    1 large egg
    2 cups (10 ounces) all-purpose flour
    1 cup (7 ounces) sugar
    1 teaspoon salt
    1 teaspoon baking powder
    ¼ teaspoon baking soda
    6 ounces (1½ cups) fresh or frozen cranberries,
       chopped coarse
    ½ cup pecans or walnuts, toasted and chopped coarse

1. Adjust oven rack to middle position and heat oven to 350 degrees. Grease 8½ by 4½-inch loaf pan. Stir buttermilk, melted butter, orange zest and juice, and egg together in bowl. In large bowl, whisk flour, sugar, salt, baking powder, and baking soda together. Stir buttermilk mixture into flour mixture with rubber spatula until just moistened. Gently stir in cranberries and pecans; do not overmix.

2. Scrape batter into prepared loaf pan and smooth top. Bake until golden brown and skewer inserted in center comes out clean, 55 minutes to 1¼ hours, rotating pan halfway through baking. Let loaf cool in pan for 10 minutes, then turn out onto wire rack and let cool for 1 hour before serving.

NOTES FROM THE TEST KITCHEN

Buttermilk Substitutions

Buttermilk is a key ingredient in many recipes—everything from pancakes to cupcakes—and for good reason. Being acidic, it not only gives baked goods a smooth tang but also provides lift when combined with a basic (or alkaline) ingredient such as baking soda.

Although we prefer real buttermilk, even in the test kitchen we occasionally find ourselves without it. Luckily, there are several easy substitutes that will work in a pinch.

SUBSTITUTES FOR 1 CUP OF BUTTERMILK

OPTION 1	OPTION 2	OPTION 3
1 cup milk + 1 tablespoon lemon juice or distilled white vinegar	¾ cup plain whole-milk or low-fat yogurt + ¼ cup milk	Shelf-stable powdered buttermilk: Follow the package instructions.

Date-Nut Bread

MAKES 1 LOAF   **TOTAL TIME** 2 HOURS
(PLUS 1 HOUR COOLING TIME)

✔ **WHY THIS RECIPE WORKS:** Date bread often suffers from unmitigated sweetness and hard, chewy dates. We wanted to make a quick bread rich with soft, sweet dates and a moist, tender crumb. Our first step was to soak the dates in hot water with a teaspoon of baking soda; the alkaline mixture softened the dates' fibers. Rather than throw out the flavorful soaking liquid, we added it to the batter. Dark brown sugar (preferred over light brown here) complemented the flavor of the dates and gave our loaf an appealingly rich, dark color. Buttermilk contributed a tanginess that balanced the sweetness of the dates. Chopped toasted nuts (pecans or walnuts) added further flavor and some crunch to our loaf. For an accurate measurement of boiling water, bring a full kettle of water to a boil, then measure out the desired amount. The test kitchen's preferred loaf pan measures 8½ by 4½ inches; if you use a 9 by 5-inch loaf pan, start checking for doneness 5 minutes early. For information on buttermilk substitutions, see above.

    10 ounces pitted dates, chopped coarse (1⅔ cups)
     1 cup boiling water
     1 teaspoon baking soda

- **2** cups (10 ounces) all-purpose flour
- **1** teaspoon baking powder
- **½** teaspoon salt
- **¾** cup packed (5¼ ounces) dark brown sugar
- **⅔** cup buttermilk
- **6** tablespoons unsalted butter, melted and cooled
- **1** large egg
- **1** cup pecans or walnuts, toasted and chopped coarse

1. Adjust oven rack to middle position and heat oven to 350 degrees. Grease 8½ by 4½-inch loaf pan. Combine dates, boiling water, and baking soda in medium bowl, cover, and let stand until dates have softened, about 30 minutes.

2. Whisk flour, baking powder, and salt together in large bowl. In medium bowl, whisk sugar, buttermilk, melted butter, and egg together until smooth, then stir in date mixture until combined. Gently fold buttermilk mixture into flour mixture until just combined; do not overmix. Gently fold in pecans.

3. Scrape batter into prepared loaf pan and smooth top. Bake until golden brown and skewer inserted in center comes out clean, 55 minutes to 1 hour, rotating pan halfway through baking.

4. Let loaf cool in pan for 10 minutes, then turn out onto wire rack and let cool for 1 hour before serving.

Chopping Dried Fruit

To prevent dried fruit from sticking to knife, coat blade with thin film of vegetable oil spray before chopping.

Pumpkin Bread

MAKES 2 LOAVES   **TOTAL TIME** 1 HOUR 40 MINUTES (PLUS 1½ HOURS COOLING TIME)

✔ **WHY THIS RECIPE WORKS:** Canned pumpkin puree often lends a raw, metallic flavor to pumpkin bread. We cook down the puree to eliminate those off-putting flavors. Instead of dirtying more dishes, we mix the quick bread right in the pot, adding cream cheese and buttermilk for their tangy flavor. A quick-to-assemble topping adds texture and keeps the loaf from getting soggy the next day. The test kitchen's preferred

Cooking the canned puree before making the batter yields full pumpkin flavor in this quick bread.

loaf pan measures 8½ by 4½ inches; if using 9 by 5-inch loaf pans, start checking for doneness 5 minutes early. For information on buttermilk substitutions, see page 577.

TOPPING
- **5** tablespoons packed (2¼ ounces) light brown sugar
- **1** tablespoon all-purpose flour
- **1** tablespoon unsalted butter, softened
- **1** teaspoon ground cinnamon
- **⅛** teaspoon salt

BREAD
- **2** cups (10 ounces) all-purpose flour
- **1½** teaspoons baking powder
- **½** teaspoon baking soda
- **1** (15-ounce) can unsweetened pumpkin puree
- **1** teaspoon salt
- **1½** teaspoons ground cinnamon
- **¼** teaspoon ground nutmeg
- **⅛** teaspoon ground cloves
- **1** cup (7 ounces) granulated sugar
- **1** cup packed (7 ounces) light brown sugar

½ cup vegetable oil

4 ounces cream cheese, cut into 12 pieces

4 large eggs

¼ cup buttermilk

1 cup walnuts, toasted and chopped fine

1. FOR THE TOPPING: Using fingers, mix all ingredients together in bowl until well combined and mixture resembles wet sand.

2. FOR THE BREAD: Adjust oven rack to middle position and heat oven to 350 degrees. Grease two 8½ by 4½-inch loaf pans. Whisk flour, baking powder, and baking soda together in bowl.

3. Cook pumpkin puree, salt, cinnamon, nutmeg, and cloves in large saucepan over medium heat, stirring constantly, until reduced to 1½ cups, 6 to 8 minutes. Off heat, stir in granulated sugar, brown sugar, oil, and cream cheese until combined. Let mixture stand for 5 minutes. Whisk until no visible pieces of cream cheese remain and mixture is homogeneous.

4. Whisk eggs and buttermilk together in separate bowl, then whisk into pumpkin mixture. Gently fold in flour mixture until combined (some small lumps of flour are OK). Fold in walnuts. Scrape batter into prepared pans, smooth tops, and sprinkle evenly with topping. Bake until skewer inserted in center comes out clean, 45 to 50 minutes, rotating pans halfway through baking.

5. Let loaves cool in pans for 20 minutes, then turn out onto wire rack and let cool for 1½ hours before serving.

VARIATION

Pumpkin Bread with Crystallized Ginger

Substitute ½ teaspoon ground ginger for cinnamon in topping. Add ⅓ cup minced crystallized ginger to batter with walnuts.

Golden Northern Cornbread

SERVES 9   **TOTAL TIME** 50 MINUTES

⚫ **WHY THIS RECIPE WORKS:** The classic Northern version of cornbread is slightly sweet, has a light texture, and stands taller than its Southern counterpart. Traditionally, Northern cornbread recipes combine white flour and yellow cornmeal, and we found that a 1:1 ratio worked best. As for cornmeal, stone-ground cornmeal outshone finer-milled degerminated varieties. For the liquid we used equal amounts of milk and buttermilk to provide rich flavor and a slight tang. To create a sweet but not dessertlike cornbread we tested honey, molasses, and light brown sugar, but in the end settled on granulated sugar. If stone-ground cornmeal is unavailable, any fine- or medium-ground cornmeal will work; do not use coarse-ground cornmeal. For information on buttermilk substitutions, see page 577.

1 cup (5 ounces) stone-ground cornmeal

1 cup (5 ounces) all-purpose flour

4 teaspoons sugar

2 teaspoons baking powder

½ teaspoon baking soda

½ teaspoon salt

2 large eggs

⅔ cup buttermilk

⅔ cup whole milk

2 tablespoons unsalted butter, melted and cooled

1. Adjust oven rack to middle position and heat oven to 425 degrees. Grease 9-inch square baking pan. Whisk cornmeal, flour, sugar, baking powder, baking soda, and salt together in large bowl, then make well in center of bowl.

2. Crack eggs into well and stir gently with wooden spoon. Add buttermilk and milk and quickly stir until batter is almost combined. Stir in melted butter until batter is just combined.

3. Pour batter into prepared pan and smooth top. Bake until top is golden brown and lightly cracked and edges have pulled away from sides of pan, about 25 minutes, rotating pan halfway through baking. Let cornbread cool in pan for 5 to 10 minutes before serving.

VARIATIONS

Golden Northern Cornbread with Cheddar

Omit sugar. After adding melted butter to batter, quickly fold in 1 cup shredded cheddar cheese.

Golden Northern Cornbread with Jalapeños

For bolder heat, use up to two jalapeños, with seeds.

Omit sugar. After adding melted butter to batter, quickly fold in 1 seeded and minced jalapeño chile.

NOTES FROM THE TEST KITCHEN

Baking Miniature Loaves

Mini loaf pans come in many forms, from the connected four-loaf pans available in gourmet shops and specialty catalogs to inexpensive decorative loaf pans and the disposable aluminum pans available at just about every supermarket. These pans turn out small loaves that make great gifts, especially around the holidays. Most of these pans hold 2 cups of batter, and therefore with our quick-bread recipes one loaf will make four mini loaves. Simply divide the batter evenly among four greased 2-cup loaf pans and bake as directed, reducing the baking time to about 35 minutes.

FLAVORED BUTTERS

A light smear of a flavored butter (also known as compound butter) can elevate the status of even the most humble baked goods. Savory butters are traditionally served with steak or fish as an alternative to sauce, but they can give a flavor boost to breads, muffins, and biscuits as well. Here are some of our favorite savory and sweet butter combinations.

DIRECTIONS: In medium bowl, whip softened butter with fork until light and fluffy, then stir in remaining ingredients.

MOLASSES-PECAN BUTTER `FAST`

- 8 tablespoons unsalted butter, softened
- ¼ cup pecans, toasted and chopped fine
- 4 teaspoons molasses
- 2 teaspoons sugar
- ¼ teaspoon vanilla extract
  Pinch salt

SWEET ORANGE BUTTER `FAST`

- 8 tablespoons unsalted butter, softened
- 2 teaspoons sugar
- 1 teaspoon grated orange zest
- ⅛ teaspoon vanilla extract
  Pinch salt

HONEY BUTTER `FAST`

- 8 tablespoons unsalted butter, softened
- ¼ cup honey
  Pinch salt

CHIPOTLE-CILANTRO BUTTER `FAST`

- 8 tablespoons unsalted butter, softened
- 4 teaspoons minced fresh cilantro
- 1 tablespoon minced canned chipotle chile in adobo sauce
- 2 garlic cloves, minced
- 2 teaspoons honey
- 2 teaspoons grated lime zest
  Pinch salt

PARSLEY-LEMON BUTTER `FAST`

- 8 tablespoons unsalted butter, softened
- ¼ cup minced fresh parsley
- 4 teaspoons grated lemon zest
  Pinch salt

Southern-Style Skillet Cornbread

SERVES 12   **TOTAL TIME** 1 HOUR

✔ **WHY THIS RECIPE WORKS:** Savory skillet-baked Southern-style cornbread should boast hearty corn flavor, a sturdy, moist crumb, and a dark brown crust. For the right texture, we used stone-ground cornmeal. Toasting it in the oven for a few minutes intensified the corn flavor. Buttermilk added a sharp tang that worked well with the corn, and soaking the cornmeal in the buttermilk helped to soften it so our cornbread was moist and tender. When it came to the fat, a combination of butter (for flavor) and vegetable oil (which can withstand high heat without burning) worked best, and greasing the pan with both delivered the crisp crust we were after. We prefer a cast-iron skillet here, but any ovensafe 10-inch skillet will work fine. You can substitute any type of fine- or medium-ground cornmeal here; do not use coarse-ground cornmeal.

- 2¼ cups (11¼ ounces) stone-ground cornmeal
- 2 cups buttermilk
- ¼ cup vegetable oil
- 4 tablespoons unsalted butter, cut into 4 pieces
- 1 teaspoon baking powder
- 1 teaspoon baking soda
- ¾ teaspoon salt
- 2 large eggs

1. Adjust oven racks to lower-middle and middle positions and heat oven to 450 degrees. Heat 10-inch cast-iron skillet on middle rack for 10 minutes. Spread cornmeal over rimmed baking sheet and bake on lower rack until fragrant and color begins to deepen, about 5 minutes. Transfer hot cornmeal to large bowl, whisk in buttermilk, and set aside.

2. Carefully add oil to hot skillet and continue to heat in oven until oil is just smoking, about 5 minutes. Remove skillet from oven, add butter, and carefully swirl pan until butter is melted. Pour all but 1 tablespoon hot oil mixture into cornmeal mixture. Whisk baking powder, baking soda, and salt into cornmeal mixture until combined, then whisk in eggs.

3. Quickly pour cornmeal mixture into hot skillet with remaining fat. Bake on upper rack until top begins to crack and sides are golden brown, 12 to 16 minutes, rotating pan halfway through baking. Let cornbread cool in pan for 5 minutes before serving.

SOUTHERN-STYLE SKILLET CORNBREAD

Southern-style cornbread, which contains neither sugar nor flour, has a stronger corn flavor than Northern versions and is baked in a preheated cast-iron skillet, giving it a crisp crust. However, many recipes yield cornbread that is flat as a pancake or dripping in grease, and most lack any flavor at all. Our recipe makes cornbread that has a moist interior, a dark brown crust, and hearty corn flavor, and is savory enough to join the dinner table.

1. PREHEAT THE SKILLET: Heat the oven to 450 degrees. Heat a 10-inch cast-iron skillet on the middle rack until hot, about 10 minutes.

WHY? Preheating the cast-iron skillet, which has great heat retention, ensures that the cornbread will have a crunchy, brown crust. If you don't preheat the skillet, the cornbread will be soft and pale.

2. TOAST THE CORNMEAL: Spread the cornmeal on a rimmed baking sheet and toast it in the oven on the lower-middle rack (while the skillet is heating up) until it's fragrant and lightly golden, about 5 minutes.

WHY? Toasting the cornmeal for a few minutes deepens its flavor.

3. SOFTEN THE CORNMEAL WITH BUTTERMILK: Transfer the toasted cornmeal to a bowl, whisk in the buttermilk, and let it soften for several minutes before making the batter.

WHY? Buttermilk adds a lot of flavor and a nice tang. Combining the hot cornmeal and the buttermilk softens the cornmeal, resulting in a tender, moist crumb in the finished cornbread.

4. USE OIL AND BUTTER: Carefully add the oil to the hot skillet and continue to heat in the oven until the oil is just smoking. Using a pot holder (the skillet handle will be very hot), remove the skillet from the oven and swirl in the butter until it is melted. Pour all but 1 tablespoon of the hot fat into the cornmeal mixture. Whisk in the remaining ingredients.

WHY? We use a combination of oil, which can withstand high heat without burning, and butter for flavor. We leave a table-spoon in the pan to ensure a crisp crust.

5. ADD THE BATTER TO THE HOT SKILLET: Quickly pour the batter into the hot skillet and bake until the top begins to crack, 12 to 16 minutes, rotating the skillet halfway through baking.

WHY? The hot skillet is what gives this bread its crunchy crust, so we make sure it doesn't cool off before adding the batter. Rotating the skillet ensures that the cornbread cooks evenly.

6. COOL THE CORNBREAD IN THE SKILLET, THEN FLIP IT OUT: Carefully remove the skillet from the oven. Let the cornbread cool for 5 minutes, then gently flip out the cornbread onto a wire rack.

WHY? If you try to flip the cornbread out of the skillet before letting it cool slightly, it will crumble apart.

Skillet Olive Bread

SERVES 8 TO 10   **TOTAL TIME** 45 MINUTES **FAST**

✔ **WHY THIS RECIPE WORKS:** For a quick rustic loaf of olive bread, we turned to our cast-iron skillet. We made a thick batter using all-purpose flour, milk, egg, and a little sour cream for richness, and leavened it with baking powder. We used a full cup of briny kalamata olives and for a rugged texture, we halved them. Chopped fresh basil and shredded Parmesan both contributed bold flavors that stood up to the assertive olives, but the loaf needed more dimension. Garlic was a natural fit; to tame its pungent bite, we sautéed it in a generous amount of olive oil right in the skillet we would be using to bake the bread. The garlic and flavored oil infused the loaf with flavor, and the hot, greased skillet helped produce a crisp, golden-brown crust. Use the large holes of a box grater to shred the Parmesan. Do not substitute finely grated or pregrated Parmesan. We prefer to use a cast-iron skillet here because it makes the best crust; however, a 10-inch ovensafe skillet will also work.

2½   **cups (12½ ounces) all-purpose flour**
¼   **cup chopped fresh basil**
1   **tablespoon baking powder**
½   **teaspoon salt**
4½   **ounces Parmesan cheese, shredded (1½ cups)**
1   **cup whole milk**
½   **cup sour cream**
1   **large egg**
5   **tablespoons olive oil**
3   **garlic cloves, minced**
1   **cup pitted kalamata olives, halved**

1. Adjust oven rack to middle position and heat oven to 450 degrees. Whisk flour, basil, baking powder, and salt together in large bowl. Stir in 1 cup Parmesan, breaking up any clumps, until coated with flour. In separate bowl, whisk milk, sour cream, and egg together until smooth.

2. Heat oil in 10-inch cast-iron skillet over medium-high heat until shimmering. Add garlic and cook until fragrant, about 30 seconds. Pour all but 1 tablespoon of oil mixture into milk mixture and whisk to incorporate. Gently fold milk mixture into flour mixture until just combined, then fold in olives. Batter will be heavy and thick; do not overmix.

3. Quickly scrape batter into hot skillet and smooth top. Sprinkle with remaining ½ cup Parmesan. Bake until golden brown and toothpick inserted in center comes out clean, 15 to 20 minutes, rotating pan halfway through baking. Let bread cool in pan for 5 minutes, then turn out onto wire rack. Serve warm or at room temperature.

Cheddar Cheese Bread

MAKES 1 LOAF   **TOTAL TIME** 1 HOUR 15 MINUTES
(PLUS 45 MINUTES COOLING TIME)

✔ **WHY THIS RECIPE WORKS:** Run-of-the-mill cheese bread is at once dry and greasy, with almost no cheese flavor at all. We wanted a rich, moist loaf topped with a bold, cheesy crust. We started with all-purpose flour and added whole milk and sour cream for a clean, creamy flavor and moist texture. Just a few tablespoons of butter added enough richness without greasiness. Keeping the butter to a minimum also gave the bread a heartier texture. Most recipes for cheese bread call for shredded cheese, but we preferred our cheese cut into small chunks, which, when baked, created luscious, cheesy pockets throughout the bread. For added cheesy flavor and a crisp crust, we coated the pan and sprinkled the top of the loaf with shredded Parmesan. The texture of the bread improves as it cools, so resist the urge to slice the loaf while it is piping hot. The test kitchen's preferred loaf pan measures 8½ by 4½ inches; if you use a 9 by 5-inch loaf pan, start checking for doneness 5 minutes early.

3   **ounces Parmesan cheese, shredded (1 cup)**
2½   **cups (12½ ounces) all-purpose flour**
1   **tablespoon baking powder**
1   **teaspoon salt**
⅛   **teaspoon cayenne pepper**
⅛   **teaspoon pepper**
4   **ounces extra-sharp cheddar cheese, cut into ½-inch cubes (1 cup)**
1   **cup whole milk**
½   **cup sour cream**
3   **tablespoons unsalted butter, melted and cooled**
1   **large egg**

1. Adjust oven rack to middle position and heat oven to 350 degrees. Grease 8½ by 4½-inch loaf pan, then sprinkle ½ cup Parmesan evenly in bottom of pan.

2. In large bowl, whisk flour, baking powder, salt, cayenne, and pepper to combine. Mix in cheddar, breaking up clumps, until coated with flour. In medium bowl, whisk milk, sour cream, melted butter, and egg together. Gently fold milk mixture into flour mixture until just combined. Batter will be heavy and thick; do not overmix.

3. Scrape batter evenly into prepared loaf pan, smooth top, and sprinkle with remaining ½ cup Parmesan. Bake until deep golden brown and skewer inserted in center comes out clean (skewer will be wet if inserted into cheese pocket), 45 to 50 minutes, rotating pan halfway through baking.

4. Let loaf cool in pan for 5 minutes, then transfer loaf to wire rack and let cool until warm, about 45 minutes. Serve.

Cheese Bread with Bacon and Gruyère

Omit butter and substitute Gruyère for cheddar. Cook 5 slices finely chopped bacon in 12-inch skillet over medium-high heat until crisp, about 8 minutes; transfer to paper towel–lined plate. Pour off all but 3 tablespoons fat left in pan, add ½ cup finely chopped onion, and cook over medium heat until softened, about 5 minutes; let cool. Add cooked bacon and onion to flour mixture with cheese.

Brown Soda Bread

MAKES 1 LOAF   **TOTAL TIME** 1 HOUR 10 MINUTES
(PLUS 1 HOUR COOLING TIME)

✓ **WHY THIS RECIPE WORKS:** For a brown soda bread with good wheaty flavor but without a gummy, dense texture, we started by finding the right ratio of whole-wheat to all-purpose flour. Toasted wheat germ played up the sweet, nutty flavor of the whole wheat. To keep the texture light, we needed plenty of leavening; baking soda alone gave the bread a soapy taste, so we used a combination of baking soda and baking powder. Just a touch of sugar and a few tablespoons of butter didn't overwhelm the wholesomeness of our bread, but they did keep it from tasting "health food-y." Brushing a portion of the melted butter on the loaf after baking gave it a rich crust.

      2   **cups (10 ounces) all-purpose flour**
   1½   **cups (8¼ ounces) whole-wheat flour**
      ½   **cup toasted wheat germ**
      3   **tablespoons sugar**
   1½   **teaspoons salt**
      1   **teaspoon baking powder**
      1   **teaspoon baking soda**
   1¾   **cups buttermilk**
      3   **tablespoons unsalted butter, melted**

1. Adjust oven rack to lower-middle position and heat oven to 400 degrees. Line rimmed baking sheet with parchment paper.

2. Whisk all-purpose flour, whole-wheat flour, wheat germ, sugar, salt, baking powder, and baking soda together in large bowl. Combine buttermilk and 2 tablespoons melted butter in 2-cup liquid measuring cup. Add buttermilk mixture to flour mixture and stir with rubber spatula until dough just comes together.

3. Turn out dough onto lightly floured counter and knead until cohesive mass forms, about 8 times. Pat dough into 7-inch round and transfer to prepared sheet. Using sharp serrated knife, make ¼-inch-deep cross about 5 inches long on top of loaf.

4. Bake until skewer inserted in center comes out clean and loaf registers 195 degrees, 45 to 50 minutes, rotating sheet halfway through baking. Remove bread from oven. Brush with remaining 1 tablespoon melted butter. Transfer loaf to wire rack and let cool for at least 1 hour. Serve.

Brown Soda Bread with Currants and Caraway

Add 1 cup dried currants and 1 tablespoon caraway seeds to flour mixture before adding buttermilk.

Making Brown Soda Bread

1. MIX BUTTER INTO BUTTERMILK: Combine buttermilk and 2 tablespoons melted butter in 2-cup liquid measuring cup.

2. KNEAD BY HAND: Add buttermilk mixture to flour mixture and stir with rubber spatula until dough comes together. Turn out dough onto lightly floured counter and knead until cohesive mass forms, about 8 times.

3. SHAPE AND SLASH: Pat dough into 7-inch round and transfer to prepared sheet. Using sharp serrated knife, make ¼-inch-deep cross about 5 inches long on top of loaf.

4. BAKE: Bake until skewer inserted in center comes out clean and loaf registers 195 degrees, 45 to 50 minutes, rotating sheet halfway through baking.

Yeast Breads

Savory Breads

Sweet Breads

Easy Refrigerator Jams

Fluffy Dinner Rolls

MAKES 15 ROLLS **TOTAL TIME** 3 TO 3½ HOURS

✔ **WHY THIS RECIPE WORKS:** Soft, rich, homemade dinner rolls beat store-bought versions any day. The key to rich flavor and tender texture was using butter for richness, and shortening to keep our rolls light and tender. We found that lining a baking dish with a foil sling made it especially easy to get these tightly packed rolls out of the pan without flipping the pan over and damaging the tops. See page 635 for more information on how to make a foil sling. We do not recommend mixing this sticky dough by hand.

1½ **cups whole milk, heated to 110 degrees**
⅓ **cup honey, warmed**
¼ **cup vegetable shortening, melted**
3 **tablespoons unsalted butter, melted**
2 **large eggs**
5–5½ **cups (25 to 27½ ounces) all-purpose flour**
2¼ **teaspoons instant or rapid-rise yeast**
2 **teaspoons salt**
Vegetable oil spray

1. Whisk milk, honey, melted shortening, and melted butter together in large liquid measuring cup, then whisk in 1 egg. Combine 5 cups flour, yeast, and salt in bowl of stand mixer. Using dough hook on low speed, add milk mixture and mix until dough comes together, about 2 minutes. Increase speed to medium-low and knead until dough is smooth and elastic, about 8 minutes. (If after 4 minutes more flour is needed, add remaining ½ cup flour, 2 tablespoons at a time, until dough clears sides of bowl but sticks to bottom.)

2. Transfer dough to lightly floured counter and knead by hand to form smooth, round ball, about 15 seconds. Place dough in large, lightly greased bowl, cover tightly with greased plastic wrap, and let rise until doubled in size, 1 to 1½ hours.

3. Line 13 by 9-inch baking dish with foil sling and grease foil. Transfer dough to clean counter and stretch into even 15-inch log. Cut log into 15 equal pieces and cover with greased plastic.

4. Working with 1 piece of dough at a time, dimple top with fingertips, then fold short ends of dough underneath, pressing lightly to compress. Stretch dough around your thumbs into smooth, taut ball, then place seam side down on clean counter. Drag dough in small circles over counter using cupped hand until dough feels firm and round (should feel like dough is spinning underneath your hand, not turning over).

5. Arrange rolls in prepared baking dish and press lightly so they just touch. Mist rolls with oil spray, cover with plastic, and let rise until nearly doubled in size, 45 to 75 minutes.

6. Adjust oven rack to lower-middle position and heat oven to 350 degrees. Beat remaining 1 egg with 1 tablespoon water in bowl, then brush gently over rolls. Mist rolls with water. Bake until deep golden brown, 25 to 30 minutes, rotating pan halfway through baking. Let rolls cool in pan for 10 minutes, then remove from pan using foil sling. Serve warm.

TO MAKE AHEAD: Bowl of unrisen dough (step 2) can be refrigerated for up to 16 hours; let dough sit at room temperature for 30 minutes before shaping into rolls (step 3). Risen, unbaked rolls (step 5) can be frozen for up to 1 month; let frozen rolls sit at room temperature for 30 minutes before baking, and increase baking time to 30 to 35 minutes.

Shaping Fluffy Dinner Rolls

1. Working with 1 piece of dough at a time, dimple top with fingertips.

2. Fold short ends of dough underneath, pressing lightly to compress.

3. Stretch dough around your thumbs into smooth, taut ball.

4. Place dough seam side down on clean counter and turn in small circles using cupped hand until dough feels firm and round (dough should spin underneath your hand, not turn over).

Rustic Dinner Rolls

MAKES 16 ROLLS   **TOTAL TIME** 4 HOURS
(PLUS 1 HOUR COOLING TIME)

🗸 **WHY THIS RECIPE WORKS:** The remarkably crisp crust of European-style dinner rolls keeps them in the domain of professionals, who use steam-injected ovens to expose the developing crust to moisture. We wanted a reliable recipe for rustic dinner rolls with a crisp crust and a chewy crumb as good as any from an artisanal bakery. But when we tasted our first batch, we found a dense, bland crumb beneath a leathery crust. The flavor was easy to improve—we added whole-wheat flour for earthiness, and honey for sweetness. A little extra yeast improved the crumb slightly, but making the dough wetter was the best fix; the water created steam bubbles during baking, producing an airier crumb. Next we came up with a two-step process to mimic a steam-injected oven: First, we misted the rolls with water before baking. Next, we started baking them in a cake pan at a high temperature to help set their shape. Then we lowered the temperature, pulled the rolls apart, and returned them to the oven until we had golden rolls with a perfect crust and crumb. Because this dough is sticky, keep your hands well floured when handling it. We do not recommend mixing this sticky dough by hand. For more information on turning dough (step 3), see Turning Bread Dough.

1½ **cups plus 1 tablespoon water, room temperature**
2 **teaspoons honey**
1½ **teaspoons instant or rapid-rise yeast**
3 **cups plus 1 tablespoon (16½ ounces) bread flour, plus extra as needed**
3 **tablespoons whole-wheat flour**
1½ **teaspoons salt**

1. Whisk water, honey, and yeast together in bowl of stand mixer. Using dough hook on low speed, add bread flour and whole-wheat flour and mix on low speed until cohesive dough is formed, about 3 minutes. Cover bowl tightly with plastic wrap and let dough sit for 30 minutes.

2. Sprinkle salt over dough and knead on low speed for 5 minutes. Increase speed to medium and knead until dough is smooth and slightly tacky, about 1 minute. (If dough is very sticky, add 1 to 2 tablespoons flour and mix for 1 minute.) Place dough in large, lightly greased bowl, cover tightly with greased plastic, and let rise until doubled in size, about 1 hour.

3. Gently press center of dough to deflate. Using greased bowl scraper (or rubber spatula), fold partially risen dough over itself by gently lifting and folding edge of dough toward middle. Turn bowl 90 degrees and fold dough again; repeat turning bowl and folding dough 1 more time. Cover with plastic, let dough rise for 30 minutes, then repeat folding process. Cover with plastic and let dough rise until doubled in size, about 30 minutes.

4. Grease two 9-inch round cake pans. Transfer dough to floured counter, sprinkle lightly with flour, and cut in half. Stretch each half into 16-inch log, then cut each log into 8 equal pieces. With well-floured hands, gently pick up each piece and roll to coat with flour, shaking off excess. Arrange rolls in prepared pans, cut sides facing up, placing 1 in center and 7 around edges. Cover with plastic and let rise until doubled in size, about 30 minutes. Adjust oven rack to middle position and heat oven to 500 degrees.

5. Mist rolls with water. Bake until tops are brown, about 10 minutes. Remove rolls from oven and reduce oven temperature to 400 degrees. Carefully turn rolls out of pans onto baking sheet. Let rolls cool slightly, then turn right side up, pull apart, and space evenly on sheet. Continue to bake until deep golden brown, 10 to 15 minutes, rotating sheet halfway through baking. Transfer rolls to wire rack and let cool to room temperature, about 1 hour, before serving.

TO MAKE AHEAD: Baked rolls can be frozen for up to 1 month; reheat on baking sheet in 450-degree oven for 6 to 8 minutes.

Turning Bread Dough

1. Slide bowl scraper or rubber spatula under 1 side of dough. Gently lift and fold about one-third of dough toward center.

2. Repeat step 1 with opposite side of dough.

3. Fold dough in half perpendicular to first series of folds. Dough should have rough square shape.

This classic sandwich bread is among the simplest and fastest yeast breads you can make. The milk and butter add richness, while the honey adds a touch of welcome sweetness. Simple steps and two risings deliver bread in 2 hours (plus cooling time). If you don't have a stand mixer, you can mix and knead the bread dough by hand; see pages 590–91.

1. WEIGH THE FLOUR: Measure out 3½ cups bread flour using a scale.
WHY? Because the ratio of flour to liquids is critical, weighing your flour is advisable because it is more accurate. We use bread flour rather than all-purpose flour because it is higher in protein; the higher the protein, the more gluten in the dough, which produces a taller, sturdier loaf.

2. MAKE SURE THE WATER AND MILK ARE 110 DEGREES: Before combining all the wet ingredients, make sure that the milk and water are the right temperature.
WHY? If the liquids are too hot (130 degrees or more), they will kill the yeast; if too cool the yeast won't activate and the bread won't rise. We use instant yeast because it can be added without needing to proof it ahead of time.

3. KNEAD THE DOUGH: Combine the dry ingredients in a stand mixer fitted with a dough hook, and then slowly add the milk mixture until the dough comes together. Increase the speed to medium and knead until the dough is smooth.
WHY? Kneading develops gluten, which is crucial to the texture of the bread. We prefer to use a stand mixer because it is easier.

4. LET THE DOUGH RISE: Turn the dough out onto a floured counter and knead it briefly to form a round, smooth ball. Place the dough in a greased bowl, cover with greased plastic wrap, and let it rise until doubled in size, about 40 minutes.
WHY? After kneading, the dough needs to rest, relax, and rise. During this stage the yeast causes the dough to rise and fosters flavor development.

5. SHAPE THE LOAF: Press the dough into a rectangle about 1 inch thick. With the long side facing you, roll the dough into a firm cylinder. Pinch the seam closed and place the dough seam side down in a greased loaf pan. Press the dough so it touches all four sides of the pan.
WHY? Rolling the dough into a cylinder builds structure and makes a nice, tall loaf.

6. LET THE LOAF RISE: Cover the loaf pan with plastic and let the dough rise until doubled in size, 20 to 30 minutes.
WHY? This second rise, called proofing, allows the dough to regain some airiness lost during shaping, and the gluten to relax. To test if the dough is properly proofed, press on it gently with your fingertip: it should leave an indentation that slowly fills in.

7. HEAT A BAKING STONE AND CREATE A STEAMY ENVIRONMENT: Place a baking stone on the lowest oven rack and put a loaf pan on the stone. Heat the oven to 350 degrees. Pour boiling water into the hot loaf pan.
WHY? A steamy oven prevents the crust from setting and allows the maximum rise when the bread enters the oven. A baking stone ensures a well-browned bottom crust.

8. BAKE THE LOAF AND CHECK FOR DONENESS: Place the loaf pan on the baking stone and bake until the bread is golden brown and registers 195 degrees, 40 to 50 minutes, rotating the pan halfway through baking.
WHY? The use of an instant-read thermometer is recommended, but you should also follow the visual cues, as temperature alone doesn't always signify a perfectly baked loaf.

American Sandwich Bread

MAKES 1 LOAF   **TOTAL TIME** 2 HOURS
(PLUS 2 HOURS COOLING TIME)

WHY THIS RECIPE WORKS: Many people who might enjoy making terrific sandwich bread at home don't even try it because they think it takes most of a day. We wanted a good, solid sandwich bread recipe that could be prepared in 2 hours, start to finish, including baking time. We found that sandwich bread improved markedly when kneaded with a stand mixer. This method helped us resist the temptation to add extra flour in an effort to tame the sticky bread dough, as more flour tends to make the dough denser and less flavorful; it also makes it rise less. We were also surprised to find that we preferred instant yeast to active dry yeast for our sandwich bread recipe. Not only did it greatly reduce rising times, but it also made for better-tasting bread. If you don't have a stand mixer, you can mix and knead the bread dough by hand; see pages 590–91. If you don't have a baking stone, bake the bread on an overturned and preheated rimmed baking sheet.

Even beginning bakers can make our sandwich bread, which takes only 2 hours from start to finish.

1	**cup whole milk, heated to 110 degrees**
⅓	**cup warm water (110 degrees)**
3	**tablespoons honey**
2	**tablespoons unsalted butter, melted**
3½	**cups (19¼ ounces) bread flour**
2¼	**teaspoons instant or rapid-rise yeast**
2	**teaspoons salt**

1. Whisk milk, water, honey, and butter together in 4-cup liquid measuring cup. Using stand mixer fitted with dough hook, combine flour, yeast, and salt on low speed. Slowly add milk mixture and let dough come together, about 2 minutes. Increase speed to medium and knead until dough is smooth and slightly tacky, about 10 minutes.

2. Transfer dough to lightly floured counter and knead by hand to form smooth, round ball, about 15 seconds. Place dough in large, lightly greased bowl, cover tightly with greased plastic wrap, and let rise until doubled in size, 40 to 50 minutes.

3. Grease 9 by 5-inch loaf pan. Transfer dough to lightly floured counter and press into rectangle about 1 inch thick and no longer than 9 inches, with long side facing you. Roll dough toward you into firm cylinder, keeping roll taut by tucking it under itself as you go. Pinch seam closed and place seam side down in prepared pan, pressing gently into corners. Cover with plastic and let rise until nearly doubled in size, 20 to 30 minutes.

4. One hour before baking, place baking stone on lowest rack and place empty loaf pan (or other heatproof pan) on stone. Heat oven to 350 degrees. Bring 2 cups water to boil. Working quickly, pour boiling water into hot pan and place pan with loaf on baking stone. Bake until loaf is golden brown and registers 195 degrees, 40 to 50 minutes, rotating pan halfway through baking.

5. Let bread cool in pan for 5 minutes, then transfer to wire rack and let cool to room temperature, about 2 hours, before serving.

VARIATIONS
Wheat Sandwich Bread
For extra wheat flavor, we add toasted wheat germ to the dough.

Toast ¼ cup wheat germ in dry skillet until fragrant, about 5 minutes. Reduce amount of bread flour to 2 cups and combine with 1¼ cups whole-wheat flour and toasted wheat germ.

Oatmeal-Raisin Sandwich Bread
Omit warm water from milk mixture. Bring ¾ cup water to boil in small saucepan. Stir in ¾ cup old-fashioned rolled oats or quick oats (do not use instant oats) and cook until

softened slightly, about 90 seconds. Reduce flour to 2¾ cups and add cooked oatmeal to mixer with flour. Knead ¾ cup raisins, tossed in bowl with 1 tablespoon all-purpose flour, into dough after it is removed from mixer.

Buttermilk Sandwich Bread

For information on buttermilk substitutions, see page 577.

Substitute buttermilk, heated to 110 degrees, for whole milk. Increase first rise to 50 minutes to 1 hour.

Honey-Bran Sandwich Bread with Sunflower Seeds

Substitute ¼ cup wheat bran for ¼ cup bread flour, and increase honey to ¼ cup. Add ½ cup unsalted sunflower seeds to mixer during final minute of kneading.

Multigrain Bread

MAKES 2 LOAVES   **TOTAL TIME** 4 HOURS
(PLUS 2 HOURS COOLING TIME)

✔ **WHY THIS RECIPE WORKS:** Often multigrain bread either has great flavor but is as dense and as heavy as a brick, or it has a nice, light, sandwich-style texture but so little grain it might as well be white bread. We wanted a multigrain bread with both great flavor and balanced texture. Early tests showed that the whole grains impede the development of gluten, the protein that gives baked goods structure. Bread flour, with its high protein content, would seem the ideal candidate to combat this problem, but we found that it only made the bread chewier, not less dense. We switched to all-purpose flour and came up with a twofold solution: an autolyse, a resting period that gives the flour time to hydrate, followed by long kneading. The result was a loaf that baked up light yet chewy without being tough. For the whole grains, we hit upon a convenient, one-stop-shopping alternative: packaged seven-grain hot cereal. To soften the grains, we made a thick porridge with the cereal before adding it to the dough. A final step of rolling the shaped loaves in oats yielded a finished, professional look. Do not substitute instant oats in this recipe. For an accurate measurement of boiling water, bring a full kettle of water to a boil, then measure out the desired amount. If you don't have a stand mixer, you can mix and knead the bread dough by hand; see page 591 and below.

1¼	**cups (6¼ ounces) seven-grain hot cereal mix**
2½	**cups boiling water**
3	**cups (15 ounces) all-purpose flour,** **plus extra as needed**
1½	**cups (8¼ ounces) whole-wheat flour**
¼	**cup honey**
4	**tablespoons unsalted butter, melted and cooled**
2½	**teaspoons instant or rapid-rise yeast**
1	**tablespoon salt**
¾	**cup unsalted pumpkin seeds or sunflower seeds** **Vegetable oil spray**
½	**cup (1½ ounces) old-fashioned rolled oats** **or quick oats**

Kneading Bread Dough by Hand

1. MIX DOUGH: Whisk liquid ingredients together in medium mixing bowl. Whisk dry ingredients together in large mixing bowl. Stir liquid mixture into dry ingredients with rubber spatula until dough comes together and looks shaggy.

2. PRESS DOWN AND AWAY: Turn dough out onto lightly floured counter and shape with hands into rough ball. Start each stroke by gently pressing dough down and away from you with heel of hand.

3. LIFT AND FOLD: Lift edge of dough farthest away from you and fold dough in half toward you.

4. PRESS DOUGH FORWARD: Press dough forward again using heel of hand. Knead dough until smooth and elastic, 15 to 25 minutes.

1. Combine cereal mix and boiling water in bowl of stand mixer and let stand, stirring occasionally, until mixture cools to 100 degrees and resembles thick porridge, about 1 hour. In separate bowl, whisk all-purpose and whole-wheat flours together.

2. Using stand mixer fitted with dough hook, add honey, butter, and yeast to cooled cereal and mix on low speed until combined. Add flour mixture, ½ cup at a time, and knead until cohesive mass starts to form, 1½ to 2 minutes. Cover bowl tightly with plastic wrap and let dough sit for 20 minutes.

3. Sprinkle salt over dough and knead on medium-low speed until dough is smooth and clears sides of bowl, 8 to 9 minutes. (If dough is very sticky, add 1 to 2 tablespoons flour and mix for 1 minute.) Add seeds and knead for 15 seconds. Transfer dough to lightly floured counter and knead by hand to form smooth, round ball, about 1 minute. Place dough in large, lightly greased bowl, cover tightly with greased plastic, and let rise until nearly doubled in size, 45 minutes to 1 hour.

4. Grease two 9 by 5-inch loaf pans. Transfer dough to lightly floured counter and cut in half. Working with 1 piece of dough at a time, press into 9 by 6-inch rectangle, with short side facing you. Roll dough toward you into firm cylinder, keeping roll taut by tucking it under itself as you go. Pinch seam closed.

5. Mist loaves lightly with vegetable oil spray, then roll in oats. Place loaves seam side down in prepared pans, pressing gently into corners. Cover with plastic and let rise until nearly doubled in size, 30 to 40 minutes.

6. Adjust oven rack to middle position and heat oven to 375 degrees. Bake until loaves register 200 degrees, 35 to 40 minutes, rotating pans halfway through baking. Let bread cool in pan for 5 minutes, then transfer to wire rack and let cool to room temperature, about 2 hours, before serving.

VARIATION

Multigrain Dinner Rolls

Grease 13 by 9-inch baking dish. After dough has risen in step 3, transfer to lightly floured counter and cut into 18 even pieces. Working with 1 piece of dough at a time, stretch it around your thumbs into smooth, taut ball, then place seam side down on clean counter. Turn dough in small circles over counter using cupped hand until dough feels firm and round (should feel like dough is spinning underneath your hand, not turning over). Roll 1 side of each roll in oats, arrange in prepared baking dish, and cover lightly with greased plastic wrap; let rise until nearly doubled in size, 30 to 40 minutes. Bake in 375-degree oven until rolls register 200 degrees, 30 to 35 minutes. Let rolls cool in dish for 5 minutes, then transfer to wire rack and let cool to room temperature, about 2 hours, before serving.

Shaping Loaf Breads

1. Place dough on lightly floured counter. Using hands, gently press into rectangle as directed in recipe.

2. Roll dough into firm cylinder, keeping roll taut by tucking it under itself as you go.

3. Pinch seam closed.

4. Place seam side down in prepared pan, pressing gently into corners.

NOTES FROM THE TEST KITCHEN

Mixing Bread Dough by Hand

We prefer to mix dough with a stand mixer fitted with a dough hook because it's effortless and produces great bread. However, if you don't own a machine you can mix dough by hand following these instructions. Note that there are some recipes in this chapter for which a stand mixer is necessary because the dough is too sticky or wet.

Whisk the liquid ingredients together in a medium bowl or large liquid measuring cup. In a large bowl, whisk the dry ingredients together. Stir the liquid mixture into the dry ingredients until the dough comes together and looks shaggy. Turn the dough out onto a clean counter and knead to form a smooth, round ball, 15 to 25 minutes, adding extra flour as needed to prevent the dough from sticking to the counter. Transfer to a large, lightly oiled bowl, cover with greased plastic wrap, and let rise as directed.

We focused on the unique ingredients in this traditional bread—molasses and cornmeal—for a hearty, moist loaf.

NOTES FROM THE TEST KITCHEN

Yeast

Yeast is commonly available in two forms: instant and active dry. We prefer instant yeast, also called rapid-rise, because it's faster-acting and easy to use. It does not need to be "proofed" in warm water; it can simply be added to dry ingredients. Both types of yeast come in packets of 2¼ teaspoons. Active dry yeast can be substituted for instant yeast, although you will need to use more. To compensate for the greater quantity of inactive yeast cells in active dry, simply use 25 percent more of it (for example, if the recipe calls for 1 teaspoon of instant, use 1¼ teaspoons of active dry). The inverse also applies—use about 25 percent less instant yeast in a recipe that calls for active dry. Don't forget to dissolve active dry yeast in a portion of the water (heated to 110 degrees) from the recipe. Then let it stand for 5 minutes before adding it to the remaining wet ingredients. Yeast begins to die at 130 degrees, so make sure the water is not too hot.

Yeast should be stored in a cool environment, in either the fridge or the freezer. Because yeast is a living organism, the expiration date on the package should be observed.

Anadama Bread

MAKES 2 LOAVES   **TOTAL TIME** 2½ TO 3 HOURS (PLUS 2 HOURS COOLING TIME)

✓ **WHY THIS RECIPE WORKS:** We wanted a hearty, not heavy, version of this traditional New England bread, and we wanted the star ingredients—molasses and cornmeal—to have real presence. We increased the amount of molasses called for in most recipes until we landed on a full ½ cup—enough to impart a decidedly bittersweet flavor and a beautiful golden color. We found that a whole cup of cornmeal was necessary to achieve the heartiness and pleasant grit we were after, and boosting the yeast helped keep the texture light. Finally, a judicious amount of butter made for a moist, tender loaf. If you don't have a stand mixer, you can mix and knead the bread dough by hand; see pages 590–91. This recipe is easily halved if you'd like to make just one loaf.

2	cups warm water (110 degrees)
½	cup molasses
5	tablespoons unsalted butter, melted
5½	cups (27½ ounces) all-purpose flour
1	cup (5 ounces) cornmeal, plus extra for pans
1	tablespoon instant or rapid-rise yeast
2½	teaspoons salt

1. Whisk water, molasses, and melted butter together in 4-cup liquid measuring cup. Using stand mixer fitted with dough hook, mix flour, cornmeal, yeast, and salt on low speed until combined, about 5 seconds. Slowly add molasses mixture and knead until cohesive mass starts to form, about 2 minutes. Increase speed to medium-low and knead until dough is smooth and elastic, 6 to 8 minutes. (Dough should clear sides of bowl but will stick to bottom.)

2. Transfer dough to lightly floured counter and knead by hand for about 1 minute. Place dough in large, lightly greased bowl, cover tightly with greased plastic wrap, and let rise until almost doubled in size, 1 to 1½ hours.

3. Grease two 8½ by 4½-inch loaf pans and dust with cornmeal. Press on dough gently to deflate, then transfer to lightly floured counter and cut in half. Working with 1 piece of dough at a time, press into 17 by 8-inch rectangle, with short side facing you. Roll dough into firm cylinder, keeping roll taut by tucking it under itself as you go. Pinch seam closed. Place loaves seam side down in prepared pans, pressing gently into corners. Cover with plastic and let rise until nearly doubled in size, 30 to 40 minutes.

4. Twenty minutes before baking, adjust oven rack to lower-middle position and heat oven to 425 degrees.

5. Place pans in oven and reduce oven temperature to 375 degrees. Bake until loaves are brown and register 200 degrees, 35 to 45 minutes, switching and rotating pans halfway through baking. Let bread cool in pan for 5 minutes, then transfer to wire rack and let cool to room temperature, about 2 hours, before serving.

English Muffin Bread

MAKES 2 LOAVES   **TOTAL TIME** 1 HOUR 45 MINUTES (PLUS 1 HOUR COOLING TIME)

✓ **WHY THIS RECIPE WORKS:** We love English muffins for their crunchy crust, chewy interior, and many nooks and crannies. So we looked for those same great qualities in a quick, easy loaf bread. We've taken our favorite English muffin recipe and translated it into a simple bread recipe that toasts and tastes like English muffins but with half the work. We prefer bread flour in this recipe for its stronger gluten proteins, which give this loaf a chewy yet light consistency. In addition, in contrast to all-purpose flour, bread flour absorbs more water, an important aspect since this is a fairly wet and sticky batter/dough. The resulting crumb has a solid structure and consistent holes. This bread can be eaten plain, but it really shines when toasted—and buttered.

  5 **cups (27½ ounces) bread flour**
4½ **teaspoons instant or rapid-rise yeast**
  1 **tablespoon sugar**
  2 **teaspoons salt**
  1 **teaspoon baking soda**
  3 **cups whole milk, heated to 120 degrees**
     Cornmeal

1. Combine flour, yeast, sugar, salt, and baking soda in large bowl. Stir in milk until combined, about 1 minute. Cover tightly with greased plastic wrap and let rise until doubled in size and bubbly, about 30 minutes.

2. Grease two 8½ by 4½-inch loaf pans and dust with cornmeal. Stir dough, then divide between prepared pans, pushing into corners with greased rubber spatula. (Pans should be about two-thirds full.) Cover pans with greased plastic and let dough rise until it reaches edge of pans, about 30 minutes. Adjust oven rack to middle position and heat oven to 375 degrees.

3. Bake until loaves are well browned and register 200 degrees, about 30 minutes, switching and rotating pans halfway through baking. Let bread cool in pans for 5 minutes, then transfer to wire rack and let cool to room temperature, about 1 hour. Slice, toast, and serve.

EASY REFRIGERATOR JAMS

You can experience the wonders of homemade jam with these simple recipes, each of which makes 2 cups. The jams don't need to be processed, and they can be kept in the fridge for a few weeks.

STRAWBERRY REFRIGERATOR JAM
MAKES ABOUT 2 CUPS   **TOTAL TIME** 40 MINUTES (PLUS COOLING TIME)

1½ **pounds strawberries, hulled and cut into ½-inch pieces (3 cups)**
  1 **cup sugar**
  3 **tablespoons lemon juice**

1. Place metal spoon in freezer to chill. Combine strawberries, sugar, and lemon juice in large saucepan. Bring to boil over medium-high heat, then reduce heat to medium. Mash fruit with potato masher until fruit is mostly broken down. Simmer vigorously until fruit mixture thickens to jamlike consistency, 15 to 20 minutes.

2. To test for set point, remove saucepan from heat. Dip chilled spoon into jam and allow jam to run off spoon; jam should slowly fall off spoon in single thickened clump. If jam is runny, return to medium heat and simmer 2 to 4 minutes before retesting. Transfer finished jam to jar with tight-fitting lid, let cool to room temperature, then cover and refrigerate. (Jam can be refrigerated for up to 3 weeks.)

RASPBERRY REFRIGERATOR JAM
Substitute 1 pound raspberries for strawberries and leave fruit whole. Reduce sugar to ¾ cup and lemon juice to 2 tablespoons.

BLUEBERRY REFRIGERATOR JAM
Substitute 1 pound blueberries for strawberries and leave fruit whole. Reduce sugar to ¾ cup and lemon juice to 2 tablespoons. In step 1, simmer mixture for 8 to 12 minutes.

To easily shape challah bread, we top a large braid with a smaller one.

Challah

MAKES 1 LOAF   **TOTAL TIME** 3 TO 4 HOURS
(PLUS 2 HOURS 15 MINUTES COOLING TIME)

✔ WHY THIS RECIPE WORKS: The best challah is rich with eggs and lightly sweetened, and it has a dark, shiny crust and a firm but light and tender texture. For our recipe, we began with all-purpose flour (bread flour made no significant improvement) and 2¼ teaspoons of instant yeast, which gave the challah the right amount of lift. A combination of two whole eggs and an egg yolk made a loaf with good egg flavor and tender texture, without being too eggy. We kept with tradition and made the bread dairy-free, using water and oil instead of milk and butter (we found that the challah made with water had a lighter and more appealing texture). Just ¼ cup of sugar sweetened the challah and improved its flavor and color. The recommended shape for challah is a simple braid, but we found this to be a problem because the loaf rose out but not up. Some recipes call for braiding six strands for a higher loaf, but this can get complicated. Our solution was to make two braids, one large and one small, and place the smaller braid on

top. An egg white–water mixture brushed over the loaf before putting it into the oven produced an evenly brown and shiny crust. If you don't have a stand mixer, you can mix and knead the bread dough by hand; see pages 590–91. Leftover challah makes sensational French toast (page 548).

3	large eggs
½	cup warm water (110 degrees), plus 1 tablespoon
¼	cup vegetable oil
3–3½	cups (15 to 17½ ounces) all-purpose flour
¼	cup (1¾ ounces) sugar
2¼	teaspoons instant or rapid-rise yeast
1¼	teaspoons salt
1	teaspoon poppy or sesame seeds (optional)

1. Separate 1 egg; reserve white for glaze. Whisk separated yolk, remaining 2 eggs, ½ cup warm water, and oil together in liquid measuring cup. Combine 3 cups flour, sugar, yeast, and salt in bowl of stand mixer. Using dough hook on low speed, add egg-water mixture and mix until dough comes together, about 2 minutes. Increase speed to medium and knead until dough is smooth and slightly tacky, about 1 minute. (If after 4 minutes more flour is needed, add remaining ½ cup flour, 2 tablespoons at a time, until dough clears sides of bowl but sticks to bottom.)

2. Transfer dough to lightly floured counter and knead by hand to form smooth, round ball, about 1 minute. Place dough in large, lightly greased bowl, cover tightly with greased plastic wrap, and let rise until doubled in size, 1 to 1½ hours.

3. Line baking sheet with parchment paper. Transfer dough to lightly floured counter and cut into 2 pieces, one twice as large as the other. Cut doughs into 3 pieces and roll each piece out into 16-inch-long rope (3 ropes will be much thicker). Braid 2 loaves, one using 3 large ropes and one using 3 small ropes.

4. Beat reserved egg white and remaining 1 tablespoon water together in bowl. Transfer large braid to prepared sheet, brush top with egg white mixture, and place smaller braid on top. Tuck braid ends underneath. Cover with greased plastic and let rise until nearly doubled in size, 45 minutes to 1¼ hours.

5. Adjust oven rack to lower-middle position and heat oven to 375 degrees. Brush loaf with remaining egg white mixture, sprinkle with seeds, if using, and mist with water. Bake until loaf is golden and registers 200 degrees, 30 to 40 minutes, rotating sheet halfway through baking. Let bread cool on sheet for 15 minutes, then transfer to wire rack and let cool to room temperature, about 2 hours, before serving.

TO MAKE AHEAD: Bowl of unrisen dough (step 2) can be refrigerated for up to 16 hours; let dough sit at room temperature for 30 minutes before shaping into loaf (step 3).

Braiding Challah Bread

1. Transfer dough to lightly floured counter and cut into 2 pieces, one twice as large as the other.

2. Cut larger piece of dough into 3 pieces and roll out into evenly sized 16-inch ropes. Repeat with smaller piece of dough.

3. Braid 2 loaves, one using 3 large ropes and one using 3 small ropes.

4. Transfer large braid to prepared sheet, brush top with some egg white mixture, and place smaller braid on top. Tuck braid ends underneath.

NOTES FROM THE TEST KITCHEN

Storing Bread

Storing bread in the refrigerator to extend its shelf life may seem like a good idea, but this actually shortens it. The cool temperature of the fridge speeds up the staling process, and a loaf of refrigerated bread will go stale more quickly than an unrefrigerated loaf. Bread will last a few days simply stored cut side down on the counter. Do not store bread in plastic (the trapped moisture encourages mold). For longer storage, wrap the bread tightly in aluminum foil, place it in a zipper-lock bag, and store in the freezer for up to one month. To serve, bake the frozen foil-wrapped loaf directly on the rack of a 450-degree oven until warm and crisp, 10 to 30 minutes.

Almost No-Knead Bread

MAKES 1 LOAF   **TOTAL TIME** 3 HOURS 30 MINUTES
(PLUS 8 HOURS RESTING TIME AND 2 HOURS COOLING TIME)

✔ **WHY THIS RECIPE WORKS:** The no-knead method of bread making replaces kneading, the mechanical process that forms the gluten that gives bread structure, with a very high hydration level (85 percent—for every 10 ounces of flour, there are 8.5 ounces of water) and an 8- to 18-hour autolyse, or resting period, that allows the flour to hydrate and rest before the dough is briefly kneaded. The bread is baked in a covered Dutch oven; the humid environment gives the loaf a dramatic open crumb structure and a crisp crust. However, as we baked loaf after loaf, we found two big problems: The dough didn't have enough structure, and it lacked flavor. To give the dough more strength (and make it easier to handle), we lowered the hydration and added the bare minimum of kneading time (under a minute) to compensate. For flavor, we introduced two elements: an acidic tang with vinegar and a shot of yeasty flavor with beer. Use a Dutch oven that holds 6 quarts or more for this recipe. An enameled cast-iron Dutch oven with a tight-fitting lid works best, but a cast-iron Dutch oven or heavy stockpot will also work. Make sure the knob on the pot lid is ovensafe at 425 degrees; you can often buy inexpensive replacement knobs from the pot manufacturer.

> 3 cups (15 ounces) all-purpose flour
> 1½ teaspoons salt
> ¼ teaspoon instant or rapid-rise yeast
> ¾ cup water, room temperature
> ½ cup mild-flavored lager, such as Budweiser, room temperature
> 1 tablespoon distilled white vinegar
>   Vegetable oil spray

1. Whisk flour, salt, and yeast together in large bowl. Add water, beer, and vinegar. Using rubber spatula, fold mixture, scraping up dry flour from bottom of bowl, until shaggy ball forms. Cover bowl with plastic wrap and let dough sit at room temperature for at least 8 hours or up to 18 hours.

2. Lay 18 by 12-inch sheet of parchment paper on counter and coat lightly with vegetable oil spray. Transfer dough to lightly floured counter and knead by hand to form smooth, round ball, 10 to 15 times. Shape dough into ball by pulling edges into middle. Transfer loaf, seam side down, to center of greased parchment paper. Using parchment paper as sling, gently lower dough into heavy-bottomed Dutch oven. Mist dough lightly with vegetable oil spray, cover loosely with plastic, and let rise until doubled in size, about 2 hours.

This is the easiest loaf of bread you can make. Kneading is replaced with a very high hydration level and an overnight resting period, which produce gluten slowly but without any work. Before baking, the dough is kneaded for less than a minute, shaped, and allowed to rise before baking in a Dutch oven. Mild beer and vinegar amp up the malty flavor of the bread.

1. MIX THE DOUGH AND LET IT REST:
Make the dough by folding the wet ingredients into the dry until the dough comes together and looks shaggy. Cover the bowl with plastic and let the dough sit at room temperature for at least 8 hours.
WHY? Letting the dough sit for a long time actually develops the gluten, much like kneading—this is the trick to this bread. Don't skimp on the resting time, or the bread won't have enough structure and will turn out very flat.

2. KNEAD THE DOUGH JUST 10 TO 15 TIMES BY HAND: Turn the dough out onto a lightly floured counter and knead by hand to form a smooth, round ball, 10 to 15 times.
WHY? These few turns done by hand on the counter make a big difference to the texture of the final loaf, and it's very easy to do.

3. SHAPE THE LOAF: After kneading the loaf, shape the dough into a ball by pulling the edges into the middle.
WHY? The dough is very easy to handle and has plenty of structure. You just want to pull up the sides so the ball of dough is taller and narrower, rather than wider and flatter.

4. LET THE DOUGH RISE IN A DUTCH OVEN: Transfer the loaf, seam side down, to a large sheet of greased parchment and, using the paper, transfer it to a Dutch oven. Mist the bread with vegetable oil spray, cover it loosely with plastic, and let it rise until doubled in size, about 2 hours.
WHY? Since we use a Dutch oven to bake this bread, it's convenient to let it rise in it as well. During baking the Dutch oven traps steam, creating a thick, hearty crust while helping the dough keep its round shape.

5. START THE DOUGH IN A COLD OVEN:
Sprinkle the top of the dough lightly with flour and cut a ½-inch-deep X into the top of the loaf. Cover the pot, place it in the oven, and turn the oven to 425 degrees.
WHY? Most recipes for no-knead bread require preheating the pot in a superhot oven before placing the dough in the pot. Our method is easier (and will keep you from burning yourself), and, more important, it prevents the bottom of the loaf from burning.

6. BAKE COVERED, THEN UNCOVERED:
Bake the bread, covered, for 30 minutes as the oven heats up. Remove the lid and continue to bake until the center of the loaf registers 210 degrees on an instant-read thermometer and the crust is deep golden brown, 20 to 30 minutes.
WHY? By baking the bread both covered and uncovered, you get a chewy interior and a thick, hearty crust.

3. Sprinkle flour lightly over top of loaf. Using sharp serrated knife, cut ½-inch-deep X into top of loaf. Cover pot, place on middle rack in oven, turn oven to 425 degrees, and bake bread for 30 minutes while oven heats.

4. Remove lid and continue to bake until loaf is deep brown and registers 210 degrees, 20 to 30 minutes. Remove bread from pot using parchment sling and transfer to wire rack, discarding parchment. Let bread cool to room temperature, about 2 hours, before serving.

VARIATIONS

Almost No-Knead Seeded Rye Bread

Reduce all-purpose flour to 1½ cups plus 1 tablespoon. Add 1 cup plus 2 tablespoons rye flour and 2 tablespoons caraway seeds to flour mixture.

Almost No-Knead Whole-Wheat Bread

Substitute 1 cup whole-wheat flour for 1 cup all-purpose flour. Stir 2 tablespoons honey into water before adding to dry ingredients in step 1.

Almost No-Knead Cranberry-Pecan Bread

This bread makes especially good toast.

Add ½ cup dried cranberries and ½ cup toasted pecans to flour mixture.

Rosemary Focaccia

MAKES 2 LOAVES   TOTAL TIME 4 HOURS

(PLUS 8 HOURS RESTING TIME AND 35 MINUTES COOLING TIME)

✓ **WHY THIS RECIPE WORKS:** Focaccia can easily disappoint if it turns out heavy and thick. We wanted a light, airy, and crisp-crusted loaf topped with a smattering of herbs. Using a sponge—a mixture of flour, water, and yeast—gave us the flavor benefits of a long fermentation with minimal effort. But our loaves weren't tender and airy enough; kneading was developing too much gluten. For a gentler process, we used a high proportion of water to flour and a long rest to replicate the effect of kneading. To give our loaves a flavorful, crisp crust, we oiled the baking pans and added coarse salt. For more information on turning dough (step 3), see page 587. If you don't have a baking stone, bake the bread on an overturned and preheated rimmed baking sheet.

SPONGE
½   **cup (2½ ounces) all-purpose flour**
⅓   **cup warm water (110 degrees)**
¼   **teaspoon instant or rapid-rise yeast**

Types of Flour

When it comes to baking, the type of flour you use, whether all-purpose flour, bread flour, cake flour, or whole-wheat flour, matters. What are the differences? In the case of most of these flours, the main one is protein level, which varies significantly among them. Therefore, these flours will absorb water differently. Protein content also affects gluten development. More protein leads to more gluten, which, in turn, can translate to coarseness, chewiness, toughness, or crispness. Depending on the recipe, these traits may or may not be desirable.

ALL-PURPOSE FLOUR is by far the most versatile flour available. Its protein content (10 to 11.7 percent, depending on the brand; King Arthur is close to 11.7 percent, Pillsbury and Gold Medal around 10.5 percent) provides enough structure to make good sandwich bread, yet it's light enough to use for cakes of a medium-to-coarse crumb. We prefer unbleached flour. Bleached flours in our tests did not perform as well as the unbleached flours and were sometimes criticized for tasting flat or carrying off-flavors.

BREAD FLOUR has a protein content of about 12 to 14 percent, meaning it develops a lot of gluten to provide strong, chewy structure for sandwich and rustic breads.

CAKE FLOUR has a low protein content—about 6 to 8 percent—and thus yields cakes and pastries with less gluten, which translates to a finer, more delicate crumb. We use cake flour for light cakes, such as pound cake and angel food cake. One note: Most cake flour is bleached, which affects the starches in flour and enables it to absorb greater amounts of liquid and fat. Most cakes have so much sugar and fat it's very hard to detect any off-notes in the flour caused by the bleaching process. It is possible to approximate 1 cup of cake flour by using 2 tablespoons of cornstarch plus ⅞ cup of all-purpose flour.

WHOLE-WHEAT FLOUR is made from all three parts of the wheat kernel—the endosperm as well as the fiber-rich bran, or outer shell, and the tiny, vitamin-packed germ. The presence of the germ and bran in whole-wheat flour makes it more nutritious and more flavorful, but also more dense and less able to rise. We generally don't like breads or baked goods made with 100 percent whole-wheat flour; they are too dense and can be sour-tasting. Instead, we rely on a combination of all-purpose flour and whole-wheat flour.

DOUGH

2½ cups (12½ ounces) all-purpose flour

1¼ cups warm water (110 degrees)

1 teaspoon instant or rapid-rise yeast

Kosher salt

4 tablespoons extra-virgin olive oil

2 tablespoons minced fresh rosemary

1. FOR THE SPONGE: Stir all ingredients together in large bowl until uniform mass forms and no dry flour remains, about 1 minute. Cover bowl tightly with plastic wrap and let sponge sit at room temperature for at least 8 hours or up to 1 day.

2. FOR THE DOUGH: Stir flour, water, and yeast into sponge until uniform mass forms and no dry flour remains, about 1 minute. Cover with plastic and let sit for 15 minutes. Sprinkle 2 teaspoons salt over dough and stir to combine, about 1 minute. Cover with plastic and let rise for 30 minutes.

3. Gently press center of dough to deflate. Using greased bowl scraper (or rubber spatula), fold partially risen dough over itself by gently lifting and folding edge of dough toward middle. Turn bowl 90 degrees and fold dough again; repeat turning bowl and folding dough 6 more times. Cover with plastic and let dough rise for 30 minutes. Repeat folding and rising process 2 more times.

4. One hour before baking, adjust oven rack to upper-middle position, place baking stone on rack, and heat oven to 500 degrees. Coat each of two 9-inch round cake pans with 2 tablespoons oil, and sprinkle each with ½ teaspoon salt.

5. Gently transfer dough to lightly floured counter, sprinkle lightly with flour, and cut in half. Shape each half into 5-inch round by gently tucking under edges, then place in prepared pans, top sides down. Slide each dough around pan to coat bottom and sides with oil, then flip dough over. Cover pans with plastic and let rest for 5 minutes.

6. Using fingertips, press dough out toward edges of pan, taking care not to tear it. (If dough resists stretching, let it rest for 10 minutes, then try again.) Using dinner fork, poke entire surface of dough 25 to 30 times, popping any large bubbles. Sprinkle rosemary evenly over top. Let dough rest in pans until slightly bubbly, 5 to 10 minutes.

7. Place pans on baking stone and lower oven temperature to 450 degrees. Bake until tops are golden brown, 25 to 28 minutes, rotating pans halfway through baking. Let bread cool in pans for 5 minutes, then transfer to wire rack and brush with any oil left in pans. Let cool for 30 minutes before serving.

VARIATIONS

Focaccia with Kalamata Olives and Anchovies

Omit salt from pans in step 4. Substitute 1 cup pitted kalamata olives, rinsed and chopped coarse, 4 rinsed and minced anchovy fillets, and 1 teaspoon red pepper flakes for rosemary. Sprinkle each focaccia with ¼ cup finely grated Pecorino Romano cheese as soon as it is removed from oven.

Focaccia with Caramelized Red Onion, Pancetta, and Oregano

Cook 4 ounces finely chopped pancetta in 12-inch skillet over medium heat, stirring occasionally, until most of fat has rendered, about 10 minutes; transfer to paper towel–lined plate. Add 1 chopped red onion and 2 tablespoons water to fat left in skillet and cook over medium heat until onion softens and is beginning to brown, about 12 minutes; set aside. Substitute pancetta, onion, and 2 teaspoons minced fresh oregano for rosemary.

Making Focaccia

1. Shape each dough half into rounds by tucking under edges, then place in pans, top sides down. Coat with oil by sliding dough around pan and flipping. Let rest 5 minutes.

2. Using fingertips, press dough out toward edges of pan, taking care not to tear it. (If dough resists stretching, let it rest for 10 minutes, then try again.)

3. Using fork, poke surface of dough 25 to 30 times. Sprinkle rosemary evenly over top. Let dough rest until slightly bubbly, 5 to 10 minutes.

4. Place pans on baking stone and lower oven temperature to 450 degrees. Bake until tops are golden brown, 25 to 28 minutes, rotating pans halfway through baking.

A little cornstarch helps to make a tender but sturdy dough for our cinnamon and brown sugar–filled sticky buns.

Ultimate Cinnamon Buns

MAKES 8 BUNS   **TOTAL TIME** 5 HOURS

✔ **WHY THIS RECIPE WORKS:** This mammoth breed of cinnamon bun is distinguished from its more diminutive cousins by its size, yes, but also by the richness of the soft, buttery, yeasted dough, the abundance of cinnamon-sugar filling, and the thickness of the cream cheese glaze. We used dough for brioche—an eggy, buttery white bread—as the perfect soft and tender base for our buns. Looking for even more tenderness, we tried cake flour instead of all-purpose, but that just made heavy, squat buns. Cutting all-purpose flour with a little cornstarch gave us a tender, soft dough that held its structure. For a filling with a hint of caramel flavor, we combined cinnamon with brown sugar, rather than white sugar. Softened butter helped keep the filling from spilling out as we rolled up the dough. Baked together, the butter and cinnamon sugar turned into a rich, gooey filling. No bun would be complete without a thick spread of icing, so we spread the buns with a tangy glaze of confectioners' sugar, cream cheese, milk, and vanilla. We do not recommend mixing this sticky dough by hand.

DOUGH

- ¾ cup whole milk, heated to 110 degrees
- 2¼ teaspoons instant or rapid-rise yeast
- 3 large eggs, room temperature
- 4¼–4½ cups (21¼ to 22½ ounces) all-purpose flour
- ½ cup cornstarch
- ½ cup (3½ ounces) granulated sugar
- 1½ teaspoons salt
- 12 tablespoons unsalted butter, cut into 12 pieces and softened

FILLING

- 1½ cups packed (10½ ounces) light brown sugar
- 1½ tablespoons ground cinnamon
- ¼ teaspoon salt
- 4 tablespoons unsalted butter, softened

GLAZE

- 1½ cups (6 ounces) confectioners' sugar
- 4 ounces cream cheese, softened
- 1 tablespoon whole milk
- 1 teaspoon vanilla extract

1. FOR THE DOUGH: Make foil sling for 13 by 9-inch baking pan by folding 2 long sheets of aluminum foil; first sheet should be 13 inches wide and second sheet should be 9 inches wide. Lay sheets of foil in pan perpendicular to each other, with extra foil hanging over edges of pan. Push foil into corners and up sides of pan, smoothing foil flush to pan. Grease foil.

2. Whisk milk and yeast together in liquid measuring cup until yeast dissolves, then whisk in eggs. Combine 4¼ cups flour, cornstarch, sugar, and salt in bowl of stand mixer. Using dough hook on low speed, slowly add milk mixture and mix until dough comes together, about 1 minute. Increase speed to medium and add butter, 1 piece at a time, until incorporated. Continue to mix until dough is smooth and comes away from sides of bowl, about 10 minutes. (If after 5 minutes more flour is needed, add remaining ¼ cup flour, 1 tablespoon at a time, until dough clears sides of bowl but sticks to bottom.)

3. Transfer dough to lightly floured counter and knead by hand to form smooth, round ball, about 1 minute. Place dough in large, lightly greased bowl, cover tightly with greased plastic wrap, and let rise until doubled in size, about 2 hours.

4. FOR THE FILLING: Combine sugar, cinnamon, and salt in bowl. Transfer dough to lightly floured counter and roll into 18-inch square. Spread butter over dough, leaving ½-inch border at edges. Sprinkle with filling, leaving ¾-inch border at top edge, and press lightly to adhere. Roll dough away from you into firm cylinder, keeping roll taut by tucking it under itself as you go. Pinch seam closed. Using serrated knife, cut cylinder into 8 pieces and arrange, cut side down, in prepared pan. Cover with plastic and let rise until doubled in size, about 1 hour.

5. Adjust oven rack to middle position and heat oven to 350 degrees. Bake until buns are deep golden brown and filling is melted, 35 to 40 minutes, rotating pan halfway through baking.

6. FOR THE GLAZE: Whisk all ingredients together in bowl until smooth. Drizzle glaze over buns as soon as they come out of oven. Let glazed buns cool in pan for 30 minutes, then remove from pan using sling and serve.

TO MAKE AHEAD: Pan of unrisen buns (step 4) can be refrigerated for up to 1 day; let buns sit at room temperature for 1 hour before baking (step 5).

Sticky Buns with Pecans

MAKES 12 BUNS   **TOTAL TIME** 5½ TO 6 HOURS

✔ **WHY THIS RECIPE WORKS:** Sticky buns are often too sweet, too big, too rich, and just too much. We wanted sticky buns with a tender, feathery crumb and a gently gooey and chewy glaze. We made our dough with a basic mix of flour, yeast, and salt and added buttermilk, which gave the buns a complex flavor and a little acidity that balanced the sweetness. Butter and eggs enriched the dough further. Dark brown sugar worked fine in the filling, but it made for an unappealingly dark (and burnt-looking) glaze, so we stuck with light brown sugar for both components. To prevent the sticky bun glaze from hardening into a taffylike shell, we added a couple of tablespoons of heavy cream, which kept the glaze supple. Setting the pan on a baking stone in the oven helped the bottoms of the buns (which ended up on top) to bake and brown evenly. We found it was important to wait a few minutes before turning the buns out of the pan to give the glaze time to thicken and stay put; fresh out of the oven, the glaze was liquid and ran right off the buns. Although we like sticky buns with nuts, we don't like the steamed texture of nuts baked inside the buns. Our solution was to toast the nuts, add them to a lightly sweetened topping, and then spoon them over the baked buns so they stayed crisp. For information on buttermilk substitutions, see page 577. If you don't have a baking stone, bake the buns on an overturned and preheated rimmed baking sheet. We do not recommend mixing this sticky dough by hand.

DOUGH

¾ cup buttermilk, heated to 110 degrees
¼ cup (1¾ ounces) granulated sugar
2¼ teaspoons instant or rapid-rise yeast
3 large eggs, lightly beaten
6 tablespoons unsalted butter, melted and cooled
4¼ cups (21¼ ounces) all-purpose flour
1¼ teaspoons salt

CARAMEL GLAZE

6 tablespoons unsalted butter
¾ cup packed (5¼ ounces) light brown sugar
3 tablespoons corn syrup
2 tablespoons heavy cream
   Pinch salt

FILLING

¾ cup packed (5¼ ounces) light brown sugar
2 teaspoons ground cinnamon
¼ teaspoon ground cloves
   Pinch salt
1 tablespoon unsalted butter, melted and cooled

PECAN TOPPING

¼ cup packed (1¾ ounces) light brown sugar
3 tablespoons unsalted butter
3 tablespoons corn syrup
   Pinch salt
1 teaspoon vanilla extract
¾ cup pecans, toasted and chopped coarse

1. FOR THE DOUGH: Whisk buttermilk, sugar, and yeast together in liquid measuring cup until yeast dissolves, then whisk in eggs and melted butter. Combine 4 cups flour and salt in bowl of stand mixer. Using dough hook on low speed, slowly add buttermilk mixture and mix until dough comes together, about 1 minute. Increase speed to medium and knead until dough is smooth and comes away from sides of bowl, about 10 minutes. (If after 5 minutes more flour is needed, add remaining ¼ cup flour, 1 tablespoon at a time, until dough clears sides of bowl but sticks to bottom.)

2. Transfer dough to lightly floured counter and knead by hand to form smooth, round ball, about 1 minute. Place dough in large, lightly greased bowl, cover tightly with greased plastic wrap, and let rise until doubled in size, 2 to 2½ hours.

3. FOR THE CARAMEL GLAZE: Combine all ingredients in small saucepan and cook over medium heat, whisking occasionally, until butter is melted and mixture is thoroughly combined. Pour mixture into nonstick metal 13 by 9-inch baking pan and spread evenly over bottom using rubber spatula.

Sticky buns are hard to resist even though they can be too sweet and too rich. The dough for our sticky buns is moist with substantial chew, and filled with an assertive filling made with brown sugar. Crowned with a caramel glaze and toasted pecan topping, our recipe guarantees bakery success at home.

1. POUR THE CARAMEL INTO THE PAN: Pour the caramel mixture into a 13 by 9-inch nonstick metal baking pan and spread evenly over the bottom using a rubber spatula.

WHY? Baking the buns on top of the caramel in the pan helps them caramelize and get that hallmark gooey texture.

2. ROLL OUT THE DOUGH: Transfer the dough to a lightly floured counter and roll it into a 16 by 12-inch rectangle, with the long side facing you.

WHY? You need to roll out the dough into a uniform rectangle so that you can fill and assemble equally sized rolls with the filling evenly distributed throughout.

3. ADD THE FILLING: Brush melted butter over the dough, leaving a ½-inch border; brush the sides of the pan with the remaining butter on the brush. Sprinkle the filling over the dough, leaving a ¾-inch border at the top edge, and press to adhere.

WHY? The butter helps the filling adhere to the dough, and pressing on the filling helps it stay in place when rolling and cutting the buns.

4. ROLL UP THE DOUGH: Roll the dough away from you into a firm cylinder, keeping the roll taut by tucking it under itself as you go. Firmly pinch the seam closed.

WHY? Rolling the dough up tightly, with no holes or gaps, is crucial to preventing the filling from leaking out during baking.

5. STRETCH THE DOUGH AND CUT THE BUNS: Stretch the dough into an 18-inch length, pat the ends even, and use serrated knife to cut the cylinder into 12 evenly sized pieces.

WHY? Making sure the log is evenly sized before cutting ensures that the rolls will be the same size and will bake at the same rate. A serrated knife makes cutting through the dough and filling easy.

6. ARRANGE THE BUNS IN THE PAN: Arrange the rolls one cut side down in the prepared pan. Cover with plastic and let rise until puffy and pressed against one another, about 1½ hours.

WHY? Giving the rolls a little room to puff as they bake is important for their shape and texture. They will bake into each other but will be easy to pull apart when serving.

7. BAKE THE BUNS ON A BAKING STONE: Adjust an oven rack to the lowest position, place a baking stone on the rack, and heat the oven to 350 degrees. Place the pan on the baking stone and bake until the rolls are golden brown, 25 to 30 minutes, rotating the pan halfway through baking.

WHY? Baking on a baking stone ensures that the bottoms of the buns bake completely and get caramelized.

8. INVERT BUNS ONTO A BAKING SHEET AND TOP WITH NUTS AND FRESH CARAMEL: Spread the nuts and topping over the buns and let them cool until just warm, 15 to 20 minutes, before serving.

WHY? Make the pecan topping while the buns cool. Spooning the nuts and some fresh caramel over the buns before serving preserves the texture of the nuts, preventing them from tasting soggy.

4. FOR THE FILLING: Mix sugar, cinnamon, cloves, and salt together in bowl, breaking up sugar clumps. Transfer dough to lightly floured counter and roll into 16 by 12-inch rectangle, with long side facing you. Brush melted butter over dough, leaving ½-inch border at edges; brush sides of baking pan with remaining butter. Sprinkle filling over dough, leaving ¾-inch border at top edge, and press lightly to adhere.

5. Roll dough away from you into firm cylinder, keeping roll taut by tucking it under itself as you go. Pinch seam closed. Gently stretch cylinder 18 inches long, then push in on ends until cylinder is evenly thick. Using serrated knife, cut cylinder into 12 pieces and arrange, one cut side down, in prepared pan. Cover with greased plastic and let rise until puffy and pressed against one another, about 1½ hours.

6. Adjust oven rack to lowest position, place baking stone on rack, and heat oven to 350 degrees. Place baking pan on baking stone and bake until rolls are golden brown, 25 to 30 minutes, rotating pan halfway through baking. Let rolls cool in pan for 10 minutes, then invert onto rimmed baking sheet (or cutting board). Scrape any glaze stuck in baking pan onto buns using rubber spatula and let cool while making topping.

7. FOR THE PECAN TOPPING: Combine sugar, butter, corn syrup, and salt in small saucepan and bring to simmer over medium heat, whisking occasionally. Off heat, stir in vanilla and pecans. Spread topping over buns and let cool until just warm, 15 to 20 minutes, before serving.

TO MAKE AHEAD: Pan of unrisen buns (step 5) can be refrigerated for up to 14 hours. Before baking, place baking pan in warm-water bath (about 120 degrees) in kitchen sink or large roasting pan for 20 minutes. Remove pan from water bath and let buns rise until slightly puffy and pressed against one another, about 1½ hours; bake as directed.

Monkey Bread

SERVES 6 TO 8   **TOTAL TIME** 3½ TO 4 HOURS

✔ **WHY THIS RECIPE WORKS:** Monkey bread is a knotty-looking loaf of bread made from buttery balls of dough coated in cinnamon, brown sugar, and melted butter and baked in a Bundt pan. It's traditionally served hot so that the sticky baked pieces can be easily pulled apart. The older recipes we found were two-day affairs, while newer ones took the convenience road, using store-bought biscuit dough and yielding lean, dry, bland bread. We wanted a faster recipe for monkey bread that didn't compromise on its delicious flavor. To expedite the rising and proofing in this recipe we used a large amount of instant yeast and added sugar to the dough. Butter and milk helped keep the dough rich and flavorful. We rolled the dough in

We make monkey bread faster by using a large amount of instant yeast in the dough.

butter and sugar to help give it a thick, caramel-like coating. The monkey bread is best served warm. After baking, don't let the bread cool in the pan for more than 5 minutes or it will stick and come out in pieces. If you don't have a stand mixer, you can mix and knead the bread dough by hand; see pages 590–91.

DOUGH
- 1 cup milk, heated to 110 degrees
- ⅓ cup warm water (110 degrees)
- ¼ cup (1¾ ounces) granulated sugar
- 2 tablespoons unsalted butter, melted and cooled
- 2¼ teaspoons instant or rapid-rise yeast
- 3¼ cups (16¼ ounces) all-purpose flour
- 2 teaspoons salt

BROWN SUGAR COATING
- 1 cup packed (7 ounces) light brown sugar
- 2 teaspoons ground cinnamon
- 8 tablespoons unsalted butter, melted and cooled

Assembling Monkey Bread

1. Pat dough into rough 8-inch square, then cut into 4 equal pieces. Continue to divide each piece of dough into 4 even pieces twice more, for total of 64 small dough pieces.

2. Working with 1 piece of dough at a time, roll into ball, dip in melted butter, then roll in sugar mixture to coat. Place balls in Bundt pan, staggering seams where dough balls meet as you build layers.

GLAZE

1 **cup (4 ounces) confectioners' sugar**
2 **tablespoons milk**

1. FOR THE DOUGH: Whisk milk, water, sugar, melted butter, and yeast together in liquid measuring cup. Combine flour and salt in bowl of stand mixer. Using dough hook on low speed, slowly add milk mixture and mix until dough forms, about 1 minute. Increase speed to medium and knead until dough is smooth and shiny, 6 to 7 minutes.

2. Transfer dough to lightly floured counter and knead by hand to form smooth, round ball, about 15 seconds. Place dough in large, lightly greased bowl, cover tightly with greased plastic wrap, and let rise until doubled in size, 1 to 1½ hours.

3. FOR THE BROWN SUGAR COATING: Combine sugar and cinnamon together in small bowl. Place melted butter in separate small bowl. Grease Bundt pan thoroughly.

4. Transfer dough to lightly floured counter, pat into rough 8-inch square, then cut into 64 pieces. Working with 1 piece of dough at a time, roll into ball, dip in melted butter, then roll in sugar mixture to coat. Place balls in prepared Bundt pan, staggering seams where dough balls meet as you build layers. Cover pan with greased plastic and let rise until balls are puffy and have risen 1 to 2 inches over lip of pan, 1 to 1½ hours.

5. Adjust oven rack to middle position and heat oven to 350 degrees. Bake until top is deep brown and caramel begins to bubble around edges, 30 to 35 minutes. Let cool in pan for 5 minutes, then turn out on platter and let cool for 10 minutes.

6. FOR THE GLAZE: While bread cools, whisk sugar and milk together in bowl until smooth. Drizzle glaze over warm bread, letting it run down sides, and serve.

Our tender and lightly sweetened doughnuts are easy to customize.

Yeasted Doughnuts

MAKES ABOUT 16 DOUGHNUTS AND DOUGHNUT HOLES
TOTAL TIME 3½ TO 4 HOURS

✔ **WHY THIS RECIPE WORKS:** The yeasted doughnuts found in chain shops always seem to look more impressive than they taste, and the flavor always falls short. We set out to develop the ultimate yeasted doughnut that was lightly sweetened, tender on the inside, and lightly crisp on the outside. To get tender texture, we preferred all-purpose flour to bread flour, which made dense, tough doughnuts. A modest amount of sugar added enough sweetness to complement a sugary glaze without overwhelming it. The sugar also kept the doughnuts from browning too quickly in the hot oil. When we kneaded the dough by hand, the softened butter melted, resulting in greasy doughnuts. A stand mixer thoroughly kneaded the dough while allowing it to remain cool. If you don't have a doughnut cutter, you can improvise with two biscuit cutters: Use a standard-size cutter (about 2½ inches) for the doughnuts, and a smaller one (about 1¼ inches) for the holes. We do not recommend mixing this sticky dough by hand.

3-3¼ cups (15 to 16¼ ounces) all-purpose flour
   6 tablespoons (2⅔ ounces) sugar,
     plus 1 cup for rolling
2¼ teaspoons instant or rapid-rise yeast
   ½ teaspoon salt
   ⅔ cup whole milk, room temperature
   2 large eggs, lightly beaten
   6 tablespoons unsalted butter, cut into 6 pieces,
     softened but still cool
   6 cups vegetable shortening

1. Whisk 3 cups flour, 6 tablespoons sugar, yeast, and salt together in bowl of stand mixer. Using dough hook on low speed, add milk and eggs and mix until dough comes together, 3 to 4 minutes. Increase speed to medium and add butter, 1 piece at a time, until incorporated. Continue to mix until dough is smooth, about 3 minutes. (If necessary, add remaining ¼ cup flour, 1 tablespoon at a time, until dough forms soft ball.)

2. Transfer dough to large, lightly greased bowl, cover tightly with greased plastic wrap, and let rise until nearly doubled in size, 2 to 2½ hours.

3. Transfer dough to lightly floured counter and roll flat with rolling pin until ½ inch thick. Cut out doughnuts and holes using 2½- or 3-inch doughnut cutter. Gently gather dough scraps, rerolling them as necessary, and cut out additional doughnuts. Transfer doughnuts and holes to floured baking sheet, cover loosely with greased plastic, and let rise until slightly puffy, 30 to 45 minutes.

4. Meanwhile, heat shortening in large Dutch oven over medium-high heat to 375 degrees. Line baking sheet with several layers of paper towels. Place remaining 1 cup sugar in bowl; set aside for coating. Working in batches of 4 or 5 rings and holes at a time, fry until golden brown, 1 to 2 minutes, flipping halfway through cooking. Transfer to prepared baking sheet, let cool for 10 minutes, then roll in sugar to coat. Serve warm or at room temperature.

VARIATIONS
Cinnamon-Sugared Doughnuts
Add 1 tablespoon ground cinnamon to rolling sugar in step 4.

Vanilla-Glazed Doughnuts
Omit 1 cup sugar for rolling. While doughnuts cool, whisk 3 cups sifted confectioners' sugar, ½ cup half-and-half, and 1 teaspoon vanilla extract together in medium bowl. Dip 1 side of cooled doughnut into glaze, letting excess drip off, and transfer to wire rack; let glaze set before serving.

Chocolate-Glazed Doughnuts
Omit 1 cup sugar for rolling. While doughnuts cool, whisk 4 ounces finely chopped semisweet or bittersweet chocolate and ½ cup hot half-and-half together in medium bowl until chocolate is melted and mixture is smooth. Whisk in 2 cups sifted confectioners' sugar. Dip 1 side of cooled doughnut into glaze, letting excess drip off, and transfer to wire rack; let glaze set before serving.

Making Yeasted Doughnuts

1. Place dough on lightly floured counter and, using rolling pin, roll out to thickness of ½ inch.

2. Cut dough using 2½- or 3-inch doughnut cutter, gathering scraps and rerolling them as necessary. Transfer to floured baking sheet, cover with plastic wrap, and let rise.

3. Heat shortening in large Dutch oven over medium-high heat to 375 degrees. Place rings and holes carefully in hot fat, 4 or 5 at a time.

4. Using skimmer, slotted spoon, or tongs, remove rings and holes from hot fat and drain on paper towel–lined baking sheet or wire rack. Let cool and roll in sugar.

This easy, make-at-home version of a New Orleans classic jump-starts the yeast rise with warm water and sugar.

Beignets

MAKES 24 BEIGNETS   **TOTAL TIME** 2 HOURS 10 MINUTES

✔ **WHY THIS RECIPE WORKS:** The squares of fried sweet dough called *beignets* are the object of desire of every tourist in New Orleans. We wanted access to these delicate, lightly sweet, yeasty doughnuts without a trip to the Morning Call café, and we wanted to limit the rising time to 1 hour. We started with a basic recipe of flour, eggs, oil, milk, and yeast. For the slight chewiness desirable in a good beignet, we swapped out the milk, which contains gluten-weakening peptides, for water, and upped the amount until we had a very wet dough. To develop enough flavor in our short rising time, we increased the amount of yeast and warmed the water to jump-start the fermentation process; we also added sugar to feed the yeast. A short stint in the refrigerator made our dough less sticky and easier to work with. After cutting the beignets and deep-frying them until golden brown, we gave them a dusting of confectioners' sugar. This dough is very wet and sticky, so flour the counter and parchment-lined baking sheet generously. Use a Dutch oven that holds 6 quarts or more for this recipe.

1 cup warm water (110 degrees)
3 tablespoons granulated sugar
1 tablespoon instant or rapid-rise yeast
3 cups (15 ounces) all-purpose flour
¾ teaspoon salt
2 large eggs
2 tablespoons plus 2 quarts vegetable oil
Confectioners' sugar

1. Combine water, 1 tablespoon granulated sugar, and yeast in large bowl and let sit until foamy, about 5 minutes. In separate bowl, combine flour, salt, and remaining 2 tablespoons granulated sugar. Whisk eggs and 2 tablespoons oil into yeast mixture. Add flour mixture and stir vigorously with rubber spatula until dough comes together. Cover tightly with plastic wrap and refrigerate until dough has nearly doubled in size, about 1 hour.

2. Set wire rack in rimmed baking sheet. Line second sheet with parchment paper and dust heavily with flour. Transfer dough to generously floured counter and cut in half. Working with 1 piece of dough at a time, pat into rough rectangle with floured hands, flipping to coat with flour. Roll dough into ¼-inch-thick rectangle roughly 12 by 9 inches in size. Using pizza wheel, cut dough into twelve 3-inch squares and transfer to floured sheet.

3. Add remaining 2 quarts oil to large Dutch oven until it measures about 1½ inches deep, and heat over medium-high heat to 350 degrees. Working in batches of 6 beignets at a time, fry until golden brown, about 3 minutes, flipping halfway through frying; transfer to prepared wire rack. Dust with confectioners' sugar and serve warm.

Shaping Beignets

1. Place half of dough on well-floured counter and pat into rough rectangle with floured hands, flipping dough to coat. Using well-floured rolling pin, roll dough into ¼-inch-thick rectangle (about 12 by 9 inches).

2. Using pizza wheel, cut dough into twelve 3-inch squares and transfer to floured sheet. Repeat with remaining dough.

Cookies and Bars

Drop Cookies and More

Rolled and Cut Cookies

Bar Cookies

■ SIGNIFIES A **FAST** RECIPE (45 MINUTES OR LESS)

Browning some of the butter gives our chocolate chip cookies nutty, toffeelike flavor.

Chocolate Chip Cookies

MAKES 16 LARGE COOKIES **TOTAL TIME** 1 HOUR
(PLUS COOLING TIME)

✔ WHY THIS RECIPE WORKS: We wanted to refine the classic Toll House recipe to create a moist and chewy chocolate chip cookie with crisp edges and deep notes of toffee and butterscotch. The foundation for building both the right texture and the right flavor turned out to be melted butter. After browning a portion of the butter for nutty flavor, we stirred in the remaining butter until it was melted and then added brown and white sugar. The sugar dissolved in the liquid butter, which enhanced its caramelization as the cookies baked. The freed-up liquid in the fat also encouraged a bit of gluten development, making our cookies chewier. Using two egg yolks, but only one white, added richness to the cookies but not a cakey texture. Knowing they would continue to firm up as they cooled, we made sure to bake the cookies just until

they were golden brown and set, but still soft in the center. Studded with gooey chocolate and boasting a complex medley of buttery caramel and toffee flavors, these cookies are as close as you can get to chocolate chip cookie perfection. Avoid using a nonstick skillet to brown the butter; the dark color of the nonstick coating makes it difficult to gauge when the butter is sufficiently browned. Light brown sugar can be used in place of the dark, but the cookies won't be as full-flavored; make sure the brown sugar is fresh and moist.

1¾ cups (8¾ ounces) all-purpose flour
½ teaspoon baking soda
14 tablespoons unsalted butter
¾ cup packed (5¼ ounces) dark brown sugar
½ cup (3½ ounces) granulated sugar
2 teaspoons vanilla extract
1 teaspoon salt
1 large egg plus 1 large yolk
1¼ cups (7½ ounces) semisweet or bittersweet chocolate chips
¾ cup pecans or walnuts, toasted and chopped (optional)

1. Adjust oven rack to middle position and heat oven to 375 degrees. Line 2 baking sheets with parchment paper. Whisk flour and baking soda together in bowl.

2. Melt 10 tablespoons butter in 10-inch skillet over medium-high heat. Continue cooking, swirling pan constantly, until butter is dark golden brown and has nutty aroma, 1 to 3 minutes.

3. Transfer browned butter to large bowl and stir in remaining 4 tablespoons butter until melted. Whisk in brown sugar, granulated sugar, vanilla, and salt until incorporated. Whisk in egg and yolk until smooth with no lumps, about 30 seconds.

4. Let mixture stand for 3 minutes, then whisk for 30 seconds. Repeat process of resting and whisking 2 more times until mixture is thick, smooth, and shiny. Using rubber spatula, stir in flour mixture until just combined, about 1 minute. Stir in chocolate chips and pecans, if using.

5. Working with 3 tablespoons dough at a time, roll into balls and space 2 inches apart on prepared sheets. (Raw cookies can be frozen for up to 1 month; bake frozen cookies in 300-degree oven for 30 to 35 minutes.)

6. Bake cookies, 1 sheet at a time, until golden brown and edges have begun to set but centers are still soft and puffy, 10 to 14 minutes, rotating sheet halfway through baking. Let cookies cool completely on sheet and serve.

For the ultimate chocolate chip cookies, we tinkered with the back-of-the-package recipe in order to get more flavor and an improved chewy texture. The best part of our recipe is that you can leave your electric mixer in the cupboard and just pull out some big mixing bowls.

1. BROWN SOME OF THE BUTTER: Melt 10 tablespoons butter over medium-high heat. Cook, swirling constantly, until the butter is dark golden brown with a nutty aroma.
WHY? Browning creates more complex flavor. Use a light-colored skillet to accurately gauge the color as the butter browns.

2. MELT IN THE REMAINING BUTTER: Transfer the browned butter to a large bowl and stir in the remaining butter until it's melted.
WHY? Using melted butter gives the cookies a superchewy texture because it frees up the water in the butter to bond with the proteins in the flour.

3. DISSOLVE THE SUGARS BY WHISKING: Whisk the sugars, vanilla, and salt into the butter, then add the egg and yolk. Alternate 30 seconds whisking with 3 minutes rest 3 times until mixture is thick and shiny.
WHY? Dissolving the sugars into the butter leads to crisp edges and deep toffee flavor.

4. ADD THE FLOUR, THEN THE CHIPS: Use a rubber spatula to stir the flour mixture into the sugar-egg mixture until just combined. Then add the chocolate chips and, if desired, the pecans.
WHY? Folding in the flour before the chips prevents flour pockets inside the cookies.

5. ROLL THE DOUGH INTO BALLS: Working with 3 tablespoons of dough at a time, roll the dough into balls and space 2 inches apart on 2 parchment-lined baking sheets.
WHY? Portioning the dough into even balls ensures that the cookies bake at the same rate and fit onto the sheet. Lining the sheets with parchment helps the cookies spread the right amount during baking and makes it easy to remove them once they've cooled—plus, cleanup's a breeze.

6. BAKE THE COOKIES 1 TRAY AT A TIME: Bake the cookies, 1 sheet at a time, on the middle rack of a 375-degree oven.
WHY? For evenly baked cookies with crisp edges and soft centers, it's important to bake them just one tray at a time. When there is another baking sheet in the oven, it blocks the flow of heat to the cookies and prevents them from baking evenly. Consequently, the cookies on the bottom rack will spread too much, often resulting in overly thin, scorched edges.

7. BAKE THE COOKIES UNTIL THE EDGES ARE SET: Bake the cookies until they're golden brown and the edges have begun to set but the centers are still soft and puffy, rotating the sheet halfway through baking.
WHY? If you overbake the cookies, the centers will be hard and crumbly rather than chewy. A timer is helpful, but the best way to determine doneness is to poke the cookies; the edges should be set but the centers should still be slightly soft.

8. LET THE COOKIES COOL ON THE SHEET: Let the cookies cool completely on the baking sheet before serving.
WHY? As the cookies cool on the baking sheet, they will continue to bake through thanks to the residual heat of the baking sheet. The cookies will also set up as they cool, making it easy to remove them from the baking sheet without breaking.

ALL ABOUT **CHOCOLATE**

All chocolate begins as cacao beans, which are seeds found in large pods that grow on cacao trees in regions around the equator. These beans are fermented, dried, and roasted and then the inner meat (or nib) of the bean is removed from the shell and ground into a paste. This paste is called chocolate liquor (although it contains no alcohol) and consists of cocoa solids and cocoa butter. Chocolate liquor is then further processed and mixed with sugar and flavorings to make the various types of chocolate. White chocolate is made from just the cocoa butter and doesn't contain any cocoa solids. Sweet, semisweet, and bittersweet chocolate go through a refining process known as conching where the chocolate liquor and the other ingredients are smeared against rollers until smooth. This conching action also drives off some of the volatile compounds responsible for chocolate's natural bitterness. Since unsweetened chocolate is rarely conched, it has a coarse texture and bitter flavor.

Using the right type and brand of chocolate in baking can make a big difference. After tasting and cooking with hundreds of pounds of chocolate in the test kitchen, we came up with what you really need to know. For more information and our buying recommendations, see Shopping for Ingredients on page 808–809. Never store chocolate in the refrigerator or freezer, as cocoa butter can easily pick up off-flavors from other foods.

Cocoa Powder

Cocoa powder is chocolate liquor that is processsed to remove all but 10 to 24 percent of the cocoa butter. Cocoa powder comes in natural and Dutched versions. Dutching, which was invented in the 19th century by a Dutch chemist and chocolatier, raises the powder's pH, which neutralizes its acids and astringent notes and rounds out its flavor. (It also darkens the color.) We often "bloom" cocoa powder in a hot liquid such as water or coffee. This dissolves the remaining cocoa butter and disperses water-soluble flavor compounds for a deeper, stronger flavor.

Unsweetened Chocolate

Unsweetened chocolate is the traditional choice for recipes in which a bold hit of chocolate flavor is more important than a smooth or delicate texture (think brownies). If you don't have unsweetened chocolate, you can replace 1 ounce of unsweetened chocolate with 3 tablespoons of cocoa powder and 1 tablespoon of butter or oil. This substitution, however, is best for small quantities, because it ignores the many important differences between butter, oil, and cocoa butter.

Semisweet and Bittersweet Chocolate

Semisweet and bittersweet chocolates, also called dark chocolate, must contain at least 35 percent chocolate liquor, although most contain more than 55 percent and some go as high as 99 percent. Our favorite brands, Ghirardelli Bittersweet Chocolate and Callebaut Intense Dark, both contain 60 percent cacao. (Chocolates containing 70 percent or more cacao usually require recipe adjustments to get good results.)

For substitutions, we found that you can replace 1 ounce of bittersweet or semisweet chocolate with ⅔ ounce of unsweetened chocolate and 2 teaspoons of granulated sugar, yet because the unsweetened chocolate has not been conched it will not provide the same smooth, creamy texture as bittersweet or semisweet chocolate.

Milk Chocolate

Milk chocolate must contain at least 10 percent chocolate liquor and 12 percent milk solids, with sweeteners and flavorings making up the balance. The result is a mellow, smooth flavor. Yet because of its relatively weak chocolate flavor (milk chocolate is usually more than 50 percent sugar), we don't use it in many recipes. We reserve milk chocolate for frostings and for eating out of hand.

White Chocolate

White chocolate is technically not chocolate since it contains no cocoa solids. Authentic white chocolate contains at least 20 percent cocoa butter, which provides its meltingly smooth texture. Note that many brands rely on palm oil in place of some or all of the cocoa butter and can't be labeled "chocolate." If the product is called "white chips" or "white confection," it is made with little or no cocoa butter. That said, since both styles derive their flavor from milk and sugar, not the fat, we find this distinction makes little difference in recipes.

Chocolate and White Chocolate Chips

Chocolate and white chocolate chips contain less cocoa butter than bar chocolate. The lower fat content means that chips don't melt as readily, which is a good thing—they hold their shape better when baked. In taste tests, our tasters picked up big differences in creaminess, awarding extra points to brands that were especially smooth melters. Smoothness is more a function of conching than cocoa butter content.

Oatmeal-Raisin Cookies

MAKES 20 LARGE COOKIES   **TOTAL TIME** 50 MINUTES
(PLUS COOLING TIME)

✓**WHY THIS RECIPE WORKS:** For oatmeal cookies with hearty oat flavor and a sturdy, not crumbly, texture, we settled on a ratio of 2 parts oats to 1 part flour—far more oats than most recipes use. Brown sugar added flavor and helped the cookies retain moisture. Most recipes for oatmeal cookies use (or abuse) cinnamon; we preferred the subtler notes of nutmeg. With a stiff dough, courtesy of all those oats, these cookies needed a relatively long stint in the oven, which tended to dry them out. Increasing the portions to a generous quarter-cup gave us oversized cookies that remained moist and chewy in the center. Quick oats will work in this recipe, but the cookies will be less chewy and flavorful. Do not use instant oats.

- 1½ cups (7½ ounces) all-purpose flour
- ½ teaspoon baking powder
- ½ teaspoon salt
- ¼ teaspoon nutmeg
- 16 tablespoons unsalted butter, softened
- 1 cup packed (7 ounces) light brown sugar
- 1 cup (7 ounces) granulated sugar
- 2 large eggs
- 3 cups (9 ounces) old-fashioned rolled oats
- 1½ cups (7½ ounces) raisins

1. Adjust oven racks to upper-middle and lower-middle positions and heat oven to 325 degrees. Line 2 baking sheets with parchment paper. Whisk flour, baking powder, salt, and nutmeg together in bowl.

2. Using stand mixer fitted with paddle, beat butter, brown sugar, and granulated sugar at medium speed until light and fluffy, about 3 minutes. Beat in eggs, one at a time, until combined, about 30 seconds, scraping down bowl as needed.

3. Reduce speed to low and slowly add flour mixture until combined, about 30 seconds. Mix in oats and raisins until just incorporated. Give dough final stir by hand to ensure that no flour pockets remain.

4. Working with ¼ cup dough at a time, roll into balls and space 2 inches apart on prepared sheets. Flatten dough slightly using your palm. (Raw cookies can be frozen for up to 1 month; bake frozen cookies in 300-degree oven for 30 to 35 minutes.)

5. Bake cookies until tops are lightly golden but centers are still soft and puffy, 22 to 25 minutes, switching and rotating sheets halfway through baking. Let cookies cool on sheets for 10 minutes. Serve warm or transfer to wire rack and let cool completely.

Chocolate-Chunk Oatmeal Cookies with Pecans and Dried Cherries

MAKES 16 LARGE COOKIES   **TOTAL TIME** 50 MINUTES
(PLUS COOLING TIME)

✓**WHY THIS RECIPE WORKS:** When it comes to chunky oatmeal cookies, many recipes take a kitchen-sink approach, resulting in a crazy jumble of flavors and textures. We instead chose a carefully balanced trio of bittersweet chocolate chunks, fragrant toasted pecans, and tart, chewy dried cherries. Old-fashioned rolled oats gave us the right hearty texture for the dough base, and using all dark brown sugar made for moist, chewy cookies with a rich color and flavor. We found that two leaveners were better than one in these cookies; baking soda helped produce a crisp exterior while baking powder kept the center soft. Walnuts or skinned hazelnuts can be substituted for the pecans, and dried cranberries can be used in place of the cherries. Quick oats will work in this recipe, but the cookies will be less chewy and flavorful. Do not use instant oats.

- 1¼ cups (6¼ ounces) all-purpose flour
- ¾ teaspoon baking powder
- ½ teaspoon baking soda
- ½ teaspoon salt
- 1¼ cups (3¾ ounces) old-fashioned rolled oats
- 1 cup pecans, toasted and chopped
- 1 cup dried sour cherries, chopped coarse
- 4 ounces bittersweet chocolate, chopped fine
- 12 tablespoons unsalted butter, softened
- 1½ cups packed (10½ ounces) dark brown sugar
- 1 large egg
- 1 teaspoon vanilla extract

1. Adjust oven racks to upper-middle and lower-middle positions and heat oven to 350 degrees. Line 2 baking sheets with parchment paper. Whisk flour, baking powder, baking soda, and salt together in bowl. In second bowl, stir oats, pecans, cherries, and chocolate together.

2. Using stand mixer fitted with paddle, beat butter and sugar together on medium speed until light and fluffy, about 3 minutes. Beat in egg and vanilla until incorporated, about 30 seconds, scraping down bowl as needed.

3. Reduce speed to low and slowly add flour mixture until combined, about 30 seconds. Gradually mix in oat-chocolate mixture until incorporated. Give dough final stir by hand to ensure that no flour pockets remain.

4. Working with ¼ cup dough at a time, roll into balls and space 2½ inches apart on prepared sheets. Flatten dough to 1-inch thickness with your palm. (Raw cookies can be frozen

Baking with Butter

We use unsalted butter exclusively in the test kitchen. On average, a stick of salted butter contains ⅓ teaspoon of salt, but that can vary from brand to brand, making managing the amount of salt in a recipe difficult, so it's best to stick with unsalted. We also like its sweet, delicate flavor. Margarine, although butterlike in appearance and usage, should never be substituted in baking. As for low-fat butter, the reduction in fat and calories is simply not worth the trade-off in taste and texture.

BUTTER TEMPERATURE: The temperature of butter makes a big difference and can dramatically affect the texture of finished baked goods. For example, pie dough made with warm or room-temperature butter will be nearly impossible to roll out, and the resulting crust will be tough rather than flaky. On the other hand, many cakes and cookies require softened butter for creaming since it blends easily with the sugar, creating tender baked goods. Generally, recipes will call for butter chilled, softened, or melted and cooled. Chilled butter (about 35 degrees) should be unyielding when pressed. To chill quickly, cut butter into small pieces and freeze for 10 to 15 minutes. Softened butter (65 to 67 degrees) bends easily without breaking and gives slightly when pressed. To soften quickly, place cold butter in a plastic bag and use a rolling pin to pound it to the desired consistency, or cut it into small pieces and let sit until softened. For melted and cooled butter (85 to 90 degrees), melt on the stovetop or in the microwave, then cool for about 5 minutes.

SOFTENING BUTTER IN THE MICROWAVE: To keep butter from melting, microwave 4 tablespoons in one piece for 1 minute at 10 percent power. Press the butter with your finger to see if it is sufficiently softened; if not, heat for an additional 20 seconds at 10 percent power. For each additional 2 tablespoons of butter, increase the second microwave interval by 10 seconds.

RESCUING OVERSOFTENED BUTTER: When butter is properly softened to 65 or 70 degrees, tiny fat crystals surround and stabilize the air bubbles that are generated during creaming. When heated to the melting point, however, these crystals are destroyed. They can be reestablished if the butter is rapidly chilled. Mix the partially melted butter with a few ice cubes. Once the butter has cooled to a softened stage, remove the ice.

STORING BUTTER: In the back of the fridge where it's coldest (not in the door compartment), butter will keep for 2½ weeks. Any longer and it can turn rancid. For longer storage (up to 4 months), freeze it. Also, since butter quickly picks up odors and flavors, we slip the sticks into a zipper-lock bag.

for up to 1 month; bake frozen cookies in 300-degree oven for 30 to 35 minutes.)

5. Bake cookies until edges are set and beginning to brown but centers are still soft and puffy (cookies will look raw between cracks and seem underdone), 20 to 25 minutes, switching and rotating sheets halfway through baking. Let cookies cool on sheets for 10 minutes. Serve warm or transfer to wire rack and let cool completely.

Two Ways to Chop Chocolate

A. WITH A KNIFE: Hold knife at 45-degree angle to corner of block of chocolate and bear down evenly. After cutting about 1 inch from corner, repeat with other corners.

B. WITH A LARGE FORK: Alternatively, use sharp 2-tined meat fork to break chocolate into smaller pieces.

Peanut Butter Cookies

MAKES 24 COOKIES   **TOTAL TIME** 40 MINUTES (PLUS COOLING TIME)

✓ **WHY THIS RECIPE WORKS:** Our ideal peanut butter cookie is soft and chewy, with a strong peanut flavor. The problem is, the more peanut butter added to the dough, the sandier and crumblier the cookies become. After hitting the limit with 1 cup of extra-crunchy, we packed extra peanut flavor into our dough by adding a cup of salted, dry-roasted peanuts, which we processed to fine crumbs. A generous amount of softened butter provided lightness and a chewy texture. To sweeten the cookies, we included both granulated and brown sugars—the former yielded crisp-edged cookies, while the latter underscored the peanut flavor. We prefer extra-crunchy peanut butter for these cookies, but crunchy peanut butter or creamy peanut butter also work.

2½ cups (12½ ounces) all-purpose flour
1 teaspoon salt
½ teaspoon baking soda
½ teaspoon baking powder
1 cup dry-roasted salted peanuts
16 tablespoons unsalted butter, softened
1 cup packed (7 ounces) light brown sugar
1 cup (7 ounces) granulated sugar
1 cup extra-crunchy peanut butter
2 teaspoons vanilla extract
2 large eggs

1. Adjust oven racks to upper-middle and lower-middle positions and heat oven to 350 degrees. Line 2 baking sheets with parchment paper. Whisk flour, salt, baking soda, and baking powder together in bowl. Pulse peanuts in food processor to fine crumbs, about 14 pulses.

2. Using stand mixer fitted with paddle, beat butter, brown sugar, and granulated sugar on medium speed until light and fluffy, about 3 minutes. Beat in peanut butter until fully incorporated, about 30 seconds. Beat in vanilla, then eggs, one at a time, until combined, about 30 seconds, scraping down bowl as needed.

3. Reduce speed to low and slowly mix in flour mixture until combined, about 30 seconds. Mix in ground peanuts until incorporated. Give dough final stir by hand to ensure that no flour pockets remain.

4. Working with 3 tablespoons dough at a time, roll into balls and space 2 inches apart on prepared sheets. Using fork, make crosshatch design on cookies. (Raw cookies can be frozen for up to 1 month; bake frozen cookies in 300-degree oven for 17 to 22 minutes.)

5. Bake cookies until edges are golden and centers have puffed but are beginning to deflate, 10 to 12 minutes, switching and rotating sheets halfway through baking. Let cookies cool on sheets for 10 minutes. Serve warm or transfer to wire rack and let cool completely.

Making a Crosshatch Design

Using fork, press crosshatch design into cookies before baking.

These cookies combine chocolate flavor from cocoa and bittersweet chocolate with chewiness from dark corn syrup.

Chewy Chocolate Cookies

MAKES 16 COOKIES   **TOTAL TIME** 1 HOUR
(PLUS COOLING TIME)

✔WHY THIS RECIPE WORKS: We set out to make an exceptionally rich chocolate cookie we could sink our teeth into without it falling apart. Our first batch, with modest amounts of cocoa and melted chocolate, baked up too cakey and tender. The chocolate was the culprit—its fat softened the dough. To keep chocolate flavor without adding too much fat, we increased the cocoa powder and reduced the flour. Using an egg white rather than a whole egg gave us the structure we wanted. Adding dark corn syrup gave the cookies a nice chewiness and lent a hint of caramel flavor. For more richness, we folded in chopped bittersweet chocolate; the chunks stayed intact and added intense flavor. After rolling the dough into balls, we dipped them in granulated sugar to give the cookies a sweet crunch and an attractive crackled appearance. Use a high-quality bittersweet or semisweet chocolate here. Light brown sugar can be used in place of the dark, but the cookies won't be as full-flavored; make sure the brown sugar is fresh and moist.

- 1½ cups (7½ ounces) all-purpose flour
- ¾ cup (2¼ ounces) Dutch-processed cocoa powder
- ½ teaspoon baking soda
- ⅜ teaspoon salt
- ½ cup dark corn syrup
- 1 large egg white
- 1 teaspoon vanilla extract
- 12 tablespoons unsalted butter, softened
- ⅓ cup packed (2⅓ ounces) dark brown sugar
- ⅓ cup (2⅓ ounces) granulated sugar, plus ½ cup for rolling
- 4 ounces bittersweet or semisweet chocolate, chopped into ½-inch pieces

1. Adjust oven racks to upper-middle and lower-middle positions and heat oven to 375 degrees. Line 2 baking sheets with parchment paper. Whisk flour, cocoa, baking soda, and salt together in bowl. Whisk corn syrup, egg white, and vanilla together in second bowl.

2. Using stand mixer fitted with paddle, beat butter, brown sugar, and ⅓ cup granulated sugar on medium speed until light and fluffy, about 3 minutes. Reduce speed to medium-low, add corn syrup mixture, and beat until fully incorporated, about 20 seconds, scraping down bowl as needed. Reduce speed to low, add flour mixture and chopped chocolate, and mix until just incorporated, about 30 seconds. Give dough final stir by hand to ensure that no flour pockets remain. Refrigerate dough for 30 minutes to firm slightly.

3. Place remaining ½ cup granulated sugar in shallow dish. Working with 2 tablespoons dough at a time, roll into balls, then roll in sugar to coat; space 2 inches apart on prepared baking sheets. (Raw cookies can be frozen for up to 1 month; bake frozen cookies in 325-degree oven for 25 minutes.)

4. Bake cookies until edges have begun to set but centers are still soft, puffy, and cracked (cookies will look raw between cracks and seem underdone), 10 to 11 minutes, switching and rotating sheets halfway through baking. Let cookies cool on sheets for 5 minutes, then transfer to wire rack and let cool completely before serving.

NOTES FROM THE TEST KITCHEN

Spacing Out Cookies

When scoops of dough are placed too close together on the sheet, the cookies can fuse together. To ensure enough space between cookies, alternate the rows. For example, place three cookies in the first row, two in the second, three in the third, and so on.

To keep these cookies soft and chewy, we used butter, vegetable oil, and a surprise ingredient—cream cheese.

Chewy Sugar Cookies

MAKES 24 COOKIES   **TOTAL TIME** 50 MINUTES (PLUS COOLING TIME)

WHY THIS RECIPE WORKS: Traditional sugar cookie recipes can be surprisingly fussy: If the butter temperature is wrong or the measurements a bit off, the cookies spread too much or become brittle. We wanted an approachable recipe for great, chewy sugar cookies that anyone could make anytime. The right proportions of saturated and unsaturated fats can enhance chewiness in baked goods, so we replaced some of the butter with vegetable oil. Rather than trying to cream the small amount of butter left in the recipe, we simply melted it. This made a mixer unnecessary and, as a bonus, the liquid butter made for chewier cookies. A small amount of cream cheese added rich flavor and a bit of acidity that enabled us to include baking soda as an additional leavener, which gave the cookies a beautiful crackly surface. The final dough will be slightly softer than most cookie doughs. For the best results, handle the dough as briefly and as gently as possible. Overworking the dough will result in flatter cookies.

2¼ cups (11¼ ounces) all-purpose flour
1 teaspoon baking powder
½ teaspoon baking soda
½ teaspoon salt
1½ cups (10½ ounces) sugar, plus ⅓ cup for rolling
2 ounces cream cheese, cut into 8 pieces
6 tablespoons unsalted butter, melted and still warm
⅓ cup vegetable oil
1 large egg
1 tablespoon whole milk
2 teaspoons vanilla extract

1. Adjust oven rack to middle position and heat oven to 350 degrees. Line 2 baking sheets with parchment paper. Whisk flour, baking powder, baking soda, and salt together in bowl.

2. Place 1½ cups sugar and cream cheese in large bowl. Whisk in warm melted butter (some lumps of cream cheese will remain). Whisk in oil until incorporated. Whisk in egg, milk, and vanilla until smooth. Fold in flour mixture with rubber spatula until soft, homogeneous dough forms.

3. Place remaining ⅓ cup sugar in shallow dish. Working with 2 tablespoons dough at a time, roll into balls, then roll in sugar to coat; space 2 inches apart on prepared baking sheets. Using bottom of greased measuring cup, flatten dough balls until 3 inches in diameter. Using sugar left in dish, sprinkle 2 teaspoons sugar over each sheet of cookies; discard extra sugar. (Raw cookies can be frozen for up to 1 month; bake frozen cookies in 350-degree oven for 17 to 22 minutes.)

4. Bake cookies, 1 sheet at a time, until edges are set and beginning to brown, 11 to 13 minutes, rotating sheet halfway through baking. Let cookies cool on sheet for 5 minutes, then transfer to wire rack and let cool completely before serving.

VARIATIONS
Chewy Hazelnut–Browned Butter Sugar Cookies

Nutty browned butter gives these cookies a toffeelike flavor.

Increase milk to 2 tablespoons and omit vanilla. Add ¼ cup finely chopped toasted hazelnuts to bowl with sugar and cream cheese. Substitute browned butter for melted butter; melt butter in 10-inch skillet over medium-high heat, then continue to cook, swirling pan constantly, until butter is dark golden brown and has nutty aroma, 1 to 3 minutes; add immediately to bowl with sugar and cream cheese.

Making Sugar Cookies

1. MAKE DOUGH: Fold flour mixture into liquid ingredients with rubber spatula until soft, homogeneous dough forms.

2. ROLL DOUGH INTO BALLS AND COAT IN SUGAR: Working with 2 tablespoons dough at a time, roll into balls, then roll in sugar to coat; space 2 inches apart on prepared baking sheets.

3. FLATTEN BALLS: Using bottom of greased measuring cup, flatten dough balls until 3 inches in diameter. Sprinkle tops of cookies evenly with some of remaining sugar.

4. BAKE: Bake cookies, 1 sheet at a time, until edges are set and beginning to brown, 11 to 13 minutes, rotating sheet halfway through baking.

Chewy Chai-Spice Sugar Cookies

Add ¼ teaspoon ground cinnamon, ¼ teaspoon ground ginger, ¼ teaspoon ground cardamom, ¼ teaspoon ground cloves, and pinch pepper to bowl with sugar and cream cheese. Reduce vanilla to 1 teaspoon.

Chewy Coconut-Lime Sugar Cookies

Whisk ½ cup finely chopped sweetened shredded coconut into flour mixture. Add 1 teaspoon finely grated lime zest to bowl with sugar and cream cheese. Substitute 1 tablespoon lime juice for vanilla.

This cookie's rich and nutty flavor comes from a combination of browned butter, dark brown sugar, vanilla, and salt.

Brown Sugar Cookies

MAKES 24 COOKIES   **TOTAL TIME** 1 HOUR 10 MINUTES
(PLUS COOLING TIME)

✔ **WHY THIS RECIPE WORKS:** We wanted to turn up the volume on the sugar cookie by switching out the granulated sugar in favor of brown sugar. We had in mind an oversized cookie with big flavor to match. Browning the butter was a given; it produced a range of butterscotch and toffee flavors in our dough. For the deepest flavor we chose dark brown sugar over light. We supported its sweet caramel notes with a full tablespoon of vanilla and balanced it with a dash of salt. By itself, baking soda gave the cookies a nice, crackly top but made the crumb coarse. Baking powder tightened up the texture of the cookies' interiors. For the signature crystalline coating, we stuck with brown sugar but added a little granulated sugar to prevent clumping. The right baking technique proved crucial to the success of this recipe; we baked the cookies one sheet at a time and pulled them from the oven when a light touch from our fingers produced a slight indentation in the surface of the

cookie. Avoid using a nonstick skillet to brown the butter; the dark color of the nonstick coating makes it difficult to gauge when the butter is sufficiently browned. Using fresh, moist brown sugar is crucial to the texture of these cookies.

14	tablespoons unsalted butter
2	cups plus 2 tablespoons (10⅔ ounces) all-purpose flour
½	teaspoon baking soda
¼	teaspoon baking powder
1¾	cups packed (12¼ ounces) dark brown sugar, plus ¼ cup for rolling
½	teaspoon salt
1	large egg plus 1 large yolk
1	tablespoon vanilla extract
¼	cup (1¾ ounces) granulated sugar

1. Melt 10 tablespoons butter in 10-inch skillet over medium-high heat. Continue cooking, swirling pan constantly, until butter is dark golden brown and has nutty aroma, 1 to 3 minutes. Transfer browned butter to large bowl and stir in remaining 4 tablespoons butter until melted; let cool for 15 minutes.

Making Browned Butter

1. Place butter chunks in heavy-bottomed skillet or saucepan with light-colored interior. Turn heat to medium-high and cook, swirling pan occasionally, until butter melts and begins to foam.

2. Continue to cook, swirling pan constantly, until butter is dark golden brown and has nutty aroma, 1 to 3 minutes.

3. Immediately transfer browned butter to heatproof bowl.

2. Meanwhile, adjust oven rack to middle position and heat oven to 350 degrees. Line 2 baking sheets with parchment paper. Whisk flour, baking soda, and baking powder together in separate bowl.

3. Whisk 1¾ cups brown sugar and salt into cooled butter until smooth with no lumps, about 30 seconds. Whisk in egg and yolk and vanilla until incorporated, about 30 seconds. Using rubber spatula, stir in flour mixture until just combined, about 1 minute.

4. Combine remaining ¼ cup brown sugar and granulated sugar in shallow dish. Working with 2 tablespoons dough at a time, roll into balls, then roll in sugar to coat; space 2 inches apart on prepared baking sheets. (Raw cookies can be frozen for up to 1 month; bake frozen cookies on 1 rimmed baking sheet nestled inside a second sheet in 325-degree oven for 20 to 25 minutes.)

5. Bake cookies, 1 sheet at a time, until edges have begun to set but centers are still soft, puffy, and cracked (cookies will look raw between cracks and seem underdone), 12 to 14 minutes, rotating sheet halfway through baking. Let cookies cool on baking sheet for 5 minutes, then transfer to wire rack and let cool completely before serving.

Snickerdoodles

MAKES 24 COOKIES **TOTAL TIME** 50 MINUTES (PLUS COOLING TIME)

☑ WHY THIS RECIPE WORKS: With their crinkly tops, slightly tangy flavor, and liberal dusting of cinnamon sugar, chewy snickerdoodles are a New England favorite. We quickly determined that cream of tartar is essential to these cookies. Not only is it responsible for their characteristic subtle tang, but, combined with baking soda, it creates a short-lived leavening effect that causes the cookies to rise and fall quickly while baking, leaving them with a distinctive crinkly appearance. Some traditional snickerdoodle recipes contain vegetable shortening, and with good reason: Unlike butter, shortening contains no water, so cookies made with shortening tend to hold their shape rather than spread out. We found that using equal amounts of shortening and butter gave us the best of both worlds—thick, nicely shaped cookies that were chewy and buttery-tasting. Vanilla proved to be a distraction, so we left it out. Rolling the balls of dough in cinnamon sugar—we liked a full tablespoon for warm spice flavor—imparted a spicy sweet crunch to the cookies. For the best results, we baked the cookies one sheet at a time and pulled them from the oven just as they were beginning to brown but were still soft and puffy in the middle. They continued to cook as they cooled on the baking sheet, and were perfectly done and chewy once cooled.

Cream of tartar is the secret to our snickerdoodles' characteristic tang and their crinkly look.

2½ cups (12½ ounces) all-purpose flour
2 teaspoons cream of tartar
1 teaspoon baking soda
½ teaspoon salt
8 tablespoons unsalted butter, softened
8 tablespoons vegetable shortening
1½ cups (10½ ounces) sugar, plus ¼ cup for rolling
2 large eggs
1 tablespoon ground cinnamon

1. Adjust oven rack to middle position and heat oven to 375 degrees. Line 2 baking sheets with parchment paper. Whisk flour, cream of tartar, baking soda, and salt together in bowl.

2. Using stand mixer fitted with paddle, beat butter, shortening, and 1½ cups sugar together on medium speed until light and fluffy, about 3 minutes. Beat in eggs, one at a time, until incorporated, about 30 seconds, scraping down bowl as needed.

3. Reduce speed to low and slowly add flour mixture until combined, about 30 seconds. Give dough final stir by hand to ensure that no flour pockets remain.

4. Combine remaining ¼ cup sugar and cinnamon in shallow dish. Working with 2 tablespoons dough at a time, roll into balls, then roll in sugar to coat; space 2 inches apart on prepared baking sheets. (Raw cookies can be frozen for up to 1 month; bake frozen cookies in 300-degree oven for 18 to 20 minutes.)

5. Bake cookies, 1 sheet at a time, until edges are just set and beginning to brown but centers are still soft, puffy, and cracked (cookies will look raw between cracks and seem underdone), 10 to 12 minutes, rotating sheet halfway through baking. Let cookies cool on sheet for 10 minutes, then transfer to wire rack and let cool completely before serving.

Molasses Spice Cookies

MAKES 24 COOKIES   **TOTAL TIME** 50 MINUTES
(PLUS COOLING TIME)

✔ **WHY THIS RECIPE WORKS:** The best molasses spice cookies combine a homespun crinkled appearance with a chewy texture and a deep, gently spiced molasses flavor. We tested the three main kinds of molasses in our dough and liked two of them equally: Light or mild molasses imparted a milder flavor, while dark or robust molasses had a stronger presence, so the choice is up to you. (We found blackstrap molasses overpowering and bitter.) A modest amount of dark brown sugar boosted the sweetness and added strong caramel notes. To complement these assertive sweeteners, we needed a strong yet balanced team of spices. Cinnamon, ginger, cloves, allspice, and black pepper provided warmth with just a little bite, and a spoonful of vanilla smoothed out any rough edges. While many older molasses cookie recipes call for shortening, we liked the richness of butter. When rolling the balls of dough, we found that dipping our hands in water prevented the dough from sticking to our hands while also helping the granulated sugar stick to the dough. For the best texture and appearance, be sure to bake the cookies one sheet at a time and pull them from the oven when they look substantially underdone. They will continue to bake and harden as they cool, with the insides remaining soft and moist.

2¼   **cups (11¼ ounces) all-purpose flour**
  1   **teaspoon baking soda**
1½   **teaspoons ground cinnamon**
1½   **teaspoons ground ginger**
  ½   **teaspoon ground cloves**
  ¼   **teaspoon ground allspice**
  ¼   **teaspoon pepper**
  ¼   **teaspoon salt**
 12   **tablespoons unsalted butter, softened**
  ⅓   **cup packed (2⅓ ounces) dark brown sugar**
  ⅓   **cup (2⅓ ounces) granulated sugar,
        plus ½ cup for rolling**
  1   **large egg yolk**
  1   **teaspoon vanilla extract**
  ½   **cup light or dark molasses**

1. Adjust oven rack to middle position and heat oven to 375 degrees. Line 2 baking sheets with parchment paper. Whisk flour, baking soda, cinnamon, ginger, cloves, allspice, pepper, and salt together in bowl.

2. Using stand mixer fitted with paddle, beat butter, brown sugar, and ⅓ cup granulated sugar on medium speed until light and fluffy, about 3 minutes. Reduce speed to medium-low and beat in egg yolk and vanilla until combined, about 30 seconds. Beat in molasses until incorporated, about 30 seconds, scraping down bowl as needed.

3. Reduce speed to low and slowly add flour mixture until combined, about 30 seconds (dough will be soft). Give dough final stir by hand to ensure that no flour pockets remain.

4. Place remaining ½ cup granulated sugar in shallow dish. Working with 2 tablespoons dough at a time, roll into balls, then roll in sugar to coat; space 2 inches apart on prepared baking sheets. (Raw cookies can be frozen for up to 1 month; bake frozen in 300-degree oven for 30 to 35 minutes.)

5. Bake cookies, 1 sheet at a time, until edges are set but centers are still soft, puffy, and cracked (cookies will look raw between cracks and seem underdone), 10 to 12 minutes, rotating sheet halfway through baking. Let cookies cool on sheet for 10 minutes. Serve warm or transfer to wire rack and let cool completely.

VARIATIONS

Molasses Spice Cookies with Dark Rum Glaze
Whisk 1 cup confectioners' sugar and 3 tablespoons dark rum together until smooth. Drizzle glaze over cooled cookies and let set for 10 to 15 minutes before serving.

Molasses Spice Cookies with Orange Essence
Add 1 teaspoon grated orange zest to dough with molasses. Process ⅔ cup granulated sugar with 2 teaspoons grated orange zest in food processor until fragrant, about 10 seconds; substitute orange sugar for granulated sugar when rolling in step 4.

These cookies are made with instant espresso powder and vanilla for serious coffee flavor.

Coffee Toffee Cookies

MAKES 24 COOKIES   **TOTAL TIME** 45 MINUTES
(PLUS COOLING TIME)

WHY THIS RECIPE WORKS: To build intense coffee flavor, we started with the strong stuff: espresso. The concentrated flavor and fine texture of instant espresso powder gave us a huge shot of coffee flavor without the coffee; in fact, we found that we needed only 1 tablespoon of hot water to dissolve the espresso before whisking it into the melted butter (since espresso is water-soluble, it wouldn't dissolve directly in the warm butter), and a full 2 tablespoons of espresso powder were necessary to satisfy our java craving. Surprisingly, coffee-flavored liqueur added neither flavor nor complexity, but vanilla extract helped balance and soften the espresso's bite. You can substitute espresso granules for the espresso powder; however, they might not dissolve as readily in the water.

2   **cups (10 ounces) all-purpose flour**
¾   **teaspoon baking soda**
½   **teaspoon salt**
2   **tablespoons instant espresso powder**
1   **tablespoon hot water**
10 **tablespoons unsalted butter, melted**
1¼ **cups (8¾ ounces) sugar**
2   **large eggs**
1   **teaspoon vanilla extract**
¾   **cup toffee chips**

1. Adjust oven racks to upper-middle and lower-middle positions and heat oven to 350 degrees. Line 2 baking sheets with parchment paper. Whisk flour, baking soda, and salt together in bowl.

2. Whisk espresso powder and water together in large bowl until espresso dissolves, then whisk in melted butter and sugar until incorporated. Whisk in eggs and vanilla until smooth. Gently stir in flour mixture with rubber spatula until soft dough forms. Fold in toffee chips.

3. Working with 2 tablespoons dough at a time, roll into balls and space 2 inches apart on prepared baking sheets.

4. Bake cookies until edges are set but centers are still soft and puffy, about 16 minutes, switching and rotating sheets halfway through baking. Let cookies cool on sheets for 10 minutes. Serve warm or transfer to wire rack and let cool completely.

NOTES FROM THE TEST KITCHEN

Freezing Cookie Dough

Keeping frozen cookie dough on hand means that you can bake as many, or as few, cookies as you like (note that this technique applies only to drop cookies). To freeze the dough, form it into balls, arrange the balls on a baking sheet, and place the sheet in the freezer. Once the individual balls of dough are frozen, place them in a zipper-lock bag and store them in the freezer. To bake, line a baking sheet with parchment paper. Arrange the frozen cookies (do not thaw) on the prepared sheet and bake as directed, adjusting the temperature and the baking time as indicated.

Using both butter and shortening keeps these streusel cookies crisp and perfect for dunking.

Cinnamon Streusel Cookies

MAKES 24 COOKIES **TOTAL TIME** 40 MINUTES
(PLUS COOLING TIME)

✓ **WHY THIS RECIPE WORKS:** While we love a chewy cookie, we wanted this cinnamon streusel cookie to have a crispier, slightly crunchy texture. With a flavor profile reminiscent of a warm cinnamon roll, this cookie was designed to be a dunker. To achieve this crisp texture, we focused on fat. While melted butter contributes great flavor, it also contributes moisture and chew to cookies (butter is only 80 percent fat; the remaining 20 percent is liquid). For a crispier cookie, we needed to cut down on moisture by replacing some of the butter with pure fat. We substituted shortening for almost half of the butter and ended up with a stiffer dough that was easier to shape and less likely to spread. The cookies still had plenty of buttery flavor, but now they had just the crisp texture we were seeking. Other nuts, such as walnuts or almonds, can be substituted for the pecans.

⅔ cup pecans, chopped fine
¾ teaspoon ground cinnamon
1¼ cups (8¾ ounces) plus 1 tablespoon sugar
7 tablespoons unsalted butter, melted
2¼ cups (11¼ ounces) all-purpose flour
1½ teaspoons cream of tartar
¾ teaspoon baking soda
½ teaspoon salt
5 tablespoons vegetable shortening, cut into 1-inch pieces
2 large eggs

1. Adjust oven racks to upper-middle and lower-middle positions and heat oven to 375 degrees. Line 2 baking sheets with parchment paper. Combine pecans, ½ teaspoon cinnamon, and 1 tablespoon sugar in bowl, then stir in 1 tablespoon melted butter. In separate bowl, whisk flour, cream of tartar, baking soda, salt, and remaining ¼ teaspoon cinnamon together.

2. Place remaining 1¼ cups sugar and shortening in large bowl. Whisk in remaining 6 tablespoons melted butter until incorporated. Whisk in eggs until smooth. Gently stir in flour mixture with rubber spatula until soft dough forms.

3. Working with 1½ tablespoons dough at a time, roll into balls and space 2 inches apart on prepared sheets. Using wet thumb, make small indentation in center of each dough ball, then fill with generous 1 teaspoon pecan mixture.

4. Bake cookies until edges are set but centers are still soft and puffy, about 12 minutes, switching and rotating sheets halfway through baking. Let cookies cool on baking sheets for 10 minutes. Serve warm or transfer to wire rack and let cool completely.

Putting Streusel on a Cookie

1. Working with 1½ table-spoons dough at a time, roll into balls and space 2 inches apart on prepared sheets. Using wet thumb, make small indentation in center of each ball.

2. Fill each indentation with generous 1 teaspoon pecan mixture.

Finely ground pecans or walnuts mixed in with the flour gives these cookies their nutty shortbread flavor.

Mexican Wedding Cookies

MAKES 48 SMALL COOKIES   **TOTAL TIME** 1 HOUR (PLUS COOLING TIME)

✓ **WHY THIS RECIPE WORKS:** Mexican wedding cookies, also known as Russian tea cakes or nut crescents (when shaped accordingly), have a delicate, fine texture much like shortbread. In order to really drive home the nut flavor, we found it necessary to use equal amounts of nuts and flour. The trick to helping these cookies hold together with all those nuts and no eggs (eggs made the cookies too cakey) was to grind half of the nuts very finely into crumbs to release their natural oil—almost to a butter. When we tried grinding all of the nuts this fine, the cookies turned out too dense. Finally, we found it best to roll the cookies in powdered sugar twice—after cooling and again just before serving—so that the sugar doesn't melt or brush off. If you can't find superfine sugar in the supermarket, simply process ½ cup granulated sugar in a food processor for 30 seconds and then measure out ⅓ cup.

2 cups pecans or walnuts
2 cups (10 ounces) all-purpose flour
¾ teaspoon salt
16 tablespoons unsalted butter, softened
⅓ cup (2⅓ ounces) superfine sugar
1½ teaspoons vanilla extract
1½ cups (6 ounces) confectioners' sugar

1. Adjust oven racks to upper-middle and lower-middle positions and heat oven to 325 degrees. Line 2 baking sheets with parchment paper. Process 1 cup nuts in food processor until texture of coarse cornmeal, 10 to 15 seconds; transfer to medium bowl. Process remaining 1 cup nuts in now-empty food processor until coarsely chopped, about 5 seconds; transfer to bowl with ground nuts. Stir flour and salt into nuts.

2. Using stand mixer fitted with paddle, beat butter and superfine sugar at medium speed until light and fluffy, about 3 minutes. Beat in vanilla. Reduce speed to low and slowly add nut mixture until combined, about 30 seconds. Scrape bowl with rubber spatula and continue to beat on low speed until dough is cohesive, about 7 seconds. Give dough final stir by hand to ensure that no flour pockets remain.

3. Working with 1 tablespoon dough at a time, roll into balls and space 1 inch apart on prepared sheets.

4. Bake cookies until tops are pale golden and bottoms are just beginning to brown, about 18 minutes, switching and rotating sheets halfway through baking. Let cookies cool on sheets for 5 minutes, then transfer to wire rack and let cool completely. Place confectioners' sugar in shallow dish. Working with several cookies at a time, roll in sugar to coat. Just before serving, reroll cookies in confectioners' sugar and gently shake off excess.

Rolling Cookies in Confectioners' Sugar

Working with several cookies at a time, roll in confectioners' sugar to coat. Before serving, reroll cookies in sugar or dust lightly with sugar.

Sweetening with Sugar

Sugar not only adds sweetness to baked goods, it affects texture too. The amount or type of sugar can make a cookie crisp or chewy. Here are the most common types of sugar for baking.

WHITE GRANULATED SUGAR: Made from either sugar cane or sugar beets, this is the type of sugar used most often in our recipes. It has a clean flavor, and its evenly ground, loose texture ensures that it incorporates well with butter when creaming, and dissolves easily into batters.

CONFECTIONERS' SUGAR: Also called powdered sugar, this is the most finely ground sugar. It is commonly used for dusting cakes and cookies and for making quick glazes and icings. To prevent clumping, confectioners' sugar contains a small amount of cornstarch. You can also approximate confectioners' sugar: For 1 cup of confectioners' sugar, process 1 cup of granulated sugar with 1 tablespoon of cornstarch in a blender (not a food processor) until fine, 30 to 40 seconds.

TURBINADO AND DEMERARA SUGAR: These "raw" sugars have large crystals that do not readily dissolve—a reason to avoid them in dough. Instead, we sprinkle them on muffin tops to create crunch or use them in the crust on Crème Brûlée (page 768).

BROWN SUGAR: Brown sugar is simply granulated white sugar combined with molasses. (When necessary, we indicate "light" or "dark" brown sugar. If either can be used, we simply list "brown sugar.") To approximate 1 cup of light brown sugar, blend 1 cup of granulated sugar with 1 tablespoon of mild molasses in a food processor. Use 2 tablespoons molasses for dark brown sugar.

Store brown sugar in an airtight container to keep it from drying out. If it does dry out, place the sugar in a zipper-lock bag, add a slice of bread, and set it aside overnight until the sugar is soft again. Or, quicker yet, put the sugar in a bowl with the bread and cover. Microwave until the sugar is moist, 15 to 30 seconds.

MEASURING SUGAR: Weighing sugar is the most accurate, but if you're measuring by volume it's important to use the best method. For white sugar, use the dip-and-sweep method: Dip the measuring cup into the sugar and sweep away the excess with a straight-edged object like the back of a butter knife. Brown sugar is moist and clumpy so it must be packed into the measuring cup to get an accurate measurement. Fill the dry measure with brown sugar and use the next smallest cup to pack it down. When properly packed, 1 cup of brown sugar should weigh the same as 1 cup of granulated sugar: 7 ounces.

Cornmeal Olive Oil Cookies

MAKES 24 COOKIES   **TOTAL TIME** 40 MINUTES (PLUS COOLING TIME)

✔ **WHY THIS RECIPE WORKS:** The success of this unusual cookie lies in the interplay between sweet and savory ingredients. Using a modest amount of granulated sugar in the dough enabled the cornmeal and rosemary flavors to shine through. A full teaspoon of baking powder and two whole eggs contributed to the cookies' cakey quality. A double dusting of confectioners' sugar—once while warm and again just before serving—further balanced the flavors and ensured that the sugar wouldn't melt or brush off. Extra-virgin olive oil can be substituted for the regular olive oil; however, the cookies will have a more pronounced olive oil flavor.

1½ cups (7½ ounces) all-purpose flour
½ cup (2½ ounces) cornmeal
1 teaspoon baking powder
¼ teaspoon salt
½ cup (3½ ounces) granulated sugar
½ cup olive oil
2 eggs
1 teaspoon minced fresh rosemary
1 cup (4 ounces) confectioners' sugar, plus extra as needed

1. Adjust oven racks to upper-middle and lower-middle positions and heat oven to 375 degrees. Line 2 baking sheets with parchment paper. Whisk flour, cornmeal, baking powder, and salt together in medium bowl.

2. Whisk granulated sugar and oil together in large bowl. Whisk in eggs and rosemary until smooth. Gently stir in flour mixture with rubber spatula until soft dough forms.

3. Scoop 1-tablespoon portions of dough and space 2 inches apart on prepared sheets.

4. Bake cookies until edges are lightly golden and centers are puffy and split open, about 13 minutes, switching and rotating sheets halfway through baking. Let cookies cool on sheets for 5 minutes. Place confectioners' sugar in shallow dish. Working with several warm cookies at a time, roll in sugar to coat. Just before serving, dust with extra confectioners' sugar. Serve warm or let cool completely.

For serious coconut flavor, we use cream of coconut along with both sweetened and unsweetened shredded coconut.

Macaroons

MAKES 48 COOKIES   **TOTAL TIME** 1 HOUR
(PLUS COOLING TIME)

✓ WHY THIS RECIPE WORKS: We set out to create a great coconut macaroon with a pleasing texture and real, honest coconut flavor. Our first move was to include both unsweetened coconut, for a less-sticky, more appealing texture, and sweetened shredded coconut, for more intense coconut flavor. On a whim, we tried cream of coconut and hit the jackpot, with macaroons with deeply layered coconut flavor. A few egg whites and some corn syrup ensured that the macaroons held together well and baked up moist and pleasantly chewy. Be sure to use cream of coconut and not coconut milk here. Unsweetened desiccated coconut is commonly sold in natural foods stores and Asian markets. If you are unable to find any, use all sweetened flaked or shredded coconut, but reduce the amount of cream of coconut to ½ cup, omit the corn syrup, and toss 2 tablespoons cake flour with the coconut before adding the liquid ingredients.

1 cup cream of coconut
2 tablespoons light corn syrup
4 large egg whites
2 teaspoons vanilla extract
½ teaspoon salt
3 cups (9 ounces) unsweetened shredded coconut
3 cups (9 ounces) sweetened shredded coconut

1. Adjust oven racks to upper-middle and lower-middle positions and heat oven to 375 degrees. Line 2 baking sheets with parchment paper.

2. Whisk cream of coconut, corn syrup, egg whites, vanilla, and salt together in small bowl. Toss unsweetened and sweetened coconuts together in large bowl, breaking up any clumps. Pour liquid ingredients over coconut and mix until evenly moistened. Refrigerate for 15 minutes.

3. Scoop 1-tablespoon portions of dough and space 1 inch apart on prepared sheets. Using moistened fingertips, form dough into loose haystacks. Bake cookies until light golden brown, about 15 minutes, switching and rotating sheets halfway through baking.

4. Let macaroons cool on sheets for 5 minutes, then transfer to wire rack and let cool completely before serving.

VARIATION
Chocolate-Dipped Macaroons
Let baked macaroons cool completely; line 2 baking sheets with parchment paper. Microwave 8 ounces chopped semisweet chocolate in bowl at 50 percent power for 2 minutes. Stir chocolate and continue heating until melted, stirring once every additional minute. Stir in 2 ounces of chopped semisweet chocolate until smooth. Working with 1 macaroon at a time, dip bottom of cookie in chocolate ½ inch up sides, scrape off excess, and place on prepared baking sheet. Refrigerate until chocolate sets, about 15 minutes, before serving.

NOTES FROM THE TEST KITCHEN

Storing Cookies

Many cookies taste best the day they are baked, but you may want to keep cookies for several days. We suggest storing them in an airtight container at room temperature. You can restore that just-baked freshness to cookies (with the exception of cookies that have been glazed or dusted with confectioners' sugar) by recrisping them in a 425-degree oven for 4 to 5 minutes. Let the cookies cool on the baking sheet for a couple of minutes before removing them and serving them warm.

A little sour cream helps make our black and white cookies tender and rich.

Black and White Cookies

MAKES 12 COOKIES   **TOTAL TIME** 1 HOUR
(PLUS COOLING AND GLAZING TIME)

✔ **WHY THIS RECIPE WORKS:** These gigantic, tender, cakey cookies, a mainstay of New York City bakeries, are flavored with vanilla or lemon and sport a two-toned coat of icing—half chocolate and half vanilla or lemon. To create a black and white cookie worthy of its iconic status, we started with a basic creamed batter and swapped in sour cream for the milk to add tenderness and rich flavor. Cake flour took the tenderness factor too far; all-purpose made the cookies just sturdy enough to hold together. We dialed back on the baking soda and baking powder to produce just enough lift and keep the texture fine and even. Our final step in fine-tuning this recipe was to abandon the lemon and stick with vanilla—and lots of it. For the icing, we had two major decisions to make: Should it be creamy or hard, and should it coat the round tops or flat undersides of the cookies? The second question was quickly settled; the flat undersides were far simpler and neater to frost. And to address the texture issue, we made a simple icing with confectioners' sugar, milk, vanilla, and corn syrup that formed a crisp shell as it dried, yet stayed creamy underneath. Creating the chocolate icing was as simple as adding cocoa to the vanilla icing. Twelve cookies doesn't sound like much, but these cookies are huge. You'll get neater cookies if you spread on the vanilla glaze first. This recipe provides a little extra glaze, just in case.

COOKIES

1¾ cups (8¾ ounces) all-purpose flour
 ½ teaspoon baking powder
 ¼ teaspoon baking soda
 ⅛ teaspoon salt
 10 tablespoons unsalted butter, softened
  1 cup (7 ounces) granulated sugar
  1 large egg
  2 teaspoons vanilla extract
 ⅓ cup sour cream

GLAZE

  5 cups (20 ounces) confectioners' sugar, sifted
  7 tablespoons whole milk
  2 tablespoons corn syrup
  1 teaspoon vanilla extract
 ½ teaspoon salt
  3 tablespoons Dutch-processed cocoa powder, sifted

1. FOR THE COOKIES: Adjust oven racks to upper-middle and lower-middle positions and heat oven to 350 degrees. Line 2 baking sheets with parchment paper. Combine flour, baking powder, baking soda, and salt in bowl.

Glazing Black and White Cookies

1. Working with 1 cookie at a time, spread 1 tablespoon vanilla glaze over half of flat side of cookie. Refrigerate until glaze is set, about 15 minutes.

2. Glaze other half of cookie with 1 tablespoon chocolate glaze. Let glaze set for 1 hour before serving.

2. Using stand mixer fitted with paddle, beat butter and sugar on medium speed until light and fluffy, about 3 minutes. Add egg and vanilla and beat until combined. Reduce speed to low and add flour mixture in 3 additions, alternating with sour cream in 2 additions, scraping down bowl as needed. Give dough final stir by hand to ensure that no flour pockets remain.

3. Using greased ¼-cup dry measuring cup, drop mounds of dough 3 inches apart on prepared sheets. Bake until edges are lightly browned, 15 to 18 minutes, switching and rotating sheets halfway through baking. Let cookies cool on sheets for 5 minutes, then transfer to wire rack to cool completely, about 1 hour.

4. FOR THE GLAZE: Whisk sugar, 6 tablespoons milk, corn syrup, vanilla, and salt together in bowl until smooth. Transfer 1 cup glaze to small bowl; reserve. Whisk cocoa and remaining 1 tablespoon milk into remaining glaze until combined.

5. Working with 1 cookie at a time, spread 1 tablespoon vanilla glaze over half of flat side of cookie. Refrigerate until glaze is set, about 15 minutes. Glaze other half of cookie with 1 tablespoon chocolate glaze. Let glaze set for 1 hour before serving.

Whoopie Pies

MAKES 6 WHOOPIE PIES   **TOTAL TIME** 1 HOUR 15 MINUTES (PLUS COOLING TIME)

✓WHY THIS RECIPE WORKS: Made of two cookielike chocolate cakes stuffed to the gills with fluffy marshmallow filling, the whoopie pie is our idea of a perfect sweet snack. For the cake component, we drew inspiration from devil's food cake, creaming butter with sugar, adding eggs and buttermilk for tenderness, and using all-purpose flour and baking soda for the right amount of structure. For the chocolate flavor, we preferred the darker color and flavor that Dutched cocoa provided. One-half cup delivered a balanced flavor, especially when boosted with a splash of vanilla extract. We tried replacing some of the granulated sugar with brown sugar and liked the results so much, we wound up using all brown sugar in the recipe. This substitution deepened the flavor and added moisture. Using a ⅓-cup dry measuring cup, we portioned the batter onto two baking sheets to give the cakes room to spread. For the filling, we eschewed the traditional sugar and lard in favor of marshmallow crème, which we enriched with butter to make the mixture fluffy yet firm. Don't be tempted to bake all the cakes on one baking sheet; the batter needs room to spread in the oven while it bakes. For information on buttermilk substitutions, see page 577.

A fluffy filling made with marshmallow crème is the perfect complement to the chocolaty cakes in this classic snack.

CAKES

  2 cups (10 ounces) all-purpose flour
  ½ cup (1½ ounces) Dutch-processed cocoa powder
  1 teaspoon baking soda
  ½ teaspoon salt
  8 tablespoons unsalted butter, softened but still cool
  1 cup packed (7 ounces) light brown sugar
  1 large egg, room temperature
  1 teaspoon vanilla extract
  1 cup buttermilk

FILLING

  12 tablespoons unsalted butter, softened but still cool
  1¼ cups (5 ounces) confectioners' sugar
  1½ teaspoons vanilla extract
  ⅛ teaspoon salt
  2½ cups marshmallow crème

1. FOR THE CAKES: Adjust oven racks to upper-middle and lower-middle positions and heat oven to 350 degrees. Line 2 baking sheets with parchment paper. Whisk flour, cocoa, baking soda, and salt together in medium bowl.

2. Using stand mixer fitted with paddle, beat butter and sugar on medium speed until light and fluffy, about 3 minutes. Beat in egg until incorporated, scraping down bowl as needed. Beat in vanilla. Reduce speed to low and beat in flour mixture in 3 additions, alternating with buttermilk in 2 additions. Give batter final stir by hand to ensure that no flour pockets remain.

3. Using ⅓-cup dry measuring cup, scoop 6 mounds of batter onto each prepared sheet, spaced about 3 inches apart. Bake until centers spring back when lightly pressed, 15 to 18 minutes, switching and rotating sheets halfway through baking. Let cakes cool on sheets to room temperature.

4. FOR THE FILLING: Using stand mixer fitted with paddle, beat butter and sugar on medium speed until fluffy, about 3 minutes. Beat in vanilla and salt. Beat in marshmallow crème until incorporated, about 2 minutes. Refrigerate filling until slightly firm, about 30 minutes. (Filling can be refrigerated for up to 2 days.)

5. Dollop ⅓ cup filling in center of flat side of 6 cakes. Top with flat side of remaining 6 cakes and gently press until filling spreads to edge of cake. Serve. (Whoopie pies can be refrigerated for up to 3 days.)

Baking and Filling a Whoopie Pie

1. Using ⅓-cup measuring cup, scoop 6 mounds of batter onto each prepared sheet, spaced about 3 inches apart.

2. Once baked and cooled, dollop ⅓ cup filling in center of flat side of 6 cakes. Top with flat side of remaining 6 cakes and gently press until filling spreads to edge of cake.

The tender but crisp texture of these cookies comes from the combination of granulated and confectioners' sugar.

Vanilla Icebox Cookies

MAKES 48 COOKIES   **TOTAL TIME** 45 MINUTES
(PLUS 2 HOURS CHILLING TIME PLUS COOLING TIME)

WHY THIS RECIPE WORKS: Also known as slice-and-bake or refrigerator cookies, icebox cookies are a classic thin, crisp American cookie. The trick is making them tender and "snappy" without making them hard. We found the key to a tender texture was to use two types of sugar: granulated and confectioners'. The granulated sugar gave the cookie some structure and a good snap, while the confectioners' sugar ensured tenderness. Some recipes call for baking powder, but we found it made the cookies either too soft or too cakey. For a rich cookie that stayed thin, we added two yolks rather than whole eggs. Once the dough was fully chilled, we sliced it thin, making sure to rotate the dough log every few slices to avoid creating a flat side. If the dough becomes soft while slicing the cookies, return it to the refrigerator until firm.

- 2¼ cups (11¼ ounces) all-purpose flour
- ½ teaspoon salt
- 16 tablespoons unsalted butter, softened
- ¾ cup (5¼ ounces) granulated sugar
- ½ cup (2 ounces) confectioners' sugar
- 2 large egg yolks
- 2 teaspoons vanilla extract

1. Whisk flour and salt together in bowl. Using stand mixer fitted with paddle, beat butter, granulated sugar, and confectioners' sugar together on medium speed until light and fluffy, about 3 minutes. Beat in egg yolks and vanilla until incorporated, about 30 seconds, scraping down bowl as needed. Reduce speed to low, slowly add flour mixture, and beat until combined, about 30 seconds.

2. Transfer dough to clean counter and divide into 2 equal pieces. Roll each piece of dough into log 6 inches long and 2 inches thick. Wrap dough tightly in plastic wrap and refrigerate until firm, about 2 hours.

3. Adjust oven racks to upper-middle and lower-middle positions and heat oven to 325 degrees. Line 2 baking sheets with parchment paper.

4. Working with chilled dough log at a time, slice dough into ¼-inch-thick rounds, turning log every few slices to prevent sides from flattening; space cookies ¾ inch apart on prepared sheets.

5. Bake cookies until edges are just beginning to brown, 12 to 15 minutes, switching and rotating sheets halfway through baking. Let cookies cool on sheets for 3 minutes, then transfer to wire rack and cool completely before glazing or serving. Repeat with remaining dough.

VARIATIONS

Butterscotch Icebox Cookies
Substitute brown sugar for granulated sugar.

Chocolate Icebox Cookies
Substitute ¼ cup unsweetened cocoa powder for ¼ cup flour. Add 2 ounces melted and cooled semisweet chocolate to batter with egg yolks and vanilla.

Nutty Icebox Cookies
Add ½ cup finely chopped nuts to flour mixture.

Making Slice-and-Bake Cookies

1. Scrape dough onto counter and divide into 2 equal pieces. Roll each piece into 6-inch-long cylinder, about 2 inches thick. If desired, roll each cylinder in colored sugar, chopped nuts, or sprinkles.

2. Tightly wrap each log of dough in plastic wrap, twisting wrap to help square off ends of dough. Chill dough in refrigerator until firm, at least 2 hours or up to 2 days.

3. Working with 1 piece of chilled dough at a time, slice dough into ¼-inch-thick rounds, turning log every few slices to prevent sides from flattening.

4. Divide rounds of dough between 2 parchment paper–lined baking sheets, spacing rounds about ¾ inch apart.

Pecan Sandies

MAKES 32 COOKIES   **TOTAL TIME** 50 MINUTES
(PLUS 2 HOURS CHILLING TIME PLUS COOLING TIME)

✓ **WHY THIS RECIPE WORKS:** Pecan sandies run the gamut from greasy and bland to dry and crumbly. We wanted cookies with a tender but crisp texture and a sandy melt-in-the-mouth character. Some recipes use oil in place of butter for a sandy texture. We found that the flavor of oil was abysmal, so we stuck with butter. We settled on light brown sugar, and to tenderize our cookies we swapped out some for confectioners' sugar. A whole egg made the dough too sticky, so we used just the yolk. Toasting the pecans and then grinding them ensured that rich processor running, add egg yolk and process until dough comes together into rough ball, about 20 seconds.

3. Transfer dough to clean counter, knead briefly, and divide into 2 equal pieces. Roll each piece of dough into 6-inch log. Wrap dough tightly with plastic wrap and refrigerate until firm, at least 2 hours or up to 5 days. (Dough can be frozen for up to 1 month.)

4. Adjust oven racks to upper-middle and lower-middle positions and heat oven to 325 degrees. Line 2 baking sheets with parchment paper.

5. Working with 1 dough log at a time, slice dough into ⅜-inch-thick rounds, turning log every few slices to prevent sides from flattening; space cookies 1 inch apart on prepared baking sheets. Gently press pecan half in center of each cookie.

6. Bake cookies until edges are golden brown, 20 to 25 minutes, switching and rotating sheets halfway through baking. Let cookies cool on sheets for 3 minutes, then transfer to wire rack and let cool completely before serving.

Keeping Dough Round

To help icebox cookie logs keep their shape in the refrigerator, place each wrapped log in a paper towel tube that's been cut open to form a large semicircle. This keeps the dough from flattening out on the refrigerator shelf.

Holiday Cookies

MAKES ABOUT 36 COOKIES   **TOTAL TIME** 1 HOUR 45 MINUTES (PLUS COOLING TIME)

✔ **WHY THIS RECIPE WORKS:** We wanted a simple recipe that would produce cookies sturdy enough to decorate yet tender enough to be worth eating. Superfine sugar helped to achieve a delicate texture, while a little cream cheese made the dough workable without turning the cookies tough. Using the reverse-creaming method of beating the butter into the flour-sugar mixture made for flat cookies that didn't have any air pockets and that were easy to decorate. Baking them one sheet at a time ensured that they all baked evenly. If you can't find superfine sugar, simply process 1 cup granulated sugar in a food processor for about 30 seconds, and then measure out ¾ cup. The dough scraps can be patted together, chilled, and rerolled one time only. This recipe can easily be doubled.

Adding confectioners' sugar and ground pecans to these cookies helps to create their sandy consistency.

pecan flavor. While we were grinding the nuts, we realized we might as well use the food processor to mix the dough as well. After briefly kneading it, we shaped the dough into logs to chill so that we could slice and bake pecan sandies with clean, crisp edges. Don't substitute another type of sugar for the confectioners' sugar—it is important for a tender, sandy texture.

   2 **cups pecans, toasted**
  ½ **cup packed (3½ ounces) light brown sugar**
  ¼ **cup (1 ounce) confectioners' sugar**
1½ **cups (7½ ounces) all-purpose flour**
  ¼ **teaspoon salt**
 12 **tablespoons unsalted butter, cut into ½-inch pieces and chilled**
  1 **large egg yolk**

1. Reserve 32 pretty pecan halves for garnish. Process remaining pecans, brown sugar, and confectioners' sugar in food processor until nuts are finely ground, about 20 seconds. Add flour and salt and process to combine, about 10 seconds.

2. Add butter pieces and process until mixture resembles damp sand and rides up sides of bowl, about 20 seconds. With

There are three qualities of a great holiday cookie. The first quality, of course, is taste and texture; the cookie should have a clean, buttery flavor and a crisp, melt-in-your-mouth texture. The second quality is flatness; a cookie with bumps and cracks is hard to decorate and will look sloppy. The third quality is a minimal spread during baking; the cookie should not melt dramatically as it bakes but rather it should hold a nice, clean edge so that the shape of the cookie resembles that of the cookie cutter.

1. BEAT THE BUTTER AND FLOUR TOGETHER: Whisk the flour, sugar, and salt together in a stand mixer. Fit the mixer with the paddle and beat in the butter, 1 piece at a time, on medium-low speed until the dough is crumbly and slightly wet.
WHY? This process, called "reverse creaming," makes these cookies bake up nice and flat, with no air pockets and a minimum of spreading. This ensures that the cookies hold their shape and are easy to decorate.

2. ADD THE CREAM CHEESE: Beat the cream cheese and vanilla into the dough until it begins to form large clumps, about 30 seconds. Knead the dough by hand a few times until it forms a cohesive mass.
WHY? The cream cheese helps give the cookies flavor and makes the dough particularly easy to work with. Make sure that the cream cheese is softened before adding it to the mixer or else it won't incorporate into the dough evenly.

3. REST THE DOUGH AND CHILL: Press each piece of dough into a 4-inch disk, wrap tightly in plastic wrap, and refrigerate until the dough is firm yet malleable, at least 30 minutes or up to 2 days.
WHY? Resting the dough allows for the flour to hydrate and the gluten to relax, which make the dough easier to roll out into a thin sheet. Be sure to wrap the dough tightly in plastic wrap so that it doesn't dry out in the refrigerator.

4. ROLL THE DOUGH OUT THIN AND CHILL AGAIN: Roll the dough out between 2 sheets of parchment paper to an even ⅛-inch thickness. Slide the dough, still between the parchment, onto a baking sheet and refrigerate until the dough is firm, about 10 minutes.
WHY? If the dough is too thick, the cookies will be tough. Rolling the dough out between two sheets of parchment makes rolling and chilling it super easy.

5. STAMP OUT THE COOKIES: Working with 1 sheet of dough at a time, remove the top piece of parchment and stamp out cookies using cookie cutters. Using a thin offset spatula, transfer the cookies to a parchment-lined baking sheet, spaced about 1 inch apart.
WHY? Working with chilled dough helps the cookie cutting process go much more smoothly. You can gather and chill the leftover dough scraps for one more batch.

6. DON'T OVERBAKE: Bake the cookies, 1 sheet at a time, until they're light golden brown, about 10 minutes, rotating the sheet halfway through baking.
WHY? These thin cookies go from perfectly baked to overbaked in a matter of minutes, so it's important to watch—they should show a slight resistance to touch and be starting to brown along the edges. Baking them one sheet at a time ensures that they all bake evenly.

Decorating cutout cookies is the place to express your creativity. We've outlined general tips and techniques here, but feel free to go your own way. Always let cookies cool completely before starting the decorating process. You will likely want to start with a good glaze (page 631).

A. GET ORGANIZED: Place your cookie decorations in a muffin tin, using each cup to hold a different decoration. **WHY?** During the holidays you may find yourself making cookies several times over a period of several weeks. A muffin tin keeps sprinkles, colored sugars, and other decorations organized and reusable. Just cover the muffin tin with plastic wrap between uses.

B. GLAZE FROM THE CENTER OUT: Spoon a small amount of glaze in the center of the cookie, then spread it into an even layer using the back of a spoon. **WHY?** Spreading the glaze outward from the center is the best way to ensure even coverage. The back of a spoon will work; you can also use a small offset spatula. For the lightest touch, use a very small paintbrush. Be sure to let the glaze set before storing or serving.

C. PIPE A BORDER OR DESIGN: Place the glaze in a small zipper-lock bag and snip off a tiny piece from one corner with scissors. Pipe the glaze through the hole in the bag and onto the cookies. **WHY?** Glaze can be used to add detail to a cutout cookie. A small zipper-lock bag works just as well as a pastry bag. Just snip a very small hole and push the glaze down into that corner of the bag; exert even pressure to ensure even flow of the glaze.

D. ADD EMBELLISHMENTS: While the glaze is still soft, place decorations on the glaze and allow them to set. **WHY?** Small confections, often shiny silver or gold balls known as dragées, can be used to dress up cookies. Other small candies—gumdrops, mini chocolate morsels, jelly beans—can be used in a similar fashion. Add these candies immediately after applying the glaze. As the glaze hardens, it will affix the candies in place.

E. DRAG TWO GLAZES TOGETHER: Glaze the entire cookie (see step B), then pipe small drops of a second glaze in a decorative pattern. Drag a toothpick through the glazes to create a design. **WHY?** As long as both glazes are still wet, you can create a range of designs, everything from hearts (shown here) to stars, wiggly lines, and swirls. This idea works best with glazes that are two different colors.

F. DIP IN CHOCOLATE: Melt chocolate in a small bowl, then gently dip part of the cookie (such as one end, or the bottom) in the chocolate to coat. Transfer the cookie to a wire rack and cool completely. **WHY?** Any kind of chocolate and any kind of cookie will work here. Using a small bowl makes it easier to have a deep pool of chocolate in which to dip the cookies. Alternatively, use a brush or the back of a spoon to coat the cookie with chocolate.

2½ cups (12½ ounces) all-purpose flour

¾ cup (5¼ ounces) superfine sugar

¼ teaspoon salt

16 tablespoons unsalted butter, cut into ½-inch pieces and softened

2 tablespoons cream cheese, softened

2 teaspoons vanilla extract

1. Whisk flour, sugar, and salt together in bowl of stand mixer. Fit mixer with paddle and beat in butter, 1 piece at a time, on medium-low speed until dough looks crumbly and slightly wet, 1 to 2 minutes.

2. Beat in cream cheese and vanilla until dough just begins to form large clumps, about 30 seconds. Knead dough in bowl by hand several times until it forms large, cohesive mass.

3. Transfer dough to clean counter and divide into 2 equal pieces. Press each piece into 4-inch disk, wrap tightly in plastic wrap, and refrigerate until dough is firm yet malleable, at least 30 minutes or up to 2 days. (Dough can be frozen for up to 2 weeks; defrost in refrigerator before using.)

4. Working with 1 piece of dough at a time, roll dough out between 2 large sheets of parchment paper to even ⅛-inch thickness. Slide dough, still between parchment, onto baking sheet and refrigerate until firm, about 10 minutes.

5. Adjust oven rack to middle position and heat oven to 375 degrees. Line 2 baking sheets with parchment paper. Working with 1 sheet of dough at a time, remove top piece of parchment and stamp out cookies using cookie cutters. Using thin offset spatula, transfer cookies to prepared baking sheet, spaced about 1 inch apart.

6. Bake cookies, 1 sheet at a time, until light golden brown, about 10 minutes, rotating sheet halfway through baking. Let cookies cool on sheet for 3 minutes, then transfer to wire rack and let cool completely before glazing or serving. Repeat with remaining dough using freshly lined baking sheets.

Gingerbread People

MAKES ABOUT 20 PEOPLE   **TOTAL TIME** 1 HOUR
(PLUS COOLING TIME)

✔**WHY THIS RECIPE WORKS:** To make the process of rolling out gingerbread cookies even easier, we altered the usual mixing method. Instead of creaming softened butter and sugar, then adding the dry and liquid ingredients, we used a food processor and mixed the dry ingredients first, adding the butter and finally the molasses and a little milk. This method produced a dough that was firm enough to be rolled out at once. To further ensure that the cookies would maintain a perfect

---

GLAZES FOR COOKIES

Glazes are an easy way to decorate flat cookies, such as Vanilla Icebox Cookies (page 626), Holiday Cookies (page 628), and Gingerbread People. To make the glaze, just whisk all the ingredients together in a bowl until smooth. Spread the glaze onto completely cooled cookies using the back of a spoon, or pipe the glaze onto cookies to form a pattern or design (see page 630). Let the glaze dry completely, about 30 minutes, before serving. (Each glaze makes about 1 cup.)

EASY ALL-PURPOSE GLAZE `FAST`

2 cups (8 ounces) confectioners' sugar

3 tablespoons milk

2 tablespoons cream cheese, softened

Food coloring, as needed (optional)

CITRUS GLAZE `FAST`

2 cups (8 ounces) confectioners' sugar

3 tablespoons lemon, lime, or orange juice

2 tablespoons cream cheese, softened

NUTTY GLAZE `FAST`

2 cups (8 ounces) confectioners' sugar

3 tablespoons milk

2 tablespoons cream cheese, softened

½ teaspoon almond or coconut extract

COFFEE GLAZE `FAST`

2 cups (8 ounces) confectioners' sugar

3 tablespoons milk

2 tablespoons cream cheese, softened

1¼ teaspoons instant espresso powder or instant coffee

BITTERSWEET CHOCOLATE GLAZE `FAST`

5 ounces bittersweet chocolate, melted

4 tablespoons unsalted butter, melted

2 tablespoons corn syrup

1 tablespoon vanilla extract

shape, we rolled the dough between sheets of parchment and then chilled it briefly before cutting. For this recipe, we used 5-inch gingerbread people cookie cutters, but any cookie cutter will work; the baking time may be slightly different for larger or smaller cookies. Be careful not to overbake the cookies or they will be dry. When storing these cookies, layer them between sheets of parchment to prevent them from sticking together.

3 cups (15 ounces) all-purpose flour
¾ cup packed (5¼ ounces) dark brown sugar
¾ teaspoon baking soda
1 tablespoon ground cinnamon
1 tablespoon ground ginger
½ teaspoon ground cloves
½ teaspoon salt
12 tablespoons unsalted butter,
    cut into pieces and softened
¾ cup light molasses
2 tablespoons milk

1. Process flour, sugar, baking soda, cinnamon, ginger, cloves, and salt in food processor until combined, about 10 seconds. Add butter and process until mixture is very fine and sandy, about 15 seconds. With processor running, add molasses and milk in steady stream and continue to process until dough comes together, about 10 seconds.

2. Divide dough into 2 even pieces and roll each out to ¼-inch thickness between 2 pieces of parchment paper. Slide dough, still between parchment, onto baking sheet and freeze until firm, 15 to 20 minutes.

3. Adjust oven racks to upper-middle and lower-middle positions and heat oven to 375 degrees. Line 2 baking sheets with parchment paper. Working with 1 sheet of dough at a time, remove top piece of parchment and stamp out cookies using cookie cutters. Using thin offset spatula, transfer cookies to prepared baking sheet, spaced about 1 inch apart. (Dough scraps can be rerolled and cut out as many times as necessary.)

4. Bake cookies until light golden brown and edges are set, 8 to 11 minutes, switching and rotating sheets halfway through baking. Let cookies cool on sheets for 5 minutes, then transfer to wire rack and let cool completely before glazing or serving. Repeat with remaining dough using freshly lined baking sheets.

NOTES FROM THE TEST KITCHEN

Types of Molasses

Molasses is a byproduct of the cane sugar refining process; it is the liquid drawn off after the cane juice has been boiled and has undergone crystallization. The resulting molasses is then subjected to subsequent boilings, and with each it grows increasingly dark, bitter, and potent as more sugar is extracted. There are three types of molasses: light or mild molasses (from the first boiling), dark or robust molasses (from the second boiling), and blackstrap (from the third boiling). Which molasses you use is largely a matter of personal preference, though we find the bitter flavor of blackstrap molasses to be overpowering for most baked goods.

VARIATION
Thin and Crispy Gingerbread Cookies
MAKES ABOUT 34 GINGERBREAD PEOPLE OR 54 COOKIES
These gingersnap-like cookies are very sturdy and are great for making Christmas tree ornaments; use a drinking straw to punch holes in the cookies (for threading) when they're just out of the oven and still soft.

Divide dough into 4 even pieces in step 2, and roll each piece out to even ⅛-inch thickness. Stamp out cookies and bake in 325-degree oven until slightly darkened and firm in center when pressed with finger, 15 to 20 minutes. Let cool as directed.

Shortbread Cookies
MAKES 16 WEDGES   **TOTAL TIME** 1 HOUR 45 MINUTES
(PLUS COOLING TIME)

✔**WHY THIS RECIPE WORKS:** The basics of shortbread making haven't changed much over the past five centuries: Combine flour, sugar, butter, and salt, then pat the dough into a round and bake. But even with this simple, time-honored formula, it can turn out greasy, bland, tough, or cakelike. We wanted shortbread that crumbled in the mouth with a pure, buttery richness. We tinkered with the ratio of butter to flour, settling on slightly less butter than flour by weight, which yielded rich-tasting but not greasy shortbread. Swapping in confectioners' sugar for granulated gave us a smoother texture. Reverse creaming (mixing the flour and sugar before adding the butter) created less aeration and produced substantial shortbread. To solve the persistent problem of toughness, we needed to reduce gluten formation. Replacing some of the flour with a combination of cornstarch and ground oats tenderized the shortbread and added a hint of nutty depth. We patted the dough into a circle, using a springform pan collar for a mold, then baked it for about 20 minutes, after which we turned off the oven and let it finish cooking. An hour later, our shortbread was perfectly golden brown and crisp throughout.

½ cup (1½ ounces) old-fashioned rolled oats
1½ cups (7½ ounces) all-purpose flour
⅔ cup (2⅔ ounces) confectioners' sugar
¼ cup cornstarch
½ teaspoon salt
14 tablespoons unsalted butter, cut into ⅛-inch-thick
    slices and chilled

1. Adjust oven rack to middle position and heat oven to 450 degrees. Pulse oats in spice grinder or blender to fine powder, about 10 pulses. Whisk processed oats, flour, sugar, cornstarch, and salt together in bowl of stand mixer. Fit mixer with paddle and beat in butter, 1 piece at a time, on low speed until dough just forms and pulls away from sides of bowl, 5 to 10 minutes.

2. Place collar of 9- or 9½-inch springform pan on parchment paper–lined rimmed baking sheet (do not use springform pan bottom). Press dough evenly into collar, smoothing top of dough with back of spoon. Cut out center of dough using 2-inch biscuit cutter, place extracted 2-inch cookie on sheet next to collar, and replace cutter in center of dough. Open springform collar, but leave it in place.

3. Bake shortbread for 5 minutes. Reduce oven temperature to 250 degrees and continue to bake until edges turn pale golden, 10 to 15 minutes.

4. Remove baking sheet from oven and turn off oven. Remove springform pan collar. Using knife, score surface of shortbread into 16 even wedges, cutting halfway through shortbread. Using wooden skewer, poke 8 to 10 holes in each

Making Shortbread Cookies

1. Press dough evenly into collar of springform pan, smoothing top of dough with back of spoon.

2. Cut out center of dough using 2-inch biscuit cutter.

3. Place extracted 2-inch cookie on sheet next to collar, then replace cutter in center of dough. Open springform collar, but leave it in place.

4. After baking, remove collar and score surface of shortbread into 16 wedges, cutting halfway through. Using wooden skewer, poke 8 to 10 holes in each wedge.

wedge. Return shortbread to oven, prop door open with handle of wooden spoon, and let shortbread dry in turned-off oven until pale golden in center and is firm but giving to touch, about 1 hour.

5. Remove shortbread from oven and let cool completely, about 2 hours. Cut shortbread at scored marks and serve. (Shortbread can be stored at room temperature for up to 1 week.)

Almond Biscotti

MAKES 30 COOKIES   **TOTAL TIME** 1 HOUR 40 MINUTES
(PLUS COOLING TIME)

✔ WHY THIS RECIPE WORKS: Our ideal biscotti is somewhere in between the dry, hard Italian original and the buttery, tender American version. We wanted nut-filled cookies that were crisp enough for dunking, yet not tooth-shattering. Knowing that the crunch depended, in part, on the amount of butter, we settled on just enough to give us a dough that was neither too hard nor too lean. Without enough butter to effectively cream with the sugar, we needed to find another way to aerate the dough. Whipping the eggs until they were light in color and then adding the sugar did the trick. To moderate the crunchiness we ground part of the nuts (lightly toasted) in a food processor and substituted them for a portion of the flour. With less gluten formed, the biscotti were more tender—and they had nutty flavor in every bite. We baked the dough in two neat rectangles, then sliced them and baked the slices on a wire rack set in a baking sheet, flipping them halfway through baking. The rack allowed air circulation around the cookies, making them evenly crisp. Be sure to toast the almonds just until fragrant; they will continue to toast while the biscotti bake.

1¼ **cups whole almonds, lightly toasted**
1¾ **cups (8¾ ounces) all-purpose flour**
 2 **teaspoons baking powder**
 ¼ **teaspoon salt**
 2 **large eggs, plus 1 large white beaten with pinch salt**
 1 **cup (7 ounces) sugar**
 4 **tablespoons unsalted butter, melted and cooled**
1½ **teaspoons almond extract**
 ½ **teaspoon vanilla extract**
    Vegetable oil spray

1. Adjust oven rack to middle position and heat oven to 325 degrees. Using ruler and pencil, draw two 8 by 3-inch rectangles, spaced 4 inches apart, on piece of parchment paper. Grease baking sheet and place parchment on it, pencil side down.

2. Pulse 1 cup almonds in food processor until coarsely chopped, 8 to 10 pulses; transfer to bowl. Process remaining ¼ cup almonds in now-empty food processor until finely ground, about 45 seconds. Add flour, baking powder, and salt and process to combine, about 15 seconds; transfer to separate bowl.

3. Process 2 eggs in now-empty food processor until lightened in color and almost doubled in volume, about 3 minutes. With processor running, slowly add sugar until thoroughly combined, about 15 seconds. Add melted butter, almond extract, and vanilla and process until combined, about 10 seconds. Transfer egg mixture to medium bowl. Sprinkle half of flour mixture over top and fold gently with rubber spatula until just combined. Add remaining flour mixture and chopped almonds and gently fold until just combined.

4. Divide batter in half. With floured hands, form each half into 8 by 3-inch rectangle, using lines on parchment as guide. Spray each loaf lightly with vegetable oil spray. Using rubber spatula lightly coated with oil spray, smooth tops and sides of rectangles. Gently brush tops of loaves with egg white wash. Bake loaves until golden and just beginning to crack on top, 25 to 30 minutes, rotating sheet halfway through baking.

5. Let loaves cool on sheet for 30 minutes. Transfer loaves to cutting board. Using serrated knife, slice each loaf on slight bias into ½-inch-thick slices. Space slices, with one cut side down, about ¼ inch apart on wire rack set in rimmed baking sheet. Bake until crisp and golden brown on both sides, about 35 minutes, flipping slices halfway through baking. Let cool completely before serving. (Biscotti can be stored at room temperature for up to 1 month.)

VARIATIONS

Pistachio-Spice Biscotti

Substitute shelled pistachios for almonds. Add 1 teaspoon ground cardamom, ½ teaspoon ground cloves, ½ teaspoon pepper, ¼ teaspoon ground cinnamon, and ¼ teaspoon ground ginger to food processor with flour. Substitute 1 teaspoon water for almond extract, and increase vanilla extract to 1 teaspoon.

Hazelnut-Orange Biscotti

Substitute lightly toasted and skinned hazelnuts for almonds. Add 2 tablespoons minced fresh rosemary to food processor with flour. Substitute orange-flavored liqueur for almond extract, and add 1 tablespoon grated orange zest to food processor with butter.

Hazelnut-Lavender Biscotti

Substitute lightly toasted and skinned hazelnuts for almonds. Add 2 teaspoons dried lavender flowers to food processor with flour. Substitute 1½ teaspoons water for almond extract, and add 2 tablespoons grated lemon zest to food processor with butter.

Anise Biscotti

Add 1½ teaspoons anise seeds to food processor with flour. Substitute anise-flavored liqueur for almond extract.

Making Biscotti

1. Using ruler and pencil, draw two 8 by 3-inch rectangles, spaced 4 inches apart, on piece of parchment paper. Place parchment marked side down on greased baking sheet.

2. After preparing batter, divide in half and with floured hands form each half into 8 by 3-inch loaf on parchment-lined sheet, using lines as guide.

3. Transfer partially baked loaves to cutting board. Using serrated knife, slice each loaf on slight bias into ½-inch-thick slices.

4. Space slices, with one cut side down, about ¼ inch apart on wire rack set in rimmed baking sheet. Bake until crisp and golden brown on both sides, about 35 minutes, flipping slices halfway through baking.

These decadent brownies are packed with three different forms of chocolate.

Ultimate Fudgy Brownies

MAKES 36 SMALL BROWNIES   **TOTAL TIME** 1 HOUR
(PLUS COOLING TIME)

✔ **WHY THIS RECIPE WORKS:** To make sinfully rich brownies that would be a chocolate lover's dream, we used three forms of chocolate: unsweetened chocolate for intensity, cocoa powder to offset any sourness from the unsweetened chocolate and add complexity, and bittersweet or semisweet chocolate for slightly mellower notes. Melting butter along with the chocolate was the key to a fudgy texture, and a generous three eggs added body. In addition to providing pure sweetness, granulated sugar gave the baked brownies a delicate, shiny, crackly top crust. We found it best to cut these brownies into small bites, rather than big bake-sale squares—a little goes a long way. Tasters preferred the more complex flavor of bittersweet chocolate over semisweet chocolate, but either type works well here, as does 5 ounces of bittersweet or semisweet chocolate chips in place of the bar chocolate.

5   **ounces bittersweet or semisweet chocolate, chopped**
2   **ounces unsweetened chocolate, chopped**
8   **tablespoons unsalted butter, cut into 4 pieces**
3   **tablespoons unsweetened cocoa powder**
1¼   **cups (8¾ ounces) sugar**
3   **large eggs**
2   **teaspoons vanilla extract**
½   **teaspoon salt**
1   **cup (5 ounces) all-purpose flour**

1. Adjust oven rack to middle position and heat oven to 350 degrees. Make foil sling for 8-inch square baking pan by folding 2 long sheets of aluminum foil so each is 8 inches wide. Lay sheets of foil in pan perpendicular to each other, with extra foil hanging over edges of pan. Push foil into corners and up sides of pan, smoothing foil flush to pan, and grease foil.

2. Microwave bittersweet and unsweetened chocolates in bowl at 50 percent power for 2 minutes. Stir in butter and continue to microwave until melted, stirring often. Whisk in cocoa and let mixture cool slightly.

3. Whisk sugar, eggs, vanilla, and salt together in large bowl until combined. Whisk in melted chocolate mixture until smooth. Stir in flour until no streaks remain. Scrape batter into prepared pan and smooth top. Bake brownies until toothpick inserted into center comes out with few crumbs attached, 35 to 40 minutes, rotating pan halfway through baking.

4. Let brownies cool completely, about 2 hours. Using foil overhang, lift brownies from pan. (Uncut brownies can be refrigerated for up to 3 days.) Cut into small squares and serve.

Making a Foil Sling

1. Line pan with 2 folded sheets of foil (or parchment) placed perpendicular to each other, with extra foil hanging over edges of pan. Push foil into corners and smooth flush to pan.

2. Use foil handles to lift baked bar cookies or cake from pan.

Chewy Brownies

MAKES 24 BROWNIES **TOTAL TIME** 55 MINUTES
(PLUS COOLING TIME)

✔ **WHY THIS RECIPE WORKS:** While box-mix brownies may not offer superior chocolate flavor, there's no denying their chewy appeal. We cracked the code for perfectly chewy brownies, and the key was fat—specifically, the right amounts of saturated and unsaturated fats. Once we figured out that an almost 1:3 ratio of saturated fat (butter) to unsaturated fat (vegetable oil) produced the chewiest brownies, we fine-tuned the other sources of fat (eggs and chocolate) to preserve the balance. Two extra egg yolks, along with two whole eggs, provided emulsification that prevented the brownies from turning greasy. We whisked unsweetened cocoa, along with some espresso powder, into boiling water, and then stirred in unsweetened chocolate. The heat unlocked the chocolate's flavor compounds, increasing its impact. Looking for even more chocolate punch, we realized that we could stir chunks of chocolate into the batter without affecting the balance of fats we'd worked hard to achieve. Our brownies now had pockets of gooey chocolate in a delicious, chewy base. For the chewiest texture, it is important to let the brownies cool thoroughly before cutting. If your baking dish is glass, cool the brownies 10 minutes, then remove them promptly from the pan (otherwise, the superior heat retention of glass can lead to overbaking).

⅓ cup (1 ounce) Dutch-processed cocoa
1½ teaspoons instant espresso powder (optional)
½ cup plus 2 tablespoons boiling water
2 ounces unsweetened chocolate, chopped fine
½ cup plus 2 tablespoons vegetable oil
4 tablespoons unsalted butter, melted
2 large eggs plus 2 large yolks
2 teaspoons vanilla extract
2½ cups (17½ ounces) sugar
1¾ cups (8¾ ounces) all-purpose flour
¾ teaspoon salt
6 ounces bittersweet chocolate, cut into ½-inch pieces

1. Adjust oven rack to lowest position and heat oven to 350 degrees. Make foil sling for 13 by 9-inch baking pan by folding 2 long sheets of aluminum foil; first sheet should be 13 inches wide, and second sheet should be 9 inches wide. Lay sheets of foil in pan perpendicular to each other, with extra foil hanging over edges of pan. Push foil into corners and up sides of pan, smoothing foil flush to pan, and grease foil.

2. Whisk cocoa, espresso powder, if using, and boiling water together in large bowl until smooth. Add unsweetened chocolate and whisk until chocolate is melted. Whisk in oil and melted butter. (Mixture may look curdled.) Whisk in eggs, yolks, and vanilla until smooth and homogeneous. Whisk in sugar until fully incorporated. Add flour and salt and mix with rubber spatula until combined. Fold in chocolate pieces.

3. Scrape batter into prepared pan and smooth top. Bake brownies until toothpick inserted halfway between edge and center comes out with few moist crumbs attached, 30 to 35 minutes, rotating pan halfway through baking. Let brownies cool in pan for 1½ hours.

4. Using foil overhang, lift brownies from pan. Transfer to wire rack and let cool completely, about 1 hour. Cut into squares and serve.

VARIATIONS
Frosted Brownies

Our chewy brownies are also sturdy enough to be frosted. Use one of our frostings below, or try some of the cake frostings on pages 691–694; you will need about 1½ cups of frosting.

Chocolate Frosted Brownies

After brownies have cooled for 1 hour, microwave ⅔ cup chocolate chips and 1 tablespoon vegetable oil together in bowl at 50 percent power, stirring often, until chocolate is melted, 1 to 3 minutes. Cool mixture until barely warm, about 5 minutes, then spread over brownies with spatula. Continue to cool brownies until topping sets, 1 to 2 hours.

White Chocolate and Peppermint Brownies

Pulse ⅓ cup peppermint candies in food processor until finely chopped. When brownies come out of oven, sprinkle with 6 ounces white chocolate chips and let sit until chocolate softens but is not melted, about 5 minutes. Smooth softened chocolate into even layer, then sprinkle with chopped peppermint candies. Let brownies cool until topping sets, 1 to 2 hours.

German Chocolate Brownies

When brownies come out of oven, sprinkle with 6 ounces butterscotch chips and let sit until chips soften but are not melted, about 5 minutes. Smooth softened chips into even layer, then sprinkle with ½ cup toasted coconut. Let brownies cool until topping sets, 1 to 2 hours.

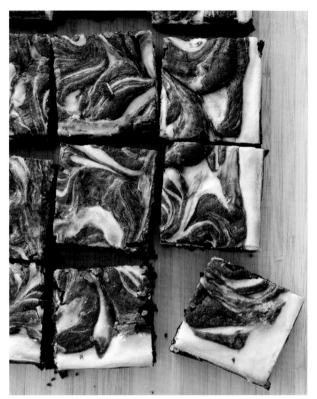

The key to the perfect balance between fudgy brownies and rich cheesecake is our layer-and-swirl technique.

Cream Cheese Brownies

MAKES 16 BROWNIES   **TOTAL TIME** 1 HOUR
(PLUS COOLING TIME)

✓ **WHY THIS RECIPE WORKS:** At their best, cream cheese brownies serve up a perfectly matched duet of velvety cheesecake and fudgy brownie, swirled together yet each maintaining their distinct identity. Because we knew the cream cheese filling would be adding plenty of moisture to the mix, we decided to make the brownie base slightly cakey. We combined unsweetened chocolate with a modest amount of sugar and included ½ teaspoon of baking powder for lift. Mixed with just an egg and a bit of sugar, the cream cheese was too muted to hold its own against the brownie's chocolaty sweetness. A half-cup of sour cream provided a refreshing tang without any sour notes. To compensate for the increased moisture from the sour cream, we ditched the egg and stirred in a tablespoon of flour. Spooned over the brownie batter and swirled in, the cream cheese weighed down the chocolate in spots, creating

Pure Vanilla versus Imitation Vanilla

Pure vanilla extract is made by soaking vanilla beans in a solution of water and alcohol and then aging the mixture in holding tanks—sometimes for a few months—prior to bottling. This lengthy production process contributes to the high cost of pure vanilla extract. The less-expensive imitation extract, on the other hand, relies primarily on the synthetic compound vanillin to mimic the smell and taste of real vanilla.

We compared batches of chocolate chip cookies and pastry cream made with each extract. When the extract was baked into the cookies, most of the tasters actually preferred the artificial vanilla, claiming that its "mild, natural" flavor melded nicely with the buttery, chocolaty cookies. In the pastry cream (where the extracts were added after cooking), the opinions were more varied. Some tasters lauded the "clean, floral" aroma of the pure vanilla, but others found it to be "too strong" and "boozy."

Ultimately, since both extracts were deemed acceptable in both recipes, the choice comes down to cost and personal philosophy about using imitation products. Imitation vanilla certainly will not ruin your baked goods.

a lumpy pan of brownies. Instead, we spread most of the brownie batter in the pan and then spread the cream cheese filling evenly over it. Finally, we dolloped the last bit of brownie batter on top and swirled everything together with a knife. This gave us even brownies, with cream cheese in every bite. To accurately test the doneness of the brownies, be sure to stick the toothpick through part of the brownie and not the cream cheese.

CREAM CHEESE FILLING
- 4 ounces cream cheese, cut into 8 pieces
- ½ cup sour cream
- 2 tablespoons sugar
- 1 tablespoon all-purpose flour

BROWNIES
- ⅔ cup (3⅓ ounces) all-purpose flour
- ½ teaspoon baking powder
- ½ teaspoon salt
- 4 ounces unsweetened chocolate, chopped fine
- 8 tablespoons unsalted butter
- 1¼ cups (8¾ ounces) sugar
- 2 large eggs
- 1 teaspoon vanilla extract

1. Adjust oven rack to middle position and heat oven to 325 degrees. Make foil sling for 8-inch square baking pan by folding 2 long sheets of aluminum foil so each is 8 inches wide. Lay sheets of foil in pan perpendicular to each other, with extra foil hanging over edges of pan. Push foil into corners and up sides of pan, smoothing foil flush to pan, and grease foil.

2. **FOR THE FILLING:** Microwave cream cheese in bowl until soft, 20 to 30 seconds. Whisk in sour cream, sugar, and flour.

3. **FOR THE BROWNIES:** Whisk flour, baking powder, and salt together in bowl. Microwave chocolate and butter together in separate bowl at 50 percent power, stirring often, until melted, 1 to 2 minutes. In medium bowl, whisk sugar, eggs, and vanilla together. Whisk in melted chocolate mixture until incorporated. Fold in flour mixture with rubber spatula.

4. Spread all but ½ cup of brownie batter in prepared pan. Spread cream cheese mixture evenly over top. Microwave remaining brownie batter until warm and pourable, 10 to 20 seconds. Using spoon, dollop softened batter over cream cheese filling (6 to 8 dollops). Using knife, swirl brownie batter through cream cheese topping, making marbled pattern, leaving ½-inch border around edges.

5. Bake brownies until toothpick inserted in center comes out with few moist crumbs attached, 35 to 40 minutes, rotating pan halfway through baking. Let brownies cool in pan for 1 hour.

6. Using foil overhang, lift brownies from pan. Transfer to wire rack and let cool completely, about 1 hour. Cut into squares and serve.

Mississippi Mud Brownies

MAKES 24 BROWNIES   **TOTAL TIME** 1 HOUR (PLUS COOLING TIME)

✅ **WHY THIS RECIPE WORKS:** This pecan-laced brownie is usually topped with mini marshmallows once the base is set but still moist, briefly returned to the oven, and then covered with chocolate frosting once cooled. We wanted to make this dense, rich concoction without causing sugar overload. Cocoa powder was the natural choice as a low-sugar source of chocolate flavor in our brownie base. Three-quarters of a cup of chopped pecans added plenty of textural interest without being distracting. Next, rather than using mini marshmallows, we found that a thin layer of marshmallow crème evenly coated the brownies and kept the sugar quotient in check. Moving on to the frosting, we decided the brownies needed just a drizzle of chocolate for an impressive, dressed-up look. We melted a few chocolate chips and added a little oil to keep the chocolate flowing from the spoon as we waved it over the brownies. Be careful not to overbake these brownies; they should be moist and fudgy.

 6 **ounces unsweetened chocolate, chopped**
16 **tablespoons unsalted butter, cut into 16 pieces**
1½ **cups (7½ ounces) all-purpose flour**
⅓ **cup (1 ounce) Dutch-processed cocoa powder**
½ **teaspoon salt**
 3 **cups (21 ounces) sugar**
 5 **large eggs**
¾ **cup pecans, chopped**
¾ **cup marshmallow crème**
¼ **cup (1½ ounces) semisweet chocolate chips**
 2 **teaspoons vegetable oil**

Making Cream Cheese Brownies

1. Spread all but ½ cup of brownie batter in prepared pan. Spread cream cheese mixture evenly over top.

2. Microwave remaining brownie batter until warm and pourable, 10 to 20 seconds.

3. Using spoon, dollop softened batter over cream cheese filling (6 to 8 dollops).

4. Using knife, swirl brownie batter through cream cheese topping, making marbled pattern, leaving ½-inch border around edges.

To maximize the chocolate flavor in these moist brownies, we add cocoa powder and keep the amount of sugar in check.

oil together in small bowl at 50 percent power until melted and smooth, 30 to 60 seconds. Spread softened marshmallow crème evenly over brownies, and then drizzle with chocolate. Let brownies cool completely, about 2 hours. Using foil overhang, lift brownies from pan. Cut into squares and serve.

Blondies

MAKES 36 BARS   **TOTAL TIME** 45 MINUTES
(PLUS COOLING TIME)

✓ **WHY THIS RECIPE WORKS:** Although blondies are baked in a pan like brownies, the flavorings are more similar to those in chocolate chip cookies—vanilla, butter, and brown sugar. Blondies should be chewy but not dense, sweet but not cloying, and loaded with nuts and chocolate. We found that the secret to chewy blondies was using melted, not creamed, butter because the creaming process incorporates too much air into the batter. For sweetening, light brown sugar lent the right amount of earthy molasses flavor. And combined with a substantial amount of vanilla extract and salt, the light brown sugar developed a rich butterscotch flavor. To add both texture and flavor to the cookies, we included chocolate chips and pecans. We also tried butterscotch chips, but we found that they did little for this recipe. On a whim, we included white chocolate chips with the semisweet chips, and we were surprised that they produced the best blondies yet. Walnuts can be substituted for the pecans.

1½ **cups (7½ ounces) all-purpose flour**
1 **teaspoon baking powder**
½ **teaspoon salt**
1½ **cups packed (10½ ounces) light brown sugar**
12 **tablespoons unsalted butter, melted and cooled**
2 **large eggs**
1½ **teaspoons vanilla extract**
1 **cup pecans, toasted and chopped coarse**
½ **cup (3 ounces) semisweet chocolate chips**
½ **cup (3 ounces) white chocolate chips**

1. Adjust oven rack to middle position and heat oven to 350 degrees. Make foil sling for 13 by 9-inch baking pan by folding 2 long sheets of aluminum foil; first sheet should be 13 inches wide, and second sheet should be 9 inches wide. Lay sheets of foil in pan perpendicular to each other, with extra foil hanging over edges of pan. Push foil into corners and up sides of pan, smoothing foil flush to pan, and grease foil.

1. Adjust oven rack to middle position and heat oven to 325 degrees. Make foil sling for 13 by 9-inch baking pan by folding 2 long sheets of aluminum foil; first sheet should be 13 inches wide, and second sheet should be 9 inches wide. Lay sheets of foil in pan perpendicular to each other, with extra foil hanging over edges of pan. Push foil into corners and up sides of pan, smoothing foil flush to pan, and grease foil.

2. Microwave unsweetened chocolate and butter together in large bowl at 50 percent power, stirring occasionally, until melted and smooth, 1 to 2 minutes; let cool slightly. In separate bowl, whisk flour, cocoa, and salt together.

3. In medium bowl, whisk sugar and eggs together. Whisk into melted chocolate mixture until uniform. Stir in flour mixture until no streaks remain. Stir in pecans.

4. Scrape batter into prepared pan and smooth top. Bake until toothpick inserted in center comes out with few moist crumbs attached, about 35 minutes, rotating pan halfway through baking.

5. Transfer pan to wire rack, gently spoon marshmallow crème over top of hot brownies, and let sit until softened, about 1 minute. Meanwhile, microwave chocolate chips and

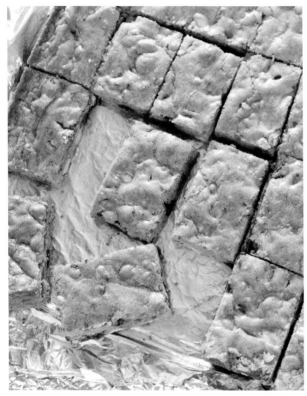
Adding white chocolate chips plus semisweet chocolate chips gives our blondies a rich, full flavor.

2. Whisk flour, baking powder, and salt together in bowl. In medium bowl, whisk sugar and melted butter together until combined. Whisk in eggs and vanilla. Using rubber spatula, fold in flour mixture until just combined. Fold in pecans and semisweet and white chocolate chips.

3. Scrape batter into prepared pan and smooth top. Bake until top is shiny and cracked and feels firm to touch, 22 to 25 minutes, rotating pan halfway through baking.

4. Let blondies cool completely, about 2 hours. Using foil overhang, lift blondies from pan. Cut into bars and serve.

VARIATION

Congo Bars

Keep a close eye on the toasting coconut, as it can burn easily.

Toast 1½ cups unsweetened shredded coconut on rimmed baking sheet in 350-degree oven, stirring occasionally, until light golden, 4 to 5 minutes. Let cool, then add to batter with chocolate chips and nuts.

Lemon Bars

MAKES 16 BARS   **TOTAL TIME** 1 HOUR (PLUS COOLING TIME)

✔**WHY THIS RECIPE WORKS:** Successful lemon bars, with bright lemon flavor, depend on ample amounts of fresh lemon juice and lemon zest. We used four lemons in our lemon curd filling, along with two whole eggs and seven yolks for thickening. To tame the curd's pucker power and make it creamy, we added a small dose of heavy cream and some butter. Confectioners' sugar contributed a tender texture to the crust. We found that it was important to pour the warm filling over a still-hot crust to ensure that the filling cooked through evenly; you can prepare the filling while the crust bakes. Humidity tends to make the sugar melt and turn splotchy, so if you live in a humid climate dust the lemon bars with the confectioners' sugar right before serving. Any leftover bars can be sealed in plastic wrap and refrigerated for up to two days.

CRUST

- 1¼ cups (6¼ ounces) all-purpose flour
- ½ cup (2 ounces) confectioners' sugar
- ½ teaspoon salt
- 8 tablespoons unsalted butter, cut into 8 pieces and softened

FILLING

- 2 large eggs plus 7 large yolks
- 1 cup (7 ounces) plus 2 tablespoons granulated sugar
- ¼ cup grated lemon zest plus ⅔ cup juice (4 lemons) Pinch salt
- 4 tablespoons unsalted butter, cut into 4 pieces
- 3 tablespoons heavy cream Confectioners' sugar

1. Adjust oven rack to middle position and heat oven to 350 degrees. Make foil sling for 9-inch square baking pan by folding 2 long sheets of aluminum foil so each is 9 inches wide. Lay sheets of foil in pan perpendicular to each other, with extra foil hanging over edges of pan. Push foil into corners and up sides of pan, smoothing foil flush to pan, and grease foil.

2. FOR THE CRUST: Process flour, confectioners' sugar, and salt in food processor until combined, about 3 seconds. Sprinkle butter over top and pulse until mixture is pale yellow and resembles coarse cornmeal, about 8 pulses. Sprinkle mixture into prepared pan and press firmly into even layer using your fingers. Bake until crust starts to brown, about 20 minutes, rotating pan halfway through baking.

3. FOR THE FILLING: Meanwhile, whisk eggs and yolks together in medium saucepan. Whisk in granulated sugar until combined, then whisk in lemon zest and juice and salt. Add butter and cook over medium-low heat, stirring constantly, until butter is melted and mixture thickens slightly and registers 170 degrees, about 5 minutes.

4. Strain mixture immediately into bowl and stir in cream. Pour warm lemon curd over hot crust. Bake until filling is shiny and opaque and center jiggles slightly when shaken, rotating pan halfway through baking, 10 to 15 minutes.

5. Let bars cool completely, about 2 hours. Using foil overhang, lift bars from pan. Cut into squares, dust with confectioners' sugar, and serve.

Making Lemon Bars

1. MAKE CRUST: Sprinkle crust mixture into prepared pan and press firmly into even layer. Bake until crust starts to brown, about 20 minutes, rotating pan halfway through baking.

2. COOK FILLING: Cook lemon curd over medium-low heat, stirring constantly, until mixture thickens slightly and registers 170 degrees, about 5 minutes.

3. STRAIN FILLING: Strain curd mixture immediately into bowl and stir in cream.

4. BAKE: Pour warm lemon curd over hot crust and bake until filling is shiny and opaque and center jiggles slightly when shaken, 10 to 15 minutes.

Adding cream cheese to the usual condensed milk and egg yolk ensures our lime filling stands up in bar form.

Key Lime Bars

MAKES 16 BARS   **TOTAL TIME** 1 HOUR (PLUS COOLING TIME)

✔ **WHY THIS RECIPE WORKS:** To get big, fresh lime flavor into our lime bars we avoided bottled lime juice in favor of fresh. The convenience of bottled juice is negated by its bitterness and weak lime flavor. We also added fresh lime zest. We found that regular supermarket, or Persian, limes worked just fine in the filling, and it took only four (as opposed to 20 Key limes) to yield the right amount of juice. For these bars, we needed the filling to be firmer than that for a Key lime pie, so we supplemented the usual sweetened condensed milk and egg yolk with cream cheese. Our crust needed to be sturdier, too, and since this meant using more crumbs, we found the flavor of graham cracker crumbs too assertive. Animal crackers had just the right flavor, and light brown sugar added mild caramel notes. Key limes can be substituted for the regular limes here, although they have a more delicate flavor; you'll need about 20 to make ½ cup of juice. Do not substitute bottled Key lime juice. Be sure to zest the limes before juicing them.

CRUST

- **5** ounces (2½ cups) animal crackers
- **3** tablespoons packed light brown sugar
  Pinch salt
- **4** tablespoons unsalted butter, melted and cooled

FILLING

- **2** ounces cream cheese, softened
- **1** tablespoon grated lime zest plus ½ cup juice (4 limes)
  Pinch salt
- **1** (14-ounce) can sweetened condensed milk
- **1** large egg yolk
- **¾** cup (2¼ ounces) sweetened shredded coconut, toasted (optional)

1. Adjust oven rack to middle position and heat oven to 325 degrees. Make foil sling for 8-inch square baking pan by folding 2 long sheets of aluminum foil so each is 8 inches wide. Lay sheets of foil in pan perpendicular to each other, with extra foil hanging over edges of pan. Push foil into corners and up sides of pan, smoothing foil flush to pan, and grease foil.

2. FOR THE CRUST: Process animal crackers, sugar, and salt in food processor to fine crumbs, about 15 seconds. Drizzle melted butter over crumbs and pulse to incorporate, about 10 pulses. Sprinkle mixture into prepared pan and press into even layer with bottom of dry measuring cup. Bake until crust is fragrant and deep golden brown, 18 to 20 minutes, rotating pan halfway through baking.

3. FOR THE FILLING: Stir cream cheese, lime zest, and salt together in medium bowl until combined. Whisk in

NOTES FROM THE TEST KITCHEN

Juicing Lemons and Limes

We've tried countless methods and gizmos for juicing lemons and limes and have dismissed most of them. However, we do endorse rolling lemons vigorously on a hard surface before slicing them open to be juiced. Why? Rolling a lemon on a hard surface bruises, breaks up, and softens the rind's tissues while it tears the membranes of the juice vesicles (tear-shaped juice sacs), thereby filling the inside of the lemon with juice before it is squeezed. Once the lemon is rolled, we recommend either a wooden reamer or a juicer, which we found to be especially easy and fast, and equally effective.

However you squeeze them, we strongly recommend that you squeeze lemon or lime juice at the last minute; testing has proven that the flavor mellows quickly and will taste bland in a short time.

condensed milk until smooth. Whisk in egg yolk and lime juice until combined.

4. Pour filling evenly over crust. Bake until bars are set and edges begin to pull away slightly from sides of pan, 15 to 20 minutes, rotating pan halfway through baking.

5. Let bars cool completely, about 2 hours, then refrigerate until thoroughly chilled, at least 2 hours. Using foil overhang, lift bars from pan. Cut into squares, sprinkle with toasted coconut, if using, and serve. (Uncut bars can be frozen for up to 1 month; let wrapped bars thaw at room temperature for 4 hours before serving.)

VARIATION

Triple-Citrus Bars

Be sure to zest all of the citrus before juicing.

Reduce lime zest to 1½ teaspoons and combine with 1½ teaspoons grated lemon zest and 1½ teaspoons grated orange zest. Reduce lime juice to 6 tablespoons and combine with 1 tablespoon lemon juice and 1 tablespoon orange juice.

Peach Squares

MAKES 24 BARS   **TOTAL TIME** 1 HOUR 10 MINUTES (PLUS COOLING TIME)

✓ **WHY THIS RECIPE WORKS:** The combination of juicy fruit and tender shortbread is a winning one, but when we tried this concept with peaches we found that they needed precooking or the bars would be too wet. Frozen peaches were more convenient than fresh (no peeling and pitting), and their quality proved more consistent. We spread the thawed peaches on a dish towel to rid them of excess moisture, then processed them with peach jam and cooked them in a large skillet to rapidly drive off moisture. The jam intensified the peach flavor, and a little lemon zest and juice brightened it further. Almonds are a natural pairing with peaches; we ground a generous amount for the crust and added sliced almonds to the streusel topping. Our recipe worked so well that we made a version with frozen cherries, and also adapted it for dried apricots.

- **1½** cups (7½ ounces) all-purpose flour
- **1¾** cups sliced almonds
- **⅓** cup (2⅓ ounces) granulated sugar
- **⅓** cup packed (2⅓ ounces) plus 1 tablespoon packed light brown sugar
  Salt
- **12** tablespoons unsalted butter, cut into 12 pieces and softened

These fruity squares rely on frozen peaches, so you can make them any time of the year.

1½ pounds (6 cups) frozen peaches, thawed and drained
½ cup peach jam
½ teaspoon grated lemon zest plus 1 teaspoon juice

1. Adjust oven rack to middle position and heat oven to 375 degrees. Make foil sling for 13 by 9-inch baking pan by folding 2 long sheets of aluminum foil; first sheet should be 13 inches wide, and second sheet should be 9 inches wide. Lay sheets of foil in pan perpendicular to each other, with extra foil hanging over edges of pan. Push foil into corners and up sides of pan, smoothing foil flush to pan, and grease foil.

2. Process flour, 1¼ cups almonds, granulated sugar, ⅓ cup brown sugar, and ½ teaspoon salt together in food processor until combined, about 5 seconds. Add butter and pulse until mixture resembles coarse meal with few pea-size pieces, about 20 pulses. Reserve ½ cup mixture separately in medium bowl for topping.

3. Sprinkle remaining flour mixture into prepared pan and press into even layer with bottom of dry measuring cup. Bake until crust is fragrant and golden brown, about 15 minutes, rotating pan halfway through baking.

4. Meanwhile, mix remaining 1 tablespoon brown sugar and reserved flour mixture together, and pinch mixture between your fingers into clumps of streusel.

5. Pulse peaches and jam together in food processor until peaches are rough ¼-inch chunks, 5 to 7 pulses. Transfer peach mixture to 12-inch nonstick skillet and cook over high heat until thickened and jamlike, about 10 minutes. Off heat, stir in lemon zest and juice and pinch salt.

6. Spread cooked peach mixture evenly over hot crust, then sprinkle with streusel and remaining ½ cup almonds. Bake until almonds are golden brown, about 20 minutes, rotating pan halfway through baking. Let bars cool completely, about 2 hours. Using foil overhang, lift bars from pan. Cut into squares and serve.

VARIATIONS

Apricot Squares
Substitute 1 pound dried apricots for frozen peaches, and apricot jam for peach jam. Add 1 cup water to food processor with apricots in step 5.

Cherry Squares
Substitute frozen pitted cherries for frozen peaches and cherry jam for peach jam. Omit lemon zest and reduce lemon juice to ½ teaspoon. Add ¼ teaspoon vanilla extract to peach mixture with lemon juice.

Raspberry Streusel Bars
MAKES 24 BARS   **TOTAL TIME** 55 MINUTES
(PLUS COOLING TIME)

✔ **WHY THIS RECIPE WORKS:** We wanted the right balance of bright, tangy fruit filling and rich, buttery shortbread crust for these bars—and we wanted an easy topping. For a fresh-tasting fruity filling, we combined fresh raspberries with raspberry jam. Adding a dash of lemon juice to the berries brightened the filling further. We made a butter-rich shortbread dough that did double duty as both the bottom crust and the base for our streusel topping. After pressing part of the mixture into the pan, we added oats, brown sugar, nuts, and a little extra butter to the rest, and pinched it into clumps. To prevent soggy-bottomed bars, we baked the bottom crust on its own before adding the raspberries and streusel and baking it all together. Frozen raspberries can be substituted for fresh, but be sure to defrost them before using. Quick oats will work in this recipe, but the bars will be less chewy and flavorful. Do not use instant oats.

The shortbread crust on our raspberry bars does double duty as part of the buttery streusel topping.

2½ cups (12½ ounces) all-purpose flour

⅔ cup (4⅔ ounces) granulated sugar

½ teaspoon salt

18 tablespoons (2¼ sticks) unsalted butter, cut into 18 pieces and softened

½ cup (1½ ounces) old-fashioned rolled oats

½ cup pecans, toasted and chopped fine

¼ cup packed (1¾ ounces) light brown sugar

¾ cup raspberry jam

3¾ ounces (¾ cup) fresh raspberries

1 tablespoon lemon juice

1. Adjust oven rack to middle position and heat oven to 375 degrees. Make foil sling for 13 by 9-inch baking pan by folding 2 long sheets of aluminum foil; first sheet should be 13 inches wide, and second sheet should be 9 inches wide. Lay sheets of foil in pan perpendicular to each other, with extra foil hanging over edges of pan. Push foil into corners and up sides of pan, smoothing foil flush to pan, and grease foil.

2. Whisk flour, granulated sugar, and salt together in bowl of stand mixer. Fit mixer with paddle and beat in 16 tablespoons butter, 1 piece at a time, on medium-low speed until mixture

resembles damp sand, 1 to 1½ minutes. Reserve 1¼ cups mixture separately in medium bowl for topping.

3. Sprinkle remaining mixture into prepared pan and press into even layer with bottom of dry measuring cup. Bake until edges of crust begin to brown, 14 to 18 minutes, rotating pan halfway through baking.

4. Meanwhile, stir oats, nuts, and brown sugar into reserved topping mixture. Add remaining 2 tablespoons butter and pinch mixture between your fingers into clumps of streusel. In small bowl, mash jam, raspberries, and lemon juice together with fork until few berry pieces remain.

5. Spread berry mixture evenly over hot crust, then sprinkle with streusel. Bake bars until filling is bubbling and topping is deep golden brown, 22 to 25 minutes, rotating pan halfway through baking.

6. Let bars cool completely, about 2 hours. Using foil overhang, lift bars from pan. Cut into squares and serve. (Uncut bars can be frozen for up to 1 month; let wrapped bars thaw at room temperature for 4 hours before serving.)

VARIATIONS

Strawberry Streusel Bars

Thawed frozen strawberries will also work here.

Substitute strawberry jam and chopped fresh strawberries for the raspberry jam and raspberries.

Blueberry Streusel Bars

Thawed frozen blueberries will also work here.

Substitute blueberry jam and fresh blueberries for the raspberry jam and raspberries.

NOTES FROM THE TEST KITCHEN

Storing Nuts

We use all manner of nuts in this book. For many recipes we toast nuts before baking to intensify their flavor (see page 59). What's the best way to keep nuts tasting fresh? All nuts are high in oil and will become rancid rather quickly. In the test kitchen, we store all nuts in the freezer in sealed freezer-safe zipper-lock bags. Frozen nuts will keep for months, and there's no need to defrost before toasting or chopping. If you use toasted nuts in recipes such as cookies or brownies, but become impatient when it comes to toasting small amounts for each dish, you can toast them in large batches and, when the nuts are cool, transfer them to a zipper-lock bag, then freeze them. Do not use pretoasted frozen nuts for recipes in which a crisp texture is desired, such as salads.

Dutch Apple Pie Bars

MAKES 24 BARS   **TOTAL TIME** 1 HOUR 15 MINUTES
(PLUS COOLING TIME)

✓ WHY THIS RECIPE WORKS: To translate Dutch apple pie into snack bar form, we needed an easy crust whose flavor wouldn't compete with the other ingredients. An animal cracker–crumb crust was the perfect foil for our spiced apple filling. Using raw apples for our bars led to a crunchy filling and a soggy crust. In order to get the apples tender and keep the crust crisp, it was necessary to precook the apples before baking. Cooking them in a large nonstick skillet helped evaporate their moisture before baking and softened the apples just enough to make them tender right out of the oven. Just ½ teaspoon of cinnamon provided warm spice notes without being overwhelming. We sprinkled the filling with an easy streusel, which included a tablespoon of cornmeal, for an appealing light crunch. We like the tart flavor of Granny Smith apples here, but other apples, such as Empire, Cortland, Golden Delicious, Jonagold, or Braeburn can also be used.

CRUST

- 8 ounces (4 cups) animal crackers
- ⅓ cup packed (2⅓ ounces) light brown sugar
- ⅛ teaspoon salt
- 6 tablespoons unsalted butter, melted and cooled

STREUSEL

- 1 cup (5 ounces) all-purpose flour
- ⅓ cup packed (2⅓ ounces) light brown sugar
- ⅓ cup (2⅓ ounces) granulated sugar
- 1 tablespoon cornmeal
- 6 tablespoons unsalted butter, melted and cooled

FILLING

- 2 tablespoons unsalted butter
- 2 pounds Granny Smith apples, peeled, cored, and sliced ¼ inch thick
- ¼ cup (1¾ ounces) granulated sugar
- ½ teaspoon ground cinnamon
- ⅛ teaspoon salt
- ½ cup golden raisins (optional)

1. Adjust oven rack to middle position and heat oven to 375 degrees. Make foil sling for 13 by 9-inch baking pan by folding 2 long sheets of aluminum foil; first sheet should be 13 inches wide, and second sheet should be 9 inches wide. Lay sheets of foil in pan perpendicular to each other, with extra foil hanging over edges of pan. Push foil into corners and up sides of pan, smoothing foil flush to pan, and grease foil.

An easy crust made from animal crackers makes the perfect support for these apple-filled bars.

2. FOR THE CRUST: Process animal crackers, sugar, and salt together in food processor to fine crumbs, about 15 seconds. Drizzle melted butter over crumbs and pulse to incorporate, about 10 pulses. Sprinkle mixture into prepared pan and press into even layer with bottom of dry measuring cup. Bake until crust is fragrant and deep golden brown, 10 to 13 minutes, rotating pan halfway through baking.

3. FOR THE STREUSEL: Whisk flour, brown sugar, granulated sugar, and cornmeal together in bowl. Drizzle with melted butter and toss with fork to combine.

4. FOR THE FILLING: Melt butter in 12-inch nonstick skillet over medium-high heat. Add apples, sugar, cinnamon, and salt and cook, stirring occasionally, until apples have softened and all of liquid has evaporated, 8 to 10 minutes. Stir in raisins, if using.

5. Spread apple mixture over warm crust and sprinkle with streusel. Bake bars until streusel has browned, 25 to 30 minutes, rotating pan halfway through baking.

6. Let bars cool completely, about 2 hours. Using foil overhang, lift bars from pan. Cut into squares and serve.

This pecan filling is boosted by vanilla, bourbon, and salt to hold up against its generous pecan shortbread crust.

Pecan Bars

MAKES 16 SQUARES   **TOTAL TIME** 1 HOUR 15 MINUTES (PLUS COOLING TIME)

☑ **WHY THIS RECIPE WORKS:** We wanted the best qualities of pecan pie—buttery crust, gooey filling, and nutty topping—packed into bite-size squares. Starting from the bottom up, we made a substantial shortbread crust, with chopped toasted pecans for flavor and tenderness. Since the ratio of filling to crust is proportionately less in bars than pie, our filling needed to be intensely flavored. To boost the flavor, we added vanilla as well as a hint of bourbon (dark rum works, too) to cut through the sweetness. A half-teaspoon of salt sharpened the sweetness and intensified the pecan flavor. As for the pecans, while halves look attractive, they made the bars difficult to cut. Coarsely chopped pecans were much easier to handle, and to eat.

CRUST
1 cup (5 ounces) all-purpose flour
⅓ cup packed (2⅓ ounces) light brown sugar
¼ cup pecans, toasted and chopped coarse

1 teaspoon salt
¼ teaspoon baking powder
6 tablespoons unsalted butter, cut into ¼-inch pieces and chilled

FILLING
½ cup packed (3½ ounces) light brown sugar
⅓ cup light corn syrup
4 tablespoons unsalted butter, melted and cooled
1 tablespoon bourbon or dark rum
2 teaspoons vanilla extract
½ teaspoon salt
1 large egg, lightly beaten
1¾ cups pecans, toasted and chopped coarse

1. FOR THE CRUST: Adjust oven rack to middle position and heat oven to 350 degrees. Make foil sling for 8-inch square baking pan by folding 2 long sheets of aluminum foil so each is 8 inches wide. Lay sheets of foil in pan perpendicular to each other, with extra foil hanging over edges of pan. Push foil into corners and up sides of pan, smoothing foil flush to pan, and grease foil.

2. Process flour, sugar, pecans, salt, and baking powder in food processor until mixture resembles coarse cornmeal, about 5 pulses. Sprinkle butter over top and pulse until mixture is pale yellow and resembles coarse cornmeal, about 8 pulses.

3. Sprinkle mixture into prepared pan and press firmly into even layer using your fingers. Bake until crust starts to brown, 20 to 24 minutes, rotating pan halfway through baking.

4. FOR THE FILLING: As soon as crust finishes baking, whisk sugar, corn syrup, melted butter, bourbon, vanilla, and salt together in bowl until just combined. Whisk in egg until incorporated. Pour mixture over hot crust and sprinkle with pecans. Bake until top is brown and cracks start to form across surface, 25 to 30 minutes.

5. Let bars cool completely, about 2 hours. Using foil overhang, lift bars from pan. Cut into squares and serve.

Oatmeal Butterscotch Bars

MAKES 36 BARS   **TOTAL TIME** 45 MINUTES (PLUS COOLING TIME)

☑ **WHY THIS RECIPE WORKS:** "Oatmeal scotchies" often appeal more to our sense of nostalgia than to our taste buds, thanks to overwhelming sweetness and waxy, orange chips. We wanted moist, chewy oatmeal bars with gentle butterscotch flavor and dialed-back sweetness. The obvious first step was to cut back on sugar; using dark brown sugar gave the bars a more

Dark brown sugar gives these old-fashioned bars a nuanced sweetness while rolled oats make them chewy.

nuanced sweetness. We browned the butter to add a nutty depth of flavor. Unable to find a substitute for butterscotch chips, we solved their texture problem by melting them so they blended smoothly into the batter. Quick oats will work in this recipe, but the bars will be less chewy and flavorful; do not use instant oats.

BARS

- 1¼ **cups (6¼ ounces) all-purpose flour**
- 2 **cups (6 ounces) old-fashioned rolled oats**
- ½ **teaspoon baking soda**
- ½ **teaspoon salt**
- ¾ **cup (4½ ounces) butterscotch chips**
- 16 **tablespoons unsalted butter**
- 1 **cup packed (7 ounces) dark brown sugar**
- 2 **teaspoons vanilla extract**
- 1 **large egg**

GLAZE

- ¼ **cup (1½ ounces) butterscotch chips**
- 2 **tablespoons packed dark brown sugar**
- 1 **tablespoon water**
- ⅛ **teaspoon salt**

1. FOR THE BARS: Adjust oven rack to middle position and heat oven to 350 degrees. Make foil sling for 13 by 9-inch baking pan by folding 2 long sheets of aluminum foil; first sheet should be 13 inches wide, and second sheet should be 9 inches wide. Lay sheets of foil in pan perpendicular to each other, with extra foil hanging over edges of pan. Push foil into corners and up sides of pan, smoothing foil flush to pan, and grease foil.

2. Mix flour, oats, baking soda, and salt together in bowl. Place butterscotch chips in large bowl. Melt butter in 12-inch skillet over medium-high heat. Continue cooking, swirling pan constantly, until butter is dark golden brown and has nutty aroma, 1 to 5 minutes. Add browned butter to butterscotch chips and whisk until smooth. Whisk in sugar until dissolved, then whisk in vanilla and egg until combined. Stir in flour mixture in 2 additions until combined.

3. Spread mixture into prepared pan and bake until edges are golden brown and toothpick inserted in center comes out with few crumbs attached, 17 to 19 minutes, rotating pan halfway through baking. Transfer pan to wire rack.

4. FOR THE GLAZE: Place butterscotch chips in small bowl. Bring sugar, water, and salt to simmer in small saucepan. Pour hot sugar mixture over butterscotch chips and whisk until smooth. Drizzle glaze over warm bars and let cool until warm to touch, about 1½ hours.

5. Using foil overhang, lift bars from pan and transfer to wire rack. Remove foil and let cool completely before cutting and serving.

Crunchy Granola Bars

MAKES 36 BARS   **TOTAL TIME** 1 HOUR 30 MINUTES
(PLUS COOLING TIME)

✓**WHY THIS RECIPE WORKS:** Great granola bars put the flavor of the oats at the forefront and support them with a mellow sweetness. We found that toasting the oats with a little oil and salt before mixing them with the other ingredients really amped up their oaty presence. Honey provided classic granola bar flavor as well as a cohesive quality. We kept the other flavors simple: a little brown sugar to add depth to the sweetness, generous amounts of vanilla and cinnamon, and chopped nuts for extra crunch. After many crumbly attempts at baking the bars, we realized the key to making ones that held their shape was to spread the mixture into a rimmed baking sheet and then press firmly on it with a greased metal spatula or with another, slightly smaller, pan (greased on the bottom). Quick-cooking oats cannot be substituted for the old-fashioned oats

We press these bars into a rimmed baking sheet before baking for the perfect sliceable consistency.

here because their texture becomes too sandy when toasted. Don't use a baking sheet smaller than 18 by 13 inches or the bars will be too thick and won't bake evenly. Be sure to allow the granola bars to cool for 15 minutes before cutting. If any of the bars should fall apart during cutting, just press them back together, and as they cool they will firm up and stick together.

  7   **cups (21 ounces) old-fashioned rolled oats**
  ½   **cup vegetable oil**
  ½   **teaspoon salt**
  ¾   **cup honey**
  ¾   **cup packed (5¼ ounces) light brown sugar**
  1   **tablespoon vanilla extract**
  2   **teaspoons ground cinnamon (optional)**
  1½ **cups whole almonds, pecans, peanuts, or walnuts, chopped coarse**

1. Adjust oven rack to middle position and heat oven to 375 degrees. Toss oats, oil, and salt together in medium bowl. Spread mixture out over rimmed baking sheet and toast, stirring often, until pale golden, 20 to 25 minutes.

2. Meanwhile, line 18 by 13-inch rimmed baking sheet with aluminum foil and grease foil. Cook honey and sugar together in small saucepan over medium heat, stirring frequently, until sugar is fully dissolved, about 5 minutes. Off heat, stir in vanilla and cinnamon, if using.

3. Transfer toasted oat mixture to large bowl. Reduce oven temperature to 300 degrees. Add honey mixture and nuts to toasted oat mixture and toss until well combined. Spread mixture out over prepared sheet and press into even layer using greased spatula. Bake granola bars until golden, 35 to 40 minutes, rotating sheet halfway through baking.

4. Let granola bars cool in sheet for 15 minutes, then cut into bars. Let bars cool completely, then remove individual bars from sheet using spatula. Serve. (Bars can be stored at room temperature for up to 2 weeks.)

VARIATIONS

Crunchy Granola Bars with Dried Cranberries and Ginger

Microwave 1 cup dried cranberries with ½ cup water in bowl until softened, about 4 minutes; drain and pat dry. Add softened cranberries and ¼ cup chopped crystallized ginger to granola mixture with nuts.

Crunchy Granola Bars with Coconut and Sesame

Add ½ cup sesame seeds and ½ cup unsweetened shredded coconut to granola mixture with nuts.

Pressing Granola Bars

Spread granola mixture out over prepared sheet and press into even layer using greased spatula.

Cheesecake Bars

MAKES 16 BARS   **TOTAL TIME** 1 HOUR 20 MINUTES (PLUS COOLING TIME)

✓ **WHY THIS RECIPE WORKS:** We gave our cheesecake bars a rich, creamy texture by thoroughly beating the softened cream cheese in a stand mixer and scraping down the bowl and paddle—this ensured a light, lump-free filling. Adding sour cream and a modest amount of lemon juice to the filling gave our bars a slight tang without making them mouth-puckering. We saw little need for improvement in the traditional graham cracker crust, but it did benefit from the addition of a couple tablespoons of flour, which made it sturdier. Make sure to scrape the paddle and the sides of the bowl regularly when making the cheesecake filling in order to achieve a silky, smooth texture.

CRUST

- **7** whole graham crackers, broken into 1-inch pieces
- **6** tablespoons unsalted butter, melted and cooled
- **3** tablespoons packed light brown sugar
- **2** tablespoons all-purpose flour
- **⅛** teaspoon salt

FILLING

- **1** pound cream cheese, softened
- **⅔** cup (4⅔ ounces) granulated sugar
- **2** large eggs
- **¼** cup sour cream
- **2** teaspoons lemon juice
- **1** teaspoon vanilla extract

1. Adjust oven rack to middle position and heat oven to 325 degrees. Make foil sling for 8-inch square baking pan by folding 2 long sheets of aluminum foil so each is 8 inches wide. Lay sheets of foil in pan perpendicular to each other, with extra foil hanging over edges of pan. Push foil into corners and up sides of pan, smoothing foil flush to pan, and grease foil.

2. **FOR THE CRUST:** Process graham cracker pieces in food processor to fine, even crumbs, about 30 seconds. Sprinkle butter, sugar, flour, and salt over crumbs and pulse to incorporate, about 10 pulses. Sprinkle mixture into prepared pan and press into even layer with bottom of dry measuring cup. Bake until crust is fragrant and beginning to brown, 12 to 15 minutes, rotating pan halfway through baking.

3. **FOR THE FILLING:** Using stand mixer fitted with paddle, beat cream cheese on medium speed until smooth, 1 to 3 minutes, scraping down bowl as needed. Gradually beat in sugar until incorporated, about 1 minute. Beat in eggs, one at a time, until combined, about 30 seconds. Beat in sour cream, lemon juice, and vanilla until incorporated, about 30 seconds.

4. Pour filling over crust. Bake until edges are set but center still jiggles slightly, 35 to 40 minutes, rotating pan halfway through baking.

The cheesecake filling in these bars is carefully engineered for perfect texture and tang.

5. Let bars cool completely, about 2 hours, then refrigerate until thoroughly chilled, at least 3 hours or up to 1 day. Using foil overhang, lift bars from pan. Cut into squares and serve. (Uncut bars can be frozen for up to 1 month; let wrapped bars thaw at room temperature for 4 hours before serving.)

VARIATIONS
Chocolate Swirl Cheesecake Bars
Before baking bars, microwave 3 ounces semisweet chocolate and 2 tablespoons heavy cream together in bowl at 50 percent power, stirring often, until melted and smooth, 1 to 3 minutes. Spoon small dollops of melted chocolate over filling and run butter knife through to create swirls.

Strawberry Cheesecake Bars
Before serving, toss 1¼ cups coarsely chopped strawberries with 2 tablespoons warm apricot jam, 1 teaspoon lemon juice, 1 teaspoon sugar, and pinch salt in bowl. Spoon strawberry mixture over bars and let set for 15 minutes before cutting and serving.

Cakes

■ SIGNIFIES A **FAST** RECIPE (45 MINUTES OR LESS)

Chocolate Chip Snack Cake

SERVES 9   **TOTAL TIME** 1 HOUR
(PLUS 1 TO 2 HOURS COOLING TIME)

✓**WHY THIS RECIPE WORKS:** This sweet and tender cake, studded with chocolate chips, is the perfect afterschool snack or a last-minute homey dessert. This cake gets its richness from a full stick of butter and two eggs. A cup of sour cream contributes tanginess and ensures that even adults will be asking for more.

> 2 cups (10 ounces) all-purpose flour
> 2½ teaspoons baking powder
> ¼ teaspoon salt
> 8 tablespoons unsalted butter, softened
> 1¼ cups (8¾ ounces) sugar
> 2 large eggs, room temperature
> 1 cup sour cream, room temperature
> ⅓ cup whole milk, room temperature
> 1 teaspoon vanilla extract
> 1 cup (6 ounces) semisweet chocolate chips

1. Adjust oven rack to middle position and heat oven to 350 degrees. Make foil sling for 8-inch square baking pan by folding 2 long sheets of aluminum foil so each is 8 inches wide. Lay sheets of foil in pan perpendicular to each other, with extra foil hanging over edges of pan. Push foil into corners and up sides of pan, smoothing foil flush to pan.

2. Whisk flour, baking powder, and salt together in bowl. Using stand mixer fitted with paddle, beat butter and sugar on medium-high speed until pale and fluffy, about 3 minutes. Add eggs, 1 at a time, and beat until combined. Beat in sour cream, milk, and vanilla until combined, about 30 seconds.

3. Whisk in flour mixture by hand until just incorporated. Stir in chocolate chips. Give batter final stir with rubber spatula. Scrape batter into prepared pan, smooth top, and gently tap pan on counter to settle batter.

4. Bake cake until toothpick inserted in center comes out with a few crumbs attached, 40 to 50 minutes, rotating pan halfway through baking. Let cake cool completely in pan, 1 to 2 hours. Remove cake from pan using foil sling and serve. (Cake can be stored at room temperature for 2 days.)

VARIATIONS

Chocolate Chip–Cherry Snack Cake
Add 1 cup dried cherries to batter with chocolate chips.

Chocolate Chip–Banana Snack Cake
Substitute 2 very ripe large bananas, peeled and mashed, for sour cream.

Applesauce Snack Cake

SERVES 9   **TOTAL TIME** 1 HOUR 20 MINUTES
(PLUS 1 TO 2 HOURS COOLING TIME)

✓**WHY THIS RECIPE WORKS:** We wanted a moist and tender applesauce cake that actually tasted like its namesake. It was easy to achieve the looser, more casual crumb that is best suited to a rustic snack cake. Since this texture is similar to that of quick breads and muffins, we used the same technique, mixing the wet ingredients separately and then gently adding the dry ingredients by hand. The harder challenge was to develop more apple flavor; simply adding more applesauce made for a gummy cake, and fresh apples added too much moisture. But two other sources worked well. Apple cider contributed a pleasing sweetness and tang, and plumping dried apples in the cider while it was reducing added even more apple taste without making the cake chunky. With such great apple flavor, we didn't want the cake to be too rich, so we rejected the idea of topping the cake with a glaze. But we found we liked a simple sprinkling of spiced granulated sugar. The cake is very moist, so it is best to err on the side of overdone when testing its doneness. The test kitchen prefers the rich flavor of cider, but apple juice can be substituted.

> ¾ cup dried apples, cut into ½-inch pieces
> 1 cup apple cider
> 1 cup unsweetened applesauce, room temperature
> ⅔ cup (4⅔ ounces) sugar
> ½ teaspoon ground cinnamon
> ¼ teaspoon ground nutmeg
> ⅛ teaspoon ground cloves
> 1½ cups (7½ ounces) all-purpose flour
> 1 teaspoon baking soda
> 1 large egg, room temperature
> ½ teaspoon salt
> 8 tablespoons unsalted butter, melted and cooled
> 1 teaspoon vanilla extract

1. Adjust oven rack to middle position and heat oven to 325 degrees. Make foil sling for 8-inch square baking pan by folding 2 long sheets of aluminum foil so each is 8 inches wide. Lay sheets of foil in pan perpendicular to each other, with extra foil hanging over edges of pan. Push foil into corners and up sides of pan, smoothing foil flush to pan.

2. Simmer dried apples and cider in small saucepan over medium heat until liquid evaporates and mixture appears dry, about 15 minutes. Let mixture cool to room temperature, then process with applesauce in food processor until smooth, 20 to 30 seconds.

3. Whisk sugar, cinnamon, nutmeg, and cloves together in bowl; set 2 tablespoons mixture aside separately for topping. In separate bowl, whisk flour and baking soda together.

4. Whisk egg and salt together in large bowl. Whisk in sugar mixture until well combined and light-colored, about 20 seconds. Whisk in melted butter in 3 additions, whisking after each addition until incorporated. Whisk in applesauce mixture and vanilla. Using rubber spatula, fold in flour mixture until just combined.

5. Scrape batter into prepared pan, smooth top, and gently tap pan on counter to settle batter. Sprinkle reserved sugar mixture over top. Bake cake until toothpick inserted in center comes out clean, 35 to 40 minutes, rotating pan halfway through baking. Let cake cool completely in pan, 1 to 2 hours. Remove cake from pan using foil sling and serve. (Cake can be stored at room temperature for up to 2 days.)

VARIATIONS
Ginger-Cardamom Applesauce Snack Cake
Substitute ½ teaspoon ground ginger and ¼ teaspoon ground cardamom for cinnamon, nutmeg, and cloves. Add 1 tablespoon finely chopped crystallized ginger to sugar mixture set aside for topping.

Applesauce Snack Cake with Oat-Nut Streusel
Add 2 tablespoons brown sugar, ⅓ cup chopped pecans or walnuts, and ⅓ cup old-fashioned rolled oats or quick oats to sugar mixture set aside for topping, then add 2 tablespoons softened unsalted butter and pinch with fingers to incorporate and form mixture into hazelnut-size clumps.

Easy Chocolate Cake
SERVES 9   **TOTAL TIME** 50 MINUTES
(PLUS 1 TO 2 HOURS COOLING TIME)

✓**WHY THIS RECIPE WORKS:** Many old-fashioned chocolate snack cakes are made with mayonnaise—which adds moisture and richness—instead of eggs. For our take on this simple cake, which can be assembled quickly, we "bloomed" unsweetened cocoa powder in coffee to intensify its flavor and supplemented the cocoa with bittersweet chocolate. And although most of the old recipes are made with mayonnaise only, we found that adding an egg to the batter gave it moisture and a springy texture that we loved. Instead of confectioners' sugar, the cake can also be served plain or with Whipped Cream (page 712).

1½   **cups (7½ ounces) all-purpose flour**
 1   **cup (7 ounces) sugar**
 ½   **teaspoon baking soda**
 ¼   **teaspoon salt**
 ⅔   **cup mayonnaise**
 1   **large egg**
 2   **teaspoons vanilla extract**
 ½   **cup (1½ ounces) Dutch-processed cocoa powder**
 2   **ounces bittersweet chocolate, chopped fine**
 1   **cup black coffee, hot**
    Confectioners' sugar (optional)

1. Adjust oven rack to middle position and heat oven to 350 degrees. Grease and flour 8-inch square baking pan. Whisk flour, sugar, baking soda, and salt together in large bowl. In separate bowl, whisk mayonnaise, egg, and vanilla together.

2. Combine cocoa and chocolate in medium bowl, pour hot coffee over top, and whisk until smooth; let cool slightly. Whisk in mayonnaise mixture until combined. Stir chocolate mixture into flour mixture until combined.

3. Scrape batter into prepared pan, smooth top, and gently tap pan on counter to settle batter. Bake cake until toothpick inserted into center of cake comes out with few crumbs attached, 30 to 35 minutes, rotating pan halfway through baking. Let cake cool completely in pan, 1 to 2 hours. Dust with confectioners' sugar, if using, before serving.

Testing Cake for Doneness

To check cake for doneness, insert toothpick into center; it should come out either with few crumbs attached or clean, depending on recipe.

If you see raw batter, continue to bake cake, checking every few minutes.

The batter and streusel topping for this easy coffee cake can be made up to a day ahead of time.

Easy Coffee Cake

MAKES TWO 9-INCH CAKES, EACH SERVING 6
TOTAL TIME 50 MINUTES (PLUS 30 MINUTES COOLING TIME)

✓ **WHY THIS RECIPE WORKS:** Towering Bundt-style coffee cakes and yeasted Danish rings are impressive, but sometimes we just want a simple cake we can whip up at the last minute for unexpected company or a weekend breakfast. We had in mind a rich yellow cake blanketed with crunchy, nutty streusel. To add to the convenience factor, we decided to make enough batter for two 9-inch cakes, which could be refrigerated or frozen and baked anytime. Starting from the top, we mixed a basic streusel, including a generous tablespoon of cinnamon, and then stirred in a cup of chopped nuts. For a sturdy batter that could support the topping, thick, tangy sour cream worked better than milk, and three whole eggs added structure and richness. Granulated sugar alone yielded a rather one-dimensional flavor, so we swapped in brown sugar for half of the white, and added a teaspoon of cinnamon to echo the spicy notes in the topping. Mixed by hand (no heavy equipment

needed), the batter came together quickly, and divided into two cake pans it baked quickly, too—in just half an hour. Do not try to put all of the batter into one large cake pan because it will bake very unevenly.

TOPPING

⅓ cup packed (2⅓ ounces) light brown sugar
⅓ cup (2⅓ ounces) granulated sugar
⅓ cup (1⅔ ounces) all-purpose flour
4 tablespoons unsalted butter, softened
1 tablespoon ground cinnamon
1 cup pecans or walnuts, chopped coarse

CAKE

3 cups (15 ounces) all-purpose flour
1 tablespoon baking powder
1 teaspoon baking soda
1 teaspoon ground cinnamon
¼ teaspoon salt
1¾ cups sour cream, room temperature
1 cup packed (7 ounces) light brown sugar
1 cup (7 ounces) granulated sugar
3 large eggs, room temperature
7 tablespoons unsalted butter, melted and cooled

1. FOR THE TOPPING: Using your fingers, mix brown sugar, granulated sugar, flour, butter, and cinnamon together in bowl until mixture resembles wet sand. Stir in pecans.

2. FOR THE CAKE: Adjust oven rack to middle position and heat oven to 350 degrees. Grease two 9-inch cake pans. Whisk flour, baking powder, baking soda, cinnamon, and salt together in large bowl. In separate bowl, whisk sour cream, brown sugar, granulated sugar, eggs, and melted butter together until smooth. Gently fold egg mixture into flour mixture until smooth.

3. Scrape batter into prepared pans, smooth tops, and sprinkle with topping. Gently tap pans on counter to settle batter. Bake cakes until tops are golden and toothpick inserted in centers comes out with few crumbs attached, 25 to 30 minutes, rotating pans halfway through baking.

4. Let cakes cool in pans for 30 minutes. Serve slightly warm or at room temperature.

TO MAKE AHEAD: Portion batter and topping into cake pans but do not bake. Wrap cake pans tightly with plastic wrap and refrigerate for up to 1 day, or freeze for up to 1 month. Bake cakes as directed, increasing baking time to 30 to 35 minutes if refrigerated, or 40 to 45 minutes if frozen (do not thaw cakes before baking).

VARIATIONS
Easy Lemon-Blueberry Coffee Cake

Add 1 teaspoon grated lemon zest to flour mixture. Toss 2 cups fresh or frozen blueberries (do not thaw if frozen) with 1 tablespoon flour in bowl, then gently fold into batter.

Easy Apricot-Orange Coffee Cake

Add 1 teaspoon grated orange zest to flour mixture, and gently fold 1 cup chopped dried apricots into batter.

Easy Cranberry-Orange Coffee Cake

Dried cherries can be substituted for the cranberries. Add 1 teaspoon grated orange zest to flour mixture, and gently fold 1 cup dried cranberries into batter.

Making Easy Coffee Cake

1. Using your fingers, mix brown sugar, granulated sugar, flour, butter, and cinnamon together in bowl until mixture resembles wet sand. Stir in pecans.

2. Gently fold egg mixture into flour mixture until smooth.

3. Scrape batter into 2 greased 9-inch cake pans and smooth tops.

4. Sprinkle evenly with topping.

Gingerbread

SERVES 8   **TOTAL TIME** 1 HOUR
(PLUS 1 TO 2 HOURS COOLING TIME)

✔**WHY THIS RECIPE WORKS:** Most gingerbread recipes that are moist also suffer from a dense, sunken center, and from flavors that range from barely gingery to addled with enough spices to make a curry fan cry for mercy. Focusing on flavor first, we bumped up the ginger by using a hefty dose of ground ginger and then folding in grated fresh ginger. Cinnamon and fresh-ground pepper helped produce a warm, complex, lingering heat. As for the liquid components, dark stout, gently heated to minimize its booziness, had a bittersweet flavor that brought out the caramel undertones of the molasses. Finally, swapping out the butter for vegetable oil, and replacing some of the brown sugar with granulated, let the spice flavors come through. To prevent a sunken center, we looked at our leaveners first. Baking powder isn't as effective at leavening if too many other acidic ingredients are present in the batter. In this case, we had three—molasses, brown sugar, and stout—so we decided to buck the usual protocol for cakes and incorporated the baking soda with the wet ingredients instead of the other dry ones. This change helped to neutralize those acidic ingredients before they were incorporated into the batter and allowed the baking powder to do a better job. And while stirring develops flour's gluten, which is typically the enemy of tenderness, our batter was so loose that vigorous stirring actually gave our cake the structure necessary to further ensure the center didn't collapse. This cake packs potent yet well-balanced, fragrant, and spicy heat. If you are particularly sensitive to spice, you can decrease the amount of ground ginger to 1 tablespoon. Avoid opening the oven door until the minimum baking time has elapsed. Serve plain or with Whipped Cream or Brown Sugar Whipped Cream (page 712).

¾ **cup stout, such as Guinness**
½ **teaspoon baking soda**
⅔ **cup molasses**
¾ **cup packed (5¼ ounces) light brown sugar**
¼ **cup (1¾ ounces) granulated sugar**
1½ **cups (7½ ounces) all-purpose flour**
2 **tablespoons ground ginger**
½ **teaspoon baking powder**
½ **teaspoon salt**
¼ **teaspoon ground cinnamon**
¼ **teaspoon pepper**
2 **large eggs, room temperature**
⅓ **cup vegetable oil**
1 **tablespoon grated fresh ginger**

1. Adjust oven rack to middle position and heat oven to 350 degrees. Grease 8-inch square baking pan, line with parchment paper, grease parchment, and flour pan.

2. Bring stout to boil in medium saucepan over medium heat, stirring occasionally. Remove from heat and stir in baking soda (mixture will foam vigorously). When foaming subsides, stir in molasses, brown sugar, and granulated sugar until dissolved. In large bowl, whisk flour, ground ginger, baking powder, salt, cinnamon, and pepper together.

3. Transfer stout mixture to second large bowl and whisk in eggs, oil, and grated ginger until combined. Whisk stout mixture into flour mixture in thirds, stirring vigorously after each addition until completely smooth.

4. Scrape batter into prepared pan, smooth top, and gently tap pan on counter to settle batter. Bake cake until top is just firm to touch and toothpick inserted in center comes out clean, 35 to 45 minutes. Let cake cool completely in pan, 1 to 2 hours. Serve. (Cake can be stored at room temperature for up to 2 days.)

Bringing Eggs to Room Temperature

To bring eggs to room temperature quickly, place whole eggs (still in their shells) in bowl and cover with hot (but not boiling) tap water. Allow to stand for about 5 minutes.

Almond Cake

SERVES 8 TO 10   **TOTAL TIME** 1 HOUR 30 MINUTES
(PLUS 2 HOURS COOLING TIME)

✔**WHY THIS RECIPE WORKS:** To create an almond cake with a great appearance and superior almond flavor, we used finely ground almonds, which had more pronounced almond flavor than almond paste, which is used in most cake recipes. And to create a light cake with a moist, open crumb, we used the protein structure of eggs in place of the denser gluten structure created from using only all-purpose flour. To perfect this elegant European dessert, we deepened its flavor and lightened its texture—and did it all in a food processor. If you can't find blanched sliced almonds, grind slivered almonds for the batter and use unblanched sliced almonds for the topping.

For superior almond flavor, we used finely ground almonds in the cake and toasted sliced almonds on top.

1½   cups plus ⅓ cup blanched sliced almonds, toasted
¾   cup (3¾ ounces) all-purpose flour
¾   teaspoon salt
¼   teaspoon baking powder
⅛   teaspoon baking soda
4   large eggs
1¼   cups (8¾ ounces) plus 2 tablespoons sugar
1   tablespoon plus ½ teaspoon grated lemon zest
      (2 lemons)
¾   teaspoon almond extract
5   tablespoons unsalted butter, melted
⅓   cup vegetable oil

1. Adjust oven rack to middle position and heat oven to 300 degrees. Grease 9-inch round cake pan and line with parchment paper. Pulse 1½ cups almonds, flour, salt, baking powder, and baking soda in food processor until almonds are finely ground, 5 to 10 pulses; transfer to bowl.

2. Process eggs, 1¼ cups sugar, 1 tablespoon lemon zest, and almond extract in now-empty processor until very pale yellow, about 2 minutes. With processor running, add melted butter and oil in steady stream until incorporated. Add almond mixture and pulse to combine, 4 to 5 pulses.

3. Transfer batter to prepared pan and sprinkle with remaining ⅓ cup almonds. Using your fingers, combine remaining 2 tablespoons sugar and remaining ½ teaspoon lemon zest in bowl until fragrant, 5 to 10 seconds, then sprinkle evenly over cake.

4. Bake cake until center is set and bounces back when gently pressed, and toothpick inserted in center comes out clean, 55 to 65 minutes, rotating pan after 40 minutes.

5. Let cake cool in pan for 15 minutes. Run paring knife around edge of cake to loosen. Place greased wire rack over cake pan and, holding rack tightly, invert cake onto rack. Discard parchment and reinvert cake onto second wire rack. Let cake cool completely, about 2 hours. Serve. (Cake can be stored at room temperature for up to 3 days.)

Apple Upside-Down Cake

SERVES 8   **TOTAL TIME** 2 HOURS

✅ **WHY THIS RECIPE WORKS:** Precooking some of the apples before placing them in the bottom of the cake pan gave us plentiful fruit infused with caramel flavor for our best apple upside-down cake recipe. For a coarse-crumbed cake that wouldn't buckle under the weight of the fruit, we used the quick-bread method, melting the butter and mixing the liquid and dry ingredients separately before combining them.

The melted butter introduced less air into the batter, creating a sturdier crumb. You will need a 9-inch nonstick cake pan with sides that are at least 2 inches high for this cake. Alternatively, you can use a 10-inch ovensafe stainless steel skillet (don't use cast iron) to both cook the apples and bake the cake, with the following modifications: Cook the apples in the skillet and set them aside while mixing the batter (it's OK if the skillet is still warm when the batter is added), and increase the baking time by 7 to 9 minutes. You will need a 9-inch nonstick cake pan with sides that are at least 2 inches high for this cake.

TOPPING

- 2 **pounds Granny Smith or Golden Delicious apples, peeled and cored**
- 4 **tablespoons unsalted butter, cut into 4 pieces**
- ⅔ **cup packed (4⅔ ounces) light brown sugar**
- 2 **teaspoons lemon juice**

CAKE

- 1 **cup (5 ounces) all-purpose flour**
- 1 **tablespoon cornmeal (optional)**
- 1 **teaspoon baking powder**
- ½ **teaspoon salt**
- ¾ **cup (5¼ ounces) granulated sugar**
- ¼ **cup packed (1¾ ounces) light brown sugar**
- 2 **large eggs**
- 6 **tablespoons unsalted butter, melted and cooled slightly**
- ½ **cup sour cream**
- 1 **teaspoon vanilla extract**

Making Apple Upside-Down Cake

1. PRECOOK THICKER-CUT APPLES: Cook ½-inch-thick apple slices in butter in hot skillet, stirring occasionally, until they begin to caramelize, 4 to 6 minutes. (Do not fully cook apples.)

2. ADD THINNER-CUT APPLES: Add ¼-inch-thick apple slices, brown sugar, and lemon juice. Cook, stirring constantly, until sugar dissolves and apples are coated, about 1 minute.

3. PRESS APPLES INTO PAN AND ADD BATTER: Transfer apple mixture to pan and press into even layer. Assemble batter, then pour into pan and spread evenly over apples.

4. BAKE AND COOL: Bake cake about 35 minutes. Let cool in pan for 20 minutes. Remove cake from pan, replace any fruit on top of cake, and let cool for another 20 minutes.

1. Adjust oven rack to lowest position and heat oven to 350 degrees. Grease 9-inch round nonstick cake pan.

2. **FOR THE TOPPING:** Cut half of apples into ¼-inch-thick slices. Cut remaining apples into ½-inch-thick slices. Melt butter in 12-inch skillet over medium-high heat. Add ½-inch-thick apple slices and cook, stirring occasionally, until they begin to caramelize, 4 to 6 minutes. (Do not fully cook apples.)

3. Add ¼-inch-thick apple slices, sugar, and lemon juice. Cook, stirring constantly, until sugar dissolves and apples are coated, about 1 minute. Transfer apple mixture to prepared pan and lightly press into even layer.

4. **FOR THE CAKE:** Whisk flour, cornmeal, if using, baking powder, and salt together in bowl. In large bowl, whisk granulated sugar, brown sugar, and eggs together until thick and homogeneous, about 45 seconds. Slowly whisk in melted butter until combined. Whisk in sour cream and vanilla until combined. Add flour mixture and whisk until just combined.

5. Pour batter into pan and spread evenly over apples. Bake until cake is golden brown and toothpick inserted into center comes out clean, 35 to 40 minutes, rotating pan halfway through baking.

6. Let cake cool slightly in pan, about 20 minutes. Run paring knife around edge of cake to loosen. Place wire rack over cake pan and, holding rack tightly, invert cake onto rack and let sit until cake releases itself from pan, about 1 minute. Place rack over baking sheet to catch drips. Remove cake pan and gently scrape off any fruit stuck in pan and arrange on top of cake. Let cake cool for at least 20 minutes before serving.

Pineapple Upside-Down Cake

SERVES 8   **TOTAL TIME** 1 HOUR 30 MINUTES
(PLUS 2 HOURS COOLING TIME)

✓**WHY THIS RECIPE WORKS:** The ideal pineapple upside-down cake has a glistening, caramelized, deep amber topping encasing plump fruit on top of a flavorful, tender butter cake. The classic version, made with canned pineapple, lacked true pineapple flavor, so we had higher hopes for a cake made with fresh fruit. However, while the flavor was certainly better, the fresh pineapple's juices turned the cake soggy. We alleviated this problem by making sure the pineapple was well drained before arranging it on top of a brown sugar–melted butter mixture in a tall cake pan. For a cake batter that could stand up to its topping without becoming a gummy mess, we started with a classic butter cake, then cut back on the milk to alleviate gumminess and added an egg white, which lightened the texture without compromising the structure. Reducing the amount of sugar ensured our final pineapple-topped cake wasn't too sweet. We find it easiest to buy fresh pineapple that has already been peeled and cored, but you can also buy a whole medium pineapple and prep it yourself. If the pineapple is very juicy, pat it dry. You will need a 9-inch nonstick cake pan with sides that are at least 2 inches high for this cake.

| 12 | tablespoons unsalted butter, cut into 12 pieces and softened |
| ¾ | cup packed (5¼ ounces) light brown sugar |

Assembling a Pineapple Upside-Down Cake

1. Stir brown sugar into melted butter in cake pan. Using spatula, pat sugar mixture into even layer.

2. Press pineapple into pan on top of sugar mixture.

3. Spoon batter over pineapple and gently spread into even layer.

1½ **pounds peeled and cored fresh pineapple,
cut into ½-inch pieces (4 cups)**
1½ **cups (7½ ounces) all-purpose flour**
1½ **teaspoons baking powder**
½ **teaspoon salt**
¾ **cup (5¼ ounces) granulated sugar**
2 **large eggs plus 1 large white**
1 **teaspoon vanilla extract**
⅓ **cup whole milk**

1. Adjust oven rack to lower-middle position and heat oven to 350 degrees. Place 4 tablespoons butter in 9-inch round nonstick cake pan and let melt in oven, 2 to 4 minutes. Stir brown sugar into melted butter in cake pan. Using spatula, pat sugar mixture into even layer and top evenly with pineapple.

2. Whisk flour, baking powder, and salt together in bowl. Using stand mixer fitted with paddle, beat remaining 8 tablespoons butter and granulated sugar on medium-high speed until pale and fluffy, about 3 minutes. Add eggs and egg white, 1 at a time, and beat until combined. Add vanilla. Reduce speed to low and add flour mixture in 3 additions, alternating with milk in 2 additions, scraping down bowl as needed. Give batter final stir by hand (batter will be thick).

3. Spoon batter over pineapple and gently spread into even layer. Gently tap pan on counter to settle batter. Bake cake until toothpick inserted in center comes out clean, 45 to 50 minutes, rotating pan halfway through baking.

4. Let cake cool slightly in pan, about 10 minutes. Run paring knife around edge of cake to loosen. Place wire rack over cake pan and, holding rack tightly, invert cake onto rack and let sit until cake releases itself from pan, about 1 minute. Place rack over baking sheet to catch drips. Remove cake pan and gently scrape off any fruit stuck in pan and arrange on top of cake. Let cake cool completely, about 2 hours. Serve.

Summer Peach Cake

SERVES 8   **TOTAL TIME** 2 HOURS 45 MINUTES
(PLUS 2 TO 3 HOURS COOLING TIME)

✓**WHY THIS RECIPE WORKS:** This dessert, which marries cake with fresh summer peaches, is a bakery favorite, but most versions are plagued by soggy cake and barely noticeable peach flavor. We wanted a buttery cake that was moist yet not at all soggy, with a golden-brown exterior and plenty of peach flavor. Roasting chunks of peaches, tossed in sugar and a little lemon juice, helped concentrate their flavor and expel moisture before we combined them with our cake batter. However, during roasting, the peach chunks became swathed in a flavorful but unpleasantly gooey film. Coating our roasted peaches in panko bread crumbs before combining them with the batter ensured the film was absorbed by the crumbs, which then dissolved into the cake during baking. To amplify the

Making Peach Cake

1. Gently toss 24 peach wedges with 2 tablespoons schnapps, 2 teaspoons lemon juice, and 1 tablespoon granulated sugar in bowl; set aside for topping.

2. Cut remaining wedges crosswise into 3 chunks and toss with schnapps, lemon juice, and sugar. Spread onto prepared baking sheet and bake until exuded juices begin to thicken and caramelize, 20 to 25 minutes.

3. Sprinkle crushed panko over roasted peaches and toss gently to combine. Arrange peaches evenly in pan and press gently into batter.

4. Gently spread remaining batter over peaches, smooth top, and arrange reserved peaches attractively over top, also placing wedges in center.

peach flavor we tossed the fruit with peach schnapps before roasting, and a little almond extract added to the batter lent a subtle complementary note. Fanning peach slices (macerated with a little more of the schnapps) over the top, then sprinkling everything with some almond extract–enhanced sugar for a light glaze, ensured our cake looked as good as it tasted. To crush the panko bread crumbs, place them in a zipper-lock bag and smash them with a rolling pin. If you can't find panko, ¼ cup plain, unseasoned bread crumbs can be substituted. Orange liqueur can be substituted for the peach schnapps. If using peak-of-season farm-fresh peaches, omit the peach schnapps.

PEACHES

2½   **pounds peaches, halved, pitted, and cut into ½-inch wedges**
5   **tablespoons peach schnapps**
4   **teaspoons lemon juice**
3   **tablespoons granulated sugar**

CAKE

1   **cup (5 ounces) all-purpose flour**
1¼   **teaspoons baking powder**
¾   **teaspoon salt**
½   **cup packed (3½ ounces) light brown sugar**
⅓   **cup (2⅓ ounces) plus 3 tablespoons granulated sugar**
2   **large eggs, room temperature**
8   **tablespoons unsalted butter, melted and cooled**
¼   **cup sour cream**
1½   **teaspoons vanilla extract**
¼   **teaspoon plus ⅛ teaspoon almond extract**
⅓   **cup panko bread crumbs, crushed fine**

1. FOR THE PEACHES: Adjust oven rack to middle position and heat oven to 425 degrees. Line rimmed baking sheet with aluminum foil and spray with vegetable oil spray. Grease and flour 9-inch springform pan. Gently toss 24 peach wedges with 2 tablespoons schnapps, 2 teaspoons lemon juice, and 1 tablespoon sugar in bowl; set aside for topping.

2. Cut remaining peach wedges crosswise into 3 chunks and gently toss in separate bowl with remaining 3 tablespoons schnapps, remaining 2 teaspoons lemon juice, and remaining 2 tablespoons sugar. Spread peach chunks onto prepared baking sheet and bake until exuded juices begin to thicken and caramelize at edges of pan, 20 to 25 minutes. Let peaches cool on pan to room temperature, about 30 minutes. Reduce oven temperature to 350 degrees.

3. FOR THE CAKE: Whisk flour, baking powder, and salt together in bowl. In large bowl, whisk brown sugar, ⅓ cup granulated sugar, and eggs together until thick and thoroughly combined, about 45 seconds. Slowly whisk in melted butter until combined. Whisk in sour cream, vanilla, and ¼ teaspoon almond extract until combined. Add flour mixture and whisk until just combined.

4. Pour half of batter into prepared pan and spread evenly to pan edges using spatula. Sprinkle crushed panko over roasted peaches and toss gently to combine. Arrange peaches evenly in pan and press gently into batter. Gently spread remaining batter over peaches, smooth top, and arrange reserved peaches attractively over top, also placing wedges in center. Combine remaining 3 tablespoons granulated sugar and remaining ⅛ teaspoon almond extract together in bowl, then sprinkle over top.

5. Bake cake until golden brown and toothpick inserted in center comes out clean, 50 minutes to 1 hour, rotating pan halfway through baking. Let cake cool in pan for 5 minutes. Run paring knife around edge of cake to loosen, then remove sides of pan. Let cake cool completely, 2 to 3 hours. Serve.

Easy Pound Cake

SERVES 8   **TOTAL TIME** 1 HOUR 30 MINUTES
(PLUS 2 HOURS COOLING TIME)

☑ **WHY THIS RECIPE WORKS:** Classic pound cake recipes tend to be very particular, requiring ingredients at certain temperatures as well as finicky mixing methods. For a simpler pound cake that was also foolproof, we discovered that hot melted (rather than softened) butter and the food processor were key. The fast-moving blade of the processor plus the hot melted butter emulsified the liquid ingredients quickly before they had a chance to curdle. Sifting the dry ingredients over our emulsified egg mixture in three additions, and whisking them in after each addition, allowed us to incorporate the dry ingredients easily and ensured no pockets of flour marred our final cake. The test kitchen's preferred loaf pan measures 8½ by 4½ inches; if you use a 9 by 5-inch loaf pan, start checking for doneness 5 minutes early.

1½   **cups (6 ounces) cake flour**
1   **teaspoon baking powder**
½   **teaspoon salt**
1¼   **cups (8¾ ounces) sugar**
4   **large eggs, room temperature**
1½   **teaspoons vanilla extract**
16   **tablespoons unsalted butter, melted and hot**

This old-fashioned classic never goes out of style, and we reimagined it to make it utterly foolproof. We use melted butter and the food processor to ensure perfect emulsification. And unlike pound cakes that rely solely on eggs for leavening, ours uses baking powder, which provides just the right amount of lift—and does so reliably. We also use cake flour, which has less protein than all-purpose flour and ensures a tender crumb.

1. GREASE AND FLOUR THE LOAF PAN: Grease an 8½ by 4½-inch loaf pan with butter, then dust it with flour, making sure to thoroughly coat both the bottom and the sides of the pan. Dump out any excess flour.
WHY? A dusting of flour helps the pound cake climb the sides of the pan and prevents the edges from forming a hard, crusty lip. Make sure to grease the pan well to avoid any sticking.

2. START THE BATTER IN A FOOD PROCESSOR: Process the sugar, eggs, and vanilla together in a food processor until combined, about 10 seconds.
WHY? The food processor ensures that the liquid ingredients (the sugar dissolves, so it's considered a liquid) are evenly combined. Let the eggs come to room temperature on the counter (this will take about an hour), or place them in a bowl of warm tap water for 5 minutes.

3. ADD HOT MELTED BUTTER: With the processor running, add the hot melted butter in a steady stream until incorporated. Pour the mixture into a large bowl.
WHY? The blade of the food processor plus the hot melted butter emulsifies the liquid ingredients before they curdle.

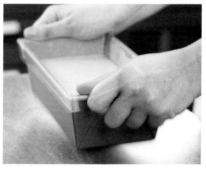

4. SIFT IN THE DRY INGREDIENTS: Sift the flour mixture over the egg mixture in three additions, whisking to combine after each addition until just a few streaks of flour remain. Whisk the batter gently until almost no lumps remain (do not overmix).
WHY? Because overmixing the heavy batter will lead to a dense cake, it's best to sift the dry ingredients over the batter, as this prevents them from clumping together and forming lumps as you mix.

5. TAP THE PAN ON THE COUNTER: Scrape the batter into the prepared pan, smooth the top, and gently tap the pan on the counter to settle the batter.
WHY? Tapping the loaf pan on the counter releases large air bubbles from the batter that could cause tunneling (large holes) in the crumb of the finished cake.

6. BAKE, THEN COOL BRIEFLY IN THE PAN: Bake the cake about 50 minutes, rotating the pan halfway through baking. Let the cake cool in the pan for 10 minutes. After removing it from the pan, let it cool completely on a wire rack.
WHY? Rotating the cake ensures even heating. Cooling the cake briefly in the pan allows it to firm up so that it won't break apart when removed from the pan.

GLAZES FOR CAKES

MAKES ABOUT ¾ CUP   **TOTAL TIME** 30 MINUTES   **FAST**

Bundt, tube, and pound cakes all look pretty on their own, and many of them can be simply dusted with confectioners' sugar. But we think they will always look (and taste) better when drizzled with a little glaze. Here are some easy glazes that will jazz up any of these cakes (you will have some glaze left over if glazing a pound cake).

DIRECTIONS: Whisk all glaze ingredients together in bowl until smooth, then let sit until thickened, about 25 minutes. Pour glaze over top of completely cooled cake, letting it drip down sides. Let glaze set for 25 minutes before serving.

CITRUS GLAZE

- 1¾ **cups (7 ounces) confectioners' sugar**
- ¼ **cup lemon or orange juice**
- 1 **teaspoon grated lemon or orange zest**
  Pinch salt

NUTTY GLAZE

- 1¾ **cups (7 ounces) confectioners' sugar**
- ¼ **cup milk**
- ¼ **teaspoon almond or coconut extract**
  Pinch salt

CREAM CHEESE GLAZE

- 1½ **cups (6 ounces) confectioners' sugar**
- 3 **tablespoons cream cheese, softened**
- 3 **tablespoons milk**
- 1 **teaspoon lemon juice**
  Pinch salt

COFFEE GLAZE

- 1¾ **cups (7 ounces) confectioners' sugar**
- ¼ **cup milk**
- 1 **tablespoon instant espresso powder or instant coffee powder**
  Pinch salt

CHOCOLATE GLAZE

- 4 **ounces bittersweet chocolate, melted**
- ⅓ **cup heavy cream, hot**
- 2 **tablespoons light corn syrup**
- ¼ **teaspoon vanilla extract**
  Pinch salt

1. Adjust oven rack to middle position and heat oven to 350 degrees. Grease and flour 8½ by 4½-inch loaf pan. Whisk flour, baking powder, and salt together in bowl.

2. Process sugar, eggs, and vanilla in food processor until combined, about 10 seconds. With processor running, add hot melted butter in steady stream until incorporated. Pour mixture into large bowl.

3. Sift flour mixture over egg mixture in 3 additions, whisking to combine after each addition until few streaks of flour remain. Continue to whisk batter gently until almost no lumps remain (do not overmix).

4. Scrape batter into prepared pan, smooth top, and gently tap pan on counter to settle batter. Bake cake until toothpick inserted in center comes out with few crumbs attached, 50 to 60 minutes, rotating pan halfway through baking.

5. Let cake cool in pan for 10 minutes. Run paring knife around edge of cake to loosen. Gently turn cake out onto wire rack and let cool completely, about 2 hours. Serve.

VARIATIONS

Easy Lemon Pound Cake

Add 2 tablespoons grated lemon zest (2 lemons) and 2 teaspoons juice to food processor with sugar, eggs, and vanilla.

Easy Orange Pound Cake

Add 1 tablespoon grated orange zest and 1 tablespoon juice to food processor with sugar, eggs, and vanilla.

Easy Almond Pound Cake

Add 1 teaspoon almond extract and ¼ cup slivered almonds to food processor with sugar, eggs, and vanilla. Sprinkle 2 tablespoons slivered almonds over cake before baking.

Easy Ginger Pound Cake

Add 3 tablespoons minced crystallized ginger, 1½ teaspoons ground ginger, and ½ teaspoon ground mace to food processor with sugar, eggs, and vanilla.

Chocolate Pound Cake

SERVES 8   **TOTAL TIME** 1 HOUR 40 MINUTES (PLUS 2 HOURS COOLING TIME)

✔ **WHY THIS RECIPE WORKS:** We retooled classic pound cake to make it ultra-chocolaty. We found that room-temperature eggs worked best because they didn't deflate the batter. For chocolate flavor we used two types of chocolate: Dutch-processed cocoa powder and milk chocolate. By blooming both in hot water, we got big chocolate flavor without the harshness

Two sources of chocolate, cocoa powder and chopped milk chocolate, helped deepen this pound cake's chocolate flavor.

of just plain cocoa powder. For an accurate measurement of boiling water, bring a full kettle of water to a boil, then measure out the desired amount. The test kitchen's preferred loaf pan measures 8½ by 4½ inches; if you use a 9 by 5-inch loaf pan, start checking for doneness 5 minutes early.

- ¾ cup (2¼ ounces) Dutch-processed cocoa powder
- 2 ounces milk chocolate, chopped fine
- ⅓ cup boiling water
- 1 cup (5 ounces) all-purpose flour
- 1 teaspoon salt
- 16 tablespoons unsalted butter, softened
- 1 cup (7 ounces) granulated sugar
- ¼ cup packed (1¾ ounces) light brown sugar
- 2 teaspoons vanilla extract
- 5 large eggs, room temperature

1. Adjust oven rack to lower-middle position and heat oven to 325 degrees. Grease and flour 8½ by 4½-inch loaf pan. Combine cocoa and chocolate in medium bowl, pour boiling water over top, and stir until smooth; let cool slightly. In separate bowl, combine flour and salt.

2. Using stand mixer fitted with paddle, beat chocolate mixture, butter, granulated sugar, brown sugar, and vanilla on medium-high speed until fluffy, 2 to 3 minutes. Add eggs, 1 at a time, and beat until combined. Reduce speed to low and add flour mixture in 3 additions, scraping down bowl as needed, until just combined. Give batter final stir by hand (batter may look curdled).

3. Scrape batter into prepared pan, smooth top, and gently tap pan on counter to settle batter. Bake cake until toothpick inserted in center comes out clean, 60 to 70 minutes, rotating pan halfway through baking.

4. Let cake cool in pan for 10 minutes. Run paring knife around edge of cake to loosen. Gently turn cake out onto wire rack and let cool completely, about 2 hours. Serve.

Classic Yellow Bundt Cake

SERVES 12   **TOTAL TIME** 1 HOUR 30 MINUTES
(PLUS 2 HOURS COOLING TIME)

✔ **WHY THIS RECIPE WORKS:** Most Bundt cakes have a dry texture that is too crumbly and coarse. Creaming the butter was critical for a light crumb, and while most recipes call for 1 cup, we found that upping the amount gave us a richer, more tender crumb. Likewise, using buttermilk instead of the usual milk gave our cake a lighter, more tender crumb as well as a nice, mild tang. Adding lemon juice and baking soda ensured the heavy batter would rise properly. See page 577 for more information on buttermilk substitutes. Serve this cake as is or dress it up with lightly sweetened berries or a glaze (see page 662) or soaking syrup (see page 664).

- 3 cups (15 ounces) all-purpose flour
- 1 teaspoon salt
- 1 teaspoon baking powder
- ½ teaspoon baking soda
- ¾ cup buttermilk, room temperature
- 1 tablespoon vanilla extract
- 1 tablespoon lemon juice
- 18 tablespoons (2¼ sticks) unsalted butter, cut into chunks and softened
- 2 cups (14 ounces) sugar
- 3 large eggs plus 1 large yolk

1. Adjust oven rack to lower-middle position and heat oven to 350 degrees. Grease and flour 12-cup nonstick Bundt pan. Whisk flour, salt, baking powder, and baking soda together in bowl. In separate bowl, whisk buttermilk, vanilla, and lemon juice together.

SOAKING SYRUPS FOR CAKES

MAKES ABOUT ¾ CUP   **TOTAL TIME** 40 MINUTES **FAST**

Soaking syrups—made of sugar, water and/or juice, and flavorings—are a great way to moisten a simple Bundt cake, tube cake, or pound cake, as well as to brighten its flavor. Syrups are different from glazes in that they are meant to soak into the cake; therefore, they're brushed over cakes that are still warm from the oven. In our tests we found that thick syrups (made with more sugar than liquid) are better because they add moisture to cakes without making them soggy, and they cool to an attractive glossy sheen on the crust.

AMARETTO SOAKING SYRUP
- ½ **cup (3½ ounces) sugar**
- ¼ **cup amaretto or other almond-flavored liqueur**
- 2 **tablespoons water**

KAHLÚA SOAKING SYRUP
- ½ **cup (3½ ounces) sugar**
- ¼ **cup Kahlúa**
- 2 **tablespoons water**

LEMON SOAKING SYRUP
- ½ **cup (3½ ounces) sugar**
- ¼ **cup lemon juice**
- 2 **tablespoons water**

ORANGE SOAKING SYRUP
- ½ **cup (3½ ounces) sugar**
- 6 **tablespoons orange juice**

GINGER SOAKING SYRUP
- ½ **cup (3½ ounces) sugar**
- 6 **tablespoons water**
- 1 **tablespoon grated fresh ginger**

Bring all ingredients to boil in small saucepan over high heat and cook, stirring often, until sugar is dissolved, 1 to 2 minutes. Remove pan from heat, strain if necessary, and let syrup cool for 30 minutes. After turning warm cake out onto wire rack, poke top and sides with wooden skewer and brush with syrup. Let cake cool as directed.

2. Using stand mixer fitted with paddle, beat butter and sugar on medium-high speed until pale and fluffy, about 3 minutes. Add eggs and yolk, 1 at a time, and beat until combined. Reduce speed to low and add flour mixture in 3 additions, alternating with buttermilk mixture in 2 additions, scraping down bowl as needed. Give batter final stir by hand.

3. Scrape batter into prepared pan, smooth top, and gently tap pan on counter to settle batter. Bake cake until wooden skewer inserted in center comes out with few crumbs attached, 50 to 60 minutes, rotating pan halfway through baking.

4. Let cake cool in pan for 10 minutes. Gently turn cake out onto wire rack and let cool completely, about 2 hours. Serve.

VARIATIONS
Lemon Bundt Cake
Increase lemon juice to 3 tablespoons and add 3 tablespoons grated lemon zest (3 lemons) to buttermilk mixture.

Orange Bundt Cake
Add 2 tablespoons grated orange zest (2 oranges) and 2 tablespoons juice to buttermilk mixture.

Marble Bundt Cake
Microwave 3 ounces chopped bittersweet chocolate, 2 tablespoons unsalted butter, and 2 tablespoons Dutch-processed cocoa powder together in bowl, stirring often, until smooth, 1 to 3 minutes; let cool slightly. Divide cake batter evenly into 2 bowls and stir chocolate mixture into 1 bowl. Scrape plain cake batter into prepared Bundt pan first, then scrape chocolate cake batter over top. Using butter knife, swirl batters together; bake as directed.

NOTES FROM THE TEST KITCHEN

Storing Bundt, Tube, and Pound Cakes

Cooled cakes, even glazed or soaked cakes, can be stored in an airtight container or wrapped in plastic wrap for up to three days. To freeze, wrap the cooled cake in plastic wrap, then aluminum foil, and freeze for up to one month. If you plan on freezing your cake, avoid glazing or applying a soaking syrup until it is defrosted. To defrost a frozen cake, thaw it completely at room temperature (do not unwrap), about 4 hours. (Thawing the cake while still wrapped ensures a nice, firm crust.) For cakes that will be brushed with soaking syrup, it is best to reheat the cake before applying the syrup. To reheat the cake, place it on a baking sheet in a 350-degree oven for 10 to 15 minutes. We do not recommend freezing angel food or chiffon cakes, as their texture is too delicate.

Tunnel of Fudge Cake

SERVES 12   **TOTAL TIME** 1 HOUR 30 MINUTES
(PLUS 3 HOURS 30 MINUTES COOLING TIME)

✓ **WHY THIS RECIPE WORKS:** We wanted to resurrect the classic childhood favorite, Tunnel of Fudge Cake, without resorting to a prepackaged cake mix. To do this, we sweetened the cake by using Dutch-processed cocoa instead of more-acidic natural cocoa powder. Adding melted chocolate to the batter made our cake more moist and contributed big chocolate punch. Slightly underbaking the cake in our recipe was the first step toward achieving the ideal consistency for the tunnel. Replacing some of the granulated sugar with brown sugar, and cutting back on the flour and butter, provided the perfect environment for the fudgy interior to form. We also found that the only way to judge when our Tunnel of Fudge Cake was done was to remove the cake from the oven when the sides just began to pull away from the pan and the surface of the cake sprang back when pressed gently with a finger. Our usual method for testing cake doneness using a toothpick or skewer just doesn't work here since the fudgy interior won't give an accurate reading. For an accurate measurement of boiling water, bring a full kettle of water to a boil, then measure out the desired amount.

CAKE

- ¾ cup (2¼ ounces) Dutch-processed cocoa powder, plus extra for pan
- 2 ounces bittersweet chocolate, chopped
- ½ cup boiling water
- 2 cups (10 ounces) all-purpose flour
- 2 cups pecans or walnuts, chopped fine
- 2 cups (8 ounces) confectioners' sugar
- 1 teaspoon salt
- 5 large eggs, room temperature
- 1 tablespoon vanilla extract
- 20 tablespoons (2½ sticks) unsalted butter, softened
- 1 cup (7 ounces) granulated sugar
- ¾ cup packed (5¼ ounces) light brown sugar

Preparing a Bundt Pan

If you don't have baking spray with flour, make paste from 1 tablespoon melted butter and 1 tablespoon flour (or cocoa powder for chocolate cakes) and use pastry brush to coat pan, including all nooks and crannies.

Melted chocolate and brown sugar help to create the soft, fudgy tunnel in this chocolate Bundt cake.

CHOCOLATE GLAZE

- ¾ cup heavy cream
- ¼ cup light corn syrup
- 8 ounces bittersweet chocolate, chopped
- ½ teaspoon vanilla extract

1. FOR THE CAKE: Adjust oven rack to lower-middle position and heat oven to 350 degrees. Grease 12-cup nonstick Bundt pan and dust with cocoa powder. Place chocolate in medium bowl, pour boiling water over top, and whisk smooth; let cool to room temperature. In large bowl, whisk ¾ cup cocoa, flour, nuts, confectioners' sugar, and salt together. Beat eggs and vanilla together in large measuring cup.

2. Using stand mixer fitted with paddle, beat butter, granulated sugar, and brown sugar on medium-high speed until pale and fluffy, about 3 minutes. Reduce speed to low and add egg mixture until combined, about 30 seconds. Mix in melted chocolate until combined, about 30 seconds. Mix in flour mixture until just combined, about 30 seconds.

3. Scrape batter into prepared pan, smooth top, and gently tap pan on counter to settle batter. Bake cake until edges are beginning to pull away from pan and surface springs back when pressed gently, about 45 minutes.

4. Let cake cool in pan for 1½ hours. Gently turn cake out onto wire rack and let cool completely, about 2 hours.

5. **FOR THE GLAZE:** Cook cream, corn syrup, and chocolate in small saucepan over medium heat, stirring constantly, until smooth. Off heat, stir in vanilla and let sit until slightly thickened, about 30 minutes. Drizzle glaze over cake and let set for 10 minutes. Serve. (Cake can be stored at room temperature for up to 2 days.)

Magic Chocolate Flan Cake

SERVES 16   **TOTAL TIME** 2 HOURS
(PLUS 2 HOURS COOLING TIME AND 8 HOURS CHILLING TIME)

✔ **WHY THIS RECIPE WORKS:** This hybrid dessert has a layer of chocolate cake and a layer of caramel-coated flan that "magically" switch places as they bake. We started with a simple dump-and-stir chocolate cake recipe. At first, the flan added too much moisture to the cake, making it soggy. A drier cake was key, and removing some of the buttermilk and sugar did the trick. To help our flan stand tall rather than slump when sliced, we used some whole eggs (instead of just yolks) and added cream cheese as a stabilizer. We opted for store-bought caramel sauce to top it all off—much easier than homemade. If your blender doesn't hold 2 quarts, process the flan in two batches. The cake needs to chill for at least 8 hours before you can unmold it. See page 577 for more information on buttermilk substitutes.

CAKE
- ½ cup caramel sauce or topping
- ½ cup plus 2 tablespoons (3⅛ ounces) all-purpose flour
- ⅓ cup (1 ounce) unsweetened cocoa powder
- ½ teaspoon baking soda
- ⅛ teaspoon salt
- 4 ounces bittersweet chocolate, chopped
- 6 tablespoons unsalted butter
- ½ cup buttermilk
- ½ cup (3½ ounces) sugar
- 2 large eggs
- 1 teaspoon vanilla extract

FLAN
- 2 (14-ounce) cans sweetened condensed milk
- 2½ cups whole milk

The cake and the flan switch places in the pan during baking in this magical layered dessert.

- 6 ounces cream cheese
- 6 large eggs plus 4 large yolks
- 1 teaspoon vanilla extract

1. **FOR THE CAKE:** Adjust oven rack to middle position and heat oven to 350 degrees. Grease 12-cup nonstick Bundt pan. Microwave caramel until easily pourable, about 30 seconds, then pour into prepared pan to coat bottom. Whisk flour, cocoa, baking soda, and salt together in bowl.

2. Microwave chocolate and butter in large bowl at 50 percent power, stirring occasionally, until melted, 2 to 4 minutes. Whisk in buttermilk, sugar, eggs, and vanilla until incorporated. Stir in flour mixture until just combined. Pour batter over caramel in prepared pan and wipe away any drips.

3. **FOR THE FLAN:** Process all ingredients in blender until smooth, about 1 minute. Gently pour flan over cake batter. Place Bundt pan in large roasting pan. Place roasting pan on oven rack and pour warm water into roasting pan until it reaches halfway up sides of Bundt pan. Bake cake until toothpick inserted in center comes out clean and flan registers 180 degrees, 75 to 90 minutes.

4. Transfer Bundt pan to wire rack and let cake cool for 2 hours, then refrigerate cake until set, at least 8 hours or up to 1 day. To serve, place bottom third of Bundt pan in bowl of hot tap water for 1 minute; remove and pat pan dry. Place large serving platter over cake pan and, holding platter tightly, invert cake onto platter. Slowly remove pan, allowing caramel to drizzle over top of cake.

Baking a Magic Flan Cake

Place Bundt pan in large roasting pan. Place on oven rack and pour in warm water until halfway up sides of Bundt pan. Bake until toothpick inserted in cake comes out clean and flan registers 180 degrees, 75 minutes.

Holiday Rum Cake

SERVES 10 TO 12   **TOTAL TIME** 1 HOUR 45 MINUTES (PLUS 3 HOURS 20 MINUTES COOLING TIME)

✓**WHY THIS RECIPE WORKS:** Despite the name, most rum cakes lack any real rum flavor. We decided to change this unfortunate trend and treated our cake to a triple helping of dark rum. We first mixed rum into the cake batter, which was layered in a Bundt pan along with a sweet and nutty streusel. After the cake finished baking, we poked it full of holes and brushed it with a rum syrup that slowly saturated the cooling cake. To give the final punch of rum flavor, we whisked some reserved syrup with confectioners' sugar to form a smooth glaze. Once the glaze had been drizzled over the cake and had cooled, this dessert earned the right to be called a rum cake. See page 577 for more information on buttermilk substitutes.

STREUSEL
- 1 **cup pecans, toasted and chopped fine**
- ½ **cup packed (3½ ounces) light brown sugar**
- 2 **tablespoons unsalted butter, softened**

CAKE
- 3 **cups (15 ounces) all-purpose flour**
- 1 **teaspoon salt**
- 1 **teaspoon baking powder**
- ½ **teaspoon baking soda**
- ½ **cup buttermilk**
- ¼ **cup dark rum**
- 1 **tablespoon vanilla extract**
- 1 **tablespoon lemon juice**
- 18 **tablespoons (2¼ sticks) unsalted butter, cut into 18 pieces and softened**
- 2 **cups (14 ounces) sugar**
- 3 **large eggs plus 1 large yolk**

SYRUP AND GLAZE
- ⅔ **cup (4⅔ ounces) granulated sugar**
- ½ **cup dark rum**
- 2 **tablespoons water**
- 4 **tablespoons unsalted butter, softened**
- 1 **cup (4 ounces) confectioners' sugar**
- 2 **tablespoons pecans, toasted and chopped fine**

1. FOR THE STREUSEL: Pinch all ingredients together with fingers in bowl until uniform.

2. FOR THE CAKE: Adjust oven rack to lower-middle position and heat oven to 350 degrees. Grease and flour 12-cup nonstick Bundt pan. Combine flour, salt, baking powder, and baking soda in bowl. In separate bowl, whisk buttermilk, rum, vanilla, and lemon juice together.

3. Using stand mixer fitted with paddle, beat butter and sugar on medium-high speed until pale and fluffy, about 3 minutes. Add eggs and yolk, 1 at a time, and beat until combined. Reduce speed to low and add flour mixture in 3 additions, alternating with 2 additions of buttermilk mixture, scraping down bowl as needed.

4. Scrape two-thirds of batter into prepared pan, sprinkle with even layer of streusel, and top with remaining batter. Bake cake until toothpick inserted in center comes out clean, 50 to 60 minutes, rotating pan halfway through baking. Let cake cool in pan for 20 minutes before brushing and glazing.

5. FOR THE SYRUP AND GLAZE: Bring granulated sugar, rum, and water to boil in small saucepan and simmer over medium-low heat until sugar dissolves, about 2 minutes. Whisk in butter until smooth, then let cool to room temperature, about 30 minutes.

6. Gently turn cake out onto wire rack, prick all over with wooden skewer or fork, and brush with ¾ cup rum syrup. Let cake cool completely, about 2 hours. Whisk confectioners' sugar into remaining rum syrup until smooth, then drizzle over top of cake and sprinkle with pecans. Let sit until glaze is firm, about 30 minutes. Serve.

Angel Food Cake

SERVES 10 TO 12   **TOTAL TIME** 1 HOUR 25 MINUTES
(PLUS 2 TO 3 HOURS COOLING TIME)

✔**WHY THIS RECIPE WORKS:** Making a great angel food cake requires a delicate balance of ingredients and proper technique. First, we found it key to create a stable egg-white base, starting the whites at medium-low speed just to break them up into a froth, and then increasing the speed to medium-high to form soft, billowy mounds. Next, we added the sugar gradually. Once all the sugar was incorporated, the whites became shiny and formed soft peaks when the whisk was lifted. A delicate touch was required when incorporating the flour, which we sifted over the batter and gently folded in. We like to use a tube pan with a removable bottom, but a pan without one can be lined with parchment paper. Do not grease the pan; greasing prevents the cake from climbing up and clinging to the sides as it bakes, and a greased pan will produce a disappointingly short cake. If your tube pan has a removable bottom, you do not need to line it with parchment. Serve this cake as is or dust with confectioners' sugar.

- ¾ **cup (3 ounces) cake flour**
- 1½ **cups (10½ ounces) sugar**
- 12 **large egg whites, room temperature**
- 1 **teaspoon cream of tartar**
- ¼ **teaspoon salt**
- 1½ **teaspoons vanilla extract**
- 1½ **teaspoons lemon juice**
- ½ **teaspoon almond extract**

1. Adjust oven rack to lower-middle position and heat oven to 325 degrees. Line 16-cup tube pan with parchment paper but do not grease. Whisk flour and ¾ cup sugar together in bowl.

2. Using stand mixer fitted with whisk, whip egg whites, cream of tartar, and salt on medium-low speed until foamy, about 1 minute. Increase speed to medium-high and whip to soft, billowy mounds, about 1 minute. Gradually add remaining ¾ cup sugar and whip until soft, glossy peaks form, 1 to 2 minutes. Add vanilla, lemon juice, and almond extract and beat until just blended.

3. Sift flour mixture over egg whites, about 3 tablespoons at a time, gently folding mixture into whites after each addition using large rubber spatula.

4. Gently scrape batter into prepared pan, smooth top, and wipe away any drips. Bake cake until golden brown and top springs back when pressed firmly, 50 to 60 minutes, rotating pan halfway through baking.

Making an impressive angel food cake is easy if you pay attention to important details like folding with a light touch.

5. If cake pan has prongs around rim for elevating cake, invert pan on them. If not, invert pan over neck of bottle or funnel so that air can circulate all around it. Let cake cool in pan completely, 2 to 3 hours.

6. Run paring knife around edge of cake to loosen, then gently tap pan upside down on counter to release cake. Peel off parchment, turn cake right side up onto serving platter, and serve. (Cake can be stored at room temperature for up to 2 days or refrigerated for up to 4 days.)

Chiffon Cake

SERVES 10 TO 12   **TOTAL TIME** 1 HOUR 25 MINUTES
(PLUS 2 TO 3 HOURS COOLING TIME)

✔**WHY THIS RECIPE WORKS:** With the airy height of angel food cake (from using whipped egg whites) and the richness of pound cake (from incorporating egg yolks and oil), chiffon cake is a win-win. Our starting point for this classic was the original version, as first put before the public by General Mills in *Better Homes and Gardens* in 1948. Sadly, we were disappointed to find this cake was a bit dry—cottony and fluffy rather than moist and foamy, the way we thought chiffon cakes should be—and it lacked flavor. Decreasing the flour meant a moister, more flavorful cake but also less structure. Increasing the amount of egg yolks was a step closer, but our cake still wasn't perfect. In the end, instead of whipping all of the egg whites, we found that mixing some of them (unbeaten) into the dry ingredients along with the yolks, water, and oil, provided the structure our cake needed. If your tube pan has a removable bottom, you do not need to line it with parchment. Serve this cake as is or dust with confectioners' sugar.

1½ cups (10½ ounces) sugar
1⅓ cups (5⅓ ounces) cake flour
2 teaspoons baking powder
½ teaspoon salt
7 large eggs (2 whole, 5 separated), room temperature
¾ cup water
½ cup vegetable oil
1 tablespoon vanilla extract
½ teaspoon almond extract
½ teaspoon cream of tartar

1. Adjust oven rack to lower-middle position and heat oven to 325 degrees. Line 16-cup tube pan with parchment paper but do not grease. Whisk sugar, flour, baking powder, and salt together in large bowl. Whisk in whole eggs and yolks, water, oil, vanilla, and almond extract until batter is just smooth.

2. Using stand mixer fitted with whisk, whip egg whites and cream of tartar on medium-low speed until foamy, about 1 minute. Increase speed to medium-high and whip until stiff peaks form, 3 to 4 minutes. Using large rubber spatula, fold whites into batter, smearing any stubborn pockets of egg white against side of bowl.

3. Pour batter into prepared pan, smooth top, and gently tap pan on counter to settle batter. Bake cake until skewer inserted in center comes out clean, 55 to 65 minutes, rotating pan halfway through baking.

4. If cake has prongs around rim for elevating cake, invert pan on them. If not, invert pan over neck of bottle or funnel so that air can circulate all around it. Let cake cool in pan completely, 2 to 3 hours.

5. Run paring knife around edge of cake to loosen, then gently tap pan upside down on counter to release cake. Peel off parchment, turn cake right side up onto serving platter, and serve. (Cake can be stored at room temperature for up to 2 days or refrigerated for up to 4 days.)

NOTES FROM THE TEST KITCHEN

Whipping Egg Whites

Perfectly whipped egg whites begin with a scrupulously clean bowl—fat will inhibit egg whites from whipping properly. Choosing the right bowl is essential too. Bowls made from plastic, a petroleum product with a porous surface, retain an oily film even when washed carefully and should not be used for whipping egg whites. Glass and ceramic should be avoided as well, as their slippery surfaces make it harder for whites to billow up. The two best choices are stainless steel and, for those who have it, copper. First wash the bowl in soapy, hot-as-you-can-stand-it water, rinse with more hot water, and dry with paper towels. (A dish towel may have traces of oil within its fibers that could be transferred to the bowl.) Start with eggs straight from the fridge—these will separate more easily than eggs at room temperature. Be careful not to puncture the yolk as you separate the eggs. With your whites and cream of tartar (for stabilization) in the bowl, start with the mixer on low speed and whip the whites until foamy, about 1 minute. Then increase the mixer speed (adding sugar if required) and continue to whip the whites to their desired consistency (soft peaks or stiff peaks).

VARIATIONS
Lemon Chiffon Cake

Substitute ½ teaspoon baking soda for baking powder. Reduce water to ⅔ cup, reduce vanilla to 1 teaspoon, and omit almond extract. Add 3 tablespoons grated lemon zest plus 2 tablespoons juice (3 lemons) to batter with vanilla.

Orange Chiffon Cake

Substitute 2 tablespoons grated orange zest plus ¾ cup juice (2 oranges) for water. Reduce vanilla to 1 teaspoon and omit almond extract.

Mocha-Nut Chiffon Cake

Substitute ¾ cup brewed espresso or strong coffee for water and omit almond extract. Add ½ cup finely chopped toasted walnuts and 1 ounce unsweetened grated chocolate to batter before folding in whites.

Classic Yellow Sheet Cake

SERVES 15 TO 18   **TOTAL TIME** 1 HOUR 10 MINUTES
(PLUS 2 HOURS COOLING TIME)

✅ **WHY THIS RECIPE WORKS:** Perfect for everything from birthday parties to potlucks and cookouts, sheet cake is easy to make, doesn't require a lot of ingredients, and is a crowd-pleaser because of its simplicity. We started by using lower-protein cake flour instead of all-purpose flour because it would give the cake an ultralight texture. Creaming the butter incorporated some air and thus gave our cake lift, and it also ensured the other ingredients would easily incorporate into the batter. To keep our batter from curdling, we mixed in the eggs one at a time. Then we added our dry ingredients and milk, alternating between the two in a few increments to ensure our batter stayed smooth. We stopped the mixer as soon as we incorporated the last addition of the dry ingredients to avoid overbeating and creating a dry, tough cake. Taking the baked and cooled cake out of the pan was as easy as flipping it onto a rack, peeling off the parchment, and inverting it onto a platter. All it needed was our frosting of choice and our sheet cake was ready to go. You can serve the cake right out of the pan, in which case you'll need only 3 cups of frosting for the top of the cake.

2¾ cups (11 ounces) cake flour
2 teaspoons baking powder
¾ teaspoon salt
16 tablespoons unsalted butter, softened
1¾ cups (12¼ ounces) sugar
4 large eggs, room temperature
1 tablespoon vanilla extract
1½ cups whole milk, room temperature
4 cups frosting or buttercream (page 691–694)

1. Adjust oven rack to middle position and heat oven to 350 degrees. Grease 13 by 9-inch baking pan, line with parchment paper, grease parchment, then flour pan.

2. Whisk flour, baking powder, and salt together in bowl. Using stand mixer fitted with paddle, beat butter and sugar on medium-high speed until light and fluffy, about 3 minutes. Add eggs, 1 at a time, then vanilla, and beat until combined.

3. Reduce speed to low and add flour mixture in 3 additions, alternating with milk in 2 additions, scraping down bowl as needed. Give batter final stir by hand.

4. Scrape batter into prepared pan, smooth top, and gently tap pan on counter to settle batter. Bake until toothpick inserted in center comes out with few crumbs attached, 25 to 30 minutes, rotating pan halfway through baking.

5. Let cake cool completely in pan, about 2 hours. Run paring knife around edge of cake and flip cake out onto wire rack. Peel off parchment, then flip cake right side up onto serving platter. Spread frosting evenly over top and sides of cake and serve.

VARIATION
Classic Yellow Cupcakes
This recipe yields 24 cupcakes; you will need only 3 cups of frosting.

Line two 12-cup muffin tins with paper liners. Prepare batter as directed, then portion into tins using greased ¼-cup measure. Bake cupcakes on upper-middle and lower-middle racks until toothpick inserted in center comes out with few crumbs attached, 15 to 20 minutes, switching and rotating muffin tins halfway through baking. Let cupcakes cool in pans for 15 minutes, then carefully transfer to wire rack and let cool to room temperature, about 30 minutes. Spread frosting evenly over cupcakes and serve.

Making a Yellow Sheet Cake

1. CREAM BUTTER AND SUGAR: In stand mixer, beat butter and sugar on medium-high until light and fluffy. Add eggs, 1 at a time, then vanilla.

2. ALTERNATE ADDING DRY INGREDIENTS AND MILK: Reduce speed to low and add dry ingredients in 3 additions, alternating with milk in 2 additions.

3. FILL PAN AND BAKE: Scrape batter into prepared pan, smooth top, then tap on counter to settle batter. Bake in 350-degree oven for 25 to 30 minutes.

4. COOL AND FLIP: Flip cooled cake onto wire rack. Peel parchment off bottom and place large inverted platter over cake. Holding platter and rack, flip cake right side up.

Classic White Sheet Cake

SERVES 15 TO 18　　**TOTAL TIME** 1 HOUR 10 MINUTES (PLUS 2 HOURS COOLING TIME)

✔ **WHY THIS RECIPE WORKS:** White cake is an old-fashioned classic, but while straightforward in appearance it comes with its own unique set of challenges. White cake is simply a basic butter cake made with egg whites rather than whole eggs (as you would find in yellow cake). Theoretically, the whites should make the cake soft and fine-grained. But most white cakes come out dry and chewy (or cottony) and usually riddled with tunnels and small holes. Reverse creaming—beating the butter into the dry ingredients and then adding the liquid ingredients—delivered a fine crumb and a tender texture. And while most white cake recipes call for folding stiffly beaten whites into the batter at the end, we found that combining the whites with the milk before adding them to the batter produced a cake that actually was lighter and had a greater rise—plus, the method was dead simple. You can serve the cake right out of the pan, in which case you'll need only 3 cups of frosting for the top of the cake.

  1　cup whole milk, room temperature
  6　large egg whites, room temperature
  2　teaspoons almond extract (optional)
  1　teaspoon vanilla extract
2¼　cups (9 ounces) cake flour
1¾　cups (12¼ ounces) sugar
  4　teaspoons baking powder
  1　teaspoon salt
12　tablespoons unsalted butter, cut into
    12 pieces and softened
  4　cups frosting or buttercream (page 691–694)

1. Adjust oven rack to middle position and heat oven to 350 degrees. Grease 13 by 9-inch baking pan, line with parchment paper, grease parchment, then flour pan. Whisk milk, egg whites, almond extract, if using, and vanilla together in bowl.

2. Mix flour, sugar, baking powder, and salt together in bowl of stand mixer. Using paddle on low speed, add butter, 1 piece at a time, until only pea-size pieces remain, about 1 minute.

3. Add half of milk mixture, increase speed to medium-high and beat until light and fluffy, about 1 minute. Reduce speed to medium-low, add remaining milk mixture, and beat until incorporated, about 30 seconds (batter will look slightly curdled). Give batter final stir by hand.

4. Scrape batter into prepared pan, smooth top, and gently tap pan on counter to settle batter. Bake until toothpick inserted in center comes out with few crumbs attached, 25 to 30 minutes, rotating pan halfway through baking.

5. Let cake cool completely in pan, about 2 hours. Run paring knife around edge of cake and flip cake out onto wire rack. Peel off parchment, then flip cake right side up onto serving platter. Spread frosting evenly over top and sides of cake and serve.

VARIATION

Classic White Cupcakes

This recipe yields 24 cupcakes; you will need only 3 cups of frosting.

Line two 12-cup muffin tins with paper liners. Prepare batter as directed, then portion into tins using greased ¼-cup measure. Bake cupcakes on upper-middle and lower-middle racks until toothpick inserted in center comes out with few crumbs attached, 15 to 20 minutes, switching and rotating muffin tins halfway through baking. Let cupcakes cool in pans for 15 minutes, then carefully transfer to wire rack and let cool to room temperature, about 30 minutes. Spread frosting evenly over cupcakes and serve.

Simple Chocolate Sheet Cake

SERVES 15 TO 18　　**TOTAL TIME** 1 HOUR 30 MINUTES (PLUS 1 HOUR COOLING TIME)

✔ **WHY THIS RECIPE WORKS:** Sheet cakes, for all their simplicity, can still turn out dry, sticky, or flavorless and, on occasion, can even sink in the middle. We wanted a simple, dependable recipe, one that was moist yet also light and chocolaty. We started with the mixing method, testing everything from creaming butter to beating egg yolks, whipping egg whites, and gently folding together everything in the end. The best of the lot was the most complicated to make, so we took a step back. The simplest technique we tried was simply whisking all the ingredients together without beating, creaming, or whipping. The recipe needed work, but the approach was clearly what we were after. We added buttermilk and baking soda to lighten the batter, and we reduced the sugar, flour, and butter to increase the chocolate flavor. To further deepen the chocolate taste, we used semisweet chocolate in addition to cocoa powder. We baked the cake at a low temperature for a long time—40 minutes—to produce a perfectly baked cake with a lovely flat top. See page 577 for more information on buttermilk substitutes. You can serve the cake right out of the pan, in which case you'll need only 3 cups of frosting for the top of the cake.

A longer baking time at a lower temperature keeps our chocolate sheet cake moist and perfectly flat.

1¼ cups (6¼ ounces) all-purpose flour
¾   cup (2¼ ounces) Dutch-processed cocoa powder
¼   teaspoon salt
8   ounces semisweet chocolate, chopped
12 tablespoons unsalted butter, cut into 12 pieces
4   large eggs
1½ cups (10½ ounces) sugar
1   teaspoon vanilla extract
1   cup buttermilk
½   teaspoon baking soda
4   cups frosting or buttercream (page 691–694)

1. Adjust oven rack to middle position and heat oven to 325 degrees. Grease 13 by 9-inch baking pan, line with parchment paper, grease parchment, then flour pan. Sift flour, cocoa, and salt together into bowl.

2. Microwave chocolate at 50 percent power for 2 minutes. Stir chocolate, add butter, and continue to microwave until melted, stirring often.

3. In large bowl, whisk eggs, sugar, and vanilla together. Whisk in chocolate mixture until combined. Whisk buttermilk and baking soda together in separate bowl, then whisk mixture into batter. Whisk in flour mixture until batter is smooth and glossy.

4. Scrape batter into prepared pan and smooth top. Bake cake until firm in center when lightly pressed and toothpick inserted in center comes out clean, about 40 minutes.

5. Let cake cool completely in pan, about 1 hour. Run paring knife around edge of cake and flip cake out onto wire rack. Peel off parchment, then flip cake right side up onto serving platter. Spread frosting evenly over top and sides of cake and serve.

VARIATION
Chocolate Cupcakes
This recipe yields 24 cupcakes; you will need only 3 cups of frosting.

Line two 12-cup muffin tins with paper liners. Prepare batter as directed, then portion into tins using greased ¼-cup measure. Bake cupcakes on upper-middle and lower-middle racks until toothpick inserted in center comes out clean, 15 to 20 minutes, switching and rotating muffin tins halfway through baking. Let cupcakes cool in pans for 15 minutes, then carefully transfer to wire rack and let cool to room temperature, about 30 minutes. Spread frosting evenly over cupcakes and serve.

Melting Chocolate

When melting chocolate, it is best to be gentle because chocolate can burn easily. We've found two methods to be the best for melting chocolate: using a double boiler or microwaving it on 50 percent power.

STOVETOP: Chop the chocolate (so it melts evenly) and place it in a heatproof bowl set over a pot of barely simmering water, but be sure the bowl is not touching the water or the chocolate could scorch. Stir occasionally.

MICROWAVE: Microwave the chopped chocolate at 50 percent power for 2 minutes. Stir the chocolate and continue microwaving until melted, stirring once every additional minute.

Carrot Sheet Cake

SERVES 15 TO 18   **TOTAL TIME** 1 HOUR 30 MINUTES
(PLUS 2 HOURS COOLING TIME)

✅ **WHY THIS RECIPE WORKS:** Carrot cake was once heralded for its use of vegetable oil in place of butter, and carrots as a natural sweetener. Sure, the carrots add sweetness, but they also add a lot of moisture. And oil? It makes this cake dense and, well, oily. We wanted a moist, not soggy, cake that was rich, with a tender crumb and balanced spice. Cake flour proved too delicate to support the grated carrots, so we started with all-purpose. Some carrot cakes use a heavy hand with the spices; we took a conservative approach and used modest amounts of cinnamon, nutmeg, and cloves. We settled on 1 pound of grated carrots for a pleasantly moist texture, and 1½ cups of vegetable oil for a rich, but not greasy, cake. For a simple mixing method, we mixed the dry ingredients separately from the wet ingredients before slowly whisking them together and then stirring in the carrots. You can serve the cake right out of the pan, in which case you'll need only 3 cups of frosting for the top of the cake.

This perfectly spiced cake gets its rich, moist texture from the right amount of grated carrots and vegetable oil.

2½   **cups (12½ ounces) all-purpose flour**
1¼   **teaspoons ground cinnamon**
1¼   **teaspoons baking powder**
 1   **teaspoon baking soda**
½   **teaspoon salt**
½   **teaspoon ground nutmeg**
⅛   **teaspoon ground cloves**
 4   **large eggs**
1½   **cups (10½ ounces) granulated sugar**
½   **cup packed (3½ ounces) light brown sugar**
1½   **cups vegetable oil**
 1   **pound carrots, peeled and grated**
 4   **cups Cream Cheese Frosting (page 693)**

1. Adjust oven rack to middle position and heat oven to 350 degrees. Grease 13 by 9-inch baking pan and line bottom with parchment paper. Whisk flour, cinnamon, baking powder, baking soda, salt, nutmeg, and cloves together in bowl.

2. In large bowl, whisk eggs, granulated sugar, and brown sugar together until sugars are mostly dissolved and mixture is frothy. Continue to whisk while slowly drizzling in oil until thoroughly combined and emulsified. Whisk in flour mixture until just incorporated. Stir in carrots. Give batter final stir by hand.

3. Scrape batter into prepared pan, smooth top, and gently tap pan on counter to settle batter. Bake cake until toothpick inserted in center comes out clean, 35 to 40 minutes, rotating pan halfway through baking.

4. Let cake cool completely in pan, about 2 hours. Run paring knife around edge of cake and flip cake out onto wire rack. Peel off parchment, then flip cake right side up onto serving platter. Spread frosting evenly over top and sides of cake and serve.

VARIATION
Carrot Cupcakes
This recipe yields 24 cupcakes; you will need only 3 cups of frosting.

Line two 12-cup muffin tins with paper liners. Prepare batter as directed, then portion into tins using greased ¼-cup measure. Bake cupcakes on upper-middle and lower-middle racks until toothpick inserted in center comes out clean, 25 to 30 minutes, switching and rotating muffin tins halfway through baking. Let cupcakes cool in pans for 15 minutes, then carefully transfer to wire rack and let cool to room temperature, about 30 minutes. Spread frosting evenly over cupcakes and serve.

Yellow Cupcakes

MAKES 12 CUPCAKES   **TOTAL TIME** 1 HOUR 40 MINUTES

✔ **WHY THIS RECIPE WORKS:** We wanted a yellow cupcake so delicious that the cake itself would be savored as much as its rich frosting, a grown-up cupcake good enough to satisfy the mothers and fathers at a kid's birthday party. The answer was easier than we could have hoped. We started with a simple ingredient list of all-purpose flour (pastry flour and cake flour produced too fine a crumb), a combination of a whole egg and two yolks (fewer whites meant richer flavor), sugar, butter, and sour cream (for tangy richness). After pitting the classic creaming method against the two-stage method (cutting the butter into the dry ingredients, then adding the eggs and liquid), we couldn't tell much difference, but when we used a less methodical approach (throwing everything into the mixer together in no particular order), we had the best cupcakes of the bunch. Why? One possible answer is that egg yolks contain emulsifiers that hold the fat and liquid together even when mixed in such a haphazard fashion. Once portioned into muffin tins and baked, these cupcakes emerged from the oven lightly golden and tender.

1½	**cups (7½ ounces) all-purpose flour**
1	**cup (7 ounces) sugar**
1½	**teaspoons baking powder**
½	**teaspoon salt**
8	**tablespoons unsalted butter, softened**
½	**cup sour cream**
1	**large egg plus 2 large yolks**
1½	**teaspoons vanilla extract**
3	**cups frosting or buttercream (page 691–694)**

1. Adjust oven rack to middle position and heat oven to 350 degrees. Line 12-cup muffin tin with paper liners.

2. Mix flour, sugar, baking powder, and salt together in bowl of stand mixer. Using paddle on medium speed, add butter, sour cream, egg and yolks, and vanilla and beat until smooth and satiny, about 30 seconds. Scrape down sides of bowl with rubber spatula and mix by hand until smooth and no flour pockets remain.

3. Divide batter evenly among muffin cups. Bake cupcakes until tops are pale gold and toothpick inserted into center comes out clean, 20 to 24 minutes. Let cupcakes cool in muffin pan for 15 minutes, then carefully transfer to wire rack and let cool to room temperature, about 30 minutes.

4. Mound about 2 tablespoons icing in center of each cupcake. Using small icing spatula or butter knife, spread icing to edge of cupcake, leaving slight mound in center.

Melting the butter in these chocolate cupcakes instead of creaming it saves time and improves texture.

Dark Chocolate Cupcakes

MAKES 12 CUPCAKES   **TOTAL TIME** 1 HOUR 50 MINUTES

✔ **WHY THIS RECIPE WORKS:** We wanted the consummate chocolate cupcake—one with a rich, buttery flavor, a light, moist, cakey texture, and just the right amount of sugar—but we wanted it to be almost as quick and easy to make as the cupcakes that come from a box. For the mixing method, we found that the melted-butter method often used for mixing muffins, quick breads, and brownies—a method that requires no mixer and no time spent waiting for butter to soften—worked best. This procedure won out over the more conventional creaming method for our cupcakes, delivering a light texture with a tender, fine crumb. Moving on to tackle our desire for deep chocolate flavor, we found that a combination of cocoa powder and bittersweet chocolate delivered intense chocolate flavor and that mixing the cocoa powder with the butter and chocolate as they melted (rather than adding the cocoa to the dry ingredients) made the chocolate flavor even stronger and richer. Sour cream gave our cupcakes moistness and a little tang. This recipe does not double very well.

8 tablespoons unsalted butter, cut into 4 pieces
2 ounces bittersweet chocolate, chopped
½ cup (1½ ounces) Dutch-processed cocoa powder
¾ cup (3¾ ounces) all-purpose flour
¾ teaspoon baking powder
½ teaspoon baking soda
2 large eggs
¾ cup (5¼ ounces) sugar
1 teaspoon vanilla extract
½ teaspoon salt
½ cup sour cream
3 cups frosting or buttercream (page 691–694)

1. Adjust oven rack to lower-middle position and heat oven to 350 degrees. Line 12-cup muffin tin with paper liners. (If making Chocolate Cream Cupcakes, grease and flour muffin tin; do not use liners.)

2. Combine butter, chocolate, and cocoa in medium heat-proof bowl. Set bowl over saucepan filled with 1 inch of barely simmering water. Cook, stirring occasionally, until butter and chocolate are melted. Whisk smooth and let cool slightly.

3. Whisk flour, baking powder, and baking soda together in bowl. In medium bowl, whisk eggs until combined, then whisk in sugar, vanilla, and salt until fully incorporated. Whisk in cooled chocolate mixture until combined. Sift about one-third of flour mixture over chocolate mixture and whisk until combined. Whisk in sour cream until combined. Sift remaining flour mixture over batter and whisk until batter is homogeneous and thick.

4. Divide batter evenly among muffin cups. Bake cupcakes until toothpick inserted into center comes out with few crumbs attached, 18 to 20 minutes. Let cupcakes cool in pan for 15 minutes, then carefully transfer to wire rack and let cool to room temperature, about 30 minutes.

5. Mound about 2 tablespoons icing in center of each cupcake. Using small icing spatula or butter knife, spread icing to edge of cupcake, leaving slight mound in center.

NOTES FROM THE TEST KITCHEN

Baking Outside the Tin

If you don't own a muffin tin, we have found that foil liners are sturdy enough to hold our cupcake batter. Simply arrange the liners on a rimmed baking sheet and then fill them with batter. Note that cupcakes baked in a muffin tin brown on both the bottom and the sides. If the cupcakes are baked without a muffin tin, only the bottoms (and not the sides) will brown.

Chocolate Cream Cupcakes

MAKES 12 CUPCAKES   **TOTAL TIME** 1 HOUR 50 MINUTES

✓ **WHY THIS RECIPE WORKS:** We wanted to recreate—and improve upon—this childhood favorite with a moist-tender chocolate cake, a buttery filling that wouldn't dribble out, and a shiny, fudgy glaze. First, we tried simply plopping a marshmallow into the chocolate cupcake batter, but this created moonlike craters in our cupcakes. Combining marshmallow crème and the right amount of gelatin gave us the perfect creamy filling. The chocolate cupcakes were too delicate to allow us to inject the filling with a pastry bag. Instead, we used a paring knife to cut inverted cones from the tops of the cupcakes, added the frosting, and plugged the holes. We prefer a stiffer marshmallow crème in this filling, such as Jet-Puffed or Fluff.

1 recipe Dark Chocolate Cupcakes (page 674),
    baked, cooled, and unfrosted
3 tablespoons water
¾ teaspoon unflavored gelatin
7 tablespoons unsalted butter, 4 tablespoons softened
1 teaspoon vanilla extract
    Pinch salt
1¼ cups marshmallow crème
½ cup (3 ounces) semisweet chocolate chips

1. While cupcakes cool, combine water and gelatin in large bowl and let gelatin soften, about 5 minutes. Microwave until mixture is bubbling around edges and gelatin dissolves, about 30 seconds. Stir in 4 tablespoons softened butter, vanilla, and salt. Let mixture cool until just warm to touch, about 5 minutes. Whisk in marshmallow crème until smooth, then refrigerate until set, about 30 minutes.

2. Microwave chocolate chips and remaining 3 tablespoons butter in bowl, stirring occasionally, until smooth, about 30 seconds. Cool glaze to room temperature, about 10 minutes. Transfer ⅓ cup marshmallow crème mixture to pastry bag fitted with small, plain tip for decorating, and reserve remaining mixture for cupcake filling.

3. Using paring knife, cut out cone-shaped wedge from top of each cupcake, about ⅛ inch in from cupcake edge and 1-inch deep into center of cupcake. Trim off and discard pointed end of cone, leaving ¼-inch-thick cupcake top. Fill each cupcake with 1 tablespoon filling, then replace trimmed cupcake top. Frost top of cupcakes with 2 teaspoons cooled glaze, and let set for 10 minutes. Using pastry bag, pipe curlicues across glazed cupcakes and serve.

Whipped egg whites are the secret to a tall and fluffy, beautiful yellow layer cake.

Yellow Layer Cake

SERVES 10 TO 12   **TOTAL TIME** 1 HOUR 20 MINUTES
(PLUS 2 HOURS COOLING TIME)

✓ WHY THIS RECIPE WORKS: For a layer cake with an ultralight texture, we adapted a chiffon cake technique (using whipped egg whites to get a high volume and a light texture) to combine the ingredients from our butter cake recipe. This gave us a light, porous cake that was sturdy enough to hold the frosting's weight. We used both butter and vegetable oil to keep the butter flavor intact while improving the moistness of the cake. For extra tenderness, we increased the sugar and substituted buttermilk for milk. Be sure to use cake pans with at least 2-inch-tall sides. See page 577 for more information on buttermilk substitutes.

2½   cups (10 ounces) cake flour
1¼   teaspoons baking powder
¼   teaspoon baking soda
¾   teaspoon salt

1¾   cups (12¼ ounces) sugar
10   tablespoons unsalted butter, melted and cooled
1   cup buttermilk, room temperature
3   tablespoons vegetable oil
2   teaspoons vanilla extract
3   large eggs, separated, plus 3 large yolks, room temperature
   Pinch cream of tartar
4   cups frosting or buttercream (page 691–694)

1. Adjust oven rack to middle position and heat oven to 350 degrees. Grease two 9-inch round cake pans, line with parchment paper, grease parchment, and flour pans. Whisk flour, baking powder, baking soda, salt, and 1½ cups sugar together in bowl. In separate bowl, whisk melted butter, buttermilk, oil, vanilla, and egg yolks together.

2. Using stand mixer fitted with whisk, whip egg whites and cream of tartar on medium-low speed until foamy, about 1 minute. Increase speed to medium-high and whip whites to soft billowy mounds, about 1 minute. Gradually add remaining ¼ cup sugar and whip until glossy, stiff peaks form, 2 to 3 minutes; transfer to third bowl.

3. Add flour mixture to now-empty stand mixer bowl. With mixer on low speed, gradually add melted butter mixture and mix until almost incorporated (a few streaks of dry flour will remain), about 15 seconds. Scrape down bowl, then beat on medium-low speed until smooth and fully incorporated, 10 to 15 seconds.

4. Using rubber spatula, stir one-third of whites into batter. Gently fold remaining whites into batter until no white streaks remain. Divide batter evenly between prepared pans, smooth tops, and gently tap pans on counter to settle batter. Bake cakes until toothpick inserted in centers comes out clean, 20 to 22 minutes, switching and rotating pans halfway through baking.

5. Let cakes cool in pans for 10 minutes. Remove cakes from pans, discard parchment, and let cool completely on wire rack, about 2 hours. (Cakes can be stored at room temperature for up to 1 day or frozen for up to 1 month; defrost cakes at room temperature.)

6. Line edges of cake platter with 4 strips of parchment paper to keep platter clean, and place small dab of frosting in center of platter to anchor cake. Place 1 cake layer on platter. Spread 1½ cups frosting evenly over top, right to edge of cake. Top with second cake layer, press lightly to adhere, then spread remaining 2½ cups frosting evenly over top and sides of cake. To smooth frosting, run edge of offset spatula around cake sides and over top. Carefully remove parchment strips before serving. (Frosted cake can be refrigerated for up to 1 day; bring to room temperature before serving.)

Everyone should have a simple, foolproof yellow layer cake in their repertoire, and this one fits the bill perfectly. To make a sturdy yet tender yellow layer cake with a buttery flavor, we turned to a chiffon-style cake that uses whipped egg whites for lift and extra yolks for richness. Swapping buttermilk for the milk added a nice flavor and gave the cake a slightly more tender texture, and swapping oil for some of the butter made the cake supermoist.

1. BRING THE EGGS TO ROOM TEMPERATURE: Separate 3 eggs, then separate 3 more eggs, discarding the whites. Let the yolks and whites come to room temperature. **WHY?** In order for all the ingredients to blend properly and produce maximum rise, they have to be at room temperature. Separating the eggs straight from the refrigerator is easier because the yolks are firmer.

2. USE MELTED BUTTER AND OIL: Melt butter in the microwave, let it cool to room temperature, then whisk it together with the buttermilk, oil, vanilla, and egg yolks. **WHY?** In order to give the cake a moist texture, we swapped in some oil for some of the butter. Melting the butter makes it easier to incorporate into the batter.

3. WHIP THE EGG WHITES: Whip the egg whites and cream of tartar on medium-low speed until foamy, about 1 minute. Increase the speed to medium-high and whip until billowy, about 1 minute. Gradually add ¼ cup sugar and whip until glossy, stiff peaks form; transfer to a bowl. **WHY?** For maximum cake height, it's important to whip the egg whites to stiff peaks. Cream of tartar helps produce a stable, voluminous foam.

4. COMBINE THE FLOUR MIXTURE AND MELTED BUTTER MIXTURE: Mix the flour mixture and melted butter mixture on low speed until almost incorporated. Then beat the mixture on medium-low speed until smooth. **WHY?** Combining the liquid and dry ingredients in the mixer slowly prevents lumps from forming. Once they're combined, it's important to increase the mixer speed and beat the batter until smooth.

5. FOLD IN THE WHIPPED WHITES: Stir one-third of the egg whites into the batter. Gently fold in the remaining whites until no white streaks remain. **WHY?** To loosen the thick batter, we first add a portion of the whipped egg whites. Then we fold in the remaining whites gently to preserve their fluffy texture.

6. PORTION THE BATTER: Divide the batter between the 2 prepared cake pans, smooth the tops, and tap the pans on the counter. **WHY?** Dividing the batter evenly ensures that the cake layers will be the same size and will bake at the same rate. Tapping the pans releases any air bubbles trapped in the batter.

7. BAKE AND TEST FOR DONENESS: Bake until a toothpick inserted into the cakes comes out clean, 20 to 22 minutes, switching and rotating the pans halfway through baking. **WHY?** We've found the toothpick test to be the most foolproof. Also, if the cake is pulling away from the sides of the pan, it is likely done.

8. LET THE CAKES COOL: Let the cakes cool in the pans for 10 minutes, then unmold them onto a wire rack and let them cool completely, about 2 hours, before frosting. **WHY?** Letting the cakes cool in the pan briefly helps them set up so that they are less likely to break apart when removing them.

Most home cooks think a bakery-smooth frosted cake is well beyond their ability, so they make do with a cake that "looks home-made." The truth is that a polished appearance is easy if you have the right tools and use the right technique. Starting with flat layers (and a cool cake) is absolutely essential.

1. REMOVE THE DOME: Using a serrated knife, gently slice back and forth with a sawing motion to remove the domed portion from each cake layer.
WHY? Cake layers with a domed top are difficult to stack and frost. If your layers dome, trim enough of the top to ensure a flat surface. Brush the crumbs off the cake since they can mar the frosting.

2. KEEP THE PLATTER CLEAN: Cover the edges of the cake stand or platter with strips of parchment paper.
WHY? The strips of parchment paper ensure that extra frosting doesn't end up on the platter. Once the cake is frosted, you can slide out and discard the parchment.

3. FROST THE FIRST LAYER: Dollop a small amount of frosting in the center of the cake stand, then place a cake layer on top. Dollop a large portion of frosting in the center of the cake layer. Spread the frosting evenly to the edge of the cake.
WHY? The dollop of frosting on the platter will anchor the cake. An offset spatula, with its thin, flexible blade, makes it easy to push the frosting out from the center of the cake layer to the edges.

4. ALIGN THE SECOND LAYER: Place the second layer on top, making sure it is aligned with the first layer. As you place the top layer, don't push down on it or you risk squeezing the frosting out the sides of the cake.
WHY? Careful placement of the top layer ensures that the sides line up and allows you to frost the cake properly with smooth sides.

5. FROST THE TOP, THEN THE SIDES: Spread more frosting over the top layer, pushing it over the edge of the cake. Gather several tablespoons of frosting with the tip of an offset spatula and gently smear it onto the side of the cake. Repeat until the side is covered with frosting.
WHY? You need a gentler approach to frosting the side of the cake. If you spread a large amount of frosting, you risk getting crumbs in the frosting or causing the layers to shift. Clean off the spatula in a glass filled with warm water as needed.

6. SMOOTH OUT THE ROUGH SPOTS: Gently run the edge of the spatula around the sides to smooth out bumps and tidy areas where the frosting on the top and sides merge.
WHY? The superthin edge of an offset spatula will pick up excess blobs of frosting and fill any holes. You can run the edge of the spatula over the top of the cake to give it a smooth look, too. Remove the strips of parchment. (If decorating the frosted cake, leave the parchment in place.)

Classic White Layer Cake

SERVES 10 TO 12   **TOTAL TIME** 1 HOUR 20 MINUTES
(PLUS 2 HOURS COOLING TIME)

✓**WHY THIS RECIPE WORKS:** White layer cakes have been the classic birthday cake for more than 100 years. White cake is simply a butter cake made with egg whites instead of whole eggs (using the latter would make it a yellow cake). The whites are supposed to make the cake soft and fine-grained. Unfortunately, most white cakes fall short, coming out dry and cottony and riddled with tunnels and small holes. Traditional recipes call for folding stiffly beaten egg whites into the batter at the end. We suspected that it was the beaten whites that were forming the large air pockets and holes in the baked cakes. We solved the problem by mixing the whites with the milk before beating them into the flour-butter mixture. This cake not only was fine-grained and free from holes, it was also larger and lighter than the ones made with beaten whites. And the method couldn't be simpler, quicker, or more foolproof.

      1   cup whole milk, room temperature
      6   large egg whites, room temperature
      2   teaspoons almond extract
      1   teaspoon vanilla extract
  2¼   cups (9 ounces) cake flour
  1¾   cups (12¼ ounces) sugar
      4   teaspoons baking powder
      1   teaspoon salt
    12   tablespoons unsalted butter, cut into
          12 pieces and softened
      4   cups frosting or buttercream (page 691–694)

1. Adjust oven rack to middle position and heat oven to 350 degrees. Grease two 9-inch round cake pans, line with parchment paper, grease parchment, and flour pans. Whisk milk, egg whites, almond extract, and vanilla together in bowl.

2. Stir flour, sugar, baking powder, and salt together in bowl of stand mixer. Using paddle on low speed, beat in butter, 1 piece at a time, until only pea-size pieces remain, about 1 minute. Add all but ½ cup milk mixture, increase speed to medium-high, and beat until light and fluffy, about 1 minute.

3. Reduce speed to medium-low, add remaining ½ cup milk mixture, and beat until incorporated, about 30 seconds (batter may look curdled). Give batter final stir by hand.

4. Divide batter evenly between prepared pans, smooth tops, and gently tap pans on counter to settle batter. Bake cakes until toothpick inserted in centers comes out with few crumbs attached, 23 to 25 minutes, switching and rotating pans halfway through baking.

5. Let cakes cool in pans for 10 minutes. Remove cakes from pans, discard parchment, and let cool completely on wire rack, about 2 hours. (Cakes can be stored at room temperature for up to 1 day or frozen for up to 1 month; defrost cakes at room temperature.)

6. Line edges of cake platter with 4 strips of parchment paper to keep platter clean, and place small dab of frosting in center of platter to anchor cake. Place 1 cake layer on platter. Spread 1½ cups frosting evenly over top, right to edge of cake. Top with second cake layer, press lightly to adhere, then spread remaining 2½ cups frosting evenly over top and sides of cake. To smooth frosting, run edge of offset spatula around cake sides and over top. Carefully remove parchment strips before serving. (Frosted cake can be refrigerated for up to 1 day; bring to room temperature before serving.)

Old-Fashioned Chocolate Layer Cake

SERVES 10 TO 12   **TOTAL TIME** 1 HOUR 30 MINUTES
(PLUS 2 HOURS COOLING TIME)

✓**WHY THIS RECIPE WORKS:** Over the years, chocolate cakes have become denser, richer, and squatter. We wanted an old-style, mile-high chocolate layer cake with a tender, airy, open crumb and a soft, billowy frosting. The mixing method was the key to getting the right texture. After trying a variety of techniques, we turned to a popular old-fashioned method called ribboning. Ribboning involves whipping eggs with sugar until they double in volume, then adding the butter, dry ingredients, and milk. The egg foam aerated the cake, giving it both structure and tenderness. To achieve a moist cake with rich chocolate flavor, we once again looked to historical sources, which suggested using buttermilk and making a "pudding" with a mixture of chocolate, water, and sugar. We simply melted unsweetened chocolate and dissolved cocoa powder in hot water over a double boiler, then stirred in sugar until it dissolved. Be sure to use cake pans with at least 2-inch-tall sides. See page 577 for more information on buttermilk substitutes.

      4   ounces unsweetened chocolate, chopped coarse
    ¼   cup (¾ ounce) Dutch-processed cocoa powder
    ½   cup hot water
  1¾   cups (12¼ ounces) sugar
  1¾   cups (8¾ ounces) all-purpose flour
  1½   teaspoons baking soda

1 **teaspoon salt**
1 **cup buttermilk**
2 **teaspoons vanilla extract**
4 **large eggs plus 2 large yolks, room temperature**
12 **tablespoons unsalted butter, cut into 12 pieces and softened**
4 **cups frosting or buttercream (page 691–694)**

1. Adjust oven rack to middle position and heat oven to 350 degrees. Grease two 9-inch round cake pans, line with parchment paper, grease parchment, and flour pans. Combine chocolate, cocoa, and hot water in medium heatproof bowl. Set bowl over saucepan filled with 1 inch of barely simmering water. Cook, stirring occasionally, until chocolate is melted, about 2 minutes. Stir in ½ cup sugar and cook until mixture is thick and glossy, 1 to 2 minutes. Remove from heat and let cool.

2. Whisk flour, baking soda, and salt together in bowl. In separate bowl, combine buttermilk and vanilla. Using stand mixer fitted with whisk, whip eggs and yolks on medium-low speed until combined, about 10 seconds. Add remaining 1¼ cups sugar, increase speed to high, and whip until light and fluffy, 2 to 3 minutes.

3. Fit stand mixer with paddle. Add cooled chocolate mixture to egg mixture and mix on medium speed until thoroughly combined, 30 to 45 seconds, scraping down bowl as needed.

Add butter, 1 piece at a time, mixing about 10 seconds after each addition. Reduce speed to low and add flour mixture in 3 additions, alternating with buttermilk mixture in 2 additions, scraping down bowl as needed (batter may look curdled). Mix batter at medium-low speed until thoroughly combined, about 15 seconds. Give batter final stir by hand.

4. Divide batter evenly between prepared pans, smooth tops, and gently tap pans on counter to settle batter. Bake cakes until toothpick inserted in centers comes out with few crumbs attached, 25 to 30 minutes, switching and rotating pans halfway through baking.

5. Let cakes cool in pans for 10 minutes. Remove cakes from pans, discard parchment, and let cool completely on wire rack, about 2 hours. (Cakes can be stored at room temperature for up to 1 day or frozen for up to 1 month; defrost cakes at room temperature.)

6. Line edges of cake platter with 4 strips of parchment paper to keep platter clean, and place small dab of frosting in center of platter to anchor cake. Place 1 cake layer on platter. Spread 1½ cups frosting evenly over top, right to edge of cake. Top with second cake layer, press lightly to adhere, then spread remaining 2½ cups frosting evenly over top and sides of cake. To smooth frosting, run edge of offset spatula around cake sides and over top. Carefully remove parchment strips before serving. (Frosted cake can be refrigerated for up to 1 day; bring to room temperature before serving.)

Preparing Cake Pans

The steps below show how to prepare a round cake pan; however, the same method can be used to prepare square or 13 by 9-inch cake pans. Don't skip this crucial step. If the pan is improperly prepared, the cake will stick and break into pieces as you attempt to remove it.

1. Place cake pan on sheet of parchment paper and trace around bottom of pan with pencil or pen. Cut out parchment circle.

2. Evenly spray bottom and sides of cake pan with vegetable oil spray.

3. Fit trimmed piece of parchment into pan.

4. Spray parchment with vegetable oil spray, then sprinkle with several tablespoons of flour. Shake and rotate pan to coat evenly. Shake out excess flour.

Buttermilk and vinegar react with the baking soda in this cake to deliver an extra-tender crumb.

Red Velvet Layer Cake

SERVES 10 TO 12   **TOTAL TIME:** 1 HOUR 20 MINUTES
(PLUS 2 HOURS COOLING TIME)

✓**WHY THIS RECIPE WORKS:** Although the shockingly bright color seems to get most of the attention, red velvet layer cake is more than just a novelty. The cake itself is extra-tender, light, and moist, which we achieved through the use of two unexpected ingredients: buttermilk and vinegar. This combination formed a reaction with our recipe's baking soda to create a fine and tender crumb. Another challenge was to give this cake enough cocoa to lend a pleasant chocolate flavor without overpowering the fluffy cream cheese frosting sandwiched between the layers. The natural cocoa powder itself does more than provide good flavor; part of the rich color and airy texture come from this ingredient. Be sure to use natural cocoa powder; do not substitute Dutch-processed cocoa. See page 577 for more information on buttermilk substitutions.

2¼ cups (11¼ ounces) all-purpose flour
1½ teaspoons baking soda
     Pinch salt
 1 cup buttermilk
 2 large eggs
 1 tablespoon distilled white vinegar
 1 teaspoon vanilla extract
 2 tablespoons unsweetened cocoa powder
 2 tablespoons (1 ounce) red food coloring
12 tablespoons unsalted butter, cut into
     12 pieces and softened
1½ cups (10½ ounces) sugar
 4 cups Cream Cheese Frosting (page 693)

1. Adjust oven rack to middle position and heat oven to 350 degrees. Grease two 9-inch round cake pans, line with parchment paper, grease parchment, and flour pans. Whisk flour, baking soda, and salt together in bowl. In separate bowl, whisk buttermilk, eggs, vinegar, and vanilla together. In third bowl, mix cocoa and red food coloring together to smooth paste.

2. Using stand mixer fitted with paddle, beat butter and sugar on medium-high speed until pale and fluffy, about 3 minutes. Reduce speed to low and add flour mixture in 3 additions, alternating with buttermilk mixture in 2 additions, scraping down bowl as needed. Beat in cocoa mixture until batter is uniform. Give batter final stir by hand.

3. Divide batter evenly between prepared pans, smooth tops, and gently tap pans on counter to settle batter. Bake cakes until toothpick inserted in centers comes out clean, about 25 minutes, switching and rotating pans halfway through baking.

4. Let cakes cool in pans for 10 minutes. Remove cakes from pans, discard parchment, and let cool completely on wire rack, about 2 hours. (Cakes can be stored at room temperature for up to 1 day or frozen for up to 1 month; defrost cakes at room temperature.)

5. Line edges of cake platter with 4 strips of parchment paper to keep platter clean, and place small dab of frosting in center of platter to anchor cake. Place 1 cake layer on platter. Spread 1½ cups frosting evenly over top, right to edge of cake. Top with second cake layer, press lightly to adhere, then spread remaining 2½ cups frosting evenly over top and sides of cake. To smooth frosting, run edge of offset spatula around cake sides and over top. Carefully remove parchment strips before serving. (Frosted cake can be refrigerated for up to 1 day; bring to room temperature before serving.)

Even simple decorations can give a frosted layer cake a professional look. Note that for all but the first technique below, it's imperative to create a smooth finish on the frosted cake. To do this, use the edge of an offset spatula to create a level surface for decorating (see the last step on page 678). When decorating a cake, leave the strips of parchment used to protect the platter during the frosting process in place. Any excess decoration will fall onto the parchment rather than onto the platter. Once you're finished decorating, carefully remove and discard the parchment.

A. GIVE THE FROSTING TEXTURE:
Press the back of a soupspoon into the frosting, then twirl the spoon as you lift it away.
WHY? One of the simplest ways to decorate a cake is to give the frosting some texture. To make wavy lines or a stripe pattern, simply drag a cake comb (or fork) around the cake's sides.

B. ADORN JUST THE BOTTOM EDGE:
Use your fingers to gently press toasted sliced nuts, 1 at a time, around the bottom edge of the cake.
WHY? This simple trick makes the cake look elegant and also camouflages any messiness at the base of the cake. Instead of nuts, you can also use fruit, sprinkles, candies, or even cookies.

C. COVER THE SIDES COMPLETELY: Press a small handful of crushed candies into the sides of the frosted cake.
WHY? This is a great way to hide a messy or uneven frosting job, and it also looks great. You can also use sprinkles, toasted nuts, shredded coconut (toasted or plain), chocolate shavings, or crushed cookies (choose something fairly plain like chocolate wafer cookies).

D. MARK EACH SLICE: Mark each slice of cake with a small garnish, such as 2 raspberries and a sprig of fresh mint.
WHY? Marking each slice helps guide your knife as you slice the cake. Cut between the garnishes so that each slice has a garnish in the center. The garnish can represent the flavors inside the cake (such as fruit or nuts) or simply be decorative.

E. COVER THE TOP COMPLETELY:
Cover the top of the cake completely with shavings made by running a sharp vegetable peeler over a block of chocolate.
WHY? Covering the top can hide imperfections in the frosting and will make a short cake look taller and more impressive. Instead of chocolate shavings, also try fruit or shaved coconut.

F. MAKE A BORDER WITH A PIPING BAG:
Use a closed star tip and hold the bag perpendicular to the surface of the cake. Slowly pipe out the frosting while directing the tip in a tight, circular motion, then stop piping and pull the bag straight away from the cake.
WHY? A shell (or ruffled) border along the bottom and top edges is a festive finish, and it's also ideal for covering the space between the cake and the platter.

Coconut Layer Cake

SERVES 10 TO 12   **TOTAL TIME** 1 HOUR 40 MINUTES
(PLUS 2 HOURS COOLING TIME)

✓ **WHY THIS RECIPE WORKS:** Coconut cake should be perfumed inside and out with the cool, subtle essence of coconut. Its layers should be moist and tender, with a delicate, yielding crumb, and the icing a silky, gently sweetened coat covered with a deep drift of downy coconut. For this moist and tender cake, we prefer a rich and moist butter cake made with low-protein cake flour. To infuse it with maximum coconut flavor, we rely on coconut extract and cream of coconut. We tried coconut milk but found that the fat content among brands varies too much, and cream of coconut simply delivered fuller coconut flavor in our cake. In lieu of seven-minute frosting, which is too sweet with this cake, we turned to a related frosting—an egg-white buttercream. We flavored it with coconut extract and cream of coconut. We also gave our cake a woolly coating of shredded coconut for more coconut flavor and textural interest. Be sure to use cream of coconut and not coconut milk here. One 15-ounce can is enough for both the cake and the icing.

CAKE

- 1 large egg plus 5 large whites
- ¾ cup cream of coconut
- ¼ cup water
- 1 teaspoon vanilla extract
- 1 teaspoon coconut extract
- 2¼ cups (9 ounces) cake flour
- 1 cup (7 ounces) sugar
- 1 tablespoon baking powder
- ¾ teaspoon salt
- 12 tablespoons unsalted butter, cut into 12 pieces and softened
- 2 cups (6 ounces) sweetened shredded coconut

ICING

- 4 large egg whites
- 1 cup (7 ounces) sugar
  Pinch salt
- 1 pound (4 sticks) unsalted butter, each stick cut into 6 pieces and softened
- ¼ cup cream of coconut
- 1 teaspoon coconut extract
- 1 teaspoon vanilla extract

1. FOR THE CAKE: Adjust oven rack to lower-middle position and heat oven to 325 degrees. Grease two 9-inch round cake pans, line with parchment paper, grease parchment, and flour pans. Whisk egg and whites together in large liquid measuring cup. Whisk in cream of coconut, water, vanilla, and coconut extract.

2. Mix flour, sugar, baking powder, and salt in bowl of stand mixer. Using paddle on low speed, beat in butter, 1 piece at a time, until only pea-size pieces remain, about 1 minute. Add half of egg mixture, increase speed to medium-high, and beat until light and fluffy, about 1 minute. Reduce speed to medium-low, add remaining egg mixture, and beat until incorporated, about 30 seconds. Give batter final stir by hand.

3. Divide batter evenly between prepared pans, smooth tops, and gently tap pans on counter to settle batter. Bake cakes until toothpick inserted in centers comes out clean, about 30 minutes, switching and rotating pans halfway through baking.

4. Let cakes cool in pans for 10 minutes. Remove cakes from pans, discard parchment, and let cool completely on wire rack, about 2 hours. (Cakes can be stored at room temperature for up to 1 day or frozen for up to 1 month; defrost cakes at room temperature.) Meanwhile, spread shredded coconut on rimmed baking sheet and toast in oven until shreds are mix of golden brown and white, 15 to 20 minutes, stirring 2 or 3 times; let cool.

5. FOR THE ICING: Combine egg whites, sugar, and salt in bowl of stand mixer and set over medium saucepan filled with 1 inch of barely simmering water (do not let bottom of bowl touch water). Cook, whisking constantly, until mixture is opaque and registers 120 degrees, about 2 minutes.

6. Remove bowl from heat. Using whisk on high speed, whip egg white mixture until glossy, sticky, and barely warm (80 degrees), about 7 minutes. Reduce speed to medium-high and whip in butter, 1 piece at a time, followed by cream of coconut, coconut extract, and vanilla, scraping down bowl as needed. Continue to whip at medium-high speed until combined, about 1 minute.

7. Cut 1 horizontal line around sides of each layer. Following scored lines, cut each layer into 2 even layers with long serrated knife.

8. Line edges of cake platter with 4 strips of parchment paper to keep platter clean, and place small dab of frosting in center of platter to anchor cake. Place 1 cake layer on platter. Spread ¾ cup frosting evenly over top, right to edge of cake. Top with second cake layer, aligning cuts so that layers are even, and press lightly to adhere. Repeat with more frosting and remaining cake layers. Spread remaining frosting evenly over top and sides of cake. To smooth frosting, run edge of offset spatula around cake sides and over top. Sprinkle top of cake evenly with toasted coconut, then press remaining toasted coconut into sides of cake. Carefully remove parchment strips before serving. (Frosted cake can be refrigerated for up to 1 day; bring to room temperature before serving.)

German Chocolate Cake

SERVES 10 TO 12   **TOTAL TIME** 2 HOURS
(PLUS 4 HOURS CHILLING AND COOLING TIME)

✔**WHY THIS RECIPE WORKS:** Most German chocolate cake recipes are similar, if not identical, to the one on the German's Sweet Chocolate box. Our tasters found several shortcomings in this recipe. It produced a cake that was too sweet, with chocolate flavor that was too mild and a texture so listless that the filling and cake together formed a soggy, sweet mush. We wanted a cake that was less sweet and more chocolaty than the original, but we didn't want to sacrifice the overall blend of flavors and textures that make German chocolate cake so appealing in the first place. The first order of business was to scale back the recipe by one quarter, which allowed us to fit the batter into two cake pans, thereby producing a cake with four thinner layers rather than three thicker layers. This adjustment would make the cake, with its thick coconut filling, easier to slice. German chocolate cake typically calls for German's Sweet Chocolate, but its flavor is too sweet. Mixing a combination of cocoa powder and semisweet or bittersweet chocolate with boiling water intensified their flavor for a cake with full, not faint, chocolate flavor. Both brown and white sugars gave this cake the right level of caramel-like sweetness and a tender texture. The filling base, made with egg yolks, evaporated milk, sugar (both brown and white), and butter, needed to be boiled—when we followed traditional recipes that called for just simmering the filling, it came out too loose. After we cooked the filling, we refrigerated it to allow it to chill and firm up further. We stirred sweetened shredded coconut into the filling before chilling, followed by the toasted pecans just before assembling the cake to preserve their crunch. For an accurate measurement of boiling water, bring a full kettle of water to a boil, then measure out the desired amount. Be sure to use cake pans with at least 2-inch-tall sides.

FILLING

- 4 **large egg yolks**
- 1 **(12-ounce) can evaporated milk**
- 1 **cup (7 ounces) granulated sugar**
- ¼ **cup packed (1¾ ounces) light brown sugar**
- 6 **tablespoons unsalted butter, cut into 6 pieces**
- ⅛ **teaspoon salt**
- 2 **teaspoons vanilla extract**
- 2⅓ **cups (7 ounces) sweetened shredded coconut**
- 1½ **cups pecans, toasted and chopped fine**

CAKE

- 4 **ounces semisweet or bittersweet chocolate, chopped fine**
- ¼ **cup (¾ ounce) Dutch-processed cocoa powder**
- ½ **cup boiling water**
- 2 **cups (10 ounces) all-purpose flour**
- ¾ **teaspoon baking soda**
- 12 **tablespoons unsalted butter, softened**
- 1 **cup (7 ounces) granulated sugar**
- ⅔ **cup packed (4⅔ ounces) light brown sugar**
- ¾ **teaspoon salt**
- 4 **large eggs**
- 1 **teaspoon vanilla extract**
- ¾ **cup sour cream**

Cutting a Cake into Layers

1. Measure height of cake. Use paring knife to mark midpoint at several places around sides of cake.

2. Using marks as guide, score entire circumference of cake with long serrated knife.

3. Following score lines, run knife around cake several times, cutting inward. Once knife is inside cake, use back-and-forth motion. Make sure knife remains aligned with scoring around sides.

4. Once knife cuts through cake, separate layers, gently inserting your fingers between them. Lift top layer and place it on counter.

1. FOR THE FILLING: Whisk egg yolks in medium saucepan, then gradually whisk in evaporated milk. Whisk in granulated sugar, brown sugar, butter, and salt and cook over medium-high heat, whisking constantly, until mixture is boiling, frothy, and slightly thickened, about 6 minutes. Transfer mixture to bowl, whisk in vanilla, then stir in coconut. Let cool until just warm, then refrigerate until cool, at least 2 hours or up to 3 days. (Pecans are added later.)

2. FOR THE CAKE: Adjust oven rack to lower-middle position and heat oven to 350 degrees. Grease two 9-inch round cake pans, line with parchment paper, grease parchment, and flour pans. Combine chocolate and cocoa in bowl, add boiling water, cover, and let sit for 5 minutes. Whisk chocolate mixture until smooth, then let cool to room temperature. In separate bowl, whisk flour and baking soda together.

3. Using stand mixer fitted with paddle, beat butter, granulated sugar, brown sugar, and salt on medium-high speed until light and fluffy, about 3 minutes. Add eggs, 1 at a time, and beat until combined. Add vanilla, increase speed to medium-high, and beat until light and fluffy, about 45 seconds. Reduce speed to low, add chocolate mixture, then increase speed to medium and beat until combined, about 30 seconds, scraping down bowl once (batter may look curdled). Reduce speed to low, add flour mixture in 3 additions, alternating with sour cream in 2 additions, scraping down bowl as needed. Give batter final stir by hand (batter will be thick).

4. Divide batter evenly between prepared pans, smooth tops, and gently tap pans on counter to settle batter. Bake until toothpick inserted in centers comes out clean, about 30 minutes, switching and rotating pans halfway through baking.

5. Let cakes cool in pans for 10 minutes. Remove cakes from pans, discard parchment, and let cool completely on wire rack, about 2 hours. (Cakes can be stored at room temperature for up to 1 day or frozen for up to 1 month; defrost cakes at room temperature.)

6. Cut 1 horizontal line around sides of each layer. Following scored lines, cut each layer into 2 even layers with long serrated knife. Stir toasted pecans into chilled filling.

7. Line edges of cake platter with 4 strips of parchment paper to keep platter clean, and place small dab of frosting in center of platter to anchor cake. Place 1 cake layer on platter. Spread 1 cup filling evenly over top, right to edge of cake. Top with second cake layer, aligning cuts so that layers are even, and press lightly to adhere. Repeat with more filling and remaining cake layers. Spread remaining filling evenly over top of cake, leaving sides unfrosted. Carefully remove parchment strips before serving. (Frosted cake can be refrigerated for up to 1 day; bring to room temperature before serving.)

A mixture of fresh and frozen strawberries enhance the batter, filling, and frosting for a cake that lives up to its name.

Strawberry Dream Cake

SERVES 10 TO 12   **TOTAL TIME** 1 HOUR 40 MINUTES
(PLUS 2 HOURS COOLING TIME)

✔**WHY THIS RECIPE WORKS:** Strange as it may seem, the vast majority of existing strawberry cake recipes turn to strawberry Jell-O for flavor. Hoping to avoid this artificial solution, we performed test after test to figure out the best way to season our cake with actual strawberries. Any strawberry solids wreaked havoc on the tender cake, but strained and reduced strawberry juices kept our cake light and packed a strawberry punch. Not to be left behind, the reserved strawberry solids made for the perfect studded addition to the frosting.

CAKE

10 ounces frozen whole strawberries (2 cups)
¾ cup whole milk
6 large egg whites
2 teaspoons vanilla extract
2¼ cups (9 ounces) cake flour

- 1¾ cups (12¼ ounces) granulated sugar
- 4 teaspoons baking powder
- 1 teaspoon salt
- 12 tablespoons unsalted butter, cut into 12 pieces and softened

FROSTING
- 10 tablespoons unsalted butter, softened
- 2¼ cups (9 ounces) confectioners' sugar
- 12 ounces cream cheese, cut into 12 pieces and softened
- Pinch salt
- 8 ounces fresh strawberries, hulled and sliced thin (1½ cups)

1. FOR THE CAKE: Adjust oven rack to middle position and heat oven to 350 degrees. Grease two 9-inch round cake pans, line with parchment paper, grease parchment, and flour pans.

2. Microwave frozen strawberries in covered bowl until softened and they have released their juice, about 5 minutes. Strain berries through fine-mesh strainer set over small saucepan, pressing on berries to extract as much liquid as possible; reserve strawberry solids for frosting. Bring juice to boil over medium-high heat and cook, stirring occasionally, until syrupy and reduced to ¼ cup, 6 to 8 minutes. Off heat, whisk in milk. Transfer mixture to clean bowl and whisk in egg whites and vanilla until combined.

3. Stir flour, sugar, baking powder, and salt together in bowl of stand mixer. Using paddle on low speed, beat in butter, 1 piece at a time, until only pea-size pieces remain, about 1 minute. Add half of milk mixture, increase speed to medium-high, and beat until light and fluffy, about 1 minute. Reduce speed to medium-low, add remaining milk mixture, and beat until incorporated, about 30 seconds. Give batter final stir by hand.

4. Divide batter evenly between prepared pans, smooth tops, and gently tap pans on counter to settle batter. Bake cakes until toothpick inserted in centers comes out clean, 20 to 25 minutes, switching and rotating pans halfway through baking.

5. Let cakes cool in pans for 10 minutes. Remove cakes from pans, discard parchment, and let cool completely on wire rack, about 2 hours. (Cakes can be stored at room temperature for up to 2 days.)

6. FOR THE FROSTING: Using stand mixer fitted with paddle, mix butter and sugar on low speed until combined, about 30 seconds. Increase speed to medium-high and beat until pale and fluffy, about 2 minutes. Add cream cheese, 1 piece at a time, and beat until incorporated, about 1 minute. Add reserved strawberry solids and salt and mix until combined, about 30 seconds. Refrigerate until ready to use or up to 2 days.

7. Pat sliced strawberries dry with paper towels. Line edges of cake platter with 4 strips of parchment paper to keep platter clean, and place small dab of frosting in center of platter to anchor cake. Place 1 cake layer on platter. Spread ¾ cup frosting evenly over top, press 1 cup strawberries into frosting, then spread ¾ cup frosting over top. Top with second cake layer, press lightly to adhere, and spread remaining frosting evenly over top and sides of cake. Garnish with remaining strawberries. Carefully remove parchment strips before serving. (Frosted cake can be refrigerated for up to 2 days; bring to room temperature before serving.)

Glazed Chocolate Cream Roll

SERVES 8 TO 10   **TOTAL TIME** 1 HOUR 40 MINUTES
(PLUS 1 HOUR CHILLING TIME)

✔ **WHY THIS RECIPE WORKS:** A spiral of chocolate sponge cake rolled up around a creamy filling is an eye-catching centerpiece. Rolled cakes depend on light, airy sponge cake that is thin, even, and "rollable," but even though sponge cake isn't typically rich, we still wanted our cake to pack serious chocolate flavor and remain moist and tender. We found the number of eggs was key. Too few and the cake was not supple. Too many and we got either a wet chocolate sponge or dry chocolate matting. Five eggs provided the proper support, lift to help the cake rise, and flexibility needed to roll it. We found that rolling the cake up while it was still warm, cooling it briefly, and then unrolling it resulted in a cake that retained its rolled "memory" and that could be easily filled and rolled again. When it came to filling, we settled on marshmallow crème beaten with butter, sugar, and vanilla. A rich layer of chocolate glaze on the exterior was the perfect finish. You'll need an 18 by 13-inch rimmed baking sheet for this cake. We prefer a stiffer marshmallow crème in this filling, such as Jet-Puffed or Fluff. Be sure to have the filling ready by the time the cake is finished baking; if the baked cake sits around for longer than 15 minutes before filling, it will become too stiff to roll.

CAKE
- ¾ cup (3¾ ounces) all-purpose flour
- ¼ cup (¾ ounce) Dutch-processed cocoa powder
- 1 teaspoon baking powder
- ¼ teaspoon salt
- 5 large eggs, room temperature
- ¾ cup (5¼ ounces) granulated sugar
- ½ teaspoon vanilla extract

FILLING

- 6 tablespoons unsalted butter, softened
- ⅔ cup (2⅔ ounces) confectioners' sugar
- 1¼ cups marshmallow crème
- ¾ teaspoon vanilla extract
- ⅛ teaspoon salt

GLAZE

- ⅓ cup heavy cream
- 2 tablespoons light corn syrup
- 4 ounces bittersweet chocolate, chopped fine
- ¼ teaspoon vanilla extract

1. FOR THE CAKE: Adjust oven rack to lower-middle position and heat oven to 350 degrees. Grease 18 by 13-inch rimmed baking sheet, line bottom with parchment paper, and grease parchment. Whisk flour, cocoa, baking powder, and salt together in bowl.

2. Using stand mixer fitted with whisk, whip eggs on medium-high speed and gradually add sugar and vanilla, about 1 minute. Continue to whip mixture until very thick and voluminous, about 4 minutes. Sift flour mixture over egg mixture and fold in with rubber spatula until just incorporated.

3. Spread batter evenly into prepared baking sheet and gently tap pan on counter to settle batter. Bake cake until it feels firm and springs back when touched, 12 to 17 minutes, rotating pan halfway through baking.

4. FOR THE FILLING: Using stand mixer fitted with paddle, mix butter and sugar on low speed until combined, about

30 seconds. Increase speed to medium-high and beat until pale and fluffy, about 2 minutes. Add marshmallow crème, vanilla, and salt and mix until incorporated, about 2 minutes.

5. After removing cake from oven, run paring knife around edge of cake to loosen. Flip hot cake out onto large sheet of greased parchment paper. Peel off and discard parchment paper baked onto cake. Starting from short end of cake, roll cake and parchment snugly into log and let cool for 15 minutes.

6. Gently unroll cake. Spread filling over cake, leaving ½-inch border at edges. Reroll cake gently but snugly around filling, leaving parchment behind as you roll. Trim ends of cake, then let it cool completely, about 30 minutes.

7. FOR THE GLAZE: Transfer cake to wire rack set over parchment-lined rimmed baking sheet. Microwave glaze ingredients together in bowl, whisking often, until melted and smooth, 1 to 2 minutes. Pour warm glaze evenly over cake, letting it drip down sides. Refrigerate until glaze has set, about 1 hour, before serving.

VARIATIONS

Glazed Chocolate–Peanut Butter Cream Roll
Add ½ cup peanut butter to filling with marshmallow crème.

Glazed Chocolate-Mocha Cream Roll
Melt 2 ounces chopped bittersweet or semisweet chocolate with 2 teaspoons instant espresso powder in bowl in microwave, stirring often, about 1 minute. Let mixture cool slightly, then add to filling with marshmallow crème.

Making a Chocolate Cream Roll

1. Run paring knife around edge of cake to loosen. Flip hot cake out onto large sheet of greased parchment paper.

2. Peel off and discard parchment paper baked onto cake. Starting from short end of cake, roll cake and parchment snugly into log and let cool for 15 minutes.

3. Gently unroll cake. Spread filling over cake, leaving ½-inch border at edges.

4. Reroll cake gently but snugly around filling, leaving parchment behind as you roll.

Foolproof New York-Style Cheesecake

SERVES 12 TO 16   **TOTAL TIME** 4 HOURS
(PLUS 8 HOURS 30 MINUTES COOLING AND CHILLING TIME)

✔ **WHY THIS RECIPE WORKS:** We set out to find the secret to New York cheesecake with the creamy, dense filling, impressive stature, and browned top that characterize this style. The texture of New York cheesecake should be plush and velvety rather than silky and light. We wanted a recipe that was guaranteed to produce a perfect cake with a firm crust every time. This style of cheesecake is baked without a water bath, since that often causes it to crack across the top. Baking the cheesecake at a low temperature ensures that it will not crack; it also means that it takes more than 12 hours from start to finish, though most of that time is hands-off. An accurate oven thermometer is essential in this recipe. Check the thermometer occasionally to make sure the oven is holding steady at 200 degrees. When cutting the cake, have a pitcher of hot tap water nearby; dipping the blade of the knife into the water and wiping it clean with a dish towel after each cut helps make neat slices.

CRUST
- 6 whole graham crackers (3 ounces), broken into pieces
- ⅓ cup packed (2⅓ ounces) dark brown sugar
- ½ cup (2½ ounces) all-purpose flour
- ¼ teaspoon salt
- 7 tablespoons unsalted butter, melted

FILLING
- 2½ pounds cream cheese, softened
- ⅛ teaspoon salt
- 1½ cups (10½ ounces) granulated sugar
- ⅓ cup sour cream
- 2 teaspoons lemon juice
- 2 teaspoons vanilla extract
- 6 large eggs plus 2 large yolks

1. FOR THE CRUST: Adjust oven racks to upper-middle and lower-middle positions and heat oven to 325 degrees. Process crackers and sugar in food processor until finely ground, about 30 seconds. Add flour and salt and pulse to combine, 2 pulses. Add 6 tablespoons melted butter and pulse until crumbs are evenly moistened, about 10 pulses. Brush bottom of 9-inch springform pan with ½ tablespoon melted butter. Using hands, press crumb mixture evenly over pan bottom. Using bottom of dry measuring cup, firmly pack crust into pan. Bake on lower-middle rack until fragrant and beginning to brown around edges, about 13 minutes. Transfer to rimmed baking sheet.

2. FOR THE FILLING: Using stand mixer fitted with paddle, beat cream cheese, salt and ¾ cup sugar at medium-low speed until combined, about 1 minute. Beat in remaining ¾ cup sugar until combined, about 1 minute. Scrape down beater and bowl thoroughly. Add sour cream, lemon juice, and vanilla and beat on low speed until combined, about 1 minute. Add egg yolks and beat at medium-low speed until thoroughly combined, about 1 minute. Scrape bowl and beater. Add whole eggs, beating until thoroughly combined, about 30 seconds after each addition. Strain filling through fine-mesh strainer into bowl using rubber spatula to help batter pass through strainer.

3. Spread ⅓ cup filling over crust, leaving ¼-inch border at edges. Return pan, on baking sheet, to lower-middle rack and bake until filling is set, 12 to 15 minutes. Remove cake from oven and reduce oven temperature to 200 degrees.

4. Brush sides of springform pan with remaining ½ tablespoon melted butter. Pour remaining filling into crust and let sit at room temperature for 10 minutes to allow air bubbles to rise to top. Gently draw tines of fork across surface of cake to pop air bubbles that have risen to surface. When oven is 200 degrees, bake cheesecake on lower-middle rack until center registers 165 degrees, 3 to 3½ hours.

5. Remove cake from oven and increase oven temperature to 500 degrees. When oven is 500 degrees, bake cheesecake on upper-middle rack until top is evenly browned, about 12 minutes.

6. Let cheesecake cool for 5 minutes, then run paring knife between cake and side of pan. Let cheesecake cool until barely warm, 2½ to 3 hours. Refrigerate until cold and firmly set, at least 6 hours or up to 4 days. To unmold cheesecake, wrap hot, damp dish towel around pan and let stand for 1 minute. Remove sides of pan. Slide thin metal spatula between crust and pan bottom to loosen, then slide cake onto serving platter. Serve.

Lemon Cheesecake

SERVES 12 TO 16   **TOTAL TIME** 2 HOURS
(PLUS 7 HOURS COOLING AND CHILLING TIME)

✔ **WHY THIS RECIPE WORKS:** The fresh flavor of citrus can take cheesecake to a refreshing new level. We aimed to develop a creamy cheesecake with a bracing lemon flavor. We found graham crackers were too overpowering for the filling's lemon flavor. Instead, we turned to biscuit-type cookies, such as animal crackers, for a mild-tasting crust that allowed the lemon flavor to shine. For maximum lemon flavor, we ground lemon zest with a portion of the sugar, a step that released its flavorful oils. Heavy cream provided richness, and vanilla rounded out the flavors. For ultimate creaminess, we baked the cake in a water bath. And finally, for an additional layer of bright lemon flavor, we topped off the cake with lemon curd. When cutting the cake, have a pitcher of hot tap water nearby; dipping the blade of the knife into the water and wiping it clean with a dish towel after each cut helps make neat slices.

CRUST

- 5 ounces Nabisco Barnum's Animals Crackers or Social Tea Biscuits
- 3 tablespoons sugar
- 5 tablespoons unsalted butter, melted

FILLING

- 1¼ cups (8¾ ounces) sugar
- 1 tablespoon grated lemon zest plus ¼ cup juice (2 lemons)
- 1½ pounds cream cheese, softened
- ¼ teaspoon salt
- ½ cup heavy cream
- 2 teaspoons vanilla extract
- 4 large eggs, room temperature

LEMON CURD

- ⅓ cup lemon juice (2 lemons)
- 2 large eggs plus 1 large yolk
- ½ cup (3½ ounces) sugar
- 2 tablespoons unsalted butter, cut into ½-inch pieces and chilled
- 1 tablespoon heavy cream
- ¼ teaspoon vanilla extract
  Pinch salt

1. FOR THE CRUST: Adjust oven rack to lower-middle position and heat oven to 325 degrees. Process cookies and sugar in food processor until finely ground, about 30 seconds. Add 4 tablespoons melted butter and pulse until crumbs are evenly moistened, about 10 pulses. Using hands, press crumb mixture evenly over bottom of 9-inch springform pan. Using bottom of measuring cup, firmly pack crust into pan. Bake crust until fragrant and golden brown, 15 to 18 minutes.

2. Transfer to wire rack, let cool, then wrap outside of pan with two 18-inch square pieces heavy-duty aluminum foil. Being careful not to disturb baked crust, brush inside of pan with melted butter. Set springform pan in large roasting pan and bring kettle of water to boil.

3. FOR THE FILLING: Process ¼ cup sugar and lemon zest in food processor until sugar is yellow and zest is broken down, about 15 seconds; transfer to small bowl and stir in remaining 1 cup sugar.

Preparing a Water Bath

1. Line bottom of large roasting pan with dish towel to insulate bottom of pan and prevent cake from sliding around.

2. To prevent water from leaking into springform cake pan, cover bottom and sides of pan with 2 pieces heavy-duty aluminum foil before placing in roasting pan.

3. Place roasting pan with springform pan on oven rack, then carefully pour boiling water into roasting pan until it reaches halfway up sides of cake pan.

4. Using stand mixer fitted with paddle, beat cream cheese, salt, and half of lemon-sugar mixture at medium-low speed until combined, about 1 minute. Beat in remaining lemon-sugar mixture until combined, about 1 minute. Scrape down beater and bowl thoroughly. Add heavy cream, lemon juice, and vanilla and beat on low speed until combined and smooth, 1 to 3 minutes. Add eggs, two at a time, beating until thoroughly combined, about 30 seconds after each addition.

5. Pour filling into prepared pan. Set roasting pan on oven rack and pour enough boiling water into roasting pan to come halfway up sides of springform pan. Bake cake until center jiggles slightly, sides just start to puff, surface is no longer shiny, and center of cake registers 150 degrees, 55 minutes to 1 hour.

6. Turn off oven and prop open oven door with potholder or wooden spoon handle; allow cake to cool in water bath in oven for 1 hour. Transfer springform pan to wire rack, discarding foil. Run paring knife between cake and side of pan, then let cake cool for 2 hours.

7. FOR THE LEMON CURD: While cheesecake bakes, heat lemon juice in small saucepan over medium heat until hot but not boiling. Whisk eggs and yolk together in medium bowl, then gradually whisk in sugar. Whisking constantly, slowly pour hot lemon juice into eggs, then return mixture to saucepan and cook over medium heat, stirring constantly with wooden spoon, until mixture is thick enough to cling to spoon and registers 170 degrees, about 3 minutes. Immediately remove pan from heat and stir in cold butter until incorporated. Stir in cream, vanilla, and salt, then pour curd through fine-mesh strainer into small bowl. Place plastic wrap directly on surface of curd and refrigerate until needed.

8. When cheesecake is cool, scrape lemon curd onto cheesecake still in springform pan. Using offset spatula, spread curd evenly over top of cheesecake. Cover tightly with plastic and refrigerate for at least 4 hours or up to 1 day. To unmold cheesecake, wrap hot, damp dish towel around pan and let stand for 1 minute. Remove sides of pan. Slide thin metal spatula between crust and pan bottom to loosen, then slide cake onto serving platter. Serve.

Flourless Chocolate Cake

SERVES 12 TO 16   **TOTAL TIME** 55 MINUTES
(PLUS 14 HOURS COOLING AND CHILLING TIME)

WHY THIS RECIPE WORKS: All flourless chocolate cake recipes share common ingredients, but you can end up with anything from a fudgy brownie to a chocolate soufflé. We wanted something dense and ultra-chocolaty, but with some textural finesse. Cake made with both bittersweet and semisweet chocolate delivered deep chocolate flavor and a smooth texture. We found that batter made with chilled rather than room-temperature eggs produced denser foam and that the resulting cake boasted a smooth, velvety texture. The gentle, moist heat of a water bath further preserved the cake's lushness. Even though the cake may not look done, pull it from the oven when it registers 140 degrees. It will continue to firm up as it cools. If you use a 9-inch springform pan instead of the preferred 8-inch, reduce the baking time to 18 to 20 minutes.

  8 **large eggs, chilled**
  1 **pound bittersweet or semisweet chocolate, chopped**
 16 **tablespoons unsalted butter, cut into ½-inch pieces**
  ¼ **cup strong brewed coffee, room temperature**
     Confectioners' sugar or unsweetened cocoa powder (optional)

1. Adjust oven rack to lower-middle position and heat oven to 325 degrees. Grease 8-inch springform pan bottom, line with parchment paper, then grease pan sides. Wrap outside of pan with two 18-inch square pieces of aluminum foil and set in large roasting pan. Bring kettle of water to boil.

We beat whole eggs to a foam and used bittersweet chocolate for the perfect taste and texture in this rich cake.

2. Using stand mixer fitted with whisk, whip eggs on medium speed until doubled in volume, about 5 minutes.

3. Meanwhile, combine chocolate, butter, and coffee in large heatproof bowl. Set bowl over saucepan filled with 1 inch of barely simmering water. Cook, stirring occasionally, until smooth and very warm (about 115 degrees). Using large rubber spatula, fold one-third of whipped eggs into chocolate mixture until few streaks of egg are visible. Fold in remaining eggs in 2 additions until mixture is totally homogeneous.

4. Scrape batter into prepared pan and smooth top. Set roasting pan on oven rack and pour enough boiling water into roasting pan to come halfway up sides of springform pan. Bake until cake has risen slightly, edges are just beginning to set, thin glazed crust (like brownie crust) has formed on surface, and cake registers 140 degrees, 22 to 25 minutes.

5. Remove pan from water bath and let cool to room temperature. Cover and refrigerate for at least 12 hours, or up to 4 days.

6. Thirty minutes before serving, run paring knife around edge of cake to loosen, then remove sides of pan. Invert cake onto sheet of parchment paper. Peel off and discard parchment baked onto cake. Turn cake right side up onto serving platter. Dust with confectioners' sugar or cocoa, if using, and serve.

Vanilla Frosting

MAKES ABOUT 4 CUPS   **TOTAL TIME** 15 MINUTES **FAST**

✔**WHY THIS RECIPE WORKS:** We use unsalted butter in our vanilla frosting and add a precisely measured amount of salt ourselves because different brands of salted butter contain varying amounts of salt. Just ¼ teaspoon salt heightens the flavors without making the frosting salty. We cut the butter into pieces and let them soften—but not too much, or the frosting will be greasy. Many recipes for vanilla frosting call for milk; we prefer heavy cream, which gives the frosting a silky quality. For fun, consider adding some color to the frosting by stirring in a few drops of food coloring; be sure to add the food coloring sparingly because a little goes a long way.

- 24 **tablespoons (3 sticks) unsalted butter, cut into chunks and softened**
- 3 **tablespoons heavy cream**
- 2½ **teaspoons vanilla extract**
- ¼ **teaspoon salt**
- 3 **cups (12 ounces) confectioners' sugar**

1. Using stand mixer fitted with paddle, beat butter, cream, vanilla, and salt together on medium-high speed until smooth, about 1 minute. Reduce speed to medium-low, slowly add confectioners' sugar, and beat until incorporated and smooth, about 4 minutes.

2. Increase mixer speed to medium-high and beat until frosting is light and fluffy, about 5 minutes. (Frosting can be refrigerated for up to 3 days; let soften at room temperature, about 2 hours, then rewhip using mixer on medium speed until smooth, 2 to 5 minutes.)

VARIATIONS
Coffee Frosting
Add 2 tablespoons instant espresso powder or instant coffee powder to mixer with butter.

Peppermint Frosting
Add 2 teaspoons peppermint extract to mixer with butter.

Orange Frosting
Add 2 teaspoons grated orange zest and 2 tablespoons juice to mixer with butter.

Almond Frosting
Add 2 teaspoons almond extract to mixer with butter.

Coconut Frosting
Add 1 tablespoon coconut extract to mixer with butter.

MAKING SMALLER OR LARGER BATCHES OF VANILLA FROSTING

INGREDIENT	3 CUPS (24 CUPCAKES OR TOP OF SHEET CAKE)	5 CUPS (3-LAYER CAKE)
Butter	2½ sticks	4 sticks
Cream	2 tablespoons	¼ cup
Vanilla Extract	2 teaspoons	1 tablespoon
Salt	⅛ teaspoon	¼ teaspoon
Confectioners' Sugar	2½ cups	4 cups

TO MAKE THE VARIATIONS: ADD ANY OF THE FOLLOWING AS DESIRED

Instant Espresso Powder or Instant Coffee Powder	1 tablespoon	3 tablespoons
Peppermint Extract	1½ teaspoons	2½ teaspoons
Orange Juice	4 teaspoons	7 teaspoons
Grated Orange Zest	1½ teaspoons	1 tablespoon
Almond Extract	1¼ teaspoons	1 tablespoon
Coconut Extract	2¼ teaspoons	1 tablespoon

Chocolate Frosting

MAKES ABOUT 4 CUPS   **TOTAL TIME** 10 MINUTES   **FAST**

✔ **WHY THIS RECIPE WORKS:** We combined a hefty amount of cocoa powder with melted chocolate to give this frosting deep chocolate flavor. A combination of confectioners' sugar and corn syrup made it smooth and glossy. To keep the frosting from separating and turning greasy, we moved it out of the stand mixer and into the food processor. The faster machine minimized any risk of overbeating, as it blended the ingredients quickly without melting the butter or incorporating too much air. The result was a thick, fluffy chocolate frosting that spread like a dream. Bittersweet, semisweet, or milk chocolate can be used in this recipe.

26 tablespoons (3¼ sticks) unsalted butter, softened
1⅓ cups (5⅓ ounces) confectioners' sugar
  1 cup (3 ounces) Dutch-processed cocoa powder
     Pinch salt
  1 cup light corn syrup
1½ teaspoons vanilla extract
 10 ounces chocolate, melted and cooled

Process butter, sugar, cocoa, and salt in food processor until smooth, about 30 seconds, scraping down bowl as needed. Add corn syrup and vanilla and process until just combined, 5 to 10 seconds. Scrape down bowl, then add chocolate and process until smooth and creamy, 10 to 15 seconds. (Frosting can be kept at room temperature for up to 3 hours or refrigerated for up to 3 days; if refrigerated, let stand at room temperature for 1 hour before using.)

MAKING SMALLER OR LARGER BATCHES OF CHOCOLATE FROSTING

INGREDIENT	3 CUPS (24 CUPCAKES OR TOP OF SHEET CAKE)	5 CUPS (3-LAYER CAKE)
Butter	2½ sticks	3¾ sticks
Confectioners' Sugar	1 cup	1½ cups
Dutch-Processed Cocoa	¾ cup	1 cup
Salt	pinch	⅛ teaspoon
Light Corn Syrup	¾ cup	1 cup
Vanilla Extract	1 teaspoon	1½ teaspoons
Chocolate	8 ounces	12 ounces

Peanut Butter Frosting

MAKES ABOUT 4 CUPS   **TOTAL TIME** 15 MINUTES   **FAST**

✔ **WHY THIS RECIPE WORKS:** Peanut butter and chocolate are an inspired combination, so we wanted a frosting that would be good on chocolate cake, cupcakes, and even brownies. This peanut butter frosting balances peanutty flavor against sweetness; it is sweet but not too sweet. The butter and heavy cream contributed to a smooth and creamy texture that wasn't greasy. We mixed the cream with the butter and peanut butter before adding the sugar in order to lighten the butter and make incorporating the sugar easier. Do not use crunchy, old-fashioned, or natural peanut butter in this recipe.

20 tablespoons (2½ sticks) unsalted butter, cut into chunks and softened
1⅓ cups creamy peanut butter
  3 tablespoons heavy cream
2½ teaspoons vanilla extract
     Pinch salt
2¼ cups (9 ounces) confectioners' sugar

1. Using stand mixer fitted with paddle, beat butter, peanut butter, cream, vanilla, and salt together on medium-high speed until smooth, about 1 minute. Reduce speed to medium-low, slowly add confectioners' sugar, and beat until incorporated and smooth, about 4 minutes.

2. Increase mixer speed to medium-high and beat until frosting is light and fluffy, about 5 minutes. (Frosting can be refrigerated for up to 3 days; let soften at room temperature, about 2 hours, then rewhip using mixer on medium speed until smooth, 2 to 5 minutes.)

MAKING SMALLER OR LARGER BATCHES OF PEANUT BUTTER FROSTING

INGREDIENT	3 CUPS (24 CUPCAKES OR TOP OF SHEET CAKE)	5 CUPS (3-LAYER CAKE)
Butter	2 sticks	3 sticks
Peanut Butter	1 cup	1⅔ cups
Heavy Cream	2 tablespoons	4 tablespoons
Vanilla Extract	2 teaspoons	1 tablespoon
Salt	pinch	⅛ teaspoon
Confectioners' Sugar	1½ cups	3 cups

Cream Cheese Frosting

MAKES ABOUT 4 CUPS   **TOTAL TIME** 15 MINUTES **FAST**

☑ **WHY THIS RECIPE WORKS:** Cream cheese frosting is the perfect partner for carrot cake, and we enriched our version with sour cream for extra tang, and vanilla for depth of flavor. We found that first mixing the ingredients together on a lower speed, until they were well combined, and then turning up the speed gave us more control of the texture, ultimately producing a pleasing fluffy frosting. Do not use low-fat or nonfat cream cheese or the frosting will turn out too soupy to work with. This frosting has a softer, looser texture than other frostings; it won't work with a three-layer cake. If the frosting becomes too soft to work with, let it chill in the refrigerator until firm.

- 1 pound cream cheese, softened
- 10 tablespoons unsalted butter, cut into chunks and softened
- 2 tablespoons sour cream
- 1½ teaspoons vanilla extract
- ¼ teaspoon salt
- 2 cups (8 ounces) confectioners' sugar

1. Using stand mixer fitted with paddle, beat cream cheese, butter, sour cream, vanilla, and salt together on medium-high speed until smooth, about 2 minutes. Reduce speed to medium-low, slowly add confectioners' sugar, and beat until incorporated and smooth, about 4 minutes.

2. Increase mixer speed to medium-high and beat until frosting is light and fluffy, about 4 minutes. (Frosting can be refrigerated for up to 3 days; let soften at room temperature, about 1 hour, then rewhip using mixer on medium speed until smooth, about 2 minutes.)

**MAKING A SMALLER BATCH
OF CREAM CHEESE FROSTING**

INGREDIENT	3 CUPS (24 CUPCAKES OR TOP OF SHEET CAKE)
Cream Cheese	12 ounces
Butter	6 tablespoons
Sour Cream	4 teaspoons
Vanilla Extract	1 teaspoon
Salt	¼ teaspoon
Confectioners' Sugar	1¾ cups

Seven-Minute Frosting

MAKES ABOUT 5 CUPS   **TOTAL TIME** 15 MINUTES **FAST**

☑ **WHY THIS RECIPE WORKS:** Some quick frostings are too sweet or too gritty—but not this one. Our recipe produces a thick, glossy frosting made from egg whites and sugar that are cooked together. Taking its name from the time it takes to beat the frosting over simmering water, our easy recipe is the perfect finishing touch to any cake or cupcake. This frosting should be spread on very thick, then swept into big, billowy swirls using the back of a spoon.

- 1½ cups (10½ ounces) sugar
- 2 large egg whites
- 6 tablespoons cold water
- 1½ tablespoons light corn syrup
- ¼ teaspoon cream of tartar
  Pinch salt
- 1 teaspoon vanilla extract

1. Combine sugar, egg whites, water, corn syrup, cream of tartar, and salt in bowl of stand mixer. Set bowl over saucepan filled with 1 inch of barely simmering water (do not let bottom of bowl touch water). Cook, whisking constantly, until mixture registers 160 degrees, 5 to 10 minutes.

2. Remove bowl from heat. Using stand mixer fitted with whisk, whip warm egg mixture on medium speed until it forms soft peaks, about 5 minutes. Add vanilla, increase speed to medium-high, and continue to whip until mixture has cooled to room temperature and forms stiff, glossy peaks, 5 to 7 minutes. Use immediately.

Vanilla Buttercream

MAKES 4 CUPS   **TOTAL TIME** 25 MINUTES **FAST**

☑ **WHY THIS RECIPE WORKS:** Classic French recipes rely on sugar alone, but we discovered substituting corn syrup for some of the sugar gave our buttercream a fluid but stable consistency and also made it easy to melt the sugar. Some recipes also call for whole eggs, but we preferred the richer texture from using only yolks. It was key to heat the sugar syrup at the same time that the yolks were whipping so that the hot syrup was ready once the yolks were done. Pouring hot syrup into the egg yolks was essential to raise their temperature to a safe level; make sure to pour the syrup into the eggs slowly to avoid scrambling the eggs. We whipped the yolk-syrup mixture to both aerate it and cool it off before adding softened butter; we didn't want the butter to melt into pools of grease. Because you need to pour the hot sugar syrup into the bowl with the eggs with the mixer on, we find this operation is much, much simpler in a stand mixer. If you don't have a stand mixer, you will need to stabilize the mixing bowl with a dish towel so that you can operate the handheld mixer with one hand while pouring in the hot syrup with the other. For colored frosting, stir in drops of food coloring at the end; this buttercream has a natural pale yellow color, but if stored in the refrigerator the buttercream will become yellower over time.

6	large egg yolks
¾	cup (5¼ ounces) sugar
½	cup light corn syrup
2½	teaspoons vanilla extract
¼	teaspoon salt
1	pound (4 sticks) unsalted butter, each stick cut into quarters and softened

1. Using stand mixer fitted with whisk, whip egg yolks on medium speed until slightly thickened and pale yellow, 4 to 6 minutes.

2. Meanwhile, bring sugar and corn syrup to boil in small saucepan over medium heat, stirring occasionally to dissolve sugar, about 3 minutes.

3. Without letting hot sugar mixture cool off, turn mixer to low and slowly pour hot sugar syrup into whipped egg yolks without hitting side of bowl or whisk. Increase speed to medium-high and whip until mixture is light and fluffy and bowl is no longer warm, 5 to 10 minutes.

4. Reduce speed to medium-low and add vanilla and salt. Gradually add butter, 1 piece at a time, and whip until completely incorporated, about 2 minutes. Increase speed to medium-high and whip until buttercream is smooth and silky, about 2 minutes. If mixture looks curdled, wrap hot, wet dish towel around bowl and continue to whip until smooth, 1 to 2 minutes. (Buttercream can be refrigerated for up to 3 days; let soften at room temperature, about 2 hours, then rewhip using mixer on medium speed until smooth, about 2 minutes.)

VARIATIONS
Chocolate Buttercream
After buttercream has become smooth and silky in step 4, add 8 ounces melted and cooled bittersweet or semisweet chocolate and continue to mix on medium-low speed until completely incorporated, about 1 minute.

Almond Buttercream
Add 2 teaspoons almond extract with vanilla.
Coconut Buttercream
Add 1 tablespoon coconut extract with vanilla.

MAKING SMALLER OR LARGER BATCHES OF VANILLA BUTTERCREAM

INGREDIENT	2 CUPS (20 SANDWICH COOKIES)	3 CUPS (24 CUPCAKES OR TOP OF SHEET CAKE)	5 CUPS (3-LAYER CAKE)
Egg Yolks	3 yolks	4 yolks	8 yolks
Sugar	½ cup	⅔ cup	1 cup
Light Corn Syrup	⅓ cup	⅓ cup	¾ cup
Vanilla Extract	1½ teaspoons	2 teaspoons	1 tablespoon
Salt	pinch	⅛ teaspoon	¼ teaspoon
Butter	2½ sticks	3½ sticks	5 sticks

TO MAKE THE VARIATIONS: ADD ANY OF THE FOLLOWING AS DESIRED

Bittersweet or Semisweet Chocolate melted and cooled	4 ounces	6 ounces	10 ounces
Almond Extract	¾ teaspoon	1¼ teaspoons	1 tablespoon
Coconut Extract	1¼ teaspoons	2¼ teaspoons	1 tablespoon

Buttercream takes a little more time to make than frosting, but it has a far smoother and silkier texture because it's made with melted sugar and egg yolks. In order to make buttercream, you need to pour a hot sugar syrup into a bowl of whipped egg yolks while the mixer is still running. This is far simpler when you use a stand mixer. If you don't have a stand mixer, you will need to stabilize the mixing bowl with a dish towel so that you can operate the handheld mixer with one hand while pouring in the hot syrup with the other.

1. WHIP THE EGG YOLKS: Using a stand mixer fitted with a whisk, whip the egg yolks on medium speed until they're slightly thickened and pale yellow, 4 to 6 minutes.

WHY? You want to make sure that the egg yolks are thick and pale before you pour the sugar mixture into the mixing bowl or else the mixture won't come together properly. While some recipes call for whole eggs, we prefer the richer texture achieved by using just the yolks.

2. COOK THE SUGAR AND CORN SYRUP: Bring the sugar and corn syrup to a boil in a small saucepan over medium heat, stirring occasionally to dissolve the sugar, about 3 minutes.

WHY? It's important to heat the sugar syrup at the same time the yolks are whipping so that the hot syrup will be ready once the yolks are done. Don't let the syrup cool off. The corn syrup gives the finished buttercream a fluid but stable consistency. The corn syrup also makes it easy to melt the sugar.

3. SLOWLY ADD THE HOT SYRUP: With the mixer turned to low speed, pour the hot sugar syrup into the whipped egg yolks without hitting the sides of the bowl or the whisk.

WHY? Pouring the hot syrup into the egg yolks gently raises their temperature to a safe level. If you dump the syrup into the bowl all at once you can scramble the eggs. Aim to pour the syrup into the bowl so that it avoids both the whisk and the sides of the bowl (where it can seize up).

4. WHIP THE MIXTURE UNTIL COOL: Increase the mixer speed to medium-high and whip the mixture until it's light and fluffy and the bowl is no longer warm, 5 to 10 minutes.

WHY? Whipping aerates the yolk mixture and makes it easier to add the butter.

5. BEAT IN THE SOFTENED BUTTER: Reduce the mixer speed to medium-low and add the vanilla and salt. Gradually add the softened butter until it's completely incorporated.

WHY? Cold butter will clump up and you will have to overbeat the frosting to smooth it back out. Softened butter incorporates quickly and smoothly.

6. WHIP THE FROSTING UNTIL SILKY: Increase the mixer speed to medium-high and whip the buttercream until it's smooth and silky.

WHY? Stop the mixer once the texture is right. If the finished frosting looks curdled, the butter was probably too cold. Wrap a hot wet towel around the mixing bowl and continue to whip until smooth.

Pies and Tarts

■ SIGNIFIES A **FAST** RECIPE (45 MINUTES OR LESS)

Foolproof Single-Crust Pie Dough

MAKES ENOUGH FOR ONE 9-INCH PIE   **TOTAL TIME** 1 HOUR
(PLUS 1½ HOURS CHILLING TIME)

✔ **WHY THIS RECIPE WORKS:** Since water bonds with flour to form gluten, too much water makes a crust tough. But rolling out dry dough is difficult. For a pie dough recipe that baked up tender and flaky and rolled out easily every time, we found a magic ingredient: vodka. Using vodka, which is just 60 percent water, gave us an easy-to-roll crust recipe with less gluten and no alcohol flavor, since the alcohol vaporizes in the oven. Vodka is essential to the tender texture of this crust and imparts no flavor—do not substitute water. This dough is moister than most standard pie doughs and will require lots of flour to roll out (up to ¼ cup). A food processor is essential to making this dough—we don't recommend making it by hand. For more information on making a single-crust pie shell, see page 701.

1¼ **cups (6¼ ounces) all-purpose flour**
1 **tablespoon sugar**
½ **teaspoon salt**
6 **tablespoons unsalted butter, cut into
   ¼-inch pieces and chilled**
4 **tablespoons vegetable shortening, cut into
   2 pieces and chilled**
2 **tablespoons vodka, chilled**
2 **tablespoons ice water**

1. Process ¾ cup flour, sugar, and salt in food processor until combined, about 5 seconds. Scatter butter and shortening pieces over top and process until incorporated and mixture begins to form uneven clumps with no remaining floury bits, about 10 seconds.

2. Scrape down sides of bowl and redistribute dough evenly around processor blade. Sprinkle remaining ½ cup flour over dough and pulse until mixture has broken up into pieces and is evenly distributed around bowl, 4 to 6 pulses.

3. Transfer mixture to large bowl. Sprinkle vodka and ice water over mixture. Stir and press dough together, using stiff rubber spatula, until dough sticks together.

4. Turn dough onto sheet of plastic wrap and flatten into 4-inch disk. Wrap tightly and refrigerate for 1 hour. Before rolling dough out, let it sit on counter to soften slightly, about 10 minutes. (Dough can be refrigerated for up to 2 days or frozen for up to 1 month. If frozen, let dough thaw completely on counter before rolling it out.)

5. Lay dough on generously floured counter and roll dough outward from its center into 12-inch circle. Loosely roll dough around rolling pin and gently unroll it over 9-inch pie plate. Lift dough and gently press it into pie plate, letting excess hang over plate's edge.

6. Trim all but ½ inch of dough overhanging edge of pie plate. Tuck dough underneath itself to form tidy, even edge that sits on lip of pie plate. Crimp dough evenly around edge of pie using fingers. Wrap dough-lined pie plate loosely in plastic and freeze until dough is firm, about 30 minutes.

7. Adjust oven rack to middle position and heat oven to 375 degrees. Line chilled pie crust with double layer of aluminum foil, covering edges to prevent burning, and fill with pie weights or pennies.

8A. FOR A PARTIALLY BAKED CRUST: Bake until pie dough looks dry and is pale in color, 25 to 30 minutes. Transfer pie plate to wire rack and remove weights and foil. Following particular pie recipe, use crust while it is still warm or let it cool completely.

8B. FOR A FULLY BAKED CRUST: Bake until pie dough looks dry and is pale in color, 25 to 30 minutes. Remove weights and foil and continue to bake crust until deep golden brown, 10 to 12 minutes. Transfer pie plate to wire rack. Following particular pie recipe, use crust while it is still warm or let it cool completely.

VARIATION
Foolproof Double-Crust Pie Dough

MAKES ENOUGH FOR ONE 9-INCH PIE
TOTAL TIME 40 MINUTES (PLUS 1½ HOURS CHILLING TIME)

Vodka is essential to the tender texture of this crust and imparts no flavor—do not substitute water. This dough is moister than most standard pie doughs and will require lots of flour to roll out (up to ¼ cup). A food processor is essential to making this dough—we don't recommend making it by hand.

2½ **cups (12½ ounces) all-purpose flour**
2 **tablespoons sugar**
1 **teaspoon salt**
12 **tablespoons unsalted butter, cut into ¼-inch pieces
   and chilled**
8 **tablespoons vegetable shortening, cut into 4 pieces
   and chilled**
¼ **cup vodka, chilled**
¼ **cup ice water**

1. Process 1½ cups flour, sugar, and salt in food processor until combined, about 5 seconds. Scatter butter and shortening pieces over top and process until incorporated and mixture begins to form uneven clumps with no remaining floury bits, about 15 seconds.

Pie dough seems easy enough to prepare. Yet it can all go wrong so easily, resulting in tough dough that is hard to roll out. This foolproof version uses a few tricks that ensure success, including replacing some of the water with vodka. The result is a dough that has enough moisture to roll out easily but still bakes up flaky and tender.

1. CUT AND CHILL THE BUTTER AND SHORTENING: Cut the butter and shortening into pieces and chill in the freezer.
WHY? Shortening makes the crust tender and flaky, while butter provides flavor. Cutting them into pieces helps to minimize the processing time, and chilling them allows them to be cut into the dough without softening.

2. CHILL 2 LIQUIDS: Fill a liquid measuring cup with ice and cold water. Chill ¼ cup of vodka.
WHY? While gluten forms readily in water, it doesn't form in ethanol. Vodka is 60 percent water and 40 percent ethanol. We use equal parts water and vodka for a tender, easy-to-roll-out dough. The ethanol vaporizes in the oven during baking.

3. PROCESS SOME OF THE FLOUR WITH THE CHILLED FAT: Scatter butter and shortening over a portion of the flour (combined with the sugar and salt in the food processor). Process until the mixture forms uneven clumps with no floury bits.
WHY? As the flour and fat are processed, the fat coats the flour, which will prevent it from absorbing liquid and forming gluten.

4. PULSE IN THE REMAINING FLOUR: Add the remaining flour and pulse until evenly distributed.
WHY? Adding flour in two steps allows better control over how much liquid is needed to make a malleable dough. This addition of flour does not get coated with fat, so it will absorb the liquid, form gluten, and help the dough hold together.

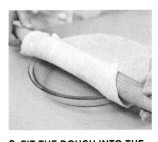

5. ADD THE CHILLED VODKA AND ICE WATER BY HAND: Transfer the mixture to a large bowl and sprinkle with the chilled vodka and ¼ cup ice water. Stir and press the dough together, using a stiff rubber spatula, until the dough sticks together.
WHY? It's easier to incorporate the liquid by hand. If this step is done in a food processor, there's a tendency to overwork the dough.

6. CHILL THE DOUGH: Turn the dough onto a sheet of plastic wrap and flatten into a 4-inch disk. (If making a double crust, divide the dough into 2 even pieces). Wrap the dough tightly with plastic and refrigerate for at least 1 hour.
WHY? Since cold fat is essential to creating a flaky texture, the dough must be chilled before rolling. Also, the gluten in the flour relaxes a bit as the dough chills, ensuring that the dough isn't tough.

7. ROLL OUT THE DOUGH WITH LOTS OF FLOUR: Let the dough soften before rolling it out. Roll out the dough on a well-floured counter, and toss additional flour underneath the dough to keep it from sticking.
WHY? Chilled dough is quite stiff and hard to roll out. Letting it warm up means less work and less risk of overworking the dough. Keeping the counter well floured enables you to roll out the dough without it sticking or tearing.

8. FIT THE DOUGH INTO THE PIE PLATE: Loosely roll the dough around the rolling pin and gently unroll it over the pie plate. Then lift the dough and gently press it into the pie plate, letting the excess hang over the edge.
WHY? You want to gently fit the dough into the pie plate to ensure it doesn't rip or tear, and you want to avoid any gaps between the plate and the dough.

2. Scrape down sides of bowl and redistribute dough evenly around processor blade. Sprinkle remaining 1 cup flour over dough and pulse until mixture has broken up into pieces and is evenly distributed around bowl, 4 to 6 pulses.

3. Transfer mixture to large bowl. Sprinkle vodka and ice water over mixture. Stir and press dough together, using stiff rubber spatula, until dough sticks together.

4. Divide dough into 2 even pieces. Turn each piece of dough onto sheet of plastic wrap and flatten each into 4-inch disk. Wrap each piece tightly and refrigerate for 1 hour. Before rolling dough out, let it sit on counter to soften slightly, about 10 minutes. (Dough can be refrigerated for up to 2 days or frozen for up to 1 month. If frozen, let dough thaw completely on counter before rolling it out.)

5. FOR THE BOTTOM CRUST: Lay 1 piece of dough on generously floured counter and roll dough outward from its center into 12-inch circle. Loosely roll dough around rolling pin and gently unroll it over 9-inch pie plate. Lift dough and gently press it into pie plate, letting excess hang over plate's edge. Wrap loosely in plastic and refrigerate until dough is firm, about 30 minutes.

6A. FOR A TRADITIONAL TOP CRUST: Roll second piece of dough into 12-inch circle on generously floured counter, transfer to parchment paper–lined baking sheet, cover with plastic, and refrigerate for 30 minutes.

6B. FOR A LATTICE TOP CRUST: Roll second piece of dough into 13½ by 10½-inch rectangle on generously floured counter, then transfer to parchment paper–lined baking sheet. Trim dough to 13 by 10-inch rectangle and slice lengthwise into eight 13-inch-long strips. Separate strips slightly, cover with plastic, and freeze until very firm, about 30 minutes.

All-Butter Single-Crust Pie Dough

MAKES ENOUGH FOR ONE 9-INCH PIE **TOTAL TIME** 1 HOUR
(PLUS 1 HOUR 45 MINUTES CHILLING TIME)

✔ **WHY THIS RECIPE WORKS:** All-butter pie doughs possess great flavor, but they often fail to be flaky and are notoriously difficult to work with. We wanted an all-butter dough that was easier to mix, handle, and roll, with all the tenderness and flavor that "all-butter" promises. For easier handling, we tried reducing the amount of butter, but this resulted in bland flavor and dry texture. Instead, we experimented with other forms of fat, including heavy cream, cream cheese, and sour cream. In the end, we found that sour cream not only added flavor to the crust but, because acid reduces gluten development, it also helped keep the dough tender and flaky. To distribute the sour cream evenly, mix it first with the water. Freezing the butter is

crucial to the flaky texture of this crust—do not skip this step. If preparing the dough in a very warm kitchen, refrigerate all of the ingredients (including the flour) before making the dough. For more information on making a single-crust pie shell, see page 701.

3 tablespoons ice water, plus extra as needed
4 teaspoons sour cream
1¼ cups (6¼ ounces) all-purpose flour
1½ teaspoons sugar
½ teaspoon salt
8 tablespoons unsalted butter, cut into ¼-inch pieces and frozen for 10 to 15 minutes

1. Whisk ice water and sour cream together in bowl. Process flour, sugar, and salt in food processor until combined, about 3 seconds. Scatter frozen butter over top and pulse mixture until butter is size of large peas, about 10 pulses.

2. Pour half of sour cream mixture over flour mixture and pulse until incorporated, about 3 pulses. Repeat with remaining sour cream mixture. Pinch dough with your fingers; if dough feels dry and does not hold together, sprinkle 1 to 2 tablespoons more ice water over mixture and pulse until dough forms large clumps and no dry flour remains, 3 to 5 pulses.

3. Turn dough onto sheet of plastic wrap and flatten into 4-inch disk. Wrap tightly and refrigerate for 1 hour. Before rolling dough out, let it sit on counter to soften slightly, about 10 minutes. (Dough can be refrigerated for up to 2 days or frozen for up to 1 month. If frozen, let dough thaw completely on counter before rolling it out.)

4. Roll dough between 2 large sheets parchment paper to 12-inch circle. (If dough is soft and/or sticky, refrigerate until firm.) Remove parchment on top of dough round and flip into 9-inch pie plate; peel off second layer parchment. Lift dough and gently press it into pie plate, letting excess hang over plate's edge. Cover loosely with plastic and refrigerate until firm, about 30 minutes.

5. Trim all but ½ inch of dough overhanging edge of pie plate. Tuck dough underneath itself to form tidy, even edge that sits on lip of pie plate. Crimp dough evenly around edge of pie using fingers. Wrap dough-lined pie plate loosely in plastic and refrigerate until firm, about 15 minutes.

6. Adjust oven rack to middle position and heat oven to 400 degrees. Line chilled pie crust with double layer of aluminum foil, covering edges to prevent burning, and fill with pie weights or pennies.

7A. FOR A PARTIALLY BAKED CRUST: Bake until pie dough looks dry and is pale in color, 25 to 30 minutes. Transfer pie plate to wire rack and remove weights and foil. Following particular pie recipe, use crust while it is still warm or let it cool completely.

7B. FOR A FULLY BAKED CRUST: Bake until pie dough looks dry and is pale in color, 25 to 30 minutes. Remove weights and foil and continue to bake crust until deep golden brown, 5 to 10 minutes. Transfer pie plate to wire rack. Following particular pie recipe, use crust while it is still warm or let it cool completely.

VARIATION
All-Butter Double-Crust Pie Dough
MAKES ENOUGH FOR ONE 9-INCH PIE
TOTAL TIME 40 MINUTES (PLUS 2 HOURS CHILLING TIME)

Freezing the butter for 10 to 15 minutes is crucial to the flaky texture of this crust—do not skip this step. If preparing the dough in a very warm kitchen, refrigerate all of the ingredients (including the flour) before making the dough.

⅓ cup ice water, plus extra as needed
3 tablespoons sour cream
2½ cups (12½ ounces) all-purpose flour
1 tablespoon sugar
1 teaspoon salt
16 tablespoons unsalted butter, cut into ¼-inch pieces and frozen for 10 to 15 minutes

1. Whisk ice water and sour cream together in bowl. Process flour, sugar, and salt in food processor until combined, about 5 seconds. Scatter frozen butter over top and pulse mixture until butter is size of large peas, about 10 pulses.

2. Pour half of sour cream mixture over flour mixture and pulse until incorporated, about 3 pulses. Repeat with remaining sour cream mixture. Pinch dough with your fingers; if dough feels dry and does not hold together, sprinkle 1 to 2 tablespoons more ice water over mixture and pulse until dough forms large clumps and no dry flour remains, 3 to 5 pulses.

3. Divide dough into 2 even pieces. Turn each piece of dough onto sheet of plastic wrap and flatten each into 4-inch disk. Wrap each piece tightly and refrigerate for 1 hour. Before rolling dough out, let it sit on counter to soften slightly, about 10 minutes. (Dough can be refrigerated for up to 2 days or frozen for up to 1 month. If frozen, let dough thaw completely on counter before rolling it out.)

4. FOR THE BOTTOM CRUST: Roll 1 piece of dough between 2 large sheets parchment paper to 12-inch circle. (If dough is soft and/or sticky, refrigerate until firm.) Remove parchment on top of dough round and flip into 9-inch pie plate; peel off second layer parchment. Lift dough and gently press it into pie plate, letting excess hang over plate's edge. Cover loosely with plastic and refrigerate until firm, about 30 minutes.

5A. FOR A TRADITIONAL TOP CRUST: Roll second piece of dough between 2 large sheets parchment paper to 12-inch circle. Slide dough, still between parchment sheets, onto rimmed baking sheet and refrigerate for 30 minutes.

5B. FOR A LATTICE TOP CRUST: Roll second piece of dough between 2 large sheets parchment paper to 13½ by 10½-inch rectangle. Slide dough, still between parchment sheets, onto rimmed baking sheet. Remove parchment on top of dough. Trim dough to 13 by 10-inch rectangle and slice lengthwise into eight 13-inch-long strips. Separate strips slightly, cover with plastic, and freeze until very firm, about 30 minutes.

Making a Single-Crust Pie Shell

1. TRIM AND FOLD EDGE OF DOUGH: Trim all but ½ inch of dough overhanging edge of pie plate. Tuck dough underneath itself to form tidy, even edge that sits on lip of pie plate.

2. CRIMP EDGE OF CRUST: Use index finger of one hand and thumb and index finger of other hand to create fluted ridges perpendicular to edge of pie plate.

3. CHILL CRUST: Wrap dough-lined pie plate loosely in plastic and refrigerate or freeze until firm, 15 or 30 minutes depending on the dough recipe used.

4. FILL WITH PIE WEIGHTS BEFORE BAKING: Before baking crust, line chilled pie crust with double layer of aluminum foil, covering edges to prevent burning, and fill with pie weights or pennies.

Graham Cracker Crust

MAKES ENOUGH FOR ONE 9-INCH PIE

TOTAL TIME 30 MINUTES `FAST`

✅ **WHY THIS RECIPE WORKS:** Saving time is always a good idea—just as long as you're not sacrificing quality. But while store-bought graham cracker pie crusts are tempting (all you have to do is fill, chill, then serve), they taste stale and bland. We wanted a fresh-tasting homemade crust that wasn't too sweet and that had a crisp texture. Turns out, a classic graham cracker crust couldn't be easier to make: Combine crushed crumbs with sugar and a little melted butter to bind them, then use a measuring cup to pack the crumbs into the pie plate. And producing a perfect graham cracker crust has a lot to do with the type of graham crackers used. After experimenting with the three leading brands, we discovered subtle but distinct differences among them and found that these differences carried over into crumb crusts made with each kind of cracker. In the end, we preferred Keebler Grahams Crackers Original in our crust. We don't recommend using store-bought graham cracker crumbs here, as they can often be stale.

8 whole graham crackers, broken into 1-inch pieces
3 tablespoons sugar
5 tablespoons unsalted butter, melted and cooled

1. Adjust oven rack to middle position and heat oven to 325 degrees. Process graham cracker pieces and sugar in food processor to fine, even crumbs, about 30 seconds. Sprinkle melted butter over crumbs and pulse to incorporate, about 5 pulses.

2. Sprinkle mixture into 9-inch pie plate. Using bottom of dry measuring cup, press crumbs into even layer on bottom and sides of pie plate. Bake until crust is fragrant and beginning to brown, 12 to 18 minutes; transfer to wire rack. Following particular pie recipe, use crust while it is still warm or let it cool completely.

Pressing Crumbs into a Pie Shell

Sprinkle crumb mixture into 9-inch pie plate. Using bottom of dry measuring cup, press crumbs into even layer on bottom and sides of pie plate.

Chocolate Cookie Crust

MAKES ENOUGH FOR ONE 9-INCH PIE

TOTAL TIME 30 MINUTES `FAST`

✅ **WHY THIS RECIPE WORKS:** For pies like Grasshopper Pie (page 722) and Snickers Icebox Pie (page 722), it's nice to have an alternative for the usual graham cracker pie crust. Looking for just the right source for making these crumbs, we found the answer right in the cookie aisle: Oreo cookies, the childhood favorite, offered just the right balance of dark, rich chocolate crumbs with a texture, once processed, that was neither too dry nor too moist. Other brands of chocolate sandwich cookies may be substituted, but avoid "double-filled" cookies because the proportion of cookie to filling won't be correct.

16 Oreo cookies, broken into rough pieces
4 tablespoons unsalted butter, melted and cooled

1. Adjust oven rack to middle position and heat oven to 325 degrees. Pulse cookies in food processor until coarsely ground, about 15 pulses, then process to fine, even crumbs, about 15 seconds. Sprinkle melted butter over crumbs and pulse to incorporate.

2. Sprinkle mixture into 9-inch pie plate. Using bottom of dry measuring cup, press crumbs into even layer on bottom and sides of pie plate. Bake until crust is fragrant and looks set, 13 to 18 minutes; transfer to wire rack. Following particular pie recipe, use crust while it is still warm or let it cool completely.

VARIATIONS

Mint Chocolate Cookie Crust

Substitute 16 Cool Mint Creme Oreo cookies for Oreo cookies.

Nutter Butter Cookie Crust

Substitute 16 Nutter Butter cookies for Oreo cookies.

Free-Form Tart Dough

MAKES ENOUGH FOR ONE 9-INCH TART

TOTAL TIME 25 MINUTES (PLUS 1 HOUR CHILLING TIME)

✅ **WHY THIS RECIPE WORKS:** A free-form tart—a single layer of buttery pie dough folded up around fresh fruit—is a simpler take on pie. But without the support of a pie plate, tender crusts are prone to leaking juice, and this can result in a soggy bottom. For our crust, we used a high proportion of butter to flour, which provided the most buttery flavor and tender texture without compromising the structure. We then turned to the French *fraisage* method to make the pastry: Chunks of butter are pressed into long, thin sheets that create lots of flaky layers when the dough is baked.

  1½ **cups (7½ ounces) all-purpose flour**
  ½ **teaspoon salt**
  10 **tablespoons unsalted butter, cut into ½-inch pieces and chilled**
  4–6 **tablespoons ice water**

1. Process flour and salt in food processor until combined, about 5 seconds. Scatter butter pieces over top and pulse until mixture resembles coarse sand and butter pieces are about size of small peas, about 10 pulses. Continue to pulse, adding water 1 tablespoon at a time, until dough begins to form small curds that hold together when pinched with fingers, about 10 pulses.

2. Turn mixture onto lightly floured counter and gather into rectangular-shaped pile. Starting at farthest end, use heel of hand to smear small amount of dough against counter. Continue to smear dough until all crumbs have been worked. Gather smeared crumbs together in another rectangular-shaped pile and repeat process.

3. Press dough into 6-inch disk, wrap tightly in plastic wrap, and refrigerate for 1 hour. Before rolling dough out, let it sit on counter to soften slightly, about 10 minutes. (Dough can be refrigerated for up to 2 days or frozen for up to 1 month. If frozen, let dough thaw completely on counter before rolling it out.)

Making Free-Form Tart Dough

1. Turn butter mixture onto lightly floured counter and gather into rectangular-shaped pile.

2. Starting at farthest end, use heel of hand to smear small amount of dough against counter. Continue to smear dough until all crumbs have been worked.

Classic Tart Dough

MAKES ENOUGH FOR ONE 9-INCH TART
TOTAL TIME 1 HOUR (PLUS 2 HOURS CHILLING TIME)

✓ **WHY THIS RECIPE WORKS:** While regular pie crust is tender and flaky, classic tart crust should be fine textured, buttery rich, crisp, and crumbly—it is often described as being shortbreadlike. We set out to achieve the perfect tart dough, one that we could use in a number of tart recipes. We found that using a whole stick of butter made tart dough that tasted great and was easy to handle, yet still had a delicate crumb. Instead of using the hard-to-find superfine sugar and pastry flour that many other recipes call for, we used confectioners' sugar and all-purpose flour to achieve a crisp texture. Rolling the dough and fitting it into the tart pan was easy, and we had ample dough to patch any holes.

  1 **large egg yolk**
  1 **tablespoon heavy cream**
  ½ **teaspoon vanilla extract**
  1¼ **cups (6¼ ounces) all-purpose flour**
  ⅔ **cup (2⅔ ounces) confectioners' sugar**
  ¼ **teaspoon salt**
  8 **tablespoons unsalted butter, cut into ¼-inch pieces and chilled**

1. Whisk egg yolk, cream, and vanilla together in bowl. Process flour, sugar, and salt together in food processor until combined, about 5 seconds. Scatter butter pieces over top and pulse until mixture resembles coarse cornmeal, about 15 pulses. With machine running, add egg yolk mixture and continue to process until dough just comes together around processor blade, about 12 seconds.

2. Turn dough onto sheet of plastic wrap and flatten into 6-inch disk. Wrap tightly and refrigerate for 1 hour. Before rolling dough out, let it sit on counter to soften slightly, about 10 minutes. (Dough can be refrigerated for up to 2 days or frozen for up to 1 month. If frozen, let dough thaw completely on counter before rolling it out.)

3. Roll dough into 11-inch circle on lightly floured counter. (If dough is soft and/or sticky, slide onto baking sheet and refrigerate until firm.) Place dough round on baking sheet, cover with plastic, and refrigerate for 30 minutes.

4. Loosely roll dough around rolling pin and gently unroll it onto 9-inch tart pan with removable bottom, letting excess dough hang over edge. Lift dough and gently press it into corners and fluted sides of pan. Run rolling pin over top of pan to remove any excess dough. Wrap loosely in plastic, place on large plate, and freeze until dough is fully chilled and firm, about 30 minutes. (Dough-lined tart pan can be frozen for up to 1 month.)

5. Adjust oven rack to middle position and heat oven to 375 degrees. Set dough-lined tart pan on rimmed baking sheet, line with double layer of aluminum foil, and fill with pie weights or pennies.

6A. FOR A PARTIALLY BAKED SHELL: Bake until tart shell is golden and set, about 30 minutes, rotating baking sheet halfway through baking. Transfer tart shell with baking sheet to wire rack and carefully remove weights and foil. Following particular tart recipe, use crust while it is still warm or let it cool completely.

Making a Tart Shell

1. GENLTY CENTER DOUGH OVER TART PAN: Loosely roll dough around rolling pin and gently unroll it onto 9-inch tart pan with removable bottom, letting excess dough hang over edge.

2. LIFT AND PRESS DOUGH INTO PAN: Lift dough and gently press it into corners and fluted sides of pan.

3. MAKE CLEAN EDGES USING ROLLING PIN: Run rolling pin over top of pan to remove any excess dough.

4. FILL TART WITH PIE WEIGHTS BEFORE BAKING: Before baking, set dough-lined tart pan on rimmed baking sheet, line with double layer of aluminum foil, and fill with pie weights or pennies.

6B. FOR A FULLY BAKED SHELL: Bake until tart shell is golden and set, about 30 minutes, rotating baking sheet halfway through baking. Carefully remove weights and foil and continue to bake tart shell until it is fully baked and golden brown, 5 to 10 minutes. Transfer tart shell with baking sheet to wire rack. Following particular tart recipe, use crust while it is still warm or let it cool completely.

Ultimate Blueberry Pie

SERVES 8   **TOTAL TIME** 1 HOUR 45 MINUTES (PLUS 4 HOURS COOLING TIME)

✔ **WHY THIS RECIPE WORKS:** If the filling in blueberry pie doesn't gel, a wedge can collapse into a soupy puddle topped by a sodden crust. But use too much thickener, and the filling can be so dense that cutting into it is a challenge. We wanted a pie that had a firm, glistening filling full of fresh, bright flavor and still-plump berries. To thicken the pie, we favored tapioca, which allowed the fresh yet subtle blueberry flavor to shine through. Too much of it, though, and we had a congealed mess. Cooking and reducing half of the berries helped us cut down on the tapioca required, but not enough. A second inspiration came when we remembered that apples are high in pectin, a type of carbohydrate that acts as a thickener when cooked. Along with a modest 2 tablespoons of tapioca, a peeled and shredded Granny Smith apple thickened the filling to a soft, even consistency that was neither gelatinous nor slippery. Baking the pie on a baking sheet on the bottom oven rack produced a crisp, golden bottom crust. To vent the steam from the berries, we found a faster, easier alternative to a lattice top: a biscuit cutter, which we used to cut out circles in the top crust. This recipe was developed using fresh blueberries, but unthawed frozen blueberries will work as well. In step 1, cook half the frozen berries over medium-high heat, without mashing, for 12 to 15 minutes, until reduced to 1¼ cups. Use a coarse grater to shred the apple.

Making the Top Crust of a Blueberry Pie

Using 1¼-inch round cookie cutter, cut round from center of dough. Cut 6 more rounds from dough, 1½ inches from edge of center hole and equally spaced around center hole.

We found that a peeled and grated apple, rich in pectin, helps to thicken and flavor the blueberries in our pie.

Grind the tapioca to a powder in a spice grinder or a mini food processor. You can use the Foolproof Double-Crust Pie Dough (page 698), the All-Butter Double-Crust Pie Dough (page 701), or store-bought pie dough in this recipe; depending on which dough you use, the method for rolling it out and transferring it to the pie plate will be different.

30 ounces (6 cups) blueberries
1 Granny Smith apple, peeled, cored, and shredded
¾ cup (5¼ ounces) sugar
2 tablespoons instant tapioca, ground
2 teaspoons grated lemon zest plus 2 teaspoons juice
   Pinch salt
1 recipe double-crust pie dough, bottom crust fitted into 9-inch pie plate and top crust rolled out into 12-inch round
2 tablespoons unsalted butter, cut into ¼-inch pieces
1 large egg white, lightly beaten

1. Place 3 cups berries in medium saucepan and set over medium heat. Using potato masher, mash berries several times to release juices. Continue to cook, stirring often and mashing occasionally, until about half of berries have broken down and mixture is thickened and reduced to 1½ cups, about 8 minutes; let cool slightly.

2. Adjust oven rack to lowest position and heat oven to 400 degrees. Line rimmed baking sheet with aluminum foil.

3. Place shredded apple in dish towel and wring dry. Transfer apple to large bowl and stir in cooked berries, remaining 3 cups uncooked berries, sugar, tapioca, lemon zest and juice, and salt until combined. Spread mixture into dough-lined pie plate and scatter butter over top.

4. Using 1¼-inch round cookie cutter, cut hole in center of top crust. Cut 6 more holes evenly around edge of crust, about 1½ inches from edge of center hole. Loosely roll top crust round around rolling pin, then gently unroll it over filling.

5. Trim overhanging dough ½ inch beyond lip of pie plate. Pinch edges of top and bottom dough crusts firmly together. Tuck overhang under itself; folded edge should be flush with edge of pie plate. Crimp dough evenly around edge of pie using your fingers. Brush surface with beaten egg white.

6. Place pie on prepared sheet and bake until crust is light golden brown, about 25 minutes. Reduce oven temperature to 350 degrees, rotate baking sheet, and continue to bake until juices are bubbling and crust is deep golden brown, 35 to 50 minutes longer. Let pie cool on wire rack to room temperature, about 4 hours. Serve.

Deep-Dish Apple Pie

SERVES 8   **TOTAL TIME** 2 HOURS 20 MINUTES
(PLUS 2 HOURS COOLING TIME)

✔ **WHY THIS RECIPE WORKS:** The problem with deep-dish apple pie is that the apples are often unevenly cooked and the exuded juice leaves the apples swimming in liquid, producing a bottom crust that is pale and soggy. Then there is the huge gap left between the shrunken apples and the top crust, making it impossible to slice neatly. We wanted our piece of deep-dish pie to be a towering wedge of tender, juicy apples, fully framed by a buttery, flaky crust. Precooking the apples solved the shrinking problem, helped the apples hold their shape, and prevented a flood of juices from collecting in the bottom of the pie plate, thereby producing a nicely browned bottom crust. We learned that when the apples are gently heated, their pectin is converted to a heat-stable form that keeps them from becoming mushy when cooked further in the oven. This allowed us to boost the quantity of apples to 5 pounds. A little brown sugar, salt, lemon, and cinnamon contributed flavor and sweetness. You can substitute Empire or Cortland apples for the Granny Smith apples, and Jonagold, Fuji, or Braeburn for the Golden

Despite what many think, making a delicious and well-formed deep-dish apple pie is not as easy as tossing some apples with sugar and spices and piling them into a pie shell. To begin with, you must select the right apples for a balance of sweet-tart flavor. And most important, we found that precooking the apples on the stovetop ensured that the pie emerged from the oven with no gap between the top crust and the filling.

1. USE 2 TYPES OF APPLES: Peel, core, and cut 2½ pounds each of Granny Smith and Golden Delicious apples into ¼-inch-thick slices.
WHY? Firm apples hold their shape—an important point since the filling is pre-cooked. A mix of tart and sweet apples provides the right flavor.

2. COOK THE APPLES: Cover and cook the apples, sugars, and seasonings until the apples are tender but still hold their shape, 15 minutes.
WHY? Precooking the apples helps them hold their shape. When gently heated, the apples' pectin converts to a stable form that prevents the apples from becoming mushy.

3. LET THE APPLES COOL: Transfer the cooked apples and their juices to a rimmed baking sheet and let them cool to room temperature.
WHY? If you make a double-crust pie with a hot filling, the dough will melt into a mushy mess. Spreading out the apples helps them cool quickly and shed excess liquid.

4. DRAIN THE COOLED APPLES, RESERVING JUICE: Drain the apples in a colander set over a bowl. Reserve ¼ cup of the drained juice and mix it with the lemon juice.
WHY? Adding just ¼ cup of the apple juices, with lemon juice for flavor, helps control the moisture inside the pie.

5. PACK THE APPLES INTO A DOUGH-LINED PIE PLATE AND COVER WITH THE TOP CRUST: Spread the apples into a dough-lined pie plate, mounding them slightly in the middle. Drizzle the apple juice mixture over them, then center the top crust over the pie.
WHY? Since the apples are slightly softened, you can pack them firmly into the dough-lined pie plate, making sure there are no big gaps or holes, before you add the top crust.

6. CRIMP THE EDGES OF THE TOP AND BOTTOM CRUSTS: Trim the top crust to ½ inch beyond the edge of the pie plate. Pinch the top and bottom crusts together, and tuck the overhanging dough under flush with the edge of the pie plate. Use your fingers to crimp the dough evenly around the edge of the pie.
WHY? Making sure the edges are properly pinched, folded, and crimped together helps ensure that the pie juices won't leak out during baking.

7. CUT VENT HOLES: Cut four 2-inch vent holes in the top crust with a paring knife. Brush the pie with a beaten egg white, and sprinkle evenly with 1 tablespoon sugar.
WHY? The vent holes in the top crust allow steam to escape from the pie during baking. This prevents the top crust from turning soggy and helps the pie juices evaporate so they don't puddle around the edge and leak out.

8. BAKE AT 2 TEMPERATURES: Bake the pie in a 425-degree oven until the crust is light golden brown, about 25 minutes. Reduce the oven to 375 degrees, rotate the baking sheet, and bake until the crust is deep golden brown, about 30 minutes.
WHY? The baking sheet con-ducts heat and helps the bot-tom crust bake through and turn brown. Starting the pie in a hot oven helps the crust set and brown; lowering the tem-perature enables the pie to bake through without burning at the edges.

Delicious apples. You can use the Foolproof Double-Crust Pie Dough (page 698), the All-Butter Double-Crust Pie Dough (page 701), or store-bought pie dough in this recipe; depending on which dough you use, the method for rolling it out and transferring it to the pie plate will be different.

2½ pounds Granny Smith apples, peeled, cored, and sliced ¼ inch thick
2½ pounds Golden Delicious apples, peeled, cored, and sliced ¼ inch thick
½ cup (3½ ounces) plus 1 tablespoon granulated sugar
¼ cup packed (1¾ ounces) light brown sugar
½ teaspoon grated lemon zest plus 1 tablespoon juice
¼ teaspoon salt
⅛ teaspoon ground cinnamon
1 recipe double-crust pie dough, bottom crust fitted into 9-inch pie plate and top crust rolled out into 12-inch round
1 large egg white, lightly beaten

1. Toss apples, ½ cup granulated sugar, brown sugar, lemon zest, salt, and cinnamon together in Dutch oven. Cover and cook over medium heat, stirring often, until apples are tender when poked with fork but still hold their shape, 15 to 20 minutes. Transfer apples and their juices to rimmed baking sheet and let cool to room temperature, about 30 minutes.

2. Adjust oven rack to lowest position and heat oven to 425 degrees. Line clean rimmed baking sheet with aluminum foil. Drain cooled apples thoroughly in colander set over bowl, reserving ¼ cup of juice. Stir lemon juice into reserved apple juice.

3. Spread apples into dough-lined pie plate, mounding them slightly in middle, and drizzle with apple juice mixture. Loosely roll top crust round around rolling pin, then gently unroll it over filling.

4. Trim overhanging dough ½ inch beyond lip of pie plate. Pinch edges of top and bottom dough crusts firmly together. Tuck overhang under itself; folded edge should be flush with edge of pie plate. Crimp dough evenly around edge of pie using your fingers. Cut four 2-inch slits in top of dough. Brush surface with beaten egg white and sprinkle evenly with remaining 1 tablespoon granulated sugar.

5. Place pie on prepared sheet and bake until crust is light golden brown, about 25 minutes. Reduce oven temperature to 375 degrees, rotate baking sheet, and continue to bake until juices are bubbling and crust is deep golden brown, 30 to 40 minutes longer. Let pie cool on wire rack until filling has set, about 2 hours. Serve slightly warm or at room temperature.

Lattice-Top Cherry Pie

SERVES 8   **TOTAL TIME** 2 HOURS 30 MINUTES (PLUS 2 HOURS COOLING TIME)

✓ WHY THIS RECIPE WORKS: For a cherry pie with plenty of fresh cherry flavor, we found that sour cherries were a must, as sweet cherries lost their flavor once cooked. Among the varieties of light and dark cherries, Morellos were our favorite. For flavorings, almond extract complemented the flavor of the cherries, while a little cinnamon added a hint of warmth. Making a lattice top for the pie ensured maximum evaporation from the filling as the fruit released its juices. Do not use canned cherry pie filling because it has added sugars and thickeners. You can use the Foolproof Double-Crust Pie Dough (page 698), the All-Butter Double-Crust Pie Dough (page 701), or store-bought pie dough in this recipe; depending on which dough you use, the method for rolling it out and transferring it to the pie plate will be different.

2½ pounds fresh sour cherries, pitted
1–1¼ cups (7–8¾ ounces) plus 1 tablespoon sugar
¼ cup cornstarch
¼ teaspoon ground cinnamon
¼ teaspoon almond extract
   Pinch salt
1 recipe double-crust pie dough, bottom crust fitted into 9-inch pie plate and top crust rolled out and cut into lattice strips (see page 708)
1 large egg white, lightly beaten

1. Toss cherries with 1 cup sugar in large bowl and let sit, tossing occasionally, until cherries release their juice, about 1 hour. Adjust oven rack to lowest position and heat oven to 425 degrees. Line rimmed baking sheet with aluminum foil.

2. Drain cherries thoroughly in colander set over bowl, reserving ¼ cup juice. In large bowl, toss drained cherries, reserved juice, cornstarch, cinnamon, almond extract, and salt together until well combined. (If cherries taste too tart, add up to ¼ cup more sugar.)

3. Spread cherries into dough-lined pie plate. Lay 4 parallel strips of chilled dough evenly over filling. Weave remaining strips in opposite direction, one at a time, to create lattice (if dough becomes too soft to work with, refrigerate pie and dough strips until firm). Let strips soften for 5 to 10 minutes.

4. Trim overhanging dough ½ inch beyond lip of pie plate. Pinch edges of bottom crust and lattice strips together, then tuck overhang under itself; folded edge should be flush with edge of pie plate. Crimp dough evenly around edge of pie using fingers. Brush lattice with beaten egg white and sprinkle evenly with remaining 1 tablespoon sugar.

5. Bake pie on prepared sheet until crust is light golden brown, about 25 minutes. Reduce oven temperature to 375 degrees, rotate baking sheet, and continue to bake until juices are bubbling and crust is deep golden brown, 30 to 45 minutes longer. Let pie cool on wire rack until filling has set, about 2 hours. Serve slightly warm or at room temperature.

Making a Lattice-Top Pie

1. ROLL OUT DOUGH AND CUT INTO STRIPS: Roll dough into 13 by 10-inch rectangle, then slice lengthwise into eight 13 by 1¼-inch strips. Cover with plastic and freeze until very firm, 30 minutes.

2. START WITH FOUR STRIPS RUNNING IN SAME DIRECTION: Lay 4 strips of chilled dough evenly parallel over filling.

3. WEAVE REMAINING STRIPS: Weave remaining strips in opposite direction, one at a time (if dough becomes too soft to work with, refrigerate pie with strips until firm).

4. TRIM EDGES AND CRIMP: Trim crust to ½ inch beyond lip of pie plate, pinch edges together, and tuck overhang under itself; folded edge should be flush with plate. Crimp dough evenly around edge of pie using fingers.

A lattice crust is not just decorative; it allows moisture to evaporate, keeping pies from becoming soggy.

Lattice-Top Peach Pie

SERVES 8   **TOTAL TIME** 2 HOURS 30 MINUTES (PLUS 2 HOURS COOLING TIME)

✔ **WHY THIS RECIPE WORKS:** Fresh peach pies are often soupy and/or overly sweet, with a bottom crust that is soggy or undercooked. We wanted to create a pie with filling that was juicy but not swimming in liquid and that had flavors that were neither muscled out by spices nor overwhelmed by thickeners, and with a crust that was well browned on the bottom. We peeled and sliced the peaches and found that all they needed in the way of flavor was sugar, lemon juice, cinnamon, nutmeg, and a dash of salt. To thicken the juices, we used a little cornstarch, but by itself it didn't solve the liquid problem. A lattice-top pie crust was our solution—it required a bit more work than making a regular double-crust pie, but we found that it was worth the effort. Not only is it pretty and very traditional on peach pies, but it serves an important purpose: The structure of a lattice top allows for maximum evaporation while the pie cooks—the juices released by the fruit cook down slowly while baking so the filling isn't soupy.

For easy assembly, after we rolled and cut the dough for the lattice, we froze it so the strips were firm and easy to handle. See below for more information on peeling peaches. You can use the Foolproof Double-Crust Pie Dough (page 698), the All-Butter Double-Crust Pie Dough (page 701), or store-bought pie dough in this recipe; depending on which dough you use, the method for rolling it out and transferring it to the pie plate will be different.

2½ **pounds peaches, peeled, halved, pitted, and sliced ⅓ inch thick**
1 **cup (7 ounces) plus 1 tablespoon sugar**
1 **tablespoon cornstarch**
1 **tablespoon lemon juice**
   Pinch ground cinnamon
   Pinch ground nutmeg
   Pinch salt
1 **recipe double-crust pie dough, bottom crust fitted into 9-inch pie plate and top crust rolled out and cut into lattice strips (see page 708)**
1 **large egg white, lightly beaten**

1. Toss peaches with 1 cup sugar in large bowl and let sit, tossing occasionally, until peaches release their juice, about 1 hour. Adjust oven rack to lowest position and heat oven to 425 degrees. Line rimmed baking sheet with aluminum foil.

2. Drain peaches thoroughly in colander set over bowl, reserving ¼ cup juice. In large bowl, toss drained peaches, reserved juice, cornstarch, lemon juice, cinnamon, nutmeg, and salt together until well combined.

3. Spread peaches into dough-lined pie plate. Lay 4 parallel strips of chilled dough evenly over filling. Weave remaining strips in opposite direction, one at a time, to create lattice (if dough becomes too soft to work with, refrigerate pie and dough strips until firm). Let strips soften for 5 to 10 minutes.

4. Trim overhanging dough ½ inch beyond lip of pie plate. Pinch edges of bottom crust and lattice strips together, then tuck overhang under itself; folded edge should be flush with edge of pie plate. Crimp dough evenly around edge of pie using fingers. Brush lattice with beaten egg white and sprinkle evenly with remaining 1 tablespoon sugar.

5. Bake pie on prepared sheet until crust is light golden brown, about 25 minutes. Reduce oven temperature to 375 degrees, rotate baking sheet, and continue to bake until juices are bubbling and crust is deep golden brown, 30 to 40 minutes longer. Let pie cool on wire rack until filling has set, about 2 hours. Serve slightly warm or at room temperature.

Pecan Pie

SERVES 8   **TOTAL TIME** 1 HOUR 15 MINUTES
(PLUS 2 HOURS COOLING TIME)

✓ **WHY THIS RECIPE WORKS:** Pecan pies can be overwhelmingly sweet, with no real pecan flavor. And they too often turn out curdled and separated. What's more, the weepy filling makes the bottom crust soggy and leathery. The fact that the crust usually seems underbaked at the outset doesn't help matters. We wanted to create a recipe for a not-too-sweet pie with a smooth-textured filling and a properly baked bottom crust. We tackled this pie's problems by using brown sugar for rich, deep flavor, and reducing the amount, so the pecan flavor could take center stage. We also partially baked

Peeling Peaches

If your peaches are firm, you should be able to peel them with a sharp vegetable peeler. If they are too soft to withstand the pressure of a peeler, you'll need to blanch them in a pot of simmering water for 30 seconds and then shock them in a bowl of ice water before peeling.

1. Score small X at base of each peach with paring knife.

2. Lower peaches into boiling water and simmer until skins loosen, 30 to 60 seconds.

3. Transfer peaches immediately to ice water and let cool for 1 minute.

4. Using paring knife, remove strips of loosened peel, starting at X on base of each peach.

the crust, which kept it crisp. We found that it's important to add the hot filling to a warm pie crust, as this helps keep the crust from getting soggy. In addition, we discovered that simulating a double boiler when you're melting the butter and making the filling is an easy way to maintain gentle heat, which helps ensure that the filling doesn't curdle. You can use the Foolproof Single-Crust Pie Dough (page 698), the All-Butter Single-Crust Pie Dough (page 700), or store-bought pie dough in this recipe. The crust must still be warm when the filling is added.

- **6 tablespoons unsalted butter, cut into 6 pieces**
- **1 cup packed (7 ounces) dark brown sugar**
- **½ teaspoon salt**
- **3 large eggs**
- **¾ cup light corn syrup**
- **1 tablespoon vanilla extract**
- **2 cups pecans, toasted and chopped fine**
- **1 recipe single-crust pie dough, partially baked and still warm**

1. Adjust oven rack to lower-middle position, place aluminum foil–lined rimmed baking sheet on rack, and heat oven to 275 degrees. Melt butter in heatproof bowl set in skillet of water maintained at just below simmer. Remove bowl from skillet and stir in sugar and salt until butter is absorbed. Whisk in eggs, then corn syrup and vanilla until smooth. Return bowl to hot water and stir until mixture is shiny and hot to touch and registers 130 degrees. Off heat, stir in pecans.

2. Pour pecan mixture into warm prebaked pie crust. Bake pie on heated sheet until filling looks set but yields like Jell-O when gently pressed with back of spoon, 50 minutes to 1 hour. Let pie cool on wire rack until filling has set, about 2 hours. Serve slightly warm or at room temperature.

VARIATIONS
Maple Pecan Pie
More liquid than corn syrup, maple syrup yields a softer, more custardlike pie. Toasted walnuts can be substituted for pecans. We prefer to use grade B or grade A dark amber maple syrup for this recipe.

Reduce butter to 4 tablespoons and pecans to 1½ cups. Substitute ½ cup granulated sugar for brown sugar and 1 cup maple syrup for corn syrup and vanilla.

Buttermilk Pecan Pie with Raisins
Substitute 1½ cups granulated sugar for brown sugar and ⅔ cup buttermilk for corn syrup and vanilla. Reduce pecans to ½ cup and stir into filling with ½ cup finely chopped raisins.

We use dark brown sugar and light corn syrup to create a not-too-sweet pecan pie with classic praline flavor.

NOTES FROM THE TEST KITCHEN

Freezing Holiday Pies

For longer-term storage options, we tested freezing two common holiday pies. Apple pie can be fully assembled and frozen before baking, though the crust will be slightly less crisp once baked. To freeze, follow the recipe all the way through sealing the pie crust, but do not brush with egg wash. Freeze the pie for 2 to 3 hours, then wrap it tightly in a double layer of plastic wrap, followed by a layer of aluminum foil, and return it to the freezer for up to one month. On serving day, brush egg wash onto the frozen pie, sprinkle it with sugar, and bake it straight from the freezer, adding 10 minutes to the baking time.

Pecan pie can also be frozen for up to one month before baking. Fill the pie, then wrap it and freeze it using the same method as the apple pie and bake it straight from the freezer, adding 30 minutes to the baking time. (This pie is denser than apple pie and requires more time to cook through.)

Pumpkin Pie

SERVES 8 **TOTAL TIME** 1 HOUR 15 MINUTES
(PLUS 2 TO 3 HOURS COOLING TIME)

✓ **WHY THIS RECIPE WORKS:** Too often, pumpkin pie appears at the end of a Thanksgiving meal as a grainy, overspiced, canned-pumpkin custard encased in a soggy crust. We wanted to create a pumpkin pie destined to be a new classic: velvety smooth, packed with pumpkin flavor, and redolent of just enough fragrant spices. To concentrate its flavor, we cooked canned pumpkin with sugar and spices, then whisked in heavy cream, milk, and eggs. This improved the flavor, and the hot filling helped the custard firm up quickly in the oven, preventing it from soaking into the crust. For spices, we chose nutmeg, cinnamon, and, surprisingly, freshly grated ginger. Sugar and maple syrup sweetened things, but for more complex flavor we added mashed roasted yams to the filling (switching to canned candied yams streamlined the procedure). To keep the custard from curdling, we started the pie at a high temperature for 10 minutes, followed by a reduced temperature for the remainder of the baking time. This cut the baking time to less than an hour, and the dual temperatures produced a creamy pie fully and evenly cooked from edge to center. Make sure to buy unsweetened canned pumpkin. If candied yams are unavailable, regular canned yams can be substituted. The crust must still be warm when the filling is added. When properly baked, the center 2 inches of the pie should look firm but jiggle slightly. The pie finishes cooking with residual heat; to ensure that the filling sets, let it cool at room temperature and not in the refrigerator. You can use the Foolproof Single-Crust Pie Dough (page 698), the All-Butter Single-Crust Pie Dough (page 700), or store-bought pie dough in this recipe.

1 cup heavy cream
1 cup whole milk
3 large eggs plus 2 large yolks
1 teaspoon vanilla extract
1 (15-ounce) can unsweetened pumpkin puree
1 cup canned candied yams, drained
¾ cup (5¼ ounces) sugar
¼ cup maple syrup
2 teaspoons grated fresh ginger
1 teaspoon salt
½ teaspoon ground cinnamon
¼ teaspoon ground nutmeg
1 recipe single-crust pie dough, partially baked and still warm

Our creamy pumpkin pie is packed with flavor from using sweet potatoes, fresh ginger, and maple syrup.

1. Adjust oven rack to lowest position and heat oven to 400 degrees. Line rimmed baking sheet with aluminum foil. Whisk cream, milk, eggs and yolks, and vanilla together in bowl. Bring pumpkin, yams, sugar, maple syrup, ginger, salt, cinnamon, and nutmeg to simmer in large saucepan and cook, stirring constantly and mashing yams against sides of pot, until thick and shiny, 15 to 20 minutes.

2. Remove saucepan from heat and whisk in cream mixture until fully incorporated. Strain mixture through fine-mesh strainer into bowl, using rubber spatula to help work puree through strainer. Whisk mixture, then pour into warm prebaked pie crust.

3. Place pie on prepared sheet and bake for 10 minutes. Reduce oven temperature to 300 degrees and continue to bake until edges of pie are set and center registers 175 degrees, 20 to 35 minutes longer. Let pie cool on wire rack to room temperature, 2 to 3 hours. Serve.

WHIPPED CREAM

MAKES ABOUT 2 CUPS **TOTAL TIME** 10 MINUTES **FAST**

The lightly sweetened flavor and creamy texture of whipped cream make it the perfect partner to numerous desserts, especially pies. For lightly sweetened whipped cream, reduce the sugar to 1½ teaspoons. For the best results, chill the mixer bowl and the whisk in the freezer for 20 minutes before whipping the cream.

- 1 **cup heavy cream, chilled**
- 1 **tablespoon sugar**
- 1 **teaspoon vanilla extract**
  Pinch salt

Using stand mixer fitted with whisk, whip all ingredients together on medium-low speed until foamy, about 1 minute. Increase speed to high and whip until soft peaks form, 1 to 3 minutes. (Whipped cream can be refrigerated in fine-mesh strainer set over small bowl and covered with plastic wrap for up to 8 hours.)

BOURBON WHIPPED CREAM

Reduce vanilla to ¼ teaspoon and add ¼ cup bourbon or dark rum with other ingredients.

BROWN SUGAR WHIPPED CREAM

MAKES ABOUT 2½ CUPS **TOTAL TIME** 4 HOURS 10 MINUTES

Refrigerating the mixture in step 1 gives the brown sugar time to dissolve. This whipped cream pairs well with any dessert that has lots of nuts, warm spices, or molasses, like gingerbread, pecan pie, or pumpkin pie.

- 1 **cup heavy cream, chilled**
- ½ **cup sour cream**
- ½ **cup packed (3½ ounces) light brown sugar**
- ⅛ **teaspoon salt**

1. Whisk all ingredients together in bowl of stand mixer until combined. Cover with plastic wrap and refrigerate until ready to serve, at least 4 hours or up to 1 day, stirring once or twice during chilling to ensure that sugar dissolves.

2. Before serving, using stand mixer fitted with whisk, whip mixture on medium-low speed until foamy, about 1 minute. Increase speed to high and whip until soft peaks form, 1 to 3 minutes.

BROWN SUGAR AND BOURBON WHIPPED CREAM

Add 2 teaspoons bourbon with other ingredients.

Our fudgy Tar Heel pie uses brown sugar to help it stay moist and to bolster the flavor of the semisweet chocolate chips.

Fudgy Tar Heel Pie

SERVES 8   **TOTAL TIME** 50 MINUTES
(PLUS 1½ HOURS COOLING TIME)

✓ **WHY THIS RECIPE WORKS:** Tar Heel Pie is named for its roots in North Carolina and possibly its resemblance to a certain sticky natural resource from that state. To correct the cloying sweetness of this brownie pie, we replaced the white sugar with dark brown sugar, adding depth. Upping the vanilla and salt and adding cocoa powder finished the job. To make the pie fudgy, we backed the flour down to just ¼ cup, and used half butter and half oil (making for a softer, chewier crumb). Finally, prebaking the pie crust and toasting the nuts ensured that both stayed crisp. You can use the Foolproof Single-Crust Pie Dough (page 698), the All-Butter Single-Crust Pie Dough (page 700), or store-bought pie dough in this recipe. Serve with vanilla ice cream.

- 1 **cup (6 ounces) semisweet chocolate chips**
- 4 **tablespoons unsalted butter**
- ¼ **cup vegetable oil**
- 2 **tablespoons unsweetened cocoa powder**

¾ cup packed (5¼ ounces) dark brown sugar
2 large eggs
1 tablespoon vanilla extract
¾ teaspoon salt
¼ cup (1¼ ounces) all-purpose flour
1¼ cups pecans, toasted and chopped coarse
1 recipe single-crust pie dough, fully baked and cooled

1. Adjust oven rack to middle position and heat oven to 325 degrees. Microwave ⅔ cup chocolate chips and butter in bowl at 50 percent power, stirring often, until melted, 60 to 90 seconds. Whisk in oil and cocoa until smooth.

2. In separate bowl, whisk sugar, eggs, vanilla, and salt together until smooth. Whisk chocolate mixture into sugar mixture until incorporated. Stir in flour and remaining ⅓ cup chocolate chips until just combined.

3. Spread pecans in bottom of pie shell, then pour batter over top and smooth top. Bake pie until toothpick inserted in center comes out with thin coating of batter attached, 30 to 35 minutes.

4. Let pie cool on wire rack until filling has set, about 1½ hours. Serve slightly warm or at room temperature.

NOTES FROM THE TEST KITCHEN

Using Disposable Pie Plates

We prefer baking pies in Pyrex plates because the glass evenly distributes heat (for great browning) while providing a clear view (so we can easily judge when the crust is done). We place our glass pie plates on a baking sheet for an extra-crisp, golden bottom crust that doesn't get soggy when filled.

Initially, we assumed that disposable aluminum pie plates would absorb and conduct heat too quickly, leading to burnt crusts, so we omitted the baking sheet. But after blind-baking a few pie shells, we found the opposite to be true—the bottoms were still pale and damp long after the fluted edges had browned. Placing them on a baking sheet helped, but the sides were still undercooked and tended to slump after we removed the pie weights to let the insides of the shells brown.

It turns out that, due to their thin walls, aluminum plates can't hold or transfer a significant amount of heat from the oven to the crust. Crusts bake more slowly in aluminum, so they need to spend more time in the oven. For prebaking empty crusts, you'll need to increase the time that the crust bakes with weights by up to 10 minutes or until you see any visual doneness cues indicated by the recipe. For filled double-crust pies, increase the baking time by up to 10 minutes and cover the top of the pie with aluminum foil if it starts to get too dark. Place aluminum pie plates on a baking sheet for a well-browned bottom crust and for added stability when moving pies in and out of the oven.

Thoroughbred Pie

SERVES 8   TOTAL TIME 1 HOUR (PLUS 4 HOURS COOLING TIME)

WHY THIS RECIPE WORKS: What better way to top off the Kentucky Derby than with a slice of chocolate-walnut-bourbon pie? None, as long as you rein in the runaway sweetness. Since the majority of Thoroughbred Pie recipes we tried were far too sweet, we started by reducing the amount of sugar. Brown sugar contributed spice and depth, while more neutral white sugar ensured that the nuts and chocolate weren't eclipsed. To bring more balance to the pie, we replaced semisweet chocolate chips with chopped bittersweet chocolate. To give the top of our pie its trademark crunch, we went with cornstarch instead of flour as a thickener. Sprinkling the chocolate over the crust provided intense chocolate in every bite. You can use the Foolproof Single-Crust Pie Dough (page 698), the All-Butter Single-Crust Pie Dough (page 700), or store-bought pie dough in this recipe. The crust must still be hot when you sprinkle on the chocolate—otherwise it will not soften sufficiently.

3 ounces bittersweet chocolate, chopped fine
1 recipe single-crust pie dough, baked and still hot
8 tablespoons unsalted butter, cut into 8 pieces
3 tablespoons bourbon
¾ cup (5¼ ounces) granulated sugar
½ cup packed (3½ ounces) light brown sugar
2 tablespoons cornstarch
½ teaspoon salt
2 large eggs plus 1 large yolk, lightly beaten
1 teaspoon vanilla extract
1½ cups walnuts, toasted and chopped
1 recipe Bourbon Whipped Cream (page 712)

1. Sprinkle chocolate evenly over hot pie crust, let sit until softened, about 5 minutes, then smooth into even layer. Adjust oven rack to lowest position and heat oven to 400 degrees. Line rimmed baking sheet with aluminum foil.

2. Melt butter in small saucepan over medium-low heat. Cook, stirring constantly, until butter is nutty brown, 5 to 7 minutes. Off heat, slowly stir in bourbon (mixture will bubble vigorously). Let mixture cool for 5 minutes.

3. Whisk granulated sugar, brown sugar, cornstarch, and salt together in large bowl until combined. Whisk in eggs and yolk and vanilla until smooth. Slowly whisk in butter mixture until incorporated. Stir in walnuts.

4. Pour filling into chocolate-lined crust. Bake pie until filling is puffed and center jiggles slightly when pie is gently shaken, 35 to 40 minutes. Let pie cool completely on wire rack, about 4 hours. Serve with Bourbon Whipped Cream.

Lemon Meringue Pie

SERVES 8   **TOTAL TIME** 1 HOUR
(PLUS 2 HOURS COOLING TIME)

✔ **WHY THIS RECIPE WORKS:** The most controversial part of lemon meringue pie is the meringue. It can shrink, bead, puddle, deflate, burn, sweat, break down, or turn rubbery. We wanted a pie with a flaky crust and a rich filling that was soft but not runny and firm but not gelatinous, and that balanced the airy meringue. Most important, we wanted a meringue that didn't break down and puddle on the bottom or "tear" on the top. We learned that the puddling underneath the meringue was from undercooking, the beading on top from overcooking. We discovered that if the filling is piping hot when the meringue is applied, the underside of the meringue will not undercook; if the oven temperature is relatively low, the top of the meringue won't overcook. Baking the pie in a relatively cool oven also produced the best-looking, most evenly baked meringue. To further stabilize the meringue and keep it from weeping, we beat in a small amount of cornstarch. Make the pie crust, let it cool, and then begin work on the filling. As soon as the filling is made, cover it with plastic wrap to keep it hot and then start working on the meringue topping. You want to add hot filling to the cooled pie crust and then apply the meringue topping and quickly get the pie into the oven. You can use the Foolproof Single-Crust Pie Dough (page 698), the All-Butter Single-Crust Pie Dough (page 700), or store-bought pie dough in this recipe.

FILLING

1½ cups water
1 cup (7 ounces) sugar
¼ cup cornstarch
⅛ teaspoon salt
6 large egg yolks
1 tablespoon grated lemon zest plus ½ cup juice
   (3 lemons)
2 tablespoons unsalted butter, cut into 2 pieces

MERINGUE

⅓ cup water
1 tablespoon cornstarch
4 large egg whites
½ teaspoon vanilla extract
¼ teaspoon cream of tartar
½ cup (3½ ounces) sugar

1 recipe single-crust pie dough, fully baked and cooled

1. FOR THE FILLING: Adjust oven rack to middle position and heat oven to 325 degrees. Bring water, sugar, cornstarch, and salt to simmer in large saucepan, whisking constantly. When mixture starts to turn translucent, whisk in egg yolks, two at a time. Whisk in lemon zest and juice and butter. Return mixture to brief simmer, then remove from heat. Lay sheet of plastic wrap directly on surface of filling to keep warm and prevent skin from forming.

2. FOR THE MERINGUE: Bring water and cornstarch to simmer in small saucepan and cook, whisking occasionally, until thickened and translucent, 1 to 2 minutes. Remove from heat and let cool slightly.

Topping a Pie with Meringue

1. Using stand mixer fitted with whisk, whip egg whites with vanilla and cream of tartar, then add sugar and, finally, cornstarch mixture until glossy, stiff peaks form.

2. Using rubber spatula, immediately distribute meringue evenly around edge and then center of pie, attaching meringue to pie crust to prevent shrinking.

3. Using back of spoon, create attractive swirls and peaks in meringue.

4. Bake until meringue is light golden brown, about 20 minutes.

3. Using stand mixer fitted with whisk, whip egg whites, vanilla, and cream of tartar on medium-low speed until foamy, about 1 minute. Increase speed to medium-high and beat in sugar, 1 tablespoon at a time, until incorporated and mixture forms soft, billowy mounds. Add cornstarch mixture, 1 tablespoon at a time, and continue to beat to glossy, stiff peaks, 2 to 3 minutes.

4. Meanwhile, remove plastic from filling and return to very low heat during last minute or so of beating meringue (to ensure filling is hot).

5. Pour warm filling into cooled prebaked pie crust. Using rubber spatula, immediately distribute meringue evenly around edge and then center of pie, attaching meringue to pie crust to prevent shrinking. Using back of spoon, create attractive swirls and peaks in meringue. Bake until meringue is light golden brown, about 20 minutes. Let pie cool on wire rack until filling has set, about 2 hours. Serve.

Summer Berry Pie

SERVES 8   **TOTAL TIME** 45 MINUTES
(PLUS 3 HOURS CHILLING TIME)

WHY THIS RECIPE WORKS: A fresh berry pie might seem like an easy-to-pull-off summer dessert, but most of the recipes we tried buried the berries in gluey thickeners or embedded them in bouncy gelatin. Our goal was to make a pie with great texture and flavor—and still keep it simple. We started with the test kitchen's quick and easy graham cracker crust, which relies on crushed graham crackers (store-bought graham cracker crumbs often taste stale). For the filling, we used a combination of raspberries, blackberries, and blueberries. After trying different methods, we found a solution that both bound the berries in the graham cracker crust and intensified their bright flavor. We processed a portion of berries in a food processor until they made a smooth puree, then we thickened the puree with cornstarch. Next, we tossed the remaining berries with warm jelly for a glossy coat and a shot of sweetness. Pressed gently into the puree, the berries stayed put and tasted great. Feel free to vary the amount of each berry as desired as long as you have 6 cups of berries total; do not substitute frozen berries here. Serve with Whipped Cream (page 712).

10 ounces (2 cups) raspberries
10 ounces (2 cups) blackberries
10 ounces (2 cups) blueberries
½ cup (3½ ounces) sugar
3 tablespoons cornstarch
⅛ teaspoon salt

Processing some of the berries and thickening the puree with cornstarch gives this pie great texture and flavor.

1 tablespoon lemon juice
1 recipe Graham Cracker Crust (page 702), baked and cooled
2 tablespoons red currant or apple jelly

1. Gently toss berries together in large bowl. Process 2½ cups of berries in food processor until very smooth, about 1 minute (do not underprocess). Strain puree through fine-mesh strainer into small saucepan, pressing on solids to extract as much puree as possible (you should have about 1½ cups); discard solids.

2. Whisk sugar, cornstarch, and salt together in bowl, then whisk into strained puree. Bring puree mixture to boil, stirring constantly, and cook until it is as thick as pudding, about 7 minutes. Off heat, stir in lemon juice and let cool slightly.

3. Pour warm berry puree into cooled prebaked pie crust. Melt jelly in clean small saucepan over low heat, then pour over remaining 3½ cups berries and toss to coat. Spread berries evenly over puree and lightly press them into puree. Cover pie loosely with plastic wrap and refrigerate until filling is chilled and set, at least 3 hours or up to 1 day. Serve chilled or at room temperature.

We fold fresh strawberries into a mixture of heated frozen berries and gelatin for a pie that sets up beautifully.

Icebox Strawberry Pie

SERVES 8   **TOTAL TIME** 1 HOUR 30 MINUTES
(PLUS 4 HOURS CHILLING TIME)

WHY THIS RECIPE WORKS: We used frozen berries for part of our Icebox Strawberry Pie (which worked well for cooking and cost less than fresh) and cooked them down until they released their juices and became thick, concentrated, and flavorful. Because strawberries are low in pectin (the natural thickener found in citrus fruits and many other plants), we added some lemon juice, which perked up the flavor and tightened the texture of the filling a little. To thicken the filling further, we added a bit of unflavored gelatin, which produced a clean-slicing, not-too-bouncy pie. After stirring in the gelatin—which we combined with the lemon juice and a little water—along with sugar and salt, we then mixed in fresh strawberries off the heat. This gave us the big berry flavor we

wanted. In step 1, it is imperative that the cooked strawberry mixture measures 2 cups; any more and the filling will be loose. If your fresh berries aren't fully ripe, you may want to add extra sugar to taste in step 2. You can use the Foolproof Single-Crust Pie Dough (page 698), the All-Butter Single-Crust Pie Dough (page 700), or store-bought pie dough in this recipe.

PIE
- 2 pounds (7 cups) frozen strawberries
- 2 tablespoons lemon juice
- 2 tablespoons water
- 1 tablespoon unflavored gelatin
- 1 cup (7 ounces) sugar
  Pinch salt
- 1 pound fresh strawberries, hulled and sliced thin
- 1 recipe single-crust pie dough, fully baked and cooled

TOPPING
- 4 ounces cream cheese, softened
- 3 tablespoons sugar
- ½ teaspoon vanilla extract
- 1 cup heavy cream, chilled

1. FOR THE PIE: Cook frozen berries in large saucepan over medium-low heat until they begin to release juice, about 3 minutes. Increase heat to medium-high and cook, stirring often, until thickened and measures 2 cups, about 25 minutes.

2. Combine lemon juice, water, and gelatin in small bowl and let sit until gelatin softens, about 5 minutes. Stir gelatin mixture, sugar, and salt into cooked berries, bring to simmer over medium heat, and cook for 2 minutes. Transfer mixture to large bowl and let cool to room temperature, about 30 minutes.

3. Gently fold fresh berries into cooled gelatin mixture. Spread filling into cooled prebaked pie crust, cover loosely with plastic wrap, and refrigerate for at least 4 hours or up to 1 day.

4. FOR THE TOPPING: Using stand mixer fitted with whisk, whip cream cheese, sugar, and vanilla together on medium speed until smooth, about 30 seconds. Add heavy cream and whip until stiff peaks form, about 2 minutes. Serve pie with topping.

Key Lime Pie

SERVES 8   TOTAL TIME 1 HOUR
(PLUS 4 HOURS COOLING AND CHILLING TIME)

✓ WHY THIS RECIPE WORKS: Key lime pie often disappoints us with a harsh and artificial flavor. We wanted a recipe for classic Key lime pie with a fresh flavor and a silky filling. Traditional Key lime pie is usually not baked; instead, the combination of egg yolks, lime juice, and sweetened condensed milk firms up when chilled because the juice's acidity causes the proteins in the eggs and milk to bind. We found that just one simple swap—from bottled, reconstituted lime juice to juice and zest from fresh limes—gave us a pie that was pungent and refreshing, cool yet creamy, and very satisfying. We also discovered that while the pie filling will set without baking (most recipes call only for mixing and then chilling), it set much more nicely after being baked for only 15 minutes. We tried more dramatic departures from the "classic" recipe—folding in egg whites, substituting heavy cream for condensed milk—but they didn't work. Just two seemingly minor adjustments to the classic recipe made all the difference. Despite this pie's name, we found that most tasters could not tell the difference between pies made with regular supermarket limes (called Persian limes) and true Key limes. Since Persian limes are easier to find and juice, we recommend them. The timing here is different from that for other pies; you need to make the filling first, then prepare the crust.

4   large egg yolks
4   teaspoons grated lime zest plus ½ cup juice (5 limes)
1   (14-ounce) can sweetened condensed milk
1   recipe Graham Cracker Crust (page 702), baked and still warm
1   cup heavy cream, chilled
¼   cup (1 ounce) confectioners' sugar

1. Adjust oven rack to middle position and heat oven to 325 degrees. Whisk egg yolks and lime zest together in medium bowl until mixture has light green tint, about 2 minutes. Whisk in condensed milk until smooth, then whisk in lime juice. Cover mixture and let sit at room temperature until thickened, about 30 minutes.

2. Pour thickened filling into warm prebaked pie crust. Bake pie until center is firm but jiggles slightly when shaken, 15 to 20 minutes. Let pie cool slightly on wire rack, about 1 hour. Cover pie loosely with plastic wrap and refrigerate until filling is chilled and set, at least 3 hours or up to 1 day.

3. Before serving, use stand mixer fitted with whisk to whip cream and sugar on medium-low speed until foamy, about 1 minute. Increase speed to high and whip until soft peaks form, 1 to 3 minutes. Spread whipped cream attractively over top of pie and serve.

Making a Key Lime Pie

1. WHISK FILLING AND LET THICKEN: Whisk egg yolks and lime zest together until mixture has light green tint, about 2 minutes. Whisk in condensed milk, then whisk in lime juice. Cover mixture and let sit at room temperature until thickened, about 30 minutes.

2. POUR FILLING INTO PIE SHELL AND BAKE: Pour thickened filling into warm prebaked pie crust. Bake pie until center is firm but jiggles slightly when shaken, 15 to 20 minutes.

3. CHILL BAKED PIE: Cover pie loosely with plastic wrap and refrigerate until filling is chilled and set, at least 3 hours or up to 1 day.

4. TOP WITH WHIPPED CREAM: Before serving, make whipped cream and spread attractively over top of pie.

The pastry cream for our banana pie is made with banana-infused half-and-half for big flavor.

Banana Cream Pie

SERVES 8   **TOTAL TIME** 2 HOURS 20 MINUTES
(PLUS 5 HOURS CHILLING TIME)

WHY THIS RECIPE WORKS: This layered concoction of pastry cream and sliced bananas topped with whipped cream is often delicious and sometimes sliceable, but very rarely both. Using starch for stability resulted in a chalky, stodgy pastry cream, but we found we could get a sliceable texture by trading starch for more egg yolk and a bit of butter. Instead of banana extract (artificial) or liqueur (impractical), we got banana flavor by infusing half-and-half with sautéed bananas. To slow down browning of the fresh banana slices, we tossed them in orange juice. You can use the Foolproof Single-Crust Pie Dough (page 698), the All-Butter Single-Crust Pie Dough (page 700), or store-bought pie dough in this recipe.

5	ripe bananas
4	tablespoons unsalted butter
2½	cups half-and-half
½	cup (3½ ounces) plus 2 tablespoons granulated sugar
6	large egg yolks
¼	teaspoon salt
2	tablespoons cornstarch
1½	teaspoons vanilla extract
1	recipe single-crust pie dough, fully baked and cooled
2	tablespoons orange juice
1	cup heavy cream, chilled
2	tablespoons confectioners' sugar

1. Peel 2 bananas and slice into ½-inch-thick pieces. Melt 1 tablespoon butter in medium saucepan over medium-high heat. Add sliced bananas and cook until beginning to soften, about 2 minutes. Add half-and-half, bring to boil, and boil for 30 seconds. Remove from heat, cover, and let sit for 40 minutes.

2. Whisk granulated sugar, egg yolks, and salt together in large bowl until smooth. Whisk in cornstarch. Strain cooled half-and-half mixture through fine-mesh strainer into yolk mixture—do not press on bananas—and whisk until incorporated; discard cooked bananas.

3. Transfer mixture to clean medium saucepan and cook over medium heat, whisking constantly, until thickened to consistency of warm pudding (180 degrees), 4 to 6 minutes. Off heat, whisk in remaining 3 tablespoons butter and 1 teaspoon vanilla. Transfer mixture to clean bowl, lay sheet of plastic wrap directly on surface, and refrigerate pastry cream for 1 hour.

4. Peel and slice remaining 3 bananas into ¼-inch-thick pieces and toss with orange juice in bowl. Whisk pastry cream briefly. Spread half of pastry cream over bottom of cooled pre-baked pie crust, arrange sliced bananas over top, then spread remaining pastry cream over bananas.

5. Using stand mixer fitted with whisk, whip cream, confectioners' sugar, and remaining ½ teaspoon vanilla on medium-low speed until foamy, about 1 minute. Increase speed to high and whip until stiff peaks form, 1 to 3 minutes. Spread whipped cream evenly over top of pie. Refrigerate pie until filling is chilled and set, at least 5 hours or up to 1 day. Serve.

For this custard pie, coconut milk and shredded coconut provide unmistakable coconut flavor.

Coconut Cream Pie

SERVES 8   **TOTAL TIME** 35 MINUTES
(PLUS 4 HOURS CHILLING TIME)

✓ **WHY THIS RECIPE WORKS:** Most recipes for this diner dessert are nothing more than a redecorated vanilla cream pie. We wanted a coconut cream pie with the exotic and elusive flavor of tropical coconut rather than a thinly disguised vanilla custard. We found that a not-too-sweet graham cracker crust provided a delicate, cookielike texture that didn't overshadow the coconut filling. For the filling, we started with a basic custard, using a combination of unsweetened coconut milk and whole milk. And for more coconut flavor, we stirred in unsweetened shredded coconut and cooked it so the shreds softened slightly in the hot milk. To top it all off, we added a little rum to our whipped cream, slathered it over the top of the pie, and then dusted the top with crunchy shreds of toasted coconut for one more layer of coconut flavor. Do not use light coconut milk here because it does not have enough flavor. Also, do not confuse coconut milk with cream of coconut. The filling should be warm when poured into the cooled pie crust.

To toast the coconut, place it in an 8-inch skillet over medium heat and cook, stirring often, for 3 to 5 minutes. It burns quite easily, so keep a close eye on it.

PIE

     1 **(13.5-ounce) can coconut milk**
     1 **cup whole milk**
    ⅔ **cup (4⅔ ounces) sugar**
    ½ **cup (1½ ounces) unsweetened shredded coconut**
    ¼ **teaspoon salt**
     5 **large egg yolks**
    ¼ **cup cornstarch**
     2 **tablespoons unsalted butter, cut into 2 pieces**
   1½ **teaspoons vanilla extract**
     1 **recipe Graham Cracker Crust (page 702), baked and cooled**

TOPPING

   1½ **cups heavy cream, chilled**
   1½ **tablespoons sugar**
   1½ **teaspoons dark rum (optional)**
    ½ **teaspoon vanilla extract**
     1 **tablespoon unsweetened shredded coconut, toasted**

1. FOR THE PIE: Bring coconut milk, whole milk, ⅓ cup sugar, shredded coconut, and salt to simmer in medium saucepan, stirring occasionally.

2. As coconut milk mixture begins to simmer, whisk egg yolks, cornstarch, and remaining ⅓ cup sugar together in medium bowl until smooth. Slowly whisk 1 cup simmering coconut milk mixture into yolk mixture to temper, then slowly whisk tempered yolk mixture back into remaining coconut milk mixture. Reduce heat to medium and cook, whisking vigorously, until mixture is thickened and few bubbles burst on surface, about 30 seconds. Off heat, whisk in butter and vanilla. Let mixture cool until just warm, stirring often, about 5 minutes.

3. Pour warm filling into cooled prebaked pie crust. Lay sheet of plastic wrap directly on surface of filling. Refrigerate pie until filling is chilled and set, at least 4 hours or up to 1 day.

4. FOR THE TOPPING: Before serving, use stand mixer fitted with whisk to whip cream, sugar, rum, if using, and vanilla on medium-low speed until foamy, about 1 minute. Increase speed to high and whip until soft peaks form, 1 to 3 minutes. Spread whipped cream attractively over top of pie, sprinkle with shredded toasted coconut, and serve.

VARIATION
Lime-Coconut Cream Pie
Whisk 1½ teaspoons grated lime zest into filling with butter and vanilla.

Chocolate Cream Pie

SERVES 8   **TOTAL TIME** 35 MINUTES
(PLUS 4 HOURS CHILLING TIME)

✔ **WHY THIS RECIPE WORKS:** Chocolate cream pies can look superb, but they're often gluey, overly sweet, and impossible to slice. We wanted a creamy pie with a well-balanced chocolate flavor and a delicious, easy-to-slice crust. After testing every type of cookie on the market, we hit on pulverized Oreos and a bit of melted butter for the tastiest, most tender and sliceable crumb crust. We found that the secret to perfect chocolate cream pie filling was to combine two different types of chocolate for a deeper, more complex flavor. Bittersweet or semisweet chocolate provided the main thrust of flavor, and intensely flavored unsweetened chocolate lent depth—one ounce of unsweetened chocolate may not seem like much, but it gave this pie great flavor. We also discovered that the custard's texture depended upon carefully pouring the egg yolk mixture into simmering half-and-half, then whisking in butter. Do not combine the egg yolks and sugar in advance of making the filling—the sugar will begin to break down the yolks, and the finished cream will be pitted.

PIE

2½   **cups half-and-half**
⅓   **cup (2⅓ ounces) sugar**
    Pinch salt
6   **large egg yolks**
2   **tablespoons cornstarch**
6   **tablespoons unsalted butter, cut into 6 pieces**
6   **ounces semisweet or bittersweet chocolate, chopped fine**
1   **ounce unsweetened chocolate, chopped fine**
1   **teaspoon vanilla extract**
1   **recipe Chocolate Cookie Crust (page 702), baked and cooled**

TOPPING

1½   **cups heavy cream, chilled**
2   **tablespoons sugar**
½   **teaspoon vanilla extract**

1. FOR THE PIE: Bring half-and-half, 3 tablespoons sugar, and salt to simmer in medium saucepan, stirring occasionally. As half-and-half mixture begins to simmer, whisk egg yolks, cornstarch, and remaining sugar together in medium bowl until smooth. Slowly whisk 1 cup of simmering half-and-half mixture into yolk mixture to temper, then slowly whisk tempered yolk mixture back into remaining half-and-half mixture.

2. Reduce heat to medium and cook, whisking vigorously, until mixture is thickened and few bubbles burst on surface, about 30 seconds. Off heat, whisk in butter, semisweet chocolate, and unsweetened chocolate until completely smooth and melted. Stir in vanilla.

3. Pour warm filling into cooled prebaked pie crust. Lay sheet of plastic wrap directly on surface of filling. Refrigerate pie until filling is chilled and set, at least 4 hours or up to 1 day.

4. FOR THE TOPPING: Before serving, use stand mixer fitted with whisk to whip cream, sugar, and vanilla on medium-low speed until foamy, about 1 minute. Increase speed to high and whip until soft peaks form, 1 to 3 minutes. Spread whipped cream attractively over top of pie and serve.

NOTES FROM THE TEST KITCHEN

Storing Pies

Because of their high dairy content, leftover custard- and cream-filled pies (including pumpkin) must be wrapped tightly in plastic wrap and stored in the refrigerator. They will generally last for a day or two stored this way. If you're planning on serving only a few slices from a whipped cream–topped pie, top each slice individually with whipped cream and save the rest of the pie for later.

Double-crust and lattice-topped fruit pies such as apple, peach, blueberry, and cherry can safely be stored at room temperature because of their high sugar content and acidity, which retard the growth of bacteria. To find out if fruit pies fare better when refrigerated or stored at room temperature, we held a baking marathon, then stored pies both ways. In all cases, refrigeration turned the crisp crusts on fruit pies gummy. This occurs as a result of retrogradation, or the process by which the structure of the starch changes and becomes stale. So when it comes to fruit pies, room temperature is the way to go. Wrapped well in foil and stored at room temperature, pies made with cooked fruit will last up to two days.

Note that pies made with fresh, uncooked fruit such as strawberries are a different story. These delicate pies often contain gelatin and should be stored in the refrigerator for up to one day.

A layer of chopped honey-roasted peanuts on top of the crust of our peanut butter pie adds crunch and flavor.

Peanut Butter Pie

SERVES 8 **TOTAL TIME** 25 MINUTES
(PLUS 2 HOURS CHILLING TIME)

✓ **WHY THIS RECIPE WORKS:** For a pie with the intense, nutty flavor of peanut butter but not its dense texture, we started by whipping smooth peanut butter with cream cheese (for tang and sliceability), confectioners' sugar, and just a touch of cream until it was light and fluffy; we then folded in more whipped cream to lighten it even further. To enhance our basic graham cracker pie shell, we swapped out granulated sugar for brown—its caramel notes complemented the peanut flavor. We sprinkled the baked crust with candied peanuts before layering in the filling, and then topped the whole thing with still more whipped cream before chilling. Before serving, a second dose of crunchy nuts was the finishing touch. All-natural peanut butters will work in this recipe. You can use our Homemade Candied Peanuts in place of the honey-roasted peanuts.

HOMEMADE CANDIED PEANUTS

MAKES ABOUT ½ CUP   **TOTAL TIME** 20 MINUTES **FAST**

½   **cup dry-roasted peanuts**
2   **tablespoons sugar**
2   **tablespoons water**
¼   **teaspoon salt**

1. Line baking sheet with parchment paper. Bring all ingredients to boil in medium saucepan over medium heat. Cook, stirring constantly, until water evaporates and sugar appears dry and somewhat crystallized and evenly coats peanuts, about 5 minutes.

2. Reduce heat to low and continue to cook, stirring constantly, until sugar turns amber color, about 2 minutes. Spread peanuts out evenly over prepared sheet. Let cool completely, about 10 minutes.

½   **cup honey-roasted peanuts, chopped**
1   **recipe Graham Cracker Crust (page 702), baked and cooled**
¾   **cup creamy peanut butter**
6   **ounces cream cheese, softened**
¾   **cup (3 ounces) plus 2 tablespoons confectioners' sugar**
1¾ **cups heavy cream**
1   **teaspoon vanilla extract**

1. Spread ⅓ cup chopped peanuts evenly over bottom of cooled crust.

2. Using stand mixer fitted with whisk, mix peanut butter, cream cheese, ¾ cup confectioners' sugar, and 3 tablespoons cream on low speed until combined, about 1 minute. Increase speed to medium-high and whip until fluffy, about 1 minute. Transfer to large bowl.

3. In now-empty mixer bowl, whip ¾ cup cream on medium-low speed until foamy, about 1 minute. Increase speed to high and whip until stiff peaks form, 1 to 3 minutes. Gently fold whipped cream into peanut butter mixture in 2 additions until no white streaks remain. Spread filling evenly into crust on top of nuts.

4. In now-empty mixer bowl, whip vanilla, remaining cream, and remaining 2 tablespoons confectioners' sugar on medium-low speed until foamy, about 1 minute. Increase speed to high and whip until stiff peaks form, 1 to 3 minutes. Spread whipped cream evenly over filling. Refrigerate pie until filling is chilled and set, at least 2 hours or up to 1 day. Sprinkle with remaining chopped peanuts before serving.

Grasshopper Pie

SERVES 8   **TOTAL TIME** 50 MINUTES
(PLUS 6 HOURS CHILLING TIME)

✓ **WHY THIS RECIPE WORKS:** For the mint-flavored crust in our Grasshopper Pie recipe, we crushed minty Oreo cookies. The food processor made quick work of this task, but smashing them with a rolling pin worked just as well. Mint liqueur lent an intensely minty flavor to our filling, which we thickened with gelatin. The perfect texture of our pie relied on carefully beating the cream: To avoid a grainy texture, we started beating the cream slowly, and then increased the mixer's speed once the cream began to build in volume.

2¼ teaspoons unflavored gelatin
½ cup (3½ ounces) sugar
2 cups heavy cream
  Pinch salt
3 large egg yolks
¼ cup green crème de menthe
¼ cup white crème de cacao
1 Mint Chocolate Cookie Crust (page 702),
  baked and cooled
  Chocolate shavings, for decorating

1. Combine gelatin, sugar, ½ cup cream, and salt in medium saucepan and let sit until gelatin softens, about 5 minutes.

2. Beat egg yolks in medium bowl. Cook gelatin mixture over medium heat until gelatin dissolves and mixture is very hot but not boiling, about 2 minutes. Whisking vigorously, slowly add gelatin mixture to beaten egg yolks. Return mixture to saucepan and cook, stirring constantly, until slightly thickened, about 2 minutes. Off heat, add crème de menthe and crème de cacao. Pour into clean bowl and refrigerate, stirring occasionally, until wobbly but not set, about 20 minutes.

3. Using stand mixer fitted with whisk, whip remaining 1½ cups cream on medium-low speed until foamy, about 1 minute. Increase speed to high and whip until stiff peaks form, 1 to 3 minutes. Whisk 1 cup whipped cream into gelatin mixture until completely incorporated. Using rubber spatula, gently fold gelatin mixture into remaining whipped cream until no streaks of white remain.

4. Scrape mixture into cooled prebaked pie crust and smooth top. Cover loosely with plastic wrap and refrigerate until firm, at least 6 hours or up to 2 days. Before serving, garnish with chocolate shavings.

A stiff marshmallow crème is key to creating the perfect nougat layer in our pie version of a Snickers candy bar.

Snickers Icebox Pie

SERVES 8   **TOTAL TIME** 1 HOUR
(PLUS 2 HOURS CHILLING TIME)

✓ **WHY THIS RECIPE WORKS:** In creating the ultimate Snickers Icebox Pie we wanted a simple pie that tasted just like the candy bar. Focusing first on the nougat layer, we found that a combination of marshmallow crème, cream cheese, cream, peanut butter, and butter provided the perfect balance of flavor and texture. The cream cheese took the edge off the sweetness of the marshmallow crème, while the cream helped to make it fluffy and light, rather than sticky and gooey. To this mixture we added a touch of melted caramel to round out the nougat flavor. With a chocolate cookie crust, a layer each of caramel and chocolate, and some roasted peanuts, this icebox pie is a perfect rendition of a Snickers candy bar. We prefer a stiffer marshmallow crème in this filling, such as Jet-Puffed or Fluff; other brands may be too runny. We like to use either Kraft Caramels or Brach's Milk Maid Caramels for this recipe, but any brand of soft caramels will do. The crust must still be hot when you sprinkle the chocolate chips over it—otherwise they will not soften sufficiently.

  1 cup (6 ounces) semisweet chocolate chips
  1 recipe Chocolate Cookie Crust (page 702),
    baked and still hot
1½ cups marshmallow crème
  4 ounces cream cheese, softened
  ½ cup heavy cream
  ½ cup creamy peanut butter
  2 tablespoons unsalted butter, softened
  7 ounces soft caramels (about 26 candies)
  ¼ cup water
  ¼ cup unsalted roasted peanuts, chopped
    Chocolate shavings, for decorating

1. Sprinkle chocolate chips evenly over hot pie crust; let sit until softened but not melted, about 5 minutes. Smooth chocolate into even layer, then refrigerate until chocolate is set, 20 to 25 minutes.

2. Using stand mixer fitted with paddle, beat marshmallow crème, cream cheese, heavy cream, peanut butter, and butter on medium-high speed until light and fluffy, about 2 minutes.

3. Cook caramels and water together in small saucepan over medium-high heat, stirring occasionally, until melted and smooth, 8 to 10 minutes. Stir 1 tablespoon hot caramel into marshmallow crème mixture. Spread remaining hot caramel evenly over chilled chocolate layer in pie crust. Sprinkle with peanuts and refrigerate until caramel is just set, about 10 minutes.

4. Dollop marshmallow crème mixture on top of caramel and spread into even layer. Refrigerate pie, uncovered, until chilled and set, at least 2 hours or up to 1 day. Before serving, garnish with chocolate shavings.

Making Chocolate Shavings

Scrape vegetable peeler against block of room-temperature (or slightly warm) chocolate to make chocolate shavings.

Our rustic fruit tart combines stone fruits and berries for appealing flavor and texture.

Free-Form Summer Fruit Tart

SERVES 6   **TOTAL TIME** 2 HOURS
(PLUS 25 MINUTES COOLING TIME)

✔ **WHY THIS RECIPE WORKS:** For a simple summer fruit tart that's as good as harder-to-prepare pie, we started with a foolproof free-form tart dough. To keep the delicate dough from breaking, we rolled it out between parchment sheets and chilled it until firm. Rolling the dough into a 12-inch circle produced a crust that was thick enough to contain a lot of fruit but thin enough to bake evenly. A mix of stone fruits and berries produced an especially nice contrast in flavors and textures. We placed the fruit in the middle, then lifted the dough over the fruit (leaving the center exposed). To prevent the tart from leaking, we found it crucial to leave a small swath about ½ inch wide between the fruit and the edge of the tart to act as a barrier. Taste the fruit before adding sugar; use less sugar if the fruit is very sweet, more if it is tart. Do not add the sugar to the fruit until you are ready to fill and form the tart. Serve with vanilla ice cream or Whipped Cream (page 712).

Free-form tarts are a rustic and beautiful alternative to a traditional fruit pie. But there are pitfalls, namely dough that leaks in the oven because it isn't sturdy enough to contain the fruit. Our Free-Form Tart Dough (page 702), which we make in the food processor, is especially flaky and strong, making the process more foolproof. Two other tricks help the tart turn out perfectly. First, be sure to pile the fruit in the very center of the dough, leaving plenty of room around the edge in order to fashion a crust. Second, leave a swath between the fruit and the edge of the tart to help prevent the juice from the filling from leaking out during baking.

1. SMEAR THE DOUGH AGAINST THE COUNTER: Turn the dough out onto a floured counter and make a rectangular pile. Starting at the farthest end, smear the dough against the counter, away from you. Repeat until all the buttery crumbs have been worked.
WHY? Smearing the dough pushes the butter chunks into long, thin sheets that make the dough flaky and sturdy, and far less prone to leaking in the oven.

2. SMEAR THE DOUGH AGAIN: Gather the smeared bits of dough back into a rectangular pile and repeat the smearing process until all the crumbs have been worked a second time.
WHY? This second round of smearing ensures that the butter is evenly worked into the dough; note that this will result in large flakes of dough that stick to your palms.

3. CHILL THE DOUGH: Press the flakes of smeared dough together and form into a 6-inch disk. Wrap the disk tightly in plastic wrap and refrigerate for 1 hour.
WHY? Since cold fat is essential to creating a flaky texture, the dough must go into the fridge to chill before rolling. Also, the gluten in the flour will relax a bit as the dough chills, ensuring that the dough isn't tough.

4. ROLL OUT THE DOUGH: Roll the chilled dough between sheets of floured parchment into a 12-inch circle, flipping the dough over and loosening the parchment as needed. Slide the dough, still between parchment, onto a rimmed baking sheet and refrigerate until firm.
WHY? Rolling this fragile dough between parchment prevents tearing; if the dough sticks to the parchment it doesn't matter because the tart is baked on the paper.

5. ARRANGE THE FRUIT: Remove the top sheet of parchment from the dough and arrange the fruit in the center, leaving a 2½-inch border around the edge.
WHY? It's important to leave the outer edge of the dough free of fruit. Also, piling the fruit in the center of the tart makes for a prettier, full-looking tart.

6. FOLD AND PLEAT THE DOUGH: Fold the outermost 2 inches of the dough over the fruit, pleating every 2 to 3 inches as needed; be sure to leave a ½-inch border of dough between the fruit and edge of the tart. Gently pinch the pleated dough to secure it.
WHY? The gap between the fruit and tart's edge keeps the fruit juices from leaking.

7. BAKE THE TART: Brush the dough with water and sprinkle with sugar. Bake the tart in a 375-degree oven until the crust is golden brown and the fruit is tender, about 1 hour, rotating the baking sheet halfway through baking.
WHY? Brushing the tart with water helps the sugar to stick. A rimmed baking sheet catches any juices that leak.

8. COOL THE TART: Cool the tart on the baking sheet for 10 minutes. Use the parchment to transfer it to a wire rack, then remove the paper with the help of a thin metal spatula. Let the tart cool 25 minutes before serving.
WHY? Cooling the tart on the baking sheet first allows the crust to set up so that you can safely transfer it to a wire rack.

1 recipe Free-Form Tart Dough (page 702)
1 pound peaches, nectarines, apricots, or plums, halved, pitted, and cut into ½-inch wedges
5 ounces (1 cup) blackberries, blueberries, or raspberries
¼ cup (1¾ ounces) plus 1 tablespoon sugar

1. Roll dough into 12-inch circle between 2 large sheets of floured parchment paper. (If dough sticks to parchment, gently loosen dough with bench scraper and dust parchment with additional flour.) Slide dough, still between parchment sheets, onto rimmed baking sheet and refrigerate until firm, 15 to 30 minutes.

2. Adjust oven rack to middle position and heat oven to 375 degrees. Gently toss fruit and ¼ cup sugar together in bowl.

3. Remove top sheet of parchment paper from dough. Mound fruit in center of dough, leaving 2½-inch border around edge of fruit. Fold outermost 2 inches of dough over fruit, pleating it every 2 to 3 inches as needed; be sure to leave ½-inch border of dough between fruit and edge of tart. Gently pinch pleated dough to secure, but do not press dough into fruit.

4. Brush top and sides of dough lightly with water and sprinkle with remaining 1 tablespoon sugar. Bake until crust is golden brown and fruit is bubbling, about 1 hour, rotating baking sheet halfway through baking.

5. Let tart cool on baking sheet for 10 minutes. Use parchment to transfer tart to wire rack, then discard parchment and let tart cool until filling thickens, about 25 minutes. Serve slightly warm or at room temperature.

A mix of Granny Smith and McIntosh apples gives this free-form tart complex flavor.

the edge of the dough around the apples before baking the tart until golden brown. To prevent the tart from leaking, it is crucial to leave a ½-inch-wide border of dough around the fruit. Serve with vanilla ice cream or Whipped Cream (page 712).

Free-Form Apple Tart

SERVES 6   **TOTAL TIME** 2 HOURS
(PLUS 25 MINUTES COOLING TIME)

✔ **WHY THIS RECIPE WORKS:** For our free-form apple tart, we started by rolling out our Free-Form Tart Dough between two sheets of parchment paper to keep the delicate dough from breaking. Then we transferred the dough sandwich to a baking sheet and chilled it until firm. A mix of Granny Smith and McIntosh apples gave us complex flavor, and just ½ cup of sugar, a squeeze of lemon juice, and a pinch of cinnamon perfected the filling. We stacked the apples in a ring, then filled the ring in with more apples to give the finished tart a neater, fuller appearance. Finally, we just folded and pleated

1 recipe Free-Form Tart Dough (page 702)
1 pound Granny Smith apples, peeled, cored, and sliced ¼ inch thick
1 pound McIntosh apples, peeled, cored, and sliced ¼ inch thick
½ cup (3½ ounces) plus 1 tablespoon sugar
1 tablespoon lemon juice
⅛ teaspoon ground cinnamon

1. Roll dough into 12-inch circle between 2 large sheets of floured parchment paper. (If dough sticks to parchment, gently loosen dough with bench scraper and dust parchment with additional flour.) Slide dough, still between parchment sheets, onto rimmed baking sheet and refrigerate until firm, 15 to 30 minutes.

2. Adjust oven rack to middle position and heat oven to 375 degrees. Toss apples, ½ cup sugar, lemon juice, and cinnamon together in large bowl.

3. Remove top sheet of parchment paper from dough. Stack some apple slices into circular wall around dough, leaving 2½-inch border around edge of fruit. Fill in middle of tart with remaining apples. Fold outermost 2 inches of dough over fruit, pleating it every 2 to 3 inches as needed; be sure to leave ½-inch border of dough between fruit and edge of tart. Gently pinch pleated dough to secure, but do not press dough into fruit.

4. Brush top and sides of dough lightly with water and sprinkle with remaining 1 tablespoon sugar. Bake until crust is golden brown and apples are tender, about 1 hour, rotating baking sheet halfway through baking.

5. Let tart cool on baking sheet for 10 minutes. Use parchment to transfer tart to wire rack, then discard parchment and let tart cool until apple juices have thickened, about 25 minutes. Serve slightly warm or at room temperature.

Easy Caramel Apple Tart

SERVES 6   **TOTAL TIME** 2 HOURS

✅ **WHY THIS RECIPE WORKS:** For an impressive yet effortless French-style apple and caramel tart, we used jarred caramel sauce to give the apples a sweet, glazed coating. For complexity, we added a bit of vanilla, plus a rather unexpected ingredient: garam masala. Microwaving the apples drove off moisture that would have made the bottom of the crust soggy. Glazing our baked tart with more caramel gave it an elegant shine, and serving it with vanilla ice cream was the final touch: As the ice cream melted, it seeped in between the apples, adding its rich, sweet flavor into the mix. Any brand of high-quality jarred caramel sauce will work fine here.

- 2 **pounds Granny Smith apples, peeled, cored, and sliced ¼ inch thick**
  Pinch salt
- 1 **recipe Classic Tart Dough (page 703), fully baked and cooled**
- ¾ **cup caramel sauce**
- 1 **teaspoon vanilla extract**
- ½ **teaspoon garam masala**
- 1½ **pints vanilla ice cream**

1. Adjust oven rack to middle position and heat oven to 375 degrees. Toss apples with salt in bowl, cover, and microwave at 50 percent power, stirring occasionally, until apples begin to soften, 10 to 12 minutes; drain well.

2. Starting at edge of cooled tart shell and working toward center, shingle apples in overlapping rows. Repeat with remaining apples to form second layer on top of first layer.

3. Microwave ½ cup caramel sauce, vanilla, and garam masala together in bowl until sauce liquefies, about 20 seconds. Pour caramel mixture evenly over apples. Bake until filling is bubbling at edges and topping is golden, about 35 minutes, rotating baking sheet halfway through baking.

4. Let tart cool on baking sheet, at least 30 minutes or up to 8 hours. Heat 1 tablespoon caramel sauce in bowl in microwave to liquefy, about 10 seconds. Brush warm caramel over tart and let set slightly, about 15 minutes. To serve, remove outer ring of tart pan, slide thin metal spatula between tart and tart pan bottom, and carefully slide tart onto serving platter or cutting board. Garnish individual portions with small scoops of ice cream and remaining caramel sauce.

Arranging Apples in a Tart

Starting at edge and working toward center, shingle apples in overlapping rows over tart shell. Repeat with remaining apples to form second layer on top of first. Use any very soft or broken apples in bottom layer.

Fresh Fruit Tart

SERVES 8 TO 10   **TOTAL TIME** 40 MINUTES
(PLUS 3 HOURS CHILLING TIME)

✅ **WHY THIS RECIPE WORKS:** Beyond their dazzling beauty, fresh fruit tarts usually offer little substance: rubbery or puddinglike fillings, soggy crusts, and underripe, flavorless fruit. We set out to create a buttery, crisp crust filled with rich, lightly sweetened pastry cream and topped with fresh fruit. We started with our Classic Tart Dough and baked it until it was golden brown. We then filled the tart with pastry cream made with half-and-half that was enriched with butter and thickened with just enough cornstarch to keep its shape without becoming gummy. For the fruit, we chose a combination of sliced kiwis, raspberries, and blueberries. We found that it was important not to wash the berries, as washing caused them to bruise and bleed and made for a less-than-attractive tart. (Buy organic if you're worried about pesticide residues.) The finishing touch: a drizzle of jelly glaze for a glistening presentation. Do not fill the prebaked tart shell until just before serving. Once filled, the tart should be topped with fruit, glazed, and served within 30 minutes or so.

2 cups half-and-half
½ cup (3½ ounces) sugar
Pinch salt
5 large egg yolks
3 tablespoons cornstarch
4 tablespoons unsalted butter, cut into 4 pieces
1½ teaspoons vanilla extract
1 recipe Classic Tart Dough (page 703), fully baked and cooled
2 large kiwis, peeled, halved lengthwise, and sliced ⅜ inch thick
10 ounces (2 cups) raspberries
5 ounces (1 cup) blueberries
½ cup red currant or apple jelly

1. Bring half-and-half, 6 tablespoons sugar, and salt to simmer in medium saucepan, stirring occasionally. As half-and-half mixture begins to simmer, whisk egg yolks, cornstarch, and remaining 2 tablespoons sugar together in medium bowl until smooth.

2. Slowly whisk 1 cup simmering half-and-half mixture into yolk mixture to temper, then slowly whisk tempered yolk mixture back into remaining half-and-half mixture. Reduce heat to medium and cook, whisking vigorously, until mixture is thickened and few bubbles burst on surface, about 30 seconds. Off heat, whisk in butter and vanilla.

3. Transfer mixture to clean bowl, lay sheet of plastic wrap directly on surface, and refrigerate pastry cream until chilled and firm, at least 3 hours or up to 2 days.

4. Whisk pastry cream briefly, then spread evenly over bottom of cooled prebaked tart shell. Shingle kiwi slices on top of pastry cream around edge of tart, then arrange 3 rows of raspberries inside kiwi row. Finally, arrange mound of blueberries in center.

5. Melt jelly in small saucepan over medium-high heat, stirring occasionally to smooth out any lumps. Using pastry brush, dab melted jelly over fruit. To serve, remove outer ring of tart pan, slide thin metal spatula between tart and tart pan bottom, and carefully slide tart onto serving platter or cutting board.

Making a Fresh Fruit Tart

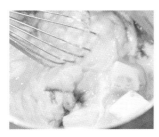   

1. MAKE PASTRY CREAM: Cook pastry cream on stovetop until thickened, about 30 seconds. Off heat, whisk in butter and vanilla.

2. SPREAD CHILLED PASTRY CREAM INTO PREBAKED TART SHELL: Chill pastry cream in refrigerator until firm, about 3 hours. Whisk pastry cream briefly, then spread evenly over bottom of cooled prebaked tart shell.

3. ARRANGE FRUIT ATTRACTIVELY OVER TOP: Shingle kiwi slices around edge of tart, then arrange 3 rows of raspberries inside kiwi row. Finally, arrange mound of blueberries in center.

4. GLAZE TART: Melt jelly in small saucepan over medium-high heat, stirring occasionally. Using pastry brush, dab melted jelly over fruit.

Baked Raspberry Tart

SERVES 8 TO 10   **TOTAL TIME** 1 HOUR 10 MINUTES
(PLUS 2 HOURS COOLING TIME)

✔ **WHY THIS RECIPE WORKS:** To perfect our baked berry tart—using a partially baked tart shell loaded with raspberries and topped with a simple butter, egg, sugar, and flour filling—we focused on the filling, since we were happy with our classic tart crust. We heightened the filling's flavor by browning the butter instead of simply melting it, and by substituting Wondra instant flour for all-purpose flour, for a smooth and silky texture. Wondra is sold in the baking aisle. To minimize waste, reserve the egg white left from making the tart pastry for use in the filling. If your raspberries are either very tart or very sweet, adjust the amount of sugar by about a tablespoon or so.

6	**tablespoons unsalted butter**
1	**large egg plus 1 large white**
½	**cup (3½ ounces) plus 1 tablespoon sugar**
¼	**teaspoon salt**
1	**teaspoon vanilla extract**
¼	**teaspoon grated lemon zest plus 1½ teaspoons juice**
1	**teaspoon kirsch or framboise (optional)**
2	**tablespoons instant flour (such as Wondra)**
2	**tablespoons heavy cream**
10	**ounces (2 cups) raspberries**
1	**recipe Classic Tart Dough (page 703), partially baked and cooled**

1. Adjust oven rack to middle position and heat oven to 375 degrees. Melt butter in small saucepan over medium heat, swirling occasionally, until butter is browned and releases nutty aroma, about 7 minutes; transfer to bowl and let cool slightly.

2. Whisk egg and white together in medium bowl, then vigorously whisk in sugar and salt until light-colored, about 1 minute. Whisk in browned butter until combined. Whisk in vanilla, lemon zest and juice, and kirsch, if using. Whisk in instant flour. Whisk in cream until thoroughly combined.

3. Distribute raspberries in single tightly packed layer in bottom of cooled partially baked tart shell. Pour filling mixture evenly over raspberries. Bake tart on baking sheet until fragrant, filling is set (does not jiggle when shaken) and bubbling lightly around edges, and surface is puffed and deep golden brown, about 30 minutes, rotating baking sheet halfway through baking.

4. Let tart cool on baking sheet to room temperature, about 2 hours. To serve, remove outer ring of tart pan, slide thin metal spatula between tart and tart pan bottom, and carefully slide tart onto serving platter or cutting board.

A simple lemon curd enriched with cream is easy to make on the stovetop and is the filling for this bracing lemon tart.

Lemon Tart

SERVES 8 TO 10   **TOTAL TIME** 40 MINUTES
(PLUS 2 HOURS COOLING TIME)

✔ **WHY THIS RECIPE WORKS:** Despite its apparent simplicity, there is much that can go wrong with a lemon tart. It can slip over the edge of sweet into cloying; its tartness can grab at your throat; it can be gluey or eggy or, even worse, metallic-tasting, and its crust can be too hard, too soft, too thick, or too sweet. We wanted a proper tart, one with filling that is baked with the shell. For us, that meant only one thing: lemon curd. For just enough sugar to offset the acid in the lemons, we used 3 parts sugar to 2 parts lemon juice, plus a whopping ¼ cup of lemon zest. To achieve a curd that was creamy and dense with a vibrant lemony yellow color, we used a combination of whole eggs and egg yolks, and then cooked the curd over direct heat. And for a smooth, light texture, we strained the curd and then stirred in heavy cream just before baking. Once the lemon curd ingredients have been combined, cook the curd immediately; otherwise, its finished texture will be grainy. The shell should still be warm when the filling is added. We dusted the tart with confectioners' sugar before serving; you can also serve it with Whipped Cream (page 712).

2 large eggs plus 7 large yolks
1 cup (7 ounces) sugar
¼ cup grated lemon zest plus ⅔ cup juice (4 lemons)
Pinch salt
4 tablespoons unsalted butter, cut into 4 pieces
3 tablespoons heavy cream
1 recipe Classic Tart Dough (page 703), partially baked and still warm
Confectioners' sugar

1. Adjust oven rack to middle position and heat oven to 375 degrees. Whisk eggs and yolks together in medium saucepan. Whisk in sugar until combined, then whisk in lemon zest and juice and salt. Add butter and cook over medium-low heat, stirring constantly, until mixture thickens slightly and registers 170 degrees, about 5 minutes. Immediately pour mixture through fine-mesh strainer into bowl. Stir in cream.

2. Pour warm lemon filling into warm partially baked tart shell. Bake tart on baking sheet until filling is shiny and opaque and center jiggles slightly when shaken, 10 to 15 minutes, rotating baking sheet halfway through baking.

3. Let tart cool on baking sheet to room temperature, about 2 hours. To serve, remove outer ring of tart pan, slide thin metal spatula between tart and tart pan bottom, and carefully slide tart onto serving platter or cutting board. Dust with confectioners' sugar.

Nutella Tart

SERVES 8 TO 10   **TOTAL TIME** 50 MINUTES
(PLUS 1 HOUR 30 MINUTES CHILLING TIME)

✓ WHY THIS RECIPE WORKS: Nutella is the surprise base for the no-bake filling of this easy-to-make chocolate tart featuring the irresistible combination of rich chocolate and hazelnuts. For a dense and velvety filling, we included Nutella in a simple ganache made of chocolate and cream. Adding butter to the mixture proved important because it helped make the filling sliceable once it was chilled. To assemble the filling, we found the microwave was the easiest method as long as we used a low power and stirred the mixture often as the chocolate and butter melted. If the microwave power is too high, you'll risk breaking the ganache, which then cools into a grainy texture. Adding a layer of chopped toasted hazelnuts to the tart, underneath the ganache, added both flavor and crunch. A garnish of whole toasted hazelnuts completed the look, but we had to add them after the filling had firmed slightly or else they sank down in the filling.

1 cup hazelnuts
1 recipe Classic Tart Dough (page 703), fully baked and cooled
2 ounces bittersweet chocolate, finely chopped
1¼ cups Nutella
½ cup heavy cream
2 tablespoons unsalted butter
1 recipe Whipped Cream (page 712) (optional)

Making a Lemon Tart

1. COOK LEMON CURD: Cook lemon curd in medium saucepan over medium-low heat, stirring constantly, until it thickens slightly and registers 170 degrees, about 5 minutes.

2. STRAIN LEMON CURD: Immediately pour mixture through fine-mesh strainer into bowl. Use rubber spatula to help work curd through strainer. Stir in cream.

3. POUR CURD INTO PREBAKED TART SHELL: Pour warm lemon filling into warm partially baked tart shell.

4. BAKE TART BRIEFLY: Bake tart on baking sheet until filling is shiny and opaque and center jiggles slightly when shaken, 10 to 15 minutes, rotating baking sheet halfway through baking.

We make a rich, no-bake chocolate and hazelnut filling for this easy tart in the microwave using Nutella.

1. Adjust oven rack to middle position and heat oven to 375 degrees. Toast hazelnuts on rimmed baking sheet until skins begin to blister and crack, 15 to 20 minutes. Wrap warm nuts in dish towel and rub gently to remove skins. Reserve 24 whole nuts for garnish, then chop remaining nuts coarsely. Sprinkle chopped nuts into cooled prebaked tart shell.

2. Microwave chocolate, Nutella, cream, and butter in covered bowl at 30 percent power, stirring often, until mixture is smooth and glossy, about 1 minute (do not overheat).

3. Pour warm chocolate mixture evenly into tart shell. Refrigerate tart, uncovered, until filling is just set, about 15 minutes. Arrange reserved whole nuts around edge of tart, cover loosely with plastic wrap, and continue to refrigerate until filling is firm, at least 1½ hours or up to 1 day.

4. To serve, remove outer ring of tart pan, slide thin metal spatula between tart and tart pan bottom, and carefully slide tart onto serving platter or cutting board. Serve with whipped cream, if desired.

Garnishing a Nutella Tart

After tart has chilled 15 minutes to allow filling to set slightly, arrange reserved whole nuts around edge of tart. Cover tart loosely with plastic wrap, and continue to refrigerate until filling is firm, about 1½ hours.

Chocolate Truffle Tart

SERVES 8 TO 10   **TOTAL TIME** 25 MINUTES
(PLUS 2 HOURS CHILLING TIME)

✔ **WHY THIS RECIPE WORKS:** The simplicity of this chocolate tart's filling belies its rich flavor and dense but silky texture. We learned that the choice of chocolate really mattered here and that it is worth tracking down good-quality bittersweet chocolate. The addition of cognac (or brandy) in the recipe rounded out the chocolate's flavor and added further dimension to it. During testing, we also learned that stirring the chocolate, cream, and butter together required a light hand. Vigorous stirring aerated the mixture, causing unattractive bubbles in the filling once it set. Brandy or Grand Marnier may be substituted for the cognac. This tart is extremely rich and is best served with fresh berries and unsweetened whipped cream.

- 1 **cup heavy cream**
- 12 **ounces bittersweet chocolate, chopped fine**
- 6 **tablespoons unsalted butter, softened**
- 1 **tablespoon cognac**
- 1 **recipe Classic Tart Dough (page 703), fully baked and cooled**

1. Bring cream to brief simmer in small saucepan over medium-high heat. Off heat, stir in chocolate and butter, cover pan, and let stand until chocolate is mostly melted, about 2 minutes. Gently stir mixture until smooth. Stir in cognac.

2. Pour warm chocolate mixture evenly into cooled prebaked tart shell. Refrigerate tart, uncovered, until filling is firm, at least 2 hours or up to 1 day.

3. To serve, remove outer ring of tart pan, slide thin metal spatula between tart and tart pan bottom, and carefully slide tart onto serving platter or cutting board.

VARIATIONS

Espresso Truffle Tart

Omit cognac. Add 2 teaspoons instant espresso powder (or instant coffee) to hot cream with chocolate.

Peanut Butter Truffle Tart

Spread ½ cup smooth peanut butter evenly over bottom of tart shell and refrigerate while preparing chocolate filling. Pour warm chocolate filling over peanut butter; chill as directed.

Rustic Walnut Tart

SERVES 8 TO 10   **TOTAL TIME** 50 MINUTES
(PLUS 2 HOURS COOLING TIME)

☑ **WHY THIS RECIPE WORKS:** This elegant nut tart is surprisingly easy to prepare, thanks to the very simple filling. For the filling, we used a pecan pie base but swapped in walnuts, reduced the amount of sugar, and added a hefty amount of vanilla as well as a hit of bourbon (or rum). The liquor cuts through the sweetness and intensifies the flavor of the nuts. Pecans can be substituted for the walnuts if desired.

A little bourbon cuts the sweetness of this elegant nut tart.

½	**cup packed (3½ ounces) light brown sugar**
⅓	**cup light corn syrup**
4	**tablespoons unsalted butter, melted and cooled**
1	**tablespoon bourbon or dark rum**
2	**teaspoons vanilla extract**
½	**teaspoon salt**
1	**large egg**
1	**recipe Classic Tart Dough (page 703), fully baked and cooled**
1¾	**cups (7 ounces) walnuts, chopped coarse**
1	**recipe Bourbon Whipped Cream (page 712) (optional)**

1. Adjust oven rack to middle position and heat oven to 375 degrees. Whisk sugar, corn syrup, butter, bourbon, vanilla, and salt in large bowl until sugar dissolves. Whisk in egg until combined. Pour filling evenly into cooled prebaked tart shell and sprinkle with walnuts. Bake tart on baking sheet until filling is set and walnuts begin to brown, 30 to 40 minutes, rotating baking sheet halfway through baking.

2. Let tart cool on baking sheet to room temperature, about 2 hours. (Tart can be refrigerated for up 2 days; bring to room temperature before serving.)

3. To serve, remove outer ring of tart pan, slide thin metal spatula between tart and tart pan bottom, and carefully slide tart onto serving platter or cutting board. Serve with whipped cream, if desired.

Removing a Tart from a Tart Pan

1. Holding tart steady with one hand, gently remove outer ring from tart.

2. Slide thin metal spatula between tart and tart pan bottom, and carefully slide tart onto serving platter or cutting board.

CHAPTER 20

Fruit Desserts

Crisps, Cobblers, Shortcakes, and More

Trifles and More

Roasted Fruit, Poached Fruit, and Compotes

Our stovetop-to-oven method concentrates the apple flavor and produces a topping that's truly crisp.

Skillet Apple Crisp

SERVES 6 TO 8 **TOTAL TIME** 1 HOUR 25 MINUTES

✔ **WHY THIS RECIPE WORKS:** We wanted an exemplary apple crisp—a lush (but not mushy) sweet-tart apple filling covered with truly crisp morsels of topping. Our first few crisps contained unevenly cooked apples; stirring the fruit helped solve the texture problem, but reaching into a hot oven to do so was a hassle. Instead, we softened the apples on the stovetop—in a skillet. The shallow, flared pan also encouraged evaporation, browning, and better flavor overall. To improve the flavor further, we turned to apple cider, reducing it to a syrupy consistency. As for the topping, we added brown sugar to the white to play up the apples' caramel notes, and swapped out some flour for rolled oats to give the topping character and chew. Chopped pecans not only improved the crunch factor, but added a rich flavor as well. If your skillet is not ovensafe, prepare the recipe through step 3 and then transfer the filling to a 13 by 9-inch baking dish; top the filling as directed and bake for 5 minutes longer than the times given in the recipe. We like Golden Delicious apples in this recipe, but Honeycrisp or Braeburn apples can be substituted; do not use Granny Smith apples. While old-fashioned rolled oats are preferable in this recipe, quick oats can be substituted; do not use instant oats. Serve with vanilla ice cream.

TOPPING

- ¾ **cup (3¾ ounces) all-purpose flour**
- ¾ **cup pecans, chopped fine**
- ¾ **cup (2¼ ounces) old-fashioned rolled oats**
- ½ **cup packed (3½ ounces) light brown sugar**
- ¼ **cup (1¾ ounces) granulated sugar**
- ½ **teaspoon ground cinnamon**
- ½ **teaspoon salt**
- 8 **tablespoons unsalted butter, melted**

FILLING

- 3 **pounds Golden Delicious apples, peeled, cored, halved, and cut into ½-inch wedges**
- ¼ **cup (1¾ ounces) granulated sugar**
- ¼ **teaspoon ground cinnamon**
- 1 **cup apple cider**
- 2 **teaspoons lemon juice**
- 2 **tablespoons unsalted butter**

1. FOR THE TOPPING: Adjust oven rack to middle position and heat oven to 450 degrees. Line rimmed baking sheet with aluminum foil. Combine flour, pecans, oats, brown sugar, granulated sugar, cinnamon, and salt in bowl. Stir in melted butter until mixture is thoroughly moistened and crumbly.

2. FOR THE FILLING: Toss apples, sugar, and cinnamon together in large bowl. Bring cider to simmer in 12-inch ovensafe skillet over medium heat and cook until reduced to ½ cup, about 5 minutes. Transfer reduced cider to liquid measuring cup and stir in lemon juice.

3. Melt butter in now-empty skillet over medium heat. Add apple mixture and cook, stirring frequently, until apples begin to soften and become translucent, 12 to 14 minutes. (Do not fully cook apples.) Off heat, gently stir in cider mixture until apples are coated.

4. Sprinkle topping evenly over fruit, breaking up any large chunks. Place skillet on prepared baking sheet and bake until fruit is tender and topping is deep golden brown, 15 to 20 minutes, rotating baking sheet halfway through baking. Transfer to wire rack and let cool for 15 minutes. Serve warm.

VARIATIONS
Skillet Apple Crisp with Raspberries and Almonds

Substitute slivered almonds for pecans. Add ⅛ teaspoon almond extract to reduced cider with lemon juice. Stir 1 cup raspberries into apple mixture with reduced cider.

Skillet Apple Crisp with Vanilla, Cardamom, and Pistachios

For more information on removing seeds from a vanilla bean, see page 770.

Substitute ½ cup shelled pistachios and ¼ cup walnuts for pecans. Substitute ½ teaspoon ground cardamom for cinnamon in filling, and add seeds from 1 vanilla bean to apple, sugar, and cardamom mixture.

Apple-Cranberry Crisp for a Crowd

SERVES 8 TO 10   **TOTAL TIME** 1 HOUR 40 MINUTES

✓ **WHY THIS RECIPE WORKS:** Although it's hard to imagine that apple crisp needs much improvement, we liked the tartness and texture that cranberries added to one of our favorite standard dessert recipes. The challenges were balancing the fruit flavors and making sure that the filling baked evenly while the topping stayed crisp. We achieved the perfect fruit mix by combining fresh and dried cranberries, and we precooked all the fruit and added tapioca to thicken the juices. This step shortened the oven time and ensured that the classic butter, flour, sugar, cinnamon, and oat topping lived up to the name "crisp." The result was a nice fall dessert perfect for a large gathering. If you can't find Braeburn apples, Golden Delicious will work. While old-fashioned rolled oats are preferable in this recipe, quick oats can be substituted; do not use instant oats. Serve with vanilla ice cream or Whipped Cream (page 712).

TOPPING

- ¾ cup (3¾ ounces) all-purpose flour
- ½ cup packed (3½ ounces) light brown sugar
- ½ cup (3½ ounces) granulated sugar
- 1 teaspoon ground cinnamon
- 12 tablespoons unsalted butter, cut into ½-inch pieces and chilled
- ¾ cup (2¼ ounces) old-fashioned rolled oats

FILLING

- 1 pound (4 cups) fresh or frozen cranberries
- 1¼ cups (8¾ ounces) granulated sugar
- ¼ cup water
- 2½ pounds Granny Smith apples, peeled, cored, and cut into ½-inch pieces
- 2½ pounds Braeburn apples, peeled, cored, and cut into ½-inch pieces
- 1 cup sweetened dried cranberries
- 3 tablespoons instant tapioca

1. FOR THE TOPPING: Adjust oven rack to middle position and heat oven to 400 degrees. Pulse flour, brown sugar, granulated sugar, cinnamon, and butter in food processor until mixture has texture of coarse crumbs (some pea-size pieces of butter will remain), about 12 pulses. Transfer mixture to medium bowl, stir in oats, and use fingers to pinch topping into peanut-size clumps. Refrigerate while making filling.

2. FOR THE FILLING: Bring cranberries, ¾ cup sugar, and water to simmer in Dutch oven over medium-high heat, and cook until cranberries are completely softened and mixture is jamlike, about 10 minutes. Scrape mixture into bowl. Add apples, remaining ½ cup sugar, and dried cranberries to now-empty pot and cook over medium-high heat until apples begin to release their juices, about 5 minutes. Off heat, stir cranberry mixture and tapioca into apple mixture.

3. Pour into 13 by 9-inch baking dish set in rimmed baking sheet and smooth surface evenly with spatula. Scatter topping evenly over filling and bake until juices are bubbling and topping is deep golden brown, about 30 minutes, rotating pan halfway through baking. (If topping is browning too quickly, loosely cover with piece of aluminum foil.) Transfer to wire rack and let cool for 15 minutes. Serve warm.

TO MAKE AHEAD: Topping and dish of cooked filling can be refrigerated separately for up to 2 days. To bake, sprinkle chilled topping evenly over chilled filling, loosely cover with foil, and bake for 20 minutes. Uncover and bake until juices are bubbling and topping is deep golden brown, 15 to 20 minutes longer.

Cooking Cranberries

Bring fresh cranberries, ¾ cup sugar, and water to simmer in Dutch oven over medium-high heat, and cook until cranberries are completely softened and mixture is jamlike, about 10 minutes.

Pear Crisp

SERVES 6   **TOTAL TIME** 1 HOUR 15 MINUTES

✔ **WHY THIS RECIPE WORKS:** Pears exude so much moisture that simply substituting pears for apples in a classic crisp is a recipe for disaster. We wanted a classic crisp using pears, with tender fruit and a crunchy, sweet topping. To compensate for the liquid they released in the oven, we added a slurry of cornstarch mixed with lemon juice. Even with the thickened juices, our standard crisp topping sank into the filling, so we switched to a streusel-like topping, which proved sturdier and kept its crunch. Adding nuts to the topping provided more crunch, and keeping the topping to a modest amount prevented it from sinking into the fruit. We prefer a crisp made with Bartlett pears, but Bosc pears can also be used. The pears should be ripe but firm, which means the flesh at the base of the stem should give slightly when gently pressed. Bartlett pears will turn from green to greenish-yellow when ripe.

TOPPING

- ¾ cup almonds or pecans, chopped coarse
- ½ cup (2½ ounces) all-purpose flour
- ¼ cup packed (1¾ ounces) light brown sugar
- 2 tablespoons granulated sugar
- ¼ teaspoon ground cinnamon
- ⅛ teaspoon ground nutmeg
- ⅛ teaspoon salt
- 5 tablespoons unsalted butter, melted and cooled

FILLING

- 2 tablespoons granulated sugar
- 2 teaspoons lemon juice
- 1 teaspoon cornstarch
  Pinch salt
- 3 pounds ripe but firm Bartlett pears, peeled, halved, cored, and cut into 1½-inch pieces

1. FOR THE TOPPING: Adjust oven rack to lower-middle position and heat oven to 425 degrees. Pulse almonds, flour, brown sugar, granulated sugar, cinnamon, nutmeg, and salt in food processor until nuts are finely chopped, about 9 pulses. Drizzle melted butter over flour mixture and pulse until mixture resembles crumbly wet sand, about 5 pulses, scraping down bowl as needed.

2. FOR THE FILLING: Whisk sugar, lemon juice, cornstarch, and salt together in large bowl. Add pears and toss to coat. Transfer mixture to 8-inch square baking dish and place on aluminum foil–lined baking sheet.

Pears might resemble apples, but they require different treatment for a crisp with tender fruit and a crunchy topping.

3. Sprinkle topping evenly over fruit, breaking up any large chunks. Bake until fruit is bubbling around edges and topping is deep golden brown, about 30 minutes, rotating baking sheet halfway through baking. Transfer to wire rack and let cool for 15 minutes. Serve warm.

VARIATIONS

Pear Crisp with Oat Topping

Reduce nuts to ½ cup and increase melted butter to 6 tablespoons. After incorporating butter into flour mixture in food processor, add ½ cup old-fashioned rolled oats and process until evenly incorporated, about 3 pulses.

Triple-Ginger Pear Crisp

Use almonds for nuts. Substitute ¾ teaspoon ground ginger for cinnamon and nutmeg. Add 2 tablespoons coarsely chopped crystallized ginger to food processor with nuts. Reduce lemon juice to 1 teaspoon and add 1 teaspoon grated fresh ginger to sugar-cornstarch mixture.

Peach Crumble

SERVES 6   **TOTAL TIME** 2 HOURS

✔ **WHY THIS RECIPE WORKS:** A soggy topping and a watery, flavorless filling are the norm for a simple, humble peach crumble. The problem is the peaches—you never know just how juicy or how flavorful they will be until you cut them open. We wanted a peach crumble that consisted of fresh-tasting, lightly sweetened peaches topped with a buttery, crisp, and nutty-tasting crumble—no matter how sweet the peaches were (or weren't). Solving the peach problem involved letting the peeled, sliced peaches macerate in sugar before draining them and measuring out the amount of peach juice that would be added back to the filling: always ¼ cup. The sweetness of the filling was then adjusted by adding more or less lemon juice as needed. One challenge remained: Getting a crisp, well-browned topping required too much oven time for the peaches, which turned to mush. Instead, we baked the topping separately and then added it to the filling, baking the combination just until the fruit bubbled around the edges. Add the lemon juice to taste in step 2 according to the sweetness of your peaches. See page 709 for more information on peeling peaches. Serve with vanilla ice cream.

FILLING

- 3½ **pounds peaches, peeled, halved, pitted, and cut into ¾-inch wedges**
- ⅓ **cup (2⅓ ounces) granulated sugar**
- 1¼ **teaspoons cornstarch**
- 3–5 **teaspoons lemon juice**
  Pinch salt
  Pinch ground cinnamon
  Pinch ground nutmeg

TOPPING

- 1 **cup (5 ounces) all-purpose flour**
- ¼ **cup (1¾ ounces) plus 1 tablespoon granulated sugar**
- ¼ **cup packed (1¾ ounces) brown sugar**
- ⅛ **teaspoon salt**
- 2 **teaspoons vanilla extract**
- 6 **tablespoons unsalted butter, cut into 6 pieces and softened**
- ½ **cup sliced almonds**

1. FOR THE FILLING: Gently toss peaches and sugar together in large bowl and let sit for 30 minutes, gently stirring several times. Drain peaches in colander, reserving ¼ cup drained juice.

2. Whisk reserved juice, cornstarch, lemon juice to taste, salt, cinnamon, and nutmeg together in now-empty bowl. Add drained peaches and toss to coat. Transfer mixture to 8-inch square baking dish.

3. FOR THE TOPPING: Meanwhile, adjust oven racks to lowest and middle positions and heat oven to 350 degrees. Line rimmed baking sheet with parchment paper. Pulse flour, ¼ cup granulated sugar, brown sugar, and salt in food processor until combined, about 5 pulses. Drizzle vanilla over top and pulse until incorporated, about 5 pulses. Scatter butter pieces and ¼ cup almonds over top and process until mixture clumps together into large, crumbly balls, about 30 seconds, scraping down bowl as needed. Sprinkle remaining ¼ cup almonds over mixture and pulse 2 times to combine.

4. Transfer mixture to prepared baking sheet and spread into even layer (mixture should break up into roughly ½-inch chunks, with some smaller, loose bits). Bake on middle rack until chunks are lightly browned and firm, 18 to 22 minutes, rotating baking sheet halfway through baking. (Baked topping

Making a Crumble Topping

1. Transfer mixture to prepared baking sheet and spread into even layer (mixture should break up into roughly ½-inch chunks with some smaller, loose bits).

2. Bake on middle rack until chunks are lightly browned and firm, 18 to 22 minutes, rotating baking sheet halfway through baking.

3. Grasp edges of parchment paper firmly.

4. Slide topping off paper and over peaches.

Prebaking the rich, buttery crumble ensures a well-browned topping over juicy peach filling.

can be stored at room temperature for up to 2 days.) Increase oven temperature to 375 degrees.

5. Grasp edges of parchment and slide topping off paper and over peaches. Spread topping into even layer, breaking up any very large pieces and packing it lightly. Sprinkle with remaining 1 tablespoon granulated sugar. Place dish on aluminum foil–lined rimmed baking sheet. Bake on lowest rack until well browned and filling is bubbling around edges, 25 to 35 minutes, rotating baking sheet halfway through baking. Transfer to wire rack and let cool for 15 minutes. Serve warm.

VARIATION

All-Season Peach Crumble

Start defrosting the peaches about 2 hours before assembling and baking the crumble.

Substitute 3 pounds frozen peaches for fresh peaches. Let frozen peaches thaw completely in colander, 2 to 3 hours, reserving ¼ cup juice.

Blueberry Cobbler with Biscuit Topping

SERVES 8   **TOTAL TIME** 1 HOUR 25 MINUTES

✔ **WHY THIS RECIPE WORKS:** Too often, blueberry cobbler means a filling that is too sweet, overspiced, and unappealingly thick. We wanted a not-too-thin, not-too-thick filling with blueberry flavor that was front and center. And over the fruit we wanted a light, tender biscuit topping that could hold its own against the fruit filling. We started by preparing a filling using 6 cups of fresh berries and just enough sugar to sweeten them. Cornstarch worked well to thicken the fruit's juices. A little lemon juice and cinnamon enhanced the filling without masking the blueberry flavor. Parbaking the biscuit topping ensured that the biscuits wouldn't become soggy once placed on top of the fruit, and precooking the fruit filling meant all we had to do was top it with the parbaked biscuits and heat them together for 15 minutes until the fruit was bubbling. Before preparing the filling, taste the fruit, adding a smaller amount of sugar if the fruit is on sweet side, and more if the fruit is tart. Do not let the biscuit batter sit for longer than 5 minutes or so before baking. If you don't have a deep-dish glass pie plate, use a round baking dish of similar size; the round shape of the dish makes it easy to fit the biscuits on top. For information on buttermilk substitutions, see page 577.

FRUIT FILLING

⅓–⅔ **cup (2⅓ to 4⅔ ounces) sugar**
  4 **teaspoons cornstarch**
 30 **ounces (6 cups) blueberries**
  1 **tablespoon lemon juice**
 ½ **teaspoon ground cinnamon**

BISCUIT TOPPING

1½ **cups (7½ ounces) all-purpose flour**
 ¼ **cup (1¾ ounces) plus 2 teaspoons sugar**
1½ **teaspoons baking powder**
 ¼ **teaspoon baking soda**
 ¼ **teaspoon salt**
 ¾ **cup buttermilk, chilled**
  6 **tablespoons unsalted butter, melted and hot**
 ⅛ **teaspoon ground cinnamon**

1. FOR THE FRUIT FILLING: Adjust oven rack to middle position and heat oven to 400 degrees. Whisk sugar and cornstarch together in large bowl. Add blueberries, lemon juice, and cinnamon and toss gently to combine. Transfer fruit mixture to 9-inch deep-dish glass pie plate, cover with aluminum foil, and set on foil-lined rimmed baking sheet. (Fruit filling can be held at room temperature for up to 4 hours.)

The appeal of a cobbler is hard to deny, especially when made with fresh, height-of-the-season fruit. Plus, it is easy to make: Drop biscuits and a simple fruit filling take little time. Since one problem that plagues cobblers is soggy-bottomed biscuits, we parbake our simple drop biscuits as well as the filling.

1. MAKE THE DROP BISCUITS: Using a greased ¼-cup measure, scoop out and drop 8 mounds of dough onto the prepared baking sheet, spaced about 1½ inches apart.

WHY? The key to great drop biscuits is to mix cold buttermilk with melted butter until it clumps—this clumpy butter gives the biscuits a flaky texture. Using a greased ¼-cup measure makes portioning out evenly sized biscuits very easy.

2. PARBAKE THE BISCUITS: Bake the biscuits until they're puffed and lightly browned on the bottom, about 10 minutes. (They will not be fully baked.)

WHY? Parbaking the biscuits prevents them from becoming soggy on the bottom when they're placed on top of the fruit filling. Also, parbaking the biscuits, rather than baking them through completely, prevents them from tasting dry.

3. PARBAKE THE FRUIT FILLING: After parbaking the biscuits, parbake the fruit filling in a covered dish until the fruit is just hot and has released its juices, 20 to 25 minutes.

WHY? Giving the fruit a head start in the oven ensures that when the cobbler is assembled, the biscuits and filling will finish cooking at same time. A foil-lined rimmed baking sheet will catch any juices that bubble up and out of the dish.

4. PUT THE FRUIT AND BISCUITS TOGETHER: Remove the fruit from the oven and stir it gently. Arrange the parbaked biscuits over the top, squeezing them slightly as needed to fit into the dish.

WHY? Stirring the filling ensures its temperature is uniform before adding the biscuits. In order to arrange the biscuits evenly over the filling, you may need to squeeze them slightly in order to fit since they're parbaked.

5. BAKE UNTIL THE FILLING IS BUBBLING: Bake the cobbler until the biscuits are golden brown and the fruit is bubbling, about 15 minutes, rotating the dish halfway through baking.

WHY? The biscuit-topped cobbler is then returned to the oven so that the two components can finish baking through together, which makes the dish more cohesive. The short baking time prevents the biscuits from overbaking and becoming dry and tough.

6. COOL THE COBBLER: Transfer the cobbler to a wire rack and let it cool for 15 minutes. Serve the cobbler warm.

WHY? Letting the cobbler cool a bit before serving ensures that you won't burn the roof of your mouth, and this also gives the fruit juices time to cool and thicken into a glossy sauce.

2. FOR THE BISCUIT TOPPING: Line rimmed baking sheet with parchment paper. Whisk flour, ¼ cup sugar, baking powder, baking soda, and salt together in large bowl. In separate bowl, stir buttermilk and melted butter together until butter forms small clumps. Using rubber spatula, stir buttermilk mixture into flour mixture until just incorporated and dough pulls away from sides of bowl.

3. Using greased ¼-cup measure, scoop out and drop 8 mounds of dough onto prepared baking sheet, spaced about 1½ inches apart. Combine remaining 2 teaspoons sugar with cinnamon in bowl, then sprinkle over biscuits. Bake biscuits until puffed and lightly browned on bottom, about 10 minutes. Remove biscuits from oven and set aside. (Parbaked biscuits can be held at room temperature for up to 4 hours.)

4. Place fruit in oven and bake until fruit is hot and has released its juices, 20 to 25 minutes. Remove fruit from oven, uncover, and stir gently. Arrange parbaked biscuits over top, squeezing them slightly as needed to fit into dish. Bake cobbler until biscuits are golden brown and fruit is bubbling, about 15 minutes, rotating dish halfway through baking. Transfer to wire rack and let cool for 15 minutes. Serve warm.

VARIATIONS

Blackberry Cobbler with Biscuit Topping
Substitute 6 cups blackberries for blueberries and omit cinnamon. Reduce cornstarch to 1 tablespoon, sugar to ⅓ to ½ cup, and lemon juice to 1 teaspoon. Add 1 teaspoon vanilla extract to bowl with blackberries.

Peach or Nectarine Cobbler with Biscuit Topping
Substitute 3 pounds peaches or nectarines, peeled, halved, pitted, and cut into ½-inch-thick wedges, for blueberries. Omit cinnamon. Reduce cornstarch to 1 tablespoon and lemon juice to 1 teaspoon. Add 1 teaspoon vanilla extract to bowl with fruit.

Sour Cherry Cobbler with Biscuit Topping
Substitute 3 pounds pitted fresh sour cherries or 72 ounces drained jarred or canned sour cherries for blueberries. Omit lemon juice and cinnamon. Increase cornstarch to 4½ teaspoons and sugar to ⅔ to ¾ cup. Add 2 tablespoons red wine and ¼ teaspoon almond extract to bowl with cherries.

Strawberry Cobbler with Biscuit Topping
Substitute 8 cups hulled strawberries for blueberries (halve large strawberries), and omit cinnamon. Increase cornstarch to 5 teaspoons and lemon juice to 2 teaspoons. Add 1 teaspoon vanilla extract to bowl with strawberries.

Maximizing the berry-to-cake ratio is key to the taste and texture of this classic.

Blueberry Buckle

SERVES 8   **TOTAL TIME** 1 HOUR 45 MINUTES
(PLUS 1 HOUR COOLING TIME)

☑ **WHY THIS RECIPE WORKS:** The classic blueberry buckle can be regarded as a streusel-topped blueberry coffee cake, but that description sells it short—the substance of the blueberry buckle should be the blueberries. We wanted to keep the emphasis on the berries yet also keep the berry-to-cake ratio in balance so the moisture released from the fruit during baking wouldn't create a soggy cake. We used an ample amount of blueberries—4 cups—to keep them as headliner, then built more structure into the batter to support them. In the end, the batter resembled a cookie dough more than a cake batter. For a flavorful and crisp yet crumbly streusel, we turned to a combination of flour, light brown and granulated sugars, softened butter, and cinnamon. The batter is extremely thick and heavy, and some effort will be required to spread it into the prepared pan. Be sure to use a cake pan with at least 2-inch-high sides. Do not use frozen blueberries. Serve with vanilla ice cream.

STREUSEL

½   **cup (2½ ounces) all-purpose flour**
½   **cup packed (3½ ounces) light brown sugar**
2   **tablespoons granulated sugar**
¼   **teaspoon ground cinnamon**
    Pinch salt
4   **tablespoons unsalted butter, cut into 8 pieces and softened**

CAKE

1½   **cups (7½ ounces) all-purpose flour**
1½   **teaspoons baking powder**
10   **tablespoons unsalted butter, softened**
⅔   **cup (4⅔ ounces) granulated sugar**
½   **teaspoon salt**
½   **teaspoon grated lemon zest**
1½   **teaspoons vanilla extract**
2   **large eggs, room temperature**
1¼   **pounds (4 cups) blueberries**

1. FOR THE STREUSEL: Using stand mixer fitted with paddle, beat flour, brown sugar, granulated sugar, cinnamon, and salt on low speed until well combined and no large brown sugar lumps remain, about 45 seconds. Add butter and beat on low speed until mixture resembles wet sand and no large butter pieces remain, about 2½ minutes. Transfer to bowl.

2. FOR THE CAKE: Adjust oven rack to lower-middle position and heat oven to 350 degrees. Grease 9-inch round, 2-inch-deep cake pan, line bottom with parchment paper, grease parchment, then flour pan.

Assembling a Blueberry Buckle

1. Scrape batter into prepared pan, smooth top, and gently tap pan on counter to settle batter. Batter will be very thick.

2. Working with handfuls of streusel at a time, squeeze streusel in hand to form large cohesive clump, then break up clump with fingers and sprinkle over batter.

3. Whisk flour and baking powder together in bowl. Using stand mixer fitted with paddle, beat butter, sugar, salt, and lemon zest on medium-high speed until light and fluffy, about 3 minutes. Beat in vanilla until combined, about 30 seconds. Add eggs, 1 at a time, and beat until combined (mixture will appear broken).

4. Reduce speed to low and add flour mixture, scraping down bowl as needed, until almost fully incorporated, about 20 seconds. Give batter final stir by hand (batter will be thick). Gently fold in blueberries.

5. Scrape batter into prepared pan, smooth top, and gently tap pan on counter to settle batter. Working with handfuls of streusel at a time, squeeze streusel in hand to form large cohesive clump, then break up clump with fingers and sprinkle over batter. Bake until cake is deep golden brown and toothpick inserted in center comes out clean, about 55 minutes, rotating pan halfway through baking. Let cake cool in pan 15 to 20 minutes (cake will fall slightly as it cools).

6. Run paring knife around edge of cake to loosen. Gently turn cake out onto plate, remove parchment, then flip onto serving platter. Let cake cool for at least 1 hour. Serve warm or at room temperature. (Buckle can be stored at room temperature for up to 2 days.)

VARIATION

Blueberry Buckle with Ginger and Cardamom

Add 3 tablespoons minced crystallized ginger and ¼ teaspoon ground cardamom to mixer with sugar, salt, and lemon zest.

NOTES FROM THE TEST KITCHEN

Washing and Storing Berries

Washing berries before you use them is always a safe practice, and we think that the best way to wash them is to place the berries in a colander and rinse them gently under running water for at least 30 seconds. As for drying berries, we've tested a variety of methods and have found that a salad spinner lined with a buffering layer of paper towels is the best approach.

It's particularly important to store berries carefully, because they are prone to growing mold and rotting quickly. If the berries aren't to be used immediately, we recommend cleaning them with a mild vinegar solution (3 cups water mixed with 1 cup distilled white vinegar), which will destroy the bacteria, then drying them and storing them in a paper towel–lined airtight container.

Fresh Berry and Croissant Gratins

SERVES 8   **TOTAL TIME** 40 MINUTES   **FAST**

✓ WHY THIS RECIPE WORKS: Quicker than a crisp, a gratin is a layer of fresh fruit piled into a baking dish and dressed up with crumbs. The topping browns and the fruit is warmed just enough to release a bit of juice. We wanted to find the quickest, easiest route to this pleasing dessert. For the topping, we borrowed a page from the French, grinding croissants with sugar, cinnamon, and butter in a food processor. Using brown sugar, instead of granulated sugar, added extra flavor, and a small splash of kirsch made the dessert really sparkle. In addition to being ridiculously easy, the croissant topping was ridiculously good. Though a mixture of berries is a wonderful combination, we also like adding sliced peaches or nectarines when in season. Just make sure you have about 2 pounds of fruit in total; do not use frozen fruit. You will need eight (6-ounce) ramekins for this recipe. Serve with vanilla ice cream or Whipped Cream (page 712).

- 2 **tablespoons unsalted butter, softened**
- 3 **croissants, torn into pieces**
- ⅓ **cup packed (2⅓ ounces) brown sugar**
- **Pinch ground cinnamon**
- 30 **ounces (6 cups) blueberries, blackberries, raspberries, and/or hulled and quartered strawberries**
- **Pinch salt**
- 1 **tablespoon kirsch or other eau-de-vie (optional)**

1. Adjust oven rack to lower-middle position and heat oven to 400 degrees. Pulse butter, croissants, ¼ cup sugar, and cinnamon in food processor until mixture resembles coarse crumbs, about 10 pulses.

2. Gently toss berries with remaining sugar, salt, and kirsch, if using, in bowl. Divide mixture evenly among eight 6-ounce ramekins. Place ramekins on rimmed baking sheet and sprinkle evenly with crumbs.

3. Bake gratins until crumbs are deep golden brown and fruit is hot, 15 to 20 minutes. Transfer to wire rack and let cool for 5 minutes before serving.

Processing Croissants into a Topping

Pulse butter, croissants, brown sugar, and cinnamon in food processor until mixture resembles coarse crumbs, about 10 pulses.

For the juiciest filling, we like to crush a portion of the berries before combining them with the sugar.

Strawberry Shortcakes

SERVES 8   **TOTAL TIME** 1 HOUR

✓ WHY THIS RECIPE WORKS: Strawberry shortcake is the perfect summer dessert, but most of the time it looks far better than it tastes. Often the berries aren't ripe enough or they slip and slide from beneath the biscuit. We wanted a juicy strawberry filling that would stay put in between our biscuits. The solution? We chose the ripest berries we could find (for the best flavor), then mashed some of them into a chunky sauce and sliced the rest. Left to sit for a bit with a little sugar, the berry mixture macerated, exuding even more flavorful juice, making for a thick, chunky filling that soaked into, and didn't slip off, our tender biscuits. Preparing the fruit first gave it a chance to become truly juicy—just what you want on the fresh-made biscuits. This recipe will yield six biscuits plus scraps that can be gathered and patted out to yield another biscuit or two; these, though, will not be as tender as the first.

FRUIT

2½ pounds strawberries, hulled (8 cups)

6 tablespoons sugar

BISCUITS

2 cups (10 ounces) all-purpose flour

5 tablespoons (2¼ ounces) sugar

1 tablespoon baking powder

½ teaspoon salt

8 tablespoons unsalted butter, cut into ½-inch pieces and chilled

⅔ cup half-and-half

1 large egg plus 1 large white

1 recipe Whipped Cream (page 712)

1. FOR THE FRUIT: Crush 3 cups strawberries with potato masher in bowl. Slice remaining berries and stir into crushed berries with sugar. Let sit at room temperature until sugar has dissolved and berries are juicy, at least 30 minutes or up to 2 hours.

2. FOR THE BISCUITS: Meanwhile, adjust oven rack to lower-middle position and heat oven to 425 degrees. Pulse flour, 3 tablespoons sugar, baking powder, and salt in food processor until combined, about 5 pulses. Scatter butter pieces over top and process until mixture resembles coarse cornmeal, about 15 pulses. Transfer to large bowl.

3. In separate bowl, whisk half-and-half and whole egg together. Add half-and-half mixture to flour mixture and stir with rubber spatula until large clumps form. Turn mixture onto lightly floured counter and knead lightly until dough comes together.

4. Using your fingertips, pat dough into 9 by 6-inch rectangle about 1 inch thick. Cut out 6 biscuits using floured 2¾-inch biscuit cutter. Pat remaining dough into 1-inch-thick

pieces and cut out 2 more biscuits. Place biscuits on parchment paper–lined baking sheet, spaced 1 inch apart. (Raw biscuits can be refrigerated for up to 2 hours before baking.)

5. Brush top of biscuits with lightly beaten egg white and sprinkle with remaining 2 tablespoons sugar. Bake biscuits until golden brown, 12 to 14 minutes, rotating sheet halfway through baking. Let biscuits cool on sheet for at least 10 minutes. (Baked biscuits can be stored at room temperature for up to 1 day.)

6. Split each biscuit in half and place bottoms on individual serving plates. Spoon portion of fruit over each bottom, then top with dollop of whipped cream. Cap with biscuit tops and serve immediately.

Peach Shortcakes

SERVES 6   **TOTAL TIME** 1 HOUR 35 MINUTES

✅ **WHY THIS RECIPE WORKS:** If you're lucky enough to have access to ripe farm stand peaches, making peach short-cake is not that challenging. But try making shortcake with hard, mealy peaches that are the typical supermarket offering and you'll end up with a flavorless filling and a dry, crumbly biscuit. For a peach shortcake recipe that would work with any peach, regardless of quality, we found that macerating sliced peaches didn't adequately moisten and sweeten the fruit. Microwaving some of the peaches with peach schnapps until they were tender, and then mashing them to create a jam that we added to the remaining uncooked peaches, gave the fruit the moisture and sweetness we were looking for. For more information on peeling peaches, see page 709. For information on buttermilk substitutions, see page 577. Orange juice or orange liqueur can be used in place of the peach schnapps.

Making Strawberry Shortcakes

1. Turn dough mixture onto lightly floured counter and knead lightly until dough comes together.

2. Using your fingertips, pat dough into 9 by 6-inch rectangle about 1 inch thick.

3. Cut out 6 biscuits using floured 2¾-inch biscuit cutter. Pat remaining dough into 1-inch-thick pieces and cut out 2 more biscuits.

4. Bake biscuits until golden brown, 12 to 14 minutes. Let shortcakes cool on baking sheet for at least 10 minutes.

2 pounds peaches, peeled, halved, pitted, and cut into ¼-inch-thick wedges
6 tablespoons sugar
2 tablespoons peach schnapps

BISCUITS
2 cups (10 ounces) all-purpose flour
2 teaspoons baking powder
2 tablespoons sugar
¾ teaspoon salt
⅔ cup cold buttermilk
1 large egg
8 tablespoons unsalted butter, melted and hot
1 recipe Whipped Cream (page 712)

1. FOR THE FRUIT: Gently toss three-quarters of peaches with 4 tablespoons sugar in large bowl and let sit at room temperature for 30 minutes. In separate bowl, microwave remaining peaches, remaining 2 tablespoons sugar, and schnapps until bubbling, 1 to 1½ minutes, stirring twice during cooking. Using potato masher, crush microwaved peaches into coarse pulp, then let cool at room temperature for 30 minutes.

2. FOR THE BISCUITS: Meanwhile, adjust oven rack to middle position and heat oven to 475 degrees. Line rimmed baking sheet with parchment paper. Whisk flour, baking powder, 1 tablespoon sugar, and salt in large bowl.

3. In medium bowl, whisk buttermilk and egg together until combined. Stir in hot melted butter until butter forms small clumps. Using rubber spatula, stir buttermilk mixture into flour mixture until just incorporated and dough pulls away from sides of bowl.

4. Using greased ⅓-cup dry measure, scoop out and drop 6 mounds of dough onto prepared sheet, spaced about 1½ inches apart. Sprinkle with remaining 1 tablespoon sugar. Bake until tops are golden brown and crisp, about 15 minutes, rotating baking sheet halfway through baking. Let biscuits cool on sheet for 15 minutes. (Biscuits can be stored at room temperature for up to 1 day.)

5. Split each biscuit in half and place bottoms on individual serving plates. Spoon portion of mashed fruit over each bottom, followed by peach slices and any exuded juices. Top with dollop of whipped cream, cap with biscuit tops, and dollop with remaining whipped cream. Serve immediately.

Apple Fritters

SERVES 10   **TOTAL TIME** 1 HOUR

✔ **WHY THIS RECIPE WORKS:** Apple fritters should be crisp on the outside and moist within, and they should sing out with apple flavor. However, the amount of liquid in the fruit is a big problem for a fried recipe. We found that the best solution was to dry the apples with paper towels before mixing them with the dry ingredients. This soaked up the moisture that would otherwise have leached out during frying, ensuring that the final fritters were light and fluffy but still fully cooked. Apple cider in both the batter and the glaze added to the strong apple flavor. Do not substitute apple juice or you'll lose that flavor. We like Granny Smith apples in these fritters because they are tart and crisp.

FRITTERS
2 Granny Smith apples, peeled, cored, halved, and cut into ¼-inch pieces
2 cups (10 ounces) all-purpose flour
⅓ cup (2⅓ ounces) granulated sugar
1 tablespoon baking powder
1 teaspoon salt
1 teaspoon ground cinnamon
¼ teaspoon ground nutmeg
¾ cup apple cider
2 large eggs, lightly beaten
2 tablespoons unsalted butter, melted and cooled
3 cups vegetable oil

GLAZE
2 cups (8 ounces) confectioners' sugar
¼ cup apple cider
½ teaspoon ground cinnamon
¼ teaspoon ground nutmeg

1. FOR THE FRITTERS: Spread apples in single layer on paper towel–lined baking sheet and pat dry thoroughly with more paper towels. Whisk flour, sugar, baking powder, salt, cinnamon, and nutmeg together in large bowl. In separate bowl, whisk cider, eggs, and melted butter together. Add apples to flour mixture to coat, then stir in cider mixture until incorporated.

2. Heat oil in large Dutch oven over medium-high heat to 350 degrees. Set wire rack inside clean rimmed baking sheet. Using ⅓-cup dry measure, transfer 5 heaping portions of batter to oil. Press batter lightly with back of spoon to flatten. Fry, adjusting burner as necessary to maintain oil temperature between 325 and 350 degrees, until deep golden brown, 2 to 3 minutes per side.

3. Transfer fritters to prepared wire rack. Return oil to 350 degrees and repeat with remaining batter.

4. FOR THE GLAZE: Whisk all ingredients together in bowl until smooth. Top each fritter with 1 heaping tablespoon glaze. Let glaze set for 10 minutes before serving.

Making Apple Fritters

1. Heat oil in large Dutch oven over medium-high heat to 350 degrees.

2. Using ⅓-cup dry measure, transfer 5 heaping portions of batter to oil. Press batter lightly with back of spoon to flatten.

3. Fry, adjusting burner as necessary to maintain oil temperature between 325 and 350 degrees, until deep golden brown, 2 to 3 minutes per side.

4. Top each fritter with 1 heaping tablespoon glaze. Let glaze set for 10 minutes before serving.

Substituting store-bought phyllo dough for homemade pastry makes this a truly easy take on classic apple strudel.

Easy Apple Strudel

SERVES 6 TO 8   **TOTAL TIME** 45 MINUTES
(PLUS 40 MINUTES COOLING TIME)

✓ WHY THIS RECIPE WORKS: Classic apple strudel is an all-day affair. We wanted to see if we could get full apple flavor, a moist filling, and a crisp, flaky crust in less than an hour. From the outset, we shelved the notion of a homemade strudel dough, finding that store-bought phyllo dough was a decent substitute. For a strudel with a crisp, flaky crust that held its shape and didn't dislodge or fly off when approached with a fork, we brushed melted butter and sprinkled sugar between layers of phyllo dough. For the filling, we used a combination of thinly sliced McIntosh and Golden Delicious apples for maximum flavor and tender bites of fruit. Raisins and walnuts added textural interest; plumping the raisins first in apple brandy deepened the apple flavor overall. We incorporated bread crumbs into our filling to help absorb some of the moisture and prevent the pastry from turning soggy, and we first browned the bread crumbs in butter to lend additional rich flavor to the filling. We cut vents in the dough to allow steam to escape during baking—without the vents, the pastry burst open in the oven. Be sure to use phyllo that is fully thawed or it will crack and flake apart when handled. Phyllo dough is also available in 18 by 14-inch sheets; if using, cut them in half to make 14 by 9-inch sheets. Don't thaw the phyllo in the microwave; let it sit in the refrigerator overnight or on the counter for 4 to 5 hours. If the phyllo sheets have small cuts or tears in the same location, alternate their orientation when assembling the strudel in step 4 so that the cuts will not line up and cause a weak spot in the crust. To make fresh bread crumbs, pulse one slice of white sandwich bread (with crust) in a food processor to fine crumbs, about 6 pulses; you will have 1 cup of fresh bread crumbs. Serve with Whipped Cream (page 712).

Working with Phyllo Dough

Phyllo dough, tissue-thin layers of pastry dough, can be used in a variety of recipes, sweet and savory. Phyllo is available in two sizes: full-size sheets that are 18 by 14 inches (about 20 per box), and half-size sheets that are 14 by 9 inches (about 40 per box). The smaller sheets are more common, so we use those in our recipes. If you buy the large sheets, simply cut them in half. Here are some other pointers that make working with this delicate dough easier:

THAW THE PHYLLO DOUGH COMPLETELY BEFORE USING: Frozen phyllo must be thawed before using, and microwaving doesn't work—the sheets of dough stick together. We prefer thawing in the refrigerator for at least 12 hours. When completely thawed, the dough unfolds easily without tearing.

KEEP THE PHYLLO COVERED WHEN USING: Paper-thin phyllo dries out very quickly. As soon as the phyllo is removed from its plastic sleeve, unfold the dough and carefully flatten it with your hands. Cover with plastic wrap, then a damp kitchen towel.

THROW OUT BADLY TORN SHEETS OF DOUGH: Usually each box has one or two badly torn sheets of phyllo that can't be salvaged. If the sheets have just small cuts or tears, however, you can still work with them—put them in the middle of the pastry, where any imperfections will go unnoticed. If all of the sheets have the exact same tear, alternate the orientation of each sheet when assembling the pastry to avoid creating a weak spot.

DON'T REFREEZE LEFTOVER DOUGH: Leftover sheets can be rerolled, wrapped in plastic wrap, and stored in the refrigerator for up to five days. Don't refreeze phyllo; it will become brittle and impossible to work with.

½   cup golden raisins
2   tablespoons Calvados or apple cider
¼   cup fresh white bread crumbs
8   tablespoons unsalted butter, melted and cooled
1   pound Golden Delicious apples, peeled, cored, and sliced ¼ inch thick
1   McIntosh apple, peeled, cored, and sliced ¼ inch thick
⅓   cup walnuts, toasted and chopped fine (optional)
6   tablespoons (2⅔ ounces) granulated sugar
1   teaspoon lemon juice
¼   teaspoon ground cinnamon
⅛   teaspoon salt
10   (14 by 9-inch) phyllo sheets, thawed
1½   teaspoons confectioners' sugar

1. Adjust oven rack to lower-middle position and heat oven to 475 degrees. Line rimmed baking sheet with parchment paper. Microwave raisins and Calvados in covered bowl until simmering, about 1 minute. Let sit, covered, until needed.

2. Toast bread crumbs with 1 tablespoon melted butter in 8-inch skillet over medium heat, stirring often, until golden brown, about 2 minutes; transfer to large bowl.

3. Drain raisins, discarding liquid. Add raisins, apples, walnuts, if using, ¼ cup granulated sugar, lemon juice, cinnamon, and salt to bowl with bread crumbs and toss to combine.

4. Place large sheet of parchment on counter with long side facing you. Lay 1 phyllo sheet on left side of sheet of parchment, then brush with melted butter and sprinkle with ½ teaspoon granulated sugar. Place second phyllo sheet on right side of parchment, overlapping sheets by 1 inch, then brush with butter and sprinkle with ½ teaspoon granulated sugar. Repeat with remaining 8 phyllo sheets, brushing each layer with butter and sprinkling with granulated sugar.

5. Mound filling along bottom edge of phyllo, leaving 2½-inch border on bottom and 2-inch border on sides. Fold dough on sides over apples. Fold dough on bottom over apples and continue to roll dough tightly around filling to form strudel. Gently transfer strudel, seam side down, to prepared baking sheet. Brush with remaining butter and sprinkle with remaining 1 teaspoon granulated sugar.

6. Cut four 1½-inch vents on diagonal across top of strudel and bake until golden brown, about 15 minutes, rotating baking sheet halfway through baking. Transfer strudel and baking sheet to wire rack and let cool until warm, about 40 minutes. Dust with confectioners' sugar before serving. Slice with serrated knife and serve warm or at room temperature.

Making a classic apple strudel from scratch requires a major time commitment and some skill to make the dough. Our quicker version uses phyllo dough to simplify the process, while our easy filling features a combination of two types of apples, raisins (which we soften in the microwave with Calvados), and toasted bread crumbs (which keep the filling from getting soggy).

1. OVERLAP THE SHEETS OF PHYLLO:
Place a piece of parchment paper on the counter, with the long side facing you. Lay 1 phyllo sheet on the left side of the paper, then brush with melted butter and sprinkle with sugar. Place a second phyllo sheet on the right side of the parchment, overlapping the sheets by 1 inch, then brush with butter and sprinkle with sugar. Repeat with the remaining 8 phyllo sheets.
WHY? Overlapping the sheets and gluing them together with butter creates a larger strudel. Sprinkling sugar between the layers adds flavor and crunch.

2. TOSS FILLING WITH TOASTED BREAD CRUMBS AND MOUND ON PHYLLO: Make filling and mound it along the bottom edge of the phyllo, leaving a 2½-inch border on the bottom and a 2-inch border on the sides.
WHY? Adding toasted bread crumbs to the filling prevents it from becoming too wet and making the delicate pastry soggy. Make sure to pack the filling into an evenly shaped log when assembling the strudel so that it will have an even shape once rolled.

3. FOLD UP THE SIDES, THEN ROLL UP THE STRUDEL: Fold the dough on the sides over the apples. Fold the dough on the bottom over the apples and continue to roll the dough tightly around the filling to form the strudel.
WHY? First folding up the sides keeps the filling from falling out. Rolling the strudel as tightly as possible helps it hold together during baking and when serving.

4. GENTLY TRANSFER THE STRUDEL:
After the strudel has been assembled and rolled, gently lay it seam side down on the prepared baking sheet.
WHY? Transferring the strudel at this point can be a little tricky because the dough is delicate—we find it easiest to use our hands. Lining the baking sheet with parchment helps prevent the strudel from sticking to the baking sheet.

5. CUT VENTS: Brush the strudel with butter and sprinkle it with sugar, then cut four 1½-inch diagonal vents across the top of the strudel with a small knife.
WHY? A final brush of butter and sprinkling of sugar ensures that the exterior of the strudel will be nicely browned. The vents allow the steam to escape the pastry during baking—without vents, the pastry will burst open in the oven and make a mess.

6. LET THE STRUDEL COOL BEFORE SLICING: Bake the strudel in a 475-degree oven until golden brown, about 15 minutes, then let it cool until it is just warm, about 40 minutes, before serving.
WHY? Baking the strudel quickly in a very hot oven prevents the delicate phyllo dough from drying out and cracking apart as it bakes. Cooling the strudel for 40 minutes is very important, as it will fall apart if you try to slice it too soon.

Cherry Clafouti

SERVES 6 TO 8   **TOTAL TIME** 1 HOUR 10 MINUTES

✓ **WHY THIS RECIPE WORKS:** Clafouti is a classic French dessert of fresh fruit, usually cherries, baked in a creamy custard. The beauty of this recipe lies in its rustic simplicity: a rich and eggy custard infused with vanilla and amaretto and just a little sugar allows the sweetness of the cherries to shine through. Many clafouti recipes call for flour to act as a binder, but we found that flour produced a thick, overly heavy clafouti. Instead, we used 2 tablespoons of cornstarch, which was enough to bind the custard without weighing it down, yielding a light and creamy texture. The simple flavors of this dish make using fresh fruit a must; we found the texture and flavor of jarred, canned, or frozen cherries very disappointing here.

⅓ cup (2⅓ ounces) granulated sugar
2 tablespoons cornstarch
   Pinch salt
1¼ cups heavy cream
2 large eggs plus 2 large yolks, room temperature
1 tablespoon amaretto
2 teaspoons vanilla extract
1½ cups (10½ ounces) fresh sour cherries, pitted and halved
   Confectioners' sugar

1. Adjust oven rack to middle position and heat oven to 350 degrees. Whisk granulated sugar, cornstarch, and salt together in large bowl. Whisk in cream, eggs and yolks, amaretto, and vanilla until smooth and thoroughly combined.

2. Arrange cherries in single layer in 9-inch pie plate and pour cream mixture over top. Bake clafouti until toothpick inserted in center comes out clean, 35 to 40 minutes, rotating dish halfway through baking.

3. Transfer to wire rack and let cool until custard has set, about 15 minutes. Dust with confectioners' sugar and serve.

VARIATION

Plum Clafouti

For a nice presentation, fan the plum slices out attractively over the bottom of the dish before pouring in the custard.

Substitute 2 plums, pitted and sliced into ¼-inch wedges, for cherries, and 1 tablespoon cognac for amaretto.

You can make this beautiful layered trifle in less than half an hour by using gingersnaps and whipping up an easy custard.

Speedy Trifle with Cookies and Berries

SERVES 8   **TOTAL TIME** 25 MINUTES   **FAST**

✓ **WHY THIS RECIPE WORKS:** Trifle is a classic British dessert of sponge cake layered with fresh fruit, custard, liquor, and jam. However, trifle, with all its components, tends to take a good deal of time to prepare. Our goal was to trim as much prep time as we could. Since making the cake takes the greatest amount of time, we began looking for an alternative. We discovered that crumbled store-bought cookies were a great substitute. We preferred the crisp texture and flavor of gingersnaps. A combination of mascarpone whipped with heavy cream and sugar worked well as a simple custard filling, and we paired it with mixed fresh berries, which needed little preparation. Jam and liquor were both deemed unnecessary because they made the trifle too heavy and overly sweet. You can substitute an equal amount of amaretti or chocolate wafer cookies for the gingersnaps. You can use any combination of berries here; just be sure to have 30 ounces of fruit in total. Do not use frozen berries.

8 ounces (1 cup) mascarpone cheese
½ cup (3½ ounces) sugar
1 teaspoon vanilla extract
⅛ teaspoon salt
2 cups heavy cream, chilled
30 ounces (6 cups) blackberries, blueberries, raspberries, and/or hulled and quartered strawberries
12 ounces gingersnap cookies, crumbled (4 cups)

1. Using stand mixer fitted with whisk, whip mascarpone, sugar, vanilla, and salt together on medium-high speed until smooth, about 1 minute, scraping down bowl as needed. Reduce speed to low and gradually add cream until combined. Increase speed to medium-high and whip until stiff peaks form, about 2 minutes.

2. Measure out and reserve ½ cup of mascarpone mixture for garnish. Gently toss berries together in bowl.

3. Arrange 2 cups berries in bottom of 14- to 16-cup trifle bowl. Spread half of remaining mascarpone mixture evenly over top, then sprinkle with 2 cups crumbled cookies. Repeat with 2 cups berries, remaining mascarpone mixture, and remaining 2 cups cookies. Sprinkle remaining 2 cups berries over top. Dollop reserved mascarpone mixture attractively on top. Serve. (Trifle can be refrigerated for up to 4 hours before serving.)

Sour cream and thickened fruit puree give this berry fool its rich body and crumbled cookies add textural interest.

Berry Fool

SERVES 6   **TOTAL TIME** 45 MINUTES
(PLUS 2 HOURS CHILLING TIME)

 WHY THIS RECIPE WORKS: For a berry fool recipe with intense fruitiness and rich body, we used gelatin to thicken the fruit and combined whipped cream with sour cream for just the right touch of richness with a tangy undertone. Topping the dessert with crumbled sweet wheat crackers added a pleasant, nutty contrast. Blueberries or blackberries can be substituted for the raspberries in this recipe. You may also substitute frozen fruit for the fresh, but it will slightly compromise the texture. If using frozen fruit, reduce the amount of sugar in the puree by 1 tablespoon. We like the granular texture and nutty flavor of Carr's Whole Wheat Crackers, but graham crackers or gingersnaps will also work. You will need six tall parfait or sundae glasses.

30 ounces strawberries, hulled (6 cups)
12 ounces (2⅓ cups) raspberries
¾ cup (5¼ ounces) sugar
2 teaspoons unflavored gelatin
1 cup heavy cream, chilled
¼ cup sour cream, chilled
½ teaspoon vanilla extract
4 Carr's Whole Wheat Crackers, crushed fine (¼ cup)
6 sprigs fresh mint (optional)

1. Process half of strawberries, half of raspberries, and ½ cup sugar in food processor until mixture is completely smooth, about 1 minute. Strain berry puree through fine-mesh strainer into large liquid measuring cup (you should have about 2½ cups puree; reserve excess for another use). Transfer ½ cup puree to bowl, sprinkle gelatin over top, and let sit until gelatin softens, about 5 minutes; stir to combine.

2. Heat remaining 2 cups puree in small saucepan over medium heat until it begins to bubble, 4 to 6 minutes. Off heat, stir in gelatin mixture until dissolved. Transfer mixture to clean bowl, cover with plastic wrap, and refrigerate until well chilled, at least 2 hours or up to 4 hours.

3. Meanwhile, chop remaining strawberries into rough ¼-inch pieces. Toss chopped strawberries, remaining raspberries, and 2 tablespoons sugar together in separate bowl and let sit at room temperature for 1 hour.

4. Using stand mixer fitted with whisk, whip heavy cream, sour cream, vanilla, and remaining 2 tablespoons sugar on low speed until bubbles form, about 30 seconds. Increase speed to medium and whip until whisk leaves trail, about 30 seconds. Increase speed to high and whip until mixture has nearly doubled in volume and holds stiff peaks, about 30 seconds. Transfer ⅓ cup whipped cream mixture to small bowl; set aside for topping.

5. Whisk chilled berry puree until smooth. With mixer on medium speed, slowly add two-thirds of puree to remaining whipped cream mixture until incorporated, about 15 seconds. Using spatula, gently fold in remaining puree, leaving streaks of puree.

6. Transfer uncooked berries to fine-mesh strainer and shake gently to remove excess juice. Divide two-thirds of uncooked berries evenly among 6 tall parfait or sundae glasses. Divide creamy berry mixture evenly among glasses, followed by remaining uncooked berries. Top with reserved whipped cream, sprinkle with crushed crackers, and garnish with mint sprigs, if using. Serve immediately.

Assembling a Berry Fool

1. Divide two-thirds of uncooked berries evenly among 6 tall parfait or sundae glasses.

2. Divide creamy berry mixture evenly among glasses.

3. Spoon remaining berries into glasses and dollop with reserved whipped cream.

4. Sprinkle with crushed crackers.

Summer Berry Pudding

SERVES 6   **TOTAL TIME** 1 HOUR (PLUS 8 HOURS CHILLING TIME)

WHY THIS RECIPE WORKS: For our version of this traditional British dessert, we used four different kinds of berries, and we cooked only a portion of them in order to retain the freshness of the fruit. To avoid a soggy pudding, we drained the berries and used their sweet juices to moisten the bread. Rich, eggy challah was the best choice for this dessert, and "staling" it in the oven made it even sturdier. To prevent the pudding from slumping, we thickened the filling with a combination of unflavored gelatin and apricot preserves. Fill in any gaps in the pudding crusts with the toast trimmings.

  8 (¼-inch-thick) slices challah, crusts removed
 12 ounces strawberries, hulled and chopped (2½ cups)
  8 ounces (1½ cups) blackberries, halved
  8 ounces (1½ cups) blueberries
  5 ounces (1 cup) raspberries
  ½ cup (3½ ounces) granulated sugar
  1 teaspoon unflavored gelatin
  2 tablespoons cold water
  ½ cup (5½ ounces) apricot preserves
  1 cup heavy cream, chilled
  1 tablespoon confectioners' sugar

1. Adjust oven rack to middle position and heat oven to 350 degrees. Line 8½ by 4½-inch loaf pan with plastic wrap, pushing plastic into corners and up sides of pan and allowing excess to overhang long sides. Make cardboard cutout just large enough to fit inside pan.

2. Place challah on wire rack set in rimmed baking sheet. Bake challah until dry, about 10 minutes, flipping challah and rotating sheet halfway through baking. Let challah cool completely.

3. Combine strawberries, blackberries, blueberries, and raspberries in bowl. Transfer half of mixture to medium saucepan, add granulated sugar, and bring to simmer over medium-low heat, stirring occasionally. Reduce heat to low and continue to cook until berries release their juices and raspberries begin to break down, about 5 minutes. Off heat, stir in remaining berries and let sit for 2 minutes. Strain berries through fine-mesh strainer set over medium bowl for 10 minutes, stirring berries once halfway through straining (do not press on berries). Reserve berry juice. (You should have ¾ to 1 cup.)

4. Sprinkle gelatin over water in bowl and let sit until gelatin softens, about 5 minutes. Microwave gelatin mixture until bubbling around edges and gelatin has dissolved, about 30 seconds. Whisk preserves and warm gelatin mixture together in large bowl. Fold in strained berries.

5. Trim 4 slices of challah to fit snugly side by side in bottom of loaf pan (you may have extra challah). Dip slices in reserved berry juice until saturated, about 30 seconds per side, then place in bottom of pan. Spoon berry mixture over challah. Trim remaining 4 slices of challah to fit snugly side by side on top of berries (you may have extra challah). Dip slices in reserved berry juice until saturated, about 30 seconds per side, then place on top of berries. Cover pan loosely with plastic and place in 13 by 9-inch baking dish. Place cardboard cutout on top of pudding. Top with 3 soup cans to weigh down pudding. Refrigerate pudding for at least 8 hours or up to 1 day.

6. Using stand mixer fitted with whisk, whip cream and confectioners' sugar on medium-low speed until foamy, about 1 minute. Increase speed to high and whip until soft peaks form, 1 to 3 minutes. Transfer to serving bowl. Remove cans,

Assembling a Berry Pudding

1. Trim challah slices to fit snugly side by side in loaf pan (you may have extra challah). Dip slices in reserved berry juice until saturated, about 30 seconds per side, then place in bottom of pan.

2. Spoon berry mixture over challah, then top with another layer of dipped challah.

3. Cover pan loosely with plastic and place in 13 by 9-inch baking dish. Place cardboard cutout on top of pudding.

4. Top with 3 soup cans to weigh down pudding. Refrigerate pudding for at least 8 hours or up to 1 day.

cardboard, and plastic from top of pudding. Loosen pudding by pulling up on edges of plastic. Place inverted platter over top of loaf pan and flip platter and pan upside down to unmold pudding. Discard plastic. Slice pudding with serrated knife and serve with whipped cream.

Individual Pavlovas with Tropical Fruit

SERVES 6   **TOTAL TIME** 2 HOURS
(PLUS 2 HOURS DRYING TIME)

WHY THIS RECIPE WORKS: Pavlova is simple to prepare, yet it's often plagued by soggy, sickly sweet meringue and unripe fruit—and cutting it for serving is a messy proposition. We were seeking a pavlova made of pure white, perfectly crisped meringue, its texture softened by whipped cream and its sweetness balanced by a fresh fruit topping. First, we opted to take a restaurant approach and make individual pavlovas for a tidier presentation. Then we focused on making and baking the meringue. Whipping room-temperature egg whites with a small amount of cream of tartar and vanilla before slowly adding the sugar gave us a voluminous, billowy, stable meringue. To shape the meringues, we portioned ½ cup of the mixture into small mounds on a baking sheet, then used the back of a spoon to create indentations for holding the whipped cream and fruit. Baking the meringues at 200 degrees for an hour and a half yielded perfectly dry, crisp, white shells. Gradually cooling them in a turned-off oven ensured their crispness. While we especially liked the flavors of tropical fruit on pavlovas, fresh berries made a fine option too. For the whipped cream topping, we added sour cream for a slight tang that provided a cool, refreshing counterpoint to the sweet fruit and meringue (the sour cream can be omitted if you prefer simple whipped cream). Be mindful that the fruit is garnish here, so it's worth taking the time to cut it into tidy pieces. Avoid making the pavlovas on humid days, or the meringue shells will turn out sticky.

MERINGUES AND FRUIT
  4 **large egg whites, room temperature**
  ¾ **teaspoon vanilla extract**
  ¼ **teaspoon cream of tartar**
  1 **cup (7 ounces) plus 1 tablespoon sugar**
  1 **mango, peeled, pitted, and cut into ¼-inch pieces**
  2 **kiwis, peeled, quartered, and sliced thin**
1½ **cups ½-inch pineapple pieces**

We focused on making the meringue base for this dessert crisp, stable, and easy to serve.

TOPPING

- 1 cup heavy cream, chilled
- ½ cup sour cream, chilled
- 1 tablespoon sugar
- 1 teaspoon vanilla extract

1. FOR THE MERINGUES AND FRUIT: Adjust oven rack to middle position and heat oven to 200 degrees. Line baking sheet with parchment paper.

2. Using stand mixer fitted with whisk, whip egg whites, vanilla, and cream of tartar on medium-low speed until foamy, about 1 minute. Increase speed to medium-high and whip whites to soft, billowy mounds, about 1 minute. Gradually add 1 cup sugar and whip until glossy, stiff peaks form, 1 to 2 minutes.

3. Scoop six ½-cup mounds of meringue onto prepared sheet, spacing them about 1 inch apart. Gently make small, bowl-like indentation in each meringue using back of spoon. Bake until meringues have smooth, dry, and firm exteriors,

about 1½ hours. Turn oven off and leave meringues in oven until completely dry and hard, about 2 hours. (Meringue shells can be stored at room temperature in airtight container for up to 2 weeks.)

4. Gently toss mango, kiwis, and pineapple with remaining 1 tablespoon sugar in large bowl. Let sit at room temperature until sugar has dissolved and fruit is juicy, about 30 minutes.

5. FOR THE TOPPING: Using stand mixer fitted with whisk, whip heavy cream, sour cream, sugar, and vanilla on medium-low speed until foamy, about 1 minute. Increase speed to high and whip until soft peaks form, 1 to 3 minutes.

6. To serve, place meringue shells on individual plates and spoon about ⅓ cup whipped cream mixture into each shell. Top each with about ½ cup fruit (some fruit and juice will fall onto plate). Serve immediately.

VARIATION

Individual Pavlovas with Mixed Berries

Substitute 1½ cups each raspberries and blueberries, and 1 cup blackberries, for mango, kiwis, and pineapple.

Making Pavlovas

1. Scoop six ½-cup mounds of meringue onto prepared sheet, spacing them 1 inch apart. Gently make small, bowl-like indentation in each using back of spoon.

2. Bake until meringues have smooth, dry, and firm exteriors, about 1½ hours. Turn oven off and leave meringues in oven until completely dry and hard, about 2 hours.

3. Spoon about ⅓ cup whipped cream mixture into each shell, then top with about ½ cup fruit.

Chocolate-Covered Strawberries

SERVES 6   **TOTAL TIME** 45 MINUTES **FAST**

👨‍🍳 **WHY THIS RECIPE WORKS:** Chocolate-covered strawberries are hugely popular at specialty shops, but they can get quite pricey. Fortunately, it's very easy to make these elegant treats at home. We've found that a microwave is actually the perfect way to melt chopped chocolate. Use strawberries with long stems attached if you can find them—the stem makes a convenient handle. Although strawberries are classic, this recipe also works well with cherries, banana pieces, or pineapple chunks. Dried apricots are good, too. For fruits without stems, use a skewer to avoid dunking your fingers in the melted chocolate.

- **8** ounces bittersweet chocolate, chopped
- **1** quart strawberries, rinsed and thoroughly dried

1. Line baking sheet with parchment paper. Microwave chocolate in bowl at 50 percent power, whisking often, until melted, 1 to 3 minutes.

2. Dip fruit into chocolate and transfer to prepared baking sheet. Refrigerate strawberries until completely cool, at least 30 minutes or up to 8 hours, before serving.

Coating Fruit with Chocolate

1. Dip fruit into chocolate and coat evenly. For fruits without stems, use a skewer.

2. Transfer chocolate-covered strawberries or other fruit to parchment-lined baking sheet and refrigerate until chocolate is set, about 30 minutes.

3. If desired, use spoon to drizzle melted white chocolate over cooled chocolate-coated strawberries.

VARIATION

Chocolate-Covered Strawberries Drizzled with White Chocolate

White chocolate chips do not melt well, so use bar white chocolate.

Microwave 3 ounces white chocolate, whisking often, until melted and smooth, 1 to 3 minutes. Using spoon, drizzle white chocolate over cooled chocolate-coated strawberries. If white chocolate seems too stiff to drizzle, stir in vegetable oil, ½ teaspoon at a time, to loosen it. Refrigerate strawberries again until white chocolate is set before serving.

CARAMEL APPLES

MAKES 6 APPLES   **TOTAL TIME** 30 MINUTES **FAST**

While we prefer Granny Smith apples for their crisp texture and tart flavor, you can substitute your favorite apples here with great success. You will need 6 Popsicle sticks for this recipe. If you can't find Popsicle sticks at your local grocery store, check a craft store.

- **6** Granny Smith apples, stems removed
- **1** (14-ounce) bag caramel candies
- **2** tablespoons water
- **1** cup dry-roasted peanuts, chopped (optional)

1. Insert Popsicle stick into bottom of each apple and set aside. Line rimmed baking sheet with parchment paper, coat parchment with vegetable oil spray, and set aside.

2. Combine caramels and water in double boiler or in bowl set over saucepan filled with inch of water. Cook over medium-low heat, stirring occasionally, until caramels have melted to smooth consistency, about 10 minutes.

3. Dip apples, 1 at a time, into caramel, spooning caramel over apple to ensure even coverage. Allow excess caramel to drip back into double boiler. Transfer apples to prepared baking sheet and sprinkle with peanuts, if using. Let cool for 15 minutes before serving.

TO MAKE AHEAD: Coated apples can be refrigerated for up to 3 days.

Pan-Roasted Peaches

SERVES 4   **TOTAL TIME** 40 MINUTES   FAST

✓ **WHY THIS RECIPE WORKS:** In most recipes for roasted peaches, the peaches are cooked in the oven on a baking sheet, but this method makes it hard to achieve good caramelization. Instead, we switched to a skillet and started the peaches on the stovetop, cooking them until the cut sides were just browned. Then we transferred the skillet to the oven, where they finished cooking gently and could caramelize, soften, and turn incredibly juicy. You will need a 12-inch ovenproof nonstick skillet for this recipe. Use firm but ripe peaches for this recipe; either rock-hard or overly ripe peaches will not work well here.

- 4   **large peaches, halved and pitted**
- 1   **tablespoon sugar**
- 2   **tablespoons unsalted butter**

1. Adjust oven rack to middle position and heat oven to 400 degrees. Sprinkle cut sides of peaches with sugar. Melt butter in 12-inch ovenproof nonstick skillet over medium heat. Add peaches cut side down and cook until beginning to brown, about 2 minutes.

2. Transfer skillet to oven and roast peaches until tender when pierced with paring knife or skewer and cut sides are caramelized, 25 to 35 minutes.

3. Using potholders (skillet handle will be hot), remove skillet from oven. Remove peaches from skillet and serve.

VARIATION

Pan-Roasted Plums

Substitute 4 plums, halved and pitted, for peaches, and reduce baking time to 15 to 25 minutes.

Halving and Pitting Peaches

Cut peach in half, pole to pole, using crease in peach skin as guide. Grasp both halves of fruit and twist apart. Halves will come apart cleanly so pit can be easily removed.

Removing the skin from everywhere but the top of the apple keeps the flesh from steaming and turning into mush.

Baked Apples

SERVES 6   **TOTAL TIME** 1 HOUR

✓ **WHY THIS RECIPE WORKS:** This homey (and typically dowdy) dessert is often plagued by a mushy texture and one-dimensional, cloyingly sweet flavor. We wanted baked apples that were tender yet firm and had a filling that perfectly complemented their sweet-tart flavor. Granny Smith, with its firm flesh and tart, fruity flavor, was the best apple for the job. To avoid even the occasional collapse, we peeled the apples after cutting off the top to allow steam to escape, ensuring the apples retained their tender-firm texture. Our filling base of tangy dried cranberries, brown sugar, and pecans benefited from some finessing by way of cinnamon, orange zest, and butter. To punch up the flavor even more, we intensified the nuttiness with chewy rolled oats, and dicing one of the apples and mixing it into the filling added substance. A melon baller helped us scoop out a spacious cavity for the filling. We then capped the filled apples with the tops we had lopped off. Once in the oven, the apples were basted with an apple cider and maple syrup sauce and emerged full of flavor that was far from frumpy. If you don't have an ovensafe skillet, transfer the browned apples to a 13 by 9-inch baking dish and bake as directed. While old-fashioned rolled oats are preferable in this recipe, quick oats can be substituted; do not use instant oats. Serve with vanilla ice cream, if desired.

- 7 **large Granny Smith apples (8 ounces each)**
- 6 **tablespoons unsalted butter, softened**
- ⅓ **cup dried cranberries, chopped coarse**
- ⅓ **cup pecans, toasted and chopped coarse**
- ¼ **cup packed (1¾ ounces) brown sugar**
- 3 **tablespoons old-fashioned rolled oats**
- 1 **teaspoon finely grated orange zest**
- ½ **teaspoon ground cinnamon**
  Pinch salt
- ⅓ **cup maple syrup**
- ⅓ **cup plus 2 tablespoons apple cider**

1. Adjust oven rack to middle position and heat oven to 375 degrees. Peel, core, and cut 1 apple into ¼-inch dice. Combine diced apple, 5 tablespoons butter, cranberries, pecans, sugar, oats, orange zest, cinnamon, and salt in bowl.

2. Shave thin slice off bottom of remaining 6 apples to allow them to sit flat. Cut top ½ inch off stem end of apples and reserve. Peel apples and use melon baller or small measuring spoon to remove 1½-inch-diameter core, being careful not to cut through bottom of apples.

3. Melt remaining 1 tablespoon butter in 12-inch ovensafe nonstick skillet over medium heat. Add apples, stem side down, and cook until cut surface is golden brown, about 3 minutes. Flip apples, reduce heat to low, and spoon filling inside, mounding excess filling over cavities. Top with reserved apple caps.

4. Add maple syrup and ⅓ cup cider to skillet. Transfer skillet to oven and bake until skewer inserted into apples meets little resistance, 35 to 40 minutes, basting every 10 minutes with juices in skillet.

5. Transfer apples to individual plates or serving platter. Stir up to 2 tablespoons remaining cider into sauce in skillet to adjust consistency. Pour sauce over apples and serve.

VARIATIONS
Baked Apples with Dried Cherries and Hazelnuts
Substitute coarsely chopped dried cherries for cranberries, coarsely chopped toasted hazelnuts for pecans, and pepper for cinnamon.

Baked Apples with Dried Figs and Macadamia Nuts
Substitute coarsely chopped dried figs for cranberries, coarsely chopped toasted macadamia nuts for pecans, lemon zest for orange zest, and ¼ teaspoon ground ginger for cinnamon.

Baked Apples with Raisins and Walnuts
Substitute coarsely chopped raisins for cranberries, coarsely chopped toasted walnuts for pecans, lemon zest for orange zest, and ¼ teaspoon ground nutmeg for cinnamon.

Making Baked Apples

1. Peel apples and use melon baller or small measuring spoon to remove 1½-inch-diameter core, being careful not to cut through bottom of apples.

2. Melt 1 tablespoon butter in 12-inch ovensafe nonstick skillet over medium heat. Add apples, stem side down, and cook until cut surface is golden brown, about 3 minutes.

3. Flip apples, reduce heat to low, and spoon filling inside, mounding excess filling over cavities. Top with reserved apple caps.

4. Add maple syrup and ⅓ cup cider to skillet. Transfer skillet to oven and bake until skewer inserted into apples meets little resistance, 35 to 40 minutes, basting every 10 minutes with juices in skillet.

Skillet-Roasted Pears with Caramel Sauce

SERVES 6   **TOTAL TIME** 35 MINUTES   **FAST**

✔ **WHY THIS RECIPE WORKS:** Pears are an excellent fruit to cook because they hold their shape and texture well. We tried cooking pears in varying states of ripeness and ended up preferring moderately ripe pears, which were the most flavorful and tender once cooked. To make an elegant yet uncomplicated dessert, we cooked the pears in caramel for a sauce that clung to the fruit. We added halved pears to the hot water and sugar mixture and let them cook slowly in the browning caramel, finishing the sauce with heavy cream before removing the pears. We chose Bosc or Bartlett pears for their flavor and because they are readily available. This dish is quite rich, so plan on serving just half of a pear per person. The pears should be ripe but firm, which means the flesh at the base of the stem should give slightly when gently pressed with a finger. Trimming ¼ inch off the bottom of each pear half allows them to stand up straight when serving, making a beautiful presentation.

    3 ripe but firm Bosc or Bartlett pears, halved and cored
    ⅓ cup water
    ⅔ cup sugar
    ⅔ cup heavy cream
       Salt

1. Set wire rack inside aluminum foil–lined rimmed baking sheet. Shave thin slice off bottom of pears to allow them to sit flat.

2. Add water to 12-inch nonstick skillet, then pour sugar into center of pan (don't let it hit pan's sides). Gently stir sugar with clean spatula to moisten it thoroughly. Bring to boil over high heat and cook, stirring occasionally, until sugar has dissolved completely and liquid is bubbling, about 2 minutes.

3. Add pears to skillet cut side down. Cover, reduce heat to medium-high, and cook until pears are almost tender (a fork inserted into center of pears meets slight resistance), 13 to 15 minutes, reducing heat as needed to prevent caramel from getting too dark.

4. Uncover, reduce heat to medium, and cook until sauce is golden brown and cut sides of pears are beginning to brown, 3 to 5 minutes. Pour heavy cream around pears and cook, shaking pan until sauce is smooth and deep caramel color and cut sides of pears are golden brown, 3 to 5 minutes.

5. Off heat, transfer pears cut side up to prepared wire rack and let cool slightly. Season sauce left in pan with salt to taste, then transfer sauce to bowl. Carefully (the pears will still be hot) stand each pear half upright on individual plates or serving platter, drizzle with caramel sauce, and serve.

Our pan-poaching method simmers raw pears in vanilla sugar syrup for a rich but never mushy fruit dessert.

Poached Pears with Vanilla

SERVES 4 TO 6   **TOTAL TIME** 45 MINUTES
(PLUS 2 HOURS CHILLING TIME)

✔ **WHY THIS RECIPE WORKS:** Poaching is one of the simplest ways to cook fruit. Pears are perfect for poaching because they retain both their shape and their texture. But how long do you cook the fruit so that it is tender but not mushy? We experimented with a variety of methods and learned that the trick was to not cook the fruit at all but rather submerge the raw fruit in simmering syrup and allow it to steep off the heat for 30 minutes. This method worked perfectly; the fruit was tender, sweet, and permeated with the syrup's flavor. Use pears that are ripe but firm, which means the flesh at the base of the stem should give slightly when gently pressed with a finger. For more information on removing seeds from a vanilla bean, see page 770. Although these poached pears taste great on their own, you can serve them with ice cream, lightly sweetened and whipped crème fraîche, or cheese, such as a blue.

1½ cups water

½ cup sugar

½ vanilla bean, halved lengthwise, seeds scraped out and reserved

4 ripe but firm pears, peeled, halved, and cored

1. Bring water, sugar, and vanilla seeds and pod to boil in medium saucepan, stirring occasionally, until sugar dissolves completely, about 5 minutes.

2. Add fruit to pan, turn off heat, and cover. Let sit until mixture cools to room temperature, about 30 minutes.

3. Remove vanilla bean pod and refrigerate pan until fruit mixture is well chilled, at least 2 hours or up to 3 days. To serve, spoon portions of fruit and syrup into individual bowls.

VARIATION

Poached Pears in Spiced Red Wine

Substitute 1½ cups fruity red wine for water. Add 1 cinnamon stick, 2 cloves, and 1 long strip lemon zest to pot with wine and sugar.

Peeling a Strip of Citrus Zest

Wash fruit well. Using vegetable peeler, remove long, wide strips of zest from peel. Try not to remove bitter-tasting white pith beneath zest.

Bananas Foster

SERVES 4   TOTAL TIME 15 MINUTES   **FAST**

✓ **WHY THIS RECIPE WORKS:** With only a few ingredients (butter, brown sugar, rum, and bananas), bananas Foster should be quick and easy to make, but things can go wrong. We wanted a quick, reliable dessert with tender bananas and a flavorful but not boozy sauce. Traditionally flambéed before serving, the alcohol in the sauce is allowed to burn until the flames die down. Is this pyromaniacal method really necessary? We compared a flambéed batch with an un-flambéed batch and were surprised at how different they tasted. The un-flambéed bananas Foster tasted unpleasant and bitter in comparison. The flames served to burn off the raw alcohol flavor of the rum, resulting in a much rounder flavor and

NOTES FROM THE TEST KITCHEN

Tips For Fearless Flambéing

Flambéing is more than just tableside theatrics: As dramatic as it looks, igniting alcohol actually helps develop a more complex flavor in sauces—thanks to flavor-boosting chemical reactions that occur only at the high temperatures reached during flambéing. But accomplishing this feat at home can be daunting. The temperature on the surface of the alcohol can jump to over 500 degrees almost instantly, which makes many home cooks wary of trying this technique in their own kitchens. Here are some tips for successful—and safe—flambéing at home.

BE PREPARED: Turn off the exhaust fan, tie back long hair, and have a lid at the ready to smother flare-ups.

USE THE PROPER EQUIPMENT: A pan with flared sides (such as a skillet) rather than straight sides will allow more oxygen to mingle with the alcohol vapors, increasing the chance that you'll spark the desired flame. If possible, use long chimney matches, and light the alcohol with your arm extended to full length.

IGNITE WARM ALCOHOL: If the alcohol becomes too hot, the vapors can rise to dangerous heights, causing large flare-ups once lit. Inversely, if the alcohol is too cold, there won't be enough vapors to light at all. We found that heating alcohol to 100 degrees Fahrenheit (best achieved by adding alcohol to a hot pan off the heat and letting it sit for five to 10 seconds) produced the most moderate, yet long-burning, flames.

IF A FLARE-UP SHOULD OCCUR: Simply slide the lid over the top of the skillet (coming in from the side of, rather than over, the flames) to put out the fire quickly. Let the alcohol cool down and start again.

IF THE ALCOHOL WON'T LIGHT: If the pan is full of other ingredients, the potency of the alcohol can be diminished as it becomes incorporated. For a more foolproof flame, ignite the alcohol in a separate small skillet or saucepan; once the flame has burned off, add the reduced alcohol to the other ingredients.

better-tasting bananas Foster. While the bananas cook, scoop the ice cream into individual bowls so that the desserts are ready to serve once the sauce has been flambéed. Before flambéing, be sure to roll up long shirtsleeves, tie back long hair, and turn off the exhaust fan and any lit burners.

- ½ cup packed (3½ ounces) dark brown sugar
- 4 tablespoons unsalted butter
- 1 cinnamon stick
- 1 (2-inch) strip lemon zest
- ¼ cup dark rum
- 2 large, firm, ripe bananas, peeled, halved lengthwise, and then halved crosswise
- 1 pint vanilla ice cream

1. Combine sugar, butter, cinnamon stick, lemon zest, and 1 tablespoon rum in heavy-bottomed 12-inch skillet. Heat mixture over medium-high heat, stirring constantly, until sugar dissolves and mixture is thick, about 2 minutes.

2. Reduce heat to medium and add bananas, spooning some sauce over each piece. Cook until bananas are glossy and golden on both sides, about 3 minutes.

3. Off heat, add remaining 3 tablespoons rum and wait until rum has warmed slightly, about 5 seconds. Wave lit match over pan until rum ignites. Return skillet to heat, shaking pan to distribute flame over entire pan. When flame subsides (this will take 15 to 30 seconds), divide bananas and sauce among four bowls of ice cream, discarding cinnamon stick and lemon zest.

Flambéing Bananas

1. Off heat, add 3 tablespoons rum and wait until rum has warmed slightly, about 5 seconds.

2. Wave lit match over pan until warmed rum ignites.

3. Return skillet to heat, shaking pan to distribute flame over entire pan.

This compote makes a sweet topping for ice cream, as suggested here, or for other desserts, such as pound cake.

Strawberry-Rhubarb Compote with Ice Cream

SERVES 6   **TOTAL TIME** 35 MINUTES   FAST

✔ **WHY THIS RECIPE WORKS:** We set out to turn the classic pie duo of rhubarb and strawberries into a sweet, jammy compote, perfect for serving over ice cream or pound cake. The rhubarb is easily peeled, cut, and cooked to soften; the strawberries cook off the heat as the compote cools. To prevent the compote from overcooking, be sure to transfer it to a bowl to cool. Also, take care not to overcook the rhubarb or it will become stringy. For more information on removing seeds from a vanilla bean, see page 770.

- 6 tablespoons honey
- ¼ cup water
- ½ vanilla bean, halved lengthwise, seeds scraped out and reserved
- Pinch salt

8 ounces rhubarb, peeled and cut into 1-inch lengths
20 ounces strawberries, hulled and quartered (4 cups)
1 tablespoon unsalted butter
3 cups vanilla ice cream or frozen yogurt
1 tablespoon minced fresh mint

1. Bring honey, water, vanilla seeds and pod, and salt to simmer in 12-inch nonstick skillet over medium heat. Stir in rhubarb and cook until it begins to soften and sauce thickens slightly, 4 to 6 minutes.

2. Off heat, gently stir in strawberries and butter until butter has melted. Discard vanilla bean pod, transfer compote to bowl, and let cool to room temperature, 10 to 15 minutes. (Compote can be refrigerated for up to 1 day; return to room temperature before serving.)

3. Scoop ice cream into individual bowls and top with about ½ cup of compote. Sprinkle with mint and serve immediately.

VARIATIONS
Plum-Blackberry Compote with Ice Cream
SERVES 6 **TOTAL TIME** 35 MINUTES **FAST**

Try to buy plums of similar ripeness so that they cook evenly. To prevent the compote from overcooking, be sure to transfer it to a bowl to cool. For more information on removing seeds from a vanilla bean, see page 770.

6 tablespoons water
¼ cup honey
½ vanilla bean, halved lengthwise, seeds scraped
   out and reserved
   Pinch salt
1½ pounds plums, pitted, sliced ⅓ inch thick, then halved
   crosswise
2 cups (10 ounces) blackberries
1 tablespoon unsalted butter
3 cups vanilla ice cream or frozen yogurt
1 tablespoon minced fresh mint

1. Bring water, honey, vanilla seeds and pod, and salt to simmer in 12-inch nonstick skillet over medium heat. Stir in plums and cook until they begin to soften and sauce thickens slightly, 5 to 7 minutes.

2. Stir in blackberries and continue to cook until they begin to soften, about 1 minute. Off heat, stir in butter until melted. Discard vanilla bean pod, transfer compote to bowl, and let cool to room temperature, 10 to 15 minutes. (Compote can be refrigerated for up to 1 day; return to room temperature before serving.)

3. Scoop ice cream into individual bowls and top with about ½ cup of compote. Sprinkle with mint and serve immediately.

Blueberry-Nectarine Compote with Ice Cream
SERVES 6 **TOTAL TIME** 35 MINUTES **FAST**

Try to buy nectarines of similar ripeness so that they cook evenly. To prevent the compote from overcooking, be sure to transfer it to a bowl to cool. For more information on removing seeds from a vanilla bean, see page 770.

3 tablespoons honey
2 tablespoons water
½ vanilla bean, halved lengthwise, seeds scraped
   out and reserved
   Pinch salt
1½ pounds nectarines, pitted, sliced ⅓ inch thick,
   then halved crosswise
2 cups (10 ounces) blueberries
1 tablespoon lemon juice
1 tablespoon unsalted butter
3 cups vanilla ice cream or frozen yogurt
1 tablespoon minced fresh mint

1. Bring honey, water, vanilla seeds and pod, and salt to simmer in 12-inch nonstick skillet over medium heat. Stir in nectarines and cook until they begin to soften and sauce thickens slightly, 3 to 5 minutes. Stir in blueberries and continue to cook until they begin to release their juice, 2 to 4 minutes.

2. Off heat, stir in lemon juice and butter until butter has melted. Discard vanilla bean pod, transfer compote to bowl, and let cool to room temperature, 10 to 15 minutes. (Compote can be refrigerated for up to 1 day; return to room temperature before serving.)

3. Scoop ice cream into individual bowls and top with about ½ cup of compote. Sprinkle with mint and serve immediately.

Peeling Rhubarb

1. Trim ends of stalk. Working from bottom, slice thin disk off stalk, being careful not to cut through stalk entirely. Gently pull partially attached disk away from stalk to peel off fibrous outer layers.

2. Working from bottom of stalk again, repeat in reverse direction to remove peel on opposite side.

CHAPTER 21

Puddings, Custards, and More

Puddings and Custards

Ice Cream and More

■ SIGNIFIES A **FAST** RECIPE (45 MINUTES OR LESS)

A careful balance of bittersweet chocolate and cocoa powder gives our pudding rich flavor and a creamy texture.

Creamy Chocolate Pudding

SERVES 6   **TOTAL TIME** 25 MINUTES
(PLUS 4 HOURS CHILLING TIME)

WHY THIS RECIPE WORKS: Homemade chocolate pudding often suffers from either lackluster chocolate flavor, caused by a dearth of chocolate, or a grainy texture, caused by too much cocoa butter. We were after chocolate pudding that tasted deeply of chocolate and was thickened to a perfectly silky, creamy texture. We found that using a moderate amount of bittersweet chocolate in combination with unsweetened cocoa powder and espresso powder helped us achieve maximum chocolate flavor. Cornstarch proved the right thickener for our pudding; using mostly milk and just half a cup of heavy cream, along with three egg yolks, ensured that our pudding had a silky-smooth texture. Salt and vanilla enhanced the chocolate flavor even more. We prefer this recipe when made with 60 percent bittersweet chocolate. Using a chocolate with a higher cacao percentage will result in a thicker pudding. Low-fat milk may be substituted for the whole milk with a small sacrifice in richness; do not substitute skim milk.

2 teaspoons vanilla extract
½ teaspoon instant espresso powder
½ cup (3½ ounces) sugar
3 tablespoons Dutch-processed cocoa powder
2 tablespoons cornstarch
¼ teaspoon salt
3 large egg yolks
½ cup heavy cream
2½ cups whole milk
5 tablespoons unsalted butter, cut into 8 pieces
4 ounces bittersweet chocolate, chopped fine

1. Combine vanilla and espresso powder in bowl. Whisk sugar, cocoa, cornstarch, and salt together in large saucepan. Whisk in egg yolks and cream until fully incorporated, making sure to scrape corners of saucepan. Whisk in milk until incorporated.

2. Place saucepan over medium heat and cook, whisking constantly, until mixture is thickened and bubbling over entire surface, 5 to 8 minutes. Cook for 30 seconds longer, then remove from heat. Whisk in butter and chocolate until melted and fully incorporated. Whisk in vanilla-espresso mixture.

3. Strain pudding through fine-mesh strainer into bowl. Place lightly greased parchment paper against surface of pudding and refrigerate until cold, at least 4 hours or up to 2 days. Whisk pudding until smooth before serving.

VARIATIONS
Creamy Mexican Chocolate Pudding
Add ½ teaspoon ground cinnamon, ¼ teaspoon chipotle chile powder, and pinch cayenne pepper to saucepan with cocoa.

Creamy Mocha Pudding
Increase instant espresso powder to 1 teaspoon. Add 1 tablespoon Kahlúa to vanilla-espresso mixture. Substitute ¼ cup brewed coffee for ¼ cup milk.

Preventing a Pudding Skin

To prevent unsavory (and unseemly) pudding skin from forming on top of pudding as it cools, press lightly greased parchment paper flush to surface of pudding.

Best Butterscotch Pudding

SERVES 8   **TOTAL TIME** 45 MINUTES
(PLUS 3 HOURS CHILLING TIME)

✓ **WHY THIS RECIPE WORKS:** For butterscotch pudding with a rich, bittersweet flavor, we made butterscotch sauce by cooking butter, brown and white sugar, corn syrup, lemon juice, and salt together into a dark caramel. We made the process more foolproof by first boiling the caramel to jump-start it and then reducing the heat to a low simmer to provide a large window to take the temperature and stop the cooking at the right moment. To turn our butterscotch into pudding, we ditched the classical (yet time-consuming) tempering method in favor of a revolutionary technique that calls for pouring the boiling caramel sauce directly over the thickening agents (egg yolks and cornstarch thinned with a little milk). A final addition of vanilla extract and dark rum enhanced the deep caramel notes of the butterscotch. The result is the sophisticated bittersweet flavor of traditional butterscotch with less mess and fuss. When taking the temperature of the caramel in step 1 and step 2, tilt the pan and move the thermometer back and forth to equalize hot and cool spots. Work quickly when pouring the caramel mixture over the egg mixture in step 5 to ensure proper thickening. Two percent low-fat milk may be substituted for the whole milk with a small sacrifice in richness; do not substitute 1 percent low-fat or skim milk. Serve with Whipped Cream (page 712).

12	tablespoons unsalted butter, cut into ½-inch pieces
½	cup (3½ ounces) granulated sugar
½	cup packed (3½ ounces) dark brown sugar
¼	cup water
2	tablespoons light corn syrup
1	teaspoon lemon juice
¾	teaspoon salt
1	cup heavy cream
2¼	cups whole milk
4	large egg yolks
¼	cup cornstarch
2	teaspoons vanilla extract
1	teaspoon dark rum

1. Bring butter, granulated sugar, brown sugar, water, corn syrup, lemon juice, and salt to boil in large saucepan over medium heat, stirring occasionally to dissolve sugar and melt butter. Once boiling, continue to cook, stirring occasionally, for 5 minutes (caramel will register about 240 degrees).

2. Immediately reduce heat to medium-low and simmer gently (caramel should maintain steady stream of lazy bubbles—if not, adjust heat accordingly), stirring often, until mixture is color of dark peanut butter, 12 to 16 minutes longer (caramel will register about 300 degrees and have slight burnt smell).

3. Remove pan from heat, carefully pour ¼ cup cream into caramel mixture, and swirl to incorporate (mixture will bubble and steam); let bubbling subside. Whisk vigorously and scrape

Making Butterscotch Pudding

1. SIMMER CARAMEL: Simmer caramel mixture gently, stirring often, until mixture is color of dark peanut butter, 12 to 16 minutes (caramel will register about 300 degrees and have slight burnt smell).

2. ADD CREAM TO CARAMEL: Remove pan from heat, carefully pour ¼ cup cream into caramel, and swirl to incorporate (mixture will bubble and steam); let bubbling subside.

3. WHISK IN REST OF CREAM AND MILK: Vigorously whisk caramel mixture until completely smooth. Return pan to medium heat and gradually whisk in remaining ¾ cup cream and 2 cups milk until mixture is smooth.

4. ADD BOILING CARAMEL TO YOLK MIXTURE: Whisk ¼ cup hot milk into egg yolks and cornstarch. Return caramel mixture to full rolling boil, then immediately pour into yolk mixture in one motion. Whisk thoroughly for 10 seconds. Whisk in vanilla and rum.

We whisk hot caramel sauce into an egg yolk-cornstarch-milk mixture to streamline turning butterscotch into pudding.

corners of pan until mixture is completely smooth, at least 30 seconds. Return pan to medium heat and gradually whisk in remaining ¾ cup cream until smooth. Whisk in 2 cups milk until mixture is smooth, making sure to scrape corners and edges of pan to remove any remaining bits of caramel.

4. Meanwhile, microwave remaining ¼ cup milk until simmering, 30 to 45 seconds. Whisk egg yolks and cornstarch together in large bowl until smooth. Gradually whisk in hot milk until smooth.

5. Return saucepan to medium-high heat and bring mixture to full rolling boil, whisking frequently. When mixture is boiling rapidly, immediately pour into bowl with yolk mixture in one motion (do not add gradually). Whisk thoroughly for 10 to 15 seconds (mixture will thicken after a few seconds).

6. Whisk in vanilla and rum. Place lightly greased parchment paper against surface of pudding and refrigerate until cold, at least 3 hours or up to 2 days. Whisk pudding until smooth before serving.

Creamy Tapioca Pudding

SERVES 4   **TOTAL TIME** 30 MINUTES
(PLUS 1 HOUR CHILLING TIME)

✓ **WHY THIS RECIPE WORKS:** Tapioca pudding is as much about texture as it is about flavor, which may be why people feel so passionately about it. At its best, it's a simple, homey dish with warm vanilla flavor and a creamy, yielding custard. It's often underrated, and if you don't like it maybe you've never tasted it made right. Many recipes we found had intricate directions for cooking the tapioca that, despite the work, failed to produce anything special. Happily, we had the best luck with the easiest method: We combined all the ingredients in a saucepan and let them sit at room temperature for 5 minutes (to soften the tapioca), brought the mixture slowly to a boil, stirred, stirred, stirred, and then removed the pan from the heat. That's it—the pudding thickened as it cooled. To arrive at just the right firm yet supple texture, we tried batches with varying amounts of tapioca and found that ¼ cup thickened 2½ cups of milk admirably. To make the pudding richer, we added an egg plus a yolk, then lightened the entire mixture with some whipped cream. Using a combination of white and brown sugar gave the pudding an extra boost of flavor. This recipe uses Minute tapioca (also labeled "quick-cooking") and cooks in a fraction of the time of traditional pearl tapioca; do not substitute traditional pearl tapioca here.

2½ **cups whole milk**
 1 **large egg plus 1 large yolk, lightly beaten**
 ¼ **cup (1¾ ounces) plus 1 tablespoon granulated sugar**
 1 **tablespoon packed light brown sugar**
 ¼ **teaspoon salt**
 ¼ **cup Minute tapioca**
 1 **teaspoon vanilla extract**
 ½ **cup heavy cream, chilled**

1. Combine milk, egg and yolk, ¼ cup granulated sugar, brown sugar, salt, and tapioca in medium saucepan and let sit for 5 minutes. Bring mixture to boil over medium heat, then reduce heat and simmer, stirring constantly for 2 minutes.

2. Off heat, stir in vanilla and scrape pudding into medium bowl. Place lightly greased parchment paper against surface of pudding and refrigerate until set, at least 1 hour or up to 2 days.

3. Using stand mixer fitted with whisk, whip cream and remaining 1 tablespoon granulated sugar together on medium-low speed until foamy, about 1 minute. Increase speed to high and whip until stiff peaks form, 1 to 3 minutes.

4. Gently fold half of whipped cream into pudding. Serve, garnishing with remaining whipped cream.

For rice pudding with perfect texture, we use double the usual amount of milk and add more milk just before serving.

Old-Fashioned Rice Pudding

SERVES 4 TO 6 **TOTAL TIME** 1 HOUR
(PLUS 2 HOURS CHILLING TIME)

✓ **WHY THIS RECIPE WORKS:** Recipes for rice pudding vary dramatically, calling for different types of rice or different liquids, or even adding eggs. Techniques vary as well. After making and tasting a variety of styles, we found that we preferred a simple stovetop method using uncooked rice. We simply combined everything and gently simmered it all, uncovered, until the rice was tender. Not only was this method simple, but the finished pudding also had the creamiest texture. Long-grain rice proved far better than short-grained, which turned inedibly stodgy once it cooled. For the liquid, we liked milk, which reduced and sweetened as the pudding cooked. The richer flavor of cream or half-and-half didn't suit this simple pudding. Using a steep ratio of milk to rice (12 to 1) resulted in the best-tasting sweet, milky flavor. We reserved ½ cup of the milk to help loosen the pudding before serving. Two percent low-fat milk may be substituted for the whole milk with a small sacrifice in richness; do not substitute 1 percent low-fat or skim milk.

6 **cups whole milk**
½ **cup (3½ ounces) sugar**
½ **teaspoon salt**
½ **cup long-grain white rice**
2 **teaspoons vanilla extract**

1. Bring 5½ cups milk, sugar, and salt to boil in large saucepan over medium-high heat. Stir in rice, reduce heat to low, and cook, stirring occasionally and adjusting heat as needed to maintain gentle simmer, until rice is soft and pudding has thickened to consistency of yogurt, 50 to 60 minutes.

2. Off heat, stir in vanilla and scrape pudding into bowl. Place lightly greased parchment paper against surface of pudding and refrigerate until cold, at least 2 hours or up to 2 days. Before serving, stir in remaining ½ cup milk.

VARIATIONS

Cinnamon-Raisin Rice Pudding

Add 1 cinnamon stick to saucepan with milk. While pudding cooks, microwave ⅓ cup raisins and ⅓ cup water in covered bowl for 1 minute; let sit until raisins are softened, about 5 minutes, then drain. Discard cinnamon stick and add plumped raisins to pudding with vanilla.

Coconut Rice Pudding

In step 1, reduce milk to 3¾ cups and add 1¾ cups canned coconut milk. Add ½ teaspoon ground cardamom to pudding with vanilla.

Lemony Rice Pudding

Add 1 teaspoon grated lemon zest to pudding with vanilla.

Latin American–Style Flan

SERVES 8 TO 10 **TOTAL TIME** 2 HOURS 30 MINUTES
(PLUS 8 HOURS CHILLING TIME)

✓ **WHY THIS RECIPE WORKS:** Flan is a sweet custard baked in a pan that is lined with caramel. The rich caramel cascades out over the top and sides of the custard when it is unmolded for serving. The Latin American version is a sweet, rich, and creamy dessert, but without the correct ingredients and proper handling it can become rubbery, with an uneven texture and lackluster flavor. To ensure even baking and great texture we baked our flan gently at a low temperature, and we covered it to keep any skin from forming. We also relied on the heavy protein content of canned sweetened condensed and evaporated milks to provide a firmer structure, and their unique flavors enhanced the caramel notes. Borrowing from

Three different kinds of milk—sweetened condensed, evaporated, and whole—make our flan rich and creamy.

European custards, we added some fresh milk, which helped our flan stay creamy. Finally, adding extra water to the finished caramel facilitated an easier release of plenty of caramel sauce. Baking the flan in a narrow loaf pan, rather than in a wide cake pan, made it easier to unmold without cracking. We recommend an 8½ by 4½-inch loaf pan for this recipe. If your pan is 9 by 5 inches, begin checking for doneness after 1 hour. Cook the caramel in a pan with a light-colored interior, since a dark surface makes it difficult to judge the color of the syrup. Two percent low-fat milk may be substituted for the whole milk with a small sacrifice in richness; do not substitute 1 percent low-fat or skim milk. Use a platter with a raised rim for serving.

- ¼ **cup plus 2 tablespoons warm water**
- ⅔ **cup (4⅔ ounces) sugar**
- 2 **large eggs, plus 5 large yolks**
- 1 **(14-ounce) can sweetened condensed milk**
- 1 **(12-ounce) can evaporated milk**
- ½ **cup whole milk**
- 1½ **tablespoons vanilla extract**
- ½ **teaspoon salt**

1. Place ¼ cup water in large saucepan. Pour sugar into center of pan, taking care not to let sugar crystals touch pan sides. Gently stir with spatula to moisten sugar thoroughly. Bring mixture to boil over medium heat, without stirring, until it begins to turn golden, 4 to 7 minutes. Gently swirling pan, continue to cook until sugar is color of peanut butter, 1 to 2 minutes.

2. Remove pan from heat and continue to swirl pan until sugar is reddish-amber and fragrant, 15 to 20 seconds. Immediately add remaining 2 tablespoons water (mixture will bubble) and swirl pan until water is incorporated. Pour caramel into 8½ by 4½-inch loaf pan; do not scrape out saucepan.

3. Adjust oven rack to middle position and heat oven to 300 degrees. Line bottom of 13 by 9-inch baking pan with dish towel, folding towel to fit smoothly. Bring kettle of water to boil.

4. Whisk eggs and yolks together in bowl. Whisk in sweetened condensed milk, evaporated milk, whole milk, vanilla, and salt until incorporated. Strain mixture through fine-mesh strainer into loaf pan with caramel. Cover loaf pan tightly with aluminum foil, place in prepared baking pan, and transfer to oven. Carefully pour enough boiling water into dish to reach halfway up sides of pan. Bake until center of custard jiggles slightly when shaken and registers 180 degrees, 1¼ to 1½ hours.

5. Transfer roasting pan to wire rack and remove foil. Let custard cool in water bath until loaf pan has cooled to room temperature. Cover loaf pan tightly with plastic wrap and refrigerate until chilled, at least 8 hours or up to 4 days.

6. To serve, slide paring knife around edges of pan. Invert serving platter on top of pan, and turn pan and platter over. When flan is released, remove loaf pan. Use rubber spatula to scrape residual caramel onto flan. Slice and serve.

VARIATIONS
Coffee Flan
Whisk 4 teaspoons instant espresso powder into egg-milk mixture until dissolved.

Orange-Cardamom Flan
Whisk 2 tablespoons orange zest and ¼ teaspoon ground cardamom into egg-milk mixture.

Almond Flan
Reduce vanilla to 1 tablespoon and whisk 1 teaspoon almond extract into egg-milk mixture.

Crème Caramel

SERVES 8   **TOTAL TIME** 2 HOURS

✓ **WHY THIS RECIPE WORKS:** What many people love about crème caramel is the caramel. While we can't deny its appeal, what most concerned us when we set out to make a really great crème caramel was the custard. We wanted custard that was creamy and tender enough to melt in our mouths, yet firm enough to unmold without collapsing. We also wanted a mellow flavor that was neither too rich nor too eggy. We discovered that the proportion of egg whites to yolks in the custard was critical for the right texture. Too many whites caused the custard to solidify too much, and too few left it almost runny. We settled on three whole eggs and two yolks. Light cream and milk for the dairy provided the proper amount of richness. For contrast with the sweet caramel, we kept the amount of sugar in the custard to a minimum. Baking the ramekins in a water bath was essential for even cooking and ensured a delicate custard; a dish towel on the bottom of the pan stabilized the ramekins and prevented the bottoms of the custards from overcooking. When we unmolded our crème caramel on serving plates, the sweet caramel sauce bathed the rounds of perfectly cooked custard. You can vary the amount of sugar in the custard to suit your taste. Most tasters preferred the full ⅔ cup, but you can reduce that amount to as little as ½ cup to create a greater contrast between the custard and the caramel. Cook the caramel in a pan with a light-colored interior, since a dark surface makes it difficult to judge the color of the syrup. Caramel can leave a real mess in the pan, but it is easy to clean; simply boil water in the pan for 5 to 10 minutes to loosen the hardened caramel.

Unmolding Crème Caramel

1. Slide small knife around custard to loosen, pressing it against side of dish.

2. Hold individual serving plate over top of ramekin and swiftly invert.

3. Set plate on counter and shake ramekin gently to release custard and caramel. Let caramel drip over custard to coat (some caramel will remain in ramekin).

CARAMEL

- ⅓ cup water
- 2 tablespoons light corn syrup
- ¼ teaspoon lemon juice
- 1 cup (7 ounces) sugar

CUSTARD

- 1½ cups whole milk
- 1½ cups light cream
- 3 large eggs plus 2 large yolks
- ⅔ cup (4⅔ ounces) sugar
- 1½ teaspoons vanilla extract
  Pinch salt

1. FOR THE CARAMEL: Combine water, corn syrup, and lemon juice in medium saucepan. Pour sugar into center of pan, taking care not to let sugar crystals touch pan sides. Gently stir with spatula to moisten sugar thoroughly. Bring to boil over medium-high heat and cook, without stirring, until sugar is completely dissolved and liquid is clear, 6 to 10 minutes. Reduce heat to medium-low and continue to cook, gently swirling pan, until mixture is color of honey, 4 to 5 minutes. Working quickly, carefully divide caramel among eight 6-ounce ramekins. Let caramel cool and harden, about 15 minutes.

2. FOR THE CUSTARD: Adjust oven rack to middle position and heat oven to 350 degrees. Combine milk and cream in medium saucepan and heat over medium heat, stirring occasionally, until steam appears and mixture registers 160 degrees, 6 to 8 minutes; remove from heat. Meanwhile, gently whisk eggs and yolks and sugar in large bowl until just combined. Gently whisk warm milk mixture, vanilla, and salt into egg mixture until just combined but not foamy. Strain mixture through fine-mesh strainer into 4-cup liquid measuring cup or bowl.

3. Bring kettle of water to boil. Place dish towel in bottom of large baking dish or roasting pan and set ramekins with caramel on towel (ramekins should not touch). Divide custard evenly among ramekins and transfer to oven. Taking care not to splash water into ramekins, pour enough boiling water into dish to reach halfway up sides of ramekins; cover dish loosely with aluminum foil. Bake until paring knife inserted halfway between center and edge of custards comes out clean, 35 to 40 minutes. Transfer ramekins to wire rack and let cool to room temperature. (Custards can be refrigerated for up to 2 days.)

4. To unmold, run paring knife around perimeter of each ramekin. Invert serving plate over top of each ramekin and turn plate and ramekin over; set plate on counter and gently shake ramekin to release custard and caramel. Let caramel drip over custard to coat. Serve.

VARIATION
Espresso Crème Caramel
Crush the espresso beans lightly with the bottom of a skillet; don't use a coffee grinder or else the beans will be ground too fine.

Heat ½ cup lightly crushed espresso beans with milk and cream mixture until steam appears and mixture registers 160 degrees, 6 to 8 minutes. Off heat, cover and let steep until coffee flavor has infused milk and cream, about 15 minutes. Strain mixture through fine-mesh strainer and proceed as directed, discarding crushed espresso beans. Reduce vanilla extract to 1 teaspoon.

Crème Brûlée

SERVES 8   **TOTAL TIME** 1 HOUR 10 MINUTES
(PLUS 6 HOURS 30 MINUTES COOLING AND CHILLING TIME)

✔ **WHY THIS RECIPE WORKS:** Crème brûlée is all about the contrast between the crisp crust and the silky custard. But too often the crust is either stingy or rock-hard, and the custard is heavy and tasteless. We found that the secret to perfect custard was using yolks rather than whole eggs. Heavy cream added a luxurious richness. Sugar, a vanilla bean, and salt were the only other additions. Many recipes use scalded cream, but we found that this made for overcooked custard. However, we needed heat to extract flavor from the vanilla bean and dissolve the sugar. Our compromise was to heat half of the cream with the sugar and vanilla bean, and add the remaining cream cold. For the crust, we used a kitchen torch, which worked better than the broiler, and because the blast of heat inevitably warms the custard, we chilled our crèmes brûlées once more before serving. Separate the eggs and whisk the yolks after the cream has finished steeping; if left to sit, the yolks will dry and form a film. A vanilla bean gives the deepest flavor, but 2 teaspoons of vanilla extract, whisked into the yolks in step 3, can be used instead. While we prefer turbinado or Demerara sugar for the sugar crust, regular granulated sugar will work, but use only a scant 1 teaspoon on each ramekin or 1 teaspoon on each shallow fluted dish.

To achieve the desired richness, our recipe for crème brûlée uses 10 egg yolks.

1	vanilla bean
4	cups heavy cream
⅔	cup (4⅔ ounces) granulated sugar
	Pinch salt
10	large egg yolks
8–12	teaspoons turbinado or Demerara sugar

1. Adjust oven rack to lower-middle position and heat oven to 300 degrees. Cut vanilla bean in half lengthwise. Using tip of paring knife, scrape out vanilla seeds. Combine vanilla bean and seeds, 2 cups cream, granulated sugar, and salt in medium saucepan. Bring mixture to boil over medium heat, stirring occasionally to dissolve sugar. Off heat, cover and let steep for 15 minutes.

2. Meanwhile, place dish towel in bottom of large baking dish or roasting pan; set eight 4- or 5-ounce ramekins (or shallow fluted dishes) on towel (ramekins should not touch). Bring kettle of water to boil.

3. After cream has steeped, stir in remaining 2 cups cream. Whisk egg yolks in large bowl until uniform. Whisk about 1 cup cream mixture into yolks until combined; repeat with 1 cup more cream mixture. Add remaining cream

Making Crème Brûlée

1. STEEP VANILLA BEAN IN CREAM: Combine vanilla, 2 cups cream, granulated sugar, and salt in saucepan. Bring mixture to boil, stirring occasionally. Off heat, cover and let steep for 15 minutes.

2. MAKE AND STRAIN CUSTARD: Whisk egg yolks in bowl. Add in cream mixture 1 cup at a time until combined. Pour custard through fine-mesh strainer into large liquid measuring cup.

3. BAKE IN WATER BATH: Divide mixture among ramekins set inside towel-lined baking dish. Set dish on oven rack. Pour boiling water into dish to reach two-thirds up sides of ramekins.

4. CARAMELIZE SUGAR TOPPING: Sprinkle each ramekin with 1 to 1½ teaspoons turbinado sugar. Distribute sugar evenly, then dump out excess and wipe rims clean. Ignite torch and caramelize sugar.

mixture and whisk until evenly colored and thoroughly combined. Strain mixture through fine-mesh strainer into large liquid measuring cup or bowl; discard solids in strainer. Divide mixture evenly among ramekins.

4. Set baking dish on oven rack. Taking care not to splash water into ramekins, pour enough boiling water into dish to reach two-thirds up sides of ramekins. Bake until centers of custards are just barely set and register 170 to 175 degrees, 25 to 35 minutes; depending on ramekin type, check temperature 5 minutes early.

5. Transfer ramekins to wire rack and let cool to room temperature, about 2 hours. Set ramekins on baking sheet, cover tightly with plastic wrap, and refrigerate until cold, at least 4 hours or up to 3 days.

6. Uncover ramekins and gently blot tops dry with paper towels. Sprinkle each with 1 to 1½ teaspoons turbinado sugar (amount depends on ramekin type). Tilt and tap each ramekin to distribute sugar evenly, then dump out excess sugar and wipe rims of ramekins clean. Ignite torch and caramelize sugar. Refrigerate ramekins, uncovered, to rechill custard before serving, 30 to 45 minutes.

VARIATIONS
Espresso Crème Brûlée
Crush the espresso beans lightly with the bottom of a skillet; don't use a coffee grinder or else the beans will be ground too fine.

Substitute ¼ cup lightly crushed espresso beans for vanilla bean. Whisk 1 teaspoon vanilla extract into yolks before adding cream.

Tea-Infused Crème Brûlée
Substitute 10 Irish Breakfast tea bags, tied together, for vanilla bean; after steeping, squeeze bags with tongs or press into fine-mesh strainer to extract all liquid. Whisk 1 teaspoon vanilla extract into yolks before adding cream.

Family-Style Crème Brûlée
Substitute 11 by 7-inch baking dish for ramekins and bake for 40 to 50 minutes. Let cool to room temperature, 2½ to 3 hours, before chilling completely in refrigerator.

Panna Cotta
SERVES 8   **TOTAL TIME** 35 MINUTES
(PLUS 4 HOURS CHILLING TIME)

✔ **WHY THIS RECIPE WORKS:** Although the literal translation of its name is "cooked cream," panna cotta is not actually cooked at all. It is a simple, refined dessert where sugar and gelatin are dissolved in cream and milk, and the mixture is poured into individual ramekins and chilled. Panna cotta is frequently found on restaurant menus, but we wanted a version for the home cook with the rich flavor of cream and vanilla and a delicate texture. After trying several different recipes, we concluded that we needed a higher proportion of cream to milk. We used a light hand with the gelatin, adding just enough to make the dessert firm enough to unmold. And because gelatin sets more quickly at cold temperatures, we minimized the heat. A vanilla bean gives the deepest flavor, but 2 teaspoons of vanilla extract can be used instead. Serve the panna cotta with lightly sweetened berries or a pureed berry coulis. Though traditionally unmolded, panna cotta may be chilled and served in wineglasses with the sauce on top. If you would like to make the panna cotta a day ahead, reduce the amount of gelatin by ½ teaspoon and chill the filled ramekins or wineglasses for at least 18 hours and up to 1 day.

1 cup whole milk
2¾ teaspoons unflavored gelatin
3 cups heavy cream
1 vanilla bean
6 tablespoons (2⅔ ounces) sugar
  Pinch salt

1. Pour milk into medium saucepan, sprinkle gelatin over top, and let sit until gelatin softens, about 10 minutes. Meanwhile, place cream in large measuring cup. Cut vanilla bean in half lengthwise. Using tip of paring knife, scrape out seeds. Add vanilla bean and seeds to cream. Set eight 4-ounce ramekins on rimmed baking sheet. Fill large bowl with ice water.

2. Heat milk and gelatin mixture over high heat, stirring constantly, until gelatin is dissolved and mixture registers 135 degrees, about 1½ minutes. Off heat, stir in sugar and salt until dissolved, about 1 minute.

3. Stirring constantly, slowly pour cream into milk mixture. Transfer mixture to clean bowl and set over bowl of ice water. Stir mixture often until slightly thickened and mixture registers 50 degrees, about 10 minutes. Strain mixture through fine-mesh strainer into large liquid measuring cup, then distribute evenly among ramekins.

4. Cover baking sheet with plastic wrap and refrigerate until custards are just set (mixture should wobble when shaken gently), at least 4 hours or up to 12 hours.

5. To unmold, run paring knife around perimeter of each ramekin. (If shape of ramekin makes this difficult, quickly dip ramekin into hot water bath to loosen custard.) Invert

Removing Vanilla Seeds

1. Cut vanilla bean in half lengthwise.

2. Using tip of paring knife, scrape out vanilla seeds.

serving plate over top of each ramekin and turn ramekin and plate over; set plate on counter and gently shake ramekin to release custard. Serve.

VARIATION
Lemon Panna Cotta
For more information on making a strip of zest, see page 757.

Add four 2-inch strips lemon zest, cut into thin strips, to cream with vanilla bean. Add ¼ cup lemon juice (2 lemons) to strained cream mixture before dividing among ramekins.

Lemon Yogurt Mousse with Blueberry Sauce
SERVES 6   **TOTAL TIME** 1 HOUR
(PLUS 6 HOURS CHILLING TIME)

✔ **WHY THIS RECIPE WORKS:** With its sunny flavor, lemon mousse is a creamy and refreshing dessert. But while its texture is light, its egg yolk–enriched base combined with whipped cream and sugar is heavy on the fat. We turned to Greek yogurt and gelatin for a new take on this chilled dessert. The gelatin held the mousse together without the added fat of egg yolks. Greek yogurt, which is thicker and creamier than American-style yogurt and has a mild, slightly tangy flavor, is an ideal companion for fruit and so was perfect for our fresher recipe. A sauce of sweet blueberries complemented the bright citrus flavor of the mousse and became the first layer in the chilled ramekins. You can substitute 1 cup frozen blueberries for the fresh berries. Do not substitute 2 percent or nonfat Greek yogurt in this recipe.

BLUEBERRY SAUCE
¾ cup (3¾ ounces) blueberries
2 tablespoons sugar
2 tablespoons water
  Pinch salt

MOUSSE
3 tablespoons water
¾ teaspoon unflavored gelatin
½ cup plain whole-milk Greek yogurt
¼ cup heavy cream
1½ teaspoons grated lemon zest plus 3 tablespoons juice
1 teaspoon vanilla extract
⅛ teaspoon salt
3 large egg whites
¼ teaspoon cream of tartar
6 tablespoons (2⅔ ounces) sugar

Thick and tangy Greek yogurt and unflavored gelatin combine for a light, fresh take on chilled lemon mousse.

NOTES FROM THE TEST KITCHEN

Making Vanilla Extract

Most of vanilla's flavor compounds are soluble in either water or alcohol, so the most shelf-stable form of vanilla is vanilla extract, produced by soaking vanilla beans in a solution of 65 percent water and at least 35 percent alcohol. We wondered if we could make our own vanilla extract by soaking a split vanilla bean in heated vodka (which would contribute very little of its own flavor). After testing several ratios of vanilla beans to vodka, we arrived at 1 bean per ¾ cup of vodka as the proportion most closely resembling the potency of our recommended store-bought brand, McCormick Pure Vanilla Extract. We then tested our homemade extract against this supermarket product in sugar cookies, crème brûlée, and vanilla buttercream frosting. In each case, our extract outperformed the commercial version, boasting cleaner, more intense vanilla flavor.

To make vanilla extract, split a fresh bean lengthwise and scrape out the seeds. Place the seeds and split pod in a 1-cup sealable container. Add ¾ cup hot vodka (we used Smirnoff—a premium brand is not necessary) and let the mixture cool to room temperature. Seal the container and store at room temperature for one week, shaking gently every day. Strain the extract, if desired, and store in a cool, dark place. The extract should keep indefinitely.

1. FOR THE BLUEBERRY SAUCE: Bring blueberries, sugar, water, and salt to simmer in medium saucepan over medium heat, stirring occasionally. Cook until sugar is dissolved and fruit is heated through, 2 to 4 minutes.

2. Transfer blueberry mixture to blender and puree until smooth, about 20 seconds. Strain puree through fine-mesh strainer, pressing on solids to extract as much puree as possible. Spoon sauce evenly into six 4-ounce ramekins and refrigerate until chilled, at least 20 minutes or up to 2 days.

3. FOR THE MOUSSE: Meanwhile, pour water into bowl, sprinkle gelatin over top, and let sit until gelatin softens, about 10 minutes. In separate bowl, whisk yogurt, heavy cream, lemon zest and juice, vanilla, and salt together until smooth.

4. Whisk egg whites, cream of tartar, and sugar together in bowl of standing mixer. Set bowl over large saucepan of barely simmering water, making sure water does not touch bottom of bowl. Heat mixture, whisking constantly, until it has tripled in size and registers about 160 degrees, 5 to 10 minutes.

5. Off heat, quickly whisk in hydrated gelatin until dissolved. Using stand mixer fitted with whisk, whip mixture on medium-high speed until it forms stiff, shiny peaks, 4 to 6 minutes. Add yogurt mixture and continue to whip until just combined, 30 to 60 seconds.

6. Divide mousse evenly among chilled ramekins with blueberry sauce, cover tightly with plastic wrap, and refrigerate until chilled and set, at least 6 hours or up to 1 day. Serve chilled.

VARIATIONS
Lemon Yogurt Mousse with Raspberry Sauce
You can substitute 1 cup frozen raspberries for the fresh berries.

Substitute 1 cup raspberries for blueberries.

Lemon Yogurt Mousse with Strawberry Sauce
You can substitute 1 cup frozen strawberries for the fresh berries.

Substitute 1 cup hulled strawberries, halved, for blueberries and reduce amount of water to 2 teaspoons.

Diced fresh strawberries add a punch of bright fruit flavor (and color) to this creamy mousse.

Strawberry Mousse

SERVES 4 TO 6   **TOTAL TIME** 1 HOUR 30 MINUTES (PLUS 4 HOURS CHILLING TIME)

WHY THIS RECIPE WORKS: There's a good reason why strawberry mousse recipes aren't very prevalent: The berries contain lots of juice, which can ruin the texture of a mousse. Plus, the fruit flavor produced by most strawberry mousse recipes is too subtle. We started by processing berries into small pieces and macerating them with sugar and a little salt. This caused them to release liquid, which we then reduced to a syrup before adding it to the mousse—a technique that not only limited the amount of moisture in the dessert but also concentrated the berry flavor. Then we fully pureed the juiced berries, which contributed bright, fresh berry flavor. Finally, we chose our stabilizers carefully: gelatin for structure and cream cheese, an unusual addition, for richer, creamier body. This recipe works well with supermarket strawberries or farmers' market strawberries. Be careful not to overprocess the berries in step 1. For more complex berry flavor, replace the 3 tablespoons

LEMON WHIPPED CREAM

MAKES ABOUT 1 CUP   **TOTAL TIME** 10 MINUTES   **FAST**

Lime zest and juice can be substituted for the lemon, if desired.

- ½ **cup heavy cream**
- 2 **tablespoons sugar**
- 1 **teaspoon finely grated lemon zest plus 1 tablespoon juice**

Using stand mixer fitted with whisk, whip cream on medium-low speed until foamy, about 1 minute. Add sugar and lemon zest and juice, increase speed to medium-high, and whip until soft peaks form, 1 to 3 minutes.

of raw (not reduced) strawberry juice in step 2 with strawberry or raspberry liqueur. In addition to the diced berries, serve the mousse with Lemon Whipped Cream.

- 2 **pounds strawberries, hulled (6½ cups)**
- ½ **cup (3½ ounces) sugar**
- **Pinch salt**
- 1¾ **teaspoons unflavored gelatin**
- 4 **ounces cream cheese, cut into 8 pieces and softened**
- ½ **cup heavy cream, chilled**

1. Cut enough strawberries into ¼-inch dice to measure 1 cup; refrigerate until serving. Working in 2 batches, pulse remaining strawberries in food processor until most pieces measure ¼ to ½ inch (some larger pieces are fine), 6 to 10 pulses; transfer to bowl. Stir in ¼ cup sugar and salt, cover, and let strawberries stand for 45 minutes, stirring occasionally. (Do not clean processor.)

2. Strain processed strawberries through fine-mesh strainer into bowl. Measure 3 tablespoons of drained juice into small bowl, sprinkle gelatin over top, and let sit until gelatin softens, about 5 minutes. Pour remaining drained juice into small saucepan and cook over medium-high heat until reduced to 3 tablespoons, about 10 minutes. Off heat, stir in softened gelatin mixture until dissolved. Whisk in cream cheese until smooth. Transfer mixture to large bowl.

3. Return drained strawberries to now-empty processor and process until smooth, 15 to 20 seconds. Strain puree through fine-mesh strainer into bowl, pressing on solids to extract as much puree as possible; discard solids left in strainer. Whisk strawberry puree into cream cheese mixture to combine.

Dicing Strawberries

1. Cut out stem of strawberry using paring knife.

2. Using chef's knife, slice strawberries ¼ inch thick.

3. Cut sliced strawberries lengthwise into ¼-inch-wide strips, then crosswise into ¼-inch dice.

4. Using stand mixer fitted with whisk, whip cream on medium-low speed until foamy, about 1 minute. Increase speed to high and whip until soft peaks form, 1 to 3 minutes. Gradually add remaining ¼ cup sugar and whip until stiff peaks form, 1 to 2 minutes.

5. Whisk whipped cream into strawberry mixture until no white streaks remain. Portion into dessert dishes and chill for at least 4 hours or up to 2 days. (If chilled longer than 6 hours, let mousse sit at room temperature for 15 minutes before serving.) Serve, garnishing with reserved diced strawberries.

VARIATION

All-Season Strawberry Mousse

Frozen strawberries cannot be diced for garnish. Instead, garnish this mousse with Lemon Whipped Cream (page 772). Substitute 5¼ cups frozen strawberries for fresh strawberries. Skip step 1 (do not process berries) and let frozen berries thaw completely in colander set over bowl to catch juices. Add all of sugar and salt to whipped cream in step 4.

Our mousse is light in texture but heavy on flavor thanks to bittersweet chocolate, cocoa powder, and espresso powder.

Chocolate Mousse

SERVES 6 TO 8   **TOTAL TIME** 30 MINUTES
(PLUS 2 HOURS CHILLING TIME)

✓ **WHY THIS RECIPE WORKS:** Rich, creamy, and dense, chocolate mousse can be delicious but too filling after a few mouthfuls. On the other hand, a light and airy mousse usually lacks deep chocolate flavor. We wanted chocolate mousse that had both a light, meltingly smooth texture and a substantial chocolate flavor. To start, we addressed the mousse's dense, heavy texture. Most recipes for chocolate mousse contain butter. Could we do without it? We eliminated the butter and found that our mousse tasted less heavy. We further lightened the mousse's texture by reducing the number of egg whites and yolks. To make up for the lost volume of the eggs, we whipped the heavy cream to soft peaks before adding it to the chocolate. Next we tackled the mousse's flavor. We maximized the chocolate flavor with a combination of bittersweet chocolate and cocoa powder. To further deepen the chocolate flavor,

The best chocolate mousse has a unique texture halfway between pudding and soufflé. It's light but rich, with deep chocolate flavor. We wanted to take the chocolate seriously while also achieving the perfect balance between creaminess and airiness. Whipping both the egg whites and the heavy cream helped keep things smooth and silky, but not too heavy. We also made some small but crucial additions to the melted chocolate for chocolate flavor to match the perfect texture.

1. CHOP THE CHOCOLATE:
Using a chef's knife, finely chop 8 ounces of bittersweet chocolate.
WHY? Good bittersweet chocolate (roughly 60 percent cacao) creates ideal flavor and texture. A sweeter chocolate (such as semisweet) will taste cloying and one-dimensional. Chopping helps the chocolate melt evenly without scorching.

2. MELT THE CHOCOLATE:
Heat the chocolate, water, cocoa, brandy, and espresso in a heatproof bowl over a saucepan of barely simmering water, stirring frequently until smooth.
WHY? The additions deepen the chocolate flavor. Using a double boiler ensures that the final texture of the mousse will be silky and that the chocolate won't burn or scorch.

3. ADD THE CHOCOLATE TO THE EGG YOLKS: Whisk the yolks, sugar, and salt together until the mixture lightens in color and thickens. Whisk in the chocolate until combined.
WHY? Whisking the melted chocolate mixture into the yolks helps loosen up the chocolate so that it's easier to fold in the whipped egg whites and whipped cream.

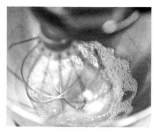

4. WHIP THE EGG WHITES:
Using a stand mixer fitted with a whisk, whip the egg whites at medium-low speed until foamy, about 1 minute.
WHY? The whipped egg whites are crucial to the structure of the mousse, adding light, airy texture. Beating the eggs to soft peaks ensures that the mousse will be light and creamy.

5. ADD THE EGG WHITES TO THE CHOCOLATE MIXTURE:
Whisk one-quarter of the egg whites into the chocolate. Fold in the remaining egg whites with a rubber spatula until just a few white streaks remain.
WHY? Whisking some of the whites into the chocolate mixture helps to loosen it up, so that you can more easily incorporate the rest of the whites without ruining their airy texture. Be sure to scrape along the bottom of the bowl for unmixed batter.

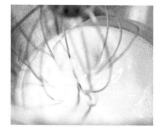

6. WHIP THE CREAM: In the now-empty mixer bowl, whip the cream on medium speed until it begins to thicken. Increase the speed to high until soft peaks form.
WHY? The richness of the whipped cream rounds out the chocolate flavor, and its soft, whipped texture makes the mousse smooth and silky. Much like the egg whites, whipping the cream just to soft peaks (not stiff peaks) ensures that the final mousse will be soft and creamy.

7. FOLD THE CREAM INTO THE MOUSSE: Using a rubber spatula, fold the whipped cream into the mousse until no white streaks remain.
WHY? Using a stiff rubber spatula is key when folding in the whipped cream. You need to fold in the whipped cream completely so that there are no streaks in the final mousse, but be gentle so as not to deflate its airy texture.

8. CHILL THE MOUSSE:
Spoon the mousse into 6 to 8 individual serving dishes, cover them with plastic wrap, and refrigerate until the mousse is set and firm, at least 2 hours or up to 1 day.
WHY? Chilling the mousse is crucial to help it set. Covering the dishes tightly with plastic wrap will prevent the mousse from picking up any other flavors in the refrigerator.

we found that a small amount of instant espresso powder, salt, and brandy did the trick. When developing this recipe, we used Ghirardelli Bittersweet Chocolate Baking Bar, which contains about 60 percent cacao. If you want to use a chocolate with a higher percentage of cacao, see our variation, Premium Dark Chocolate Mousse. If you choose to make the mousse a day in advance, let it sit at room temperature for 10 minutes before serving. Serve with Whipped Cream (page 712) and Chocolate Shavings (page 723) if desired.

- 8 **ounces bittersweet chocolate, chopped fine**
- 5 **tablespoons water**
- 2 **tablespoons Dutch-processed cocoa powder**
- 1 **tablespoon brandy**
- 1 **teaspoon instant espresso powder**
- 2 **large eggs, separated**
- 1 **tablespoon sugar**
- ⅛ **teaspoon salt**
- 1 **cup plus 2 tablespoons heavy cream, chilled**

1. Place chocolate, water, cocoa, brandy, and espresso powder in medium heatproof bowl set over saucepan filled with 1 inch barely simmering water, stirring frequently until chocolate is melted, cocoa powder is dissolved, and mixture is smooth. Remove from heat.

2. Whisk egg yolks, 1½ teaspoons sugar, and salt in medium bowl until mixture lightens in color and thickens slightly, about 30 seconds. Whisk in melted chocolate mixture until combined. Let cool until just warmer than room temperature, 3 to 5 minutes.

3. Using stand mixer fitted with whisk, whip egg whites at medium-low speed until foamy, about 1 minute. Add remaining 1½ teaspoons sugar, increase speed to medium-high, and whip until soft peaks form, about 1 minute. Using whisk, stir about one-quarter of whipped egg whites into chocolate mixture to lighten it. Gently fold in remaining egg whites with rubber spatula until few white streaks remain.

4. In now-empty mixer bowl, whip cream on medium speed until it begins to thicken, about 30 seconds. Increase speed to high and whip until soft peaks form, about 15 seconds longer. Using rubber spatula, fold whipped cream into mousse until no white streaks remain. Spoon mousse into 6 to 8 individual serving dishes. Cover with plastic wrap and refrigerate until set and firm, at least 2 hours or up to 1 day. Serve.

VARIATIONS
Premium Dark Chocolate Mousse
This recipe is designed to work with a boutique chocolate that contains a higher percentage of cacao than that in our master recipe.

Use 62 percent to 70 percent cacao bittersweet chocolate, increase water to 7 tablespoons, and increase eggs to 3. Increase sugar to 3 tablespoons, adding extra 2 tablespoons to chocolate mixture in step 1.

Chocolate-Raspberry Mousse
Chambord is our preferred brand of raspberry-flavored liqueur for this recipe. Serve the mousse with fresh raspberries, if desired.

Reduce water to 4 tablespoons, omit brandy, and add 2 tablespoons raspberry-flavored liqueur to melted chocolate mixture in step 1.

Chocolate Pots de Crème
SERVES 8   **TOTAL TIME** 1 HOUR 30 MINUTES
(PLUS 4 HOURS CHILLING TIME)

✔ **WHY THIS RECIPE WORKS:** Classic *pots de crème* can be finicky and laborious, requiring a hot water bath that threatens to splash the custards every time the pan is moved. We wanted a user-friendly recipe that delivered a decadent dessert with a satiny texture and intense chocolate flavor. First we moved the dish out of the oven, concentrating on an unconventional approach in which the custard is cooked on the stovetop in a saucepan, then poured into ramekins. Our next challenge was developing the right amount of richness and body, which we did by choosing a combination of heavy cream and half-and-half, along with egg yolks only, for maximum richness. For intense chocolate flavor, we focused on bittersweet chocolate—and a lot of it. Our chocolate content was at least 50 percent more than in any other recipe we had encountered. When developing this recipe, we used Ghirardelli Bittersweet Chocolate Baking Bar, which contains about 60 percent cacao. If you want to use a chocolate with a higher percentage of cacao, see our variation Premium Dark Chocolate Pots de Crème.

POTS DE CRÈME
- 10 **ounces bittersweet chocolate, chopped fine**
- 1 **tablespoon vanilla extract**
- 1 **tablespoon water**
- ½ **teaspoon instant espresso powder**
- 5 **large egg yolks**
- 5 **tablespoons (2¼ ounces) sugar**
- ¼ **teaspoon salt**
- 1½ **cups heavy cream**
- ¾ **cup half-and-half**

WHIPPED CREAM AND GARNISH

½ cup heavy cream, chilled

2 teaspoons sugar

½ teaspoon vanilla extract

Cocoa powder and/or chocolate shavings (page 723) (optional)

1. FOR THE POTS DE CRÈME: Place chocolate in medium bowl and set fine-mesh strainer over top. Combine vanilla, water, and espresso powder in small bowl.

2. Whisk egg yolks, sugar, and salt together in separate bowl until combined. Whisk in cream and half-and-half. Transfer mixture to medium saucepan and cook over medium-low heat, stirring constantly and scraping bottom of pot with wooden spoon, until thickened and silky and registers 175 to 180 degrees, 8 to 12 minutes. (Do not let custard overcook or simmer.)

3. Immediately pour custard through fine-mesh strainer over chocolate. Let mixture stand to melt chocolate, about 5 minutes. Add espresso-vanilla mixture and whisk mixture until smooth. Divide mixture evenly among eight 5-ounce ramekins. Gently tap ramekins against counter to settle custard.

4. Let pots de crème cool to room temperature, then cover with plastic wrap and refrigerate until chilled, at least 4 hours or up to 3 days. Before serving, let pots de crème stand at room temperature for 20 to 30 minutes.

5. FOR THE WHIPPED CREAM AND GARNISH: Using stand mixer fitted with whisk, whip cream, sugar, and vanilla on medium-low speed until foamy, about 1 minute. Increase speed to high and whip until stiff peaks form, 1 to 3 minutes. Dollop each pot de crème with about 2 tablespoons whipped cream and garnish with cocoa and/or chocolate shavings, if using. Serve.

VARIATIONS

Milk Chocolate Pots de Crème

Milk chocolate behaves differently than bittersweet chocolate in this recipe, and more of it must be used to ensure that the custard sets. Because of the increased amount of chocolate, it's necessary to cut back on the amount of sugar so that the custard is not overly sweet.

Substitute 12 ounces milk chocolate, chopped fine, for bittersweet chocolate, and reduce sugar to 2 tablespoons (in pots de crème).

Premium Dark Chocolate Pots de Crème

This recipe is designed to work with a boutique chocolate that contains a higher percentage of cacao than that in our master recipe.

Use 62 percent to 70 percent cacao bittersweet chocolate, and reduce chocolate amount to 8 ounces.

Making Pots de Crème

1. MAKE CUSTARD: Cook egg yolks, sugar, salt, cream, and half-and-half over medium-low heat, stirring constantly and scraping bottom of pot with wooden spoon, until custard is thickened and registers 175 to 180 degrees.

2. STRAIN CUSTARD INTO BOWL OF CHOCOLATE: Immediately pour custard through fine-mesh strainer set over bowl of chopped chocolate. Let mixture stand to melt chocolate, about 5 minutes.

3. ADD FLAVORS AND WHISK SMOOTH: Add espresso-vanilla mixture and whisk mixture until smooth.

4. PORTION INTO RAMEKINS AND CHILL: Divide mixture evenly among ramekins. Gently tap ramekins against counter to settle custard, cover with plastic wrap, and refrigerate until chilled, at least 4 hours or up to 3 days.

Tiramisù

SERVES 10 TO 12   **TOTAL TIME** 35 MINUTES
(PLUS 6 HOURS CHILLING TIME)

✓ **WHY THIS RECIPE WORKS:** Although it's a recent invention, the Italian dessert tiramisù has quickly become a modern classic. The layers of creamy mascarpone filling and ladyfinger cookies infused with alcohol, coffee, and chocolate have proven an irresistible combination. We wanted to find a streamlined approach to tiramisù—one that highlighted the luxurious combination of flavors and textures that have made this dessert so popular while avoiding labor-intensive preparation and overly soggy ladyfingers. Instead of making a fussy custard-based filling (called *zabaglione*), we instead simply whipped egg yolks, sugar, salt, rum (our preferred spirit), and mascarpone together. Salt is not traditional, but we found that it heightened the filling's subtle flavors. To lighten the filling, we chose whipped cream instead of egg whites. For the coffee soaking mixture, we combined strong brewed coffee and espresso powder (along with more rum). To moisten the ladyfingers so that they were neither too dry nor too saturated, we dropped them one at a time into the spiked coffee mixture and, once they were moistened, rolled them over to moisten the other side for just a couple of seconds. For the best flavor and texture, we discovered that it was important to allow the tiramisù to chill in the refrigerator for at least 6 hours. Brandy and even whiskey can be substituted for the dark rum. The test kitchen prefers a tiramisù with a pronounced rum flavor; for a less potent rum flavor, reduce the amount of rum in the coffee mixture. Do not let the mascarpone warm to room temperature before whipping, or else it might break. Dried ladyfingers are also called *savoiardi*; you will need between 42 and 60 savoiardi, depending on their size and brand.

2½ cups strong brewed coffee, room temperature
1½ tablespoons instant espresso powder
 9 tablespoons dark rum
 6 large egg yolks
⅔ cup (4⅔ ounces) sugar
¼ teaspoon salt
1½ pounds (3 cups) mascarpone, chilled
¾ cup heavy cream, chilled
14 ounces dried ladyfingers (savoiardi)
3½ tablespoons unsweetened cocoa powder, preferably Dutch-processed
¼ cup grated semisweet or bittersweet chocolate (optional)

We simplify the filling for tiramisù by using whipped egg yolks, mascarpone, and whipped cream.

1. Stir coffee, espresso powder, and 5 tablespoons rum together in wide bowl or baking dish until espresso dissolves.

2. Using stand mixer fitted with whisk, beat yolks at low speed until just combined. Add sugar and salt and beat at medium-high speed until pale yellow, 1½ to 2 minutes, scraping down bowl as needed. Reduce speed to medium, add remaining 4 tablespoons rum, and beat until just combined, 20 to 30 seconds; scrape down bowl. Add mascarpone and beat on medium speed until no lumps remain, 30 to 45 seconds, scraping down bowl as needed. Transfer mixture to large bowl.

3. Return now-empty bowl to mixer and beat cream at medium speed until frothy, 1 to 1½ minutes. Increase speed to high and continue to beat until stiff peaks form, 1 to 1½ minutes. Using rubber spatula, fold one-third whipped cream into mascarpone mixture to lighten, then gently fold in remaining whipped cream until no white streaks remain.

4. Working with 1 ladyfinger at a time, drop half of ladyfingers into coffee mixture, roll, remove, and transfer to 13 by 9-inch dish. (Do not submerge ladyfingers in coffee mixture; entire process should take no longer than 2 to 3 seconds for each cookie.) Arrange soaked cookies in single layer in baking dish, breaking or trimming ladyfingers as needed to fit neatly into dish.

5. Spread half of mascarpone mixture over ladyfingers, spreading mixture to sides and into corners of dish, and smooth top. Place 2 tablespoons cocoa in fine-mesh strainer and dust cocoa over mascarpone.

6. Repeat with remaining ladyfingers, mascarpone mixture, and 1½ tablespoons cocoa to make second layer. Wipe edges of dish clean, cover with plastic wrap, and refrigerate until set, at least 6 hours or up to 1 day. Before serving, sprinkle with grated chocolate, if using.

Assembling Tiramisù

1. Working with 1 ladyfinger at a time, drop into coffee mixture, roll, remove, and transfer to baking dish. Arrange in single layer, trimming cookies as needed to fit neatly in dish.

2. Spread half of mascarpone mixture over ladyfingers, spreading it to sides and into corners of dish, and smooth top.

3. Place 2 tablespoons cocoa in fine-mesh strainer and dust cocoa over mascarpone.

Roasting Bananas

Place 3 unpeeled bananas on baking sheet and bake until skins are completely black, about 20 minutes. Let cool, about 5 minutes, then peel.

Banana Pudding

SERVES 12   **TOTAL TIME** 1 HOUR 40 MINUTES
(PLUS 8 HOURS CHILLING TIME)

✔ **WHY THIS RECIPE WORKS:** Traditional banana pudding is made by layering vanilla pudding with sliced bananas and vanilla wafers. Not only does this risk brown, slimy bananas and soggy cookies, but the pudding also tastes plain-Jane vanilla—which it is. We wanted a banana pudding that put the banana into the pudding itself. We wanted it to be rich and creamy, so we opted for half-and-half instead of milk. Roasting the bananas that were going directly into the pudding intensified their flavor and helped break them down so we could incorporate them more easily. Adding a squeeze of lemon juice to the roasted bananas prevented them from browning in the refrigerator while the pudding set. When building the pudding, we used whole cookies, since crushed cookies disintegrated in the finished dessert. To keep the cookies from getting sodden and pasty, we waited until the pudding cooled a little before layering them into the dish. If your food processor bowl holds less than 11 cups, puree half the pudding with the roasted bananas and lemon juice in step 3, transfer it to a large bowl, and whisk in the rest of the pudding.

PUDDING

- 7 **slightly underripe large bananas**
- 1½ **cups (10½ ounces) sugar**
- 8 **large egg yolks**
- 6 **tablespoons cornstarch**
- 6 **cups half-and-half**
- ½ **teaspoon salt**
- 3 **tablespoons unsalted butter**
- 1 **tablespoon vanilla extract**
- 3 **tablespoons lemon juice**
- 1 **(12-ounce) box vanilla wafers**

WHIPPED TOPPING

- 1 **cup heavy cream, chilled**
- 1 **tablespoon sugar**
- ½ **teaspoon vanilla extract**

1. FOR THE PUDDING: Adjust oven rack to upper-middle position and heat oven to 325 degrees. Place 3 unpeeled bananas on baking sheet and bake until skins are completely black, about 20 minutes. Let cool, about 5 minutes, then peel.

2. Meanwhile, whisk ½ cup sugar, egg yolks, and cornstarch in medium bowl until smooth. Bring half-and-half, remaining 1 cup sugar, and salt to simmer in large saucepan over medium heat. Whisk ½ cup simmering half-and-half mixture

The rich pudding in this sweet and creamy trifle gets its flavor from roasted bananas.

Classic Bread Pudding

SERVES 8 TO 10   **TOTAL TIME** 2 HOURS
(PLUS 45 MINUTES COOLING TIME)

☑ **WHY THIS RECIPE WORKS:** Bread pudding started as a frugal way to transform stale, old loaves of bread into an appetizing dish. But contemporary versions vary from mushy, sweetened porridge to chewy, desiccated cousins of holiday stuffing. We wanted a refined bread pudding, with a moist, creamy (but not eggy) interior and a crisp top crust. For the bread, we chose challah for its rich flavor. We cut it into cubes, toasted them, and soaked the cubes in a batch of basic custard. Once the cubes were saturated, we transferred them to a baking dish and slid our pudding into a low-temperature oven to prevent curdling. The custard turned out creamy and smooth, but not as set as we'd have liked. Adding another egg or two helped, but tasters complained that the pudding tasted somewhat eggy. It turns out that eggy flavor comes from the sulfur compounds in egg whites, so we just used just the yolks. We now had a luscious, silky custard. Brushing the surface with melted butter and sprinkling sugar over the top prior to baking gave the pudding a crunchy, buttery, sugary crust. Challah is an egg-enriched bread that can be found in most bakeries and supermarkets. Hearty white sandwich bread can be substituted for the challah. Serve with Bourbon Brown Sugar Sauce (page 780).

1 **(14-ounce) loaf challah, cut into ¾-inch cubes (12 cups)**
9 **large egg yolks**
¾ **cup (5¼ ounces) plus 1 tablespoon granulated sugar**
4 **teaspoons vanilla extract**
¾ **teaspoon salt**
2½ **cups heavy cream**
2½ **cups milk**
2 **tablespoons light brown sugar**
2 **tablespoons unsalted butter, melted**

1. Adjust oven racks to middle and lower-middle positions and heat oven to 325 degrees. Spread challah in single layer over 2 rimmed baking sheets. Bake, tossing occasionally, until just dry, about 15 minutes; let cool for about 15 minutes. Measure out 2 cups dried challah and set aside for topping.

2. Whisk egg yolks, ¾ cup granulated sugar, vanilla, and salt together in large bowl. Whisk in cream and milk until combined. Add remaining dried challah and toss to combine. Transfer mixture to 13 by 9-inch baking dish and let stand, occasionally pressing on challah to submerge, until bread is well saturated, about 30 minutes.

into egg yolk mixture. Slowly whisk tempered yolk mixture into saucepan. Cook, whisking constantly, until mixture is thick and large bubbles appear on surface, about 2 minutes. Off heat, stir in butter and vanilla.

3. Transfer pudding to food processor, add warm roasted bananas and 2 tablespoons lemon juice, and process until smooth, 30 to 60 seconds. Scrape pudding into large bowl, place lightly greased parchment paper against surface of pudding, and refrigerate until slightly cool, about 45 minutes.

4. Cut remaining bananas into ¼-inch slices and toss in bowl with remaining 1 tablespoon lemon juice. Spoon one-quarter of pudding into 3-quart trifle dish and top with layer of cookies, layer of sliced bananas, and another layer of cookies. Repeat twice more, ending with pudding. Place lightly greased parchment paper against surface of pudding and refrigerate until wafers have softened, at least 8 hours or up to 2 days.

5. FOR THE WHIPPED TOPPING: Using stand mixer fitted with whisk, whip cream, sugar, and vanilla on medium-low speed until foamy, about 1 minute. Increase speed to high and whip until stiff peaks form, 1 to 3 minutes. Dollop whipped cream over top of banana pudding and serve.

3. Combine brown sugar and remaining 1 tablespoon granulated sugar in bowl. Sprinkle reserved challah evenly over top of bread pudding and press gently into custard. Brush with melted butter and sprinkle with sugar mixture. Place dish with bread pudding on rimmed baking sheet and bake on middle rack until custard is just set and center of pudding registers 170 degrees, 45 to 50 minutes, rotating pan halfway through baking.

4. Transfer to wire rack and let cool until pudding is set and just warm, about 45 minutes. Serve.

VARIATIONS

Pecan Bread Pudding with Bourbon and Orange

Add ⅔ cup chopped toasted pecans, 1 tablespoon all-purpose flour, and 1 tablespoon softened unsalted butter to sugar mixture in step 3 and mix until crumbly. Add 1 tablespoon bourbon and 2 teaspoons finely grated orange zest to egg yolk mixture.

Rum Raisin Bread Pudding with Cinnamon

Add ⅛ teaspoon ground cinnamon to sugar mixture in step 3. Microwave ⅔ cup golden raisins and 5 teaspoons dark rum in covered bowl until hot, about 20 seconds; let cool, then add to custard with dried challah.

BOURBON BROWN SUGAR SAUCE

MAKES ABOUT 1 CUP   **TOTAL TIME** 10 MINUTES **FAST**

Rum can be substituted for the bourbon.

- ½ **cup packed (3½ ounces) light brown sugar**
- 7 **tablespoons heavy cream**
- 2½ **tablespoons unsalted butter**
- 1½ **tablespoons bourbon**

Whisk brown sugar and heavy cream in small saucepan until combined. Cook over medium heat, whisking frequently, until mixture comes to boil, about 5 minutes. Whisk in butter and return mixture to boil, about 1 minute. Off heat, whisk in bourbon. Let cool slightly and serve with any of our bread puddings.

Cocoa powder, chocolate sauce, and ganache on top make this a bread pudding that's really all about the chocolate.

Chocolate Bread Pudding

SERVES 12   **TOTAL TIME** 2 HOURS 15 MINUTES

✓ **WHY THIS RECIPE WORKS:** Adding chocolate to a traditional bread pudding sounds like a winning proposition, but the reality isn't so rosy. It wasn't as simple as just adding cocoa powder or melted chocolate to an existing recipe. Recipes that just stirred cocoa powder into the custard base were pale and lacking chocolate punch. Those that added melted chocolate tasted better, but the dense chocolate thickened the base so it never fully permeated the bread, making for bland, dry bread cubes suspended in chocolate custard. In the end, the answer was to use both cocoa powder and melted chocolate at different stages, so that the bread cubes were not only soaked in a "hot cocoa" mixture but also baked in a rich chocolate custard (and topped with extra chocolate sauce for good measure). We toasted the challah cubes in the oven until crisp and golden; the extra browning helps to deepen the chocolate flavor in the finished pudding. Challah is an egg-enriched bread that can be found in most bakeries and supermarkets. Hearty white sandwich bread can be substituted for the challah. Be sure to use Dutch-processed cocoa in this recipe; natural cocoa powder will make the pudding taste bitter.

1 (14-ounce) loaf challah, cut into ½-inch cubes (12 cups)
4 cups heavy cream
2 cups whole milk
½ cup (1½ ounces) Dutch-processed cocoa powder
1 tablespoon instant espresso powder
1 cup (7 ounces) sugar
8 ounces semisweet chocolate, chopped
10 large egg yolks

1. Adjust oven rack to middle position and heat oven to 300 degrees. Spread challah in single layer over rimmed baking sheet. Bake, tossing occasionally, until golden and crisp, about 30 minutes. Transfer to large bowl.

2. Increase oven temperature to 325 degrees. Grease 13 by 9-inch baking dish. Heat 1½ cups cream, milk, cocoa, espresso powder, and ½ cup sugar in saucepan over medium-high heat, stirring occasionally, until steaming and sugar dissolves. Pour warm cream mixture over toasted bread and let stand, tossing occasionally, until liquid has been absorbed, about 10 minutes.

3. Meanwhile, bring 1 cup cream to simmer in saucepan over medium-high heat. Off heat, stir in chocolate until melted and smooth. Transfer 1 cup chocolate mixture to bowl, let cool 5 minutes, then whisk in egg yolks, remaining 1½ cups cream, and remaining ½ cup sugar. Cover pan and reserve remaining chocolate mixture for serving.

4. Transfer soaked bread mixture to prepared pan and pour chocolate custard evenly over bread. Bake until pudding is just set and surface is slightly crisp, about 45 minutes, rotating pan halfway through baking. Let cool 30 minutes. Warm reserved chocolate mixture over low heat, then pour over bread pudding and serve.

Ultimate Vanilla Ice Cream

MAKES ABOUT 1 QUART   TOTAL TIME 50 MINUTES
(PLUS 7 HOURS FREEZING AND CHILLING TIME)

✓ **WHY THIS RECIPE WORKS:** Homemade vanilla ice cream is never as creamy or smooth as the "super-premium" ice creams. We wanted a creamy, custard-based vanilla that would rival any pricey artisanal batch. A combination of heavy cream and whole milk, along with egg yolks, yielded the right richness. Creating smooth ice cream means reducing the size of the ice crystals. Our first move was to replace some of the

For super-premium texture, we swapped out some of the sugar in the custard base of this ice cream for corn syrup.

sugar in our custard with corn syrup, which interfered with crystal formation for a supersmooth texture. To speed up the freezing process, we froze a portion of the custard prior to churning, then mixed it with the remaining refrigerated custard. Freezing the churned ice cream in a thin layer on a cold metal baking pan allowed the ice cream to firm up more quickly. Two teaspoons of vanilla extract can be substituted for the vanilla bean; stir the extract into the cold custard in step 4. An instant-read thermometer is critical for the best results. If using a canister-style ice cream maker, be sure to freeze the empty canister for at least 1 day and preferably 2 days before churning. For a self-refrigerating ice cream maker, prechill the canister by running the machine for 5 to 10 minutes before pouring in the custard.

1 vanilla bean
1¾ cups heavy cream
1¼ cups whole milk
½ cup (3½ ounces) plus 2 tablespoons sugar
⅓ cup light corn syrup
¼ teaspoon salt
6 large egg yolks

To avoid the problems associated with homemade ice cream, we replaced some of the sugar with corn syrup, which interferes with ice crystal formation and helps keep ice cream smooth. Faster freezing also helps, so we froze a small portion of the custard and used it to superchill the rest of our mix before churning, and then we chilled the churned ice cream in a flat metal pan. Just these few humble steps—all of which helped freeze the custard quickly—delivered superpremium smoothness in a homemade ice cream.

1. ADD THE CORN SYRUP:
Combine the vanilla, cream, milk, 6 tablespoons sugar, corn syrup, and salt. Cook over medium-high heat, stirring occasionally, until the mixture registers 175 degrees.
WHY? The chemical makeup of corn syrup keeps water molecules from combining and forming large ice crystals.

2. TEMPER THE EGGS: While the cream mixture heats, whisk the egg yolks and remaining sugar until smooth. Slowly add 1 cup of the heated cream mixture into the egg yolk mixture to temper.
WHY? If you simply dump the yolk mixture into the cream mixture it will curdle and you will have to start over.

3. COOK THE CUSTARD TO 180 DEGREES: Cook the new mixture over medium-low heat, stirring constantly, until it thickens and registers 180 degrees.
WHY? To ensure that you don't overcook the custard and scramble the eggs, use medium-low heat and stir constantly while cooking.

4. FREEZE 1 CUP OF THE CUSTARD: After the custard cools, transfer 1 cup to a small bowl. Cover both bowls with plastic wrap. Refrigerate the large bowl and freeze the small bowl for at least 4 hours or up to 1 day.
WHY? The frozen portion will be used to superchill the custard for churning, to avoid ice crystal formation.

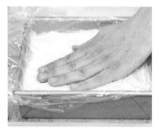

5. COMBINE THE CHILLED AND FROZEN CUSTARDS:
Remove the custards from the refrigerator and the freezer. Scrape the frozen custard into the large bowl of custard and let it dissolve completely, stirring often.
WHY? Adding the frozen custard to the chilled custard brings the overall temperature down substantially. Having the custard as cold as possible before going into the ice cream maker reduces the churning time and produces the creamiest texture.

6. STRAIN THE CUSTARD:
Strain the custard through a fine-mesh strainer into a clean bowl.
WHY? Once the frozen portion of custard has been incorporated back into the batch, the custard must be strained to remove any clumps of eggs and, of course, the vanilla bean pod.

7. MAKE SOFT-SERVE ICE CREAM: Transfer the chilled and strained custard to the ice cream maker. Churn the custard until it resembles thick soft-serve ice cream and registers about 21 degrees.
WHY? The ice cream maker, which constantly stirs the custard while freezing it, is what turns the custard into actual ice cream. Having the custard superchilled and using a well-chilled ice cream canister makes this step fairly quick, which is ideal for the finished texture.

8. FINISH CHILLING THE ICE CREAM IN A CHILLED METAL PAN: Transfer the ice cream to a frozen baking pan and cover with plastic wrap. Once the ice cream is frozen around the edges, transfer to an airtight container and again press plastic wrap on the surface. Freeze until firm, at least 2 hours or up to 5 days.
WHY? Speed of freezing is the most critical factor in ice cream making. Metal conducts heat better than glass or plastic, and a larger, flatter surface area expedites freezing.

1. Place 8- or 9-inch square metal baking pan in freezer. Cut vanilla bean in half lengthwise. Using tip of paring knife, scrape out vanilla seeds. Combine vanilla bean and seeds, cream, milk, 6 tablespoons sugar, corn syrup, and salt in medium saucepan. Heat over medium-high heat, stirring occasionally, until mixture is steaming steadily and registers 175 degrees, 5 to 10 minutes. Remove saucepan from heat.

2. While cream mixture heats, whisk egg yolks and remaining ¼ cup sugar in bowl until smooth, about 30 seconds. Slowly whisk 1 cup heated cream mixture into egg yolk mixture to temper, then whisk egg yolk mixture into cream mixture and cook over medium-low heat, stirring constantly, until mixture thickens and registers 180 degrees, 7 to 14 minutes.

3. Immediately pour custard into large bowl and let cool until no longer steaming, 10 to 20 minutes. Transfer 1 cup custard to small bowl. Cover both bowls with plastic wrap. Place large bowl in refrigerator and small bowl in freezer and let cool completely, at least 4 hours or up to 1 day. (Small bowl of custard will freeze solid.)

4. Remove custards from refrigerator and freezer. Scrape frozen custard from small bowl into large bowl and let dissolve completely, stirring often. Strain custard through fine-mesh strainer and transfer to ice cream maker. Churn until mixture resembles thick soft-serve ice cream and registers about 21 degrees, 15 to 25 minutes.

5. Transfer ice cream to frozen baking pan and press plastic wrap on surface. Return to freezer until firm around edges, about 1 hour. Transfer ice cream to airtight container, press firmly to remove any air pockets, and press plastic wrap on surface. Freeze until firm, at least 2 hours or up to 5 days. Serve.

VARIATIONS

Triple Ginger Ice Cream

Freeze the crystallized ginger for at least 15 minutes before adding it to the churning ice cream.

Substitute one 3-inch piece fresh ginger, peeled and sliced into thin rounds, and 2 teaspoons ground ginger for vanilla bean. Add ½ cup chopped crystallized ginger to ice cream during last minute of churning.

Coffee Crunch Ice Cream

Look for chocolate-covered cocoa nibs (roasted pieces of the cocoa bean) in chocolate shops or well-stocked supermarkets. Freeze the cocoa nibs for at least 15 minutes before adding them to the churning ice cream.

Substitute ½ cup coarsely ground coffee for vanilla bean. Add ¾ cup chocolate-covered cocoa nibs to ice cream during last minute of churning.

HOT FUDGE SAUCE

MAKES ABOUT 2 CUPS   **TOTAL TIME** 15 MINUTES **FAST**

Sifting the cocoa powder prevents lumps from forming in the sauce.

- 10 ounces semisweet chocolate, chopped
- ⅓ cup (1 ounce) Dutch-processed cocoa powder, sifted
- ¾ cup light corn syrup
- ⅓ cup (2⅓ ounces) sugar
- ⅓ cup heavy cream
- ⅓ cup water
  Pinch salt
- 3 tablespoons unsalted butter, cut into ¼-inch pieces
- 1 teaspoon vanilla extract

1. Microwave chocolate in bowl at 50 percent power, stirring occasionally, until melted, 2 to 4 minutes. Whisk in cocoa until dissolved.

2. Meanwhile, heat corn syrup, sugar, cream, water, and salt in medium saucepan over low heat without stirring until sugar dissolves. Increase heat to medium-high and simmer mixture, stirring often, about 4 minutes. Off heat, whisk in butter and vanilla. Let cool slightly, about 2 minutes, then whisk in melted chocolate mixture. Serve warm. (Sauce can be refrigerated for up to 2 weeks; reheat gently in microwave before serving.)

Magic Vanilla Ice Cream

MAKES ABOUT 1 QUART   **TOTAL TIME** 15 MINUTES
(PLUS 6 HOURS FREEZING TIME)

✓ **WHY THIS RECIPE WORKS:** Making your own ice cream is delicious, impressive, and fun, but it has one giant drawback: You need a bulky, hard-to-store, kitchen-cluttering ice cream maker. The machine incorporates air, reduces ice crystals, and lightens the texture. In order to find a way to make ice cream at home without that technology, we had to figure out how to replicate the taste and texture created by the machine. The magic ingredients turned out to be sweetened condensed milk and folded-in whipped cream; these kept our ice cream light but velvety even after freezing. To perfect our vanilla flavor, we started by microwaving sweetened condensed milk with white chocolate chips (for structure and silkiness). Next, we added a surprising ingredient—sour cream—for richness,

The addition of sour cream adds richness and tang and counters the sweetness in this vanilla ice cream.

body, and tartness to counter the sweetness of the condensed milk and white chocolate, plus a generous tablespoon of vanilla extract for a strong vanilla taste. Finally, we folded in the billowy whipped cream, which made the ice cream light and rich, and put the mixture in the freezer. Note that white chocolate varies greatly in quality; we like Guittard Choc-O-Lait Chips or Ghirardelli Classic White Chips. If you use a bar instead of chips, be sure to chop it fine before melting. If you plan to store the ice cream for more than a few days, place plastic wrap directly on its surface before you freeze it.

- ½ **cup sweetened condensed milk**
- 3 **tablespoons white chocolate chips**
- ¼ **cup sour cream**
- 1 **tablespoon vanilla extract**
  Pinch salt
- 1¼ **cups heavy cream, chilled**

1. Microwave condensed milk and chocolate chips in large bowl at 50 percent power until chips soften, 60 to 75 seconds, stirring halfway through. Stir mixture, smearing chips against

---

EASY CARAMEL SAUCE FOR ICE CREAM

MAKES ABOUT 1½ CUPS   **TOTAL TIME** 20 MINUTES **FAST**

Be careful when stirring in the cream because the hot mixture may splatter. Use a heavy-bottomed saucepan with a capacity of at least 3 quarts. An instant-read thermometer is especially helpful here. The addition of butter makes for a richer sauce.

- ½ **cup water**
- 1 **cup (7 ounces) sugar**
- 1 **cup heavy cream**
- ½ **teaspoon vanilla extract**
- ⅛ **teaspoon salt**
- 2 **tablespoons unsalted butter (optional)**

1. Pour water into saucepan. Pour sugar into center of saucepan, taking care not to let sugar touch sides of pan. Gently stir with clean spatula to moisten sugar thoroughly.

2. Cover pan and bring to boil over medium-high heat. Cook, without stirring, until sugar is completely dissolved and liquid is clear, 3 to 5 minutes. Uncover and continue to cook, without stirring, until liquid has faint golden color, 3 to 5 minutes. Reduce heat to medium-low and cook, swirling pan occasionally, until caramel is amber-colored and registers 350 to 360 degrees, 1 to 2 minutes.

3. Remove pan from heat and slowly whisk in cream until combined (mixture will bubble and steam). Stir in vanilla and salt. Add butter, if using, and stir until smooth. Serve warm. (Sauce can be refrigerated for up to 2 weeks; reheat gently in microwave before serving.)

---

side of bowl, until chocolate has melted completely, about 2 minutes. Stir in sour cream, vanilla, and salt until uniform.

2. Using stand mixer fitted with whisk, whip cream on medium-low speed until foamy, about 1 minute. Increase speed to high and whip until soft peaks form, 1 to 3 minutes. Stir one-third whipped cream into chocolate mixture until combined. Gently fold in remaining whipped cream until no white streaks remain. Transfer mixture to airtight container and press plastic wrap on surface. Freeze until firm, at least 6 hours or up to 2 weeks. Serve.

VARIATIONS

Magic Vanilla with Chocolate Swirl Ice Cream
Place 2 ounces finely chopped bittersweet chocolate in 2-cup liquid measuring cup. Heat ¼ cup heavy cream, 1 tablespoon light corn syrup, 1½ teaspoons vegetable oil, and ⅛ teaspoon

EASY ICE CREAM TREATS

PISTACHIO ICE CREAM WITH LIMONCELLO AND PIZZELLE `FAST`

Portion 3 cups (1½ pints) pistachio ice cream into 4 individual bowls. Drizzle with ½ cup limoncello, then top with ½ cup sweetened whipped cream and chopped pistachios. Serve with pizzelle cookies. (Serves 4)

ICE CREAM SOCIAL SANDWICHES `FAST`

Place 1 tablespoon dulce de leche ice cream (¾ cup total) between 2 Nabisco Social Tea Biscuits (16 cookies total). Squeeze gently until ice cream is even with edge of cookies, smoothing sides with knife. Freeze until firm, at least 30 minutes, then dip sides into ½ cup mini chocolate chips or sprinkles. (Makes 8)

ICE CREAM TRUFFLES `FAST`

Combine ½ cup chopped toasted almonds and ¼ cup rainbow nonpareils in shallow dish. Drop 1-tablespoon balls of strawberry ice cream (1 cup total) into mixture and roll to coat. Transfer truffles to mini muffin liners and freeze until firm, at least 30 minutes. (Makes 12)

The right ratio of water to sugar is key to a velvety-smooth sorbet that is easy to scoop.

salt in small saucepan over medium heat, stirring constantly, until steaming, about 3 minutes. Pour hot mixture over chocolate, let sit for 5 minutes to melt chocolate, then stir until well combined and smooth. Before freezing, slowly pour chocolate mixture into center of vanilla ice cream base in container. Dip butter knife through chocolate to bottom of container and repeatedly lift up and swirl until chocolate is evenly swirled through; do not overmix.

Magic Strawberry Ice Cream

You can substitute 6 ounces thawed frozen berries for fresh berries.

Process 8 ounces hulled strawberries in food processor until smooth, about 30 seconds; you should have about ¾ cup puree. Omit sour cream and reduce vanilla to ½ teaspoon. Add strawberry puree and 1 tablespoon vodka to melted chocolate mixture with vanilla and salt.

Magic Chocolate Ice Cream

Substitute 4 ounces finely chopped bittersweet chocolate for white chocolate chips. Dissolve 1 teaspoon instant coffee (or espresso powder) in 1 tablespoon hot water, then add to chocolate–condensed milk mixture before microwaving. Reduce vanilla to ½ teaspoon.

Raspberry Sorbet

MAKES 1 QUART   **TOTAL TIME** 45 MINUTES
(PLUS 6 HOURS FREEZING AND CHILLING TIME)

✔ **WHY THIS RECIPE WORKS:** In order to engineer a batch of raspberry sorbet almost as creamy and smooth as ice cream, we had to overcome the jagged, unpleasant ice crystals that often develop on homemade sorbets and avoid the tendencies toward crumbly, dull results. The key was finding the right balance of water and sugar in the base to keep the fruit puree delicately icy, velvety smooth, and easily scoopable once it was churned. The addition of corn syrup helped to create a smooth texture without over-sweetening. Separating out a small amount of the base and freezing it separately, then adding it back into the rest helped superchill the mix, making it freeze faster and more smoothly. We also added some additional pectin to bump up the raspberries' natural pectin, which helped keep the whole thing from turning into a juice puddle too quickly at room temperature. Extensive testing was done to determine the ideal amount of churning

FLAVORED ICES AND POPSICLES

Our flavorful frozen ices use very few ingredients and take no time to put together. If your tap water has off-flavors, filter it, if possible, for this recipe. Better still, use bottled water; tasters preferred ices made with spring or mineral water. The addition of vodka yields the best texture, but it can be omitted if desired. Texture is also improved by placing the serving bowls in the freezer until ready to serve. For the processed ice option, process only as many of the ice cubes as needed because, once processed, the ice must be eaten within an hour or two. Plan to process three to four ice cubes per person for dessert.

DIRECTIONS: Stir all the ingredients together in a nonreactive bowl (stainless steel, glass, or ceramic) to dissolve the sugar. Pour the mixture into 16 (4-ounce) popsicle molds or into paper cups for Italian ice and freeze until solid. Make multiflavored popsicles by freezing different layers of flavors, one at a time. Alternatively, pour the mixture into 2 ice cube trays and freeze for about 2½ hours; to serve, pulse the cubes from each tray in a food processor until smooth and creamy, then transfer to serving bowls.

Lemon or Lime
MAKES ABOUT 1 QUART

- 2¼ cups water, preferably spring water
- 1 cup lemon or lime juice (6 lemons, or 8 limes)
- 1 cup sugar
- 2 tablespoons vodka (optional)
- ⅛ teaspoon salt

Grapefruit
MAKES ABOUT 1 QUART

- 1¼ cups water, preferably spring water
- 2½ cups grapefruit juice (3 grapefruits)
- ½ cup sugar
- 1 tablespoon Campari (optional)
- ⅛ teaspoon salt

Orange
MAKES ABOUT 1 QUART

- 2¼ cups water, preferably spring water
- ¾ cup orange juice (2 oranges)
- ¾ cup sugar
- 2 tablespoons lemon juice
- 2 tablespoons vodka (optional)
- ⅛ teaspoon salt

Cranberry or Pomegranate
MAKES ABOUT 1 QUART

- 4 cups cranberry or pomegranate juice
- ½ cup sugar
- 2 tablespoons lemon or lime juice
- 2 tablespoons vodka (optional)
- ⅛ teaspoon salt

Grape
MAKES ABOUT 1 QUART

- 4 cups grape juice
- ¼ cup sugar
- 2 tablespoons lemon juice
- 2 tablespoons vodka (optional)
- ⅛ teaspoon salt

Minted Earl Grey
MAKES ABOUT 1 QUART

- 4 cups Earl Grey tea steeped with 4 fresh mint leaves
- ½ cup honey
- 2 tablespoons lemon juice
- 2 tablespoons vodka (optional)
- ⅛ teaspoon salt

FOR ADULTS ONLY

These margarita and mimosa variations are fun offerings during a hot summer picnic or barbecue.

Margarita
MAKES ABOUT 1 QUART

- 2¼ cups water, preferably spring water
- ½ cup lemon juice (3 lemons)
- ½ cup lime juice (4 limes)
- 1 cup sugar
- 2 tablespoons tequila
- ⅛ teaspoon salt

Mimosa
MAKES ABOUT 1 QUART

- 2¼ cups orange juice (5 oranges)
- 1½ cups champagne
- ½ cup sugar
- 1 tablespoon lime juice
- ⅛ teaspoon salt

required to produce a perfect final product; look for the color of the mix to lighten up and the consistency to approach that of a milkshake, a sure sign that it is beginning to take on air and is in need of a transfer to the freezer. If using a canister-style ice cream maker, be sure to freeze the empty canister for at least 1 day and preferably 2 days before churning. For a self-refrigerating ice cream maker, prechill the canister by running the machine for 5 to 10 minutes before pouring in the sorbet mixture. Fresh or frozen berries may be used. If using frozen berries, thaw them before proceeding. For fruit pectin, we recommend both Sure-Jell for Less or No Sugar Needed Recipes and Ball RealFruit Low or No-Sugar Needed Pectin.

- 1 **cup water**
- 1 **teaspoon low- or no-sugar-needed fruit pectin**
- ⅛ **teaspoon salt**
- 1¼ **pounds (4 cups) raspberries**
- ½ **cup (3½ ounces) plus 2 tablespoons sugar**
- ¼ **cup light corn syrup**

1. Heat water, pectin, and salt in medium saucepan over medium-high heat, stirring occasionally, until pectin is fully dissolved, about 5 minutes. Remove from heat and let mixture cool slightly, about 10 minutes.

2. Process pectin mixture, raspberries, sugar, and corn syrup in blender or food processor until smooth, about 30 seconds. Strain mixture through fine-mesh strainer, pressing on solids to extract as much liquid as possible. Transfer 1 cup raspberry puree to small bowl and place remaining mixture in large bowl. Cover both bowls with plastic wrap. Place large bowl in refrigerator and small bowl in freezer and cool completely, at least 4 hours or up to 1 day. (Small bowl of base will freeze solid.)

Super-Chilling Raspberry Sorbet

1. Transfer 1 cup berry puree to small bowl. Cover bowls; freeze small bowl and refrigerate large bowl for at least 4 hours or up to 1 day.

2. Scrape frozen base into large bowl. Stir until completely combined. Transfer to ice cream maker and churn until color lightens.

3. Remove mixtures from refrigerator and freezer. Scrape frozen base from small bowl into large bowl of base. Stir occasionally until frozen base has fully dissolved. Transfer mixture to ice cream maker and churn until mixture has consistency of thick milkshake and color lightens, 15 to 25 minutes.

4. Transfer sorbet to airtight container, press firmly to remove any air pockets, and press plastic wrap on surface. Freeze until firm, at least 2 hours or up to 5 days. Let sorbet sit at room temperature for 5 minutes before serving.

VARIATIONS
Raspberry-Port Sorbet
Substitute ruby port for water.

Raspberry–Lime Rickey Sorbet
Reduce water to ¾ cup. Add 2 teaspoons grated lime zest and ¼ cup lime juice (2 limes) to blender with raspberries.

Chocolate-Dipped Frozen Bananas
MAKES 8 HALF BANANAS   **TOTAL TIME** 20 MINUTES
(PLUS 1 HOUR 30 MINUTES FREEZING TIME)

✔ **WHY THIS RECIPE WORKS:** The key to these frozen banana treats is the perfect chocolate coating. Adding a bit of vegetable oil to the melted chocolate kept it from becoming tough and brittle when frozen. For best results, use firm, slightly underripe bananas. The dipped bananas can be kept in the freezer, wrapped tightly in plastic wrap, for up to two weeks. We like to sprinkle the chocolate-coated bananas with chopped peanuts, but feel free to substitute sprinkles, crushed cookies, or shredded coconut.

- 2 **cups semisweet chocolate chips**
- 2 **tablespoons vegetable oil**
- 4 **bananas, peeled and halved crosswise**
- 1 **cup dry-roasted peanuts, chopped fine**

1. In wide, shallow bowl, heat chocolate chips and oil in microwave on 50 percent power until chocolate melts, 1 to 3 minutes, stirring often. Let mixture cool and thicken for 5 minutes.

2. Meanwhile, insert one popsicle stick through center of each banana half. Spread peanuts out over dinner plate.

3. Tipping bowl slightly, dip bananas, 1 at a time, into melted chocolate and spin to coat evenly. Allow excess chocolate to drip off banana and back into bowl. Roll bananas in chopped peanuts and transfer to parchment paper– or wax paper–lined plates. Freeze until firm, about 1½ hours.

The America's Test Kitchen Shopping Guide

Shopping for Equipment

With a well-stocked kitchen, you'll be able to take on any recipe. But with so much equipment out there on the market, how do you figure out what's what? Price often correlates with design, not performance. Over the years, our test kitchen has evaluated thousands of products. We've gone through copious rounds of testing and have identified the most important attributes in every piece of equipment, so when you go shopping you'll know what to look for. And because our test kitchen accepts no support from product manufacturers, you can trust our ratings. Prices in this chart are based on shopping at online retailers and will vary. See AmericasTestKitchen.com for updates to these testings.

KNIVES AND MORE	ITEM	WHAT TO LOOK FOR	TEST KITCHEN FAVORITES
	CHEF'S KNIFE	• High-carbon stainless steel knife • Thin, curved 8-inch blade • Lightweight • Comfortable grip and nonslip handle	**Victorinox 8-Inch Swiss Army Fibrox Chef's Knife** $39.95
	PARING KNIFE	• 3- to 3½-inch blade • Thin, slightly curved blade with pointed tip • Comfortable grip	**Wüsthof Classic with PEtec 3½-Inch Paring Knife** $39.95 Best Buy: **Victorinox Fibrox 3¼-Inch Paring Knife** $4.95
	SERRATED KNIFE	• 10- to 12-inch blade • Long, somewhat flexible, slightly curved blade • Pointed serrations that are uniformly spaced and moderately sized	**Wüsthof Classic 10-Inch Bread Knife** $89.95 Best Buy: **Victorinox 10¼-Inch Fibrox Serrated Bread Knife** $49.95
	SLICING KNIFE	• Tapered 12-inch blade for slicing large cuts of meat • Oval scallops (called granton edge) carved into blade • Fairly rigid blade with rounded tip	**Victorinox Fibrox 12-Inch Granton Edge Slicing Knife** $49.95
	CARVING BOARD	• Heavy, sturdy board • Deep, wide trench to trap juices • Central well to hold meat snugly	**Williams-Sonoma Medium Reversible Carving Board** $58

KNIVES AND MORE	ITEM	WHAT TO LOOK FOR	TEST KITCHEN FAVORITES
	CUTTING BOARD	• Roomy work surface at least 20 by 15 inches • Teak board for minimal maintenance • Durable edge-grain construction (wood grain runs parallel to surface of board)	**Proteak Edge Grain Teak Cutting Board** $84.99 Best Buy: **OXO Good Grips Carving and Cutting Board** $21.99
	KNIFE SHARPENER	• Diamond sharpening material for electric sharpeners • Easy to use and comfortable • Clear instructions	Electric: **Chef'sChoice Model 130 Professional Sharpening Station** $139.99 Manual: **AccuSharp Knife and Tool Sharpener** $9.95

POTS AND PANS	ITEM	WHAT TO LOOK FOR	TEST KITCHEN FAVORITES
	TRADITIONAL SKILLET	• Stainless steel interior and fully clad for even heat distribution • 12-inch diameter and flared sides • Comfortable, ovensafe handle • Cooking surface of at least 9 inches • Good to have smaller (8- or 10-inch) skillets too	**All-Clad 12-Inch Stainless Fry Pan** $154.95
	NONSTICK SKILLET	• Dark, nonstick surface • 12- or 12½-inch diameter, thick bottom • Comfortable, ovensafe handle • Cooking surface of at least 9 inches • Good to have smaller (8- or 10-inch) skillets too	**T-Fal Professional Total Non-Stick 12½-Inch Fry Pan** $34.99
	CAST-IRON SKILLET	• Thick bottom and straight sides • Roomy interior (cooking surface of 9¼ inches or more) • Preseasoned	**Lodge 12-Inch Cast Iron Skillet** $33.95
	DUTCH OVEN	• Enameled cast iron or stainless steel • Capacity of at least 6 quarts • Diameter of at least 9 inches • Tight-fitting lid • Wide, sturdy handles	**Le Creuset 7¼-Quart Round French Oven** $304.95 **All-Clad Stainless 8-Quart Stockpot** $279.95 Best Buy: **Lodge Color Enamel 6-Quart Dutch Oven** $49.97

POTS AND PANS	ITEM	WHAT TO LOOK FOR	TEST KITCHEN FAVORITES
	SAUCEPAN	• Large saucepan with 3- to 4-quart capacity and small nonstick saucepan with 2- to 2½-quart capacity • Tight-fitting lids • Pans with rounded corners that whisk can reach into • Long, comfortable handles that are angled for even weight distribution	Large: **All-Clad Stainless 4-Quart Saucepan with Lid and Loop** $224.95 Best Buy: **Cuisinart MultiClad Unlimited 4-Quart Saucepan** $69.99 Small: **Calphalon Contemporary Nonstick 2½-Quart Shallow Saucepan** $39.95
	RIMMED BAKING SHEET	• Light-colored surface (heats and browns evenly) • Thick, sturdy pan • Dimensions of 18 by 13 inches • Good to have at least two	**Wear-Ever 13-Gauge Half Size Heavy Duty Sheet Pan by Vollrath (formerly Lincoln Foodservice)** $14.99
	ROASTING PAN	• At least 15 by 11 inches • Stainless steel interior with aluminum core for even heat distribution • Upright handles for easy gripping • Light interior for better food monitoring	**Calphalon Contemporary Stainless Roasting Pan with Rack** $99.99

HANDY TOOLS	ITEM	WHAT TO LOOK FOR	TEST KITCHEN FAVORITES
	KITCHEN SHEARS	• Take-apart scissors (for easy cleaning) • Super-sharp blades • Sturdy construction • Work for both right- and left-handed users	**Kershaw 1120M TaskMaster Kitchen Shears** $49.95 Best Buy: **J. A. Henckels International Kitchen Shears—Take Apart** $14.95
	TONGS	• Scalloped edges • Slightly concave pincers • Length of 12 inches (to keep your hand far from heat) • Open and close easily	**OXO Good Grips 12-Inch Locking Tongs** $12.09
	WOODEN SPOON	• Slim yet broad bowl • Stain-resistant bamboo • Comfortable handle	**SCI Bamboo Wood Cooking Spoon** $2.40
	SLOTTED SPOON	• Deep bowl • Long handle • Enough holes for quick draining	**OXO Good Grips Nylon Slotted Spoon** $6.99

HANDY TOOLS	ITEM	WHAT TO LOOK FOR	TEST KITCHEN FAVORITES
	ALL-AROUND SPATULA	• Head about 3 inches wide and 5½ inches long • 11 inches in length (tip to handle) • Long, vertical slots • Good to have metal spatula to use with traditional cookware and plastic for nonstick cookware	Metal: **Wüsthof Gourmet Fish Turner/Spatula** $44.95 Plastic: **Matfer Bourgeat Pelton Spatula** $8.23
	RUBBER SPATULA	• Wide, stiff blade with thin edge that's flexible enough to conform to curve of mixing bowl • Heat-resistant	**Rubbermaid Professional 13½-Inch High Heat Scraper** $18.99
	OFFSET SPATULA	• Flexible blade offset from handle • Good to have small spatula for icing cookies and cupcakes and large one for layer cakes and sheet cakes	Large: **Ateco Offset Spatula** $5.75 Small: **Wilton 9-Inch Angled Spatula** $4.79
	COOKIE SPATULA	• Small, silicone blade with thin, flexible edge • Angled handle	**OXO Good Grips Cookie Spatula** $6.99
	ALL-PURPOSE WHISK	• At least 10 wires • Wires of moderate thickness • Comfortable rubber handle • Balanced, lightweight feel	**OXO Good Grips 11-Inch Balloon Whisk** $9.99
	PEPPER MILL	• Easy-to-adjust, clearly marked grind settings • Efficient, comfortable grinding mechanism • Generous capacity	**Cole & Mason Derwent Gourmet Precision Pepper Mill** $40
	LADLE	• Stainless steel • Hook handle • Pouring rim to prevent dripping • Handle 9 to 10 inches in length	**Rösle Hook Ladle with Pouring Rim** $34 Best Buy: **OXO Good Grips Brushed Stainless Steel Ladle** $9.99

HANDY TOOLS	ITEM	WHAT TO LOOK FOR	TEST KITCHEN FAVORITES
	CAN OPENER	• Intuitive and easy to attach • Smooth turning motions • Dishwasher safe	**Kuhn Rikon Slim Safety Lidlifter** $11.95
	GARLIC PRESS	• Conical holes that press garlic through efficiently • Solid, stainless steel construction • Comfortable handle • Easy to clean	**Kuhn Rikon Stainless Steel Epicurean Garlic Press** **$39.95** Best Buy: **Trudeau Garlic Press** $11.99
	VEGETABLE PEELER	• Sharp, carbon steel blade • 1-inch space between blade and peeler to prevent jamming • Lightweight and comfortable	**Kuhn Rikon Original Swiss Peeler** $3.50
	RASP GRATER	• Sharp teeth (require little effort or pressure when grating) • Maneuverable over round shapes • Comfortable handle	**Microplane Classic Zester Grater** $12.95
	GRATER	• Paddle-style grater • Sharp, extra-large holes and generous grating plane • Rubber-lined feet for stability • Comfortable handle	**Microplane Specialty Series 4-Sided Box Grater** $34.95
	MANUAL JUICER	• Hand-held squeezer with comfortable handle • Sturdy, enameled aluminum construction • Sized specifically for lemons, limes, and oranges	**Amco Houseworks Enameled Citrus Squeezer** $11.95, lemon
	ICE CREAM SCOOP	• Stainless steel • Slim, comfortable handle • Thin bowl edge for easier scooping	**Rösle Ice Cream Scoop** $20

HANDY TOOLS	ITEM	WHAT TO LOOK FOR	TEST KITCHEN FAVORITES
	MEAT POUNDER	• At least 1½ pounds in weight • Vertical handle for better leverage and control	**Norpro Grip-EZ Meat Pounder** $17.50
	ROLLING PIN	• Moderate weight (1 to 1½ pounds) • 19-inch straight barrel • Slightly textured wooden surface to grip dough for easy rolling	**J.K. Adams Plain Maple Rolling Dowel** $13.95
	MIXING BOWLS Stainless Steel	• Lightweight and easy to handle • Durability • Conducts heat well for double boiler	**Vollrath Economy Stainless Steel Mixing Bowls** $2.90, 1.5 quart $4.50, 3 quart $6.90, 5 quart
	Glass	• Tempered to increase impact and thermal resistance • Can be used in microwave • Durability	**Pyrex Smart Essentials Mixing Bowl Set with Colored Lids** $13.19 for four-bowl set
	OVEN MITT	• Form-fitting and not overly bulky for easy maneuvering • Machine washable • Flexible, heat-resistant material	**Kool-Tek 15-Inch Oven Mitt by KatchAll** $44.95
	COOKIE CUTTERS	• Metal cutters • Thin, sharp cutting edge and round or rubber-grip top • Depth of at least 1 inch	**Little difference among various brands**
	PASTRY BRUSH	• Silicone bristles (heat-resistant, durable, and easy to clean) • Perforated flaps (to trap liquid) • Angled head to reach tight spots • Comfortable handle	**OXO Good Grips Silicone Pastry Brush** $6.99
	BOUILLON STRAINER/ CHINOIS	• Conical shape • Depth of 7 to 8 inches • At least one hook on rim for stability	**Winco Reinforced Extra Fine Mesh Bouillon Strainer** $33.78

HANDY TOOLS	ITEM	WHAT TO LOOK FOR	TEST KITCHEN FAVORITES
	COLANDER	• 4- to 7-quart capacity • Metal ring attached to bottom for stability • Many holes for quick draining • Small holes so pasta doesn't slip through	**RSVP International Endurance Precision Pierced 5-Quart Colander** $25.99
	FINE-MESH STRAINER	• At least 6 inches in diameter (measured from inside edge to inside edge) • Sturdy construction	**CIA Masters Collection 6¾-Inch Fine Mesh Strainer** $27.49
	FAT SEPARATOR	• Pitcher-style • Wide-shaped spout for pouring • Strainer for catching solids • 4-cup capacity	**Trudeau Gravy Separator with Integrated Strainer** $11.41
	POTATO MASHER	• Solid mashing disk with small holes • Comfortable grip	**WMF Profi Plus Masher** $15.99
	SALAD SPINNER	• Ergonomic and easy-to-operate hand pump • Wide base for stability • Flat lid for easy cleaning and storage	**OXO Good Grips Salad Spinner** $29.99

MEASURING EQUIPMENT	ITEM	WHAT TO LOOK FOR	TEST KITCHEN FAVORITES
	DRY MEASURING CUPS	• Stainless steel cups (hefty and durable) • Measurement markings that are visible even once cup is full • Evenly weighted and stable • Long handles that are level with rim of cup	**Amco Houseworks Professional Performance 4-Piece Measuring Cup Set** $14.95
	LIQUID MEASURING CUP	• Crisp, unambiguous markings that include ¼ and ⅓ cup measurements • Heatproof, sturdy cup with handle • Good to have in variety of sizes (1, 2, and 4 cups)	**Pyrex 2-Cup Measuring Cup** $5.99

MEASURING EQUIPMENT	ITEM	WHAT TO LOOK FOR	TEST KITCHEN FAVORITES
	ADJUSTABLE MEASURING CUP	• Plungerlike bottom (with tight seal between plunger and tube) that you can set to correct measurement, then push up to cleanly extract sticky ingredients (such as shortening or peanut butter) • 1- or 2-cup capacity • Dishwasher-safe	**KitchenArt Adjust-A-Cup Professional Series, 2-Cup** $12.95
	MEASURING SPOONS	• Long, comfortable handles • Rim of bowl flush with handle (makes it easy to "dip" into dry ingredient and "sweep" across top for accurate measuring) • Slim design	**Cuisipro Stainless Steel Measuring Spoons Set** $11.95
	KITCHEN RULER	• Stainless steel and easy to clean • 18 inches in length • Large, easy-to-read markings	**Empire 18-Inch Stainless Steel Ruler** $8.49
	DIGITAL SCALE	• Easy-to-read display not blocked by weighing platform • At least 7-pound capacity • Accessible buttons • Gram-to-ounce conversion feature • Roomy platform	**OXO Food Scale** $49.99 Best Buy: **Soehnle 65055 Digital Scale** $29.75

THERMOMETERS AND TIMERS	ITEM	WHAT TO LOOK FOR	TEST KITCHEN FAVORITES
	INSTANT-READ THERMOMETER	• Digital model with automatic shut-off • Quick-response readings in 10 seconds or less • Wide temperature range (-40 to 450 degrees) • Long stem that can reach interior of large cuts of meat • Water resistant	**ThermoWorks Splash-Proof Super-Fast Thermapen** $89 Best Buy: **ThermoWorks Super-Fast Pocket Thermometer** $24 **CDN ProAccurate Quick-Read Thermometer** $16.95
	OVEN THERMOMETER	• Clearly marked numbers for easy readability • Hang model or stable base • Large temperature range (up to 600 degrees)	**Cooper-Atkins Oven Thermometer** $5.95

THERMOMETERS AND TIMERS	ITEM	WHAT TO LOOK FOR	TEST KITCHEN FAVORITES
	CANDY/ DEEP FRY THERMOMETER	• Digital model • Easy-to-read console • Mounting clip (to attach probe to pan)	**Thermoworks ChefAlarm** $59
	REFRIGERATOR/ FREEZER THERMOMETER	• Clear digital display • Wire probe for monitoring refrigerator and freezer simultaneously	**Maverick Cold-Chek Digital Refrigerator/Freezer Thermometer** $19.99
	KITCHEN TIMER	• Lengthy time range (1 second to at least 10 hours) • Ability to count up after alarm goes off • Easy to use and read	**Polder 3-in-1 Clock, Timer, and Stopwatch** $16.99

BAKEWARE	ITEM	WHAT TO LOOK FOR	TEST KITCHEN FAVORITES
	GLASS BAKING DISH	• Dimensions of 13 by 9 inches • Large enough to hold casseroles and large crisps and cobblers • Handles	**Pyrex Bakeware 9 x 13-Inch Baking Dish** $9.09
	BROILER-SAFE BAKING DISH	• Dimensions of 13 by 9 inches • Broiler-safe • Large handles for secure gripping • Straight sides for easy serving	**HIC Porcelain Lasagna Baking Dish** $37.49
	METAL BAKING PAN	• Dimensions of 13 by 9 inches • Straight sides • Nonstick coating for even browning and easy release of cakes and bar cookies	**Williams-Sonoma 9 x 13-Inch Goldtouch Nonstick Rectangular Cake Pan** $32.95
	SQUARE BAKING PAN	• Straight sides • Light gold or dark nonstick surface for even browning and easy release of cakes • Good to have both 9-inch and 8-inch square pans	**Williams-Sonoma Goldtouch Nonstick Square Cake Pan** $21, 8-inch

BAKEWARE	ITEM	WHAT TO LOOK FOR	TEST KITCHEN FAVORITES
	ROUND CAKE PAN Best all-around	• Best for cake • Straight sides • Light finish for tall, even baking • Nonstick surface for easy release	**Nordic Ware Naturals Nonstick 9-Inch Round Cake Pan** $14.32
	Best for browning	• Dark finish is ideal for pizza and cinnamon buns • Nonstick	**Chicago Metallic Non-Stick 9-Inch Round Cake Pan** $10.97
	PIE PLATE	• Glass promotes even browning and allows progress to be monitored • ½-inch rim (makes it easy to shape decorative crusts) • Shallow angled sides prevent crusts from slumping • Good to have two	**Pyrex Bakeware 9-Inch Pie Plate** $8.16
	LOAF PAN	• Light gold or dark nonstick surface for even browning and easy release • Good to have both 8½ by 4½-inch and 9 by 5-inch pans	**Williams-Sonoma 8½ x 4½-Inch Goldtouch Nonstick Loaf Pan** $21 Best Buy: **Baker's Secret 9 x 5-Inch Nonstick Loaf Pan** $5
	SPRINGFORM PAN	• Nonstick coated base • Tight seal between band and bottom of pan (prevents leakage) • Even browning	**Nordic Ware Pro Form 9-Inch Leak-Proof Springform Pan** $17
	MUFFIN TIN	• Nonstick surface for even browning and easy release • Wide, extended rims and raised lip for easy handling • Cup capacity of ½ cup	**Wilton Avanti Everglide Metal-Safe Non-Stick 12-Cup Muffin Pan** $13.99
	COOLING RACK	• Grid-style rack with tightly woven, heavy-gauge bars • Should fit inside standard 18 by 13-inch rimmed baking sheet • Dishwasher-safe	**CIA Bakeware 12 x 17-Inch Cooling Rack** $15.95

BAKEWARE	ITEM	WHAT TO LOOK FOR	TEST KITCHEN FAVORITES
	BISCUIT CUTTERS	• Sharp edges • Set with variety of sizes	**Ateco 11-Piece Plain Round Cutter Set** $15
	BUNDT PAN	• Heavyweight cast aluminum • Silver platinum nonstick surface for even browning and easy release • Clearly defined ridges • 15-cup capacity	**Nordic Ware Platinum Collections Anniversary Bundt Pan** $26.95
	TART PAN	• Tinned steel for even browning and easy release • Removable bottom • If you bake frequently, it's good to have multiple sizes, though 9 inches is standard	**Kaiser Tinplate 9½-Inch Quiche Pan with Removable Bottom** $9
	TUBE PAN	• Heavy pan (at least 1 pound) • Heavy bottom for leak-free seal • Dark nonstick surface for even browning and easy release • 16-cup capacity • Feet on rim	**Chicago Metallic Professional Nonstick Angel Food Cake Pan with Feet** $19.95
	RAMEKINS	• Sturdy, high-fired porcelain (chip-resistant and safe for use in oven, broiler, microwave, and dishwasher) • For one all-purpose set, capacity of 6 ounces and diameter of 3 inches	**Apilco 6-Ounce Ramekins** $29 for set of four
	BAKING STONE	• Substantial but not too heavy to handle • Dimensions of 16 by 14 inches • Clay, not cement, for evenly browned crusts	**Old Stone Oven Pizza Baking Stone** $38.69

SMALL APPLIANCES	ITEM	WHAT TO LOOK FOR	TEST KITCHEN FAVORITES
	FOOD PROCESSOR	• 14-cup capacity • Sharp and sturdy blades • Wide feed tube • Should come with basic blades and discs: steel blade, dough blade, shredding/slicing disc	**Cuisinart Custom 14-Cup Food Processor** $199
	STAND MIXER	• Planetary action (stationary bowl and single mixing arm) • Powerful motor • Bowl size of at least 4½ quarts • Slightly squat bowl to keep ingredients in beater's range • Should come with basic attachments: paddle, dough hook, metal whisk	**KitchenAid Pro Line Series 7-quart Bowl Lift Stand Mixer** $549.95 Best Buy: **KitchenAid Classic Plus Stand Mixer** $199.99
	HAND-HELD MIXER	• Lightweight model • Slim wire beaters without central post • Variety of speeds	**KitchenAid 5-Speed Ultra Power Hand Mixer** $69.99 Best Buy: **Cuisinart PowerSelect™ 3-Speed Hand Mixer** $26.77
	BLENDER	• Mix of straight and serrated blades at different angles • Jar with curved base • At least 44-ounce capacity • Heavy base for stability	**Vitamix 5200** $449 Best Buy: **Breville The Hemisphere Control** $199.99
	ICE CREAM MAKER	• Minimum 1½-quart capacity • Removable canister and blade for easy cleaning	**Whynter SNÖ Professional Ice Cream Maker** $330.99 Best Buy: **Cuisinart Automatic Frozen Yogurt, Ice Cream, and Sorbet Maker** $49.95

GRILLING EQUIPMENT	ITEM	WHAT TO LOOK FOR	TEST KITCHEN FAVORITES
	GAS GRILL	• Large grilling area (at least 350 square inches) • Built-in thermometer • Two burners for varying heat levels (three is even better) • Attached table • Fat drainage system	**Weber Spirit E-210** $399
	CHARCOAL GRILL	• Sturdy construction to efficiently maintain heat • Well-designed cooking grate, handles, lids, and wheels • Generous cooking surface • Large charcoal capacity • Well-positioned air vents • Gas ignition to instantly and easily light coals • Ash catcher for easy cleanup	**Weber Performer Platinum 22.5-Inch Charcoal Grill with Touch-n-Go Gas Ignition** $349 Best Buy: **Weber One-Touch Gold 22.5-Inch Charcoal Grill** $149
	CHIMNEY STARTER	• 6-quart capacity • Holes in canister so air can circulate around coals • Sturdy construction • Heat-resistant handle • Dual handle for easy control	**Weber Rapidfire Chimney Starter** $14.99
	GRILL TONGS	• 16 inches in length • Scalloped, not sharp and serrated, edges • Open and close easily • Lightweight • Moderate amount of springy tension	**OXO Good Grips 16-Inch Locking Tongs** $14.99
	GRILL BRUSH	• Long handle • Replaceable, long-lasting steel pads for scrubbing	**Grill Wizard 18-inch China Grill Brush** $31.50

GRILLING EQUIPMENT	ITEM	WHAT TO LOOK FOR	TEST KITCHEN FAVORITES
	GRILL SPATULA	• Handle at least 12 inches in length • Sharp cutting edge	**Weber Original Stainless Steel Spatula** $14.99
	BASTING BRUSH	• Silicone bristles • Angled brush head • Handle between 8 and 13 inches • Heat-resistant	**Elizabeth Karmel's Grill Friends Super Silicone Angled Barbecue Brush** $9.95
	BARBECUE GLOVES	• Excellent heat protection • Gloves, rather than mitts, for dexterity • Long sleeves to protect forearms	**Steven Raichlen Ultimate Suede Grilling Gloves** $29.99 per pair
	SKEWERS	• Flat and metal • $3/16$ inch thick	**Norpro 12-Inch Stainless Steel Skewers** $6.85 for set of six

KITCHEN SUPPLIES	ITEM	WHAT TO LOOK FOR	TEST KITCHEN FAVORITES
	PLASTIC WRAP	• Clings tightly and resticks well • Packaging with sharp teeth that aren't exposed (to avoid snags on clothing and skin) • Adhesive pad to hold cut end of wrap	**Glad Cling Wrap Clear Plastic** $1.20
	FREEZER STORAGE BAGS	• Low porosity plastic to keep moisture in • Airtight seal (zippers are better than sliders) • Best for both freezing and storing foods	**Ziploc Brand Double Zipper Gallon Freezer Bags with the Smart Zip Seal** $3.99 for 30 bags

Shopping for Ingredients

Using the best ingredients is one way to guarantee success in the kitchen. But how do you know what to buy? Shelves are filled with a dizzying array of choices—and price does not equal quality. Over the years, the test kitchen's blind tasting panels have evaluated thousands of ingredients, brand by brand, side by side, plain and in prepared applications, to determine which brands you can trust and which brands to avoid. In the chart that follows, we share the results, revealing our top-rated choices and the attributes that made them stand out among the competition. And because our test kitchen accepts no support from product manufacturers, you can trust our ratings. See AmericasTestKitchen.com for updates to these tastings.

	ITEM	TEST KITCHEN FAVORITE	WHY WE LIKE IT
	ANCHOVIES	**Ortiz Oil Packed**	• Pleasantly fishy, salty flavor, not overwhelming or bland • Firm, meaty texture, not mushy • Already filleted and ready to use, unlike salt-packed variety
	APPLESAUCE	**Musselman's Lite**	• Unusual ingredient, sucralose, sweetens applesauce without overpowering its fresh, bright apple flavor • Pinch of salt boosts flavor above weak, bland, and too-sweet competitors • Coarse, almost chunky texture, not slimy like applesauces sweetened with corn syrup
	BACON, SUPERMARKET	**Farmland Thick Sliced** and **Plumrose Premium Thick Sliced**	• Good balance of saltiness and sweetness • Smoky and full flavored, not one-dimensional • Very meaty, not too fatty or insubstantial • Crisp yet hearty texture, not tough or dry
	BAKING POWDER	**Davis**	• Provides good lift for baking • No metallic or unpleasant aftertaste or off-flavors
	BARBECUE SAUCE	**Bull's-Eye Original**	• Spicy, fresh tomato taste • Good balance of tanginess, smokiness, and sweetness • Robust flavor from molasses • Sweetened with sugar and molasses, not high-fructose corn syrup, which caramelizes and burns quickly

ITEM	TEST KITCHEN FAVORITE	WHY WE LIKE IT
BEANS, CANNED BLACK	**Bush's Best**	• Clean, mild, and slightly earthy flavor • Firm, almost al dente texture, not mushy or pasty • Good amount of salt
BEANS, CANNED CHICKPEAS	**Pastene**	• Firm yet tender texture bests pasty and dry competitors • Clean chickpea flavor • Enough salt to enhance but not overwhelm flavor
BEANS, CANNED WHITE	**Goya Cannellini**	• Clean, earthy flavor • Smooth, creamy interior with tender skins • Not full of broken beans like some competitors
BEANS, REFRIED	**Taco Bell Home Originals**	• Well-seasoned mixture • Super-smooth texture, not overly thick, pasty, or gluey
BLUEBERRIES, FROZEN	**Wyman's Frozen Wild Blueberries**	• Intense color and flavor • Pleasing balance of sweetness and tanginess • Clean, fresh berry finish
BREAD, WHITE SANDWICH	**Arnold Country Classics**	• Subtle sweetness, not tasteless or sour • Perfect structure, not too dry or too soft
BREAD, WHOLE-WHEAT SANDWICH	**Pepperidge Farm 100% Natural** NOTE: Available only east of the Mississippi River.	• Whole-grain, nutty, earthy flavor • Dense, chewy texture, not gummy or too soft • Not too sweet, contains no corn syrup and has low sugar level (unlike competitors)

ITEM	TEST KITCHEN FAVORITE	WHY WE LIKE IT
BREAD CRUMBS, PANKO	**Ian's Original Style**	• Crisp, with substantial crunch • Not too delicate, stale, sandy, or gritty • Oil-free and without seasonings or undesirable artificial flavors
BROTH, BEEF	**Rachael Ray Stock-in-a-Box All-Natural Beef Flavored Stock**	• Deep beefy profile with rich notes and gelatin-like body • Flavor-enhancing ingredients such as tomato paste and yeast extract
BROTH, CHICKEN	**Swanson Chicken Stock** Best Buy: **Better Than Bouillon Chicken Base**	• Strong chicken flavor, not watery, beefy, or vegetal • Hearty and pleasant aroma • Roasted notes, not sour, rancid, or salty like some competitors • Flavor-boosting ingredients include carrots, celery, and onions
BROTH, VEGETABLE	**Swanson Vegetarian** NOTE: Despite this broth's high concentration of artificial additives and salt, it is the only broth we found with acceptable flavor.	• Balanced vegetable flavor with carrot and celery nuances • High concentration of vegetable product not found in competitors • High sodium content enhances vegetable flavors
BUTTER, UNSALTED	**Plugrá European-Style**	• Sweet and creamy • Complex tang and grassy flavor • Moderate amount of butterfat so that it's decadent and glossy but not so rich that baked goods are greasy
CHEESE, AMERICAN, PRESLICED	**Land O'Lakes**, **Sara Lee**, and **Kraft Deli Deluxe**	• Strong cheesy flavor, unlike some competitors • Slightly rubbery but pleasantly gooey when melted • Higher content of cheese culture contributes to better flavor

ITEM	TEST KITCHEN FAVORITE	WHY WE LIKE IT
CHEESE, ASIAGO	**BelGioioso**	• Sharp, tangy, and complex flavor, not mild • Firm and not too dry • Melts, shreds, and grates well
CHEESE, CHEDDAR, EXTRA-SHARP	**Cabot Private Stock** Runner-Up: **Cabot**	• Balance of salty, creamy, and sweet flavors • Considerable but well-rounded sharpness, not overwhelming • Firm, crumbly texture, not moist, rubbery, or springy • Aged at least 12 months for complex flavor
CHEESE, CHEDDAR, PRESLICED	**Tillamook Sharp**	• Slightly crumbly, not rubbery or processed, texture characteristic of block cheddar • Strong, tangy, and salty flavor, not bland or too mild
CHEESE, CHEDDAR, PREMIUM	**Milton Creamery Prairie Breeze** Runner-Up: **Cabot Cellars at Jasper Hill Clothbound**	• Earthy complexity with nutty, buttery, and fruity flavors • Dry and crumbly with crystalline crunch, not rubbery or overly moist • Aged no more than 12 months to prevent overly sharp flavor
CHEESE, CHEDDAR, REDUCED-FAT	**Cracker Barrel Reduced Fat Sharp**	• Ample creaminess • Strong cheesy flavor • Good for cooking
CHEESE, CHEDDAR, SHARP	**Cabot Sharp Vermont**	• Sharp, clean, and tangy flavor • Firm, crumbly texture, not moist, rubbery, or springy • Aged for minimum of 12 months for complex flavor
CHEESE, COTTAGE	**Hood Country Style**	• Rich, well-seasoned, and buttery flavor • Velvety, creamy texture • Pillowy curds
CHEESE, CREAM	**Philadelphia**	• Rich, tangy, and milky flavor • Thick, creamy texture, not pasty, waxy, or chalky

ITEM	TEST KITCHEN FAVORITE	WHY WE LIKE IT
CHEESE, FETA	**Mt. Vikos Traditional Feta**	• Strong tangy, salty flavor • Creamy, dense texture • Pleasing crumbly texture
CHEESE, FONTINA For eating out of hand	**Fontina Val d'Aosta**	• Strong, earthy aroma • Somewhat elastic texture with small irregular holes • Grassy, nutty flavor—but can be overpowering in cooked dishes
For cooking	**BelGioioso**	• Semisoft, super-creamy texture • Mildly tangy, nutty flavor • Melts well
CHEESE, GOAT	**Laura Chenel's Chèvre**	• Rich-tasting, grassy, tangy flavor • Smooth and creamy both unheated and baked • High salt content
CHEESE, GRUYÈRE	**Gruyère Reserve Wheel**	• Grassy, salty flavor, not bland • Creamy yet dry texture, not plasticky like some competitors • Aged for minimum of 10 months for strong and complex flavor • Melts especially well
CHEESE, MOZZARELLA	**Galbani Whole Milk (formerly Sorrento)**	• Creamy and buttery with clean dairy flavor • Soft, not rubbery, chew
CHEESE, PARMESAN	**Boar's Head Parmigiano-Reggiano**	• Rich and complex flavor balances tanginess and nuttiness • Dry, crumbly texture yet creamy with crystalline crunch, not rubbery or dense • Aged for minimum of 12 months for better flavor and texture
CHEESE, PEPPER JACK	**Boar's Head Monterey Jack Cheese with Jalapeño**	• Buttery, tangy cheese • Clean, balanced flavor with assertive spice

	ITEM	TEST KITCHEN FAVORITE	WHY WE LIKE IT
	CHEESE, PROVOLONE	**Provolone Vernengo**	• Bold, nutty, and tangy flavor, not plasticky or bland • Firm, dry texture
	CHEESE, RICOTTA, PART-SKIM	**Calabro**	• Clean, fresh flavor, not rancid or sour from addition of gums or stabilizers • Creamy texture with perfect curds, unlike chalky, grainy, and soggy competitors
	CHEESE, SWISS For eating out of hand	**Edelweiss Creamery Emmentaler**	• Subtle flavor with sweet, buttery, nutty, and fruity notes • Firm yet gently giving texture, not rubbery • Aged longer for better flavor, resulting in larger eyes • Mildly pungent yet balanced
	For cooking	**Emmi Emmentaler Cheese AOC** Runners-Up for eating out of hand or cooking: **Sargento Baby**, **Sargento Deli Style Aged**, and **Boar's Head Gold Label Imported**	• Creamy texture • Salty mildness preferable for grilled cheese sandwiches
	CHICKEN, WHOLE	**Mary's Free Range Air-Chilled** Runner-Up: **Bell & Evans Air Chilled Premium Fresh**	• Great, savory chicken flavor • Very tender • Air-chilled for minimum water retention and cleaner flavor
	CHICKEN, BREASTS, BONELESS, SKINLESS	**Bell & Evans Air-Chilled**	• Juicy and tender with clean chicken flavor • Not salted or brined • Air-chilled • Aged on bone for at least six hours after slaughter for significantly more tender meat
	CHILI POWDER	**Morton & Bassett**	• Bold, full-flavored heat • Multidimensional flavor from blend of cayenne and other chiles • Spices that complement but don't overwhelm chiles

	ITEM	TEST KITCHEN FAVORITE	WHY WE LIKE IT
	CHOCOLATE, DARK	**Ghirardelli 60% Cacao Bittersweet Chocolate Premium Baking Bar** Runner-Up: **Callebaut Intense Dark L-60-40NV (60% Cacao)**	• Creamy texture, not grainy or chalky • Complex flavor with notes of cherry and wine with slight smokiness • Balance of sweetness and bitterness
	CHOCOLATE, DARK CHIPS	**Ghirardelli 60% Cacao Bittersweet**	• Intense, complex flavor beats one-dimensional flavor of competitors • Low sugar content highlights chocolate flavor • High amount of cocoa butter ensures creamy, smooth texture, not gritty and grainy • Wider, flatter shape and high percentage of fat help chips melt better in cookies
	CHOCOLATE, MILK	**Dove Silky Smooth**	• Intense, full, rich chocolate flavor • Super-creamy texture from abundant milk fat and cocoa butter • Not overwhelmingly sweet
	CHOCOLATE, MILK CHIPS	**Hershey's**	• Bold chocolate flavor outshines too-sweet, weak chocolate flavor of other chips • Complex with caramel and nutty notes • Higher fat content makes texture creamier than grainy, artificial competitors
	CHOCOLATE, UNSWEETENED	**Hershey's Unsweetened Baking Bar**	• Well-rounded, complex flavor • Assertive chocolate flavor and deep notes of cocoa
	CHOCOLATE, WHITE CHIPS	**Guittard Choc-Au-Lait**	• Creamy texture, not waxy or crunchy • Silky smooth meltability from high fat content • Complex flavor like high-quality real chocolate, no artificial or off-flavors
	CINNAMON	**Penzeys Extra Fancy Vietnamese Cassia** NOTE: Available through mail order, Penzeys (800-741-7787, www.penzeys.com).	• Warm, fragrant aroma with clove, fruity, and slightly smoky flavors • Mellow start with spicy finish • Strong yet not overpowering • Not harsh, bitter, dusty, or gritty

ITEM	TEST KITCHEN FAVORITE	WHY WE LIKE IT
CLAM JUICE	**Bar Harbor** Runner-Up: **Look's Atlantic**	• Fresh, bright, clean flavor • Amplifies seafood flavor in dishes
COCOA POWDER	**Hershey's Natural Unsweetened**	• Full, strong chocolate flavor • Complex flavor with notes of coffee, cinnamon, orange, and spice
COCONUT MILK For savory recipes	**Chaokoh**	• Strong coconut flavor • Smooth and creamy texture superior to competitors • Not very sweet, ideal for savory recipes like soups and stir-fries
For sweet recipes	**Ka-Me**	• Rich, velvety texture, not too thin or watery • Fruity and complex flavor, not mild or bland • Ideal sweetness for desserts
COFFEE, WHOLE BEAN, SUPERMARKET Dark roast	**Millstone Colombian Supremo**	• Deep, complex, and balanced flavor without metallic, overly acidic, or otherwise unpleasant notes • Smoky and chocolaty with bitter, not burnt, finish
Medium roast	**Peet's Coffee Café Domingo** and **Millstone Breakfast Blend**	• Extremely smooth but bold-tasting with strong finish • Rich chocolate and toast flavors • Few defective beans, low acidity, and optimal moisture
COFFEE, DECAFFEINATED	**Maxwell House Decaf Original Roast**	• Smooth, mellow flavor without being acidic or harsh • Complex, with a slightly nutty aftertaste • Made with only flavorful Arabica beans

ITEM	TEST KITCHEN FAVORITE	WHY WE LIKE IT
CORNMEAL	**Arrowhead Mills Whole Grain**	• Clean, pure corn flavor comes from using whole-grain kernels • Ideal texture resembling slightly damp, fine sand, not too fine or too coarse
CURRY POWDER	**Penzeys Sweet** NOTE: Available through mail order, Penzeys (800-741-7787, www.penzeys.com).	• Balanced, neither too sweet nor too hot • Complex and vivid earthy flavor, not thin, bland, or one-dimensional
FISH SAUCE	**Tiparos**	• Dark and pungent sauce • Aggressive flavor
FIVE-SPICE POWDER	**Frontier Natural Products Co-op**	• Nice depth, not one-dimensional • Balanced heat and sweetness
FLOUR, ALL-PURPOSE	**King Arthur Unbleached Enriched**	• Fresh, toasty flavor • No metallic taste or other off-flavors • Consistent results across recipes • Made tender, flaky pie crust, hearty biscuits, crisp cookies, and chewy, sturdy bread
	Pillsbury Unbleached Enriched	• Clean, toasty, and hearty flavor • No metallic or other off-flavors • Consistent results across recipes • Made flaky pie crust, chewy cookies, and tender biscuits, muffins, and cakes
FLOUR, WHOLE-WHEAT	**King Arthur Premium**	• Finely ground for hearty but not overly coarse texture in bread and pancakes • Sweet, nutty flavor

ITEM	TEST KITCHEN FAVORITE	WHY WE LIKE IT
GARAM MASALA	**McCormick Gourmet Collection**	• Core garam masala ingredients • Pungent flavors with subtle heat • Mellow and well-balanced spice mix
GIARDINIERA	**Pastene**	• Sharp, vinegary tang • Crunchy mix of vegetables • Mellow heat that's potent but not overpowering
GNOCCHI	**Gia Russa Gnocchi with Potato**	• Tender, pillowlike texture • Nice potato flavor • Slightly sour taste that disappears when paired with tomato sauce
GRAHAM CRACKERS	**Keebler Original**	• Great graham taste and smooth texture • Hold up well in cakes and pie crusts
HAM, BLACK FOREST DELI For cooking	**Dietz & Watson Smoked**	• Good texture • Nice ham flavor
For eating on its own	**Abraham's Black Forest Prosciutto Ham**	• Concentrated, silky texture • Intense ham flavor with bold smokiness
HOISIN SAUCE	**Kikkoman**	• Balances sweet, salty, pungent, and spicy flavors • Initial burn mellows into harmonious and aromatic blend without bitterness
HORSERADISH	**Boar's Head Pure Horseradish**	• No preservatives, just horseradish, vinegar, and salt (found in refrigerated section) • Natural flavor and hot without being overpowering
HOT DOGS	**Nathan's Famous Beef Franks**	• Meaty, robust, and hearty flavor, not sweet, sour, or too salty • Juicy but not greasy • Firm, craggy texture, not rubbery, mushy, or chewy

	ITEM	TEST KITCHEN FAVORITE	WHY WE LIKE IT
	HOT FUDGE SAUCE	**Hershey's Hot Fudge Topping**	• True fudge flavor, not weak or overly sweet • Thick, smooth, and buttery texture
	HOT SAUCE	**Huy Fong Sriracha Hot Chili Sauce** Runner-Up: **Frank's RedHot Original Cayenne Pepper Sauce**	• Right combination of punchy heat, saltiness, sweetness, and garlic • Full, rich flavor • Mild heat that's not too hot
	ICE CREAM, CHOCOLATE	**Ben & Jerry's**	• Deep, concentrated chocolate flavor, not too light or sweet • Dense and creamy texture
	ICE CREAM, VANILLA	**Ben & Jerry's**	• Complex yet balanced vanilla flavor from real vanilla extract • Sweetness solely from sugar, rather than corn syrup • Creamy richness from both egg yolks and small amount of stabilizers
	KETCHUP	**Heinz Organic** Best Buy: **Hunt's**	• Clean, pure sweetness from sugar, not high-fructose corn syrup • Bold, harmonious punch of saltiness, sweetness, tang, and tomato flavor
	MAPLE SYRUP	**Maple Grove Farms 100% Pure Grade A Dark Amber**	• Clean yet rich maple flavor, not too mild, harsh, or artificial in flavor • Moderate sweetness bests overwhelmingly sugary competitors • Ideal consistency, neither too thin nor too thick like pancake syrups made from corn syrup
	MAYONNAISE	**Blue Plate Real** Runner-Up: **Hellmann's Real** NOTE: Hellmann's is known as Best Foods west of the Rockies.	• Great balance of taste and texture • Richer, deeper flavor from using egg yolks alone (no egg whites) • Short ingredient list that's close to homemade

ITEM	TEST KITCHEN FAVORITE	WHY WE LIKE IT
MAYONNAISE, LIGHT	**Hellmann's Light** NOTE: Hellmann's is known as Best Foods west of the Rockies.	• Bright, balanced flavor close to full-fat counterpart, not overly sweet like other light mayos • Not as creamy as full-fat but passable texture
MIRIN (JAPANESE RICE WINE)	**Mitoku Organic Mikawa Mirin Sweet Rice Seasoning** Best Buy: **Eden Mirin Rice Cooking Wine**	• Roasted flavor that is caramel-like and rich • Subtle salty-sweet and balanced flavor
MOLASSES	**Brer Rabbit All Natural Unsulphured Mild Flavor**	• Acidic yet balanced • Strong and straightforward raisin-y taste • Pleasantly bitter bite
MUSTARD, DIJON	**Grey Poupon** Runners-Up: **Maille Originale Traditional** and **Roland Extra Strong**	• Potent, bold, and very hot, not weak or mild • Good balance of sweetness, tanginess, and sharpness • Not overly acidic, sweet, or one-dimensional like competitors
MUSTARD, COARSE-GRAIN	**Grey Poupon Harvest Coarse Ground** and **Grey Poupon Country Dijon**	• Spicy, tangy burst of mustard flavor • High salt content amplifies flavor • Contains no superfluous ingredients that mask mustard flavor • Big, round seeds add pleasant crunch • Just enough vinegar, not too sour or thin
OATS, QUICK	**Quaker**	• More oat flavor than other quick oats brands • Creamy texture • Quick oats will never have complexity of rolled or steel-cut varieties, but these have pleasant nutty, buttery taste

	ITEM	TEST KITCHEN FAVORITE	WHY WE LIKE IT
	OATS, ROLLED	**Bob's Red Mill Organic Extra Thick**	• Rich oat flavor with nutty, barley, and toasty notes • Creamy, cohesive texture • Plump grains with decent chew
	OATS, STEEL-CUT	**Bob's Red Mill Organic** Runners-Up: **Arrowhead Mills Organic Hot Cereal**, **Country Choice Organic**, and **Hodgson's Mill Premium**	• Rich and complex oat flavor with buttery, earthy, nutty, and whole-grain notes • Creamy yet toothsome texture • Moist but not sticky NOTE: Not recommended for baking
	OLIVE OIL, EXTRA-VIRGIN	**Columela**	• Buttery flavor that is sweet and full with peppery finish • Aromatic and fruity, not bland or bitter • Clean taste, comparable to fresh-squeezed olive, outshines bland, greasy competitors
	OLIVE OIL, REGULAR	**Colavita**	• Peppery, fruity flavors • Bold flavor, not too bland or mild like some competitors • Loses most flavor when heated to 300 degrees, so not specifically recommended for cooking
	OYSTER SAUCE	**Lee Kum Kee's Premium Oyster Flavored Sauce**	• Intense and fishy, with depth of flavor • Perfect balance of saltiness and sweet caramel undertones
	PAPRIKA	**The Spice House Hungarian Sweet** NOTE: Available only through mail order, The Spice House (312-274-0378, www.thespicehouse.com).	• Complex flavor with earthy, fruity notes • Bright and bold, not bland and boring • Rich, toasty aroma

ITEM	TEST KITCHEN FAVORITE	WHY WE LIKE IT
PASTA, CHEESE RAVIOLI	**Rosetto**	• Creamy, plush, and rich blend of ricotta, Romano, and Parmesan cheeses • Pasta with nice, springy bite • Perfect dough-to-filling ratio
PASTA, CHEESE TORTELLINI	**Barilla Three Cheese**	• Robustly flavored filling from combination of ricotta, Emmentaler, and Grana Padano cheeses • Tender pasta that's sturdy enough to withstand boiling but not so thick that it becomes doughy
PASTA, EGG NOODLES	**Pennsylvania Dutch Wide**	• Balanced, buttery flavor with no off-flavors • Light and fluffy texture, not gummy or starchy
PASTA, ELBOW MACARONI	**Barilla**	• Rich flavor from egg yolks • Firm, chewy bite • Wide corkscrew shape
PASTA, FRESH	**Buitoni Fettuccine**	• Firm but yielding, slightly chewy texture, not too delicate, gummy, or heavy • Faint but discernible egg flavor with no chemical, plasticky, or otherwise unpleasant flavors • Rough, porous surface absorbs sauce better than dried pasta
PASTA, LASAGNA NOODLES No-boil	**Barilla**	• Taste and texture of fresh pasta • Delicate, flat noodles
Whole-wheat	**Bionaturae Organic 100% Whole Wheat**	• Complex nutty, rich wheat flavor • Substantial chewy texture without any grittiness
PASTA, PENNE	**Mueller's**	• Hearty texture, not insubstantial or gummy • Wheaty, slightly sweet flavor, not bland

	ITEM	TEST KITCHEN FAVORITE	WHY WE LIKE IT
	PASTA, SPAGHETTI	**De Cecco No. 12**	• Rich, nutty, wheaty flavor • Firm, ropy strands with good chew, not mushy, gummy, or mealy • Semolina flour for resilient texture • Dried at moderately low temperature for 18 hours to preserve flavor
	PASTA, SPAGHETTI, WHOLE-WHEAT	**Bionaturae 100% Whole Wheat**	• Chewy, firm, and toothsome, not mushy or rubbery • Full and nutty wheat flavor
	PASTA SAUCE	**Bertolli Tomato and Basil**	• Fresh-cooked, balanced tomato flavor, not overly sweet • Pleasantly chunky, not too smooth or pasty • Not overseasoned with dry herbs like competitors
	PASTA SAUCE, PREMIUM	**Victoria Marinara Sauce**	• Nice, bright acidity that speaks of real tomatoes • Robust flavor comparable to homemade
	PEANUT BUTTER, CREAMY	**Skippy**	• Smooth, creamy, and spreadable • Good balance of sweet and salty flavors
	PEPPERCORNS, BLACK Artisan	**Kalustyan's Indian Tellicherry** NOTE: Available only by mail order, Kalustyan's (800-352-3451, www.kalustyans.com).	• Enticing and fragrant, not musty, aroma with flavor to back it up and moderate heat • Fresh, complex flavor at once sweet and spicy, earthy and smoky, fruity and floral
	Supermarket	**Morton & Bassett Organic Whole**	• Spicy but not too hot • Sharp, fresh, classic pepper flavor

	ITEM	TEST KITCHEN FAVORITE	WHY WE LIKE IT
	PEPPERONI, SLICED	**Margherita Italian Style**	• Nice balance of meatiness and spice • Tangy, fresh flavor with hints of fruity licorice and peppery fennel • Thin slices with right amount of chew
	PEPPERS, ROASTED RED	**Dunbars Sweet**	• Balance of smokiness and sweetness • Mild, sweet, and earthy red pepper flavor • Firm texture, not slimy or mushy • Packed in simple yet strong brine of salt and water without distraction of other strongly flavored ingredients
	PICKLES, BREAD-AND-BUTTER	**Bubbies**	• Subtle, briny tang • All-natural solution that uses real sugar, not high-fructose corn syrup
	PIE CRUST, READY-MADE	**Wholly Wholesome 9″ Certified Organic Traditional Bake at Home Rolled Pie Dough**	• Palm oil gives it tender, flaky texture without artificial taste • Sold in sheets so you can use your own pie plate • Slightly sweet, rich flavor
	POTATO CHIPS	**Lay's Kettle Cooked Original**	• Big potato flavor, no offensive off-flavors • Perfectly salted • Slightly thick chips that aren't too delicate or brittle • Not too greasy
	PRESERVES, RASPBERRY	**Smucker's**	• Clean, strong raspberry flavor, not too tart or sweet • Not overly seedy • Ideal, spreadable texture, not too thick, artificial, or overprocessed
	PRESERVES, STRAWBERRY	**Welch's**	• Big, distinct strawberry flavor • Natural-tasting and not overwhelmingly sweet • Thick and spreadable texture, not runny, slimy, or too smooth

ITEM	TEST KITCHEN FAVORITE	WHY WE LIKE IT
RICE, ARBORIO	**RiceSelect** Runner-Up: **Riso Baricella Superfino**	• Creamier than competitors • Smooth grains • Characteristic good bite of Arborio rice in risotto where al dente is ideal
RICE, BASMATI	**Tilda Pure**	• Very long grains expand greatly with cooking, result of being aged for minimum of one year, as required in India • Ideal, fluffy texture, not dry, gummy, or mushy • Nutty taste with no off-flavors • Sweet aroma
RICE, BROWN	**Goya Natural Long Grain**	• Firm yet tender grains • Bold, toasty, nutty flavor
RICE, LONG-GRAIN WHITE	**Lundberg Organic**	• Nutty, buttery, and toasty flavor • Distinct, smooth grains that offer some chew without being overly chewy
RICE, READY	**Minute Ready to Serve White Rice**	• Parboiled long-grain white rice that is ready in less than 2 minutes • Toasted, buttery flavor • Firm grains with al dente bite
SALSA, HOT	**Pace Hot Chunky**	• Good balance of bright tomato, chile, and vegetal flavors • Chunky, almost crunchy texture, not mushy or thin • Spicy and fiery but not overpowering
SALSA, GREEN	**Frontera Tomatillo**	• Complex, roasted tomatillo taste • Nuanced sweet and smoky flavor • Good amount of heat
SALT	**Maldon Sea Salt**	• Light and airy texture • Delicately crunchy flakes • Not so coarse as to be overly crunchy or gritty nor so fine as to disappear

ITEM	TEST KITCHEN FAVORITE	WHY WE LIKE IT
SOY SAUCE For cooking	**Lee Kum Kee Table Top Premium**	• Pleasantly salty yet sweet with high sodium and sugar content • Depth of flavor balances salty, sweet, roasted, and fruity notes • Aromatic in rice and teriyaki
For dipping	**Ohsawa Nama Shoyu Organic Unpasteurized**	• Lower sodium content allows clean, mellow taste to shine in uncooked applications • Rich and nuanced flavor with sweet, floral, and caramel notes resulting from traditional, slow-brewed production
SWEETENED CONDENSED MILK	**Borden Eagle Brand Whole Milk** and **Nestlé Carnation**	• Made with whole milk; creamier in desserts and balances more assertive notes from other ingredients
TERIYAKI SAUCE	**Annie Chun's All Natural**	• Distinct teriyaki flavor without offensive or dominant flavors, unlike competitors • Smooth, rich texture, not too watery or gluey
TOMATOES, CANNED CRUSHED	**Tuttorosso in Thick Puree with Basil** NOTE: Available only in New England, Mid-Atlantic region, and Florida.	• Chunky texture, not pasty, mushy, or watery • Bright, fresh tomato taste • Balance of saltiness, sweetness, and acidity
TOMATOES, CANNED DICED	**Hunt's**	• Bright, fresh tomato flavor that balances sweet and tart • Firm yet tender texture
TOMATOES, CANNED PUREED	**Muir Glen Organic**	• Full tomato flavor without any bitter, sour, or tinny notes • Pleasantly thick, even consistency, not watery or thin

ITEM	TEST KITCHEN FAVORITE	WHY WE LIKE IT
TOMATOES, CANNED WHOLE	**Muir Glen Organic**	• Pleasing balance of bold acidity and fruity sweetness • Firm yet tender texture, even after hours of simmering
TOMATO PASTE	**Goya**	• Bright, robust tomato flavors • Balance of sweet and tart flavors
TORTILLA CHIPS	**Santitas Authentic Mexican Style White Corn**	• Mild and pleasantly salty flavor, not bland, artificial, or rancid • Sturdy yet crunchy and crisp texture, not brittle, stale, or cardboardlike
TORTILLAS, CORN	**Maria and Ricardo's Handmade Style Soft**	• Light, fresh corn flavor • Hint of sweetness but no added sugar • Extra protein keeps them pliable and strong
TORTILLAS, FLOUR	**Old El Paso 6-Inch**	• Thin and flaky texture, not doughy or stale • Made with plenty of fat and salt
TOSTADAS, CORN	**Mission Estilo Casero**	• Crisp, crunchy texture • Good corn flavor • Flavor and texture that are substantial enough to stand up to hearty toppings
TUNA, CANNED	**Wild Planet Wild Albacore**	• Rich, fresh-tasting, and flavorful, but not fishy • Hearty, substantial chunks of tuna
TUNA, CANNED PREMIUM	**Nardin Bonito Del Norte Ventresca Fillets** Best Buy: **Tonnino Tuna Ventresca Yellowfin in Olive Oil**	• Creamy, delicate meat and tender yet firm fillets • Full, rich tuna flavor

ITEM	TEST KITCHEN FAVORITE	WHY WE LIKE IT
TURKEY, WHOLE	**Empire Kosher**	• Moist and dense texture without being watery, chewy, or squishy • Meaty, full turkey flavor • Buttery white meat • Koshering process renders brining unnecessary
VANILLA BEANS	**McCormick Madagascar**	• Moist, seed-filled pods • Complex, robust flavor with caramel notes
VANILLA EXTRACT	**McCormick Pure**	• Strong, rich vanilla flavor where others are weak and sharp • Complex flavor with spicy, caramel notes and sweet undertone
VEGETABLE OIL	**Crisco Natural Blend**	• Unobtrusive, mild flavor for stir-frying and sautéing and for use in baked goods and in uncooked applications such as mayonnaise and vinaigrette • Neutral taste and absence of fishy or metallic flavors when used for frying
VINEGAR, APPLE CIDER	**Spectrum Naturals Organic Unfiltered**	• Deep, warm profile with sweet, mellow, and smooth cider flavor • Balance of richness and tanginess • Complex with notes of honey and caramel with clear apple flavor
VINEGAR, BALSAMIC	**Lucini Gran Riserva Balsamico**	• Sweet, nuanced flavor lacking any harshness or astringency • Smooth and thick like traditional balsamic, not too thin or light • Balance of tanginess and sweetness with complexity and slight acidic zing

	ITEM	TEST KITCHEN FAVORITE	WHY WE LIKE IT
	VINEGAR, RED WINE	**Laurent Du Clos**	• Crisp red wine flavor balanced by stronger than average acidity and subtle sweetness • Complex yet pleasing taste from multiple varieties of grapes
	VINEGAR, WHITE WINE For cooking	**Colavita Aged**	• Balance of tanginess and subtle sweetness, not overly acidic or weak • Fruity, bright, and perfumed
	For vinaigrettes	**Spectrum Naturals Organic**	• Rich, dark flavor tastes fermented and malty, not artificial or harsh • Fruity flavor with caramel, earthy, and nutty notes
	YOGURT, GREEK FULL-FAT	**Olympus Traditional Strained, Plain 10% Fat** Runners-Up: **Greek Gods Traditional Plain, Fage Total Strained Plain**, and **Voskos Plain Original**	• Rich taste and satiny texture, not thin, watery, or soupy • Buttery, tangy flavor
	YOGURT, GREEK LOW-FAT	**Fage Total 2% Strained, Plain** Runners-Up: **Chobani Lowfat Plain, Olympus Lowfat Plain**, and **Voskos Lowfat Plain**	• Super-creamy • Great dairy flavor
	YOGURT, GREEK NONFAT	**Olympus Traditional Strained, Plain** Runners-Up: **Voskos Plain, Brown Cow Plain, Dannon Plain, Oikos Organic**, and **Fage Total Strained**	• Smooth, creamy consistency, not watery or puddinglike from added thickeners, such as pectin or gelatin • Pleasantly tangy, well-balanced flavor, not sour or metallic
	YOGURT, WHOLE-MILK	**Brown Cow Cream Top Plain**	• Rich, well-rounded flavor, not sour or bland • Especially creamy, smooth texture, not thin or watery • Higher fat content contributes to flavor and texture

Conversions and Equivalencies

Some say cooking is a science and an art. We would say that geography has a hand in it, too. Flour milled in the United Kingdom and elsewhere will feel and taste different from flour milled in the United States. So we cannot promise that the loaf of bread you bake in Canada or England will taste the same as a loaf baked in the States, but we can offer guidelines for converting weights and measures. We also recommend that you rely on your instincts when making our recipes. Refer to the visual cues provided. If the bread dough hasn't "come together in a ball," as described, you may need to add more flour—even if the recipe doesn't tell you to. You be the judge.

The recipes in this book were developed using standard U.S. measures following U.S. government guidelines. The charts below offer equivalents for U.S., metric, and imperial (U.K.) measures. All conversions are approximate and have been rounded up or down to the nearest whole number.

EXAMPLE:

1 teaspoon	=	4.9292 milliliters, rounded up to 5 milliliters
1 ounce	=	28.3495 grams, rounded down to 28 grams

VOLUME CONVERSIONS

U.S.	METRIC
1 teaspoon	5 milliliters
2 teaspoons	10 milliliters
1 tablespoon	15 milliliters
2 tablespoons	30 milliliters
¼ cup	59 milliliters
⅓ cup	79 milliliters
½ cup	118 milliliters
¾ cup	177 milliliters
1 cup	237 milliliters
1¼ cups	296 milliliters
1½ cups	355 milliliters
2 cups (1 pint)	473 milliliters
2½ cups	591 milliliters
3 cups	710 milliliters
4 cups (1 quart)	0.946 liter
1.06 quarts	1 liter
4 quarts (1 gallon)	3.8 liters

WEIGHT CONVERSIONS

OUNCES	GRAMS
½	14
¾	21
1	28
1½	43
2	57
2½	71
3	85
3½	99
4	113
4½	128
5	142
6	170
7	198
8	227
9	255
10	283
12	340
16 (1 pound)	454

Baking is an exacting science. Because measuring by weight is far more accurate than measuring by volume, and thus more likely to achieve reliable results, in our recipes we provide ounce measures in addition to cup measures for many ingredients. Refer to the chart below to convert these measures into grams.

INGREDIENT	OUNCES	GRAMS
1 cup all-purpose flour*	5	142
1 cup cake flour	4	113
1 cup whole-wheat flour	5½	156
1 cup granulated (white) sugar	7	198
1 cup packed brown sugar (light or dark)	7	198
1 cup confectioners' sugar	4	113
1 cup cocoa powder	3	85
4 tablespoons butter[†] (½ stick, or ¼ cup)	2	57
8 tablespoons butter[†] (1 stick, or ½ cup)	4	113
16 tablespoons butter[†] (2 sticks, or 1 cup)	8	227

* U.S. all-purpose flour, the most frequently used flour in this book, does not contain leaveners, as some European flours do. These leavened flours are called self-rising or self-raising. If you are using self-rising flour, take this into consideration before adding leavening to a recipe.

[†] In the United States, butter is sold both salted and unsalted. We generally recommend unsalted butter. If you are using salted butter, take this into consideration before adding salt to a recipe.

OVEN TEMPERATURES

FAHRENHEIT	CELSIUS	GAS MARK (IMPERIAL)
225	105	¼
250	120	½
275	135	1
300	150	2
325	165	3
350	180	4
375	190	5
400	200	6
425	220	7
450	230	8
475	245	9

CONVERTING FAHRENHEIT TO CELSIUS

We include doneness temperatures in many of the recipes in this book. We recommend an instant-read thermometer for the job. Refer to the above table to convert Fahrenheit degrees to Celsius. Or, for temperatures not represented in the chart, use this simple formula:

Subtract 32 degrees from the Fahrenheit reading, then divide the result by 1.8 to find the Celsius reading.

EXAMPLE:

"Roast chicken until thighs register 175 degrees."
To convert:

$$175°F - 32 = 143°$$
$$143° ÷ 1.8 = 79.44°C, \text{ rounded down to } 79°C$$

Index

C

Cabbage
-Apple Slaw, Tangy, *81,* 81–82
Asian Beef and Noodle Soup, 96
Buttermilk Coleslaw; var., 80–81
California-Style Fish Tacos, 256
Chipotle-Grilled Pork Tacos, 319–20
Corned Beef and, *210,* 210–11
Cream-Braised, Simple, ■ 465
Drunken Noodles with Chicken, *429,* 429–30
Napa, and Shiitakes, Pork Lo Mein with, 424
Red, Sweet and Sour, 465–66
Salad, Warm, with Crispy Fried Tofu, ■ *293,* 293–94
and Sausage, Hearty Tuscan Bean Stew with, 115
Vegetable and Bean Tostadas; var., ■ *292,* 292–93
see also Bok Choy

Cajun Red Beans, 517–18
Cajun Spice Rub, ■ 332
Cake flour, about, 597
Cake pans
Bundt, preparing, 665
Bundt, ratings of, 798
metal, ratings of, 796
preparing, 680
round, ratings of, 797
square, ratings of, 796
tube, ratings of, 798

Cakes
Almond, *656,* 656–57
Angel Food, *668, 668*
Applesauce Snack; var., 652–53
Apple Upside-Down, 657–58
Blueberry Buckle; var., *740,* 740–41
Bundt, storing, 664
Carrot Sheet; var., *673, 673*
Chiffon; var., 668–69
Chocolate
  Chip Snack; var., 652
  Cream Roll, Glazed; var., 686–87

Cakes, Chocolate *(cont.)*
Easy, 653
Flan, Magic, *666,* 666–67
Flourless, 690, *690*
German, 684–85
Layer, Old-Fashioned, 679–80
Pound, 662–63, *663*
Red Velvet Layer, 681, *681*
Sheet, Simple; var., 671–72, *672*
Tunnel of Fudge, *665,* 665–66
Coconut Layer, 683
Coffee, Easy; var., *654,* 654–55
cutting into layers, 684
decorating, 682
Foolproof New York–Style Cheesecake, 688
Gingerbread, 655–56
Glazes for, ■ 662
layer, applying frosting to, 678
Lemon Cheesecake, 688–90
making a foil sling for, 635
Peach, Summer, 659–60
Pineapple Upside-Down, 658–59
Pound, Chocolate, 662–63, *663*
Pound, Easy; var., 660–62
pound, storing, 664
preparing water bath for, 689
Rum, Holiday, 667
Soaking Syrups for, ■ 664
Strawberry Dream, *685,* 685–86
testing for doneness, 653
tube, storing, 664
White Layer, Classic, 679
White Sheet, Classic; var., 671
Yellow Bundt, Classic; var., 663–64
Yellow Layer, *676,* 676–77
Yellow Sheet, Classic; var., 670
see also Cupcakes; Frostings

California Barbecued Tri-Tip, *317,* 317–18
California Burger, 304
California-Style Fish Tacos, 256
Calzones, Ricotta and Spinach; var., 444–45
Campanelle with Sautéed Mushrooms and Thyme, ■ 415–16, *416*

Canadian bacon
Eggs Benedict, ■ 529

Candied Peanuts, Homemade, ■ 721
Candy/deep fry thermometers, 13
Can openers, ratings of, 792

Caper(s)
about, 399
and Anchovies, Creamy Egg Salad with, 74
Baked Manicotti Puttanesca, 364
Chicken Piccata; var., ■ *132, 132*
and Herb Vinaigrette Poached Salmon with; var., ■ *236,* 236–38
-Lemon Butter, Prosciutto-Wrapped Cod with, ■ 245
-Lemon Sauce, Grilled Salmon Steaks with, 338
-Lemon Sauce, Sautéed Pork Cutlets with, 212
and Olives, Pasta alla Norma with, ■ 398–99, *399*
-Parsley Compound Butter, ■ 244
Persillade Relish, ■ 203
Radishes, and Cornichons, French Potato Salad with, 78
and Roasted Red Peppers, Tuna Salad with, ■ 76
Smoked Salmon, and Dill, Easy Salmon Cakes with, 241
"Smoked Salmon Platter" Sauce, ■ 339
Spaghetti Puttanesca, ■ 396–97
Tomato, and Basil Sauce, ■ 128

Caprese Skewers, ■ 31, *31*

Caramel
Apples, ■ 753
Apple Tart, Easy, 726
doneness temperatures, 15
Sauce, Skillet-Roasted Pears with, ■ 756
Sauce for Ice Cream, Easy, ■ 784
Snickers Icebox Pie, 722–23, *723*

Caraway
Almost No-Knead Seeded Rye Bread, 597
and Currants, Brown Soda Bread with, 583

S